TORT LAW

How to use your Connected Casebook

Step 1: Go to **www.CasebookConnect.com** and redeem your access code to get started.

Access Code:

Step 2: Go to your **BOOKSHELF** and select your Connected Casebook to start reading, highlighting, and taking notes in the margins of your e-book.

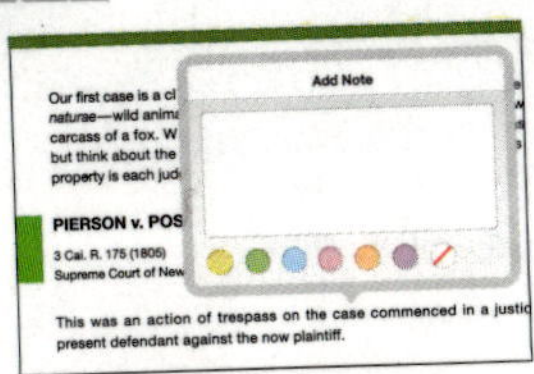

Step 3: Select the **STUDY** tab in your toolbar to access a variety of practice materials designed to help you master the course material. These materials may include explanations, videos, multiple-choice questions, flashcards, short answer, essays, and issue spotting.

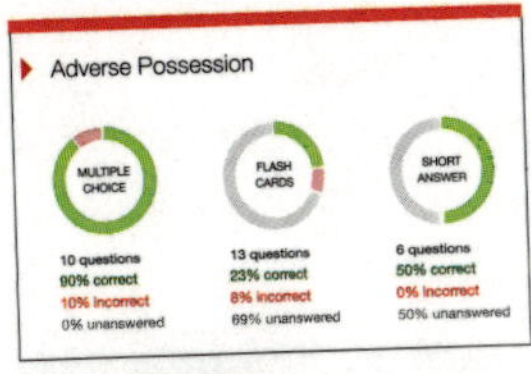

Step 4: Select the **OUTLINE** tab in your toolbar to access chapter outlines that automatically incorporate your highlights and annotations from the e-book. Use the My Notes area for copying, pasting, and editing your book notes or creating new notes.

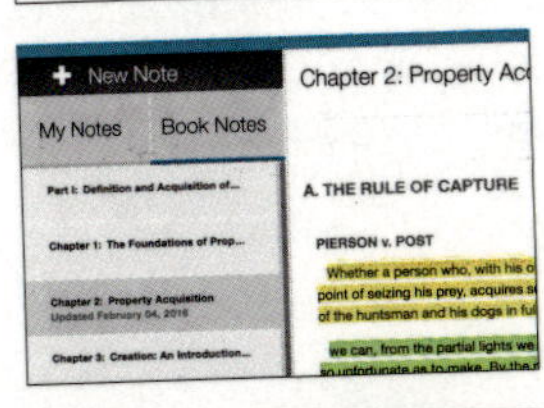

Step 5: If your professor has enrolled your class, you can select the **CLASS INSIGHTS** tab and compare your own study center results against the average of your classmates.

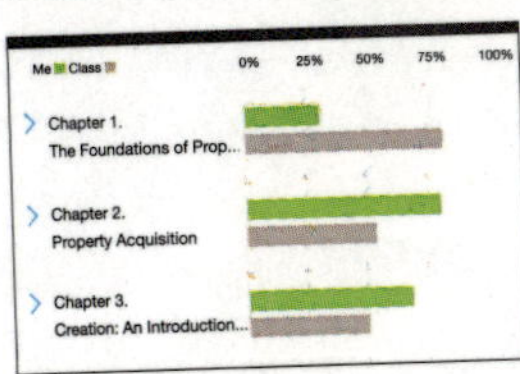

Is this a used casebook? Access code already scratched off?

You can purchase the Digital Version and still access all of the powerful tools listed above. Please visit CasebookConnect.com and select Catalog to learn more.

EDITORIAL ADVISORS

ASPEN CASEBOOK SERIES

TORT LAW

PRINCIPLES IN PRACTICE

Second Edition

James Underwood
Professor of Law
Baylor University

Published by Wolters Kluwer in New York.

Wolters Kluwer Legal & Regulatory U.S. serves customers worldwide with CCH, Aspen Publishers, and Kluwer Law International products. (www.WKLegaledu.com)

To contact Customer Service, e-mail customer.service@wolterskluwer.com, call 1-800-234-1660, fax 1-800-901-9075, or mail correspondence to:

Wolters Kluwer
Attn: Order Department
PO Box 990
Frederick, MD 21705

Printed in the United States of America.

4 5 6 7 8 9 0

ISBN 978-1-4548-9386-8

Library of Congress Cataloging-in-Publication Data

Names: Underwood, James M., author.
Title: Tort law : principles in practice / James Underwood, Professor of Law, Baylor University.
Description: Second edition. | New York : Wolters Kluwer, [2018] | Series: Aspen casebook series | Includes bibliographical references and index.
Identifiers: LCCN 2018000475 | ISBN 9781454893868
Subjects: LCSH: Torts–United States. | LCGFT: Casebooks
Classification: LCC KF1250 .U53 2018 | DDC 346.7303 — dc23
LC record available at https://lccn.loc.gov/2018000475

About Wolters Kluwer Legal & Regulatory U.S.

Wolters Kluwer Legal & Regulatory U.S. delivers expert content and solutions in the areas of law, corporate compliance, health compliance, reimbursement, and legal education. Its practical solutions help customers successfully navigate the demands of a changing environment to drive their daily activities, enhance decision quality and inspire confident outcomes.

Serving customers worldwide, its legal and regulatory portfolio includes products under the Aspen Publishers, CCH Incorporated, Kluwer Law International, ftwilliam.com and MediRegs names. They are regarded as exceptional and trusted resources for general legal and practice-specific knowledge, compliance and risk management, dynamic workflow solutions, and expert commentary.

To

Carol — the love of my life

Travis, Lindsey, Tyler & Tanner — the joy of my life

SUMMARY OF CONTENTS

CONTENTS

4 Negligence: Breach of Duty of Reasonable Care 157

12 Defamation 827

PREFACE

Allow me to briefly summarize some features of this casebook that I believe make it unique:

- **What's in a name?** The title "Torts: Principles in Practices" captures my belief that the supposed divide between legal theory and legal practice is a false dichotomy. I have now taught for nearly as long as I practiced law. One cannot truly understand how to apply the law solely based upon memorizing numerous black-letter legal rules. Circumstances are too varied and rules of law too ambiguous and conflicting to permit such ease of application. It is deep understanding and appreciation for the principles that permits a practitioner to represent clients in tort cases effectively. This book approaches the subject of Torts with a view toward capturing the spirit of the law of Torts at the dual levels of both its lofty principles and its actual implementation on the ground. To stay consistent with this theme, the book is filled with textboxes labeled either "*Principles*" or "*In Practice*" to supplement the material in the cases.
- **Vibrant mix of cases.** I love many of the old classic cases and a student of Tort law would be considered illiterate without some familiarity with these cases. This book retains many of the old standards. The book also adds many modern cases in contemporary factual circumstances so that students can appreciate how nimbly the law can be applied to new situations. For example, I have included a very recent case permitting the seat-belt defense as a form of comparative fault — a topic that courts every day continue to wrestle with. Other recent cases included one analyzing the liability of the sender of a text message for distracting a driver and causing an accident. The principles used to decide this case have been in play for decades (and to an extent, for several hundred years). Where possible, this book tries to include both the old and the new.
- **Helpful textual guidance.** The law of Torts is sufficiently robust and challenging so that artificial barriers to its understanding are not necessary. This book introduces every major section and subsection with text designed to provide context and to alert students to themes that will be important in the cases they are about to read. The concise, restrained notes following the cases elaborate on these themes and observations. Further, most major sections include a recapitulation titled "*Upon Further Review.*"
- **Useful notes and problems.** I have included short hypothetical problems after almost each subsection in the book. These problems can be utilized in class for group discussion and debate or in the private study by individual students. A pet peeve of mine regarding some casebooks is when a short case is followed by ten pages of notes where the author tries to look under every rock in the legal field. I understand a first-year Torts class will only be the beginning of a lifetime of study for many students.

- **Charts, diagrams, pictures, checklists, etc.** This book tries wherever possible to include textboxes with summaries, visual depictions, charts, and checklists for students to focus their attention on core points. Textboxes with useful or provocative quotations germane to the material are also included to capture the imagination of students and, at times, to offer a glimpse into the academic debates often accompanying various issues. Pictures are included to help students remember that these cases involved actual events that transformed the lives of real people.
- **Pattern jury instructions.** As another method of illustrating and restating core legal concepts, where possible the book includes form jury instructions from various jurisdictions, introduced with the heading "*Ladies and Gentlemen of the Jury.*" In terms of the real world application of most Tort concepts, the jury instructions embody the law as it is used in the courtrooms across the United States.
- **Practice essay questions.** Included at the end of many chapters in the book are longer-form practice essay questions entitled "*Pulling It All Together.*" These are typically made up of two to four paragraphs of hypothetical facts with a prompt question at the end and an indication of how long a student might want to spend in attempting to write an answer to the question. Students are constantly seeking such hypothetical questions for their use in exam preparation. Teachers can use these essays in class as a summary of material or students on their own can utilize them.
- **Coverage.** My goal was to avoid a 1,500-page twenty-pound book that tried to include every conceivable Tort issue. But I wanted the book to be useful for just about any first-year Torts class. It begins with coverage of the classic intentional torts and defenses to them. The book then spends several chapters exploring negligence (including causation). The book also covers general defenses (e.g., comparative fault, immunities, statutes of limitation), damages, and apportionment. These subjects alone may be all that many Torts classes will have time to cover. But for the professor who has additional time, I have also included chapters on strict liability, products liability, defamation, and business torts. The exclusion of any mention of business torts has always struck me as a serious deficiency that results in the misimpression that all Tort claims involve physical or mental injury. While entire law school electives are devoted to inquiry into some of these later chapters of this book, many Torts professors enjoy introducing these areas of the law in the first-year curriculum. In any event, this book is structured to be flexible enough to be used in many different ways.

This second edition includes all of these features from the first edition and adds to them. For example, I have now included at the beginning of each chapter an explicit list of learning objectives for that chapter. I have shown this to some of my students who love the idea of such a "checklist" that they can use as a reference point to be sure they're learning the primary lessons. I have added (and in some cases modified) problems to enhance the classroom experience. I have also added some new cases, being judicious about not getting carried away with this. For example, the original edition had a note in the mitigation of damages section about the "seat-belt defense." I thought this was not only too interesting to remain just a note but that including a recent case wrestling with this issue provided a nice review of analytical differences between a failure to mitigate and comparative fault. The new case additions also include two cases dealing with the "but-for" causation test. The original edition had one case only (*Cay v. Louisiana*) on but-for causation and then substantial material dealing with alternatives. I thought this was misleading since most causation issues are resolved by resort to the but-for test. Students were so distracted by the alternatives that they failed to appreciate the importance of the primary test for actual causation. So I have included two additional cases where the court rejected actual causation based upon the inability of the plaintiff to demonstrate but-for causation.

This book is designed to be an effective tool, for both professor and student, in offering insight into the rich and multifaceted law of Torts. I hope that you find this book provides a catalyst for your further learning.

James Underwood

March 2018

ACKNOWLEDGMENTS

I had no idea when I first agreed with Aspen to write the first edition of this book how much I was biting off. That project took two years to complete — much of it written in a hospital at my ailing son's bedside. The last five years has been swift and I am now given the chance to offer thanks for those who have helped me bring forth a second edition.

First, I am indebted to Aspen, both for having the faith in me to approach me about the initial project and in giving me a chance to produce a second edition so that I can fix all of the errors in the first. I also want to thank the editors who have shown meticulous attention to detail.

I am also thankful to teach at Baylor Law School which strives to produce the next generation of professionals dedicated to impacting others' lives. Dean Toben continues to keep our ship steered in the right direction and supports scholarly efforts like this. I have also had the chance to teach alongside Prof. Jill Lens and our lively debates about tort law have helped to inform my views in ways that impact these materials. I will miss Jill as she departs Waco for the mountains of northwest Arkansas to take up teaching duties at the University of Arkansas.

I am always grateful to my wife Carol who shows me grace and patience on a daily basis.

My son Travis and daughter-in-law Lindsey were the first of my family to be exposed to these materials as my students. They are now young, successful practicing lawyers in Dallas. I'd like to claim partial credit for the great futures they hold before them. In reality, they have had far more impact upon me and my teaching. My son Tyler was a budding theoretical mathematician in graduate school at the University of California Santa Barbara until he read one chapter of this book — he's now applying to law school. I cannot wait to see where his legal career will take him. My youngest son Tanner (now 19) was, of course, on my mind nearly every minute as I worked on the first edition of this book. He had just suffered a severe traumatic brain injury when he was the victim of a tort on an interstate highway in Waco. Miraculously, he has since graduated from high school with stellar grades. He still daily goes to therapy to work on speech, walking, and left-side movement of his body. But he has a sharp wit and an even more amazing attitude about life. If he does not complain, who am I to ever do so?

Five years ago, I wrote here that we "live in the moment with hope fueled by our faith and gratitude for our blessings." I cannot add to or improve upon that sentiment. I pray daily that these words are not just sweet sentiments but reality. Some days are easier than others. Honestly, I look forward to drafting the Acknowledgements for the third edition of this book years from now and being able to report on Tanner's continued progress.

Special thanks are also owed to Joanna Raines, my terrific research assistant at Baylor Law School who provided invaluable help in trying to limit the number of my errors.

Finally, I also wish to express my sincere gratitude to the copyright holders for granting permission to include certain excerpts in this book:

- American Law Institute, Restatement, Second, Torts: §§16, 19 (comment a), 46 (comments d & j), 65, 163 (comment b), 283 (comment c), 288A, 291, 314, 315, 339 (comment j), 401A, 433(2), 766, 768, 876 (comment d), 892, and 918; Restatement, Third, Torts: Apportionment: §8; Restatement, Third, Torts: Liability for Physical and Emotional Harm: §§2, 3, 6, 7 (comment j), 10(b), 20, 6, 27, 29, (comment j), 33 (illstr. 2), and 37 (comment c); Restatement, Second, Agency: §§219, 220 and 228. Copyright ©1965, 2000, 2006, 2009 by the American Law Institute. Reproduced by permission. All rights reserved.
- Augustus Noble Hand, illustration. Courtesy of Harvard Law School Library.
- C.V. "Buster" Kern, photograph. Courtesy of WhisperToMe/Wikimedia Commons.
- Donald Trump at CPAC 2011 in Washington, D.C., photograph. Courtesy of Gage Skidmore/Flickr.
- Gavel, photograph. Courtesy of Stoked/Media Bakery.
- Hiller, Aaron, "Rule 11 and Tort Reform: Myth, Reality, and Legislation," 18 Geo. J. Legal Ethics 809 (2005). Copyright ©2005 by the Georgetown Journal of Legal Ethics. Reproduced by permission. All rights reserved.
- Pen, photograph. Courtesy of Antonio Litterio/Wikimedia Commons
- Phil Busch, photograph. Copyright ©2010 by the Dallas Observer. Reproduced by permission. All rights reserved.
- Piedmont Driving Club, photograph. Copyright ©2018 by Ben Rose Photography. Reproduced by permission. All rights reserved.
- Spring gun, photograph. Courtesy of Throwawayhack/Wikimedia Commons.
- Westboro Baptist Church members demonstrate at the Virginia Holocaust Museum in 2010. Courtesy of J.C. Wilmore/Wikimedia Commons.
- Witherspoon, Tommy, "Waco Man Wrongly Jailed For 83 Days May Sue County," Waco Tribune-Herald (February 1, 2012). Copyright ©2012 by the Waco Tribune-Herald. Reproduced by permission. All rights reserved.

TORT LAW

CHAPTER 1

Introduction to Torts

I TORTS DEFINED

Non-lawyers typically respond with amusement when hearing of a law school course titled "Torts." A frequent refrain is either "what is that?" or "isn't that something you get at a bakery?" No, the subject you will be studying has nothing to do with food. A tort is a civil cause of action that seeks to right a wrong, historically for a claim recognized under the common law, for something other than the enforcement of a contractual promise. That is, at least, a fairly classic legal definition of a tort.

CHAPTER GOALS

- ☑ Understand the definition of a tort claim and the general scope of scenarios that might involve such causes of action.
- ☑ Introduce core tort goals that will play a role in coverage of material later in the book.
- ☑ Appreciate that there may actually be two sides to the ongoing debate over whether a tort crisis exists and whether reform of the system is warranted.
- ☑ Understand basic procedural aspects of a typical tort case from pleadings through trial and appeal.
- ☑ Facilitate preparation for first day of class through the introduction of the basics of preparing a case brief.

From a tort victim's perspective, the above definition seems somewhat dry. A child suffers a serious injury while riding in the back seat of his parents' car when it is hit from behind on the highway. A patient receives dental implants that are not placed securely and have to be removed. A schoolyard bully runs up behind a boy walking home from school and hits him over the head with a tree branch. A stalker repeatedly makes phone calls to a young lady at her home late at night threatening to break into the house to cause her bodily harm. Vandals throw paint against someone's new automobile ruining its exterior finish. A homeowner fails to secure a gate and inadvertently permits a child from next door to wander into their yard and drown in their swimming pool. A security

Tort:

The word is derived from the Latin "tortus" which meant twisted or crooked. In the common law, a tort is a "private or civil wrong or injury, other than breach of contract, for which the court will provide a remedy in the form of an action for damages."

Black's Law Dictionary

guard detains a shopper at a department store just because the customer is wearing gang attire. A husband witnesses the violent death of his wife as she crosses a street and is hit by a careless and drunk driver who has careened out of control on the city street. A mental patient confides to his psychiatrist that he is going to kill his girlfriend and the doctor fails to warn her and her death results. A jilted lover falsely tells others that his former girlfriend had a venereal disease. Or perhaps a lawyer entrusted with a new client's potential lawsuit fails to file it on time. Under the right circumstances, any of these true-to-life instances can qualify as a legitimate tort cause of action. These scenarios involve the potential violation of another citizen's civil right to be protected from certain types of harm under circumstances where the victim's rights are not defined pursuant to any contract with the defendant-tortfeasor. A tort may have occurred. A major part of your current undertaking is to acquire the knowledge and skill to look at a set of facts, and to reach an informed opinion on the question of whether a tort claim exists.

II GOALS AND CRITICISMS

From the above examples, the victims' lives might have been forever changed by these incidents. Tort law cannot undo all of these wrongs, but it can attempt to provide some civil redress, typically in the form of damages. While it is true that in exceptional circumstances the law will permit an extraordinary equitable remedy — such as for injunction — to prevent the commission of a threatened tort, most tort claims involve a request for monetary relief by the plaintiff. The subject of torts speaks in dollars and cents.

As you work through these materials, you should consider for each tort theory or doctrine the principle behind the rule of law. One fascinating aspect of legal study is the realization that the rules are not arbitrary. You may not agree with a particular doctrine — and often courts among different states will disagree about particular tort doctrines — but you can be certain that every tort doctrine had a reason for its adoption initially. As times and circumstances change, and as values evolve in our society, there are frequent occasions when a tort doctrine needs to be revisited. You will see numerous examples in the cases of courts revisiting old tort doctrines to decide if they should continue to be recognized, abandoned, or modified in some fashion. These determinations are driven by perceptions of the principles.

Likely you have heard in recent public forums debate on whether our tort system is broken and in need of serious reform. During the last few decades there have been tremendous efforts undertaken to modify common law tort doctrines either through the courts themselves or, more significantly, through legislative action. You will encounter various manifestations of judicial and legislative tort reform as you work through various portions of this book. When we get to Chapter 8 on Damages, we will encounter the tort reform movement directly. You are free to make your own assessment on the legitimacy of a torts crisis, but these materials will ask that you consider all of the evidence before reaching a conclusion. As a new lawyer (or law student) you will be asked your opinion by many laypersons about these matters. Further, if you practice tort law, you will encounter appeals to judges based upon notions that our system is broken and in need of repair. Being thoughtful in your approach to such matters will serve you well. One useful exercise for you will be to keep this issue — how well our current system is working — in the back of your mind as you read the hundreds of cases in this book. As you read each case, ask yourself, "Does it appear the current doctrines and procedural rules are already in place to avoid outrageous results?"

A. What Are the Purposes Behind Tort Law?

From a macro perspective, it is worth considering at the inception of our study the broad objectives that tort law seeks to vindicate. These objectives can be isolated and identified in many instances as we study the various tort causes of action. You may ask yourself, "what difference does it make?" There are multiple layers of response to that question. First, understanding the purposes behind tort law and its many doctrines and rules makes the study fascinating. Second, knowing the purposes behind the rules that you will discover in this book will increase the depth of your knowledge regarding those rules. A parrot might be trained to repeat certain tort phrases, but this does not make the bird into a lawyer. Being a good lawyer (or law student) is much more than memorizing a list of rules or laws. The rules themselves are very basic in terms of your education of tort law. Being able to articulate not only how a rule of law applies, but also when it applies, why it applies, and perhaps when it needs to be changed is the stuff of a torts master. Third, if you understand the rationale behind tort doctrines it will help you to articulate answers to questions that have not yet been addressed by courts. As you will see, the common law of torts evolves with every case decided because the unique facts of each case become a part of the law. Because factual circumstances underlying a tort claim are always potentially unique, judges and lawyers constantly have to determine if certain tort doctrines still apply as the facts are modified from one case to the next.

You might divide the world of tort scholars into two camps — roughly, those that believe the primary purpose of tort law is to regulate conduct by deterring (through the punishment of awards of damages) certain antisocial behavior, and those interested in "corrective justice" between the particular litigants. When a judge requires a tortfeasor who has beaten the plaintiff with a stick to pay for the harm caused, the thought is that this tortfeasor (and others who are aware of our system of civil justice) will think twice before whacking another with a stick. In addition, when the judge awards damages in favor of the victim and against the tortfeasor, the judge is implementing justice by providing compensation in favor of a worthy victim. Some torts scholars argue that these purposes stand in conflict with one another. They assert that if you push deterrence as the principal goal, then you will be more demanding of proof of fault by the defendant before you enter judgment. On the other hand, they assert that if compensation is the chief goal then a system that rewards plaintiffs without too many legal hurdles is superior. The truth is that these rather large and general goals are not in conflict but work together:

> Identifying the goals of tort law seemed to be a relatively easy task. Reduced to its essentials and stripping away all that is unnecessary, the consequence of a successful tort lawsuit is to invoke the power of the state (in the form of a judgment) to compel one person (the defendant) to compensate another (the plaintiff) for injuries for which the defendant may be judged "responsible" in some way. As a result of this invocation of sovereign power, the injured person is compensated, and the tortfeasor (and all who might find themselves in a situation similar to that of the tortfeasor in the future) is deterred from engaging in whatever conduct caused the injury. The twin pillars of tort law — compensation and deterrence — were born of the legal realist movement and the simple act of describing the most obvious consequences of a successful tort lawsuit.

J. Clark Kelso, *Sixty Years of Torts: Lessons for the Future*, 29 Torts & Ins. L.J. 1 (1993).

Beyond these rather noble goals of regulating conduct and seeking justice, there is another important goal of tort law — resolving civil disputes in a peaceable manner. The truth is that when one person is perceived to misbehave and cause harm to another, it is important that the parties believe there is a civil justice system prepared to resolve their dispute in what is perceived to be a fair and non-arbitrary manner. It is possible to simply have a referee flip a coin to resolve such disputes, but the parties would quickly realize there was no point taking their dispute to the local government to do this. Short of a civil and peaceable system to resolve these disputes, the fear is that the parties would simply engage in violent acts to get even or extract some payment for the initial injury. At this very basic level, the civil justice system is designed to avoid gunfights in the town square. If it can regulate conduct and thereby reduce injuries or at least provide justice after an injury has occurred, that's icing on the cake.

> "To me, a lawyer is basically the person that knows the rules of the country. We're all throwing the dice, playing the game, moving our pieces around the board, but if there is a problem, the lawyer is the only person who has read the inside of the top of the box."
>
> *Jerry Seinfeld*

B. Has Tort Law Gotten Out of Control?

There is a good chance that you had already heard the word "torts" before starting law school because "tort reform" has pervaded the public forum in terms of political debate for several decades. You may have even formed an opinion about whether tort lawsuits are "out of control" and the "system broken." Such is the common assertion of many partisan candidates for elected office today. Patience should be urged before forming a closed mind on this controversial issue. At the end of your study of torts you will be in a much better position to opine on that topic. Nevertheless, it is worth at least introducing the topic of tort reform at the outset because it is the elephant in the room. It is something that you should keep in the back of your mind as you begin your study of tort law. And the media's coverage of tort reform is not always conducted at a sophisticated, academic level. Because there is a good chance you have already, therefore, become familiar with some of the arguments in favor of tort reform, you should at least be aware of some serious counterarguments. The following excerpt is a good example of such scholarship.

RULE 11 AND TORT REFORM: MYTH, REALITY, AND LEGISLATION

*Aaron Hiller, 18 Geo. J. Legal Ethics 809 (2005)**

Amending modern civil procedure is a process of balance and deliberation. When any claim can be made in a federal courtroom, the system may seem overwhelmed by "frivolous" lawsuits. When heavy restrictions act as a deterrent, even legitimate claims might not have access to the system. The evolution of Rule 11 [a Federal Rule of Civil Procedure that sanctions groundless lawsuits] illustrates the need to consider both the abuse and the access ends of the equation and the dangers of mistaking harsher sanctions for genuine improvement. Good litigation reform requires poised formulation and attention to real historical trends. Moreover, good litigation reform requires good lawyers — attorneys who act, not only within the proscribed bounds of ethical codes, but to help shape those standards and conventions in a safe and responsible manner.

But American culture is saturated with the stereotyping of lawyers, and lawmakers have a tendency to cry wolf at a litigation crisis to garner easy praise and campaign support. Historical fact and current data demonstrate the folly in this approach.

Tort reform rhetoric feeds into lawyer stereotypes and is itself stereotypical. Worse than the relative predictability of the tort reform narrative, the single-minded obsession with an American litigation crisis blinds lawmakers to real

---

problems and effective solutions. All empirical evidence suggests that lawsuits are declining, that jury awards are shrinking, and that the costs of litigation to the overall American economy are slight if at all significant. House Resolution 4571 [proposed as an aid to strengthen Rule 11's application] stems from, and lends authority to, a cultural bias and a mythological emergency, but it does not reflect reality or offer a desired outcome.

A. THE MYTH

The American public does not like lawyers. Maybe it never has. The cultural roots of modern anti-lawyer sentiment run deep. In 1770, the citizens of Grafton, New Hampshire, dispatched the following census report to George III:

> Your Royal Majesty, Grafton County . . . contains 6,489 souls, most of whom are engaged in agriculture, but included in that number are 69 wheelwrights, 8 doctors, 29 blacksmiths, 87 preachers, 20 slaves and 90 students at the new college. There is not one lawyer, for which fact we take no personal credit, but thank an Almighty and Merciful God.

About three-quarters of surveyed individuals believe that the United States has too many lawyers and over half believe that lawyers file too many lawsuits. It is true that the number of attorneys in America has nearly tripled over the last three decades, a statistic approaching 900,000 practicing lawyers. But complaints about the number of lawyers, metaphors used to describe the profession, and even lawyer jokes have been part of American social values for centuries.

[The tort reformers behind the proposed amendment to Rule 11] certainly tapped into the anti-lawyer tradition. In explaining the need for direct amendment of Rule 11, the tort reformers couch their argument in personal, anecdotal appeals to the American public. Doctors cannot help but be enraged at the story of the C.E.O. of San Antonio's Methodist Children's Hospital, who "was sued after he stepped into a patient's hospital room and asked how he was doing." Parents and community volunteers must be appalled by the tale of a New Jersey little league coach who "had to settle the case for $25,000" when angry parents sued over their son's black eye. Americans should be dismayed — even if somewhat amused — by the narrative of the Pennsylvania man who "sued the Frito Lay Company, claiming that Doritos chips were inherently dangerous after one stuck in his throat." Such storytelling is captivating, entertaining, and resonates with the anti-lawyer undercurrents of American culture.

As engaging as the frivolous lawsuit narratives can be, they also follow a predictable pattern and tend to be somewhat misleading. The premise and conclusion of every storyline is that the onslaught of "frivolous lawsuits" threatens to destroy the American way of life. Very little hard data is ever presented to substantiate the claim; the basis for this rather frightening statement is almost entirely anecdotal. The public has almost always heard these stories, or stories like them, before. Of course, they are increasingly recognizable because cases like the ones described by the tort reformers receive disproportionate media attention. In the modern media culture, the line between news and entertainment is not often clear; serious coverage of the court system struggles to be heard over the din of talk radio, cable punditry, stump speeches, and election coverage. The stories that do surface are "anecdotal glimpses of atypical cases." Cognitive biases only reinforce public misperception of the overall system — because vivid incidents are easier to recall, people tend to overestimate how frequently the most outrageous stories occur. And not even these cases are the straightforward abuses of the system they may seem.

Many Americans are familiar with the multi-million dollar punitive damages award against McDonald's for serving coffee at scalding temperatures. Less are familiar with the facts of the case. The plaintiff, a seventy-nine-year-old woman, received acutely painful third degree burns from coffee heated to over 180 degrees. She only brought suit when McDonald's refused to reimburse her medical expenses; at trial, the jury learned of at least 700 other McDonald's burn victims who had been summarily dismissed by McDonald's safety experts. The $2.3 million jury verdict was later reduced to $640,000, but the original sum represented exactly two days of coffee sales revenues for McDonald's nationwide. Reasonable people can disagree as to whether this lawsuit was vindictive or vindication, but "what qualifies as a frivolous claim depends on the eye of the beholder." Given all the facts, the line between frivolous lawsuit and defensible argument is harder to draw.

Lawmakers must know that the definition of "frivolous" is not straightforward when it comes to litigation — but they hammer home the perpetual crisis of legal hypochondria anyway. By characterizing the problem as too many lawyers, the tort reformers miss a more important question — not whether or not there are too many lawyers, but whether or not the legal profession is serving the American public as it should. By obscuring the facts with extravagant, yet predictable, storytelling, they miss an even larger problem — not why the American people are terrified of tort litigation, but why large numbers of Americans lack the information and resources to assert legitimate claims. Why do they do it? Says one briefing book for House Republicans: "attacking trial lawyers is admittedly a cheap applause line, but it works. It's almost impossible to go too far when it comes to demonizing lawyers." The tort reformers might be moved by collecting campaign contributions from corporate America or by garnering popular support by tapping into a stereotypical position, but they do not appear to be motivated by reality.

B. THE REALITY

By all available data, the litigation crisis depicted by the authors of H.R. 4571 simply does not exist. In fact, the Justice Department Bureau of Justice Statistics tracked more than a decade of litigation in the seventy-five largest counties in the United States and found the exact opposite trends. From 1992 to 2001, the overall number of civil lawsuits filed in America dropped by 47%. The number of tort suits fell by 31.8% and the number of medical malpractice claims — an area of litigation often cited by tort reformers and insurance companies for increasing abuse — declined by 14.2%.

As the amount of litigation on the docket has declined, so have the jury awards so often decried as outrageous and skyrocketing by the tort reformers. The median jury award in 2001 was $ 37,000, representing a 43.1% decrease over the previous decade. Limiting that analysis to only tort cases, the median jury award stood at $ 28,000, a 56.3% drop since 1992. Moreover, juries rarely award punitive damages at all — less than 3% of all plaintiff winners in tort trials were awarded punitive damages; the median award was $38,000. If litigation rates are decreasing nationwide and jury awards are more conservative than they have been in twenty years, it is difficult to see where the litigation crisis exists. Not even the baseline mythology of a naturally litigious American culture is really accurate. Comparatively, the United States is far from the most litigious country in the world.

When the data contradicts their immediate claims, the tort reformers often turn to an alternative economic argument — because of frivolous lawsuits, whatever their number may be, "small businesses and workers suffer." Consider one anecdote presented to the House Judiciary Committee in support of H.R. 4571:

> This year, the nation's oldest ladder manufacturer, family-owned John S. Tilley Ladders Co. of Watervilet, New York, near Albany, filed for bankruptcy protection and sold off most of its assets due to litigation costs. Founded in 1855, the Tilley firm could not handle the cost of liability insurance, which had risen from 6% of sales a decade ago to 29%, even though the company never lost an actual court judgment. "We could see the handwriting on the wall and just want to end this whole thing," said Robert Howland, a descendant of company founder John Tilley.

Neither "sales" nor the reasons behind the proportional rise in insurance costs have been explained, but the statistics quoted in the story are probably technically correct.

The economic argument takes the same narrative form as the excessive litigation claim — a personal anecdote about respected, small town folks whose hard work has been swept away by lawyers and lawsuits. But these concerns about the overall cost of litigation to the American economy are based on storytelling and dubious statistics, not hard data. One Brookings Institute expert estimates that tort liability could comprise at most 2% of the total costs of United States goods and services. At that rate, he estimates that it is "highly doubtful" legal expenditures could significantly affect the competitiveness of American products. Other experts place the total estimated business liability for all legal claims at about twenty-five cents for every one hundred dollars in revenue. The legal definition of "small business" may shift, and individual stories might invoke sympathy, but there appears to be no apparent economic facet to the litigation crisis either.

The reality is that the United States does not face a litigation crisis. Even if insurance premiums are excessively high, America's litigation rates are neither excessive nor increasing. The most significant problems with the system involve, not too many cases or unreasonably high jury awards, but too little access to justice and unreasonably few legal services available to the general public. The "Frivolous Lawsuit Reduction Act" might dovetail nicely with a cultural bias or score well with a given political base, but it does not address any actual immediate emergency.

III CASE PROCEDURE AND DEFINITIONS

The Typical Life of a Civil Tort Suit

Pleadings → Discovery → Motion Practice → Trial → Judgment → Appeal

Cases tend to follow a certain pathway as they wind their way through our civil judicial system. You will be reading tort cases that are written at different points in time. Some opinions are rulings upon motions attacking the plaintiff's initial pleading because the defendant contends that no legitimate claim is possible under existing law. Other court opinions are written after some period of discovery has transpired and immediately before trial. These are in response to motions that argue that the evidence is so one-sided that no trial is necessary. Appellate courts write other opinions in this book, after a trial court's entry of judgment. These procedural nuances are often important in understanding a court's opinion. You will be learning more about these procedures in your civil procedure class. An initial overview here, however, will be helpful to you in deciphering the torts cases we will be encountering in a few pages.

A. Pleadings and Attacks on Pleadings

A tort victim who files a suit is called the "plaintiff." The alleged tortfeasor is the "defendant." The plaintiff initiates a civil tort case by filing a so-called short and plain statement of the claim. This is essentially a formal pleading that identifies the parties, states the court's power or "jurisdiction" over the type of claims filed and over the parties, and then articulates the factual and legal basis for the claims asserted. In short, the complaint tells the legal story of what the defendant did that was wrong and how this hurt the plaintiff. The complaint ends with a "prayer" for relief that identifies the legal remedies (e.g., the damages) plaintiff seeks against the defendant at the conclusion of the case.

"It won't do to have truth and justice on his side, he must have law and lawyers."

Charles Dickens

The defendant is permitted to file an initial attack on the adequacy of this pleading, denominated a "motion to dismiss." Typically, in ruling upon these foundational attacks on the lawsuit, the court is supposed to assume that every fact plaintiff has alleged is true. The focus of the motion is not arguing the facts but arguing whether the law might possibly recognize a valid claim assuming the facts are as alleged. In run-of-the-mill cases where the law is quite settled, the defendant may not bother to file a motion to dismiss. But when the complaint asserts a tort cause of action whose existence or contour is uncertain, a motion to dismiss gives the court an early opportunity to examine the case and make an early legal ruling on a potentially dispositive matter. Some of the cases contained in this book are appeals from trial court dismissals of cases at this early stage.

B. Formal Discovery

If the trial court recognizes a legitimate claim has been stated by the plaintiff and permits the plaintiff's claim to proceed, a period of often time-consuming and expensive pretrial practice occurs called formal discovery. Modern rules of civil procedure permit great latitude to both parties to a dispute to transmit formal requests for information and documents to which the other party is obligated to respond within a particular period of time — often 30 days. In addition, parties will frequently take oral depositions of parties and non-party witnesses. The formal purposes of this discovery are to prepare both sides for trial so that there are no ambushes in the courtroom, and to facilitate a later peek at the merits of the case before trial by the judge, typically in a motion for summary judgment. Informally, discovery of the facts also facilitates settlement by permitting the parties to gain a clearer view of how the case might appear at a trial. Such perspective often clarifies the merits of each side's positions.

C. Motions for Summary Judgment

Often the last formal barrier to getting its jury trial that a plaintiff faces is a defendant's motion for summary judgment arguing that no trial is needed because plaintiff lacks sufficient evidentiary support for its tort cause of action.

(Less frequently, a plaintiff can file a motion for summary judgment arguing that its claims are undisputed and that it is entitled to judgment without need for trial, in whole or part.) The parties will argue about the application of the law to the facts in a motion for summary judgment. In essence, the trial court is asking itself when ruling on such a motion, whether there is any need to convene a jury of citizens to rule upon disputed questions of fact. If not, summary judgment might well be granted and final judgment entered in an expedited fashion. Many of the cases in this book are appellate opinions reviewing the propriety of trial courts' granting of summary judgment motions.

D. Trial

At trial, the plaintiff has the opportunity to present evidence to demonstrate the merit of the particular tort cause(s) of action being pursued. This proof will come both from the witness stand in the form of live testimony from witnesses under oath, and from other tangible forms of evidence such as photographs, documents, videotapes, or other objects (e.g., an allegedly defective tire) relevant to the matter. The defendant has a chance to cross-examine each of the plaintiff's witnesses. After the plaintiff rests, the defendant is given an additional opportunity to challenge the sufficiency of the plaintiff's evidence in the form of a motion for directed (or instructed) verdict. This is an odd name for a motion. Its roots lie in an ancient practice: After granting a motion, the judge would direct the jury to enter a particular finding. Nowadays, courts granting the motion do not direct the jury to do anything other than to go home because their service is no longer necessary. Theoretically, the same basis for a directed verdict motion should have been available prior to trial in the form of a motion for summary judgment. A defendant whose motion for summary judgment was denied is often undeterred in arguing the same points later during the trial in the directed verdict motion. If this motion is denied, the defendant has the same opportunity as the plaintiff to call witnesses and introduce exhibits that support the defendant's position. At the conclusion of all of the evidence being submitted, the lawyers present closing arguments to the jury and the court instructs the jury on the law they are to apply in reaching its verdict. Trials are the pinnacle of both exhilaration and stress for both the litigants and their lawyers. Other cases in this book are appellate opinions concerning alleged errors that occurred at trial, such as ruling on evidentiary matters; the validity of the trial court's instructions on the law to the jury; and the sufficiency of the evidence to support the jury's verdict.

E. Entry of Judgment

If the jury cannot reach a verdict (in federal court a unanimous verdict is required) the trial judge declares a "mistrial" and resets the case for a new trial in the future. If the jury does render a verdict, the court will entertain motions by the prevailing party to enter judgment in conformity with that verdict, and motions by the losing party to disregard the verdict as against the great weight of the evidence. Once the trial court enters a final judgment, it loses jurisdiction over the case and the case becomes an appellate matter.

F. Appeal

Appeals are subject to their own unique procedures and rules, and many lawyers specialize in handling appeals. Litigants are typically entitled to one appeal as of right from a final judgment to an intermediate court of appeals. Beyond that, review is typically discretionary at the highest court — usually, but not always, referred to as a "supreme court."

The losing party filing the appeal is referred to as the "appellant" and the prevailing party at the trial court level is called the "appellee." The appellant is given a certain number of days after the final judgment to file an appellate brief with the appeals court pointing out reversible errors made by the trial judge in either granting or denying a motion, or in failing to enter judgment in conformity with the verdict, or in failing to disregard the verdict. Further, trials are filled with many evidentiary objections, which can be the subject of a possible appeal. Appeals can take months to years to resolve.

IV CASE BRIEFING

Your professor may expect you to prepare and bring to class a "case brief" for each of the cases you are assigned to read from these materials. Whether formally assigned this task or not, it is a wise practice, particularly for a beginning law student. A case brief is a summary or synopsis of the important aspects of a case and should reflect your thoughtful reflections on the court's analysis.

A. Reasons for Briefing a Case

There are two reasons you should brief your cases even if not required by your professor. First, case briefing will help you to understand the case better by focusing your attention upon important aspects of the court's written opinion. Second, the case brief will be a useful tool during class as well as later during the term, when you are preparing your course "outline."

Even beyond law school, good lawyers brief cases they read as they practice law. Their case brief may not be as formal as what you will likely prepare as a law student, but the lawyer's notes on the cases she reads in the firm library will generally contain similar categories to your case briefs, and help to focus the lawyer's attention on key components of the case. Doing so helps the lawyer utilize the case either in a written brief or in preparing for oral arguments at a motion hearing or on appeal.

B. Preparation of a Case Brief

The most important aspect of briefing a case is reading the case carefully and repeatedly. Particularly for the new law student, it is likely impossible to write a good case brief as you are reading through the case the very first time. If you attempt to do so you will include unnecessary information. This is because information in the opinion that might appear to be highly important at first may turn out to have no bearing on the court's analysis or holding. *The best tip is to simply read the case through the first time without attempting to write the brief,* and perhaps without even marking the case or taking any notes. This first read should be to give you general familiarity with the case and the court's ultimate outcome. Once you have completed this first careful read of the case, you are ready to re-read the case and to draft your case brief.

Case briefs generally having the following sections: Facts, Procedural History, Issue, Rule, Analysis, and Holding. Variations and additional categories are added by some but are not always necessary. Let's explore each briefly.

1. Facts

The goal in this section of the brief is to recite the most critically important factual details providing the backdrop for the court's legal discussion. The goal is not to sharpen your typing skills by simply being a scrivener and re-writing all the facts that are already contained in the opinion. After all, you already have the case on the printed page with all the facts to begin with. Including all the facts in your case brief would serve no purpose.

Which facts to include depends upon the issues and analysis in the court's opinion. Some basic information is almost always helpful, such as the identity of the key parties, the nature of the case, and the basic story behind the issues. Whether the events took place on a Tuesday or Wednesday might be irrelevant. The dates of the events may or may not be important. The color of the car might be irrelevant while the color of a traffic light might be essential to recall, at least in a traffic intersection tort case.

2. Procedural History

It is useful to note the procedural posture of the case when the trial court ruled upon the issue that is the subject of the appellate opinion. Was it a preliminary motion to dismiss for failure to state a claim? Did the case come up for appeal following a summary judgment order? Did the trial court grant a judgment notwithstanding the jury's verdict? Is the appeal just an attack upon the sufficiency of the evidence underlying a final judgment following the jury trial? This should be succinctly stated in your case brief.

3. *Issue*

There is a reason the case was appealed. There is also a reason the author of your casebook included the case in the book. And there is a reason your professor assigned the case to read and cover in class. Identifying the primary legal issues in the opinion should help to reveal these reasons. Sometimes the court in its opinion will simply say, "The issue for resolution in this case is. . . ." In these cases, identifying and articulating the legal issue should be quite easy. But even if the court has not given you this cheat for your case brief writing, your careful reading of the case and understanding of the court's analysis should enable you to identify the question, or questions, the court is trying to resolve on appeal. It might be a purely legal question, such as "what level of intent is necessary in the State of Indiana to give rise to a cause of action for battery?" Other times it might involve the application of facts to the law, such as "did the defendant have a reasonable basis for his belief that force was necessary to defend himself from the threats of the plaintiff?"

4. *Rule*

Legal analysis necessarily involves applying legal principles or rules to the facts of the case. These rules of law may or may not be disputed in a particular case. In order to permit the analysis to proceed, the court must articulate the applicable legal rule that will guide the court's decision. What rule of law does the court invoke as the foundation for declaring the litigation winner and loser? In the context of a tort claim, often the legal rule involves some statement of the elements of the particular tort cause of action involved. For example, in the context of a tort claim for battery, a legal rule might be that one is not liable for battery unless she intends to cause a harmful contact to the plaintiff. Once the court has identified, clarified, or found the applicable legal rule it can then continue its analysis by applying the circumstances (i.e., the facts) of the case to that rule. Your brief should reference the guiding legal principle or rule used by the court.

5. *Analysis*

The analysis is arguably the most important aspect of the brief. It really answers the implicit question, "*why* did the court reach its holding in this case?" All law professors will spend considerable time during class addressing the court's analysis in a case, trying to understand the rationale for the court's opinion and for any rule of law or doctrine adopted or applied by the court. This is the most interesting aspect of case briefing and will provide the most help to you in understanding any given area of the law. The analysis will be critical to the course outline you prepare on a later date. Focusing upon the courts' analyses in the cases as you read through this book will also prepare you for your final exam, because a traditional torts essay exam demands that you be able to analyze in hypothetical factual contexts how a court would reach particular conclusions. You will do this by demonstrating familiarity with the rules of law and dexterity at using the facts to reach particular reasoned conclusions. Thus, at the intersection of the rules and the facts you find legal analysis.

6. Holding

The holding should provide the answer to the issue you articulated earlier in your case brief. It can often be stated as a "yes" or "no" with explanation. There can be two aspects to correctly stating the case holding. First, who prevails on the appeal on the primary issues? Second, what rule of law is the court choosing to provide the foundation for declaring the winner and loser of the appeal? For example, your statement of the holding to the issue from the preceding paragraph about the self-defense case might be: "Yes, the court ruled that the defendant did have a reasonable belief that his force was necessary, because the court held that information that was unavailable to the defendant at the time he acted cannot be used to undermine his assertion of self-defense."

How long your case brief needs to be depends upon the case. In general, your case brief should be substantially shorter than the court's opinion you are studying. Almost always it should comfortably fit on one typed page. But remember, the length of the effective case brief is not proportional to its quality. A good case brief should be as short as possible while communicating the basic information outlined above.

Upon Further Review

Despite its ancient roots, tort law continues to evolve as times and circumstances change. These changes can take many forms, from newly created causes of action, to discarded theories of liability and constantly tweaked doctrines and claims. These changes tend to occur at the intersection where relatively constant tort principles meet changed values, experiences, and even technology. This book will present both the *principles* underlying tort doctrines as well as demonstrate how these doctrines impact litigants seeking justice in the courtroom — the modern *practice* of tort law. Key concepts like the desire to compensate worthy victims, to punish wrongdoers, and to deter future harm can be seen throughout the many tort concepts you will study in this book. Look for these themes particularly when courts face difficult choices between competing doctrines.

While understanding core concepts and their application should strike you as worthy goals, your primary concern as you embark on this journey may be more practical. How do I read these cases? How do I prepare my case briefs? How do I avoid getting embarrassed on the first day of class when I hear my professor call my name? Although the above materials attempt to help answer some of these questions with detailed information, the *best advice is simply to pour yourself into the academic inquiry.* Try to absorb the law at both the macro and micro levels — be able to restate the elements of each tort cause of action quickly but, even more importantly, be prepared to explain the thought behind each of these elements. This will all take practice. Be patient with yourself and pay close attention to your professor. She has spent considerable time absorbing the material. Most importantly, enjoy the learning process. Law school should be a fascinating entry to your new, chosen profession.

CHAPTER 2

Intentional Torts

I OVERVIEW

Many torts classes begin with a study of a category of tort claims entitled "intentional torts." And this book will do likewise. This chapter will explore many of the classic intentional tort claims. These stalwarts of tort law include battery, assault, false imprisonment, and trespass. Another important, though relatively new, tort cause of action will also be covered in this chapter — intentional infliction of emotional distress.

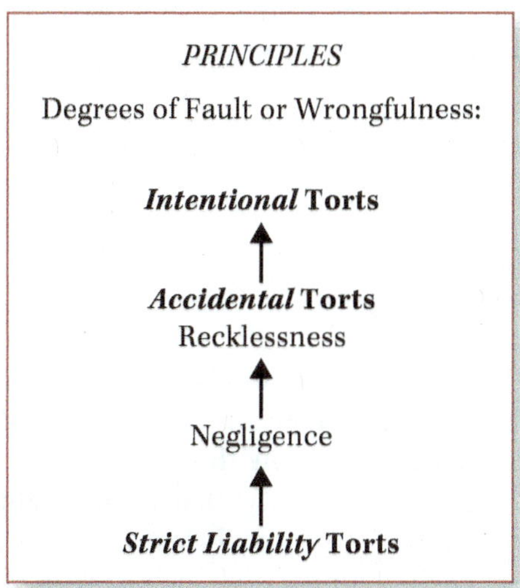

CHAPTER GOALS

- ☑ Become introduced to some of the oldest tort causes of action that involve a defendant who has intentionally engaged in certain behavior or intended a certain type of harm to the plaintiff's interests.
- ☑ Learn how to analyze the elements of a cause of action in varying factual circumstances to determine whether liability attaches.
- ☑ Appreciate the two-fold definition of intent that is employed in some manner in every intentional tort claim covered in this chapter.
- ☑ Understand for each intentional tort claim the different underlying interest at stake and why this is deemed worthy of the law's protection.

Beyond this category of intentional torts, two other general categories of tort claims exist: accidental torts (divided between claims involving recklessness and ordinary negligence) and strict liability torts (often called a "no fault" cause of action). These other varieties of tort claims will be covered in subsequent chapters.

Of the three broad categories of tort claims, intentional tort claims are *generally* considered to involve the worst, most reprehensible misconduct, though as you will see, this does not always ring true. This category is referred to as "intentional" because the tortfeasor must *intend something specific*, subjectively, in order to trigger liability. But exactly what it is that has to be intended by the tortfeasor varies widely among the various intentional tort claims. Some intentional tort claims require that something relatively bad be intended, such as "outrageous conduct," but others do not require such malevolent intent. The point is that for each intentional tort claim, as you are learning the elements of the claim, you need to pay close attention to what exactly must be intended, and what elements need not be intended.

Because intentional tort claims often involve quite reprehensible misconduct, in addition to claims for recovery of actual, "compensatory" damages, plaintiffs suing on intentional tort theories often include an additional prayer for "punitive" or exemplary damages. Such damages are covered extensively later in this book but, for now, just be aware that punitive damages are exceptional, awarded only in a small percentage of tort claims, and are designed specifically to punish the tortfeasor rather than to provide compensation to the tort victim.

II BATTERY

A. Introduction

Battery is a classic intentional tort. You have probably heard the phrase "assault and battery." Assault is technically a different, though related, tort from battery. You will need to learn how they are related but separate. Battery is designed to protect our bodily integrity; that is, our right to be free from certain unwanted physical contacts. We are daily faced with physical contacts from others, most of which are desired, unnoticed, or harmless. But certain other contacts might be physically harmful to us or unpleasant and disagreeable. The tort of battery recognizes that we are entitled to some level of autonomy over our own bodies. It provides redress where that autonomy is violated in certain ways. Pay close attention to the elements of this cause of action as you read the next set of cases. Also remember that the same notion of autonomy that gives rise to a tort claim for battery when we are subjected to unwanted contacts, also necessarily gives rise to the consent defense where we have permitted contacts to occur, even where they later turn out to be harmful. The separate defense of consent is covered along with other defenses to intentional torts in the next chapter.

B. Intent

The elements of a civil cause of action are those things that the plaintiff bears the burden of proving that are considered essential to the claim. If any element is lacking, the plaintiff's cause of action fails. You might consider the elements of a tort claim to be analogous to the necessary ingredients in a recipe. Leaving out one key ingredient means that you have not succeeded in preparing your dish. For each tort cause of action, you should look within the case opinions you are reading for some indication of the elements or key ingredients. In most of the cases the parties are disputing whether the factual record supports the existence of a particular element.

As already mentioned, every intentional tort claim requires something specific to be intended. How courts interpret and apply the word "intent" in the context of intentional torts is not entirely intuitive for law students. Battery is an intentional tort and our first case will begin to delineate what is meant in tort law by the word *intent.* One meaning — a desire to bring about a certain result — is the definition of intent you have used in your pre-law school life. There is an additional definition that might surprise you. The *Garratt* case below discusses these two traditional meanings of the word "intent." *These dual meanings apply with equal force to any intentional tort claim.* Thus, while different intentional tort claims involve something different being intended, once you grasp the concept of intent you will be equipped to analyze any intentional tort. With respect to the claim for battery, begin to focus upon what exactly must be intended. This will be a subject revisited within this section, as the final case on battery — *White v. Muniz* — will come back and provide an important final clarification.

GARRATT v. DAILEY

270 P.2d 1091 (Wash. 1955)

Hill, J.

The liability of an infant for an alleged battery is presented to this court for the first time. Brian Dailey (age five years, nine months) was visiting with Naomi Garratt, an adult and a sister of the plaintiff, Ruth Garratt, likewise an adult, in the backyard of the plaintiff's home, on July 16, 1951. It is plaintiff's contention that she came out into the backyard to talk with Naomi and that, as she started to sit down in a wood and canvas lawn chair, Brian deliberately pulled it out from under her. The only one of the three persons present so testifying was Naomi Garratt. (Ruth Garratt, the plaintiff, did not testify as to how or why she fell.) The trial court, unwilling to accept this testimony, adopted instead Brian Dailey's version of what happened, and made the following findings:

> III. . . . that while Naomi Garratt and Brian Dailey were in the back yard the plaintiff, Ruth Garratt, came out of her house into the back yard. Some time subsequent thereto defendant, Brian Dailey, picked up a lightly built wood and canvas lawn chair which was then and there located in the back yard of the above described premises, moved it sideways a few feet and seated himself therein, at which time he discovered the plaintiff, Ruth Garratt, about to sit down at the place where the lawn chair had formerly been, at which time he hurriedly got up from the chair and attempted to move it toward Ruth Garratt to aid her in sitting down in the chair; that due to the defendant's small size and lack of dexterity he was unable to get the lawn chair under the plaintiff in time to prevent her from falling to the ground. That plaintiff fell to the ground and sustained a fracture of her hip, and other injuries and damages as hereinafter set forth.
>
> IV. That the preponderance of the evidence in this case establishes that when the defendant, Brian Dailey, moved the chair in question *he did not have any wilful or unlawful purpose* in doing so; that *he did not have any intent to injure the plaintiff, or any intent to bring about any unauthorized or offensive contact with her person* or any objects appurtenant thereto; that the circumstances which immediately preceded the fall of the plaintiff established that the defendant, *Brian Dailey, did not have purpose, intent or design to perform a prank or to effect an assault and battery upon the person of the plaintiff.* (Italics ours, for a purpose hereinafter indicated.)

It is conceded that Ruth Garratt's fall resulted in a fractured hip and other painful and serious injuries. To obviate the necessity of a retrial in the event this court determines that she was entitled to a judgment against Brian Dailey, the amount of her damage was found to be eleven thousand dollars. Plaintiff appeals from a judgment dismissing the action and asks for the entry of a judgment in that amount or a new trial.

The authorities generally, but with certain notable exceptions (*See* Bohlen, *"Liability in Tort of Infants and Insane Persons,"* 23 Mich. L. Rev. 9), state that, when a minor has committed a tort with force, he is liable to be proceeded against as any other person would be. *Paul v. Hummel* (1868), 43 Mo. 119, 97 Am. Dec. 381; *Huchting v. Engel* (1863), 17 Wis. 237, 84 Am. Dec. 741; *Briese v. Maechtle* (1911), 146 Wis. 89, 130 N. W. 893; 1 Cooley on Torts (4th ed.) 194, §66; Prosser on Torts 1085, §108; 2 Kent's Commentaries 241; 27 Am. Jur. 812, Infants, §90.

In our analysis of the applicable law, we start with the basic premise that Brian, whether five or fifty-five, must have committed some wrongful act before he could be liable for appellant's injuries.

It is urged that Brian's action in moving the chair constituted a battery. A definition (not all-inclusive but sufficient for our purpose) of a battery is the intentional infliction of a harmful bodily contact upon another. The rule that determines liability for battery is given in 1 Restatement, Torts, 29, §13, as:

> An act which, directly or indirectly, is the legal cause of a harmful contact with another's person makes the actor liable to the other, if
>
> (a) the act is done with the intention of bringing about a harmful or offensive contact to the other, and
> (b) the contact is not consented to by the other [or the other's consent thereto is procured by fraud or duress], and
> (c) the contact is not otherwise privileged.

We have in this case no question of consent or privilege. We therefore proceed to an immediate consideration of intent and its place in the law of battery. In the comment on clause (a), the Restatement says:

> *Character of actor's intention.* In order that an act may be done with the intention of bringing about a harmful or offensive contact or an apprehension thereof to a particular person, either the other or a third person, the act must be done for the purpose of causing the contact or apprehension or with knowledge on the part of the actor that such contact or apprehension is substantially certain to be produced.

We have here the conceded volitional act of Brian, *i.e.*, the moving of a chair. Had the plaintiff proved to the satisfaction of the trial court that Brian moved the chair while she was in the act of sitting down, Brian's action would patently have been for the purpose or with the intent of causing the plaintiff's bodily contact with the ground, and she would be entitled to a judgment against him for the resulting damages. *Vosburg v. Putney* (1891), 80 Wis. 523, 50 N. W. 403; *Briese v. Maechtle, supra.*

The plaintiff based her case on that theory, and the trial court held that she failed in her proof and accepted Brian's version of the facts rather than that given by the eyewitness who testified for the plaintiff. After the trial court determined that the plaintiff had not established her theory of a battery (*i.e.*, that Brian had pulled the chair out from under the plaintiff while she was in the act of sitting down), it then became concerned with whether a battery was established under the facts as it found them to be.

In this connection, we quote another portion of the comment on the "Character of actor's intention," relating to clause (a) of the rule from the Restatement heretofore set forth:

> It is not enough that the act itself is intentionally done and this, even though the actor realizes or should realize that it contains a very grave risk of bringing about the contact or apprehension. Such realization may make the actor's conduct negligent or even reckless but unless he realizes that to a substantial certainty, the contact or apprehension will result, the actor has not that intention which is necessary to make him liable under the rule stated in this Section.

A battery would be established if, in addition to plaintiff's fall, it was proved that, when Brian moved the chair, he knew with substantial certainty that the plaintiff would attempt to sit down where the chair had been. If Brian had any of the intents which the trial court found, in the italicized portions of the findings of fact quoted above, that he did not have, he would of course have had the knowledge to which we have referred. The mere absence of any intent to injure the plaintiff or to play a prank on her or to embarrass her, or to commit an assault and battery on her would not absolve him from liability if in fact he had such knowledge. *Mercer v. Corbin* (1889), 117 Ind. 450, 20 N.E. 132, 3 L. R.A. 221. Without such knowledge, there would be nothing wrongful about Brian's act in moving the chair, and, there being no wrongful act, there would be no liability.

While a finding that Brian had no such knowledge can be inferred from the findings made, we believe that before the plaintiff's action in such a case should be dismissed there should be no question but that the trial court had passed upon that issue; hence, the case should be remanded for clarification of the findings to specifically cover the question of Brian's knowledge, because intent could be inferred therefrom. If the court finds that he had such knowledge, the necessary intent will be established and the plaintiff will be entitled to recover, even though there was no purpose to injure or embarrass the plaintiff. *Vosburg v. Putney, supra.* If Brian did not have such knowledge, there was no wrongful act by him, and the basic premise of liability on the theory of a battery was not established.

It will be noted that the law of battery as we have discussed it is the law applicable to adults, and no significance has been attached to the fact that Brian was a child less than six years of age when the alleged battery occurred. The only circumstance where Brian's age is of any consequence is in determining what he knew, and there his experience, capacity, and understanding are of course material.

From what has been said, it is clear that we find no merit in plaintiff's contention that we can direct the entry of a judgment for eleven thousand dollars in her favor on the record now before us.

Nor do we find any error in the record that warrants a new trial.

The cause is remanded for clarification, with instructions to make definite findings on the issue of whether Brian Dailey knew with substantial certainty that the plaintiff would attempt to sit down where the chair which he moved had been, and to change the judgment if the findings warrant it.

Remanded for clarification.

In Practice

Courts routinely hold that children can be liable for torts that they commit. More often than not, however, a child does not possess his own funds to pay a tort judgment. A homeowner's insurance policy can sometimes be required to pay, at least for accidental torts. Beyond this, parents under some circumstances, and in some states, can also be held accountable for the torts of their children. Often this is not automatic but might be triggered by the child acting in a willful or wanton manner. In any event, for now do not assume that parents are automatically liable for all tortious misbehavior by their children.

NOTES AND PROBLEMS

1. ***Intent.*** The court's opinion enumerates the elements of a common law civil tort claim for battery. Which of these elements was in dispute? The court describes two meanings to the word "intent" as used in tort law. What are those two meanings? Why did the court remand the case to the trial court? If you were the attorney for the plaintiff cross-examining Brian Garratt, what additional lines of inquiry might you pursue to prove he had the requisite intent?

2. ***Restatements.*** The court found certain passages from the Restatement of Torts persuasive in explaining the law of battery. The Restatement of Torts is not a statute that is controlling on the courts. It is written by scholars to try to explain common law principles as an aid to courts and the legal profession. Courts are free to accept its contents or reject it, and there are many examples of each such treatment. The Restatement of Torts (Second) has been highly persuasive. A third version has appeared in print but has not yet been as widely accepted by courts.

3. ***Problems.*** In which of the following circumstances do you think the evidence demonstrates the necessary intent to be liable for battery?

A. Tommy was a high school student who loved to play in the snow but was not very athletic. One day as he was having a snowball fight with some friends by the side of a highway, he noticed a car coming toward him with the driver's window down. On an impulsive whim he decided to throw a snowball at the driver, assuming there was no way he could hit an open window on a car driving so fast. To his surprise and horror, his snowball flew through the car's open window, hit the driver in the face and caused the car to crash into a tree.

B. A drunk driver was speeding through a school zone distracted as she attempted to find better tunes on the radio, when she struck a young child attempting to cross the street.

C. A pedestrian was walking on an elevated bridge that went over a busy interstate highway during rush hour traffic. As the pedestrian finished drinking his bottled beverage, he nonchalantly tossed it over the bridge railing. It fell and hit a motorist in a convertible, causing an irreparable eye injury.

WATERS v. BLACKSHEAR

591 N.E.2d 184 (Mass. 1992)

Wilkins, J.

On June 6, 1987, the minor defendant placed a firecracker in the left sneaker of the unsuspecting minor plaintiff Maurice Waters and lit the firecracker.

Maurice, who was then seven years old, sustained burn injuries. The defendant, also a minor, was somewhat older than Maurice [the court inferred he was one or two years older]. The defendant had been lighting firecrackers for about ten minutes before the incident, not holding them but tossing them on the ground and watching them ignite, jump, and spin.

Maurice and his mother now seek recovery in this action solely on the theory that the minor defendant was negligent. The judge instructed the jury, in terms that are not challenged on appeal, that the plaintiffs could recover only if the defendant's act was not intentional or purposeful and was negligent. The jury found for the plaintiffs, and judgment was entered accordingly. The trial judge then allowed the defendant's motion for judgment notwithstanding the verdict on the ground that the evidence showed intentional and not negligent conduct. We allowed the plaintiffs' application for direct appellate review and now affirm the judgment for the defendant.

We start with the established principle that intentional conduct cannot be negligent conduct and that negligent conduct cannot be intentional conduct. *Sabatinelli v. Butler*, 363 Mass. 565, 567 (1973). The only evidence of any conduct of the defendant on which liability could be based, on any theory, is that the defendant intentionally put a firecracker in one of Maurice's sneakers and lit the firecracker.

"Even a dog knows the difference between being tripped over and being kicked."

Oliver Wendell Holmes

The defendant's conduct was a battery, an intentional tort. *See Restatement (Second) of Torts §13* (1965) ("An actor is subject to liability to another for battery if [a] he acts intending to cause a harmful or offensive contact with the person of the other, and [b] a harmful contact with the person of the other directly or indirectly results"); 1 F.V. Harper, F. James, Jr., & O.S. Gray, Torts §3.3, at 272-273 (2d ed. 1986) ("to constitute a battery, the actor must have intended to bring about a harmful or offensive contact. A result is intended if the act is done for the purpose of accomplishing the result or with knowledge that to a substantial certainty such a result will ensue" [footnote omitted]); W.L. Prosser & W.P. Keeton Torts, §9, at 41 (5th ed. 1984) ("The act [of the defendant] must cause, and must be intended to cause, an unpermitted contact").

The intentional placing of the firecracker in Maurice's sneaker and the intentional lighting of the firecracker brought about a harmful contact that the defendant intended. The defendant may not have intended to cause the injuries that

Maurice sustained. The defendant may not have understood the seriousness of his conduct and all the harm that might result from it. These facts are not significant, however, in determining whether the defendant committed a battery. *See Horton v. Reaves,* 186 Colo. 149, 155 (1974) ("the extent of the resulting harm need not be intended, nor even foreseen"). The only permissible conclusion on the uncontroverted facts is that the defendant intended an unpermitted contact.

If the jury believed, as they must have, that the defendant did what the uncontroverted testimony indicated he did, as a matter of law the defendant acted intending to cause a harmful contact with Maurice. In short, there was no room for the jury to believe the uncontroverted evidence and to conclude nevertheless that the contact with Maurice was not intentionally harmful but was merely negligent.

NOTES AND PROBLEMS

In Practice

The one-bite-at-the-apple legal doctrine of *res judicata* (or "claim preclusion") prevents a plaintiff who has lost on one alleged cause of action from re-filing another related case based upon a different legal cause of action — so long as the claims arose out of the same incident.

1. ***Legal Theory.*** The plaintiff gets to choose which legal theory, or theories, to pursue for her claim. That theory may or may not prevail. In this case, the plaintiff chose to pursue a theory of an accidental tort, a negligence claim. The court inferred elsewhere in the opinion that this was due to the fact that the defendant had an insurance policy that provided for coverage for accidents but not for intentional torts. Plaintiff's strategy was based upon the pragmatic consideration that the defendant might not have sufficient assets to recover against other than a potentially applicable insurance policy. The court rejected the attempt to apply the theory of negligence because the court found that the defendant had, as a matter of law, committed an intentional tort instead.

2. ***Liability for Unintended Results.*** The court held that defendant might not have appreciated or intended the actual full results of his conduct — the severity of the burns. Nevertheless, the court held that his conduct would still constitute a battery. How does the court find that he had the requisite intent to be liable on an intentional tort theory even though the actual result obtained was possibly accidental?

3. ***Problem.*** What would be the result in *Waters* if the firecracker was a dud and failed to explode? Obviously this would reduce the damages obtainable, but would there still have been a battery? Consider the types of contacts that give rise to battery liability in light of the cases below.

C. Offensive, Indirect, and Intangible Contacts

The prior cases involve claims of wrongful conduct that resulted in harmful contacts. Courts have long held, however, that a battery would be recognized where the resulting contact involved offensive contacts as well. Even if the actor intends an offensive contact but physical harm results, liability will attach. There are some instances where a contact might be characterized as either harmful or offensive and the plaintiff's counsel might have strategic reasons to characterize it as one or the other. Finally, case law has also developed around instances where the contact involved was somewhat intangible or indirect, yet still harmful or offensive. Consider the nature of each of the types of contacts in the following three cases and whether it makes sense to hold the defendant liable for battery in each instance.

FISHER v. CARROUSEL MOTOR HOTEL, INC.

424 S.W.2d 627 (Tex. 1967)

GREENHILL, J.

This is a suit for actual and exemplary damages growing out of an alleged . . . battery. The plaintiff Fisher was a mathematician with the Data Processing Division of the Manned Spacecraft Center, an agency of the National Aeronautics and Space Agency, commonly called NASA, near Houston. The defendants were the Carrousel Motor Hotel, Inc., located in Houston, the Brass Ring Club, which is located in the Carrousel, and Robert W. Flynn, who as an employee of the Carrousel was the manager of the Brass Ring Club. Flynn died before the trial, and the suit proceeded as to the Carrousel and the Brass Ring. Trial was to a jury which found for the plaintiff Fisher. The trial court rendered judgment for the defendants notwithstanding the verdict. The Court of Civil Appeals affirmed. The question before this Court [is] whether there was evidence that an actionable battery was committed.

The plaintiff Fisher had been invited by Ampex Corporation and Defense Electronics to a one day's meeting regarding telemetry equipment at the Carrousel. The invitation included a luncheon. The guests were asked to reply by telephone whether they could attend the luncheon, and Fisher called in his acceptance. After the morning session, the group of 25 or 30 guests adjourned to the Brass Ring Club for lunch. The luncheon was buffet style, and Fisher stood in line with others and just ahead of a graduate student of Rice University who testified at the trial. As Fisher was about to be served, he was approached by Flynn, who snatched the plate from Fisher's hand and shouted that he, a Negro, could not be served in the club. Fisher testified that he was not actually touched, and did not testify that he suffered fear or apprehension of physical injury; but he did testify that he was highly embarrassed and hurt by Flynn's conduct in the presence of his associates.

The jury found that Flynn "forcibly dispossessed plaintiff of his dinner plate" and "shouted in a loud and offensive manner" that Fisher could not be served there, thus subjecting Fisher to humiliation and indignity. It was stipulated that Flynn was an employee of the Carrousel Hotel and, as such, managed the Brass Ring Club. The jury also found that Flynn acted maliciously and awarded Fisher $400 actual damages for his humiliation and indignity and $500 exemplary damages for Flynn's malicious conduct.

The Court of Civil Appeals held that there was no [battery] because there was no physical contact. However, it has long been settled . . . that actual physical contact is not necessary to constitute a battery, so long as there is contact with clothing or an object closely identified with the body. 1 Harper & James, The Law of Torts 216 (1956); *Restatement of Torts 2d, §§18* and *19.* In Prosser, Law of Torts 32 (3d Ed. 1964), it is said:

> The interest in freedom from intentional and unpermitted contacts with the plaintiff's person is protected by an action for the tort commonly called battery. The protection extends to any part of the body, or to anything which is attached to it and practically identified with it. Thus contact with the plaintiff's clothing, or with a cane, a paper, or any other object held in his hand will be sufficient. . . . The plaintiff's interest in the integrity of his person includes all those things which are in contact or connected with it.

Under the facts of this case, we have no difficulty in holding that the intentional grabbing of plaintiff's plate constituted a battery. The intentional snatching of an object from one's hand is as clearly an offensive invasion of his person as would be an actual contact with the body. "To constitute an assault and battery, it is not necessary to touch the plaintiff's body or even his clothing; knocking or snatching anything from plaintiff's hand or touching anything connected with his person, when done in an offensive manner, is sufficient." *Morgan v. Loyacomo,* 1 So. 2d 510 (Miss. 1941).

Such holding is not unique to the jurisprudence of this State. In *S.H. Kress & Co. v. Brashier,* 50 S.W.2d 922 (Tex. Civ. App. 1932, no writ), the defendant was held to have committed "an assault and trespass upon the person" by snatching a book from the plaintiff's hand. The jury findings in that case were that the defendant "dispossessed plaintiff of the book" and caused her to suffer "humiliation and indignity."

The rationale for holding an offensive contact with such an object to be a battery is explained in 1 Restatement of Torts 2d §18 (Comment p. 31) as follows:

> Since the essence of the plaintiff's grievance consists in the offense to the dignity involved in the unpermitted and intentional invasion of the inviolability of his person and not in any physical harm done to his body, it is not necessary that

> the plaintiff's actual body be disturbed. Unpermitted and intentional contacts with anything so connected with the body as to be customarily regarded as part of the other's person and therefore as partaking of its inviolability is actionable as an offensive contact with his person. There are some things such as clothing or a cane or, indeed, anything directly grasped by the hand which are so intimately connected with one's body as to be universally regarded as part of the person.

We hold, therefore, that the forceful dispossession of plaintiff Fisher's plate in an offensive manner was sufficient to constitute a battery, and the trial court erred in granting judgment notwithstanding the verdict on the issue of actual damages.

Damages for mental suffering are recoverable without the necessity for showing actual physical injury in a case of willful battery because the basis of that action is the unpermitted and intentional invasion of the plaintiff's person and not the actual harm done to the plaintiff's body. Restatement of Torts 2d §18. Personal indignity is the essence of an action for battery; and consequently the defendant is liable not only for contacts which do actual physical harm, but also for those which are offensive and insulting. Prosser, supra; *Wilson v. Orr*, 97 So. 133 (Ala. 1923). We hold, therefore, that plaintiff was entitled to actual damages for mental suffering due to the willful battery, even in the absence of any physical injury.

The judgments of the courts below are reversed, and judgment is here rendered for the plaintiff for $900 with interest from the date of the trial court's judgment, and for costs of this suit.

RICHARDSON v. HENNLY

434 S.E.2d 772 (Ga. 1993)

SMITH, J.

[Plaintiff Bonnie Richardson filed suit against her former employer and a co-worker alleging battery. The co-worker, J.R. Hennly, Jr., was successful in obtaining a summary judgment in the trial court. Plaintiff appeals from that order.]

The record reveals that Richardson had been working as a receptionist at First Federal for a number of years when Hennly, an administrative officer, began working at her branch. Richardson's work station was in the lobby of First Federal, and Hennly worked in an office approximately 30 feet from her desk. Hennly had been a pipe smoker for a number of years, and continued to smoke his pipe at work. Richardson immediately began to have difficulty with Hennly's pipe smoke, to which she apparently had an allergic reaction that caused nausea, stomach pain, loss of appetite, loss of weight, headaches, and anxiety. She discussed this problem with her superiors, and several air cleaners were purchased, which were placed in the interior of Hennly's office and adjacent to his door. For a time Hennly switched to cigarettes, which did not bother Richardson as much, but he resumed smoking his pipe, stating that he wished to avoid becoming addicted to cigarettes. Richardson was twice hospitalized because of her adverse reactions. Shortly after Richardson returned to work from her second hospitalization her employment was terminated, primarily for excessive absenteeism.

In opposition to the motion for summary judgment Richardson presented medical evidence attributing her adverse reactions to the pipe smoke. This evidence was not rebutted. It is uncontroverted that Hennly was aware of Richardson's adverse reactions to his pipe smoke and that she was twice hospitalized. The evidence is in conflict regarding whether Hennly ever smoked anywhere at work other than in his office; whether he intentionally smoked around Richardson to annoy her; and whether he made teasing or offensive remarks regarding his smoking.

Hennly moved for summary judgment as to Richardson's claim of battery on the ground that pipe smoke is an immaterial substance incapable of battering another. Richardson maintains the trial court erred by granting partial summary judgment to Hennly on this claim.

Our courts have recognized an interest in the inviolability of one's person and, along with most other jurisdictions have followed the common law rule that any unlawful touching is actionable as a battery. *Haile v. Pittman*, 389 S.E.2d 564 (Ga. 1989). Such a cause of action will lie even in the absence of direct physical contact between the actor and the injured party: "'The unlawful touching need not be direct, but may be indirect, as by the precipitation upon the body of a person of any material substance.'" *Hendricks v. Southern Bell Tel. &c. Co.*, 387 S.E.2d 593 (Ga. 1989).

We note that Richardson has not alleged that *any* or *all* smoke with which she came into contact would constitute battery. Instead, she has alleged that Hennly, knowing it would cause her to suffer an injurious reaction, intentionally and deliberately directed his pipe smoke at her *in order* to injure her or with conscious disregard of the knowledge that it would do so. We decline to hold that this allegation must fail as a matter of law. We are not prepared to accept Hennly's argument that pipe smoke is a substance so immaterial that it is incapable of being used to batter indirectly. Pipe smoke is visible; it is detectable through the senses and may be ingested or inhaled. It is capable of "touching" or making contact with one's person in a number of ways. Since no other element of the tort has been conclusively negated, Hennly has not shown as a matter of law that he is entitled to judgment. Moreover, a jury question remains regarding whether Hennly actually directed his pipe smoke at Richardson. We conclude . . . the trial court erred in granting summary judgment in favor of Hennly on the battery claim.

LEICHTMAN v. WLW JACOR COMMUNICATIONS, INC.

634 N.E.2d 697 (Ohio Ct. App. 1994)

Per Curiam.

The plaintiff-appellant, Ahron Leichtman, appeals from the trial court's order dismissing his complaint against the defendants-appellees, WLW Jacor Communications ("WLW"), William Cunningham and Andy Furman, for battery. . . . In his single assignment of error, Leichtman contends that his complaint was sufficient to state a claim upon which relief could be granted and, therefore, the trial court was in error when it granted the defendants' motion. We agree in part.

In his complaint, Leichtman claims to be "a nationally known" antismoking advocate. Leichtman alleges that, on the date of the Great American Smokeout, he was invited to appear on the WLW Bill Cunningham radio talk show to discuss the harmful effects of smoking and breathing secondary smoke. He also alleges that, while he was in the studio, Furman, another WLW talk-show host, lit a cigar and repeatedly blew smoke in Leichtman's face "for the purpose of causing physical discomfort, humiliation and distress."

Under the rules of notice pleading, Civ. R. 8(A)(1) requires only "a short and plain statement of the claim showing that the pleader is entitled to relief." When construing a complaint for failure to state a claim, under Civ. R. 12(B)(6), the court assumes that the factual allegations on the face of the complaint are true. Because it is so easy for the pleader to satisfy the standard of Civ. R. 8(A), few complaints are subject to dismissal.

Leichtman contends that Furman's intentional act constituted a battery. The Restatement of the Law 2d, Torts (1965), states:

> An actor is subject to liability to another for battery if:
>
> (a) he acts intending to cause a harmful or offensive contact with the person of the other, and
>
> (b) a harmful contact with the person of the other directly or indirectly results[; or]
>
> [c] an offensive contact with the person of the other directly or indirectly results.

In determining if a person is liable for a battery, the Supreme Court has adopted the rule that "[c]ontact which is offensive to a reasonable sense of personal dignity is offensive contact." *Love v. Port Clinton* (1988) 524 N.E.2d 166, 167. It has defined "offensive" to mean "disagreeable or nauseating or painful because of outrage to taste and sensibilities or affronting insultingness." *State v. Phipps* (1979), 389 N.E.2d 1128, 1131. Furthermore, tobacco smoke, as "particulate matter," has the physical properties capable of making contact.

As alleged in Leichtman's complaint, when Furman intentionally blew cigar smoke in Leichtman's face, under Ohio common law, he committed a battery. No matter how trivial the incident, a battery is actionable, even if damages are only one dollar. *Lacey v. Laird* (1956), 139 N.E.2d 25. The rationale is explained by Roscoe Pound in his essay "Liability": "[I]n civilized society men must be able to assume that others will do them no intentional injury — that others will commit no intentioned aggressions upon them." Pound, An Introduction to the Philosophy of Law (1922) 169.

Other jurisdictions also have concluded that a person can commit a battery by intentionally directing tobacco smoke at another. *Richardson v. Hennly* (Ga. App. 1993), 871, 434 S.E.2d 772, 774-775. We do not, however, adopt or lend credence to the theory of a "smoker's battery," which imposes liability if there is substantial certainty that exhaled smoke will predictably contact a nonsmoker. Ezra, *Smoker Battery: An Antidote to Second-Hand Smoke* (1990), 63 S. Cal. L. Rev. 1061, 1090. [W]hether the "substantial certainty" prong of intent from the Restatement of Torts translates to liability for secondary smoke via the intentional tort doctrine in employment cases as defined by the Supreme Court in *Fyffe v. Jeno's, Inc. (Ohio 1991),* 570 N.E.2d 1108, need not be decided here because Leichtman's claim for battery is based exclusively on Furman's commission of a deliberate act.

Arguably, trivial cases are responsible for an avalanche of lawsuits in the courts. They delay cases that are important to individuals and corporations and that involve important social issues. The result is justice denied to litigants and their counsel who must wait for their day in court.

This case emphasizes the need for some form of alternative dispute resolution operating totally outside the court system as a means to provide an attentive ear to the parties and a resolution of disputes in a nominal case. Some need a forum in which they can express corrosive contempt for another without dragging their antagonist through the expense inherent in a lawsuit. Until such an alternative forum is created, Leichtman's battery claim, previously knocked out by the trial judge in the first round, now survives round two to advance again through the courts into round three.

Judgment accordingly.

NOTES AND PROBLEMS

1. ***Harmful vs. Offensive Contacts Defined.*** The cases in the preceding section involved harmful or offensive contacts. Harmful contacts are defined by the Restatement as "any physical impairment of the condition of another's body, or physical pain or illness." Restatement (Second) of Torts §16. This is a fairly easy test for evaluating whether the resulting contact qualifies for a battery. Except in cases where the only claimed harm is the plaintiff's experience of pain, most harmful contacts are confirmed through objective evidence of the

harm — the bruised knee, the cut on the arm, the black eye, the missing limb, the burnt skin, or the gunshot wound. The test for an offensive contact is easily stated but tends to cause a bit more controversy in terms of its application. The test is considered to be objective rather than subjective, because it is generally insufficient if the only person to consider the contact offensive is the plaintiff. The Restatement indicates a contact is offensive only if it "offends a reasonable sense of dignity." The comments add that:

> In order that a contact be offensive to a reasonable sense of personal dignity, it must be one which would offend the ordinary person and as such one not unduly sensitive as to his personal dignity. It must, therefore, be a contact which is unwarranted by the social usages prevalent at the time and place at which it is inflicted.

Restatement (Second) of Torts §19, cmt. a (1965). Under these standards, would the contact involved in the preceding cases meet the test for a harmful or offensive contact, or both? As the courts have held, a battery can also be established by proof that the contact was offensive rather than harmful. Further, the *Fisher* court held that a battery was possible even with no actual physical contact with the plaintiff so long as contact occurred with an object closely associated and connected with the plaintiff. Can you imagine any contacts that might constitute both harmful and offensive contacts?

2. ***Indirect and Intangible Contacts.*** Deciding that smoke has physical properties and is capable of touching someone, the courts in *Hennley* and *Leichtman* permitted potential recoveries. Is there any risk of recognizing such intangible contacts as sufficient to impose battery liability? What about breathing on another person? While imposing liability for blowing smoke may seem a fair result in one case, do you recognize how expanding the tort in this manner creates uncertainty in terms of the potential application to other intangible contacts? Is this uncertainty and lack of predictability an acceptable price to pay for reaching what seems to be a fair result in one case?

3. ***Problems.***

A. Would the following contacts give rise to a claim for battery, assuming the other elements were satisfied? Might there be circumstances that might change your opinion?

1. Being spit upon.
2. A handshake.
3. A kiss upon the cheek.
4. A slap to the face.
5. A pat on the back.

B. In early 2017, a journalist received a Twitter message that read, "You deserve a seizure for your posts." When the message was clicked on, it triggered a blinding strobe light. The journalist was known to suffer from a form of epilepsy that is triggered by such lights. The man who sent the message apparently was aware of the journalist's condition and advised others of his desire to cause the journalist to suffer such a reaction. Reports indicate that the victim had been critical of President Trump and the man accused of sending the tweet was a vocal Trump supporter. Authorities explored criminal charges while the journalist filed a tort claim for battery. Should this type of behavior qualify as a battery? What barriers to recovery exist?

D. Scope of Liability for Battery

We have already seen in the *Waters v. Blackshear* case that courts will hold intentional tortfeasors liable even where the harm is greater in degree from that which was originally intended. A slightly more difficult question is whether liability for a battery will result when the *nature* of the contact intended is *qualitatively* different from that which actually occurs as a consequence of the defendant's action. In such an instance, does it even make sense to consider application of an intentional tort theory rather than an accidental tort such as negligence? The following case tackles this problem.

NELSON v. CARROLL

735 A.2d 1096 (Md. Ct. App. 1999)

Chasanow, J.

This case requires that we determine the extent to which a claim of accident may provide a defense to a civil action for battery arising out of a gunshot wound. Charles A. Nelson, the plaintiff in this case . . . asserts that the trial court should have held Albert Carroll . . . liable for the tort of battery as a matter of law, sending to the jury only the issue of damages. We agree with Nelson that a claim of "accident" provides no defense to a battery claim where the evidence is undisputed that Nelson was shot by Carroll as Carroll threatened and struck him on the side of his head with the handgun.

[The court summarized the facts as follows:]

Carroll shot Nelson in the stomach in the course of an altercation over a debt owed to Carroll by Nelson. The shooting occurred on the evening of July 25, 1992, in a private nightclub in Baltimore City that Nelson was patronizing. Carroll, who was described as being a 'little tipsy,' entered the club and demanded repayment by Nelson of the $3,800 balance of an $8,000 loan that Carroll had made to Nelson. Nelson immediately offered to make a payment on account but that was unsatisfactory to Carroll. At some point Carroll produced a handgun from his jacket.

Carroll did not testify. There were only two witnesses who described how the shooting came about, Nelson and Prestley Dukes (Dukes), a witness called by Carroll. Dukes testified that when Nelson did not give Carroll his money Carroll hit Nelson on the side of the head with the handgun and that, when Nelson did not 'respond,' Carroll 'went to hit him again, and when [Carroll] drawed back, the gun went off.' Nelson, in substance, testified that he tendered $2,300 to Carroll, that Carroll pulled out his pistol and said that he wanted all of his money, and that the next thing that Nelson knew, he heard a shot and saw that he was bleeding."

Carroll never testified. Because Prestley Dukes' testimony was the only evidence supporting Carroll's argument that his shooting of Nelson was an accident, we quote the relevant parts:

"**[Carroll's attorney]:** Tell me what happened [when Carroll entered the nightclub]?

[Dukes]: Well, when [Carroll] came in, he walked up and told [Nelson], asked him to give him his money. He didn't give it to him, so he hit him.

* * *

[Carroll's attorney]: Okay. Now, did [Carroll] have the gun out when he came into the club?

[Dukes]: Yes.

[Carroll's attorney]: Okay. And you say he hit him on the side of the head?

[Dukes]: Yeah.

[Carroll's attorney]: All right, and said, give me my money?

[Dukes]: Yeah.

[Carroll's attorney]: All right. And what happened then?

[Dukes]: Well. He didn't respond to that.

* * *

[Carroll's attorney]: Okay. [Nelson] didn't respond to it at all?

[Dukes]: No. He said, 'didn't you hear[] me; give me my money.'

[Carroll's attorney]: Okay.

[Dukes]: And went to hit him again, and when he drawed back, the gun went off."

On cross-examination, Dukes further testified:

"**[Nelson's attorney]:** How much had Mr. Carroll had to drink that evening?

[Dukes]: He had a little.

[Nelson's attorney]: He was drunk at that time, wasn't he?

[Dukes]: He was a little tipsy.

[Nelson's attorney]: And he was angry, too, wasn't he?

[Dukes]: I imagine he was. He hit him aside the head with that gun.

[Nelson's attorney]: All right. He was angry from the time he saw him, wasn't he? Is that correct?

[Dukes]: Yes.

Nelson testified to undergoing extensive medical treatment resulting from his gunshot wound. Immediately after being shot, Nelson lost consciousness as a result of blood loss and did not fully regain consciousness for three or four months, until November 1992. He continued to spend months in various hospitals and rehabilitation facilities, undergoing multiple operations. He testified to the nearly complete loss of his eyesight.

Nelson's sole contention before this Court is that he was entitled to a motion for judgment on the issue of liability for battery. He contends that the evidence that Carroll committed a battery is uncontested. Specifically, Nelson asserts that Carroll's primary defense on the issue of liability — that the discharge of the handgun was accidental — is unavailable under the circumstances of this case.

Preliminarily, it should be emphasized that the only defense raised by Carroll as to liability was that the actual shooting of the handgun was accidental. No evidence was produced to contest the other evidence relating to the course of events leading to the shooting. Carroll does not dispute the testimony that he was at the nightclub the night Nelson was shot, that he openly carried the handgun and confronted Nelson about a debt owed him, and that, out of anger, he struck Nelson with the handgun on the side of Nelson's head at least once. Nor did Carroll present any evidence that would conflict with the testimony that Carroll was responsible for firing the shot that struck Nelson. The only point made in Carroll's defense (and which apparently the jury believed) was that the actual gunshot occurred accidentally. Carroll's counsel specifically conceded in his closing argument that Carroll "shouldn't have gone in there with a gun. He was wrong. But what he intended to do was to scare him."

Since the only disputed fact relates to whether Carroll shot Nelson accidentally as he was striking him, we need only address the narrow question of whether, under the facts of this case, the defense that the shot was fired accidentally is capable of exonerating Carroll of liability.

A battery occurs when one intends a harmful or offensive contact with another without that person's consent. *See* Restatement (Second) of Torts §13 & cmt. *d* (1965). "The act in question must be some positive or affirmative action on the part of the defendant." *Saba v. Darling*, 575 A.2d 1240, 1242 (Md. 1990). *See also* Prosser & Keeton, The Law of Torts §9, at 39 (5th ed. 1984). A battery may occur through a defendant's direct or indirect contact with the plaintiff. In this case, Carroll unquestionably committed a battery when he struck Nelson on the side of his head with his handgun. Likewise, an indirect contact, such as occurs when a bullet strikes a victim, may constitute a battery. "It is enough that the defendant sets

Principles

In torts, the word "intent" means that the actor in question had either the subjective

- *Desire* (or motive) to bring about a result, or
- *Knowledge to a substantial certainty* that his actions would bring about such a result.

a force in motion which ultimately produces the result. . . ." Prosser & Keeton, The Law of Torts §9, at 40 (5th ed. 1984). Thus, if we assume the element of intent was present, Carroll also committed a battery when he discharged his handgun, striking Nelson with a bullet.

Nelson's action in the instant case focuses on the indirect contact of the bullet and not the battery that occurred when Carroll struck him on the head. It is the bullet that allegedly caused the harm for which Nelson seeks damages. As the analysis that follows suggests, however, the circumstances surrounding the gunshot are relevant in determining whether a battery occurred.

Carroll's defense that he accidentally discharged the handgun requires us to examine the "intent" requirement for the tort of battery. It is universally understood that some form of intent is required for battery. *See* Restatement (Second) of Torts §13 (1965) ("An actor is subject to liability to another for battery if . . . he acts *intending* to cause a harmful or offensive contact. . . ." (Emphasis added)); Prosser & Keeton, The Law of Torts §9, at 39 (5th ed. 1984) (Battery requires "an act *intended* to cause the plaintiff . . . to suffer such a contact. . . ." (Emphasis added)); Harper, James & Gray, The Law of Torts §3.3, at 3:9 (3d ed. 1996) ("To constitute a battery, the actor must have *intended* to bring about a harmful or offensive contact or to put the other party in apprehension thereof." (Emphasis added) (footnote omitted)). It is also clear, however, that the intent required is not a specific intent to cause the type of harm that occurred:

> The defendant's liability for the resulting harm extends, as in most other cases of intentional torts, to consequences which the defendant did not intend, and could not reasonably have foreseen, upon the obvious basis that it is better for unexpected losses to fall upon the intentional wrongdoer than upon the innocent victim.

Prosser & Keeton, The Law of Torts §9, at 40 (5th ed. 1984).

On the other hand, a purely accidental touching, or one caused by mere inadvertence, is not enough to establish the intent requirement for battery. *See, e.g., Steinman v. Laundry Co.*, 71 A. 517, 518 (Md. 1908) (finding a lack of intent for battery where "there [was] no pretense here that this contact of his knee with hers was wilful, angry or insolent, *and the only inference from her testimony is that it was purely accidental*, as in the case of one stumbling, and, in his fall coming in contact with the person of another." (Emphasis added).

The intent element of battery requires not a specific desire to bring about a certain result, but rather a general intent to unlawfully invade another's physical well being through a harmful or offensive contact or an apprehension of such a contact.

Thus, innocent conduct that accidentally or inadvertently results in a harmful or offensive contact with another will not give rise to liability, but one will be liable for such contact if it comes about as a result of the actor's volitional conduct where there is an intent to invade the other person's legally protected interests.

The only reasonable inference that can be drawn from the circumstances of this shooting, which in essence are uncontested, is that Carroll's actions evidenced an intent to commit a battery. Carroll presented no evidence disputing the fact that he carried a loaded handgun and that he struck Nelson on the head with the gun. The merely speculative evidence upon which Carroll claims the shot was an accident was Dukes' testimony that when Carroll "went to hit him again . . . the gun went off." In contrast, the evidence is undisputed that Carroll possessed a handgun which he openly carried into the nightclub, that Carroll struck Nelson with the handgun, and that the handgun discharged simultaneously as Carroll went to strike Nelson again. Indeed, taking every possible inference in favor of Carroll, the gunshot occurred as he attempted to strike Nelson with the gun. Under such circumstances, no reasonable inference can be drawn that Carroll lacked the required intent to commit the battery.

The law imposes upon Carroll the responsibility for losses associated with his wrongful actions. It is of no import that he may not have intended to actually shoot Nelson since the uncontested facts demonstrate that he did intend to invade Nelson's legally protected interests in not being physically harmed or assaulted. He violated those interests by committing an assault and battery when he threatened Nelson with the handgun and struck Nelson on the head. Even assuming as we must that Carroll did not intend to inflict the particular damages arising from the gunshot wound, it is more appropriate that those losses fall to Carroll as the wrongdoer than to Nelson as the innocent victim. Therefore, the motion for judgment as to liability should have been granted, with the only question remaining for the jury being the damages resulting from the discharge of the gun.

NOTES AND PROBLEMS

1. ***Intentional Torts and Accidents.*** The court believed the evidence was undisputed that the defendant intended to cause a harmful contact even though the favorable evidence also showed that the defendant did not intend to shoot the plaintiff. How can these observations be reconciled?

2. ***Liability for Unforeseen Results.*** To a certain extent the holding in this case is consistent with the holding in the *Blackshear* case involving the firecracker. If you represented the plaintiff in this case, how would you use the holding from *Blackshear* to argue for full liability here? If you represented the defendant in the *Nelson* case, how would you try to distinguish the *Blackshear* holding from this one? Lawyers make a living making such arguments, and recognizing when a new case presents an extension of prior law is a valuable skill to possess.

3. ***Proximate Cause Not Applicable.*** One of the traditional tests for proximate cause is a test of foreseeability — that one is only liable for harm that was reasonably foreseeable at the time of the defendant's misconduct. Chapter 5

will discuss this, and other, tests for proximate or "legal" causation in detail. The defendant in *Nelson* was, in effect, arguing for application of these proximate cause principles to the battery claim. However, proximate cause is historically not applied to intentional torts, at least not in the same manner as it is with claims for negligence. The court appropriately rejected this argument. The important concept is to remember when tort doctrines apply, and when they do not apply. We will explore proximate cause in some detail in the chapter on negligence. The Third Restatement reaffirms this principle of holding intentional tortfeasors liable for even unanticipated harms caused by their misconduct, stating that "An actor who intentionally . . . causes harm is subject to liability for a broader range of harms than the harms for which that actor would be liable if only acting negligently." Restatement (Third) of Torts §33(b). Illustration 2 to §33(b) provides an example of such broad liability:

> Mike, who suffered from manic depression, was injured while walking through a high-school parking lot by a bomb that exploded. The homemade bomb was placed there by Dick and Anna with the intent that it explode and harm those in the vicinity. A year after he was injured by the bomb, Mike committed suicide. Damages for Mike's death may be found by the factfinder to be within the scope of Dick's and Anna's liability for their intentional conduct. However, before Dick and Anna may be found liable for Mike's death, the factfinder must determine that the injury from the bomb was a factual cause of Mike's suicide.

Restatement (Third) of Torts, §33, Ill. 2 (2011). Notwithstanding these express rejections of such proximate cause limitations on liability for intentional torts, one can find some authorities that suggest that in some instances, a consequence of willful misconduct might be too far removed to create liability for the intentional tortfeasor. *See e.g.,* Thompson v. Hodges, 237 S.W.2d 757, 759 (Tex. Civ. App. — San Antonio, 1951) ("The law will presume that a person willfully assaulting another intends the direct and immediate consequences of his acts."); C.J.S., Damages §25b ("In the case of willful torts the wrongdoer is responsible for the direct and immediate consequences regardless of whether they might have been contemplated, foreseen, or expected.").

4. ***Problems.*** Should the actors below be liable under a theory of battery for the harms they caused?

- **A.** Alfonso, a renowned chef, bangs some pans together while cooking in his commercial kitchen, spilling boiling hot water onto another chef standing beside him.
- **B.** Meg, while driving under the influence of alcohol one evening, swerves too sharply around a corner and loses control of her car, causing it to crash into a small child running a lemonade stand by the sidewalk.
- **C.** Richard is upset with his brother-in-law, and in the heat of an argument, slaps him across the face. The brother-in-law is so upset by this that he immediately suffers a fatal heart attack.

E. The Single vs. Dual Intent Debate

As stated multiple times in the cases above, battery requires intent by the defendant to cause a harmful or offensive contact. But is it sufficient if the defendant intended to cause a non-harmful contact that turns out to be harmful? There is a whole category of cases involving benign hugs or other contacts where the defendant intends something like a harmless pat on the back of the plaintiff. But so long as the pat on the back is not consented to by the plaintiff, should the defendant be liable for any unforeseen ill effects of the touching? The following case highlights and discusses what is referred to as the debate between single intent and dual intent battery.

WHITE v. MUNIZ

999 P.2d 814 (Colo. 2000)

Kourlis, J.

Petitioner, Barbara White, as personal representative of the estate of Helen Everly [who died after the events in this case], appeals the decision of the court of appeals . . . which determined that a mentally incapacitated adult should be held liable for her intentional tort even if she was unable to appreciate the wrongfulness of her actions. We disagree with the court of appeals. Rather, we conclude that under the facts present in this case, in order to recover on a theory of intentional tort, the plaintiff, Sherry Lynn Muniz, was required to prove that Everly intended to commit an act and that Everly intended the act to result in a harmful or offensive contact.

In October of 1993, Barbara White placed her eighty-three-year-old grandmother, Helen Everly, in an assisted living facility, the Beatrice Hover Personal Care Center. Within a few days of admission, Everly started exhibiting erratic behavior. She became agitated easily, and occasionally acted aggressively toward others.

On November 21, 1993, the caregiver in charge of Everly's wing asked [plaintiff] Sherry Lynn Muniz, a shift supervisor at Hover, to change Everly's adult diaper. The caregiver informed Muniz that Everly was not cooperating in that effort. This did not surprise Muniz because she knew that Everly sometimes acted obstinately. Indeed, initially Everly refused to allow Muniz to change her diaper, but eventually Muniz thought that Everly relented. However, as Muniz reached toward the diaper, Everly struck Muniz on the jaw and ordered her out of the room.

The next day, Dr. Haven Howell, M.D. examined Everly at Longmont United Hospital. Dr. Howell deduced that "she [had] a progressive dementia with characteristic gradual loss of function, loss of higher cortical function including immediate and short term memory, impulse control and judgement." She diagnosed Everly with "primary degenerative dementia of the Alzheimer type, senile onset, with depression."

In November of 1994, Muniz filed suit alleging . . . battery against Everly, and negligence against Barbara and Timothy White. [The trial court dismissed the negligence claims before trial.] The case proceeded to a jury trial on March 17, 1997. While arguing outside the presence of the jury for specific jury instructions, the parties took differing positions on the mental state required to commit the alleged intentional torts. Muniz requested the following instruction: "A person who has been found incompetent may intend to do an act even if he or she lacked control of reason and acted unreasonably." White tendered a different instruction:

> A person intends to make a contact with another person if he or she does an act for the purpose of bringing about such a contact, whether or not he or she also intends that the contact be harmful or offensive. The intent must include some awareness of the natural consequences of intentional acts, and the person must appreciate the consequences of intentional acts, and the person must appreciate the offensiveness or wrongfulness of her acts.

The trial court settled on a slightly modified version of White's instruction. It read:

> A person intends to make a contact with another person if she does an act for the purpose of bringing about such a contact, whether or not she also intends that the contact be harmful or offensive.
>
> The fact that a person may suffer from Dementia, Alzheimer type, does not prevent a finding that she acted intentionally. You may find that she acted intentionally if she intended to do what she did, even though her reasons and motives were entirely irrational. *However, she must have appreciated the offensiveness of her conduct.*

(Emphasis added.) In selecting the instruction on intent, the trial court determined that Everly's condition rendered her mental state comparable to that of a child.

Muniz's counsel objected to the last sentence of the instruction, claiming that it misstated the law. He argued that the instruction improperly broadened the holding in *Horton v. Reaves,* 526 P.2d 304 (Colo. 1974), where the supreme court held that an infant must appreciate the offensiveness or wrongfulness of her conduct to be liable for an intentional tort. The jury rendered verdicts in favor of defendants Everly and White.

Principles

Even where an actor has been found not guilty of a crime by reason of insanity, this does not necessarily preclude a finding in a civil tort case that the same person had the sufficient mental capacity to be liable for an intentional tort. Criminal intent and civil intent are not necessarily the same thing in all contexts.

The court of appeals reversed the decision of the trial court and remanded the case for a new trial. The court of appeals reasoned that most states continue to hold mentally deficient plaintiffs liable for their intentional acts regardless of their ability to understand the offensiveness of their actions. The court of appeals reasoned that insanity may not be asserted as a defense to an intentional tort, and thus, concluded that the trial court erred in "instructing the jury that Everly must have appreciated the offensiveness of her conduct." Id. at 26.

The question we here address is whether an intentional tort requires some proof that the tortfeasor not only intended to contact another person, but also intended that the contact be harmful or offensive to the other person.

Historically, the intentional tort of battery required a subjective desire on the part of the tortfeasor to inflict a harmful or offensive contact on another. Thus, it was not enough that a person intentionally contacted another *resulting* in a harmful or offensive contact. Instead, the actor had to understand that his contact would be harmful or offensive. *See* Keeton, *supra,* §8; Dobbs, *supra,* §29. The actor need not have intended, however, the harm that actually resulted from his action. Thus, if a slight punch to the victim resulted in traumatic injuries, the actor would be liable for all the damages resulting from the battery even if he only intended to knock the wind out of the victim.

Juries may find it difficult to determine the mental state of an actor, but they may rely on circumstantial evidence in reaching their conclusion. No person can pinpoint the thoughts in the mind of another, but a jury can examine the facts to conclude what another must have been thinking. For example, a person of reasonable intelligence knows with substantial certainty that a stone thrown into a crowd will strike someone and result in an offensive or harmful contact to that person. Hence, if an actor of average intelligence performs such an act, the jury can determine that the actor had the requisite intent to cause a harmful or offensive contact, even though the actor denies having such thoughts.

More recently, some courts around the nation have abandoned this dual intent requirement in an intentional tort setting, that being an intent to contact and an intent that the contact be harmful or offensive, and have required only that the tortfeasor intend a contact with another that *results* in a harmful or offensive touching. *See Brzoska v. Olson,* 668 A.2d 1355, 1360 (Del. 1995) (stating that battery is an intentional, unpermitted contact on another which is harmful or offensive; and that the intent necessary for battery is the intent to contact the person); *White v. University of Idaho,* 797 P.2d 108, 111 (Idaho 1990) (determining that battery requires an intent to cause an unpermitted contact, not an intent to make a harmful or offensive contact). Under this view, a victim need only prove that a voluntary movement by the tortfeasor resulted in a contact which a reasonable person would find offensive [and] to which the victim did not consent. *See University of Idaho,* 797 P.2d at 111. These courts would find intent in contact to the back of a friend that results in a severe, unexpected injury even though the actor did not intend the contact to be harmful or offensive. The actor thus could be held liable for battery because a reasonable person would find an injury offensive or harmful, irrespective of the intent of the actor to harm or offend.

Courts occasionally have intertwined these two distinct understandings of the requisite intent. *See Brzoska,* 668 A.2d at 1360 (approving the Restatement view of the intent element of a battery, but summarizing the rule as "the intentional, unpermitted contact upon the person of another which *is* harmful or offensive") (emphasis added). In most instances when the defendant is a mentally alert adult, this commingling of definitions prejudices neither the plaintiff nor the defendant. However, when evaluating the culpability of particular classes of defendants, such as the very young and the mentally disabled, the intent required by a jurisdiction becomes critical.

In *Horton v. Reaves,* 526 P.2d 304 (Colo. 1974), we examined the jury instructions used to determine if a four-year-old boy and a three-year-old boy intentionally battered an infant when they dropped a baby who suffered skull injuries as a result. We held that although a child need not intend the resulting harm, the child must understand that the contact may be harmful in order to be held liable. Our conclusion comported with the Restatement's definition of intent; it did not state a new special rule for children, but applied the general rule to the context of an intentional tort of battery committed by a child. Because a child made the contact, the jury had to examine the objective evidence to determine if the child actors intended their actions to be offensive or harmful. This result complied with both the Colorado jury instruction at the time, and the definition of battery in the Restatement.

In this case, we have the opportunity to examine intent in the context of an injury inflicted by a mentally deficient, Alzheimer's patient. White seeks an extension of *Horton* to the mentally ill, and Muniz argues that a mere voluntary movement by Everly can constitute the requisite intent. We find that the law of Colorado requires the jury to conclude that the defendant both intended the contact and intended it to be harmful or offensive.

Because Colorado law requires a dual intent, we apply here the Restatement's definition of the term. As a result, we reject the arguments of Muniz and find that the trial court delivered an adequate instruction to the jury.

Operating in accordance with this instruction, the jury had to find that Everly appreciated the offensiveness of her conduct in order to be liable for the intentional tort of battery. It necessarily had to consider her mental capabilities in making such a finding, including her age, infirmity, education, skill, or any other characteristic as to which the jury had evidence. We presume that the jury "looked into the mind of Everly," and reasoned that Everly did not possess the necessary intent to commit an assault or a battery. *See Hall v. Walter,* 969 P.2d 224, 238 (Colo. 1998) (stating that the court presumes the jury followed instructions in reaching its verdict).

In Practice

Sometimes where an intentional theory is unavailing, a plaintiff might be able to craft a negligence cause of action — alleging that the defendant acted carelessly in causing the plaintiff's harm. The Federal Rules of Civil Procedure expressly permit pleading multiple claims as well as pleading claims in the alternative.

Fed. R. Civ. P. 8(d)(3).

A jury can, of course, find a mentally deficient person liable for an intentional tort, but in order to do so, the jury must find that the actor intended offensive or harmful consequences. As a result, insanity is not a defense to an intentional tort according to the ordinary use of that term, but is a characteristic, like infancy, that may make it more difficult to prove the intent element of battery. Our decision today does not create a special rule for the elderly, but applies Colorado's intent requirement in the context of a woman suffering the effects of Alzheimer's.

Contrary to Muniz's arguments, policy reasons do not compel a different result. Injured parties consistently have argued that even if the tortfeasor intended no harm or offense, "where one of two innocent persons must suffer a loss, it should be borne by the one who occasioned it." Keeton, *supra*, §135. Our decision may appear to erode that principle. Yet, our decision does not bar future injured persons from seeking compensation. Victims may still bring intentional tort actions against mentally disabled adults, but to prevail, they must prove all the elements of the alleged tort. Furthermore, because the mentally disabled are held to the reasonable person standard in negligence actions, victims may find relief more easily under a negligence cause of action. *See Johnson v. Lambotte,* 363 P.2d 165, 166 (1961).

With regard to the intent element of the intentional torts of assault and battery, we hold that regardless of the characteristics of the alleged tortfeasor, a plaintiff must prove that the actor desired to cause offensive or harmful consequences by his act. The plaintiff need not prove, however, that the actor intended the harm that actually results. Accordingly, we reverse the decision of the court of appeals and remand the case to that court for reinstatement of the jury verdict in favor of White and consideration of any remaining issues.

NOTES AND PROBLEMS

1. ***The Implications for the Debate.*** The court in *White* states that "in most instances when the defendant is a mentally alert adult," the choice between single and dual intent "prejudices neither the plaintiff nor the defendant." Is this statement more likely to be accurate when one is analyzing a claim involving a harmful contact or an offensive contact?

2. ***Friendly Unsolicited Hug Cases.*** If a piano professor walks up behind a student of his playing a piano at a social event and begins to tap on her shoulders, as if to demonstrate the proper technique to use in playing the instrument, and inadvertently hurts the student's back, will the professor be liable for battery? *See* White v. University of Idaho, 768 P.2d 827 (Idaho Ct. App. 1989), *aff'd,* 797 P.2d 108 (Idaho 1990). This case is analogous to the so-called friendly unsolicited hug cases, where one intends a benign, though unconsented, contact with another and causes harm. Do policy reasons support applying an intentional tort theory to such cases or would it make more sense to apply negligence law instead?

3. ***Irrational Intent.*** Another aspect of the trial court's instruction that was not challenged in *White* was the explanation that one could intend a result even if her motives were irrational. This is consistent with case law holding insane people liable for battery where they clearly intended to cause a harmful contact based upon the delusion that the victim was someone else. Polmatier v. Russ, 537 A.2d 468 (Conn. 1988) (holding defendant liable for battery where he shot his father-in-law multiple times based upon the delusion that the victim was a "spy for the red Chinese" sent to assassinate the defendant).

4. ***Problem: Interpreting a Jury Charge.*** Consider whether the following pattern of jury instruction seems to be describing a dual or single intent standard for battery liability: "A person commits a battery if he intentionally causes bodily injury to another." It's not always entirely clear, but the above charge infers that what must be intended is not just contact but bodily injury — dual intent. If a charge leaves the issue open it invites counsel for the parties to argue the case according to their own interpretation. Part of the job of judges in approving and submitting the charge to the jury is to avoid such debates from playing out during closing arguments by drafting instructions that clarify what the jury must find to impose liability.

5. ***Criminal Law vs. Civil Law Regarding Insanity.*** The law is fairly settled that in a civil tort suit, the defendant's status as insane is not a per se defense to a tort claim. So long as the defendant's mental status makes it possible for the elements of the cause of action to be satisfied, the defendant can remain fully liable for damages in tort. In criminal law, the opposite is often the case with legal insanity being a defense to many crimes.

Upon Further Review

Battery is designed to protect one's bodily integrity. Specifically, it provides redress for intentional invasions of one's bodily integrity that take the form of harmful or offensive contacts. Whether the contact is harmful or offensive is judged according to objective standards. Instances of harmful contact are usually obvious — cuts, bruises, broken bones, painful touching, or worse. Offensive contact requires not only that the plaintiff consider the touching distasteful, but also that a reasonable person under the circumstances would similarly find the contact distasteful. Every state requires that the defendant at least intended to bring about the physical contact. Accidental bumping, no matter how disastrous the consequences, is not a battery. Some states require also that the defendant must have intended for the contact to be harmful or appreciate that it would be considered offensive — the dual intent jurisdictions. But no jurisdiction requires that the defendant must have intended (or foreseen) all of the resulting harm that actually occurs. So long as the defendant intended any harm she is liable for all the harm that results.

III ASSAULT

A. Introduction

The torts of *assault* and *battery* go together like peas and carrots, being related but not identical. An assault can occur without a battery and vice versa. But often a tortfeasor's conduct will be actionable as both an assault and a battery. Unlike the interest in bodily integrity that is protected by a battery cause of action, the tort of assault is designed to protect the plaintiff's mind—specifically to provide redress for the defendant having created in the mind of the plaintiff an apprehension of an impending battery. Whether or not a battery occurs is of no consequence. If the apprehension occurs the defendant may be liable for assault in addition or in lieu of a battery cause of action.

B. The Elements

1. *Intent*

CULLISON v. MEDLEY

570 N.E.2d 27 (Ind. 1991)

KRAHULIK, J.

[Plaintiff] Dan R. Cullison petitions this Court to . . . reverse the trial court's entry of summary judgment against him and in favor of the [defendants] (collectively "the Medleys"). The Court of Appeals affirmed the entry of summary judgment. For the reasons set forth below, we . . . reverse the entry of summary judgment and remand to the trial court.

According to Cullison's deposition testimony, on February 2, 1986, he encountered Sandy, the 16-year-old daughter of Ernest, in a Linton, Indiana, grocery store parking lot. They exchanged pleasantries and Cullison invited her to have a Coke with him and to come to his home to talk further. A few hours later, someone knocked on the door of his mobile home. Cullison got out of bed and answered the door. He testified that he saw a person standing in the darkness who said that she wanted to talk to him. Cullison answered that he would have to get dressed because he had been in bed. Cullison went back to his bedroom, dressed, and returned to the darkened living room of his trailer. When he entered the living room and turned the lights on, he was confronted by Sandy Medley, as well as by father Ernest, brother Ron, mother Doris, and brother-in-law Terry Simmons. Ernest was on crutches due to knee surgery and had a revolver in a holster strapped to his thigh. Cullison testified that Sandy called him a "pervert" and told him he was "sick," mother Doris berated him while keeping her hand in her pocket, convincing Cullison that she also was carrying a pistol. Ron and Terry said nothing to Cullison, but their presence in his trailer home further intimidated him. Primarily, however, Cullison's attention was riveted to the gun carried by Ernest. Cullison testified that, while Ernest never withdrew the gun from his holster, he "grabbed for the gun a few times and shook the gun" at plaintiff while threatening to "jump astraddle" of Cullison if he did not leave Sandy alone. Cullison testified that Ernest "kept grabbing at it with his hand, like he was going to take it out," and "took it to mean he was going to shoot me" when Ernest threatened to "jump astraddle" of Cullison. Although no one actually touched Cullison, his testimony was that he feared he was about to be shot throughout the episode because Ernest kept moving his hand toward the gun as if to draw the revolver from the holster while threatening Cullison to leave Sandy alone.

As the Medleys were leaving, Cullison suffered chest pains and feared that he was having a heart attack. Approximately two months later, Cullison testified that Ernest glared at him in a menacing manner while again armed with a handgun at a restaurant in Linton. On one of these occasions, Ernest stood next to the booth where Cullison was seated while wearing a pistol and a holster approximately one foot from Cullison's face. Shortly after the incident at his home, Cullison learned that Ernest had previously shot a man. This added greatly to his fear and apprehension of Ernest on the later occasions when Ernest glared at him and stood next to the booth at which he was seated while armed with a handgun in a holster.

Cullison testified that as a result of the incident, he sought psychological counseling and therapy and continued to see a therapist for approximately 18 months. Additionally, Cullison sought psychiatric help and received prescription medication which prevented him from operating power tools or driving an automobile, thus injuring Cullison in his sole proprietorship construction business. Additionally, Cullison testified that he suffered from nervousness, depression, sleeplessness, inability to concentrate and impotency following his run-in with the Medleys.

In count two of his complaint, Cullison alleged an assault. The Court of Appeals decided that, because Ernest never removed his gun from the holster, his threat that he was going to "jump astraddle" of Cullison constituted conditional language which did not express any present intent to harm Cullison and, therefore, was not an assault. Further, the Court of Appeals decided that even if it were to find an assault, summary judgment was still appropriate because Cullison alleged only emotional distress and made no showing that the Medleys' actions were malicious, callous, or willful or that the alleged injuries he suffered were a foreseeable result of the Medleys' conduct. We disagree.

It is axiomatic that assault, unlike battery, is effectuated when one acts intending to cause a harmful or offensive contact with the person of the other or an imminent apprehension of such contact. Restatement (Second) of Torts §21 (1965). It is the right to be free from the apprehension of a battery which is protected by the tort action which we call an assault. As this Court held approximately 90 years ago in *Kline v. Kline*, 64 N.E. 9 (Ind. 1901), an assault constitutes "a touching of the mind, if not of the body." Because it is a touching of the mind, as opposed to the body, the damages which are recoverable for an assault are damages for mental trauma and distress. "Any act of such a nature as to excite an apprehension of a battery may constitute an assault. It is an assault to shake a fist under another's nose, to aim or strike at him with a weapon, or to hold it in a threatening position, to rise or advance to strike another, to surround him with a display of force. . . ." W. Prosser & J. Keaton, Prosser and Keaton on Torts §10 (5th ed. 1984). Additionally, the apprehension must be one which would normally be aroused in the mind of a reasonable person. Id. Finally, the tort is complete with the invasion of the plaintiff's mental peace.

The facts alleged and testified to by Cullison could, if believed, entitle him to recover for an assault against the Medleys. A jury could reasonably conclude that the Medleys intended to frighten Cullison by surrounding him in his trailer and threatening him with bodily harm while one of them was armed with a revolver, even if that revolver was not removed from the its holster. Cullison testified that Ernest kept grabbing at the pistol as if he were going to take it out, and that Cullison thought Ernest was going to shoot him. It is for the jury to determine whether Cullison's apprehension of being shot or otherwise injured was one which would normally be aroused in the mind of a reasonable person. It was error for the trial court to enter summary judgment on the count two allegation of assault.

For all of the reasons stated above, we hereby . . . reverse the entry of summary judgment . . . and remand this cause to the trial court.

NOTES AND PROBLEMS

1. ***Elements.*** Assault requires the defendant's voluntary action, coupled with an intent to cause the victim to suffer apprehension of an imminent harmful or offensive contact. As some courts have stated it less formally, an assault occurs when the defendant intends to cause the plaintiff to believe he is about to be battered.

2. ***Interest Protected.*** The interest protected by an assault claim is the victim's peace of mind. The tort provides a remedy for the intentional invasion of the victim's mind, which occurs when the defendant intentionally causes apprehension of an invasion of the plaintiff's bodily integrity. It is the touching of the mind, rather than the body, that distinguishes this tort from the related tort of battery. Given this interest, why was the intermediate court of appeals' reservation regarding the primary harm of the plaintiff misplaced? In terms of a recovery of actual damages, courts recognize the right of the assault victim to recover for the emotional harms caused by the assault, as well as any physical consequences of that emotional disturbance. For example, a plaintiff assaulted

by a defendant might incur psychiatric expenses, expenses for purchasing pharmaceutical products to contend with the emotional harm, and other medical expenses incurred due to physical ailments brought on by the fright.

3. ***Conditional Language.*** The court of appeals had ruled that the mere verbal threat to "jump astraddle" the plaintiff "if he did not leave Sandy alone" could not constitute an assault. There are many assault cases where courts have stated as black letter law that "words alone cannot constitute an assault." This is misleading because if there are sufficient surrounding circumstances, the defendant's utterance of certain words might actually meet the elements of assault. Suppose the defendant is holding a gun toward the plaintiff and then says "prepare to die!" Do you see how invoking the mantra "words alone cannot constitute an assault" would not satisfactorily lead to a defense for the defendant in that scenario? Words are always accompanied by some circumstances. The real test is whether, given the totality of the circumstances, including any words spoken by the defendant, the elements of the tort might be satisfied. The answer necessarily varies by the circumstances. Why did the Indiana Supreme Court find that the defendants' conduct, including the conditional threat, might satisfy the elements of the common law tort of assault? Was it a mere "future threat"?

4. ***Problem.*** Despising the plaintiff, and wanting to frighten him, the defendant stands behind the plaintiff and fires a weapon at his head but misses. The plaintiff is deaf and does not find out about the incident until another observer informs him of it. Upon confronting the defendant about the prior incident, the defendant states her plan to shoot the plaintiff the next time she sees him alone. Has an assault occurred?

"LADIES AND GENTLEMEN OF THE JURY . . ."

New Jersey Model Civil Jury Instructions

3.10 Assault

"An assault is an attempt or offer to touch or strike the person of another with unlawful force or violence."

Delaware Pattern Civil Jury Instructions

13.1 Assault

"If you find that [defendant] intentionally, and without [plaintiff's] consent, caused [plaintiff] to be in fear of an immediate harmful or offensive contact, then [defendant] is liable for assault. It is not necessary for any actual contact to have been made between the parties."

2. Reasonable Apprehension

For most courts, it is not enough that the plaintiff actually experiences apprehension of a battery. They also require that the plaintiff's apprehension be reasonable — that a reasonable person under their circumstances would likewise have experienced such apprehension. Thus both a subjective (the plaintiff's actual state of mind) and an objective (the hypothetical reasonable person's supposed state of mind) apprehension must be found before liability for an assault will attach. As you read the following spooky case, consider why courts would impose this additional qualification.

BOUTON v. ALLSTATE INS. CO.

491 So. 2d 56 (La. Ct. App. 1986)

SHORTESS, J.

This suit arose from the unfortunate events of Halloween night in 1981. Jeffrey Scott Trammel, aged 15, Robert Martin Landry, Jr., aged 13, and Daniel Breaux, aged 13, went trick-or-treating that evening. About 6:30 p.m., Trammel and Breaux rang Robert Bouton's (plaintiff) front door bell while Landry waited at the sidewalk. Plaintiff opened the door and saw Breaux standing before him. Breaux was dressed in military fatigues and was holding a plastic model submachine gun. Plaintiff shut the door immediately and locked it, then armed himself with a .357 magnum pistol. He returned to the door, opened it, and saw a flash of light, caused, he alleges, by Trammel's triggering a photographic flash. Plaintiff's pistol then discharged, the bullet striking and killing Breaux.

Plaintiff brought this suit against Allstate Insurance Company (Allstate), insurer of Landry and Breaux, and Independent Fire Insurance Company (Independent), insurer of Trammel. He alleged that the three boys' actions were tortious and caused him to be indicted and tried for second-degree murder, incur substantial attorney fees, lose his job, and suffer unfavorable publicity. [Plaintiff was ultimately acquitted in the criminal case. After filing his complaint in this civil case, defendants moved for summary judgment arguing that Plaintiff had no cause of action for assault. The trial court granted their motion.] From that action plaintiff brings this appeal.

Plaintiff claims that the boys committed an assault, causing him to become frightened and triggering the tragic series of events which ensued. Plaintiff must prove an intentional act by the defendants which would have put a person in reasonable apprehension of receiving a battery. *See Castiglione v. Galpin,* 325 So. 2d 725 (La. App. 4th Cir. 1976); *F. Stone, Tort Doctrine,* §§159 and 160 in 12 *Louisiana Civil Law Treatise* 206-207 (1977). We find that the pleadings and evidence fail to establish any right to relief because, under the facts as set out by the plaintiff, he could not have had a *reasonable* apprehension of an

In Practice

In the context of any tort claim, whenever you see the word "reasonable" used, it alludes to an objective determination based upon the fact finder's speculation about how a hypothetical, reasonable person would react to something. This reasonable person is discussed in length in Chapter 4 under the topic of Negligence. Even though the reasonable person is primarily a creation of negligence law, it is borrowed in multiple places even for intentional torts.

impending battery or physical harm. Although it is *possible* for one who opens his door to trick-or-treaters on Halloween to become so frightened that he believes a battery is imminent, under the circumstances here, such an apprehension is not reasonable. Any reasonable person expects to see an endless array of ghouls, beasts, and characters on this evening, especially when he is, as was plaintiff, passing out candy at his doorstep.

Plaintiff contends that "the sole determining issue in this case" is whether we judge the boys' actions from their point of view or from his. We do neither. Instead, "we place the average reasonable [man] in the very situation which confronted the plaintiff and ask of him oracularly" if an apprehension of a battery could be reasonably expected to follow from such a situation. *Stone*, at 209, §165. We do not believe that a reasonable person acting reasonably would have been apprehensive of a battery when confronted with this situation on Halloween. Therefore, we hold that plaintiff was not the victim of an assault.

[The court ruled that it need not address the issue of the boys' intent because the element of reasonable apprehension was lacking.]

For the foregoing reasons, the judgment of the trial court is affirmed at plaintiff's cost.

NOTES AND PROBLEMS

1. ***Reasonable Apprehension.*** This element of the assault cause of action actually contains two components — the actual (subjective) apprehension of the impending battery by the victim, and the conclusion that this apprehension was reasonable (objective) — that an ordinary person would have likewise experienced such a reaction. Which of the two was lacking according to the court in the *Bouton* case?

2. ***Fear vs. Apprehension.*** While many judicial opinions loosely use the words "fear" and "apprehension" as synonyms, technically an assault only requires the latter and not the former. This might seem to be mere semantics, but it is conceivable for an assault victim to have some apprehension, or appreciation of an impending battery, without actually being frightened by it. Perhaps the victim does not believe the battery will inflict significant harm. Or perhaps the victim feels confident in their ability to defend themselves. Perhaps they are like Jack Bauer from the television show "24" and possess great courage

and are afraid of no amount of physical pain. Nevertheless, Professor Prosser's view has been that an assault might still occur without fear: "Apprehension is not the same thing as fear, and the plaintiff is not deprived of his action merely because he is too courageous to be frightened or intimidated." Prosser, *The Law of Torts* §10 (5th ed. 1984). By the same token, an assault victim who admits to having no fear of the impending battery will not likely be awarded significant actual damages. While they may possess a claim based upon a technical violation of their rights and have a legal injury, their lack of actual harm will impact the amount of the award the defendant will have to pay. Indeed, their claim might be for nominal damages only — a token amount that signifies a wrongful violation of the plaintiff's right.

3. ***Problems.*** Consider whether the following situations would likely involve an assault:

A. Two high school students are attending the prom together. It is their first date. During one slow dance, the girl leans forward to kiss the boy unasked. He is repulsed and runs away.

B. Lucia is hiking in Rocky Mountain National Park when she sees a burly, bearded man named Jacques standing across a valley on the summit of the mountain she is hiking. He is yelling insults to "get off my mountain" and throwing rocks in her direction. The rocks fall harmlessly short by approximately one quarter of a mile. Lucia decides to abandon her hike rather than get any closer to the wild man.

3. Imminent Apprehension

The final qualification with respect to the elements of assault is that the apprehension must have been of an imminent battery. Courts universally dismiss assault claims based upon threats of a future battery. But just how imminent must the threatened battery be in order to qualify? The following case shows how strictly courts construe this final requirement. Consider the possible reasons for such a strict application of this element.

BROWER v. ACKERLY

943 P.2d 1141 (Wash. Ct. App. 1997)

Becker, J.

Jordan Brower, who alleges that Christopher and Theodore Ackerley made anonymous threatening telephone calls to him, appeals from a summary judgment dismissal of his claims against them. Because the threatened harm was insufficiently imminent to be actionable as civil assault, we hold the assault claim was appropriately dismissed.

The plaintiff, Jordan Brower, is a Seattle resident active in civic affairs. Christopher and Theodore Ackerley, in their early twenties at the time of the alleged telephone calls, are two sons of the founder of Ackerley Communications, Inc., a company engaged in various activities in Seattle including billboard advertising. Brower perceived billboard advertising as a visual blight. Based on his own investigation, he concluded that Ackerley Communications had erected numerous billboards without obtaining permits from the City of Seattle; had not given the City an accurate accounting of its billboards; and was maintaining a number of billboards that were not on the tax rolls. In January, 1991, Brower presented his findings to the City. When the City did not respond, Brower filed suit in October of 1991 against the City and Ackerley Communications seeking enforcement of the City's billboard regulations.

Within two days an anonymous male caller began what Brower describes as "a campaign of harassing telephone calls" to Brower's home that continued over a period of 20 months. The first time, the caller shouted at Brower in an aggressive, meanspirited voice to "get a life" and other words to that effect. Brower received at least one more harassing telephone call by January of 1992.

When the City agreed to pursue Brower's complaints about the billboard violations, Brower dropped his suit. In April of 1992, the City made a public announcement to the effect that Ackerley Communications had erected dozens of illegal billboards. Within a day of that announcement, Brower received an angry telephone call from a caller he identified as the same caller as the first call. In a loud, menacing voice, the caller told Brower that he should find a better way to spend his time. Two days later there was another call telling Brower to "give it up."

In July of 1992, shortly after the City Council passed a moratorium on billboard activity, Brower received another angry anonymous call. The male voice swore at him and said, "You think you're pretty smart, don't you?" Brower says he seriously wondered whether he was in any danger of physical harm from the caller. Over the following months Brower continued to receive calls from an unidentified male who he says "belittled me, told me what a rotten person I was, and who used offensive profanity."

On July 19, 1993, the City Council passed a new billboard ordinance. At about 6:30 that evening an angry-voiced man telephoned Brower and said "dick" in a loud voice and hung up. At about 7:30 p.m. the same caller called and said, "I'm going to find out where you live and I'm going to kick your ass." At 9:43 p.m. Brower received another call from a voice disguised to sound, in Brower's words, "eerie and sinister." The caller said "Ooooo, Jordan, oooo, you're finished; cut you in your sleep, you sack of shit." Brower recorded the last two calls on his telephone answering machine.

Brower made a complaint to the police, reporting that he was very frightened by these calls. Because Brower had activated a call trapping feature of his telephone service after the third telephone call, the police were able to learn that the call had originated in the residence of Christopher Ackerley. When contacted by the police, Christopher Ackerley denied making the calls. He said

Brower's telephone number was in his apartment, and that his brother Ted Ackerley had been in the apartment at the time and perhaps had made the calls.

The City filed no criminal charges based on the police report. Brower then brought this civil suit against Christopher and Theodore Ackerley seeking compensation for the emotional distress he suffered as the result of the telephone calls. According to Brower, he interpreted the calls of July 19 as a death threat, and felt "hunted down." He experienced feelings of panic, terror, and insecurity as well as a rising pulse, light-headedness, sweaty palms, sleeplessness, and an inability to concentrate that lasted for some time afterward: "Every day I come home, I worry that someone has burned our house down, or if my wife is late from work, whether she has been harmed."

The elements of civil assault have not been frequently addressed in Washington cases. The gist of the cause of action is "the victim's apprehension of imminent physical violence caused by the perpetrator's action or threat." In the 1910 case of *Howell v. Winters*, the Supreme Court relied on a definition provided in Cooley, Torts (3d ed.):

> An assault is an attempt, with unlawful force, to inflict bodily injuries upon another, accompanied with the apparent present ability to give effect to the attempt if not prevented. Such would be the raising of the hand in anger, with an apparent purpose to strike, and sufficiently near to enable the purpose to be carried into effect; the pointing of a loaded pistol at one who is in its range; the pointing of a pistol not loaded at one who is not aware of that fact and making an apparent attempt to shoot; shaking a whip or the fist in a man's face in anger; riding or running after him in threatening and hostile manner with a club or other weapon; and the like. The right that is invaded here indicates the nature of the wrong. Every person has a right to complete and perfect immunity from hostile assaults that threaten danger to his person; "A right to live in society without being put in fear of personal harm."

According to §31 of the Restatement, words alone are not enough to make an actor liable for assault "unless together with other acts or circumstances they put the other in reasonable apprehension of an imminent harmful or offensive contact with his person."

The Ackerleys argue that dismissal of Brower's assault claim was appropriate because the threatening words were unaccompanied by any physical acts or movements. Brower acknowledges that words alone cannot constitute an assault, but he contends the spoken

Principles

Courts frequently say that "words alone cannot constitute an assault," but then indicate that words, *coupled with the right circumstances*, might fulfill the elements of this claim. Of course, words are never uttered in a vacuum but in a particular set of circumstances. Interestingly, there are quite a few instances in tort law where the spoken word can become actionable as a tort cause of action. Beyond assault, where spoken threats might be actionable, words harming another's reputation might be considered defamation; false promises or representations might constitute fraud; intentional infliction of emotional distress might arise from repeated outrageous taunts directed at another; and even bad advice spoken by a lawyer to her client might constitute legal malpractice (a type of negligence).

threats became assaultive in view of the surrounding circumstances including the fact that the calls were made to his home, at night, creating the impression that the caller was stalking him.

Whether the repeated use of a telephone to make anonymous threats constitutes acts or circumstances sufficient to render the threats assaultive is an issue we need not resolve because we find another issue dispositive: the physical harm threatened in the telephone calls to Brower was not imminent.

To constitute civil assault, the threat must be of imminent harm. The Restatement's comment is to similar effect: "The apprehension created must be one of imminent contact, as distinguished from any contact in the future." [Restatement (Second) of Torts §29, comment b.] The Restatement gives the following illustration: "*A* threatens to shoot *B* and leaves the room with the express purpose of getting his revolver. *A* is not liable to *B*." [Restatement (Second) of Torts §29, comment c, illus. 4.]

The telephone calls received by Brower on July 19 contained two explicit threats: "I'm going to find out where you live and I'm going to kick your ass," and later, "you're finished; cut you in your sleep." The words threatened action in the near future, but not the imminent future. The immediacy of the threats was not greater than in the Restatement's illustration where *A* must leave the room to get his revolver. Because the threats, however frightening, were not accompanied by circumstances indicating that the caller was in a position to reach Brower and inflict physical violence "almost at once," we affirm the dismissal of the assault claim.

NOTES AND PROBLEMS

1. ***Imminent Battery.*** The court in *Brower* uses an illustration from the Restatement to find that the apprehension of the plaintiff was not of an imminent harmful contact, but one too remote to be actionable as assault. This case demonstrates that even a reasonable threat of a possible future battery will not be actionable as assault. Why would courts insist upon an imminent threat in order to provide a remedy? Aren't there some threats of such harm in the future that would cause an ordinary person to suffer great emotional distress?

2. ***Intentional Infliction of Emotional Distress.*** A tort we will be covering later in this chapter—intentional infliction of emotional distress—was also alleged by the plaintiff in this case. In a separate portion of the opinion, the court held that the plaintiff might be able to recover under that theory.

3. ***Highly Sensitive Plaintiff.*** Perhaps the plaintiffs in *Bouton* and *Brower* were unusually prone to being easily frightened. If so, under black letter law they would fail the test for having a "reasonable" apprehension of an imminent battery and be denied recovery. But what if a defendant acted on purpose to

cause such fright, with full knowledge of the plaintiff's unusual skittishness and with the desire to take advantage of the plaintiff's unusual sensitivity? Is it fair to deny recovery in such circumstances? If, for example, an associate of the eccentric Howard Hughes made an idle comment about planning to kiss him on the cheek to instill fear and cause Howard Hughes to give him a job promotion, should it be a defense that a reasonable person would have perceived no real threat and suffered no apprehension? While there are no reported cases involving such scenarios, some commentators believe that when the actor engages in conduct with full knowledge of the unusual sensitivity of the victim and for the purpose of instilling an apprehension of an imminent battery, liability for assault should be permitted as an exception to the normal rule requiring the apprehension to be reasonable. *See* Restatement of Torts (Second) §27, cmt. a (1965).

3. ***Problems.*** In which of the following scenarios can the plaintiff prove a reasonable apprehension of an imminent battery?

- **A.** Within a post office, one employee sitting at his desk looks up to see another enraged co-employee running toward him shouting, "I can't stand seeing you look at me anymore."
- **B.** A teenager finds a post on his Facebook page one evening from a jealous schoolmate saying, "you will not awake in the morning."
- **C.** An angry father threatens a boy dropping off his date on her front porch by saying, "If I ever see you on this property again you're going to get a whooping."
- **D.** As a senior citizen walks down a dark alley, a shadowy figure with a sinister smile steps in front of the senior citizen, brandishing a wooden stick.

C. Transfer of Intent

We have already seen how the intent generally associated with the torts of battery and assault are somewhat different — the former involving an intention to make harmful contact, and the latter involving the intention to cause the imminent apprehension of such contact. What happens if one intends a harmful contact and misses, but the other still experiences a reasonable apprehension of the near miss? Or what if the contact occurs but the victim, seeing the contact about to occur, experiences this apprehension? What about the person who merely intends to scare someone with such contact but accidentally hits the victim? Finally, what liability attaches if the defendant intends to hit Joe, but misses and hits Jane standing nearby instead? The following case helps to answer each of these hypothetical situations by discussing and applying the tort doctrine of transferred intent.

HALL v. MCBRYDE

919 P.2d 910 (Colo. Ct. App. 1996)

Hume, J.

Plaintiff, Eric Hall, appeals from a judgment entered in favor of defendant, Marcus McBryde (Marcus), on a claim of battery. . . .

On January 14, 1993, Marcus was at his parents' home with another youth after school. Although, at that time, Marcus was, pursuant to his parents' wishes, actually living in a different neighborhood with a relative and attending a different high school in the hope of avoiding gang-related problems, he had sought and received permission from his father to come to the McBryde house that day to retrieve some clothing. Prior to that date, Marcus had discovered a loaded gun hidden under the mattress of his parents' bed. James McBryde had purchased the gun sometime earlier.

Soon after midday, Marcus noticed some other youths in a car approaching the McBryde house, and he retrieved the gun from its hiding place. After one of the other youths began shooting towards the McBryde house, Marcus fired four shots toward the car containing the other youths.

During the exchange of gunfire one bullet struck plaintiff, who lived next to the McBryde residence, causing an injury to his abdomen that required extensive medical treatment. Although plaintiff testified that it was Marcus who shot him, the trial court made no finding as to whether plaintiff was struck by a bullet fired by Marcus.

[P]laintiff contends that the trial court erred in entering judgment for Marcus on the claim of battery. We agree.

An actor is subject to liability to another for battery if he or she acts intending to cause a harmful or offensive contact with the person of the other or a third person, or an imminent apprehension of such a contact, and a harmful or offensive contact with the person of the other directly or indirectly results. Restatement (Second) of Torts §§13, 18 (1965); W. Keeton, D. Dobbs, R. Keeton, D. Owen, Prosser & Keeton on the Law of Torts §9 (5th ed. 1985); *See Whitley v. Andersen,* 551 P.2d 1083 (Colo. App. 1976), aff'd, 570 P.2d 525 (Colo. 1977).

Principles

Battery = harmful touching of the *body*
Assault = harmful touching of the *mind*

Here, the trial court found that there was no evidence indicating that Marcus intended to shoot at plaintiff. Furthermore, based upon statements by Marcus that he was not purposely trying to hit the other youths but, instead, was shooting at their car, the trial court also determined that plaintiff had failed to prove Marcus intended to make contact with any person other than plaintiff. Based upon this second finding . . . the trial court concluded that the doctrine of transferred intent could not apply to create liability for battery upon plaintiff. We conclude that, in reaching its determination that no battery occurred, the trial court did not properly analyze the intent required for battery or the transferability of such intent.

As set forth above, the intent element for battery is satisfied if the actor either intends to cause a harmful or offensive contact or if the actor intends to cause an imminent apprehension of such contact. Moreover, with respect to the level of intent necessary for a battery and the transferability of such intent, Restatement (Second) of Torts §16 (1965) provides as follows:

> (1) If an act is done with the intention of inflicting upon another an offensive but not a harmful bodily contact, or of putting another in apprehension of either a harmful or offensive bodily contact, and such act causes a bodily contact to the other, the actor is liable to the other for a battery although the act was not done with the intention of bringing about the resulting bodily harm.
>
> (2) If an act is done with the intention of affecting a third person in the manner stated in Subsection (1), but causes a harmful bodily contact to another, the actor is liable to such other as fully as though he intended so to affect him. *See also* Restatement (Second) of Torts §20 (1965); *Alteiri v. Colasso,* 362 A.2d 798 (Conn. 1975) (when one intends an assault, then, if bodily injury results to someone other than the person whom the actor intended to put in apprehension of harm, it is a battery actionable by the injured person).

Here, the trial court considered only whether Marcus intended to inflict a contact upon the other youths. It did not consider whether Marcus intended to put the other youths in apprehension of a harmful or offensive bodily contact.

However, we conclude, as a matter of law, that by aiming and firing a loaded weapon at the automobile for the stated purpose of protecting his house, Marcus did intend to put the youths who occupied the vehicle in apprehension of a harmful or offensive bodily contact. Hence, pursuant to the rule set forth in Restatement (Second) of Torts §16(2) (1965), Marcus' intent to place other persons in apprehension of a harmful or offensive contact was sufficient to satisfy the intent requirement for battery against plaintiff.

Accordingly, we conclude that the cause must be remanded for additional findings as to whether the bullet that struck plaintiff was fired by Marcus. If the trial court finds that the bullet was fired by Marcus, it shall find in favor of plaintiff on the battery claim and enter judgment for damages as proven by plaintiff on that claim.

NOTES AND PROBLEMS

1. ***Transfer Between Torts and Persons.*** The transfer of intent doctrine helps to solve two different potential problems a victim might have, both illustrated by the *Hall* case. One problem was that the defendant did not intend to shoot anyone, yet was being sued for battery. The other problem was that the

defendant's conduct (i.e., trying to frighten those in the car) was directed toward someone other than the plaintiff.

2. ***Transfer of Intent Between Victims.*** Courts generally will apply the transfer of intent doctrine to permit the unintended victim to recover, so long as the defendant has the intent to commit the tort against another. You have seen several cases already where the court mentioned the policy of permitting the innocent victim to recover against someone who had the requisite bad intent. This policy is embodied in the transfer of intent doctrine as well.

3. ***Transfer of Intent Between Torts.*** Certainly courts will permit the intent to commit an assault to transfer to a battery cause of action, and vice versa. This makes sense because assault and battery are such related causes of action. Although there is some historic precedent for permitting this doctrine to apply among other intentional torts, modern application of this doctrine between torts other than assault and battery is very rare.

4. ***Self-defense.*** If the original intent was not wrongful there is no wrongful bad intent to transfer to another tort cause of action. The facts in *Hall* indicate a possible argument by the defendant of self-defense or defense of property. If such a defense were found valid on these facts, the plaintiff would be unable to recover against the defendant because the original action would have been justified. The defendant in *Hall* did not apparently raise such any such defense. These defenses, among others, are covered in the next chapter.

Watch "Office Prank" video on Casebook Connect.

Upon Further Review

The tort of assault protects one's particular state of mind — the right to be free from the imminent apprehension of being battered. This claim is often coupled with a battery cause of action when the apprehension is followed by the harmful or offensive contact. Because victims are often aware of the impending battery, assault claims are frequently coupled with battery claims; this coupling occurs so frequently that courts and lawyers commonly use the phrase "assault and battery." But remember that one claim might exist without the other. If you are on the receiving end of a harmful contact but did not know it was about to happen, you have a battery without an assault. And any time there is an attempted, but unsuccessful battery, there still might be an assault if the intended victim was aware of the near miss. The close relationship between these two particular torts is at the heart of the doctrine of transfer of intent.

 FALSE IMPRISONMENT

A. Introduction

The tort of false imprisonment is designed to protect and address intrusions on the victim's autonomy — specifically, threats to the victim's freedom to physically move from place to place. This tort claim has been recognized for a long time. We all face certain limitations on our movement. Twelve-year-olds cannot drive the family car, and must be physically present at school in their seat at 8:00 a.m. on Monday mornings. A mid-level manager has to arrive for work in a timely manner and stay at his desk except for lunch and bathroom breaks. You must generally stop at a red light and cannot proceed through the intersection, until granted permission by the green light. These intrusions are not the subject of this tort cause of action. As you read the following cases, try to distill the key elements of a false imprisonment claim that help to differentiate between inconveniences that our society tolerates, and misconduct that so threatens one's liberty interest as to give rise to a common law cause of action for false imprisonment.

B. The Elements

As you read the *Kern* case below, ask yourself what are the key ingredients in a claim for false imprisonment. Much of the dispute on appeal in *Kern* relates to a dispute as to what the tort involves. Specifically, the defendant sheriff asserts that his good faith precludes a finding of a false imprisonment. Plaintiff argues that the sheriff's good or bad faith is not material to the claim. Defendant contends that because he did not intend to commit any wrongful conduct, he cannot be liable for an intentional tort. Pay close attention to what must be intended for the tort of false imprisonment.

1. Intent to Detain

WILLIAM WHIRL v. C.V. (BUSTER) KERN

407 F.2d 781 (5th Cir. 1968)

GOLDBERG, J.

We review here, in an action for false imprisonment under Texas law the custodial derelictions of a Texas sheriff. The sheriff is accused of wrongfully overextending to an inmate of his jail the hospitality of his hostelry and the pleasure of his cuisine. The jury in the court below found for the sheriff. We reverse.

Harris County Sheriff C.V. "Buster" Kern, who served in office from 1949-1972, oversaw several large county jails.

The evidence in this case is largely undisputed. On September 9, 1962, the appellant, William Whirl, was arrested on suspicion of felony theft by the City of Houston police and placed in the Houston city jail. Two days later Whirl was transferred to the Harris County jail where he was booked, identified, and deprived, of the use of his artificial leg. On September 20, 1962, an examining trial was held and Whirl was bound over to the Harris County Grand Jury. Some weeks later the Grand Jury returned two indictments against him, one for burglary and one for theft.

On November 4, 1962, on the motion of the Harris County District Attorney, the indictments pending against Whirl were dismissed by a [criminal court] judge. The District Attorney had sought and obtained dismissal of the indictments on the grounds that the evidence against Whirl was "insufficient to obtain and sustain a conviction." The minutes of the court for November 5, 1962, recited the dismissal of the indictments, and a list of dismissals was then sent to the Sheriff's office, but the Sheriff who keeps the county jail testified that he was not apprised of these proceedings. As a result, Whirl languished in jail for almost nine months after all charges against him were dismissed, and was not restored to his freedom until July 25, 1963.

The breakdown in communication which led to Whirl's prolonged detention is not easy to trace. Documents are constantly transmitted among the courts, the District Clerk's office, the District Attorney's office, and the Sheriff's office, and recollection as to what happened in any particular instance is necessarily vague. Nevertheless, it is clear that the communication failure in Whirl's case occurred primarily between the District Clerk's office and the Sheriff's office.

Ordinarily, when charges are dismissed by a nolle prosequi, a member of the District Clerk's staff prepares a dismissal slip and forwards it to the Warrant Division of the Sheriff's office. Since the two offices are in the same building along with the jail, such communications are routinely made several times a day.

"*Nolle prosequi*" is a Latin phrase used to describe a formal entry upon the record by the prosecutor declaring that she "will not further prosecute" the matter — a voluntary dismissal of charges.

A record of the dismissals is also recorded in a journal or ledger kept in the District Clerk's office. This journal is sent to the Sheriff's office regularly, either separately or in conjunction with the dismissal slips, and receipt of the journal is acknowledged in writing by a sheriff's deputy. It is also customary for deputies in the Sheriff's office to make trips to the District Clerk's office in order to check the dismissal book themselves.

On the occasion following termination of charges against Whirl, dismissals had been rather numerous. As a result the Clerk's office prepared a list of cases which had been dismissed instead of the usual individual dismissal slip for each prisoner. This procedure, though rare, had been used before on similar occasions. Whirl's name was unquestionably included on that list, and the list was duly received by the Sheriff's office. Whirl's name was also entered in the dismissal book.

For some reason never adequately explained, the list of dismissals was not processed, and Whirl's freedom was lost in a shuffle of papers. Being too poor to raise bail, he was forced to remain in the courthouse lockup. Months later when attempts to set his case for trial prompted the District Attorney to check his file, it was discovered that all charges against him had been dismissed. Following his release, Whirl filed this suit.

Whirl brought his action against C.V. (Buster) Kern, the Sheriff of Harris County, Texas. Trial was to a jury. At the close of all the evidence, plaintiff moved for a directed verdict, and when his motion was denied, the case was submitted to the jury on special interrogatories as to negligence, contributory negligence, proximate cause, and damages. The jury found that Kern was not negligent in detaining Whirl in custody. It also found that Whirl was not contributorily negligent in failing to seek his own release, and that he had suffered no damages as a result of his imprisonment. On this appeal, Whirl contends that the district court erred in not granting his motion for a directed verdict and in denying his motion for a new trial as to damages. Appellant argues that all the elements of his cause of action under the Texas law of false imprisonment were established as a matter of law by the undisputed evidence, and that no fact issue apart from damages remained for the jury. He further argues that the jury's finding of no damages was contrary to the weight of the evidence and that the district court erred in instructing the jury to disregard the removal of appellant's artificial leg in assessing the extent of his injury.

Appellee, Kern, responds to these allegations of error by defending each act of the district court [by contending] that his incarceration of Whirl was entirely free of improper motive or unlawful intent.

We turn to appellant's contention that he was entitled as a matter of law to a directed verdict on the question of liability. Appellant's argument in brief is that the common law of false imprisonment [does not] require that a jailer have actual knowledge that his prisoner's incarceration is contrary to law. Whirl contends that negligence is not an element of false imprisonment and that the "good faith" of a jailer is neither a defense to nor a justification for an unlawful restraint.

While the issue of Sheriff Kern's "good faith" in confining Whirl in prison was never in so many words presented to the jury, we do not involve ourselves in the semantics of whether or not a finding of non-negligence is tantamount to a finding of good faith. As we read [prior case law] neither good faith nor non-negligence can exculpate Kern from liability.

[Cases relied upon by Sheriff Kern] were on their facts, false arrest cases and not false imprisonment cases. While it is certainly true that false arrest cases are often denominated actions for false imprisonment, false imprisonment deriving from an arrest and false imprisonment where no arrest has occurred are in substance quite different. Admittedly, a person who is falsely arrested is at the same time falsely imprisoned, *Fox v. McCurnin*, 1928, 218 N.W. 499, yet "it is not necessary, to commit false imprisonment, either to intend to make an arrest or actually to make an arrest." 32 Am. Jur. 2d, False Imprisonment, §2 (1968). "False arrest is merely one means of committing a false imprisonment." *Harrer v. Montgomery Ward & Co.*, 1950, 221 P.2d 428, 433.

In ascertaining whether the Supreme Court intended the defense of "good faith" to apply to false imprisonment as well as to false arrest, we must not allow a superficial similarity between essentially different causes of action to dictate the purpose which the good faith defense is meant to serve. There can be no quarrel with the fact that "good faith" in the circumstances of an arrest is a necessary and historically validated defense. As said by the Supreme Court, "A policeman's lot is not so unhappy that he must choose between being charged with dereliction of duty if he does not arrest when he has probable cause, and being mulcted in damages if he does." 386 U.S. at 555.

The reasons for this broad protection are clear. An arrest is often a stressful and unstable situation calling for discretion, speed, and on-the-spot evaluation. As a result, constabulary latitudinarianism is important, and peace officers are and must be endowed with privileges not accorded to ordinary citizens. In the words of the editors of the Restatement of Torts, Second:

> The additional privilege is given because the peace officer has a duty to the public to prevent crime and arrest criminals; the performance of these duties would be seriously impaired unless peace officers were given considerable discretion in their performance and protected from liability for the consequences of honest and reasonable mistakes.

§121, Comment (b) and (c) at 206.

Appellees urge that the above rule is their shield and protection. However, the breadth of a peace officer's privilege in an arrest situation is not necessarily the test of the breadth of a jailer's privilege in the context of a false imprisonment. There is no privilege in a jailer to keep a prisoner in jail beyond the period of his lawful sentence. While a jailer cannot be held liable for errors in a warrant of commitment fair and valid on its face, it is also the law that where a prisoner is held in jail without a court order or written mittimus, the jailer is liable for false imprisonment. The fact that the jailer is without personal knowledge that the prisoner is held unlawfully does not constitute a defense to an action for false imprisonment. In fact, "An illegal imprisonment must be treated as a wrong from its very inception, and it matters not on what date knowledge of such illegality is acquired." *Emanuele v. State*, 1964, 250 N.Y.S.2d 361, 366.

The case at bar is not, as appellees would have us view it, a case of justifiable reliance upon a warrant of commitment valid on its face. Cf. *Francis v. Lyman, supra*; *Peterson v. Lutz, supra*. The sheriff relied on nothing and his actions were not informed actions. Nor is this a situation where the dismissal of an indictment by a grand jury still leaves questions for judicial determination. Cf. *Lowry v. Thompson*, 1936, 184 S.E. 891 (Ga. App. 1936). Proceedings against Whirl were terminated by the actions of a court of competent jurisdiction. While not easily characterized, the case at bar seems to us closest to the situation where the jailer keeps a prisoner beyond the lawful term of his sentence. In such circumstance, as in the one before us, ignorance of the law is no excuse.

We do not find any cases nor are we referred to any by counsel which provide that "good faith" is a defense to an imprisonment that is not only without valid process, but contrary to it. Nor do we believe as a matter of federal policy that such a defense should be available to a jailer in circumstances like those before us. The responsibility for a failure of communication between the courts and the jailhouse cannot justifiably be placed on the head of a man immured in a lockup when the action of the court has become a matter of public record. Ignorance and alibis by a jailer should not vitiate the rights of a man entitled to his freedom. A jailer, unlike a policeman, acts at his leisure. He is not subject to the stresses and split second decisions of an arresting officer, and his acts in discharging a prisoner are purely ministerial. Moreover, unlike his prisoner, the jailer has the means, the freedom, and the duty to make necessary inquiries. While not a surety for the legal correctness of a prisoner's commitment, he is most certainly under an obligation, often statutory, to carry out the functions of his office. Those functions include not only the duty to protect a prisoner, but also the duty to effect his timely release.

The central issue in this case is one of privilege, not of intent; one of law, not of fact. The tort of false imprisonment is an intentional tort. Restatement of Torts, Second, §44. It is committed when a man intentionally deprives another of his liberty without the other's consent and without adequate legal justification. *Roberts v. Hecht Co.*, 280 F. Supp. 639, 640 (D. Md. 1968); *Browning v. Pay-Less Self Service Shoes, Inc.*, 373 S.W.2d 71 (1963 Tex. Civ. App., no writ). Failure to know of a court proceeding terminating all charges against one held in custody is not, as a matter of law, adequate legal justification for an unauthorized restraint. Were the law otherwise, Whirl's nine months could easily be nine years, and those nine years, ninety-nine years, and still as a matter of law no redress would follow. The law does not hold the value of a man's freedom in such low regard.

The sheriff, of course, must have some protection too. His duty to his prisoner is not breached until the expiration of a reasonable time for the proper ascertainment of the authority upon which his prisoner is detained. We are not to be interpreted as holding that a sheriff commits an instant tort at the moment when his prisoner should have been released. However, in the present case what is or is not a reasonable time is not at issue. It may safely be said that Kern's ignorance for nine long months after the termination of all proceedings against Whirl was, as a matter of law, ignorance for an unreasonable time.

The Texas law of false imprisonment zealously safeguards the rights of citizens to be free of unlawful arrest and unlawful prison detention. Persons found guilty of false imprisonment are subject to both criminal and civil penalties.

Good faith may clear the conscience, but it does not redeem or purge the act. [T]he duty to release is absolute if no such authority exists, and such duty cannot be conditioned on notice, solicitation, ignorance or blindness. Ignorance of the law is traditionally no excuse, even when a man's own liberty is at stake. Should it be a defense for officers of the law whose sworn duty it is to protect the liberty of others? Are a sheriff's statutory obligations to be effective only when he acts in willful disobedience of his official responsibilities?

The evidence is undisputed that Kern could have known of the dismissal of charges against Whirl had he only made inquiry. But inquiry he did not make, and as a consequence Whirl, quasi-literate and one-legged, languished in jail for nine months after he was entitled to be free of his fetters. Unfortunately, non-malicious restraint is no sweeter than restraint evilly motivated, and we cannot sanction chains without legal justification even if they be forged by the hand of an angel. Neither the sheriff's tears of regret nor explanations keyed the lock to unmanacle Whirl. Though we apply all the benign adjectives in our lexicon to Kern's watchmanship — these do not make Whirl a November to July free man.

As we understand the Texas law of false imprisonment, read in conjunction with the statutory duties of the sheriff as keeper of the county jail, non-negligence is no modifier of liability. Sheriff Kern had an unyielding duty to know his prisoner's sentence time, and this duty was not discharged.

Viewed on one level, the facts of this case involve nothing more grandiloquent than paper pushing between officers in the Harris County Courthouse. Yet we must never forget that we are dealing with a man's liberty, and a game of who has the paper and who saw the paper is not constitutionally playable. This must be borne in mind in the assessment of damages. Traditionally the fact of an illegal restraint creates the right to recover at least *nominal* damages. Perhaps in some circumstances that is all a man's freedom is worth, but though the price tag be a bargain, freedom is never valueless. A jury finding that a man's freedom is worthless is clearly erroneous. It is an impossible judgment to render against a sentient person, be he one legged, unschooled, friendless or without earning capacity.

There is the promise outstanding that the courts will redress the false imprisonment of any man, "no matter how poor or obscure, and no matter what may be his station in life." *McBeath v. Campbell, supra*, 12 S.W.2d at 122. Let that promise be fulfilled.

Reversed and remanded.

"LADIES AND GENTLEMEN OF THE JURY . . ."

Texas Pattern Jury Charge 6.1: False Imprisonment

Did Don David falsely imprison Paul Payne?

"Falsely imprison" means to willfully detain another person without legal justification, against his consent, whether such detention be effected by violence, by threat, or by any other means that restrains a person from moving from one place to another.

Texas Pattern Jury Charge 6.2: Unlawful Detention by Threat

"Detention by threat, violence, or other means" requires proof that the threat was such as would inspire in an ordinary person just fear of injury to his person, reputation or property.

NOTES AND PROBLEMS

1. ***Roles of Judges and Juries.*** Most tort cases that survive the pretrial motion process are submitted to juries for final resolution. Juries are considered the "judges of the facts," which means that they are to determine the true facts that gave rise to a claim. In fact, their job is somewhat broader than this sounds. In reality, they are charged with applying the law to the evidence to determine if a cause of action should prevail or not. So long as the trial judge believes that a rational jury might find for either party, there exists what is called in Civil Procedure a "genuine issue of material fact." This is why parties have trials — to determine what really happened. Where the important facts are undisputed, the judge can declare the litigation winner by applying the law to those facts. In submitting a case to a jury, the judge will often rely upon pattern jury instructions that attempt to summarize the law to the jury. In the *Kern* case, above, the court decided that the elements of the tort claim of false imprisonment did not require any attention from the jury because the important facts were not disputed. At the end of the opinion, the court reverses the judgment that had been rendered for the defendant and remands the case solely for a new trial on the issue of damages.

2. ***Criminal vs. Civil Law.*** One potential area of confusion from this case is the interplay between criminal law and procedure, and our civil tort system. How does the status of the criminal charges impact the accrual of a civil cause of action in this case for false imprisonment? Further, how might the same conduct give rise to both a criminal prosecution and a civil cause of action? What would be the purpose of permitting both criminal and civil cases to proceed against the same person?

3. ***Timing.*** The sequence of events is important in this case. At what point was plaintiff first detained? Did he have a tort cause of action at this moment? If not, at what point in his detention does the tort claim arise? Notice that the court characterizes the *Whirl* case as being one about "privilege." While it was clear that the defendant intended to detain the plaintiff, this was privileged for so long as charges were pending.

In Practice

Lawyers and judges alike often place great reliance upon published "pattern" jury instructions. Lawyers tend to pull proposed instructions from such published materials to submit to the court as proposed instructions. They are not authoritative statements of the law, but a pretty reliable source of how the law should be explained to the jury. Judges routinely place great value on their accuracy in preparing the final instructions to give to the jury.

4. ***Good Faith.*** Why does the availability of a "good faith" defense exist in a false arrest claim but not in a false imprisonment claim? The arresting officer has a privilege to detain in order to make the arrest, which is something that must occur at once. As a matter of public policy, do we want officers to be able to detain others even where there is the possibility of innocence? Consider the different functions of the arresting officer and the prison warden, and to what extent each is under time pressure to make the decision of whether to effectuate or continue detention.

5. ***Accidents as Intentional Torts.*** It may be difficult to comprehend how someone like the plaintiff could simply fall between the cracks for nine months. Of course, the Harris County Sheriff's Office is a very large operation. It is the third largest sheriff's office in the United States, behind Los Angeles and Cook County (Illinois), and currently employs over 3,500 staff overseeing 11,000 prisoners at any one time. This might help to explain the accidental over-detention of the plaintiff. Since all indications are that the defendant in this case was not trying to do any wrong, why was an intentional tort theory applicable? For any particular intentional tort claim, you must be precise in your understanding as to what exactly must be intended. For the intentional tort of false imprisonment, courts agree that all that must be intended is the detention. There is no requirement that the detention occur maliciously or with some evil intent. The Restatement (Second) of Torts §8(A) defines the intent, or degree of willfulness, needed in an intentional tort claim as follows: "Intent . . . [is when] the actor desires to cause consequences of his act, or . . . believes that the consequences are substantially certain to result from it." Why are the facts undisputed with regard to the defendant's intent to detain the plaintiff in *Whirl*?

6. ***Damages.*** The subject of awarding damages, whether compensatory, nominal, or punitive, is covered in Chapter 8 of this book. Many damage principles apply across the lines of various tort causes of action. But sometimes there are particular damage rules that uniquely apply to a particular cause of action. In another portion of the *Kern* opinion, the court indicated that the different type of damages that might be recoverable for false imprisonment could include pain and suffering, emotional distress, and lost earnings while incarcerated. In addition, the court mentions the availability of *nominal damages*—damages in "name only" that are a token award in the absence of actual harm to at least provide some philosophical vindication of the plaintiff's rights. These damage concepts are covered in substantial detail later in Chapter 8 of this book.

7. ***Problem.*** Before you begin thinking that the facts in *Kern* are so bizarre that the case has little real-world application, consider the facts from the more recent incident at the McLennan County jail in Waco, Texas in 2012. At the end of the newspaper story set forth on the following page, the lawyer for the wrongly incarcerated gentlemen indicates he will consider exploring a possible civil tort claim for false imprisonment. If you were the lawyer, after reading the *Kern* decision, what would your advice be?

Waco Tribune-Herald

Waco Man Wrongly Jailed for 83 Days May Sue County

By TOMMY WITHERSPOON

A Waco man is deciding if he will sue the county because he was wrongfully detained for 83 days after the district attorney's office declined his case for prosecution but failed to notify the McLennan County Jail.

Damion Wayne Evans, 33, stayed in the county jail with no other charges pending against him for almost three months after the district attorney's office declined to prosecute him on a tampering with physical evidence charge.

District Attorney Abel Reyna said Evans' improperly extended incarceration was the fault of his office. His staff did not fax a case disposition report to the sheriff's office so it would know to release Evans.

"I will accept responsibility for the error in my office, and my apologies go to Mr. Evans," Reyna said. "Though it doesn't change what happened to him, the only thing I can do is work hard to make sure it doesn't happen again."

The decision to refuse the case was made Oct. 25, two weeks after Evans' arrest. Once that decision was made, the disposition report should have been sent to the jail and Evans should have been released, Reyna said.

But the error was not discovered until Jan. 17, after Evans' attorney, David Bass, filed a motion asking Judge Ralph Strother to set a bail Evans could afford because he had been in jail more than 90 days and had not been indicted.

"The normal thing that happens is they send over a disposition report to the jail that the case was not accepted on this particular date, and if there are no other holds on him, they turn him loose," Bass said.

"That is what is supposed to happen in a perfect world, but that is not what happened in Mr. Evans' world. He spent Halloween, Thanksgiving, Christmas and New Year's locked up when he shouldn't have been," Bass said.

He said he referred Evans to Waco attorney James Rainey for possible civil legal action.

"I am going to investigate the matter to determine what happened, why it happened and figure out what recourse, if any, Mr. Evans has for his civil rights violations and his false imprisonment," Rainey said Tuesday.

(February 1, 2012)

2. Detention

In *Kern*, the fact that the defendant had "detained" the plaintiff was pretty obvious — if actual imprisonment will not suffice for false imprisonment, then nothing would. In the following case, the plaintiff argues that he was detained when defendant made it difficult for him to be transported in the time and manner he desired. Consider the implications if the court were to rule in favor of the plaintiff.

SMITH v. COMAIR, INC.

134 F.3d 254 (4th Cir. 1998)

WILKINSON, C.J.

James Smith sued Comair, Inc. and Delta Airlines, Inc. for false imprisonment. The district court granted summary judgment in favor of Comair on the grounds that Smith's claim must be dismissed for failure to state a claim. Smith appeals. We agree that Smith's tort claim should be dismissed. Accordingly, we affirm the judgment of the district court.

Because the instant case comes to us at the summary judgment stage, we review the evidence in the light most favorable to Smith, the nonmoving party. On the morning of October 5, 1995, Smith boarded a 6:40 a.m. Comair flight in Roanoke, Virginia to travel to Minneapolis, Minnesota, with a layover in the Cincinnati airport. Comair representatives did not ask Smith for proof of identification when he boarded the flight in Roanoke. In Cincinnati, Smith met some business associates and together they attempted to board the 9:00 a.m. connecting flight to Minneapolis. When Smith began to board, however, the Comair representative asked him "to step aside." After complying with this request and watching the rest of the flight's passengers board, Smith asked why he was not permitted to board. A Comair representative told Smith that a supervisor would be called. The supervisor, Mr. Price, arrived approximately thirty minutes after the Minneapolis flight's departure. According to Smith, Price would not explain why Smith could not fly out of the Cincinnati airport. Meanwhile, Smith also noticed for the first time two security guards standing approximately fifty and seventy feet away observing him. Smith testified that these officers watched him throughout the rest of his stay in the Cincinnati airport.

Three hours later, Price finally told Smith he was denied permission to board the Minneapolis flight because he did not match the physical description contained in his Delta frequent-flyer account. Smith, however, called his company's travel agent and learned that Delta did not maintain a record of physical descriptions in connection with frequent-flyer accounts. Smith, therefore, located Price and confronted him with this information. Price continued to insist that the dissimilar physical description was the reason Smith was not permitted to board.

At approximately 1:00 or 2:00 p.m., Price returned to Smith and told him the real reason he was refused permission to board was that the Roanoke Comair representatives had failed to ask for photo identification, as shown by the absence of pink highlighting on his boarding pass. At some point, Price explained that the Federal Aviation Administration ("FAA") required photo identification pursuant to security regulations. Smith replied that he could not produce his driver's license because he had left it in the glove compartment of his car, which was parked at the Roanoke airport. Price then asked Smith instead for his birth certificate and social security card, neither of which Smith had at the time. Smith offered to have his physical description faxed by the Virginia Department of Motor Vehicles ("DMV") or to pay Comair's expenses if they would enter his car, retrieve his driver's license, and fly it to Cincinnati on the next available flight. Price refused both options, as DMV could not fax a photo and entering Smith's car might expose Comair to liability.

Finally, sometime after 3:00 p.m., Price gave Smith a ticket to Roanoke and told him Comair would return him there. While waiting to board the flight, Smith spoke to Price again and stated that he was so angry he "would like to punch [Price] in the mouth." In response, Price motioned for the two security guards Smith previously had observed, one of whom was a Cincinnati police officer. When the two approached and restrained Smith, Price asked them to remove Smith from the terminal. After Smith explained his situation to the guard and police officer, the officer intervened on Smith's behalf and convinced Price to permit Smith to fly to Roanoke. Smith then returned to Roanoke.

Smith filed [this case in Virginia state court alleging false imprisonment]. After the case was removed to the United States District Court for the Western District of Virginia, the district court granted summary judgment in favor of Comair. The court found that Smith's tort causes of action failed to state a claim. Smith now appeals.

[W]e agree with the district court that he failed to state a claim. Because Virginia follows a lex loci delicti standard, and the incidents underlying Smith's claims occurred in the Cincinnati airport located in northern Kentucky, his tort claims are governed by Kentucky law.

Smith argues he was falsely imprisoned primarily because Comair flew him to the Cincinnati airport and stranded him there. These allegations, however, fail to state a claim for this tort. Kentucky defines false imprisonment as "'any exercise of force, by which in fact the other person is deprived of his liberty and compelled to remain where he does not wish to remain or to go where he does not wish to go.'" *Wal-Mart Stores, Inc. v. Mitchell*, 877 S.W.2d 616, 617 (Ky. App. 1994) (quoting *Great Atlantic & Pacific Tea Co. v.*

In Practice

You will encounter many instances in this book where courts from different states will follow different rules of law. Lawyers are strategic about the position they take on choice of law issues — which state's law should be applied to their case. Sometimes these considerations lead lawyers to file a case in one state rather than another, in cases where multiple venues might be appropriate.

Smith, 281 Ky. 583, 136 S.W.2d 759, 767 (Ky. 1940)). Smith's evidence simply does not show that he was compelled either to remain or to go anywhere he did not wish. He conceded that no Comair representative told him that he must remain in any specific part of the airport or that he was not free to leave the airport. Price told Smith only that Comair would not permit him to board the flight out of Cincinnati. Smith was therefore free at all times to leave the airport or leave Cincinnati altogether by any means he could arrange other than a Comair flight. False imprisonment results only if "the restraint be a total one, rather than a mere obstruction of the right to go where the plaintiff pleases." W. Page Keeton et al., *Prosser and Keeton on the Law of Torts* §11, at 47 (5th ed. 1984). Smith also briefly asserts that restraint by the security officers constituted false imprisonment. However, even he admits that the officers grabbed his arms only momentarily and nonforcefully, and then immediately interceded on his behalf by convincing Price to permit Smith to board a flight back to Roanoke. Smith's evidence thus fails to support a claim for false imprisonment.

For the foregoing reasons, we affirm the judgment of the district court.

NOTES AND PROBLEMS

1. ***Choice of Law.*** Observe that a federal court judge sitting in Virginia wrote this opinion but applied Kentucky law to decide the case. In Civil Procedure, you will learn that federal courts are required to apply state law to claims that originate under state rather than federal law. That explains the vertical dichotomy between the federal court choosing to apply state law. There is also a horizontal dichotomy as the Virginia court chooses to apply the law of a sister state. States employ recognized "conflicts of law" principles to help make a reasonable determination of which state's law ought to be applied to a multistate dispute. The *lex loci delicti* standard (roughly, the law of the place of the wrong) is commonly used in a tort suit and explains why Kentucky law applied here (since the Cincinnati airport is actually across the Ohio River in Kentucky).

2. ***Detention.*** Is it fair to say that the defendant in this case inhibited the plaintiff's freedom of movement? Courts historically demand physical confinement to a bounded area in order to find a detention. If the principle underlying recognition of the tort of false imprisonment is to promote individual autonomy, why restrict the tort's application to more egregious forms of limitation? Courts consider even highly coercive yet not immediate threats as similarly insufficient to constitute a detention. *See e.g.,* Snyder v. Evangelical Orthodox Church, 216 Cal. App. 3d 297 (1989) (bishop not falsely imprisoned when church members demanded he meditate in isolation for seven days under threat of exposing his adulterous acts, since he was subject to no physical restraint).

3. ***Consciousness of Detention.*** One minor issue that has received some focus from courts is whether the victim of false imprisonment must be aware of their confinement during the applicable time in order to have a valid claim. For example, some claims involve young children or others who are incompetent and are not aware they are being wrongly held. Many courts are willing to recognize a claim under these circumstances so long as the victim has some actual harm arising out of their detention.

4. ***Problems.*** Consider whether the element of detention needed for a false imprisonment claim is satisfied in each of the following scenarios:

A. A woman heading back home after a long business trip has taken her seat upon a commercial flight. The plane pulls back from the terminal but then sits for two hours before ever taking off, due to weather delays in the destination city. The woman was adamant about wanting to be allowed off of the plane but the flight attendant refuses to permit her to do so.

B. A teenager is about to leave his home, when he sees a bully from his school standing at the end of his driveway holding a big stick in his hand and staring at him in a menacing manner. Frightened, the boy stays inside of his home for several hours until the other finally leaves.

C. At a college party, to ensure that she is not left without a ride home, Sarah takes the keys from her friend Rosita's purse and refuses to give them back until Sarah is ready to return home.

D. Garrard leaves a big box home improvement store when, as he nears his car, he is approached by a store employee. The employee yells at him, "Sir, I think you left the store without paying for some merchandise. You have to come with me right now!" Garrard feels humiliated by this ungrounded public accusation of theft but wants to avoid any further confrontation in the parking lot and so proceeds to walk back into the store with the employee. He sits in a back room answering questions for ten minutes before the store employee realizes his error and tells Garrard he is free to go.

C. Shopkeeper's Privilege

In all likelihood, there are probably more modern false imprisonment cases that arise in the context of shoppers detained for suspected shoplifting than any other scenario. While the common law places great value on individual liberty, it also recognizes the importance of property rights and the need to permit people to engage in certain reasonable behavior to protect their property interests. Balancing these sometimes competing concerns, tort law has created a *shopkeeper's privilege,* which creates a legal justification for retailers to detain a shopper under certain circumstances and in a certain manner. In the following case, a Wal-Mart security guard has stopped one suspected shoplifter on her way out of the store and required her to remain. As you read this opinion, look for the prerequisites for application of this privilege and for the limitations on its use by the retailer. Also, compare this privilege with that of the jailer discussed in *Whirl.* Why are they so fundamentally different?

WAL-MART STORES, INC. v. RESENDEZ

962 S.W.2d 539 (Tex. 1998)

PER CURIAM.

This case involves the proper scope of authority of law in a false imprisonment case. The court of appeals affirmed the trial court's judgment against Wal-Mart Stores, Inc. ("Wal-Mart") on a jury finding of false imprisonment. We hold that, on the facts in this case, Wal-Mart established as a matter of law that it detained Lucia Resendez for a reasonable period of time, in a reasonable manner, and upon a reasonable belief that she had stolen store merchandise. Accordingly, we reverse the court of appeals' judgment and render judgment for Wal-Mart.

On January 20, 1986, Resendez went shopping at Wal-Mart during her lunch break. While browsing through the store, she began to eat from a bag of peanuts marked with a Wal-Mart price sticker. Raul Salinas, a security guard for Wal-Mart, followed Resendez and observed her place the empty bag under a rose bush. He then watched her purchase some items and leave the store. After determining that Resendez had not paid for a bag of peanuts, Salinas followed her into the parking lot. He accused her of taking the bag of peanuts without paying and asked her to accompany him back into the store. Resendez objected that she bought the peanuts the day before at another Wal-Mart store and could provide the receipt to prove it. She then accompanied Salinas to the back of the store. Within about ten to fifteen minutes a police officer arrived and arrested Resendez. Resendez posted bail and was released about one hour later.

A jury convicted Resendez of misdemeanor theft. Later, the court of appeals overturned her conviction because of a defect in the charging instrument. She then sued Wal-Mart for malicious prosecution, false imprisonment, [and] intentional infliction of emotional distress. The jury awarded Resendez $100,000 for the false imprisonment claim and $25,000 for the negligence claim. The court of appeals modified the judgment, eliminating the $25,000 recovery because it was a double recovery, and affirmed the judgment as modified.

In a false imprisonment case, if the alleged detention was performed with the authority of law, then no false imprisonment occurred. *See Sears, Roebuck & Co. v. Castillo*, 693 S.W.2d 374, 375 (Tex. 1985) (listing the elements of false imprisonment as a willful detention performed without consent and without the authority of law). The "shopkeeper's privilege" expressly grants an employee the authority of law to detain a customer to investigate the ownership of property in a reasonable manner and for a reasonable period of time if the employee has a reasonable belief that the customer has stolen or is attempting to steal store merchandise. Tex. Civ. Prac & Rem. Code Ann. §124.001.

In Practice

Legal justifications or privileges are typically considered *affirmative defenses.* This means that, rather than the plaintiff having to negate a privilege, as part of proving her case, the defendant must assert and prove the existence of the privilege.

There was no evidence to support the contention that the detention occurred for an unreasonable period of time. Without deciding the outer parameters of a permissible period of time under section 124.001, the ten to fifteen minute detention in this case was not unreasonable as a matter of law. *See Dominguez v. Globe Discount City, Inc.*, 470 S.W.2d 919, 920 (Tex. Civ. App. — El Paso 1971, no writ) (finding a five- to six-minute detention reasonable even where the plaintiff was ultimately released by the security guard who detained her); *Meadows v. F.W. Woolworth Co.*, 254 F. Supp. 907, 909 (N.D. Fla. 1966) (finding a ten-minute detention reasonable under a similar statute). Also, no evidence exists that the detention occurred in an unreasonable manner. The only question is whether it was reasonable for Salinas to believe that Resendez had stolen the peanuts. It was.

Based upon the undisputed facts — Resendez looked for peanuts immediately upon entering the Wal-Mart store, she was later seen eating from a bag of peanuts marked with a Wal-Mart price sticker, and she did not pay for the peanuts on leaving the store — probable cause existed to believe that the peanuts were stolen property. In fact, in response to the question on Resendez's malicious prosecution claim, the jury found that Salinas had probable cause to commence criminal proceedings against Resendez. If Salinas had probable cause to initiate criminal proceedings, his belief that Resendez stole the peanuts was necessarily reasonable. *See Wal-Mart Stores, Inc. v. Odem*, 929 S.W.2d 513, 520 (Tex. App. — San Antonio 996, writ denied) (finding that reasonable belief for an investigative detention is something less than that required to establish probable cause); *Berly v. D & L Security Servs. & Investigations, Inc.*, 876 S.W.2d 179, 183 (Tex. App. — Dallas 1994, writ denied) (noting that the "shopkeeper's privilege" under section 124.001 embodies the law of probable cause for the purpose of detaining a suspected shoplifter). As a matter of law, the undisputed facts of this case establish that Salinas had the authority of law to detain Resendez and therefore she was not falsely imprisoned.

The court of appeals' discussion of the proper scope of the authority of law to detain fails to recognize the full extent of the privilege granted to persons who suspect shoplifting. First, the court of appeals reasoned that the jury implicitly found that Wal-Mart exceeded the scope of its privilege to detain Resendez. To support this theory, the court of appeals cited one of its own opinions for the principle that compliance with a store's internal policies is informative in the jury's determination of whether there was a detention without authority of law. We disagree that the internal policies of a private business define the permissible scope of a detention authorized under the law.

Second, the court of appeals erred in its interpretation of the shopkeeper's privilege. The privilege does not require the detainer to confirm or refute the detainee's claims, nor does it prevent the detainer from holding the suspected shoplifter for a reasonable time in order to deliver her to the police. *See* Tex. Civ. Prac. & Rem. Code Ann. §124.001; *see also* Tex. Crim. Proc. Code Ann. §18.16 (granting to any person the privilege to seize and detain a person suspected of theft and deliver them to a peace officer).

Therefore, the court grants Wal-Mart's application for writ of error and, without hearing oral argument, reverses the court of appeals' judgment and renders judgment for Wal-Mart.

"LADIES AND GENTLEMEN OF THE JURY . . ."

Texas Pattern Jury Charge 6.3: Instruction on Defense of Privilege to Investigate Theft

"When a person reasonably believes that another has stolen or is attempting to steal property, that person has legal justification to detain the other in a reasonable manner and for a reasonable time to investigate ownership of the property."

NOTES AND PROBLEMS

1. ***Privileges.*** In most cases involving the detention of a customer by a security guard, the basic elements of a willful detention without consent are undisputed. In such instances, whether the plaintiff or defendant will prevail will turn on the primary issue of whether there was legal justification for the detention. Such affirmative defenses typically switch the burden of proof from the plaintiff to the defendant. How does the privilege asserted in this case compare with the privilege in *Whirl* (at the time of the initial incarceration)?

2. ***Good Faith.*** What does the phrase "reasonable belief" mean as a basis for the shopkeeper's privilege? Did the Sheriff's good faith act as a shield or defense in the prior case? What's the difference between these two cases?

3. ***Reasonableness.*** The shopkeeper's privilege is dependent upon three different things being found reasonable by the trier of fact. Reasonableness is the essential test for a negligence cause of action. In the prior case involving the prisoner, was negligence of the defendant considered relevant to the claim? Why is negligence, or reasonableness, relevant when a false imprisonment claim is being defended with the shopkeeper's privilege?

4. ***Evidence.*** What facts supported the court's conclusion that the defendant in Wal-Mart had a reasonable belief that the plaintiff was stealing peanuts?

5. ***Problems.***

A. *Ordinary Citizens.* Despite the phrase "shopkeeper's privilege," does either the Pattern Jury Charge set forth above or the Texas statute referred to at the end of the opinion limit the privilege to shopkeepers? What if you were shopping at a Wal-Mart and witnessed another customer attempting to steal some merchandise and walk out the door? What rights, if any, would you have to detain that other customer? How should the privilege apply here, if at all?

B. *Reasonable Manner.* The shopkeeper's privilege is limited to instances where the method of detention used is considered reasonable. What would you say about a security guard who broke a suspect's leg while tackling the suspect as the suspect tried to run out of the store with a stereo? *See* Watkins v. Sears Roebuck & Co., 735 N.Y.S.2d 75 (App. Div. 2001).

6. ***Citizen's Arrest.*** Many states, either as a matter of common law or by statutory modification to the common law, recognize a justification or privilege for ordinary citizens to detain those who have, in the presence of the citizen, committed either a felony criminal offense or a misdemeanor involving a "breach of the peace" (e.g., fighting or even driving while intoxicated).

Watch "Shopkeeper's Privilege" video on Casebook Connect.

Upon Further Review

Though classified as an intentional tort, the only thing that must be intended by the defendant in a false imprisonment case is the detention of the plaintiff. And detention does not require prison bars — simply using force or threats to keep someone from being able to move from place to place as they wish. On the other hand, merely inconveniencing someone's movement is not sufficient to count as detention. Beyond these two issues of intent and actual detention, many false imprisonment cases turn on whether or not the defendant has pled and proven either consent or a legal justification. Be aware that justifications are not all the same. Note that the officer's good faith was insufficient to create a privilege in *Whirl*, whereas with respect to the shopkeeper's privilege, a good faith belief by the defendant that the plaintiff has attempted to steal property is imperative for the application of the justification defense.

V TRESPASS

A. Introduction

The tort of trespass is ancient and historically has been highly revered due to the law's concern for protecting property rights. While it is properly classified as an intentional tort, pay close attention to what specifically must be intended, and what need not be, by the defendant in order to be a trespasser. The *Thomas* case demonstrates confusion by the litigants as to the appropriate standard. The scope of liability of a trespasser for even unforeseen harm caused during a trespass by her actions is considered in the *Baker* case. The law of trespass encompasses not only encroachments onto another's land, but also coming into unpermitted contact with another's personal property. The *Sears* and *Arora* cases set forth the various distinctions the law makes in such instances between intermeddling, dispossession, and conversion of another's personal property.

B. Land

1. Intent

THOMAS v. HARRAH'S VICKSBURG CORP.

734 So. 2d 312 (Miss. Ct. App. 1999)

PAYNE, J.

Appellants, C.N. Thomas and Surplus City, U.S.A. sought damages for common law trespass against appellees, Harrah's Vicksburg Corporation and W.G. Yates and Sons Construction Co.

This litigation stems from the development of Harrah's gambling facility in Vicksburg, Mississippi, beginning over five years ago and acts of trespass admittedly committed by Harrah's and Yates for an approximate six-month period beginning in July 1993 and continuing through December 1993. The property in question is a vacant lot . . . wholly owned by Thomas [and leased to Surplus]. Thomas and Surplus repeatedly asked Harrah's and Yates to refrain from trespassing on the Thomas/Surplus property; however, these requests were ignored by Harrah's and Yates. After realizing that his attempts to protect his property from trespass clearly were futile, Thomas instituted this litigation.

Thomas and Surplus contend that the intent of the common law trespasser is irrelevant. They cite *Kelley v. Sportsmen's Speedway*, 80 So. 2d 785, 791 (1955) as support for their contention. *Kelley* was a premises liability case and defined "trespasser" as "a person who enters the premises of another without license, invitation, or other right, and intrudes for some definite purpose of his own, or at his convenience, or merely as an idler with no apparent purpose, other than, perhaps, to satisfy his curiosity." Harrah's and Yates present *Berry v. Player*, 542 So. 2d 895 (Miss. 1989) in support of their position that negligence is the proper standard to apply. *Berry* dealt with a jury instruction under *Miss. Code Ann. §95-5-3* concerning recoverable damages for cutting timber from private property. In that case the Mississippi Supreme Court found a negligence instruction proper.

We think it instructive to briefly look at the historical basis for the trespass to land action. Professors Prosser and Keeton note that "historically, the requirements for trespass to land under the common law action of trespass were an invasion (a) which interfered with the right of exclusive possession of the land, and (b) which was the direct result of some act committed by the defendant." W. Page Keeton et al., Prosser and Keeton on Torts, §13 at 67 (5th ed. 1984). Further, the tort of trespass to land can be committed by other than simply entering on the land; trespass occurs by placing objects on the property, by causing a third party to go onto the property, or by remaining on property after the expiration of a right of entry. Keeton §13 at 72-73.

With regard to the requisite intent for trespass to land, the Restatement (Second) of Torts §163 comment (b) addresses this issue:

> b. Intention. If the actor intends to be upon the particular piece of land, it is not necessary that he intend to invade the other's interest in the exclusive possession of his land. The intention which is required to make the actor liable under the rule stated in this Section is *an intention to enter upon the particular piece of land in question*, irrespective of whether the actor knows or should know that he is not entitled to enter. It is, therefore, immaterial whether or not he honestly and reasonably believes that the land is his own, or that he has the consent of the possessor or of a third person having power to give consent on his behalf, or that he has a mistaken belief that he has some other privilege to enter. (Emphasis added.)

Thus, as Professors Prosser and Keeton point out, "the intent required as a basis for liability as a trespasser is simply an intent to be at the place on the land where the trespass occurred." Keeton §13 at 73.

With this historical basis, we now turn to the merits of the parties' arguments. Clearly, there is no negligence required for liability for trespass, and we therefore reject Harrah's and Yates' invitation to apply a negligence standard to ordinary trespass.

The Thomas and Surplus position is correct in asserting that negligence is not necessary for common law trespass liability. Furthermore, while there is an intent requirement, it is very broad in definition as demonstrated in the Restatement (Second) §163 above. Common law trespass is an intrusion upon the

"The great end for which men entered into society was to secure their property. That right is preserved sacred and incommunicable in all instances where it has not been taken away or abridged by some public law for the good of the whole."

Lord Camden (1765)

land of another without a license or other right for one's own purpose. The testimony establishes that is exactly the case here.

Two key witnesses, Charles Wells, Harrah's construction manager for this project, and Jim Smith, the construction superintendent for Yates, admitted that there were trespasses that occurred on Thomas' property. First, Wells testified that he worked on the project from July 1993 until July 1994, and that he understood that there was a continuing dispute with Thomas over the property lines. Further, Wells admitted that he, as well as Yates, were involved in the decision to move the north wall because it encroached on Thomas' property. The plans for the facility, according to Wells, called for the building to extend "right up to the property line. . . ." Questioning by appellants' counsel also established that the trespass was inevitable:

By Mr. Lotterhos [counsel for appellants]: Now, as a practical matter, if you were going to construct that [building] absolutely on the property line, it would have been necessary to get on the adjacent property to work on the exterior. Isn't that true?

By Mr. Wells: On that ten-foot face, yes, sir.

By Mr. Lotterhos: Alright and that happened, didn't it?

By Mr. Wells: Yes, sir.

Wells later testified that Harrah's Vice-President of Design and Construction, Pat Monson, approved of moving the encroaching wall.

Second, Jim Smith, the construction superintendent for Yates on Harrah's Vicksburg project, testified for the appellees. On direct examination, Smith took great pains to detail how careful Yates was in constructing special scaffolding to avoid trespassing on the Thomas/Surplus property and emphasized the fact that he had personally fired three employees of Yates for trespassing. Additionally, Smith, in a strained and futile effort, attempted to disassociate Yates from the various subcontractors employed by Yates, while admitting that Yates had control over the subcontractors. Yet, on cross-examination, Smith admitted that scaffolding erected by Yates in conjunction with the construction of the facility was indeed on the Thomas/Surplus property and that they received permission from Thomas to enter the property for the *specific* purpose of removing the scaffolding to halt the trespass. Further, Smith admitted to repeated airspace violations on the Thomas/Surplus property with the boom swinging over the property. As did Wells, Smith also admitted that the trespass on the Thomas/Surplus property was unavoidable after the construction reached a certain point and when the wall was ultimately moved:

By Mr. Lotterhos: And you were aware that . . . it was to be — a portion of that north wall was to be right on the Thomas property line, isn't that true?
By Mr. Smith: Yes, sir.
By Mr. Lotterhos: Now, you have been involved in construction a lot of years, haven't you?
By Mr. Smith: Yes, sir.

* * *

By Mr. Lotterhos: . . . based on your experience, when you build right upon the line or wall, it is necessary to get on the outside of the wall to work on it, isn't that true?
By Mr. Smith: Yes, sir, it is.

* * *

By Mr. Lotterhos: In order to break out that wall, you had to get on Mr. Thomas' property, didn't you?
By Mr. Smith: Yes, sir, we did.

This *uncontroverted* testimony established that there were trespasses on the Thomas/Surplus property.

In this case, the testimony of Charles Wells and Jim Smith established that the construction of the Harrah's facility was on a fast-tract, and it was known that the north wall of the shoreside facility would be very close to the Thomas/Surplus property line and that trespass was unavoidable in the construction process. Appellees go to great lengths to describe the precautions made by the construction personnel to avoid the trespasses. But this is quite simply irrelevant. A picture, or in this case, pictures, are worth thousands of words. It was obvious that deliveries were made, building supplies were stacked, and scaffolding was erected for construction purposes on the Thomas/Surplus property. As indicated by the photographs and the testimony of Wells, the trespass on the Thomas/Surplus property was inevitable. Undoubtedly, trespass occurred at the hands of Harrah's and Yates during the course of completing this project. While some of the photographs were unable to be directly tied to the appellees, a quantum more proved that the trespasses complained of occurred on the subject property for which Harrah's was responsible. Appellees' arguments to the contrary are spurious and not well taken.

NOTES AND PROBLEMS

1. ***Intent.*** The court describes the varying arguments of the plaintiffs and defendants in *Thomas,* with the plaintiff essentially arguing that no intention

need be established in a trespass case and the defendant arguing that a negligence standard must apply — that the defendant must have failed to exercise reasonable care in coming onto the owner's land in order to be liable. Where does the court come down as between these two extreme arguments?

2. ***Good Faith Not a Defense.*** Courts and the Restatement have clearly stated that so long as the minimal intent necessary for trespass exists, the good faith motivations or beliefs of the defendant are not a defense. The Restatement offers an extreme, though well accepted, example:

> If the actor is and intends to be upon the particular piece of land in question, it is immaterial that he honestly and reasonably believes that he has the consent of the lawful possessor to enter, or indeed, that he himself is the possessor. Unless the actor's mistake was induced by the conduct of the possessor, it is immaterial that the mistake is one such as a reasonable man . . . would have made. One who enters any piece of land takes the risk. . . . So, too, the actor cannot escape liability by showing that his mistaken belief in the validity of his title is due to the advice of the most eminent of counsel. Indeed, even though a statute expressly confers title upon him, he takes the risk that the statute may thereafter be declared unconstitutional.

Restatement (Second) of Torts §163, cmt. b (1965).

3. ***Acts Constituting Trespass.*** The *Thomas* court alludes to various types of contact with another's land that can constitute a trespass, and concludes that the defendants' actions constituted trespass against the plaintiffs. In what specific ways did the defendants commit a trespass?

4. ***Liability for Damages.*** One may maintain an action for nominal damages for trespass or, where actual harm is demonstrated, for compensatory damages. In *Thomas* the court rejected any award of damages for Thomas, however, because it had leased the land in question to Surplus and was not in possession of the land. So long as no permanent harm had occurred to the land (beyond the terms of the lease), Thomas as the owner/lessor could not recover. However, its lessee, who was in possession, could maintain an action for its actual damages.

5. ***Problems.*** Which of the following actors are trespassers?

A. One who decides to do his neighbor (who is away on vacation) a favor by mowing his neighbor's yard?

B. A child who sees a basketball goal on another's driveway and decides to enter the property to shoot hoops for a few minutes while waiting for a school bus?

C. A drunk driver who hits a patch of ice and slides onto another's front yard?

D. A blind man who walks across another's property line without realizing that he has done so?

E. One who changes the natural drainage on their property in order to cause standing water to flow into their neighbor's yard instead?

6. ***Airspace Trespass.*** A landowner has generally been understood to own the airspace of her own land up to the sky (as well as below the ground). Since the invention of modern air flight, this understanding has been altered to permit aircraft to fly over property without becoming liable to all whose property is below. With regard to intangible airspace violations, such as causing smoke or pollutants to enter over another's property, courts have come up with varying tests for determining liability. A common approach involves creating trespass liability only when actual harm is caused to the landowner's property. *See, e.g.,* Public Service Co. of Colorado v. Van Wyk, 27 P.3d 377 (Colo. 2001) (defendant not subject to trespass liability for causing radiation and electromagnetic fields to cross plaintiff's property without evidence of actual harm).

> **"LADIES AND GENTLEMEN OF THE JURY . . ."**
>
> **Idaho Civil Jury Instruction 3.19.1 — Trespasser, definition**
>
> "A trespasser is a person who goes or remains upon the premises of another without permission, invitation or lawful authority. Permission or invitation may be express or implied."

2. Scope of Liability

BAKER v. SHYMKIV

451 N.E.2d 811 (Ohio 1983)

The parties, on appeal, agreed to the following statement of facts:

"1. On March 22, 1978, at 8:00 p.m. [Mr. Baker] and his wife were returning home and turned into the driveway leading to their home.

"2. They observed a car was parked in the driveway blocking their access, and they observed Mr. and Mrs. Shymkiv throwing tools and other equipment in the trunk of their car, close the trunk lid and jump into their car.

"3. Mr. and Mrs. Baker got out of their car and observed a trench with dimensions of approximately 1 foot in width and 1 ½ feet in depth and more than 10 feet in length had been dug across their driveway and that a drain tile had been placed in the trench so that water from the Shymkiv property could drain through the trench and onto the property of an adjoining landowner.

"4. Mr. Baker was angry and visibly upset over the actions of the Shymkivs and approached the Shymkiv automobile.

"5. Mr. Shymkiv got out of the car and an argument concerning the trench followed. Mary Baker interceded and pushed herself between Homer Baker and John Shymkiv and told her husband to calm down.

"6. Mary Baker indicated that she had never seen her husband so upset or angry in all the years they had been married.

"7. Mrs. Baker then left the scene to call the police.

"8. When Mrs. Baker returned approximately 3 minutes later she found her husband laying face-down in the mud puddle while the Shymkivs were driving away.

"9. Emergency squad arrived approximately 10-15 minutes later, worked on Homer Baker and transported him to Grant Hospital where he was pronounced dead at 9:20 p.m.

"10. Mary Baker has described her husband as a very easygoing person, very friendly, and not easily prone to argue or get upset.

"11. Mary Baker has indicated that Homer Baker took great pride in the maintenance and upkeep of the driveway, home and yard."

In the court of common pleas, Mrs. Baker filed several claims against the Shymkivs: (1) as administratrix, for the wrongful death of Mr. Baker, and for her own pecuniary loss; and (2) for trespass seeking both compensatory and punitive damages. At trial, two medical experts testified. One concluded that the events of March 22, 1978, could have caused Mr. Baker's death. The other determined that there was no evidence upon which one could reach that conclusion.

The trial court instructed the jury, in part:

> Now, the test then [of proximate cause] is whether in the light of all the circumstances a reasonably prudent person would have *anticipated* that injury was likely to result to someone from the preponderance of the evidence or performance of the evidence or act. In other words, before liability attaches to the defendants in this case, the damages claimed by Mrs. Baker must have been *foreseen or reasonably anticipated* by the wrongdoer as likely to follow the trespass and the digging of the trench or the digging of the hole or whatever. (Emphasis added.)

The jury found against the Shymkivs on the trespass claim, but assessed [only] $300 in compensatory damages and $1,100 in punitive damages against Mr. Shymkiv only. [The court of appeals reversed the jury's award, ruling that the trial court's instruction that only foreseeable damages could be awarded was erroneous and may have resulted in the jury's award being too low.]

Locher, J.

This case presents one issue: whether the trial court erred by instructing the jury that only foreseeable damages could result in liability. Appellants, the Shymkivs, contend that the trial court properly charged the jury on foreseeability. We disagree.

Intentional trespassers are within that class of less-favored wrongdoers. For example, under the Restatement of Torts 2d, intentional conduct is an element of trespass: "One is subject to liability to another for trespass, irrespective of whether he thereby causes harm to any legally protected interest of the other, if he *intentionally* enters land in the possession of the other or causes a thing or a third person to do so." (Emphasis added.) Restatement of Torts 2d §158. The Restatement also articulates the scope of liability for a trespass in Section 162, which states: "A trespass on land subjects the trespasser to liability for physical harm to the possessor of the land at the time of the trespass, or to the land or to his things, or to members of his household or to their things, caused by any act done, activity carried on, or condition created by the trespasser, irrespective of whether his conduct is such as would subject him to liability were he not a trespasser." *Id.*, at pages 291-292. Comment *f* to Section 162 of the Restatement explains the intended effect of that provision:

> *f. Peculiar position of trespasser.* This Section states the peculiar liability to which a trespasser is subject for bodily harm caused to the possessor of land or the members of his family by the conduct of a trespasser while upon the land, irrespective of whether his conduct if it occurred elsewhere would subject him to liability to them. Thus, one who trespasses upon the land of another incurs the risk of becoming liable for any bodily harm which is cause [*sic*] to the possessor of the land or to members of his household by any conduct of the trespasser during the continuance of his trespass, no matter how otherwise innocent such conduct may be.

Id., at page 293.

Accordingly, we hold that damages caused by an intentional trespasser need not be foreseeable to be compensable.

We affirm the judgment of the court of appeals.

NOTES AND PROBLEMS

1. ***Foreseeability as Damage Limitation.*** As mentioned previously, foreseeability is a traditional limitation on recovery in a claim for negligence. We will discuss this test for proximate cause in Chapter 5. Courts historically reject any such requirement for proximate cause in an intentional tort cause of action, such as in the *Baker* case. So long as the harm caused is considered compensable for the particular intentional tort and actual causation is established, the scope of liability is not typically limited by notions of foreseeability. We saw this same principle applied in the *Nelson v. Carroll* case involving the battery by the debt collector. However, as the Restatement provision quoted by the court indicates, traditionally the law of trespass has limited liability to those damages caused "during the continuance" of the trespass.

2. ***Problems.***

A. Would it make a difference if Mr. Baker had died of a heart attack the next morning upon discovering that his neighbors had trespassed upon his land the night before? Think about what constitutes a trespass and the Restatement's reference to being liable for all damages caused "during the continuance" of a trespass.

B. If a neighbor trespasses on another's property, causing no actual harm at the time, but the owner sees the trespass occur while watching surveillance videotape later and suffers a heart attack, will trespass support recovery for the owner's death?

C. While a landowner is in the hospital having his hernia repaired, a kindly next-door neighbor comes upon his property to surprise him by mowing the lawn. The next morning when the landowner returns home he is incensed to discover what his neighbor has done. That afternoon the two have a confrontation — each standing upon their own property — which involves much yelling and waving of arms. The landowner falls dead from a heart attack in the heat of the debate.

C. Personal Property

In addition to recognizing trespass for encroaching upon another's land, the common law has long recognized the related cause of action for intentional touching of another's personal property without permission — trespass to chattels. As the *Koepnick* case discusses below, a trespass to chattels can take the form of either a *dispossession* or an *intermeddling*. Either variety can permit the recovery of compensatory damages when the trespass causes actual demonstrable harm to either the personal property or to the owner. As you read the following opinion, therefore, try to discern when the distinction between the two varieties of trespass to chattel claims makes a difference. Following that, we will next encounter a related cause of action to trespass to chattels — a claim for *conversion*. In the *Prince Kumar Arora* case we will see the court distinguish between these two very related claims in the context of a mad scientist caught destroying another's science experiment.

1. Trespass to Chattels

KOEPNICK v. SEARS ROEBUCK & CO.

762 P.2d 609 (Ct. App. Az. 1988)

Koepnick was stopped in the Fiesta Mall parking lot by Sears security guards Lessard and Pollack on December 6, 1982, at approximately 6:15 p.m. Lessard and Pollack suspected Koepnick of shoplifting a wrench and therefore detained him for approximately 15 minutes until the Mesa police arrived. Upon arrival of the police, Koepnick and a police officer became involved in an altercation in which Koepnick was injured. The police officer handcuffed Koepnick, placed a call for a backup, and began investigating the shoplifting allegations. Upon investigation it was discovered that Koepnick had receipts for the wrench and for all the Sears merchandise he had been carrying. Additionally, the store clerk who sold the wrench to Koepnick was located. He verified the sale and informed Lessard that he had put the wrench in a small bag, stapled it shut, and then placed that bag into a large bag containing Koepnick's other purchases. The small bag was not among the items in Koepnick's possession in the security room. To determine whether a second wrench was involved, the police and Lessard searched Koepnick's truck which was in the mall parking lot. No stolen items were found. Having completed their investigation, the police cited Koepnick for disorderly conduct and released him. The entire detention lasted approximately 45 minutes.

Koepnick sued Sears for false [imprisonment], assault, trespass to chattel, invasion of privacy and malicious prosecution. The trial court directed a verdict in favor of Sears on all charges except false [imprisonment] and trespass to chattel. After a trial on these claims, a jury awarded Koepnick $25,000 compensatory damages and $500,000 punitive damages for false [imprisonment], and $100 compensatory damages and $25,000 punitive damages for trespass to chattel.

[The trial court granted a new trial on the false imprisonment claim because of the facts indicating Sears' privilege to detain the plaintiff under the shopkeeper's privilege. The court of appeals affirmed the grant of a new trial on that claim. The trial court also granted a judgment notwithstanding the verdict to Sears on the trespass to chattels claim.]

Arizona courts follow the *Restatement (Second) of Torts* absent authority to the contrary. The *Restatement* provides that the tort of trespass to a chattel may be committed by intentionally dispossessing another of the chattel or using or intermeddling with a chattel in the possession of another. *Restatement (Second) of Torts* §217 (1965).

The *Restatement (Second) of Torts* §221 (1965) defines dispossession as follows:

> A dispossession may be committed by intentionally taking a chattel from the possession of another without the other's consent or . . . barring the possessor's access to a chattel. . . .

Comment b to §221 provides that dispossession may occur when someone intentionally assumes physical control over the chattel and deals with the chattel in a way which will be destructive of the possessory interest of the other person. Comment b further provides that "on the other hand, an intermeddling with the chattel is not a dispossession unless the actor intends to exercise a dominion and control over it inconsistent with a possession in any other person other than himself."

The *Restatement (Second) of Torts* §218 (1965) provides:

> One who commits a trespass to a chattel is subject to liability to the possessor of the chattel if, but only if,
>
> (a) he dispossesses the other of the chattel, or
>
> (b) the chattel is impaired as to its condition, quality, or value, or
>
> (c) the possessor is deprived of the use of the chattel for a substantial time, or
>
> (d) bodily harm is caused to the possessor, or harm is caused to some person or thing in which the possessor has a legally protected interest.

Koepnick argued at trial that Lessard's participation in searching his truck constituted an actionable trespass to the truck. He was awarded $100 damages by the jury which he characterizes as damages for a dispossession pursuant to subsection (a) or deprivation of use pursuant to subsection (c) of §218.

The *Restatement* recognizes that an award of nominal damages may be made, even in the absence of proof of actual damages, if a trespass to chattel involves a dispossession. *See §218, comment d.* However, both parties have agreed that the $100 compensatory award is not nominal.

Sears' actions with respect to the trespass consisted of Steve Lessard accompanying a Mesa police officer out to the parking lot and looking in the truck. There is no evidence in the record of an intent on the part of Sears' employee to claim a possessory interest in the truck contrary to Koepnick's interest. No lien or ownership interest claim of any kind was made. Further, there is no evidence that Sears intentionally denied Koepnick access to his truck.

Koepnick was in the City of Mesa's custody at the time of the search and Sears had no control over how the police department conducted its investigation or the disposition of Koepnick during that investigation. There is no evidence that Sears' employees objected to any request by Koepnick to accompany them down to the vehicle.

Comment e to the *Restatement* §218 discusses the requirement of proof of actual damage for an actionable trespass to chattel claim.

> The interest of a possessor of chattel in its inviolability, unlike the similar interest of a possessor of land, is not given legal protection by an action for nominal damages for harmless intermeddlings with the chattel. In order that an actor who interferes with another's chattel may be liable, his conduct must affect some other and more important interest of the possessor. Therefore, one who intentionally intermeddles with another's chattel is subject to liability only if his intermeddling is harmful to the possessor's materially valuable interest in the physical condition, quality, or value of the chattel, or if the possessor is deprived of the use of the chattel for a substantial time, or some other legally protected interest of the possessor is affected as stated in Clause (c). Sufficient legal protection of the possessor's interest in the mere inviolability of his chattel is afforded by his privilege to use reasonable force to protect his possession against even harmless interference.

The search in question took approximately two minutes. Neither the truck nor its contents were damaged in any manner by the police or Sears' employee. As a matter of law, Sears' action did not constitute an actionable trespass under *§218(c)*.

In arguing that Sears should not have been given a [judgment] in its favor on the trespass to chattel claim, Koepnick asserts that the search of his truck caused him to remain in custody longer than he would otherwise have been detained. While this may be true, there was no evidence showing any connection between $100 and the few minutes that Koepnick was detained as a result of waiting for that search to be completed — apparently 15 minutes. For a deprivation of use caused by a trespass to chattel to be actionable, the time must be so substantial that it is possible to estimate the loss that is caused. The record in the present case lacks any evidence to permit a jury to estimate any loss caused to Koepnick. It is well settled that conjecture and speculation cannot provide the basis for an award of damages. The evidence must make an approximately accurate estimate possible.

Even if a [judgment] on the claim of trespass could be affirmed on the basis that a dispossession occurred, the award . . . would necessarily be limited to nominal damages. As discussed above, both parties agree that the $100 award was not nominal. Furthermore, punitive damages were erroneously awarded because punitive damages cannot be awarded absent evidence of actual damages.

We conclude that there was no dispossession of the vehicle as contemplated under §218 of the *Restatement* nor was Koepnick deprived of its use for a substantial period of time. Any increase in the length of detention caused by the search is not the kind of interest protected by the tort of trespass to chattel. Accordingly, we affirm the trial court's [judgment] in favor of Sears on this issue.

NOTES AND PROBLEMS

1. ***Determining Intermeddling vs. Dispossession.*** The court in *Sears* describes two branches, or types, of trespass to chattels claims: an intermeddling and a dispossession. Referencing a test involving whether the defendant intends an act of interference with the chattel in a way that is inconsistent with the plaintiff's true ownership, the court concludes that the defendant's conduct amounted to an intermeddling. What facts support that? What might defendant have done differently with plaintiff's truck to change the court's conclusion?

2. ***Significance of the Intermeddling vs. Dispossession Dichotomy.*** The court indicates that the label can impact the damages recoverable and, in certain cases, can deny any recovery altogether. For example, for which of the two types of claim may a plaintiff recover nominal damages? How did this impact the appellate court's holding in *Sears*?

3. ***Problems.*** Billy and Sara are first-year law students. Sara owns a Chevrolet Camaro. In each of the following circumstances, does Sara have a valid claim for trespass to chattels? How would you characterize the type of trespass claim — an intermeddling or a dispossession? Will that distinction matter?

A. After class one afternoon, Billy is talking with some other 1L law students in the parking lot when he rests by leaning against Sara's Camaro.

B. During a break in his first year classes, Billy decides he should polish his golf game in anticipation of being a rich lawyer. He begins hitting golf balls in a grassy field adjacent to the parking lot. He carelessly hits an errant shot that breaks the windshield of Sara's Camaro.

C. Billy gets sick to his stomach after being called upon to recite the facts of *Pennoyer v. Neff* in Civil Procedure class and decides he needs to go home early. Because his car was in the shop undergoing repairs, he finds Sara's Camaro unlocked and hot wires it and drives it home. After resting for two hours, he returns it to the parking lot unscathed. Sara was in class the entire time but learns of the incident from another law student.

D. Billy is crazy with rage and jealousy after Sara demonstrates her superior knowledge of Property law in class one day, correcting a mistake Billy made in front of the entire class. Vowing revenge, Billy sneaks into the parking lot a few days later and cuts the hydraulic brake lines on Sara's Camaro. When she attempts to drive it home later that day, the brakes fail and she loses control over the car, ending up in a river suffering severe injuries and with her Camaro destroyed.

E. Billy is struggling financially given the high tuition of his law school. He has no transportation and decides to steal Sara's car. Sarah searches for her car to no avail and finally purchases a BMW to replace her Camaro. A month later when Billy gets a student loan check he decides to purchase another older vehicle, and he secretly returns Sara's Camaro to the school parking lot. Sara finds the car and surveillance videotape permits her to identify Billy as the culprit.

2. Conversion

UNITED STATES v. PRINCE KUMAR ARORA

860 F. Supp. 1091 (D. Md. 1994)

Messitte, J.

In this civil suit for conversion and trespass, the United States contends that Doctor Prince Kumar Arora intentionally tampered with and destroyed cells in a research project at the National Institutes of Health in Bethesda, Maryland.

Dr. Arora denies tampering and in any case responds that the Government sustained no damages by reason of the cell deaths.

The Court, sitting without a jury, received testimony and exhibits over several days and has considered the parties' post-trial briefs. On the basis of the evidence and pleadings, the Court concludes that Dr. Arora did tamper with, destroy, and convert Alpha 1-4 cells; that he is liable for the cost of the flasks and materials associated with the creation of the cells as well as the reasonable value of the time it took a laboratory assistant to re-create the cells; and that, while not liable in compensatory damages for the delay he caused in the completion of the research project, he must respond in punitive damages, as to which the effect his actions had on the research project is a relevant consideration.

The Court will award the United States $450.20 in compensatory damages and $5,000.00 in punitive damages.

The National Institutes of Health (NIH), part of the United States Department of Health and Human Services, is a world-renowned research and educational facility with extensive laboratories, located in Bethesda, Maryland. NIH conducts research in a number of critical scientific areas.

In 1978, after receiving his Ph.D. in microbiology from Michigan State University, Prince Kumar Arora joined NIH as a Visiting Fellow in the Laboratory of Immunodiagnosis at the National Cancer Institute. There and later as a Staff Fellow in the Laboratory of Developmental and Molecular Immunology at the National Institute of Child Health and Development, he conducted research in immunology, collaborated with other scientists, published his research in scientific journals, and supervised and trained younger researchers working in his laboratories. In 1987, Dr. Phil Skolnick, Chief of the Laboratory of Neuroscience in the National Institute of Diabetes and Digestive and Kidney Diseases (NIDDK), invited Dr. Arora to conduct immunology research at that institute. From approximately 1987 through 1992, Dr. Arora pursued his research at NIDDK, publishing papers, editing articles for scientific journals, collaborating with other scientists, and continuing his supervision of younger scientists working in the laboratory.

In 1989, Dr. Arora hired a post-doctoral student from Japan, Dr. Yoshitatsu Sei. Dr. Arora served as Dr. Sei's mentor and together they published several papers setting forth the results of their collaborative research. Consistent with laboratory policy, however, Dr. Sei was free to engage in collaborative projects with other researchers without Dr. Arora's involvement. Thus, in December 1990, Dr. Sei, who had special expertise in cell culturing, joined Dr. Skolnick and Dr. Garry Wong in a pioneering research project designed to study the immune properties of certain cell receptors. The purpose of the project was to attempt to develop, through a complex method, a brand new line of cells which could be transfected into human cells, which could then be cloned into a sufficient number of the newly created cell line. The cell line, if successful, would have significant implications for studies of alcohol, Alzheimer's disease, neurotoxicity, and — in the words of Dr. Wong — "just about anything that has to do with regulation of brain cells."

Between December 1990 and the beginning of 1992, working from several cell line possibilities, one of which they dubbed "Alpha 1-4," Drs. Wong and Sei sought to develop a stable cell line. By February 1992, they were successful in creating the Alpha 1-4 cell line and were able to maintain a supply of the line in a deep freeze. What remained, before preparing the manuscript announcing their research to the public and donating the cell line to a national cell bank for use by scientists around the world, were scientific assays, *i.e.* experiments, to describe the characteristics of the cell line. To perform these assays, multiple flasks, each containing millions of Alpha 1-4 cells, were required.

Against this scientific background, however, as often happens in life, human passion slowly began to overtake cool reason. [Dr. Sei and Dr. Arora began to have professional jealousy regarding each other's recognition for certain accomplishments. In addition, their relationship became strained after Dr. Arora was accused of sexually harassing a female graduate assistant later re-assigned to Dr. Sei. Eventually, Dr. Sei discovered that the Alpha 1-4 cells had been tampered with and destroyed. The police were contacted and began an investigation.]

Dr. Arora testified that Detective Miller suddenly began accusing him of killing Dr. Sei's cells, which Dr. Arora said he vigorously denied. Detective Miller, on the other hand, testified that when he asked Dr. Arora how he killed the cells, Dr. Arora answered "with 2-mercaptoethanol."

Following his interview with Dr. Arora, Detective Miller immediately asked his supervisor, Captain Timothy Pickett, to reinterview Dr. Arora out of Miller's presence. Although Dr. Arora denied saying it, Captain Pickett testified that Dr. Arora clearly admitted to him that he had adulterated cell tissues with "2-merca-something," a word Captain Pickett could neither remember nor pronounce. Captain Pickett further testified that Dr. Arora stated in effect that "it was the first time I did it; I'll never do it again."

When Dr. Arora left the police interview, he attempted to locate Dr. Skolnick but did not succeed until the following morning. When they finally met, Dr. Skolnick, who had already talked to Detective Miller, immediately confronted Dr. Arora with the question: "Why did you do it?" to which he testified Dr. Arora replied: "To teach Yoshi (Dr. Sei) and Abha (Ms. Saini) a lesson," suggesting that the two of them were "conspiring against me." Dr. Skolnick then testified that he went on to say: "You know you can't work here anymore," to which Dr. Arora replied "Yes, I know that."

Dr. Arora denies that he adulterated Dr. Sei's cells and suggests that if he touched the flasks, it would only have been to move them in the course of getting at other flasks in the incubator where the flasks were located. But the evidence to the contrary is considerable. Only Dr. Sei's flasks were in the incubator at the time he placed them inside. Dr. Arora's fingerprints were found on the flasks despite his lack of official authorization to handle them. An adulterating substance with a quick toxic effect, #2-mercaptoethanol, was found in several of the fake experiment flasks, whereas Dr. Sei testified he placed no such chemical in with the "Alpha 1-4" or other cells. Dr. Arora also had a potential animus, which is to say motive, against Dr. Sei — professional rivalry as well as possible resentment over Ms. Saini's shift of allegiance from Dr. Arora to Dr. Sei. Most importantly, three separate witnesses testified that, when confronted with the alleged wrongdoing, Dr. Arora in one fashion or another admitted his culpability.

The Court concludes, in this most unhappy affair, that Dr. Arora did in fact tamper with and cause the death of the Alpha 1-4 cells at the NIH laboratory in Bethesda in the Spring of 1992.

Was there a conversion or trespass?

It is not necessary to recount here the historical development of the torts of trespass and conversion, a matter more than adequately explored in Prosser and Keeton on *The Law of Torts,* §§14-15 (5th ed. 1984). For present purposes, it suffices to observe that the difference between the two torts is fundamentally one of degree, trespass constituting a lesser interference with another's chattel, conversion a more serious exercise of dominion or control over it. *See Restatement (Second) of Torts,* §222A, Comment (1965).

Thus a trespass has been defined as an intentional use or intermeddling with the chattel in possession of another, *Restatement (Second) of Torts,* §217(b), such intermeddling occurring, *inter alia,* when "the chattel is impaired as to its condition, quality, or value." *Restatement (Second) of Torts,* §218(b). *See also Walser v. Resthaven Memorial Gardens, Inc.,* 633 A.2d 466 (Md. 1993).

A "conversion," on the other hand, has been defined as:

> An intentional exercise of dominion or control over a chattel which so seriously interferes with the right of another to control it that the actor may justly be required to pay the other the full value of the chattel.

Restatement (Second) of Torts, §222A(1). Whereas impairing the condition, quality or value of a chattel upon brief interference can constitute a trespass, intentional destruction or material alteration of a chattel will subject the actor to liability for conversion. *Restatement (Second) of Torts,* §226.

A number of factors are considered in determining whether interference with a chattel is serious enough to constitute a conversion as opposed to a trespass. These include:

> a) the extent and duration of the actor's exercise of dominion or control;
> b) the actor's intent to assert a right in fact inconsistent with the other's right of control;
> c) the actor's good faith;
> d) the extent and duration of the resulting interference with the other's right of control;
> e) the harm done to the chattel;
> f) the inconvenience and expense caused to the other.

Staub, 37 Md. App. at 143-144, quoting *Restatement (Second) of Torts,* §222A(2).

Assuming for the moment that a cell line is a chattel capable of being converted or trespassed upon, it is clear that the United States owned the Alpha 1-4 cell line, and that Dr. Arora's dominion or control it, while brief, was total. He intended to act inconsistently with Dr. Sei's right to control the cells, he did not act in good faith, and he committed the ultimate harm — he destroyed the cells. While certain easily identifiable expense was caused by Dr. Arora's inappropriate acts, it is also apparent that he caused serious inconvenience to what was a critically important research project. By this analysis, if any tort was committed, it was unquestionably a conversion, not a mere trespass.

But what exactly did Dr. Arora convert? It is undoubtedly fair to conclude that by his wrongful act he caused the loss of the flasks, pipets and other materials used to culture the cells, a total value of $176.68.

But did he convert the cell line?

The fact is that the United States Supreme Court has recognized that a living cell line is a property interest capable of protection. *See Diamond v. Chakrabarty,* 447 U.S. 303 (1980) (inventor of a genetically-engineered organism could obtain protection of ownership interests under patent laws). Other courts have likewise acknowledged the cell line's status as property, *see e.g. Pasteur v. United States,* 814 F.2d 624 (Fed. Cir. 1987) (donated cell line assumed to be property but transfer held not subject to Contract Disputes Act). The Court thus sees no reason why a cell line should not be considered a chattel capable of being converted. Indeed, if such a cause of action is not recognized, it is hard to conceive what civil remedy would ever lie to recover a cell line that might be stolen or destroyed, including one with immense potential commercial value, as this one apparently had and has. *See generally,* Catherine M. Valerio Barrad, "*Genetic Information and Property Theory,*" 87 Nw. U. L. Rev. 1037 (1992). The Court is satisfied, therefore, under the circumstances of this case, that the Alpha 1-4 cell line was capable of being converted and that in fact Dr. Arora converted it. The more difficult question, perhaps, is how to assess damages, the next question before the Court.

What compensatory damages, if any, should be assessed?

The Government claims a broad array of damages by reason of Defendant's acts, including the costs of the flasks, materials and supplies used to create the cells, the reasonable value of the wages paid to the laboratory assistant who cultured the cells, and a sizeable amount for the delay in the research project occasioned by the conversion. Defendant, in sharp contrast, maintains that the Government has sustained no damage at all; indeed he has sought throughout to dismiss these proceedings by reason of that alleged fact.

The conventional rule in cases of conversion, it is true, fixes damages for a totally destroyed chattel at the market value as of the date of the conversion, plus interest to the date of judgment. *See Checkpoint Foreign Car Service, Inc. v. Sweeney,* 242 A.2d 148 (Md. 1968). To the extent that the chattel is a discrete tangible item of discernible market value, the calculation is fairly straightforward and presents little problem. The matter becomes more difficult when property of limited extrinsic or uncertain market value is involved. *See generally,* Dan B. Dobbs, *Law of Remedies,* §5.13(1) (2d ed. 1993).

But mere difficulty in ascertaining damages is not a basis for denying them. While the market value measure is the traditional rule in conversion cases, it is also the case, as stated by the Maryland Court of Appeals in *Staub v. Staub* that:

> [A]s in other tort actions, additional damages adequate to compensate an owner for other injurious consequences which result in a loss greater than the diminished or market value of the chattel at the time of the trespass or conversion may be allowed unless such claimed damages are so speculative as to create a danger of injustice to the opposite party.

37 Md. App. at 145-146.

See also Restatement (Second) of Torts, §927(2) (owner of converted chattel, in addition to diminished value, may recover "any further pecuniary loss of which the deprivation has been a legal cause"); *Amstar Corp. v. M/V Alexandros T,* 472 F. Supp. 1289 (D. Md. 1979) (awarding expenses of handling and testing damaged cargo of sugar, as well as loss of value of cargo). As observed by the United States District Court for the Eastern District of Pennsylvania in *American East India Corp. v. Ideal Shoe Co.,* 400 F. Supp. 141 (E.D. Pa. 1975):

> [T]he general purpose of damages in conversion is to provide indemnity for all actual losses or injuries sustained as a natural and proximate result of the converter's wrong. The measure of damages, generally employed, is the value of the property, with interest from the time of conversion, at the time and place of the conversion. However, it is appropriate to use whatever measure of damages accomplishes the general objective of indemnity under the particular circumstances. (Citations omitted.)

400 F. Supp. at 169.

For this reason, in a number of cases involving chattels of limited extrinsic or market value, courts have allowed as damages the original or replacement cost or cost of repair of the chattel. *See generally, Dobbs* at §5.13(1). And, where, as here, the converted chattel is essentially a product of creative effort as to which no original or replacement cost can fairly be assigned — for example, manuscripts or professional drawings — courts have also fixed damages based upon the value of the time that it took or would take to create the chattel. *See e.g., Wood v. Cunard,* 192 F. 293 (2d Cir. 1911) (taking into account the value of two years of intermittent labor required to reproduce lost manuscript); *Rajkovich v. Alfred Mossner Co.,* 557 N.E.2d 496 (Ill. App. 1990) (compensating for

172 hours of architectural time at specified rate necessary to redo damaged architectural drawings).

These principles find relatively easy application in the present case. The tangible chattels converted consist of the Alpha 1-4 cells and the flasks and related materials which contained them. The latter have a market value of some $176.68, while the value of the former is essentially unascertainable. But the evidence in the record also establishes the cost of creating or recreating the Alpha 1-4 cells at $273.52, the amount attributable to the services of a laboratory assistant necessary to culture the cells. The total of these two sums, $450.20, while modest, is nevertheless nontrivial. It is an amount properly awardable in this case and the Court has determined to award it.

On the other hand, the Court acknowledges the caveat of *Staub* that consequential damages may not be "so speculative as to create a danger of injustice." The Court, therefore, is inclined to agree with Defendant that any effort to quantify with precision damages for delay in the research project would run counter to that principle.

In Practice

At the core of claims for trespass to chattels and conversion is the unpermitted touching or taking of another's personal property. Whether the lawyer bringing a claim for such misconduct labels it as trespass or conversion may only affect the typical measure of damages. In some cases, such as in *Arora*, where the court could not utilize a market value theory of damages, the distinction between the two claims is not particularly important.

[The court went on to rule that the award of $5,000 in exemplary damages to punish the defendant was appropriate given the circumstances of the case.]

The Court, therefore, will enter judgment on . . . the conversion count, in favor of the United States, in the sum of $450.20 compensatory damages and $5,000.00 punitive damages and Defendant will also be directed to pay court costs.

NOTES AND PROBLEMS

1. ***Conversion vs. Trespass to Chattels.*** In *Arora*, the court spends considerable time determining whether the defendant's conduct amounted to a trespass or a conversion. What difference does this conclusion normally make? On the facts of *Arora*, and given the court's conclusion about the normal remedy for conversion being inapplicable, did the conversion vs. trespass distinction actually matter?

2. ***Forced Sale.*** With the normal remedy for conversion being for the plaintiff to recover the actual fair market value of the chattel at the time of the conversion, many courts refer to this remedy as a "forced sale," whereby

a defendant is, in effect, required to pay for the item whether the defendant wants to keep the chattel or not.

Upon Further Review

Whether analyzing a trespass to real estate or trespass to chattels claim, the key is the intentional contact made by the defendant with another's property without the owner's permission. The permission in either instance may either be express or implied from the circumstances. But even the defendant's good faith belief that he had permission (or consent) for the contact with the property is not a defense, unless the owner has acted in a way that would provide a reasonable manifestation of such consent. Reflecting the judgment that real estate is of greater import than personal property, while courts will also entertain a claim for at least nominal damages in a trespass to land case, courts will only permit a claim for nominal damages in a trespass to chattels if it characterizes the trespass as a dispossession rather than a mere harmless intermeddling. But regardless of label, where actual harm to the property is demonstrated, recovery for the intentional unpermitted touching is available.

INTENTIONAL INFLICTION OF EMOTIONAL DISTRESS

Of all of the intentional torts covered in this chapter, the newcomer to the tort block is the claim for intentional infliction of emotional distress. This is oftentimes referred to as the tort of "Outrage" because one of its chief elements — outrageous conduct by the defendant — is often the primary focus of a court's analysis of this claim. Sometimes a defendant's conduct is extreme and causes real harm, but other existing theories of recovery might be unavailing or provide a less than satisfactory response. In such situations, smart lawyers are able to draw upon existing legal principles to help courts craft a new cause of action. Our first case below involves one state's decision to recognize this new claim. This cause of action is designed primarily to protect one's right to be free from severe emotional distress caused by particularly reprehensible conduct. It is quite expansive in that it can be applied to a myriad of different fact patterns. This flexibility is both a benefit and a potential curse — courts are loathe to make it too easy for people to sue for hurt feelings, or else everyone could be considered a tortfeasor. Notice how the elements of this claim are designed to set relatively high hurdles for a claimant to clear in order to have a valid claim under this cause of action.

A. Outrageous Conduct Intending Emotional Distress

DOMINGUEZ v. EQUITABLE LIFE ASSURANCE

438 So. 2d 58 (Fla. App. 1983)

PEARSON, J.

This is an appeal from an order which, *inter alia*, dismissed with prejudice one count of the appellant's complaint which sought damages for severe emotional distress alleged to have been caused by outrageous conduct unconnected to any other identifiable tort. We are called upon to decide whether we recognize such a cause of action and, if so, whether the appellant's allegations, taken as true at this stage of the proceedings, bring him within the cause of action.

A cause of action for "intentional infliction of severe mental or emotional distress," more appropriately called "outrageous conduct causing severe emotional distress," essentially involves the deliberate or reckless infliction of mental suffering on another, even if unconnected to any other actionable wrong. Restatement (Second) of Torts §46 (1965). The elements of this cause of action are (1) the wrongdoer's conduct was intentional or reckless, that is, he intended his behavior when he knew or should have known that emotional distress would likely result; (2) the conduct was outrageous, that is, as to go beyond all bounds of decency, and to be regarded as odious and utterly intolerable in a civilized community; (3) the conduct caused the emotional distress; and (4) the emotional distress was severe.

Although the Florida Supreme Court has not yet definitively recognized the existence of this cause of action, it has not, on the other hand, definitively precluded courts of this state from doing so. *Ford Motor Credit Co. v. Sheehan*, 373 So. 2d 956, 960 (Fla. 1st DCA 1979). Thus, unimpeded by the dictates of *Hoffman v. Jones*, 280 So. 2d 431 (Fla. 1973), the district courts of appeal have forged ahead, and the First, Fourth and Fifth Districts, joining the majority view in this country, have concluded that the cause of action exists. *See Kirkpatrick v. Zitz*, 401 So. 2d 850 (Fla. 1st DCA 1981) (cause of action allowed); *Lay v. Roux Laboratories, Inc.*, 379 So. 2d 451 (Fla. 1st DCA 1980) (same); *Ford Motor Credit Co. v. Sheehan*, 373 So. 2d at 960 (same); *Dowling v. Blue Cross of Florida, Inc.*, 338 So. 2d 88 (Fla. 1st DCA 1976) (same); *Metropolitan Life Insurance Co. v. McCarson*, 429 So. 2d 1287 (Fla. 4th DCA 1983) (cause of action allowed); *Boyles v. Mid-Florida Television Corp.*, 431 So. 2d 627 (Fla. 5th DCA 1983) (cause of action recognized, but not properly pleaded); *Habelow v. Travelers Insurance Co.*, 389 So. 2d 218 (Fla. 5th DCA 1980) (cause of action recognized, but not applicable where outrageous conduct directed at another); *Food Fair, Inc. v. Anderson*, 382 So. 2d 150 (Fla. 5th DCA 1980) (cause of action recognized, but conduct not outrageous). The Second District has concluded otherwise. *See Gmuer v. Garner*, 426 So. 2d 972 (Fla. 2d DCA 1982).

We are of the opinion that the majority view is the correct one and conclude that we are not only free to adopt it, but are bound to do so by our own precedent. We recognize that in *Gellert v. Eastern Air Lines, Inc.*, 370 So. 2d 802 (Fla. 3d DCA 1979), cert. denied, 381 So. 2d 766 (Fla. 1980), and *Sacco v. Eagle Finance Corp. of North Miami Beach*, 234 So. 2d 406 (Fla. 3d DCA 1970), this court stated that a cause of action for emotional distress based on outrageous conduct will lie only where it is coupled with other recognized tortious conduct. It appears, however, that in *Sacco*, we completely overlooked our earlier contrary precedent of *Korbin v. Berlin*, 177 So. 2d 551 (Fla. 3d DCA 1965), cert. dismissed, 183 So. 2d 835 (Fla. 1966), and in *Gellert*, although paying lip service to *Korbin*, we incorrectly categorized *Korbin* as being a case where the outrageous conduct was coupled with an independent tort. *Korbin*, however, in which the court held that a child's cause of action for emotional distress lay against a defendant who told the child of her mother's alleged adultery, is not, as was pointed out in *Ford Motor Credit Co. v. Sheehan*, susceptible of the reading given it in *Gellert*:

> Gellert suggests that Korbin did not permit an independent action for severe emotional distress since the action for emotional damages was connected with the slander of the child's mother. We find this analysis unpersuasive for two reasons: First, no cause of action was brought for slander, and second, the slander, if proved, would have resulted in a tortious act against the mother, not the child. The two causes of action must be considered separate and personal to two different people.

373 So. 2d at 959 n.3.

Therefore, in our view, *Korbin*, never overruled, receded from, discredited or adequately distinguished, is clear precedent for our holding today that a cause of action for emotional distress brought about by outrageous conduct lies notwithstanding the absence of another tort. Indeed, *Korbin* is the only authority in this court which is undiluted by an alternative holding that the conduct involved was not outrageous. Neither *Gellert* nor *Sacco*, as the courts there recognized, involved conduct which would qualify as outrageous, and thus, these cases could have been decided on that ground without reaching the question of the existence *vel non* of the cause of action.

We turn now to the question of whether the allegations of Dominguez's complaint bring him within this cause of action.

The complaint alleges that in 1973, Equitable issued Dominguez a disability income policy of insurance which, in pertinent part, provided for $500 per month income for accidental total disability for the insured's lifetime. Shortly after the policy issued, Dominguez was involved in an automobile accident which "caused severe injuries to his body and extremities, including both eyes being knocked out of their sockets, brain damage, multiple large scars, psychiatric problems, periodic incontinence, paralysis of nerve in eye and other physical and mental problems, and mental injuries as well, which resulted in his total disability." Equitable paid Dominguez the disability income through August 1979 and then stopped making payments.

The heart of the complaint comes next:

> 16. On or about April 21, 1980, the Defendant, EQUITABLE, sent an agent to the home of the Plaintiff in Miami, Florida. . . . Said agent was Millie Dirube, who, at all times relevant hereto was acting for either or both Defendants, in the course and scope of her agency and employment. Said Millie Dirube falsely represented to Plaintiff that she had received a letter from the eye doctor saying that his eye(s) were OK now and that Plaintiff was no longer disabled and falsely represented to Plaintiff that he was no longer totally disabled, that he was not longer covered under the policy, that the policy was no longer in force, that he had to sign a paper agreeing that no further payments were due under the policy, that it no longer covered him, that he was no longer entitled to receive benefits under the policy and that he was giving up the policy voluntarily. At the time said Millie Dirube made said misrepresentation she knew them to be false and they were in fact false and she made them with the intention and expectation and intention that Plaintiff be deceived and defrauded thereby and that the [sic] sign said paper and surrender the subject policy. Defendants well knew that Plaintiff was suffering both physical and mental total disability and was entitled to benefits under the policy and that the representations of Millie Dirube were false. The foregoing acts were all in violation of their fiduciary relationship and duty of good faith and in an effort to use their superior knowledge skill and position to take advantage of this debilitated Plaintiff. A relative of Plaintiff overheard and intervened at the last minute and prevented Plaintiff from signing the paper and surrendering the policy.
>
> . . .
>
> 21. Defendant, EQUITABLE'S, acts and omissions set forth in this Complaint were done intentionally in order to inflict emotional distress upon the Plaintiff and/or were done in reckless disregard of the probability of causing emotional distress, and said acts and omissions did in fact cause severe and extreme emotional distress to the Plaintiff.

In our view, these allegations state a cause of action and fall well within comments e and f to *Section 46 of the Restatement,* which provide:

> e. The extreme and outrageous character of the conduct may arise from an abuse by the actor of a position, or a relation with the other, which gives him actual or apparent authority over the other, or power to affect his interests. . . .
>
> f. The extreme and outrageous character of the conduct may arise from the actor's knowledge that the other is peculiarly susceptible to emotional distress, by reason of some physical or mental condition or peculiarity. The conduct may be heartless, flagrant and outrageous when the actor proceeds in the face of such knowledge, where it would not be so if he did not know. . . .

The complaint alleges the defendants to be not only in a position to affect the plaintiff's interests, but actually having asserted their power by cutting off the plaintiff's disability payments without justification. It alleges further that the defendants were, as is obvious, aware of the plaintiff's disabilities and thus his susceptibility to emotional distress when they acted. This combination of the unjustified assertion of power by one party, and impotence of the other, would, we think, be viewed by a civilized community as outrageous and not as an indignity, annoyance or petty oppression for which the law affords no relief. Our conclusion that the conduct alleged is outrageous is amply supported by case law.

Accordingly, the trial court's order dismissing the plaintiff's complaint for failure to state a cause of action is reversed and the cause remanded for further proceedings.

NOTES AND PROBLEMS

1. ***Recognizing New Causes of Action.*** This cause of action is relatively new compared to the other intentional tort claims we have covered. In this opinion, the court determines whether or not to accept this new tort theory of recovery. This is an example of how the common law evolves to recognize new claims and doctrines. Why is the court inclined to accept this new independent theory without showing any other related tort claim?

2. ***Elements.*** What are the elements of this cause of action? How is the name "intentional infliction of emotional distress" a bit of a misnomer? What must be intended by the defendant to be potentially liable under this cause of action?

3. ***Objective Test for Outrageous Conduct.*** The Restatement (Second) of Torts §46, cmt. d (1965) describes the commonly accepted test of what is "outrageous" as follows:

> Generally, the case is one in which the recitation of the facts to an average member of the community would arouse his resentment against the actor, and lead him to exclaim, "Outrageous!"

What would be considered outrageous obviously can change under the circumstances of each case and from one community, and time, to another. What is it about the defendant's misconduct in the foregoing case that led the court to the conclusion that it might be considered outrageous?

4. ***Problems.*** Might the victims of the following conduct have a viable claim for intentional infliction of emotional distress?

A. Teenage mega-star Justine Bleeper cannot do any normal activities without being followed by paparazzi, insistent on taking unflattering photographs of her and selling them for profit. She has begun to break down, sobbing tears of anguish every time she fails in an attempt to go shopping and ends up being photographed against her will. Now she is afraid to leave her home.

B. Boo is a reclusive sort of man who lives with his father on a relatively quiet street in a small southern town. Local kids refuse to grant him any peace as they insist upon repeatedly ringing the doorbell and running away from the home. It's driving Boo mad.

C. Paula is a "gunner" in her first-year law school class, choosing to sit in the front row, diligently briefing every case, and raising her hand constantly to answer questions and pose her own hypothetical questions. Behind her back, her fellow students make fun of her, calling her names, giggling whenever she attempts to participate in class, and mocking her in the hallways in between class sessions. She cannot handle the intimidation, drops out of law school and now wants to recover from her classmates her lost future earnings as a lawyer.

ZALNIS v. THOROUGHBRED DATSUN CAR CO.

645 P.2d 292 (Colo. Ct. App. 1982)

KELLY, J.

Plaintiff, Christiane Zalnis, appeals the partial summary judgment dismissing her outrageous conduct claim against defendants. We reverse.

The following facts appear from viewing the record in a light most favorable to the plaintiff. In January 1978, Zalnis contracted with defendant Thoroughbred Datsun for the purchase of a 1978 Datsun automobile. She took possession of the car on that day, and paid the balance of the purchase price two days later. Zalnis dealt directly with Linnie Cade, a salesperson employed by Thoroughbred Datsun. Defendant Trosper, President of Thoroughbred Datsun, approved the transaction based on representations by Cade which were later determined to be based upon erroneous calculations. When Trosper discovered several days later that Cade had sold the car at a loss of approximately $1,000, he instructed Cade and the sales manager to make good the loss by either demanding more money from Zalnis, retrieving the car, or repaying the difference out of Cade's salary.

Cade refused to follow any of Trosper's alternative instructions, but another sales employee, defendant Anthony, telephoned Zalnis and told her to return her car to the dealership because it was being recalled. When Zalnis arrived at Thoroughbred Datsun, she refused to give up possession of her car without a work order explaining the need for the recall. Nevertheless, her car was taken from her. During the next few hours, Zalnis alleges that Anthony called her a "French whore," followed her throughout the showroom, told her they were keeping her automobile, yelled, screamed, used abusive language, grabbed her by the arm in a threatening manner, and continually threatened and intimidated her when she attempted to secure the return of her automobile by telling her to "shut up."

During this period, Zalnis telephoned her attorney, who then telephoned Trosper and eventually obtained the return of her car. During their conversation, Trosper told the attorney that Zalnis had "been sleeping with that nigger salesman and that's the only reason she got the deal she got." Trosper had known Zalnis for many years, and had told Cade and the sales manager that she was crazy and she had watched her husband kill himself.

Thoroughbred Datsun and Trosper moved for partial summary judgment on the outrageous conduct claim [also known as "intentional infliction of emotional distress"]. The trial court granted the motion, determining that, although the conduct was "almost shocking to the conscience and person of anyone observing that behavior," it did not amount to outrageous conduct under Colorado precedent.

In *Rugg. v. McCarty,* 476 P.2d 753 (Colo. 1970*),* the Supreme Court recognized the tort of outrageous conduct and adopted the definition set forth in the Restatement (Second) of Torts §46: "One who by extreme and outrageous conduct intentionally or recklessly causes severe emotional distress to another is subject to liability for such emotional distress, and if bodily harm to the other results from it, for such bodily harm." Although the question whether conduct is sufficiently outrageous is ordinarily a question for the jury, the court must determine in the first instance whether reasonable persons could differ on the outrageousness issue.

The defendants argue that their actions here were no more than "mere insults, indignities, threats, annoyances, petty oppressions, and other trivialities." Restatement (Second) of Torts §46, Comment d. However, the defendants did not merely threaten and insult Zalnis; they took away her car and repeatedly harassed her. Conduct, otherwise permissible, may become extreme and outrageous if it is an abuse by the actor of a position in which he has actual or apparent authority over the other, or the power to affect the other's interests. Restatement (Second) of Torts §46, Comment e; *See, e.g., Rugg v. McCarty, supra.*

The conduct here is not a mere insistence on rights in a permissible manner. *See Restatement (Second) of Torts §46, Comment g.* Rather, the defendants' recall of the car was to avoid a bad bargain, and accordingly, the conduct was not privileged. *Meiter, supra; see Enright v. Groves,* 560 P.2d 851 (Colo. 1977).

Defendants assert that their actions must be judged by the impact they would have on an ordinary person with ordinary sensibilities. We disagree. The outrageous character of the conduct may arise from the actor's knowledge that the other is peculiarly susceptible to emotional distress by reason of some physical or mental condition or peculiarity. Restatement (Second) of Torts §46, Comment f. In *Enright, supra,* outrageous conduct was found where a police officer effecting an illegal arrest grabbed and twisted the plaintiff's arm even after she told him her arm was easily dislocated. In the instant case, plaintiff was peculiarly susceptible to emotional distress because she had witnessed her husband's suicide, and Trosper and Anthony knew about her susceptibility. Here, as in *Enright,* the defendants' knowledge exacerbated the conduct.

Here, Zalnis has sufficiently alleged that Trosper and Anthony acted with the intent to bully her into giving up her car. In view of their knowledge of her emotional susceptibility, they could be considered to have acted intentionally or recklessly in causing her severe emotional distress.

The defendants argue that we should observe a distinction between a single outrageous occurrence and an outrageous course of conduct. While it is true that "the courts are more likely to find outrageous conduct in a series of incidents or a 'course of conduct' than in a single incident," it is the totality of conduct that must be evaluated to determine whether outrageous conduct has occurred. Our evaluation of the totality of the conduct leads to the conclusion that reasonable persons could differ on the question whether there was outrageous conduct, and thus, summary judgment was improper.

The judgment is reversed and the cause is remanded for further proceedings.

NOTES AND PROBLEMS

1. ***Intentional or Reckless Standard.*** The *Zalnis* case involves conduct alleged to have been intentional in causing severe emotional distress. In fact, as the court reads the allegations in that case, the defendants' plan was to cause so much stress to plaintiff that she would yield to their unreasonable and non-privileged demands to undo the transaction. The court mentions in its statement of the elements that, notwithstanding the name of the cause of action, reckless infliction of emotional distress will also suffice.

2. ***Other Causes of Action.*** Sometimes the facts in a case for intentional infliction of emotional distress might permit the plaintiff to plead another tort cause of action. Considering some of the intentional tort claims already covered in this book, can you spot any such possible claims the plaintiff might have attempted in *Zalnis*? Rule 18 of the Federal Rules of Civil Procedure permits a plaintiff pleading one claim against an opposing party to plead as many other claims as the plaintiff might have at the same time.

STRAUSS v. CILEK

418 N.W.2d 378 (Iowa 1987)

SACKETT, J.

The sole issue in this interlocutory appeal is whether the trial court erred in denying defendant's motion for summary judgment on plaintiff's claim of intentional infliction of emotional distress arising from defendant's romantic and sexual relationship with plaintiff's wife.

Defendant's affair with plaintiff's wife lasted one year. Plaintiff did not learn about the affair until after it was over. Plaintiff and his wife were in the process of obtaining a divorce at the time plaintiff initiated the present action for actual and punitive damages. The issue whether plaintiff in this case can maintain a claim for intentional infliction of emotional distress that arises out of a failed marital relationship may be appropriately resolved upon presentation of evidence through summary judgment. *Van Meter v. Van Meter,* 328 N.W.2d 497, 498 (Iowa 1983).

Summary judgment is appropriate if the moving party shows that there is no genuine issue as to any material fact and that the moving party is entitled to judgment as a matter of law. Iowa R. Civ. P. 237(c). The resisting party must set forth specific facts showing there is a genuine issue for trial. Iowa R. Civ. P. 237(e). Our task on appeal is to determine only whether a genuine issue of material fact exists and whether the law was correctly applied. *Adam v. Mt. Pleasant Bank & Trust Co.,* 355 N.W.2d 868, 872 (Iowa 1984).

The elements of the tort of intentional infliction of emotional distress are as follows:

> (1) Outrageous conduct by the defendant;
>
> (2) The defendant's intention of causing, or reckless disregard of the probability of causing emotional distress;
>
> (3) The plaintiff's suffering severe or extreme emotional distress; and
>
> (4) Actual causation of the emotional distress by the defendant's outrageous conduct.

Amsden v. Grinnell Mut. Reinsurance Co., 203 N.W.2d 252, 255 (Iowa 1972).

In overruling defendant's motion for summary judgment, the trial court declined to rule as a matter of law that defendant's actions were not outrageous. We find the evidence in the summary judgment record insufficient to demonstrate a genuine issue of fact on the outrageous conduct element.

It is for the court to determine in the first instance whether the relevant conduct may reasonably be regarded as outrageous. *Roalson v. Chaney,* 334 N.W.2d 754, 756 (Iowa 1983). To be outrageous the conduct must be so extreme in degree as to go beyond all possible bounds of decency to be regarded as atrocious and utterly intolerable in a civilized community. *Vinson v. Lin-Mar Community School Dist.,* 360 N.W.2d 108, 118 (Iowa 1984) (citations omitted).

In *Roalson v. Chaney,* 334 N.W.2d at 755, Chaney asked Roalson's wife to marry him while she and Roalson were still married. The Iowa Supreme Court held no trier of fact could reasonably find Chaney's conduct outrageous. *Id.* at 757. More recently, in *Kunau v. Pillers, Pillers & Pillers,* 404 N.W.2d 573, 576 (Iowa App. 1987), we held the facts of a case in which Kunau's wife had a lengthy sexual and romantic affair with her dentist could not support a conclusion the dentist's conduct was outrageous.

Plaintiff claims defendant's conduct in the present case is outrageous because plaintiff and defendant had known each other since elementary school and were good friends. We do not say that sexual relations between a plaintiff's friend and spouse would never give rise to a finding of outrageous conduct. We find the facts in this case, however, do not support a conclusion defendant's conduct is outrageous.

Defendant and plaintiff's wife kept their relationship secret until after it was over. Personal letters written by defendant to plaintiff's wife reveal defendant's genuine intention to leave his wife and children and to create a permanent relationship with plaintiff's wife. Plaintiff did not discover these letters discussing defendant's plans for the future until after he knew the affair had occurred. The record also reveals plaintiff's wife was unhappy in her marriage. She had previously engaged in an extramarital affair that lasted for five years with another of plaintiff's good friends.

We do not condone promiscuous sexual conduct. *See Fundermann v. Mickelson,* 304 N.W.2d 790, 794 (Iowa 1981). However, we do not find defendant's conduct in participating in a sexual relationship with a married woman, his friend's wife, who willingly continued the affair over an extended period, is atrocious and utterly intolerable conduct so extreme in degree as to go beyond all possible bounds of decency. *Vinson,* 360 N.W.2d at 118. The parties are residents of Iowa City, a community of 50,000 and the home of the University of Iowa. A recitation of the facts of this case to an average member of the community would not lead him to exclaim, "Outrageous!"

The trial court erred in overruling defendant's motion for summary judgment. We reverse and remand the case for entry of an order granting defendant's motion for summary judgment.

NOTES AND PROBLEMS

1. ***Determination of Outrageousness.*** In order to recover on a challenged claim for intentional infliction of emotional distress, one of the biggest hurdles a plaintiff must overcome is demonstrating that the challenged conduct meets the Restatement definition for "outrageous" conduct. There are a lot of different people in the audience a plaintiff must convince. First, the plaintiff must get the trial judge to accept the possibility that the alleged conduct might be considered outrageous — otherwise defendant's motion to dismiss will be granted. At trial the plaintiff must continue to convince the trial judge of the viability of the claim, or else face a motion for directed verdict. Even after doing so, the plaintiff will then have to convince a jury (in federal court by a unanimous verdict) that the conduct is outrageous. Even if the plaintiff has succeeded with each of these audiences, the plaintiff may have to convince a three-judge panel on an appellate court that the conduct might be considered outrageous.

2. ***Other Previously Recognized Claims.*** Earlier in the twentieth century, courts in most states used to recognize so-called "heart balm" torts related to

various acts of home-wrecking. For example, many states recognized a claim for "alienation of affection" or "criminal conversation" when someone seduced another's spouse into having an affair. For various reasons, most states have decided to get out of the business of regulating the morality of such conduct and have abandoned these causes of action. Does this explain, in any way, the reluctance by the *Strauss* court to even submit the issue of outrageousness to the jury?

3. ***Intent.*** Recall that this tort claim can be committed by either one intending to cause the plaintiff's severe emotional distress or through acts that recklessly cause such distress. Given our coverage of the definitions for intentional misconduct, do the facts in *Strauss* seem to be more a case of intentionally causing emotional distress or recklessly causing it?

B. Severe Emotional Distress

The final significant obstacle that every plaintiff faces when trying to recover for the tort of outrage is to prove that the plaintiff's emotional distress is *severe.* What standard courts use to measure the degree of emotional distress required to prove this element, and the type of proof demanded, are two principal subjects of the *Miller* and the *Clinton* cases. You should focus both on the definition of severe emotional distress, as well as upon the types of evidence available to a plaintiff to meet this standard.

MILLER v. WILLBANKS, M.D.

8 S.W.3d 606 (Tenn. 1999)

BARKER, J.

We granted this appeal to decide whether the Court of Appeals erred in holding that expert medical or scientific proof of a serious mental injury is required to support the plaintiffs' claims for intentional infliction of emotional distress. The trial court granted the defendants' motion for summary judgment because the plaintiffs failed to have available expert proof to corroborate their claims of having sustained serious mental injuries. The Court of Appeals affirmed the trial court's dismissal of the case.

[The Millers sued Dr. Willbanks for intentional infliction of emotional distress. Shortly after Elizabeth Ann Miller gave birth to her daughter, defendant suspected Miller of being a drug abuser. The baby had symptoms of Drug Withdrawal Syndrome. The defendant spread his suspicions among hospital staff and even Miller's parents before confronting her. She agreed to a drug test, which came back negative. Undaunted, defendant continued with his accusations and reported Miller to the local health department, which visited Miller's home for inspection and examination of Miller over her objections.]

The Millers sued Dr. Willbanks [and others] for the tort of intentional infliction of emotional distress. The defendants then moved for dismissal or summary judgment, which the trial court granted due to the plaintiffs' lack of expert evidence to support their claims of serious mental injury. The Court of Appeals affirmed the decision of the trial court.

We granted the plaintiffs' appeal to decide whether the Court of Appeals erred in holding that expert medical or scientific proof of a serious mental injury was required to support the plaintiffs' claim for the intentional infliction of emotional distress.

[The court summarized the history in Tennessee of courts' initial reluctance to recognize claims where the primary injury was mental distress. Courts began permitting such claims by stretching certain tort doctrines. Eventually the Tennessee Supreme Court adopted the tort of intentional infliction of emotional distress based upon the exacting requirements of the Restatement for proving such a claim.]

In the brief history of the tort of intentional infliction of emotional distress, this Court has not examined whether expert testimony is required to establish the existence of a serious mental injury. Other courts, however, that have examined this issue have come to markedly different conclusions.

A minority of jurisdictions requires expert medical or scientific proof of serious mental injury to maintain a claim for intentional infliction of emotional distress. *See*, e.g., *Kazatsky v. King David Mem'l Park, Inc.*, 515 Pa. 183, 527 A.2d 988 (Pa. 1987). These courts reason that expert proof is necessary to prevent the tort from being reduced to a single element of outrageousness, so by requiring expert proof, the elements of outrageous conduct and serious mental injury remain distinct. *See Kazatsky*, 527 A.2d at 995. Moreover, courts expressing the minority view contend that because expert proof can be easily obtained, it must be used to prove serious mental injury. These courts assert that due to the wide availability of expert proof, plaintiffs will encounter "little difficulty in procuring reliable testimony as to the nature and extent of their injuries." *Id.*

A majority of courts that have examined this issue, however, have concluded that expert proof is generally not necessary to establish the existence of a serious mental injury. The flagrant and outrageous nature of the defendant's conduct, according to these courts, adds weight to a plaintiff's claim and affords more assurance that the claim is serious. Moreover, expert testimony is not essential because other reliable forms of evidence, including physical manifestations of distress and subjective testimony, are available. Courts following the majority approach also contend that expert testimony is normally not necessary because a jury is generally capable of determining whether a claimant has sustained a serious mental injury as a proximate result of the intentional conduct of another person. *See McKnight*, 358 S.E.2d at 109. Additionally, courts expressing the majority view reason that the very nature of the tort of intentional infliction of emotional distress "makes it impossible to quantify damages mainly on expert medical evidence." *Chandler,* 741 P.2d at 867.

We conclude that the majority approach is consistent with our precedents and the underlying policies governing the law of intentional infliction of emotional distress. As previously discussed, the Court in Medlin examined and rejected arguments traditionally used to justify limiting actions for mental distress. Additionally, through our interpretation of intentional infliction of emotional distress, this Court has also rejected a second argument — the requirement of an accompanying physical injury. *See Medlin,* 398 S.W.2d at 273-74. The policy underlying development of the tort is that legitimate claims for emotional distress should be actionable and should be judged on their merits. With our decision today, we reject a third argument — the requirement of expert testimony. In so doing, we ensure that a plaintiff with a legitimate claim for intentional infliction of emotional distress will have an opportunity to seek redress for that claim, unburdened by the historical limits imposed by law.

We recognize that legitimate concerns of fraudulent and trivial claims are implicated when a plaintiff brings an action for a purely mental injury. Thus, safeguards are needed to ensure the reliability of claims for intentional and negligent infliction of emotional distress. These safeguards, however, differ based on the kind of conduct, rather than the kind of injury, for which a plaintiff seeks a remedy.

With regard to intentional infliction of emotional distress, the added measure of reliability, *i.e.*, the insurance against frivolous claims, is found in the plaintiff's burden to prove that the offending conduct was outrageous. This is an exacting standard requiring the plaintiff to show that the defendant's conduct is "so outrageous in character, and so extreme in degree, as to go beyond all possible bounds of decency and to be regarded as atrocious, and utterly intolerable in a civilized community." Restatement (Second) of Torts §46 cmt. d (1965). Such conduct is "important evidence that the distress has existed," id. §45 cmt. j, and from such conduct, more reliable indicia of a severe mental injury may arise. The outrageous nature of the conduct, therefore, vitiates the need for expert testimony in a claim for intentional infliction of emotional distress. The risk of frivolous litigation, then, is alleviated in claims for intentional infliction of emotional distress by the requirement that a plaintiff prove that the offending conduct was so outrageous that it is not tolerated by a civilized society.

Although we adopt the majority approach and hold that plaintiffs normally will not be required to support their claims of serious mental injury by expert proof in order to recover damages in a suit based upon the intentional infliction of emotional distress, we certainly do not discredit the use of expert testimony at trial. We are fully aware that there will be many cases in which a judge or jury may not appreciate the full extent and disabling effects of a plaintiff's emotional injury without expert evidence.

Our decision today merely recognizes that in most cases other forms of proof may also be used to establish a claim for intentional infliction of emotional distress. Such proof may include a claimant's own testimony, *See Peery,* 897 P.2d at 1191, as well as the testimony of other lay witnesses acquainted with the claimant, *see Uebelacker,* 549 N.E.2d at 1220. Physical manifestations of emotional distress may also serve as proof of serious mental injury. Moreover, evidence that a plaintiff has suffered from nightmares, insomnia, and depression or has sought psychiatric treatment may support a claim of a serious mental injury. *See Medlin,* 398 S.W.2d at 272; *Johnson v. Woman's Hosp.*, 527 S.W.2d 133, 140 (Tenn. Ct. App. 1975). The intensity and duration of the mental distress are also factors that may be considered in determining the severity of the injury.

Such proof, however, is no guarantee that a plaintiff will prevail. The weight, faith, and credibility afforded to any witness's testimony lies in the first instance with the trier of fact who is free to conclude that the subjective testimony of a plaintiff or other lay witnesses is not sufficient to prove a serious mental injury. Thus, although not legally required, "expert testimony may be the most effective method of demonstrating the existence of severe emotional distress." *Richardson,* 705 P.2d at 457 n.6.

In summary, we hold that expert medical or scientific proof of a serious mental injury is generally not required to maintain a claim for intentional infliction of emotional distress. Accordingly, we reverse the judgments of the trial court and the Court of Appeals and remand to the trial court for further proceedings.

NOTES AND PROBLEMS

1. ***Restatement Test for Severe Emotional Distress.*** In trying to differentiate *severe* emotional distress from ordinary emotional distress, courts frequently cite to the following explanation from the Restatement:

> Emotional distress passed under various names, such as mental suffering, mental anguish, mental or nervous shock, or the like. It includes all highly unpleasant mental reactions, such as fright, horror, grief, shame, humiliation, embarrassment, anger, chagrin, disappointment, worry, and nausea. It is only where it is extreme that the liability arises. Complete emotional tranquility is seldom attainable in this world, and some degree of transient and trivial emotional distress is a part of the price of living among people. The law intervenes only where the distress inflicted is so severe that no reasonable man could be expected to endure it. The *intensity* and *duration* of the distress are factors to be considered in determining its severity.

Restatement (Second) of Torts §46, comment j (1965) (emphasis added).

2. ***Reluctance to Water Down the Severity Element.*** The *Miller* court mentions that the minority of courts that demand expert witness proof of severe emotional distress do so out of a concern that otherwise this final hurdle will

become practically meaningless. In other words, that proof of this tort will be reduced essentially to showing that the defendant's conduct was outrageous. The *Miller* court finds this unpersuasive. Nevertheless it too resorts to reliance upon the element of outrageousness to help support its decision to refrain from requiring expert testimony. After this decision, in the majority of states, how difficult will it be for plaintiffs to survive dismissal when they have proof of sufficiently outrageous misconduct?

JONES v. CLINTON

990 F. Supp. 657 (W.D. Ark. 1998)

WRIGHT, J.

The plaintiff in this lawsuit, Paula Corbin Jones, seeks civil damages from William Jefferson Clinton, President of the United States . . . for alleged actions beginning with an incident in a hotel suite in Little Rock, Arkansas. [The U.S. Supreme Court had already decided in this case that the president had no immunity from suit despite his office. Thereafter the federal district court dismissed plaintiff's claims for defamation and due process violations for failure to state a claim. The current motion is by the president seeking summary judgment of, among other things, plaintiff's claim for intentional infliction of emotional distress.]

This lawsuit is based on an incident that is said to have taken place on the afternoon of May 8, 1991, in a suite at the Excelsior Hotel in Little Rock, Arkansas. President Clinton was Governor of the State of Arkansas at the time, and plaintiff was a State employee with the Arkansas Industrial Development Commission ("AIDC"), having begun her State employment on March 11, 1991. Ferguson was an Arkansas State Police officer assigned to the Governor's security detail. [Plaintiff alleged that a member of Clinton's security detail relayed a message to her that Clinton wanted to meet her at his suite and gave her his room number. She went to the room thinking that meeting the Governor of Arkansas might be a good career move and an honor.]

Plaintiff states that upon arriving at the suite and announcing herself, the Governor shook her hand, invited her in, and closed the door. She states that a few minutes of small talk ensued. . . . Plaintiff states that the Governor then "unexpectedly reached over to [her], took her hand, and pulled her toward him, so that their bodies were close to each other." She states she removed her hand from his and retreated several feet, but that the Governor approached her again and, while saying, "I love the way your hair flows down your back" and "I love your curves," put his hand on her leg, started sliding it toward her pelvic area, and bent down to attempt to kiss her on the neck, all without her consent. Plaintiff states that she exclaimed, "What are you doing?" told the Governor that she was "not that kind of girl," and "escaped" from the Governor's reach "by walking away from him." She states she was extremely upset and confused and, not knowing what to do, attempted to distract the Governor by chatting about his wife. Plaintiff states that she sat down at the end of the sofa nearest the door, but that the Governor approached the sofa where she had taken a seat and, as he sat down, "lowered his trousers and underwear, exposed his penis (which was erect) and told [her] to 'kiss it.'" She states that she was "horrified" by this and that she "jumped up from the couch" and told the Governor that she had to go, saying something to the effect that she had to get back to the registration desk. Plaintiff states that the Governor, "while fondling his penis," said, "Well, I don't want to make you do anything you don't want to do," and then pulled up his pants and said, "If you get in trouble for leaving work, have Dave [a member of his detail] call me immediately and I'll take care of it." She states that as she left the room (the door of which was not locked), the Governor "detained" her momentarily, "looked sternly" at her, and said, "You are smart. Let's keep this between ourselves."

Plaintiff states that the Governor's advances to her were unwelcome, that she never said or did anything to suggest to the Governor that she was willing to have sex with him, and that during the time they were together in the hotel suite, she resisted his advances although she was "stunned by them and intimidated by who he was." She states that from that point on, she was "very fearful" that her refusal to submit to the Governor's advances could damage her career and even jeopardize her employment.

Plaintiff voluntarily terminated her employment with AIDC on February 20, 1993, in order to move to California with her husband, who had been transferred. . . . Thereafter, on May 6, 1994, plaintiff filed this lawsuit.

Plaintiff's amended complaint contains . . . a state law claim in which plaintiff asserts a claim of intentional infliction of emotional distress or outrage against Governor Clinton, based primarily on the alleged incident at the hotel but also encompassing subsequent alleged acts.

The President moves for summary judgment on the following grounds: . . . plaintiff's claim of intentional infliction of emotional distress or outrage fails because (a) by plaintiff's own testimony, the conduct at issue does not constitute intentional infliction of emotional distress or outrage under Arkansas law, and (b) plaintiff did not as a result of the alleged conduct suffer emotional distress so severe that no reasonable person could endure it.

Arkansas recognizes a claim of intentional infliction of emotional distress based on sexual harassment. To establish a claim of intentional infliction of emotional distress, a plaintiff must prove that: (1) the defendant intended to inflict emotional distress or knew or should have known that emotional distress was the likely result of his conduct; (2) the conduct was extreme and outrageous and utterly intolerable in a civilized community; (3) the defendant's conduct was the cause of the plaintiff's distress; and (4) the plaintiff's emotional distress was so severe in nature that no reasonable person could be expected to endure it.

The President argues that the alleged conduct of which plaintiff complains was brief and isolated; did not result in any physical harm or objective symptoms of the requisite severe distress; did not result in distress so severe that no reasonable person could be expected to endure it; and he had no knowledge of any special condition of plaintiff that would render her particularly susceptible to distress. He argues that plaintiff has failed to identify the kind of clear cut proof that Arkansas courts require for a claim of outrage and that he is therefore entitled to summary judgment. The Court agrees.

One is subject to liability for the tort of outrage or intentional infliction of emotional distress if he or she wilfully or wantonly causes severe emotional distress to another by extreme and outrageous conduct. In *M.B.M. Co. v. Counce,* 268 Ark. 269, 596 S.W.2d 681, 687 (Ark. 1980), the Arkansas Supreme Court stated that "by extreme and outrageous conduct, we mean conduct that is so outrageous in character, and so extreme in degree, as to go beyond all possible bounds of decency, and to be regarded as atrocious, and utterly intolerable in civilized society." Whether conduct is "extreme and outrageous" is determined by looking at "the conduct at issue; the period of time over which the conduct took place; the relation between plaintiff and defendant; and defendant's knowledge that plaintiff is particularly susceptible to emotional distress by reason of some physical or mental peculiarity." *Doe v. Wright,* 82 F.3d 265, 269 (8th Cir. 1996) (citing *Hamaker,* 51 F.3d at 111). The tort is clearly not intended to provide legal redress for every slight insult or indignity that one must endure. *Manning,* 127 F.3d at 690 (citing *Hamaker,* 51 F.3d at 110). The Arkansas courts take a strict approach and give a narrow view to claims of outrage and merely describing conduct as outrageous does not make it so. *Ross,* 817 S.W.2d at 420.

Plaintiff seems to base her claim of outrage on her erroneous belief that the allegations she has presented are sufficient to constitute criminal sexual assault. She states that "Mr. Clinton's outrageous conduct includes offensive language, an offensive proposition, offensive touching (constituting sexual assault under both federal and state definitions), and actual exposure of intimate private body part," and that "there are few more outrageous acts than a criminal sexual assault followed by unwanted exposure, coupled with a demand for oral sex by the most powerful man in the state against a very young, low-level employee."

While the Court will certainly agree that plaintiff's allegations describe offensive conduct, the Court, as previously noted, has found that the Governor's alleged conduct does not constitute sexual assault. Rather, the conduct as alleged by plaintiff describes a mere sexual proposition or encounter, albeit an odious one, that was relatively brief in duration, did not involve any coercion or threats of reprisal, and was abandoned as soon as plaintiff made clear that the advance was not welcome. The Court is not aware of any authority holding that such a sexual encounter or proposition of the type alleged in this case, without more, gives rise to a claim of outrage. *Cf. Croom,* 323 Ark. 95, 913 S.W.2d 283 at 287 (use of wine and medication by a vastly older relative to foist sex on a minor cousin went "beyond a mere sexual encounter" and offended all sense of decency).

Moreover, notwithstanding the offensive nature of the Governor's alleged conduct, plaintiff admits that she never missed a day of work following the alleged incident, she continued to work at AIDC another nineteen months (leaving only because of her husband's job transfer), she continued to go on a daily basis to the Governor's Office to deliver items and never asked to be relieved of that duty, she never filed a formal complaint or told her supervisors of the incident while at AIDC, she never consulted a psychiatrist, psychologist, or incurred medical bills as a result of the alleged incident, and she acknowledges that her two subsequent contacts with the Governor involved comments made "in a light vein" and nonsexual contact that was done in a "friendly fashion." Further, despite earlier claiming that she suffered marital discord and humiliation, plaintiff stated in her deposition that she was not claiming damages to her marriage as a result of the Governor's alleged conduct. . . . Plaintiff's actions and statements in this case do not portray someone who experienced emotional distress so severe in nature that no reasonable person could be expected to endure it.

In sum, plaintiff's allegations fall far short of the rigorous standards for establishing a claim of outrage under Arkansas law and the Court therefore grants the President's motion for summary judgment on this claim.

NOTES AND PROBLEMS

1. ***Outrage in the Context of Sexual Harassment.*** Courts are reluctant in many instances to recognize the application of the tort of intentional infliction of emotional distress when they believe that other causes of action have already been fashioned with special requirements. To recognize this new tort when other claims are unavailing might undermine the law in those other areas. The court in *Clinton* already determined that the plaintiff did not have a good cause of action for employment discrimination. How might this impact the court's view of the plaintiff's ability to state a claim for intentional infliction of emotional distress?

2. ***The Rest of the Story.*** While the above case was still pending, plaintiff's counsel took President Clinton's deposition and inquired about other alleged sexual affairs involving other women. He was asked, famously, whether he "ever had sexual relations with Monica Lewinsky . . . ?" President Clinton denied any such activities. When a witness named Linda Tripp provided tangible evidence (in the form of a stained blue dress) of such a possible relationship, charges of perjury were drawn up and this led to the House of Representatives voting to impeach the President. The Republican-controlled Senate was never able to garner the required two-thirds votes to convict, with only 45 senators voting guilty on the charges. Despite the dismissal of the above case on summary judgment, President Clinton later agreed to a monetary payment to the plaintiff in exchange for her agreement to drop her possible appeal of this summary judgment order. If nothing else, the *Clinton* case demonstrates that even

scandalous activity may not clear the high hurdles courts have established for maintaining a claim for intentional infliction of emotional distress.

3. ***Problems.*** Would the following plaintiffs appear to show severe emotional distress in response to outrageous conduct?

A. Plaintiff screamed, yelled at the defendant, and went home fuming for most of the rest of the evening.

B. Plaintiff's blood pressure became elevated, requiring chronic medication to keep it under control.

C. Plaintiff fell to the ground with despair, required months of counseling, and still battles with insomnia.

"LADIES AND GENTLEMEN OF THE JURY . . ."

3.30F New Jersey Model Civil Jury Charges

INTENTIONAL INFLICTION OF EMOTIONAL DISTRESS

The plaintiff is (also) bringing an action based on intentional infliction of emotional distress allegedly caused by the defendant. To recover, plaintiff must establish the following elements:

First, the plaintiff must prove that the defendant acted intentionally or recklessly. For an intentional act to result in liability, the defendant must intend both to do the act and to produce emotional distress. For a reckless act to result in liability, a defendant must act in deliberate disregard of a high degree of probability that emotional distress will follow.

Second, the defendant's conduct must be extreme and outrageous. The conduct must be so outrageous in character and so extreme in degree as to go beyond all possible bounds of decency and to be regarded as atrocious and utterly intolerable in a civilized community. The liability clearly does not extend to mere insults, indignities, threats, annoyances, petty oppressions or other trivialities.

Third, the defendant's actions must have been the proximate cause of plaintiff's emotional distress.

Fourth, the emotional distress suffered by plaintiff must be so severe that no reasonable person could be expected to endure such distress. Defendant's conduct must be sufficiently severe to cause genuine and substantial emotional distress or mental harm to the average person. This average person must be one similarly situated to the plaintiff. The plaintiff cannot recover for his/her emotional distress if that emotional distress would not have been experienced by an average person.

C. Constitutional Protection of Outrageous Speech

Where a claim for intentional infliction of emotional distress relies primarily upon a form of speech to demonstrate the requisite outrageous conduct, there arises the potential that a court's entry of a judgment for damages against the defendant could be viewed as an unconstitutional restriction on free speech. In Chapter 12 we will see courts having significant concerns with the application of the law of defamation to the First Amendment's protection of freedom of speech. The United States Supreme Court has been sensitive to balancing a state's legitimate interest in providing remedies for victims of torts, while not permitting such civil actions to unduly infringe a citizen's right to express even "outrageous" views. Consider how the Supreme Court in the recent *Snyder* case has attempted to strike this balance in the context of a claim for intentional infliction of emotional distress against a church engaging in what many consider to be highly offensive speech-based conduct.

SNYDER v. PHELPS

562 U.S. 443 (2011)

A jury held members of the Westboro Baptist Church liable for millions of dollars in damages for picketing near a soldier's funeral service. The picket signs reflected the church's view that the United States is overly tolerant of sin and that God kills American soldiers as punishment. The question presented is whether the First Amendment shields the church members from tort liability for their speech in this case.

Fred Phelps founded the Westboro Baptist Church in Topeka, Kansas, in 1955. The church's congregation believes that God hates and punishes the United States for its tolerance of homosexuality, particularly in America's military. The church frequently communicates its views by picketing, often at military funerals. In the more than 20 years that the members of Westboro Baptist have publicized their message, they have picketed nearly 600 funerals. Marine Lance Corporal Matthew Snyder was killed in Iraq in the line of duty. Lance Corporal Snyder's father selected the Catholic church in the Snyders' hometown of Westminster, Maryland, as the site for his son's funeral. Local newspapers provided notice of the time and location of the service.

Phelps became aware of Matthew Snyder's funeral and decided to travel to Maryland with six other Westboro Baptist parishioners (two of his daughters and four of his grandchildren) to picket. On the day of the memorial service, the Westboro congregation members picketed on public land adjacent to public streets near the Maryland State House, the United States Naval Academy, and Matthew Snyder's funeral. The Westboro picketers carried signs that were largely the same at all three locations. They stated, for instance: "God Hates the USA/Thank God for 9/11," "America is Doomed," "Don't Pray for the USA," "Thank God

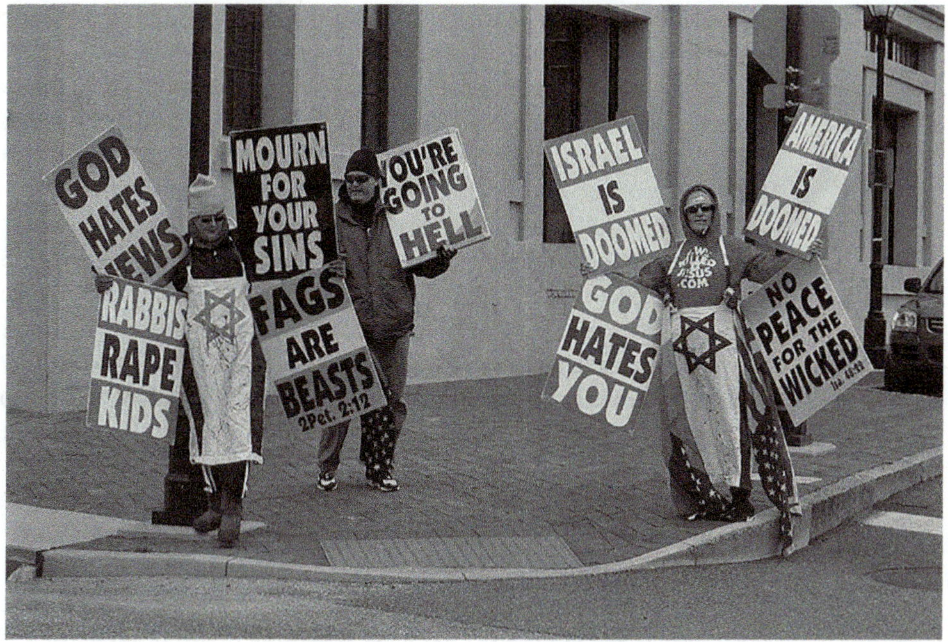

for IEDs," "Thank God for Dead Soldiers," "Pope in Hell," "Priests Rape Boys," "God Hates Fags," "You're Going to Hell," and "God Hates You."

The church had notified the authorities in advance of its intent to picket at the time of the funeral, and the picketers complied with police instructions in staging their demonstration. The picketing took place within a 10-by-25-foot plot of public land adjacent to a public street, behind a temporary fence. That plot was approximately 1,000 feet from the church where the funeral was held. Several buildings separated the picket site from the church. The Westboro picketers displayed their signs for about 30 minutes before the funeral began and sang hymns and recited Bible verses. None of the picketers entered church property or went to the cemetery. They did not yell or use profanity, and there was no violence associated with the picketing.

The funeral procession passed within 200 to 300 feet of the picket site. Although Snyder testified that he could see the tops of the picket signs as he drove to the funeral, he did not see what was written on the signs until later that night, while watching a news broadcast covering the event.

Snyder filed suit against Phelps, Phelps's daughters, and the Westboro Baptist Church (collectively Westboro or the church) in the United States District Court for the District of Maryland under that court's diversity jurisdiction. Snyder alleged . . . intentional infliction of emotional distress. Westboro moved for summary judgment contending, in part, that the church's speech was insulated from liability by the First Amendment.

To succeed on a claim for intentional infliction of emotional distress in Maryland, a plaintiff must demonstrate that the defendant intentionally or recklessly engaged in extreme and outrageous conduct that caused the plaintiff to suffer severe emotional distress. *See Harris v. Jones*, 380 A.2d 611, 614 (Md. 1977). The Free Speech Clause of the First Amendment — "Congress shall make no law . . . abridging the freedom of speech" — can serve as a defense in state tort suits, including suits for intentional infliction of emotional distress. *See, e.g., Hustler Magazine, Inc. v. Falwell*, 485 U.S. 46, 50-51 (1988).

Whether the First Amendment prohibits holding Westboro liable for its speech in this case turns largely on whether that speech is of public or private concern, as determined by all the circumstances of the case. "[S]peech on 'matters of public concern' . . . is 'at the heart of the First Amendment's protection.'" *Dun & Bradstreet, Inc. v. Greenmoss Builders, Inc.*, 472 U.S. 749, 758-759 (1985) (opinion of Powell, J.). The First Amendment reflects "a profound national commitment to the principle that debate on public issues should be uninhibited, robust, and wide-open." *New York Times Co. v. Sullivan*, 376 U.S. 254, 270 (1964). That is because "speech concerning public affairs is more than self-expression; it is the essence of self-government." *Garrison v. Louisiana*, 379 U.S. 64, 74-75 (1964). Accordingly, "speech on public issues occupies the highest rung of the hierarchy of First Amendment values, and is entitled to special protection." *Connick v. Myers*, 461 U.S. 138 (1983). "[N]ot all speech is of equal First Amendment importance," however, and where matters of purely private significance are at issue, First Amendment protections are often less rigorous. *Hustler, supra*, at 56.

We noted a short time ago, in considering whether public employee speech addressed a matter of public concern, that "the boundaries of the public concern test are not well defined." *San Diego v. Roe*, 543 U.S. 77, 83 (2004) (*per curiam*). Although that remains true today, we have articulated some guiding principles, principles that accord broad protection to speech to ensure that courts themselves do not become inadvertent censors.

Speech deals with matters of public concern when it can "be fairly considered as relating to any matter of political, social, or other concern to the community," *Connick, supra*, at 146, or when it "is a subject of legitimate news interest; that is, a subject of general interest and of value and concern to the public," *San Diego, supra*, at 83-84. The arguably "inappropriate or controversial character of a statement is irrelevant to the question whether it deals with a matter of public concern." *Rankin v. McPherson*, 483 U.S. 378, 387 (1987).

> "Congress shall make no law . . . abridging the freedom of speech."
>
> *First Amendment*

Our opinion in *Dun & Bradstreet*, on the other hand, provides an example of speech of only private concern. In that case we held, as a general matter, that information about a particular individual's credit report "concerns no public issue." 472 U.S., at 762. The content of the report, we explained, "was speech solely in the individual interest of the speaker and its specific business audience." *Ibid.* That was confirmed by the fact that the particular report was sent to only five subscribers to the reporting service, who were bound not to disseminate it further. *Ibid.*

Deciding whether speech is of public or private concern requires us to examine the "content, form, and context" of that speech, "as revealed by the whole record." *Dun & Bradstreet, supra,* at 761. As in other First Amendment cases, the court is obligated "to 'make an independent examination of the whole record' in order to make sure that 'the judgment does not constitute a forbidden intrusion on the field of free expression.'" *Bose Corp. v. Consumers Union of United States, Inc.,* 466 U.S. 485, 499.

The "content" of Westboro's signs plainly relates to broad issues of interest to society at large, rather than matters of "purely private concern." *Dun & Bradstreet, supra,* at 759, 105 S.Ct. 2939. The placards read "God Hates the USA/Thank God for 9/11," "America is Doomed," "Don't Pray for the USA," "Thank God for IEDs," "Fag Troops," "Semper Fi Fags," "God Hates Fags," "Maryland Taliban," "Fags Doom Nations," "Not Blessed Just Cursed," "Thank God for Dead Soldiers," "Pope in Hell," "Priests Rape Boys," "You're Going to Hell," and "God Hates You." While these messages may fall short of refined social or political commentary, the issues they highlight — the political and moral conduct of the United States and its citizens, the fate of our Nation, homosexuality in the military, and scandals involving the Catholic clergy — are matters of public import. The signs certainly convey Westboro's position on those issues, in a manner designed, unlike the private speech in *Dun & Bradstreet,* to reach as broad a public audience as possible. And even if a few of the signs — such as "You're Going to Hell" and "God Hates You" — were viewed as containing messages related to Matthew Snyder or the Snyders specifically, that would not change the fact that the overall thrust and dominant theme of Westboro's demonstration spoke to broader public issues.

Apart from the content of Westboro's signs, Snyder contends that the "context" of the speech — its connection with his son's funeral — makes the speech a matter of private rather than public concern. The fact that Westboro spoke in connection with a funeral, however, cannot by itself transform the nature of Westboro's speech. Westboro's signs, displayed on public land next to a public street, reflect the fact that the church finds much to condemn in modern society. Its speech is "fairly characterized as constituting speech on a matter of public concern," *Connick,* 461 U.S., at 146, and the funeral setting does not alter that conclusion.

Westboro believes that America is morally flawed; many Americans might feel the same about Westboro. Westboro's funeral picketing is certainly hurtful and its contribution to public discourse may be negligible. But Westboro addressed matters of public import on public property, in a peaceful manner, in full compliance with the guidance of local officials. The speech was indeed planned to coincide with Matthew Snyder's funeral, but did not itself disrupt that funeral, and Westboro's choice to conduct its picketing at that time and place did not alter the nature of its speech.

Speech is powerful. It can stir people to action, move them to tears of both joy and sorrow, and — as it did here — inflict great pain. On the facts before us, we cannot react to that pain by punishing the speaker. As a Nation we have chosen a different course — to protect even hurtful speech on public issues to ensure that we do not stifle public debate. That choice requires that we shield Westboro from tort liability for its picketing in this case.

NOTES AND PROBLEMS

1. ***First Amendment Defense to Tort Claims.*** In *Snyder,* the court indicated that any state law tort claim that relied upon the defendant's expression of ideas might be subject to a first amendment defense, at least where the defendant was engaged in "public speech." We will encounter significant First Amendment defenses in Chapter 12 when we cover the law of defamation, which has been changed significantly by substantial first amendment jurisprudence.

2. ***Public vs. Private Speech.*** Utilizing the Supreme Court's test from *Snyder* for distinguishing public and private speech, what facts were helpful to the defendants in establishing their first amendment defense? What facts, if changed, might result in the opposite conclusion — that the speech was private and unprotected?

3. ***Westboro Finds Opposition Online.*** "Hacktivist" organizations targeted the Westboro Baptist Church in December 2012 after church members threatened to picket the funerals of Newtown shooting victims. These hacktivist groups brought down the WBC website in conjuction with "#OpWestBor," took over Fred Phelps' Twitter account, and used it to distribute a petition to name the WBC as a hate group. Free speech can work both directions.

Upon Further Review

Other intentional tort claims we have studied are designed to protect people's mental and emotional states. The tort of assault is complete, so the courts say, upon the "touching of the mind." The tort of false imprisonment fundamentally is designed to protect our sense of personal freedom to move. Significant harm may occur without any physical injury with such a claim. Even a battery cause of action will often provide for recovery of emotional distress or pain and suffering damages. But intentional infliction of emotional distress is a unique tort because its primary focus is upon emotional and mental tranquility upset by a potentially infinite variety of different types of outrageous conduct. In this sense it is the broadest applicable claim designed primarily to protect our mental peace. Though it is so broad and flexible, rigorous prerequisites have been established before it will arise: (1) mere carelessness will not suffice, as the defendant must either intend or be reckless about causing emotional distress; (2) perhaps the highest hurdle is the requirement that the defendant's conduct in bringing about the distress be labeled "outrageous" or "utterly intolerable in a civilized society"; and (3) the requirement that the plaintiff's emotional distress be "severe"; that is, qualitatively greater than anyone should have to endure, and long-lasting rather than fleeting.

Pulling It All Together

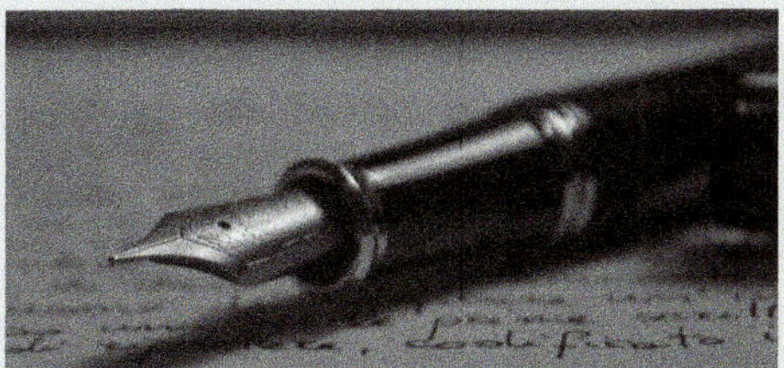

Sara and Dennis are fellow first-year law students and bitter academic rivals. Each one believes that they are the smarter, more promising lawyer than the other. One day in class while Sara is on her feet being questioned by the professor about the *Palsgraf* case, Dennis starts blurting out the correct answers to the professor's questions when Sara hesitates — Sara is horribly embarrassed by this conduct, feeling humiliated by what Dennis has done in front of her fellow students. (As it turns out, she cried the entire way home.) As she leaves the room, she puts her hand on Dennis' shoulder and says "you'll wish you never did this to me!"

That night, Dennis thinks about Sara's statement and decides that he should do something else to interrupt Sara's obsessive outlining of Torts. He plans to park near her house in the middle of the night and start honking his horn to wake her up, hoping she will be too tired the next day to do any outlining. Shortly after midnight, Dennis pulls up in his car and parks in the driveway of a house owned by Carlos, who lives directly across the street from Sara (Dennis thought he was in Sara's driveway, but was confused about Sara's address). After about thirty seconds of Dennis honking his horn, Carlos becomes outraged at the incessant honking, and, to make Dennis stop and leave, fires his shotgun toward Dennis, who is seated inside his car. Some shot from the gun impacts the car, but misses Dennis. Other shot from the shotgun goes past the car, across the street, and into Sara's living room window and her bedroom window. Some of the shot demolished her new high definition television. Other shot hit Sara in her leg causing significant medical injuries. She tries to get up out of bed but is unable to do so because of her injuries. She is forced to remain in bed until the next day when her housekeeper arrives inside her home and discovers Sara lying in bed hurt. Dennis subsequently scores the highest grade on the Torts exam.

Analyze any potential intentional tort causes of action — 30 minutes.

CHAPTER 3

Defenses to Intentional Torts

I. Introduction
II. Consent
III. Defense of Self, Others, and Property
IV. Necessity

I INTRODUCTION

CHAPTER GOALS

- ☑ Discover how the same principle of autonomy that underlies most intentional tort claims also necessarily gives rise to the affirmative defense of consent.
- ☑ Learn that, just like an intentional tortfeasor takes the risk of being liable for injuries far greater than could have been imagined, when one consents to an intentional tort she likewise runs the risk of suffering greater than anticipated but non-compensable injuries.
- ☑ Identify the common standard of reasonable belief that triggers a right to engage in otherwise wrongful conduct in order to protect oneself, others, or one's property.
- ☑ Appreciate the proportionality principle that is at the heart of limitations on the scope of harm one may intend to inflict in defense of protected interests.

There are certain universally acknowledged defenses that work to defeat any of the intentional torts we have already covered. While Chapter 7 will cover other general defenses to tort claims, the defenses covered here are unique to intentional torts. For example, *consent* is a defense that, in essence, acknowledges that the plaintiff's interest in each of these intentional torts involves the autonomy to make certain decisions regarding his own body, his peace of mind, his property and/or his freedom of movement. We have learned, for example, that battery involves unpermitted contacts and trespass involves unpermitted entry upon another's land. If the plaintiff has in some manner extended permission to the actor in question, this negates the essence of the cause of action. Even a cause of action for intentional infliction of emotional distress seems incompatible with a defendant's conduct to which the plaintiff has consented. After all, how can you characterize the invited conduct as "outrageous"? The law similarly acknowledges that this same concept of autonomy over one's own body, peace of mind, and property sometimes permits that person to engage in defensive conduct directed at the plaintiff in order to protect his own interests, or even the interests of others from the plaintiff's own threatening misconduct. Such circumstance can give rise to the affirmative defenses of self-defense, defense of others, and defense of property. Finally, this chapter will also explore briefly the common law defense of *necessity*—that sometimes the law will look more favorably upon conduct otherwise considered tortious when the purpose is to protect other valuable property rights from sources of danger unrelated to the plaintiff.

Because these defenses are generally considered to be in the nature of *affirmative* defenses, the burden in these areas is upon the defendant to plead and prove such defenses by a preponderance of the evidence. This is a departure from the *elements* of a cause of action, which the plaintiff must plead and prove.

II CONSENT

One of the fundamental questions when a defendant has raised the defense of consent is how to determine when consent has been given. What form must it take and how do courts determine its validity? Further, must the plaintiff actually consent to the infliction of the harm suffered or is something less than that sufficient? The *McQuiggan* case illustrates some of the fundamentals regarding the defense of consent.

A. Standard and Effect

McQUIGGAN v. BOY SCOUTS OF AMERICA

536 A.2d 137 (Md. Ct. App. 1988)

GILBERT, J.

The main question presented in this case is whether a twelve-year-old boy should be barred from recovery for an eye injury he sustained when he voluntarily participated in a paper clip shooting "game."

Nicholas Alexander McQuiggan, by and through his guardian, Jerome Keith Bradford, brought an action in tort against: the Boy Scouts of America (BSA) . . . , Billy Hamm and Kevin McDonnell, fellow Boy Scouts. Nicholas alleged that [BSA was liable for the negligent supervision by its scoutmasters and that] the minor defendants, Billy and Kevin, are liable for assault and battery.

The trial was held in the Circuit Court for Montgomery County where, at the conclusion of Nicholas's case, the court granted a motion for judgment in favor of all the defendants. Aggrieved by the trial court's action, Nicholas has appealed to this Court.

The events giving rise to this litigation date from April 8, 1981, when sometime between 7:10 and 7:15 p.m. Nicholas was dropped off by his mother at the Epworth Methodist Church in Montgomery County to attend a Boy Scout meeting. The meeting was scheduled to start at 7:30 p.m. When Nicholas arrived, he noticed several of the other scouts engaged in a game in which they shot paper clips at each other from rubber bands they held in their hands. The paper clips were pulled apart on one end and squeezed closed on the other. At trial, Nicholas demonstrated how the clip was shot by placing the closed end of the clip in a rubber band stretched between two upright fingers in the form of a "v" and pulling back on the open end of the paper clip and releasing it. Nicholas testified that when he arrived at the church, two Assistant Scoutmasters, William H. Hamm Sr. and Keith D. Rush, were present in the meeting room. Another Assistant Scoutmaster, Edmund Copeland, arrived after Nicholas but before the meeting actually started.

Upon arriving at the meeting room, Nicholas sat at a table and began to read his Boy Scout Handbook. Between four and eight other scouts had been playing the paper clip shooting game and running in and out of the hallway leading to the meeting room for about ten minutes before Nicholas decided to join them. Prior to his joining the game, no one had shot paper clips at him. When one of the boys asked Nicholas to join in the game, he did so freely, feeling no pressure to participate. Nicholas further related that he knew that the object of the game was to shoot paper clips; he knew that paper clips would be shot at him; he knew that there was a chance he would be hit with a paper clip.

When he decided to join in the game, Nicholas looked through some material on a shelf, and he located an elastic hair band with which he intended "to chase" the other boys. Nicholas and an unidentified Boy Scout then chased Billy Hamm Jr. and Kevin McDonnell up the hallway. Nicholas said he had no paper clips, but the boy with him was shooting them. Nicholas admitted at trial that his actions were such as to lead Kevin or Billy to believe that he had a paper clip in his possession. Nicholas further narrated that he was actively "participating" in the game.

After Nicholas had chased Billy and Kevin down the hallway for about ten feet, the two boys turned around and chased Nicholas back down the hall. Nicholas said that he dropped the hair band and entered the meeting room. He then stopped running, "split apart" from the unidentified boy, and started to walk toward a table. He told the court that at that point he "stopped playing," but he did not communicate that fact in any way to the other boys. Approximately five seconds later and five feet into the meeting room, Nicholas felt something in his right eye. When he brushed the eye, a paper clip dropped to the floor. According to Nicholas, his entire involvement in the game consumed approximately thirty seconds.

The trial judge [held] that Nicholas could not prevail on his assault and battery counts because by his actions "not only in participating in the game but pursuing . . . Billy Hamm [and Kevin McDonnell] down the hallway . . . as a matter of law he consented to the infliction of the injury upon him." We agree.

A battery consists of the unpermitted application of trauma by one person upon the body of another person. Gilbert, §3.1; *Ghassemieh v. Schafer*, 447 A.2d 84, cert. denied, 294 Md. 543 (1982). The gist of the action is not hostile intent but the absence of consent to the contact on plaintiff's part. When a plaintiff "manifests a willingness that the defendant engage in conduct and the defendant acts in response to such a manifestation," Prosser, §18 at 113, "his consent negatives the wrongful element of the defendant's act, and prevents the existence of a tort."*Id.* at 112.

The circumstances leading to Nicholas's injury do not constitute an assault and battery. As stated in Prosser, §18 at 114:

> "One who enters into a sport, game or contest may be taken to consent to physical contacts consistent with the understood rules of the game. *It is only when notice is given that all such conduct will no longer be tolerated that the defendant is no longer free to assume consent.*" (Emphasis supplied.)

Nicholas's willful joining in the game, without any notice of his withdrawal from participation, bars recovery from either Billy or Kevin.

NOTES AND PROBLEMS

1. ***Affirmative Defenses and Elements.*** You may recall that courts often state that a battery involves the defendant engaging in intentional, *unpermitted* harmful or offensive contacts. Such a statement suggests that the plaintiff must prove the lack of consent as part of the elements of the cause of action. In reality, *most* courts indicate that consent — or permission for the contact — is an affirmative defense. Affirmative defenses must be pled and proved by the defendant, or else they are waived under the Federal Rules of Civil Procedure. This means that rather than require the plaintiff to prove a negative, the defendant has the obligation to prove by a preponderance of the evidence that plaintiff consented to the contact.

2. ***Express and Implied Consent.*** While certain instances may involve express consent ("of course you may kiss me") more often consent is implied by the plaintiff's conduct amid the parties' circumstances. When the *McQuiggan* court references the fact that individuals may "manifest a willingness that the defendant engage in conduct," this refers to both express and implicit manifestations. Which type of consent did the plaintiff in *McQuiggan* manifest and how? In cases of doubt, courts typically look to see if the plaintiff's words or

conduct led the defendant to have a "reasonable belief" that permission was given to engage in the conduct or make the contact. Because a plaintiff can both give and withdraw consent the same way, the same test — "reasonable belief" — is the standard for both giving and withdrawing consent. Prof. Prosser has offered the following observations concerning implied consent:

> In a crowded world, a certain amount of personal contact is inevitable and must be accepted. Absent expression to the contrary, consent is assumed to all those ordinary contacts which are customary and reasonably necessary to the common intercourse of life, such as a tap on the shoulder to attract attention, a friendly grasp of the arm, or a casual jostling to make a passage.

Prosser and Keeton on the Law of Torts, §8. The Restatement (Third) of Torts outlines these concepts of express and implied consent as follows:

> (1) Consent is willingness in fact for conduct to occur. It may be manifested by action or inaction and need not be communicated to the actor.
>
> (2) If words or conduct are reasonably understood by another to be intended as consent, they constitute apparent consent and are as effective as consent in fact.

Restatement (Third) of Torts §892 (2011).

3. ***Consent to Contact Rather Than Injury.*** The court in *McQuiggan* found only that the plaintiff had consented to participate in the game, and that the commonly understood rules of the game involved being hit with a paper clip. Because the *contact* that the defendants caused involved exactly this type of contact, the defense of consent prevailed. But note that the court did not find that the plaintiff consented to the particular devastating eye injury. The fact that the consented to contact results in a certain injury, even one not foreseen, does not invalidate the consent otherwise properly given. Rather than his eye being hurt by a flying paper clip, what if one of the other boys had grabbed a chair and hit the plaintiff over the head with it? Unless the boys' game of paper clip frenzy typically involved such escalation, there would clearly be no consent in this scenario.

4. ***Causation.*** Another potential stumbling block faced by the plaintiff in *McQuiggan*, beyond the defense of consent, was proving which of the two other boys playing the game actually shot him in the eye. He sued both because apparently it was unclear which boy shot the paper clip. He was only hit with one clip, which could have come from only one of the two other boys. In Chapter 5 we will look into various tort doctrines designed to come to the aid of a plaintiff unable to prove causation in just such an instance. We will explore the doctrine, in particular, of *alternative liability* when we confront a hunter shot in the eye while on a hunting trip with two friends.

5. ***Application to Other Intentional Torts.*** While many cases involving consent arise in the context of battery claims, courts apply the defense to any intentional tort. One might be taken to consent, for example, to being assaulted by purchasing admission to a Halloween ghost house. An invitation to a colleague at work to come over for dinner obviously provides consent for the colleague to enter upon your land at the appointed time and date.

6. ***Consent vs. Assumption of the Risk.*** In Chapter 7 we will delve into the doctrine of *express assumption of the risk*—where one by contract expressly releases (in advance) a negligence claim against another and instead assumes the risk of incurring such injuries. This seems closely connected to consent but consent is limited to intentional torts and most courts likewise limit express assumption of the risk to accidental torts.

7. ***Problems.*** Is there consent in the following instances?

A. Two boys agree to meet at a swing near their homes at an appointed hour to engage in a fistfight. One boy is punched in the eye near the end of the fight and sustained a serious eye injury.

B. A man stands in the path of another and says, "I'm not moving. If you want to proceed further, you'll have to try to push me out of the way." The other immediately shoves the man to the side, causing the man to fall down and fracture his hip.

C. A boy and a girl are dancing when the boy asks for permission to kiss the girl. She closes her eyes and smiles and he kisses her.

D. A grandmother living in a rough neighborhood decides she is not going to be deterred by the gang violence and walks on the sidewalk toward the grocery store, right through the middle of the assembled thugs. One of them trips her, causing her to break her wrist.

E. A woman is driving down a rural farm-to-market road on her tractor and wants to take a shortcut to a portion of her own property by cutting through a corner of a neighbor's vacant property. She calls the neighbor on her cell phone as she is approaching the neighbor's property. In response to her inquiry, the neighbor is silent but makes a sweeping gesture with his arm, appearing to acquiesce to her request. In fact, he does not want the woman to do so, but she proceeds anyway.

F. Jethro asks a neighbor, Jed, who owns a "cement pond," for permission for any of the neighbors to use Jed's pool during the upcoming Fourth of July holiday. Jed readily agrees. On the Fourth of July, without knowledge of Jed's consent to Jethro, another neighbor, named Elly May, sees the swimming activities, comes over, and plunges into the pool as well.

B. Limitations on Consent

1. Exceeding the Scope

KOFFMAN v. GARNETT

574 S.E.2d 258 (Va. 2003)

Lacy, J.

In this case we consider whether the trial court properly dismissed the plaintiffs' second amended motion for judgment for failure to state [a cause of action for] assault and battery.

In the fall of 2000, Andrew W. Koffman, a 13-year-old middle school student at a public school in Botetourt County, began participating on the school's football team. It was Andy's first season playing organized football, and he was positioned as a third-string defensive player. James Garnett was employed by the Botetourt County School Board as an assistant coach for the football team and was responsible for the supervision, training, and instruction of the team's defensive players.

The team lost its first game of the season. Garnett was upset by the defensive players' inadequate tackling in that game and became further displeased by what he perceived as inadequate tackling during the first practice following the loss.

Garnett ordered Andy to hold a football and "stand upright and motionless" so that Garnett could explain the proper tackling technique to the defensive players. Then Garnett, without further warning, thrust his arms around Andy's body, lifted him "off his feet by two feet or more," and "slammed" him to the ground. Andy weighed 144 pounds, while Garnett weighed approximately 260 pounds. The force of the tackle broke the humerus bone in Andy's left arm. During prior practices, no coach had used physical force to instruct players on rules or techniques of playing football.

In [their pleading the Koffmans] alleged that Andy was injured as a result of Garnett's . . . intentional acts of assault and battery. Garnett filed a demurrer . . . asserting that the [pleading] did not allege sufficient facts to support a lack of consent to the tackling demonstration and, therefore, did not plead causes of action for . . . assault or battery. The trial court dismissed the action, finding that . . . the facts alleged were insufficient to state [claims for] assault or battery because the instruction and playing of football are "inherently dangerous and always potentially violent."

In this appeal, the Koffmans . . . assert that they pled sufficient facts . . . to sustain their claims of . . . assault and battery.

The trial court held that the second amended motion for judgment was insufficient as a matter of law to establish causes of action for the torts of assault and battery. We begin by identifying the elements of these two independent torts. The tort of assault consists of an act intended to cause either harmful or offensive contact with another person or apprehension of such contact, and that creates in that other person's mind a reasonable apprehension of an imminent battery. Restatement (Second) of Torts §21 (1965).

The tort of battery is an unwanted touching which is neither consented to, excused, nor justified. Although these two torts "go together like ham and eggs," the difference between them is "that between physical contact and the mere apprehension of it. One may exist without the other." W. Page Keeton, Prosser and Keeton on Torts §10 at 46.

The Koffmans' [pleading] does not include an allegation that Andy had any apprehension of an immediate battery. This allegation cannot be supplied by inference because any inference of Andy's apprehension is discredited by the affirmative allegations that Andy had no warning of an imminent forceful tackle by Garnett. The Koffmans argue that a reasonable inference of apprehension can be found "in the very short period of time that it took the coach to lift Andy into the air and throw him violently to the ground." At this point, however, the battery alleged by the Koffmans was in progress. Accordingly, we find that the pleadings were insufficient as a matter of law to establish a cause of action for civil assault.

The [Koffmans' pleading] is sufficient, however, to establish a cause of action for the tort of battery. The Koffmans pled that Andy consented to physical contact with players "of like age and experience" and that neither Andy nor his parents expected or consented to his "participation in aggressive contact tackling by the adult coaches." Further, the Koffmans pled that, in the past, coaches had not tackled players as a method of instruction. Garnett asserts that, by consenting to play football, Andy consented to be tackled, by either other football players or by the coaches.

Whether Andy consented to be tackled by Garnett in the manner alleged was a matter of fact. Based on the [Koffmans' allegations], reasonable persons could disagree on whether Andy gave such consent. Thus, we find that the trial court erred in holding that the Koffmans' [pleading] was insufficient as a matter of law to establish a claim for battery.

DISSENT

Justice Kinser, concurring in part and dissenting in part.

I agree with the majority opinion except with regard to the issue of consent as it pertains to the intentional tort of battery.

The thrust of the plaintiffs' allegations is that they did not consent to "Andy's participation in aggressive contact tackling by the adult coaches" but that they consented only to Andy's engaging "in a contact sport with other children of like age and experience."

It is notable, in my opinion, that the plaintiffs admitted in their pleading that Andy's coach was "responsible . . . for the supervision, training and instruction of the defensive players." It cannot be disputed that one responsibility of a football coach is to minimize the possibility that players will sustain "something more than slight injury" while playing the sport. A football coach cannot be expected "to extract from the game the body clashes that cause bruises, jolts and hard falls." *Id.* Instead, a coach should ensure that players are able to "withstand the shocks, blows and other rough treatment with which they would meet in actual play" by making certain that players are in "sound physical condition," are issued proper protective equipment, and are "taught and shown how to handle [themselves] while in play." *Id.* The instruction on how to handle themselves during a game should include demonstrations of proper tackling techniques. *Id.* By voluntarily participating in football, Andy and his parents necessarily consented to instruction by the coach on such techniques. The alleged battery occurred during that instruction.

Additionally, the plaintiffs did not allege that the tackle itself violated any rule or usage of the sport of football. Nor did they plead that Andy could not have been tackled by a larger, physically stronger, and more experienced player either during a game or practice. Tackling and instruction on proper tackling techniques are aspects of the sport of football to which a player consents when making a decision to participate in the sport.

In sum, I conclude that the plaintiffs did not sufficiently plead a claim for battery. We must remember that acts that might give rise to a battery on a city street will not do so in the context of the sport of football.

NOTES AND PROBLEMS

1. ***Rules of the Game.*** The dissenting judge had a difference of opinion from the majority as to whether the coach's conduct was a part of the understood activity in which the plaintiff had agreed to participate. The dissent argues that, because the plaintiff could have been hurt by a large player by being tackled either in practice or a game, his consent was broad enough to cover the coach's conduct. Do you see the difference, though, between consenting to other teenage *players* hitting you, and consenting to a large adult *coach* tackling you?

2. ***Problems.*** Do you believe that consent destroys the following battery claims?

A. After the *Koffman* case, the same coach from Virginia continues tackling players on his team in order to demonstrate proper tackling techniques. One of these student athletes gets hurt. Is this student in any worse position than the plaintiff in *Koffman* to sue for battery?

B. A defensive lineman in a football game commits a late hit on a quarterback and dislocates the quarterback's collarbone. He draws a 15-yard penalty for the late hit.

C. Another defensive lineman, after the whistle blows the play dead, intentionally stomps on the face of the downed offensive player, breaking his nose.

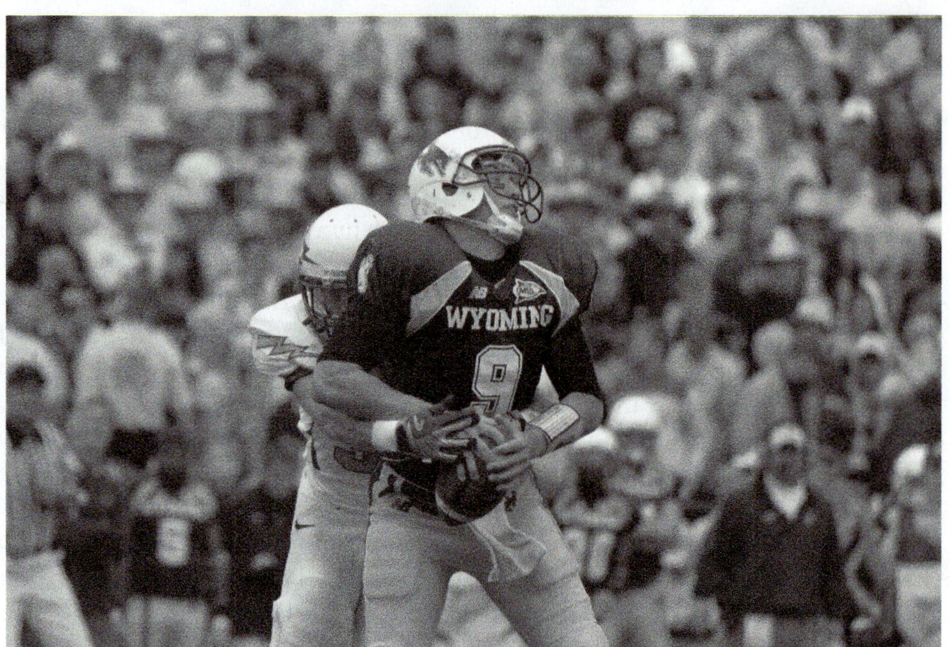

2. *Fraud*

HOGAN v. TAVZEL

660 So. 2d 350 (Fl. Dist. Ct. App. 1995)

Sharp, W., J.

Hogan appeals from a Final Judgment which dismissed her second amended complaint with prejudice. She sued her former husband, Tavzel, for negligence, battery, fraudulent concealment, and the intentional infliction of emotional distress. The substance of her complaint was that in 1989-90, through consensual sex, Tavzel infected her with genital warts (condylomhea acuminata) at a time he knew of his disease, but she did not, and she was not warned. The trial court held . . . that there is no tort of battery for consensual sex which results in the transmission of a sexually transmitted disease. We reverse.

Hogan and Tavzel were married for fifteen years but encountered marital problems which caused them to separate. During a period of attempted reconciliation between October of 1989 and January 1990, Tavzel infected Hogan with genital warts. He knew of his condition but failed to warn Hogan or take any precaution against infecting her. The parties were divorced on May 8, 1990. Hogan brought this suit in 1993. The trial court . . . dismissed the battery count because he found that consensual sexual intercourse fails as a matter of law to establish the element of unconsented to touching which is required to sustain the tort of battery. The trial judge noted that Florida law has not, as yet, recognized a cause of action for battery due to the transmission of a sexually communicable disease. With regard to this issue, we agree this is a case of first impression in this state.

We . . . turn our attention to dismissal of the battery count. Since this is a case of first impression in Florida, it is appropriate to look to other jurisdictions for guidance. A case similar to the one presented here is *Kathleen K. v. Robert B.*, 150 Cal. App. 3d 992 (Cal. 2d Dist. 1984). There, a cause of action in battery was approved when one partner contracted genital herpes from the other partner. The facts indicated that the infecting partner had represented he was free from any sexually infectious disease, and the infected partner would not have engaged in sexual relations if she had been aware of the risk of infection. The court held that one party's consent to sexual intercourse is vitiated by the partner's fraudulent concealment of the risk of infection with venereal disease (whether or not the partners are married to each other). This is not a new theory. *See, De Vall v. Strunk*, 96 S.W.2d 245 (Tx. App. 1936); *Crowell v. Crowell*, 105 S.E. 206 (1920).

The *Kathleen K.* court recognized that:

> [a] certain amount of trust and confidence exists in any intimate relationship, at least to the extent that one sexual partner represents to the other that he or she is free from venereal or other dangerous contagious disease.

Kathleen K. at 150 Cal. App. 3d 996.

The Restatement of Torts Second (1977) also takes the view that consent to sexual intercourse is not the equivalent of consent to be infected with a venereal disease. Specifically, it provides the following example:

> *A* consents to sexual intercourse with *B*, who knows that *A* is ignorant of the fact that *B* has a venereal disease. *B* is subject to liability to *A* for battery.

Illus. 5 §892B. Other authorities also conclude that a cause of action in battery will lie, and consent will be ineffective, if the consenting person was mistaken about the nature and quality of the invasion intended. *See*, Prosser and Keeton, n. 105, §18 at 119-20.

We see no reason, should the facts support it, that a tortfeasor could not be held liable for battery for infecting another with a sexually transmissible disease in Florida. In so holding, we align ourselves with the well established, majority view which permits lawsuits for sexually transmitted diseases. Hogan's consent, if without the knowledge that Tavzel was infected with a sexually transmitted disease, was the equivalent of no consent, and would not be a defense to the battery charge if successfully proven.

McPHERSON v. McPHERSON

712 A.2d 1043 (Me. 1988)

DANA, J.

Nancy McPherson appeals from the judgment of the Superior Court denying her [cause of action for] battery [arising] from her claim that her husband, Steven McPherson, infected her with a sexually transmitted disease he acquired through an extramarital affair.

Nancy filed a complaint against Steven, after their divorce, claiming that he had infected her with a sexually transmitted disease, Human Papilloma Virus (HPV). Nancy alleged that Steven acquired HPV through a clandestine extramarital affair with Jane Doe. The complaint further alleges that Steven transmitted the disease to her, prior to their divorce, through sexual intercourse.

Following a jury-waived trial, the court made the following factual findings: that Nancy "has been and may still be infected with HPV"; that it is more likely than not that she was infected with HPV through sexual contact with another individual; that Steven was the only sexual partner that Nancy has ever had; and that it was more likely than not that Steven infected Nancy with HPV. The court also noted that, even though Steven did not then exhibit evidence of the HPV infection, "this is in no way proof that he is not now in a latent stage nor does it demonstrate or have any probative value as to whether or not he was a carrier" at the time he allegedly infected Nancy. The court found further that Steven had a sexual relationship with Doe, that he had sexual intercourse with Nancy after having intercourse with Doe, that he did not disclose his sexual relationship with Doe to Nancy, and that he took no steps to protect Nancy from possible infection with a sexually transmitted disease. Finally, the court found that Steven "did not know or have reason to know" that he might have HPV at the time he infected Nancy because he had no physical symptoms of HPV infection, he had no knowledge of any other partner having symptoms of HPV, and he had no medical diagnosis of any kind of a sexually transmitted disease.

Nancy . . . challenges the court's judgment with regard to the assault and battery claim. The court found that no assault and battery occurred because the sexual intercourse between Steven and Nancy was consensual. She argues that her consent to have sexual intercourse with Steven was vitiated by the fact that he failed to inform her of his extramarital affair.

"One who effectively consents to conduct of another intended to invade his interests cannot recover in an action of tort for the conduct or for harm resulting from it." Restatement (Second) of Torts §892A(1) (1977). Consent may be vitiated, however by misrepresentation:

> If the person consenting to the conduct of another is induced to consent by a substantial mistake concerning the nature of the invasion of his interests or the extent of the harm to be expected from it and the mistake is known to the other or

> is induced by the other's misrepresentation, the consent is not effective for the unexpected invasion or harm.

Id. §892B(2). By way of illustration, the Restatement provides: "A consents to sexual intercourse with B, who knows that A is ignorant of the fact that B has a venereal disease. B is subject to liability to A for battery." *Id.* §892B(2) cmt. e, illus. 5.

Nancy argues only that Steven misled her concerning his fidelity. Given the court's finding that Steven neither knew nor should have known of his infection with HPV, however, Nancy cannot argue that Steven misled her "concerning the nature of the invasion of [her] interest or the extent of the harm to be expected" therefrom. If the defendant, ignorant of the fact that he was infected with a sexually transmitted disease, has sexual intercourse with the plaintiff, "the defendant will not be liable, because the plaintiff consented to the kind of touch intended by the defendant, and both were ignorant of the harmful nature of the invasion." Prosser & Keeton, The Law of Torts §18 at 119 (5th Ed. 1984); *see Hogan v. Tavzel*, 660 So. 2d 350 (Fla. Dist. Ct. App. 1995). Thus, Steven may not be held liable for assault and battery.

NOTES AND PROBLEMS

1. ***Fraud.*** The *Hogan* court held that the defendant's fraud tainted the consent, rendering it inoperable. Fraud plays a major role in tort litigation. In both *Hogan* and *McPherson*, plaintiffs invoked fraud to attempt to render the affirmative defense of consent void. Later, in Chapter 7, we will explore some general defenses available in any tort case. Specifically, in the context of exploring the defense of the statute of limitations (i.e., the untimely filing of a lawsuit) we will see that the related doctrine of *fraudulent concealment* similarly renders inoperable that defense. Further, fraud can be used as its own stand-alone cause of action when someone is induced to enter into a business transaction through the defendant's misrepresentation of some fact. This cause of action is covered in Chapter 13 Business Torts. Beyond torts, fraud is relevant in many areas of the law. It plays a major role in the field of contracts as a defense to contract enforcement, and in bankruptcy law it can be invoked to avoid protection of a debtor who defrauded a creditor.

2. ***Problems.*** Based upon the courts' opinions in *Hogan* and *McPherson*, would the plaintiff's consent in the following scenarios be vitiated by the defendant's fraudulent misconduct?

   A. John and Susan are unmarried. John knows he has an STD but fails to inform Susan of this fact. After they have sex, Susan discovers she has been infected.

B. John and Susan are married but John is secretly having an affair with another woman. Susan does not know about this affair and she and John continue to have sex. Susan eventually discovers the infidelity and is upset.

C. John and Susan are unmarried. After the prom, John tells Susan that he loves her and then they have sex. John never calls again and Susan is upset. During discovery in the lawsuit, Susan finds an entry in John's diary where he admits he never loved Susan.

D. If you do not believe that Susan should recover for battery in each of the above scenarios, how can you articulate a clear rule as to when the plaintiff's consent is invalid, and when the consent refutes the battery claim?

3. ***Seduction.*** At common law, many states recognized a cause of action brought by the father of a young, previously virtuous woman who had been induced to have sexual relations with the defendant based upon a false promise of marriage. In effect, the law treated the woman as tainted property and provided for recovery to aid in providing financial support on the theory that she was no longer suitable as a wife for another. There are many conceptual problems with this, in addition to the offensive presumptions underlying such a tort, and all courts have abandoned this cause of action.

III DEFENSE OF SELF, OTHERS, AND PROPERTY

The common thread holding together the tapestry of the various intentional torts is the principle of individual autonomy and freedom. We get to decide, generally, who touches our bodies, our castle, and our toys. When tortfeasors threaten those rights, the law certainly affords a court-driven remedy in terms of recognizing causes of action that provide monetary recovery to alleviate the violation. But in an effort to promote more efficient responses, ameliorate the consequences of the violation of our rights, and reflect the reality of our human nature, tort law also recognizes certain self-service rights. That is, the law permits us to take action that would otherwise be tortious in order to defend our legitimate interests in autonomy and freedom. When another's misconduct constitutes a legitimate threat of harm to our bodies (or our stuff), the law permits us to cause harmful contacts to the source of our threat; that is, the law permits us to engage in acts of self-defense. Similarly, the law permits us to defend others who are threatened. Of course, not every perceived threat validates causing harm to others. And not every legitimate threat permits unlimited response. We will begin with perhaps the most instinctive reaction to a threat to our own physical well being — the urge to lash out at others to protect ourselves.

A. Self-Defense

SLAYTON v. McDONALD

690 So. 2d 915 (La. Ct. App. 1997)

Williams, J.

The plaintiff, Slayton, appeals a trial court judgment rendered in favor of the defendant, McDonald, rejecting plaintiff's claim for personal injuries sustained as the result of a shooting incident. For the reasons assigned below, we affirm the trial court's judgment.

On the afternoon of May 20, 1994, fourteen-year-old Daniel McDonald and fourteen-year-old James Slayton had a disagreement while riding the school bus to their neighboring Dubach homes. Slayton was the larger of the two boys and was attending high school. McDonald was attending junior high school. The disagreement began when Slayton threw a piece of paper at McDonald. After McDonald threw the paper back at Slayton, Slayton threatened to come to McDonald's house. McDonald told Slayton not to come to his house. When asked about Slayton's reputation as a fighter, McDonald testified he had heard that Slayton had won fights against people larger than himself, and that Slayton could "take care of himself pretty good."

Later that afternoon, after McDonald arrived at home, he went outside his house and saw Slayton walking up the long driveway toward him. Slayton testified that he went to McDonald's house because he wanted to talk to McDonald about "kicking and punching on little kids and about messing with me and stuff." There were no adults present at McDonald's home when Slayton arrived at the residence. McDonald yelled at Slayton to go home. However, Slayton kept walking up McDonald's driveway. Slayton testified that he did not hear McDonald's warning. After shouting the warning to Slayton, McDonald went into his house, got his twelve-gauge shotgun, came back outside and loaded the gun with #7 1/2 shot shells. McDonald testified that Slayton saw him load the gun; Slayton said that he did not. Again, McDonald asked Slayton to leave and Slayton refused.

McDonald then retreated into his home and called 911 to request help. McDonald testified that he closed the front door of his house after retreating inside. Slayton testified that the door was open. However, it is undisputed that the front door of the McDonald home did not have a lock and anyone could open it from the outside.

As McDonald spoke to the 911 operator, Slayton came inside McDonald's house. The transcript of the 911 conversation reveals that McDonald told Slayton to leave several times, to no avail. McDonald can be heard to say: "I think he's like sixteen. He's a lot bigger than me and he's in my house"; "Don't take another step towards me"; and, "If he keeps coming toward me I'm going to shoot him."

McDonald testified that Slayton pointed at his own leg, dared McDonald to shoot, and said that McDonald "didn't have the guts" to shoot. McDonald also stated that Slayton told him he was going to teach him a lesson and "kick my [McDonald's] ass." Slayton testified that after McDonald threatened to shoot him, he told McDonald that if McDonald shot him, he would get up and beat McDonald.

When asked if he was afraid when Slayton came into his house, McDonald testified that Slayton frightened him because "he [Slayton] had a crazy look in his eye. I didn't know what he was going to do after he didn't stop for the gun, I thought he must have been crazy." McDonald also told the 911 operator that "he's kinda crazy, I think." McDonald testified that Slayton "asked me if I could get him before he got to me and got the gun first. I was afraid that if he came past the gun that he was crazy enough to kill me."

At some point during the encounter, Slayton's younger sister, Amanda, arrived at the McDonald home and asked Slayton to leave because McDonald was armed. According to McDonald, Slayton refused to leave by saying "he's too scared to shoot me. He's about to cry." The 911 operator told McDonald several times not to shoot Slayton; McDonald said "I ain't gonna shoot him but in the leg. But I have to defend myself." Slayton testified that McDonald never pointed the shotgun at his head or chest.

What happened next was a matter of some dispute. On the 911 transcript, McDonald tells Slayton that "I might just count to three." Slayton testified that he was kneeling down because he was "resting waiting for the cops to get there so I could tell my story." However, Amanda Slayton and McDonald testified that Slayton was standing. Both Amanda and James Slayton testified that Slayton did not make a move toward McDonald, and Slayton testified that at all times during the incident, he was never more than two feet inside the McDonald home. However, McDonald testified that Slayton then began to count and to move "eight feet at least" into the home. On the tape of the 911 conversation, most of what Slayton says is inaudible, but, at the point where McDonald's states that he might count to three, Slayton can be heard to count "one — two — three." McDonald then shot Slayton once in the left knee. Slayton's grandmother arrived shortly thereafter, pulled Slayton out of the McDonald home and waited for the paramedics and law enforcement authorities to arrive.

McDonald testified that from his experience, a load of #7½ shot did not do a great deal of damage to animals at ordinary hunting distance, but he had never fired his shotgun at anything so close before. On the 911 tape, McDonald can be heard saying, "I ain't got but squirrel shot in here. . . ."

Nevertheless, according to one of Slayton's doctors, Dr. Richard I. Ballard, the shot charge caused Slayton a "devastating" and "severe" injury that will require knee fusion rendering his knee permanently stiff and the injured leg at least a inch shorter than the other leg. Slayton and his parents testified that the injury had caused Slayton tremendous pain and had drastically reduced or eliminated his ability to engage in activities he used to enjoy.

The trial court rejected [plaintiff's claim finding that] Slayton, "a much larger opponent who had a reputation for fighting," was the aggressor in the encounter and that McDonald acted reasonably under the circumstances in protecting himself' using only that force necessary to prevent a forcible offense against his person. From this adverse judgment, plaintiff appeals.

The plaintiff contends the trial court erred in finding that the defendant's son acted reasonably under the circumstances surrounding this incident, and thus, was justified in shooting the plaintiff's son in the leg. We do not find that the trial court erred.

[Tort doctrines preclude] tort recovery where the plaintiff acts in such a way to provoke a reasonable person to use physical force in fear or anticipation of further injury at the hand of the aggressor plaintiff, unless the person retaliating has used excessive force to repel the aggression. *Baugh v. Redmond*, 565 So. 2d 953, 958 (La. App. 2d Cir. 1990); *Perkins v. Certa*, 469 So. 2d 359, 361 (La. App. 2d Cir. 1985).

Generally, one is not justified in using a dangerous weapon in self-defense if the attacking party is not armed but only commits battery with his fists or in some manner not inherently dangerous to life. However, resort to dangerous weapons to repel an attack may be justifiable in certain cases when the fear of danger of the person attacked is genuine and founded on facts likely to produce similar emotions in reasonable men. Under this rule, it is only necessary that the actor have grounds which would lead a reasonable man to believe that the employment of a dangerous weapon is necessary, and that he actually so believes. All facts and circumstances must be taken into account to determine the reasonableness of the actor's belief, but detached reflections or a pause for consideration cannot be demanded under circumstances which by their nature require split second decisions. Various factors relied upon by the courts to determine the reasonableness of the actions of the party being attacked are the character and reputation of the attacker, the belligerence of the attacker, a large difference in size and strength between the parties, an overt act by the attacker, threats of serious bodily harm, and the impossibility of a peaceful retreat. *Levesque v. Saba*, 402 So. 2d 266, 270 (La. App. 4th Cir. 1981).

In the instant case, McDonald testified that he believed that Slayton had beaten up people larger than himself, and, in essence, was capable of giving McDonald a beating as well; Slayton admitted that he had been in two fights while attending junior high school but gave no details of those altercations. Moreover, Slayton exhibited marked belligerence by refusing to leave McDonald's home despite repeated demands by McDonald while the latter was on the telephone with law enforcement authorities and was armed with a loaded twelve-gauge shotgun. This combination of reputation and belligerence evidence provides support for the trial court's conclusion that "the presence of the shotgun and defendant's threats were insufficient to thwart plaintiffs advances." It is undisputed that Slayton was considerably physically larger than McDonald, and the trial court accepted McDonald's testimony that Slayton had threatened to harm him. Indeed, Slayton himself admitted that he told McDonald that if McDonald shot him, he was going to get up and beat McDonald.

The trial court's finding that McDonald shot Slayton "to stop the plaintiff's advance" is a decision based upon the court's judgment of the credibility of the witnesses. Although both Slayton and his sister contradicted McDonald's testimony that Slayton was advancing when he was shot, Slayton's testimony that he was kneeling down when he was shot is contradicted by that of his sister and McDonald. Additionally, Slayton's testimony that he never came more than two feet into the house is contradicted by A.S. McDonald's testimony that he found blood about ten feet inside his home. Finally, the 911 tape, on which Slayton's voice became clearly audible only seconds before McDonald shot him, is further support for the conclusion that Slayton was advancing upon McDonald when shot. From its reasons for judgment, it is apparent that the trial court chose to credit McDonald's version of events over Slayton's version. Because the record supports this decision, it will not be disturbed on appeal.

Finally, it is evident that McDonald was simply unable to retreat from the encounter. While retreat is not a condition precedent for a finding of self-defense using justifiable force, in our opinion, the retreat of a lawful occupant of a home into a position in his home from which he cannot escape an attacker except by the use of force is strong evidence that the occupant's use of force to prevent the attack is proper. Although a shotgun may be a deadly weapon, McDonald used the gun in a way that he calculated would stop the attack without fatally injuring Slayton. Further, as recited above, McDonald testified that he was "afraid that if he [Slayton] came past the gun that he was crazy enough to kill me." Under these circumstances, where McDonald was on the telephone with law enforcement authorities and had repeatedly demanded that Slayton leave, and Slayton continued to advance and threaten McDonald, we cannot disagree with the trial court's conclusion that McDonald used reasonable force to repel Slayton's attack.

NOTES AND PROBLEMS

1. ***Deadly Force.*** The court notes that deadly force is usually unjustified in self-defense when the attacker is unarmed. Circumstances would often yield this result but there is no per se rule to this effect. Rather, the principle is that deadly force is permissible when a defendant has a *reasonable belief* that such force is necessary to prevent serious bodily injury to himself threatened by the plaintiff. What circumstances convinced the court in *Slayton* that the use of a shotgun was appropriate against an unarmed teenager? How important to the court's conclusion was the fact that the defendant only shot at the plaintiff's leg rather than attempting to shoot to kill?

2. ***Duty to Retreat.*** In *Slayton,* the court notes that "retreat is not a condition precedent for a finding of self-defense" but rather one factor to consider in determining if the defendant's reaction to the threat was justified. Courts have not been consistent in their view of whether one must first attempt to retreat from a threat before using deadly force. The Second Restatement offered the following compromise position:

> [T]he interest of society in the life and efficiency of its members and in the prevention of the serious breaches of the peace involved in bloody affrays requires one attacked with a deadly weapon, except within his own dwelling place, to retreat before using force intended or likely to inflict death or serious bodily harm upon his assailant, unless he reasonably believes that there is any chance that retreat cannot be safely made. But even the slightest doubt, if reasonable, is enough to justify his standing his ground, and in determining whether his doubt is reasonable every allowance must be made for the predicament in which his assailant has placed him.

Restatement (Second) of Torts §65, cmt. g (1965).

"LADIES AND GENTLEMEN OF THE JURY . . ."

3.10 New Jersey Model Civil Jury Charges Self Defense

Fundamentally, no person has a lawful right to lay hostile and menacing hands on another. However, the law does not require anyone to submit meekly to the unlawful infliction of violence upon him/her. He/She may resist the use or threatened use of force upon him/her. He/She may meet force with force, but he/she may use only such force as reasonably appears to him/her to be necessary under all the circumstances for the purpose of self-protection. Accordingly, if you find that the defendant in this case has succeeded in proving that he/she was under attack by the plaintiff, and that the injury sustained by the plaintiff was inflicted by the defendant's having used only such force as, under all the circumstances, was necessary or reasonably appeared to have been necessary for his/her own protection, then the defense of self-defense has been proven, and you must find in favor of the defendant and against the plaintiff. Should you find, however, that the defendant was not under attack, or, if he/she was under attack, that he/she used more force than reasonably appeared necessary to defend himself/herself, or that he/she continued the use of force after the apparent necessity for self-defense had ceased, then the defense of self-defense has not been proven.

B. Defense of Others

The law generally does not require us to come to the aid of others who are imperiled. But if an actor does choose to intervene on behalf of another facing danger at the hands of the plaintiff, may the actor be justified in causing harm to the plaintiff to protect the interests of the other? If so, what standard should apply to determine *when* such a privilege exists and the *extent* of the privilege? *Young v. Warren* discusses and applies the privilege of defense of others.

YOUNG v. WARREN

383 S.E.2d 381 (N.C. App. 1989)

GREENE, J.

In this civil action the plaintiff appeals from a final judgment entered by the trial court, pursuant to a jury verdict, denying any recovery on a wrongful death action.

The evidence introduced at trial showed that defendant shot and killed Lewis Reid Young ("Young") on 12 May 1986. The death occurred as a result of a 20-gauge shotgun blast fired at close range into the deceased's back. On 14 October 1986, the defendant pled guilty to involuntary manslaughter.

Prior to the shooting, in the early morning hours of 12 May 1986, Young, who had been dating defendant's daughter for several months, went to the home of defendant's daughter who lived with her two children within sight of the defendant's residence. Upon arriving at the defendant's daughter's home, Young threw a large piece of wood through the glass in the front door. He then entered the home by reaching through the broken window and unlocking the door. Once inside the house Young argued with the defendant's daughter and "jerked" her arm. At that point, the defendant arrived with his loaded shotgun, having been awakened by a telephone call from a neighbor, his ex-wife, who had told him "something bad is going on" at his daughter's house. When the defendant arrived at his daughter's house, he heard screaming and saw Young standing inside the door. The defendant then testified:

A. I told him like, 'Come on out. This doesn't make any sense,' and he kind of came forward, you know, kind of had his hands up like that. (Indicating) I backed away from the door and I told him to get on out. 'This can be taken care of tomorrow,' or something to that effect.

Q. You told him to get the hell out, didn't you?

A. Well, okay; something like that.

Q. Okay. And then what happened?

A. Then he walked out the door and I just backed up like he came out the door and he walked over about six feet. There is a cement porch there, and he stepped right there, and I was behind him anywhere from a foot to eighteen inches, maybe even two foot, and he stopped. And in my opinion, he started to turn around . . . .

Q. What did he do?

A. He stopped and started to lower his hands and started to turn around.

Q. What did you do?

A. I prodded him with the gun and told him to get on out, and that's when it went off.

The trial judge submitted [a question to the jury, to which the plaintiff objected]:

> Did the defendant, William S. Warren, act in the lawful defense of his daughter, Autumn Stanley, and her children, his grandchildren?
> Answer: Yes.

The determinative issue is whether the trial court erred in submitting the defense of family issue to the jury.

We first determine whether a defendant in a civil action may assert defense of family to justify assault on a third party. While self-defense and defense of family are seen more often in the context of criminal law, these defenses are nonetheless appropriate in civil actions. *See Harris v. Hodges*, 291 S.E.2d 346, disc. rev. denied, 294 S.E.2d 208 (1982); S. Spieser, C. Krause & A. Gans, *The American Law of Torts* Sec. 5:8 at 802 (1983) (self-defense and defense of others recognized in both criminal and civil law); *22A Am. Jur. 2d Death* Sec. 163 at 237 (1988) (the "defense of self-defense is available in a wrongful death action").

If the defenses apply, the defendant's conduct is considered "privileged" and the defendant is not subject to tort liability for actions taken within the privilege. The defenses, as they result in avoidance of liability, are considered affirmative defenses and must be affirmatively pled. The burden of proof is on the defendant to prove the defenses by a preponderance of the evidence.

An assault on a third party in defense of a family member is privileged only if the "defendant had a well-grounded belief that an assault was about to be committed by another on the family member. . . ." *State v. Hall*, 366 S.E.2d 527, 529 (1988). However, in no event may defendant's action be in excess of the privilege of self-defense granted by law to the family member. *Id.*; Spieser, *The American Law of Torts* Sec. 5:10 at 810. The privilege protects the defendant from liability only to the extent that the defendant did not use more force than was necessary or reasonable. Prosser & Keeton, *The Law of Torts* Sec. 20 at 130 (5th ed. 1984); *Hall*, 89 N.C. App. 366 S.E.2d at 528. Finally, the necessity for the defense must "be immediate, and attacks made in the past, or threats for the future, will not justify" the privilege. Prosser & Keeton, *The Law of Torts* at 130.

[T]he record contains no evidence that the defendant reasonably believed his daughter was, at the time of the shooting of the plaintiff, in peril of death or serious bodily harm. At that time, the plaintiff stood outside the house with his back to the defendant. Defendant's daughter and children were inside the house, removed from any likely harm from plaintiff. Accordingly, assuming *arguendo* the "defense of family" had been adequately pled or tried by consent, the evidence in this trial did not support the submission of the issue to the jury, and the plaintiff is entitled to a new trial.

NOTES AND PROBLEMS

1. ***Reasonable Belief.*** The ultimate standard for defense of others is the same standard we have already seen in self-defense — the "well grounded" or *reasonable belief* of the actor dictates the contours of the privilege. There are two parts to this privilege: (1) the defendant's actual *subjective* state of mind must be that the force used is necessary to protect the life or well-being of others from the plaintiff; and (2) the *objective* reasonableness of the defendant's belief based upon all of the circumstances and information available to the defendant. In this regard, in another portion of the *Young* opinion the court addressed the trial court's admission of certain volatile evidence:

> "Plaintiff first contends the trial court erred in denying his *in limine* motion seeking to prevent the admission of testimony concerning Young's possession of a firearm and his blood/alcohol level. We agree. An autopsy report indicated Young's blood/alcohol level at the time of his death was .23 and that a detective removed a .22 caliber pistol from plaintiff's pocket after his death. However, no testimony exists on record that the defendant knew Young had a handgun in his possession or that he was aware that Young had consumed any alcohol. Accordingly, we determine this evidence was not relevant . . . and the motion *in limine* should have been allowed." 383 S.E.2d at 384.

Can you understand why this evidence was irrelevant?

2. ***Triggering of the Privilege.*** In *Young*, the court holds that the evidence fails to establish any evidentiary basis for invocation of the defense of others privilege on the part of the father and that the jury should not have even had the issue submitted to them for their determination. When you read the testimony of the defendant, is it clear that he intended to fire his gun or just to nudge the decedent with it? What could possibly justify holding the defendant liable for the battery if the evidence suggests firing the weapon was not intentional?

3. ***Defense of Family or Others.*** The court refers to the privilege to protect a family member from a perceived threat. Originally this privilege was so limited. However, because it makes no sense to provide a qualified legal privilege solely for the protection of family members, courts have enlarged the *defense of family* into a *defense of others privilege*. Now any person may use force (or the threat of imminent harm) to deter or protect any third party whom the person reasonably believes to endangered.

4. ***Judging the Reasonableness of the Force.*** When the defendant has a reasonable belief that either they or another faces an imminent attack, they are permitted to use a reasonably proportional degree of force in response. The amount of force they are permitted to use is judged not by the results of their conduct, but by the intended force. If a defendant intends only to push the plaintiff aside but causes great harm, the action might be justified based upon the slight contact intended. In *Young*, did the court invalidate the privilege based upon the fact that the defendant ended up using deadly force? Or was the defendant's legal problem that he was entitled to use no force whatsoever under the circumstances? Note that the defendant testified that he intended to "prod" the decedent and that the gun "went off." What facts in *Young* were most essential to the court's conclusion that the defendant's conduct was unjustified?

C. Defense of Property

WOODARD v. TURNIPSEED

784 So. 2d 239 (Miss. Ct. App. 2000)

IRVING, J.

Kenwyon Woodard, a minor, by his father and next friend, filed a complaint against John Turnipseed in the Choctaw County Circuit Court seeking personal injury damages. The complaint arises from an assault and battery committed with a broom against him by Turnipseed, a large dairy farmer who, along with his two sons and brother, owned seventeen hundred acres of dairy land. [Turnipseed was 57 years old and weighed 145 pounds. He had a very large dairy operation, milking 450 cows daily. Kenwyon was 17 years old, 4′9″ tall and weighed ninety-five pounds.]

[The trial court denied Kenwyon's motion for a directed verdict on liability and submitted the case to the jury.] The jury returned a verdict for Turnipseed. We find merit in Kenwyon's argument that his motion for a directed verdict as to liability should have been granted. Accordingly, we reverse and render as to liability but remand for a new trial on damages only.

On September 7, 1996, Kenwyon was employed as a minimum wage milker with Turnipseed Dairy Farms of Ackerman, Mississippi. He had been working for Turnipseed Dairy Farms approximately six months during his latest employment but had worked for the dairy once before. His first employment with the dairy ended when he, according to Turnipseed, was fired by Turnipseed for not cleaning the cows prior to attaching the milker. On September 7, he was fired again for the same reason. According to Kenwyon, he did not know why he was fired the first time.

On September 7, according to Turnipseed, Kenwyon, along with two other boys, were preparing cows to be milked. One boy was driving the cows into the stalls, another was dipping the cows' udders in disinfectant, and Kenwyon was using paper towels to clean the udders. Turnipseed observed that Kenwyon had passed over three filthy cows. Upon making this observation, Turnipseed told Kenwyon, "you are fired, and go punch out."

Turnipseed claims that when he fired Kenwyon the first time Kenwyon had threatened to get him. Specifically, Kenwyon had said at that time, "I will get you for this." Remembering the previous threat, Turnipseed "thought this boy may vandalize my time clock." Because of this, Turnipseed decided to escort Kenwyon to the time clock. According to Turnipseed, Kenwyon started with a verbal assault as they walked out of the barn. Turnipseed heard the same threat he had heard upon the first firing of Kenwyon. In any event, Turnipseed escorted Kenwyon to the time clock, and Kenwyon changed clothes and telephoned his father to get a ride home.

Turnipseed gave this account of the physical assault:

> And now listen to this. Shirley is my foreman. I told her Shirley, I don't care if the cows go dry, don't allow this boy back on the farm. I passed him off to her and went back to the barn and milked . . . . Ten minutes later I step out of the barn and there is Kenwyon. I said Kenwyon, didn't I tell you not to come back on my farm. *Which wasn't quite the truth because I didn't address him.* I addressed her in his presence.
>
> Kenwyon didn't say anything. I said Kenwyon I am telling you to get off of my property. Kenwyon said I am not going anywhere. I stood there a minute. I looked down. There was a broom leaning against the barn. I picked the broom up. I said Kenwyon, you see this broom. I am telling you to get off my property. Kenwyon didn't respond in any way. *I walked the eight steps to Kenwyon, and I hit him three times with the broom. The last lick I hit him, the broom handle cracked. Didn't break. Cracked.* Kenwyon decided he wanted to leave my farm, and he did.

As a result of the attack, Kenwyon suffered a hematoma of the right flank, a contusion of the left forearm and some contusion to the kidney. Michelle Parsons, a family nurse practitioner, testified that Kenwyon was kept in the hospital for observations for eight hours because blood was detected in his urine. Parsons testified that the blood in the urine was consistent with the bruised kidney suffered by Kenwyon in the attack.

Turnipseed contends that he attacked Kenwyon in defense of self and property. Turnipseed argues that because Kenwyon had threatened to get him on a previous occasion as well as on the occasion giving rise to this appeal, he reasonably feared for his safety and the safety of his property. He contends that this is particularly true in light of the fact that he told Kenwyon to leave, but Kenwyon refused to do so.

We first recognize that if the facts showed that Turnipseed or his property were imperiled by Kenwyon, he would have had a legitimate right to defend himself and his property, but using only such force as would have been reasonably necessary to accomplish the task. Did the facts show any such peril? The answer is an emphatic "no."

We look to the evidence in the light most favorable to Turnipseed. Turnipseed testified that, while he was escorting Kenwyon out of the barn to the time clock, Kenwyon repeated over and over again that Kenwyon was going to get Turnipseed. Kenwyon did nothing other than make this threat. Turnipseed went back into the barn and began to assist with the milking operation. Ten minutes later, Turnipseed sees Kenwyon sitting on a car parked on Turnipseed's property. Kenwyon has nothing in his hands and is doing nothing other than sitting on the car. Turnipseed says to Kenwyon, "didn't I tell you not to come back on my farm," and Kenwyon did not say anything. Turnipseed then tells Kenwyon to get off Turnipseed's property. Kenwyon says, "I am not going anywhere." Turnipseed picks up a broom and again tells Kenwyon to get off Turnipseed's property. Kenwyon does not respond. Turnipseed then walks eight steps to Kenwyon and hits him three times with the broom.

This evidence clearly shows that neither Turnipseed nor his milking operation was in any danger of being attacked by Kenwyon, the ninety-five pound minor. Turnipseed knew that Kenwyon had not been able to reach anyone to get a ride off the property because Turnipseed was there when the unsuccessful calls were made. Further, Turnipseed knew that Kenwyon did not possess his own transportation and that Kenwyon's father or mother transported him to and from work at Turnipseed's Dairy Farm.

When Turnipseed approached Kenwyon just before the attack, Kenwyon was not near any of the milking operations. He had not come back into the barn or given any indications that he was attempting to do so. It had been at least ten minutes since he had been escorted out of the barn. Surely, that was enough time for him to return and launch any attack he wanted to make if indeed he had planned to do so.

The record is unclear as to how far Kenwyon lived from Turnipseed's dairy farm, but there is some indication that it was at least between five and ten miles. Having failed to reach anyone at his home or his grandmother's house, Kenwyon was left with the options of walking the distance, however far, or waiting until his friend got off work. Under these circumstances, it was not unreasonable for Kenwyon to wait for a ride home. Granted, when he was accosted by Turnipseed and told to leave, he should have left, but his failing to do so did not justify the brutal attack by Turnipseed, especially considering the fact that Kenwyon was a minor with no available means of leaving except on foot.

Moreover, the record is clear that Turnipseed really never viewed Kenwyon as a threat to either his person or his property. Consider this testimony:

Q. And when you struck him, did he get off your property?
A. The first two times he stood there and glared at me. After the third blow he started off my property.
Q. And he — did he run off the property?
A. I just observed the first few steps. I was satisfied that he was no longer an immediate threat, and I went back to work.

Surely, if Turnipseed had been concerned that Kenwyon had intentions of attacking him or sabotaging his milking operations, he would have observed Kenwyon for more than "the first few steps," and he certainly would not have gone immediately back to work. He would have stayed around to see just what Kenwyon was going to do.

The evidence leads us to the inevitable conclusion that the trial court erred in not granting Kenwyon's motion for a directed verdict. Viewing the evidence in the light most favorable to Turnipseed, as we are required to do and have done in the preceding discussion, we are convinced that reasonable and fair-minded persons could not have concluded that Turnipseed, a fifty-seven-year-old mature man weighing one hundred forty-five pounds, believed himself or his property in danger of attack from 4′9″, ninety-five pound Kenwyon. Accordingly, we reverse and render on the question of Turnipseed's liability but remand the case for a new trial on damages only.

KATKO v. BRINEY

183 N.W.2d 657 (Iowa 1971)

Moore, J.

The primary issue presented here is whether an owner may protect personal property in an unoccupied boarded-up farm house against trespassers and thieves by a spring gun capable of inflicting death or serious injury.

We are not here concerned with a man's right to protect his home and members of his family. Defendants' home was several miles from the scene of the incident to which we refer.

Plaintiff's action is for damages resulting from serious injury caused by a shot from a 20-gauge spring shotgun set by defendants in a bedroom of an old farm house which had been uninhabited for several years. Plaintiff and his companion, Marvin McDonough, had broken and entered the house to find and steal old bottles and dated fruit jars which they considered antiques.

At defendants' request plaintiff's action was tried to a jury consisting of residents of the community where defendants' property was located. The jury returned a verdict for plaintiff and against defendants for $20,000 actual and $10,000 punitive damages.

After careful consideration of defendants' motions for judgment notwithstanding the verdict and for new trial, the experienced and capable trial judge overruled them and entered judgment on the verdict. Thus we have this appeal by defendants.

Most of the facts are not disputed. In 1957 defendant Bertha L. Briney inherited her parents' farm land in Mahaska and Monroe Counties. Included was an 80-acre tract in southwest Mahaska County where her grandparents and parents had lived. No one occupied the house thereafter. Her husband, Edward, attempted to care for the land. He kept no farm machinery thereon. The outbuildings became dilapidated.

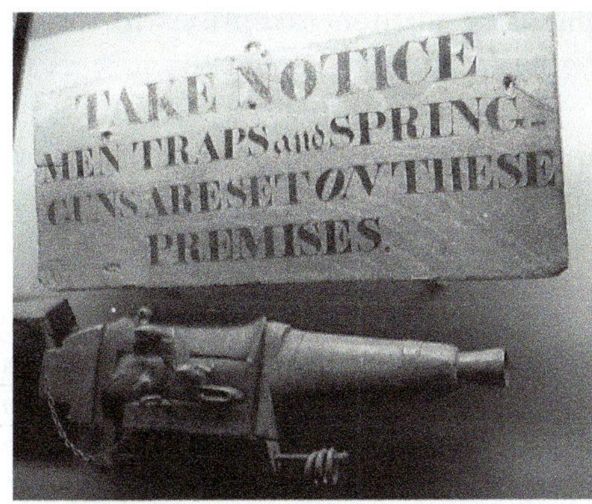

For about 10 years, from 1957 to 1967, there occurred a series of trespassing and housebreaking events with loss of some household items, the breaking of windows and "messing up of the property in general." The latest occurred June 8, 1967, prior to the event on July 16, 1967 herein involved.

Defendants through the years boarded up the windows and doors in an attempt to stop the intrusions. They had posted "no trespass" signs on the land several years before 1967. On June 11, 1967 defendants set "a shotgun trap" in the north bedroom. It was rigged with wire from the doorknob to the gun's trigger so it would fire when the door was opened. He admitted he did so "because I was mad and tired of being tormented" but "he did not intend to injure anyone." He gave no explanation of why he used a loaded shell and set it to hit a person already in the house. No warning of its presence was posted.

Plaintiff lived . . . seven miles from the old house. He had observed it for several years while hunting in the area and considered it as being abandoned. Plaintiff and McDonough had been to the premises and found several old bottles and fruit jars which they took and added to their collection of antiques. On [the date of the incident] they made a second trip to the Briney property. They entered the old house by removing a board from a porch window which was without glass. While McDonough was looking around the kitchen area plaintiff went to another part of the house. As he started to open the north bedroom door the shotgun went off striking him in the right leg above the ankle bone. Much of his leg, including part of the tibia, was blown away.

Plaintiff testified he knew he had no right to break and enter the house with intent to steal bottles and fruit jars therefrom. He further testified he had entered a plea of guilty to larceny in the nighttime of property of less than $20 value from a private building.

The main thrust of defendants' defense in the trial court and on this appeal is that "the law permits use of a spring gun in a dwelling or warehouse for the purpose of preventing the unlawful entry of a burglar or thief." They repeated this contention in their exceptions to the trial court's instructions. . . .

[The trial court instructed the jury as follows:]

> You are hereby instructed that one may use reasonable force in the protection of his property, but such right is subject to the qualification that one may not use such means of force as will take human life or inflict great bodily injury. Such is the rule even though the injured party is a trespasser and is in violation of the law himself. [and]
>
> An owner of premises is prohibited from willfully or intentionally injuring a trespasser by means of force that either takes life or inflicts great bodily injury; and therefore a person owning a premise is prohibited from setting out "spring guns" and like dangerous devices which will likely take life or inflict great bodily injury, for the purpose of harming trespassers. The fact that the trespasser may be acting in violation of the law does not change the rule. The only time when such conduct of setting a "spring gun" or a like dangerous device is justified would be when the trespasser was . . . endangering human life by his act.

The overwhelming weight of authority, both textbook and case law, supports the trial court's statement of the applicable principles of law.

Prosser on Torts, Third Edition, pages 116-118, states:

> [T]he law has always placed a higher value upon human safety than upon mere rights in property, it is the accepted rule that there is no privilege to use any force calculated to cause death or serious bodily injury to repel the threat to land or chattels, unless there is also such a threat to the defendant's personal safety as to justify self-defense. . . . spring guns and other man-killing devices are not justifiable against a mere trespasser, or even a petty thief. They are privileged only against those upon whom the landowner, if he were present in person would be free to inflict injury of the same kind.

The legal principles stated by the trial court in [these] instructions are well established and supported by the authorities cited and quoted supra. There is no merit in defendants' objections and exceptions thereto. Defendants' various motions based on the same reasons stated in exceptions to instructions were properly overruled.

NOTES AND PROBLEMS

1. ***Proportional Defense.*** Both of the foregoing cases acknowledge property owners' right to defend themselves and their property. For either, the privilege is triggered by "reasonable belief" that the plaintiff imperils the interest in question. A reasonable amount of force necessary to protect the interest is qualified, but in no event can force designed to cause death or serious bodily injury be used to justify protection of mere property rights. Cases refer to

Rule

moderate force being permitted to protect property but not deadly force. Given that in both cases there is evidence of wrongdoing by the plaintiffs, why were defendants' uses of force not privileged in either?

2. ***The Rest of the Story.*** The *Katko* case became an instant classic of torts students since it first appeared in Prosser's torts casebook in 1976; students debate whether the plaintiff or the defendants were justified in each seeking their own form of justice. Some find the result perverse, with the property owners having to pay both compensatory and punitive damages to a thief. Indeed, during oral arguments before the Iowa Supreme Court counsel for the appellants, the Brineys, consistently referred to Mr. Katko as the "plaintiff-thief." Plaintiff's counsel felt that the law was clearly on his side, however, and so he did not even demand a jury (it was defendants who did so). The all-female jury apparently connected with the plaintiff, who readily admitted his own wrongdoing, made no attempt to justify his attempted thievery, and was reportedly a likeable, pleasant fellow with a strong religious background. Perhaps the jury also did not like the antics of defense counsel, who, to demonstrate the point that nobody likes their possessions to be taken from them, reached into the jury box during closing arguments to snatch a juror's purse. After the rather sizable verdict was upheld by the Iowa Supreme Court, the Brineys were forced to sell some of their farmland in order to pay the judgment. Afterward Mrs. Briney sued Katko for the underlying trespass (one wonders why this was not a compulsory counterclaim in the first suit and waived) and was awarded $150 in actual and $1,000 in punitive damages. Apparently there was wrongdoing on both sides of this dispute, though, consistent with the proportionality principle, the respective juries viewed the property owners' sins as far worse. Counsel for Katko, Garold Heslinga, thought to himself upon first meeting his new client, "Damn this will be fun." *See* interview of Katko's trial counsel at coverageopinions.info/Vol6Issue1/GaroldHeslinga.html (accessed October 23, 2017).

"Among the natural rights of the colonists are these: First a right to life, secondly to liberty, and thirdly to property; together with the right to defend them in the best manner they can."
Samuel Adams

3. ***Use of Force to Expel Trespasser.*** A concurring opinion in *Turnipseed* acknowledges another potential right that might have been available to the large dairy farmer — the right to use "reasonable force" to eject a trespasser who refuses to leave the premises. Under the facts of

that case, however, the judge acknowledged that this defense was not pled and that it would not have justified the type of force the farmer employed. Can you think what different amount of force the farmer might have used that would have been considered reasonable?

4. ***Relationship to Shopkeeper's Privilege.*** Recall from the last chapter under the topic of "False Imprisonment" that the law permits persons to detain suspected shoplifters when their suspicions are based upon a "reasonable belief." We discovered that this privilege was limited, and that the detention would be protected only so long as it involved "reasonable means" and for a "reasonable time." There is a nice symmetry between the shopkeeper's privilege and the common law's recognition of a privilege to use a reasonably limited amount of force to protect one's property.

5. ***Statutory Modifications to Common Law.*** The foregoing materials all apply the common law regarding defenses. A legislature is always free to modify these doctrines by either granting defendant landowners greater or lesser rights. A recent trend in many legislatures has been to enact statutes designed to make it easier for a homeowner to justify the use of deadly force when the plaintiff is wrongfully on their property to commit a felony involving threatened bodily injury. For example, it is not unusual to find such a statute that creates a presumption that deadly force is reasonable when someone breaks into another's home to commit a felony offense. A good lawyer needs to always be on the lookout for such statutory modifications to these common law principles.

6. ***Problem.*** Defendant liquor storeowner is fed up with all of the criminal activity in the neighborhood. His store has been robbed after closing at night multiple times. To deter this from continuing, he purchases a vicious watchdog and sets it loose in the store every night at closing. He has posted a sign on the front door warning, "Caution: The Premises Are Protected by a Deadly Dog. Enter at Your Own Risk!" A few months later a burglar enters the store through a window and is mauled to death by the guard dog. Should the store owner be liable for the wrongful death of the burglar?

IV NECESSITY

Further reflecting the need to balance one right against another, the common law doctrine of necessity sometimes permits the intentional violation of another's right. The consequences of so acting vary depending upon whether one is deemed to be doing so to protect the public at large, or to protect only one's own individual interest. As you read the following classic cases involving *public necessity* and *private necessity*, consider whether the common law's balance of these competing interests makes sense.

SUROCCO v. GEARY

3 Cal. 69 (1853)

MURRAY, C.J.

This was an action, commenced in the court below, to recover damages for blowing up and destroying the plaintiff's house and property, during the fire of the 24th of December, 1849.

Geary, justified on the ground that it had been blown up by him to stop the progress of the conflagration then raging.

It was in proof, that the fire passed over and burned beyond the building of the plaintiffs, and that at the time said building was destroyed, they were engaged in removing their property, and could, had they not been prevented, have succeeded in removing more, if not all of their goods.

The cause was tried by the Court sitting as a jury, and a verdict rendered for the plaintiffs, from which the defendant prosecutes this appeal.

The only question for our consideration is, whether the person who tears down or destroys the house of another, in good faith, and under apparent necessity, during the time of a conflagration, for the purpose of saving the buildings adjacent, and stopping its progress, can be held personally liable in an action by the owner of the property destroyed.

The right to destroy property, to prevent the spread of a conflagration, has been traced to the highest law of necessity, and the natural rights of man, independent of society or civil government. "It is referred by moralists and jurists to the same great principle which justifies the exclusive appropriation of a plank in a shipwreck, though the life of another be sacrificed; with the throwing overboard goods in a tempest, for the safety of a vessel; with the trespassing upon the lands of another, to escape death by an enemy. It rests upon the maxim, *Necessitas inducit privilegium quod jura privata.*"

The common law adopts the principles of the natural law, and places the justification of an act otherwise tortious precisely on the same ground of necessity.

This principle has been familiarly recognized by the books from the time of the saltpetre case, and the instances of tearing down houses to prevent a conflagration, or to raise bulwarks for the defence of a city, are made use of as illustrations, rather than as abstract cases, in which its exercise is permitted. At such times, the individual rights of property give way to the higher laws of impending necessity.

A house on fire, or those in its immediate vicinity which serve to communicate the flames, becomes a nuisance, which it is lawful to abate, and the private rights of the individual yield to the considerations of general convenience and the interests of society. Were it otherwise, one stubborn person might involve a whole city in ruin, by refusing to allow the destruction of a building which would cut off the flames and check the progress of the fire, and that, too, when it was perfectly evident that his building must be consumed.

[The court also rejected the constitutional argument that the burning of his house to protect the city constituted a taking of private property for public use without just compensation. The court stated that application of this public necessity doctrine historically was not considered a taking of property, as that term is used in the Constitution.]

"*Necessitas inducit privilegium quod jura private*" is a Latin phrase referring to the doctrine that necessity gives a privilege with reference to private rights.

The evidence in this case clearly establishes the fact that the blowing up of the house was necessary, as it would have been consumed had it been left standing. The plaintiffs cannot recover for the value of the goods which they might have saved: they were as much subject to the necessities of the occasion as the house in which they were situate; and if in such cases a party was held liable, it would too frequently happen, that the delay caused by the removal of the goods would render the destruction of the house useless.

The Court below clearly erred as to the law applicable to the facts of this case. The testimony will not warrant a verdict against the defendant.

Judgment reversed.

VINCENT v. LAKE ERIE TRANSP. CO.

124 N.W. 221 (Minn. 1910)

O'Brien, J.

The steamship Reynolds, owned by the defendant, was for the purpose of discharging her cargo on November 27, 1905, moored to plaintiffs' dock in Duluth. While the unloading of the boat was taking place a storm from the northeast developed, which at about ten o'clock p.m., when the unloading was completed, had so grown in violence that the wind was then moving at fifty miles per hour and continued to increase during the night. There is some evidence that one, and perhaps two, boats were able to enter the harbor that night, but it is plain that navigation was practically suspended from the hour mentioned until the morning of the twenty-ninth, when the storm abated, and during that time no master would have been justified in attempting to navigate his vessel, if he could avoid doing so. After the discharge of the cargo the Reynolds signaled for a tug to tow her from the dock, but none could be obtained because of the severity of the storm. If the lines holding the ship to the dock had been cast off, she would doubtless have drifted away; but, instead, the lines were kept fast, and as soon as one parted or chafed it was replaced, sometimes with a larger one. The vessel lay upon the outside of the dock, her bow to the east, the wind and waves striking her starboard quarter with such force that she was constantly being lifted and thrown against the dock, resulting in its damage, as found by the jury, to the amount of $500.

We are satisfied that the character of the storm was such that it would have been highly imprudent for the master of the Reynolds to have attempted to leave the dock or to have permitted his vessel to drift away from it. One witness testified upon the trial that the vessel could have been warped into a slip, and that, if the attempt to bring the ship into the slip had failed, the worst that could have happened would be that the vessel would have been blown ashore upon a soft and muddy bank. The witness was not present in Duluth at the time of the storm, and, while he may have been right in his conclusions, those in charge of the dock and the vessel at the time of the storm were not required to use the highest human intelligence, nor were they required to resort to every possible experiment which could be suggested for the preservation of their property. Nothing more was demanded of them than ordinary prudence and care, and the record in this case fully sustains the contention of the appellant that, in holding the vessel fast to the dock, those in charge of her exercised good judgment and prudent seamanship.

It is claimed by the respondent that it was negligence to moor the boat at an exposed part of the wharf, and to continue in that position after it became apparent that the storm was to be more than usually severe. We do not agree with this position. The part of the wharf where the vessel was moored appears to have been commonly used for that purpose. It was situated within the harbor at Duluth, and must, we think, be considered a proper and safe place, and would undoubtedly have been such during what would be considered a very severe storm. The storm which made it unsafe was one which surpassed in violence any which might have reasonably been anticipated.

The appellant contends by ample assignments of error that, because its conduct during the storm was rendered necessary by prudence and good seamanship under conditions over which it had no control, it cannot be held liable for any injury resulting to the property of others, and claims that the jury should have been so instructed. An analysis of the charge given by the trial court is not necessary, as in our opinion the only question for the jury was the amount of damages which the plaintiffs were entitled to recover, and no complaint is made upon that score.

The situation was one in which the ordinary rules regulating property rights were suspended by forces beyond human control, and if, without the direct intervention of some act by the one sought to be held liable, the property of another was injured, such injury must be attributed to the act of God, and not to the wrongful act of the person sought to be charged. If during the storm the Reynolds had entered the harbor, and while there had become disabled and been thrown against the plaintiffs' dock, the plaintiffs could not have recovered. Again, if while attempting to hold fast to the dock the lines had parted, without any negligence, and the vessel carried against some other boat or dock in the harbor, there would be no liability upon her owner. But here those in charge of the vessel deliberately and by their direct efforts held her in such a position that the damage to the dock resulted, and, having thus preserved the ship at the expense of the dock, it seems to us that her owners are responsible to the dock owners to the extent of the injury inflicted.

In *Depue v. Flatau*, 111 N.W. 1, this court held that where the plaintiff, while lawfully in the defendants' house, became so ill that he was incapable of traveling with safety, the defendants were responsible to him in damages for compelling him to leave the premises. If, however, the owner of the premises had furnished the traveler with proper accommodations and medical attendance, would he have been able to defeat an action brought against him for their reasonable worth?

In *Ploof v. Putnam*, 71 Atl. 188, the supreme court of Vermont held that where, under stress of weather, a vessel was without permission moored to a private dock at an island in Lake Champlain owned by the defendant, the plaintiff was not guilty of trespass, and that the defendant was responsible in damages because his representative upon the island unmoored the vessel, permitting it to drift upon the shore, with resultant injuries to it. If, in that case, the vessel had been permitted to remain, and the dock had suffered an injury, we believe the shipowner would have been held liable for the injury done.

Theologians hold that a starving man may, without moral guilt, take what is necessary to sustain life; but it could hardly be said that the obligation would not be upon such person to pay the value of the property so taken when he became able to do so. And so public necessity, in times of war or peace, may require the taking of private property for public purposes; but under our system of jurisprudence compensation must be made.

Let us imagine in this case that for the better mooring of the vessel those in charge of her had appropriated a valuable cable lying upon the dock. No matter how justifiable such appropriation might have been, it would not be claimed that, because of the overwhelming necessity of the situation, the owner of the cable could not recover its value.

This is not a case where life or property was menaced by any object or thing belonging to the plaintiffs, the destruction of which became necessary to prevent the threatened disaster. Nor is it a case where, because of the act of God, or unavoidable accident, the infliction of the injury was beyond the control of the defendant, but is one where the defendant prudently and advisedly availed itself of the plaintiffs' property for the purpose of preserving its own more valuable property, and the plaintiffs are entitled to compensation for the injury done.

Order affirmed.

NOTES AND PROBLEMS

1. ***Public Necessity.*** Public necessity is an absolute defense that completely shields an actor from all liability for conduct that would otherwise be considered an intentional tort — whether the conduct involves a trespass to land, a trespass to chattels, or even a total conversion of another's property. The privilege applies when the defendant acts with a reasonable belief that his conduct is needed to prevent a threat to the community posed by someone or something other than the plaintiff. Do you find this doctrine to be fair? Without this doctrine, what might the law be afraid would be the reaction of the defendant in *Geary* to the oncoming fire? In other words, would the defendant be willing to take on individual liability to the plaintiff in order to protect third parties rather than his own personal interests? Some jurisdictions have provided by statute for some public compensation in certain instances where the common law doctrine of public necessity would shield the citizen from individual liability.

2. ***Private Necessity.*** When one engages in otherwise intentionally tortious behavior to protect her own individual interests rather than the public generally, the privilege is incomplete. The doctrine of private necessity will still protect the actor from liability for nominal damages or punitive damages, but the actor will be liable to the injured party for actual compensatory damages. Traditionally, the law has only recognized private necessity in instances where the actor is facing a threat of a serious imminent harm. Restatement (Second) of Torts §263 (1965). The captain of the *Reynolds* faced a choice — either he could sacrifice his own ship, or he could save it by sacrificing certain property belonging to the plaintiff. While the law does not condemn his economically efficient choice, his property rights do not trump those of the plaintiff. For this reason, he must account to the plaintiff for actual harm caused to the dock. Further, if the landowner interferes with the action taken during time of necessity, the landowner can be liable for actual harm thereby caused to the other party.

3. ***Problems.***

A. Edna takes great pride in the old live oak trees on her property. The entire neighborhood contains many such specimens, providing needed shade in the hot southern climate as well as aesthetic charm. One day, Edna looks at an oak tree on adjacent land owned by Mildred and sees what appears to be a fungus on its leaves. Edna is alarmed by her fear that this could be a symptom of a fatal disease for oak trees, known as oak wilt. Without wasting a moment's time, she retreats to her garage, powers up her chain saw, and promptly cuts down Mildred's tree. Mildred wants to sue Edna for actual and punitive damages for this willful conduct.

B. Atticus sees what appears from a distance to be a mad dog coming down the street of his neighborhood. After telling his children to go inside the house, he pulls out a rifle and shoots the dog dead. The dog's owner is incensed, claims the dog was not rabid, and seeks actual and punitive damages from Atticus.

Pulling It All Together

Lucinda is a high school honors student riding her bicycle home from school one day after her chess club meeting. She hears the sound of a young male voice screaming from inside of a home in her neighborhood. She rides upon the front yard of the home, sneaks up to the living room window, and peers inside. She sees a man swinging a sword at a young boy approximately ten years in age. He is screaming "no, don't kill me!" Lucinda remembers hearing recent reports of a serial murderer in the small town breaking into homes and killing the homeowners. Fearing for the life of the boy and wanting to abduct the possible serial killer, Lucinda quickly goes into the garage of the same home and retrieves a golf club from a bag in the corner. She then proceeds to enter the home through an open kitchen door in the back, sneaks through the home toward the living room, and whacks the sword-wielding man over the head with great force. The boy sees this and begins screaming at her, "you've killed my Daddy." The man was only holding a toy sword, as was the boy, and they were playing a game. Fortunately Lucinda did not actually kill the man but did cause him to have a concussion. Lucinda ran out of the house and encountered another teenager beginning to pick up her bicycle. Fearing that he was trying to steal her bike, she ran up to him, pushed him onto the ground, and sped off on her bike as quickly as possible. He suffered minor cuts and scratches but was humiliated. Analyze all the possible claims and defenses — 30 minutes.

CHAPTER 4

Negligence: Breach of Duty of Reasonable Care

I INTRODUCTION

The tort of negligence is undoubtedly the most important, and most pervasive, tort cause of action today. Unlike most other tort claims that tend to be self-limiting to certain particular circumstances (e.g., battery claims generally involve someone getting hit by another on purpose), the tort of negligence has great flexibility — it can be, and is, applied to an infinite variety of differing factual circumstances. Examples of negligence claims include the motor vehicle accident when a car runs a red light; the skier who hits an object left on the slope; the house that burns after the furnace is poorly repaired; the doctor who forgets about a disastrous drug interaction; the radiologist who misses the tumor; and the hunter who fails to notice another hunter in the woods. These examples barely begin to scratch the surface of an area of the law whose potential application is only limited by one's imagination.

The only thing common in each of these instances may be the fact that the injuries were not caused on purpose. They were all accidents rather than intentional torts. Tort law evolved long ago to provide a cause of action for these accidental scenarios. While not all accidents create negligence liability, if the court finds the defendant to be at fault, the defendant can be ordered to pay the plaintiff's damages legally caused by the negligent conduct. A claim for negligence involves four easily stated elements: *Duty, Breach, Cause,* and *Damage*. This chapter will focus upon the duty and breach elements. Chapter 5 will consider the element of causation in a tort case. These seemingly

CHAPTER GOALS

- ☑ Understand how tort law has defined the concept of fault in cases of accidental harms.
- ☑ Learn the basic traits of the hypothetical "reasonably prudent person."
- ☑ Identify what character traits from the actor in question are borrowed by the reasonable person in analyzing claims of negligence.
- ☑ Appreciate the flexibility in the reasonable care proposition and how it can be used to fairly determine fault regardless of the circumstances.
- ☑ Become familiar with the Learned Hand analytical formula for determining the behavior of the reasonable person — the primary method for determining breach of the duty of reasonable care.
- ☑ Learn the role in breach analysis of statutory violations, industry customs, personal habits, and circumstantial evidence (in scenarios where the actor's conduct is unknown by the claimant).
- ☑ Recognize the fundamental differences between ordinary negligence and gross negligence or recklessness.

straightforward elements have been the grist for thousands upon thousands of judicial opinions in which courts have grappled with the conceptual and legal wrinkles involved in applying this cause of action to particular circumstances in a way that promotes just results, while providing clear enough rules so that citizens and litigants can modify and plan their behavior. We begin in this chapter with a look at what is meant by the duty of reasonable care.

II THE DUTY OF REASONABLE CARE

Fundamental to negligence analysis is understanding and applying the duty of reasonable care. This model for finding fault in an accidental tort case is so ingrained in common law tort jurisprudence that it is often assumed that no other alternatives were ever possible. The following classic English case presented the court with the opportunity to choose different standards for application in a case of alleged negligence. As you read it, consider the arguments of the defendant as to why his proposed standard should be utilized instead of the one chosen by the trial court. Would there be anything wrong with picking the defendant's model?

A. The Objective Standard

VAUGHAN v. MENLOVE

132 Eng. Rep. 490 (C.P. 1837)

[Plaintiff sued the defendant for negligently burning down cottages on the plaintiff's land. Defendant was an adjacent property owner who built a hayrick on his own property. The hayrick caught fire on its own and spread across the property lines causing the plaintiff's damages. Plaintiff alleged in his suit that the defendant had been negligent in the manner in which he built the hayrick, and that this permitted the hayrick to catch on fire. At trial, the jury was instructed by the court that the defendant owed a duty to act as a prudent man would have acted under the circumstances. The jury found in the plaintiff's favor, but the defendant obtained a new trial order from the trial court arguing that the court had used the wrong standard. The defendant had urged that the jury was instead to have been instructed to consider the defendant's possible negligence judged not by the standard of ordinary prudence, but with reference to whether the defendant had acted bona fide to the best of his judgment. If he had, he was not responsible for the plaintiff's damages just because he did not possess the "highest order of intelligence." Upon review of the trial court's order granting the new trial request, the Court of Common Pleas stated as follows:]

It is contended that the question ought to have been whether the defendant had acted honestly and bona fide to the best of his own judgment. That, however, would leave so vague a line as to afford no rule at all, the degree of judgment belonging to each individual being infinitely various; and though it has been urged that the care which a prudent man would take is not an intelligible proposition as a rule of law, yet such has always been the rule adopted in cases of bailment. The care taken by a prudent man has always been the rule laid down; and as to the supposed difficulty of applying it, a jury has always been able to say, whether, taking that rule as their guide, there has been negligence on the occasion in question.

Instead, therefore, of saying that the liability for negligence should be co-extensive with the judgment of each individual, which would be as variable as the length of the foot of each individual, we ought rather to adhere to the rule which requires in all cases a regard to caution such as a man of ordinary prudence would observe. That was in substance the criterion presented to the jury in this case, and therefore the present rule must be discharged.

NOTES AND PROBLEMS

1. ***Standards of Care.*** The trial court initially instructed the jury on one standard for analysis in negligence, but was persuaded by the defendant that it should have applied a different standard. What are the differences between these two standards?

2. ***Why Does It Matter?*** Think of the implications for these two differing standards. Which of the two is more objective? In a case where the bona fide standard would be applied, what kind of evidence would become the focal point for determining liability? In a case where the standard originally used by the trial court applied, how would the focus be different? What do these differences suggest about which standard is more appropriate?

3. ***Restatement's Modern Formulation.*** We will spend more time exploring the "reasonable person," but the following explanation from the Restatement (Second) of Torts is instructive for now. It provides as follows:

> Sometimes this person is called a reasonable man of ordinary prudence, or an ordinarily prudent man, or a man of average prudence, or a man of reasonable sense exercising ordinary care. It is evident that all such phrases are intended to mean very much the same thing. The actor is required to do what this ideal individual would do in his place. The reasonable man is a fictitious person, who is never negligent, and whose conduct is always up to standard. He is not to be identified with the members of the jury, individually or collectively. It is therefore error to instruct the jury that the conduct of a reasonable man is to be determined by what they would themselves have done.

Restatement (Second) of Tort §283 cmt. c. (1965). Does this description sound more like the standard adopted by the appellate court in *Vaughan*, or that advocated by the defendant? Note that the reasonable person is a hypothetical creature who is always prudent and never negligent. Does such a person exist, in fact? If not, is it fair to impose this standard to determine fault?

B. Actual and Constructive Knowledge

PARROT v. WELLS, FARGO & CO.

82 U.S. 524 (1873)

Parrot brought an action in the court below against certain defendants who composed the well-known firm of Wells, Fargo & Co., express carriers, to recover damages for injuries to certain large buildings owned by him in the city of San Francisco, caused in April, 1866, by the explosion of nitroglycerine whilst in charge of the said defendants.

[Defendant agreed to ship a 329-pound crate for an individual from New York City to San Francisco for a fee, in the ordinary course of defendant's business. Upon arrival in San Francisco, as the crate was being moved to the wharf defendant discovered that it appeared to be leaking some fluid. The fluid had the appearance of sweet oil. An adjacent box had stains on its outside and defendant believed it too was leaking its contents due to the damage. Defendant's standard business practice was to take any damaged crates into a nearby building for inspection of the contents. Both the crate and the box were, therefore, taken inside for this purpose. Defendants' agents, in the presence of other persons, took a mallet and chisel to the crate and began to open it. In the process of doing so, the contents of the crate exploded killing all present, and causing significant damage to that building as well as other nearby buildings occupied by defendant. It was later determined that the crate contained nitroglycerine. The other box contained silverware. In 1866 the properties and dangers of nitroglycerine were not well known or understood. Although the substance was discovered 20 years earlier, few experiments had been conducted with it and those were confined to certain laboratories. Merely eight days before the accident involved in this case, another steamer travelling from Hamburg exploded while carrying the same substance, though news of this had not yet reached San Francisco. These two accidents attracted the attention of scientists to the subject and led to more careful investigation and experiments regarding the substance and to greater industrial uses for it. On plaintiff's claim for negligence, the trial court held that defendant had no tort liability for the accident and plaintiff sought review.]

Mr. Justice FIELD: It appears from the record that the court finds, that neither the defendants, nor any of their employees . . . who had anything to do with the case of nitroglycerine, knew the contents of the case, or had any means of such knowledge, or had any reason to suspect its dangerous character, and that they did not know anything about nitroglycerine, or that it was dangerous. And it also appears that the court finds, that there was no negligence on the part of the defendants in receiving the case, or in their failure to ascertain the dangerous character of the contents; and in view of the condition of their knowledge, of the want of means of knowledge, and the absence of any reasonable ground of suspicion, that there was no negligence in the handling of the case at the time of the explosion.

The question presented to us is, whether upon this state of facts the plaintiff is entitled to recover for the injuries caused by the explosion to his buildings, outside of that portion occupied by the defendants under their lease.

To fasten a further liability on the defendants, and hold them for injuries to that portion of the buildings not covered by their lease, it was contended in the court below, and it is urged here, that, as matter of law, they were chargeable with notice of the character and properties of the merchandise in their possession, and of the proper mode of handling and dealing with it, and were consequently guilty of negligence in receiving, introducing, and handling the box containing the nitroglycerine.

If express carriers are thus chargeable with notice of the contents of packages carried by them, they must have the right to refuse to receive packages offered for carriage without knowledge of their contents. It would, in that case, be unreasonable to require them to accept, as conclusive in every instance, the information given by the owner. They must be at liberty, whenever in doubt, to require, for their satisfaction, an inspection even of the contents as a condition of carrying the packages. This doctrine would be attended in practice with great inconvenience, and would seldom lead to any good. Fortunately the law is not so unreasonable. It does not exact any such knowledge on the part of the carrier, nor permit him, in cases free from suspicion, to require information as to the contents of the packages offered as a condition of carrying them.

[Cases cited from other courts] recognize the right of the carrier to refuse to receive packages offered without being made acquainted with their contents, when there is good ground for believing that they contain anything of a dangerous character. It is only when such ground exists, arising from the appearance of the package or other circumstances tending to excite his suspicions, that the carrier is authorized, in the absence of any special legislation on the subject, to require a knowledge of the contents of the packages offered as a condition of receiving them for carriage.

It not, then, being his duty to know the contents of any package offered to him for carriage, when there are no attendant circumstances awakening his suspicions as to their character, there can be no presumption of law that he had such knowledge in any particular case of that kind, and he cannot accordingly be charged as matter of law with notice of the properties and character of packages thus received. The first proposition of the plaintiff, therefore, falls, and the second, which depends upon the first, goes with it.

The defendants, being innocently ignorant of the contents of the case, received in the regular course of their business, were not guilty of negligence in introducing it into their place of business and handling it in the same manner as other packages of similar outward appearance were usually handled. "Negligence" has been defined to be "the omission to do something which a reasonable man, guided by those considerations which ordinarily regulate the conduct of human affairs, would do, or doing something which a prudent and reasonable man would not do." It must be determined in all cases by reference to the situation and knowledge of the parties and all the attendant circumstances. What would be extreme care under one condition of knowledge, and one state of circumstances, would be gross negligence with different knowledge and in changed circumstances. The law is reasonable in its judgments in this respect. It does not charge culpable negligence upon any one who takes the usual precautions against accident, which careful and prudent men are accustomed to take under similar circumstances.

[T]he gist of the action is the negligence of the defendants: unless that be established, they are not liable. The mere fact that injury has been caused is not sufficient to hold them. No one is responsible for injuries resulting from unavoidable accident, whilst engaged in a lawful business. A party charging negligence as a ground of action must prove it. He must show that the defendant, by his act or by his omission, has violated some duty incumbent upon him, which has caused the injury complained of.

Here no such proof was made, and the case stands as one of unavoidable accident, for the consequences of which the defendants are not responsible. The consequences of all such accidents must be borne by the sufferer as his misfortune.

This principle is recognized and affirmed in a great variety of cases — in cases where fire originating in one man's building has extended to and destroyed the property of others; in cases where injuries have been caused by fire ignited by sparks from steamboats or locomotives, or caused by horses running away, or by blasting rocks, and in numerous other cases which will readily occur to every one. The rule deducible from them is, that the measure of care against accident, which one must take to avoid responsibility, is that which a person of ordinary prudence and caution would use if his own interests were to be affected, and the whole risk were his own.

[As Mr. Justice Nelson has declared previously] "[n]o case or principle can be found, or, if found, can be maintained, subjecting an individual to liability for an act done without fault on his part;" and in this conclusion we all agree.

Judgment affirmed.

NOTES AND PROBLEMS

1. ***Reasonable Person's Knowledge.*** Is it fair to say, from the above opinion, that a reasonable person (a) knows all risks of harm from the conduct in question, (b) knows only those risks that the defendant was actually aware of, (c) knows only those risks that a reasonable person would have known, regardless of the actual knowledge of the defendant, or (d) some combination of the foregoing?

2. ***Catalyst for Change.*** The events that gave rise to the above case were well known. This incident, and another one happening at about the same time, led to significant general knowledge throughout the world regarding the dangerous propensities of nitroglycerine and led to widespread changes regarding its safe use, transportation, and storage. The reasonable person, as this case illustrates, does not run ahead of society but keeps pace with such awareness and changes.

3. ***Problems.*** Would Wells Fargo have been more likely to be found negligent with the following modifications to the facts in the foregoing case?

   A. The shipper of the nitroglycerine advised Wells Fargo when it delivered the crate that the contents were dangerous and needed extra care.

   B. Immediately next to the warehouse where Wells Fargo opened the crate stood an elementary school filled with young children.

   C. The Wells Fargo employee who opened the crate had special expertise with chemicals and thought to herself, just before she applied the mallet and chisel to the crate, "Hmm, this smells a lot like nitroglycerine!"

"LADIES AND GENTLEMEN OF THE JURY . . ."

Iowa Pattern Jury Charge 700.8

The mere fact an accident occurred or a party was injured does not mean a party was negligent [or at fault].

III THE REASONABLE PERSON UNDER THE CIRCUMSTANCES

The standard of the *reasonable person under the circumstances* has proven to be a very flexible standard, useful in many different contexts for determining whether an actor in question (typically the defendant, but sometimes a plaintiff too) is at fault for an accidental injury. But how does this reasonable person act under different sorts of recurring circumstances? Is reasonable care the same under emergencies as in other instances? When an activity involves a greater degree of inherent danger, does the reasonable person act the same? And what about actors that have different types of character traits? Does the reasonable person have ordinary knowledge, intelligence, and experience even if the defendant does not? Is the reasonable person sometimes blind, disabled, or mentally infirm if the actor we are judging has such a condition? The following cases answer these questions. Consider as you read these cases to what extent the answers to these questions are intellectually cohesive and consistent.

A. Extraordinary Knowledge and Skill

Given the holding in *Vaughan*, now accepted without question by courts everywhere, that an actor's below-average intelligence, skills, and experience will not excuse behavior, you might guess that for the sake of consistency an actor's above-average intelligence, skills, and experience would also be disregarded. In fact, courts hold otherwise, for the reasons explained in the following case.

CERVELLI v. GRAVES

661 P.2d 1032 (Wyo. 1983)

RAPER, J.

This case arose when Larry B. Cervelli [plaintiff] filed a personal injury suit for injuries he sustained when a pickup truck driven by him collided with a cement truck owned by DeBernardi Brothers, Inc. [and driven by its employee, Kenneth H. Graves, both defendants]. After trial, a jury found no negligence on the part of [defendants]. [Plaintiff] argues the jury was incorrectly instructed and, as a result, found as it did thereby prejudicing him. He raises the following issues on appeal: Did the court err in instructing the jury that it was not to consider a person's skills in determining whether that person is negligent?

We will reverse and remand.

Around 7:30 a.m., February 22, 1980, a collision occurred approximately nine miles west of Rock Springs, Wyoming in the westbound lane of Interstate

Highway 80 involving a pickup driven by [plaintiff] and [defendant's] cement truck. At the time of the accident, the road was icy and very slick; witnesses described it as covered with "black ice." Just prior to the accident [plaintiff] had difficulty controlling his vehicle and began to "fishtail" on the ice. He eventually lost control of his vehicle and started to slide. Graves, who had been approaching appellant from behind at a speed of 35-40 m.p.h., attempted to pass appellant's swerving vehicle first on the left side, then the right. He too, thereafter, lost control of his cement truck and the two vehicles collided. It was from that accident that [plaintiff] brought suit to recover damages for the numerous injuries he suffered.

By his own admission, Graves at the time of the accident was an experienced, professional truck driver with over ten years of truck driving experience. He possessed a class "A" driver's license which entitled him to drive most types of vehicles including heavy trucks. He had attended the Wyoming Highway Patrol's defensive driver course and had kept up-to-date with various driving safety literature. He was the senior driver employed by DeBernardi Brothers, Inc.

The suit was tried to a jury on the issues of [defendant's] negligence as well as the degree, if any, of [plaintiff's] own negligence. After a four-day trial, the jury was instructed and received the case for their consideration. They found no negligence on the part of [defendants]. Judgment was entered on the jury verdict and [plaintiff] moved for a new trial claiming the jury was improperly instructed. The district court took no action on the motion; it was deemed denied in sixty days. This appeal followed.

[Plaintiff] calls our attention to and alleges as error [that] the district court . . . instructed the jury that:

> Negligence is the lack of ordinary care. It is the failure of a person to do something a reasonable, careful person would do, or the act of a person in doing something a reasonable, careful person would not do, under circumstances the same or similar to those shown by the evidence. The law does not say how a reasonable, careful person would act under those circumstances, as that is for the Jury to decide.
>
> A reasonable, careful person, whose conduct is set up as a standard, is not the extraordinarily cautious person, nor the exceptionally skillful one, but rather a person of reasonable and ordinary prudence.

In chambers, [plaintiff's] counsel made timely and specific objections to [these] instructions. . . . [Plaintiff's] counsel . . . argued the jury is at least allowed to take cognizance of any knowledge and skill he possesses; therefore, the instruction's second paragraph should be deleted.

We agree.

That language is an apparent attempt to enlarge upon the reasonable man standard. In that attempt to explain the reasonable man concept, however, the instruction goes too far. It contradicts the correct statement of the law contained in the first paragraph of the instruction. Simply put, the first paragraph of the instruction correctly states that negligence is the failure to exercise ordinary care where ordinary care is that degree of care which a reasonable person is expected to exercise under the same or similar circumstances. The trial court's instruction first allows the jury to consider the parties' acts as compared to how the reasonable person would act in similar circumstances and then limits the circumstances the jury can consider by taking out of their purview the circumstances of exceptional skill or knowledge which are a part of the totality of circumstances.

Our view that negligence should be determined in view of the circumstances is in accord with the general view. The *Restatement, Torts 2d §283* (1965) defines the standard of conduct in negligence actions in terms of the reasonable man under like circumstances. Professor Prosser, discussing the reasonable man, likewise said that "negligence is a failure to do what the reasonable man would do 'under the same or similar circumstances.'" He contended a jury must be instructed to take the circumstances into account. Prosser, Law of Torts §32, p. 151 (4th ed. 1971). Prosser also went on to note that under the latitude of the phrase "under the same or similar circumstances," courts have made allowance not only for external facts but for many of the characteristics of the actor himself.

Principles

The reasonable person, who is the central focus in negligence analysis, actually permeates tort law. Examples we have already seen of the employment of the reasonable person have included:

- Self-Defense (reasonable belief)
- Shopkeeper's Privilege (reasonable belief)
- Assault (reasonable apprehension)
- IIED (test of outrageousness)
- Battery (test for offensive contact)

At a minimum, as Justice Holmes once said, the reasonable man is required to know what every person in the community knows. Holmes, Common Law p. 57 (1881). In a similar vein, Professor Prosser notes there is, at least, a minimum standard of knowledge attributable to the reasonable man based upon what is common to the community. Prosser, supra at pp. 159-160. Prosser went on to say, however, that although the reasonable man standard provides a minimum standard below which an individual's conduct will not be permitted to fall, the existence of knowledge, skill, or even intelligence superior to that of an ordinary man will demand conduct consistent therewith. Along that same line, *Restatement, Torts 2d §289* (1965) provides:

> The actor is required to recognize that his conduct involves a risk of causing an invasion of another's interest if a reasonable man would do so while exercising
>
> (a) such attention, perception of the circumstances, memory, knowledge of other pertinent matters, intelligence, and judgment as a reasonable man would have; and
>
> (b) such superior attention, perception, memory, knowledge, intelligence, and judgment as the actor himself has.

Section 289 comment m expands further on the effect of superior qualities of an individual when it states:

> *m. Superior qualities of actor.* The standard of the reasonable man requires only a minimum of attention, perception, memory, knowledge, intelligence, and judgment in order to recognize the existence of the risk. If the actor has in fact more than the minimum of these qualities, he is required to exercise the superior qualities that he has in a manner reasonable under the circumstances. The standard becomes, in other words, that of a reasonable man with such superior attributes.

The instruction given by the trial court could easily have been construed by the jury to preclude their consideration of exceptional skill or knowledge on the part of either party which the evidence may have shown. In determining negligence the jury must be allowed to consider all of the circumstances surrounding an occurrence, including the characteristics of the actors in reaching their decision. Where, as here, there was evidence from which the jury could have concluded appellee Graves was more skillful than others as a result of his experience as a driver, they should be allowed to consider that as one of the circumstances in reaching their decision. The second paragraph of [the challenged instruction], as [plaintiff] points out, could easily have misled the jury into disregarding what they may have found from the evidence regarding [defendant's] skill and as such prejudiced appellant. The objectionable language of the instruction is surplus language which, rather than clarifying the fictional concept of the reasonable person, actually unduly limited it. Therefore, because [this] instruction was both an incorrect statement of the law and more importantly very probably misleading, we hold that the trial court committed reversible error in using it to instruct the jury.

B. Physical Disability

Are the physical attributes of the actor in question one of the circumstances taken into account in analyzing "reasonable care under the circumstances"? We have just explored differing rules regarding how *below* versus *above* average intelligence is considered. One potential argument against considering the actor's physical attributes (or disability) is that this trends toward a variable standard of care dependent upon the actor in question. The more such idiosyncratic variables factor into the analysis, the greater the shift is toward a subjective standard. On the other hand, is it reasonable to assume that a blind person will act the same as someone without a vision disability?

POYNER v. LOFTUS

694 A.2d 69 (D.C. Ct. App. 1997)

SCHWELB, J.

This action for personal injuries was brought by William J. Poyner, who is legally blind, after he fell from an elevated walkway. The trial judge granted summary judgment in favor of the defendants, concluding that Mr. Poyner was contributorily negligent as a matter of law. On appeal, Mr. Poyner contends that, in light of his handicap, a genuine issue of material fact existed as to whether he exercised reasonable care, and that the entry of summary judgment was therefore erroneous. We affirm.

The essential evidentiary facts are undisputed. Mr. Poyner suffers from glaucoma and retrobulbar neuritis. He testified that he is able to see approximately six to eight feet in front of him. Notwithstanding his handicap, Mr. Poyner does not use a cane or a seeing eye dog in pursuing his daily activities.

On August 24, 1993, Mr. Poyner was proceeding from his home to Parklane Cleaners, a dry cleaning establishment located on the west side of the 4300 block of Connecticut Avenue, N.W. in Washington, D.C. The entrance to Parklane Cleaners is adjacent to an inclined platform which is located approximately four feet above street level. Mr. Poyner testified that he had walked by the area on three or four previous occasions, and that he was aware of the general layout. He stated that there were bushes along the edge of the platform, and that these bushes provided a natural barrier which would prevent him from falling if he attempted to walk too far. On the day of the accident, however, and unbeknownst to Mr. Poyner, one of the bushes was missing, and there was thus nothing to restrain him from falling off the platform.

Mr. Poyner testified that as he was walking along the elevated area, he heard someone call "Billy!" from Connecticut Avenue. He turned his head to the right, but continued to walk forward to the location at the end of the platform where he thought that a bush would be. There was no bush, however, and Mr. Poyner fell, suffering personal injuries.

Mr. Poyner brought suit against several defendants, including the owners of the building, the property manager in charge of its maintenance, and the proprietor of Parklane Cleaners. After the parties had conducted discovery, the defendants moved for summary judgment, contending, *inter alia*, that Mr. Poyner had been contributorily negligent as a matter of law. The trial judge granted the motion, and she stated her reasons, in pertinent part, as follows:

> Here we have a plaintiff who is partially visually impaired, legally blind, who can see some in front of him and gets about without the assistance of any mechanical or other disability aids.
>
> He was aware, as he was approaching this area to enter the cleaners, that he was on an elevated surface. He was not paying full attention, having been distracted

> by a call from someone out in the street. And according to the plaintiff's own testimony at his deposition, [he] continued to proceed forward and went over the edge into the lower — falling from the part where the bushes were, into the lower stairwell, and sustained injuries.
>
> Mr. Poyner's actions, in the court's judgment, clearly violate an objective reasonableness standard. . . . No reasonable jurors could conclude that the plaintiff was not negligent when he continued to walk on an elevated surface with limited vision while his head was turned away from the direction of his travel in an area in which he was not very familiar.

Ordinarily, questions of negligence and contributory negligence must be decided by the trier of fact. A party asserting the defense of contributory negligence is required to establish, by a preponderance of the evidence, that the plaintiff failed to exercise reasonable care. "Only in the exceptional case is evidence so clear and unambiguous that contributory negligence should be found as a matter of law." *Tilghman v. Johnson*, 513 A.2d 1350, 1351 (D.C. 1986) (citations omitted).

The trial judge concluded that this was one of those rare cases in which contributory negligence — a defense with respect to which the defendants had the burden of proof — had been established as a matter of law. We agree. Indeed, we are satisfied, as was the trial judge, that Mr. Poyner's own testimony established that he did not exercise reasonable care and that his own contributory negligence proximately caused the accident.

It is undisputed that, at the time of the accident, a shrub at the end of the elevated platform was missing. A photograph which is a part of the record demonstrates that this was readily apparent, at least to any sighted person who chose to look. "[A] person must see what is reasonably there to be seen." *Jackson v. Schenick*, 174 A.2d 353, 355 (D.C. 1961) (citation omitted). In this case, Mr. Poyner acknowledged that his attention was distracted when someone called his name, and that he turned his head to the right, but continued to walk forward. At the critical moment, according to his own testimony, Mr. Poyner, who could see six to eight feet in front of him and was aware of his handicap, did not look where he was going.

Mr. Poyner argues, however, that he is not a sighted person, and that "it is reasonable *for a legally blind person* . . . as a response to his name being called, [to] turn towards the direction of his caller, reach for the handle and continue his step towards the door." (Emphasis added.) He claims that those actions "do not constitute contributory negligence." He contends, in other words, that on account of his visual impairment, his conduct should be tested against a different standard of care.

The parties have cited no authority on this issue, and we have found no applicable case law in the District of Columbia. The precedents in other jurisdictions, however, support affirmance of the trial court's order. "It seems to be the general rule that a blind or otherwise handicapped person, in using the public ways, must exercise for his own safety due care, or care commensurate with the known or reasonably foreseeable dangers. Due care is such care as an ordinarily prudent person with the same disability would exercise under the same or similar circumstances." *Cook v. City of Winston-Salem*, 85 S.E.2d 696, 700-01 (N.C. 1955) (citing, *inter alia, Keith v. Worcester & Blackstone Valley St. Ry. Co.*, 82 N.E. 680 (Mass. 1907)). As the court explained in *Keith*, however,

> [I]t is also correct to say that in the exercise of common prudence one of defective eyesight must usually as a matter of general knowledge take more care and employ keener watchfulness in walking upon the streets and avoiding obstructions than the same person with good eyesight, in order to reach the standard established by the law for all persons alike, whether they be weak or strong, sound or deficient.

82 N.E. at 681.

In *Smith v. Sneller*, 26 A.2d 452 (Pa. 1942), the Supreme Court of Pennsylvania considered a situation similar to the one before us, and its disposition is instructive. Sneller, a plumbing contractor, had removed a portion of the sidewalk and had dug a trench in order to make a sewer connection. On the north side of the trench, Sneller constructed a barricade. On the south side, however, Sneller simply left a pile of earth two feet high. The plaintiff, Smith, was walking north along the sidewalk towards the trench. As a result of defective eyesight, he failed to see the pile of earth. Mr. Smith fell into the trench, and sustained personal injuries. A jury returned a verdict in his favor.

The intermediate appellate court expressed sympathy for Mr. Smith "in his effort to make a living in spite of his physical handicap," but nevertheless felt constrained to reverse the decision and enter judgment n.o.v. in Sneller's favor. Smith appealed to the Pennsylvania Supreme Court, which affirmed the judgment. Noting that Mr. Smith's vision was so defective that he could not see a dangerous condition immediately in front of him, and that the accident could have been avoided if he had used "one of the common well-known compensatory devices for the blind, such as a cane, a 'seeing eye' dog, or a companion," the court concluded:

> Plaintiff's conduct was not equal to the degree of care required of him. The Superior Court very properly said: "A blind man may not rely wholly upon his other senses to warn him of danger but must use the devices usually employed, to compensate for his blindness. Only by so doing can he go about with comparative safety to himself." We are in accord with that learned court, that plaintiff was guilty of contributory negligence as a matter of law, and we must, therefore, affirm the judgment.

26 A.2d at 454.

The reasoning of the court in *Smith* applies equally to the present case. Here, as in *Smith*, the plaintiff was walking alone, and he did not use a guide dog or a cane. As a result, he fell from the walkway. Indeed, the evidence of contributory negligence is stronger here than in *Smith*, for Mr. Poyner, who could see six to eight feet in front of him, acknowledged that, at the moment that he fell, he was not looking where he was going.

In *Coker v. McDonald's Corp.*, 537 A.2d 549 (Del. Super. 1987), the legally blind plaintiff was walking to the entrance of a McDonald's restaurant from the parking lot. Unlike the plaintiffs in *Smith* and in the present case, however, she was carrying a cane in her right hand, and she was holding on to a companion with her left hand. Ms. Coker lost her balance while attempting to navigate around an obstruction, and she sustained injuries. The defendant claimed that the obstruction was "open and obvious," and that the plaintiff was contributorily negligent as a matter of law. The court disagreed:

> A blind person is not bound to discover *everything* which a person of normal vision would. He is bound to use due care under the circumstances. Due care for a blind person includes a reasonable effort to compensate for his unfortunate affliction by use of artificial aids for discovery of obstacles in his path. When an effort in this direction is made, it will ordinarily be a jury question whether or not such effort was a reasonable one.

Id. at 550-51 (emphasis in original) (citations and internal quotation marks omitted). Characterizing the issue presented as being whether Ms. Coker acted reasonably under the circumstances, the court concluded that "where the blind plaintiff is not using any aid, . . . as in *Smith v. Sneller, supra*, a court could rule as a matter of law that the plaintiff was contributorily negligent." *Id.* at 551. Because Ms. Coker was using two different aids, however — the cane and the companion — the question of contributory negligence was for the jury, and the defendant was not entitled to summary judgment. *Id.*

We agree with the analysis of the courts both in *Smith v. Sneller* and in *Coker*. Like the plaintiff in *Smith*, but unlike the plaintiff in *Coker*, Mr. Poyner was alone, and he used neither a cane nor a seeing eye dog. He also looked away at the critical moment. Under these circumstances, he was contributorily negligent as a matter of law, and summary judgment was properly granted.

C. Mental Disability

Just as one's immutable physical disabilities must, in all fairness, be taken into account as a "circumstance" in analyzing our expectations for reasonable care, one would expect that mental disabilities of the actor would likewise be factored into the analysis. Yet as we will see below, courts have long held that mental impairment is not an excuse for conduct that would otherwise be considered careless. Interestingly, the original philosophical impetus for the rule — that those with mental impairment should be institutionalized — has fallen into disfavor. Yet the rule remains the same. Consider whether the modern justification for this old rule is sufficiently compelling. Notwithstanding its acceptance of this rule of law, the court below nevertheless finds in favor of the defendant for reasons more fundamental than our definition of reasonable care — it ultimately concludes that the actor owed no duty of care whatsoever.

CREASY v. RUSK

730 N.E.2d 659 (Ind. 2000)

SULLIVAN, J.

Carol Creasy, a certified nursing assistant, sued Lloyd Rusk, an Alzheimer's patient, for injuries she suffered when he kicked her while she was trying to put him to bed. We hold that adults with mental disabilities have the same general duty of care toward others as those without. But we conclude that the relationship between the parties and public policy considerations here are such that Rusk had no such duty to Creasy.

Background

In July, 1992, Lloyd Rusk's wife admitted Rusk to the Brethren Healthcare Center ("BHC") because he suffered from memory loss and confusion and Rusk's wife was unable to care for him. Rusk's primary diagnosis was Alzheimer's disease. Over the course of three years at BHC, Rusk experienced periods of anxiousness, confusion, depression, disorientation, and agitation. Rusk often resisted when staff members attempted to remove him from prohibited areas of the facility. On several occasions, Rusk was belligerent with both staff and other residents. In particular, Rusk was often combative, agitated, and aggressive and would hit staff members when they tried to care for him.

BHC had employed Creasy as a certified nursing assistant for nearly 20 months when the incident at issue occurred. Creasy's responsibilities included caring for Rusk and other patients with Alzheimer's disease. Residents with Alzheimer's had bruised Creasy during the course of her work for BHC, and Creasy knew that Rusk had Alzheimer's disease.

On May 16, 1995, Creasy and another certified nursing assistant, Linda Davis, were working through their routine of putting Rusk and other residents to bed. Creasy knew that Rusk had been "very agitated and combative that evening." By Creasy's account:

> [Davis] was helping me put Mr. Rusk to bed. She was holding his wrists to keep him from hitting us and I was trying to get his legs to put him to bed. He was hitting and kicking wildly. During this time, he kicked me several times in my left knee and hip area. My lower back popped and I yelled out with pain from my lower back and left knee.

Creasy filed a civil negligence suit against Rusk, seeking monetary damages for the injuries she suffered as a result of Rusk's conduct. Rusk moved for summary judgment and the trial court granted his motion. Creasy appealed. The Court of Appeals reversed, holding "that a person's mental capacity, whether that person is a child or an adult, must be factored [into] the determination of whether a legal duty exists," and that a genuine issue of material fact existed as to the level of Rusk's mental capacity.

This case requires us to decide two distinct questions of Indiana common law:

(1) Whether the general duty of care imposed upon adults with mental disabilities is the same as that for adults without mental disabilities?

(2) Whether the circumstances of Rusk's case are such that the general duty of care imposed upon adults with mental disabilities should be imposed upon him?

In many, if not most, jurisdictions, the general duty of care imposed on adults with mental disabilities is the same as that for adults without mental disabilities. *See Restatement (Second) of Torts §283B* (1965). Adults with mental disabilities are held to the same standard of care as that of a reasonable person under the same circumstances without regard to the alleged tortfeasor's capacity to control or understand the consequences of his or her actions.

Judge Kirsch, writing for the Court of Appeals in this case, found that Indiana law does not follow the Restatement rule. The Court of Appeals held "that a person's mental capacity, whether that person is a child or an adult, must be factored [into] the determination of whether a legal duty exists." *Creasy v. Rusk*, 696 N.E.2d 442, 446 (Ind. Ct. App. 1998*)*. We believe that the Court of Appeals accurately stated Indiana law but that the law is in need of revision.

[T]he generally accepted rule in jurisdictions other than Indiana is that mental disability does not excuse a person from liability for "conduct which does not conform to the standard of a reasonable man under like circumstances." *Restatement (Second) of Torts §283B*; *accord* Restatement (Third) of Torts §9(c) (Discussion Draft Apr. 5, 1999) ("Unless the actor is a child, the actor's mental or emotional disability is not considered in determining whether conduct is negligent."). People with mental disabilities are commonly held liable for their intentional and negligent torts. No allowance is made for lack of intelligence, ignorance, excitability, or proneness to accident.

The public policy reasons most often cited for holding individuals with mental disabilities to a standard of reasonable care in negligence claims include the following.

(1) Allocates losses between two innocent parties to the one who caused or occasioned the loss.

(2) Provides incentive to those responsible for people with disabilities and interested in their estates to prevent harm and "restrain" those who are potentially dangerous.

(3) Removes inducements for alleged tortfeasors to fake a mental disability in order to escape liability. The Restatement mentions the ease with which mental disability can be feigned as one possible basis for this policy concern.

(4) Avoids administrative problems involved in courts and juries attempting to identify and assess the significance of an actor's disability.

(5) Forces persons with disabilities to pay for the damage they do if they [are to live in the world.]. The Restatement adds that it is better that the assets, if any, of the one with the mental deficiency be used "to compensate innocent victims than that [the assets] remain in their hands."

To assist in deciding whether Indiana should adopt the generally accepted rule, we turn to an examination of contemporary public policy in Indiana as embodied in enactments of our state legislature.

Since the 1970's, Indiana law has strongly reflected policies to deinstitutionalize people with disabilities and integrate them into the least restrictive environment. National policy changes have led the way for some of Indiana's enactments in that several federal acts either guarantee the civil rights of people with disabilities or condition state aid upon state compliance with desegregation and integrationist practices.

These legislative developments reflect policies consistent with those supporting the Restatement rule generally accepted outside Indiana in that they reflect a determination that people with disabilities should be treated in the same way as non-disabled persons.

We pause for a moment to consider in greater detail . . . that the Restatement rule may very well have been grounded in a policy determination that persons with mental disabilities should be institutionalized or otherwise confined rather than "live in the world." It is clear from our recitation of state and federal legislative and regulatory developments that contemporary public policy has rejected institutionalization and confinement for a "strong professional consensus in favor of . . . community treatment . . . and integration into the least restrictive . . . environment." We observe that it is a matter of some irony that public policies favoring the opposite ends — institutionalization and confinement on the one hand and community treatment and integration into the least restrictive environment on the other — should nevertheless yield the same common law rule: that the general duty of care imposed on adults with mental disabilities is the same as that for adults without mental disabilities.

In balancing the considerations presented in the foregoing analysis, we reject the Court of Appeals' approach and adopt the Restatement rule. We hold that a person with mental disabilities is generally held to the same standard of care as that of a reasonable person under the same circumstances without regard to the alleged tortfeasor's capacity to control or understand the consequences of his or her actions.

We turn now to the question of whether the circumstances of Rusk's case are such that the general duty of care imposed upon adults with mental disabilities should be found to run from him to Creasy.

In asking this question, we recognize that exceptions to the general rule will arise where the factual circumstances negate the factors supporting imposition of a duty particularly with respect to the nature of the parties' relationship and public policy considerations.

We find that the relationship between Rusk and Creasy and public policy concerns dictate that Rusk owed no duty of care to Creasy. *See Webb v. Jarvis*, 575 N.E.2d 992, 995 (Ind. 1991) (balancing three factors to determine whether an individual owes a duty to another: (1) the relationship between the parties; (2) the reasonable foreseeability of harm to the person injured; and (3) public policy concerns).

Unlike the typical victim supporting the Restatement rationale, Creasy was not a member of the public at large, unable to anticipate or safeguard against the harm she encountered. Creasy knew of Rusk's violent history. She could have changed her course of action or requested additional assistance when she recognized Rusk's state of mind on the evening when she received the alleged injury. Rusk's inability to comprehend the circumstances of his relationship with Creasy and others was the very reason Creasy was employed to support Rusk. The nursing home and Creasy, through the nursing home, were "employed to encounter, and knowingly did encounter, just the dangers which injured" Creasy. *Anicet*, 580 So. 2d at 276.

The second Restatement policy rationale creates an inducement for those responsible for a person with a mental disability to prevent harm to others. By placing Rusk in a nursing home, we presume Rusk's wife made a difficult decision based on her desire to prevent Rusk from being violent and harming himself, herself, or others. Mrs. Rusk entrusted her husband's care, including prevention of the harm he might bring to others, to the nursing home staff and the nursing home. And as a business enterprise, the nursing home received compensation for its services.

With respect to the third policy rationale, "it is virtually impossible to imagine circumstances under which a person would feign the symptoms of mental disability and subject themselves to commitment to an institution in order to avoid some future civil liability." To the extent that such circumstances exist, there is no evidence whatsoever that they are present under the facts in this case.

Finally, there are no administrative difficulties in this case with respect to determining the degree and existence of Rusk's mental disability. Under the relationship analysis set forth above and the present policy analysis, it is unnecessary to determine the degree of Rusk's mental disability. We need only conclude that Rusk had a mental disability which served as the reason for his presence in the nursing home and the foundation of his relationship with Creasy.

We agree with Judge Friedlander . . . that there was no material question of fact as to the existence, let alone the advanced stage, of Rusk's Alzheimer's disease and his inability to appreciate or control his violent behavior. Rusk was admitted to the nursing home because he was confused and suffering from memory loss such that his wife could not care for him. By May 1995, when Creasy was injured by Rusk, Rusk had been a resident of the nursing home for three years and his condition had deteriorated. He regularly displayed behaviors characteristic of a person with advanced Alzheimer's disease such as aggression, belligerence, and violence.

In addition to the public policy concerns behind the Restatement rule, we find that it would be contrary to public policy to hold Rusk to a duty to Creasy when it would place "too great a burden on him because his disorientation and potential for violence is the very reason he was institutionalized and needed the aid of employed caretakers."

Rusk was entitled to summary judgment because public policy and the nature of the relationship between Rusk, Creasy, and the nursing home preclude holding that Rusk owed a duty of care to Creasy under these factual circumstances.

NOTES AND PROBLEMS

1. ***Inferior vs. Superior Knowledge and Skills.*** In *Vaughan*, the court rejected the defendant hayrick builder's proposed alternative standard that would have evaluated his conduct in light of his, apparently, inferior intelligence or skill. The court rejected this because, among other things, it would adopt a standard infinitely variable with each case. But isn't this also the result of the decision by courts, such as in *Cervelli*, to hold gifted and talented actors to a higher standard of care? In other words, if the reasonable person does not take on inferior knowledge and skills, why does the reasonable person take on superior knowledge and skills? Consider tort law's purpose of deterring accidents. How might this purpose be fulfilled with the dichotomy courts have adopted?

2. ***Physical Disabilities vs. Mental Disabilities.*** While it is often true that there is a physical explanation for or cause of many mental disabilities, the mental versus physical dichotomy courts recognize focuses upon the manifestation of the disability itself in applying the rules. Thus, while a traumatic brain injury is certainly a physical problem, the actor's mental disability caused by the physical condition will be considered a mental disability for purposes of applying negligence rules. Can the decisions by the majority of courts, as demonstrated in *Poyner* and *Creasy*, to treat physical and mental disabilities differently in negligence cases be reconciled? What differences exist between such disabilities that would justify having the reasonable person take on the physical disabilities, but not the mental ones? With consideration for the Restatement's five justifications for not considering mental disability (discussed in *Creasy*), which of these would point toward a different rule for physical disabilities?

3. ***Mental Impairment as a Defense for Intentional and Accidental Tort Claims.*** One must be careful about the context where we encounter various doctrines and rules of law. In the unit on *battery* we encountered an elderly patient at a nursing home with mental deficits. In that case, the court was asked whether the law of Colorado required the plaintiff to prove merely that the defendant had intended contact, or whether the defendant had also intended for the contact to be harmful or offensive — the single v. dual intent debate. The court there ruled in favor of the dual intent requirement, and affirmed the jury's fact determination that the particular defendant sued did not appreciate that her slapping the plaintiff was an offensive contact. But the court also said there was no special rule for the mentally infirm — just that such persons were less likely to meet the dual intent requirement. In *Creasy*, the court rules first that the mentally infirm will have the same standard applied to them in a negligence claim as a person of sound mind (i.e., that the reasonable person was of sound

mind). But then the court negates the law's imposition of *any* duty of care under the facts of the case. In what ways, therefore, is the *Creasy* decision either consistent or inconsistent with the prior battery case of *White v. Muniz*?

4. ***Problems.*** How does tort law say that we should analyze the tort liability of the following persons?

- **A.** A person with a mental impairment finds the keys to an automobile, gets in it, and drives down the road, causing an accident when he swerves out of his lane.
- **B.** A person with a mental impairment is a patient at a nursing home. Sitting on the front porch of the facility in a rocking chair, he decides to start randomly throwing rocks into the street. He hits the mailman making a delivery to the mailbox of the facility at the curb.
- **C.** A blind man finds the keys to an automobile, gets in it, and drives down the road, causing an accident when he fails to notice a red light and hits a pedestrian crossing the street.
- **D.** A blind man is walking down a busy sidewalk when he accidentally bumps into a young mother pushing a stroller and injures her infant.
- **E.** A college student drinks too much at a football tailgate event, becomes intoxicated, and loses control over his scooter in a crowd of people.

D. Children

It is sometimes unclear whether courts' recognition of certain legal doctrines set a path for society or merely follows the expectations of society. When a court needs to determine the reasonableness of a child's conduct, however, it is clear that the law follows the expectations of the citizenry. Most people unschooled in the law would find it monstrous to hold a child to the same expectations for care as an adult. Tort law follows this school of thought by creating a *child standard of care* for use in analyzing children's conduct in many scenarios. But this standard does not apply to any and all conduct by children.

ROBINSON v. LINDSAY

598 P.2d 392 (Wash. 1979)

Utter, J.

An action seeking damages for personal injuries was brought on behalf of Kelly Robinson who lost full use of a thumb in a snowmobile accident when she was 11 years of age. Billy Anderson, 13 years of age at the time of the accident, was the driver of the snowmobile. After a jury verdict in favor of Anderson, the trial court ordered a new trial.

The single issue on appeal is whether a minor operating a snowmobile is to be held to an adult standard of care. The trial court failed to instruct the jury as to that standard and ordered a new trial because it believed the jury should have been so instructed. We agree and affirm the order granting a new trial.

The trial court instructed the jury under WPI 10.05 that:

> In considering the claimed negligence of a child, you are instructed that it is the duty of a child to exercise the same care that a reasonably careful child of the same age, intelligence, maturity, training and experience would exercise under the same or similar circumstances.

[Plaintiff] properly excepted to the giving of this instruction and to the court's failure to give an adult standard of care.

The question of what standard of care should apply to acts of children has a long historical background. Traditionally, a flexible standard of care has been used to determine if children's actions were negligent. Under some circumstances, however, courts have developed a rationale for applying an adult standard.

> "All men make mistakes, but only wise men learn from their mistakes."
>
> *Winston Churchill*

In the courts' search for a uniform standard of behavior to use in determining whether or not a person's conduct has fallen below minimal acceptable standards, the law has developed a fictitious person, the "reasonable man of ordinary prudence." That term was first used in *Vaughan v. Menlove*, 132 Eng. Rep. 490 (1837).

Exceptions to the reasonable person standard developed when the individual whose conduct was alleged to have been negligent suffered from some physical impairment, such as blindness, deafness, or lameness. Courts also found it necessary, as a practical matter, to depart considerably from the objective standard when dealing with children's behavior. Children are traditionally encouraged to pursue childhood activities without the same burdens and responsibilities with which adults must contend. *See* Bahr, *Tort Law and the Games Kids Play*, 23 S.D.L. Rev. 275 (1978). As a result, courts evolved a special standard of care to measure a child's negligence in a particular situation.

In *Roth v. Union Depot Co.*, 13 Wash. 525, 43 P. 641 (1896), Washington joined "the overwhelming weight of authority" in distinguishing between the capacity of a child and that of an adult.

The current law in this state is fairly reflected in WPI 10.05, given in this case. In the past we have always compared a child's conduct to that expected of a reasonably careful child of the same age, intelligence, maturity, training and experience. This case is the first to consider the question of a child's liability for injuries sustained as a result of his or her operation of a motorized vehicle or participation in an inherently dangerous activity.

Courts in other jurisdictions have created an exception to the special child standard because of the apparent injustice that would occur if a child who caused injury while engaged in certain dangerous activities were permitted to defend himself by saying that other children similarly situated would not have exercised a degree of care higher than his, and he is, therefore, not liable for his tort. Some courts have couched the exception in terms of children engaging in an activity which is normally one for adults only. *See, e.g., Dellwo v. Pearson*, 259 Minn. 452, 107 N.W.2d 859, 97 A.L.R.2d 866 (1961) (operation of a motorboat). We believe a better rationale is that when the activity a child engages in is inherently dangerous, as is the operation of powerful mechanized vehicles, the child should be held to an adult standard of care.

Such a rule protects the need of children to be children but at the same time discourages immature individuals from engaging in inherently dangerous activities. Children will still be free to enjoy traditional childhood activities without being held to an adult standard of care. Although accidents sometimes occur as the result of such activities, they are not activities generally considered capable of resulting in "grave danger to others and to the minor himself if the care used in the course of the activity drops below that care which the reasonable and prudent adult would use . . ." *Daniels v. Evans*, 107 N.H. 407, 408, 224 A.2d 63 (1966).

Other courts adopting the adult standard of care for children engaged in adult activities have emphasized the hazards to the public if the rule is otherwise. We agree with the Minnesota Supreme Court's language in its decision in *Dellwo v. Pearson*, supra at 457-58:

> Certainly in the circumstances of modern life, where vehicles moved by powerful motors are readily available and frequently operated by immature individuals, we should be skeptical of a rule that would allow motor vehicles to be operated to the hazard of the public with less than the normal minimum degree of care and competence.

Dellwo applied the adult standard to a 12-year-old defendant operating a motorboat. Other jurisdictions have applied the adult standard to minors engaged in analogous activities. *Goodfellow v. Coggburn*, 560 P.2d 873 (1977) (minor operating tractor); *Williams v. Esaw*, 522 P.2d 950 (1974) (minor operating motorcycle); *Perricone v. DiBartolo*, 302 N.E.2d 637 (1973) (minor operating gasoline-powered minibike); *Krahn v. LaMeres*, 483 P.2d 522, 525-26 (Wyo. 1971) (minor operating automobile). The holding of minors to an adult standard of care when they operate motorized vehicles is gaining approval from an increasing number of courts and commentators.

The operation of a snowmobile likewise requires adult care and competence. Currently 2.2 million snowmobiles are in operation in the United States. Studies show that collisions and other snowmobile accidents claim hundreds of casualties each year and that the incidence of accidents is particularly high among inexperienced operators.

At the time of the accident, the 13-year-old petitioner had operated snowmobiles for about 2 years. When the injury occurred, petitioner was operating a 30-horsepower snowmobile at speeds of 10 to 20 miles per hour. The record indicates that the machine itself was capable of 65 miles per hour. Because petitioner was operating a powerful motorized vehicle, he should be held to the standard of care and conduct expected of an adult.

The order granting a new trial is affirmed.

NOTES AND PROBLEMS

1. ***Adult vs. Child Standard of Care.*** What is the difference between the adult versus child standard of care discussed by the court in *Robinson*? If the child standard is typically applied to children in order to avoid "monstrous" results, why do courts revert back to the adult standard for certain dangerous activities? What does this say about the law's regard for the importance of allowing children to participate in such conduct (by encouraging it)?

2. ***Objective vs. Subjective.*** To the extent that the child standard takes so many of the child-actor's own traits into consideration, what is left of the objective standard? Is the child standard a repudiation of the *Vaughan* decision to employ an objective standard for negligence analysis? Are we simply asking if the child acted in a bona fide manner? Even under the child standard of care, there is one attribute that is held inviolate — the trait of reasonableness. While the child standard of care takes on many of the particular traits of the actor — age, intelligence, and experience — the reasonably prudent child always remains careful under the circumstances. The age, intelligence, and experience may impact the perceptions of danger but, once perceived, the reasonably prudent child still makes prudent decisions.

3. ***Mentally Impaired Children.*** Unlike mentally impaired adults, under the child standard of care, the mental impairment of a child is factored into the analysis of reasonable care. In other words, the reasonably prudent child will have the same mental acuity as the actor in question.

4. ***Maximum and Minimum Ages for Child Actors.*** At what age should an actor no longer be considered a "child" and eligible for application of the more lenient (and subjective) child standard of care — 21, 18, 16? While courts are not uniform, many courts use the age of 15 or 16 as defining when an adult standard of care will be applied to determine the issue of breach. On the other end of the spectrum, courts and commentators have disagreed over whether a child may be considered too young to be considered negligent at all (even applying the child standard of care). There have actually been courts embracing one of three

different views regarding the minimum age at which a child can be held accountable in a negligence cause of action:

A. Majority view (incorporated into the Restatement (Second) of Torts §283A) — that the jury should consider on a case-by-case basis, utilizing the child standard of care, whether the child actor was too young to have any appreciation for a risk of harm.

B. "Illinois Rule" — a number of states have determined that, as a matter of law, a child younger than the age of seven years is incapable of being negligent.

C. Third Restatement Rule — Section 10(b) of the Restatement (Third) of Torts provides that: "A child less than five years of age is incapable of negligence" (citing the lack of moral blame of such a child and the reality that holding such a child liable for negligence will in fact serve no deterrent function).

5. ***Problems.*** Which standard should be applied to children involved in the following activities?

A. Bowling — the ball comes off the child's hands injuring a bystander.

B. One child handing over the keys to mom's car to another underage driver — the driver carelessly causes an accident. Consider the negligence of the children separately.

C. Playing golf — the child hits an errant shot without yelling "fore" and injures another golfer.

D. Hunting — the child accidentally shoots another hunter in the woods.

> **"LADIES AND GENTLEMEN OF THE JURY . . ."**
>
> **Idaho JI 2.02 Duty of Care — Minor Child**
>
> "A minor child has a duty to exercise the degree of care which would reasonably be expected of an ordinary child of the same age, maturity, experience and knowledge when acting under similar circumstances."

E. Extraordinarily Dangerous Activities

We have already witnessed how the "reasonable care under the circumstances" standard is quite malleable, performing capably in the requisite analysis of many different scenarios. But maybe some circumstances are so dangerous that the reasonable care standard itself needs adjustment. Should the foreseeability of great harm demand something beyond reasonable care? And if so, how would this be articulated? In *Stewart*, the court rejects the plaintiff's demands for an altered standard under the circumstance of great danger. The court believes that this is more than semantics. Do you agree?

STEWART v. MOTTS

654 A.2d 535 (Pa. 1995)

MONTEMURO, J.

Appellant, Jonathon Stewart, appeals from an order and memorandum opinion of the Superior Court affirming a judgment of the Court of Common Pleas of Monroe County following a verdict in favor of appellee, Martin Motts, in this action for personal injuries.

The sole issue presented before us is whether there exists a higher standard of "extraordinary care" for the use of dangerous instrumentalities over and above the standard of "reasonable care" such that the trial court erred for failing to give an instruction to the jury that the Appellee should have used a "high degree of care" in handling gasoline. Because we believe that there is but one standard of care, the standard of "reasonable care," we affirm.

The pertinent facts of this case are simple and were ably stated by the trial court:

> On July 15, 1987, Plaintiff, Jonathon Stewart, stopped at Defendant, Martin Motts' auto repair shop and offered assistance to the Defendant in repairing an automobile fuel tank. In an effort to start and move the car with the gasoline tank unattached, the Plaintiff suggested and then proceeded to pour gasoline into the carburetor. The Defendant was to turn the ignition key at a given moment. While the exact sequence of events was contested, the tragic result was that the car backfired, caused an explosion and resulted in Plaintiff suffering severe burns to his upper body. On October 8, 1992, following a two-day trial, a jury returned a verdict for the defendant thus denying the Plaintiff's claim for damages.

The only issue raised before this Court is the refusal of the trial court to read Stewart's requested point for charge No. 4. This point for charge reads:

> We are instructing you that gasoline due to its inflammability is a very dangerous substance if not properly handled. . . . With an appreciation of such danger, and under conditions where its existence reasonably should have been known, there follows a high degree of care which circumscribes the conduct of everyone about the danger, and whether the parties . . . acted as reasonable men under the circumstances is for you the jury to decide.

The trial court denied this point of charge finding that it was "cumulative with respect to the standard charge given by the Court. . . ." In this appeal, Stewart argues that the trial court erred in failing to read point of charge No. 4 to the jury because Pennsylvania law applies an "extraordinary" or "heightened duty of care" to those employing a dangerous agency.

We begin our discussion by reaffirming the principle that there is but one standard of care to be applied to negligence actions involving dangerous instrumentalities in this Commonwealth. This standard of care is "reasonable care" as well stated in the Restatement (Second) of Torts:

> The care required is always reasonable care. The standard never varies, but the care which it is reasonable to require of the actor varies with the danger involved in his act and is proportionate to it. The greater the danger, the greater the care which must be exercised. . . .

Restatement (Second) of Torts §298 comment b (1965).

Properly read, our cases involving dangerous agencies reaffirm these well accepted principles found in the Restatement. In *Konchar v. Cebular*, 3 A.2d 913 (Pa. 1939), . . . the plaintiff drove into a gas station and ordered a gallon of gasoline. The defendant began pumping gas into the motorcycle, but when three-quarters of a gallon was placed in the tank, the gasoline overflowed and ran into the hot cylinders of the engine. The plaintiff, sitting on the motorcycle, was burned when the gasoline exploded. . . . In deciding the case, this Court noted that gasoline was a dangerous substance requiring a "high duty of care." *Konchar*, 3 A.2d at 914. We affirmed, holding that, "it was for the jury to decide whether, under all of the circumstances, [the plaintiff] had acted as a reasonably prudent man." *Id.* Thus, we recognized that the question of the plaintiff's contributory negligence was to be determined using the reasonable care standard in light of the particular circumstances of the case. One such circumstance, we acknowledged, was that gasoline, a dangerous substance, was involved requiring that the reasonably prudent person exercise a higher degree of care under these circumstances. Taken in context, our statement that the plaintiff was under a "high duty of care" did nothing more than reaffirm the general principle that the care employed by a reasonable man must be proportionate to the danger of the activity.

Admittedly, this notion of a heightened level of "extraordinary care" for the handling of dangerous agencies has crept into our jurisprudence. In *Kuhns v. Brugger*, 135 A.2d 395 (Pa. 1957), this Court considered the proper standard of care for negligence involving a handgun. The defendant in this case was a grandfather who had left a loaded handgun in an unlocked dresser drawer. While alone in the house, his grandchild found the gun and inadvertently shot another child. [W]e found that the possession of a loaded handgun placed upon the defendant the duty of, "exercising not simply ordinary, but extraordinary care so that no harm might be visited upon others." This language in *Kuhns* on its face unfortunately suggests that this Commonwealth recognizes a separate standard of care, "extraordinary care," for dangerous instrumentalities above and beyond "ordinary care." We reject this suggestion.

[T]he *Kuhns* Court did not create a standard of "extraordinary care" for all dangerous instrumentalities as advocated by the appellant. Instead, we believe that the *Kuhns* Court considered the danger of an unattended handgun under the circumstances of this case and fashioned a standard of care proportionate to that danger.

In summation, this Commonwealth recognizes only one standard of care in negligence actions involving dangerous instrumentalities — the standard of reasonable care under the circumstances. It is well established by our case law that the reasonable man must exercise care in proportion to the danger involved in his act. *See MacDougall*, 166 A. at 592 ("Vigilance must always be commensurate with danger. A high degree of danger always calls for a high degree of care").

With these principles in mind we must next examine the jury instructions in this case. Reviewing the charge as a whole, we cannot conclude that it was inadequate. The trial judge explained to the jury that negligence is "the absence of ordinary care which a reasonably prudent person would exercise in the circumstances here presented." The trial judge further explained:

> It is for you to determine how a reasonably prudent person would act in those circumstances. Ordinary care is the care a reasonably prudent person would use under the circumstances presented in this case. It is the duty of every person to use ordinary care not only for his own safety and the protection of his property, but also to avoid serious injury to others. What constitutes ordinary care varies according to the particular circumstances and conditions existing then and there. The amount of care required by law must be in keeping with the degree of danger involved.

Id. at 158-59.

We find that this charge, when read as a whole, adequately instructed the jury. The charge informed the jury that the proper standard of care was "reasonable" or "ordinary" care under the circumstances in accordance with the law of this Commonwealth. The charge properly instructed the jury that the level of care required changed with the circumstances. The charge also informed the jury that the level of care required increased proportionately with the level of danger in the activity. We find nothing in this charge that is confusing, misleading, or unclear. From these instructions, the jury had the tools to examine the circumstances of the case and determine that the defendant was required to exercise a "higher degree of care" in using the dangerous agency of gasoline.

For the reasons set forth above, we affirm the order of the Superior Court.

NOTES AND PROBLEMS

1. ***One Standard of Care.*** The court above summarizes its position by declaring that it "recognizes only one standard of care." Notwithstanding this position, in two prior cases the court had applied a standard of "extraordinary care" and a standard of "high duty of care." Given the loose use of such language, one can understand the frustration of the plaintiff's counsel. Nevertheless, while the court indicates that the circumstance of extraordinary

danger does not necessitate a change in the standard, the court does affirm that the regular standard of care is flexible enough to demand greater care in the face of such danger. How exactly does this work? What instructions did the trial court give the jury to facilitate the jury's understanding of this proportionality principle?

2. ***Problems.*** How should the following circumstances impact a jury's expectations for care, utilizing the flexible concept of a "duty of reasonable care under the circumstances?" Remember that the inquiry must focus upon the nature of the foreseeable risk of harm at the time of the actor's conduct, and is not to be viewed with hindsight.

- **A.** A shipper of goods notices a liquid leaking from a crate. Without realizing that the liquid is nitroglycerine, the shipper attempts to open the crate and an explosion occurs hurting bystanders.
- **B.** A clown is riding a motorcycle in a parade. The parade route is flanked by large crowds of spectators clustered close to the street on both sides. The clown decides to show off by popping wheelies, loses control, and runs over several spectators.
- **C.** A motorist is driving to the top of the Continental Divide on Trail Ridge Road in Colorado's Rocky Mountain National Park. There is no guardrail along the curves, and the exposure near some of the curves is several thousand feet. The motorist decides to show off for a passenger by driving as close to the edge as possible. A wheel catches the lip of the cliff and the driver loses control, causing them to plummet to their deaths.
- **D.** A motorist is travelling on a state highway near Lawton, Oklahoma (where things are relatively flat). The driver is bored and decides to see how close he can come to the edge of the pavement. His tires veer off the edge of the highway and the car spins out in the dirt, clipping the edge of a billboard and causing some damage to it.

F. Sudden Emergency

Finally, given the reaffirmation that the reasonable care standard can take into account circumstances of grave danger without any adjustment, you might predict that this stalwart standard would need no elaboration when applied to an emergency scenario. However, many courts have traditionally felt it appropriate to enhance the normal reasonable care jury instruction in cases where the actor faced a sudden emergency. The *sudden emergency* instruction highlights for the jury the circumstance in which an actor has decreased time for attention and deliberation when facing an emergency not of his own making. Whether this truism necessitates additional jury instructions is a matter hotly debated by courts today, with mixed results.

MYHAVER v. KNUTSON

942 P.2d 445 (Ariz. 1997)

FELDMAN, J.

In November 1990, Elmo Knutson was driving north on 43rd Avenue near Bell Road in Phoenix when Theresa Magnusson entered 43rd Avenue from a shopping center driveway and headed south in Knutson's lane. Seeing Magnusson's car in his lane, Knutson accelerated and swerved left, avoiding what he perceived to be an impending head-on collision. In doing this, he crossed the double yellow line into oncoming traffic and collided with Bruce Myhaver's pickup. Magnusson continued south not realizing she was involved. A police officer who saw the accident stopped her a short distance away and asked her to return to the scene.

Myhaver was seriously injured as a result of the collision and brought a damage action against both Knutson and Magnusson. Magnusson settled and was named as a non-party at fault, and the Myhavers proceeded to trial against Knutson.

At trial, [the] judge instructed the jury as follows:

> In determining whether a person acted with reasonable care under the circumstances, you may consider whether such conduct was affected by an emergency. An "emergency" is defined as a sudden and unexpected encounter with a danger which is either real or reasonably seems to be real. If a person, without negligence on his or her part, encountered such an emergency and acted reasonably to avoid harm to self or others, you may find that the person was not negligent. This is so even though, in hindsight, you find that under normal conditions some other or better course of conduct could and should have been followed.

The jury found Knutson not liable. On appeal, the Myhavers argued that the sudden emergency doctrine [embodied in the above instruction] should be abandoned. Alternatively, they urged that the trial judge erred in giving the instruction under the facts of the case and that it constituted an impermissible comment on the evidence....

We granted review to consider the propriety of giving the instruction in this or any case.

[The] sudden emergency instruction tells the jury that in the absence of antecedent negligence, a person confronted with a sudden emergency that deprives him of time to contemplate the best reaction cannot be held to the same standard of care and accuracy of choice as one who has time to deliberate. Criticism of this doctrine has focused on its ability to confuse a jury as to whether the reasonable person standard of care or some lower standard, applies in an emergency.... [A] few jurisdictions have abolished sudden emergency instructions, either generally or just in automobile accident cases, while others have discouraged their use, sometimes placing specific restrictions on which cases are appropriate for their use. However, several jurisdictions still explicitly retain the sudden emergency doctrine, either generally or with the qualification that sudden emergency instructions are allowed but not required.

Commentators on Arizona's negligence law have described the problem and the present state of our law as follows:

> Conceptually, the emergency doctrine is not an independent rule. It is merely an application of the general standard of reasonable care; the emergency is simply one of the circumstances faced. Arguably, giving a separate instruction on sudden emergency focuses the jury's attention unduly on that aspect of a case.

Jefferson L. Lankford & Douglas A. Blaze, The Law of Negligence in Arizona §3.5(1), at 43 (1992).

Although criticizing the instruction and holding that it need not be given, other states leave it to the judge's discretion. Massachusetts has held that a judge may instruct the jury that emergency conditions "are a factor in determining" whether a party acted with reasonable care. A number of states have carefully analyzed the issue and concluded that the instruction should not be routinely given in every claim of emergency. By definition, most accidents involve an emergency. These courts have concluded that the instruction should be discouraged because of the factors already mentioned, though it may be given, in the judge's discretion, in the few cases presenting true, unanticipated emergencies.

One of the more careful analyses of the subject was made in *McKee v. Evans*, 551 A.2d 260 (Pa. Super. 1988). The Pennsylvania court found that the instruction had been improperly given in favor of a driver involved in a ten-mile pursuit. The court concluded that the instruction was not favored and should be given only in those cases in which evidence showed that (1) the party seeking the instruction had not been negligent prior to the emergency, (2) the emergency had come about suddenly and without warning, and (3) reaction to the emergency was spontaneous, without time for reflection. While these factors are certainly not all inclusive, we believe they help describe the situations to which the instruction should be confined.

Having noted that the instruction is but a factor to be considered in determining reasonable care, is subsumed within the general concept of negligence, is a matter of argument rather than a principle of law and can single out and unduly emphasize one factor and thus mislead a jury, we join those courts that have discouraged use of the instruction and urge our trial judges to give it only in the rare case. The instruction should be confined to the case in which the emergency is not of the routine sort produced by the impending accident but arises from events the driver could not be expected to anticipate.

We do not, however, join those courts that absolutely forbid use of the instruction. There are cases in which the instruction may be useful or may help to explain the need to consider a sudden emergency and the consequent reflexive actions of a party when determining reasonable care. We believe, however, that in those few cases in which the instruction is given, it would be important to explain that the existence of a sudden emergency and reaction to it are only some of the factors to be considered in determining what is reasonable conduct under the circumstances. Even though a judge may exercise his discretion and give a sudden emergency instruction in a particular case, it will rarely, if ever, be error to refuse to give it.

Applying these principles to the case at bench, we conclude that the trial judge did not abuse his discretion in giving the instruction. This is a case in which there was no evidence of antecedent negligence by Knutson, in whose favor the instruction was given. In light of the testimony of the various witnesses, there was no question about the existence of an emergency. Knutson was faced with a situation not ordinarily to be anticipated and one of imminent peril when Magnusson pulled out of the shopping center and suddenly turned toward him in the wrong lane of traffic. Finally, Knutson's reaction — swerving across the center line into the path of Myhaver's oncoming vehicle — was probably both reflexive in nature and the type of conduct that absent a sudden emergency would almost automatically be found as negligence, if not negligence per se. Given these facts, the real and only issue was whether Knutson's conduct was reasonable under the circumstances of the emergency. We believe, therefore, the trial judge had discretion to instruct on the sudden emergency as a factor in the determination of negligence.

NOTES AND PROBLEMS

1. ***Sudden Emergencies.*** As the above case illustrates, the sudden emergency instruction may be permitted, but is not viewed as indispensible. Other courts believe it should never be given because it is simply unnecessary. At best then, the instruction might be viewed as a luxury option for the actor whose conduct under an emergency is being analyzed under the traditional reasonable person analysis. The good advocate should be armed with plenty of persuasive arguments for a finding of reasonableness, depending on the actual circumstances. When the actor is facing a possible significant injury to himself, and his ability to perceive the potential danger of his conduct is lessened, the actor's conduct is then an understandable attempt to save his own life. If another car is about to hit you head on, you may not have the luxury of time to look around you to plot out your best options. Rather, fueled by a legitimate desire to avoid your own death, you reflexively swerve in one direction or another without a chance to look where you are turning. Without the emergency, such behavior would be obviously careless, maybe even reckless. But the sudden emergency circumstance, which is already permitted to be considered as part of the "under the circumstances" description of reasonable care, changes our expectations for reasonableness.

2. ***Problem.*** After pulling out of the shopping center and into the wrong lane, Magnusson suddenly finds herself facing traffic coming directly at her.

Reflexively, she swerves to the left and hits a child selling lemonade at a sidewalk stand. In the negligence suit against her, she seeks to invoke the sudden emergency instruction. Should she be entitled to it?

Upon Further Review

The foregoing materials portray a mixed bag in terms of how tort law treats various circumstances. With respect to the mental state of the actor, the reasonable person takes on the trait only of above average intelligence and experience while rejecting consideration of mental disability or below average mental acuity. Physical disabilities are considered on the other hand. Further, while the same standard applies equally (permitting consideration of both grave danger and a sudden emergency), courts will only consider a modified instruction with respect to the latter. The standard seems to change most fundamentally in the case of children, but only when the child is engaged in an activity to which society deems it appropriate for such a child to engage. These various rules seem chaotic at first blush, but there are sound rationales behind each of them. Whether the lawyer agrees or disagrees with such distinctions, competent representation nevertheless demands recognition and awareness of how such circumstances are factored into the analysis of reasonable care.

PROVING BREACH OF DUTY

In a sense, by looking at case law discussing the meaning of the duty of reasonable care, we have already seen discussions of whether particular actors, in the factual contexts of those cases, had *breached* the applicable duty. The courts, and juries, were simply applying the reasonable person standard and theorizing how the hypothetical reasonable person would have acted. By then comparing that theoretical conduct with the actual conduct of the defendant (or plaintiff, where contributory negligence has been alleged), the fact finder can determine if the actor lived up to that reasonable person standard. But analysis of breach can be more sophisticated than what we have seen thus far. First, we will consider the famous *Learned Hand Formula*, which offers a mathematical formula for analyzing the care that a reasonable person would undertake to prevent an accident. Most negligence cases are analyzed, either explicitly or often implicitly, by reference to this formula. This formula allows for an express consideration of the most important factors in analyzing reasonable care, so that the process becomes somewhat less vaguely intuitive. But there are other potential tools, often considered short cuts, available for analyzing a possible breach of the duty of reasonable care. We will consider the impact of an actor's violation of a statutory duty as evidence of breach of the duty of care. We will also see what role evidence of an actor's compliance with, or violation of, applicable industry customs will play in the breach determination. Finally, in certain instances where we lack information about the defendant's actual conduct, but circumstances strongly suggest a negligent act, the doctrine of *res ipsa loquitur* will be available to assist an otherwise out-of-luck plaintiff.

A. The Learned Hand Formula

McCARTY v. PHEASANT RUN, INC.

826 F.2d 1554 (7th Cir. 1987)

Posner, J.

The high crime rate in the United States has interacted with expanding notions of tort liability to make suits charging hotel owners with negligence in failing to protect their guests from criminal attacks increasingly common. Dula McCarty, a guest at the Pheasant Run Lodge in St. Charles, Illinois, was assaulted by an intruder in her room, and brought suit against the owner of the resort. The suit charges negligence, and bases federal jurisdiction on diversity of citizenship. The parties agree that Illinois law governs the substantive issues. The jury brought in a verdict for the defendant, and Mrs. McCarty appeals on a variety of grounds.

In 1981 Mrs. McCarty, then 58 years old and a merchandise manager for Sears Roebuck, checked into Pheasant Run — a large resort hotel on 160 acres outside Chicago — to attend a Sears business meeting. In one wall of her second-floor room was a sliding glass door equipped with a lock and a safety chain. The door opens onto a walkway that has stairs leading to a lighted courtyard to which there is public access. The drapes were drawn and the door covered by them. Mrs. McCarty left the room for dinner and a meeting. When she returned, she undressed and got ready for bed. As she was coming out of the bathroom, she was attacked by a man with a stocking mask. He beat and threatened to rape her. She fought him off, and he fled. He has never been caught. Although Mrs. McCarty's physical injuries were not serious, she claims that the incident caused prolonged emotional distress which, among other things, led her to take early retirement from Sears.

Investigation of the incident by the police revealed that the sliding glass door had been closed but not locked, that it had been pried open from the outside, and that the security chain had been broken. The intruder must have entered Mrs. McCarty's room by opening the door to the extent permitted by the chain, breaking the chain, and sliding the door open the rest of the way. Then he concealed himself somewhere in the room until she returned and entered the bathroom.

Mrs. McCarty argues that the judge should have granted her motion for judgment notwithstanding the jury's verdict for the defendant.

[As one] ground for denying the motion for judgment n.o.v., the district judge correctly pointed out that the case was not so one-sided in the plaintiff's favor that the grant of a directed verdict or judgment n.o.v. in her favor would be proper. Her theories of negligence are that the defendant should have made sure the door was locked when she was first shown to her room; should have warned her to keep the sliding glass door locked; should have equipped the door with a better lock; should have had more security guards (only two were on duty, and the hotel has more than 500 rooms); should have made the walkway on which the door opened inaccessible from ground level; should have adopted better procedures for preventing unauthorized persons from getting hold of keys to guests' rooms; or should have done some combination of these things. The suggestion that the defendant should have had better procedures for keeping keys away from unauthorized persons is irrelevant, for it is extremely unlikely that the intruder entered the room through the front door. The other theories were for the jury to accept or reject, and its rejection of them was not unreasonable.

There are various ways in which courts formulate the negligence standard. The analytically (not necessarily the operationally) most precise is that it involves determining whether the burden of precaution is less than the magnitude of the accident, if it occurs, multiplied by the probability of occurrence. (The product of this multiplication, or "discounting," is what economists call an expected accident cost.) If the burden is less, the precaution should be taken. This is the famous "Hand Formula" announced in *United States v. Carroll Towing Co.*, 159 F.2d 169, 173 (2d Cir. 1947) (L. Hand, J.), an admiralty case, and since applied in a variety of cases not limited to admiralty.

We are not authorized to change the common law of Illinois, however, and Illinois courts do not cite the Hand Formula but instead define negligence as failure to use reasonable care, a term left undefined. But as this is a distinction without a substantive difference, we have not hesitated to use the Hand Formula in cases governed by Illinois law. The formula translates into economic terms the conventional legal test for negligence. This can be seen by considering the factors that the Illinois courts take into account in negligence cases: the same factors, and in the same relation, as in the Hand Formula. Unreasonable conduct is merely the failure to take precautions that

Principles

Third Restatement Description of *Learned Hand Formula:*

> A person acts negligently if the person does not exercise reasonable care under all the circumstances. Primary factors to consider in ascertaining whether the person's conduct lacks reasonable care are the foreseeable likelihood that the person's conduct will result in harm, the foreseeable severity of any harm that may ensue, and the burden of precautions to eliminate or reduce the risk of harm.
>
> *Restatement (Third) of Torts §3 (2011).*

would generate greater benefits in avoiding accidents than the precautions would cost.

Ordinarily, and here, the parties do not give the jury the information required to quantify the variables that the Hand Formula picks out as relevant. That is why the formula has greater analytic than operational significance. Conceptual as well as practical difficulties in monetizing personal injuries may continue to frustrate efforts to measure expected accident costs with the precision that is possible, in principle at least, in measuring the other side of the equation — the cost or burden of precaution. For many years to come juries may be forced to make rough judgments of reasonableness, intuiting rather than measuring the factors in the Hand Formula; and so long as their judgment is reasonable, the trial judge has no right to set it aside, let alone substitute his own judgment.

Having failed to make much effort to show that the mishap could have been prevented by precautions of reasonable cost and efficacy, Mrs. McCarty is in a weak position to complain about the jury verdict. No effort was made to inform the jury what it would have cost to equip every room in the Pheasant Run Lodge with a new lock, and whether the lock would have been jimmy-proof. And since the door to Mrs. McCarty's room was unlocked, what good would a better lock have done? No effort was made, either, to specify an optimal security force for a resort the size of Pheasant Run. No one considered the fire or other hazards that a second-floor walkway not accessible from ground level would create. A notice in every room telling guests to lock all doors would be cheap, but since most people know better than to leave the door to a hotel room unlocked when they leave the room — and the sliding glass door gave on a walkway, not a balcony — the jury might have thought that the incremental benefits from the notice would be slight. Mrs. McCarty testified that she didn't know there was a door behind the closed drapes, but the jury wasn't required to believe this. Most people on checking into a hotel room, especially at a resort, are curious about the view; and it was still light when Mrs. McCarty checked in at 6:00 p.m. on an October evening.

AFFIRMED.

NOTES AND PROBLEMS

1. ***Learned Hand Formula.*** The formula discussed by Judge Posner, famous himself as a pioneer in the scholarship regarding "law and economics," was fashioned originally by Judge Learned Hand, a famous Second Circuit federal appellate judge. Judge Hand — once nicknamed the "Tenth man on the Supreme Court" — described his own algebraic formula as a function of three variables (in a case involving a barge breaking free and causing physical damage to other property):

> (1) the probability that she will break away; (2) the gravity of the resulting injury, if she does; (3) the burden of adequate precautions. Possibly it serves to bring this notion into relief to describe it in algebraic terms: if the probability be called P; the

> injury, L; and the burden, B; liability depends upon whether B is less than L multiplied by P; i.e., whether $B < P \times L$.

United States v. Carroll Towing, 159 F.2d 169, 173 (2d Cir. 1947) (L. Hand, J.). What does this formula suggest about the concern the reasonable person has for the welfare of others, that such person would be willing to incur a cost for the benefit of others? Does this reflect how our society actually functions or is it aspirational?

Judge B. Learned Hand

2. ***Flexible Standard.*** We have just finished looking at what "reasonable care is under the circumstances" in the context of such variables as *sudden emergencies* and *highly dangerous activities.* Now armed with the Learned Hand formula, go back and consider how you might quantify the logic behind those two doctrines algebraically.

3. ***Analytically but Not Operationally Significant.*** For various reasons, Judge Posner mentions that the formula is more useful as an analytical tool than in actual operation. Why is this the case? In what ways might the formula be useful analytically? First, when an appellate court (or trial judge) is reviewing a jury's decision on the issue of breach, this formula permits an enlightened review of the evidence to see if the decision appears to have a rational basis in the facts. Further, when a trial judge is listening to objections as to the relevancy of proposed evidence offered at trial, this formula permits analysis as to whether the evidence tends to make a material fact true or not. In other words, as to the issue of breach of duty, any evidence offered must relate to either the Burden,

Probability of an accident, or the size of the Loss, in order to be admitted. It also makes sense for lawyers to at least allude to these factors in making closing arguments before a jury on the issue of breach. On the other hand, the court does not instruct the jury on this algebraic equation and the verdict form is not a math quiz.

4. *Law and Economics.* While the Learned Hand formula has proven to have enduring value, and doubtlessly refines the analysis of breach of duty in a negligence case, it nevertheless has to be "taken with a grain of salt." This is true primarily because a mathematical formula cannot capture all of a society's contemporary values effectively. For example, under the Learned Hand formula, which circumstance would call for heightened care? Scenario A, where a homeless man's life might be put in jeopardy by the defendant's conduct? Or Scenario B, where a wealthy corporate executive's life would be placed in jeopardy? A purely cold-blooded mathematical calculation would suggest that Scenario B requires greater care, as the injury to a high-income earner would yield greater damages than the injury to a homeless person. A lawyer trying to advance such a comparative argument to a jury would be a lawyer with an unhappy client. Despite such real world limits, the field of inquiry plowed by the discipline of law and economics is rich. A good example of the debate over the utility of law and economics can be found in Christine Jolls, Cass Sunstein & Richard Thaler, *A Behavioral Approach to Law and Economics*, 50 Stanford L. Rev. 1471 (1998).

> "Economics is the painful elaboration of the obvious."
>
> *Anonymous*

5. *Burden/Utility.* The left side of the Learned Hand formula asks, with respect to the plaintiff's theory of how a reasonable person would have acted, what the costs of this alternative conduct would have entailed. The other side of the same coin might involve placing a value to the defendant on the defendant's actual chosen activity. The Restatement frames this other perspective in terms of the *Utility* of the defendant's conduct:

> Where an act is one which a reasonable man would recognize as involving a risk of harm to another, the risk is unreasonable and the act is negligent if the risk is of such magnitude as to outweigh what the law regards as the utility of the act or of the particular manner in which it is done.

Restatement (Second) of Torts §291. (1965)

6. *Problems.* Judge Posner indicated that the Learned Hand formula was more "analytically (not necessarily . . . operationally)" useful. With that in mind, address the questions below in light of this scenario: Plaintiff was injured when, as a pedestrian crossing a rural highway early one morning to obtain his mail from the box, he was hit by a car coming around a bend in the road, driven by the defendant. The car was not exceeding the speed limit of 45 mph, but the visibility around the curve was limited.

A. If you are the lawyer for the plaintiff, and you have the chance to take the deposition of the defendant driver, what lines of inquiry might you want to pursue in light of the components to the Learned Hand formula?

B. Would inquiries into whether the defendant had paid his taxes in the past yield any information relevant to this Learned Hand formula? If not, the trial court would likely rule such evidence as irrelevant and exclude it from being offered into evidence before a jury. In this way, the Learned Hand formula offers parameters on the scope of discoverable information and on the admissibility of evidence at trial.

B. Negligence Per Se — Violation of Statutes

Sometimes the challenged conduct of the actor in question may appear to violate a statute, government regulation, or municipal ordinance. This may strike the claimant's counsel as a wonderful observation. But what role, if any, should this circumstance play in the analysis of whether the defendant breached a legal duty of care? Is this circumstance even relevant to determining breach? And, if relevant, how much weight should be attached to the fact that the challenged conduct was prohibited by an act of either the legislative or executive branches of government? *Martin v. Herzog* is the classic case involving an actor whose challenged conduct violated a statute. The trial court was apparently confused as to the significance of this circumstance, as you will see from the vague jury instructions, thereby requiring Judge Cardozo to demonstrate and apply the doctrine of *Negligence Per Se.* Pay special attention to the prerequisites for this doctrine and its impact on the issue of demonstrating breach of duty.

1. Origins and Rationale

MARTIN v. HERZOG

126 N.E. 814 (N.Y. 1920)

CARDOZO, J.

The action is one to recover damages for injuries resulting in death.

Plaintiff and her husband, while driving toward Tarrytown in a buggy on the night of August 21, 1915, were struck by the defendant's automobile coming in the opposite direction. They were thrown to the ground, and the man was killed. At the point of the collision the highway makes a curve. The car was rounding the curve when suddenly it came upon the buggy, emerging, the defendant tells us, from the gloom. Negligence is charged against the defendant, the driver of the car, in that he did not keep to the right of the center of the highway (*Highway Law*, sec. 286, *subd. 3*; sec. 332; Consol. Laws, ch. 25). Negligence is charged against the plaintiff's intestate, the driver of the wagon, in that he was traveling without lights (*Highway Law*, sec. 329a, as amended by L. 1915, ch. 367). There is no evidence that the defendant was moving at an excessive speed. There is none of any defect in the equipment of his car. The beam of light from his lamps pointed to the right as the wheels of his car turned along the curve toward the left; and looking in the direction of the plaintiff's approach, he was peering into the shadow. The case against him must stand, therefore, if at all, upon the divergence of his course from the center of the highway. The jury found him delinquent and his victim blameless. The Appellate Division reversed, and ordered a new trial.

We agree with the Appellate Division that the charge to the jury was erroneous and misleading. The case was tried on the assumption that the hour had arrived when lights were due. It was argued on the same assumption in this court. In such circumstances, it is not important whether the hour might have been made a question for the jury (*Todd v. Nelson*, 109 N.Y. 316, 325). A controversy put out of the case by the parties is not to be put into it by us. We say this by way of preface to our review of the contested rulings. In the body of the charge the trial judge said that the jury could consider the absence of light "in determining whether the plaintiff's intestate was guilty of contributory negligence in failing to have a light upon the buggy as provided by law. I do not mean to say that the absence of light necessarily makes him negligent, but it is a fact for your consideration." The defendant requested a ruling that the absence of a light on the plaintiff's vehicle was "*prima facie* evidence of contributory negligence." This request was refused, and the jury were again instructed that they might consider the absence of lights as some evidence of negligence, but that it was not conclusive evidence. The plaintiff then requested a charge that "the fact that the plaintiff's intestate was driving without a light is not negligence in itself," and to this the court acceded. The defendant saved his rights by appropriate exceptions.

We think the unexcused omission of the statutory signals is more than some evidence of negligence. It *is* negligence in itself. Lights are intended for the guidance and protection of other travelers on the highway (*Highway Law*, sec. 329a). By the very terms of the hypothesis, to omit, willfully or heedlessly, the safeguards prescribed by law for the benefit of another that he may be preserved in life or limb, is to fall short of the standard of diligence to which those who live in organized society are under a duty to conform. That, we think, is now the established rule in this state. Whether the omission of an absolute duty, not willfully or heedlessly, but through unavoidable accident, is also to be characterized as negligence, is a question of nomenclature into which we need not enter, for it does not touch the case before us. There may be times, when if jural niceties are to be preserved, the two wrongs, negligence and breach of statutory duty, must be kept distinct in speech and thought. In the conditions here present they come together and coalesce. A rule less rigid has been applied where the one who complains of the omission is not a member of the class for whose protection the safeguard is designed. Courts have been reluctant to hold that the police regulations of boards and councils and other subordinate officials create rights of action beyond the specific penalties imposed. This has led them to say that the violation of a statute is negligence, and the violation of a like ordinance is only evidence of negligence. An ordinance, however, like a statute, is a law within its sphere of operation, and so the distinction has not escaped criticism. Whether it has become too deeply rooted to be abandoned, even if it be thought illogical, is a question not now before us. What concerns us at this time is that even in the ordinance cases, the omission of a safeguard prescribed by statute is put upon a different plane, and is held not merely some evidence of negligence, but negligence in itself. In the case at hand, we have an instance of the admitted violation of a statute intended for the protection of travelers on the highway, of whom the defendant at the time was one. Yet the jurors were instructed in effect that they were at liberty in their discretion to treat the omission of lights either as innocent or as culpable. They were allowed to "consider the default as lightly or gravely" as they would (Thomas, J., in the court below). They might as well have been told that they could use a like discretion in holding a master at fault for the omission of a safety appliance prescribed by positive law for the protection of a workman. Jurors have no dispensing power by which they may relax the duty that one traveler on the highway owes under the statute to another. It is error to tell them that they have. The omission of these lights was a wrong, and being wholly unexcused was also a negligent wrong. No license should have been conceded to the triers of the facts to find it anything else.

We must be on our guard, however, against confusing the question of negligence with that of the causal connection between the negligence and the injury. A defendant who travels without lights is not to pay damages for his fault unless the absence of lights is the cause of the disaster. A plaintiff who travels without them is not to forfeit the right to damages unless the absence of lights is at least a contributing cause of the disaster. To say that conduct is negligence is not to say that it is always contributory negligence. "Proof of negligence in the air, so to speak, will not do" (Pollock Torts [10th ed.], p. 472). We think, however, that evidence of a collision occurring more than an hour after sundown between a car and an unseen buggy, proceeding without lights, is evidence from which a causal connection may be inferred between the collision and the lack of signals. If nothing else is shown to break the connection, we have a case, *prima facie* sufficient, of negligence contributing to the result.

We are persuaded that the tendency of the charge and of all the rulings following it, was to minimize unduly, in the minds of the triers of the facts, the gravity of the decedent's fault. Errors may not be ignored as unsubstantial when they tend to such an outcome. A statute designed for the protection of human life is not to be brushed aside as a form of words, its commands reduced to the level of cautions, and the duty to obey attenuated into an option to conform.

The order of the Appellate Division should be affirmed....

NOTES AND PROBLEMS

1. *The Reasonable Person and Statutory Violations.* The legal effect of a statutory violation in a negligence case, which Judge Cardozo described as "negligence in itself," is now referred to by courts by the name *Negligence Per Se*. It is so well established now that one might assume it was natural law. But why should the fact that the challenged conduct violated a statute necessarily lead to the inevitable conclusion that the defendant was negligent? What does this say about the attitude of the reasonable person with respect to compliance with mandatory obligations created by legislative or regulatory enactment? Also, consider whether this doctrine is necessitated by the separation of powers concept forming the foundation for our American system of government. If the trial court's charge to the jury in *Martin* had been considered appropriate, what would the judicial branch be saying about its power to disregard decisions by the legislative branch?

2. *Specificity.* In *Martin*, there was no doubt about the fact that the plaintiff had violated a statute requiring specific conduct — lights on buggies being driven at night. Not all statutes are so specific. Sometimes a statute, such as a traffic code, might demand that a driver "exercise care to yield the right of way to oncoming traffic." To the extent that a statutory obligation merely adopts the reasonable person standard, it adds nothing to the breach analysis and the doctrine of negligence per se is inapplicable.

3. *Effect of Negligence Per Se.* Which element of the negligence cause of action does negligence per se help to prove? Judge Cardozo clarified that the "unexcused violation" of the statute constituted proof of negligence — breach of duty. Yet for negligence to be something other than "negligence in the air," it must be proven to be a legal cause of the harm as well. Negligence per se clarifies the duty analysis by giving a very definite expectation for the conduct required, and the statute's violation then establishes the breach element. But negligence per se does not establish causation. This is why, near the end of his opinion, Cardozo cautioned that the jury would still need to determine causation upon remand. Legal causation is taken up in Chapter 5 of this book.

4. *Differing Roles of Law and Fact.* Negligence per se requires proof of a statutory violation. If the alleged violation is disputed the jury might be called upon to resolve that factual dispute by determining whether the actor did, in fact, violate the statute. Once the statutory violation is proven, however, there is no more work for the jury to perform in finding that a breach of duty has occurred, unless the defendant claims that the violation was excused. Often courts will instruct the jury along the lines, "if you find that defendant's conduct was a violation of [the Code], you are instructed that the defendant was negligent as a matter of law." The jury may still have to resolve fact disputes concerning the other elements (i.e., causation and damages) but the doctrine of negligence per se focuses the jury's attention, and traditionally does not permit the jury to disregard the legislature's decision with respect to what the legislature deems to be reasonable care under the circumstances present in the statutory violation.

5. ***Statutes, Ordinances, Regulations, and Codes.*** Judge Cardozo indicated that there had been, at one time, doubts about whether a party's violation of a municipal ordinance should be afforded the same effect as a statutory violation. Courts now routinely and equally (though not universally) apply negligence per se to violations of statutes, ordinances, codes, and administrative regulations.

2. Type of Harm and Membership in Protected Class

In *Martin*, Judge Cardozo noted that the statutory requirement for a light on a buggy at night was "intended for the protection of travelers on the highway. . . ." Cardozo recognized that if the purpose of the statute was unrelated to the harm suffered by the plaintiff, there was no rational reason to defer to the legislature's decision as to the prescribed course of conduct. It is only when the legislature is seeking to prevent the type of harm suffered in the tort case that we can trust its assessment as to reasonable care. Consider the following case, where the admitted violation of a statute was found not to trigger negligence per se because the harm sought to be prevented was unrelated to the harm at issue.

WAWANESA MUTUAL INS. v. MATLOCK

60 Cal. App. 4th 583 (1997)

SILLS, J.

Timothy Matlock, age seventeen, bought two packs of cigarettes from a gas station one day in April 1993. Tim gave one of the packs to his friend, Eric Erdley, age fifteen. Smoking as they walked, the two trespassed onto a private storage facility in Huntington Beach, where a couple of hundred telephone poles were stacked up high upon the ground, held in place by two vertical poles sticking out of the ground. The two had climbed on the logs many times before.

Timothy and Eric were joined by 2 younger boys, about 10 or 11 years old, who walked with them on the logs. Eric was smoking a cigarette held in his left hand. Timothy began to tease the younger boys, telling them the logs were going to fall. The boys started to run, though perhaps more out of laughter than of fear. One of the younger boys ran right into Eric's left arm. Eric dropped his cigarette down between the logs, where it landed on a bed of sand. For about 20 seconds Eric tried to retrieve the cigarette, but he couldn't reach it. He stood up and tried to extinguish it by spitting on it, and again was unsuccessful.

Then Eric caught up with Timothy, who was about 10 feet ahead. They went into some bunkers about 50 feet away; when they came out again after about 20 minutes, they saw flames at the base of the logs. They were seen running from the location.

The Woodman Pole Company suffered considerable property damage because of the fire. [Eric's insurance company, Wawanesa, paid $100,000 to settle the tort claims on behalf of Eric. It then filed this lawsuit against Timothy seeking partial reimbursement, or contribution, based upon Timothy's tortious misconduct being an additional cause of the fire and the property damage. For purposes of this lawsuit, Wawanesa is subrogated to the rights of Eric in seeking contribution against a fellow tortfeasor.]

After a bench trial, the court [found in favor of Wawanesa holding that Timothy was liable, in part, based upon the doctrine of negligence per se]. The judge stated that the statute that makes it unlawful to give cigarettes to minors, *Penal Code section 308*, had to have been enacted in 1891 with "more than health concerns" in mind, "since the health issues on tobacco are of considerably more recent concern."

Timothy and his father Paul now appeal, arguing that there is no basis on which to hold Timothy liable for the damage caused when Eric dropped the cigarette.

We agree. There is no valid basis on which to hold Timothy liable.

Just because a statute has been violated does not mean that the violator is necessarily liable for any damage that might be ultimately traced back to the violation. As the court stated in *Olsen v. McGillicuddy* (1971) 15 Cal. App. 3d 897, 902-903 "The doctrine of negligence per se does not apply even though a statute has been violated if the plaintiff was not in the class of persons designed to be protected or the type of harm which occurred was not one which the statute was designed to prevent." Mere "but-for" causation, as is urged in Wawanesa's brief, is simply not enough. The statute must be designed to protect against the *kind of harm* which occurred.

The statute that makes it illegal to furnish tobacco to minors, *Penal Code section 308*, has nothing to do with fire suppression. As it *now* stands, it is intended to prevent early *addiction* to tobacco. It may be true, as the trial court opined, that when the first version of the statute was enacted in 1891 it was not directed primarily at protecting minors' health.[1] But it is most certainly a health statute as it exists *today*. As our Supreme Court recently noted in *Mangini v. R.J. Reynolds Tobacco Co.* (1994) 7 Cal. 4th 1057, 1060, section 308 "'reflects a statutory policy of protecting minors from addiction to cigarettes.'" The connection of *section 308* with health is emphasized by the court's specifically analogizing *section 308* to former *Health and Safety Code section 25967*, which states that preventing children from "'beginning to use tobacco products'" "is" "'among the highest priorities in *disease* prevention for the State of California.'" (*Mangini, supra*, 7 Cal. 4th at pp. 1061-1062, italics added [quoting from appellate opinion quoting statute].)

Nothing suggests that *section 308* is part of any scheme to prevent fires. Its placement in the general morals section of the Penal Code belies such an intent.

NOTES AND PROBLEMS

1. ***Negligence Per Se Elements.*** To apply the doctrine of *negligence per se*, the plaintiff has the burden of proving that (1) defendant violated a statute that prohibited certain particular conduct, (2) that the statute was intended to protect against the harm for which recovery is sought, and (3) that the victim harmed by the violation was part of the class of persons for whom the statute was intended to provide protection. In *Wawanesa*, remembering that the basis for the relief sought was the fire damage incurred by the Woodman Pole Company, which of these required prerequisites for application of the doctrine were unsatisfied?

2. ***Negligence Per Se Is Not the Exclusive Way to Prove Breach.*** Most claims of negligence are proven by persuading the jury simply that the reasonable person under the circumstances would have acted differently and that this would have prevented the harm — in other words, by resorting to the

1. Which raises the question — why *was* it originally enacted? The trial judge may have been a little hasty in concluding that health was not the reason behind the 1891 statute. The noxiousness of tobacco was known long before 1891. Back in 1604 James I called it a custom "dangerous to the lungs" in his Counterblaste to Tobacco. By 1630 (give or take a few years), Sultan Murad IV tried to ban the use of tobacco. He failed. For their part, the Puritans of the Massachusetts Bay Colony tried to prohibit smoking about the same time as Murad. They failed as well. Assuming, for sake of argument, that the Legislature did not have minors' health at heart when it prohibited giving tobacco to them in 1891, the placement of *section 308* in chapter 7 of title 9 of the Penal Code, dealing with crimes against religion, conscience, and "good morals," furnishes another answer. While we do not have the legislative history from 1891, it appears the statute was most probably enacted to protect minors from the general licentiousness associated with the consumption of cigarettes in the 1890's. (These days — though we recognize that there is altogether too much teenage tobacco smoking — cigarettes tend to be associated more with the World War II generation than with cheesy dens of iniquity.) However, we have found nothing, and certainly Wawanesa has cited to us nothing, which would show that *section 308* was ever enacted out of some concern that minors with cigarettes would pose a fire hazard.

Learned Hand methodology of analysis. Even if negligence per se is unavailable, lawyers must remember that proving ordinary negligence through the Learned Hand formula is always available. In fact, in *Wawanesa*, the plaintiff also argued that the circumstances present, apart from the statutory violation, also demonstrated a lack of due care by Timothy. In another portion of the opinion, the appellate court acknowledged such a pathway was available to proving breach. Nevertheless, it held that legal causation (a topic we take up in the next chapter) was lacking because the fire was too unforeseeable a consequence of Timothy's lack of care:

> In the present case, the connection between Timothy's initial act of giving Eric the packet of cigarettes and the later fire is simply too attenuated to show the fire was *reasonably* within the scope of the risk created by the initial act.
>
> "But-for" Timothy Matlock's illegal act of procuring tobacco for minor Eric, and "but-for" Timothy's participation as a co-conspirator in an agreement to trespass [and] to smoke these cigarettes with Eric on Woodman land, and "but-for" Timothy's act of causing the younger children to rush off of the wood pile, Eric would not have been on top of the telephone poles smoking a cigarette at the time that he was bumped by the younger children and dropped the lit cigarette which started the fire.
>
> The sentence contains no fewer than three "but-for's." In the chain, the cigarette is far less important than the jostling. Yet fires are not within the risks one foreseeably incurs by teasing youngsters, even youngsters in the general vicinity of someone smoking a cigarette. 60 Cal. App. 4th at 588-89.

3. *Other Tort Theories.* The plaintiff in *Wawanesa* also tried to hold Timothy liable for the fire caused by his trespass. The court rejected this final theory, even though Timothy clearly was a trespasser, because the court reasoned that it was not his trespass that actually caused the fire, but rather the trespass of Eric. After we cover *actual causation* in Chapter 5, you might consider coming back to the facts of this case and seeing if you agree with the court's conclusion. Looking even further ahead to Chapter 9 (Apportionment), one might also accuse Timothy of conducting himself in *concert of action* with Eric. That theory would consider the conduct of either member acting in concert to be the same as the conduct of the other member.

4. *Rationale Behind Prerequisites.* Even though Timothy admittedly violated a statute, the court refused to use that as a basis for declaring him to have breached his duty of care. Given the rationale behind the doctrine of negligence per se, why is it that courts are not comfortable utilizing the negligence per se "short cut" to declare breach, when the purpose of the statute (or the victim) is different than the harm suffered in the case? If you assume that the legislature was, in effect, trying to do its own math (utilizing the Learned Hand factors) when it crafted the statute, do you understand why, when the harm suffered is different than the harm the legislature feared, there is less reason to defer to or trust the legislature's conclusion on what is "reasonable care under the circumstances"?

5. ***Caveat Regarding Licensing Statutes.*** A subtle but important limitation upon negligence per se's application arises when the defendant has engaged in a certain course of conduct without a required license to do so. Driving a car without a license is a common example. Does the fact that the defendant has driven without a license make her negligent per se, even if the *manner* of her driving was consistent with exercising reasonable care? Courts generally say no, even though the purpose of the license may be to ensure that only qualified, trained citizens drive. The reason has more to do with causation — courts tend to find that the violation of the statute is not what caused the accident. The accident has to be caused by the method of the driving in order to establish a negligence-based liability. Another example involves a "chiropractor" who was practicing without a license. His methods allegedly caused paralysis in the plaintiff and she sued for negligence. At trial plaintiff attempted to rely upon negligence per se. The appellate court rejected negligence per se:

> Proper formulation of general standards of preliminary education and proper examination of the particular applicant should serve to raise the standards of skill and care generally possessed by members of the [chiropractic] profession in this State; but the license to practice medicine confers no additional skill upon the practitioner; nor does it confer immunity from physical injury upon a patient if the practitioner fails to exercise care. Here, injury may have been caused by lack of skill or care; it would not have been obviated if the defendant had possessed a license yet failed to exercise the skill and care required of one practicing medicine.

Brown v. Shyne, 151 N.E. 197 (N.Y. 1926). Rather than attempting to rely upon the violation of a licensing statute to prove breach through negligence per se, a lawyer needs to find the violation of a statute that mandates (or proscribes) certain specific conduct that was the cause of the plaintiff's harm.

3. *Excuse*

In *Martin*, Judge Cardozo observed that the case involved the undisputed, "unexcused" violation of the underlying statute. If the alleged tortfeasor's conduct in violating the statute is "excused," how does this impact the application of the negligence per se doctrine? And what exactly constitutes excuse? Does ignorance of the law count as an excuse? Surely not, for all of us heard before coming to law school the maxim that "ignorance of the law is no excuse." The following case helps to answer these questions and delineate when conduct forbidden by another branch of government is *excused*, and thus the doctrine of negligence per se held inapplicable.

SIKORA v. WENZEL

727 N.E.2d 1277 (Ohio 2000)

Cook, J.

[In September 1996, a deck attached to a condominium owned by Tom Wenzel collapsed during a party held by one of Wenzel's tenants. Aaron Sikora, one of the guests at the party, was injured as a result of the collapse and brought the instant negligence action. After the incident, an engineering firm hired by the city of Fairborn (the "City") concluded that the deck's collapse resulted from improper construction and design in violation of the Ohio Basic Building Code (the "OBBC").

A decade earlier, before the deck was built, Zink Road Manor Investment ("Zink") owned and was developing the property where the condominium was located as a series of condominiums. After Zink submitted plans for the condominiums to the City, Zink decided to modify the units to include decks. Documents containing the deck design were given to the City for review at a meeting between the construction company and the City. The City, however, rejected these plans because they violated the OBBC and contained insufficient information. Although the City made no further inspection of the decks during construction nor received from Zink any modified plans or other documents sufficient for it to proceed with approval, the City nevertheless issued Zink a Certificate of Occupancy.

After the City issued the certificate, Wenzel purchased the property at issue from Zink. It is undisputed that Wenzel had no knowledge, either actual or constructive, as to any defect in the deck that was attached to the condominium. The parties also agree that Wenzel was in no way involved in the discussions concerning the deck between the City, the general contractor, or the subcontractors, and that he lacked any privity of contract with these entities.

Following the deck's collapse, Sikora sued Wenzel, the contractor, and the design company, alleging that each was negligent and therefore jointly and severally liable. Sikora based his claim against Wenzel in part upon a violation of *R.C. 5321.04(A)(1)*, which requires landlords to comply with all applicable provisions of the OBBC. The trial court granted summary judgment in Wenzel's favor on the basis that he lacked notice of the defect in the deck.]

With this decision we confirm that the doctrine of negligence *per se* countenances lack of notice of a defective condition as a legal excuse. We reverse the appellate court's determination that notice is irrelevant and strict liability applies, and instead hold that a violation of *R.C. 5321.04(A)(1)* (failing to comply with the Ohio Basic Building Code) constitutes negligence *per se*, but that such liability may be excused by a landlord's lack of actual or constructive notice of the defective condition.

Negligence *per se* and strict liability, however, are not synonymous. Courts view the evidentiary value of the violation of statutes imposed for public safety in three ways: as creating strict liability, as giving rise to negligence *per se*, or as simply evidence of negligence. *See, generally,* Browder, *The Taming of a Duty—The Tort Liability of Landlords* (1982), 81 Mich. L. Rev. 99. These are three separate principles with unique effects upon a plaintiff's burden of proof and to which the concept of notice may or may not be relevant.

Strict liability is also termed "liability without fault." Black's Law Dictionary (7 Ed.1999) 926. Thus, where a statute is interpreted as imposing strict liability, the defendant will be deemed liable *per se*—that is, no defenses or excuses, including lack of notice, are applicable. Areas where the law typically imposes strict liability include liability for injuries inflicted from a dangerous instrumentality, liability for violations of certain statutes, and liability for injuries caused by a manufacturer, distributor, or vendor of certain products. *Id.*

Courts generally agree that violation of a statute will not preclude defenses and excuses—*i.e.*, strict liability—unless the statute clearly contemplates such a result. Notably, most courts refuse to impose strict liability in the context of landlord liability for defective conditions, recognizing the need for some kind of notice element prior to the imposition of liability.

More frequently, then, this sort of statutory violation either will be considered as evidence of negligence or will support a finding of negligence *per se.* As this court has consistently held, the distinction between the two depends upon the degree of specificity with which the particular duty is stated in the statute.

Where a statute contains a general, abstract description of a duty, a plaintiff proving that a defendant violated the statute must nevertheless prove each of the elements of negligence in order to prevail. Thus, proof will be necessary that the defendant failed to act as a reasonably prudent person under like circumstances, to which the defendant's lack of notice of a defective condition may be a relevant consideration.

But where a statute sets forth "a positive and definite standard of care . . . whereby a jury may determine whether there has been a violation thereof by finding a single issue of fact," a violation of that statute constitutes negligence *per se.* In such instances, the statute "serves as a legislative declaration of the standard of care of a reasonably prudent person applicable in negligence actions." Thus the "reasonable person standard is supplanted by a standard of care established by the legislature."

Furthermore, negligence *per se* and strict liability differ in that a negligence *per se* statutory violation may be "excused." As set forth in the *Restatement of Torts 2d, supra, at 37, Section 288B(1)*: "The *unexcused* violation of a legislative enactment . . . which is adopted by the court as defining the standard of conduct of a reasonable man, is negligence in itself." (Emphasis added.) But "an *excused* violation of a legislative enactment . . . is not negligence." *Restatement of Torts 2d, supra, at 32, Section 288A(1).*

Lack of notice is among the legal excuses recognized by other jurisdictions and set forth in the Restatement of Torts 2d. This excuse applies where "the actor neither knows nor should know of any occasion or necessity for action in compliance with the legislation or regulation." *Restatement of Torts 2d, supra, at 35, Section 288A(2)(b), Comment f. See also, Gore v. People's Savings Bank, supra* (applying this excuse in the context of the violation of a statutory obligation upon a landlord).

It follows, then, that a determination of liability and the relevance of notice under a statute imposed for safety depends first upon which of the above categories the statute occupies. Wenzel urges us to construe the violation of *R.C. 5321.04(A)(1)* only as evidence of his negligence and therefore to consider his lack of notice as crucial to a determination of the breach of his duty of care. Sikora, in contrast, would have us uphold the appellate court's determination that strict liability applies and that Wenzel's lack of notice is irrelevant.

We reject Sikora's argument that the statute imposes strict liability. Considering the general reluctance among courts to impose strict liability in this context, the wording of the statute fails to convince us that the General Assembly intended to create strict liability upon a violation of this statutory requirement. Absent language denoting that liability exists without possibility of excuses, we are unpersuaded that the intent behind this statute was to eliminate excuses and impose strict liability.

Nor do we agree with Wenzel that the language of that statute is so general or abstract as to constitute merely evidence of negligence. Rather, we believe the statutory requirement is stated with sufficient specificity to impose negligence *per se*. It is "fixed and absolute, the same under all circumstances and is imposed upon" all landlords. *Ornella v. Robertson (1968)*, 237 N.E.2d 140, 143. Accordingly, we conclude that the statute requires landlords to conform to a particular standard of care, the violation of which constitutes negligence *per se*.

Having determined that the statute's violation constitutes negligence *per se*, we turn now to the question of whether Wenzel's lack of notice of the defect in the deck excuses the violation. Both parties agree that Wenzel neither knew nor had any way of knowing of the defective condition. The City issued the necessary approval documents despite having failed to reinspect the situation. Because Wenzel was not involved at that point, however, he had no reason to question the validity of the City's certification. Thus, no factual circumstances existed that would have prompted or required Wenzel to investigate the process that occurred between the City and the developer prior to his involvement. Given that Wenzel neither knew nor should have known of the condition giving rise to the violation of *R.C. 5321.04(A)(1)*, his violation is excused and he is not liable to Sikora for failing to comply with the OBBC.

For the foregoing reasons, the judgment of the court of appeals is reversed.

NOTES AND PROBLEMS

1. ***Strict Liability vs. Negligence Per Se.*** The court in *Sikora* had to decide whether the building code, which imposes liability on a landlord for code violations, imposes strict liability. If so, it is essentially a statutory cause of

action being pursued rather than a common law tort claim. In that instance, the statutory claim involves strict liability — liability without regard to any showing of traditional levels of any fault. But the court recognizes that strict liability is not presumed from statutes. Because the building code in question did not clearly articulate a desire to impose strict liability, the court interpreted the statute as instead creating a specific duty to act in a certain manner. The court found the defendant in violation of the statute but recognized that negligence per se countenances a defense of *excuse* by the defendant.

2. ***Ignorance of Fact vs. Law.*** The defendant in *Sikora* was claiming that he had no notice of any defect in the deck, nor did he have any reason to know that the condition of the deck was not in compliance with the building code. The defendant was not claiming ignorance of the building code, but ignorance of the facts that revealed a violation of the building code. Plaintiff's stipulation that the defendant neither knew nor had reason to know of the defective condition enabled the court to rather easily conclude that defendant's violation of the statute was excused.

3. ***Burden of Proof in Instances Where Violations Are Excused.*** Because *excuse* is considered a defense, where the plaintiff otherwise proves the elements of negligence per se, the defendant must plead and prove its excuse. Ultimately the issue with excuse becomes whether a "reasonable person under the circumstances" would have likewise been in violation of the statute. Cases involving emergencies or loss of control of a vehicle are classic cases of excuse. One good example of the articulation of how excuse interacts with negligence per se is illustrated by the California Evidence Code, as follows:

> (a) The failure of a person to exercise due care is presumed if
>
> (1) He violated a statute, ordinance, or regulation of a public entity;
>
> (2) The violation proximately caused death or injury to person or property;
>
> (3) The death or injury resulted from an occurrence of the nature which the statute, ordinance, or regulation was designed to prevent; and
>
> (4) The person suffering the death or injury to his person or property was one of the class of persons for whose protection the statute, ordinance, or regulation was adopted.
>
> (b) This presumption may be rebutted by proof that:
>
> (1) The person violating the statute, ordinance, or regulation did what might reasonably be expected of a person of ordinary prudence, acting under similar circumstances, who desired to comply with the law.

Cal. Evid. Code §669 (2002). This statement of the law in California is helpful in demonstrating the prevailing view of the negligence per se doctrine — that it creates a presumption (or prima facie case) of negligence that is capable of being overcome or rebutted by the defendant's proof that a reasonable person would have acted the same as the defendant under the particular circumstances. This highlights the delicate balance of tort law: It defers to the assessment by its sister branches of government of preferable conduct in a general context, while retaining the flexibility to allow a jury to still find the reasonable care standard met when particular circumstances demand conduct different from that generally considered careful.

4. ***Types of Excuses.*** Ultimately, a violation of a statute may be excused when the reasonable person would have similarly been in violation of the statute under the circumstances of the case. There might be many reasons why this would be true. The Second Restatement offers the following helpful enumeration of recognized types of excuses:

> (1) An excused violation of a legislative enactment or an administrative regulation is not negligence.
>
> (2) Unless such enactment or regulation is construed not to permit such excuse, its violation is excused when
>
> (a) the violation is reasonable because of the actor's incapacity;
>
> (b) he neither knows nor should know of the occasion for compliance;
>
> (c) he is unable after reasonable diligence or care to comply;
>
> (d) he is confronted by an emergency not due to his own misconduct;
>
> (e) compliance would involve a greater risk of harm to the actor or to others.

Restatement (Second) of Torts §288A. (1965).

5. ***Alternative View on Procedural Effect of Negligence Per Se.*** While the typical procedural treatment of negligence per se is illustrated by the above California evidence code provision — where the violation creates a rebuttable presumption of breach — there are a minority of courts that treat negligence per se as merely creating an *inference of negligence.* In such courts, the plaintiff's proof of the statutory violation permits the jury to find negligence but does not mandate it, regardless of whether the defendant offers any evidence of excuse. Such courts disagree with Judge Cardozo's admonition in *Herzog* that this treatment gives the jury too much "dispensing power by which the jury may relax the duty" created by the statute. The court in *Wenzel* outlines possible procedural effects from proof of a statutory violation, ranging from supplying mere evidence of breach, to a presumption of breach, and even a type of strict liability where no excuse is permissible. Another good recent judicial discussion of the various procedural views of the effect of a statutory violation is contained in Zeni v. Anderson, 243 N.W.2d 270 (Mich. 1976) (adopting the prevailing view that the proof of a statutory violation creates a rebuttable presumption that mandates a finding of breach in the absence of proof of excuse).

"LADIES AND GENTLEMEN OF THE JURY . . ."

Texas PJC 5.2 Negligence Per Se — Excuse

The law forbids [driving the wrong way on a street designated and signposted as one-way]. A failure to comply with this law is negligence in itself, unless excused. A failure to comply is excused if [the driver was incapacitated by a heart attack immediately before the accident].

C. Custom

Often, the challenged conduct of the defendant involves an area of activity that others acting in a certain industry may tacitly or expressly recognize as appropriate or inappropriate. When the defendant is part of a particular industry, what evidentiary value is proof that the defendant has failed to comply with certain industry standards or practices? Should this be treated as tantamount to a statutory violation? Is it even relevant? Or what if a defendant's conduct conforms to an industry standard or practice? Does this constitute a silver bullet defense to any accusations of failing to observe ordinary care? Other courts commonly cite the following case of *The T.J. Hooper* for resolution of these issues.

1. Industry Custom

THE T.J. HOOPER

60 F.2d 737 (2d Cir. 1932)

L. Hand, J.

The barges No. 17 and No. 30, belonging to the Northern Barge Company, had lifted cargoes of coal at Norfolk, Virginia, for New York in March, 1928. They were towed by two tugs of the petitioner, the "Montrose" and the "Hooper," and were lost off the Jersey Coast on March tenth, in an easterly gale. [The cargo owners sued the tugboat owners for negligence, claiming that their failure to carry radio receivers by which they could have received timely warnings of the weather change caused the property loss. The trial court found in favor of the plaintiffs and this appeal followed.

Prior to the incident the weather had been fair. The barges got into serious trouble about 70 miles north of Atlantic City as the wind turned into a gale, and the barges eventually leaked in the choppy seas and lost their contents as they sank.]

The [tugs] would have had the benefit of the evening [weather] report from Arlington had they had proper receiving sets. This predicted worse weather; it read: "Increasing east and southeast winds, becoming fresh to strong, Friday night and increasing cloudiness followed by rain Friday." The bare "increase" of the morning had become "fresh to strong." To be sure this scarcely foretold a gale of from forty to fifty miles for five hours or more, rising at one time to fifty-six; but if the four tows thought the first report enough, the second ought to have laid any doubts. The master of the "Montrose" himself, when asked what he would have done had he received a substantially similar report, said that he would certainly have put in. The master of the "Hooper" was also asked for his opinion, and said that he would have turned back also, but this admission is somewhat vitiated by the incorporation in the question of the statement that it was a "storm warning," which the witness seized upon in his answer. All this seems to us to support the conclusion of the judge that prudent masters, who had received the second warning, would have found the risk more than the exigency warranted; they would have been amply vindicated by what followed. To be sure the barges would, as we have said, probably have withstood the gale, had they been well found; but a master is not justified in putting his tow to every test which she will survive, if she be fit. There is a zone in which proper caution will avoid putting her capacity to the proof; a coefficient of prudence that he should not disregard. Taking the situation as a whole, it seems to us that these masters would have taken undue chances, had they got the broadcasts.

They did not, because their private radio receiving sets, which were on board, were not in working order. These belonged to them personally, and were partly a toy, partly a part of the equipment, but neither furnished by the owner, nor supervised by it. It is not fair to say that there was a general custom among coastwise carriers so as to equip their tugs. One line alone did it; as for the rest, they relied upon their crews, so far as they can be said to have relied at all. An adequate receiving set suitable for a coastwise tug can now be got at small cost and is reasonably reliable if kept up; obviously it is a source of great protection to their tows. Twice every day they can receive these predictions, based upon the widest possible in formation, available to every vessel within two or three hundred miles and more. Such a set is the ears of the tug to catch the spoken word, just as the master's binoculars are her eyes to see a storm signal ashore. Whatever may be said as to other vessels, tugs towing heavy coal laden barges, strung out for half a mile, have little power to maneuver, and do not, as this case proves, expose themselves to weather which would not turn back stauncher craft. They can have at hand protection against dangers of which they can learn in no other way.

Is it then a final answer that the business had not yet generally adopted receiving sets? There are yet, no doubt, cases where courts seem to make the general practice of the calling the standard of proper diligence; we have indeed given some currency to the notion ourselves. Indeed in most cases reasonable prudence is in fact common prudence; but strictly it is never its measure; a whole calling may have unduly lagged in the adoption of new and available devices. It may never set its own tests, however persuasive be its usages. Courts must in the end say what is required; there are precautions so imperative that even their universal disregard will not excuse their omission. But here there was no custom at all as to receiving sets; some had them, some did not; the most that can be urged is that they had not yet become general. Certainly in such a case we need not pause; when some have thought a device necessary, at least we may say that they were right, and the others too slack. The statute (*section 484, title 46, U.S. Code* [*46 USCA §484*]) does not bear on this situation at all. It prescribes not a receiving, but a transmitting set, and for a very different purpose; to call for help, not to get news. We hold the tugs therefore because had they been properly equipped, they would have got the Arlington reports. The injury was a direct consequence of this unseaworthiness.

Decree affirmed.

NOTES AND PROBLEMS

1. ***Statutes vs. Industry Customs.*** In the famous *The T.J. Hooper* case, the defendant hoped that the tugboat industry custom was its safe harbor, but the court sunk that argument. Judge Hand, in a bit of hyperbole, stated that "there was no custom at all" yet earlier in the opinion acknowledged that only one tugboat line kept an official working radio on board; all the rest failed to have such a policy. If the doctrine of *negligence per se* is premised upon deference to legislative (and executive branch agencies') determination as to what "reasonable care under the circumstances" might sometimes require, why does the court not afford similar weight to an industry's practices? Does the court say that industry custom might provide some evidence of what ordinary prudence is? If custom is not given controlling, standard-of-care weight, why should it be relevant how an industry normally operates? How might this evidence inform the application of the Learned Hand formula?

2. ***Swords and Shields.*** In cases where the defendant's conduct has fallen short of industry practices, the plaintiff would be using the evidence of industry practice as a sword to affirmatively establish a breach of the duty of reasonable care. On the other hand, where a defendant is pointing to its adherence to an industry practice, it is using the evidence defensively as a shield to attempt to protect itself from being found liable. According to the court in *The T.J. Hooper*, and the many cases that have cited it since it was handed down, the legal effect or evidentiary weight given to industry custom is the same regardless of whether it is used as a sword or shield. Practically, however, when might a jury tend to give the industry custom more weight in its determination of the issue of breach — when the defendant company has adhered to the custom (shield) or when the plaintiff shows the defendant company has failed to live up to the custom of others within its own industry (sword)?

3. ***Custom Within the Tug Industry.*** In *The T.J. Hooper*, who was attempting to point to industry custom and for what purpose? Did the court recognize such a custom? How much weight was afforded to such evidence? Finally, if the court

had to determine the issue of breach without controlling guidance from industry customs, what tools did the court employ to determine breach? Consider that the author of the opinion is our famous Learned Hand. Notice how he observed the relative inexpensiveness of a tug's owner maintaining an operational radio on board, and, in the absence of such advance warnings of inclement weather, how exposed the slow moving barges towed by a tug would be in a storm. Do you see how this demonstrates that with a relatively small expense, a tug's owner can reduce the foreseeable risk to barges caught in all too frequent storms at sea?

2. Personal Custom

There are many instances where the defendant has chosen to adopt certain personal customs or policies for itself. Many corporations have detailed policies and procedures manuals designed to impact the conduct of its officers and employees. Do these internal policies create an alternative standard of care? Surely a defendant may not opt out of its tort duty of reasonable care through the adoption of policies. But when the defendant fails to adhere to its own policies, does this provide a shortcut method for finding a breach of the duty of reasonable care? The following case contains an insightful discussion into the problems with allowing an actor's personal customs or policies to serve as a substitute for the duty of reasonable care.

WAL-MART STORES, INC. v. WRIGHT

774 N.E.2d 891 (Ind. 2002)

BOEHM, J.

Ruth Ann Wright sued for injuries she sustained when she slipped on a puddle of water at the "Outdoor Lawn and Garden Corral" of the Carmel Wal-Mart. Wright alleged Wal-Mart was negligent in the maintenance, care and inspection of the premises, and Wal-Mart asserted contributory negligence. By stipulation of the parties, a number of Wal-Mart's employee documents assembled as a "Store Manual" were admitted into evidence at the jury trial that followed. Several of these detailed procedures for dealing with spills and other floor hazards. [The store-mandated procedures included requiring employees to "react quickly" to spills, to "never leave a spill unattended," and to "cordon off" any area containing spills.] At the end of the trial, Wright tendered the following instruction:

> There was in effect at the time of the Plaintiff's injury a store manual and safety handbook prepared by the Defendant, Wal-Mart Stores, Inc., and issued to Wal-Mart Store, Inc. employees. You may consider the violation of any rules, policies,

> practices and procedures contained in these manuals and safety handbook along with all of the other evidence and the Court's instructions in deciding whether Wal-Mart was negligent.
>
> The violation of its rules, policies, practices and procedures are a proper item of evidence tending to show the degree of care recognized by Wal-Mart as ordinary care under the conditions specified in its rules, policies, practices and procedures.

Wal-Mart objected on the ground that "you can set standards for yourself that exceed ordinary care and the fact that you've done that shouldn't be used, as this second paragraph says, as evidence tending to show the degree that you believe is ordinary. The jury decides what ordinary care is." The court overruled the objection to Final Instruction 17. The court also instructed the jury that, inter alia, (1) the jury was to consider all the instructions as a whole, and should not "single out any certain sentence or any individual point or instruction and ignore the other" instructions; (2) Wal-Mart was required to maintain its property in a reasonably safe condition suitable for use by its customers; . . . [and (3)] negligence is the failure to do what a reasonably careful and prudent person would do under the same or similar circumstances or the doing of something that a reasonably careful and prudent person would not do under the same or similar circumstances. . . .

The jury found Wal-Mart liable and assessed Wright's total damages at $600,000, reduced to $420,000 by 30% comparative fault attributed to Wright. Wal-Mart appealed, contending that the second paragraph of Final Instruction 17 was an improper statement of law that incorrectly altered the standard of care from an objective one to a subjective one. The Court of Appeals affirmed, holding the challenged paragraph of the instruction was proper because it "did not require the jury to find that ordinary care, as recognized by Wal-Mart, was the standard to which Wal-Mart should be held," and because the trial court had not "instructed the jury that reasonable or ordinary care was anything other than that of a reasonably, careful and ordinarily prudent person." This Court granted transfer.

When an instruction is challenged as an incorrect statement of the law . . . appellate review of the ruling is de novo. Here, Wal-Mart argues that the second paragraph of Final Instruction 17 incorrectly stated the law because it invited jurors to apply Wal-Mart's subjective view of the standard of care as evidenced by the Manual, rather than an objective standard of ordinary care. Wright responds that the paragraph simply allows jurors to consider Wal-Mart's subjective view of ordinary care as some evidence of what was in fact ordinary care, and does not convert the objective standard to a subjective one.

Initially, we note that implicit in each of these positions, and explicit in the second paragraph of the instruction, is the assumption that the Manual in fact "tends to show the degree of care recognized by Wal-Mart as ordinary care under the conditions specified in [the Manual]." Wal-Mart also objected to this assumption, contending "you can set standards for yourself that exceed ordinary care and the fact that you've done that shouldn't be used, as this second paragraph says, as evidence tending to show the degree that you believe is ordinary." We agree. The second paragraph of the instruction told the jurors that because Wal-Mart has established certain rules and policies, those rules and policies are evidence of the degree of care recognized by Wal-Mart as ordinary care. But Wal-Mart is correct that its rules and policies may exceed its view of what is required by ordinary care in a given situation. Rules and policies in the Manual may have been established for any number of reasons having nothing to do with safety and ordinary care, including a desire to appear more clean and neat to attract customers, or a concern that spills may contaminate merchandise.

The law has long recognized that failure to follow a party's precautionary steps or procedures is not necessarily failure to exercise ordinary care. *57 Am. Jur. 2d Negligence §187* at 239 (1998) (failure to follow company rule does not constitute negligence per se; jury may consider rule, but rule does not set standard of conduct establishing what law requires of a reasonable person under the circumstances); *1 J.D. Lee and Barry A. Lindahl, Modern Tort Law §3.29* (1996) ("Company rules are generally admissible but not conclusive on the question of the standard of care."). We think this rule is salutary because it encourages following the best practices without necessarily establishing them as a legal norm.

There is a second problem with the instruction. Even if the Manual reflected Wal-Mart's subjective view of ordinary care, the second paragraph of the instruction incorrectly states the law because it invites jurors to apply Wal-Mart's subjective view — as evidenced by the Manual — rather than an objective standard of ordinary care. It is axiomatic that in a negligence action "the standard of conduct which the community demands must be an external and objective one, rather than the individual judgment, good or bad, of the particular actor." W. Page Keeton et al., *Prosser &Keeton on the Law of Torts* §32, at 173-74 & n.3 (5th ed. 1984). An individual "actor's belief that he is using reasonable care is immaterial." *Keeton, supra*, §32, at 174 n.3. This door swings both ways. A defendant's belief that it is acting reasonably is no defense if its conduct falls below reasonable care. Similarly, a defendant's belief that it should perform at a higher standard than objective reasonable care is equally irrelevant. As one court succinctly put it, "a party's own rules of conduct are relevant and can be received into evidence with an express caution that they are merely evidentiary and not to serve as a legal standard." *Mayo v. Publix Super Mkts, Inc.*, 686 So. 2d 801, 802 (Fla. Dist. Ct. App. 1997).

Wright cites four cases in support of the instruction: *Smith v. Cleveland C.C. & St. L. Ry. Co.*, 117 N.E. 534 (Ind. 1917); *N.Y. Cent. Ry. Co. v. Wyatt*, 184 N.E.2d 657 (Ind. 1962); *Cent. Ind. Ry. Co. v. Anderson Banking Co.*, 240 N.E.2d 840 (Ind. App. 1968); and *Frankfort v. Owens*, 358 N.E.2d 184 (Ind. App. 1976). These authorities support the admissibility of the Manual, which Wal-Mart does not contest. They do not support an instruction to consider any "violation" of the Manual as "evidence tending to show the degree of care recognized by Wal-Mart as ordinary care under the conditions." We conclude that the second paragraph of Final Instruction 17 was an improper invitation to deviate from the accepted objective standard of ordinary care and therefore incorrectly stated the law.

When a jury instruction incorrectly states the law, we assume that the erroneous instruction influenced the verdict and will reverse unless the verdict would have been the same under a proper instruction. This instruction suffered from two flaws. It equated Wal-Mart's procedures with reasonable care and it asserted that Wal-Mart's subjective view of reasonable care was relevant. No other instruction corrected these problems. Accordingly, read together these instructions introduced the concept of reasonable or ordinary care, directed the jurors to consider the Manual as evidence tending to show what Wal-Mart "recognized" that ordinary care to be, and thereby implied that a violation of the Manual was a violation of ordinary care.

The judgment of the trial court is reversed. This action is remanded for a new trial.

NOTES AND PROBLEMS

1. ***A Party's Own Customs/Habits/Policies.*** In the above case, Wal-Mart (a common defense litigant in tort cases) had a written policy and procedure manual that required its employees to behave in a particular way under the circumstances of a spill on the store floor. How was the plaintiff attempting to use this manual? What did the trial court's various instructions suggest to the jury about the weight to be given this evidence?

2. ***Standard of Care vs. Admissibility as Evidence.*** Wal-Mart never disputed the admissibility of the manual into evidence. It just took exception to the particular jury instruction that became the subject of the court's opinion on appeal. Why do courts routinely hold that evidence of a party's own customs/policies/habits is relevant to the determination of breach of the duty of ordinary care? How should such evidence (whether used as a sword or shield) be relevant to the factors reflected by the Learned Hand formula? In the *Wal-Mart* case, what might the existence of such a policy indicate, if the policy is not followed by the employees?

D. Res Ipsa Loquitur

The Learned Hand formula provides a very flexible tool for determining if an actor has met the duty of reasonable care in a broad variety of circumstances. Juries often use evidence of a defendant's compliance, or lack thereof, with industry custom in their determination of what reasonable care under the circumstances might actually require. And when the legislature has done the math in advance, we presume that a party's failure to adhere to a relevant statute is a breach of the duty.

In each of these instances, we have a pretty good idea what the defendant's specific challenged conduct involved. But is it even possible for a plaintiff to persuade a jury that a defendant has breached its duty in situations where the plaintiff lacks direct evidence of the defendant's conduct? The evidentiary doctrine of *res ipsa loquitur* — which means "the thing speaks for itself" — shows that plaintiffs, even in the absence of direct proof of a breach, might still prevail. The famous case of *Byrne v. Boadle* introduces this doctrine. After reviewing this case, we will consider a more modern application of its principles.

BYRNE v. BOADLE

159 Eng. Rep. 299 (Ex. 1863)

POLLOCK, C.B.

[Plaintiff was walking alongside defendant's building when he was hit on the head by a barrel that fell from the defendant shop's second floor window. Plaintiff failed to offer direct evidence at trial as to what defendant had done, or failed to do, that permitted the barrel to fall from his shop. The trial court dismissed the plaintiff's negligence claim due to this lack of direct evidence.]

We are of the opinion that the rule must be absolute to enter the verdict for the plaintiff. The learned counsel was quite right in saying that there are many accidents from which no presumption of negligence can arise, but I think it would be wrong to lay down as a rule that in no case can presumption of negligence arise from the fact of an accident. Suppose in this case the barrel had rolled out of the warehouse and fall on the plaintiff, how could he possibly ascertain from what cause it occurred? It is the duty of persons who keep barrels in a warehouse to take care that they do not roll out, and I think that such a case would, beyond all doubt, afford prima facie evidence of negligence. A barrel could not roll out of a warehouse without some negligence, and to say that a plaintiff who is injured by it must call witnesses from the warehouse to prove negligence seems to me preposterous. So in the building or repairing a house, or putting pots on the chimneys, if a person passing along the road is injured by something falling upon him, I think the accident alone would be prima facie evidence of negligence. Or if an article calculated to cause damage is put in a wrong place and does mischief, I think that those whose duty it was to put it in the right place are prima facie responsible, and if there is any state of facts to rebut the presumption of negligence, they must prove them. The present case upon the evidence comes to this, a man in passing in front of the premises of a dealer in flour, and there falls down upon him a barrel of flour. I think it apparent that the barrel was in the custody of the defendant who occupied the premises, and who is responsible for the acts of his servants who had the control of it; and in my opinion the fact of its falling is prima facie evidence of negligence, and the plaintiff who was injured by it is not bound to shew that it could not fall without negligence, but if there are any facts inconsistent with negligence it is for the defendant to prove them.

NOTES AND PROBLEMS

1. ***Effect of Res Ipsa Loquitur's Application.*** Despite some of the language in *Byrne* about the doctrine creating a "presumption" of negligence, the vast majority of courts today hold that the doctrine merely creates a possible *inference* of the defendant's negligence — which the jury is free to accept or reject. The practical impact of the doctrine, therefore, is not to guarantee a verdict for the plaintiff but to simply give the plaintiff a chance to win. When the doctrine applies, courts recognize that the plaintiff has offered sufficient circumstantial evidence of breach to avoid a directed verdict for the defendant. This doctrine permits the plaintiff to get the issue of breach before the jury. The jury can find the circumstantial inference of breach persuasive or not. Compare this effect with that created by the doctrine of *negligence per se.*

2. ***Doctrine's Prerequisites.*** Stated simply, *res ipsa loquitur* requires evidence that (1) the nature of a particular accident suggests that it was probably due to negligence (2) the defendant had exclusive control over whatever caused the accident (such that it was the defendant's negligence) and (3) the plaintiff lacks direct evidence of the event relative to the information available to the defendant. Some courts used to say that the circumstances must also indicate that the plaintiff was not at fault, but this is misleading because item (2) already negates such a requirement and, further, because such language is more a reflection of the common law's harsh treatment of contributory negligence than an aspect of the doctrine of *res ipsa loquitur.* We will consider contributory negligence in Chapter 7 on Affirmative Defenses.

KREBS v. CORRIGAN

321 A.2d 558 (D.C. Ct. App. 1974)

YEAGLEY, J.

This is an appeal from a directed verdict entered in favor of appellees (defendants) at the conclusion of appellant's (plaintiff's) case in chief. The complaint alleged that defendant Bronson negligently caused damage to personal property belonging to plaintiff and that defendant Donald Corrigan was liable for such damage as Bronson's principal.

The evidence reflected the following. Plaintiff is an artist who creates plexiglass sculptures. On the morning of the accident he entered his studio to find a station wagon parked within, just inside of a 10' roll-back garage door. The bumper was very close to a large sculpture. The car had been placed there by defendant Bronson so that he could avoid the chill of the morning while endeavoring to fix some dents in the automobile. Although plaintiff had not given Bronson permission to put the car in the studio, he did not order him to remove the car at once. However, after giving Bronson a dent-removing tool, so as to expedite his work, and instructing him on the use of the tool, he asked him to remove the car as soon as possible. At that moment the telephone (which was on a nearby wall) rang and plaintiff proceeded to answer it. From that position he could see the studio area, but his attention was away from Bronson as he talked on the telephone. While still on the phone, plaintiff glanced back toward where Bronson was working and saw him "flying through the air . . . at least three feet off the ground — and he landed in the middle of [a plexiglass sculpture]." Four sculptures in all were destroyed.

Upon the conclusion of plaintiff's case, defendants moved for a directed verdict on the ground that plaintiff had not presented a prima facie case of negligence. After extended argument, mainly involving the doctrine of res ipsa loquitur, the court granted defendants' motion and directed a verdict in their favor. The judge, in explaining his decision to the jury, indicated that a verdict was directed because plaintiff could not show what caused defendant Bronson's body to fall or be thrown onto the sculptures.

This information was not only unknown to plaintiff but was peculiarly within the knowledge of the defendant Bronson. He, of course, never testified as to any explanation he might have had for the accident, since his motion for a directed verdict was granted. We do not believe a plaintiff ought to be held to that burden on these facts which, left unexplained, support an inference of negligence. Accordingly, we reverse and remand for a new trial.

It is well established, to the extent that a citation of authority is unnecessary, that the mere happening of an accident does not give rise to any inference of negligence. On the other hand, it is established that the circumstances of certain accidents may be such as to justify an inference that negligence was involved. In the District of Columbia an inference that defendant may have been negligent is permitted when the following three conditions exist: first, the cause of the accident is known; second, the accident-producing instrumentality is under the exclusive control of the defendant; and third, the instrumentality is unlikely to do harm without negligence on the part of the person in control. *Powers v. Coates*, D.C. App., 203 A.2d 425 (1964), citing *Washington Loan & Trust Co. v. Hickey*, 78 U.S. App. D.C. 59, 61, 137 F.2d 677, 679 (1943). The presence of these factors distinguishes such cases from the vast majority that lack those features, concerning which it is said that negligence is not to be inferred from the mere happening of an accident.

In the case before us there is no doubt that the cause of the accident was known, *i.e.*, the sculpture was damaged by Bronson's falling on it. To say that the cause of the accident was not known, because there was no evidence as to what caused Bronson to come into contact with the sculptures, "confuses the cause of the accident with the manner in which it was caused, lack of knowledge of which, in plaintiff, is a reason for the doctrine of res ipsa loquitur. . . ." *Kerlin v. Washington Gas Light Co.*, 110 F. Supp. 487, 488 (D.D.C. 1953) aff'd., 94 U.S. App. D.C. 39, 211 F.2d 649 (1954). The doctrine was applied in that case where the evidence reflected that plaintiff, while standing on the sidewalk, was struck by an object propelled from an area where defendant's employees were digging with picks.

Nor is there any doubt that the accident-producing instrumentality, Bronson's body, was within his exclusive control. While falling cans in a supermarket may not be within the owner's exclusive control, we think it to be a fair presumption that a person's body usually is within his exclusive control; such is the sub silentio presumption in most medical malpractice cases. *See also Kohner v. Capital Traction Co.*, 22 App. D.C. 181 (1903). Defendants' contention that the dent-removing tool was the accident-producing instrumentality, and that Bronson did not have exclusive control over that tool, misses the mark. Moreover, the factual assumption, being without proof on this record, is no more than speculation. As stated, *supra*, the accident-producing instrumentality was Bronson's body, the dent-removing tool, if at all involved in this case, was in the control of defendant and would only be related to the "manner in which [the accident] was caused." *Kerlin, supra.*

Lastly, as in other situations permitting the application of res ipsa loquitur, we consider it of no small significance that the accident-producing instrumentality, Bronson's body, is one which is unlikely to do harm in the absence of negligence on the part of the person in control. Such a conclusion does not ignore the possibility of other explanations for the incident, explanations which might not involve negligence; but human bodies do not generally go crashing into breakable personal property. When they do, as here, we think the facts require the court to permit an inference of negligence. The person in control of the body or instrumentality may come forth with an explanation. To have to explain the actions of one's body is certainly not unreasonable and is less burdensome than to have to explain why a barrel of flour fell out of one's warehouse onto a pedestrian, a situation to which res ipsa loquitur was held applicable in *Byrne v. Boadle*, 159 Eng. Rep. 299 (Ex. 1863).

The instant situation, plaintiff's art objects being damaged by an inexplicably falling human body, is not unlike that of a parked automobile inexplicably being hit by a moving automobile. In the latter situation a prima facie case of negligence was found to have been presented, though there was no evidence as to why defendant's car struck plaintiff's car. *Bonbrest v. Lewis*, D.C. Mun. App., 54 A.2d 751, 752 (1947); *Schwartzbach v. Thompson*, D.C. Mun. App., 33 A.2d 624 (1943).

In a case which did involve a bodily collision, *Kohner v. Capital Traction Co., supra*, plaintiff established only that as he was riding on an open summer streetcar he was injured by "the violent contact of the right hand of the conductor of the car with the face of the appellant. . . ." *Id. at 182.* Plaintiff was unable to testify as to any negligent act on the conductor's part or as to the manner in which the accident was caused. The court reversed a directed verdict for defendant finding that res ipsa loquitur was applicable.

In *Machanic v. Storey*, 115 U.S. App. D.C. 87, 317 F.2d 151 (1963), res ipsa loquitur was applied where a car driven by defendant, in which plaintiff was a sleeping passenger, went off the road causing injuries to plaintiff, although plaintiff was unable to produce any evidence as to why the car left the road.

Appellees contend that res ipsa loquitur does not apply when the accident-producing instrumentality is a human body. We find nothing in the law of this jurisdiction to indicate that res ipsa loquitur does not apply when the accident-producing instrumentality is a body rather than an inanimate object. In *Kohner, supra*, the instrumentality was a streetcar conductor's hand. Medical malpractice cases also involve bodily instrumentalities and it has been held that in a proper case res ipsa loquitur may be applied.

Appellees also contend that appellant could not rely on the doctrine of res ipsa loquitur because there was an eyewitness to the accident, *i.e.*, defendant Bronson, and that appellant should have called Bronson as a witness before being allowed to invoke res ipsa loquitur.

To our knowledge this court has never held that a plaintiff may not invoke the doctrine of res ipsa loquitur when the defendant is an eyewitness. In fact on many occasions we have noted that one of the main reasons for the doctrine is the superior, if not exclusive, knowledge which defendants sometimes have as to the cause of accidents. If requiring a plaintiff to call the defendant as an adverse witness was deemed a sufficient method of determining the cause of an accident, there would be no need for the doctrine of res ipsa loquitur. The doctrine exists because of the realization that examination of a defendant as an adverse witness is not a viable way to discover the cause of an accident.

Although there are no cases in this jurisdiction commenting on whether a plaintiff must call an eyewitness-defendant to testify before being allowed to rely on res ipsa loquitur, there have been several where res ipsa loquitur has been applied although an available eywitness-defendant was not called by plaintiff.

In deciding whether or not res ipsa loquitur is applicable, courts necessarily are mindful of the different effects which that decision will have on the parties and the trial. If res ipsa loquitur is not employed, plaintiff's case is terminated even though he suffered an injury that was caused by the defendant. If res ipsa loquitur is found applicable, defendant is put to no greater burden than to produce information peculiarly within his knowledge as to how the incident occurred. Even if that explanation is unsatisfactory or indeed even if no explanation is made, the jury is free to decline to draw an inference of negligence, and it is so instructed.

We find that the plaintiff's evidence, considered in the light most favorable to him, as must be done in ruling on the motion for a directed verdict by a defendant, was sufficient to raise an inference of negligence so as to survive the defendants' motion and to put them to their proof.

Reversed for a new trial.

NOTES AND PROBLEMS

1. ***Exclusive Control.*** What did the defendant mean in arguing that he lacked exclusive control over the instrumentality that caused the plaintiff's harm? Why did the court reject this?

2. ***Plaintiff's Lack of Information.*** Defendant argued that the plaintiff had the same access to information as the defendant, because the plaintiff could have called him as an adverse witness to testify concerning the cause of the accident, but chose not to. Because the doctrine of *res ipsa loquitur* is premised, in part, on the unfairness of requiring the plaintiff to offer direct evidence when only circumstantial evidence is available, why did the court reject this argument?

3. ***Problem.*** Using the facts from *The T.J. Hooper*, analyze whether the plaintiff could have argued for application of the doctrine of res ipsa loquitur in that case.

"LADIES AND GENTLEMEN OF THE JURY . . ."

Iowa Pattern Jury Charge 700.07: Res Ipsa Loquitur

Under the rules of general negligence, the occurrence of an injury allows you to conclude that the defendant was negligent if the plaintiff proves (1) the injury was caused by [the instrument] under the exclusive control of the defendant, and (2) the injury would not have occurred if ordinary care had been used.

The plaintiff must prove the defendant had exclusive control when the negligence occurred.

The plaintiff must also prove the occurrence would not have happened if ordinary care had been used. Proof of this requirement rests on common experience.

RECKLESSNESS AS AN ALTERNATIVE STANDARD

Throughout this chapter we have been exploring the standard of ordinary or reasonable care. And we have used the Learned Hand formula to understand how a plaintiff typically proves that the defendant has breached this duty — by failing to undertake a burden less than the foreseeable risk of harm to others. However, tort law sometimes utilizes a different standard other than reasonable care. *Recklessness* is sometimes used as an alternate standard. There can be various reasons for the utilization of a different standard. Sometimes the common law has determined in a certain situation that a defendant will only be liable if they are shown to be reckless rather than just careless. We will see such instances in Chapter 6, Special Duty Rules. Or there might be a statute that provides some degree of protection for certain actors. Chapter 6 will also have some examples of Good Samaritan statutes that sometimes provide a shield against ordinary negligence-based liability for rescuers. Instead, such actors might be liable only when they are reckless. Finally, a plaintiff might want to offer proof of recklessness in order to attempt to recover punitive damages, as in the following case. Another synonym for recklessness is *gross negligence*. This is sometimes also referred to by the phrase "*willful, wanton, or reckless.*" All of these phrases — reckless, gross negligence, or willful and wanton misconduct — refer to the same heightened showing. As you read the following case describing alleged gross negligence, consider how gross negligence or recklessness is different than ordinary negligence and how it might be displayed, by reference to the Learned Hand formula.

MOBIL v. ELLENDER

968 S.W.2d 917 (Tex. 1998)

Baker, J.

Eli Ellender worked periodically as an independent contractor millwright at Mobil's Beaumont refinery and chemical plants between 1963 and 1977. As a millwright, Ellender repaired, serviced, and cleaned pumps, product lines, and other equipment. While working at Mobil, Ellender was exposed to benzene. He was diagnosed with acute myelogenous leukemia and died in 1989. Ellender's surviving family, individually and on behalf of his estate, sued Mobil and other defendants, alleging that exposure to benzene caused Ellender's leukemia and subsequent death. Specifically, the Ellenders alleged that Mobil was negligent [and] grossly negligent in: (1) failing to warn Ellender about his exposure to benzene on Mobil's premises and the risks associated with it, and (2) failing to protect Ellender from those risks. Just before trial, all defendants, except Mobil, agreed to settle. Before the trial court submitted the case to the jury, Mobil elected a dollar-for-dollar settlement credit. *See* Tex. Civ. Prac. & Rem. Code §33.014. The jury found that Mobil's conduct was grossly negligent and awarded the Ellenders $622,888.97 in compensatory damages and $6,000,000 in punitive damages.

Mobil first argues that there is legally insufficient evidence to support the jury's findings that Mobil's conduct was grossly negligent. Gross negligence includes two elements: (1) viewed objectively from the actor's standpoint, the act or omission must involve an extreme degree of risk, considering the probability and magnitude of the potential harm to others, and (2) the actor must have actual, subjective awareness of the risk involved, but nevertheless proceed in conscious indifference to the rights, safety, or welfare of others. *See Transportation Ins. Co. v. Moriel*, 879 S.W.2d 10, 23 (Tex. 1994). Evidence of simple negligence is not enough to prove either the objective or subjective elements of gross negligence. *See Universal Servs. Co. v. Ung*, 904 S.W.2d 638, 641 (Tex. 1995); *Moriel*, 879 S.W.2d at 22-23. Under the first element, "extreme risk" is not a remote possibility of injury or even a high probability of minor harm, but rather the likelihood of serious injury to the plaintiff. *See Ung*, 904 S.W.2d at 641; *Moriel*, 879 S.W.2d at 22. Under the second element, actual awareness means that the defendant knew about the peril, but its acts or omissions demonstrated that it did not care. *See Wal-Mart Stores, Inc. v. Alexander*, 868 S.W.2d 322, 326 (Tex. 1993). Circumstantial evidence is sufficient to prove either element of gross negligence. *See Moriel*, 879 S.W.2d at 22-23; *Wal-Mart Stores*, 868 S.W.2d at 327.

Mobil asserts that there is legally insufficient evidence of an extreme risk to Ellender of serious injury from benzene exposure at Mobil's facilities. Mobil argues that the trial court and the court of appeals improperly relied on evidence of Mobil's conduct and the resultant risks arising after Ellender worked at Mobil. We conclude that legally sufficient evidence shows that, viewed objectively from Mobil's standpoint when Ellender worked at Mobil, Mobil did not warn contract workers about benzene exposure or protect them from it and this failure involved an extreme degree of risk to those workers.

There is evidence that, from Mobil's viewpoint during the period Ellender worked at Mobil in the 1960s and 1970s, the extreme degree of risk associated with benzene exposure was common knowledge in the petrochemical industry. As early as 1926, the National Safety Council reported that "the most characteristic pathological effect of [benzene] is perhaps its destructive influence upon the cells of the blood and the blood forming organs." Mobil stipulated NSC membership dating back to 1922. In 1948, the American Petroleum Institute reported that benzene could cause leukemia and that the only absolutely safe concentration for benzene was zero. The API report also warned that a person should avoid all contact with benzene if possible, but that if the hands must contact the solvent, then a person should use neoprene gloves or protective creams. Mobil stipulated API membership dating back to 1919.

> "A pinch of probability is worth a pound of perhaps."
>
> *James Thurber*

Dr. R.J. Potts, Mobil's medical director for the Western region (including Beaumont) from 1960 to 1983, testified that he believed Mobil had knowledge of benzene hazards in the 1950s. The record shows other petrochemical companies had knowledge of benzene hazards. For example, Conoco's 1953 Employee Safety Manual included information from the 1948 API report and warned that the only safe level of benzene exposure was zero. Conoco also warned that workers should use air masks in case of benzene leaks and neoprene gloves in case of hand contact. In 1948,

Exxon noted a definite correlation between benzene and cancer. A 1943 report to Shell warned that prolonged exposure to low concentrations of benzene may be very dangerous.

There is evidence that Ellender's benzene exposure was dangerously high. Mobil's own benzene samples, taken at the olefins and aromatic plant where Ellender periodically worked in the 1960s and 1970s, showed dangerous levels of benzene exposure between 1976 and 1978. These levels were many times more than levels the Occupational Safety and Health Administration considered dangerous in 1977. Roy Gatlin, one of Ellender's co-workers, testified that on many occasions he and Ellender steam-cleaned equipment containing benzene and inhaled benzene. Gatlin and other co-workers also testified that workers used benzene, furnished by Mobil, to wash their tools and hands as often as daily. Russell Witzke, an industrial hygienist at Mobil from 1973 to 1976 admitted that benzene was always being spilled on the ground when piping equipment was connected and disconnected.

Dr. Eula Bingham, a toxicologist specializing in environmental occupational health, reviewed testimony about Ellender's exposure to benzene and described it as "substantial." Dr. John M. Dement, a industrial hygienist and epidemiologist, reviewed the same testimony and described Ellender's exposure as "significant lifetime exposure that would have put him at increased risk for leukemia."

David B. Dunham, a Mobil industrial hygienist, testified that although Mobil monitored its employees, it had an "unwritten practice or policy" not to monitor contract workers and that when he attempted to monitor contract workers, he was told not to. Ellender's co-workers testified that they never saw any signs warning them of benzene hazards at Mobil and that Mobil did not monitor them for exposure or provide them with protective gear when they worked around benzene. Moreover, Mobil did not include any reference to benzene or other chemicals in its 1967 pamphlet entitled "Mobil Safety and Security Regulations for Contract Workers." Dr. Josh Esslinger, a former medical consultant for Mobil in Beaumont, testified that he knew workers washed their hands in benzene and that such a practice indicated that workers were not adequately warned of benzene hazards. Dr. Dement testified that Mobil's industrial hygiene program was poor and practically nonexistent for contractors. This is evidence from which the jury could reasonably infer that Mobil had a company policy of not monitoring contract workers for benzene exposure, not warning them of the dangers of such exposure, and not providing them with protective gear and that this policy involved an extreme degree of risk to those workers.

We conclude that there is legally sufficient evidence that Mobil's conduct, viewed objectively from Mobil's point of view when Ellender worked at Mobil, involved an extreme degree of risk to contract workers like Ellender.

Mobil also asserts that there is legally insufficient evidence of gross negligence's subjective element. Mobil argues that the court of appeals erred in relying on evidence of general knowledge of some benzene exposure risks to affirm the finding of actual awareness of an extreme risk. Mobil further argues that there is no evidence that a Mobil [executive] knew of an extreme risk to contract workers. We conclude that there is legally sufficient evidence that Mobil . . . had actual awareness of the extreme risk benzene exposure involves, but nevertheless proceeded in conscious indifference to the rights, safety or welfare of Ellender and other contract workers.

Dr. Potts, Mobil's regional medical director from 1960 to 1983, testified that even before he became medical director he knew that benzene caused, among other diseases, aplastic anemia. He knew that washing hands and tools in benzene was hazardous. He further testified that he and Dr. Stewart, a physician working directly under him at the Beaumont refinery, implemented a plan "to see that noxious agents [including benzene] were not being used in a manner that was deleterious to employee health." Dr. Esslinger testified that Mobil had a policy to conduct blood and urine tests on its own employees for benzene exposure and that he carried out that policy.

Dunham testified that Mobil had a fleet of industrial hygiene monitors who monitored employees for benzene, among other chemicals, and who sent their results to Mobil's corporate medical director. Some of these samples, including one sample of a Mobil maintenance mechanic doing work identical to the work Ellender periodically did, showed excessive levels of benzene exposure. Further, in 1969, Mobil's Employee Relations Division . . . recognized that long-term benzene inhalation is the most likely source of benzene intoxication and that continuous exposure to benzene affects the formation of red-blood cells in bone marrow. This circumstantial evidence is legally sufficient evidence that Mobil . . . knew that not providing protective gear, not monitoring and not warning workers about benzene exposure was an extreme risk to contract workers, like Ellender, who routinely came into contact with benzene at Mobil.

Furthermore, there is probative evidence that despite this knowledge, Mobil proceeded in conscious indifference to the rights, safety or welfare of contract workers like Ellender. Contrary to Mobil's policy of warning, monitoring, and protecting its employees, Mobil did not warn, monitor, or protect contract workers from benzene exposure. Dunham admitted that personal monitoring and medical surveillance are the only sure ways to assess a worker's exposure to benzene. Yet, Dunham testified that Mobil had an "unwritten practice or policy" not to monitor contract workers and that when he attempted to monitor contract workers, he was told not to. Ellender's co-workers testified that they were not warned about benzene hazards or provided benzene protective equipment and that Mobil actually furnished benzene for workers to wash their tools. Dr. Dement testified that Mobil's failure to inform workers about benzene exposure reflected Mobil's conscious disregard for worker safety. Evidence that Mobil had a policy of monitoring and protecting its own employees but chose not to do the same for contract workers provides additional facts and circumstances for the jury to infer that Mobil knew the risks of benzene exposure yet proceeded with conscious indifference toward the rights, safety or welfare of contract workers vis-a-vis that risk.

Because there is legally sufficient evidence that Mobil was grossly negligent, we affirm the jury's finding of gross negligence against Mobil.

NOTES AND PROBLEMS

1. *Recklessness Defined.* The Restatement describes gross negligence, as follows:

> A person acts with recklessness in engaging in conduct if:
> a. the person knows of the risk of harm created by the conduct . . . and
> b. the precaution that would eliminate or reduce that risk involves burdens that are so slight relative to the magnitude of the risk as to render the person's failure to adopt the precaution a demonstration of the person's indifference to the risk.

Restatement (Third) of Torts §2 (2011). Most courts would add to this definition, as the court does in *Mobil*, by also requiring that the plaintiff prove that the risk of the activity demonstrate a "high degree of probability" that a "substantial harm" will occur. If you compare this to Learned Hand's formula for ordinary negligence, how would gross negligence vary that formula?

2. *Other Instances Where Gross Negligence Is Used.* In *Mobil*, the court uses the gross negligence standard because the plaintiff sought punitive damages. This is a common instance for application of this higher degree of fault. As you will see in Chapter 6 concerning special duty rules, the common law sometimes requires a showing of gross negligence to impose liability even for actual damages. Further, there are instances where statutes mandate gross negligence rather than ordinary negligence as a prerequisite for recovery of actual damages. For example, some states provide by statute a level of immunity for charitable organizations in personal injury claims, making them responsible only for gross negligence.

3. *Problem.* Recall the defendant hayrick builder from *Vaughan v. Menlove* at the beginning of this chapter — who took the position that he lacked the "highest order of intelligence" and perhaps failed to appreciate the risk of his actions. Would it be fair to characterize his conduct as illustrating recklessness? Explain your answer.

Pulling It All Together

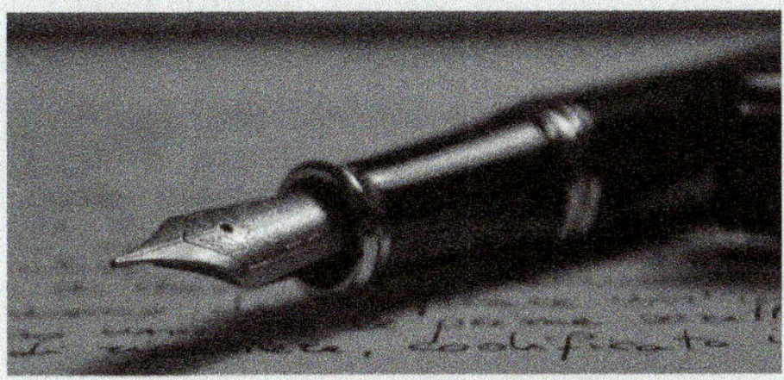

Gene owns and operates a mid-sized grocery store. Near the holidays he receives incentives from certain food manufacturers to erect special displays on the ends of the aisles in his store. This is a well-established custom in the grocery business. One brewery produces a flavorful beer called "Cheers," and Cheers pays him handsomely to display large pyramid-shaped stacks of his beer around Thanksgiving. He gets paid a greater amount depending upon the size of the display. Gene builds such a display nearly ten feet tall. Of course, as Thanksgiving approaches, the store is extra busy with customers getting ready for their feasts. The local municipality has a Fire Code that requires retailers to pass an inspection with the fire marshal prior to erecting such displays, to ensure adequate clearance for customers to retreat from a store during an emergency. Gene neglected to do this. Shania is a customer in the store during this time. She has finished filling her cart with items when, as she is passing near the Cheers display, she hears a loud noise as many six-packs of Cheers come tumbling down onto her head, giving her a concussion. She is passed out and has blood pouring from an open head wound. Nobody sees exactly how the incident occurred. Other customers come upon Shania's body and yell for Gene. Gene runs over, sees the blood on his floor, and angrily stomps to the back room to retrieve a mop to clean up the mess. He's concerned that he will lose valuable business if he doesn't clear this up fast. Nobody else intercedes on behalf of Shania and she dies before Gene returns ten minutes later.

Analyze any potential negligence causes of action — 30 minutes.

Upon Further Review

The factors considered by the Hand Formula provide an analytical construct for what is otherwise a purely intuitive method of determining whether an actor has breached the duty of reasonable care. It is a cost-benefit method of taking into account many varying circumstances confronting a particular actor. Its timeless utility lies in its flexibility. Its basic considerations can be applied to an infinite variety of circumstances to permit a reasoned analysis of whether the conduct is blameworthy or negligent. Circumstances that can easily be taken into account within the analytical confines of the Hand Formula include sudden emergencies, industry customs, the actor's adoption of policies and procedures, and certain character traits of the actor in question. As useful as the Hand Formula is, its application demands that the fact finder have some information about the actor's actual course of conduct and the availability of other alternative courses of conduct. Where that information is lacking (e.g., when barrels fall out of warehouses for unknown reasons), the doctrine of res ipsa loquitur acknowledges that circumstantial evidence may be compelling enough to permit an inference of negligence, despite the inability to scrutinize the actor's conduct in the typical manner. Finally, when a legislative or executive branch of government has made an effort to prevent particular accidental harms by mandating a specific course of conduct, this can provide a shortcut to determine breach — the reasonable person, after all, seeks to obey the law when reasonably feasible.

CHAPTER 5

Causation

I INTRODUCTION

Just because a defendant has done something wrong and a plaintiff has suffered harm does not mean that the defendant must pay damages. Tort law demands a link between the defendant's misconduct and the plaintiff's harm. *Causation* is that missing link. When we covered intentional torts an often implicit and unstated requirement was actual causation. For example, a defendant who intends a harmful contact with the plaintiff is only liable when his voluntary act *causes* a harmful or offensive contact to occur. A defendant who intends to cause emotional distress to a plaintiff is only liable when his outrageous conduct *causes* the plaintiff to suffer severe emotional distress. This causation requirement is often unstated in the arena of intentional torts because typically causation is not disputed in such cases. But when one enters the world of accidental injuries, causation often plays a vital role. We will first pick up with the test for actual causation — the "but-for" test. This is the same test that would be used both in a negligence case and any other tort cause of action. It is often straightforward and almost intuitive.

CHAPTER GOALS

- ☑ Understand why tort law demands the logical nexus of causation in order to create liability for a wrongdoer in favor of an injured party.
- ☑ Learn the but-for test for actual causation and appreciate that this does not involve a search for the sole cause.
- ☑ Identify recurring exceptional scenarios where courts have created alternative doctrines to substitute for but-for causation.
- ☑ Recognize why in cases of accidental torts, there is a need for an additional limitation on liability beyond actual causation — proximate cause.
- ☑ Become familiar with the various different tests courts have created for proximate cause.

Essentially, it asks the fact-finder to consider a world where all of the facts existing in a case remain unchanged except that the defendant's misconduct instead becomes acceptable conduct (reasonably careful conduct, in a negligence case). In the hypothesized alternative world, does the plaintiff still suffer the same harm? This test often works well. When it does not, the law of torts sometimes utilizes a different doctrine as a "Band-Aid" to fix the actual causation problem. We will explore the primary doctrines that serve as alternatives to the but-for test.

Finally, this chapter will then explore a second required test for legal causation in a negligence case — proximate cause. As it turns out, merely demanding that the defendant's conduct constitute a but-for cause often would permit imposition of liability on actors whose conduct was very remote from the plaintiff's harm. Without this additional check or limitation upon liability, the common notion is that some defendants would unfairly be found liable. We will explore the primary tests different courts use today for proximate cause.

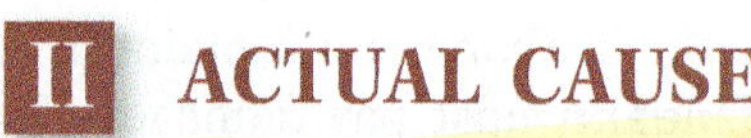

II ACTUAL CAUSE

A. The "But-For" Test

In order to demonstrate the necessary nexus between the defendant's misconduct and the plaintiff's harm, a plaintiff must prove by a preponderance of the evidence that the misconduct was essential to bringing about the harm — that without the misconduct the plaintiff would not have suffered the complained of injury. In many scenarios this is not too difficult. A hunter in the woods fires toward his prey without carefully surveying the area for other hunters and accidentally shoots a fellow hunter in the leg. It is not difficult to demonstrate actual but-for causation in this simple yet realistic scenario. Had the hunter not fired his weapon without ensuring that the coast was clear, the injury would not have likely occurred. Sometimes but-for causation is more complicated. In cases where it is not exactly clear how the accident even occurred, demonstrating actual causation might not be so intuitively obvious. *Cay* clarifies the actual burden of proving but-for causation in circumstances where the plaintiff's death is somewhat of a mystery. The *Lyons* case highlights the importance on focusing upon whether the *wrongful* conduct of the defendant was a cause of the claimant's harm rather than some other innocent conduct by the defendant. And finally the *East Texas Theatres* case shows an example where plaintiff might be able to prove defendant's negligence but it appears the harm would have occurred even had the defendant acted reasonably.

CAY v. LOUISIANA

631 So. 2d 393 (La. 1994)

LEMMON, J.

This is a wrongful death action filed by the parents of Keith Cay, who was killed in a fall from a bridge constructed and maintained by the Department of Transportation and Development (DOTD). [A] principal issue [is] whether plaintiffs proved that DOTD's construction of the bridge railing at a height lower than the minimum standard for pedestrian traffic was a cause-in-fact of Cay's fall from the bridge. . . .

Cay, a twenty-seven-year-old single offshore worker, returned to his home in Sandy Lake from a seven-day work shift on November 3, 1987. Later that afternoon his sister drove him to Jonesville, thirteen miles from his home, to obtain a hunting license and shotgun shells for a hunting trip the next day. Cay cashed a check for $60.00 and paid for the hunting items, but remained in Jonesville when his sister returned to Sandy Lake about 7:00 p.m. Around 10:00 p.m. Cay entered a barroom and stayed until about 11:00 p.m., when he left the barroom on foot after declining an offer for a ride to his home. He carried an opened beer with him.

Five days later, Cay's body was discovered on a rock bank of the Little River, thirty-five feet below the bridge across the river. Cay would have had to cross the bridge in order to travel from Jonesville to his home.

Cay's body was found in a thicket of brambles and brush. The broken brush above the body and the lack of a path through the brush at ground level indicated that Cay had fallen from the bridge. There was no evidence suggesting suicide or foul play. [Cay had just purchased a hunting license and supplies.] There was evidence, however, that Cay, who was wearing dark clothes, was walking on the wrong side of the road for pedestrian traffic and was intoxicated.

The bridge, built in 1978, was forty feet wide, with two twelve-foot lanes of travel and an eight-foot shoulder on each side. The side railings were thirty-two inches high, the minimum height under existing standards for bridges designed for vehicular traffic. There were no curbs, sidewalks or separate railings for pedestrian traffic, although it was well known that many pedestrians had used the old bridge to cross the river to communities and recreation areas on the other side.

> "Ever since the first cause brought the world into being, no event has had a single cause."
>
> *Public Citizen Health Research Group v. Young, 909 F.2d 546, 550 (D.C. Cir. 1990).*

Cay's parents filed this action against DOTD, seeking recovery on the basis that the guard railings on the sides of the bridge were too low and therefore unsafe for pedestrians whom DOTD knew were using the bridge and that DOTD failed to provide pedestrian walkways or signs warning pedestrians about the hazardous conditions.

The trial court rendered judgment for plaintiffs, concluding that Cay accidently fell from the bridge. The court held that the fall was caused in part by the inadequate railing and in part by Cay's intoxicated condition. Pointing out that DOTD had closed the old bridge to both vehicular and pedestrian traffic and should have been aware that numerous pedestrians would use the new bridge to reach a recreational park, the Trinity community and other points across the river from Jonesville, the court found that DOTD breached its duty to pedestrians by failing to build the side railings to a height of thirty-six inches, as required by the American Association of State Highway and Transportation Officials (AASHTO) standards for pedestrian railings. The court concluded that this construction deficiency was a cause of the accident in that "a higher rail would have prevented the fall." Noting that there was no evidence establishing what actually caused the incident, the court surmised that Cay was "startled by oncoming traffic, moved quickly to avoid perceived danger, tripped over the low rail, lost his balance, and with nothing to prevent the fall, fell from the Little River Bridge." The court apportioned fault sixty percent to DOTD and forty percent to Cay.

The court of appeal affirmed. The court concluded that the inadequate railing was a cause-in-fact of the accident, stating, "It is true that the accident might have occurred had the railing been higher. However, it is also true that the accident might not have happened had the railing been higher." The court further stated, "Had the railing been higher, the decedent might have been able to avoid the accident."

Because these statements are an incorrect articulation of the preponderance of the evidence standard for the plaintiffs' burden of proof in circumstantial evidence cases, we granted certiorari.

BURDEN OF PROOF

In a negligence action, the plaintiff has the burden of proving negligence and causation by a preponderance of the evidence. *Jordan v. Travelers Ins. Co.*, 245 So. 2d 151 (La. 1971). Proof is sufficient to constitute a preponderance when the entirety of the evidence, both direct and circumstantial, establishes that the fact or causation sought to be proved is more probable than not. *Boudreaux v. American Ins. Co.*, 264 So. 2d 621 (La. 1972).

One critical issue in the present case is causation, and the entirety of the evidence bearing on that issue is circumstantial. For the plaintiff to prevail in this type of case, the inferences drawn from the circumstantial evidence must establish all the necessary elements of a negligence action, including causation, and the plaintiff must sustain the burden of proving that the injuries were more likely than not the result of the particular defendant's negligence.

CAUSE-IN-FACT

Cause-in-fact is the initial inquiry in a duty-risk analysis. Cause-in-fact is usually a "but-for" inquiry which tests whether the injury would not have occurred but for the defendant's substandard conduct. The cause-in-fact issue is usually a jury question unless reasonable minds could not differ.

The principal negligence attributed to DOTD in the present case is the failure to build the bridge railings to the height required in the AASHTO standards. The causation inquiry is whether that failure caused Cay's fall or, conversely, whether the fall would have been prevented if DOTD had constructed the railing at least thirty-six inches high.

The determination of whether a higher railing would have prevented Cay's fall depends on how the accident occurred. Plaintiffs had the burden to prove that a higher railing would have prevented Cay's fall in the manner in which the accident occurred.

The circumstantial evidence did not establish the exact cause of Cay's fall from the bridge, but it is more likely than not that Cay's going over the side was not intentional, either on his part or of the part of a third party. More probably than not, Cay did not commit suicide, as evidence of plans and preparation for a hunting trip minimize this possibility. More probably than not, he was not pushed, as he had little money or valuables on his person, and the evidence from barroom patrons does not suggest any hostility toward or by him during the evening. More likely than not, he was not struck by a vehicle and knocked over the railing. It is therefore most likely that he accidently fell over the railing.

The evidence suggests that Cay moved at a sharp angle toward the railing, for some unknown reason, and stumbled over. For purposes of the cause-in-fact analysis, it matters little whether his movement toward the railing was prompted by perceived danger of an approaching automobile or by staggering in an intoxicated condition or for some other reason. Whatever the cause of Cay's movement toward the railing at a sharp angle, the cause-in-fact inquiry is whether a higher railing would have prevented the accidental fall.

The trial judge's finding that a higher railing would have prevented the fall is supported by expert testimony that the very reason for the minimum height requirement for railing on bridges intended for pedestrian use is to have a railing above the center of gravity of most persons using the bridge so that the users will not fall over.

A cause-in-fact determination is one of fact on which appellate courts must accord great deference to the trial court. We cannot say that the trial court erred manifestly in determining that a railing built to AASHTO minimum specifications would have prevented Cay's fall when he approached the railing at a sharp angle, although the exact cause of Cay's approaching the railing at a sharp angle is not known. While a higher rail would not have prevented Cay from jumping or a third party from throwing Cay over the rail, one could reasonably

Principles

The Restatement articulates the following explanation of actual cause:

> "Tortious conduct must be a factual cause of harm for liability to be imposed. Conduct is a factual cause of harm when the harm would not have occurred absent the conduct."
>
> *Restatement (Third) of Torts §26 (2011).*

conclude that a rail above Cay's center of gravity would have prevented an accidental fall.

NOTES AND PROBLEMS

1. ***The "But-For" Test.*** The *Cay* court articulates a simple test for actual causation and applies it to a case where mystery abounds. In order to determine if the defendant's negligence — building the railing on the bridge four inches too low — caused the decedent's death, the court must determine what *probably* happened on that evening. The intermediate court of appeals believed causation was present if the negligence "might have" made a difference. The Louisiana Supreme Court rejects this — because the plaintiff's burden in a civil case is to prove each element by a "preponderance" of the evidence. Once the court determines what probably happened — that the decedent stumbled toward the railing and fell over it — the application of the "but-for" test is fairly straightforward. Because the railing should have been designed to exceed a typical adult's center of gravity, there is persuasive evidence that the low railing was an essential fact that led to the death.

2. ***The Number of "But-For" Causes of an Accident.*** In *Cay*, the trial court found two essential causes: (1) the decedent's intoxication and (2) the defendant's negligence. In fact, when taken to its logical extreme there are virtually an infinite number of but-for causes for any event. In *Cay*, had the plaintiff not declined a ride from another patron of the bar he could not have fallen off the bridge. Had the plaintiff's sister not driven him to the town he would not have fallen off the bridge. Had he not made the decision to purchase a hunting license he would not have fallen off the bridge. Had his parents never been born, he would not have fallen off the bridge. The point of all of this is that but-for cause is not a search for a lone cause — there is no such thing. It is merely an analysis of whether the defendant's act or omission of negligence is *one of the essential links* in the chain of causation that led to the harm.

3. ***Problems.***

A. The appellate court in *Cay* references the trial court's surmise that another driver had probably done something to spook the decedent and cause him to stumble toward the bridge railing. If that other driver could be located and plaintiff could show that he was negligent in how he drove the car, would that other driver also be liable to the plaintiff for the negligent death of the decedent?

B. Suppose a fancy resort permits its employees to hand a key card for a guest room to anyone who requests it without any identifying information. A man requests such a card from the front desk for a particular room. The man goes into the room and assaults the occupant of the room.

However, the evidence also shows that the room's occupant left the front door unlocked. Is the hotel's negligence in handing out room keys a but-for cause of the guest's damages?

C. What if the evidence in *Cay* showed that Keith Cay, the deceased, was unusually tall — over seven feet? Might this impact the actual causation conclusion that the trial court made? What if he was instead unusually short — less than five feet?

LYONS v. MIDNIGHT SUN TRANSPORTATION SERVICES

928 P.2d 1202 (Alaska 1996)

Per Curiam.

Esther Hunter-Lyons was killed when her Volkswagen van was struck broadside by a truck driven by David Jette and owned by Midnight Sun Transportation Services, Inc. When the accident occurred, Jette was driving south in the right-hand lane of Arctic Boulevard in Anchorage. Hunter-Lyons pulled out of a parking lot in front of him. Jette braked and steered to the left, but Hunter-Lyons continued to pull out further into the traffic lane. Jette's truck collided with Hunter-Lyons's vehicle. David Lyons, the deceased's husband, filed suit, asserting that Jette had been speeding and driving negligently.

At trial, conflicting testimony was introduced regarding Jette's speed before the collision. Lyons's expert witness testified that Jette may have been driving as fast as 53 miles per hour. Midnight Sun's expert testified that Jette probably had been driving significantly slower and that the collision could have occurred even if Jette had been driving at the speed limit, 35 miles per hour. Lyons's expert later testified that if Jette had stayed in his own lane, and had not steered to the left, there would have been no collision. Midnight Sun's expert contended that steering to the left when a vehicle pulls out onto the roadway from the right is a normal response and is generally the safest course of action to follow.

Over Lyons's objection, the jury was given an instruction on the sudden emergency doctrine. The jury found that Jette, in fact, had been negligent, but his negligence was not a legal cause of the accident. [The Alaska Supreme Court decided that it no longer would approve of use of the sudden emergency instruction but that it was harmless because the jury found negligence in favor of the plaintiff anyway.]

Lyons's claims were defeated on the basis of lack of causation. Although the jury found Jette to have been negligent, it also found that this negligence was *not* the legal cause of the accident. Duty, breach of duty, causation, and harm are the separate and distinct elements of a negligence claim, all of which must be proven before a defendant can be held liable for the plaintiff's injuries.

Further, we cannot say that the jury's finding of lack of causation was unreasonable. There was evidence presented at trial from which the jury could reasonably have drawn the conclusion that even though Jette was driving negligently, his negligence was not the cause of the accident. Midnight Sun introduced expert testimony to the effect that the primary cause of the accident was Ms. Hunter-Lyons's action in pulling out of the parking lot in front of an oncoming truck. Terry Day, an accident reconstruction specialist testified that, depending on how fast Ms. Hunter-Lyons was moving, the accident could have happened even if Jette had been driving within the speed limit. Midnight Sun also introduced expert testimony to the effect that Jette responded properly to the unexpected introduction of an automobile in his traffic lane. Although all of this testimony was disputed by Lyons, a reasonable jury could have concluded that Ms. Hunter-Lyons caused the accident by abruptly pulling out in front of an oncoming truck, and that David Jette's negligence was not a contributing factor. With the element of causation lacking, even the most egregious negligence cannot result in liability.

EAST TEXAS THEATRES, INC. v. RUTLEDGE

453 S.W.2d 466 (Tex. 1970)

SMITH, J.

This is a damage suit alleging personal injuries were sustained by Sheila Rutledge, on or about September 25, 1966, while attending a midnight movie in a theatre owned and operated by East Texas Theatres, Inc. The suit was brought by Sheila, joined by her husband, against East Texas Theatres, Inc. alleging that certain acts of negligence on the part of the theatre were a proximate cause of the injuries Sheila sustained while a patron of the theatre. The jury found the defendant guilty of negligence in failing to remove certain unidentified "rowdy persons" from the theatre and that such negligence was a cause of Sheila's injuries. Damages were assessed by the jury at $31,250.00. Based upon the jury findings, the trial court entered judgment for the plaintiffs. The Court of Civil Appeals has affirmed. We reverse the judgments of both courts and here render judgment that the plaintiffs take nothing. [Defendant contends on appeal that the evidence of causation was insufficient to support this judgment.]

On September 24 and the early morning of September 25, 1966, Sheila, a paying guest, was attending a special "midnight show" at the Paramount Theatre, one of the several theatres owned by the defendant. The interior of the theatre was arranged with a lower floor and a balcony for the seating of patrons. Sheila and her friends took seats on the lower floor out beyond the overhang of the balcony. When the picture came to an end, Sheila started making her exit. As she proceeded up the aisle toward the front of the building for the purpose of leaving the theatre and just before she walked under the balcony overhang, some unidentified person in the balcony threw a bottle which struck her on the side of her head just above her left ear.

Conduct of the Theatre Patrons

Since the jury found that the patrons in the balcony were acting in a "rowdy" manner and that the defendant negligently failed to remove such rowdy persons from the premises and that such negligence caused the injuries sustained by Sheila, we deem it important to particularly point out the evidence bearing on the conduct of the patrons during the evening. The evidence favorable to the verdict is that during the progress of the show, the patrons in the theatre, both on the lower floor and in the balcony, were engaged in "hollering." Sheila, in describing the "hollering," said that "a few slang words" were used. This "hollering" was intermittent; it occurred "off and on" during "parts of" the movie. One witness testified that ". . . they would holler and maybe slack off a few minutes and then holler again." Buddy Henderson [a witness] testified that he saw paper or cold drink cups either "drifting down" or being thrown down toward the front of the theatre. Sheila did not see throwing of any type. Henderson testified that he did not recall anything drifting down or being thrown down other than the paper cold drink cups. In regard to the duration of the commotion in the theatre, the evidence shows that there was more commotion on the lower floor than in the balcony. Henderson testified that he thought that the "hollering" seemed to get worse toward the end of the show. Sheila was certain that ". . . [about] 30 minutes before the show was over it seemed to be quieter; they didn't seem to be as rowdy then." Sheila, Henderson and an officer by the name of Burt, all agreed in their testimony that before the show was over, and, thus, before the accident, all commotion in the theatre had ceased. The last disturbance of any kind before the show was over was not throwing but "hollering." Henderson further testified that nothing happened, whether "hollering" or the throwing of paper cups, to make him think that something bad was going to happen; he was not worried about the safety of himself or the safety of his friends or anybody that was there.

The balcony, which would seat 263 people, was "just about full." The witness, Burt, estimated that about 175 of the balcony seats were occupied. The disturbance in the balcony seemed to come from the balcony generally, "just all over it." The evidence does not identify any particular person as being a "rowdy person." No witness could state which persons in the balcony were rowdy and which were not. No witness could identify the person who threw the bottle. Incidentally, there is no evidence that a hard substance of any character was thrown, other than the bottle which struck Sheila. The witness, Henderson, testified that he could not identify the person who threw the bottle, but that out of the corner of his eye, he saw a "movement, a jerking motion" by someone in the balcony and then saw the bottle hit Sheila. No witness testified that the bottle thrower had been engaged in "hollering" or throwing paper cups.

Assuming without deciding that the finding of negligence is supported by evidence of probative force, we go direct to the question of whether there is in the record evidence or probative force to support the finding of cause. We hold that there is no evidence to support the finding of the jury that the failure of the defendant to remove "rowdy persons" from its premises was a cause of Sheila's injuries.

[In order to find a negligent actor liable for the claimant's injuries] there must be cause in fact — a cause which produces an event and without which the event would not have occurred. "An essential element of the plaintiff's cause of action for negligence is that there be some reasonable connection between the act or omission of the defendant and the damage which the plaintiff has suffered." Prosser, Law of Torts (3rd Ed.) 240-41 (1964). We base our decision here on the ground that the plaintiffs have failed to offer evidence of probative force to establish the cause-in-fact element of [causation]. In particular, the plaintiffs contend that the act of omission in failing to remove "rowdy persons" from the theatre was a cause of the injuries resulting from the throwing of the bottle by an unknown patron of the theatre. We recognize that cause-in-fact covers the defendant's omissions as well as its acts. However, it cannot be said from this record that had the defendant removed the "rowdy persons" from the premises, the bottle thrower would not have thrown the bottle. The record in this case clearly shows a complete lack of proof that the bottle would not have been thrown "but for" the failure of the defendant to remove "rowdy persons" from the premises. There is no evidence that the bottle thrower was one of the "rowdy persons" engaged in "hollering" and throwing paper cups from the balcony. We cannot say from this evidence what persons would have been removed.

We recognize that the theatre was under a duty to exercise reasonable care for the safety of its patrons. However, operators of theatres are not insurers of their patrons' safety.

The judgments of the Court of Civil Appeals and the trial court are reversed and judgment is here rendered that plaintiffs take nothing.

NOTES AND PROBLEMS

1. ***Connecting the Dots.*** In *Lyons,* there was both evidence that the defendant was negligent (in driving too fast) and that his veering the car to the left resulted in the collision. Given this evidence, how could the court uphold a jury finding of negligence but no causation? The point is that one must ask whether the negligent act was a but-for cause of the harm. Just because veering to the left may have been a cause of the accident, if this defensive maneuver was justified rather than negligent, its causal connection to the accident is irrelevant. Rather, if the lone act of negligence was the speeding, the focus then shifts to whether the additional speed made a difference in the outcome. In this case, it appears the jury credited the testimony of the defendant's expert witness who said that the collision would have occurred regardless of whether the defendant was going 35 m.p.h. or 53 m.p.h.

2. ***Plaintiff's Burden.*** In *East Texas Theatres,* the court also is willing to concede possible negligence by the theatre operator in failing to remove rowdy audience members from the balcony. Given that the bottle that hit the plaintiff was thrown from the balcony, why does the court affirm a summary judgment for the defendant based upon causation? Recall that the plaintiff must prove but-for causation by a preponderance of the evidence. Did the plaintiff offer such evidence to support the theory that if the defendant had removed the rowdy persons that this probably would have prevented the plaintiff's injuries? What more would the plaintiff have had to show in this scenario to avoid summary judgment?

B. Alternatives to But-For Causation

The but-for test for actual causation intuitively makes sense and resolves the issue of whether the defendant's (or plaintiff's) negligence matters. That is, was the misconduct "negligence in the air," as Judge Cardozo mentioned in *Martin v. Herzog* (i.e., lacking in causation), or did the actor's misconduct have a logical connection with the plaintiff's harm such that the party's negligence should make them responsible? If the but-for test is satisfied, a defendant is liable to the plaintiff for the plaintiff's resulting losses. If the test is not satisfied, the plaintiff loses. Normally this is the approach taken. But there are certain recurring factual scenarios where the but-for test cannot be satisfied, yet permitting the tortfeasors to escape liability would be unjust. In these few exceptional scenarios, courts have dispensed with the but-for test and utilized one of a few other doctrines to save the plaintiff's cause of action. One scenario involves *Multiple Sufficient Independent Causes* for the plaintiff's harm. A different, but related, situation involves two similarly acting tortfeasors where only one of them could have actually caused the harm, but plaintiff has no way to determine which of the two is responsible. *Alternative Liability* is a theory that applies to this instance and provides motivation for the two tortfeasors to help explain the mystery rather than facing liability. We will see a related doctrine, *Modified Alternative Liability* (a.k.a. "market share liability"), applied in scenarios where alternative liability is inapplicable but plaintiffs are still hampered in their efforts to prove causation when injured by a fungible product sold by multiple manufacturers. Finally, in the field of medical malpractice and toxic torts we will see some courts utilize a test other than but-for causation where the defendant's tortious misconduct has either decreased a plaintiff's chances for cure or increased the plaintiff's chances for illness, though the misconduct probably did not actually alter the outcome. These two related doctrines — *Loss of Chance* and *Increased Risk of Harm*—often help plaintiffs who seem to have been harmed in some sense yet cannot prove but-for causation.

1. Multiple Sufficient Independent Causes

Normally a tort victim who has been victimized by the misconduct of more than one tortfeasor would seem to be in a relatively good position as a strategic proposition. Even if one tortfeasor had insufficient assets, at least there would be another able to pay. How could it possibly be a bad thing to have two tortfeasors to go after? While this is often true, in some instances it may be that neither one can be considered a true but-for cause of the harm. Unless there is a new doctrine available to help rescue the plaintiff's tort cause of action, this *conceptual but-for dilemma* would leave a legitimately harmed plaintiff without any means of receiving compensation and the tortfeasors would go unpunished. The following is a classic case involving just such a scenario. Consider the rationale behind the court recognizing and applying an alternative means of recovery.

KINGSTON v. CHICAGO & NORTHWESTERN RAILWAY

211 N.W. 913 (Wisc. 1927)

OWEN, J.

The jury found that both fires were set by sparks emitted from locomotives on and over defendant's right of way. Appellant contends that there is no evidence to support the finding that either fire was so set. We have carefully examined the record and have come to the conclusion that the evidence does support the finding that the northeast fire was set by sparks emitted from a locomotive then being run on and over the right of way of defendant's main line. We conclude, however, that the evidence does not support the finding that the northwest fire was set by sparks emitted from defendant's locomotives or that the defendant had any connection with its origin.

We therefore have this situation: The northeast fire was set by sparks emitted from defendant's locomotive. This fire, according to the finding of the jury, constituted a proximate cause of the destruction of plaintiff's property. This finding we find to be well supported by the evidence. We have the northwest fire, of unknown origin. This fire, according to the finding of the jury, also constituted a proximate cause of the destruction of the plaintiff's property. This finding we also find to be well supported by the evidence. We have a union of these two fires 940 feet north of plaintiff's property, from which point the united fire bore down upon and destroyed the property. We therefore have two separate, independent, and distinct agencies, each of which constituted the proximate cause of plaintiff's damage, and either of which, in the absence of the other, would have accomplished such result.

It is settled in the law of negligence that any one of two or more joint tortfeasors, or one of two or more wrongdoers whose concurring acts of negligence result in injury, are each individually responsible for the entire damage resulting from their joint or concurrent acts of negligence. This rule also obtains

> where two causes, each attributable to the negligence of a responsible person, concur in producing an injury to another, either of which causes would produce it regardless of the other, . . . because, whether the concurrence be intentional, actual, or constructive, each wrongdoer, in effect, adopts the conduct of his co-actor, and for the further reason that it is impossible to apportion the damage or to say that either perpetrated any distinct injury that can be separated from the whole. The whole loss must necessarily be considered and treated as an entirety.

Cook v. M., St. P. & S.S.M.R. Co., 98 Wis. 624 (74 N.W. 561), at p. 642. That case presented a situation very similar to this. One fire, originating by sparks emitted from a locomotive, united with another fire of unknown origin and consumed plaintiffs' property. There was nothing to indicate that the fire of unknown origin was not set by some human agency. The evidence in the case merely failed to identify the agency. In that case it was held that the railroad company which set one fire was not responsible for the damage committed by the united fires because the origin of the other fire was not identified. In that case a rule of law was announced [concerning the situation where one fire is started by another's negligence but the second fire is of no known responsible origin. Either fire, had the other not existed, would have reached the property and caused the harm. Therefore, plaintiff can have no recovery].

Emphasis is placed upon the fact, especially in the opinion, that one fire had "no responsible origin." At other times in the opinion the fact is emphasized that it had no "known responsible origin." The plain inference from the entire opinion is that if both fires had been of responsible origin, or of known responsible origin, each wrongdoer would have been liable for the entire damage. The conclusion of the court exempting the railroad company from liability seems to be based upon the single fact that one fire had no responsible origin or no known responsible origin. It is difficult to determine just what weight was accorded to the fact that the origin of the fire was unknown. If the conclusion of the court was founded upon the assumption that the fire of unknown origin had no responsible origin, the conclusion announced may be sound and in harmony with well settled principles of negligence.

From our present consideration of the subject we are not disposed to criticize the doctrine which exempts from liability a wrongdoer who sets a fire which unites with a fire originating from natural causes, such as lightning, not attributable to any human agency, resulting in damage. It is also conceivable that a fire so set might unite with a fire of so much greater proportions, such as a raging forest fire, as to be enveloped or swallowed up by the greater holocaust, and its identity destroyed, so that the greater fire could be said to be an intervening or superseding cause. But we have no such situation here. These fires were of comparatively equal rank. If there was any difference in their magnitude or threatening aspect, the record indicates that the northeast fire was the larger fire and was really regarded as the menacing agency. At any rate there is no intimation or suggestion that the northeast fire was enveloped and swallowed up by the northwest fire. We will err on the side of the defendant if we regard the two fires as of equal rank.

According to well settled principles of negligence, it is undoubted that if the proof disclosed the origin of the northwest fire, even though its origin be attributed to a third person, the railroad company, as the originator of the northeast fire, would be liable for the entire damage. There is no reason to believe that the northwest fire originated from any other than human agency. It was a small fire. It had traveled over a limited area. It had been in existence but for a day. For a time it was thought to have been extinguished. It was not in the nature of a raging forest fire. The record discloses nothing of natural phenomena which could have given rise to the fire. It is morally certain that it was set by some human agency.

Now the question is whether the railroad company, which is found to have been responsible for the origin of the northeast fire, escapes liability because the origin of the northwest fire is not identified, although there is no reason to believe that it had any other than human origin. An affirmative answer to that question would certainly make a wrongdoer a favorite of the law at the expense of an innocent sufferer. The injustice of such a doctrine sufficiently impeaches the logic upon which it is founded. Where one who has suffered damage by fire proves the origin of a fire and the course of that fire up to the point of the destruction of his property, one has certainly established liability on the part of the originator of the fire. Granting that the union of that fire with another of natural origin, or with another of much greater proportions, is available as a defense, the burden is on the defendant to show that by reason of such union with a fire of such character the fire set by him was not the proximate cause of the damage. No principle of justice requires that the plaintiff be placed under the burden of specifically identifying the origin of both fires in order to recover the damages for which either or both fires are responsible.

We are not disposed to apply the doctrine of the *Cook Case* to the instant situation. There being no [proof that the northwest fire was due to an irresponsible origin], the defendant

Principles

The Restatement describes the doctrine of multiple independent sufficient causes in this way:

> "If multiple acts occur, each of which . . . alone would have been a factual cause of the physical harm at the same time in the absence of the other act(s), each act is regarded as a factual cause of the harm."
>
> *Restatement (Third) of Torts §27 (2011).*

is responsible for the entire amount of that loss. While under some circumstances a wrongdoer is not responsible for damage which would have occurred in the absence of his wrongful act . . . that doctrine does not obtain "where two causes, each attributable to the negligence of a responsible person, concur in producing an injury to another, either of which causes would produce it regardless of the other." This is because "it is impossible to apportion the damage or to say that either perpetrated any distinct injury that can be separated from the whole," and to permit each of two wrongdoers to plead the wrong of the other as a defense to his own wrongdoing would permit both wrongdoers to escape and penalize the innocent party who has been damaged by their wrongful acts.

The fact that the northeast fire was set by the railroad company . . . is sufficient to affirm the judgment.

NOTES AND PROBLEMS

1. ***Nature of But-For Problem.*** The *Kingston* case deals with a situation in which each of the two causes (i.e. the fires) would easily be considered a but-for cause of the plaintiff's property loss if the other fire never existed. But because of the two fires, each independent and sufficient to have caused all of the plaintiff's loss on its own, neither can meet the test. If the court were to insist on traditional but-for causation here the plaintiff could not recover against either tortfeasor, and both tortfeasors would escape judgment. Such a result would frustrate both the purpose of compensation and deterrence. This is a scenario where *conceptually* the but-for test seems to fail in achieving justice.

2. ***Other Instances of Multiple Causes.*** In one sense, every tort case involves the confluence of many but-for causes that result in a single, indivisible injury to the plaintiff. If a criminal assault is permitted to occur to a plaintiff in her hotel room because of the hotel's inadequate security, both the criminal and the hotel would be considered but-for causes of the one loss. The but-for causation test can be satisfied and the plaintiff can recover against either or both. Just because multiple causes exist does not mean that a but-for dilemma will be present — we saw this earlier in the *Cay v. Louisiana* case. The multiple independent sufficient causes doctrine is only applicable in situations where each tortfeasor's misconduct, on its own, would lead to the same result and thus neither is actually essential.

3. ***Natural Causes.*** Some courts have held, as the *Cook* court held, that where the second, independently sufficient cause is a natural cause of the plaintiff's loss, the multiple independent sufficient cause doctrine should not be available. This is because the chief concern cited in *Kingston* — that the but-for-test might

otherwise allow two tortfeasors to both escape liability by pointing to one another — is not present. Not all courts agree with this and will apply the doctrine even if the second cause is of natural origins.

4. *An Alternative Analysis.* After recognizing that the search for essential but-for causation in scenarios involving multiple independent sufficient causes was impossible, courts eventually began asking instead whether the defendant's role was at least a *substantial factor* in leading to the claimant's harm. We will see this employed in such an instance later in this chapter in the case of Brisboy v. Fibreboard Paper Products Corp. Such alternative analysis can be traced back to the language in *Kingston* when the court wondered about the relative size of the two fires, suggesting that if one were far greater than the other it might diminish the smaller fire being considered substantial enough to create liability. The Restatement (Third) of Torts now suggests skipping this "substantial factor" analysis in cases of multiple independent sufficient causes.

5. *Problem.* A plaintiff was exposed to a toxic substance, asbestos, from multiple different employers during a long career working at shipyards where asbestos was used for insulation. Plaintiff eventually was diagnosed with a form of cancer caused by asbestos exposure. Will this plaintiff face any difficulty proving causation in a suit against all of the former employers? What additional information would be necessary to determine if the rule from *Kingston* would apply?

2. *Alternative Liability*

Alternative liability is another doctrine intended to help repair a but-for causation problem in another instance where the but-for test would yield unsavory results. Alternative liability applies in a multiple tortfeasor scenario where there is a true but-for cause associated with the tort but the plaintiff is not in a position to identify, as between the tortfeasors, which one is responsible for causing the harm. *Summers* is the classic case cited for this doctrine. It involves three hunters in the woods. Plaintiff gets shot but cannot prove which other hunter actually shot him. The two defendants both fired the same type of weapon in plaintiff's direction. As you read this, notice that although the plaintiff suffers two injuries, as to each injury it is clear that only one of the hunters could have caused the harm. Consider how the *nature* of the but-for problem is very different here than in cases of multiple independently sufficient causes, and yet the *principle* motivating the doctrine is virtually identical. The next case, *Burke*, involves a plaintiff trying to use a causation cure (alternative liability), even though the plaintiff's real problem has more to do with proving breach of duty. For this reason, the doctrine is unavailing there.

SUMMERS v. TICE

199 P.2d 1 (Cal. 1948)

CARTER, J.

Each of the two defendants appeals from a judgment against them in an action for personal injuries. Pursuant to stipulation the appeals have been consolidated.

Plaintiff's action was against both defendants for an injury to his right eye and face as the result of being struck by bird shot discharged from a shotgun. The case was tried by the court without a jury and the court found that . . . plaintiff and the two defendants were hunting quail on the open range. Each of the defendants was armed with a 12 gauge shotgun loaded with shells containing 7 ½ size shot. Prior to going hunting plaintiff discussed the hunting procedure with defendants, indicating that they were to exercise care when shooting and to "keep in line." In the course of hunting plaintiff proceeded up a hill, thus placing the hunters at the points of a triangle. The view of defendants with reference to plaintiff was unobstructed and they knew his location. Defendant Tice flushed a quail which rose in flight to a 10-foot elevation and flew between plaintiff and defendants. Both defendants shot at the quail, shooting in plaintiff's direction. At that time defendants were 75 yards from plaintiff. One shot struck plaintiff in his eye and another in his upper lip. Finally it was found by the court that as the direct result of the shooting by defendants the shots struck plaintiff as above mentioned and that defendants were negligent in so shooting and plaintiff was not contributorily negligent.

First, on the subject of negligence, defendant Simonson contends that the evidence is insufficient to sustain the finding on that score, but he does not point out wherein it is lacking. There is evidence that both defendants, at about the same time or one immediately after the other, shot at a quail and in so doing shot toward plaintiff who was uphill from them, and that they knew his location. That is sufficient from which the trial court could conclude that they acted with respect to plaintiff other than as persons of ordinary prudence. The issue was one of fact for the trial court.

The problem presented in this case is whether the judgment against both defendants may stand. It is argued by defendants that . . . there is not sufficient evidence to show which defendant was guilty of the negligence which caused the injuries — the shooting by Tice or that by Simonson.

[W]e believe it is clear that the court sufficiently found on the issue that defendants were jointly liable and that thus the negligence of both was the cause of the injury or to that legal effect. It found that both defendants were negligent and "That as a direct and proximate result of the shots fired by *defendants, and each of them*, a birdshot pellet was caused to and did lodge in plaintiff's right eye and that another birdshot pellet was caused to and did lodge in plaintiff's upper lip." In so doing the court evidently did not give credence to the admissions of Simonson to third persons that he fired the shots, which it was justified in doing. It thus determined that the negligence of both defendants was the legal cause of the injury—or that both were responsible. Implicit in such finding is the assumption that the court was unable to ascertain whether the shots were from the gun of one defendant or the other or one shot from each of them. The one shot that entered plaintiff's eye was the major factor in assessing damages and that shot could not have come from the gun of both defendants. It was from one or the other only.

It has been held that where a group of persons are on a hunting party, or otherwise engaged in the use of firearms, and two of them are negligent in firing in the direction of a third person who is injured thereby, both of those so firing are liable for the injury suffered by the third person, although the negligence of only one of them could have caused the injury. The same rule has been applied in criminal cases, and both drivers have been held liable for the negligence of one where they engaged in a racing contest causing an injury to a third person. These cases speak of the action of defendants as being in concert as the ground of decision, yet it would seem they are straining that concept and the more reasonable basis appears in *Oliver v. Miles, supra.* There two persons were hunting together. Both shot at some partridges and in so doing shot across the highway injuring plaintiff who was travelling on it. The court stated they were acting in concert and thus both were liable. The court then stated: "We think that . . . each is liable for the resulting injury to the boy, although no one can say definitely who actually shot him. *To hold otherwise would be to exonerate both from liability, although each was negligent, and the injury resulted from such negligence.*" Dean Wigmore has this to say: "When two or more persons by their acts are possibly the sole cause of a harm, or when two or more acts of the same person are possibly the sole cause, and the plaintiff has introduced evidence that the one of the two persons, or the one of the same person's two acts, is culpable, then the defendant has the burden of proving that the other person, or his other act, was the sole cause of the harm. . . . The real reason for the rule that each joint tortfeasor is responsible for the whole damage is the practical unfairness of denying the injured person redress simply because he cannot prove how much damage each did, when it is certain that between them they did all; let them be the ones to apportion it among themselves. Since, then, the difficulty of proof is the reason, the rule should apply whenever the harm has plural causes, and not merely when they acted in conscious concert. . . ." (Wigmore, Select Cases on the Law of Torts, §153.)

When we consider the relative position of the parties and the results that would flow if plaintiff was required to pin the injury on one of the defendants only, a requirement that the burden of proof on that subject be shifted to defendants becomes manifest. They are both wrongdoers—both negligent toward plaintiff. They brought about a situation where the negligence of one of them injured the plaintiff, hence it should rest with them each to absolve himself if he can. The injured party has been placed by defendants in the unfair position of pointing to which defendant caused the harm. If one can escape the other may also and plaintiff is remediless. Ordinarily defendants are in a far better position to offer evidence to determine which one caused the injury. This reasoning has recently found favor in this court.

In addition to that, however, it should be pointed out that the same reasons of policy and justice shift the burden to each of defendants to absolve himself if he can — relieving the wronged person of the duty of apportioning the injury to a particular defendant, apply here where we are concerned with whether plaintiff is required to supply evidence for the apportionment of damages. If defendants are independent tortfeasors and thus each liable for the damage caused by him alone, and, at least, where the matter of apportionment is incapable of proof, the innocent wronged party should not be deprived of his right to redress. The wrongdoers should be left to work out between themselves any apportionment.

The judgment is affirmed.

NOTES AND PROBLEMS

1. ***Nature of Problem.*** In the instance of multiple independent sufficient causes, there is a conceptual impossibility of proving but-for causation since neither of the tortfeasors' actions is essential. How is the but-for problem different with alternative liability, as set forth in *Summers*? In alternative liability scenarios, is there a but-for cause? If so, then why do courts not insist upon placing the ordinary burden of proving this element of the cause of action? Consider that we know for sure that one of the hunters shot the plaintiff in the eye. As to that defendant, but-for causation would be easy if we could identify the source of the shot that hit the eye. But this *evidentiary problem*, through no fault of the plaintiff, would insulate both defendants from liability. Absent this doctrine, how could the plaintiff prove causation by a preponderance of the evidence? As to either defendant, what are the statistical chances that the defendant was in fact the one who shot the plaintiff? Can you say that either hunter is *probably* responsible? If not, what becomes of the plaintiff's entire case?

2. ***Concert of Action Distinguished.*** In *Summers*, the court briefly considers (and rejects) an alternative way around the causation problem — utilization of the *concert of action* doctrine. This is the civil world's corollary to criminal law's conspiracy theory. We will explore that doctrine further in Chapter 9 Apportionment.

3. ***Problem.*** You may recall the case *Boy Scouts of America* from the section on consent to intentional torts. The plaintiff minor sued two other boys for shooting him in one eye with one paper clip, even though each of the boys had been playing the game separately. Assuming the plaintiff had not consented to the battery, would he have been able to demonstrate but-for causation against either of the other boys? Would the doctrine of alternative liability be applicable to assist?

BURKE v. SCHAFFNER

683 N.E.2d 861 (Ohio Ct. App. 1996)

TYACK, J.

On October 4, 1994, Gary Burke and his wife, Tammy Burke, filed a complaint in the Franklin County Court of Common Pleas, naming Kerri Schaffner as the lone defendant. The lawsuit arose as a result of serious injuries sustained by Gary Burke on October 26, 1993, when he was struck by a pickup truck driven by Martin Malone, with whom the Burkes settled prior to commencing litigation. The incident occurred during a party held for officers of the City of Columbus Division of Police, 8th Precinct.

There is no dispute between the parties that the pickup truck accelerated suddenly, causing Mr. Burke to be pinned between it and a parked car. The Burkes' complaint alleged that Ms. Schaffner, who was seated directly beside the driver, negligently stepped on the accelerator as she moved over on the front seat to make room for two other passengers getting into the truck.

Prior to trial, counsel for Ms. Schaffner filed a motion for summary judgment. Appended to the motion was an affidavit in which she stated, "at no time while I was in the vehicle did my foot hit the accelerator. . . ." In their memorandum contra, the Burkes relied upon deposition testimony of Mr. Malone, which included his denial of fault and resulting conclusion that Ms. Schaffner must have stepped on the accelerator. In a decision rendered August 24, 1995, the trial court denied the motion, holding that there existed a genuine issue of material fact as to who hit the accelerator.

The case proceeded to a trial by jury on March 11, 1996. Essentially, plaintiffs' theory, based in large part upon the testimony of Mr. Malone, was that Ms. Schaffner stepped on the accelerator. To the evident surprise of plaintiffs' counsel, the defense rested without calling any witnesses, including Ms. Schaffner herself. Plaintiffs' counsel unsuccessfully attempted to reopen their case or, alternatively, to call the defendant as a "rebuttal" witness.

On March 14, 1996, the jury returned a verdict in favor of Ms. Schaffner. The jury's response to an interrogatory submitted with the verdict forms indicated the jury's express finding that Ms. Schaffner was not negligent.

In their first assignment of error, appellants argue that the trial court erred in failing to grant their motion for a directed verdict. Specifically, appellants

In Practice

Given the evidentiary nature of the problem in an alternative liability scenario, the doctrine provides for an evidentiary response — it shifts the burden of proof to the defendants to negate but-for causation. If one of the defendants is successful in doing so, they have in effect solved the plaintiff's riddle. Persuasive exonerating proof as to one hunter in the woods provides evidentiary support for establishing but-for causation as to the other hunter. By contrast, the doctrine of multiple independent sufficient causes does not act to shift the burden of proof because that doctrine solves a conceptual problem with but-for causation. In this way, the nature of the problem defines the nature of the doctrinal remedy.

reason as follows. They "proved" that Ms. Schaffner was one of only two persons who could have negligently harmed Mr. Burke. The only other potentially responsible person, Martin Malone, called by appellants as a witness, testified that he did not step on the accelerator. Thus, since Ms. Schaffner failed to present any evidence to overcome her burden to demonstrate that she did not cause the harm, appellants should have been granted a directed verdict.

In addressing this specific contention, appellants necessarily incorporate issues pertaining to the doctrine of alternative liability, the subject of their second assignment of error. Thus, we address these arguments jointly.

Appellants' argument relies heavily upon the testimony of Martin Malone, who, as indicated above, unequivocally denied stepping on the accelerator. Appellants contend that the doctrine of alternative liability mandates a finding that since Ms. Schaffner did not testify or otherwise present evidence, she failed to satisfy her burden to prove that she was *not* negligent. Appellees counter, and the trial court so held, that the doctrine of alternative liability is not applicable to this case.

The doctrine of alternative liability was adopted by a narrow majority of the Supreme Court of Ohio in *Minnich v. Ashland Oil Co.* (1984), 473 N.E.2d 1199, at the syllabus:

> *Where the conduct of two or more actors is tortious*, and it is proved that harm has been caused to the plaintiff by only one of them, but there is uncertainty as to which one has caused it, the burden is upon each such actor to prove that he has not caused the harm. (2 *Restatement of the Law 2d, Torts, Section 433*[*B*][*3*], adopted.) (Emphasis added.)

In this case, the trial court found alternative liability (and thus, burden-shifting) to be inappropriate based upon a narrow interpretation of *Minnich*, limiting its application to cases involving multiple defendants, *each* of whom acted tortiously. The trial court rejected the doctrine based upon appellants' theory that *only one* of two persons stepped on the accelerator either the named defendant, Kerri Schaffner, or Martin Malone, the latter of whom denied fault.

Appellants acknowledge the current status of the doctrine in Ohio, citing pertinent case law; however, they construe the case law in a manner which broadens the scope of the doctrine to include situations involving a single negligent act committed by one potentially unidentifiable person, regardless of that person's status as a party or non-party. The trial court rejected this expansion of the doctrine.

We too reject such a broad interpretation. We agree with the holding of the trial court and find its reasoning to be sound. Plain language in *Minnich* lends support to this narrow interpretation:

> It should be emphasized that under this alternative liability theory, plaintiff must still prove: (1) that *two or more defendants committed tortious acts*, and (2) that plaintiff was injured as a proximate result of the wrongdoing of one of the

> defendants. Only then will the burden shift to the defendants to prove that they were not the cause of plaintiff's injuries. *This doctrine does not apply in cases where there is no proof that the conduct of more than one defendant has been tortious. Id. at 397.* (Emphasis added.)

See, also, Goldman v. Johns-Manville Sales Corp. (1987), 33 Ohio St. 3d 40, 514 N.E.2d 691.

The rationale for the doctrine of alternative liability, and the burden-shifting exception, is not applicable in circumstances where only one person has acted tortiously. The Supreme Court of Ohio has consistently reiterated the rationale justifying the seldom-employed burden-shifting:

> The reason for the exception is the unfairness of permitting tortfeasors to escape liability simply because the nature of their conduct and of the resulting injury has made it difficult or impossible to prove which of them caused the harm.

Huston v. Konieczny, 218, 556 N.E.2d 505 (Oh. 1990).

Ms. Schaffner argues, and the trial court agreed, that the doctrine further requires that the multiple negligent persons be named as defendants in the litigation; if all negligent actors are brought before the court, then the burden shifts to each of them to disprove causation. We agree. In *Huston*, the court was careful to note:

> In order for the burden of proof to shift from the plaintiffs, *all tortfeasors should be before the court, if possible.* See *Comment h to Section 433b(3)* ('The cases thus far decided in which the rule stated in Subsection has been applied all have been cases in which all of the actors involved have been joined as defendants.'); *Sindell v. Abbott Laboratories* (Cal. 1980), 607 P.2d 924, 930-93; *Summers v. Tice* (Cal. 1948), 199 P.2d 1.

52 Ohio St. 3d at 219. The Supreme Court of Ohio has continued to limit the application of alternative liability to "unique situations," all of which have required a plaintiff to satisfy a threshold burden of proving that "*all the defendants* acted tortiously." *Horton v. Harwick Chem. Corp.* (1995), 653 N.E.2d 1196 (Oh. 1995), citing Goldman, supra.

Only upon a plaintiff's showing that *each* of the multiple defendants acted tortiously should the causation burden shift to and among the *defendants*, who have *each* created a "substantially similar risk of harm." *Horton* at 688. That rationale simply does not apply to these facts, since appellants attempted to prove that a single tortfeasor, Ms. Schaffner, committed a single tortious act, to the exclusion of the only other potentially responsible person — Martin Malone, whom appellants did

In Practice

Knowing the right context, and the rationale, for tort doctrines is more than just good for law school exams. It helps lawyers avoid serious problems trying cases.

not sue and, in fact, attempted to exculpate during trial.

While case law on this issue is scant, research reveals that our holding is generally in accord with those courts that have addressed this particular question. In *Fiorella v. Ashland Oil, Inc.*, 635 N.E.2d 1306 (Oh. 1993), the Summit County Court of Appeals, construing *Minnich, supra*, held that the failure to join as defendants all potentially responsible tortfeasors precluded the application of alternative liability. The court cited cases from numerous other jurisdictions, applying and adopting the following reasoning:

> In *Vigiolto v. Johns-Manville Corp.* (W.D. Pa. 1986), 643 F. Supp. 1454, 1457, a federal district court rejected application of the alternative liability theory in a case where all the possible wrongdoers were not before the court, supplying its reasoning as follows:
>
> The *sine qua non* of *§433B(3)* liability [alternative liability] is proof that harm has been caused to plaintiff by *at least one* of the multiple [defendants] sued by the plaintiff. If plaintiff cannot prove who caused his injuries and does not name as defendants *all* who *possibly could have*, plaintiff has not proved that *at least one* of the named defendants caused the harm. The plaintiff must "name as defendants all who could have caused the complained of injury."

Fiorella at 416.

As Ms. Schaffner was the only defendant before the court, there was no other named defendant to whom the burden could or should have shifted. The trial court properly ruled that alternative liability was inappropriate under these circumstances and, thus, properly rejected the requested jury instruction. Further, since alternative liability was not applicable, the defendant had no burden to present evidence that she did not cause the harm. As a result, the trial court did not err in overruling appellants' motion for a directed verdict, since reasonable minds could differ in concluding who, if anyone, was negligent. *Judgment affirmed.*

NOTES AND PROBLEMS

1. *Prerequisites for Doctrine.* The court in *Burke* identifies several fundamental criteria for application of the alternative liability doctrine. These include that (a) there be more than one tortfeasor, (b) all tortfeasors are engaged in similar conduct, (c) plaintiff was injured as a result of the actions of one of the tortfeasors, and (d) plaintiff name all of the tortfeasors to the action. When this doctrine applies, it acts as a burden-shifting device, which presumes that all defendants caused the plaintiff's harm unless and until one of them proves otherwise. Given these requirements, what was wrong with plaintiff's attempt in *Burke* to rely upon the doctrine? Was the doctrine designed to fix the true problem that the plaintiff faced?

2. ***Knowing When to Apply Doctrines.*** Ultimately, the *Burke* case demonstrates the importance of understanding the theory behind tort doctrines to know when they actually apply. Alternative liability applies when the plaintiff can prove that the few defendants brought before the court are tortfeasors and that either of them could have been the actual cause, but that it is impossible to prove which one. In *Burke*, plaintiff failed to win because plaintiff could not prove that the defendant passenger had stepped on the accelerator. This is the proof necessary to show that the defendant committed an act of negligence. It was a breach failure of proof. Had the plaintiff demonstrated that the defendant had carelessly stepped on the accelerator, the plaintiff would not have had any problems proving causation. Viewed this way, the case shows a plaintiff attempting to fix a breach problem with a causation cure. In a larger sense, the lesson here is to know in what context, and for what reasons, particular tort doctrines apply. This will be enormously useful to you not only on your final exam but also in the practice of law. Ignorance as to the rationale behind the alternative liability rule, and when it applies, may have led the plaintiff's lawyer in *Burke* to rest plaintiff's case without calling the defendant as an adverse witness, on the assumption that the burden of proof had shifted to the defendant.

3. ***Problems.***

A. Could the plaintiff in *Burke* have relied upon the doctrine of *res ipsa loquitur* to recover against the defendant?

B. What if, in *Burke*, the plaintiff proved that both the driver and the defendant passenger had placed their feet on the accelerator at the same time? How might this impact the liability of the defendant?

C. Could the jury in *Burke* have properly found in favor of the plaintiff based upon the evidence that was submitted?

3. Modified Alternative Liability: Market Share

When a defective product hurts a plaintiff, proving actual causation might not be too complicated. But what if there are multiple unrelated manufacturers of the same identical product and the plaintiff cannot tell whose product was the source of the injury? In these instances, alternative liability might be unavailing for various reasons, including that the plaintiff might be unable to bring all of the manufacturers into court. Further, even if the plaintiff could locate and serve complaints on every potential source of the product, is it fair to apply alternative liability? After all, when there are only two tortfeasing hunters in the woods, the odds that either is the culprit are relatively high. When the plaintiff proves that both shot in his direction, there is a 50/50 chance as to either defendant that they were the actual cause. Application of a doctrine that makes both fully liable does not seem out of the question. But when there are hundreds of manufacturers of a defective, fungible product, is the half of one percent chance that Company X is the source of the product that caused the harm a sufficiently fair basis to make them liable for 100 percent of the plaintiff's damages? In such instances, where a prevailing doctrine does not quite fit, courts will sometimes create a new doctrinal fix for the problem. The *Sindell* case below is an example of just such a phenomenon. Pay careful attention to why existing tort theories could not help the plaintiff prove actual causation and how the new doctrine — *modified alternative liability* (or *market share liability*) — is uniquely shaped to seek justice that would otherwise be unavailing.

SINDEL v. ABBOTT LABORATORIES

607 P.2d 924 (Cal. 1980)

Mosk, J.

This case involves a complex problem both timely and significant: may a plaintiff, injured as the result of a drug administered to her mother during pregnancy, who knows the type of drug involved but cannot identify the manufacturer of the precise product, hold liable for her injuries a maker of a drug produced from an identical formula?

Plaintiff Judith Sindell brought an action against eleven drug companies and Does 1 through 100, on behalf of herself and other women similarly situated.

[In her complaint, Sindell alleged that the defendants manufactured, marketed, and sold a synthetic compound of the female hormone estrogen called "DES" from 1941 until 1971. There were hundreds of manufacturers who sold the identical formulation of DES during this time period. The FDA approved DES as a miscarriage preventative but only on an experimental basis with a requirement for certain warnings to that effect. In 1971, the FDA ordered all manufacturers to discontinue marketing and selling the product for preventing miscarriages and to warn physicians and the public of its ill effects. The FDA had determined that DES caused the female offspring of mothers who ingested the drug to suffer certain forms of cervical and vaginal cancer, often one or two decades after their birth. Plaintiff named ten specific manufacturers and alleged that other John Doe companies marketed the DES even though they knew or should have known that it was a carcinogenic substance. She also alleged that they failed to adequately test the drug and failed to comply with FDA restrictions regarding DES. Plaintiff alleges that she, and other similarly situated women, were exposed to DES before their birth, but failed to have any reason to suspect any ill effects from their exposure until many years later. Plaintiff brought this suit within one year of discovering that her illness was possibly linked to DES consumption by her mother. Plaintiff suffered a malignant bladder tumor which had to be surgically removed. She now requires regular medical monitoring for a possible recurrence.]

DES was produced from a common and mutually agreed upon formula as a fungible drug interchangeable with other brands of the same product; [Plaintiff alleges] defendants knew or should have known that it was customary for doctors to prescribe the drug by its generic rather than its brand name and that pharmacists filled prescriptions from whatever brand of the drug happened to be in stock.

[Defendants obtained dismissal of the plaintiff's complaint on the grounds that the plaintiff could not prove causation due to her inability to identify which manufacturer provided the DES ingested by the plaintiff's mother. Plaintiff appeals from this dismissal.]

This case is but one of a number filed throughout the country seeking to hold drug manufacturers liable for injuries allegedly resulting from DES prescribed to the plaintiffs' mothers since 1947. According to a note in the Fordham Law Review, estimates of the number of women who took the drug during pregnancy range from 1 ½ million to 3 million. Hundreds, perhaps thousands, of the daughters of these women suffer from adenocarcinoma, and the incidence of vaginal adenosis among them is 30 to 90 percent. Most of the cases are still pending. With two exceptions, those that have been decided resulted in judgments in favor of the drug company defendants because of the failure of the plaintiffs to identify the manufacturer of the DES prescribed to their mothers. The present action is another attempt to overcome this obstacle to recovery.

We begin with the proposition that, as a general rule, the imposition of liability depends upon a showing by the plaintiff that his or her injuries were caused by the act of the defendant or by an instrumentality under the defendant's control. The rule applies whether the injury resulted from an accidental event or from the use of a defective product.

There are, however, exceptions to this rule. Plaintiff's complaint suggests several bases upon which defendants may be held liable for her injuries even though she cannot demonstrate the name of the manufacturer which produced the DES actually taken by her mother. The first of these theories, classically illustrated by *Summers v. Tice*, places the burden of proof of causation upon tortious defendants in certain circumstances. The second basis of liability emerging from the complaint is that defendants acted in concert to cause injury to plaintiff. . . . We shall conclude that these doctrines, as previously interpreted, may not be applied to hold defendants liable under the allegations of this complaint. However, we shall propose and adopt a [different] basis for permitting the action to be tried, grounded upon an extension of the *Summers* doctrine.

Plaintiff places primary reliance upon cases which hold that if a party cannot identify which of two or more defendants caused an injury, the burden of proof may shift to the defendants to show that they were not responsible for the harm. This principle is sometimes referred to as the "alternative liability" theory.

The celebrated case of *Summers v. Tice, supra*, 33 Cal. 2d 80, a unanimous opinion of this court, best exemplifies the rule. In *Summers*, the plaintiff was injured when two hunters negligently shot in his direction. It could not be determined which of them had fired the shot that actually caused the injury to the plaintiff's eye, but both defendants were nevertheless held jointly and severally liable for the whole of the damages. We reasoned that both were wrongdoers, both were negligent toward the plaintiff, and that it would be unfair to require plaintiff to isolate the defendant responsible, because if the one pointed out were to escape liability, the other might also, and the plaintiff-victim would be shorn of any remedy. In these circumstances, we held, the burden of proof shifted to the defendants, "each to absolve himself if he can." We stated that under these or similar circumstances a defendant is ordinarily in a "far better position" to offer evidence to determine whether he or another defendant caused the injury. . . .

Defendants assert that these principles are inapplicable here. First, they insist that a predicate to shifting the burden of proof under *Summers* is that the defendants must have greater access to information regarding the cause of the injuries than the plaintiff, whereas in the present case the reverse appears.

Plaintiff does not claim that defendants are in a better position than she to identify the manufacturer of the drug taken by her mother or, indeed, that they have the ability to do so at all, but argues, rather, that *Summers* does not impose such a requirement as a condition to the shifting of the burden of proof. In this respect we believe plaintiff is correct.

In *Summers*, the circumstances of the accident themselves precluded an explanation of its cause. To be sure, *Summers* states that defendants are "[ordinarily] . . . in a far better position to offer evidence to determine which one caused the injury" than a plaintiff, but the decision does not determine that this "ordinary" situation was present. Neither the facts nor the language of the opinion indicate that the two defendants, simultaneously shooting in the same direction, were in a better position than the plaintiff to ascertain whose shot caused the injury. As the opinion acknowledges, it was impossible for the trial court to determine whether the shot which entered the plaintiff's eye came from the gun of one defendant or the other. Nevertheless, burden of proof was shifted to the defendants.

Here, as in *Summers*, the circumstances of the injury appear to render identification of the manufacturer of the drug ingested by plaintiff's mother impossible by either plaintiff or defendants, and it cannot reasonably be said that one is in a better position than the other to make the identification. Because many years elapsed between the time the drug was taken and the manifestation of plaintiff's injuries she, and many other daughters of mothers who took DES, are unable to make such identification. Certainly there can be no implication that plaintiff is at fault in failing to do so — the event occurred while plaintiff was *in utero*, a generation ago.

On the other hand, it cannot be said with assurance that defendants have the means to make the identification. In this connection, they point out that drug manufacturers ordinarily have no direct contact with the patients who take a drug prescribed by their doctors. Defendants sell to wholesalers, who in turn supply the product to physicians and pharmacies. Manufacturers do not maintain records of the persons who take the drugs they produce, and the selection of the medication is made by the physician rather than the manufacturer. Nor do we conclude that the absence of evidence on this subject is due to the fault of defendants. While it is alleged that they produced a defective product with delayed effects and without adequate warnings, the difficulty or impossibility of identification results primarily from the passage of time rather than from their allegedly negligent acts of failing to provide adequate warnings.

It is important to observe, however, that while defendants do not have means superior to plaintiff to identify the maker of the precise drug taken by her mother, they may in some instances be able to prove that they did not manufacture the injury-causing substance. In the present case, for example, one of the original defendants was dismissed from the action upon proof that it did not manufacture DES until after plaintiff was born.

Thus we conclude the fact defendants do not have greater access to information that might establish the identity of the manufacturer of the DES which injured plaintiff does not per se prevent application of the *Summers* rule.

Nevertheless, plaintiff may not prevail in her claim that the *Summers* rationale should be employed to fix the whole liability for her injuries upon defendants, at least as those principles have previously been applied. There is an important difference between the situation involved in *Summers* and the present case. There, all the parties who were or could have been responsible for the harm to the plaintiff were joined as defendants. Here, by contrast, there are approximately 200 drug companies which made DES, any of which might have manufactured the injury-producing drug.

Defendants maintain that, while in *Summers* there was a 50 percent chance that one of the two defendants was responsible for the plaintiff's injuries, here since any one of 200 companies which manufactured DES might have made the product that harmed plaintiff, there is no rational basis upon which to infer that any defendant in this action caused plaintiff's injuries, nor even a reasonable possibility that they were responsible.

These arguments are persuasive if we measure the chance that any one of the defendants supplied the injury-causing drug by the number of possible tortfeasors. In such a context, the possibility that any of the five defendants supplied the DES to plaintiff's mother is so remote that it would be unfair to require each defendant to exonerate itself. There may be a substantial likelihood that none of the five defendants joined in the action made the DES which caused the injury, and that the offending producer not named would escape liability altogether. While we propose, *infra*, an adaptation of the rule in *Summers* which will substantially overcome these difficulties, defendants appear to be correct that the rule, as previously applied, cannot relieve plaintiff of the burden of proving the identity of the manufacturer which made the drug causing her injuries.

The second principle upon which plaintiff relies is the so-called "concert of action" theory. . . . With respect to this doctrine, Prosser states that "those who, in pursuance of a common plan or design to commit a tortious act, actively take part in it, or further it by cooperation or request, or who lend aid or encouragement to the wrongdoer, or ratify and adopt his acts done for their benefit, are equally liable with him. Express agreement is not necessary, and all that is required is that there be a tacit understanding. . . ." (Prosser, Law of Torts (4th ed. 1971) §46, p. 292.)

In our view, [Plaintiff's] litany of charges is insufficient to allege a cause of action under the rules stated above. The gravamen of the charge of concert is that defendants failed to adequately test the drug or to give sufficient warning of its dangers and that they relied upon the tests performed by one another and took advantage of each others' promotional and marketing techniques. These allegations do not amount to a charge that there was a tacit understanding or a common plan among defendants to fail to conduct adequate tests or give sufficient warnings, and that they substantially aided and encouraged one another in these omissions.

The complaint charges also that defendants produced DES from a "common and mutually agreed upon formula," allowing pharmacists to treat the drug as a "fungible commodity" and to fill prescriptions from whatever brand of DES they had on hand at the time. It is difficult to understand how these allegations can form the basis of a cause of action for wrongful conduct by defendants, acting in concert. The formula for DES is a scientific constant. It is set forth in the United States Pharmacopoeia, and any manufacturer producing that drug must, with exceptions not relevant here, utilize the formula set forth in that compendium.

What the complaint appears to charge is defendants' parallel or imitative conduct in that they relied upon each others' testing and promotion methods. But such conduct describes a common practice in industry: a producer avails himself of the experience and methods of others making the same or similar products. Application of the concept of concert of action to this situation would expand the doctrine far beyond its intended scope and would render virtually any manufacturer liable for the defective products of an entire industry, even if it could be demonstrated that the product which caused the injury was not made by the defendant.

There is no allegation here that each defendant knew the other defendants' conduct was tortious toward plaintiff, and that they assisted and encouraged one another to inadequately test DES and to provide inadequate warnings. Indeed, it seems dubious whether liability on the concert of action theory can be predicated upon substantial assistance and encouragement given by one alleged tortfeasor to another pursuant to a tacit understanding to fail to perform an act. Thus, there was no concert of action among defendants within the meaning of that doctrine.

If we were confined to the [theory of *Summers*], we would be constrained to hold that the judgment must be sustained. Should we require that plaintiff identify the manufacturer which supplied the DES used by her mother or that all DES manufacturers be joined in the action, she would effectively be precluded from any recovery. As defendants candidly admit, there is little likelihood that all the manufacturers who made DES at the time in question are still in business or that they are subject to the jurisdiction of the California courts. There are, however, forceful arguments in favor of holding that plaintiff has a cause of action.

In our contemporary complex industrialized society, advances in science and technology create fungible goods which may harm consumers and which cannot be traced to any specific producer. The response of the courts can be either to adhere rigidly to prior doctrine, denying recovery to those injured by such products, or to fashion remedies to meet these changing needs.

The most persuasive reason for finding plaintiff states a cause of action is that advanced in *Summers*: as between an innocent plaintiff and negligent defendants, the latter should bear the cost of the injury. Here, as in *Summers*, plaintiff is not at fault in failing to provide evidence of causation, and although the absence of such evidence is not attributable to the defendants either, their conduct in marketing a drug the effects of which are delayed for many years played a significant role in creating the unavailability of proof.

Where, as here, all defendants produced a drug from an identical formula and the manufacturer of the DES which caused plaintiff's injuries cannot be identified through no fault of plaintiff, a modification of the rule of *Summers* is warranted. As we have seen, an undiluted *Summers* rationale is inappropriate to shift the burden of proof of causation to defendants because if we measure the chance that any particular manufacturer supplied the injury-causing product by the number of producers of DES, there is a possibility that none of the five defendants in this case produced the offending substance and that the responsible manufacturer, not named in the action, will escape liability.

But we approach the issue of causation from a different perspective: we hold it to be reasonable in the present context to measure the likelihood that any of the defendants supplied the product which allegedly injured plaintiff by the percentage which the DES sold by each of them for the purpose of preventing miscarriage bears to the entire production of the drug sold by all for that purpose. Plaintiff asserts in her briefs that Eli Lilly and Company and five or six other companies produced 90 percent of the DES marketed. If at trial this is established to be the fact, then there is a corresponding likelihood that this comparative handful of producers manufactured the DES which caused plaintiff's injuries, and only a 10 percent likelihood that the offending producer would escape liability.

If plaintiff joins in the action the manufacturers of a substantial share of the DES which her mother might have taken, the injustice of shifting the burden of proof to defendants to demonstrate that they could not have made the substance which injured plaintiff is significantly diminished. While 75 to 80 percent of the market [has been suggested by some proponents of this new theory of liability] we hold only that a substantial percentage is required.

The presence in the action of a substantial share of the appropriate market also provides a ready means to apportion damages among the defendants. Each defendant will be held liable for the proportion of the judgment represented by its share of that market unless it demonstrates that it could not have made the product which caused plaintiff's injuries. In the present case, as we have seen, one DES manufacturer was dismissed from the action upon filing a declaration that it had not manufactured DES until after plaintiff was born. Once plaintiff has met her burden of joining the required defendants, they in turn may cross-complain against other DES manufacturers, not joined in the action, which they can allege might have supplied the injury-causing product.

Under this approach, each manufacturer's liability would approximate its responsibility for the injuries caused by its own products. It is probably impossible, with the passage of time, to determine market share with mathematical exactitude. But . . . the difficulty of apportioning damages among the defendant producers in exact relation to their market share does not seriously militate against the rule we adopt. As we said in *Summers* with regard to the liability of independent tortfeasors, where a correct division of liability cannot be made "the trier of fact may make it the best it can." (33 Cal. 2d at p. 88.)

We are not unmindful of the practical problems involved in defining the market and determining market share, but these are largely matters of proof which properly cannot be determined at the pleading stage of these proceedings. Defendants urge that it would be both unfair and contrary to public policy to hold them liable for plaintiff's injuries in the absence of proof that one of them supplied the drug responsible for the damage. Most of their arguments, however, are based upon the assumption that one manufacturer would be held responsible for the products of another or for those of all other manufacturers if plaintiff ultimately prevails. But under the rule we adopt, each manufacturer's liability for an injury would be approximately equivalent to the damage caused by the DES it manufactured.

NOTES AND PROBLEMS

1. ***Modifications to Alternative Liability.*** What prerequisites for application of the doctrine of alternative liability were missing in *Sindell*? The court alludes to several failings. For one thing, not all of the potential sources of the defective product were before the court. Remember that alternative liability operates to shift the burden of proof to the defendants to come forward with evidence negating causation as to them. In the absence of such proof, all tortfeasing defendants are liable. Alternative liability's operation does not work without all sources present in the courtroom. Second, there are simply too many potential sources of the problem to make application of the doctrine fair to any one defendant. Given these shortcomings, the California Supreme Court opined that the application of that doctrine to fix the but-for causation problem of the plaintiffs would be unfair. Ultimately the court adopts a variation of alternative liability, often called *market share liability*. How is this different from alternative liability, in terms of its prerequisites and its effects on any defendant's liability?

This can be answered by reference to the problems mentioned above with regard to applying alternative liability. For one thing, the court loosens the burden of bringing all tortfeasors before the court. If the plaintiff instead brings before the court defendants constituting a substantial share of the market for the product, this will be considered sufficient. At least in this instance there is a probability that the correct manufacturer is present. Second, each defendant (that fails to exonerate itself as a cause) is liable only for its percentage share of the market of the product. If a defendant sold 5 percent of the product in the relevant market at the relevant period of time, it would only be liable for 5 percent of the plaintiff's compensatory damages.

2. ***Statutes of Limitations.*** Plaintiffs in these DES cases, which were filed in abundance after the FDA's actions in 1971, typically faced significant hurdles both in terms of proving causation — due to their inability to identify the manufacturer of the pills taken by their mothers — and in terms of justifying the late filing of their claims under applicable statutes of limitations. In some states the legislature passed new laws expressly granting DES claimants additional time to pursue their litigation. While many states have now adopted modified alternative liability, in appropriate cases involving fungible goods where product identification is difficult, other states have refused to do so.

3. ***Concert of Action.*** The court also dispenses with plaintiff's additional argument that but-for causation need not be proven because all of the manufacturers were acting in unison or in concert with one another. Had that theory been applicable to the facts, the court would have treated the defendants as one and this would have mooted the product identification problem. Unfortunately, parallel conduct does not prove two manufacturers are acting in any joint fashion. Concert of action theory is dealt with later in this book in Chapter 9 under the topic of Apportionment.

4. Increased Risk of Future Harm

Another causation riddle occurs when the plaintiff has been either exposed to some toxic substance, or received some inadequate medical treatment, and this results in the plaintiff being at risk for some *future* harm. The statute of limitations may compel the plaintiff to bring suit today for a possible injury tomorrow. Further, the civil procedure doctrine of *res judicata* demands that in any suit a plaintiff seek recovery for all past, present, and future damages at once. But what if the plaintiff is less than 50 percent likely to actually experience the anticipated future ill effects of the exposure or treatment? Will the court stick with the traditional demand for proving causation by a preponderance of the evidence, and only permit recovery for likely future effects, or will the court permit the plaintiff to recover on some other novel theory? The case that follows shows one plaintiff's effort to suggest a pathway around this causation problem.

TEMPLE-INLAND PRODUCTS CORP. v. CARTER

993 S.W.2d 88 (Tex. 1999)

HECHT, J.

The sole issue in this case is whether a person who has been exposed to asbestos but does not have an asbestos-related disease may recover damages for fear of the possibility of developing such a disease in the future. The district court granted summary judgment for the defendant on plaintiff's claims for actual and punitive damages. A divided court of appeals reversed only on the actual damages claim. For reasons we explain, the district court was correct.

Temple-Inland Forest Products Corporation employed Biskamp Electric to install electric outlets and computer jacks in a laboratory at one of its paper mills. In performing the installation, two Biskamp employees, Martin Reeves Carter Sr. and Larry Wilson, drilled holes in laboratory countertops, which they did not know and were not told contained asbestos. The drilling generated dust containing asbestos fibers to which Carter and Wilson were exposed. They had no protective gear to prevent them from inhaling the dust. Carter worked on the project from four to six weeks, and Wilson worked on it about two weeks. Not until the work was almost complete did the laboratory manager warn Carter and Wilson of the asbestos, at which point they stopped work on the project. Temple-Inland then tested and decontaminated the lab.

Some eighteen months later Carter and Wilson were examined by Dr. Daniel Jenkins, to whom they had been referred by their attorney. Although Dr. Jenkins concluded that neither Carter nor Wilson had any asbestos-related disease, they sued Temple-Inland for mental anguish damages caused by its having negligently exposed them to asbestos fibers.

Dr. Jenkins testified at his deposition that . . . Wilson and Carter suffered from no disease as a result of their exposure to asbestos. . . . Dr. Jenkins, however, insisted that Wilson and Carter had been injured by their exposure to asbestos and probable inhalation of asbestos fibers at the Temple-Inland lab. He estimated that the chances of their developing a disease as a result had increased from one in a million, which he estimated to be the risk that a person would ever develop a disease from asbestos exposure not occupationally related, to about one in 500,000 for the next ten or fifteen years, and as much as one in 100 over twenty or thirty years. Dr. Jenkins characterized plaintiffs' risk as a "high possibility" but not a probability.

Based on the depositions of Dr. Jenkins, Carter, Wilson, and others, Temple-Inland moved for summary judgment on the ground that Carter and Wilson had not suffered any injury for which they could recover mental anguish damages. Temple-Inland argued that plaintiffs' claims for fear of the mere possibility of developing some disease in the future amounted to nothing more than negligent infliction of emotional distress for which they could not recover under this Court's decision in *Boyles v. Kerr* [p. 356]. Plaintiffs responded that their inhalation of asbestos fibers was a real, physical injury which could eventually lead to disease, and that they were entitled to be compensated for their anxiety over that eventuality.

The trial court granted summary judgment. The court of appeals . . . reversed the judgment on plaintiffs' actual damage claims. Relying principally on [on some recent federal courts' opinions] the court concluded that "it is well established a plaintiff may recover for mental anguish based upon fear of cancer even though the evidence shows the plaintiff does not have, and in reasonable medical probability, will not have cancer, so long as there has been exposure to the causative agent and the fear is reasonable."

We granted Temple-Inland's application for writ of error and now reverse the court of appeals' judgment insofar as it reversed the district court's judgment.

The summary judgment record establishes that Carter and Wilson were exposed to asbestos at Temple-Inland's lab but do not presently suffer from any asbestos-related disease, and that while their risk of developing such a disease was increased by their exposure to asbestos, that risk is still no higher than one chance in a hundred over twenty to thirty years. The issue is whether they can recover for their fear that they will someday develop such a disease from their work at Temple-Inland's lab.

Carter and Wilson first argue that they are entitled to recover mental anguish damages even if they sustained no physical injury, as long as their fear of developing some asbestos-related disease is reasonable. This argument conflicts with our decision in *Boyles v. Kerr*, where we held that "there is no general duty not to negligently inflict emotional distress." As we later explained in *City of Tyler v. Likes*, "it has been established for over a century that '[a] person who is placed in peril by the negligence of another, but who escapes without injury, may not recover damages simply because he has been placed in a perilous position. . . .'"

Carter and Wilson argue that they have been physically injured because of their exposure to asbestos fibers. Carter's and Wilson's testimony, as well as that of Dr. Jenkins, supports the inference that they inhaled asbestos fibers in the lab, and Temple-Inland has not refuted this inference. . . . The question comes to this: given that plaintiffs inhaled asbestos fibers, can they recover mental anguish damages for their increased risk and reasonable fear of possibly developing asbestos-related diseases that they do not currently have and may never have?

While the existence of physical injury is ordinarily *necessary* for recovery of mental anguish damages . . . , such injury may not be *sufficient* for recovery of mental anguish damages when the injury has not produced disease, despite a reasonable fear that such disease will develop. . . . [L]ike the Supreme Court and courts in most other jurisdictions, we cannot permit recovery of mental anguish damages in cases like this one. In almost all instances involving personal injury, the law allows for the recovery of accompanying mental anguish damages, even if the mental anguish is not itself physically manifested. But if bodily injury is at most latent and any eventual consequences uncertain, as when a person's exposure to asbestos has not produced disease, then the case for recovery of mental anguish damages is much weaker. A person exposed to asbestos can certainly develop serious health problems, but he or she also may not. The difficulty in predicting whether exposure will cause any disease and if so, what disease, and the long latency period characteristic of asbestos-related diseases, make it very difficult for judges and juries to evaluate which exposure claims are serious and which are not. This difficulty in turn makes liability unpredictable, with some claims resulting in significant recovery while virtually indistinguishable claims are denied altogether. Some claimants would inevitably be overcompensated when, in the course of time, it happens that they never develop the disease they feared, and others would be undercompensated when it turns out that they developed a disease more serious even than they feared. Also, claims for exposure could proliferate because in our society, as the Supreme Court observed, "contacts, even extensive contacts, with serious carcinogens are common." Indeed, most Americans are daily subjected to toxic substances in the air they breathe and the food they eat. Suits for mental anguish damages caused by exposure that has not resulted in disease would compete with suits for manifest diseases for the legal system's limited resources. If recovery were allowed in the absence of present disease, individuals might feel obliged to bring suit for such recovery prophylactically, against the possibility of future consequences from what is now an inchoate risk. This would exacerbate not only the multiplicity of suits but the unpredictability of results.

The question is not, of course, whether Carter and Wilson have themselves suffered genuine distress over their own exposure. We assume they have, and that their anxiety is reasonable. The question, rather, is whether this *type* of claim — for fear of an increased risk of developing an asbestos-related disease when no disease is presently manifest — should be permitted, regardless of any individual plaintiff's circumstances, when the effort in determining the genuineness of each claim and assuring appropriate recovery is beset with the difficulties we have described. We conclude that no such action should be recognized.

NOTES AND PROBLEMS

1. ***Increased Risk as a But-For Problem.*** The plaintiffs alleged that their exposure to asbestos placed them at an increased risk of future medical illness even though they had no present condition. Taking into account the normal burden of proof in a civil case — proving each element by a preponderance of the evidence — how does this case demonstrate a but-for causation problem? Note that this problem does not exist with regard to all cases of future harms. When a motorist's leg is mutilated in a car accident, it may be very likely that she will suffer future pain and suffering the rest of her life. So long as the future damages are likely (more than 50% chance) to occur, she can recover those damages in her trial. The plaintiffs in the foregoing case could not prove the

likelihood of such future injury. How does their redefining the injury — from cancer to the fear of cancer — attempt to circumvent the normal proof of causation? The majority of other courts to address the unlikely prospect of future harm similarly reject such claims. For example, in Potter v. Firestone Tire & Rubber Co., 863 P.2d 795 (Cal. 1993), the plaintiffs complained of the defendant dumping toxic industrial waste nearby and increasing the plaintiffs' risk of cancer. Because the plaintiffs could not prove that they probably would suffer such harm from the exposure, the California Supreme Court rejected their claims:

> We cannot say that it would never be reasonable for a person who has ingested toxic substances to harbor a genuine and serious fear of cancer where reliable medical or scientific opinion indicates that such ingestion has significantly increased his or her risk of cancer, but not to a probable likelihood. Nonetheless, we conclude, for . . . public policy reasons . . . that emotional distress caused by the fear of a cancer that is not probable should generally not be compensable in a negligence action. 863 P.2d at 811.

2. ***Alternative No-Duty Rationale.*** In *Temple-Inland,* the court holds the plaintiffs to the normal rules of proving but-for causation by a preponderance of the evidence. This is the same requirement that would be applied to any future damages — lost future wages arising from a present injury, for example. With regard to the plaintiffs' attempt to evade this causation rule by re-casting the damage as one for fear, rather than for cancer, the court also cites another legal proposition — that there is no legal duty to exercise care in preventing others from experiencing emotional distress. This no-duty rule is covered in Chapter 6, Special Duty Rules when we revisit the duty element of a negligence claim.

3. ***Minority Rule.*** Departing from the majority of courts, which refuse to recognize recovery for a future medical problem that is unlikely to occur, a minority of courts will recognize a right to recover. The amount of recovery in such instances is calculated by taking the total amount of damages, if they were to occur, and multiplying this dollar amount by the present percentage chance of ever experiencing such harm. In *Temple-Inland,* the Texas Supreme Court suggests that this alternative will always result in either overcompensating plaintiffs or undercompensating plaintiffs, but will never achieve the right level of justice. How is this true?

4. ***Problem.*** A plaintiff underwent surgery that was not done correctly. As a consequence of this malpractice, the plaintiff had to undergo a second surgical procedure to attempt to correct the first mistake. Plaintiff learned that, as a result of having to undergo the second procedure, he was placed at risk of an 8 to 16 percent chance of having a bowel obstruction in the future. To what extent can this plaintiff demonstrate but-for causation of any harm under the traditional proof requirements?

5. *Loss of Chance*

In a related circumstance unique to medical malpractice claims, courts have been even more sympathetic with the plight of plaintiffs who have suffered harm and accused the medical doctor of wrongfully denying them a chance for a cure. The *loss of chance* doctrine is applied by a majority of courts to permit a medical malpractice plaintiff to recover against a doctor who has failed to make a timely diagnosis or to treat an existing physical condition. The causation problem arises in cases where even the timely treatment of the condition would likely not change the bad outcome. For example, if a deadly cancer can only be cured 5 percent of the time, even with proper diagnosis and care, has the plaintiff been injured when the doctor's negligence deprives the plaintiff of the attempted cure? In the following case, the court adopts the majority rule of *loss of chance* to help provide some recovery in this instance. As you read this, consider why the majority of courts are more sympathetic with the plaintiff's plight in this scenario than in the related circumstance in the preceding section.

LORD v. LOVETT

770 A.2d 1103 (N.H. 2001)

NADEAU, J.

The plaintiff, Belinda Joyce Lord, appeals the Superior Court's dismissal of her "loss of opportunity" action against the defendants, James Lovett, M.D., and Samuel Aldridge, M.D. We reverse and remand.

The plaintiff suffered a broken neck in an automobile accident on July 22, 1996, and was treated at the Lakes Region General Hospital by the defendants. She contends that because the defendants negligently misdiagnosed her spinal cord injury, they failed both to immobilize her properly and to administer steroid therapy, causing her to lose the opportunity for a substantially better recovery. She alleges that she continues to suffer significant residual paralysis, weakness and sensitivity.

Upon learning that the defendants intended to move to dismiss at the close of the plaintiff's case, the trial court permitted the plaintiff to make a pre-trial offer of proof. She proffered that her expert would testify that the defendants' negligence deprived her of the opportunity for a substantially better recovery. She conceded, however, that her expert could not quantify the degree to which she was deprived of a better recovery by their negligence.

Following the plaintiff's offer of proof, the defendants moved to dismiss on two grounds: (1) New Hampshire law does not recognize the loss of opportunity theory of recovery; and (2) the plaintiff failed to set forth sufficient evidence of causation. The trial court dismissed the plaintiff's action on the basis that her case is "clearly predicated on loss of . . . opportunity" and that "there's no such theory permitted in this State." This appeal followed.

The loss of opportunity doctrine, in its many forms, is a medical malpractice form of recovery which allows a plaintiff, whose preexisting injury or illness is aggravated by the alleged negligence of a physician or health care worker, to recover for her lost opportunity to obtain a better degree of recovery. Generally, courts have taken three approaches to loss of opportunity claims.

The first approach, the traditional tort approach, is followed by a minority of courts. According to this approach, a plaintiff must prove that as a result of the defendant's negligence, the plaintiff was deprived of at least a fifty-one percent chance of a more favorable outcome than she actually received. Once the plaintiff meets this burden, she may recover damages for the entire preexisting illness or condition.

Under this approach, a patient whose injury is negligently misdiagnosed, but who would have had only a fifty percent chance of full recovery from her condition with proper diagnosis, could not recover damages because she would be unable to prove that, absent the physician's negligence, her chance of a better recovery was at least fifty-one percent. If, however, the patient could establish the necessary causal link by establishing that absent the negligence she would have had at least a fifty-one percent chance of a better outcome, not only would the patient be entitled to recover, but she would be awarded damages for her entire injury. This approach has been criticized as yielding an "all or nothing" result.

The second approach, a variation of the traditional approach, relaxes the standard of proof of causation. The causation requirement is relaxed by permitting plaintiffs to submit their cases to the jury upon demonstrating that a defendant's negligence more likely than not "increased the harm" to the plaintiff or "destroyed a substantial possibility" of achieving a more favorable outcome.

Under this approach, the patient would not be precluded from recovering simply because her chance of a better recovery was less than fifty-one percent, so long as she could prove that the defendant's negligence increased her harm to some degree. The precise degree required varies by jurisdiction. Some courts require that the defendant's negligence increase the plaintiff's harm by any degree, while other courts require that the increase be substantial. As in the traditional approach, once the plaintiff meets her burden, she recovers damages for the entire underlying preexisting condition or illness rather than simply the loss of opportunity. This approach "represents the worst of both worlds [because it] continues the arbitrariness of the all-or-nothing rule, but by relaxing the proof requirements, it increases the likelihood that a plaintiff will be able to convince a jury to award full damages." King, *"Reduction of Likelihood" Reformulation*, 28 U. Mem. L. Rev. 491 (1998).

Under the third approach, the lost opportunity for a better outcome is, itself, the injury for which the negligently injured person may recover. As with the second approach, a plaintiff may prevail even if her chances of a better recovery are less than fifty-one percent. The plaintiff, however, does not receive damages for the *entire* injury, but just for the lost opportunity.

In other words, if the plaintiff can establish the causal link between the defendant's negligence and the lost opportunity, the plaintiff may recover that portion of damages actually attributable to the defendant's negligence.

Under this approach, "by defining the injury as the loss of chance . . . , the traditional rule of preponderance is fully satisfied." *Perez v. Las Vegas Medical Center*, 805 P.2d 589, 592 (Nev. 1991).

We agree with the majority of courts rejecting the traditional "all-or-nothing" approach to loss of opportunity cases, and find the third approach most sound. *See Delaney*, 873 P.2d at 184-86; *Perez*, 805 P.2d at 591-93. The third approach permits plaintiffs to recover for the loss of an opportunity for a better outcome, an interest that we agree should be compensable, while providing for the proper valuation of such an interest.

> The loss of a chance of achieving a favorable outcome or of avoiding an adverse consequence should be compensable and should be valued appropriately, rather than treated as an all-or-nothing proposition. Preexisting conditions must, of course, be taken into account in valuing the interest destroyed. When those preexisting conditions have not absolutely preordained an adverse outcome, however, the chance of avoiding it should be appropriately compensated even if that chance is not better than even.

King, *Causation, Valuation, and Chance in Personal Injury Torts Involving Preexisting Conditions and Future Consequences*, 90 Yale L.J. 1353, 1354 (1981).

Accordingly, we hold that a plaintiff may recover for a loss of opportunity injury in medical malpractice cases when the defendant's alleged negligence aggravates the plaintiff's preexisting injury such that it deprives the plaintiff of a *substantially* better outcome. *See Delaney*, 873 P.2d at 178, 185-86; *see also Perez*, 805 P.2d at 592.

The defendants imply that the loss of opportunity doctrine is contrary to the burden of proof requirements described in *RSA 507-E:2* (1997). Specifically, the defendants argue that the loss of opportunity doctrine permits recovery based on the "possibility" that the defendant caused the plaintiff's injury, whereas *RSA 507-E:2* requires the plaintiff to establish that the alleged negligence "probably" caused the injury.

We disagree that the loss of opportunity doctrine is inconsistent with [the legal requirement of proving each element by a preponderance of the evidence]. By recognizing loss of opportunity as a cognizable injury, we refute the notion that the plaintiff would be unable to prove that the defendants' negligence "probably" caused her to suffer "injuries which would not otherwise have occurred." The right we recognize today still requires a plaintiff to prove that the injury she suffered — the lost opportunity for a better outcome — was caused, more probably than not, by the defendant's negligence.

Finally, defendant Lovett argues that we should not recognize the plaintiff's loss of opportunity injury because it is intangible and, thus, is not amenable to damages calculation. We disagree.

First, we fail to see the logic in denying an injured plaintiff recovery against a physician for the lost opportunity of a better outcome on the basis that the alleged injury is too difficult to calculate, when the physician's own conduct has caused the difficulty. *See Hicks v. United States*, 368 F.2d 626, 632 (4th Cir. 1966). Second, "we have long held that difficulty in calculating damages is not a sufficient reason to deny recovery to an injured party." *Smith v. Cote*, 513 A.2d 341 (N.H. 1986). Third, loss of opportunity is not inherently unquantifiable. A loss of opportunity plaintiff must provide the jury with a basis upon which to distinguish that portion of her injury caused by the defendant's negligence from the portion resulting from the underlying injury. *See Valliere v. Filfalt*, 266 A.2d 843 (N.H. 1970); King, *Causation, Valuation, and Chance, supra* at 1360. This can be done through expert testimony just as it is in aggravation of pre-existing injury cases.

We decline to address the defendants' arguments disputing the sufficiency of the plaintiff's evidence because the trial court has not yet considered the issue. The trial court limited its ruling to the legal question of whether New Hampshire recognizes the loss of opportunity doctrine. We likewise limit our holding to that question.

NOTES AND PROBLEMS

1. ***Loss of Chance of Recovery as a But-For Problem.*** Defendant in *Lord* argues that plaintiff cannot recover because plaintiff simply cannot prove but-for causation by a preponderance of the evidence. The court acknowledges that under traditional tort principles, plaintiff could not recover because plaintiff likely would have not recovered from the underlying condition even with proper treatment. Nevertheless, the court fashions a new theory permitting recovery. How does the court rationalize this new theory with the normal burden of proof requirements?

2. ***Damage Calculation.*** The court does not specify exactly how damages should be quantified under this new theory of recovery but concedes that the plaintiff should not receive compensation for 100 percent of the injury because plaintiff would have likely had the same result regardless of the defendant's mistreatment. In other cases, courts recognizing this theory of recovery typically provide that the jury should calculate the total damages for the injury and multiply it by a percentage reflecting the diminution in the chances for recovery.

3. ***Increased Risk of Harm vs. Loss of Chance.*** To a large extent, the increased risk of harm scenario (reflected by *Carter*) simply reflects the other side of the coin from the loss of chance scenario in *Lord*. The former involves a scenario where the plaintiff was likely not hurt by the defendant's misconduct and likely will never be. The latter involves a scenario where the plaintiff was likely not adversely affected by the defendant's negligence, although the plaintiff

does have a present injury or condition (that predates the defendant's negligence). The traditional rules are still embraced by the majority of courts in the increased risk of harm scenario but rejected by courts in the loss of chance scenario. Can you explain why? Consider how sympathetic each plaintiff is as they enter the courtroom. With the loss of chance scenario the plaintiff has suffered the harm. With increased risk of harm, the plaintiff approaches the court having suffered no harm and, in all likelihood, not ever going to suffer the harm.

III PROXIMATE CAUSE

In many instances proving the actual causal link between the defendant's misconduct and the plaintiff's harm seems to satisfy tort law's sense of fairness and justice. When an inattentive driver cruises past a stop sign into an intersection striking the plaintiff, there can be little doubt about his liability to the wounded plaintiff. But what if the driver was inattentive because he was tired, having been kept awake late at night by a neighbor hosting a loud party past midnight in violation of a noise-reduction ordinance? Perhaps the defendant driver has no liability insurance and few assets to cover the plaintiff's losses. If the plaintiff decides to sue the noisy neighbor, the plaintiff might be able to prove that the neighbor's careless partying was an actual, but-for cause of the accident. Or what if the driver was speeding through the intersection because he was late for an appointment, having overslept that morning when his defective alarm clock failed to wake him? If the defect was due to negligent design or manufacturing, can the wounded plaintiff sue the clock manufacturer because its carelessness was an additional, actual, but-for cause of the accident? For quite some time, tort law has recognized that it needs another check on liability in order to prevent what it perceives as unfair results when the defendant's negligence is too remote from the plaintiff's harm or when the accident that occurred is so surprising and unexpected. When fairness demands that the defendant prevail, despite the plaintiff's proof of breach of duty and actual causation, the only element available is tort law's concept of *proximate* causation.

Some courts have referred to proximate causation as the "ultimate issue" in a negligence case. While perhaps hyperbole, it is unquestionably a complex potential issue in many cases involving *accidental harm*, particularly where there are multiple remote actors. As you may recall, courts have fairly consistently refuted any suggestion that proximate cause plays a role in intentional tort cases. For example, we saw courts reject defendants' attempts to invoke proximate cause as a check on liability in the trespass case of *Baker v. Shymkiv* and in the battery case of *Nelson v. Carroll* in Chapter 2. In both cases of surprisingly bad harm, the courts found that the defendants satisfied the elements for the respective intentional tort and that proximate cause provided no check on liability.

Yet in cases of accidental harm, courts are more concerned with imposing liability on a mere careless defendant who did not intend to invade anyone's legal interests or to cause harm of any type. In such cases, courts have labored to articulate a framework suitable to the task of separating out cases where liability is fairly imposed, from instances where it seems unfair to make the careless actor pay for the resulting unexpected harm. How to articulate a test that ultimately is measured by a vague notion of "fairness" is something for which courts have failed to find a uniform answer — so we will delve into three different existing tests modern courts continue to use for proximate cause. But first we will begin with the seminal decision in *Palsgraf v. Long Island Railway* where the judges publicly debated what was ultimately the question of *who should decide* this question of fairness — the *judge* by ruling upon the issue under the element of "duty," or the *jury* by resolving the fairness debate under the banner of "proximate cause"?

A. Introduction

Palsgraf is one of those few tort cases that any astute lawyer or law student will instantly recall and about which will often have a strong opinion. The defendant railroad's employees carelessly jostled a passenger in an ill-advised attempt to help him squeeze onto a crowded train. But that passenger was not injured. Rather, the injury occurred seconds later across the train station to another passenger hurt by the ripples of the defendant's action. The jury found the defendant liable for negligence and judgment was entered in accordance with the verdict. The majority opinion sets aside this judgment. Set forth below are the majority opinion authored by the famous Judge Cardozo and the dissenting opinion of Judge Andrews. Pay close attention to the judges' debate about (a) the macro issue of whether the issue of liability for a surprising result should be resolved as one of duty or proximate causation, and (b) the micro issue of whether the harm that occurred on the train station was too surprising from the standpoint of the defendant to fairly create liability.

PALSGRAF v. LONG ISLAND RAILWAY CO.

162 N.E. 99 (N.Y. 1928)

CARDOZO, J.

Plaintiff was standing on a platform of defendant's railroad after buying a ticket to go to Rockaway Beach. A train stopped at the station, bound for another place. Two men ran forward to catch it. One of the men reached the platform of the car without mishap, though the train was already moving. The other man, carrying a package, jumped aboard the car, but seemed unsteady as if about to fall. A guard on the car, who had held the door open, reached forward to help him in, and another guard on the platform pushed him from behind. In this act, the package was dislodged, and fell upon the rails. It was a package of small size, about fifteen inches long, and was covered by a newspaper. In fact it contained fireworks, but there was nothing in its appearance to give notice of its contents. The fireworks when they fell exploded. The shock of the explosion threw down some scales at the other end of the platform, many feet away. The scales struck the plaintiff, causing injuries for which she sues.

The conduct of the defendant's guard, if a wrong in its relation to the holder of the package, was not a wrong in its relation to the plaintiff, standing far away. Relatively to her it was not negligence at all. Nothing in the situation gave notice that the falling package had in it the potency of peril to persons thus removed. Negligence is not actionable unless it involves the invasion of a legally protected interest, the violation of a right. "Proof of negligence in the air, so to speak, will not do" *Martin v. Herzog*, 228 N.Y. 164, 170. "Negligence is the absence of care, according to the circumstances" (Willes, J., in *Vaughan* v. *Taff Vale Ry. Co.*, 5 H. & N. 679, 688). *Parrott* v. *Wells-Fargo Co.*, 15 Wall. [U.S.] 524). The plaintiff as she stood upon the platform of the station might claim to be protected against intentional invasion of her bodily security. Such invasion is not charged. She might claim to be protected against unintentional invasion by conduct involving in the thought of reasonable men an unreasonable hazard that such invasion would ensue. These, from the point of view of the law, were the bounds of her immunity, with perhaps some rare exceptions, survivals for the most part of ancient forms of liability, where conduct is held to be at the peril of the actor. If no hazard was apparent to the eye of ordinary vigilance, an act innocent and harmless, at least to outward seeming, with reference to her, did not take to itself the quality of a tort because it happened to be a wrong, though apparently not one involving the risk of bodily insecurity, with reference to some one else. "In every instance, before negligence can be predicated of a given act, back of the act must be sought and found a duty to the individual complaining, the observance of which would have averted or avoided the injury" (McSherry, C. J., in *W. Va. Central R. Co. v. State*, 96 Md. 652, 666). The plaintiff sues in her own right for a wrong personal to her, and not as the vicarious beneficiary of a breach of duty to another.

A different conclusion will involve us, and swiftly too, in a maze of contradictions. A guard stumbles over a package which has been left upon a platform. It seems to be a bundle of newspapers. It turns out to be a can of dynamite. To the eye of ordinary vigilance, the bundle is abandoned waste, which may be kicked or trod on with impunity. Is a passenger at the other end of the platform protected by the law against the unsuspected hazard concealed beneath the waste? If not, is the result to be any different, so far as the distant passenger is concerned, when the guard stumbles over a valise which a truckman or a porter has left upon the walk? The passenger far away, if the victim of a wrong at all, has a cause of action, not derivative, but original and primary. His claim to be protected against invasion of his bodily security is neither greater nor less because the act resulting in the invasion is a wrong to another far removed. In this case, the rights that are said to have been violated, the interests said to have been invaded, are not even of the same order. The man was not injured in his person nor even put in danger. The purpose of the act, as well as its effect, was to make his person safe. If there was a wrong to him at all, which may very well be doubted, it was a wrong to a property interest only, the safety of his package. Out of this wrong to property, which threatened injury to nothing else, there has passed, we are told, to the plaintiff by derivation or succession a right of action for the invasion of an interest of another order, the right to bodily security. The diversity of interests emphasizes the futility of the effort to build the plaintiff's right upon the basis of a wrong to some one else. The gain is one of emphasis, for a like result would follow if the interests were the same. Even then, the orbit of the danger as disclosed to the eye of reasonable vigilance would be the orbit of the duty. One who jostles one's neighbor in a crowd does not invade the rights of others standing at the outer fringe when the unintended contact casts a bomb upon the ground. The wrongdoer as to them is the man who carries the bomb, not the one who explodes it without suspicion of the danger. Life will have to be made over, and human nature transformed, before prevision so extravagant can be accepted as the norm of conduct, the customary standard to which behavior must conform.

The argument for the plaintiff is built upon the shifting meanings of such words as "wrong" and "wrongful," and shares their instability. What the plaintiff must show is "a wrong" to herself, i.e., a violation of her own right, and not merely a wrong to someone else, nor conduct "wrongful" because unsocial, but not "a wrong" to any one. We are told that one who drives at a reckless speed through a crowded city street is guilty of a negligent act and, therefore, of a wrongful one irrespective of the consequences. Negligent the act is, and wrongful in the sense that it is unsocial, but wrongful and unsocial in relation to other travelers, only because the eye of vigilance perceives the risk of damage. If the same act were to be committed on a speedway or a race course, it would lose its wrongful quality. The risk reasonably to be perceived defines the duty to be obeyed, and risk imports relation; it is risk to another or to others within the range of apprehension. This does not mean, of course, that one who launches a destructive force is always relieved of liability if the force, though known to be destructive, pursues an unexpected path. "It was not necessary that the defendant should have had notice of the particular method in which an accident would occur, if the possibility of an accident was clear to the ordinarily prudent eye" (*Munsey v. Webb*, 231 U.S. 150, 156). Some acts, such as shooting, are so imminently dangerous to any one who may come within reach of the missile, however unexpectedly, as to impose a duty of prevision not far from that of an insurer. Even today, and much oftener in earlier stages of the law, one acts sometimes at one's peril. (Under this head, it may be, fall certain cases of what is known as transferred intent, an act willfully dangerous to A resulting by misadventure in injury to B. These cases aside, wrong is defined in terms of the natural or probable, at least when unintentional (*Parrot* v. *Wells-Fargo Co.* [the "Nitro-Glycerine Case"], 15 Wall. [U.S.] 524). The range of reasonable apprehension is at times a question for the court, and at times, if varying inferences are possible, a question for the jury. Here, by concession, there was nothing in the situation to suggest to the most cautious mind that the parcel wrapped in newspaper would spread wreckage through the station. If the guard had thrown it down knowingly and willfully, he would not have threatened the plaintiff's safety, so far as appearances could warn him. His conduct would not have involved, even then, an unreasonable probability of invasion of her bodily security. Liability can be no greater where the act is inadvertent.

Negligence, like risk, is thus a term of relation. Negligence in the abstract, apart from things related, is surely not a tort, if indeed it is understandable at all. Negligence is not a tort unless it results in the commission of a wrong, and the commission of a wrong imports the violation of a right, in this case, we are told, the right to be protected against interference with one's bodily security. . . . The victim does not sue derivatively, or by right of subrogation, to vindicate an interest invaded in the person of another. Thus to view his cause of action is to ignore the fundamental difference between tort and crime. He sues for breach of a duty owing to himself.

The law of causation, remote or proximate, is thus foreign to the case before us. The question of liability is always anterior to the question of the measure of the consequences that go with liability. If there is no tort to be redressed, there is no occasion to consider what damage might be recovered if there were a finding of a tort. We may assume, without deciding, that negligence, not at large or in the abstract, but in relation to the plaintiff, would entail liability for any and all consequences, however novel or extraordinary. There is room for argument that a distinction is to be drawn according to the diversity of interests invaded by the act, as where conduct negligent in that it threatens an insignificant invasion of an interest in property results in an unforseeable invasion of an interest of another order, as, *e. g.*, one of bodily security. Perhaps other distinctions may be necessary. We do not go into the question now. The consequences to be followed must first be rooted in a wrong.

The judgment of the Appellate Division and that of the Trial Term should be reversed, and the complaint dismissed, with costs in all courts.

DISSENT

ANDREWS, J. (dissenting)

Judge William S. Andrews

Assisting a passenger to board a train, the defendant's servant negligently knocked a package from his arms. It fell between the platform and the cars. Of its contents the servant knew and could know nothing. A violent explosion followed. The concussion broke some scales standing a considerable distance away. In falling they injured the plaintiff, an intending passenger.

Upon these facts may she recover the damages she has suffered in an action brought against the master? The result we shall reach depends upon our theory as to the nature of negligence. Is it a relative concept — the breach of some duty owing to a particular person or to particular persons? Or where there is an act which unreasonably threatens the safety of others, is the doer liable for all its proximate consequences, even where they result in injury to one who would generally be thought to be outside the radius of danger? This is not a mere dispute as to words. We might not believe that to the average mind the dropping of the bundle would seem to involve the probability of harm to the plaintiff standing many feet away whatever might be the case as to the owner or to one so near as to be likely to be struck by its fall. If, however, we adopt the second hypothesis we have to inquire only as to the relation between cause and effect. We deal in terms of proximate cause, not of negligence.

Negligence may be defined roughly as an act or omission which unreasonably does or may affect the rights of others, or which unreasonably fails to protect oneself from the dangers resulting from such acts. Here I confine myself to the first branch of the definition. Nor do I comment on the word "unreasonable." For present purposes it sufficiently describes that average of conduct that society requires of its members.

But we are told that "there is no negligence unless there is in the particular case a legal duty to take care, and this duty must be one which is owed to the plaintiff himself and not merely to others." (Salmond Torts [6th ed.], 24.) This, I think too narrow a conception. Where there is the unreasonable act, and some right that may be affected, there is negligence whether damage does or does not result. That is immaterial. Should we drive down Broadway at a reckless speed, we are negligent whether we strike an approaching car or miss it by an inch. The act itself is wrongful. It is a wrong not only to those who happen to be within the radius of danger but to all who might have been there — a wrong to the public at large. Such is the language of the street. . . . As was said by Mr. Justice Holmes many years ago, "the measure of the defendant's duty in determining whether a wrong has been committed is one thing, the measure of liability when a wrong has been committed is another." (*Spade v. Lynn & Boston R.R. Co.*, 172 Mass. 488.) Due care is a duty imposed on each one of us to protect society from unnecessary danger, not to protect A, B or C alone.

It may well be that there is no such thing as negligence in the abstract. "Proof of negligence in the air, so to speak, will not do." In an empty world negligence would not exist. It does involve a relationship between man and his fellows. But not merely a relationship between man and those whom he might reasonably expect his act would injure. Rather, a relationship between him and those whom he does in fact injure. If his act has a tendency to harm some one, it harms him a mile away as surely as it does those on the scene. We now permit children to recover for the negligent killing of the father. It was never prevented on the theory that no duty was owing to them. A husband may be compensated for the loss of his wife's services. To say that the wrongdoer was negligent as to the husband as well as to the wife is merely an attempt to fit facts to theory. An insurance company paying a fire loss recovers its payment of the negligent incendiary. We speak of subrogation — of suing in the right of the insured. Behind the cloud of words is the fact they hide, that the act, wrongful as to the insured, has also injured the company. Even if it be true that the fault of father, wife or insured will prevent recovery, it is because we consider the original negligence not the proximate cause of the injury.

In the well-known *Polemis Case* (1921, 3 K.B. 560), Scrutton, L.J., said that the dropping of a plank was negligent for it might injure "workman or cargo or ship." Because of either possibility the owner of the vessel was to be made good for his loss. The act being wrongful the doer was liable for its proximate results. Criticized and explained as this statement may have been, I think it states the law as it should be and as it is.

The proposition is this. Everyone owes to the world at large the duty of refraining from those acts that may unreasonably threaten the safety of others. Such an act occurs. Not only is he wronged to whom harm might reasonably be expected to result, but he also who is in fact injured, even if he be outside what would generally be thought the danger zone. There needs be duty due the one complaining but this is not a duty to a particular individual because as to him harm might be expected. Harm to some one being the natural result of the act, not only that one alone, but all those in fact injured may complain. We have never, I think, held otherwise.... Unreasonable risk being taken, its consequences are not confined to those who might probably be hurt.

If this be so, we do not have a plaintiff suing by "derivation or succession." Her action is original and primary. Her claim is for a breach of duty to herself— not that she is subrogated to any right of action of the owner of the parcel or of a passenger standing at the scene of the explosion.

The right to recover damages rests on additional considerations. The plaintiff's rights must be injured, and this injury must be caused by the negligence. We build a dam, but are negligent as to its foundations. Breaking, it injures property down stream. We are not liable if all this happened because of some reason other than the insecure foundation. But when injuries do result from our unlawful act we are liable for the consequences. It does not matter that they are unusual, unexpected, unforeseen and unforeseeable. But there is one limitation. The damages must be so connected with the negligence that the latter may be said to be the proximate cause of the former.

These two words have never been given an inclusive definition. What is a cause in a legal sense, still more what is a proximate cause, depend in each case upon many considerations, as does the existence of negligence itself. Any philosophical doctrine of causation does not help us. A boy throws a stone into a pond. The ripples spread. The water level rises. The history of that pond is altered to all eternity. It will be altered by other causes also. Yet it will be forever the resultant of all causes combined. Each one will have an influence. How great only omniscience can say. You may speak of a chain, or if you please, a net. An analogy is of little aid. Each cause brings about future events. Without each the future would not be the same. Each is proximate in the sense it is essential. But that is not what we mean by the word. Nor on the other hand do we mean sole cause. There is no such thing.

Should analogy be thought helpful, however, I prefer that of a stream. The spring, starting on its journey, is joined by tributary after tributary. The river, reaching the ocean, comes from a hundred sources. No man may say whence any drop of water is derived. Yet for a time distinction may be possible. Into the clear creek, brown swamp water flows from the left. Later, from the right comes water stained by its clay bed. The three may remain for a space, sharply divided. But at last, inevitably no trace of separation remains. They are so commingled that all distinction is lost.

As we have said, we cannot trace the effect of an act to the end, if end there is. Again, however, we may trace it part of the way. A murder at Serajevo may be the necessary antecedent to an assassination in London twenty years hence. An overturned lantern may burn all Chicago. We may follow the fire from the shed to the last building. We rightly say the fire started by the lantern caused its destruction.

A cause, but not the proximate cause. What we do mean by the word "proximate" is, that because of convenience, of public policy, of a rough sense of justice, the law arbitrarily declines to trace a series of events beyond a certain point. This is not logic. It is practical politics. Take our rule as to fires. Sparks from my burning haystack set on fire my house and my neighbor's. I may recover from a negligent railroad. He may not. Yet the wrongful act as directly harmed the one as the other. We may regret that the line was drawn just where it was, but drawn somewhere it had to be. We said the act of the railroad was not the proximate cause of our neighbor's fire. Cause it surely was. The words we used were simply indicative of our notions of public policy. Other courts think differently. But somewhere they reach the point where they cannot say the stream comes from any one source.

It is all a question of expediency. There are no fixed rules to govern our judgment. There are simply matters of which we may take account. We have in a somewhat different connection spoken of "the stream of events." We have asked whether that stream was deflected — whether it was forced into new and unexpected channels. This is rather rhetoric than law. There is in truth little to guide us other than common sense.

There are some hints that may help us. The proximate cause, involved as it may be with many other causes, must be, at the least, something without which the event would not happen. The court must ask itself whether there was a natural and continuous sequence between cause and effect. Was the one a substantial factor in producing the other? Was there a direct connection between them, without too many intervening causes? Is the effect of cause on result not too attenuated? Is the cause likely, in the usual judgment of mankind, to produce the result? Or by the exercise of prudent foresight could the result be foreseen? Is the result too remote from the cause, and here we consider remoteness in time and space. . . . Clearly we must so consider, for the greater the distance either in time or space, the more surely do other causes intervene to affect the result. When a lantern is overturned the firing of a shed is a fairly direct consequence. Many things contribute to the spread of the conflagration — the force of the wind, the direction and width of streets, the character of intervening structures, other factors. We draw an uncertain and wavering line, but draw it we must as best we can.

Once again, it is all a question of fair judgment, always keeping in mind the fact that we endeavor to make a rule in each case that will be practical and in keeping with the general understanding of mankind.

This last suggestion is the factor which must determine the case before us. The act upon which defendant's liability rests is knocking an apparently harmless package onto the platform. The act was negligent. For its proximate consequences the defendant is liable. If its contents were broken, to the owner; if it fell upon and crushed a passenger's foot, then to him. If it exploded and injured one in the immediate vicinity, to him also as to A in the illustration. Mrs. Palsgraf was standing some distance away. How far cannot be told from the record — apparently twenty-five or thirty feet. Perhaps less. Except for the explosion, she would not have been injured. We are told by the appellant in his brief "it cannot be denied that the explosion was the direct cause of the plaintiff's injuries." So it was a substantial factor in producing the result — there was here a natural and continuous sequence — direct connection. The only intervening cause was that instead of blowing her to the ground the concussion smashed the weighing machine which in turn fell upon her. There was no remoteness in time, little in space. And surely, given such an explosion as here it needed no great foresight to predict that the natural result would be to injure one on the platform at no greater distance from its scene than was the plaintiff. Just how no one might be able to predict. Whether by flying fragments, by broken glass, by wreckage of machines or structures no one could say. But injury in some form was most probable.

Under these circumstances I cannot say as a matter of law that the plaintiff's injuries were not the proximate result of the negligence. That is all we have before us. The court refused to so charge. No request was made to submit the matter to the jury as a question of fact, even would that have been proper upon the record before us.

The judgment appealed from should be affirmed, with costs.

NOTES AND PROBLEMS

1. ***Dealing with Bizarre Consequences.*** *Palsgraf* is the classic torts case in which two esteemed judges have a war of words regarding how tort law should deal with determining the scope of liability for unusual accidents. With respect to the elements of a negligence case, where does Judge Cardozo believe the unusual nature of the accident should primarily be analyzed? How does Judge Andrews disagree? Is this just a game of semantics or some philosophical debate suitable for a law school lecture? Does the issue of who should decide liability in cases of surprising outcomes make any difference? The answer may ultimately lie in where we place our trust for this question to be answered. Questions of *duty* are classically viewed as questions of law for the court to determine, while questions of *proximate cause* are generally considered questions of fact for the jury to answer. Whether you find yourself agreeing with Cardozo or Andrews may reflect upon *who* you believe should be answering the question of how far removed liability should be extended.

2. ***Torts at a Crossroads.*** Judge Cardozo decided to question the assumption that we owe a duty of reasonable care at all times to all people. Many courts in negligence cases do revisit this assumption under certain circumstances while ignoring the issue of duty in most negligence cases. In Chapter 6, Special Duty Rules, we will return to the issue of duty by visiting

these recurring instances of courts pausing at the element of "duty" and divining whether a duty of reasonable care exists or should be modified. But first, because most courts in practice routinely presume a duty of reasonable care (as we shall see in Chapter 6, Special Duty Rules) and instead handle issues of unusual accidents under the analytical framework of "proximate" or "legal" causation, we will turn to that topic in the next subsection of this chapter. Judge Andrews' dissent introduced to us several examples of *proximate cause* analysis.

3. ***And the Winner Is?*** With respect to the issue of duty, once you have covered Chapter 6, Special Duty Rules, turn back to the facts of *Palsgraf* and ask yourself if Judge Cardozo reached the right conclusion on the issue of whether the defendant owed plaintiff a duty of care. In terms of their practice, most courts today would agree with Judge Andrews on the macro issue of whether *Palsgraf* was a proximate cause or a duty case. As you will see in the next chapter, courts generally assume a duty of care in circumstances where a defendant acts. Further, due to defendant's affirmative conduct, the status of plaintiff as a business invitee, and defendant's status as a common carrier, it is doubtful any court today would bother to debate whether a duty of care existed toward Ms. Palsgraf. Yet many courts might disagree with Judge Andrews' micro conclusion that proximate cause existed on the facts of that case, depending upon the specific proximate cause test selected. As we explore the actual proximate cause tests in the next section, you should come back to the facts of *Palsgraf* and Judge Andrews' opinion, and ask yourself if he got the actual results of that case right.

4. ***Problems.***

A. With regard to the leaping passenger holding the fireworks rolled up inside the newspaper, how would Judge Cardozo and Judge Andrews each have analyzed his liability toward Ms. Palsgraf? Would he have owed her a duty of care and would proximate cause be satisfied as to him?

B. Assume that the leaping passenger was knocked down and caused to suffer a knee injury. He was taken to a nearby hospital. This delayed his delivery of important closing documents to a business transaction, which ultimately fell through due to his tardy arrival. Can the business that experienced lost profits from this failed transaction sue the Long Island Railway for its negligence? What if it was our leaping passenger who suffered the loss from this failed transaction? Can he recover for both his knee injury and his failed business loss from the Long Island Railway?

B. The Direct Cause Test

One of the older, blunter analytical tools for determining the issue of proximate cause is referred to as the *direct cause* test. Judge Andrews, in discussing possible tests for proximate cause, asked if there was "a direct connection between [the negligent act and the harm], without too many intervening causes?" The following two cases, one older and one of more recent origin, apply this direct cause test to two very different fact patterns and reach different conclusions. As you read these cases, consider whether you see any benefits to the direct cause test.

IN RE POLEMIS

3 K.B. 560 (Ct. App. 1921)

[The claimants were owners of a ship that was lost in a fire. Included among the items in the ship's cargo were benzene and petrol. While in port at Casablanca in July 1917, stevedores employed by the defendant (who had chartered the ship) were removing portions of the cargo. They had placed wooden planks across the ship's hold to assist them during the unloading of the ship. The stevedores used slings to move the cargo up from the ship's hold. Petrol vapors were in the air within the ship's cargo hold due to leaking of benzene and petrol.] In the course of heaving a sling of the cases from the hold, the rope by which the sling was being raised or the sling itself came into contact with the boards placed across the forward end of the hatch, causing one of the boards to fall into the lower hold, and the fall was instantaneously followed by a rush of flames from the lower hold, and this resulted eventually in the total destruction of the ship.

[The ship's owner alleged that the charterers were liable for the negligence of the stevedores that caused the fire and the ship's loss. The charterers took issue with these allegations, saying that there was no negligence for which they were responsible and that the damage to the ship was too remote to create liability — that no "reasonable man would have foreseen danger and/or damage of this kind resulting from the fall of the board."

The arbitrators found that the stevedores were negligent in causing the planks to fall into the ship's cargo hold and that this negligence created a spark which ignited the petrol vapors and resulted in the total loss of the ship. The arbitrators also found, however, that such loss could not reasonably have been foreseen, even though some other damage to cargo or the ship was foreseeable. An award against the charterers was levied and an appeal taken.]

BANKES, L.J.

In the present case the arbitrators have found as a fact that the falling of the plank was due to the negligence of the defendants' servants. The fire appears to me to have been directly caused by the falling of the plank. Under these circumstances I consider that it is immaterial that the causing of the spark by the falling of the plank could not have been reasonably anticipated. . . . Given the breach of duty which constitutes the negligence, and given the damages as a direct result of that negligence, the anticipations of the person whose negligent act has produced the damage appear to me to be irrelevant. I consider that the damages claimed are not too remote.

Scrutton, L.J.

The defence is that the damage is too remote from the negligence, as it could not be reasonably foreseen as a consequence. On this head we were referred to a number of well known cases in which vague language, which I cannot think to be really helpful, has been used in an attempt to define the point at which damage becomes too remote from, or not sufficiently directly caused by, the breach of duty, which is the original cause of action, to be recoverable. For instance, I cannot think it useful to say the damage must be the natural and probable result. This suggests that there are results which are natural but not probable, and other results which are probable but not natural. I am not sure what either adjective means in this connection; if they mean the same thing, two need not be used; if they mean different things, the difference between them should be defined. . . . To determine whether an act is negligent, it is relevant to determine whether any reasonable person would foresee that the act would cause damage; if he would not, the act is not negligent. But if the act would or might probably cause damage, the fact that the damage it in fact causes is not the exact kind of damage one would expect is immaterial, so long as the damage is in fact directly traceable to the negligent act, and not due the operation of independent causes having no connection with the negligent act, except that they could not avoid its results. Once the act is negligent, the fact that its exact operation was not foreseen is immaterial. . . . In the present case it was negligent in discharging cargo to known down the planks of the temporary staging, for they might easily cause some damages either to workmen, or cargo, or the ship. The fact that they did directly produce an unexpected result, a spark in an atmosphere of petrol vapour which caused a fire, does not relieve the person who was negligent from the damage which his negligent act directly caused.

LAUREANO v. LOUZOUN

560 N.Y.S.2d 337 (N.Y. App. Div. 1990)

Per Curiam.

On January 21, 1985, the plaintiff, a tenant in the defendants' premises, arose from bed at approximately 5 A.M. and put two large pots of water on her stove to boil. While in the process of pouring the boiling water from one pot into the other, the plaintiff banged the pots against each other, causing the boiling water to spill onto her knee and feet. The plaintiff commenced the instant action, alleging, *inter alia*, that the defendants' negligence in failing to provide heat and hot water to the premises and in failing to maintain the boiler in proper working condition caused the incident and her resulting injuries. The plaintiff further alleged that the defendants had constructive notice of the defective condition at least two weeks prior to the incident, as well as actual notice. The defendants moved for summary judgment on the ground that their conduct was not, as a matter of law, the proximate cause of the plaintiff's injuries. The trial court granted the motion holding that "there was no connection of proximate cause between the lack of heat and the accident." We affirm.

The defendants' failure to provide heat and hot water to the premises was not the proximate cause, as a matter of law, of the injuries sustained by the plaintiff. [T]he defendants' conduct gave rise to the plaintiff's attempt to provide a substitute supply of heat. [Yet] the intervening act of banging one pot against the other brought about the injuries sustained by the plaintiff. Those injuries would not have resulted from the failure to supply hot water alone, and cannot be classified as injuries normally to have been expected to ensue from the landlord's conduct.

NOTES AND PROBLEMS

1. *Direct Cause Test.* As enunciated in the *Polemis* case, the court looked to determine if there were any independent intervening actions that took place between the defendant's negligence and the plaintiff's harm. On the facts of *Polemis* and *Laureano,* why is there proximate cause found in the former but not the latter, utilizing this standard for determining proximate cause? Do you like the seeming simplicity of this test for proximate cause or do you think it leads to unfair results?

2. *Preference for Proximate Cause Tests.* Does the direct cause test, which does not require that the harm suffered be foreseeable from the defendant's standpoint, seem to be a pro-plaintiff test for proximate cause? If so, why does the plaintiff in *Laureano* lose? Do you see why the court believed that the tenant's need to boil water was not an *independent* intervening cause while the tenant's banging of the pans into each other was an independent intervening cause? Observe that it only takes a single independent intervening cause to put a kink in the chain of causation.

3. *Problems.*

A. Regarding *Polemis,* what if it were determined that the initial leak of petrol vapors was due to the antecedent act of negligence by someone coming on board the ship and spilling the product in the ship's cargo hold? Would that originally negligent actor be found to be a proximate cause of the loss of the ship?

B. Using the facts from *Palsgraf,* analyze proximate causation using the direct cause test.

C. The Foreseeability Test

While some courts continue to use the direct cause test to analyze proximate cause, a greater number of courts have come to embrace a *foreseeability* test for proximate cause. This test considers whether the nature of the harm or accident giving rise to the plaintiff's claim was the same general type of harm or accident that was within the scope of the original risk that permitted a finding of breach of the duty of reasonable care. There is a natural symmetry, therefore, between this proximate cause test and the Learned Hand analysis already employed in the breach determination. The following case illustrates its application to another scenario involving a rather bizarre twist of events. As you read each case in the Proximate Cause section of this book, consider whether the facts of each case would satisfy the other proximate cause tests as well. Doing so will help you conclude whether, and to what extent, the choice of proximate cause tests matters.

1. Whether the Type of Accident Was Within the Scope of the Risk

TIEDER v. LITTLE

502 So. 2d 923 (Fla. Dist. Ct. App. 1987)

HUBBART, J.

This is a consolidated appeal by the plaintiffs from (1) a final order dismissing a complaint as to one defendant, and (2) a final summary judgment entered in favor of a second defendant, in a wrongful death action. The trial court concluded that the defendants' alleged negligence was not, as a matter of law, a proximate cause of the death of the plaintiffs' decedent. For the reasons which follow, we disagree and reverse.

The facts of this case, as alleged in the operative complaint and as developed by the discovery and affidavits filed in the record, may be briefly stated as follows.

On January 7, 1983, at approximately 9:00 P.M., the plaintiffs' decedent, Trudi Beth Tieder, was struck by an automobile, pinned up against a brick wall, and killed when the wall collapsed on her — as she walked out the front door of Eaton Hall dormitory on the University of Miami campus. At the time, two students were attempting to clutch-start an automobile in the circular drive in front of Eaton Hall — one student was pushing the car while the other student was in the car behind the wheel — when, suddenly, the student behind the wheel lost control of the car. The automobile left the circular driveway, lurched over a three-inch curb onto a grassy area, and travelled some thirty-three feet across the front lawn parallel to Eaton Hall. The automobile collided with an elevated walkway leading out of the front door of Eaton Hall, jumped onto the walkway, and struck the plaintiffs' decedent as she walked out the front door of the dormitory. The automobile continued forward, pinning the decedent against a high brick wall that supported a concrete canopy at the entrance to the dormitory. Because the wall was negligently designed and constructed without adequate supports required by the applicable building code, the entire wall came off intact from its foundation and crushed her to death. Dr. Joseph Davis, the Dade County Medical Examiner, averred by affidavit that in his opinion the decedent would not have died merely from the automobile impact; in his opinion, she died as a result of the brick wall falling intact and in one piece upon her. Two affidavits of professional engineers were also filed below detailing the negligent design and construction of the subject brick wall.

The plaintiffs Sheila M. Tieder and Richard J. Tieder, administrators of the estate of Trudi Beth Tieder, brought a wrongful death action against: (1) the owner and the operator of the automobile (not parties to this appeal), (2) Robert M. Little, the architect who designed the allegedly defective brick wall, and (3) the University of Miami, which caused the said brick wall to be erected and maintained. The amended complaint charged the defendant Little and the University of Miami with various acts of negligent conduct including negligence in the design and construction of the brick wall. The defendant Little moved to dismiss the complaint against him and urged that his alleged negligence was not, as a matter of law, the proximate cause of the decedent's death because the entire accident was so bizarre as to be entirely unforeseeable; the University of Miami moved for a summary judgment in its favor and made the same argument. The trial court agreed and granted both motions. . . .

In the instant case, the parties appear to agree that, for complaint dismissal and summary judgment purposes, the first two elements of the plaintiff's negligence (wrongful death) action are shown on this record. It is solely the third element of "proximate cause" which is in dispute in this case. The defendants contended below, and the trial court agreed, that the defendants' negligence in designing and constructing the brick wall was not, as a matter of law, the proximate cause of the death of the plaintiffs' decedent. The plaintiffs, on the other hand, contend that the complaint alleges sufficient facts, and the record raises sufficient issues of material fact, that a jury issue is presented on the proximate cause element. It is therefore necessary to consult the applicable Florida law on "proximate cause" in negligence actions as applied to the facts presented herein.

At the outset, the "proximate cause" element of a negligence action embraces, as a *sine qua non* ingredient, a causation-in-fact test, that is, the defendant's negligence must be a cause-in-fact of the plaintiff's injuries. Generally speaking, Florida courts have followed a "but-for" causation-in-fact test, that is, "to constitute proximate cause there must be such a natural, direct and continuous sequence between the negligent act [or omission] and the [plaintiff's] injury that it can be reasonably said that *but for* the [negligent] act [or omission] the injury would not have occurred." There is, however, a "substantial factor" exception to the "but-for" test where two causes concur to bring about an event in fact, either one of which would have been sufficient to cause the identical result. *Stahl v. Metropolitan Dade County*, 438 So. 2d 14, 18-19 (Fla. 3d DCA 1983). In that narrow circumstance, it is settled that a "defendant's conduct in an action for personal injuries is considered a cause [in fact] of the event if it was a material and substantial factor in bringing it about." *Loftin v. Wilson*, 67 So. 2d 185, 191 (Fla. 1953).

In addition to the causation-in-fact test, the "proximate cause" element of a negligence action includes a second indispensable showing. This showing is designed to protect defendants from tort liability for results which, although caused-in-fact by the defendant's negligent act or omission, seem to the judicial mind highly unusual, extraordinary, or bizarre, or, stated differently, seem beyond the scope of any fair assessment of the danger created by the defendant's negligence. The courts here have required a common sense, fairness showing that the accident in which the plaintiff suffered his injuries was within the scope of the danger created by the defendant's negligence, or stated differently, that the said accident was a reasonably foreseeable consequence of the defendant's negligence.

It is not necessary, however, that the defendant foresee the exact sequence of events which led to the accident sued upon; it is only necessary that the general type of accident which has occurred was within the scope of the danger created by the defendant's negligence, or, stated differently, it must be shown that the said general-type accident was a reasonably foreseeable consequence of the defendant's negligence. . . . Moreover, it has long been held that "proximate cause" issues are generally for juries to decide using their common sense upon appropriate instructions, although occasionally when reasonable people cannot differ, the issue has been said to be one of law for the court.

Turning now to the instant case, we have no difficulty in concluding that the trial court erred in dismissing the complaint against the defendant Little and in entering a final summary judgment in favor of the University of Miami. This is so because the complaint sufficiently alleges the proximate cause element herein as to the defendant Little, and the record raises genuine issues of material fact with reference to the same element as to the defendant University of Miami.

> ***(P x L)***
>
> Foreseeability asks if the type of incident that hurt the plaintiff is one of those risks that permitted a finding of breach in the first instance.

Plainly, the alleged negligence in designing and constructing the brick wall adjoining the entrance way to Eaton Hall in this case was a cause-in-fact of the accident which led to the death of the plaintiffs' decedent. It is alleged that the said wall was designed and built with insufficient supports as required by the applicable building code so that, when it was impacted in this case, it fell over intact, and in one piece, on the decedent. Dr. Joseph Davis, the Dade County Medical Examiner, avers that in his opinion the decedent died as a result of the brick wall falling intact upon her. "But for" the negligent design and construction of the brick wall which led to its collapse in one piece, then, the decedent would not have died. A jury question is therefore presented on this aspect of the proximate cause element.

The foreseeability aspect of the proximate cause element is also satisfied in this case for the complaint dismissal and summary judgment purposes. The collapse of a brick wall resulting in the death of a person near such wall is plainly a reasonably foreseeable consequence of negligently designing and constructing such a wall without adequate supports in violation of applicable building codes — even though the exact sequence of events leading to the collapse of the wall — as in this case, the bizarre incident involving the clutch-started automobile leaving the circular driveway and striking the wall — may have been entirely unforeseeable. The general-type accident which occurred in this case — namely, the collapse of the brick wall resulting in the decedent's death — was entirely within the scope of the danger created by the defendants' negligence in designing and constructing the wall without adequate supports, and was a reasonably foreseeable consequence of such negligence. Just as injuries sustained by business patrons in attempting to escape a fire in a cafeteria or hotel was a reasonably foreseeable consequence of the cafeteria or hotel's negligence in failing to have adequate fire exits, even though the act of the arsonist in setting the building aflame was entirely unforeseeable — so too the death of the plaintiffs' decedent was entirely foreseeable in this case even though the exact sequence of events leading to the collapse of the wall may have been unforeseeable. This being so, a jury issue is presented on the proximate cause element as pled in the complaint and revealed by this record.

The final order of dismissal and the final summary judgment under review are both reversed and the cause is remanded to the trial court for further proceedings.

Reversed and remanded.

NOTES AND PROBLEMS

1. ***Learned Hand Formula Gets Double Duty.*** The foreseeability test for proximate cause, in effect, goes back to the same Learned Hand formula we saw courts employ in analyzing issues of breach of duty. If the accident that hurt the plaintiff was one of those possible accidents that led to the conclusion that defendant breached its duty, by failing to exercise enough care to avoid it from occurring, then the foreseeability test is satisfied. What types of events were within the scope of the foreseeable risks of harm that would have compelled the reasonable person to comply with the building code in *Tieder*?

Is what happened to the plaintiff — an insufficiently supported wall collapsing when force was applied to it — the reason for compliance with the building code?

2. *Popularity of the Foreseeability Test.* Though some courts persist in using the direct cause test, and some others have adopted a *substantial factor* test (which we will explore next), the majority of courts analyze proximate cause using the foreseeability test. Even English courts that created the direct cause test — as we saw in *Polemis* — subsequently rejected that analysis. In the case of *The Wagon Mound*, 1961 A.C. 388 (P.C.), the Privy Council opined: "Enough has been said to show that the authority of *Polemis* has been severely shaken though lip-service has from time to time been paid to it. In their Lordships' opinion it should no longer be regarded as good law." Instead, the court adopted the test of reasonable foreseeability.

3. Palsgraf *Revisited.* In dissent, Judge Andrews analyzed the plaintiff's accident in *Palsgraf* under the various proximate cause tests. With respect to the foreseeability test, he concluded that "surely, given such an explosion as here it needed no great foresight to predict that the natural result would be to injure one on the platform at no greater distance . . . than was the plaintiff". Do you agree with Judge Andrews' application of the foreseeability test for proximate cause? Was it the foreseeable risk of injury to Ms. Palsgraf that made the railway employees' decision to reach out and touch the leaping passenger negligent?

4. *Foreseeing the Type of Harm Rather Than the Extent of It.* In jurisdictions utilizing the foreseeability test, defendants have sometimes asserted that they should not be liable if the amount of harm suffered by the plaintiff is greater than could have been reasonably foreseen. For example, imagine a driver goes through a red light and hits a very frail pedestrian. This plaintiff suffers permanent, disabling injuries due to a prior history of orthopedic problems with her legs. Courts reject this attempt to limit liability, citing the *Eggshell Plaintiff* rule — that a negligent tortfeasor "takes his victim as he finds him." The Restatement of Torts (Second) §461 *comment* (a) (1965) states that, "A negligent actor must bear the risk that his liability will be increased by reason of the actual physical condition of the other toward whom his act is negligent." A related doctrine is the *Shabby Millionaire Rule,* which makes a defendant liable for unforeseeable economic losses (i.e., lost wages) of someone who appeared to have a low income. Thus, for purposes of proximate cause, the *extent* of harm need not be foreseeable. How does this compare with *breach* analysis in terms of whether the extent of harm is pertinent? Remember the Learned Hand formula in pondering this distinction. How does this formula reflect the reality that the extent of foreseeable harm is directly relevant to analyzing breach of the duty of reasonable care?

2. *Breach of Duty Does Not Necessarily Prove Proximate Cause*

CRANKSHAW v. PIEDMONT DRIVING CLUB

156 S.E.2d 208 (Ga. Ct. App. 1967)

Plaintiff Elizabeth Crankshaw seeks damages against Piedmont Driving Club, Inc. alleging that on January 15, 1966, she in company with R.M. Harris and Miss Arlene Harris patronized the dining room of the defendant; that Miss Harris ordered shrimp and began eating same at which time she noticed a peculiar odor emanating from the shrimp dish causing her to feel nauseated; that Miss Harris excused herself and proceeded toward the rest room; shortly thereafter plaintiff proceeded toward the rest room to give aid and comfort to Miss Harris and as plaintiff entered the rest room she saw Miss Harris leaning over one of the bowls; that "unbeknownst to plaintiff, Miss Harris had vomited just inside the entrance to the rest room" and that as she hurried toward her she "stepped into the vomit, and her feet flew out from under her," causing her to fall and break her hip. The petition alleged negligence of the defendant in selling unwholesome, deleterious food and in failing to clean up the floor of the rest room or to warn plaintiff of the condition of the floor.

The trial court sustained the defendant's general demurrer to the petition, from which judgment the plaintiff appeals.

JORDON, J.

Appellant in her brief properly abandons the allegation of negligence due to defendant's failure to clean the regurgitated substance from the floor since under the facts alleged the defendant had no notice, actual or constructive, of its presence on the floor prior to plaintiff's fall. Appellant contends, however, that "the heart of the legal question presented" is whether or not the negligent serving of unwholesome food to Miss Harris was the proximate cause of her (appellant's) injury. Viewing the case from this posed question we conclude that the trial court was correct in sustaining the general demurrer.

"If the damages are only the imaginary or possible result of the tortious act, or other and contingent circumstances preponderate largely in causing the injurious effect, such damages are too remote to be the basis of recovery against the wrongdoer." *Code* §105-2008. Damages must flow from the "legal and natural result of the act done." *Code* §105-2009. The question of proximate cause is one for a jury except in palpably clear and indisputable cases. We think the facts alleged in this petition bring it within the exception and subject it to be ruled upon as a matter of law. The court must assume this burden where a jury can draw but one reasonable conclusion if the facts alleged are proved, that conclusion being that the acts of the defendant were not the proximate cause of the injury. In our opinion a jury could not reasonably conclude that the plaintiff's injury was proximately caused by the defendant's negligence in serving unwholesome food to another person.

NOTES AND PROBLEMS

1. ***Foreseeability of Any Harm Not Sufficient.*** A demurrer to an original petition is a state court equivalent in Georgia to a federal court motion to dismiss for failure to state a cause of action under Fed. R. Civ. P. 12(b)(6). All facts alleged must be accepted as true. Despite this standard for reviewing the plaintiff's pleading favorably, the court still found in *Crankshaw* that plaintiff could not possibly prove proximate cause. Even though defendant might have been negligent in serving tainted seafood, the court finds that the reasonably foreseeable risks involved in serving such food do not include a slip and fall incident. Though such an outcome might be "imaginary" or "possible" this is not the same as saying that it would be reasonably foreseeable.

2. ***Problems.***

A. Assume that a country club has a policy that forbids unaccompanied children under the age of 8 years old from swimming in the club pool, even though the club has a full-time lifeguard on duty. One summer afternoon the lifeguard fails to enforce this policy and a 6-year-old boy is permitted to swim without any parental supervision or presence. Later that day the boy comes down sick from a bacterial infection he contracted during that afternoon swim in the contaminated pool. If he can prove negligence against the pool company for letting him swim without escort, will he also be able to establish proximate cause?

B. Would the *Polemis* case have had a different outcome under the foreseeability test than under the direct cause test?

C. By contrast, take the facts from the University of Miami in the *Tieder* case and apply the direct cause test for proximate cause with respect to the alleged negligence of designing the wall with improper supports. Under the foreseeability test the court finds proximate cause does potentially exist. But under the direct cause test, do you see any independent intervening actions that occurred after the design of the wall and prior to the death of the student? If so, this intervening action will put a kink in the chain of causation and cut off liability to the architect and owner.

D. Again using the facts from *Tieder*, would the direct cause test provide any protection to the students who clutch-started their car? Were there any independent intervening acts after their negligence in starting and losing control of their car?

D. The Substantial Factor Test

The final test that some courts use in their proximate cause analysis is the *substantial factor* test. This test was first employed as an alternative to the but-for test of actual cause in cases where the doctrine of multiple independent sufficient causes applies (the Florida appellate court in *Tieder* discussed this use of the substantial factor test). Multiple courts, however, have since employed the test as their primary test for proximate cause. We will first familiarize ourselves with the substantial factor test in *Brisboy*—a case involving multiple independent sufficient causes, where the court is using it as an alternative to but-for actual causation. Following that we will encounter the test as a standard for finding proximate cause in *Thorne Equipment.*

1. Introduction to the Substantial Factor Test

In its earliest inception, the substantial factor test was introduced by courts as an alternative to the but-for test for actual causation in scenarios where there were multiple independent sufficient causes—such as we saw earlier in this chapter with the two fires burning down the plaintiff's property. Understanding that it was impossible for either of the two fires to constitute a true but-for cause, courts began instead to ask whether either or both of the fires were a "substantial factor" in causing the plaintiff's harm. The *Brisboy* case below depicts just such a scenario where the court utilizes the substantial factor test as an alternative to demanding proof that any of the defendants' conduct (or here, products) was a but-for cause of the harm.

BRISBOY v. FIBREBOARD PAPER PRODUCTS CORP.

384 N.W.2d 39 (Mich. Ct. App. 1986)

Per Curiam.

Defendant appeals as of right from a jury verdict finding the defendant's negligence in failing to warn the plaintiff's decedent of the danger of working with asbestos products to be the proximate cause of his death.

Charlotte Rand filed a complaint on October 31, 1979, seeking damages for the wrongful death of her husband, Charles Rand. Plaintiff alleged that her decedent died as a result of lung cancer caused by asbestosis contracted during his 26-year career as an asbestos insulation worker. Plaintiff named as defendants the nine employers her decedent had worked for from 1951 until 1977, but three of those defendants settled with the plaintiff prior to trial. [By the end of trial the lone remaining defendant was Fibreboard.]

The testimony of a coworker of the decedent, Laurence Jean, revealed that the decedent worked for the defendant for at least six months and at most nine months as an asbestos insulator, *i.e.*, applying insulation material containing asbestos to various pipes. Mr. Jean testified that the air was "very, very dusty" while performing the work, and that there was no way to avoid breathing this dust.

The evidence presented at trial also revealed that plaintiff's decedent was a heavy cigarette user, having smoked two packs per day for 30 years. The effect of the cigarette use on the plaintiff's condition was disputed by the medical experts presented by the parties. Dr. Joseph Wagoner, appearing on behalf of the plaintiff, discounted the effect of Mr. Rand's cigarette smoking on the grounds that Mr. Rand died of adenocarcinoma, and that cigarette smoking is more related to the squamous-type cell, not the adeno type. Dr. Wagoner concluded that cigarette smoking does not increase an asbestos worker's risk of developing lung cancer.

Dr. Leighton Kong, who performed the autopsy on the decedent, admitted that cigarette smoking can be related to adenocarcinoma of the lung, and in fact could have been the sole cause of Mr. Rand's lung cancer. However, Dr. Kong believed that there is a stronger link between asbestosis and cancer than cigarette smoking and cancer.

Dr. Gerrit Scheppes also testified on plaintiff's behalf. Dr. Scheppes indicated that, in his opinion, Mr. Rand's lung cancer was caused by asbestosis. However, Dr. Scheppes admitted that Mr. Rand's history of cigarette smoking played a minor contributing role in the development of his lung cancer.

The defendant's medical evidence included the testimony of Dr. Harry Demopoulos. Dr. Demopoulos opined that Mr. Rand did not suffer from asbestosis and that Mr. Rand's adenocarcinoma was due solely to cigarette smoking. Dr. William Weiss testified that Mr. Rand had no evidence of pulmonary asbestosis and, in light of this fact, Mr. Rand's development of lung cancer was attributable to his history of cigarette smoking. Dr. Weiss also testified that, while asbestosis and cigarette smoking can combine to create a synergistic effect and thus a greater risk of developing lung cancer than the additive risk of the two factors alone, this increased risk does not exist without the presence of asbestosis.

On appeal, defendant first argues that there was insufficient evidence to establish that Mr. Rand's six-to nine-month exposure to defendant's asbestos products was a proximate cause of his death. Defendant argues that the trial court therefore improperly denied defendant's motion for a directed verdict. . . .

Under Michigan law, an actor will not be held liable for his negligent conduct unless that conduct was a legal or proximate cause of the harm to the plaintiff. There may be more than one proximate cause of an injury, and thus the mere fact that some other cause concurs, contributes, or cooperates to produce an injury does not relieve any of the parties whose negligent conduct was one of the causes of the plaintiff's harm. An actor's negligent conduct will not be a legal or proximate cause of the harm to another unless that conduct was a substantial factor in bringing about the harm. *McLean v. Rogers*, 300 N.W.2d 389 (1980). One of the considerations in determining whether an actor's conduct was a substantial factor in bringing about the harm to another is "the number of other factors which contribute in producing the harm and the extent of the effect which they have in producing it." 2 Restatement Torts, 2d, §433(a), p. 432. Where a number of events each contribute to the ultimate harm, one may have such a predominant effect as to make the effect of a particular actor's negligence insignificant. On the other hand, where none of the contributing factors has a predominant effect, their combined effect may act to dilute the effect of the actor's negligence and prevent it from becoming a substantial factor in bringing about the harm.

The plaintiff's proofs, viewed in the light most favorable to him, revealed the following. Mr. Rand's autopsy indicated that he died from cancer resulting from asbestosis and that there was a massive amount of asbestos in his lungs. The nature of the disease from which Mr. Rand suffered is that it progresses cumulatively, with each group of asbestos fibers which lodges in the lung doing damage to the area in which it is present. The exposure to asbestos need not be extensive, and, in fact, even one month of exposure may cause asbestosis and ultimately result in the victim's death. Consequently, there is no safe level of exposure to any carcinogen.

This evidence was sufficient to permit reasonable minds to conclude that Mr. Rand died, at least in part, due to the development of asbestosis in his lungs as a result of his inhalation of asbestos fibers during his working career. While plaintiff naturally could not directly prove that defendant's asbestos fibers caused the disease which led to his death (it is impossible to determine which particular fibers from the group of fibers to which Mr. Rand was exposed in his career caused the disease), plaintiff did establish that, during the time Mr. Rand worked with defendant's product, the air was extremely dusty and that, when asbestos dust is visible, it necessarily implies an extreme exposure.

Plaintiff also established that each fiber which lodges in the lung causes asbestosis in the area around that fiber. Thus, reasonable minds could conclude that Mr. Rand inhaled asbestos fibers from defendant's product and developed asbestosis. The only remaining issue, therefore, is whether the harm caused by defendant's negligent conduct was a substantial factor in bringing about the disease which led to Mr. Rand's death. While clearly a close question, we find that there was sufficient evidence in plaintiff's favor to withstand a motion for a directed verdict. Evidence was presented which showed that Mr. Rand was heavily exposed to defendant's product for six to nine months, that asbestos products were phased out in the early 1970's, and that Mr. Rand was exposed to asbestos products only 50 percent of the time at work during the years from 1954-1962. This conclusion is supported by two federal court opinions dealing with the complex problem of proof in asbestosis cases: *Borel v. Fibreboard Paper Products Corp*, 493 F.2d 1076 (C.A. 5, 1973), *cert den* 419 U.S. 869; 42 L. Ed. 2d 107 (1974); *Migues v. Fibreboard Corp*, 662 F.2d 1182 (C.A. 5, 1981). We therefore find that the trial court properly denied defendant's motion for a directed verdict.

Affirmed.

NOTES AND PROBLEMS

1. ***Substantial Factor as an Alternative to "But-For."*** Early on, the substantial factor test was utilized by some courts when the conceptual problem with the but-for test precluded its use because there were multiple, independently sufficient causes — as in *Kingston*, where there were two fires of roughly equal size which converged upon the plaintiff's property. That court discussed the fact that the defendant might prevail if it could show that the fire it started was so small and insubstantial in comparison to the fire from the northwest quadrant of Chicago. This type of analysis gave rise to courts asking in such cases whether the defendant's conduct was a "substantial factor" in causing the harm rather than a "but-for" factor in causing it. Some courts, as we will see in the next case, subsequently borrowed this test as their primary test for proximate cause rather than being used solely as a substitute test for actual cause. Used in either context, however, it is the same test.

2. ***Review: Multiple Independent Sufficient Causes.*** Under what view of the facts in *Brisboy* would that case illustrate an instance of multiple independent sufficient causes? What expert evidence suggested that the asbestos that the plaintiff was exposed to, at any of the nine employer's locations, might have been sufficient to have caused the disease without the cooperation of any other exposure? The Restatement (Third) identifies toxic tort cases as illustrating multiple independent sufficient causes where there is some threshold dose sufficient to cause the disease and the plaintiff is exposed to such doses from multiple defendants. §27 comment g. (2011).

3. ***Restatement Formulation of the Substantial Factor Test.*** The Restatement (Second) of Torts §433(2) (1965) shows how the substantial factor test should be utilized in cases of multiple independent sufficient causes:

> If two forces are actively operating, one because of the actor's negligence, the other not because of any misconduct on his part, and each of itself is sufficient to bring about the harm to another, the actor's negligence *may* be found to be a substantial factor in bringing it about. (Emphasis added.)

In the next case, we will see the court explore all of the factors to be considered in the substantial factor test in determining whether an actual cause of an event is also a proximate cause of an event.

2. Substantial Factor as a Test for Proximate Cause

Eventually, having been introduced to the substantial factor test as an alternative to but-for actual causation, some courts began to turn to the substantial factor test as a *proximate cause* test — as an alternative to either the direct cause or the foreseeability test. The *American Truck Leasing* case below is an example of a modern court's adaptation of the substantial factor test as its jurisdiction's primary test for proximate cause in a setting where but-for cause was undisputed. Notice the various criteria courts utilize in applying the modern substantial factor test.

AMERICAN TRUCK LEASING, INC. v. THORNE EQUIPMENT CO.

583 A.2d 1242 (Pa. Super. Ct. 1991)

In this case, the trial court determined as a matter of law that a property owner's alleged negligence, even if proved, was not a substantial factor in causing the plaintiff's loss. Therefore, the court sustained preliminary objections in the nature of a demurrer to those counts of the plaintiff's complaint which asserted liability on the part of the property owner. After careful review, we affirm.

Dorothy Gross was the owner of a vacant building [in] Philadelphia. On June 27, 1988, between 1:30 and 2:30 a.m., a fire started in combustible trash and debris which had been allowed to accumulate on the premises. The fire spread across a narrow street and damaged premises . . . owned by Joseph A. Tartaglia and occupied for business purposes by JATCO, Inc. The fire burned for more than eight hours before being extinguished. Pursuant to a determination made by the City of Philadelphia, Thorne Equipment was engaged thereafter to demolish a six story elevator shaft on Tartaglia's land. This elevator shaft, although still standing, had been damaged by the fire. Thorne Equipment began its demolition work on June 28, 1988, but during the course thereof a portion of the elevator shaft fell upon and damaged buildings and vehicles owned by the plaintiffs, American Truck Lines, Inc. and American Truck Leasing, Inc. (American). American thereafter filed a civil action against Thorne Equipment, the City of Philadelphia, Tartaglia, JATCO, Inc. and Dorothy Gross. All claims remain undetermined in the trial court except the claim against Dorothy Gross, which has been summarily dismissed.

American alleged in its complaint that Gross had been negligent by allowing combustible trash and debris to accumulate on her property and in otherwise failing to exercise care to prevent the occurrence of a fire. That negligence, if it existed, would be a legal cause of American's harm only if it could be shown to be a substantial factor in bringing about such harm. *Restatement (Second) of Torts §431.* Factors to be considered in determining whether an act is a substantial factor in bringing about harm to another are enumerated in *Restatement (Second) of Torts §433* as follows:

> "We . . . say in common speech, that the wrong was a cause of the injury. But to make such a standard [the but-for test] the basis of legal responsibility would soon prove very unsatisfactory; for a reduction ad absurdum may be promptly established by calling to mind, that, if the injured person had never been born, the injury would not have happened. So the courts ask another question: Was the wrong act the proximate cause?"
>
> *Justice Powell*
> *Atlantic Coast Line R. Co. v. Daniels, 70 S.E. 203 (Ga. Ct. App. 1911)*

> The following considerations are in themselves or in combination with one another important in determining whether the actor's conduct is a substantial factor in bringing about harm to another:
>
> (a) the number of other factors which contribute in producing the harm and the extent of the effect which they have in producing it;
>
> (b) whether the actor's conduct has created a force or series of forces which are in continuous and active operation up to the time of the harm, or has created a situation harmless unless acted upon by other forces for which the actor is not responsible;
>
> (c) lapse of time.

When these considerations are applied to the facts of the instant case, they demonstrate that even if Dorothy Gross had been negligent in allowing combustible trash to accumulate on her property, such accumulation was too far removed factually and chronologically from American's harm to be a legal cause thereof. Gross's negligence was passive and harmless until acted upon by an independent force. Moreover, the fire which erupted on her property was extinguished before any harm had occurred to American. The negligence for which she was responsible, if any, was not in active operation at the time when damages were caused to American's property. Those damages were caused on the day following the fire because of the manner in which the fire-weakened elevator shaft was demolished by Thorne Equipment. Because the negligent accumulation of combustible trash was too far removed from the damages to American's property and because those damages were caused by the intervening act of the demolition contractor, it cannot be said legally or factually that the alleged negligence of Dorothy Gross was a substantial factor in causing harm to American.

In *Ford v. Jeffries*, 379 A.2d 111 (Pa. 1977), the Supreme Court held that it was for the jury to determine whether a property owner's negligence in maintaining his property in a state of disrepair was a substantial factor in causing the harm to a neighbor's property damaged by fire originating on the original owner's property. In the instant case, however, American's property damage was not caused by a spreading fire. It was caused, rather, by the demolition of a fire damaged grain elevator after the fire had been extinguished. This demolition constituted an independent agency. We conclude, therefore, that the trial court correctly determined that Dorothy Gross, as a matter of law, was not legally responsible for appellant's harm.

Affirmed.

NOTES AND PROBLEMS

1. ***Actual and Proximate Cause.*** In *Thorne*, the court does not discuss actual cause, apparently because defendant Dorothy Gross did not contest that type of required causation. Do you understand how Gross's alleged negligence in letting the fire start would be considered an actual but-for cause of the plaintiff's property damage? If there had never been the fire, would there have been any demolition of the elevator shaft? And if there had been no demolition, would plaintiff's property have been hurt? Once actual causation is satisfied, however, the court has to address the challenged requirement of proximate or legal causation. This court employed the *substantial factor* test as its primary test for proximate cause. How does the court analyze the three considerations under Restatement (Second) §433 in concluding as a matter of law that Gross's negligence was not a proximate cause of the plaintiff's harm?

2. ***Commingling of Tests.*** If this choice of three different tests is not confusing enough, be forewarned that there are some courts in some jurisdictions that use more than one test for proximate cause at the same time. In such jurisdictions, for example ones that require that a cause be both a foreseeable cause of the harm and a substantial factor in bringing about the harm, would having to clear more than one proximate cause hurdle be something that would tend to favor plaintiffs or defendants? Recall who has the burden of proof on this issue.

3. ***Restatement (Third) View.*** The relatively recent Restatement (Third) states a preference for what's referred to as a "risk standard" test for proximate cause: "An actor's liability is limited to those physical harms that result from the risks that made the actor's conduct tortious." §29 (2011). Comment d to §29 further indicates that the test is designed to prevent the imposition of liability by "confining liability's scope to the reasons for holding the actor liable in the first place." If you think this sounds an awful lot like the foreseeability test for proximate cause, you are not alone. This is acknowledged in the drafts of the Third Restatement:

> Properly understood, both the risk standard and a foreseeability test exclude liability for harms that were sufficiently unforeseeable at the time of the actor's tortious conduct that they were not among the risks — potential harms — that made the actor negligent. . . . [W]hen scope of liability arises in a negligence case, the risks that make an actor negligent are limited to foreseeable ones, and the factfinder must determine whether the type of harm that occurred is among those reasonably foreseeable potential harms that made the actor's conduct negligent.

§29, cmt. j (2011). Thus, despite the change in semantics, the Third Restatement has in reality simply indicated a preference for the traditional foreseeability test for proximate cause.

4. ***Problem.*** Again, as a bit of review of the different tests we have seen for proximate cause, how would proximate cause be analyzed using the facts from *Thorne* in jurisdictions utilizing as their proximate cause test, (a) the direct cause test; and (b) the foreseeability test? Does one test seem to be easier to resolve in a rather definitive manner than the other test? What does this say about the benefits or weaknesses about each of these tests?

E. Superseding vs. Intervening Causes

In some cases, there is a final potential way that the plaintiff's effort to prove causation in a negligence claim can be derailed. Even though a plaintiff has proven that defendant's negligence was a factual but-for cause of her harm, and even though the plaintiff has been able to satisfy the jurisdiction's test for proximate cause, defendant might still be able to argue that a *superseding cause* puts a fatal kink in the chain of causation. A superseding cause is a third party's intervening act (occurring after the defendant's negligence) that was not reasonably foreseeable from the standpoint of the defendant. In *Price*, the court discusses and applies this test for distinguishing between a mere intervening cause and a fatal superseding cause. The *McCane-Sondock* case involves a court applying this same test in the context of an intentional crime as the intervening act. In each case the defendant argues that intentional misconduct by a third-party that intervened should cut off causation. As you read the following cases, pay close attention to how this test for superseding versus intervening causes has a different focal point than the foreseeability test for proximate cause.

PRICE v. BLAINE KERN ARTISTA, INC.

893 P.2d 367 (Nev. 1995)

Per Curiam.

Appellant Thomas Price filed an action sounding in . . . negligence as a result of injuries sustained when he was wearing a large manufactured "head" and was pushed or fell to the floor in a Reno club. The district court found that Price's injuries resulted from a supervening cause and entered summary judgment against him. We conclude that material factual issues precluded summary judgment and therefore reverse.

Thomas Price filed an action . . . against Blaine Kern Artista, Inc. ("BKA"), a Louisiana corporation that manufactures oversized masks in the form of caricatures resembling various celebrities and characters (hereafter "caricature mask"). The caricature mask covers the entire head of the wearer. Price alleged in his complaint that the caricature mask of George Bush which he wore during employment as an entertainer at Harrah's Club in Reno was defective due to the absence of a safety harness to support his head and neck under the heavy weight. He also alleged that his injury occurred when a Harrah's patron pushed him from behind, causing the weight of the caricature mask to strain and injure his neck as he fell to the ground.

On BKA's motion for summary judgment, the district court determined that the patron's push that precipitated Price's fall constituted an unforeseeable superseding cause absolving BKA of liability.

The focal point of this appeal is whether the unknown assailant's push that caused Price to fall to the ground is an intervening, superseding cause of Price's injuries, insulating BKA from liability. . . .

Price argues that legal causation is a question of fact to be decided by the trier of fact and that an intervening criminal or tortious act by a third party does not necessarily preclude liability as a matter of law. In so arguing, however, he concedes (rather improvidently, we suggest) that BKA, a Louisiana corporation, could not reasonably be expected to have foreseen an attack on a user of one of its products by a third-party assailant in Reno, Nevada, and relies exclusively on the prospect that a jury might reasonably infer that a performer wearing a top-heavy, oversized caricature mask may stumble, trip, be pushed, or become imbalanced for numerous reasons. That same jury, according to Price, may find that BKA proximately caused Price's injury due to its failure to equip the caricature mask of our former President with a safety harness.

BKA first counters that legal causation, although normally a jury issue, may nevertheless be resolved summarily in appropriate cases when there is no genuine issue of material fact on the issue of foreseeability. BKA next argues that this is an appropriate case for summary judgment because, by Price's own admission, the third-party attack forming the basis of his complaint was not foreseeable to BKA, and is thus a superseding cause of Price's injuries.

Contrary to BKA's assertions, we conclude for two reasons that genuine issues of material fact remain with respect to the issue of legal causation.

[W]ith respect to the negligence claim, while it is true that criminal or tortious third-party conduct typically severs the chain of proximate causation between a plaintiff and a defendant, the chain remains unbroken when the third party's intervening intentional act is reasonably foreseeable. Under the circumstances of this case, the trier of fact could reasonably find that BKA should have foreseen the possibility or probability of some sort of violent reaction, such as pushing, by intoxicated or politically volatile persons, ignited by the sight of an oversized caricature of a prominent political figure. We certainly cannot preclude such an inference as a matter of law and decline to penalize Price for his attorney's lack of acuity in conceding this issue. Indeed, while the precise force that caused Price's fall is uncertain, shortly before the fall, an irate and perhaps somewhat confused patron of Harrah's took issue with the bedecked Price over Bush's policy on abortion rights.

For the reasons discussed above, we conclude that a genuine issue of material fact remains with respect to the issue of the legal and proximate cause of Price's injuries. Accordingly, we reverse the district court's entry of summary judgment and remand for trial.

McCANE-SONDOCK PROTECTION SYSTEMS v. EMMITTEE

540 S.W.2d 764 (Tex. App. 1976)

James Roy Emmittee d/b/a Bedford Package Store sued McCane-Sondock Protection Systems, Inc. for negligently installing a burglar alarm system at his business. After a jury trial, judgment was entered awarding Emmittee $6,839 damages. McCane-Sondock appeals. We affirm.

Appellant argues in five points of error there was no evidence [or legally insufficient evidence] to support the finding that it proximately caused the loss by failing to connect the wires leading from the hold-up button to the burglar alarm control panel and that such finding was so against the great weight and preponderance of the evidence as to be manifestly wrong and unjust.

Appellant argues its action could not be a proximate cause of the loss suffered by Emmittee because it was the action of some third party which caused the loss.

The court in *Teer v. J. Weingarten, Inc.*, 426 S.W.2d 610 (Tex. Civ. App.—Houston (14th Dist.) 1968, writ ref. n.r.e.) said:

> [T]he Texas Courts are firmly committed to the proposition that the issue of foreseeability is related to the issue of proximate cause. It is also undoubtedly true, as a matter of substantive Texas law, that an intervening cause reasonably foreseeable by the defendant, is not such a new and independent cause as to break the chain of

> causation between the defendant's negligence and the injury complained of to the extent of relieving the defendant of liability for such injury. *City of Austin v. Schmedes*, 154 Tex. 416, 279 S.W.2d 326.

It is established appellant failed to connect the wires leading from the hold-up buttons to the burglar alarm control panel and failed to test the system after installation of the alarm buttons.

In the instant case, Mrs. Emmittee and the store manager pressed alarm buttons to activate the system when a robber came into the store declaring "it was a hold-up." There was testimony that if the alarm had functioned the police would have been notified within 30 to 45 seconds. The police station was located only a couple of miles from the liquor store. The robber remained in the store five to ten minutes after the alarm buttons were pressed. We hold these facts constitute some evidence that Emmittee's loss was the proximate result of McCane-Sondock's failure to properly install the alarm equipment. *Martinez v. Delta Brands, Inc.*, 515 S.W.2d 263 (Tex. 1974); *Butler v. Hanson*, 455 S.W.2d 942 (Tex. 1970). Also, we have carefully considered the entire record and find the jury's answers to the challenged special issues are not against the great weight and preponderance of the evidence so as to be manifestly wrong and unjust, nor are they factually insufficient. *In Re King's Estate*, 150 Tex. 662, 244 S.W.2d 660 (Tex. 1951).

Principles

Causation Three-Step Analysis:

1. Is there actual but-for cause (or will some alternative doctrine suffice)?
2. Is there proximate cause using the court's primary test?
3. Is there any superseding cause?

We have considered and overrule all points of error. The judgment is affirmed.

NOTES AND PROBLEMS

1. ***Foreseeable Intervening Acts.*** As both cases above illustrate, intervening third party actions that are reasonably foreseeable do not interfere with legal causation. Only if the third party conduct is unforeseeable would it negate causation. The *Price* court refers to such causes as *superseding*, while the *McCane-Sondock* court refers to them as *new and independent*. Even though one involves at least an intentional tort (a battery) and the other criminal misconduct, neither ends up negating causation. Why would intentional or criminal misconduct be more likely to satisfy the test for superseding cause? Why did the factual circumstances in these two cases not follow that pattern?

2. Tieder ***Revisited.*** Recall the facts from the case of *Tieder*, involving the crushed college student at the University of Miami. The appellate court found that there was potentially proximate cause against the owner and architect who designed the defective wall utilizing the foreseeability test of proximate cause. Should the defendants in that case have raised the defense of superseding cause instead? If defendants had raised that defense, how should the court rule?

3. ***Medical Malpractice as Superseding Cause.*** Sometimes there is an intervening act by a medical doctor who is attempting to treat the plaintiff's initial injury. In this scenario, the intervening act being analyzed comes after the plaintiff's initial injury and serves to aggravate those injuries. What if the doctor commits medical malpractice and this aggravates the initial injury caused by the defendant? Does the act by the doctor constitute an unforeseeable intervening act — a superseding cause — so that the defendant is not liable for the exacerbation of the injury? Courts typically treat this as a fact question. But generally courts hold that the mere fact that the doctor's treatment fell below the duty of care does not necessarily cut off or reduce the defendant's liability because a doctor's negligence can be foreseeable:

> "Generally, medical treatment sought by an injured person is considered a normal consequence of the tortfeasor's conduct. A defendant will be liable for the adverse results of medical treatment unless the treatment is extraordinary or the harm is outside the risks incident to the medical treatment."

Weems v. Hy-Vee Food Stores, Inc., 526 N.W.2d 571 (Iowa App. 1994); Corbett v. Weisband, 551 A.2d 1059 (Pa. App. Ct. 1988) (finding that even a doctor's undisputed negligent treatment was not necessarily a superseding cause because the "issue is whether his negligence was 'highly extraordinary.'" *Id.* at 1075).

4. ***Car Thief's Accident as Superseding Cause.*** A very interesting scenario that has been litigated in many courts involves a car thief causing a traffic accident shortly after stealing the car. As you might imagine, the thief might be difficult to either sue or to collect from on a judgment. In many instances, the aggrieved plaintiff sues instead the owner of the stolen vehicle arguing that their negligence (e.g., leaving the keys in the unlocked vehicle) was a legal cause of the accident. The defendant owners have often raised the issue of superseding cause. Most courts have been friendly toward this defense, citing either no duty, no proximate cause, or superseding cause as the reason to deny recovery:

> [A] substantial number of courts have not held owners liable for leaving the keys in their unattended vehicles and for the injuries to third persons as a result of the thefts and subsequent negligent operation of those vehicles. Those courts have concluded either that an owner owes no duty to the general public to guard against the risk of a thief's negligent operation of a vehicle . . . ; that the theft and subsequent negligence of the thief could not reasonably be foreseen by the owner . . . ; or . . . because the thief's actions constituted an independent, intervening cause.

McClenahan v. Cooley, 806 S.W.2d 767, 773 (Tenn. 1991) (quoting Prosser and Keeton, The Law of Torts, §44 (5th ed. 1984). The *Cooley* court said the issue should be analyzed as one of intervening versus superseding cause. It concluded that, at least when the accident happens shortly after the theft, there is a jury question on whether the actions of the thief could be reasonably foreseeable. It refused to affirm summary judgment for the car owner. In Chapter 6, Special Duty Rules, we will see this same scenario in *Moody v. Delta Western* (introducing the firefighter rule, but not discussing the proximate cause dilemma).

5. *Superseding Causes in a Direct Cause Jurisdiction.* At least when a court's primary test for proximate cause is the foreseeability or substantial factor test, there is no conceptual problem with the final, additional application of the superseding cause test — it is analysis that is not redundant. But would it make any sense in a direct cause jurisdiction to consider whether an intervening act is a superseding cause? After all, any independent, intervening act by a third-party negates proximate causation anyway. Asked another way, in a direct cause jurisdiction would the alarm company defendant in *McClane-Sondock* necessarily win? Do you see any room for argument by the plaintiff in a direct cause case to hold the alarm company liable as the legal cause of its harm? Consider the indispensible relationship between the alarm company's negligent conduct and the ability of the burglar to commit his intentional act of stealing from the plaintiff. Do you see how one appears to be dependent on the other, rather than constituting an *independent* intervening act?

Upon Further Review

The law of torts could dispense with the complexities of proximate cause if we were prepared to dispense justice with no concern for fairness. We could hold people liable for remote acts of negligence that caused unforeseeable ripples around the world decades after the fact. The only limitation on liability would be the courts' ability to perceive but-for causation. But there seems to be universal agreement that this is untenable when we are dealing with accidental injuries. So the trick becomes finding a way to articulate at what point we draw a line in the sand and say, "no more." As Judge Andrews observed in his famous dissent in *Palsgraf*, "[w]e may regret that the line was drawn just where it was, but drawn somewhere it had to be.... The words we used were simply indicative of our notions of public policy...."

Most courts choose between one of three tests for proximate cause, with the prevailing view preferring the test of *foreseeability*. After considering the foreseeable scope of harm in determining whether a defendant's conduct is careless, we then ask whether the nature of the accident is what we feared might happen all along. If so, then proximate cause exists even though all of the precise details might not have been foreseen. In days past, the *direct* test was more in fashion, though it is still used even today at times. Unlike the foreseeability test, which focuses upon whether the nature of the final accident was foreseeable, the direct test focuses instead upon whether any independent, intervening acts broke the chain of causation — foreseeability is not relevant to this analysis. Finally, some courts have adopted the *substantial factor* test, which considers issues of time, the number of other factors, and to what extent the defendant's carelessness unleashed a force still active when the plaintiff was harmed. Particularly in foreseeability and substantial factor jurisdictions, even if the applicable test is satisfied, in appropriate cases the defendant might still prevail by proving that an unforeseeable intervening act has made it unfair to impose liability on the defendant.

When all three tests are easily satisfied, there likely is not a very significant proximate cause issue in the case; this is very common. But when application of different proximate cause tests yields different conclusions, this is indicative of a very serious proximate cause challenge to the plaintiff's ability to hold the negligent actor liable. Considerable attention — whether on your torts final or in handling a lawsuit — is likely warranted on the matter. Whether proximate cause truly is the "ultimate issue" in a torts case likely varies with the circumstances of each case. But mastering the subject is highly useful.

Pulling It All Together

Wheels, Inc. is a manufacturer of automobile tires and rims. It supplies tires and rims in large quantities to Fjord Motors, a Norwegian automobile manufacturer. To save money and boost profits, Wheels laid off all of its quality control inspectors at its manufacturing facility. As a result, certain units of a particular model rim were shipped to Fjord despite hairline cracks that were too small to be seen by the unaided eye, but could have been revealed using an x-ray machine that other rim manufacturers typically use for this purpose. Wheels actually has the x-ray equipment and used to have a policy to inspect by x-ray each rim before it was shipped, but this practice had to stop due to the layoffs. Fjord was not told of this change in practice, was unaware of the hairline cracks in the rims, and went ahead and used them on many of its cars that were produced at this time.

Juan was a new purchaser of one of the Fjords that received a defective wheel rim. He was headed to the office, speeding at an excessive rate on the interstate freeway one sunny morning when the crack on his rim suddenly caused a complete wheel failure and his wheel came off the Fjord. Because he was running late, rather than try to pull to the side, he gripped the steering wheel hard, maintained his speed, and tried to keep going. But his efforts to control the car were in vain and a few seconds later he completely lost control of his Fjord. As he swerved from his lane of traffic, another car (driven by Roxanne) tried to pass him rather than slowing. As a result, Juan and Roxanne ran into each other, and they both spun out of control, coming to a stop in the middle lane of the freeway, blocking much of the traffic behind them. Roxanne was only mildly hurt, but the delay occasioned by the crash caused her to miss an important business meeting and she was fired from her job later that day. One of the vehicles coming up behind the accident scene a few minutes later was a truck filled with frozen meats. The driver of the truck, Frank, was distracted while texting on his cellphone and failed to notice the stoppage on the freeway. As a result, Frank crashed into the back of another car that had just come to a stop ahead of him due to the crash between Juan and Roxanne. This caused significant property damage to the car. The truck was also disabled because the front-end damage hurt its engine. The truck was stalled for hours due to both the engine problems and the delays the public authorities had in cleaning up the damaged vehicles belonging to Juan and Roxanne. Also, because the engine was not running on the truck, the refrigeration unit was also shut down and the entire shipment of frozen meat thawed and was ruined.

Please analyze the negligence claims, including the causation issues, for each claimant above — 45 minutes.

CHAPTER 6

Special Duty Rules

I INTRODUCTION

Thus far, we have been assuming that there is always a duty of reasonable care. We spent time reviewing the character traits of the reasonable person, to what extent this reasonable person took on certain attributes of the actor in question, and how the circumstances of the accident were factored into the analysis. All the while, we have implicitly assumed that a duty of reasonable care existed. This chapter will reexamine that assumption, because it turns out that such a duty is not nearly as omnipresent as this assumption. We will begin with the traditional dichotomy between a person's acts and a person's omissions. This will create certain default positions on the issue of the existence of a duty. We will also cover exceptions to such default positions. Beyond that, this chapter will address certain recurring factual situations where tort law has determined whether, and to what extent, a particular duty of care will exist. Often the circumstance of special relationships among the parties, the nature of the activity, the nature of the harm, and the status of the victim and the defendant actor influence this determination. Not only will you become familiar with these special duty rules, but you will also gain some insight into how courts go about fashioning these rules of law.

CHAPTER GOALS

- ☑ Understand the basic dichotomy between acts and omissions in terms of setting default rules for whether a duty of reasonable care exists.
- ☑ Learn when and why courts will pause at the issue of duty in different scenarios to reexamine the default duty rules and become familiar with the balancing of policies.
- ☑ Appreciate how special relationships commonly are used to create or modify a duty of care where one might otherwise not exist.
- ☑ Recognize concerns courts have with certain types of primary harms that cause them to either narrow the universe of victims owed duties of care or, in other cases, eliminate altogether a duty of care to avoid such harms.
- ☑ Become familiar with the doctrine of primary assumption of the risk.
- ☑ Discover the trichotomy of duties traditionally applied in premises liability claims.
- ☑ Reexamine *The T.J. Hooper* view on industry customs in the unique context of claims against professionals.

II DUTY TO ACT

A very fundamental proposition in negligence law is the presumption that when we act we have to act with reasonable care. Implicit within this black letter law is the rather startling corollary that we do not generally have an obligation to act, even though refusing to come to the aid of an imperiled person may seem most unreasonable and uncivilized, if not downright monstrous. If this bothers you, you can take some comfort in the fact that tort law does impose a general duty of care on all of us to take reasonable care when we do choose to undertake some activity. When we drive a car we must do so carefully. When we go hunting we must exercise care. When we mow our lawn the obligation to act with care is established. But failing to drive our car, or mow our lawn, or go hunting does not generally make us negligent regardless of the circumstances. If we do not have an obligation to rescue others, we will see that when we do undertake to lend a hand, we are obligated to act with reasonable care. A related doctrine, however, establishes that if an actor has caused a situation of peril for another and we inject ourselves into the perilous situation as a rescuer, the law also imposes the same duty of care on that original actor toward us — the *rescue doctrine.* After exploring the parameters of the right to remain inactive, and the obligation to exercise care when acting, we will delve into the rescue doctrine and a special no-duty rule that often precludes public emergency actors from suing to recover for their own injuries during a rescue.

A. Acts vs. Omissions

The *Yania* case that follows is a classic case concerning the lack of a duty to act to come to the aid of another. This fundamental rule of law is something many law students find shocking. The *Lawter* decision immediately thereafter illustrates the limits of this no-duty rule. Finally, in *Lundy*, we will begin to see some cracks in the wall of this legal dichotomy. As it turns out, when some special relationship exists between the parties, the *Yania* rule of law is modified to create a duty of care otherwise absent.

1. No General Duty to Aid Others

YANIA v. BIGAN

155 A.2d 343 (Pa. 1959)

JONES, J.

A bizarre and most unusual circumstance provides the background of this appeal.

On September 25, 1957 John E. Bigan was engaged in a coal strip-mining operation in Shade Township, Somerset County. On the property being stripped were large cuts or trenches created by Bigan when he removed the earthen overburden for the purpose of removing the coal underneath. One cut contained water 8 to 10 feet in depth with side walls or embankments 16 to 18 feet in height; at this cut Bigan had installed a pump to remove the water.

At approximately 4 p.m. on that date, Joseph F. Yania, the operator of another coal strip-mining operation, and one Boyd M. Ross went upon Bigan's property for the purpose of discussing a business matter with Bigan, and, while there, were asked by Bigan to aid him in starting the pump. Ross and Bigan entered the cut and stood at the point where the pump was located. Yania stood at the top of one of the cut's side walls and then jumped from the side wall — a height of 16 to 18 feet — into the water and was drowned.

Yania's widow, in her own right and on behalf of her three children, instituted wrongful death and survival actions against Bigan contending Bigan was responsible for Yania's death. [Bigan demurred to the complaint and the trial court dismissed the complaint. Plaintiff has appealed this dismissal.]

Summarized, Bigan stands charged with three-fold negligence: (1) by urging, enticing, taunting and inveigling Yania to jump into the water; (2) by failing to warn Yania of a dangerous condition on the land, i.e., the cut wherein lay 8 to 10 feet of water; (3) by failing to go to Yania's rescue after he had jumped into the water.

Our inquiry must be to ascertain whether the well-pleaded facts in the complaint, assumedly true, would, if shown, suffice to prove negligent conduct on the part of Bigan.

Appellant initially contends that Yania's descent from the high embankment into the water and the resulting death were caused "entirely" by the spoken words and blandishments of Bigan delivered at a distance from Yania. The complaint does not allege that Yania slipped or that he was pushed or that Bigan made any *physical* impact upon Yania. On the contrary, the only inference deducible from the facts alleged in the complaint is that Bigan, by the employment of cajolery and inveiglement, caused such a *mental* impact on Yania that the latter was deprived of his volition and freedom of choice and placed under a compulsion to jump into the water. Had Yania been a child of tender years or a person mentally deficient then it is conceivable that taunting and enticement could constitute actionable negligence if it resulted in harm. However to contend that such conduct directed to an adult in full possession of all his mental faculties constitutes actionable negligence is not only without precedent but completely without merit.

Principles

"Silence in the face of evil is evil itself. To not speak is to speak; to not act is to act."

Dietrich Bonhoeffer

The *only* condition on Bigan's land which could possibly have contributed in any manner to Yania's death was the water-filled cut with its high embankment. Of this condition there was neither concealment nor failure to warn, but, on the contrary, the complaint specifically avers that Bigan not only requested Yania and Boyd to assist him in starting the pump to remove the water from the cut but "led" them to the cut itself. If this cut possessed any potentiality of danger, such a condition was as obvious and apparent to Yania as to Bigan, both coal strip-mine operators. Under the circumstances herein depicted Bigan could not be held liable in this respect.

Lastly, it is urged that Bigan failed to take the necessary steps to rescue Yania from the water. The mere fact that Bigan saw Yania in a position of peril in the water imposed upon him no legal, although a moral, obligation or duty to go to his rescue unless Bigan was legally responsible, in whole or in part, for placing Yania in the perilous position: Restatement, Torts, §314. Cf: Restatement, Torts, §322. The language of this Court in *Brown v. French*, 104 Pa. 604, 607, 608, is apt:

> If it appeared that the deceased, by his own carelessness, contributed in any degree to the accident which caused the loss of his life, the defendants ought not to have been held to answer for the consequences resulting from that accident. . . . He voluntarily placed himself in the way of danger, and his death was the result of his own act. . . . That his undertaking was an exceedingly reckless and dangerous one, the event proves, but there was no one to blame for it but himself. He had the right to try the experiment, obviously dangerous as it was, but then also upon him rested the consequences of that experiment, and upon no one else; he may have been, and probably was, ignorant of the risk which he was taking upon himself, or knowing it, and trusting to his own skill, he may have regarded it as easily superable. But in either case, the result of his ignorance, or of his mistake, must rest with himself— and cannot be charged to the defendants.

The complaint does not aver any facts which impose upon Bigan legal responsibility for placing Yania in the dangerous position in the water and, absent such legal responsibility, the law imposes on Bigan no duty of rescue.

Recognizing that the deceased Yania is entitled to the benefit of the presumption that he was exercising due care and extending to appellant the benefit of every well pleaded fact in this complaint and the fair inferences arising therefrom, yet we can reach but one conclusion: that Yania, a reasonable and prudent adult in full possession of all his mental faculties, undertook to perform an act which he knew or should have known was attended with more or less peril and it was the performance of that act and not any conduct upon Bigan's part which caused his unfortunate death.

2. *When Acting, the Duty of Care Exists*

UNITED STATES v. LAWTER

219 F.2d 559 (5th Cir. 1955)

Hucheson, J.

[T]he suit was for damages for the death of plaintiff's wife. The claim was that the death was caused by the negligence of Coast Guard personnel in the conduct of a helicopter air-sea rescue.

[On April 18, 1953, the deceased, Loretta Jean Lawter, her husband Oren Lawter, his brother Andrew Lawter and his wife, Susan Lawter, were in a 16-foot skiff in Biscayne Bay, when a wave drowned out the outboard motor attached to the skiff and further waves resulted in the swamping of the boat. As a result, the four passengers were cast into water approximately 500 yards from the nearest shore. The water at that particular point was approximately four feet deep.

At this time a U.S. Coast Guard helicopter was making a routine patrol flight over the Biscayne Bay area. The flight by the helicopter was made for the purpose of determining if any vessels or people in the area were in the need of aid or assistance, so that such aid or assistance could be rendered before darkness set in. The crew of the helicopter included some who had experience and training in sea rescues and some completely lacking any such experience or training. The crew spotted the four Lawters in the water. There were no boats or vessels nearby to rescue them and so the crew of the helicopter proceeded to undertake the rescue. The helicopter was equipped with a cable used to raise someone from the sea. It was supposed to be secured to any rescued person prior to being lifted into the helicopter. On this occasion, an inexperienced member of the crew took charge of this rescue. The cable was lowered to the decedent but not secured to her. She merely had a hold of it with her hands. Before any crewmember could secure her, the inexperienced crewmember began hoisting her into the air toward the helicopter. She was raised until her head and shoulders were above the bottom of the door in the helicopter, when the cable was stopped. Deceased had not been raised high enough to be brought into the cabin. Before the cable could be raised further, she lost her grip and fell to her death.]

[The trial court found negligence on the part of the United States. That court held that a duty was imposed upon respondent to act with reasonable care in the performance of rescue operations once such rescue operations are undertaken. The court entered judgment for plaintiff in the sum of $10,000.]

As appellee correctly points out, the case made is not one of omission or failure on the part of the Coast Guard to act, but of a definite and affirmative act causing death, an act deliberately undertaken and negligently performed by it.

Whatever then might be said of the liability of the United States, if the case had to do with mere negligent omission or inaction of the Coast Guard, as was the case in *Indian Towing Co. v. United States*, 5th Cir., 211 F.2d 886, is not controlling here. For the uncontradicted evidence shows that the Coast Guard, pursuant to long established policy, affirmatively took over the rescue mission, excluding others therefrom, and thus not only placed the deceased in a worse position than when it took charge, but negligently brought about her death, and it is hornbook law that under such circumstances the law imposes an obligation upon everyone who attempts to do anything, even gratuitously, for another not to injure him by the negligent performance of that which he has undertaken.

The judgment is affirmed.

3. Special Relationships Compelling Action

LUNDY v. ADAMAR OF NEW JERSEY, INC.

34 F.3d 1173 (3d Cir. 1994)

STAPLETON, J.

Appellant Sidney Lundy suffered a heart attack while a patron at appellee's casino, TropWorld Casino ("TropWorld"), in Atlantic City, New Jersey. While he survived, Lundy was left with permanent disabilities. Lundy and his wife here appeal from a summary judgment entered against them by the district court. Their appeal raises [the issue of] what duty, if any, did TropWorld owe under New Jersey law to provide medical care to Lundy.

The district court held that TropWorld's duty is, at most, to provide basic first aid to the patron when the need becomes apparent and to take reasonable steps to procure appropriate medical care. Because the court found no evidence that TropWorld was negligent in carrying out this duty to Lundy, it granted TropWorld's motion for summary judgment. We will affirm.

On August 3, 1989, Lundy, a 66-year-old man with a history of coronary artery disease, was patronizing TropWorld Casino. While Lundy was gambling at a blackjack table, he suffered cardiac arrest and fell to the ground unconscious. Three other patrons quickly ran to Lundy and began to assist him. The first to reach him was Essie Greenberg ("Ms. Greenberg"), a critical care nurse. Ms. Greenberg was soon joined by her husband, Dr. Martin Greenberg ("Dr. Greenberg"), who is a pulmonary specialist. The third individual who aided Lundy did not disclose his identity, but he indicated to Dr. Greenberg that he was a surgeon. During his deposition, Dr. Greenberg stated that, when he first arrived on the scene, Lundy was unresponsive, not breathing, and without a pulse. Dr. Greenberg testified that he, his wife, and the surgeon immediately began to perform cardiopulmonary resuscitation ("CPR") on Lundy.

Meanwhile, the blackjack dealer at the table where Lundy had been gambling pushed an emergency "call" button at his table which alerted TropWorld's Security Command Post that a problem existed.

A sergeant in TropWorld's security force and a TropWorld security guard arrived at the blackjack table apparently within fifteen seconds of their receiving the radio message from the Security Command Post. The Greenbergs and the unidentified surgeon were already assisting Lundy. Upon arriving, the security guard called the Security Command Post on her hand-held radio and requested that someone contact the casino medical station, which was located one floor above the casino. Several witnesses agree that Nurse Margaret Slusher ("Nurse Slusher"), the nurse who was on-duty at the casino medical station at the time, arrived on the scene within a minute or two of being summoned. As soon as Nurse Slusher arrived, she instructed the security guards to call for an ambulance.

Nurse Slusher brought with her an ambu-bag, oxygen, and an airway. She did not, however, bring an intubation kit to the scene. Dr. Greenberg testified that he asked Nurse Slusher for one and she told him that it was TropWorld's "policy" not to have an intubation kit on the premises. Nurse Slusher testified at her deposition that some of the equipment normally found in an intubation kit was stocked in TropWorld's medical center, but that she did not bring this equipment with her because she was not qualified to use it.

Nurse Slusher proceeded to assist the three patrons in performing CPR on Lundy. Specifically, Nurse Slusher placed the ambu-bag over Lundy's face while the others took turns doing chest compressions. The ambu-bag was connected to an oxygen source. Dr. Greenberg testified that he was sure that air was entering Lundy's respiratory system and that Lundy was being adequately oxygenated during the period when he was receiving both CPR treatment and air through the ambu-bag. Dr. Greenberg went on to say that the only reason he had requested an intubation kit was "to establish an airway and subsequently provide oxygen in a more efficient manner."

Upon the arrival of the EMT unit, a technician, with the help of the two doctor patrons, attempted to intubate Lundy using an intubation kit brought by the EMT unit. Dr. Greenberg claimed that, due to Lundy's stout physique and rigid muscle tone, it was a very difficult intubation, and that there were at least a half dozen failed attempts before the procedure was successfully completed. After intubation, Lundy regained a pulse and his color improved.

[By way of granting a summary judgment motion, the] district court held that TropWorld had fulfilled its duty to Lundy under New Jersey law. The court found that TropWorld had "immediately summoned medical attention for Mr. Lundy once it became aware of his need for it." Additionally, the court stated that [TropWorld] "fulfilled its duty to aid injured patrons by having at least a registered nurse available, trained in emergency care, who could immediately size up a patron's medical situation and summon appropriate emergency medical personnel and equipment by ambulance to respond to the patrons's (sic) emergency needs."

Additionally, the court held that New Jersey's Good Samaritan Statute, *N.J. Stat. Ann. §2A:62A-1* (West 1993), shielded TropWorld and its employees from liability for any acts or omissions they took while rendering care in good faith to Lundy.

The Lundys cannot, and do not, claim that TropWorld was responsible in any way for Mr. Lundy's medical emergency. Rather, as we understand it, the Lundys advance two theories of liability against TropWorld. First, the relationship between a casino and its patrons gives rise to a duty to provide medical care, and TropWorld breached this duty when it failed to have on-site the equipment and skilled personnel necessary to perform an intubation. Second, TropWorld breached a voluntarily assumed duty by failing to provide Dr. Greenberg, upon his request, with the laryngoscope with intubation tube that was available in the medical station.

Generally, a bystander has no duty to provide affirmative aid to an injured person, even if the bystander has the ability to help. *See* W. Page Keeton et al., *Prosser and Keeton on the Law of Torts §56*, at 375 (5th ed. 1984). New Jersey courts have recognized, however, that the existence of a relationship between the victim and one in a position to render aid may create a duty to render assistance. In *Szabo v. Pennsylvania R.R. Co.*, 132 N.J.L. 331, 40 A.2d 562 (N.J. Err. & App. 1945), for example, New Jersey's highest court held that [if an employee,] while engaged in the work of his or her employer, sustains an injury rendering him or her helpless to provide for his or her own care, the employer must secure medical care for the employee. If a casino owner in New Jersey owes no greater duty to its patrons than an employer owes its employees while they are engaged in the employer's business, we think it clear that TropWorld did not fail in its duty to render assistance.

The Lundys insist, however, that TropWorld had a duty beyond that recognized in *Szabo*. They urge specifically that the Supreme Court of New Jersey would adopt the rule set forth in the *Restatement (Second) of Torts §314A* (1965). *Section 314A* states in pertinent part:

> (1) A common carrier is under a duty to its passengers to take reasonable action
>
> (a) to protect them against unreasonable risk of physical harm, and
>
> (b) to give them first aid after it knows or has reason to know that they are ill or injured, and to care for them until they can be cared for by others.
>
> (2) An innkeeper is under a similar duty to its guests.
>
> (3) A possessor of land who holds it open to the public is under a similar duty to members of the public who enter in response to his invitation.

We think it likely that the Supreme Court of New Jersey would accept the principles enunciated in *§314A* and would apply them in a case involving a casino and one of its patrons. The pertinent commentary following *§314A* indicates that the duty "to take reasonable action . . . to give . . . first aid" in times of emergency requires only that carriers, innkeepers and landowners procure appropriate medical care as soon as the need for such care becomes apparent and provide such first aid prior to the arrival of qualified assistance as the carrier's, innkeeper's or landowner's employees are reasonably capable of giving. Clearly, the duty recognized in *§314A* does not extend to providing all medical care that the carrier or innkeeper could reasonably foresee might be needed by a patron. Specifically, the commentary states:

> f. The defendant . . . in the case of an ill or injured person . . . will seldom be required to do more than give such first aid as he reasonably can, and take reasonable steps to turn the sick man over to a physician, or to those who will look after him and see that medical assistance is obtained.

Nurse Slusher was a registered, licensed nurse who had been trained in emergency care and who had fifteen years of nursing experience. The uncontradicted evidence was that, despite this training and experience, she was not competent to perform an intubation. It necessarily follows that the duty which the Lundys insist the New Jersey Supreme Court would recognize in this case would require casinos to provide a full-time on-site staff physician. Certainly, maintaining on a full-time basis the capability of performing an intubation goes far beyond any "first aid" contemplated by *§314A*. We are confident the New Jersey Supreme Court would decline to impose liability on TropWorld for failing to maintain that full-time capability.

The Lundys further claim that, even if there would otherwise be no duty to provide a level of care encompassing intubation, TropWorld voluntarily assumed a duty to provide such care and breached that duty by negligently failing to provide it. As we understand the argument, TropWorld voluntarily assumed this duty in two ways. First, by [having] a laryngoscope with intubation tube on the premises, TropWorld voluntarily assumed the duty of having it available for use on request. Second, by voluntarily undertaking to assist Mr. Lundy, TropWorld assumed a duty to use due care in providing that assistance and breached this duty when Nurse Slusher failed to bring the laryngoscope with intubation tube to Dr. Greenberg. In connection with this second argument, the Lundys rely upon the principles outlined in *§324 of the Restatement (Second) of Torts* which provides:

> One who, being under no duty to do so, takes charge of another who is helpless adequately to aid or protect himself is subject to liability to the other for any bodily harm caused to him by
>
> (a) the failure of the actor to exercise reasonable care to secure the safety of the other while within the actor's charge, or
>
> (b) the actor's discontinuing his aid or protection, if by so doing he leaves the other in a worse position than when the actor took charge of him.

As we have indicated, TropWorld's medical center, did have a laryngoscope with intubation tube as part of its inventory of equipment. Nurse Slusher did not bring this equipment with her when she was summoned to Pit 3, however. She brought only that equipment that she was qualified to use: the ambu-bag, oxygen, and an airway. At some point after her arrival on the scene, Dr. Greenberg asked for an intubation kit. While the Lundys do not expressly so state, we understand their contention to be that Nurse Slusher should have returned to the medical center at this point and retrieved the intubation tube for Dr. Greenberg's use and TropWorld is liable for her failure to do so. They suggest that her failure to do so was the result of an ill-considered TropWorld policy that she was not permitted to use intubation equipment.

We reject the notion that TropWorld voluntarily assumed a duty to Mr. Lundy it would not otherwise have had. The Lundys have referred us to no New Jersey case law supporting this proposition and we have found none.

The Lundys' argument based on *§324 of the Restatement*, ignores the fact that the principles restated therein have been materially altered by New Jersey's Good Samaritan Act, *§2A: 62A-1 N.J. Stat. Ann.* That Act provides that anyone "who in good faith renders emergency aid at the scene of an ... emergency to the victim ... shall not be liable for any civil damages as a result of acts or omissions by such person in rendering the emergency care." We believe the Supreme Court of New Jersey would hold that this mandate protects TropWorld from liability in the situation before us.

The Lundys do not, and cannot, assert that there was bad faith here. Rather, they seek to avoid the effect of New Jersey's Good Samaritan Act by relying on what is known as the "preexisting duty" exception to the Act. Under this exception, the Act provides no immunity from liability if the duty allegedly breached by the volunteer was a duty that existed prior to the voluntary activity. *E.g., Praet v. Borough of Sayreville, 218 N.J. Super.* 218, 527 A.2d 486 (1987) (police officers who have a preexisting duty to render emergency assistance to a motorist trapped in a car may be held liable for failing to extricate motorist and prevent fire). We do not believe the preexisting duty exception is applicable under New Jersey law in a situation, like the present one, where the preexisting duty is a limited one and the alleged negligence is the failure to provide a level of assistance beyond that required by the preexisting duty.

We think this becomes apparent when one focuses on the purposes of the Good Samaritan Act and the preexisting duty exception and on the nature of the preexisting duty in this case. The purpose of the Good Samaritan Act is to encourage the rendering of assistance to victims by providing that the voluntary rendering of aid will not give rise to any liability that would not otherwise exist. The preexisting duty exception recognizes that fulfillment of this objective of the statute can be accomplished without the eradication of preexisting duties.

Nurse Slusher had no preexisting duty to Lundy apart from her role as an employee of TropWorld. Nurse Slusher, if she had been a fellow patron, for example, would have had no preexisting duty obligation and she would have been fully protected by the Good Samaritan Act. Thus, the only relevant preexisting duty for purposes of applying the Act under New Jersey law is the preexisting duty owed by TropWorld to Mr. Lundy. That preexisting duty, as we have seen, was a duty limited to summoning aid and, in the interim, taking reasonable first aid measures. It did not include the duty to provide the medical equipment and personnel necessary to perform an intubation. It follows, we believe, that Nurse Slusher's conduct with respect to the providing or withholding of the intubation equipment on the premises was not conduct with respect to which she or TropWorld owed a preexisting duty to Lundy. It further follows that, if TropWorld is responsible for the assistance voluntarily provided by Nurse Slusher, it is protected by the Act from liability arising from her alleged negligence in failing to provide that intubation equipment. Accordingly, we conclude that TropWorld's motion for summary judgment was properly granted.

NOTES AND PROBLEMS

1. ***Acts vs. Omissions.*** Why does the common law make this distinction between acts and failures to act? Judge Cardozo in *Palsgraf* argued that the foreseeable orbit of danger set the contours for the duty of care. Wasn't the plaintiff in *Yania* (who drowned after jumping into the water) in foreseeable danger? Did Dr. Greenberg, in *Lundy*, have any common law obligation to come to the assistance of the ill gambler? Regardless of how slight (or reasonable) the burden might be on a bystander to come to the rescue of another, and despite how foreseeable (perhaps inevitable) the harm might be from inaction, the common law generally does not obligate one to act. What is the overriding interest that would preclude such a duty? What exceptions to this no-duty principle do we see at work or referenced in the above cases?

2. ***Restatement View of a Duty to Act.*** Restatement (Second) of Torts §314 (1965) provides: "The fact that the actor realizes or should realize that action on his part is necessary for another's aid or protection does not of itself impose upon him a duty to take such action." Illustration no. 4 to this section provides this example: "A, a strong swimmer, sees B, against whom he entertains an unreasonable hatred, floundering in deep water and obviously unable to swim. Knowing B's identity, he turns away. A is not liable to B." While this is the common law in America, many European countries disagree. Further, there is a small number of northeastern states that by legislative fiat have changed this common law rule and require an actor with actual knowledge of another's peril to render aid if such is possible without exposing the rescuer to danger.

3. ***Special Relationships Can Create an Obligation to Act.*** The court in *Lundy* references the judicial rulings requiring an employer to provide aid to an injured employee on the job. And the Restatement provision quoted in *Lundy* mentions three other instances where the default no-duty assumption is rejected — in cases involving common carriers, innkeepers, and property owners with injured customers. Do these groups have anything in common that might explain the exceptional rule demanding that they take some action to assist others? Two ideas spring to mind. First, that in these relationships the defendant seems to be in a position to profit in some manner from the presence of the plaintiff; therefore, imposing a duty of care requiring action does not seem unfair. Second, in these scenarios, the plaintiff is generally put in a

position of having to rely upon the defendant for protection. The confluence of these two general thoughts seems to be enough impetus under the common law to overcome the no-duty common law rule and to instead compel (reasonable) actions.

4. ***Good Samaritan Statutes.*** As the court in *Lundy* states, Good Samaritan statutes are designed to remove the threat of litigation as a potential disincentive to assisting gratuitously one in need. One has to be careful not to treat all such legislation as the same. The way the statute is phrased can lead to very different levels of protection. Consider the disparate levels of protection under the following two states' Good Samaritan statutes. With respect to each, who may take advantage of the statute's protection? What level of immunity from common law negligence is offered? How successful would you anticipate each statute being in removing the chill arising from the common law's imposition of a duty of reasonable care upon rescuers?

Texas Good Samaritan Statute

(a) A person who in good faith administers emergency care, including using an automated external defibrillator, is not liable in civil damages for an act performed during the emergency unless the act is wilfully or wantonly negligent.

(b) This section does not apply to care administered:

(1) for or in expectation of remuneration, provided that being legally entitled to receive remuneration for the emergency care rendered shall not determine whether or not the care was administered for or in anticipation of remuneration; or

(2) by a person who was at the scene of the emergency because he or a person he represents as an agent was soliciting business or seeking to perform a service for remuneration.

. . .

(e) This section does not apply to a person whose negligent act or omission was a producing cause of the emergency for which care is being administered.

Tex. Civ. Prac. & Rem. Code §74.151 (Tex. 2005).

Mississippi Good Samaritan Statute

No duly licensed, practicing physician, dentist, registered nurse, licensed practical nurse, certified registered emergency technician, or any other person who, in good faith and in the exercise of reasonable care, renders emergency care to any injured person at the scene of an emergency, or in transporting said injured person to a point where medical assistance can be reasonably expected, shall be liable for any civil damages to said injured person as a result of any acts committed in good faith and in the exercise of reasonable care or omissions in good faith and in the exercise of reasonable care by such persons in rendering the emergency care to said injured person.

Miss. Code Ann. §73-25-37 (1972)

5. ***Default Rules for Duty.*** This chapter will present many cases presenting special duty rules that courts have crafted for particular recurring factual

scenarios. As the foregoing cases illustrate, however, the common law generally imposes on actors a duty to act with reasonable care. In cases of *failure to act*, the default rule is that there is no duty to act with reasonable care. The Restatement (Third) of Torts does a pretty good job explaining how courts actually operate consistent with these default positions:

> Ordinarily, an actor whose conduct creates risks of physical harm to others has a duty to exercise reasonable care. Except in unusual categories of cases in which courts have developed no-duty rules, an actor's duty to exercise reasonable care does not require attention from the court.

Restatement (Third) of Torts §6, comment B. (2011). Do you see how this Restatement provision demonstrates a general judicial rejection of Judge Cardozo's limited view of duty and seems much closer to Judge Andrews' assumption that generally a duty of care exists (at least in cases involving *affirmative acts*) toward others? This does not mean that a duty always exists when an actor acts. We will see multiple examples where courts, having paused at the element of duty, have seen fit to negate or limit the duty for some other reason. Yet another provision in the Third Restatement provides the mirror image to the presumption of a duty for actors whose affirmative conduct has created a risk of harm. Section 37 provides that, with respect to actors who are not accused of affirmative conduct creating the risk of harm, no general duty is presumed: "An actor whose conduct has not created a risk of physical . . . harm to another has no duty of care to the other unless the court determines that one of the affirmative duties [otherwise found] is applicable."

In Practice

How difficult is it to distinguish between acts and omissions? The Restatement urges caution in this regard: "The distinction [between acts and omissions] can be misleading. The proper question is . . . whether the actor's entire conduct created a risk of harm. [A] failure to employ an automobile's brakes . . . is not a case of nonfeasance [because] the entirety of the actor's conduct (driving an automobile) created a risk of harm."

Restatement (Third) of Torts §37 cmt. c.

6. Palsgraf *Revisited.* Given this common law dichotomy between acts and omissions, would the law generally impose upon the employees of the Long Island Railway an obligation to act with reasonable care when they undertake to perform some task? Was the Long Island Railway accused of failing to take action or of taking some careless action? It seems that the essence of Mrs. Palsgraf's complaint in that case was that when the employees of the defendant reached out and put their hands upon the leaping passenger, they failed to exercise reasonable care. While Judge Cardozo said that some foreseeable harm particular to the plaintiff was necessary to trigger a duty, what does the Restatement provision quote above indicate? In fact, the Third

Restatement has rather directly refuted Cardozo's contention that the "orbit of danger" sets the duty of care:

> A no-duty ruling represents a determination, a purely legal question, that no liability should be imposed on actors in a category of cases. These reasons . . . do not depend on the foreseeability of harm based on the specific facts of a case. They should be articulated directly without obscuring references to foreseeability.

Restatement (Third) of Torts §7 comment j (2011). Thus, because the Long Island Railway employees affirmatively acted in a way that created a risk of harm, they presumptively owed Mrs. Palsgraf a duty of reasonable care, regardless of whether they could foresee danger to her specifically. Furthermore, as *Lundy* notes, common carriers (including railways) have special relationships with their passengers that create duties that would not otherwise even exist under the common law. The facts of *Palsgraf* indicate that Mrs. Palsgraf was a passenger of the defendant waiting for her train to arrive. Given these considerations, does it now strike you as odd that Judge Cardozo chose to deal with the issue of a surprising outcome under the rubric of duty rather than proximate cause?

7. *Exception Where Defendant Caused the Peril.* Another recognized exception to the no-duty to rescue rule is when the defendant has wrongfully created the peril in the first instance. If a defendant has caused an accident, he has a duty of reasonable care to effectuate some rescue or to at least seek help from others. This can either be understood as an exception to the no-duty to rescue rule or as a mere practical reality of his liability in the first instance. If you have wrongfully caused an accident, you will already be held legally responsible for the resulting injuries. If you fail to lessen these injuries through rescue efforts, you are already liable for the full extent of the harm by virtue of your tort in causing the accident. It is in your interest to reduce, or mitigate, the totality of the damages if possible. Regardless of the theory, a tortfeasor has every incentive to lessen his liability by reducing the ultimate harm.

8. *Problems.* Will a duty of reasonable care likely exist in the following scenarios?

- **A.** Rodney is driving his Mustang when a young girl, Amanda, strolls out into an intersection. Rodney has the green light and fails to apply his brakes, hitting Amanda and causing serious injuries.
- **B.** Jamie runs a printing shop. One afternoon, a customer of his trips and falls over a pile of booklets left on an aisle floor. She has a compound fracture and is bleeding profusely. Jamie ignores the customer's injury and gets back to work.
- **C.** Donald, who owns the TropWorld Casino, is being driven home from work one January morning when he sees a hungry, shivering, homeless person by the side of the road with a sign begging for a coat and money for

food. He instructs his driver to speed up so that Donald doesn't have to look upon the suffering for too long. The homeless man dies later that evening from hunger and exposure to the elements.

D. One late evening in the law school library, Joshua suffers a heart attack and falls to the floor unconscious. One of his more competitive classmates, Madeleine, steps over Joshua's body while she returns to her cubicle to get back to work on her torts outline. Joshua dies.

Watch "Good Samaritan" video on Casebook Connect.

4. Duty Ends at Expiration of Special Relationship

As *Lundy* shows, when there is a legally recognized special relationship, this will overcome the general default rule of no duty to act with reasonable care to assist another. Presumably Mr. Lundy had such a relationship with the casino while he was inside their business. The Restatement provision also references relationships between common carriers and innkeepers with regard to their respective customers. The following case analyzes the duration of this special relationship in terms of the issue of duty.

BOYETTE v. TRANS WORLD AIRLINES, INC.

954 S.W.2d 350 (Mo. App. 1997)

Pudlowski, J.

This is an appeal by Patricia Boyette (Appellant) from the trial court's decision granting summary judgment for Trans World Express (TWE) in her wrongful death action for the death of her son, Joseph Rutherford (Rutherford). Because TWE presented uncontested facts negating the element of duty, the judgment of the trial court is affirmed.

On April 2, 1989, Rutherford and three co-workers took TWE flight 7145 from Memphis, Tennessee to Sioux City, Iowa with a change of planes at Lambert International Airport. Andrea Lake (Lake) was the sole flight attendant on this flight. Prior to departure from Memphis, Rutherford had at least two drinks containing alcohol. During a ground delay in Memphis, and for the duration of the Memphis to St. Louis flight, Rutherford consumed six more alcoholic drinks.

Once TWE flight 7145 arrived in St. Louis, Rutherford deplaned onto the tarmac with the other passengers. While on the way to the terminal, Rutherford passed under a yellow rope and climbed onto a luggage tug that was idling on the tarmac. Britney Callier (Callier), a TWE gate agent, radioed his supervisor and requested airport security. The supervisor contacted airport security at 4:23 p.m.

Upon learning of the dispatch to airport security, Rutherford slid off the tug and entered the terminal without further incident. At 4:33 p.m. Callier's supervisor contacted airport security and informed them that their help was no longer needed.

Once inside the terminal Rutherford made his way toward the gate from which his connecting flight was departing. On the way to the gate, Rutherford stole an electric golf cart and began driving around the gate area. Callier, who at this point had returned to the terminal to begin boarding passengers on another outbound flight, chased Rutherford on foot in an effort to stop him or to maintain sight of him until security could be summoned.

Callier eventually cornered Rutherford in an alcove off of the D concourse and informed Rutherford's co-workers that Rutherford was going to jail. However, Callier was unable to locate Rutherford in the alcove [as Rutherford had escaped to Room D-231, a cleaning room that had been left unlocked. This room contained a small door leading to a trash chute that, in turn led to a trash compactor 10 feet below. Inside the compactor was an electric eye that, if blocked for more than 8 seconds, would begin to compact all "trash" inside].

[In an attempt to evade further detection, Rutherford climbed into the trash chute.] Rutherford climbed too far into the trash chute and fell into the trash compactor ten feet below, injuring himself in the fall. [A colleague of Rutherford's informed TWE personnel at 4:51 that Rutherford had fallen into the trash chute. TWE personnel radioed for assistance in finding a shut-off switch for the compactor. Before this happened, however, TWE personnel heard the compactor start. By the time they shut it off, Rutherford's body had been compacted. He was taken to a hospital and pronounced dead.]

Appellant filed a wrongful death action against TWE . . . and others. In her petition, the appellant claimed TWE acted negligently by chasing Rutherford through the concourse after he commandeered the golf cart and, once he was discovered in the trash compactor, failing to take necessary steps to ensure Rutherford's safety. On November 14, 1994, the trial court granted TWE's motion for summary judgment. From this order and judgment, the appellant appeals.

The appellant argues the trial court erred in granting the . . . motion for summary judgment on her negligence cause of action. It is well-established law that in order to maintain a negligence cause of action the appellant must establish: "1) the existence of a duty on the part of the defendant to protect [Rutherford] from injury; 2) a breach of that duty; 3) that defendant's breach proximately caused [Rutherford's] injuries." *Krause v. United States Truck Co., Inc.*, 787 S.W.2d 708, 710 (Mo. banc 1990); *Strickland v. Taco Bell Corp*, 849 S.W.2d 127, 131 (Mo. App. E.D. 1993). If the appellant fails to show the existence of a duty owed by . . . TWE to Rutherford, she cannot maintain a negligence cause of action.

The appellant contends the pursuit of Rutherford by TWE employees after he commandeered the golf cart expanded the duration of the duty of care TWE, as a common carrier, owed to Rutherford. We disagree.

Missouri has long recognized a special relationship exists between a common carrier, like TWE, and its passengers. "A common carrier has a duty to exercise the highest degree of care to safely transport its passengers and protect them while in transit." *Collier v. Bi-State Dev. Agency*, 700 S.W.2d 479, 480 (Mo. App. E.D. 1985). But this duty exists only so long as the special relationship of passenger and carrier exists. *Meyer v. St. Louis Pub. Serv. Co.*, 253 S.W.2d 525 (Mo. App. 1952). The carrier discharges its duty once the passenger reaches a reasonably safe place. *Sanford v. Bi-State Dev. Agency*, 705 S.W.2d 572 (Mo. App. E.D. 1986). In the instant case it is without dispute Rutherford safely reached the airport. Thus, TWE fulfilled the duty it owed Rutherford as a common carrier once he reached the airport terminal. At that point TWE's duty as a common carrier was discharged. [Whether a "reasonably safe place" is the tarmac or the terminal matters not in this case.]

At oral arguments the appellant suggested that even if TWE's duty as a common carrier was discharged once Rutherford reached the airport terminal, a new duty arose once TWE initiated pursuit of Rutherford. We disagree. [The court further held that even if a duty could be found, there was no proximate cause, as the crushing death was too remote a consequence to chasing someone through the airport.]

Because TWE's duty as a common carrier was discharged once Rutherford reached the airport terminal and because, even assuming a new duty arose from Callier's pursuit, there is no causal connection between Callier's pursuit and Rutherford's death, the trial court's grant of summary judgment for TWE is affirmed.

The judgment of the trial court is affirmed.

NOTE

1. ***Relationship as Basis for Duty.*** In *Boyette*, the court agreed that the relationship between the common carrier, TWE, and its customer was sufficient to create an obligation to act with care. Plaintiff attempted to rely upon this relationship to trigger an obligation to effectuate a rescue with reasonable care. What was wrong with this theory? Note that even had the court found a duty, plaintiff would have had to demonstrate that TWE failed to take reasonably prudent measures to make a timely rescue. The facts indicated TWE did make a call for help in an attempt to save the plaintiff. But the issue of breach is not faced if the court holds that no duty of care existed. How is this case different on the issue of duty from *Lawter*, where the defendant attempted a rescue, but did so carelessly?

B. Rescuers

Thus far we have dealt with whether and when someone might be obligated to act, notwithstanding the uniquely American common law rule blessing inaction. Another related special duty rule concerns how the common law should treat the rescuer who becomes a victim in the course of the rescue. That is, when one chooses to take action to aid another, should the law afford any protection in the case of the injured rescuer? To what extent does the original tortfeasor — who created the need for another's rescue — owe any duty toward the rescuer? The following cases present the *Rescue Doctrine* and its antithesis — the rather alarming *Firefighter Rule.*

1. The Rescue Doctrine

McCOY v. AMERICAN SUZUKI MOTOR CORP.

961 P.2d 952 (Wash. 1998)

SANDERS, J.

Respondent James McCoy's product liability suit against petitioners American Suzuki Motor Corporation and Suzuki Motor Company, Ltd. (Suzuki) was dismissed by summary judgment. The Court of Appeals reversed and reinstated the claim. We affirm the Court of Appeals, but on different grounds, and remand for trial.

The issues are (1) whether the rescue doctrine may be invoked in a product liability action; (2) whether a plaintiff asserting a claim as a rescuer under the rescue doctrine must still prove his injuries were proximately caused by defendant's allegedly tortious conduct; and, if so, (3) whether the alleged fault of this defendant was the proximate cause of this plaintiff's injuries.

We conclude the rescue doctrine may be invoked in a product liability action. We also conclude the rescuer must show the defendant's wrongdoing proximately caused his injuries. Lastly, we conclude the question of whether Suzuki proximately caused rescuer McCoy's injuries is a disputed one for the jury to determine on remand.

At 5:00 P.M. on a cold November evening James McCoy drove eastbound on Interstate 90 outside Spokane as the car which preceded him, a Suzuki Samurai, swerved off the roadway and rolled. McCoy stopped to render assistance, finding the driver seriously injured. Shortly thereafter a Washington State Patrol trooper arrived on the scene and asked McCoy to place flares on the roadway to warn approaching vehicles. McCoy did so, but concerned the flares were insufficient, continued further and positioned himself a quarter-mile from the accident scene with a lit flare in each hand, manually directing traffic to the inside lane.

By 6:50 P.M., almost two hours after the accident, the injured driver and passenger of the Suzuki were removed and the scene was cleared, leaving only the trooper and McCoy on the roadway. McCoy walked back on the shoulder of the roadway to his car with a lit flare in his roadside hand. When McCoy was within three or four car-lengths of the trooper, the trooper pulled away without comment. Moments later McCoy was struck from behind while still walking on the roadway's shoulder by a hit-and-run vehicle.

McCoy and his wife filed a multicount complaint against [various defendants, including the driver of the Suzuki and the State of Washington as well as against] American Suzuki Motor Corporation and its parent corporation, Suzuki Motor Company, Ltd., for its allegedly defective Samurai which allegedly caused the wreck in the first place. We presently consider only McCoy's claim against Suzuki.

McCoy alleged the Suzuki Samurai was defectively designed and manufactured, was not reasonably safe by virtue of its tendency to roll, and lacked proper warnings. McCoy also alleged these defects caused the principal accident, that he was injured while a rescuer within the purview of the "rescue doctrine," and Suzuki should therefore be held liable for his injuries.

Suzuki moved for summary judgment asserting: (1) the rescue doctrine does not apply to product liability actions; and (2) even if it does, McCoy must still, but cannot, prove Suzuki proximately caused his injuries. The trial court found the rescue doctrine applies to product liability actions but concluded any alleged defect in the Suzuki was not the proximate cause of McCoy's injuries and, accordingly, granted summary judgment of dismissal.

McCoy appealed the dismissal to the Court of Appeals which reversed in a published, split decision. The appellate court found the rescue doctrine applies in product liability actions just as it does in negligence actions. The court agreed with the trial court that McCoy's injuries were not proximately caused by Suzuki; however, it held under the rescue doctrine an injured rescuer need not prove the defendant proximately caused his injuries. Instead the court concluded the rescuer need only prove the defendant proximately caused the danger and that the rescuer was injured while rescuing.

The Court of Appeals thus concluded McCoy alleged sufficient facts to avoid summary judgment of dismissal and, accordingly, remanded for trial. We granted review.

THE RESCUE DOCTRINE

The rescue doctrine is invoked in tort cases for a variety of purposes in a variety of scenarios. The doctrine, as here asserted, allows an injured rescuer to sue the party which caused the danger requiring the rescue in the first place. As Justice Cardozo succinctly summarized, the heart of this doctrine is the notion that "danger invites rescue." *Wagner v. International Ry. Co.*, 232 N.Y. 176, 133 N.E. 437, 437, 19 A.L.R. 1 (1921). This doctrine serves two functions. First, it informs a tortfeasor it is foreseeable a rescuer will come to the aid of the person imperiled by the tortfeasor's actions, and, therefore, the tortfeasor owes the rescuer a duty similar to the duty he owes the person he imperils. Second, the rescue doctrine negates the presumption that the rescuer assumed the risk of injury when he knowingly undertook the dangerous rescue, so long as he does not act rashly or recklessly.

To achieve rescuer status one must demonstrate: (1) the defendant was negligent to the person rescued and such negligence caused the peril or appearance of peril to the person rescued; (2) the peril or appearance of peril was imminent; (3) a reasonably prudent person would have concluded such peril or appearance of peril existed; and (4) the rescuer acted with reasonable care in effectuating the rescue. The Court of Appeals found McCoy demonstrated sufficient facts of rescuer status to put the issue of whether he met the four requirements . . . to the jury. Suzuki does not question this finding. Nor will we.

DOES THE RESCUE DOCTRINE APPLY IN PRODUCT LIABILITY ACTIONS?

Suzuki argues the rescue doctrine may not be invoked in product liability actions. Suzuki contends the PLA supplants all common law remedies and contends the rescue doctrine is nothing more than a common law remedy. We disagree. The rescue doctrine is not a common law remedy. Rather, it is shorthand for the idea that rescuers are to be anticipated and is a reflection of a societal value judgment that rescuers should not be barred from bringing suit for knowingly placing themselves in danger to undertake a rescue. We can conceive of no reason why this doctrine should not apply with equal force when a product manufacturer causes the danger.

MUST PLAINTIFF SHOW PROXIMATE CAUSATION UNDER THE RESCUE DOCTRINE?

McCoy argues the rescue doctrine relieves the rescuer-plaintiff of proving the defendant's wrongdoing proximately caused his injuries. McCoy asserts a rescuer may prevail in a suit by showing the defendant proximately caused the danger and that, while serving as rescuer, the plaintiff was injured. The Court of Appeals agreed stating the rescue doctrine "varies the ordinary rules of negligence." *McCoy*, 86 Wn. App. at 110 (citing *Solgaard v. Guy F. Atkinson Co.*, 6 Cal. 3d 361, 491 P.2d 821, 99 Cal. Rptr. 29 (1971)).

The Court of Appeals erred on this point. [T]he rescuer, like any other plaintiff, must still show the defendant proximately caused his injuries.

Here, Suzuki argues, it was totally unforeseeable that a rescuer such as McCoy would be injured by a third vehicle under these particular facts and, accordingly, Suzuki asks us to rule in its favor on this issue as a matter of law. We find the issue of foreseeability of the intervening cause is sufficiently close that it should be decided by a jury, not the court. A jury might consider the position of the rescuer, the negligence of the oncoming motorist, if any, and many other factors.

In the present case, if the Suzuki Samurai is found to be defective the jury could find it foreseeable that the Suzuki Samurai would roll and that an approaching car would cause injury to either those in the Suzuki Samurai or to a rescuer, depending on the specific facts to be proved. We note sister jurisdictions have reached the same conclusion under similar facts.

Here, we do not find the alleged fault of Suzuki, if proved, to be so remote from these injuries that its liability should be cut off as a matter of law. Accordingly, we will not dismiss this case for lack of legal causation. Instead we remand the case for trial consistent with this opinion.

NOTES AND PROBLEMS

1. *Effect of* Rescue Doctrine. As the court indicates, the *Rescue Doctrine* negates any presumption of an assumption of the risk (a topic discussed later in Chapter 7 on Affirmative Defenses) and also informs a tortfeasor that the presence of a rescuer at the scene of an accident is likely. This legal boost to the foreseeability of a rescuer at the scene can help (a) remove any doubt about the defendant owing the rescuer a duty of care (to the extent, like Cardozo, the court might be reluctant to find such a duty), and (b) assist with proving proximate causation to the extent that the court is utilizing a foreseeability test for proximate cause, or analyzing whether the actions of the rescuer might constitute a superseding cause.

2. *Proximate Cause.* The court holds that the original tortfeasor owes a rescuer the same duty of care owed to the original victim. However, even a rescuer invoking the *Rescue Doctrine* must still prove proximate cause. In effect, what must the jury conclude was reasonably foreseeable in order to find proximate cause on the facts of *McCoy*?

2. The Firefighter Rule

MOODY v. DELTA WESTERN

38 P.3d 1139 (Alaska 2002)

MATTHEWS, J.

The question in this case is whether the so-called Firefighter's Rule applies in Alaska. The Firefighter's Rule holds that firefighters and police officers who are injured may not recover based on the negligent conduct that required their presence. For public policy reasons we join the overwhelming majority of states that have adopted the rule.

I. FACTS AND PROCEEDINGS

The facts of this case are undisputed. On or around July 25, 1996, a Delta Western employee left a fuel truck owned by Delta Western in a driveway in Dillingham. The keys were in the ignition, the door was unlocked, and the truck contained fuel and weighed over 10,000 pounds. Delta Western had a policy of removing the keys from the ignitions of its trucks. Delta Western enacted this policy because of past incidents involving the theft and unauthorized entry of its trucks.

Joseph Coolidge, who was highly intoxicated, entered the unlocked truck and proceeded to drive around Dillingham. He ran cars off the road, nearly collided with several vehicles, and drove at speeds exceeding seventy miles per hour. Brent Moody, the chief of the Dillingham Police Department, was one of the officers who responded to the reports of the recklessly driven fuel truck. The driver of the van in which Moody was a passenger attempted to stop the truck after moving in front of it, but Coolidge rammed the van, throwing Moody against the dashboard and windshield. Moody suffered permanent injuries.

Moody filed suit against Delta Western, alleging that the company (through its employee) negligently failed to remove the truck's keys from the ignition. In its amended answer, Delta Western argued that the "Firefighter's Rule" barred Moody's cause of action. Delta Western moved for summary judgment based on its Firefighter's Rule defense. The superior court granted Delta Western's motion, holding that the Firefighter's Rule bars police officers from recovering for injuries caused by the "negligence which creates the very occasion for their engagement."

Nearly all of the courts that have considered whether or not to adopt the Firefighter's Rule have in fact adopted it. Only one court [the Oregon Supreme Court] has rejected it.

Both [firefighters and police officers] are paid to confront crises and allay dangers by an uncircumspect citizenry, a circumstance that serves to distinguish firefighters and police from most other public employees. Citizens summon police and firefighters to confront danger. Government entities maintain police and fire departments in anticipation of those inevitable physical perils that burden the human condition, whereas most public employment posts are created not to confront dangers that will arise but to perform some other public function that may incidentally involve risk.

This fundamental concept rests on the assumption that government entities employ firefighters and police officers, at least in part, to deal with the hazards that may result from their taxpayers' own future acts of negligence. Exposing the negligent taxpayer to liability for having summoned police would impose upon him multiple burdens for that protection.

Jurisdictions adopting the Firefighter's Rule emphasize its narrowness; the doctrine bars only recovery for the negligence that creates the need for the public safety officer's service. Thus the Firefighter's Rule does not apply to negligent conduct occurring after the police officer or firefighter arrives at the scene or to misconduct other than that which necessitates the officer's presence. [*Kreski*, 415 N.W.2d 178, 189 (Mich. 1987) (recognizing exceptional cases, such as those involving willful misconduct, in which courts have refused to apply firefighter's rule to bar action).]

Modern courts stress interrelated reasons, based on public policy, for the rule. The negligent party is said to have no duty to the public safety officer to act without negligence in creating the condition that necessitates the officer's intervention because the officer is employed by the public to respond to such conditions and receives compensation and benefits for the risks inherent in such responses. Requiring members of the public to pay for injuries resulting from such responses effectively imposes a double payment obligation on them. Further, because negligence is at the root of many calls for public safety officers, allowing recovery would compound the growth of litigation.

Courts find an analogy in cases in which a contractor is injured while repairing the condition that necessitated his employment. In these cases, the owner is under no duty to protect the contractor against risks arising from the condition the contractor is hired to repair, and thus is not liable even if the condition was the product of the owner's negligence. This "contractor for repairs" exception to the general duty of reasonable care is grounded in necessity and fairness. Property owners should not be deterred by the threat of liability to the contractor from summoning experts to repair their property, regardless of why repairs are needed. Further, owners have paid for the contractor's expertise at confronting the very danger that injured him and should not have to pay again if the contractor is then injured. The same factors are found to apply with respect to the public's need to call for the services of public safety officers.

We agree with the reasoning of the modern courts and with the analogy to contractor cases. The Firefighter's Rule reflects sound public policy.

We thus conclude that the Firefighter's Rule applies in Alaska. We reach this conclusion based on the merits of the rule as accepted by the overwhelming majority of the courts of our sister states. It follows that summary judgment was properly granted.

AFFIRMED.

NOTES AND PROBLEMS

1. ***Public Policy.*** The courts' refusal to recognize a duty of care owed to public emergency personnel — police and firefighters — reflects a combination of two identified policies. What are these reasons? And speaking of the policies behind the *Firefighter Rule,* do you see any parallel between these and the rationale for the no-duty rule we encountered in Creasy v. Rusk in Chapter 4 (no duty of care owed by patient to his caregiver in nursing home)? Effective advocates identify the policies behind the rules to enable their best arguments in cases where there is a lack of clarity regarding a rule's application.

2. ***Problems.*** Would the *Firefighter Rule* preclude the following claims?

A. Officer Moody files a tort suit against the thief who broadsided the van and directly caused his injuries.

B. Officer Moody sues Delta Western on the same theory, but he is an unpaid volunteer police officer.

SNELLENBERGER v. RODRIGUEZ

760 S.W.2d 237 (Tex. 1988)

GONZALEZ, J.

This is an appeal in a wrongful death action brought by the heirs of Harold Snellenberger against Rosita Hernandez Rodriguez. The trial court granted a summary judgment for Rodriguez. The court of appeals affirmed the judgment of the trial court. We affirm the judgment of the court of appeals.

On March 23, 1983, Rodriguez drove her automobile over and critically injured a small child. At the time of the accident, Snellenberger was employed as a police officer by the City of Pecos. When he and another officer were notified of the accident, they immediately proceeded to the scene in their separate patrol cars. Upon arrival, the other officer administered CPR to the child, while officer Snellenberger moved back the crowd of people which had gathered at the scene. Included in the crowd was the grief-stricken mother of the injured child. As officer Snellenberger began controlling the crowd, he suddenly collapsed and later died of a heart attack. His widow and children brought this action relying upon the rescue doctrine.

As a matter of public policy, the rescue doctrine supports the heroic acts of individuals who rush into danger to rescue others from imminent peril. This doctrine came into being before the adoption of comparative negligence in order to relieve the all or nothing effects of contributory negligence. *See Wagner v. International Railway Co.*, 232 N.Y. 176, 133 N.E. 437 (1921); *Kelley v. Alexander*, 392 S.W.2d 790 (Tex. Civ. App. — San Antonio 1965, writ ref'd n.r.e.).

The court of appeals held that the rescue doctrine was not raised under the facts of this case because "no perilous situation existed to invite rescue." Without ruling on whether this was a proper application of the rescue doctrine, we nonetheless affirm the judgment of the court of appeals because we hold, as a matter of law, that Officer Snellenberger's heart attack was not a foreseeable result of Rodriguez's negligence.

The rescue doctrine does not dispense with the requirement of foreseeability in negligence causes of action. In establishing the requirement of proximate cause in negligence actions, this court has stated:

> [A] mere showing of negligence will not justify holding the one guilty thereof liable for damages. The evidence must go further, and show that such negligence was the proximate, and not the remote, cause of the resulting injuries. In order for it to be said that an injury proximately resulted from an act of negligence, the evidence must justify the conclusion that such injury was the natural and probable result thereof. In order to justify such a conclusion, the evidence must justify a finding that the party committing the negligent act ought to have foreseen the consequences thereof in the light of the attendant circumstances.

Carey v. Pure Distributing Corporation, 124 S.W.2d 847, 849 (Tex. 1939).

"Foreseeability means that the actor, as a person of ordinary intelligence, should have anticipated the dangers that his negligent act created for others." *Nixon v. Mr. Property Management*, 690 S.W.2d at 549-50.

In *Freeman v. City of Pasadena*, 744 S.W.2d 923, 924 (Tex. 1988) we rejected the notion that the "due care/foreseeability issue [is] totally within the jury's discretion." We held that as a matter of law it is not foreseeable that a stepfather who was not at the scene of the accident would suffer emotional harm from the negligent injury to his stepson.

The judgment of the court of appeals is affirmed.

NOTES AND PROBLEMS

1. *Rescue Doctrine Does Not Ensure Victory.* Even though the court in *Snellenberger* is willing to apply the *Rescue Doctrine* to these facts, it still holds that a necessary element — proximate cause — cannot be satisfied. If the doctrine is supposed to, in part, help bolster a plaintiff rescuer's arguments for foreseeability, why does the plaintiff still lose? Why, as a matter of law, isn't the injury here reasonably foreseeable even if "danger invites rescue?" Consider how the facts differ between *Snellenberg* and *McCoy*. If the doctrine informs the tortfeasor of the likely presence of a rescuer at the scene of an accident caused by the tortfeasor's misconduct, the courts seem to be saying that the risk of a secondary auto accident is reasonably foreseeable while the risk of a heart attack at the scene of a traffic accident is a seemingly random event that is not reasonably foreseeable. What these cases illustrate is that the *Rescue Doctrine* aids a plaintiff-rescuer by enhancing her foreseeability argument, but the doctrine has limits and does not guarantee a recovery.

2. *Problem.* Given the court's opinion in *Moody*, what is the other fatal flaw with the plaintiff's attempts to recover in *Snellenberger*?

Upon Further Review

As we have seen, a primary distinction in negligence cases exists between a defendant's acts and a defendant's omissions. While either can be the basis for a negligence claim, when the defendant has acted in a way that caused the plaintiff's injury, courts normally assume there was a duty of reasonable care, but assume no duty existed in cases of omissions. These are general rules that are subject to exceptions. Special relationships are a primary circumstance that varies this no-duty presumption, as we saw in *Lundy*. We have seen mention of employers, common carriers, hoteliers, and businesses open to the public as examples of such relationships that vary the common law blessing on inactivity. With respect to those who choose to become rescuers, the common law would impose a duty of care upon them, but Good Samaritan statutes often overcome this — subject to the language of the particular statute applicable. But unless the rescuer is a firefighter or police officer, the common law generally makes it easier for a rescuer to sue the original tortfeasor by enhancing foreseeability arguments and making clear that the duty that ran toward the original victim also runs to the rescuer.

III DUTY TO PROTECT THIRD PARTIES FROM ANOTHER'S HARM

In the prior section we saw the default rule that actions typically require due care, but that inaction owes no duty of care. We also encountered exceptions to this principle based upon a "special" relationship between the tortfeasor and the victim — relationships such as employer-employee, landowner-customer, common carrier-passenger, and innkeeper-guest. Sometimes the victim does not have any special relationship with the defendant but courts still impose a duty to act with reasonable care. These exceptions involve factual scenarios where the tortfeasor has a *special relationship* with the one who is the source of the victim's harm. This can be articulated in terms of a duty to warn the victim or, at times, a duty to control the one threatening harm. We will cover two areas where this exceptional duty rule has been applied — in the context of health care workers and employers.

A. Health Care Workers

It is clear that doctors owe a duty of care toward their patients and that, even in cases of omissions, the special nature of the relationship compels reasonable conduct. Later in this chapter we will consider the special rules applicable to such medical malpractice lawsuits. But what about a health care professional's obligation to protect third parties from harm caused by the patient? In what circumstances can the relationship between the doctor and patient obligate the doctor to take action to protect third parties at risk of harm from the patient? The *Emerich* and *Bradshaw* cases below discuss two circumstances where the patient might pose a risk of harm to others — when the patient suffers a mental illness and has manifest a desire to harm another and when the patient suffers a contagious disease.

EMERICH v. PHILADELPHIA CENTER FOR HUMAN DEVELOPMENT

720 A.2d 1032 (Pa. 1998)

Cappy, J.

We granted allocatur limited to the issues of one, whether a mental health professional has a duty to warn a third party of a patient's threat to harm the third party; two, if there is a duty to warn, the scope thereof; and finally, whether in this case a judgment on the pleadings was proper.

This admittedly tragic matter arises from the murder of Appellant's decedent, Teresa Hausler, by her former boyfriend, Gad Joseph ("Joseph"). At the time of the murder, Joseph was being treated for mental illness and drug problems. Appellant brought wrongful death and survival actions against Appellees. Judgment on the pleadings was granted in favor of Appellees by the trial court and was affirmed on appeal by the Superior Court.

A detailed recitation of the facts is necessary to analyze the complex and important issues before us. The factual allegations raised in Appellant's complaint, which we must accept as true, are as follows.

Ms. Hausler and Joseph, girlfriend and boyfriend, were cohabitating in Philadelphia. For a substantial period of time, both Ms. Hausler and Joseph had been receiving mental health treatment at Appellee Philadelphia Center for Human Development (the "Center" or "PCHD"). Appellee Anthony Scuderi was a counselor at the Center.

Joseph was diagnosed as suffering from, among other illnesses, post-traumatic stress disorder, drug and alcohol problems, and explosive and schizo-affective personality disorders. He also had a history of physically and verbally abusing Ms. Hausler, as well as his former wife, and a history of other violent propensities. Joseph often threatened to murder Ms. Hausler and suffered from homicidal ideations.

Several weeks prior to June 27, 1991, Ms. Hausler ended her relationship with Joseph, moved from their Philadelphia residence, and relocated to Reading, Pennsylvania. Angered by Ms. Hausler's decision to terminate their relationship, Joseph had indicated during several therapy sessions at the Center that he wanted to harm Ms. Hausler.

On the morning of June 27, 1991, at or about 9:25 a.m., Joseph telephoned his counselor, Mr. Scuderi, and advised him that he was going to kill Ms. Hausler. Mr. Scuderi immediately scheduled and carried out a therapy session with Joseph at 11:00 that morning. During the therapy session, Joseph told Mr. Scuderi that his irritation with Ms. Hausler was becoming worse because that day she was returning to their apartment to get her clothing, that he was under great stress, and that he was going to kill her if he found her removing her clothing from their residence.

Mr. Scuderi recommended that Joseph voluntarily commit himself to a psychiatric hospital. Joseph refused; however, he stated that he was in control and would not hurt Ms. Hausler. At 12:00 p.m., the therapy session ended, and, as stated in the complaint, Joseph was permitted to leave the Center "based solely upon his assurances that he would not harm" Ms. Hausler.

At 12:15 p.m., Mr. Scuderi received a telephone call from Ms. Hausler informing him that she was in Philadelphia en route to retrieve her clothing from their apartment, located at 6924 Large Street. Ms. Hausler inquired as to Joseph's whereabouts. Mr. Scuderi instructed Ms. Hausler not to go to the apartment and to return to Reading.

In what ultimately became a fatal decision, Ms. Hausler ignored Mr. Scuderi's instructions and went to the residence where she was fatally shot by Joseph at or about 12:30 p.m. Five minutes later, Joseph telephoned Mr. Scuderi who in turn called the police at the instruction of Director Friedrich.

Joseph was subsequently arrested and convicted of the murder of Ms. Hausler. Based upon these facts, Appellant filed [this] wrongful death and survival action, alleging that Appellees negligently failed to properly warn Ms. Hausler, and others including her family, friends and the police, that Joseph presented a clear and present danger of harm to her.

The trial court granted judgment on the pleadings in favor of Appellees finding, inter alia, that the duty of a mental health professional to warn a third party had not yet been adopted in Pennsylvania, but that even if such a legal duty existed, Mr. Scuderi's personal warning discharged that duty. The Superior Court affirmed, reiterating that mental health care providers currently have no duty to warn a third party of a patient's violent propensities, and that even if such a duty existed, Appellant failed to establish a cause of action as his decedent was killed when she ignored Mr. Scuderi's warning not to go to Joseph's apartment.

Initially, we must determine if in this Commonwealth, a mental health care professional owes a duty to warn a third party of a patient's threat of harm to that third party, and if so, the scope of such a duty. While this precise issue is one of first impression for this court, it is an issue which has been considered by a number of state and federal courts and has been the subject of much commentary. Supported by the wisdom of decisions from other jurisdictions, as well as by analogous decisions by this court and lower court case law in this Commonwealth, we determine that a mental health care professional, under certain limited circumstances, owes a duty to warn a third party of threats of harm against that third party. Nevertheless, we find that in this case, judgment on the pleadings was proper, and thus, we affirm the decision of the learned Superior Court, albeit, for different reasons.

Under common law, as a general rule, there is no duty to control the conduct of a third party to protect another from harm. However, a judicial exception to the general rule has been recognized where a defendant stands in some special relationship with either the person whose conduct needs to be controlled or in a relationship with the intended victim of the conduct, which gives to the intended victim a right to protection. *See, Restatement (Second) of Torts §315* (1965). Appellant argues that this exception, and thus, a duty, should be recognized in Pennsylvania.

Our analysis must begin with the California Supreme Court's landmark decision in *Tarasoff v. Regents of Univ. of California,* 551 P.2d 334 (1976), which was the first case to find that a mental health professional may have a duty to protect others from possible harm by their patients. In *Tarasoff,* a lawsuit was filed against, among others, psychotherapists employed by the Regents of the University of California to recover for the death of the plaintiffs' daughter, Tatiana Tarasoff, who was killed by a psychiatric outpatient.

Two months prior to the killing, the patient had expressly informed his therapist that he was going to kill an unnamed girl (who was readily identifiable as the plaintiffs' daughter) when she returned home from spending the summer in Brazil. The therapist, with the concurrence of two colleagues, decided to commit the patient for observation. The campus police detained the patient at the oral and written request of the therapist, but released him after satisfying themselves that he was rational and exacting his promise to stay away from Ms. Tarasoff. The therapist's superior directed that no further action be taken to confine or otherwise restrain the patient. No one warned either Ms. Tarasoff or her parents of the patient's dangerousness.

After the patient murdered Ms. Tarasoff, her parents filed suit alleging, among other things, that the therapists involved had failed either to warn them of the threat to their daughter or to confine the patient.

The California Supreme Court, while recognizing the general rule that a person owes no duty to control the conduct of another, determined that there is an exception to this general rule where the defendant stands in a special relationship to either the person whose conduct needs to be controlled or in a relationship to the foreseeable victim of that conduct, citing *Restatement (Second) of Torts §315-320.* Applying that exception, the court found that the special relationship between the defendant therapists and the patient could support affirmative duties for the benefit of third persons. *Tarasoff,* 551 P.2d at 343.

The court made an analogy to cases which have imposed a duty upon physicians to diagnose and warn about a patient's contagious disease and concluded that "'by entering into a doctor-patient relationship the therapist becomes sufficiently involved to assume some responsibility for the safety, not only of the patient himself, but also of any third person whom the doctor knows to be threatened by the patient.'" *Id.,* 551 P.2d at 344, quoting Fleming & Maximov, The Patient and His Victim: The Therapist's Dilemma, 62 Cal. L. Rev. 1025, 1030 (1974).

The court also considered various public policy interests determining that the public interest in safety from violent assault outweighed countervailing interests of the confidentiality of patient therapist communications and the difficulty in predicting dangerousness. *Id.,* 551 P.2d at 344-48.

The California Supreme Court ultimately held:

> When a therapist determines, or pursuant to the standards of his profession should determine, that his patient presents a serious danger of violence to another, he incurs an obligation to use reasonable care to protect the intended victim against such danger.

551 P.2d at 340.

Following *Tarasoff*, the vast majority of courts that have considered the issue have concluded that the relationship between a mental health care professional and his patient constitutes a special relationship which imposes upon the professional an affirmative duty to protect a third party against harm. Thus, the concept of a duty to protect by warning, albeit limited in certain circumstances, has met with virtually universal approval.

We believe that the *Tarasoff* decision and its progeny are consistent with, and supported by, Pennsylvania case law and properly recognize that pursuant to the special relationship between a mental health professional and his patient, the mental health professional has a duty to warn a third party of potential harm by his patient.

Further supporting the concept of a duty to warn, this court has already recognized the existence of a cause of action against a physician favoring a third person in the context of contagious disease, and, thus, has recognized certain legal duties on the part of a physician to protect another from future harm by a patient.

In *DiMarco v. Lynch Homes-Chester County, Inc.*, 583 A.2d 422 (1990), this court held that a physician may be liable to a non-patient third person who is injured because of his negligent treatment of a patient. In that case, a physician misinformed his patient, a blood technician who had been accidentally exposed to the communicable disease, hepatitis B, that if she remained symptom-free for six weeks she was not infected with the disease. While the patient was told to refrain from sexual relations for six weeks, she abstained from sex with her boyfriend for eight weeks. After eight weeks, when she was still symptom-free, the patient engaged in sexual relations. Both she and her partner were later diagnosed with hepatitis B. The patient's boyfriend brought an action against, inter alia, the patient's doctors alleging their negligence in not having warned the patient that having sexual relations within six months of exposure to hepatitis B could expose her sexual partner to the disease.

This court extended the physician's duty to encompass third parties whose health could be threatened by contact with the diseased patient.

Such precautions are taken not to protect the health of the patient, whose well being has already been compromised, rather such precautions are taken to safeguard the health of others. Thus, the duty of a physician in such circumstances extends to those "within the foreseeable orbit of risk of harm" (citation omitted). *DiMarco*, 583 A.2d at 424.

Having found that a physician owes a duty to a non-patient third party, at least in the context of a contagious disease, we believe that there is no reason why an analogous duty to warn should not be recognized when the disease of the patient is a mental illness that may pose a potentially greater and more immediate risk of severe harm or death to others. *See, Peck,* 499 A.2d at 425.

Finally, sound principles of public policy support a duty to warn. It has been stated by this court that "in determining the existence of a duty of care, it must be remembered that the concept of duty amounts to no more than 'the sum total of those considerations of policy which led the law to say that the particular plaintiff is entitled to protection' from the harm suffered." *Mazzagatti v. Everingham By Everingham,* 516 A.2d 672, 678 (1986). Thus, recognition of a duty is in essence one of policy considerations.

It is axiomatic that important policy considerations exist regarding the public's interest in safety from immediate and serious, if not deadly, harm. Countervailing policies regarding the treatment of mental health patients, specifically recognition of the difficulty in predicting violent behavior, the importance of confidential communications between therapist and patient, and the policy that patients be placed in the least restrictive environment must be acknowledged. We believe, however, that the societal interests in the protection of this Commonwealth's citizens from harm mandates the finding of a duty to warn. Simply stated, it is reasonable to impose a duty on a mental health professional to warn a third party of an immediate, known and serious risk of potentially lethal harm. This is especially so considering the very circumscribed instances in which we find such a duty to warn arises, which are more fully discussed below.

After consideration of the above, we find that the special relationship between a mental health professional and his patient may, in certain circumstances, give rise to an affirmative duty to warn for the benefit of an intended victim. We find, in accord with Tarasoff, that a mental health professional who determines, or under the standards of the mental health profession, should have determined, that his patient presents a serious danger of violence to another, bears a duty to exercise reasonable care to protect by warning the intended victim against such danger.

Mindful that the treatment of mental illness is not an exact science, we emphasize that we hold a mental health professional only to the standard of care of his profession, which takes into account the uncertainty of such treatment. Thus, we will not require a mental health professional to be liable for a patient's violent behavior because he fails to predict such behavior accurately.

Moreover, recognizing the importance of the therapist-patient relationship, the warning to the intended victim should be the least expansive based upon the circumstances.

As stated by the court in *Tarasoff,*

> We realize that the open and confidential character of psychotherapeutic dialogue encourages patients to express threats of violence, few of which are ever executed. Certainly a therapist should not be encouraged routinely to reveal such threats;

> such disclosures could seriously disrupt the patient's relationship with his therapist and with the person threatened. To the contrary, the therapist's obligations to his patient require that he not disclose a confidence unless such disclosure is necessary to avert danger to others, and even then that he do so discreetly, and in a fashion that would preserve the privacy of his patient to the fullest extent compatible with the prevention of the threatened danger.

Tarasoff, 551 P.2d at 347.

Having determined that a mental health professional has a duty to protect by warning a third party of potential harm, we must further consider under what circumstances such a duty arises. We are extremely sensitive to the conundrum a mental health care professional faces regarding the competing concerns of productive therapy, confidentiality and other aspects of the patient's well being, as well as an interest in public safety. In light of these valid concerns and the fact that the duty being recognized is an exception to the general rule that there is no duty to warn those endangered by another, we find that the circumstances in which a duty to warn a third party arises are extremely limited.

First, the predicate for a duty to warn is the existence of a specific and immediate threat of serious bodily injury that has been communicated to the professional. We believe that in light of the relationship between a mental health professional and patient, a relationship in which often vague and imprecise threats are made by an agitated patient as a routine part of the relationship, that only in those situations in which a specific and immediate threat is communicated can a duty to warn be recognized.

Moreover, the duty to warn will only arise where the threat is made against a specifically identified or readily identifiable victim. Strong reasons support the determination that the duty to warn must have some limits. We are cognizant of the fact that the nature of therapy encourages patients to profess threats of violence, few of which are acted upon. Public disclosure of every generalized threat would vitiate the therapist's efforts to build a trusting relationship necessary for progress. Moreover, as a practical matter, a mental health care professional would have great difficulty in warning the public at large of a threat against an unidentified person. Even if possible, warnings to the general public would "produce a cacophony of warnings that by reason of their sheer volume would add little to the effective protection of the public." *Thompson*, 614 P.2d at 735.

Thus, drawing on the wisdom of prior analysis, and common sense, we believe that a duty to warn arises only where a specific and immediate threat of serious bodily injury has been conveyed by the patient to the professional regarding a specifically identified or readily identifiable victim.

[With regard to Appellees' argument about the importance of confidentiality in the treatment of mental health patients, this] court is aware of the critical role that confidentiality plays in the relationship between therapist and patient, constituting, as one author has described, the "sine qua non of successful psychiatric treatment." *Commonwealth ex rel. Platt v. Platt*, 266 Pa. Super. 276, 304, 404 A.2d 410, 425 (1979). Nevertheless, we believe that the protection against disclosure of confidential information gained in the therapist-patient relationship does not bar the finding of a duty to warn.

[S]imply stated, regulations promulgated by the State Board of Psychology, which include a majority of members with license to practice psychology, recognize an exception in the case of a serious threat of harm to an identified or readily identifiable person.

Based upon the above, it is clear that the law regarding privileged communications between patient and mental health care professional is not violated by, and does not prohibit, a finding of a duty on the part of a mental health professional to warn an intended victim of a patient's threats of serious bodily harm. As succinctly stated by the court in *Tarasoff*, "The protective privilege ends where the public peril begins." *Tarasoff, 551 P.2d at 347.*

In summary, we find that in Pennsylvania, based upon the special relationship between a mental health professional and his patient, when the patient has communicated to the professional a specific and immediate threat of serious bodily injury against a specifically identified or readily identifiable third party and when the professional, determines, or should determine under the standards of the mental health profession, that his patient presents a serious danger of violence to the third party, then the professional bears a duty to exercise reasonable care to protect by warning the third party against such danger.

Finally we must decide whether judgment on the pleadings was proper in this case. Viewing the facts as averred in the complaint, with all reasonable inferences therefrom, it is clear that Joseph was a patient of Appellees and was being treated by Appellees for mental illness. Further, Joseph had a definite, established, long term and ongoing relationship with the Center, and with Mr. Scuderi in particular. Thus, sufficient facts were pled to support the existence of a special relationship between Appellees and Joseph, while Joseph was being treated as an outpatient, which is necessary for the finding of a duty to warn.

Moreover, the complaint alleges that in the course of his treatment, Joseph stated to Mr. Scuderi that if Ms. Hausler came to his apartment that day, he was going to kill her. Thus, Joseph communicated a specific and immediate threat of serious bodily harm against a specifically identified victim. The complaint alleges that Mr. Scuderi knew or should have known that Joseph was a clear and present danger of harm to Ms. Hausler. Consistent with the decision rendered by the court today, and specifically, consistent with the limitations regarding when a duty to warn arises, the facts as stated in the complaint are sufficient to support a finding of the existence of a duty to warn.

Having determined that the facts set forth in the complaint are sufficient to support a finding of the existence of a duty to warn, we turn to consider whether the instructions given by Mr. Scuderi to Ms. Hausler discharged any such duty. Both lower courts in this matter found, and Appellees argue, that Mr. Scuderi discharged any duty to warn as a matter of law.

While the existence of a duty is a question of law, whether there has been a neglect of such duty is generally for the jury. However, the issue of whether an act or a failure to act constitutes negligence may be removed from consideration by a jury and decided as a matter of law when the case is free from doubt and there is no possibility that a reasonable jury could find negligence.

Our determination as to whether Appellees breached any duty as a matter of law is really an inquiry as to whether the instruction given by Mr. Scuderi was adequate to discharge a duty to warn. A mental health care professional's warning must be reasonable under the particular circumstances. See *Tarasoff*, 551 P.2d at 345. This consideration of the reasonableness of the warning under the circumstances is eminently sound as different warnings, depending upon the attendant circumstances in each case, may be given to maintain patient confidentiality, and, at the same time, to prevent serious bodily harm.

Here, the facts as alleged in the complaint disclose that Joseph had physically and verbally abused Ms. Hausler in the past and had often threatened to murder her. Thus, Ms. Hausler knew of Joseph's history of violent propensities. It was Ms. Hausler who telephoned Mr. Scuderi on the date in question. She informed Mr. Scuderi that she was en route to pick up her clothing at their apartment and inquired as to the whereabouts of Joseph. A reasonable inference from her telephone call and inquiry as to the whereabouts of Joseph is that Ms. Hausler was concerned for her safety. Mr. Scuderi informed Ms. Hausler not to go to Joseph's residence and instructed her to return to her lodgment in Reading.

After consideration of the facts as pled regarding the circumstances surrounding the events of June 27, 1991, and after consideration of Mr. Scuderi's specific instructions designed to prevent the threatened harm, including the reasonable inferences that Ms. Hausler knew of Joseph's violent propensities and that she telephoned Mr. Scuderi in concern for her safety, we find that Mr. Scuderi's warning was reasonable as a matter of law. The warning was discreet and in accord with preserving the privacy of his patient to the maximum extent possible consistent with preventing the threatened harm to Ms. Hausler. Thus, Mr. Scuderi discharged any duty to warn.

While this matter evokes great sympathy, we agree with the lower courts that after examining the complaint in this case, it is clear that on the facts averred, as a matter of law, recovery by Appellant is not possible. Thus, judgment on the pleadings was proper.

NOTES AND PROBLEMS

1. ***Restatement Source of Duty.*** The Restatement (Second) of Torts recognizes that certain relationships can give rise to a duty to use reasonable care to protect victims from third parties:

> There is no duty so to control the conduct of a third person as to prevent him from causing physical harm to another unless
>
> (a) a special relation exists between the actor and the third person which imposes a duty upon the actor to control the third person's conduct, or
>
> (b) a special relation exists between the actor and the other which gives to the other a right to protection.

Restatement (Second) of Torts §315 (1965). Which of these provisions does the court in *Emerich* rely upon to support its decision to recognize a new duty? Under the actual facts of that case, would the other provision also arguably apply?

2. ***Role of Foreseeability.*** Special duty rules are often crafted with the concept of foreseeability. In the case of the so-called *Tarasoff* rule, there are two essential components of the doctor's duty of care. First, the doctor has a special relationship with the patient who is the source of the harm to the plaintiff. Absent this relationship, the common law default rule of no duty to act would prevail. Second, there is enhanced foreseeability of harm to the third party in situations where the patient has manifest a serious threat of immediate harm to a readily identifiable victim. Given both the special relationship and the enhanced foreseeability, most courts have determined that some duty of care to at least provide a minimal warning should be recognized, notwithstanding the legitimate concerns for doctor-patient confidentiality.

3. ***Duty to Protect Others from Contagious Diseases.*** In its decision, the court in *Emerich* relies upon its prior decisions recognizing that when a patient of a medical professional has an illness that is a source of risk to others, the doctor owes a duty of reasonable care to protect those particularly foreseeable to be at risk from the illness. Satisfaction of this duty might be accomplished through some treatment of the patient or through warnings given to the family members.

4. ***Tarasoff Rule vs. HIPAA Privacy Rights.*** The Health Insurance Portability and Accountability Act of 1996 (HIPAA) generally provides strict rules for maintaining the privacy of patient information. Patients believing healthcare providers have violated their privacy may file a complaint directly with the U.S. Department of Health and Human Services. How do these privacy rights square with the *Tarasoff* duty to warn third parties about specific threats of serious harm by the patient? Federal regulations offer many exceptions to these privacy rights, including in cases where the health care provider believes "in good faith" that the disclosure is "necessary to prevent or lessen a serious and imminent threat to the health or safety of a person or the public." The Department of Health and Human Services likewise issued a letter saying that HIPAA permitted *Tarasoff* warnings to protect both patients and third parties.

BRADSHAW v. DANIEL, M.D.

854 S.W.2d 865 (Tenn. 1993)

ANDERSON, J.

We granted this appeal to determine whether a physician has a legal duty to warn a non-patient of the risk of exposure to the source of his patient's non-contagious disease — Rocky Mountain Spotted Fever. The trial court denied the defendant physician's motion for summary judgment, but granted an interlocutory appeal on the issue of the physician's legal duty. The Court of Appeals limited the record and held that the facts were insufficient to show that the risk to the non-patient of contracting Rocky Mountain Spotted Fever was such that a legal duty arose on the part of the physician. We disagree and conclude, for the reasons stated herein, that the physician had a legal duty to warn the non-patient of the risk of exposure to the source of the patient's non-contagious disease.

On July 19, 1986, Elmer Johns went to the emergency room at Methodist Hospital South in Memphis, Tennessee, complaining of headaches, muscle aches, fever, and chills. He was admitted to the hospital under the care and treatment of the defendant, Dr. Chalmers B. Daniel, Jr. Dr. Daniel first saw Johns on July 22, 1986, at which time he ordered the drug Chloramphenicol, which is the drug of choice for a person in the latter stages of Rocky Mountain Spotted Fever. Johns' condition rapidly deteriorated, and he died the next day, July 23, 1986. An autopsy was performed, and the Center for Disease Control in Atlanta conclusively confirmed, in late September 1986, that the cause of death was Rocky Mountain Spotted fever. Although Dr. Daniel communicated with Elmer Johns' wife, Genevieve, during Johns' treatment, he never advised her of the risks of exposure to Rocky Mountain Spotted Fever, or that the disease could have been the cause of Johns' death.

A week after her husband's death, on August 1, 1986, Genevieve Johns came to the emergency roam of Baptist Memorial Hospital in Memphis, Tennessee, with similar symptoms of chills, fever, mental disorientation, nausea, lung congestion, myalgia, and swelling of the hands. She was admitted to the hospital and treated for Rocky Mountain Spotted Fever, but she died three days later, on August 4, 1986, of that disease. It is undisputed that no patient-physician relationship existed between Genevieve Johns and Dr. Daniel.

The plaintiff, William Jerome Bradshaw, is Genevieve Johns' son. He filed this suit alleging that the defendant's negligence in failing to advise Genevieve Johns that her husband died of Rocky Mountain Spotted Fever, and in failing to warn her of the risk of exposure, proximately caused her death. The defendant filed a motion to dismiss for failure to state a cause of action on the grounds that the physician owed Genevieve Johns no legal duty because of the absence of a patient-physician relationship. The trial judge denied the motion.

The defendant physician argues that he owed his patient's wife no legal duty because first, there was no physician-patient relationship, and second, Rocky

Mountain Spotted Fever is not a contagious disease and, therefore, there is no duty to warn of the risk of exposure.

We begin our analysis by examining how we determine when a legal duty may be imposed upon one for the benefit of another. While duty was not part of the early English common law jurisprudence of tort liability, it has since become an essential element in negligence cases. No claim for negligence can succeed in the absence of any one of the following elements: (1) a duty of care owed by the defendant to the plaintiff; (2) conduct falling below the applicable standard of care amounting to a breach of that duty; (3) an injury or loss; (4) causation in fact; and (5) proximate, or legal cause. *See McClenahan v. Cooley*, 806 S.W.2d 767, 774 (Tenn. 1991).

[T]he imposition of a legal duty reflects society's contemporary policies and social requirements concerning the right of individuals and the general public to be protected from another's act or conduct. Indeed, it has been stated that "'duty' is not sacrosanct in itself, but is only an expression of the sum total of those considerations of policy which lead the law to say that the plaintiff is entitled to protection." Prosser, §53 at 358.

The defendant contends that the absence of a physician-patient relationship negates the existence of a duty in this case. While it is true that a physician-patient relationship is necessary to the maintenance of a medical malpractice action, it is not necessary for the maintenance of an action based on negligence, and this Court has specifically recognized that a physician may owe a duty to a non-patient third party for injuries caused by the physician's negligence, if the injuries suffered and the manner in which they occurred were reasonably foreseeable. *Wharton Transport Corp. v. Bridges*, 606 S.W.2d 521, 526 (Tenn. 1980) (physician owed duty to third party injured by disabled truck driver's negligence, where the physician was negligent both in his physical examination and certification of the truck driver for the employer).

Here, we are asked to determine whether a physician has an affirmative duty to warn a patient's family member about the symptoms and risks of exposure to Rocky Mountain Spotted Fever, a non-contagious disease. Insofar as we are able to determine, there is no reported decision from this or any other jurisdiction involving circumstances exactly similar to those presented in this case.

We begin by observing that all persons have a duty to use reasonable care to refrain from conduct that will foreseeably cause injury to others. *See Doe v. Linder*, 845 S.W.2d 173 (Tenn. 1992); *Restatement (Second) of Torts §314* (1964).

In determining the existence of a duty, courts have distinguished between action and inaction. Professor Prosser has commented that "the reason for the distinction may be said to lie in the fact that by 'misfeasance' the defendant has created a new risk of harm to the plaintiff, while by 'nonfeasance' he has at least made his situation no worse, and has merely failed to benefit him by interfering in his affairs." Prosser, §56 at 373; *Lindsey, supra*, 689 S.W.2d at 859.

Because of this reluctance to countenance nonfeasance as a basis of liability, as a general rule, under the common law, one person owed no affirmative duty to warn those endangered by the conduct of another. Prosser, §56 at 374; *Tarasoff v. Regents of University of California.* 551 P.2d 334, 343 (Cal. 1976).

To mitigate the harshness of this rule, courts have carved out exceptions for cases in which the defendant stands in some special relationship to either the person who is the source of the danger, or to the person who is foreseeably at risk from the danger. *Lindsey,* 689 S.W.2d at 859; *Tarasoff,* 551 P.2d at 343; *Restatement (Second) of Torts §315* (1964). Accordingly,

> while an actor is always bound to prevent his acts from creating an unreasonable risk to others, he is under the affirmative duty to act to prevent another from sustaining harm only when certain socially recognized relations exist which constitute the basis for such legal duty.

Harper & Kime, *The Duty to Control the Conduct of Another,* 43 Yale L.J. 886, 887 (1934).

One of the most widely known cases applying that principle is *Tarasoff,* in which the California Supreme Court held that when a psychotherapist determines or, pursuant to the standards of his profession, should determine that his patient presents a serious danger of violence to another, the therapist has an affirmative duty to use reasonable care to protect the intended victim against such danger, and the duty may require the physician to warn the intended victim of the danger. 551 P.2d at 340. The special relationship of the patient to his psychotherapist supported imposition of the affirmative duty to act for the benefit of third persons.

Decisions of other jurisdictions have employed the same analysis and held that the relationship of a physician to his patient is sufficient to support the duty to exercise reasonable care to protect third persons against foreseeable risks emanating from a patient's physical illness. Specifically, other courts have recognized that physicians may be liable to persons infected by a patient, if the physician negligently fails to diagnose a contagious disease, or having diagnosed the illness, fails to warn family members or others who are foreseeably at risk of exposure to the disease. *See Gammill v. United States,* 727 F.2d 950, 954 (10th Cir. 1984) (physician may be found liable for failing to warn a patient's family, treating attendants, or other persons likely to be exposed to the patient of the nature of the disease and the danger of exposure).

For example, in *Hofmann,* an action was brought against a physician by a child who had contracted tuberculosis as a result of the physician's negligent failure to diagnose the disease in his patient, the child's father. Reversing a summary judgment for the physician, the Florida District Court of Appeals held

> that a physician owes a duty to a minor child who is a member of the immediate family and living with a patient suffering from a contagious disease to inform those charged with the minor's well being of the nature of the contagious disease and the

> precautionary steps to be taken to prevent the child from contracting such disease and that the duty is not negated by the physician negligently failing to become aware of the presence of such a contagious disease.

241 So. 2d at 753.

Likewise, in *Shepard, supra,* a wrongful death action was filed by the mother of a child who was infected and died of spinal meningitis after the physician failed to diagnose the disease in his patient, the mother. Again, reversing a summary judgment in favor of the defendant on the issue of legal duty, the Michigan Court of Appeals stated that the

> defendant had a physician-patient relationship with plaintiff. This was a special relationship with the one who allegedly infected Eric, leading to his death. . . . Because defendant had a special relationship with plaintiff we conclude that defendant owed a duty of reasonable care to Eric. As plaintiff's son and a member of her household, Eric was a foreseeable potential victim of defendant's conduct.

390 N.W.2d at 241.

Returning to the facts of this case, first, it is undisputed that there was a physician-patient relationship between Dr. Daniel and Elmer Johns. Second, here, as in the contagious disease context, it is also undisputed that Elmer Johns' wife, who was residing with him, was at risk of contracting the disease. This is so even though the disease is not contagious in the narrow sense that it can be transmitted from one person to another. Both Dr. Daniel and Dr. Prater, the plaintiff's expert, testified that family members of patients suffering from Rocky Mountain Spotted Fever are at risk of contracting the disease due to a phenomenon called clustering, which is related to the activity of infected ticks who transmit the disease to humans Dr. Prater also testified that Dr. Daniel negligently failed to diagnose the disease and negligently failed to warn his patient's wife, Genevieve Johns, of her risk of exposure to the source of disease. Dr. Daniel's expert disputed these conclusions, but Dr. Daniel conceded there is a medical duty to inform the family when there is a diagnosis of the disease. Thus, this case is analogous to the *Tarasoff* line of cases adopting a duty to warn of danger and the contagious disease cases adopting a comparable duty to warn. Here, as in those cases, there was a foreseeable risk of harm to an identifiable third party, and the reasons supporting the recognition of the duty to warn are equally compelling here.

We, therefore, conclude that the existence of the physician-patient relationship is sufficient to impose upon a physician an affirmative duty to warn identifiable third persons in the patient's immediate family against foreseeable risks emanating from a patient's illness. Accordingly, we hold that under the factual circumstances of this case, viewing the evidence in a light most favorable to the plaintiff, the defendant physician had a duty to warn his patient's wife of the risk to her of contracting Rocky Mountain Spotted Fever, when he knew, or in the exercise of reasonable care, should have known, that his patient was suffering from the disease. Our holding here is necessarily limited to the conclusion that the defendant physician owed Genevieve Johns a legal duty. We express no opinion on the other elements which would be required to establish a cause of action for common-law negligence in this case.

Accordingly, the judgment of the Court of Appeals granting the defendant's motion for summary judgment is reversed, and this cause is remanded to the trial court for proceedings consistent with this opinion.

NOTES AND PROBLEMS

1. ***Source of Duty.*** The court mentions the need for the special relationship in order to create an affirmative duty to act. What is the exact special relationship utilized by the court in *Bradshaw* to create this obligation on the part of the doctor? Is this case analogous to *Tarasoff* and the contagious disease cases? There is arguably less foreseeability of harm here than in *Tarasoff* because, in this instance, there is no threat of anyone intending to harm the plaintiff. Further, can you say in the *Bradshaw* case that the doctor had a special relationship with the source of the harm? Was this a case with a contagious disease? If not, it seems debatable that a duty of care should arise, absent any special relationship between the doctor and either the victim or the source of the victim's harm.

2. ***Problem.*** Suppose the plaintiff-decedent in the *Bradshaw* case lived in an apartment complex and had many neighbors who used the same common areas outside. One of those neighbors, a month after the events in *Bradshaw*, gets infected from a tick at the complex playground. Should the doctor treating the husband for Rocky Mounted Spotted Fever have had a duty to warn the residents of that apartment complex? If not, what is the principle that allows you to reject a duty here but recognize one for the plaintiff-decedent in *Bradshaw*?

B. Employer-Employee Relationships

Just as doctor-patient relationships can give rise to duties, not only to the patient, but also to those at risk from the patient, courts have long recognized duties owed by employers to protect third parties from the conduct of the employees. What happens to this duty when the employee is "off the clock"? Consider the following case and how the court approaches the recognition of a duty.

OTIS ENGINEERING CORP. v. CLARK

668 S.W.3d 307 (Tex. 1983)

KILGARLIN, J.

This is a wrongful death action instituted by Larry and Clifford Clark against Otis Engineering Corporation after the Clarks' wives were killed in an automobile accident involving an Otis employee, Robert Matheson. At the time of the accident Matheson was not in the course of his employment. The trial court granted Otis' motion for summary judgment. The court of appeals reversed and remanded the cause for trial, holding there were genuine issues of fact. We affirm the judgment of the court of appeals.

Two questions are presented. First, does the law impose any duty upon Otis under the evidence as developed? Secondly, does such evidence give rise to any genuine issues of material fact?

Matheson worked the evening shift at Otis' Carrollton plant. He had a history of drinking on the job, and was intoxicated on the night of the accident. At his dinner break that night and on other occasions that day he went to the parking lot, where he allegedly consumed alcoholic beverages in his automobile. Donald Roy was Matheson's supervisor and Rennie Pyle was a co-worker who assisted Matheson on occasion. Pyle testified that he knew of Matheson's drinking problems and that he told Roy on the day of the accident that Matheson was not acting right, was not coordinated, was slurring his words, and that "we need to get him off the machines." David Sartain, a fellow worker, testified that Matheson was either sick or drinking, was getting worse, "his complexion was blue and like he was sick," and that he was weaving and bobbing on his stool and about to fall into his machine. The supervisor testified that he observed Matheson's condition and was aware that other employees believed he should be removed from the machine. When Matheson returned from his dinner break, Roy suggested that he should go home. Roy, as he escorted Matheson to the company's parking lot, asked if he was all right and if he could make it home, and Matheson answered that he could. Thirty minutes later, some three miles away from the plant, the fatal accident occurred.

Dr. Charles S. Petty, the medical examiner, testified that Matheson had a blood alcohol content of 0.268% which indicated he had ingested a substantial quantity of alcohol, an amount representing some sixteen to eighteen cocktails if consumed over a period of one hour, or twenty to twenty-five cocktails if consumed over a period of two hours. The doctor stated that persons working around Matheson would undoubtedly have known of his condition, expressing his opinion that one hundred percent of persons with that much alcohol exhibit signs of intoxication observable to the average person.

Matheson's extreme state of intoxication was well known to his supervisor and fellow workers. The testimony indicated the supervisor knew Matheson was in no condition to drive home safely that night. When some night shift employees came to work around 10:30 p.m. and remarked there had been an accident on Belt Line Road, Roy immediately suspected Matheson was involved. Roy testified he feared Matheson might have an accident, knowing that Matheson had to drive on heavily traveled Belt Line Road to reach home. Upon hearing of the accident, Roy, acting on a hunch, voluntarily went to the police station to see if Matheson was involved.

The Clarks contend that under the facts in this case Otis sent home, in the middle of his shift, an employee whom it knew to be intoxicated. They aver this was an affirmative act which imposed a duty on Otis to act in a non-negligent manner. *Cf. Osuna v. Southern Pacific Railroad*, 641 S.W.2d 229 (Tex. 1982). This action by Otis subjected Matheson and other motorists to the dangers of an accident on the highway.

The Clarks further contend that Otis maintained a nurses' station on the premises for the benefit of ill or disabled employees. Although Otis provided this facility to aid employees in situations such as this, the supervisor chose instead to accompany Matheson to the parking lot and send him out on the highway, even though he had foreseen the possibility of an accident. The Clarks likewise maintain that Roy had other alternatives which the jury could find to be more reasonable, such as taking Matheson to the nurses' station, giving him a ride home, or calling a taxi, the police, or Matheson's wife. The Clarks state that fact questions exist as to whether Otis was negligent in sending Matheson home in an obviously intoxicated condition and whether such negligence was a proximate cause of the Clarks' deaths.

Otis' motion for summary judgment was granted on the basis that as a matter of law Otis owed no duty to the Clarks. In order to establish tort liability, a plaintiff must initially prove the existence and breach of a duty owed to him by the defendant. *Abalos v. Oil Development Co. of Texas*, 544 S.W.2d 627, 631 (Tex. 1976). As a general rule, one person is under no duty to control the conduct of another, *Restatement (Second) of Torts* §315 (1965), even if he has the practical ability to exercise such control. *Trammell v. Ramey*, 329 S.W.2d 153 (Ark. 1959). Yet, certain relationships do impose, as a matter of law, certain duties upon parties. *See e.g., Restatement (Second)* §§316-20. For instance, the master-servant relationship may give rise to a duty on the part of the master to control the conduct of his servants outside the scope of employment. This duty, however, is a narrow one. Ordinarily, the employer is liable only for the off-duty torts of his employees which are committed on the employer's premises or with the employer's chattels. *Restatement (Second)* §317.

Though the decisional law of this State has yet to address the precise issues presented by this case, factors which should be considered in determining whether the law should impose a duty are the risk, foreseeability, and likelihood of injury weighed against the social utility of the actor's conduct, the magnitude of the burden of guarding against the injury and consequences of placing that burden on the employer. *See Robertson v. LeMaster*, 301 S.E.2d 563 (W. Va. 1983); *Turner v. Grier*, 608 P.2d 356 (Colo. 1979).

While a person is generally under no legal duty to come to the aid of another in distress, he is under a duty to avoid any affirmative act which might worsen the situation. *See* W. Prosser, *The Law of Torts* §56 at 343 (4th ed. 1971). One who voluntarily enters an affirmative course of action affecting the interests of another is regarded as assuming a duty to act and must do so with reasonable care. *Colonial Savings Ass'n v. Taylor*, 544 S.W.2d 116 (Tex. 1976); *Fox v. Dallas Hotel Co.*, 240 S.W. 517 (1922); *see* W. Prosser, *supra*, §56.

Otis contends that, at worst, its conduct amounted to nonfeasance and under established law it owed no duty to the Clarks' respective wives. Otis further says that by imposing liability for the acts of its intoxicated employee, this Court would be judicially creating "dram shop" liability. We disagree. This is not a "dram shop" case. If a duty is to be imposed on Otis it would not be based on the *mere knowledge* of Matheson's intoxication, but would be based on additional factors.

Traditional tort analysis has long drawn a distinction between action and inaction in defining the scope of duty. Dean Prosser attributes this distinction to the early common law courts' preoccupation with "more flagrant forms of misbehavior [rather than] with one who merely did nothing, even though another might suffer harm because of his omission to act." W. Prosser, *supra*, at 338. However, although courts have been slow to recognize liability for nonfeasance, "during the last century, liability for 'nonfeasance' has been extended still further to a limited group of relations, in which custom, public sentiment and views of social policy have led the courts to find a duty of affirmative action." *Id.* at 339. Be that as it may, we do not view this as a case of employer nonfeasance.

What we must decide is if changing social standards and increasing complexities of human relationships in today's society justify imposing a duty upon an employer to act reasonably when he exercises control over his servants. Even though courts have been reluctant to hold an employer liable for the off-duty torts of an employee, "as between an entirely innocent plaintiff and a defendant who admittedly has departed from the social standard of conduct, if only toward one individual, who should bear the loss?" W. Prosser, *supra*, at 257. Dean Prosser additionally observed that "there is nothing sacred about 'duty,' which is nothing more than a word, and a very indefinite one, with which we state our conclusion." *Id.*

During this year, we have taken a step toward changing our concept of duty in premises cases. In *Corbin v. Safeway Stores, Inc.*, 648 S.W.2d 292 (Tex. 1983), we held that a store owner has a duty to guard against slips and falls if he has actual or constructive knowledge of a dangerous condition and it is foreseeable a fall would occur. We now leave to the jury exclusive determination of the matter if evidence exists that the store owner had the requisite knowledge of the dangerous premises condition. No longer do we require knowledge of the specific object. Following *Corbin*, why should we be reluctant to impose a duty on Otis? As Dean Prosser has observed, "changing social conditions lead constantly to the recognition of new duties. No better general statement can be made, than the courts will find a duty where, in general, reasonable men would recognize it and agree that it exists." W. Prosser, *supra*, at 327. If, as Prosser asserts should be done, we change concepts of duty as changing social conditions occur, then this case presents the Court with the opportunity to conform our conception of duty to what society demands.

Several recent cases in other jurisdictions have extended concepts of duty in the area of employer liability. In *Leppke v. Segura*, 632 P.2d 1057 (Colo. App. 1981), a tavern owner refused to serve an intoxicated man; however, a tavern employee later jump-started the man's car. Subsequently, the intoxicated man caused a fatal automobile accident. The Colorado court, in reversing a summary judgment, held that the employee's affirmative action was enough to raise an issue of breach of duty even though there was no relationship between the defendant and the intoxicated driver. *Id.* at 1059.

An employer was held liable for injuries sustained by third parties in an accident caused by its intoxicated employee in *Brockett v. Kitchen Boyd Motor Co.*, 264 Cal. App. 2d 69, 70 Cal. Rptr. 136 (1968). The employee, Huff, became intoxicated at a Christmas party given by the motor company. Although Huff was "grossly intoxicated," a representative of the company placed him in his automobile and directed him to drive home. The court recognized that the supplying of alcohol does not ordinarily make the supplier liable to an injured third party, but the affirmative acts of placing him in his car and directing him to drive home imposed a duty on the company to exercise reasonable care. 70 Cal. Rptr. at 139.

Recently, the Supreme Court of Appeals of West Virginia rendered its opinion in *Robertson v. LeMaster*, 301 S.E.2d 563 (W. Va. 1983). In that case, LeMaster's employer, The Norfolk and Western Railway Company, had required LeMaster to work twenty-seven consecutive hours to remove debris and repair a track damaged by a train derailment. After many complaints by LeMaster that he was tired and wanted to go home, LeMaster's foreman permitted him to do so. LeMaster lived some fifty miles from his place of work, and while driving his own car home, fell asleep and was involved in a collision with Robertson, causing injuries to Robertson. The West Virginia court recognized that the railroad company owed no duty to control an employee acting outside of the scope of employment, but stated that such was not the issue in the case, saying "rather it is whether the appellee's conduct prior to the accident created a foreseeable risk of harm." *Id.* at 567. The court concluded that requiring LeMaster to work such long hours and then setting him loose upon the highway in an obviously exhausted condition was sufficient to sustain a cause of action against the railroad. We are persuaded by the logic of the holdings in these three cases.

Therefore, the standard of duty that we now adopt for this and all other cases currently in the judicial process, is: when, because of an employee's incapacity, an employer exercises control over the employee, the employer has a duty to take such action as a reasonably prudent employer under the same or similar circumstances would take to prevent the employee from causing an unreasonable risk of harm to others. Such a duty may be analogized to cases in which a defendant can exercise some measure of reasonable control over a dangerous person when there is a recognizable great danger of harm to third persons. *See, e.g., Restatement (Second) of Torts*, §319; W. Prosser, *supra*, at 350. Additionally, we adopt the rule from cases in this Restatement area that the duty of the employer or one who can exercise charge over a dangerous person is not an absolute duty to insure safety, but requires only reasonable care. *See Missouri, K. & T. Ry. Co. of Texas v. Wood*, 95 Tex. 223, 66 S.W. 449 (1902); *Sylvester v. Northwestern Hospital of Minneapolis*, 236 Minn. 384, 53 N.W.2d 17 (1952).

Therefore, the trier of fact in this case should be left free to decide whether Otis acted as a reasonable and prudent employer considering the following factors: the availability of the nurses' aid station, a possible phone call to Mrs. Matheson, having another employee drive Matheson home, dismissing Matheson early rather than terminating his employment, and the foreseeable consequences of Matheson's driving upon a public street in his stuporous condition. As summary judgment proof clearly raises all of these factors questioning the reasonableness of Otis' conduct, a fact issue is present and summary judgment was improper.

For these reasons, we affirm the judgment of the court of appeals and remand to the trial court for determination of the issues.

NOTES AND PROBLEMS

1. ***Employer Liability for Torts of Employees.*** In Chapter 9, Apportionment, we will study the doctrine of *vicarious liability*, by which a master is deemed liable based upon its association with an employee who commits a tort during her course and scope of employment. Such liability is premised solely upon the fault of the employee rather than any breach of duty by the employer. One difficulty the plaintiffs faced in *Otis* was that the tort of the drunk employee was committed "off the clock." He had left the course and scope of employment prior to causing the accident. Therefore, plaintiffs needed to establish negligent conduct by the employer and, of course, this necessitated a determination that the employer owed a duty to prevent this accident from occurring.

2. ***Duty to Control Others.*** The Restatement referred to by the court above acknowledges the many court decisions imposing a duty upon certain actors to act with reasonable care when they are responsible for certain people. Specifically, §§316-318 imposes a duty of reasonable care upon actors with regard to their minor children, dangerous persons in their custody, employees, and those using their property to conduct certain activities. In view of where and when the traffic accident took place in the foregoing case, do these provisions from the Restatement clearly resolve the issue of duty in the foregoing case? If the defendant's employee was beyond their control at the time of the accident, exactly what is the source of the duty of reasonable care? Consider the dichotomy presented at the beginning of this chapter between malfeasance and nonfeasance. While the defendant may have wanted to portray the plaintiff's claim as alleging a failure to act, the court takes the opposite

view — that the defendant, while acting to remove a problem from its own worksite, instead placed that danger on the public roads of North Dallas.

Upon Further Review

Due to special relationships, the common law idea that one does not have an obligation to undertake action for the protection of others finds an exception. With regard to health care workers, the law recognizes that the combination of the special relationship between the doctor and the patient can provide an obligation to act for the benefit of third parties at risk from the patient. When the patient has transmitted a specific serious threat to intentionally injure a third party, most courts have recognized at least a duty to provide some reasonable warning. And in the contagious disease context, courts have likewise recognized that the patient presents a highly foreseeable risk of harm to other nearby health care workers and family members, which compels action for their protection. The employer-employee relationship is likewise sufficient to create an obligation to supervise employees for the protection of others. This is relatively easy to recognize when the employee is at work or at least using company property (e.g., a company car). But when the employee is not at work, finding a source of duty on the part of the employer is much more difficult. While the employee would be liable for his own torts, when does the employer separately breach a duty? Once the employee departs from work, generally the duty to supervise ends. But the careful and creative lawyer can sometimes create a persuasive argument that, while the consequences of the employer's negligence might be manifest "off the clock," the employer may have been careless while the employee was still under its control. Both the health care and the employer scenarios involve special relationships and foreseeable harms to others that combine to change the default no-duty rule to one requiring action.

IV DUTY LIMITED BY THE NATURE OF THE PRIMARY HARM

Thus far we have encountered the tort dichotomy between malfeasance (act) and nonfeasance (failure to act) and seen different relationships that change the default rules regarding duty. In this section we will find that courts have doubts about whether certain duties of care should exist to prevent *certain types of harm* from being suffered. We will first deal with instances where the defendant's negligence causes no immediate physical consequences to the plaintiff, but instead disturbs his emotional tranquility. This emotional injury may or may not have secondary physical consequences, but the non-physical accidental "touching" of the mind raises significant concerns for courts. The second area we will introduce is analogous — where the plaintiff is not physically impacted in any way by the negligence but instead suffers economic losses (i.e., lost profits). Finally, we will delve into an area some courts say is better left to philosophers and theologians rather than the courts. Entering the arena of so-called "wrongful life" claims, we will see how courts react to plaintiffs who argue that they wished they had never been born and blame the defendant for their existence. We will simultaneously consider the related claims for wrongful birth and wrongful pregnancy. In each area, think about what it is about the nature of the claimed harm that causes courts to pause at the question of duty.

A. Emotional Distress

At common law, courts have long permitted recovery of claimed emotional injuries that are secondary to physical harms. When a defendant's negligence causes a plaintiff to lose a limb, there has never been any serious difficulty recognizing that plaintiff's right to recover for the emotional consequences of the physical harm. This became known as the "*Impact Rule*" — that so long as some physical injury has occurred, emotional distress was a recoverable element of damages. Eventually this rule of recovery became stretched enough so that any physical touching — whether truly harmful or not — could support a claim for negligently inflicted emotional distress. In the following *Robb* case, the court recognizes the absurdity of this rule and transitions to a new rule for recognition of negligently inflicted emotional distress — the "*Zone of Danger*" rule. Next, in the *Dillon* case, we will see a subsequent court question the wisdom behind the zone of danger rule and transition to yet another rule — the so-called "Dillon rule of foreseeability." Whether following the *impact*, *zone of danger*, or *Dillon* rules, each of these cases grapple with when to recognize a "bystander" claim for negligent infliction of emotional distress when the plaintiff is not physically involved in an accident but still seeks compensation for her emotional injuries. In the final case in this section, *Kerr*, the court will consider a broader question — outside of the bystander area, will courts generally recognize any duty not to negligently cause emotional distress? Particularly in this area, courts worry about the ramifications of making it too easy for an emotionally upset plaintiff to sue. Ask yourself which rule, each of which is still utilized today by various courts, strikes the most effective balance between compensating victims for true harm without turning everyone into a tortfeasor for hurting others' feelings.

1. *From Impact Rule to Zone of Danger*

ROBB v. THE PENNSYLVANIA RAILROAD CO.

210 A.2d 709 (Dela. 1965)

HERMANN, J.

The question before us for decision is this: May the plaintiff recover for the physical consequences of fright caused by the negligence of the defendant, the plaintiff being within the immediate zone of physical danger created by such negligence, although there was no contemporaneous bodily impact?

Considering the record in the light most favorable to the plaintiff, the facts may be thus summarized:

A private lane leading to the home of the plaintiff, Dixie B. Robb, was intersected by a railroad right-of-way leased to the defendant, The Pennsylvania Railroad Company. On March 11, 1961, the plaintiff was driving an automobile up the lane toward her home when the vehicle stalled at the railroad grade crossing. A rut about a foot deep had been negligently permitted by the defendant to form at the crossing. The rear wheels of the automobile lodged in the rut and, although the plaintiff tried to move the vehicle for several minutes, she was unable to do so. While thus engaged in attempting to move the vehicle, the plaintiff saw the defendant's train bearing down upon her. With only seconds to spare, she jumped from the stalled vehicle and fled for her life. Immediately thereafter, the locomotive collided with the vehicle, hurled it into the air and demolished it. The plaintiff was standing within a few feet of the track when the collision occurred and her face was covered with train soot and dirt. However — and this is the nub of the problem — she was not touched by the train; there was no bodily impact; and she suffered no contemporaneous physical injury. Nevertheless, the plaintiff was greatly frightened and emotionally disturbed by the accident as the result of which she sustained shock to her nervous system. The fright and nervous shock resulted in physical injuries including cessation of lactation which interfered with the plaintiff's ability to nurse and otherwise care for her infant child. Her nervous and general physical condition resulting from the accident also obliged the plaintiff to abandon a horse breeding business and an article which she had been engaged to write for substantial compensation.

The defendant moved for summary judgment taking the position that, assuming the defendant's negligence and its proximate causation of the plaintiff's fright and nervous shock, she may not recover because there was no "impact" and contemporaneous physical injury. The trial judge agreed and granted summary judgment in the defendant's favor, stating: "In spite of a modern trend to the contrary in other jurisdictions, I feel compelled to follow the 'impact theory' in this matter by reason of well established precedents in this State."

The question is still an open one in this State. Two reported Delaware cases and one unreported case border upon the field of inquiry, but none really enter it.

There is sharp diversity of judicial opinion as to the right to recover for the physical consequences of fright in the absence of an impact and contemporaneous physical injury. . . .

The impact rule was established in America by the leading cases of *Ewing v. Pittsburgh, etc. R. Co.*, 23 A. 340 (Pa. 1892); *Mitchell v. Rochester R. Co.*, 45 N.E. 354 (N.Y. 1896); and *Spade v. Lynn & Boston R. Co.*, 47 N.E. 88 (Mass. 1897). [T]he trend favoring the impact rule . . . attained a head-start in America by reason of the *Ewing*, *Mitchell* and *Spade* cases and it spread to numerous other jurisdictions under the influence of those cases.

The impact rule is based, generally speaking, upon three propositions expounded in the *Mitchell* and *Spade* cases:

1) It is stated that since fright alone does not give rise to a cause of action, the consequences of fright will not give rise to a cause of action. This is now generally recognized to be a non-sequitur, want of damage being recognized as the reason that negligence causing mere fright is not actionable. It is now generally agreed, even in jurisdictions which have adopted the impact rule, that the gist of the action is the injury flowing from the negligence, whether operating through the medium of physical impact or nervous shock.

2) It is stated that the physical consequences of fright are too remote and that the requisite causal connection is unprovable. The fallacies of this ground of the impact rule, viewed in the light of growing medical knowledge, were well stated by Chief Justice Maltbie in *Orlo v. Connecticut Co.*, 21 A.2d 402 (Conn. 1941). It was there pointed out that the early difficulty in tracing a resulting injury back through fright or nervous shock has been minimized by the advance of medical science; and that the line of cases permitting recovery for serious injuries resulting from fright, where there has been but a trivial impact in itself causing little or no injury, demonstrate that there is no insuperable difficulty in tracing causal connection between the wrongdoing and the injury via the fright.

3) It is stated that public policy and expediency demand that there be no recovery for the physical consequences of fright in the absence of a contemporaneous physical injury. In recent years, this has become the principal reason for denying recovery on the basis of the impact rule. In support of this argument, it is said that fright is a subjective state of mind, difficult to evaluate, and of such nature that proof by the claimant is too easy and disproof by the party charged too difficult, thus making it unsafe as a practical matter for the law to deal with such claims. This school of thought concludes that to permit recovery in such cases would open a "Pandora's Box" of fictitious and fraudulent claims involving speculative and conjectural damages with which the law and medical science cannot justly cope.

It is our opinion that the reasons for rejecting the impact rule far outweigh the reasons which have been advanced in its support.

The cause of action and proximate cause grounds for the rule have been discredited in the very jurisdictions which first gave them credence. As stated by Holmes, C.J., for the Supreme Judicial Court of Massachusetts, the *Spade* decision did not result from "a logical deduction from the general principles of liability in tort, but as a limitation of those principles upon purely practical grounds." *Smith v. Postal Telegraph Cable Co.*, 55 N.E. 380 (Mass. 1899). Or, as stated by the same eminent jurist on another occasion, he deemed exemption from such damages to be "an arbitrary exception, based upon a notion of what is practicable." *Homans v. Boston Elevated R. Co.*, 62 N.E. 737 (Mass. 1902). And, referring to the *Mitchell* case and the grounds here under consideration, Lehman, J., speaking for the New York Court of Appeals, stated: "Its conclusions cannot be tested by pure logic. The court recognized that its views of public policy to some extent dictated its decision," *Comstock v. Wilson, supra.*

If more were needed to warrant a declination to follow the cause of action and the proximate cause arguments, reference to the fictional and mechanical ends to which the impact rule has been carried would suffice for the purpose. The most trivial bodily contact, itself causing little or no injury, has been considered sufficient to take a case out of the rule and permit recovery for serious physical injuries resulting from the accompanying fright. Token impact sufficient to satisfy the rule has been held to be a slight bump against the seat, dust in the eyes, inhalation of smoke, a trifling burn, jostling in an automobile, indeed any degree of physical impact, however slight.

This leaves the public policy or expediency ground to support the impact rule. We think that ground untenable.

It is the duty of the courts to afford a remedy and redress for every substantial wrong. Part of our basic law is the mandate that "every man for an injury done him in his . . . person . . . shall have remedy by the due course of law. . . ." Del. Const. Art. 1, Sec. 9, Del. C. Ann. Neither volume of cases, nor danger of fraudulent claims, nor difficulty of proof, will relieve the courts of their obligation in this regard. None of these problems are insuperable. Statistics fail to show that there has been a "flood" of such cases in those jurisdictions in which recovery is allowed; but if there be increased litigation, the courts must willingly cope with the task. As to the danger of illusory and fictional claims, this is not a new problem; our courts deal constantly with claims for pain and suffering based upon subjective symptoms only; and the courts and the medical profession have been found equal to the danger. Fraudulent claims may be feigned in a slight-impact case as well as in a no-impact case. Likewise, the problems of adequacy of proof, for the avoidance of speculative and conjectural damages, are common to personal injury cases generally and are surmountable, being satisfactorily solved by our courts in case after case.

We are unwilling to accept a rule, or an expediency argument in support thereof, which results in the denial of a logical legal right and remedy in all cases because in some a fictitious injury may be urged or a difficult problem of the proof or disproof of speculative damage may be presented. Justice is not best served, we think, when compensation is denied to one who has suffered injury through the negligence of another merely because of the possibility of encouraging fictitious claims or speculative damages in other cases. Public policy requires the courts, with the aid of the legal and medical professions, to find ways and means to solve satisfactorily the problems thus presented-not expedient ways to avoid them. We recognize that "[expediency] may tip the scales when arguments are nicely balanced," *Woolford Realty Co. v. Rose*, 286 U.S. 319, 330; but, in our view, such nice balance no longer exists as to the subject matter.

Accordingly, we decline to adopt the impact rule, as urged by the defendant in this cause. The impact rule "is almost certainly destined for ultimate extinction, although it displays surprising vitality, and the process may not be a rapid one. [I]t seems clear that the courts which deny all remedy in such cases are fighting a rearguard action." Prosser on Torts (3d Ed.) pp. 351-352.

We hold, therefore, that where negligence proximately caused fright, in one within the immediate area of physical danger from that negligence, which in turn produced physical consequences such as would be elements of damage if a bodily injury had been suffered, the injured party is entitled to recover under an application of the prevailing principles of law as to negligence and proximate causation. Otherwise stated, where results, which are regarded as proper elements of recovery as a consequence of physical injury, are proximately caused by fright due to negligence, recovery by one in the immediate zone of physical risk should be permitted.

This view has the general approval of the writers on the subject and is now distinctly the majority rule. We are satisfied that it is the better rule, supported by reason, logic and fairness.

We conclude, therefore, that the Superior Court erred in the instant case in holding that the plaintiff's right to recover is barred by the impact rule. The plaintiff claims physical injuries resulting from fright proximately caused by the negligence of the defendant. She should have the opportunity to prove such injuries and to recover therefor if she succeeds. The summary judgment granted in favor of the defendant must be reversed and the cause remanded for further proceedings.

NOTES AND PROBLEMS

1. ***Dire Prediction for Impact Rule Not Realized.*** The *Robb* court found the pragmatic principles undergirding the impact rule untenable and predicted the demise of that rule. What were the rationales and how effectively did the court repudiate them? By the way, under the facts of *Robb*, was there any argument that the plaintiff could have recovered without a new doctrinal switch by the court? Remember factually what the plaintiff experienced in the near miss and how the court referenced what types of "trivial" contact could satisfy the impact rule. Notwithstanding the court's prediction, the impact rule lives on to this day being employed by multiple courts in different jurisdictions. It is the

distinct minority rule but it still survives. Do you see any advantage, conceptual or pragmatic, to the impact rule over the zone of danger rule adopted in *Robb*?

2. ***Requirement for Physical Manifestation of Emotional Distress.*** The *Robb* court permits recovery where the negligence of the defendant does not even touch the plaintiff physically but affects the plaintiff emotionally — yet only where the emotional distress results in some physical consequences. Why limit recovery for emotional distress in this way? Do you see how even some courts embracing the newer zone of danger rule are still uncomfortable with recognizing a claim for negligently caused emotional distress? In what way does the requirement of physical consequences help courts to alleviate some of their concerns with fraudulent and fictitious claims? Is this any more effective than the old impact rule?

3. ***Zone of Danger.*** In terms of physical space, the zone of danger increases the potential for a plaintiff to recover for emotional distress — rather than demanding that the plaintiff be close enough to the calamity caused by defendant's negligence to be physically touched, now it is sufficient for the plaintiff to be merely close enough to have a legitimate fear for their own safety. How close the plaintiff must be necessarily depends upon the circumstances of the accident. In the case of a train wreck, plaintiff was surely within the zone of danger in *Robb*, as she barely escaped her car before disaster struck.

4. ***No Emotional Distress Recovery for Property Loss.*** The *Robb* court failed to acknowledge that the plaintiff suffered the loss of her vehicle due to the defendant railway's negligence. There was no doubt about the plaintiff's entitlement to recover for the negligently caused property loss. Could she have claimed to suffer emotional distress from the loss of her car? Courts have consistently refused to recognize such a claim. *See* e.g., Kleinke v. Farmers Cooperative Supply & Shipping, 549 N.W.2d 714 (Wis. 1996) ("[I]t is unlikely that a plaintiff could ever recover for the emotional distress caused by negligent damage to his or her property"). While emotional distress recovery can be a component of damages for physical injuries to oneself, courts do not allow such claims to be tacked onto a property loss claim. No matter how much you like your Camaro, it can be easily replaced.

2. *From Zone of Danger to* Dillon *Rule of Foreseeability*

Sometimes convincing a court to abandon one doctrine in favor of another requires extraordinary facts that would yield a perceived grave injustice under then-prevailing standards. Although the zone of danger rule had already become quite popular, the California Supreme Court found its application untenable under the facts of the *Dillon* case below. The repudiation of the old doctrine in favor of a new one became so tied to the following case that the new doctrine is now known as the *Dillon rule.*

DILLON v. LEGG

441 P.2d 912 (Cal. 1968)

TOBRINER, J.

That the courts should allow recovery to a mother who suffers emotional trauma and physical injury from witnessing the infliction of death or injury to her child for which the tortfeasor is liable in negligence would appear to be a compelling proposition. As Prosser points out, "All ordinary human feelings are in favor of her [the mother's] action against the negligent defendant. If a duty to her requires that she herself be in some recognizable danger, then it has properly been said that when a child is endangered, it is not beyond contemplation that its mother will be somewhere in the vicinity, and will suffer serious shock." Prosser, Law of Torts (3d ed. 1964) p. 353.

Nevertheless, past American decisions have barred the mother's recovery. Refusing the mother the right to take her case to the jury, these courts ground their position on an alleged absence of a required "duty" of due care of the tortfeasor to the mother. Duty, in turn, they state, must express public policy; the imposition of duty here would work disaster because it would invite fraudulent claims and it would involve the courts in the hopeless task of defining the extent of the tortfeasor's liability. In substance, they say, definition of liability being impossible, denial of liability is the only realistic alternative.

We have concluded that neither of the feared dangers excuses the frustration of the natural justice upon which the mother's claim rests. We shall point out that in the past we have rejected the argument that we should deny recovery upon a legitimate claim because other fraudulent ones may be urged. We shall further explain that the alleged inability to fix definitions for recovery on the different facts of future cases does not justify the denial of recovery on the specific facts of the instant case; in any event, proper guidelines can indicate the extent of liability for such future cases.

In the instant case plaintiff's first cause of action alleged that on or about September 27, 1964, defendant drove his automobile in a southerly direction on Bluegrass Road near its intersection with Clover Lane in the County of Sacramento, and at that time plaintiff's infant daughter, Erin Lee Dillon, lawfully crossed Bluegrass Road. The complaint further alleged that defendant's negligent operation of his vehicle caused it to "collide with the deceased Erin Lee Dillon resulting in injuries to decedent which proximately resulted in her death." Plaintiff, as the mother of the decedent, brought an action for compensation for the loss.

Plaintiff's second cause of action alleged that she, Margery M. Dillon, "was in close proximity to the . . . collision and personally witnessed said collision." She further alleged that "because of the negligence of defendants . . . and as a proximate cause [*sic*] thereof plaintiff . . . sustained great emotional disturbance and shock and injury to her nervous system" which caused her great physical and mental pain and suffering.

Plaintiff's third cause of action alleged that Cheryl Dillon, another infant daughter, was "in close proximity to the . . . collision and personally witnessed said collision." Because of the negligence, Cheryl Dillon "sustained great emotional disturbance and shock and injury to her nervous system" which caused her great physical and mental pain and suffering.

On December 22, 1965, defendant, after he had filed his answer, moved for judgment on the pleadings, contending that [no cause of action for emotional distress had been stated from the mere witnessing of the accident]. Even where a child, sister or spouse is the object of the plaintiff's apprehension no cause of action is stated unless the complaint alleges that the plaintiff suffered emotional distress, fright or shock as a result of fear for his own safety. The [trial] court granted a judgment on the pleadings against the mother's count, the second cause of action, and denied it as to the sister's count, the third cause of action. Margery M. Dillon, the mother, appealed from that judgment.

Thereafter, on January 26, further proceedings took place as to the third cause of action, Cheryl Dillon's claim for emotional trauma from witnessing her sister's death while "watching her sister lawfully cross Bluegrass Road." [Defendant had also moved for summary judgment as to the sister's claim for emotional distress. There was some evidence, though disputed, that the sister was on the curb and within the zone of danger.]

The trial court apparently sustained the motion for judgment on the pleadings on the second cause as to the mother because she was not within the zone of danger and denied that motion as to the third cause involving Cheryl because of the possibility that she was within such zone of danger or feared for her own safety. Thus we have before us a case that dramatically illustrates the difference in result [from the zone of danger rule] because the complaint here presents the claim of the emotionally traumatized mother, who admittedly was *not* within the zone of danger, as contrasted with that of the sister, who *may have been* within it. The case thus illustrates the fallacy of the rule that would deny recovery in the one situation and grant it in the other. In the first place, we can hardly justify relief to the sister for trauma which she suffered upon apprehension of the child's death and yet deny it to the mother merely because of a happenstance that the sister was some few yards closer to the accident. The instant case exposes the hopeless artificiality of the zone-of-danger rule. In the second place, to rest upon the zone-of-danger rule when we have rejected the impact rule becomes even less defensible. We have, indeed, held that impact is not necessary for recovery. The zone-of-danger concept must, then, inevitably collapse because the only reason for the requirement of presence in that zone lies in the fact that one within it will fear the danger of *impact.* At the threshold, then, we point to the incongruity of the rules upon which any rejection of plaintiff's recovery must rest.

We turn then to an analysis of the concept of duty, which, as we have stated, has furnished the ground for the rejection of such claims as the instant one. Normally the simple facts of plaintiff's complaint would establish a cause of action: the complaint alleges that defendant drove his car (1) negligently, as a (2) proximate result of which plaintiff suffered (3) physical injury. Proof of these facts to a jury leads to recovery in damages; indeed, such a showing represents a classic example of the type of accident with which the law of negligence has been designed to deal.

The assertion that liability must nevertheless be denied because defendant bears no "duty" to plaintiff "begs the essential question — whether the plaintiff's interests are entitled to legal protection against the defendant's conduct . . . . It [duty] is a shorthand statement of a conclusion, rather than an aid to analysis in itself . . . . But it should be recognized that 'duty' is not sacrosanct in itself, but only an expression of the sum total of those considerations of policy which lead the law to say that the particular plaintiff is entitled to protection." Prosser, Law of Torts, *supra*, at pp. 332-333.

The history of the concept of duty in itself discloses that it is not an old and deep-rooted doctrine but a legal device of the latter half of the nineteenth century designed to curtail the feared propensities of juries toward liberal awards. "It must not be forgotten that 'duty' got into our law for the very purpose of combatting what was then feared to be a dangerous delusion (perhaps especially prevalent among juries imbued with popular notions of fairness untempered by paramount judicial policy), viz., that the law might countenance legal redress for all foreseeable harm." Fleming, An Introduction to the Law of Torts (1967) p. 47.

We have pointed out that this late 19th century concept of duty, as applied to the instant situation, has led the courts to deny liability. We have noted that this negation of duty emanates from the twin fears that courts will be flooded with an onslaught of (1) fraudulent and (2) indefinable claims. We shall point out why we think neither fear justified.

In the first instance, the argument proceeds from a doubtful factual assumption. Whatever the possibilities of fraudulent claims of physical injury by disinterested spectators of an accident, a question not in issue in this case, we certainly cannot doubt that a mother who sees her child killed will suffer physical injury from shock. "It seems sufficiently obvious that the shock of a mother at danger or harm to her child may be both a real and a serious injury." Prosser, Law of Torts, *supra*, at p. 353.

In the second instance, and more fundamentally, the possibility that fraudulent assertions may prompt recovery in isolated cases does not justify a wholesale rejection of the entire class of claims in which that potentiality arises. "Certainly it is a very questionable position for a court to take, that because of the possibility of encouraging fictitious claims compensation should be denied those who have actually suffered serious injury through the negligence of another." *Orlo v. Connecticut Co.*, 21 A.2d 402 (Conn. 1941).

The possibility that some fraud will escape detection does not justify an abdication of the judicial responsibility to award damages for sound claims:

if it is "to be conceded that our procedural system for the ascertainment of truth is inadequate to defeat fraudulent claims . . . the result is a virtual acknowledgment that the courts are unable to render justice in respect to them." *Chiuchiolo v. New England Wholesale Tailors,* 150 A. 540 (N.H. 1930).

In sum, the application of tort law can never be a matter of mathematical precision. In terms of characterizing conduct as tortious and matching a money award to the injury suffered as well as in fixing the extent of injury, the process cannot be perfect. Yet we cannot let the difficulties of adjudication frustrate the principle that there be a remedy for every substantial wrong.

In the absence of "overriding policy considerations . . . foreseeability of risk [is] of . . . primary importance in establishing the element of duty." *Grafton v. Mollica,* 42 Cal.Rptr. 306 (1965). As a classic opinion states: "The risk reasonably to be perceived defines the duty to be obeyed." *Palsgraf v. Long Island R.R. Co.,* 162 N.E. 99 (N.Y. 1928). Defendant owes a duty, in the sense of a potential liability for damages, only with respect to those risks or hazards whose likelihood made the conduct unreasonably dangerous, and hence negligent, in the first instance.

Since the chief element in determining whether defendant owes a duty or an obligation to plaintiff is the foreseeability of the risk, that factor will be of prime concern in every case. Because it is inherently intertwined with foreseeability such duty or obligation must necessarily be adjudicated only upon a case-by-case basis. We cannot now predetermine defendant's obligation in every situation by a fixed category; no immutable rule can establish the extent of that obligation for every circumstance of the future. We can, however, define guidelines which will aid in the resolution of such an issue as the instant one.

We note, first, that we deal here with a case in which plaintiff suffered a shock which resulted in physical injury and we confine our ruling to that case. In determining, in such a case, whether defendant should reasonably foresee the injury to plaintiff, or, in other terminology, whether defendant owes plaintiff a duty of due care, the courts will take into account such factors as the following: (1) Whether plaintiff was located near the scene of the accident as contrasted with one who was a distance away from it. (2) Whether the shock resulted from a direct emotional impact upon plaintiff from the sensory and contemporaneous observance of the accident, as contrasted with learning of the accident from others after its occurrence. (3) Whether plaintiff and the victim were closely related, as contrasted with an absence of any relationship or the presence of only a distant relationship.

The evaluation of these factors will indicate the *degree* of the defendant's foreseeability: obviously defendant is more likely to foresee that a mother who observes an accident affecting her child will suffer harm than to foretell that a stranger witness will do so. Similarly, the degree of foreseeability of the third person's injury is far greater in the case of his contemporaneous observance of the accident than that in which he subsequently learns of it. The defendant is more likely to foresee that shock to the nearby, witnessing mother will cause . . . harm than to anticipate that someone distant from the accident will suffer more than a temporary emotional reaction. All these elements, of course, shade into each other; the fixing of obligation, intimately tied into the facts, depends upon each case.

In the instant case, the presence of all the above factors indicates that plaintiff has alleged a sufficient prima facie case. Surely the negligent driver who causes the death of a young child may reasonably expect that the mother will not be far distant and will upon witnessing the accident suffer emotional trauma. As Dean Prosser has stated: "when a child is endangered, it is not beyond contemplation that its mother will be somewhere in the vicinity, and will suffer serious shock." Prosser, *The Law of Torts, supra,* at p. 353. *See also* 2 Harper & James, *The Law of Torts, supra,* at p. 1039.

Thus we see no good reason why the general rules of tort law, including the concepts of negligence, proximate cause, and foreseeability, long applied to all other types of injury, should not govern the case now before us. Any questions that the cause raises "will be solved most justly by applying general principles of duty and negligence, and . . . mechanical rules of thumb which are at variance with these principles do more harm than good." 2 Harper & James, The Law of Torts, *supra,* p. 1039 (footnote omitted).

In short, the history of the cases does not show the development of a logical rule but rather a series of changes and abandonments. Upon the argument in each situation that the courts draw a Maginot Line to withstand an onslaught of false claims, the cases have assumed a variety of postures. At first they insisted that there be no recovery for emotional trauma at all. Retreating from this position, they gave relief for such trauma only if physical impact occurred. They then abandoned the requirement for physical impact but insisted that the victim fear for her own safety, holding that a mother could recover for fear for her children's safety if she simultaneously entertained a personal fear for herself. They stated that the mother need only be in the "zone of danger." The final anomaly would be the instant case in which the sister, who observed the accident, would be granted recovery because she was in the "zone of danger," but the *mother,* not far distant, would be barred from recovery.

The successive abandonment of these positions exposes the weakness of artificial abstractions which bar recovery contrary to the general rules. As the commentators have suggested, the problem should be solved by the application of the principles of tort, not by the creation of exceptions to them. Legal history shows that artificial islands of exceptions, created from the fear that the legal process will not work, usually do not withstand the waves of reality and, in time, descend into oblivion.

We have explained that recovery here will not expose the courts to false claims or a flood of litigation. The test that we have set forth will aid in the proper resolution of future cases. Indeed, the general principles of tort law are acknowledged to work successfully in all other cases of emotional trauma.

To deny recovery would be to chain this state to an outmoded rule of the 19th century which can claim no current credence. No good reason compels our captivity to an indefensible orthodoxy.

The judgment is reversed.

NOTES AND PROBLEMS

1. ***Further Enlargement of Duty.*** Near the end of its seminal opinion, the *Dillon* court briefly traces the evolution of tort law's acceptance of claims for primarily emotional loss. As the law transitioned from only allowing emotional distress secondary to some physical harm (or at least impact) to the zone of danger, the court then further widens the circle by permitting a plaintiff to recover for emotional distress despite not being close enough to reasonably fear for her own safety. While the decedent's sister was close enough, the mother was not. The court believed this situation illustrated the hopeless artificiality of the zone of danger rule, because surely the mother's grief was just as genuine, and foreseeable, as that of the sibling.

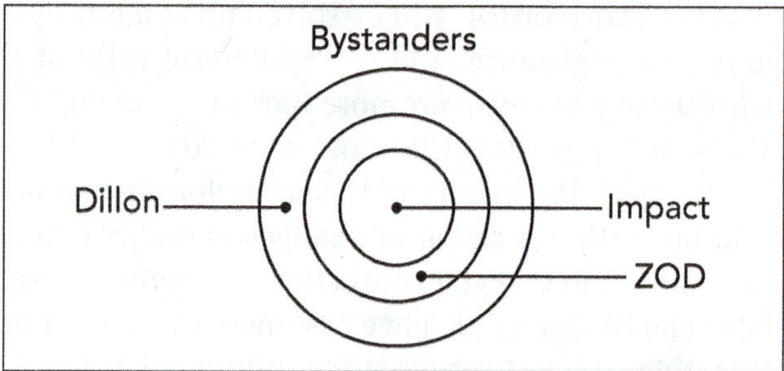

2. ***Physical Manifestation of Emotional Distress.*** In *Dillon*, as with the plaintiff in *Robb*, the plaintiff complained of being emotionally upset by witnessing the event and of this causing some physical consequences. Both courts permitted recovery for the emotional injury only because there was a physical manifestation of it. But many other courts, in applying these duty doctrines, do not demand that there be any physical manifestation of the emotional injury. As one court held, "To . . . require that, before one who is mentally injured may recover, he must at least regurgitate once seems . . . to be imposing upon the law a requirement that makes little sense." James v. Lieb, 375 N.W.2d 109, 116 (Neb. 1985) (quoting Fournell v. Usher Pest Control Co., 305 N.W.2d 605, 611 (Neb. 1981)).

3. ***Guidelines Become Prerequisites.*** The court referred to three "factors" or guidelines that were to be a proxy in the analysis for "foreseeability" of the plaintiff's emotional injury. The plaintiff in *Dillon* satisfied all three, so the court left undecided whether all three had to be present to pursue a bystander claim for emotional distress. Subsequent decisions from the California Supreme Court ultimately held that all three were requirements rather than just factors. *See* Thing v. La Chusa, 771 P.2d 814 (Cal. 1989). This is how other jurisdictions following *Dillon* have treated these three indicia of genuineness — the absence of any of the three negates any duty.

4. ***How Close Must the Plaintiff Be?*** The first requirement — that the plaintiff be "near the scene" of the accident begs the question "how close is close enough?" Surely one need not be close enough to fear for his own safety or else we would simply regress back to the zone of danger rule. Logically, the first requirement is subsumed by the second — that the plaintiff must have been close enough to have "contemporaneous" sensory observation of the accident. While this second factor seems pretty straightforward, some courts applying *Dillon* have struggled at times trying to decide whether to admit or deny a claim where the plaintiff did not actually see the accident but came upon it moments later. *See* Archibald v. Braverman, 275 Cal. App. 2d 253 (Cal. App. 1969) (mother who arrived at scene moments after accident allowed to recover because she had heard it); *cf.*, Hegel v. McMahon, 960 P.2d 424 (Wash. 1998) (permitting recovery to plaintiff father who arrived at scene ten minutes after his son was killed on his motorcycle and was able to witness son injured but still alive). In *McMahon,* the Supreme Court of Washington stated with regard to its decision to extend the rule and permit recovery: "A bright line rule that limits recovery for emotional distress to those who witnessed the accident is attractive in its simplicity. However, it draws an arbitrary line that served to exclude plaintiffs without meaningful distinction." *Id.* at 428. Courts are all over the map on how strictly to apply this requirement. The risk is that by not taking this requirement seriously, you lose the predictability of the *Dillon* approach and also create potentially greater liability than originally intended. For example, should a loved one watching the death of their relative on television be allowed to recover?

5. ***How Badly Hurt Must the Family Member Be?*** Courts applying the *Dillon* test typically require the primary victim to have suffered death or at least serious bodily injury in the accident. This can be viewed as a fourth prerequisite. In other words, a mother watching her son get knocked off his bicycle and scuffing his knees would not be entitled to recover her emotional distress damages under *Dillon.* How does this requirement comport with the underlying concern that the emotional injury be authentic and foreseeable?

GROTTS v. ZAHNER

989 P.2d 415 (Nev. 1999)

MAUPIN, J.

Appellant, Kellie Grotts ("Grotts"), and her fiance were involved in an accident with respondent Gertrude Zahner ("Zahner"). Grotts commenced her action below against Zahner seeking "bystander" emotional distress damages in connection with fatal injuries sustained by her fiance in the accident. The district court dismissed her claim of bystander emotional distress on the ground that she was not, as a matter of law, "closely related" to her fiance for these purposes. Grotts appeals.

A bystander who witnesses an accident may recover for emotional distress in certain limited situations. *See State v. Eaton*, 101 Nev. 705, 716, 710 P.2d 1370, 1377-78 (1985) (citing *Dillon v. Legg*, 68 Cal. 2d 728, 441 P.2d 912, 916, 69 Cal. Rptr. 72 (Cal. 1968)). To recover, the witness-plaintiff must prove that he or she (1) was located near the scene; (2) was emotionally injured by the contemporaneous sensory observance of the accident; and (3) was closely related to the victim.

In *State Department of Transportation v. Hill*, 114 Nev. 810, 816, 963 P.2d 480, 483 (1998), a plurality of this court determined that "whether a plaintiff can recover [damages] for NIED [negligent infliction of emotional distress] after witnessing injury to another based on the plaintiff's relationship to the victim is generally a question of fact." Acknowledging that obvious cases will exist where the issue of "closeness" can be determined as a matter of law, the plurality concluded that the fact finder in most cases should be left with the task of assessing the nature and quality of the claimant's relationship to the victim for these purposes.

We now conclude, contrary to the plurality holding in Hill, that standing issues concerning "closeness of relationship" between a victim and a bystander should, as a general proposition, be determined based upon family membership, either by blood or marriage. Immediate family members of the victim qualify for standing to bring NIED claims as a matter of law. When the family relationship between the victim and the bystander is beyond the immediate family [i.e., beyond the first degree of consanguinity] the fact finder should assess the nature and quality of the relationship and, therefrom, determine as a factual matter whether the relationship is close enough to confer standing. This latter category represents the "few close cases" where standing will be determined as an issue of fact, either by a jury or the trial court sitting without a jury. We therefore hold that any non-family "relationship" fails, as a matter of law, to qualify for NIED standing.

In this case, Grotts claims standing to lodge a "bystander" NIED claim because of her affianced relationship to the victim. Because she was not a member of his "family" by blood or marriage, we hold that she does not enjoy the type of "close relationship" required under Eaton.

For the above reasons, we affirm the trial court.

Rose, C.J., dissenting

Just a year ago, in *State Department of Transportation v. Hill*, 114 Nev. 810, 963 P.2d 480 (1998), we drafted a less rigid and more equitable framework for deciding negligent infliction of emotional distress issues. The majority's departure from the framework set forth in *Hill* prevents that procedure from being tested in our district courts to determine its validity. I believe we are discarding this precedent prematurely.

The rule adopted by the majority requires a relationship by blood or marriage before one can claim to have a close relationship for purposes of pursuing damages for negligent infliction of emotional distress. While this rule will be predictable, it will permit some people to pursue this claim who have no close relationship, and yet prohibit others who have a loving, close relationship with someone injured or killed from pursuing these claims merely because they are not related by blood or marriage.

The case at issue provides a good example. Kellie Grotts and John Colwell were very much in love and expected to marry in the near future. They were at the zenith of love and commitment. Numerous plays and novels have been written about the great loss suffered when this type of relationship ends with the death of one party. Yet the majority denies Kellie Grotts' claim for emotional distress caused as a result of witnessing the death of the love of her life and constant companion simply because their wedding date was a few months off. This same scenario could happen to an older man and woman who, for a variety of reasons, had lived together for years but were not formally married.

And the unfairness of the rule adopted today does not stop there. Anyone living in a non-traditional relationship will be denied the chance to recover emotional distress damages, while those living together with benefit of marriage will not suffer such prejudice. It is a fact of life that many gay men and lesbian women have partners with whom they have lived for decades and shared a close, loving relationship. These individuals will be denied the right to even claim damages for emotional distress for witnessing injury or death to their partner for no other reason than that they are not legally married, a status they cannot prevent. The closeness of two people should be judged by the quality and intimacy of the relationship, not by whether there is a blood relationship or whether a document has been filed at the courthouse. A segment of our population should not be denied legal redress simply because of their lifestyle.

Accordingly, I dissent.

NOTES AND PROBLEMS

1. ***Predictability and Clarity vs. Fairness.*** Of the three *Dillon* criteria, some courts concede that the most valuable indicator of foreseeable emotional injury is the family relationship. This is not to say that a family relationship necessarily predicts genuine and deep emotional distress when witnessing injury, or that the lack of a family relationship negates any emotional distress. But the thought is that, in general, witnessing the death or serious injury to a family member causes more emotional distress than to someone else. Some courts, such as the one above, require legal or blood relationship. The dissent would prefer that the closeness of the relationship just be an issue for the jury's consideration. However, the more predictable the result, the more strict the rules must be applied. This sometimes would mean the dismissal of a claim where the emotional distress was quite severe, presumably such as when a fiancé has died as the majority held above.

2. *Other Relationships.* Strictly applied, would a best friend for life be permitted to sue under *Dillon*? What about a stepmother? A father-in-law? If the dissent in *Grotts* were to prevail these would all be jury questions — whether the jury is convinced by the relationship that true emotional distress has occurred. If relationship by blood or marriage is required then the latter two instances might possibly qualify due to the legal relationship.

3. *Homosexual Relationships.* One concern that the dissent in *Grotts* mentioned involved those living in "non-traditional relationships" who were once denied the opportunity to create a legally recognized relationship such as marriage. In 2015, however, the U.S. Supreme Court ruled in Obergefell v. Hodges, 135 S. Ct. 2584 (2015), that homosexuals were constitutionally entitled to have states permit their formal marriage. As a result, homosexual couples are no longer discriminated against by virtue of the *Dillon* rule's general requirement for a legally recognized relationship involving blood or marriage.

4. *False Dichotomy?* Most jurisdictions today choose between the two most prevalent rules for recognizing negligent infliction of emotional distress — the zone of danger rule or the *Dillon* rule. Yet each of these rules permits recovery in light of a different type of emotional distress. Zone of danger permits recovery for distress associated with one's concern for oneself. The *Dillon* recovery for emotional distress is limited instead to emotional distress associated with concern for a family member. Given this difference, why should a jurisdiction feel compelled to choose between these two rules? A court could permit recovery if the plaintiff could satisfy either test. This has not yet happened, however. Should it? Perceptive counsel should always be prepared to argue for modification or expansion of existing doctrines when the circumstances reveal a hopeless artificiality in them.

5. *Problems.*

A. Of the three tests we have studied — the impact rule, the zone of danger rule, and the *Dillon* rule — which permits the broadest, most liberal scope of coverage?

B. Under the facts of *Grotts,* would the fiancée have been able to recover in either an impact rule or a zone of danger jurisdiction?

3. *Is There a General Duty Not to Cause Emotional Distress?*

All courts permit a plaintiff suffering physical injuries to recover for emotional distress associated with those injuries — to the extent the jury finds such emotional distress. And, as the prior section illustrates, courts also permit primary claims for emotional distress under whatever bystander rule is adopted by the jurisdiction. But will courts recognize a general duty not to negligently inflict emotional distress in a non-bystander scenario? The following case tries to make sense of the various rules dealing with recovery for emotional distress in the context of a plaintiff arguing that a general duty of care exists.

BOYLES v. KERR

855 S.W.2d 593 (Tex. 1993)

Phillips, C.J.

This is a suit for the negligent infliction of emotional distress. We hold that there is no general duty in Texas not to negligently inflict emotional distress. A claimant may recover mental anguish damages only in connection with defendant's breach of some other legal duty. Because Respondent proceeded below only on the theory of negligent infliction of emotional distress, we reverse the judgment of the court of appeals in her favor. However, in the interest of justice, we remand for a new trial.

On August 10, 1985, Petitioner Dan Boyles, Jr., then seventeen, covertly videotaped nineteen-year-old Respondent Susan Leigh Kerr engaging in sexual intercourse with him. Although not dating steadily, they had known each other a few months and had shared several previous sexual encounters. Kerr testified that she had not had sexual intercourse prior to her relationship with Boyles.

Kerr and Boyles, who were both home in Houston for the summer, had made plans to go out on the night of the incident. Before picking Kerr up, Boyles arranged with a friend, Karl Broesche, to use the Broesche house for sexual intercourse with Kerr. Broesche suggested videotaping the activity, and Boyles agreed. Broesche and two friends, Ray Widner and John Paul Tamborello, hid a camera in a bedroom before Kerr and Boyles arrived. After setting up the camera, the three videotaped themselves making crude comments and jokes about the activity that was to follow. They left with the camera running, and the ensuing activities were recorded. Boyles took possession of the tape shortly after it was made, and subsequently showed it on three occasions, each time at a private residence. Although he showed the tape to only ten friends, gossip about the incident soon spread among many of Kerr and Boyles' friends in Houston. Soon many students at Kerr's school, Southwest Texas State University, and Boyles' school, the University of Texas at Austin, also became aware of the story. Kerr did not learn of the video until December 1985, long after she and Boyles had stopped seeing each other. After she confronted him, Boyles eventually admitted what he had done and surrendered the tape to Kerr. No copies had been made.

Kerr alleges that she suffered humiliation and severe emotional distress from the videotape and the gossip surrounding it. At social gatherings, friends and even casual acquaintances would approach her and comment about the video, wanting to know "what [she] was going to do" or "why did [she] do it." The tape stigmatized Kerr with the reputation of "porno queen" among some of her friends, and she claimed that the embarrassment and notoriety affected her academic performance. Kerr also claimed that the incident made it difficult for her to relate to men, although she testified to having had subsequent sexually-active relationships. Eventually, she sought psychological counseling.

Kerr sued Boyles, Broesche, Widner and Tamborello, alleging intentional invasion of privacy, negligent invasion of privacy, and negligent (but not intentional) infliction of emotional distress. Before the case was submitted to the jury, however, Kerr dropped all causes of action except for negligent infliction of emotional distress. The jury returned a verdict for Kerr on that claim, assessing $500,000 in actual damages. The jury also found that all defendants were grossly negligent, awarding an additional $500,000 in punitive damages, $350,000 of which was assessed against Boyles. The trial court rendered judgment in accordance with the jury's verdict. Only Boyles appealed to the court of appeals. That court affirmed the judgment against him, concluding that Kerr established negligent infliction of emotional distress under the facts of this case.

Initially, we must determine whether negligent infliction of emotional distress constitutes an independent cause of action in Texas. Kerr claims that we recognized a broad right to recover for negligently inflicted emotional distress in *St. Elizabeth Hospital v. Garrard*, 730 S.W.2d 649 (Tex. 1987). Boyles contends that the *Garrard* holding is limited to the particular facts of that case.

In *Garrard*, a hospital negligently disposed of the Garrards' stillborn baby in an unmarked, common grave without the plaintiffs' knowledge or consent. The Garrards sued for negligent infliction of emotional distress, without alleging that they suffered any physical injury. This Court nonetheless concluded that they had stated a cause of action. We determined that "Texas first recognized the tort of negligent infliction of mental anguish in *Hill v. Kimball*, 13 S.W. 59 (Tex. 1890)." This tort, we said, had been administered under traditional tort concepts, subject only to a refinement on the element of damages: the mental suffering is not compensable unless it manifests itself physically. *Id.* After determining that the physical manifestation requirement was arbitrary because it "denies court access to persons with valid claims they could prove if permitted to do so," *id.*, we proceeded to abolish it.

The Court then proceeded, we believe, to create a general duty not to inflict reasonably foreseeable emotional distress. The Court said:

> Clearly, freedom from severe emotional distress is an interest which the law should serve to protect . . . . Having recognized that an interest merits protection, it is the duty of this court to continually monitor the legal doctrines of this state to insure the public is free from unwarranted restrictions on the right to seek redress for wrongs committed against them . . . . Thus, we hold that proof of physical injury resulting from mental anguish is no longer an element of the common law action for negligent infliction of mental anguish.

730 S.W.2d at 653-54. Four justices joined in the judgment, but concurred on the grounds that the same result could be reached under the traditional Texas rule

allowing emotional distress damages arising from the mishandling of a corpse. If the Court's holding was, as Boyles contends, limited to the mishandling of corpses, the concurring opinion would not need to have been written, as its rationale would have been incorporated in the majority opinion.

While the holding of *Garrard* was correct, we conclude that its reasoning was based on an erroneous interpretation of *Hill v. Kimball*, and is out of step with most American jurisdictions. Therefore, we overrule the language of *Garrard* to the extent that it recognizes an independent right to recover for negligently inflicted emotional distress. Instead, mental anguish damages should be compensated only in connection with defendant's breach of some other duty imposed by law. This was the basis for recovery prior to *Garrard*, which expanded the scope of liability based on a misconstruction of *Hill v. Kimball*.

In *Hill*, a pregnant woman suffered a miscarriage when she witnessed the defendant severely beating two men in her yard. The woman sued for her physical injuries under negligence, claiming that the emotional trauma of witnessing the beatings produced the miscarriage and that the defendant should have reasonably anticipated the danger to her. The Court found that the plaintiff had stated a cause of action. The basis, however, was the physical injury she had suffered, together with her allegation of foreseeability. The Court reasoned as follows:

> That a physical personal injury may be produced through a strong emotion of the mind there can be no doubt. The fact that it is more difficult to produce such an injury through the operation of the mind than by direct physical means affords no sufficient ground for refusing compensation, in an action at law, when the injury is intentionally or negligently inflicted . . . . Here, according to the allegations of the petition, the defendant has produced a bodily injury by means of that emotion, and it is for that injury that the recovery is sought.

13 S.W. at 59.

The Court considered only whether the plaintiff could recover for her physical injuries, not whether she could otherwise recover for her emotional distress or mental anguish caused by witnessing the beatings. Furthermore, the Court noted that liability would depend on "whether, under the circumstances, and with the lights before him, a reasonably prudent man would have anticipated the danger to her or not." *Id.* In other words, the defendant was negligent if he should have known that he was imposing an unreasonable risk of physical injury to the plaintiff, not if he merely should have anticipated that the plaintiff would suffer emotional distress.

Hill, therefore, did not recognize a cause of action for negligent infliction of emotional distress. It merely recognized the right to recover for physical injuries under standard negligence principles, notwithstanding that the physical injury is produced indirectly through emotional trauma. *Garrard* thus did not merely modify *Hill*, but created an entirely new cause of action. *Garrard*, however, ill deserves the lofty pedestal to which the dissent has belatedly elevated it. Even today, the justices of this Court cannot agree on the extent of *Garrard*'s reach and we have never embraced its broad holding. Thus, in *Freeman v. City of Pasadena*, 744 S.W.2d 923 (Tex. 1988), we limited the bystander cause of action to those persons meeting the criteria of *Dillon v. Legg*, 68 Cal. 2d 728, 441 P.2d 912, 920, 69 Cal. Rptr. 72 (Cal. 1968), without even citing *Garrard* as a potential basis for broader liability.

Professor Crump, one of Boyles' appellate counsel, has argued that "it is important . . . not to lose sight of the contractual relationship between hospital and patient as the source of the underlying duty [in *Garrard*]." David Crump, *Evaluating Independent Torts Based upon "Intentional" or "Negligent" Infliction of Emotional Distress: How Can We Keep the Baby from Dissolving in the Bath Water?*, 34 Ariz. L. Rev. 439, 458 (1992).

Considering our opinions and those of other Texas courts, as well as the law in most American jurisdictions, *Garrard* could fairly be characterized as an anomaly rather than a landmark. We believe the jurisprudence of our state is better served by overruling *Garrard's* broad language outright . . . .

By overruling the language of *Garrard*, we hold only that there is no general duty not to negligently inflict emotional distress. Our decision does not affect a claimant's right to recover mental anguish damages caused by defendant's breach of some other legal duty. *See, e.g., Fisher v. Coastal Transp. Co.*, 230 S.W.2d 522 (Tex. 1950) (negligent infliction of direct physical injury); *Moore v. Lillebo*, 722 S.W.2d 683 (Tex. 1986) (wrongful death); *Fisher v. Carrousel Motor Hotel, Inc.*, 424 S.W.2d 627 (Tex. 1967) (battery); *Stuart v. Western Union Tel. Co.*, 66 Tex. 580, 18 S.W. 351 (1885) (failure of telegraph company to timely deliver death message); *Billings v. Atkinson*, 489 S.W.2d 858 (Tex. 1973) (invasion of privacy); *Leyendecker & Assocs., Inc. v. Wechter*, 683 S.W.2d 369 (Tex. 1984) (defamation); *Pat H. Foley & Co. v. Wyatt*, 442 S.W.2d 904 (Tex. Civ. App.—Houston [14th Dist.] 1969, writ ref'd n.r.e.) (negligent handling of corpse).

Also, our holding does not affect the right of bystanders to recover emotional distress damages suffered as a result of witnessing a serious or fatal accident. Texas has adopted the bystander rules originally promulgated by the California Supreme Court in *Dillon v. Legg*, 441 P.2d 912, 920 (Cal. 1968).

The policy concerns that require limiting the emotional distress cause of action in the direct victim case generally do not apply in the bystander case. Before a bystander may recover, he or she must establish that the defendant has negligently inflicted serious or fatal injuries on the primary victim.

We emphasize that we are not *broadening* a claimant's right to recover mental anguish damages caused by breach of a particular duty; we leave such right unaffected.

We also are not imposing a requirement that emotional distress manifest itself physically to be compensable. As explained in *Garrard*, the sole purpose of the physical manifestation rule is to ensure the genuineness of claims for emotional distress. *Garrard* criticized this requirement as both under- and overinclusive, *id.*, and we agree. *See* Julie A. Davies, *Direct Actions for Emotional Harm: Is Compromise Possible?*, 67 Wash. L. Rev. 1, 24-25 (1992) (the physical manifestation rule "has been criticized on the ground that it has no obvious relation to emotional harm"). Where emotional distress is a recognized element of damages for breach of a legal duty, the claimant may recover without demonstrating a physical manifestation of the emotional distress.

Most other jurisdictions do not recognize a general duty not to negligently inflict emotional distress. A few jurisdictions recognize a general right to recover for negligently inflicted emotional distress, but these jurisdictions are squarely in the minority.

We therefore reverse the judgment of the court of appeals in favor of Kerr on the ground of negligent infliction of emotional distress.

In rejecting negligent infliction of emotional distress as an independent cause of action, we stated in the original opinion that "tort law cannot and should not attempt to provide redress for every instance of rude, insensitive or distasteful behavior, even though it may result in hurt feelings, embarrassment, or even humiliation." We made clear, however, that we did not consider Boyles' conduct to fall into that category, stating in part as follows:

> The tort system can and does provide a remedy against those who engage in such conduct. But an independent cause of action for negligent infliction of emotional distress would encompass conduct far less outrageous than that involved here, and such a broad tort is not necessary to allow compensation in a *truly egregious case* such as this. (Emphasis supplied).

We denied recovery not because Boyles breached no duty toward Kerr, but because the only theory which she chose to assert — negligent infliction of emotional distress — was overly broad and would encompass other cases involving merely rude or insensitive behavior. We reaffirm that conclusion today. [The court stated that Kerr might be able to recover instead on a claim for intentional infliction of emotional distress.]

Kerr cannot recover based on the cause of action under which she proceeded. It may well be, however, that she failed to assert and preserve alternative causes of action because of her reliance on our holding in *Garrard.* We have broad discretion to remand for a new trial in the interest of justice where it appears that a party may have proceeded under the wrong legal theory. Remand is particularly appropriate where the losing party may have presented his or her case in reliance on controlling precedent that was subsequently overruled. We therefore reverse the judgment of the court of appeals and remand this cause to the trial court for a new trial.

NOTES AND PROBLEMS

1. *Rejection of General Duty.* The court in *Kerr* repudiated the only prior holding in that state to suggest a general duty of care to prevent emotional distress exists. Rather, the court held that only where the defendant has breached some other independent duty might a recovery for emotional distress be recognized. Where a defendant negligently causes physical harm this is rather obvious. With regard to the prior decision involving the careless disposal of a family member's body, the court clarifies that we should be mindful of a contractual obligation's breach as being the cornerstone of the emotional distress recovery. Further, the court states that it recognizes bystander recovery under *Dillon*'s requirements. How would an emotional distress recovery under *Dillon* be consistent with this idea of there being a breach of an independent duty?

2. ***Rejection Consistent with Prior Decision.*** In *Temple-Inland*, seen earlier in Chapter 5 on Causation, the court rejected the effort by the plaintiff to recover for his fear of contracting cancer in the future. One reason for the court's decision was its rejection of a general duty not to negligently inflict emotional distress in *Kerr*. Do you see the connection between the two holdings?

3. ***The Rest of the Story.*** After the trial in *Kerr*, defense counsel was so overjoyed with what it viewed as a small jury verdict for the plaintiff that it held a party to celebrate. Unfortunately, at the party, the law firm's staff showed the video — despite a trial court order prohibiting such action. A temporary secretary was present and informed opposing counsel and the court. As a result, the law firm settled with Ms. Kerr for the additional sum of $600,000 for a release from any liability of the firm for displaying the video. Would Ms. Kerr have had a claim against the firm for negligent infliction of emotional distress? If not, what claim, if any, would she have had? Perhaps a claim for intentional infliction of emotional distress, as discussed in Chapter 2?

4. ***NIED vs. IIED.*** The reluctance by courts to recognize a general duty to avoid carelessly causing emotional distress to others makes sense when you consider the broader torts landscape. In Chapter 2, we delved into the topic of intentional infliction of emotional distress. You may recall that we saw the courts, while recognizing such a new claim, eager to create fairly high thresholds to recovery to avoid permitting too many claims for trivial matters. These barriers to recovery included: (1) the need for a defendant's "fault" to rise beyond negligence to either recklessness or intentional infliction of emotional distress; (2) outrageous conduct; and (3) conduct resulting in "severe" emotional distress — something beyond transient or trivial distress. It would make no sense to erect such barriers to recovery for the tort of IIED and then recognize a general duty to avoid carelessly causing emotional distress. Viewed this way, the court's decision in *Kerr* is very predictable.

B. "Mere" Economic Harm

After confronting the intangible nature of emotional distress damages and seeing the courts' reluctance to allow recovery for them as the primary harm in a negligence suit, one would think that financial losses would be viewed differently. In fact, courts are similarly reluctant to impose a duty of care on actors to avoid causing economic loss to others. As you read the following case, compare the nature of economic loss with emotional distress and the courts' reaction to imposing a duty of care regarding the avoidance of such economic damage.

532 MADISON AVENUE GOURMET FOODS v. FINLANDIA CENTER, INC.

750 N.E.2d 1097 (N.Y. 2001)

KAYE, C.J.

The novel issues raised by these appeals — arising from construction-related disasters in midtown Manhattan — concern a landholder's duty in negligence where plaintiffs' sole injury is lost income . . . .

Two of the three appeals involve the same event. On December 7, 1997, a section of the south wall of 540 Madison Avenue, a 39-story office tower, partially collapsed and bricks, mortar and other material fell onto Madison Avenue at 55th Street, a prime commercial location crammed with stores and skyscrapers. The collapse occurred after a construction project, which included putting 94 holes for windows into the building's south wall, aggravated existing structural defects. New York City officials directed the closure of 15 heavily trafficked blocks on Madison Avenue — from 42nd to 57th Street — as well as adjacent side streets between Fifth and Park Avenues. The closure lasted for approximately two weeks, but some businesses nearest to 540 Madison remained closed for a longer period.

In *532 Madison Ave. Gourmet Foods v. Finlandia Ctr.*, plaintiff operates a 24-hour delicatessen one-half block south of 540 Madison, and was closed for five weeks. The two named plaintiffs in the companion case, *5th Ave. Chocolatiere v. 540 Acquisition Co.*, are retailers at 510 Madison Avenue, two blocks from the building, suing on behalf of themselves and a putative class of "all other business entities, in whatever form, including but not limited to corporations, partnerships and sole proprietorships, located in the Borough of Manhattan and bounded geographically on the west by Fifth Avenue, on the east by Park Avenue, on the north by 57th Street and on the South by 42nd Street." Plaintiffs allege that shoppers and others were unable to gain access to their stores during the time Madison Avenue was closed to traffic. Defendants in both cases are Finlandia Center (the building owner), 540 Acquisition

Company (the ground lessee) and Manhattan Pacific Management (the managing agent).

On defendants' motions in both cases, Supreme Court dismissed plaintiffs' negligence claims on the ground that they could not establish that defendants owed a duty of care for purely economic loss in the absence of personal injury or property damage . . . .

Goldberg Weprin & Ustin v. Tishman Constr. involves the July 21, 1998 collapse of a 48-story construction elevator tower on West 43rd Street between Sixth and Seventh Avenues — the heart of bustling Times Square. Immediately after the accident, the City prohibited all traffic in a wide area of midtown Manhattan and also evacuated nearby buildings for varying time periods. Three actions were consolidated — one by a law firm, a second by a public relations firm and a third by a clothing manufacturer, all situated within the affected area. Plaintiff law firm sought damages for economic loss on behalf of itself and a proposed class "of all persons in the vicinity of Broadway and 42nd Street, New York, New York, whose businesses were affected and/or caused to be closed" as well as a subclass of area residents who were evacuated from their homes.

Noting the enormity of the liability sought, including recovery by putative plaintiffs as diverse as hot dog vendors, taxi drivers and Broadway productions, Supreme Court concluded that the failure to allege personal injury or property damage barred recovery in negligence.

The Appellate Division affirmed dismissal of the *Goldberg Weprin* complaint, concluding that, absent property damage, the connection between defendants' activities and the economic losses of the purported class of plaintiffs was "too tenuous and remote to permit recovery on any tort theory." The court, however, reinstated the negligence and public nuisance claims of plaintiffs *532 Madison* and *5th Ave. Chocolatiere*, holding that defendants' duty to keep their premises in reasonably safe condition extended to "those businesses in such close proximity that their negligent acts could be reasonably foreseen to cause injury" (which included the named merchant plaintiffs) and that, as such, they established a special injury distinct from the general inconvenience to the community at large. Two Justices dissented, urging application of the "economic loss" rule, which bars recovery in negligence for economic damage absent personal injury or property damage.

We now reverse in *532 Madison* and *5th Ave. Chocolatiere* and affirm in *Goldberg Weprin & Ustin.*

Plaintiffs contend that defendants owe them a duty to keep their premises in reasonably safe condition, and that this duty extends to protection against economic loss even in the absence of personal injury or property damage. Defendants counter that the absence of any personal injury or property damage precludes plaintiffs' claims for economic injury.

The existence and scope of a tortfeasor's duty is, of course, a legal question for the courts, which "fix the duty point by balancing factors, including the reasonable expectations of parties and society generally, the proliferation of claims, the likelihood of unlimited or insurer-like liability, disproportionate risk and reparation allocation, and public policies affecting the expansion or limitation of new channels of liability" (*Hamilton v. Beretta U.S.A. Corp.*, 96 N.Y.2d 222, 232 [quoting *Palka v. Servicemaster Mgt. Servs. Corp.*, 83 N.Y.2d 579, 586]). At its foundation, the common law of torts is a means of apportioning risks and allocating the burden of loss. In drawing lines defining actionable duty, courts must therefore always be mindful of the consequential, and precedential, effects of their decisions.

As we have many times noted, foreseeability of harm does not define duty. Absent a duty running directly to the injured person there can be no liability in damages, however careless the conduct or foreseeable the harm. This restriction is necessary to avoid exposing defendants to unlimited liability to an indeterminate class of persons conceivably injured by any negligence in a defendant's act.

A duty may arise from a special relationship that requires the defendant to protect against the risk of harm to plaintiff. Landowners, for example, have a duty to protect tenants, patrons and invitees from foreseeable harm caused by the criminal conduct of others while they are on the premises, because the special relationship puts them in the best position to protect against the risk. That duty, however, does not extend to members of the general public. Liability is in this way circumscribed, because the special relationship defines the class of potential plaintiffs to whom the duty is owed.

In *Strauss v. Belle Realty Co.* (65 N.Y.2d 399) we considered whether a utility owed a duty to a plaintiff injured in a fall on a darkened staircase during a citywide blackout. While the injuries were logically foreseeable, there was no contractual relationship between the plaintiff and the utility for lighting in the building's common areas. As a matter of policy, we restricted liability for damages in negligence to direct customers of the utility in order to avoid crushing exposure to the suits of millions of electricity consumers in New York City and Westchester.

Even closer to the mark is *Milliken & Co. v. Consolidated Edison Co.* (84 N.Y.2d 469), in which an underground water main burst near 38th Street and 7th Avenue in Manhattan. The waters flooded a subbasement where Consolidated Edison maintained an electricity supply substation, and then a fire broke out, causing extensive damage that disrupted the flow of electricity to the Manhattan Garment Center and interrupting the biannual Buyers Week. Approximately 200 Garment Center businesses brought more than 50 lawsuits against Con Edison, including plaintiffs who had no contractual relationship with the utility and who sought damages solely for economic loss. Relying on *Strauss*, we again held that only those persons contracting with the utility could state a cause of action. We circumscribed the ambit of duty to avoid limitless exposure to the potential suits of every tenant in the skyscrapers embodying the urban skyline.

A landowner who engages in activities that may cause injury to persons on adjoining premises surely owes those persons a duty to take reasonable precautions to avoid injuring them. We have never held, however, that a landowner owes a duty to protect an entire urban neighborhood against purely economic losses. A comparison of *Beck v. FMC Corp.* (53 A.D.2d 118, 121, aff'd 42 N.Y.2d 1027) and *Dunlop Tire & Rubber Corp. v. FMC Corp.* (53 A.D.2d 150, 154-155) is instructive. Those cases arose out of the same incident: an explosion at defendant FMC's chemical manufacturing plant caused physical vibrations, and rained stones and debris onto plaintiff Dunlop Tire's nearby factory. The blast also caused a loss of electrical power — by destroying towers and distribution lines owned by a utility — to both Dunlop Tire and a Chevrolet plant located one and one-half miles away. Both establishments suffered temporary closure after the accident. Plaintiffs in *Beck* were employees of the Chevrolet plant who sought damages for lost wages caused by the plant closure. Plaintiff Dunlop Tire sought recovery for property damage emanating from the blast and the loss of energy, and lost profits sustained during the shutdown.

In *Dunlop Tire*, the Appellate Division observed that, although part of the damage occurred from the loss of electricity and part from direct physical contact, defendant's duty to plaintiffs was undiminished. The court permitted plaintiffs to seek damages for economic loss, subject to the general rule requiring proof of the extent of the damage and the causal relationship between the negligence and the damage. The *Beck* plaintiffs, by contrast, could not state a cause of action, because, to extend a duty to defendant FMC would, "like the rippling of the waters, [go] far beyond the zone of danger of the explosion," to everyone who suffered purely economic loss (*Beck v. FMC Corp.*, 53 A.D.2d, at 121, *supra*).

Policy-driven line-drawing is to an extent arbitrary because, wherever the line is drawn, invariably it cuts off liability to persons who foreseeably might be plaintiffs. The *Goldberg Weprin* class, for example, would include all persons in the vicinity of Times Square whose businesses had to be closed and a subclass of area residents evacuated from their homes; the *5th Ave. Chocolatiere* class would include all business entities between 42nd and 57th Streets and Fifth and Park Avenues. While the Appellate Division attempted to draw a careful boundary at storefront merchant-neighbors who suffered lost income, that line excludes others similarly affected by the closures — such as the law firm, public relations firm, clothing manufacturer and other displaced plaintiffs in *Goldberg Weprin*, the thousands of professional, commercial and residential tenants situated in the towers surrounding the named plaintiffs, and suppliers and service providers unable to reach the densely populated New York City blocks at issue in each case.

As is readily apparent, an indeterminate group in the affected areas thus may have provable financial losses directly traceable to the two construction-related collapses, with no satisfactory way geographically to distinguish among those who have suffered purely economic losses. In such circumstances, limiting the scope of defendants' duty to those who have, as a result of these events, suffered personal injury or property damage — as historically courts have done — affords a principled basis for reasonably apportioning liability.

We therefore conclude that plaintiffs' negligence claims based on economic loss alone fall beyond the scope of the duty owed them by defendants and should be dismissed.

NOTES AND PROBLEMS

1. ***Mere Economic Loss and Emotional Distress.*** Like emotional distress, courts have generally held that there is no duty to avoid causing economic loss alone ("mere economic loss"). In both instances, the absence of physical harm to the plaintiff or the plaintiff's tangible property raises concern as to both the authenticity of the loss and the potential for unlimited liability far in excess of any wrongdoing. The requirement for physical harm as a general prerequisite to recovery of either type of damage certainly provides a bright line for when a court will impose a duty of care.

2. ***Imposing a Duty Only with Hindsight.*** The mere economic loss rule says to the tortfeasor, in effect, that a duty of care will only arise when the negligence causes some physical harm. Until the tort is carried out, one cannot gauge whether the actor was under any duty of care. It is only with hindsight, when we can look at the ripples of harm, that we can determine whether any duty of care was owed.

3. ***Problems.*** Consider the application of the mere economic loss rule to the following circumstances:

A. A professional soccer team had a goalie under contract who was hurt in an automobile accident caused by the defendant driver. The team had to pay additional money to a substitute goalie for the duration of the season. The team sues the driver for their losses.

B. Among the areas closed to traffic following the collapse of the building in the *Finlandia* case is a little travel bookshop with a blue door. During the accident to the tower, one of the bricks bounces across the street and hits this blue door causing a scratch. The owner of the bookshop pays $1.95 to purchase some paint to touch up the door. His shop is also closed for a significant time, due to the police closing down the street on which it sits, and he loses $15,000 in lost sales. He sues for $15,001.95 in damages.

C. English Petroleum ("EP") maintains an offshore drilling rig in the Gulf of Mexico. The crew working on the rig fails to maintain the rig properly and an explosion ensues, followed by a massive oil spill. EP fails to respond appropriately to the spill and the environmental pollution extends to beaches, wetlands, and estuaries all along the Gulf Coast. Not only are property owners impacted by the pollution, but also many other business owners in the area suffer business losses. For example, numerous seafood restaurants have trouble obtaining locally caught shrimp, lose customers, and go out of business. Local bait shops, boat charters, and even wedding planners lose money from the oil spill. They sue for these losses.

4. ***Special Relationships Altering Mere Economic Loss Rule.*** In certain situations courts do not anticipate there being any physical harm caused by a defendant's negligence but still permit recovery. For example, in most legal or accounting malpractice cases the entirety of the harm is economic. Courts do not have difficulty recognizing a duty of care owed by the professional toward their client, notwithstanding the mere economic harm rule. The special relationship trumps the concerns of the mere economic harm rule. Sometimes, even outside the professional-client relationship, courts will permit a claim for economic losses to be made against such a professional (e.g. an accountant who gives a poor financial report relied upon by a bank to extend a loan). In this scenario, courts have fashioned special rules related to whether one without privity of contract can still maintain a cause of action. In this non-physical scenario, however, courts rarely concern themselves with the mere economic harm rule.

5. ***Fishermen.*** There are a number of reported cases involving fishermen who have lost profits associated with the defendant having caused physical harm to someone else (e.g., the owner of the boats utilized by the fishermen). Courts tend to treat the fishermen as a special class of claimants and avoid application of the mere economic harm rule to their claims, as a limited exception to this rule. This exception seems to reflect traditional sympathy for such plaintiffs rather than any conceptual distinction.

C. Wrongful Pregnancy, Wrongful Life, and Wrongful Birth

There are related causes of action when there are unwanted pregnancies or births for which the defendant doctor's malpractice was a but-for cause. Courts dealing with these type of cases have had to come up with special rules either limiting recovery or refusing to recognize a duty of care based upon the unique nature of the harm alleged. Pay close attention to the difference between the claimant and the claimed harm for *wrongful pregnancy*, *wrongful birth*, and *wrongful life*.

1. *Wrongful Pregnancy*

JOHNSON v. UNIVERSITY HOSPITALS OF CLEVELAND

540 N.E.2d 1370 (Ohio 1989)

[Plaintiff Ruth Johnson sued defendant University Hospitals of Cleveland and three doctors for their negligence in performing a tubal ligation for sterilization purposes. Due to their negligence, the plaintiff became pregnant and gave birth to a healthy baby girl. Plaintiff's suit for negligence seeks damages for pain and suffering from the pregnancy and birth, the medical bills related to her pregnancy and giving birth, and the lifetime child-rearing expenses anticipated for her daughter. The trial court entered judgment in favor of the plaintiff of $12,500, which was the cost associated with her pain and suffering and the medical expenses. The court denied any recovery for the costs of raising her daughter. The court of appeals held that Ohio recognizes a claim for wrongful pregnancy but limited the costs to "damages arising from the pregnancy itself . . . delivery fees, prenatal care, loss of spousal consortium and services during pregnancy, pain and suffering during pregnancy and child birth, etc." The court upheld the trial court's refusal to permit damages for the expenses of raising a healthy child because such award would ignore the benefit the parents receive from the joys of raising a child — the court holding that, as a matter of law, these benefits outweigh the financial burdens of parenting. Further the court held that it would be a windfall to the parents to make the defendant pay these costs. Finally, the court found that the costs of raising the daughter were too speculative to permit recovery. Plaintiff appeals from this decision.]

Douglas, J.

The issue raised in this case is whether the parent of a healthy, normal child, born subsequent to a negligently performed sterilization operation, may recover, as an element of damages, the expenses of raising the child.

Numerous cases in other jurisdictions have been reported concerning the type of action before us. These cases have been variously classified as "wrongful pregnancy," "wrongful birth," or "wrongful life." However, a consensus appears to be emerging that several distinct causes of action are described in these categories. *Smith v. Gore* (Tenn. 1987), 728 S.W.2d 738, 741.

An action for "wrongful pregnancy" refers to a suit filed by a parent for proximate damages arising from the birth of a child subsequent to a doctor's failure to properly perform a sterilization procedure. The case before us now is a "wrongful pregnancy" action.

"Wrongful birth," on the other hand, refers to a cause of action whereby parents, on their own behalf, seek to recover damages for the birth of an impaired child when the impairment was caused by the defendant's failure to diagnose or discover a genetic defect in the parents or the infant through prenatal testing or counseling in time for the parent to obtain a eugenic abortion or to prevent pregnancy altogether.

[There is also a "wrongful life" action that a child might attempt to bring, complaining that the doctor's negligence caused his birth and that he would have been better off not to have been born.]

This court in *Bowman*, a five-to-two *per curiam* decision, clearly decided that Ohio recognizes a "wrongful pregnancy" action. Such a cause is "not barred by notions of public policy. The choice not to procreate, as part of one's right to privacy, has become (subject to certain limitations) a Constitutional guarantee." *Bowman* at 46, 2 O.O.3d at 135, 356 N.E.2d at 499.

Bowman did not directly address the measure of damages in a "wrongful pregnancy" action.

Thus, whether child-rearing expenses are recoverable in a "wrongful pregnancy" action in Ohio is a question of first impression. Numerous jurisdictions have already addressed this issue and four theories of recovery of damages in a "wrongful pregnancy" action have developed. We will review these four theories.

NO RECOVERY

When cases of this kind were first brought in the United States, courts were hesitant to recognize any cause of action at all. An early case, *Christensen v. Thornby* (1934), 255 N.W. 620, involved a failed vasectomy. The Minnesota Supreme Court denied any recovery in that case. Subsequently, in *Shaheen v. Knight* (1957), 11 Pa. D. & C.2d 41, a Pennsylvania common pleas court held that to permit damages for the birth of a healthy child was foreign to the popular sentiment regarding children and the family. Both of these jurisdictions now recognize an action for "wrongful pregnancy."

Recently, at least one other court has taken the position that the birth of a normal child is "an event which, of itself, is not a legally compensable injurious consequence even if the birth is partially attributable to the negligent conduct of someone purporting to be able to prevent the eventuality of childbirth." *Szekeres v. Robinson* (Nev. 1986), 715 P.2d 1076, 1078. Thus, Nevada is currently the only jurisdiction to adhere to this absolute position of no tort recovery in a "wrongful pregnancy" action, at least when a normal, healthy child is born.

THE BENEFITS RULE

Several jurisdictions recognize that an uninterrupted chain of causation exists between a negligently performed sterilization procedure and the foreseeable consequences of the conception, pregnancy and birth of a normal child. *C.S. v. Nielson* (Utah 1988), 767 P.2d 504, 510-511.

Thus, these courts believe that "it must be recognized that [rearing] costs are a direct financial injury to the parents, no different in immediate effect than the medical expenses resulting from the wrongful conception and birth of the child. Although public sentiment may recognize that to the vast majority of parents the long-term and enduring benefits of parenthood outweigh the economic costs of rearing a healthy child, it would seem myopic to declare today that those benefits exceed the costs as a matter of law." *Sherlock v. Stillwater Clinic* (Minn. 1977), 260 N.W.2d 169, 175.

[Courts adhering to the benefits rule permit] the jury to calculate the economic cost of child rearing by weighing the expense against the worth of the child's companionship, comfort and aid to the parents [opining that] the calculations of the cost of child rearing are based on well-recognized economic factors regularly made by estate planners and insurance companies and are fully appreciated by the average citizen's own family experience.

However, this approach has been criticized as essentially comparing apples to oranges because it requires the jury to compare pecuniary costs with non-pecuniary benefits and then offset the economic costs of child rearing with these intangible benefits.

LIMITED DAMAGES

The vast majority of jurisdictions which have decided the issue adheres to this theory of damages which denies all *child-rearing expenses.* Refusal to permit recovery has been based upon various considerations:

1. A parent cannot be said to have been damaged by the birth of a normal, healthy child because the benefits of having a child outweigh any economic loss which the parents might incur in rearing and educating a healthy child.

2. Child-rearing expenses will be a windfall to the parents, wholly disproportionate to the doctor's culpability.

3. Another rationale is that the cost of child-rearing would be too speculative to measure with any certainty.

"[I]t seems to us that that kind of judgment [recovery for child-rearing costs], if appropriate at all in an American Court of law, might be applied at the end of a life, after it has been lived and when the facts can be identified. But, in our view, any attempt to apply it at birth can only be an exercise in prophecy, an undertaking not within the speciality of our factfinders." *Coleman v. Garrison* (Del. 1975), 349 A.2d 8, 12.

4. Recovery should be denied to protect the mental and emotional health of the child, sometimes harshly described as an "emotional bastard."

Courts are concerned that if they grant child-rearing costs to the parents in a "wrongful pregnancy" case, that one day the child will learn that he or she was not only unwanted by his or her parents, but was reared by funds supplied by another person, and that this will greatly upset the child.

5. Damages for a "wrongful pregnancy" action should not include child-rearing costs since to allow damages would be the equivalent of allowing damages in an action for "wrongful life."

FULL RECOVERY

This rule has little, if any, support. However, at least one court considers *Custodio v. Bauer* (1967), 251 Cal. App. 2d 303, 59 Cal. Rptr. 463, to be a full recovery case. *See Smith v. Gore*, supra, at 742. A California appellate court in *Custodio*, applying general tort principles, found that a child is a foreseeable consequence of a failed sterilization procedure and stated that if a "change in the family status can be measured economically it should be as compensable as the [other] losses." *Custodio*, supra, at 323-324, 59 Cal. Rptr. at 476.

Appellant argues that she is entitled to a full recovery because all the expenses for child support are foreseeable and proximately caused by the negligent sterilization.

In regard to the extent of damages, a number of courts have discussed the reasonableness of the alternatives to rearing a child, *i.e.*, an abortion or adoption, as part of the duty to mitigate.

Appellees have contended that if this court adopts the tort benefits rule, parents would have to mitigate their damages for child rearing by adoption or abortion. Appellees further argue that if the parents choose neither to abort nor adopt and instead keep the child, the jury would have to take this lack of mitigation into consideration when calculating child-rearing expenses.

We refuse to say as a matter of law that every parent must mitigate damages by abortion or adoption as a "reasonable effort" to avoid child-rearing expenses. In fact, we find either suggestion repugnant. Many people would be opposed to either recourse. Thus, in a "wrongful pregnancy" action, the mother need not mitigate damages by abortion or adoption since a tort victim has no duty to make *unreasonable* efforts to diminish or avoid prospective damages.

We come now to decide which course of action is best for Ohio. In doing so, we comment that this has been one of the most difficult cases we have been called upon to decide. Our occupational duty continuously requires us to balance rights and responsibilities of persons regardless of their color, sex, position or station in life. We accomplish that balancing in this case while recognizing that our decision will be something less than universally accepted.

We reject the "no recovery" rule as being one that is clearly in conflict with the traditional concepts of tort law. Certainly, in the case now before us, there was a duty and a breach of that duty which was the proximate cause of damage. What damages should be allowed is the more difficult question.

Likewise, we are opposed to following the benefits rule because of the impossibility of a jury placing a price tag on a child's benefits to her parents. We are not in the business of placing a value on a smile or quantifying the negative impact of a temper tantrum. We are not qualified to judge whether a child might become President or a hopeless derelict. We cannot pretend to know what the future may hold — and neither can or may a jury!

Furthermore, we are not persuaded to adopt the full recovery rule because the strict rules of tort should not be applied to an action to which they are not suited, such as a wrongful pregnancy case, in which a doctor's tortious conduct permits to occur the birth of a child rather than the causing of an injury.

After reviewing the four theories of recovery, we find the limited damages theory is the most persuasive rule. Allowing a jury to award child-rearing costs would be to invite unduly speculative and ethically questionable assessments of such matters as the emotional effect of a birth on siblings as well as parents, and the emotional as well as the pecuniary costs of raising an unplanned and, perhaps, unwanted child in varying family environments.

Additionally, these speculative expenses for child rearing in a "wrongful pregnancy" action were not recognized at common law, just as damages were not recognized in an action for "wrongful death." We believe that if such expenses are to be recognized, it is the role of the General Assembly to establish guidelines in a "wrongful pregnancy" action as the legislature has done in allowing damages in "wrongful death" actions.

Thus, in a "wrongful pregnancy" action, Ohio recognizes the "limited damages" rule which limits the damages to the pregnancy itself and does not include child-rearing expenses. The extent of recoverable damages is limited by Ohio's public policy that the birth of a normal, healthy child cannot be an injury to her parents.

We are aware of the possible hardships that might result from today's decision and we are not blind to the economic realities that accompany the rearing of a child. However, if liability is to be extended in such cases to child-rearing expenses, then the General Assembly is the proper forum in which the competing social philosophies involved in "wrongful pregnancy" actions should be considered in establishing the law.

Accordingly, based on the foregoing reasons, the judgment of the court of appeals is affirmed.

NOTES AND PROBLEMS

1. *Wrongful Pregnancy.* The majority of courts that recognize a claim for wrongful pregnancy limit the damages to prenatal medical expenses. But courts have expressed a wide variety of views regarding the available damage and pain awards, from no recovery to a full, unlimited recovery for the costs of raising of the child. Why did the foregoing court choose the limited recovery and reject the other views?

2. *Defensive Practice of Medicine.* If medical practitioners faced liability for the costs of raising unwanted children in helping parents with their family planning medical care, what would be the repercussions of the costs and availability of such services, if any?

3. *Problem.* If a couple undergoes a sterilization procedure to avoid having another child and the doctor negligently performs the procedure resulting in an unwanted pregnancy, may the couple recover the medical costs of the abortion and for emotional distress associated with the unwanted pregnancy and abortion? Does the answer depend upon which jurisdiction's rules apply?

2. *Wrongful Birth and Wrongful Life*

The prior case involving *wrongful pregnancy* dealt with the birth of a healthy child. Even though not desired, the court had to contend with whether the birth was a cause of action or a cause for celebration. The next case deals with a very different problem. The plaintiffs gave birth to a child who, but for the defendant doctor's alleged negligence, would have never been born. The child is born with severe birth defects and the parents alleged they would have aborted the child had they been properly advised of the birth defect. Notice that parents bring both a claim on their own behalf and a claim on behalf of their disabled son. The courts treat these claims differently — can you see why?

NELSON v. KRUSEN

678 S.W.2d 918 (Tex. 1984)

[Plaintiffs Tom and Gloria Nelson brought a wrongful birth suit in their own behalf and a wrongful life suit as next friends of Mark Nelson, their minor son, against Dr. Edward Krusen and Baylor University Medical Center. Plaintiffs alleged Dr. Krusen was negligent in advising them that Mrs. Nelson was not a genetic carrier of muscular dystrophy and was no more likely than any other woman to have a child afflicted by the disease. Plaintiffs contend that had the defendant given them the proper advice, they would have terminated the pregnancy.

According to the summary judgment evidence, the Nelsons already had one child with muscular dystrophy when they learned Mrs. Nelson was pregnant again. They consulted defendant Krusen seeking to determine if Mrs. Nelson was a genetic carrier of the disease. Dr. Krusen advised them that she was not a carrier and so they proceeded with her pregnancy. Mark Nelson was born in 1976. In 1979 they began to notice tight heel cords bilaterally. A pediatric neurologist then confirmed that Mark Nelson had muscular dystrophy. Plaintiffs contend that the defendant Krusen committed negligence in giving them erroneous advice.

The trial court entered summary judgment for the defendants on the wrongful life claim of Mark Nelson, finding that no cause of action existed. On the wrongful birth claim the trial court ruled that the claim was untimely under the statute of limitations. The court of appeals affirmed.

The Supreme Court reversed the summary judgment of the wrongful birth claim, finding that the parents timely brought their wrongful birth claim. The court affirmed the summary judgment of the wrongful life claim.]

Concurring opinion by Robertson, J.

I concur in the result reached by the majority.

The reason for permitting the Nelsons a cause of action, but denying a similar cause of action to their son is simple: the claim of the parents arguably contains all the elements for a prima facie case in negligence; the claim of the child does not.

Viewing Dr. Krusen's alleged conduct from the standpoint of the parents, under the summary judgment evidence and pleadings a viable suit in negligence is presented. The elements of actionable negligence are duty, a breach of that duty, an injury to the person owed the duty, and proximate cause. *Pullman Co. v. Caviness*, 116 S.W. 410 (1909, writ ref'd). The duty to give accurate medical advice runs from the doctor to the patient. That duty was arguably breached. Since the parents allege that they would have sought an abortion had they known Mrs. Nelson was a genetic carrier of Duchenne muscular dystrophy, proximate cause must be presumed. The injury consists of medical bills that would not have been incurred by the parents, but for the birth of Mark Nelson.

The "wrongful life" cause of action must be viewed from a different perspective, that of the child. With the child as a plaintiff, a suit in negligence is difficult to conceptualize. Courts examining "wrongful life" suits have had difficulty with virtually every element of the cause of action — the nature of the duty, if any, owed to an unborn child under these circumstances, the concomitant question of breach, and the issue of proximate cause in a situation where both the child's life and his or her defective condition are due to the same negligent act.

I am most concerned by the element of injury. We cannot compare Mark Nelson's current condition, life as a victim of muscular dystrophy, with the alternative of a normal, healthy childhood. Were this so, the fact of injury would not be in issue, and the sole question would be the calculation of the extent of damages. Under the summary judgment evidence, the same medical advice that was the proximate cause of his affliction must be assumed to be the cause of his life itself. To determine whether Mark Nelson has suffered an injury in fact, then, his life with physical impairment must be compared to the alternative of nonexistence.

This calculation cannot rationally be made, as man knows nothing of nonexistence, and can assign it neither a positive nor a negative value. Unfortunately, the fact of injury is a prima facie element in a cause of action for negligence. *Johnson v. Sovereign Camp, W.O.W.*, 125 Tex. 329, 83 S.W.2d 605 (1935). It is not fatal to a cause of action in negligence that a plaintiff cannot prove the quantum of injury; but a plaintiff must always establish the *existence* of injury. This is an impossible burden for a "wrongful life" plaintiff to meet.

Since the initial burden of proof of each element of a negligence cause of action is upon the plaintiff, and one element is rationally unprovable in a "wrongful life" setting, a negligence suit cannot be maintained. The absence of any injury in fact is also a primary factor in the refusal of New York courts to recognize a "wrongful life" cause of action. *See, e.g., Becker v. Schwartz*, 46 N.Y.2d 401, 413 N.Y.S.2d 895, 900, 386 N.E.2d 807 (1978); *Alquijay v. St. Luke's-Roosevelt Hospital Center*, 99 A.D.2d 704, 472 N.Y.S.2d 2, 3 (1984).

There is no inconsistency between permitting a cause of action for the parents, but not for the child. The difference is the identity of the parties. For the parents, the alternatives to be considered in determining whether there has been any injury in fact are no child, and no medical expenses, or a child with physical impairment resulting in medical expenses the parents are obligated to pay. The fact of injury is apparent. For the child, though, the alternatives are existence in an impaired state, or nonexistence. The fact of injury is not only not apparent, but unknowable.

The distinction between the parents' and child's cause of action has also been explained in a somewhat different fashion:

> When the plaintiff alleges that his own birth was wrongful, in effect he asks the court to judicially determine that he should not have been allowed to live, but when another person such as a parent alleges that the infant should not have been born, the parent does not seek to negate his own present existence. *The parent is in reality seeking damages for injuries causally related to the fact of birth, but not for the birth itself.* Thus, the parents are not placed in the anomalous position of trying to sue themselves into oblivion, as are the children.

Comment, *Wrongful Birth: The Emerging Status of a New Tort*, 8 St. Mary's L.J. 140, 145 (1976) (emphasis added).

It is worth noting that most other jurisdictions make the same distinction as this court makes today, finding no logical inconsistency between permitting a cause of action for the parents, but not for children. As the Supreme Court of Georgia observed earlier this year:

> An action brought by a child against the parents or physician on the theory that because of his illegitimacy or birth defects he would have been better not born has found almost no support in the law. However, most jurisdictions now allow an action by parents against the physician for wrongful pregnancy or wrongful conception.

Fulton-DeKalb Hospital Authority v. Graves, 252 Ga. 441, 314 S.E.2d 653, 654 (1984). In at least three leading decisions, a cause of action for the parents has been permitted, but a similar cause of action for the child denied in the same decision. *See Becker v. Schwartz*, 386 N.E.2d 807 (1978); *Speck v. Finegold*, 408 A.2d 496 (1979), aff'd in part, rev'd in part, 439 A.2d 110 (1981); *Dumer v. St. Michael's Hospital*, 233 N.W.2d 372 (1975).

Recently, California and Washington courts have permitted a limited right of recovery for a child presenting a "wrongful life" claim. *See Turpin v. Sortini*, 31 Cal. 3d 220, 643 P.2d 954, 182 Cal. Rptr. 337 (1982); *Harbeson v. Parke-Davis, Inc.*, 98 Wash. 2d 460, 656 P.2d 483 (1983). Even more recently, New Jersey has approved the same result — permitting a child's recovery of extraordinary medical expenses — albeit on a different rationale. *Procanik v. Cillo*, 97 N.J. 339, 478 A.2d 755 (1984). It is tempting to join these courts in fashioning some relief for a severely handicapped child, when that child may be burdened with crushing medical expenses for the remainder of his natural life.

A court should not, however, discard established principles of tort law sub silentio in an attempt to reach a "right" result. Close examination of the California and Washington opinions reveals such an unexplained gap in the decisional reasoning.

> "Whether it is better never to have been born at all than to have been born with even gross deficiencies is a mystery more properly left to the philosophers and the theologians."
>
> *Becker v. Schwarts, 386 N.E.2d 807, 812 (N.Y. 1978).*

The California Supreme Court distinguished between general and special damages in a "wrongful life" setting, denying the former, yet permitting the latter. Explaining why general damages could not be assessed, the *Turpin* court observed that "the problem is not . . . simply the fixing of damages for a conceded injury, but the threshold question of determining whether the plaintiff has in fact suffered an injury by being born with an ailment as opposed to not being born at all." 643 P.2d at 963. The court also noted that "it is simply impossible to determine in any rational or reasoned fashion whether the plaintiff has in fact suffered an injury in being born impaired rather than not being born." *Id.*

Thus, the California Supreme Court, in denying general damages, seems to have explicitly conceded that a prima facie element of the tort was not established. In deciding to award special damages, however, the *Turpin* court ignored the reasoning that prevented an award of general damages. The problem of establishing the fact of injury was simply passed over, and all discussion focused on the nonspeculative nature of a recovery for medical expenses.

To reiterate, the pleadings and briefs of plaintiffs in this case are based in negligence. While this court is not adverse to reexamining and modifying traditional negligence concepts to meet changing social needs, *see Otis Eng'g Corp. v. Clark*, 668 S.W.2d 307 (Tex. 1983), it is properly unwilling to take the step required by a "wrongful life" plaintiff: complete *waiver* of the requirement of injury in a negligence cause of action. Once such a step is taken, it is difficult to envision any principled basis for refusing to extend the reasoning to other elements and other situations.

This court neither addresses nor decides the question of whether some day, under some different theory, a plaintiff might prevail under similar facts. "New and nameless torts are being recognized constantly, and the progress of the common law is marked by many cases of first impression, in which the court has struck out boldly to create a new cause of action, where none has been recognized before." W. Prosser and W. Keeton, *The Law of Torts §1* (5th ed. 1984). The claim of Mark Nelson, however, simply fails to state a cause of action in negligence and must be denied.

NOTES AND PROBLEMS

1. ***Conceptual Damage Problem.*** In effect, the *Nelson* court holds (as do most courts) that while the parents might be able to proceed with a wrongful birth claim, the child does not have a wrongful life claim. With regard to the child's cause of action, most courts find that the concept of proving that the defendant's negligence caused an injury is too difficult to fathom. Why is this a problem for the wrongful life claim of the child but not the parents' wrongful birth claim?

2. ***Right to Privacy and Wrongful Birth.*** The parents on a wrongful birth claim allege that, but for the defendant's negligence, they would have exercised their rights to terminate the pregnancy. To what extent, therefore, does the existence of this cause of action depend upon the continued validity of the Supreme Court's decision in *Roe v. Wade*?

3. ***Problems.***

A. A married couple has a strong desire to have a girl but not a boy. They seek counseling, upon the wife becoming pregnant, to determine the sex of their child. The technician wrongly informs them that they are going to have a girl. They end up giving birth to a boy and contend that, but for the wrong reading of the ultrasound, they would have terminated the pregnancy and tried again for a girl. How would the court analyze the existence of their wrongful birth cause of action? Would the birth of their healthy son be viewed as a viable wrongful birth claim? Or would the court treat it with the same view that most courts have of wrongful pregnancy claims — that generally the birth of a healthy child should be a cause for celebration?

B. A doctor's negligence during the birth of a baby boy causes the child to suffer permanent damage to his brain. The boy sues the doctor for negligence. Will his claim be recognized? How would a court measure his damages?

4. ***Odd Nature of Wrongful Birth Damages.*** In most wrongful birth claims, the parents are suing for two types of damages: (1) emotional distress damages for having a disabled child they would have never chosen to parent, and (2) economic losses associated with the extraordinary care for such a child. We just finished reading two categories of cases, one rejecting a general duty to

avoid causing emotional distress (*Kerr*) and the other rejecting a negligence claim for economic losses (*Finlandia*). Is it odd that a plaintiff can pursue a type of negligence claim that consists of both of these questionable types of damages? Consider the relationship between the plaintiffs and defendant in a wrongful birth claim that helps to avoid limitless liability to the public.

Upon Further Review

Negligence claims that are not associated with physical harm but instead with emotional or economic injuries are suspect in tort law. This is because the harm might be easily feigned and because imposing a duty to avoid such harms generally could expose defendants to far-flung, unlimited liability far beyond what courts would deem acceptable. Rather than stifle activity, courts craft small exceptions. With respect to emotional distress, courts will recognize bystander claims while rejecting any general duty to avoid causing emotional problems. For economic loss, courts essentially cling to something analogous to the impact rule — that absent physical harm to one's property or person you cannot recover purely economic losses. With respect to newborn children, courts refuse to recognize a wrongful life claim by a disabled child whose life might have been avoided by careful prenatal diagnosis and the performance of an abortion. The harm is too conjectural and problematic — courts refuse to acknowledge that one might be better off unborn than born with problems. The claim by parents is not problematic for the courts as we can identify and measure their harm.

DUTY LIMITED BY NATURE OF THE ACTIVITY: PRIMARY ASSUMPTION OF THE RISK

A. Introduction

Thus far we have seen the concept of a duty of care impacted by notions of freedom not to act or intervene in a perilous situation, by the lack of special relationships, and by concerns about the nature of the harm incurred by the plaintiff. In this section, we will see courts negate any duty of care in instances where the doctrine of primary assumption of risk applies. You may have already heard the phrase "assumption of the risk." If so, be warned that tort law has three very distinct varieties of assumption of risk. Two of these types of assumption of risk — *secondary implied* and *express* — are dealt with in Chapter 7 under the topic of Affirmative Defenses. By contrast, *primary assumption of the risk* operates to impair the plaintiff's ability to show negligence against the defendant and is not, technically speaking, an affirmative defense. We will introduce this concept with a very old opinion by Judge Cardozo in *Steeplechase Amusement,* and then consider a more modern application in *Snowbird Ski Resort.*

B. Inherent Risk

MURPHY v. STEEPLECHASE AMUSEMENT CO., INC.

166 N.E. 173 (N.Y. 1929)

CARDOZO, J.

The defendant, Steeplechase Amusement Company, maintains an amusement park at Coney Island, New York.

One of the supposed attractions is known as "The Flopper." It is a moving belt, running upward on an inclined plane, on which passengers sit or stand. Many of them are unable to keep their feet because of the movement of the belt, and are thrown backward or aside. The belt runs in a groove, with padded walls on either side to a height of four feet, and with padded flooring beyond the walls at the same angle as the belt. An electric motor supplies the needed power.

Plaintiff, a vigorous young man, visited the park with friends. One of them, a young woman, now his wife, stepped upon the moving belt. Plaintiff followed and stepped behind her. As he did so, he felt what he describes as a sudden jerk, and was thrown to the floor. His wife in front and also friends behind him were thrown at the same time. Something more was here, as every one understood, than the slowly moving escalator that is common in shops and public places. A fall was foreseen as one of the risks of the adventure. There would have been no point to the whole thing, no adventure about it, if the risk had not been there. The very name above the gate, the Flopper, was warning to the timid. If the name was not enough, there was warning more distinct in the experience of others. We are told by the plaintiff's wife that the members of her party stood looking at the sport before joining in it themselves. Some aboard the belt were able, as she viewed them, to sit down with decorum or even to stand and keep their footing; others jumped or fell. The tumbling bodies and the screams and laughter supplied the merriment and fun. "I took a chance," she said when asked whether she thought that a fall might be expected.

Plaintiff took the chance with her, but, less lucky than his companions, suffered a fracture of a knee cap. He states in his complaint that the belt was dangerous to life and limb in that it stopped and started violently and suddenly and was not properly equipped to prevent injuries to persons who were using it without knowledge of its dangers, and in a bill of particulars he adds that it was operated at a fast and dangerous rate of speed and was not supplied with a proper railing, guard or other device to prevent a fall therefrom. No other negligence is charged.

We see no adequate basis for a finding that the belt was out of order. It was already in motion when the plaintiff put his foot on it. He cannot help himself to a verdict in such circumstances by the addition of the facile comment that it threw him with a jerk. One who steps upon a moving belt and finds his heels above his head is in no position to discriminate with nicety between the successive stages of the shock, between the jerk which is a cause and the jerk, accompanying the fall, as an instantaneous effect. There is evidence for the defendant that power was transmitted smoothly, and could not be transmitted otherwise. If the movement was spasmodic, it was an unexplained and, it seems, an inexplicable departure from the normal workings of the mechanism. An aberration so extraordinary, if it is to lay the basis for a verdict, should rest on something firmer than a mere descriptive epithet, a summary of the sensations of a tense and crowded moment. But the jerk, if it were established, would add little to the case. Whether the movement of the belt was uniform or irregular, the risk at greatest was a fall. This was the very hazard that was invited and foreseen.

Volenti non fit injuria. One who takes part in such a sport accepts the dangers that inhere in it so far as they are obvious and necessary, just as a fencer accepts the risk of a thrust by his antagonist or a spectator at a ball game the chance of contact with the ball. The antics of the clown are not the paces of the cloistered cleric. The rough and boisterous joke, the horseplay of the crowd, evokes its own guffaws, but they are not the pleasures of tranquility. The plaintiff was not seeking a retreat for meditation. Visitors were tumbling about the belt to the merriment of onlookers when he made his choice to join them. He took the

Volenti non fit injuria
To the willing, no injury is done (Lat.)

chance of a like fate, with whatever damage to his body might ensue from such a fall. The timorous may stay at home.

A different case would be here if the dangers inherent in the sport were obscure or unobserved or so serious as to justify the belief that precautions of some kind must have been taken to avert them. Nothing happened to the plaintiff except what common experience tells us may happen at any time as the consequence of a sudden fall. Many a skater or a horseman can rehearse a tale of equal woe. A different case there would also be if the accidents had been so many as to show that the game in its inherent nature was too dangerous to be continued without change. The president of the amusement company says that there had never been such an accident before. A nurse employed at an emergency hospital maintained in connection with the park contradicts him to some extent. She says that on other occasions she had attended patrons of the park who had been injured at the Flopper, how many she could not say. None, however, had been badly injured or had suffered broken bones. Such testimony is not enough to show that the game was a trap for the unwary, too perilous to be endured. According to the defendant's estimate, two hundred and fifty thousand visitors were at the Flopper in a year. Some quota of accidents was to be looked for in so great a mass. One might as well say that a skating rink should be abandoned because skaters sometimes fall.

The judgment of the Appellate Division and that of the Trial Term should be reversed, and a new trial granted, with costs to abide the event.

NOTES AND PROBLEMS

1. ***Primary Assumption of the Risk vs. Contributory Negligence.*** Sometimes different tort doctrines overlap. In a case involving primary assumption of the risk, it is possible to allege as well that the plaintiff took some unreasonable risk of harm in participating in an obviously dangerous activity. But primary assumption of the risk is not focused upon blaming the plaintiff for participating voluntarily in some risky endeavor. The focal point is on the activity itself, or at least defendant's provision of that activity. What is it about the activity of riding an amusement park ride like the Flopper that causes the court to invoke the doctrine?

2. ***Foreseeability Negates Duty.*** Often, courts rely upon concepts of foreseeability in crafting special duty rules. The *Tarasoff* rule and the *Dillon* rule are both examples of this we have just covered earlier in this chapter. Do you see how with regard to primary assumption of the risk, the foreseeability of the potential harm is actually used to eliminate any duty of care? Why would this be true in this area?

C. A More Refined Test for Inherent Risks

CLOVER v. SNOWBIRD SKI RESORT

808 P.2d 1037 (Utah 1991)

HALL, J.

Plaintiff Margaret Clover sought to recover damages for injuries sustained as the result of a ski accident in which Chris Zulliger, an employee of defendant Snowbird Corporation ("Snowbird"), collided with her. From the entry of summary judgment in favor of defendants, Clover appeals.

At the time of the accident, Chris Zulliger was employed by Snowbird as a chef at the Plaza Restaurant . . . which was located at the base of the resort, and the Mid-Gad Restaurant, which was located halfway to the top of the mountain.

On December 5, 1985, the date of the accident, Zulliger was scheduled to begin work at the Plaza Restaurant. Prior to beginning work, he had planned to go skiing . . . . Snowbird preferred that their employees know how to ski because it made it easier for them to get to and from work.

[Zulliger skied four runs before heading down the mountain to work. On his final run he] took a route that was often taken by Snowbird employees to travel from the top of the mountain to the Plaza. About mid-way down the mountain, at a point above the Mid-Gad, Zulliger decided to take a jump off a crest on the side of an intermediate run. He had taken this jump many times before. A skier moving relatively quickly is able to become airborne at that point because of the steep drop off on the downhill side of the crest. Due to this drop off, it is impossible for skiers above the crest to see skiers below the crest. The jump was well known to Snowbird. In fact, the Snowbird ski patrol often instructed people not to jump off the crest. There was also a sign instructing skiers to ski slowly at this point in the run. Zulliger, however, ignored the sign and skied over the crest at a significant speed. Clover, who had just entered the same ski run from a point below the crest, either had stopped or was traveling slowly below the crest. When Zulliger went over the jump, he collided with Clover, who was hit in the head and severely injured.

Clover brought claims against Zulliger and Snowbird, alleging that [Snowbird was negligent in designing and maintaining its ski runs and Zulliger was negligent in his manner of skiing]. Zulliger settled separately with Clover. [By summary judgment,] the trial judge dismissed Clover's claims against Snowbird [because] Utah's Inherent Risk of Skiing Statute, *Utah Code Ann. §§78-27-51 to -54* (Supp. 1986), bars plaintiff's claim of negligent design and maintenance . . . .

The trial court dismissed Clover's negligent design and maintenance claim on the ground that such a claim is barred by Utah's Inherent Risk of Skiing Statute, *Utah Code Ann. §§78-27-51 to -54* (Supp. 1986). This ruling was based on the trial court's findings that "Clover was injured as a result of a collision with another skier, and/or the variation of steepness in terrain." Apparently, the trial court reasoned that regardless of a ski resort's culpability, the resort is not liable for an injury occasioned by one or more of the dangers listed in section 78-27-52(1). This reasoning, however, is based on an incorrect interpretation of sections 78-27-51 to -54.

Utah Code Ann. §§78-27-51 and *-52(1)* read in part:

> Inherent risks of skiing — Public policy
>
> The Legislature finds that the sport of skiing is practiced by a large number of residents of Utah and attracts a large number of nonresidents, significantly contributing to the economy of this state.
>
> . . . It is the purpose of this act, therefore, to clarify the law in relation to skiing injuries and the risks inherent in that sport, and to establish as a matter of law that certain risks are inherent in that sport, and to provide that, as a matter of public policy, no person engaged in that sport shall recover from a ski operator for injuries resulting from those inherent risks.
>
> Inherent risk of skiing — Definitions
>
> As used in this act:
>
> (1) "Inherent risk of skiing" means those dangers or conditions which are an integral part of the sport of skiing, including, but not limited to: changing weather conditions, variations or steepness in terrain; snow or ice conditions; surface or subsurface conditions such as bare spots, forest growth, rocks, stumps, impact with lift towers and other structures and their components; collisions with other skiers; and a skier's failure to ski within his own ability.

It is clear that [these sections] protect ski area operators from suits initiated by their patrons who seek recovery for injuries caused by an inherent risk of skiing. The statute, however, does not purport to grant ski area operators complete immunity from all negligence claims initiated by skiers. While the general parameters of the act are clear, application of the statute to specific circumstances is less certain. In the instant case, both parties urge different interpretations of the act. Snowbird claims that any injury occasioned by one or more of the dangers listed in section 78-27-52(1) is barred by the statute because, as a matter of law, such an accident is caused by an inherent risk of skiing. Clover, on the other hand, argues that a ski area operator's negligence is not an inherent risk of skiing and that if the resort's negligence causes a collision between skiers, a suit arising from that collision is not barred by [the statute].

Although the trial court apparently agreed with Snowbird, we decline to adopt such an interpretation. The basis of Snowbird's argument is that the language of section 78-27-52(1) stating that "'inherent risk of skiing means those dangers or conditions which are an integral part of the sport of skiing, including but not limited to: . . . collision with other skiers" must be read as defining all collisions between skiers as inherent risks. The wording of the statute does not compel such a reading. To the contrary, the dangers listed in section 78-27-52(1) are modified by the term "integral part of the sport of skiing." Therefore, ski area operators are protected from suits to recover for injuries caused by one or more of the dangers listed in section 78-27-52(1) only to the extent that those dangers, under the facts of each case, are integral aspects of the sport of skiing. Indeed, the list of dangers in section 78-27-52(1) is expressly nonexclusive. The statute, therefore, contemplates that the determination of whether a risk is inherent be made on a case-by-case basis, using the entire statute, not solely the list provided in section 78-27-52(1).

Inasmuch as the purpose of the statute is to "clarify the law," not to radically alter ski resort liability, it is necessary to briefly examine the relevant law at the time the statute was enacted. Although there is limited Utah case law on point, when the statute was enacted the majority of jurisdictions employed the doctrine of primary assumption of risk in limiting ski resorts' liability for injuries their patrons received while skiing. Terms utilized in the statute such as "inherent risk of skiing" and "assumes the risk" are the same terms relied upon in such cases. This language suggests that the statute is meant to achieve the same results achieved under the doctrine of primary assumption of risk. In fact, commentators suggest that the statute was passed in reaction to a perceived erosion in the protection ski area operators traditionally enjoyed under the common law doctrine of primary assumption of risk.

As we have noted in the past, the single term "assumption of risk" has been used to refer to several different, and occasionally overlapping, concepts. One concept, primary assumption of risk, is simply "an alternative expression for the proposition that the defendant was not negligent, that is, there was no duty owed or there was no breach of an existing duty." This suggests that the statute, in clarifying the "confusion as to whether a skier assumes the risks inherent in the sport of skiing," operates to define the duty ski resorts owe to their patrons.

Finally, it is to be noted that without a duty, there can be no negligence. Such an interpretation, therefore, harmonizes the express purpose of the statute, protecting ski area operators from suits arising out of injuries caused by the inherent risks of skiing, with the fact that the statute does not purport to abrogate a skier's traditional right to recover for injuries caused by ski area operators' negligence.

A similar analysis leads to the conclusion that the [duty this statute imposes] on ski resorts [includes] the duty to use reasonable care for the protection of its patrons.... [H]owever, a ski area operator is under no duty to protect its patrons from the inherent risks of skiing. The inherent risks of skiing are those dangers that skiers wish to confront as essential characteristics of the sport of skiing or hazards that cannot be eliminated by the exercise of ordinary care on the part of the ski area operator.

The term "inherent risk of skiing," refers to those risks that are essential characteristics of skiing — risks that are so integrally related to skiing that the sport cannot be undertaken without confronting these risks. Generally, these risks can be divided into two categories. The first category of risks consists of those risks, such as steep grades, powder, and mogul runs, which skiers wish to confront as an essential characteristic of skiing. Under sections 78-27-51 to -54, a ski area operator is under no duty to make all of its runs as safe as possible by eliminating the type of dangers that skiers wish to confront as an integral part of skiing.

The second category of risks consists of those hazards which no one wishes to confront but cannot be alleviated by the use of reasonable care on the part of a ski resort. It is without question that skiing is a dangerous activity. Hazards may exist in locations where they are not readily discoverable. Weather and snow conditions can suddenly change and, without warning, create new hazards where no hazard previously existed. Hence, it is clearly foreseeable that a skier, without skiing recklessly, may momentarily lose control or fall in an unexpected manner. Ski area operators cannot alleviate these risks, and under sections 78-27-51 to -54, they are not liable for injuries caused by such risks . . . . This does not mean, however, that a ski area operator is under no duty to use ordinary care to protect its patrons. In fact, if an injury was caused by an unnecessary hazard that could have been eliminated by the use of ordinary care, such a hazard is not, in the ordinary sense of the term, an inherent risk of skiing and would fall outside of sections 78-27-51 to -54.

Having established the proper interpretation of sections 78-27-51 to -54, the next step is to determine whether, given this interpretation, there is a genuine issue of material fact in regard to Clover's claim. First, the existence of a blind jump with a landing area located at a point where skiers enter the run is not an essential characteristic of an intermediate run. Therefore, Clover may recover if she can prove that Snowbird could have prevented the accident through the use of ordinary care. It is to be noted that Clover's negligent design and maintenance claim is not based solely on the allegation that Snowbird allowed conditions to exist on an intermediate hill which caused blind spots and allowed skiers to jump. Rather, Clover presents evidence that Snowbird was aware that its patrons regularly took the jump, that the jump created an unreasonable hazard to skiers below the jump, and that Snowbird did not take reasonable measures to eliminate the hazard. This evidence is sufficient to raise a genuine issue of material fact in regard to Clover's negligent design and maintenance claim.

In light of the genuine issues of material fact in regard to each of Clover's claims, summary judgment was inappropriate.

Reversed and remanded for further proceedings.

NOTES AND PROBLEMS

1. *Inherent Dangers.* The statute in Utah referred both to collisions with other skiers and changes in terrain as inherent dangers of snow skiing. The court clarified, however, that only some collisions and some changes in terrain were actually inherent dangers. The court then identifies two types of inherent dangers: positive dangers that are desirable, and negative dangers that can't reasonably be avoided without fundamentally changing the sport or activity. How does the court then decide that the allegations of negligence by the plaintiff possibly demonstrated negligence?

2. *A Necessary Doctrine?* Courts and commentators agree that primary assumption of the risk is merely an acknowledgement that the defendant either has no duty to prevent inherent risks or that the defendant has not breached any duty of care regarding such risks. Application of the Learned Hand formula for negligence is ultimately what is employed to define an inherent risk. Given this, does the doctrine really add anything to our negligence analysis?

3. ***Societal Expectations Can Change.*** The primary assumption of the risk doctrine is so associated with foul ball injuries at baseball games that some refer to the doctrine as the "baseball doctrine." For many years courts have fairly consistently denied recovery to spectators at baseball games hit by foul balls. But in recent years, Major League Baseball teams have begun extending the netting further around the stadium (past the dugout areas) after a series of well publicized and serious injuries, including one to a young child at the New York Yankees' stadium during the summer of 2017. After these changes, would a fan attending a baseball game at a stadium that had not yet extended the netting and who gets hit sitting behind the dugout, be in a better position to argue that this activity no longer constituted a primary assumption of the risk?

4. ***Problems.*** Does primary assumption of the risk preclude the following negligence claims?

- **A.** A spectator at a major league ballpark sitting along the third base side is hit with a foul ball and injured. She sues the club for negligently failing to protect her from such hazards.
- **B.** A spectator at a major league ballpark sitting directly behind home plate is hit by a foul ball and injured. The ballpark had recently decided to remove the netting that was typically used to protect fans in this portion of the park.
- **C.** A spectator at a major league ballpark is on a concourse with a peek hole built into the wall that permits someone waiting in line for hot dogs to watch the action. The spectator is not watching the action and a ball hit during batting practice comes through the opening and hits the spectator.

Upon Further Review

Primary assumption of the risk is just a particular way that a court can declare as a matter of law that the defendant is not liable to the plaintiff in negligence, either because there was no duty to prevent harms associated with inherent risks, or because there was no unreasonable conduct by the defendant. It is technically not an affirmative defense but simply another way of saying that the plaintiff has failed to prove negligence. It applies when the particular risk is either desirable or not one that can be avoided through the exercise of reasonable care. The modern inquiry focuses not so much upon the plaintiff's awareness, but more upon the nature of the activity and the defendant's conduct. In Chapter 7, we will learn about two true defenses that share a common name—secondary implied assumption of the risk and express assumption of the risk.

DUTY BASED UPON VICTIM'S STATUS

A. Introduction

In premises liability cases, tort law has traditionally altered its duty rules based upon the status of the victim who was hurt upon the defendant's land. In other words, not all claimants are treated equally. We will see at the end of this section that there has emerged a modern trend away from such disparate treatment. We begin, however, with a review of the traditional categories of *trespasser, licensee*, and *invitee*. Be careful to understand both how courts define and determine these categories, as well as how and why the duty rules vary with each.

B. Trespassers

Trespassers occupy a least-favored status among all of the entrants to another's property. This stems from the strong tradition in the common law to respect the property rights of citizens. You may recall in Chapter 2 that it was relatively easy to be labeled a trespasser (even if acting in good faith) so long as you were on the land of another without their permission. Further, as a trespasser your liability was quite broad — unburdened by any proximate cause limitations. Most jurisdictions have held that, therefore, a landowner owes only minimal duties toward a trespasser — the duty to refrain from gross negligence ("willful or wanton misconduct"). This limited duty is subject to modification. In the case of trespassers who have stepped onto the defendant's property with sinister intentions, arguably even a lesser duty applies, as we will see in the *Ryals* case below. In the case of child trespassers, however, courts will sometimes elevate the duty of care owed under the *attractive nuisance doctrine*. This is explored in the *Stanley* case.

1. Adult Trespassers

RYALS v. UNITED STATES STEEL CORP.

562 So. 2d 192 (Ala. 1990)

JONES, J.

Wilson Ryals, Jr., as administrator of the estate of his brother, David Ryals, appeals from a summary judgment in favor of the defendant, United States Steel Corporation ("U.S. Steel"). The plaintiff alleged that the defendant caused the decedent's death by negligently or wantonly failing to maintain and secure a "switch rack" [something akin to an electrical substation]. Ryals later voluntarily dismissed the negligence claim, and the trial court entered summary judgment in favor of U.S. Steel on the wantonness claim.

Because this Court, by this opinion, recognizes two distinct classes of trespassers to land — (1) mere trespassers, to whom the landowner owes the duty not to wantonly injure them; and (2) trespassers who enter upon the land of another with the manifest intent to commit a criminal act and to whom the landowner owes only the duty not to intentionally injure them — we affirm the judgment.

On March 31, 1984, Wilson and David Ryals, as trespassers, went to U.S. Steel's Muscoda Mines switch rack for the purpose of "stripping out" copper, brass, and other salvageable metals. Wilson Ryals testified at his deposition that, when they arrived at the site, they found the base of the structure to be partially stripped; that they found one rusty warning sign, detached metals lying on the ground, dangling wires, garbage in and around the fenced area and wild vegetation growing around the fence; and that they found the gate leading into the switch rack to be "wide open." David Ryals contacted a 44,000-volt copper line; he suffered third degree burns over 95% of his body and died several days later as a result.

The only issue presented here is whether U.S. Steel was entitled to a summary judgment under the appropriate standard of care owed by U.S. Steel to David Ryals, as a trespasser, who, at the time of his injury, was engaged in the crime of theft of U.S. Steel's property.

Necessarily antecedent to any evaluation of the facts, however, is a determination of the legal duty owed by a landowner to a trespasser. David Ryals was, without question, a trespasser. The standard of care that a landowner owes to a trespasser is generally recognized as the lowest standard of care owed to one who enters upon another's land. The landowner is bound only to refrain from reckless, willful, or wanton conduct toward the trespasser. *Copeland v. Pike Liberal Arts School*, 553 So. 2d 100 (Ala. 1989).

It is noteworthy that the highest degree of care imposed upon a landowner by this traditional common law rule toward a *mere* trespasser, i.e., one who wrongfully comes upon the land of another but without any motive, design, or intent to engage in further wrongful conduct, is not to recklessly or wantonly injure that person. Ryals does not contend otherwise; rather, he argues that the facts, when construed most favorably to him, support a finding of wantonness on the part of U.S. Steel, and, thus, that summary judgment was inappropriate. Admittedly, if all trespassers are to be treated equally, and if we agree that the conduct of U.S. Steel amounted to wantonness, then the summary judgment is due to be reversed.

"Wantonness" has been defined by this Court as follows:

> [Wantonness is] the conscious doing of some act or the omission of some duty under the knowledge of the existing conditions, and conscious that from the doing of such act or omission of such duty injury will likely or probably result.

Kilcrease v. Harris, 259 So. 2d 797, 801-02 (1972).

Ryals contends that a genuine issue of material fact was presented on the question whether U.S. Steel wantonly caused the death of David Ryals. Ryals bases his wantonness argument primarily on his claim that when he and his brother arrived at the site they found it in the condition hereinabove set out. He also points out that agents of U.S. Steel acknowledged in deposition and in answers to interrogatories that there had been two prior deaths at the same switch rack under similar circumstances. He maintains, in light of those alleged and admitted facts, that the factfinder could reasonably infer that U.S. Steel had actual or constructive notice that persons might come into contact with the electrical lines at the switch rack.

We agree; if reckless or wanton conduct is the appropriate standard of care applicable to these facts, then a jury question has been presented as to U.S. Steel's conduct. We believe, however, that these facts strongly demonstrate a public policy justification for lowering the requisite degree of care due from a landowner to one who, as here, wrongfully enters upon the land of another to commit a crime. For public policy reasons, therefore, we hold that the duty

owed by a landowner to an adult trespasser who comes upon the land and is injured while committing a crime is the duty not to *intentionally* injure such trespasser.

Applying this standard to the full context of the instant case, we conclude that a fact question was not presented on the issue whether U.S. Steel intentionally caused the death of David Ryals. The switch rack was surrounded by a chain link fence topped with barbed wire. On the fence surrounding the switch rack there was at least one sign warning of the electrical danger within. Given these conspicuous indications of danger, an unlocked gate would not imperil a person unless that person elected to disregard the obvious danger presented by the electricity. In summary, the evidence, as a matter of law, fails to suggest that U.S. Steel breached its duty not to intentionally injure David Ryals, who undisputedly, at the time of his injury, was an adult illegally upon U.S. Steel's property for the purpose of stealing copper wire.

Accordingly, the judgment of the trial court is due to be, and it hereby is, affirmed.

NOTES AND PROBLEMS

1. ***Justification for Lower Duty to Ordinary Trespassers.*** There are two ways to justify the lower duty owed to trespassers. First, that trespassers are simply disliked or disfavored and, as a matter of justice, should not be entitled to the same protections as one permitted to be on the property. Second, that they are less foreseeable than the invited or permitted guest. Given that they might happen onto the land at any time, day or night, and without notice, it would create an undue burden on the owner to anticipate and prepare the land for their safe entry.

2. ***Duty Not to Intentionally Harm the Criminal Trespasser.*** Most courts have not reached the issue of whether the duty of care should be lowered further for a trespasser on another's property to commit a crime. What seems to be the justification for doing so? By saying there is only a duty not to intentionally injure the trespasser, the court is really taking such liability out of the realm of accidental torts altogether. To create liability under this standard, the defendant would have to have committed a battery. On the other hand, we have previously seen in Chapter 3 that conduct that would otherwise constitute a battery can be justified to protect property. If the landowner in *Ryals* had set up the electrical substation in order to purposefully injure the plaintiff, for the protection of its property, would this have been justified? Recall the holding of the court in the *Katko* (spring gun) case in that chapter.

3. ***Gross Negligence as Typical Standard for Trespassers.*** The court in *Ryals* stated that if the typical standard applicable to trespassers were utilized then the summary judgment would have been improper. Which facts, in particular, demonstrate that the defendant might have met the standard for gross negligence?

2. Child Trespassers: The Attractive Nuisance Doctrine

When the injured plaintiff is a child trespasser, courts face countervailing feelings. On the one hand, the common law still favors landowners and disfavors those who commit trespass. These feelings justify in part the lower duty owed to such tortfeasors by landowners. But on the other hand, the law seeks to protect and promote the interests of children. So when a child trespasser is injured on another's property and sues that landowner, courts stand in the crossroads of these conflicting principles and emotions. The common law has developed the *attractive nuisance doctrine* as its compromise answer to this dilemma.

BENNETT v. STANLEY

748 N.E.2d 41 (Ohio 2001)

PFEIFER, J.

In this case we are called upon to determine what level of duty a property owner owes to a child trespasser. We resolve the question by adopting the attractive nuisance doctrine set forth in *Restatement of the Law 2d, Torts (1965), Section 339.* We also hold that an adult who attempts to rescue a child from an attractive nuisance assumes the status of the child, and is owed a duty of ordinary care by the property owner.

When Rickey G. Bennett, plaintiff-appellant, arrived home in the late afternoon of March 20, 1997, he found his two young daughters crying. The three-year-old, Kyleigh, told him that "Mommy" and Chance, her five-year-old half-brother, were "drowning in the water." Bennett ran next door to his neighbors' house to find mother and son unconscious in the swimming pool. Both died.

The Bennetts had moved next door to defendants-appellees, Jeffrey and Stacey Stanley, in the fall of 1996. The Stanleys had purchased their home the previous June. At the time of their purchase, the Stanleys' property included a swimming pool that had gone unused for three years. At that time, the pool was enclosed with fencing and a brick wall. After moving in, the Stanleys drained the pool once but thereafter they allowed rainwater to accumulate in the pool to a depth of over six feet. They removed a tarp that had been on the pool and also removed the fencing that had been around two sides of the pool. The pool became pond-like: it contained tadpoles and frogs, and Mr. Stanley had seen a snake swimming on the surface. The pool contained no ladders, and its sides were slimy with algae.

The Stanleys were aware that the Bennetts had moved next door and that they had young children. They had seen the children outside unsupervised. Stacey Stanley had once called Chance onto her property to retrieve a dog. The Stanleys testified, however, that they never had any concern about the children getting into the pool. They did not post any warning or "no trespassing" signs on their property.

Rickey Bennett testified that he had told his children to stay away from the pool on the Stanleys' property. He also stated that he had never seen the children playing near the pool.

Kyleigh told her father that she and Chance had been playing at the pool on the afternoon of the tragedy. The sheriff's department concluded that Chance had gone to the pool to look at the frogs and somehow fell into the pool. His mother apparently drowned trying to save him.

Bennett alleged [in his complaint] that appellees had negligently maintained an abandoned swimming pool on their property and that appellees' negligence proximately caused the March 20, 1997 drowning of Chance and Cher. Appellant averred that appellees had created a dangerous condition by negligently maintaining the pool and that appellees reasonably should have known that the pool posed an unreasonable risk of serious harm to others. Appellant specifically alleged that appellees' pool created an unreasonable risk of harm to children who, because of their youth, would not realize the potential danger. Appellant further asserted that appellees' conduct in maintaining the pool constituted willful and wanton misconduct such as to justify an award of punitive damages.

Appellees filed a motion for summary judgment, which the trial court granted on September 4, 1998. The trial court found that Chance and Cher were trespassers on appellees' property and that appellees therefore owed them only a duty to refrain from wanton and willful misconduct. As the complaint alleged that appellees had violated a duty of ordinary care, the court found for the Stanleys as a matter of law.

On appeal, the appellate court affirmed the trial court's granting of summary judgment. It, too, held that appellees owed the decedents only a duty to refrain from wanton and willful misconduct, and added that there was no evidence of such misconduct. The appellate court also addressed the issue of appellees' duty to Cher Bennett. The court held that even if she were on the Stanleys' property in an attempt to rescue Chance, she would still have the status only of a licensee [to whom the Stanleys would not owe a duty of reasonable care].

Ohio has long recognized a range of duties for property owners vis-a-vis persons entering their property. Currently, to an invitee the landowner owes a duty "to exercise ordinary care and to protect the invitee by maintaining the premises in a safe condition." *Light v. Ohio Univ.* (1986), 28 Ohio St. 3d 66, 68, 28 Ohio B. Rep. 165, 167, 502 N.E.2d 611, 613. To . . . trespassers, on the other hand, "a landowner owes no duty . . . except to refrain from willful, wanton or reckless conduct which is likely to injure [the trespasser]." *Gladon*, 75 Ohio St. 3d at 317, 662 N.E.2d at 293. Today, we face the issue of whether child trespassers should become another class of users who are owed a different duty of care.

This court has consistently held that children have a special status in tort law and that duties of care owed to children are different from duties owed to adults . . . .

Recognizing the special status of children in the law, this court has even accorded special protection to child trespassers by adopting the "dangerous instrumentality" doctrine:

"The dangerous instrumentality exception [to nonliability to trespassers] imposes upon the owner or occupier of a premises a higher duty of care to a child trespasser when such owner or occupier actively and negligently operates hazardous machinery or other apparatus, the dangerousness of which is not readily apparent to children." *McKinney v. Hartz & Restle Realtors, Inc.* (1987), 510 N.E.2d 386, 390.

That doctrine was developed in *Coy v. Columbus, Delaware & Marion Elec. Co.* (1932), 125 Ohio St. 283, 181 N.E. 131, a case where a six-year-old boy was injured when he touched a high voltage transformer owned by the defendant and located in a vacant lot known to be frequented by children. The court applied a negligence standard to the behavior of the company, despite the fact that the child had been trespassing.

Thus, the court adopted as early as 1932 some of the hallmarks of the attractive nuisance doctrine. Elements such as knowledge of children's presence, the maintenance of a potentially dangerous force, and an exercise of care by the owner commensurate with the danger are a part of the attractive nuisance doctrine in most states, as reflected in Section 339 of the Restatement of Torts.

Despite the fact that in premises liability cases a landowner's duty is defined by the status of the plaintiff, and that children, even child trespassers, are accorded special protection in Ohio tort law, this court has never adopted the attractive nuisance doctrine. The doctrine as adopted by numerous states is set forth in Restatement of the Law 2d, Torts (1965), Section 339:

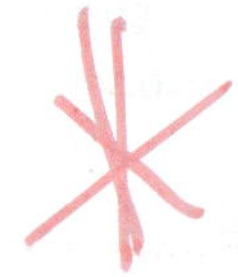

> "A possessor of land is subject to liability for physical harm to children trespassing thereon caused by an artificial condition upon land if:
>
> "(a) the place where the condition exists is one upon which the possessor knows or has reason to know that children are likely to trespass, and
>
> "(b) the condition is one of which the possessor knows or has reason to know and which he realizes or should realize will involve an unreasonable risk of death or serious bodily harm to such children, and
>
> "(c) the children because of their youth do not discover the condition or realize the risk involved in intermeddling with it or in coming within the area made dangerous by it, and
>
> "(d) the utility to the possessor of maintaining the condition and the burden of eliminating the danger are slight as compared with the risk to children involved, and
>
> "(e) the possessor fails to exercise reasonable care to eliminate the danger or otherwise to protect the children."

This court has never explicitly rejected the Restatement version of the doctrine, which was adopted in 1965. Instead, Ohio's tradition in this area of the law is based upon this court's rejection in 1907 of the "turntable doctrine."

The "turntable doctrine" was a somewhat controversial doctrine wherein railroads could be liable to children for injuries suffered on unguarded railroad turntables. The theory of liability was established in *Sioux City & Pacific RR. Co. v. Stout* (1873), 84 U.S. (17 Wall.) 657, 21 L. Ed. 745, and had been adopted by many states as of 1907. The burning question for many years was whether to apply the doctrine to non-turntable cases. Many of the states that adopted the turntable doctrine refused to apply it to cases not involving turntables. *Id.* at 245, 83 N.E. at 69-70.

However, the theory of liability has evolved since 1907. The Restatement of the Law, Torts (1934) and Restatement of the Law 2d, Torts (1965) removed legal fictions and imposed balancing factors to consider on behalf of landowners. Comment, The Restatement's Attractive Nuisance Doctrine: An Attractive Alternative for Ohio, 46 Ohio St. L.J. 135, 138-139 (1985). Ohio's refusal to recognize the turntable doctrine in 1907 was not a serious anomaly at the time; today, our failure to adopt the attractive nuisance doctrine is.

Ohio is one of only three states that have not either created a special duty for trespassing children or done away with distinctions of duty based upon a person's status as an invitee, licensee, or trespasser. *Kessler v. Mortenson* (Utah 2000), 2000 UT 95, 16 P.3d 1225, 1228; Comment, supra, 46 Ohio St. L.J. at 147; Drumheller, Maryland's Rejection of Attractive Nuisance Doctrine (1996), 55 Md. L. Rev. 807, 810, and fn. 32.

[Previously this court has rejected attempts to invoke the attractive nuisance doctrine, in part, because the foreseeability of the child's presence required by §339(a) of the Restatement (Second) was lacking.] In this case, there is at least a genuine issue of fact regarding the foreseeability of one of the Bennett children entering onto the Stanley property. [H]ere, the child resided next door. Reasonable minds could conclude that it was foreseeable that one of the Bennett children would explore around the pool.

Thus, in this case we cannot decline to adopt the attractive nuisance doctrine because of a lack of foreseeability. Any failure to adopt attractive nuisance would be to reject its philosophical underpinnings and would keep Ohio in the small minority of states that do not recognize some form of the doctrine.

Adopting the attractive nuisance doctrine would be merely an incremental change in Ohio law, not out of line with the law that has developed over time. It is an appropriate evolution of the common law. While the present case is by no means a guaranteed winner for the plaintiff, it does present a factual scenario that would allow a jury to consider whether the elements of the cause of action have been fulfilled.

We therefore use this case to adopt the attractive nuisance doctrine contained in Restatement of the Law 2d, Torts (1965) §339. In doing so, we do not abandon the differences in duty a landowner owes to the different classes of users. In this case we simply further recognize that children are entitled to a greater level of protection than adults are. We remove the "distinctions without differences" between the dangerous instrumentality doctrine and the attractive nuisance doctrine. Whether an apparatus or a condition of property is involved, the key element should be whether there is a foreseeable, "unreasonable risk of death or serious bodily harm to children." Restatement, §339(b).

The Restatement's version of the attractive nuisance doctrine balances society's interest in protecting children with the rights of landowners to enjoy their property. Even when a landowner is found to have an attractive nuisance on his or her land, the landowner is left merely with the burden of acting with ordinary care. A landowner does not automatically become liable for any injury a child trespasser may suffer on that land.

The requirement of foreseeability is built into the doctrine. The landowner must know or have reason to know that children are likely to trespass upon the part of the property that contains the dangerous condition. *See* Section 339(a). Moreover, the landowner's duty "does not extend to those conditions the existence of which is obvious even to children and the risk of which should be fully realized by them." *Id.* at Comment *i.* Also, if the condition of the property that poses the risk is essential to the landowner, the doctrine would not apply:

"The public interest in the possessor's free use of his land for his own purposes is of great significance. A particular condition is, therefore, regarded as not involving unreasonable risk to trespassing children unless it involves a grave risk to them which could be obviated without any serious interference with the possessor's legitimate use of his land." *Id.* at Comment *n.*

We are satisfied that the Restatement view effectively harmonizes the competing societal interests of protecting children and preserving property rights. In adopting the attractive nuisance doctrine, we acknowledge that the way we live now is different from the way we lived in 1907, when *Harvey* was decided. We are not a rural society any longer, our neighbors live closer, and our use of our own property affects others more than it once did.

Despite our societal changes, children are still children. They still learn through their curiosity. They still have developing senses of judgment. They still do not always appreciate danger. They still need protection by adults. Protecting children in a changing world requires the common law to adapt. Today, we make that change.

Finally, we add that on remand should the facts establish that the attractive nuisance doctrine applies in this case, that finding would also affect the duty of care the appellees owed to Cher Bennett if Cher entered the property to rescue her son.

On remand, the evidence may establish that Cher's status was that of a rescuer. This court has held pertaining to rescuers that "if the rescuer does not rashly and unnecessarily expose himself to danger, and is injured, the injury should be attributed to the party that negligently, or wrongfully, exposed to danger, the person who required assistance." *Pennsylvania Co. v. Langendorf*, 28 N.E. 172 (Ohio 1891), paragraph three of the syllabus. While the attractive nuisance doctrine is not ordinarily applicable to adults, it "may be successfully invoked by an adult seeking damages for his or her own injury if the injury was suffered in an attempt to rescue a child from a danger created by the defendant's negligence." 62 American Jurisprudence 2d (1990), Premises Liability §288. Therefore, we hold that if Cher Bennett entered the Stanleys' property to rescue her son from an attractive nuisance, the Stanleys owed her a duty of ordinary care.

Accordingly, we reverse the judgment of the court of appeals and remand the cause to the trial court.

Cook, J., dissenting

[The majority errs in deciding to change Ohio law by adopting the attractive nuisance doctrine in a case where the plaintiffs failed to preserve the issue by properly raising it in the trial court.]

Even if the Bennetts had properly preserved the attractive nuisance issue for our review, I would decline to join the majority's second syllabus paragraph. The majority holds, without citation of any supporting case law, that an *adult* may successfully invoke the attractive nuisance doctrine if the adult suffered injury "in an attempt to rescue a child from a danger created by the defendant's negligence." Yet this extension of the doctrine is unnecessary to assure recovery for an adult who sustains injury in an attempt to rescue a child placed in danger by the tortfeasor's negligence. As the majority correctly observes, a person injured during an attempted rescue may recover from the party negligently causing the danger to the same extent as the person who required assistance from the rescuer. *See Pittsburg, Cincinnati, Chicago & St. Louis Ry. Co. v. Lynch*, 68 N.E. 703 (1903). This "rescue doctrine" has long been a part of Ohio's common law. Thus, a possessor of land who is liable to a child under the attractive nuisance doctrine is also liable for injuries suffered by the adult rescuer of the child. But this liability is predicated on a straightforward application of the rescue doctrine and not on any extension of the attractive nuisance doctrine to cover adults.

NOTES AND PROBLEMS

1. ***Origins of the Attractive Nuisance Doctrine.*** The court in *Stanley* discusses the *turntable doctrine*. This was a product of the nineteenth century that arose out of a concern for children who were trespassing onto railroad property and getting hurt on turntables. These were devices designed to turn locomotives around to face a different direction. Because the children were coming onto the property "attracted" to the dangerous condition (the turntables), and the railroads were able to anticipate their presence and take precautions, courts treated these child trespassers differently than adults and required reasonable precautions to be taken.

2. ***Artificial Conditions.*** Notice that the language of the Restatement limits application of the doctrine to manmade conditions on the defendant's land. It is this limitation that has led some courts to conclude that the attractive nuisance doctrine should not apply to swimming pools because water is a natural hazard — something "reasonably to be expected to be fully understood and appreciated by any child of an age allowed at large." Restatement (Second) §339, cmt. j (1965). The *Stanley* court apparently did not agree with this comment from the Restatement.

3. ***The Rescue Doctrine.*** The majority in *Stanley* held that, in addition to the child, the parent coming to the aid of the child should also have the same duty of care extended to them. The dissent disagrees with this extension of the attractive nuisance doctrine to any adult, particularly because it believed that the traditional *rescue doctrine*, covered earlier in this chapter, would yield the same result.

4. ***Changing Status.*** Courts have held that just because someone enters land with one status does not mean they retain that status regardless of the circumstances. *See e.g.*, Gladon v. Greater Cleveland Regional Transit Authority, 662 N.E.2d 287 (Ohio 1996) (plaintiff who held a ticket to ride defendant's train was no longer an invitee when he left public areas); Restatement (Second) of Torts §336 (1965) (using illustration of a train's customer who has fallen onto the tracks and been run over, customer should be considered a trespasser because he was not permitted on the tracks). For example, if someone enters a convenience store to purchase candy but enters a back room marked "Staff Only — Not for Use by Public" — they have shifted from an invitee to a trespasser. Which set of rules to apply to their claim for personal injury would depend upon when and where their accident occurred. If in the back room, the landowner would only have to refrain from gross negligence (unless the attractive nuisance doctrine applied).

5. ***Problems.*** In each of the following scenarios, what duty of care do the target defendants owe? Why?

A. Twelve-year-old Peter is aware that his neighbors have a tree house built 20 feet off the ground in an old oak tree. Without their permission, he enters the property and climbs into the tree house. Despite seeing that it is high off the ground, he decides to jump off. After breaking his leg, his parents want to sue the neighbors.

B. Eight-year-old Sarah likes horses. Her house is in a semi-rural area and is adjacent to ranch property owned by another family. Sarah, without permission, climbs through the barbed wire fence and goes up to pet a horse on the backside. The horse becomes spooked and kicks her in the head, causing a serious injury. Her parents want to sue the ranch owners.

C. Paul is a ten-year-old boy who lives next door to the Smith family. The Smith children are all grown. Nevertheless, they still have an old rusty swing set in their unfenced yard. Paul sometimes goes onto the property when the Smiths are not around to use the swing set. One evening he decides it would be fun to use the swing set while the Smiths were asleep. He also has been thinking of playing a prank on the Smiths by toilet papering their trees. While it's dark he enters the yard armed with rolls of toilet paper and begins throwing them through the trees. He then gets on the swing and begins swinging vigorously. He failed to notice that the chain on one of the swings had loosened and the swing collapses, throwing him violently to the ground and breaking his neck. He wants to sue the Smiths.

C. Licensees

Licensees occupy a middle ground between trespassers and invitees. We have already seen that the traditional duty owed to trespassers is to avoid hurting them through gross negligence. Invitees are owed a duty of reasonable care. Consider how the duty owed to licensees takes on some attributes of each of these foregoing standards. The following case discusses this middle ground.

KNORPP v. HALE

981 S.W.2d 469 (Tex. App. 1998)

GRANT, J.

Bonita Knorpp appeals from a directed verdict in a premises liability case. Knorpp contends that the trial court erred by finding her son, Todd Erwin, to be a licensee rather than an invitee at the time of his death and by rendering a directed verdict against her claim for damages.

The decedent, Todd Erwin, was killed while cutting down a tree at the Hales' house. The evidence shows that he had moved to Texarkana to be near the Hales' daughter Autumn, who he had been dating for about a year, and that he spent a great deal of time at their house. The Hales were planning a New Year's Eve bonfire at a location in a pasture near their house around the base of a dead pine tree. They decided to cut down the tree. Erwin went to the house on December 6, 1994, took the Hales' chain saw, and began to cut down the tree. After about forty-five minutes, the tree fell in an unexpected direction and landed on Erwin, killing him.

There was evidence that Erwin had worked with his stepfather cutting and trimming trees. The stepfather testified that Erwin did not cut the tree properly. He testified that the vertical distance between Erwin's front and back cuts was too great; that Erwin should have used a rope to pull the tree in a particular direction and should have used wedges to direct the tree's fall.

When Knorpp completed the presentation of her evidence, the trial court granted the landowner's motion for a directed verdict and ruled as a matter of law that Hale was a licensee and that there was no evidence that the landowners were negligent under applicable standards for a licensee.

Knorpp . . . contends that there was evidence that Erwin was an invitee on this particular day when he came onto the property.

The owner/operator of property owes the highest degree of care to an invitee. An invitee has been described as one who enters on another's land with the owner's knowledge and for the mutual benefit of both. *Rosas v. Buddies Food Store*, 518 S.W.2d 534, 536 (Tex. 1975), citing *Restatement (Second) of Torts §332* (1965).

A licensee is a person who is privileged to enter or remain on land only by virtue of the possessor's consent. *Dominguez v. Garcia*, 746 S.W.2d 865, 867 (Tex. App. — San Antonio 1988, writ denied), quoting *Restatement (Second) of Torts §330 (1965)*. Thus, a licensee is one who enters with permission of the landowner, but does so for his own convenience or on business for someone other than the owner. *Smith v. Andrews*, 832 S.W.2d 395, 397 (Tex. App. — Fort Worth 1992, writ denied).

A landowner owes an invitee a duty to exercise ordinary care to protect him from risks of which the owner is actually aware and those risks of which the owner should be aware after reasonable inspection. *Motel 6 G.P., Inc. v. Lopez*, 929 S.W.2d 1, 3 (Tex. 1996). To recover, a plaintiff must plead and prove that the landowner (1) had actual or constructive knowledge of some condition on the premises; (2) that the condition posed an unreasonable risk of harm; (3) that the landowner did not exercise reasonable care to reduce or eliminate the risk; and (4) that the landowner's failure to use such care proximately caused the plaintiff's injuries. *Keetch v. Kroger Co.*, 845 S.W.2d 262, 264 (Tex. 1992).

The duty that an owner owes to a licensee is to not injure him by "willful, wanton or grossly negligent conduct, and that the owner use ordinary care to either warn a licensee of, or to make reasonably safe, a dangerous condition of which the owner is aware and the licensee is not." *State Dept. of Highways v. Payne*, 838 S.W.2d 235, 237 (Tex. 1992). In order to establish liability, a licensee must prove (1) that a condition of the premises created an unreasonable risk of harm to him; (2) that the owner actually knew of the condition; (3) that the licensee did not actually know of the condition; (4) that the owner failed to exercise ordinary care to protect the licensee from danger; and (5) that the owner's failure was a proximate cause of injury to the licensee.

In the present case, it is admitted by all that Erwin was a regular visitor to the Hales' house, that he had his own key to the house and came and went unsupervised, and that he was looked on as a likely son-in-law. He was clearly invited onto the property. Thus, it would appear that he should be defined as an "invitee." This is not, however, the case. In Texas, a "social guest" is classified as a licensee. *Dominguez*, 746 S.W.2d 865; *McKethan v. McKethan*, 477 S.W.2d 357, 361 (Tex. Civ. App.—Corpus Christi 1972, writ ref'd n.r.e.). As set out above, a host owes a social guest a duty not to injure him by willful, wanton or gross negligence. *Lower Neches Valley Authority v. Murphy*, 536 S.W.2d 561, 563 (Tex. 1976).

All of the evidence in the present case shows that the decedent was invited onto the premises, but also shows that he falls into the category of a "social guest." In Texas, as a matter of law, he was a licensee. The trial court did not err by finding him to be a licensee.

Knorpp . . . contends that this conclusion is erroneous and that the trial court erred by rendering a directed verdict in the Hales' favor, because regardless of the decedent's usual status, a different one existed in this particular situation. She argues that because there was a discussion, at which the decedent was present, about cutting down the tree, because Reeda Hale had asked Erwin if he was going to help her husband cut down the tree, and because Erwin was going to be present at the bonfire, then the cutting of the tree was done for the mutual advantage (or benefit) of the decedent and the landowner. This, Knorpp argues, constitutes some evidence that the decedent was an invitee and that the trial court therefore erred by finding him to be a licensee as a matter of law.

In determining whether an individual is an invitee or a licensee, the cases typically use the language "mutual benefit" or "mutual advantage." Knorpp argues that this term stretches so far as to include an intangible benefit, such as having the opportunity to attend or conduct the New Year's Eve bonfire.

The concept behind this language was originally brought into Texas cases as a paraphrase of the predecessor of *Restatement (Second) of Torts §332* (1965). *Carlisle v. J. Weingarten, Inc.*, 137 Tex. 220, 152 S.W.2d 1073, 1076 (1941); *See Spencer v. Dallas*, 819 S.W.2d 612 (Tex. App.—Dallas 1991, no writ). In *Carlisle*, the Court discussed an invitee in terms of business-related ventures exclusively, as discussed in the Restatement. Later cases discussed the necessity of determining who qualified as an invitee and cited to the Restatement and cases applying the Restatement concepts. However, instead of using the more explicit terminology contained in *Section 332*[1] to determine whether a person was an invitee, the courts instead looked to see whether an entry was one by a person invited and to the "mutual advantage" of both parties.

This language does not appear in the Restatement's description of an "invitee," but is found in 65 C.J.S. *Negligence* §63(41) (1966). The "mutual advantage" or "mutual benefit" language found in C.J.S. has been repeated by numerous cases, including the most recent premises liability cases from this court. *See Dabney*, 953 S.W.2d at 536.

The two terminologies were merged in *Cowart v. Meeks*, 131 Tex. 36, 111 S.W.2d 1105 (1938), where that court discussed the business relations between the injured person and landowner as showing the nature of his invitee status, and then stating that in "the absence of some relation which inures to the *mutual benefit* of the two, or to that of the owner, no invitation can be implied, and the injured person must be regarded as a mere licensee." *Crum v. Stasney*, 404 S.W.2d 72, 75 (Tex. Civ. App.-Eastland 1966, no writ) (emphasis added).

Thus, we have the courts using language abstracted from C.J.S. as a shorthand method of describing the analysis to be used in determining whether a party qualifies for the status of "invitee," but actually using the analysis set out in the Restatement.

It appears that the formula set out by the Restatement for analysis of invitee/licensee/trespasser status was adopted for use in Texas by *Carlisle*, 137 Tex. 220, 152 S.W.2d 1073, as reiterated in *Rosa*, 518 S.W.2d at 536, and that it remains the proper analysis to apply.

The decedent was a social guest of the landowners. He was not expecting payment for cutting down the tree, and the evidence is that no one asked him personally to do so, but that he volunteered to do so. There was no business relationship or dealing in existence or contemplated between the decedent and the landowner, and it is unquestioned that the land was not open to the public. Accordingly, as a matter of law, the decedent was not an invitee, but was a licensee on this particular occasion, and the trial court did not err by so holding.

Knorpp also argues that, in the alternative, there was evidence that the dead tree presented an unreasonable risk of harm and that there is at least some evidence that the landowners were negligent in failing to warn of the danger involved in cutting down the tree. This contention is based upon Knorpp's contention that the landowners were aware of the risk of harm and failed to use reasonable care to reduce the risk .... Even if we analyze this argument as an attempt to show liability for a licensee, the attempt fails on several grounds.

---

1. *Restatement (Second) of Torts §332* (1965) defines invitee:

> (1) An invitee is either a public invitee or a business visitor.
>
> (2) A public invitee is a person who is invited to enter or remain on land as a member of the public for a purpose for which the land is held open to the public.
>
> (3) A business visitor is a person who is invited to enter or remain on land for a purpose directly or indirectly connected with business dealings with the possessor of the land.

In the present case, the undisputed evidence is that the decedent had worked with his father trimming and felling trees and that he had at least a passing acquaintance with the dangers involved. The undisputed evidence also shows that the landowners were unaware of any special dangers involved in cutting down a dead tree. Thus, the evidence shows that the licensee was aware of the danger involved in the action that he intentionally undertook.

The evidence also shows that the tree itself was not a dangerous condition. The worry stated by the landowners was that if they burned it in the bonfire, it would fall on someone. Cutting the tree was the act that caused the danger.

Counsel attempts to compare this situation to a slip-and-fall case where the ice on the floor is not dangerous of itself — it becomes dangerous only when someone slips on it. We do not accept this basic premise. Ice on the floor is generally a dangerous condition in and of itself. A dangerous condition is one which creates a substantial risk of injury when the property is used with due care in a manner in which it is reasonably foreseeable that it will be used. It is generally foreseeable that a floor will be used by people walking, and thus, a substantial risk of injury is foreseeable. In the present case, the tree at that time was not in a condition that it was likely to fall until someone cut or burned the tree. Therefore, the dangerous condition of the tree did not occur until it was cut.

In summary, the condition did not exist until Erwin began cutting the tree, thus, it was not a "condition of the premises"; the owner did not know that the licensee was creating a dangerous condition; and the licensee was the one creating the condition. In light of those facts, there was nothing for the landowner to warn the licensee about, because no dangerous condition existed until it was created by the licensee and, therefore, no duty to warn was shown by the evidence.

The judgment is affirmed.

NOTES AND PROBLEMS

1. *Duty Owed to Licensees.* While the duty owed to trespassers (normally) is to refrain from gross negligence, the duty owed to invitees is to use reasonable care. The duty owed to licensees is a hybrid — with regard to dangerous activities (conducted by or under the control of the landowner), the duty is to avoid gross negligence. With regard to dangerous conditions on the land, the duty is triggered by actual knowledge of the condition. Only then does the landowner owe a duty of reasonable care to warn or remove the danger. Why did the plaintiff's evidence in *Knorpp* fail to show a possible violation of these hybrid standards?

2. *Social Guests as Licensees.* The plaintiff took the position that because he had a standing invitation to be on the land that he must be considered an "invitee." He also argues that because he removed the tree for the "mutual benefit" of the defendant, he must also be considered an invitee. Why does the court reject both of these arguments? As between social guests and random members of the public who are enticed to come upon your land, does the landowner have a closer or "special" relationship with one more than the other? Some believe these two categories should be the opposite, with the social guest licensee owed the greater duty. The explanation usually given by the courts for the classification of social guests as licensees is that there is a common understanding that the guest is expected to take the premises as the possessor himself uses them, and does not expect and is not entitled to expect that they will be prepared for his reception. *See* Restatement (Second) of Torts §330, cmt. (h)(3) (1965). Not all courts applying the traditional rules agree with this characterization of social guests.

3. ***Police, Firefighters, and Meter Readers.*** Most courts hold, as a matter of law, that police and firefighters coming onto your land during an emergency take the status of a licensee rather than an invitee. Of course, depending on the nature of their injury the *firefighter rule* might preclude any duty whatsoever, but remember that there are limits to that doctrine's application. Public utility meter readers are considered, by contrast, to be invitees of the landowner.

D. Invitees

Landowners owe their invitees a duty of reasonable care under the circumstances. This applies with respect to activities undertaken on the land. With respect to dangerous conditions, the duty of reasonable care is triggered by either actual or constructive knowledge. In cases of constructive knowledge, a common inquiry consists of determining the length of time that the dangerous condition existed without being dealt with by the owner. The following two cases discuss this triggering concept of constructive knowledge and time. *Commodore* deals with a scenario involving a ceiling that was permitted to deteriorate over a long period. The next case involves a slip and fall, a type of case where courts frequently struggle to determine the passage of time.

1. Time as a Trigger of Duty

RICHARDSON v. THE COMMODORE

599 N.W.2d 693 (Iowa 1999)

TERNUS, J.

Appellant, Russell Richardson, was injured at a bar owned and operated by the defendants/appellees when a portion of the ceiling fell on him. His suit against the defendants was dismissed on their motion for summary judgment. The court of appeals affirmed. On further review, we find sufficient evidence to create a jury question on Richardson's premises liability claim. Therefore, we vacate the court of appeals decision and reverse the judgment of the district court, remanding for further proceedings.

The record shows that, at the time of Richardson's injury, The Commodore Tap was a bar operated by the appellee, The Commodore, Inc. Appellees Ralph and Betty Hauerwas owned the corporation as well as the building in which the bar was located.

The accident giving rise to this action occurred on September 12, 1994. While shooting pool at the bar on that date, Richardson was suddenly struck by falling plaster. Richardson thereafter brought this action against the defendants to recover damages for his physical injuries. Richardson's claim was based on a theory of premises liability. He alleged that he was a business invitee and the collapse of the ceiling and his resulting injuries were caused by the defendants' negligence in failing to maintain the premises in a reasonably safe condition.

The record shows that the building that housed The Commodore Tap was built in 1913. Ralph and Betty Hauerwas acquired the building in 1982, and subsequently moved their tavern business into it. The tavern was on the first floor of this two-story building. Prior to opening for business, the Hauerwases contracted with Wayne Blumer to repair portions of the plaster ceiling of the first floor where the wood lath had been exposed by the removal of some partition walls. Blumer did not notice any signs of damage to or other problems with the plaster ceiling at the time of his repairs.

In 1985, the Hauerwases installed a drop ceiling on the first floor of the building to improve the efficiency of heating and cooling the premises. They did not notice any problems with the plaster ceiling at that time. Between 1985 and the date of the accident in 1994, the Hauerwases did not inspect the plaster ceiling, were unaware of any problems in that ceiling, and made no repairs to it.

It is undisputed that Richardson was struck by a portion of the original (1913) plaster ceiling when the plaster separated from the lath and fell through the drop ceiling. Blumer repaired the plaster ceiling after its collapse in 1994. He estimated that a piece of ceiling measuring two feet by five feet fell. This piece was not close to the areas he had repaired in 1982. Blumer testified that the ceiling collapsed due to its age and the effect, over time, of vibration from heavy traffic on the adjoining street. He thought this particular area of the ceiling may have fallen off because it was thicker than the rest of the plaster ceiling. While making the repairs in 1994, Blumer inspected the remainder of the plaster ceiling by looking through the drop ceiling where the tiles had been pushed off by falling plaster, and using a spotlight to view whether the plaster was sagging in any other areas.

As noted above, Richardson's suit is based on a theory of premises liability. The district court granted the defendants' motion for summary judgment, holding there was no evidence they knew or should have known of the dangerous condition of the plaster ceiling.

The general rule applicable to the liability of possessors of land for injuries caused by conditions on the land is found in the Restatement (Second) of Torts:

> A possessor of land is subject to liability for physical harm caused to his invitees by a condition on the land if, but only if, he
>
> (a) knows or by the exercise of reasonable care would discover the condition, and should realize that it involves an unreasonable risk of harm to such invitees, and
>
> (b) should expect that they will not discover or realize the danger, or will fail to protect themselves against it, and
>
> (c) fails to exercise reasonable care to protect them against the danger.

Restatement (Second) of Torts §343, at 215-16 (1965). The parties do not dispute Richardson's status as an invitee nor the defendants' status as possessors of the land. The dispute in this case centers on the requirement that the defendants know of the dangerous condition or by the exercise of reasonable care should have known of the condition.

Although Richardson does not contend that the defendants had actual knowledge of the condition of the plaster ceiling, he argues that this knowledge should be imputed to them because the defendants created the dangerous condition by installing the drop ceiling. Alternatively, he claims that if the defendants had exercised reasonable care in inspecting the plaster ceiling, they would have discovered the condition of the ceiling. We discuss these issues separately.

Knowledge of a dangerous condition is imputed to a possessor of land who has created the condition that causes the plaintiff's injury. *See Ling v. Hosts, Inc.*, 164 N.W.2d 123, 126 (Iowa 1969); *Smith v. Cedar Rapids Country Club*, 255 Iowa 1199, 1210, 124 N.W.2d 557, 564 (1963). For example, in *Smith*, the plaintiff was injured when she slipped and fell on a floor that had been waxed to an uneven and extremely slippery finish. There was no dispute that the defendant had applied the finish to the floor. We stated that when "the condition has been created by the owner[,] . . . he will not be heard to deny he had notice of it." *Id.* at 567.

This rule does not, however, help the plaintiff here. There is no evidence that the defendants created the condition in the plaster ceiling *that caused it to fall.* The defendants merely installed a drop ceiling over the plaster ceiling, and there is nothing in the record to indicate that the drop ceiling contributed in any way to the collapse of the plaster ceiling. Therefore, knowledge of the dangerous condition in the plaster ceiling cannot be imputed to the defendants.

The defendants' duty of reasonable care as possessors of the premises extends to an inspection of the premises to discover any dangerous conditions or latent defects, "'followed by such repair, safeguards, or warning as may be reasonably necessary for [the invitee's] protection under the circumstances.'" *Wieseler v. Sisters of Mercy Health Corp.*, 540 N.W.2d 445, 450 (Iowa 1995) (quoting *Restatement (Second) of Torts §343 cmt. b*, at 216). The action necessary to satisfy this duty of reasonable care depends upon "the nature of the land and the purposes for which it is used." *Restatement (Second) of Torts §343 cmt. e*, at 217.

"The duty of one who operates a place of entertainment or amusement is higher than that of the owner of private property generally." *Grall v. Meyer*, 173 N.W.2d 61, 63 (Iowa 1969).

[In this case, the facts] could support a jury finding that reasonable care warranted an inspection. Although the plaster ceiling had not collapsed in the past, the defendants were aware of the age of the ceiling (it was built in 1913), and they should have realized that a falling ceiling posed a serious danger to their patrons. Even more important, an inspection was not an onerous and impractical burden. . . . Here, with a ladder and a flashlight, the defendants could have conducted periodic inspections by simply lifting a ceiling tile in the drop ceiling and viewing the original ceiling, as Blumer did after the accident in 1994. We think these facts . . . provide an evidentiary basis for a jury finding that the defendants' duty of reasonable care included inspection for hidden defects in the plaster ceiling.

Of course, a failure to inspect is relevant only to the extent such an inspection would have revealed the defect in the ceiling. *See Restatement (Second) of Torts §343*, at 215 (imposing liability only if the possessor knew or *would have discovered* the defect in the exercise of reasonable care). The record in this case shows that the plaster ceiling fell because the plaster separated from the wood lath. In addition, the record reveals that the cause of this separation was vibration of the ceiling over many years caused by traffic outside the building. We think the jury could make a common-sense inference from this evidence that the separation would not occur instantly, but that the plaster would gradually separate over time and begin to sag, thereby resulting in an appearance observable to someone looking at the ceiling. In fact, the repairman, Blumer, testified that was exactly what he was looking for when he inspected the ceiling after Richardson's accident — signs of sagging that would indicate the need for additional repairs. Therefore, we conclude that the plaintiff generated a jury question on whether the defect in the ceiling would have been discoverable upon inspection.

We think material issues of disputed fact exist as to whether reasonable care warranted an inspection of the plaster ceiling and whether such an inspection would have alerted the defendants to the dangerous condition of the ceiling. Therefore, the district court erred in ruling that the defendants were entitled to judgment as a matter of law.

WAL-MART STORES, INC. v. GONZALEZ

968 S.W.2d 934 (Tex. 1998)

GONZALEZ, J.

The question in this slip-and-fall case is what quantum of circumstantial evidence is legally sufficient to support a finding that an unreasonably dangerous condition has existed long enough to charge a proprietor with constructive notice of the condition. The court of appeals held that there was legally sufficient evidence that some macaroni salad had existed on the Wal-Mart floor long enough to charge Wal-Mart with constructive notice of the condition. We hold that when circumstantial evidence is relied upon to prove constructive notice, the evidence must establish that it is more likely than not that the dangerous condition existed long enough to give the proprietor a reasonable opportunity to discover the condition. Because we conclude that the circumstantial evidence in this case supports only the *possibility* that the dangerous condition existed long enough to give Wal-Mart a reasonable opportunity to discover it, we reverse and render judgment for Wal-Mart.

Flora Gonzalez visited the Rio Grande City Wal-Mart with her daughter and two granddaughters. While walking in a busy aisle from the cafeteria toward a store refrigerator, Gonzalez stepped on some cooked macaroni salad that came from the Wal-Mart cafeteria. Gonzalez slipped and fell, sustaining painful injuries to her back, shoulder, and knee. Gonzalez sued Wal-Mart for negligence. A jury awarded her $100,000 and the trial court rendered judgment on the verdict. The court of appeals, with one justice dissenting, reduced Gonzalez's damages to $96,700 and affirmed the judgment as modified.

Gonzalez was Wal-Mart's invitee. As such, Wal-Mart owed her a duty to exercise reasonable care to protect her from dangerous conditions in the store known or discoverable to it. *Rosas v. Buddies Food Store*, 518 S.W.2d 534, 536-37 (Tex. 1975). However, a land possessor's duty toward its invitee does not make the possessor an insurer of the invitee's safety. *McElhenny v. Thielepape*, 155 Tex. 319, 285 S.W.2d 940, 941 (Tex. 1956). To recover damages in a slip-and-fall case, a plaintiff must prove:

> (1) Actual or constructive knowledge of some condition on the premises by the owner/operator;
> (2) That the condition posed an unreasonable risk of harm;
> (3) That the owner/operator did not exercise reasonable care to reduce or eliminate the risk; and
> (4) That the owner/operator's failure to use such care proximately caused the plaintiff's injuries.

Keetch v. Kroger Co., 845 S.W.2d 262, 264 (Tex. 1992).

The central issue in this case is whether Wal-Mart had constructive knowledge of the spilled macaroni. Wal-Mart argues that the evidence is legally insufficient to show that the macaroni had been on the floor long enough to charge Wal-Mart with constructive notice. When reviewing a legal sufficiency point, this court "must consider only the evidence and inferences tending to support the trial court's finding, disregarding all contrary evidence and inferences." *Continental Coffee Prods. Co. v. Cazarez*, 937 S.W.2d 444, 450 (Tex. 1996). However, meager circumstantial evidence from which equally plausible but opposite inferences may be drawn is speculative and thus legally insufficient to support a finding. *See Hammerly Oaks, Inc. v. Edwards*, 958 S.W.2d 387, 392 (Tex. 1997); *see also Browning-Ferris, Inc. v. Reyna*, 865 S.W.2d 925, 928 (Tex. 1993) (holding that a factual finding must be supported by more than mere surmise or suspicion).

No witnesses testified that they had seen or were aware of the spilled macaroni before Gonzalez slipped on it. However, as evidence that the macaroni had been on the floor for a prolonged period of time, Gonzalez testified that the macaroni had mayonnaise in it, was "fresh," "wet," "still humid," and contaminated with "a lot of dirt." Gonzalez's daughter testified that the macaroni had footprints and cart track marks in it and "seemed like it had been there a while." The court of appeals held this evidence legally sufficient to support the verdict, apparently calling for a relaxed burden of proof in slip-and-fall cases when the evidence is scant:

> A plaintiff has the obligation to produce the evidence that exists. If a court requires more than is possible to prove, the court has taken over the legislative function of simply deciding that there will be no negligence cause of action for slip and falls. No court has done this, and the cause of action exists. The great majority of slip-and-fall cases are lost at the trial level and, no doubt, always will be. But this court is not willing to say that an injured person must go beyond the evidence that is created by the operative facts, which would be an impossibility. Of course, there may be cases where there is simply not enough evidence to make a case, even if it is all produced. This is not such a case though.

However, "the fact that proof of causation is difficult does not provide a plaintiff with an excuse to avoid introducing some evidence of causation." *Schaefer v. Texas Employers' Ins. Ass'n*, 612 S.W.2d 199, 205 (Tex. 1980). As the dissent in the court of appeals explained, "the harsh reality is that if the plaintiff cannot prove facts to support her cause of action, there is simply no recovery. This is true not only in slip and fall cases, but in all cases."

Dirt in macaroni salad lying on a heavily-traveled aisle is no evidence of the length of time the macaroni had been on the floor. That evidence can no more support the inference that it accumulated dirt over a long period of time than it can support the opposite inference that the macaroni had just been dropped on the floor and was quickly contaminated by customers and carts traversing the aisle. In *Furr's Supermarkets, Inc. v. Arellano*, 492 S.W.2d 727 (Tex. Civ. App. — El Paso 1973, writ ref'd n.r.e.), another spilled-macaroni case, the court held that testimony that the dried macaroni noodles that caused the plaintiff's fall were "soiled, scattered and appeared as though other persons had passed through the area and had been run over presumably by another cart or carts" was no evidence of the length of time the macaroni noodles had been there. *Id.* at 728; *see also H.E. Butt Grocery Co. v. Rodriguez*, 441 S.W.2d 215, 217 (Tex. Civ. App. — Corpus Christi 1969, no writ) (holding that testimony that the grape on which plaintiff slipped was squashed and muddy, that the floor was dirty, and that pieces of paper were strewn around nearby was no evidence that the grape had been on the floor long enough to charge the store with notice); *H.E. Butt Grocery Store v. Hamilton*, 632 S.W.2d 189, 191 (Tex. App. — Corpus Christi 1982, no writ) (holding that testimony that grapes were stepped on and that the juices from both red and green grapes had blended together was no evidence of how long the grapes were on the floor). There were no comparisons between the dirt on the macaroni salad and the dirt on the surrounding floorspace that would justify the inference, relied on in *H.E. Butt Grocery Co. v. Heaton*, 547 S.W.2d 75, 76 (Tex. Civ. App. — Waco 1977, no writ), that the macaroni salad had been on the floor as long as the surrounding dirt on the floor, or that the dirt on the macaroni salad had dried, suggesting that it had been there for a prolonged period of time.

The presence of footprints or cart tracks in the macaroni salad equally supports the inference that the tracks were of recent origin as it supports the opposite inference, that the tracks had been there a long time. In *Kimbell, Inc. v. Roberson*, 570 S.W.2d 587, 590 (Tex. Civ. App. — Tyler 1978, no writ), the court rejected testimony that two or three tracks that had been made through a syrupy or jelly-like substance on which plaintiff slipped tended to show that the substance had been there long enough to charge the store with constructive notice. The court explained, "It is just as likely that the tracks were made by customers traversing the aisle only minutes or even seconds before plaintiff's fall." *Id.* at 590.

The testimony that the macaroni salad "seemed like it had been there awhile" is mere speculative, subjective opinion of no evidentiary value. The witnesses had not seen the macaroni salad prior to the fall and had no personal knowledge of the length of time it had been on the floor. *See Robledo*, 597 S.W.2d at 561 (holding that the trial court committed no error in sustaining objection to plaintiff's testimony that the water "had been there for some time" because the plaintiff had no personal knowledge of how long the puddle had been there).

We hold that the evidence that the macaroni salad had "a lot of dirt" and tracks through it and the subjective testimony that the macaroni salad "seemed like it had been there awhile" is no evidence that the macaroni had been on the floor long enough to charge Wal-Mart with constructive notice of this condition. Gonzalez had to demonstrate that it was *more likely than not* that the macaroni salad had been there for a long time; Gonzalez proved only that the macaroni salad *could possibly* have been there long enough to make Wal-Mart responsible for noticing it.

Because there is no evidence that Wal-Mart had constructive notice of the actual existence of spilled macaroni, this Court grants Wal-Mart's petition for review, and reverses the court of appeals' judgment and renders judgment that Flora Gonzalez take nothing.

NOTES AND PROBLEMS

1. ***Constructive Knowledge.*** It should not be surprising that many cases brought by invitees based upon dangerous conditions are premised upon constructive knowledge. This is because if the owner has actual knowledge and

fails to take any remedial action the breach of duty is fairly obvious. More contentious are the claims where the owner has no actual knowledge, but the claimant alleges that they *should* have known of the dangerous condition. The court in *Commodore* mentions two ways to demonstrate constructive knowledge. What are those two ways and why did they both fail in that case?

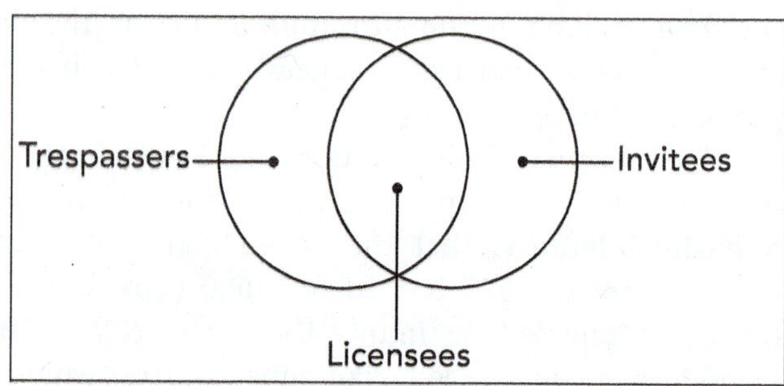

2. ***Overlapping Duties of Care.*** As the foregoing cases demonstrate, landowners owe a duty of reasonable care toward their invitees with regard to dangerous activities conducted on their land, and with regard to dangerous conditions of which the landowner has actual or constructive knowledge. With regard to licensees, they occupy a middle ground between the general duty of reasonable care owed to invitees and the duty only to avoid recklessness owed toward trespassers. There is a borrowing of the duties in the case of licensees based upon the distinction between activities and dangerous conditions. This is analogous to the general dichotomy in tort law between acts and omissions. Liability for dangerous conditions could essentially be considered a claim that the landowner failed to take action to remedy or warn about such conditions — an omission. As a hybrid of the two other sets of duties, the landowner's duties toward licensees is mixed. With regard to activities, the landowner must avoid recklessness. With regard to dangerous conditions, the landowner must exercise reasonable care (though only when the owner has actual knowledge of the condition).

3. ***Slip and Fall Cases.*** There are many slip and fall claims brought by invitees where the issue of constructive knowledge depends upon some showing that the condition existed for an unreasonably long time without being discovered and remediated. If the plaintiff can show the length of time the condition persisted, then the jury might be able to conclude that this time was more than sufficient to permit the landowner to find and fix the issue. When the plaintiff cannot demonstrate the length of time, even approximately, many courts hold that they have failed to meet their burden of proof required to trigger any duty of care. There are many cases involving slip and fall injuries in grocery stores where the issue of constructive knowledge focuses upon the various adjectives used to describe the food products on the floor as a means of

demonstrating time. This can be a difficult way to trigger the duty of care as the intermediate appellate court in *Wal-Mart* sympathized. This ruling still illustrates the majority approach to analyzing the trigger of duty when there is no evidence of actual knowledge.

2. *Open and Obvious Dangers*

O'SULLIVAN v. SHAW

726 N.E.2d 951 (Mass. 2000)

LYNCH, J.

The plaintiff seeks to recover for injuries he sustained when he dived, headfirst, into the shallow end of a swimming pool owned by the defendants and located on their residential property. His complaint alleges that the defendants were negligent in allowing visitors to dive into the shallow end of the pool and in failing to warn of the danger associated with this activity. A judge in the Superior Court allowed the defendants' motion for summary judgment, reasoning that diving into the shallow end of a swimming pool is an open and obvious danger which was known to the plaintiff, and that the defendants therefore did not owe the plaintiff a duty of care. The plaintiff timely appealed, and we transferred the case here on our own motion. We affirm.

The pool in question is an in-ground type, measuring eighteen feet in width by thirty-six feet in length, with both shallow and deep ends. The bottom of the pool is level in the shallow end, for approximately ten feet of the pool's length, after which it slopes gradually toward the deep end, the sides of which are tapered. When filled to capacity, the pool is four feet deep at its shallowest point and eight feet at its deepest. There are no markers, either in the pool or on its exterior surround, to indicate the pool's depth at various points along its length or to demarcate the separation of its shallow and deep ends. However, a diving board is affixed to the exterior of the pool at its deep end. The pool's interior is covered with a vinyl liner and there is no underwater lighting, so that the bottom of the pool is not visible at night.

The plaintiff, who was a friend of the defendants' granddaughter, had swum in the pool at least once prior to the night of the accident, during daylight hours. He had observed various swimmers dive into the pool's deep end from the diving board. He also saw swimmers dive into the pool from the shallow end by performing a flat or "racing dive," i.e., diving headfirst, with arms outstretched over their heads, landing in the water at an angle roughly parallel to the bottom of the pool, gliding just beneath the water's surface and eventually surfacing in the deep end. The plaintiff himself had previously dived into the pool's deep end from the diving board two or three times, and had made one dive into the shallow end. Although he did not know the exact dimensions of the pool, the plaintiff was aware of approximately where the shallow part ended.

Moreover, he was aware of the shallow end's approximate depth, having observed other swimmers standing in that part of the pool and having subsequently stood next to these people outside the pool.

On the evening of July 16, 1996, the plaintiff, then twenty-one years of age, was a guest of the defendants' granddaughter at the defendants' residence. The defendants were out of town, but their granddaughter had permission to be on the premises and to use the swimming pool. Sometime between 9 and 9:30 P.M. the plaintiff suffered injuries to his neck and back when he dived into the shallow end of the pool. At the time, he was attempting, in racing dive fashion, to clear the ten-foot expanse of the shallow end and surface in the deep end, but he entered the water at too steep an angle and struck his head on the pool bottom, resulting in a fracture of his cervical vertebrae. By his own admission, the plaintiff knew that he could be injured if he were to hit his head on the bottom of the pool when diving, and his purpose in trying to clear the shallow end was to avoid the sort of accident that occurred. The plaintiff's injury caused immediate paralysis in his lower extremities and required a two-day stay in the hospital, but the paralysis was not permanent.

An owner or possessor of land owes a common-law duty of reasonable care to all persons lawfully on the premises. This duty includes an obligation to "maintain[] his property in a reasonably safe condition in view of all the circumstances, including the likelihood of injury to others, the seriousness of the injury, and the burden of avoiding the risk," *Mounsey v. Ellard, 708*, 297 N.E.2d 43 (1978), and "to warn visitors of any unreasonable dangers of which the landowner is aware or reasonably should be aware." *Davis v. Westwood Group, supra*, and cases cited. However, a landowner is "not obliged to supply a place of maximum safety, but only one which would be safe to a person who exercises such minimum care as the circumstances reasonably indicate." *Lyon v. Morphew*, 424 Mass, 678 N.E.2d 1306 (1997). Moreover, it is well established in our law of negligence that a landowner's duty to protect lawful visitors against dangerous conditions on his property ordinarily does not extend to dangers that would be obvious to persons of average intelligence. *See Lyon v. Morphew, supra*. Landowners are relieved of the duty to warn of open and obvious dangers on their premises because it is not reasonably foreseeable that a visitor exercising (as the law presumes) reasonable care for his own safety would suffer injury from such blatant hazards. Stated otherwise, where a danger would be obvious to a person of ordinary perception and judgment, a landowner may reasonably assume that a visitor has knowledge of it and, therefore, "any further warning would be an empty form" that would not reduce the likelihood of resulting harm. *LeBlanc v. Atlantic Bldg. & Supply Co.*, 84 N.E.2d 10 (1949).

Although we have not previously addressed this precise issue, Massachusetts courts have continued to apply the open and obvious danger rule in cases decided after the Legislature's abolition of the assumption of risk defense, thereby at least implicitly recognizing the rule's continuing viability. Assumption of risk, along with contributory negligence, was an affirmative defense to negligence for which the defendant bore the burden of proof at trial. A plaintiff assumed the risk of harm when he voluntarily exposed himself to a known danger which had been caused by the defendant's negligence; the focus of the inquiry was thus on the plaintiff's own carelessness or negligence in failing to avoid a hazard which he knew about and appreciated. By contrast, the open and obvious danger doctrine arises in connection with the separate issue of a defendant's duty to protect others from dangerous conditions about which the defendant knows or should know. *Callahan v. Boston Edison Co.*, 24 Mass. App. Ct. 950, 953, 509 N.E.2d 1208 (1987) ("Whether a danger is open and obvious has to do with the duty of the defendant, not the negligence of the plaintiff"). Rather than evaluating a particular plaintiff's subjective reasonableness or unreasonableness in encountering a known hazard, the inquiry is an objective one that focuses, instead, on the reasonableness of the defendant's conduct: it presumes a plaintiff's exercising reasonable care for his own safety and asks whether the dangerous condition was, objectively speaking, so obvious that the defendant would be reasonable in concluding that an ordinarily intelligent plaintiff would perceive and avoid it and, therefore, that any further warning would be superfluous.

Thus, the superseded common-law defense of assumption of risk goes to a plaintiff's failure to exercise due care for his own safety, whereas the open and obvious danger rule concerns the existence of a defendant's duty of care, which the plaintiff must establish as part of his prima facie case before any comparative analysis of fault may be performed.

The remaining issue concerns whether the judge, in granting summary judgment for the defendants, correctly concluded that the open and obvious danger rule obviated any duty to warn the plaintiff not to dive headfirst into the shallow end of the defendants' swimming pool. Plain common sense, bolstered by the weight of authority in other jurisdictions where this issue has been addressed, convince us that this conclusion is indisputably correct. *See, e.g., Lederman v. Pacific Indus.*, 939 F. Supp. 619, 625 (N.D. Ill. 1996), aff'd, 119 F.3d 551 (7th Cir. 1997) (under Illinois law, manufacturer of swimming pool under no duty to warn adult of danger of quadriplegia posed by diving into water of uncertain depth); *Neff v. Coleco Indus., Inc.* 760 F. Supp. 864, 868 (D. Kan. 1991), aff'd, 961 F.2d 220 (10th Cir. 1992) (manufacturer had no duty to warn of open and obvious risk of diving headfirst into shallow swimming pool).

Finally, the plaintiff argues that, in concluding that the danger was open and obvious, the judge improperly considered subjective factors particular to this plaintiff, thus revealing that, under the guise of performing an objective inquiry about the defendant's duty, he was in reality performing an assumption of risk analysis. Admittedly, certain of the factors relied on by the judge — such as the plaintiff's prior experience and ostensible skill as a swimmer, and his awareness that serious injury could result if he were to strike his head on the bottom of the defendants' swimming pool while diving — bear on this particular plaintiff's subjective state of mind and actual knowledge of the danger of engaging in this activity, and thus should have been excluded from an objective inquiry concerning whether the risk of injury was obvious to a hypothetical "person of average intelligence." However, even when such subjective factors are excluded from the analysis, sufficient undisputed evidence remains to support the judge's conclusion.

It would be obvious to a person of average intelligence that a swimming pool must have a bottom. We have no doubt that an ordinarily intelligent adult in our society would be aware that the bottom of a swimming pool is a hard surface, liable to cause injury if one were to strike it with one's head. Moreover, the design and layout of the defendants' pool would have indicated to a person of average intelligence that the end into which the plaintiff dived was not intended for this activity: the diving board was affixed to the opposite end of the pool, making it apparent that the pool's deepest water was located at that end and that diving was intended to take place there. Finally, the plaintiff attempted his dive late in the evening, when there was little if any natural light, and the defendants' pool had no underwater lighting, such that its bottom was not visible to someone standing outside the water. The water into which the plaintiff dived, then, was of uncertain depth. A person of average intelligence would clearly have recognized that diving head first into shallow water in these circumstances posed a risk of suffering injury by striking the bottom of the pool.

We conclude that, because the danger of diving into the shallow end of a swimming pool is open and obvious to a person of average intelligence, the defendants had no duty to warn the plaintiff of this danger as a matter of law and, therefore, they could not be found liable for his injuries. The defendants' motion for summary judgment was correctly allowed.

NOTES AND PROBLEMS

1. ***Contributory Negligence vs. Open and Obvious Exception.*** The *open and obvious* doctrine utilized by the court takes an instance where the danger is so greatly foreseeable, that no duty is deemed necessary. In many instances where the open and obvious danger doctrine applies it would also be possible to assert contributory negligence against the plaintiff. Another possible defense, covered in Chapter 7, is secondary implied assumption of risk — that the plaintiff was aware of the danger and voluntarily encountered it anyway. As the court indicated, many courts have abolished the secondary implied assumption of the risk affirmative defense and contributory negligence is no longer fatal to the plaintiff's claim in many states. Beyond these pragmatic differences, why else would the doctrine applied by the court be better for a defendant than asserting some other affirmative defense?

2. ***Objective vs. Subjective Inquiry.*** The analysis of whether a danger is open and obvious is objective: Would the reasonable person under the circumstances have noticed the danger? In defense of the trial court's analysis, the appellate court suggests that it was improper to consider any specialized

knowledge or experience of the plaintiff. But if the plaintiff were considered the actor in question, why wouldn't it be appropriate to consider any elevated knowledge, gifts, or experience in utilizing the objective inquiry? Recall *Cervelli v. Graves* in Chapter 4 (actor's elevated knowledge and driving skills should be considered in applying the reasonable person, objective test).

3. *The Natural Accumulation Rule.* Some states are not willing to recognize the open and obvious danger rule because it can apply to both natural and man-made hazards. In such states they instead only apply a related doctrine — the *natural accumulation* rule. Under this rule, when natural hazards (rain, snow, wind, etc.) are obvious to a reasonable person, the defendant has no duty to eliminate the condition or warn the plaintiff about it. It works exactly like the open and obvious danger rule but is only applicable to weather-related phenomena. *See e.g.*, Klopp v. The Wackenhut Corp., 824 P.2d 292 (N. Mex. 1992).

Watch "Negligence Analysis" video on Casebook Connect.

3. *Duty to Protect Invitees from Criminal Attack*

We saw at the beginning of this chapter, in *Lundy*, that when an invitee is in peril on the land of the defendant, that the defendant's relationship with the invitee requires it to come to their aid. In other words, actual knowledge of peril demands some reasonable action. Courts have reaffirmed this principle when the invitee is attacked by someone on the defendant's land and the defendant witnesses the attack. In one case, the landowner failed to even pick up a phone and dial 911 despite watching an invitee getting battered in a brawl. Gould v. Taco Bell, 722 P.2d 511 (Kan. 1986). The tougher issue is when should the landowner have to anticipate a possible criminal attack on its invitees and exercise reasonable care in arranging for security? The following case wrestles with this issue and discusses a variety of differing approaches taken by various states.

DELTA TAU DELTA v. JOHNSON

712 N.E.2d 968 (Ind. 1999)

SELBY, J.

The present case asks us to determine whether the trial court, in a negligence action, properly denied a motion for summary judgment on the issue of duty. After being sexually assaulted in a fraternity house where she had attended a party, Tracey Johnson ("Johnson") brought a civil claim against the perpetrator, Joseph Motz ("Motz"); Delta Tau Delta, Beta Alpha Chapter ("DTD"), the fraternity at which the party and sexual assault occurred; and Delta Tau Delta, National Fraternity ("National"). Johnson claims that DTD breached a duty of care owed to her. DTD filed motions for summary judgment on the grounds that [it did not owe] Johnson a duty of care . . . [and the] motions were denied. On interlocutory appeal, the Court of Appeals reversed [this denial] of summary judgment on all issues. We . . . now address whether DTD owed Johnson a common law duty of reasonable care. [We reverse and remand on this issue.]

DTD is a fraternity on the campus of Indiana University at Bloomington; it is the local chapter of Delta Tau Delta, National Fraternity. On the evening of October 13, 1990, Johnson, an undergraduate student at Indiana University, attended a party at DTD's house. Johnson had been invited to the party by a member of DTD. She arrived at the party around 10:00 p.m. with some friends who had also been invited. At the party, beer was served in a downstairs courtyard area of the house. Pledges drew beer from a keg into pitchers, which they then poured into cups to serve to guests. The courtyard was very crowded and rather chaotic. Around midnight, Johnson and her friends were about to leave when she encountered Motz, an alumnus of the fraternity and an acquaintance of hers.

Motz had driven into Bloomington that day. After going to a football game, Motz bought a case of beer which he brought back to the chapter house. He stored his beer in room C17. Prior to meeting Johnson, Motz drank four or five of his beers.

While Johnson and Motz were talking, Johnson's friends wandered off and she was unable to find them. Motz offered to drive her home, but only after he had sobered up. Johnson accepted the offer. They waited together in room C17 where they both had some drinks of hard liquor, talked, and listened to music with other guests.

Between 3:30 a.m. and 4:00 a.m., Johnson again searched for a ride home. When she was unsuccessful, Motz reaffirmed his offer to drive her home, but only after he sobered up. Soon thereafter, Motz locked himself and Johnson in the room. He then sexually assaulted Johnson.

The . . . issue in this appeal is whether the trial court was correct to deny DTD's motion for summary judgment on Johnson's negligence claim. In this case, Johnson argues that DTD owed its guests a duty of reasonable care, for example, by providing reasonable protection, security, and supervision at the party, that DTD breached its duty, and that the breach proximately caused her injuries. DTD moved for summary judgment on the issue of duty, arguing that it owed no duty to protect Johnson from the unforeseeable criminal acts of a third party. Determining whether one party owes a duty to another is a question of law for the court. As such, we will determine, de novo, whether DTD owed a duty to Johnson and, thus, whether the trial court correctly denied DTD's motion for summary judgment.

[A member of DTD invited Johnson to the party and the assault occurred in DTD's house.] In Burrell v. Meads, this Court held that a social guest who has been invited by a landowner onto the landowner's land is to be treated as an invitee. 569 N.E.2d 637, 643 (Ind. 1991). Thus, a social host owes his guests the duty to exercise reasonable care for their protection. The issue in this case is whether a landowner may have a duty to take reasonable care to protect an invitee from the criminal acts of a third party. This issue is one that we have not addressed recently and one which has resulted in some disagreement in the Court of Appeals.

The question of whether and to what extent landowners owe any duty to protect their invitees from the criminal acts of third parties has been the subject of substantial debate among the courts and legal scholars in the past decade. *See, e.g., McClung v. Delta Square Ltd. Partnership*, 937 S.W.2d 891, 897 (Tenn. 1996) (noting that the debate caused the court to reconsider its law in this area). The majority of courts that have addressed this issue agree that, while landowners are not to be made the insurers of their invitees' safety, landowners do have a duty to take reasonable precautions to protect their invitees from foreseeable criminal attacks. Indiana courts have not held otherwise.

A further question arises, however, in that courts employ different approaches to determine whether a criminal act was foreseeable such that a landowner owed a duty to take reasonable care to protect an invitee from the criminal act. There are four basic approaches that courts use to determine foreseeability in this context: (1) the specific harm test, (2) the prior similar incidents test, (3) the totality of the circumstances test, and (4) the balancing test. *See generally, Krier v. Safeway Stores 46, Inc.*, 943 P.2d 405 (Wyo. 1997); *McClung*, 937 S.W.2d at 899-901; *Boren v. Worthen Nat'l Bank*, 921 S.W.2d 934, 940-41 (Ark. 1996); *Ann M. v. Pacific Plaza Shopping Ctr.*, 6 Cal. 4th 666, 863 P.2d 207, 215-16 (Cal. 1993); Michael J. Yelnosky, Comment, *Business Inviters' Duty to Protect Invitees from Criminal Acts*, 134 U. Pa. l. Rev. 883, 891-900 (1986).

Under the specific harm test, a landowner owes no duty unless the owner knew or should have known that the specific harm was occurring or was about to occur. *See McClung*, 937 S.W.2d at 895; *Boren*, 921 S.W.2d at 940. Most courts are unwilling to hold that a criminal act is foreseeable only in these situations. *See McClung*, 937 S.W.2d at 899 (abrogating *Cornpropst v. Sloan*, 528 S.W.2d 188, 198 (Tenn. 1975) which had employed this test); *Boren*, 921 S.W.2d at 940.

Under the prior similar incidents (PSI) test, a landowner may owe a duty of reasonable care if evidence of prior similar incidents of crime on or near the landowner's property shows that the crime in question was foreseeable. Although courts differ in the application of this rule, all agree that the important factors to consider are the number of prior incidents, their proximity in time and location to the present crime, and the similarity of the crimes. *See McClung*, 937 S.W.2d at 899; *Boren*, 921 S.W.2d at 941. Courts differ in terms of how proximate and similar the prior crimes are required to be as compared to the current crime. Compare *Baptist Mem'l Hosp. v. Gosa*, 686 So. 2d 1147 (Ala. 1996) (employing a strict PSI test; holding that, although there were 57 crimes reported over a five year period, only six involved a physical touching and, therefore, the assault of someone with a gun was unforeseeable) with *Sturbridge Partners, Ltd. v. Walker*, 482 S.E.2d 339 (Ga. 1997) (employing a liberal PSI test; holding that two prior burglaries of apartments was sufficient to make a rape in an apartment foreseeable). While this approach establishes a relatively clear line when landowner liability will attach, many courts have rejected this test for public policy reasons. *See Isaacs v. Huntington Mem'l Hosp.*, 695 P.2d 653, 658-59 (Cal. 1985), modified by *Ann M. v. Pacific Plaza Shopping Ctr.*, 863 P.2d 207 (Cal. 1993); *Maguire v. Hilton Hotels Corp.*, 899 P.2d 393, 400 (Haw. 1995); *Sharp v. W.H. Moore Inc.*, 796 P.2d 506, 510-11 (Idaho 1990); *Seibert v. Vic Regnier Builders, Inc.*, 856 P.2d 1332, 1339 (Kan. 1993); *Gans v. Parkview Plaza Partnership*, 571 N.W.2d 261, 268 (Neb. 1997); *Doud v. Las Vegas Hilton Corp.*, 864 P.2d 796, 800 (Nev. 1993); *Clohesy v. Food Circus Supermarkets, Inc.*, 694 A.2d 1017, 1023 (N.J. 1997); *Small v. McKennan*, 403 N.W.2d 410, 413 (S.D. 1987), aff'd, 437 N.W.2d 194, 201 (S.D. 1989). The public policy considerations are that under the PSI test the first victim in all instances is not entitled to recover, landowners have no incentive to implement even nominal security measures, the test incorrectly focuses on the specific crime and not the general risk of foreseeable harm, and the lack of prior similar incidents relieves a defendant of liability when the criminal act was, in fact, foreseeable.

Under the totality of the circumstances test, a court considers all of the circumstances surrounding an event, including the nature, condition, and location of the land, as well as prior similar incidents, to determine whether a criminal act was foreseeable. *See Isaacs*, 695 P.2d at 659-61; *Maguire*, 899 P.2d at 399; *Seibert*, 856 P.2d at 1339; *Whittaker v. Saraceno*, 418 Mass. 196, 635 N.E.2d 1185, 1188 (Mass. 1994); *Gans*, 571 N.W.2d at 268-69; *Doud*, 864 P.2d at 800; *Clohesy*, 694 A.2d at 1023; *Small v. McKennan*, 437 N.W.2d 194, 200-01 (S.D. 1989). Courts that employ this test usually do so out of dissatisfaction with the limitations of the prior similar incidents test. The most frequently cited limitation of this test is that it tends to make the foreseeability question too broad and unpredictable, effectively requiring that landowners anticipate crime. *See McClung*, 937 S.W.2d at 900 (adopting the balancing test); *Ann M.*, 863 P.2d at 214-15 (reconsidering and rejecting the totality of the circumstances test in favor of the balancing test).

Under the final approach, the balancing test, a court balances "the degree of foreseeability of harm against the burden of the duty to be imposed." *McClung*, 937 S.W.2d at 901; *see Ann M.*, 863 P.2d at 215. In other words, as the foreseeability and degree of potential harm increase, so, too, does the duty to prevent against it. This test still relies largely on prior similar incidents in order to ensure that an undue burden is not placed upon landowners.

We agree with those courts that decline to employ the specific harm test and prior similar incidents test. We find that the specific harm test is too limited in its determination of when a criminal act is foreseeable. While the prior similar incidents test has certain appeal, we find that this test has the potential to unfairly relieve landowners of liability in some circumstances when the criminal act was reasonably foreseeable.

As between the totality of the circumstances and balancing tests, we find that the totality of the circumstances test is the more appropriate. The balancing test seems to require that the court ask whether the precautions which plaintiff asserts should have been taken were unreasonably withheld given the foreseeability of the criminal attack. In other words, the question is whether defendant took reasonable precautions given the circumstances. We believe that this is basically a breach of duty evaluation and is best left for the jury to decide.

On the other hand, the totality of the circumstances test permits courts to consider all of the circumstances to determine duty. In our view and the view of other state supreme courts, the totality of the circumstances test does not impose on landowners the duty to ensure an invitee's safety, but requires landowners to take *reasonable* precautions to prevent *foreseeable* criminal acts against invitees. A substantial factor in the determination of duty is the number, nature, and location of prior similar incidents, but the lack of prior similar incidents will not preclude a claim where the landowner knew or should have known that the criminal act was foreseeable. The advantage of the totality of the circumstances approach is that it incorporates the specific harm and prior similar incidents tests as factors to consider when determining whether the landowner owed a duty to an injured invitee without artificially and arbitrarily limiting the inquiry. Therefore, we now explicitly state that Indiana courts confronted with the issue of whether a landowner owes a duty to take reasonable care to protect an invitee from the criminal acts of a third party should apply the totality of the circumstances test to determine whether the crime in question was foreseeable.

Applying the totality of the circumstances test to the facts of this case, we hold that DTD owed Johnson a duty of reasonable care. Within two years of this case, two specific incidents occurred which warrant consideration. First, in March 1988, a student was assaulted by a fraternity member during an alcohol party at DTD. Second, in April 1989 at DTD, a blindfolded female was made, against her will, to drink alcohol until she was sick and was pulled up out of the chair and spanked when she refused to drink. In addition, the month before this sexual assault occurred, DTD was provided with information from National concerning rape and sexual assault on college campuses. Amongst other information, DTD was made aware that "1 in 4 college women have either been raped or suffered attempted rape," that "75% of male students and 55% of female students involved in date rape had been drinking or using drugs," that "the group most likely to commit gang rape on the college campus was the fraternity," and that fraternities at seven universities had "recently experienced legal action taken against them for rape and/or sexual assault." We believe that to hold that a sexual assault in this situation was not foreseeable, as a matter of law, would ignore the facts and allow DTD to flaunt the warning signs at the risk of all of its guests.

As a landowner under these facts, DTD owed Johnson a duty to take reasonable care to protect her from a foreseeable sexual assault. It is now for the jury to decide whether DTD breached this duty, and, if so, whether the breach proximately caused Johnson's injury. While this may be the exceptional case wherein a landowner in a social host situation is held to have a duty to take reasonable care to protect an invitee from the criminal acts of another, when the landowner is in a position to take reasonable precautions to protect his guest from a foreseeable criminal act, courts should not hesitate to hold that a duty exists.

NOTES AND PROBLEMS

1. ***Social Guest as Invitee.*** You will observe that Indiana recently made the decision to treat social guests as invitees rather than licensees. While social guests have not traditionally been afforded this status, some states have been uncomfortable with giving the social guest less protection than the random member of the public who is considered an invitee on the premises of a business. Some states have simply merged licensees and invitees and afforded them both a duty of reasonable care. The *Freeland* case in the next unit discusses such reform.

2. ***Differing Tests for Foreseeable Harm from Crime.*** All courts will demand a duty of reasonable care when the premises owner witnesses an invitee being attacked; that is, when there is actual knowledge of the peril. What specifically is required of the landowner depends on the jury's view of the circumstances. But simply to stand by and attempt nothing almost certainly will constitute a breach. If you think of the duty to invitees for dangerous conditions, you might consider this circumstance one where the owner has actual knowledge of the danger. The foregoing case deals with how to tag a landowner with constructive knowledge of the dangerous condition (i.e. the relatively high potential for crime). The two most widely used tests — the *prior similar instances* test and the *totality of the circumstances* test — are different ways to ascertain just how foreseeable the potential for crime is on the land. Where it is foreseeable enough — for example, where there is greater foreseeability of crime than in other surrounding areas — courts say that this triggers a duty to take some reasonable actions to provide protection to the invitee or to deter such crime. In the foregoing case, what steps might DTD have undertaken in light of the foreseeability of date rape to protect its guests during alcohol parties?

3. ***Other Examples of This Duty.*** The foregoing case is somewhat unusual. More typical examples, where the issue of the duty to protect from or prevent criminal attack on invitees arises, involve armed robberies, fighting, or theft in shopping malls, in parking lots of retail stores, or in taverns. As between the various tests, which one would appear to be best for the landowner? Why? Considering the facts from *Delta Tau Delta*, under which tests would you conclude that a duty of care should exist? You may recall the *McCarty* case in Chapter 4 where we first confronted the Learned Hand Formula for determining reasonable conduct. The court in that opinion did not address the issue of whether the resort owed the plaintiff a duty to anticipate and prevent the

criminal attack. Do you see how that situation is analogous to the *Delta Tau Delta* case?

E. Modern Rejection of Three Categories

Now that you have rigorously studied the traditional classification system and learned the distinctions between invitees, licensees, and trespassers, you will see below that approximately half of the states have rejected this system — either in whole or part. The following case shows one such state's determination that the old system, dependent upon classifying the plaintiff to determine her rights, is flawed. Consider carefully the reason for the original system and whether the approach adopted by many states is actually better or worse in operation.

NELSON v. FREELAND

507 S.E.2d 882 (N.C. 1998)

WYNN, J.

The sole issue arising out of the case *sub judice* is whether defendant Dean Freeland's ("Freeland") act of leaving a stick on his porch constituted negligence. Indeed, this case presents us with the simplest of factual scenarios–Freeland requested that plaintiff John Harvey Nelson ("Nelson") pick him up at his house for a business meeting the two were attending, and Nelson, while doing so, tripped over a stick that Freeland had inadvertently left lying on his porch. Nelson brought this action against Freeland and his wife seeking damages for the injuries he sustained in the fall. The trial court granted summary judgment for the defendants, and the Court of Appeals affirmed.

Although the most basic principles of tort law should provide an easy answer to this case, our current premises liability trichotomy — that is, the invitee, licensee, and trespasser classifications — provides no clear solution and has created dissension and confusion amongst the attorneys and judges involved. Thus, once again, this Court confronts the problem of clarifying our enigmatic premises-liability scheme–a problem that we have addressed over fourteen times.

[W]e have repeatedly waded through the mire of North Carolina premises-liability law. Nonetheless, despite our numerous attempts to clarify this liability scheme and transform it into a system capable of guiding North Carolina landowners toward appropriate conduct, this case and its similarly situated predecessors convincingly demonstrate that our current premises-liability scheme has failed to establish a stable and predictable system of laws. Significantly, despite over one hundred years of utilizing the common-law trichotomy, we still are unable to determine unquestionably whether a man who trips over a stick at a friend/business partner's house is entitled to a jury trial — a question ostensibly answerable by the most basic tenet and duty under tort law: the reasonable-person standard of care.

Given that our current premises-liability scheme has confounded our judiciary, we can only assume that it has inadequately apprised landowners of their respective duties of care. Thus, it befalls us to examine the continuing utility of the common-law trichotomy as a means of determining landowner liability in North Carolina. In analyzing this question, we will consider the effectiveness of our current scheme of premises-liability law, the nationwide trend of abandoning the common-law trichotomy in favor of a reasonable-care standard, and the policy reasons for and against abandoning the trichotomy in this state.

Under current North Carolina law, the standard of care a landowner owes to persons entering upon his land depends upon the entrant's status, that is, whether the entrant is a licensee, invitee, or trespasser. An invitee is one who goes onto another's premises in response to an express or implied invitation and does so for the mutual benefit of both the owner and himself. The classic example of an invitee is a store customer. *See, e.g., Rives v. Great Atl. & Pac. Tea Co.*, 68 N.C. App. 594, 315 S.E.2d 724 (1984). A licensee, on the other hand, "is one who enters onto another's premises with the possessor's permission, express or implied, solely for his own purposes rather than the possessor's benefit." *Mazzacco*, 303 N.C. at 497, 279 S.E.2d at 586-87. The classic example of a licensee is a social guest. *See, e.g., Crane v. Caldwell*, 113 N.C. App. 362, 366, 438 S.E.2d 449, 452 (1994). Lastly, a trespasser is one who enters another's premises without permission or other right. *See Newton*, 342 N.C. at 559, 467 S.E.2d at 63.

In a traditional common-law premises-liability action, the threshold issue of determining the plaintiff's status at the time of the injury is of substantial import. The gravity of this determination stems from the fact that there is a descending degree of duty owed by a landowner based upon the plaintiff's status.

Although the common-law trichotomy has been entrenched in this country's tort-liability jurisprudence since our nation's inception, over the past fifty years, many states have questioned, modified, and even abolished it after analyzing its utility in modern times. At first, states believed that although the policies underlying the trichotomy — specifically those involving the supremacy of land ownership rights — were no longer viable, they nonetheless could find means to salvage it. In particular, states attempted to salvage the trichotomy by engrafting into it certain exceptions and subclassifications which would allow it to better congeal with our present-day policy of balancing land-ownership rights with the right of entrants to receive adequate protection from harm. Accordingly, North Carolina, along with the rest of the country, witnessed the burgeoning of novel jurisprudence involving entrant-protection theories such as the active-negligence . . . doctrine. Unfortunately, these exceptions and subclassifications ultimately forced courts to maneuver their way through a dizzying array of factual nuances and delineations. *See Kermarec*, 358 U.S. at 631, 3 L.

Ed. 2d at 555 (stating "the classification and subclassification bred by the common law have produced confusion and conflict").

Additionally, courts were often confronted with situations where none of the exceptions or subclassifications applied, yet if they utilized the basic trichotomy, unjust and unfair results would emerge. Therefore, these courts were forced to define terms such as "invitee" . . . in a broad or strained manner to avoid leaving an injured plaintiff deserving of compensation without redress. Although these broad or strained definitions may have led to just and fair results, they often involved rationales teetering on the edge of absurdity.

[An] example of a broad or strained reading can be found in this Court's holding in *Walker v. Randolph County*, 251 N.C. 805, 112 S.E.2d 551 (1960). In *Walker*, we held that a seventy-seven-year-old woman who went to the county courthouse to look at a notice of sale of realty was an invitee when she fell down the courthouse stairway. This case involved a strained reading of the term "invitee" given that we have always defined that term to include only those individuals who enter another's premises for the mutual benefit of the landowner and himself. That is, we were willing to implicitly conclude that the county somehow benefitted from posting notices it was statutorily required to post in order to classify the plaintiff as an invitee and hence provide compensation. Thus, . . . *Walker* demonstrate[s] how courts have made strained readings of the trichotomy classifications to reach just and fair results.

The first significant move toward abolishing the common-law trichotomy occurred in 1957 when England—the jurisdiction giving rise to the trichotomy—passed the Occupier's Liability Act which abolished the distinction between invitees, licensees and so-called contractual visitors. Shortly thereafter, the United States Supreme Court decided not to apply the trichotomy to admiralty law after concluding that it would be inappropriate to hold that a visitor is entitled to a different or lower standard of care simply because he is classified as a "licensee." *See Kermarec*, 358 U.S. at 630, 3 L. Ed. 2d at 554. In so ruling, the Court noted that "the distinctions which the common law draws between licensee and invitee were inherited from a culture deeply rooted to the land, a culture which traced many of its standards to a heritage of feudalism." *Id.* Ultimately, the Court concluded that the numerous exceptions and subclassifications engrafted into the trichotomy have obscured the law, thereby causing it to move unevenly and with hesitation toward "'imposing on owners and occupiers a single duty of reasonable care in all the circumstances.'" *Id.* at 631.

Nine years later, the Supreme Court of California decided the seminal case of *Rowland v. Christian*, 443 P.2d 561 which abolished the common-law trichotomy in California in favor of modern negligence principles. Specifically, the court in *Rowland* held that the proper question to be asked in premises-liability actions is whether "in the management of his property [the landowner] has acted as a reasonable man in view of the probability of injury to others." *Id.* at 568. Moreover, the court followed both England's and the United States Supreme Court's lead by noting that "whatever may have been the historical justifications for the common law distinctions, it is clear that those distinctions are not justified in the light of our modern society." *Id.* at 567. The court continued by stating that the trichotomy was "contrary to our modern social mores and humanitarian values . . . [, and it] obscures rather than illuminates the proper considerations which should govern determination of the question of duty." *Id.* at 568.

The *Rowland* decision ultimately served as a catalyst for similar judicial decisions across the country. Indeed, since *Rowland*, twenty-five jurisdictions have either modified or abolished their common-law trichotomy scheme—seven within the last five years.

Specifically, eleven jurisdictions have completely eliminated the common-law distinctions between licensee, invitee, and trespasser.

Further, fourteen jurisdictions have repudiated the licensee-invitee distinction while maintaining the limited-duty rule for trespassers.

In summation, nearly half of all jurisdictions in this country have judicially abandoned or modified the common-law trichotomy in favor of the modern "reasonable-person" approach that is the norm in all areas of tort law.

To assess the advantages and disadvantages of abolishing the common-law trichotomy, we first consider the purposes and policies behind its creation and current use. The common-law trichotomy traces its roots to nineteenth-century England. Indeed, it emanated from an English culture deeply rooted to the land; tied with feudal heritage; and wrought with lords whose land ownership represented power, wealth, and dominance. Even though nineteenth-century courts were aware of the threat that unlimited landowner freedom and its accompanying immunity placed upon the community, they nevertheless refused to provide juries with unbounded authority to determine premises-liability cases. Rather, these courts restricted the jury's power because juries were comprised mainly of potential land *entrants* who most likely would act to protect the community at large and thereby reign in the landowner's sovereign power over his land. Sears, *Common Law of Premises Liability*, 44 U. Kan. L. Rev. at 176. Thus, the trichotomy was created to disgorge the jury of some of its power by either allowing the judge to take the case from the jury based on legal rulings or by forcing the jury to apply the mechanical rules of the trichotomy instead of considering the pertinent issue of whether the landowner acted reasonably in maintaining his land.

Although the modern trend of premises-liability law in this country has been toward abolishing the trichotomy in favor of a reasonable-person standard, there are some jurisdictions that have refused to modify or abolish it. One of the primary reasons that some jurisdictions have retained the trichotomy is fear of jury abuse—a fear similar to the reason it was created in the first place. Specifically, jurisdictions retaining the trichotomy fear that plaintiff-oriented juries—like feudal juries composed mostly of land entrants—will impose unreasonable burdens upon defendant-landowners. This argument, however, fails to take into account that juries have properly applied negligence principles in all other areas of tort law, and there has been no indication that defendants in other areas have had unreasonable burdens placed upon them. Moreover, given that modern jurors are more likely than feudal jurors to be landowners themselves, it is unlikely that they would be willing to place a burden upon a defendant that they would be unwilling to accept upon themselves.

Lastly, opponents of abolishing the trichotomy argue that retention of the scheme is necessary to ensure predictability in the law. For example, prior to abolishing its common-law trichotomy, the Kansas Supreme Court declined an invitation to do so because it believed that the replacement of its stable and established system would result in one that is devoid of standards for liability. *See Britt v. Allen County Community Jr. College*, 230 Kan. 502, 638 P.2d 914 (1982).

The complexity and confusion associated with the trichotomy is twofold. First, the trichotomy itself often leads to irrational results not only because the entrant's status can change on a whim, but also because the nuances which alter an entrant's status are undefinable. Consider, for example, the following scenario: A real-estate agent trespasses onto another's land to determine the value of property adjoining that which he is trying to sell; the real-estate agent is discovered by the landowner, and the two men engage in a business conversation with respect to the landowner's willingness to sell his property; after completing the business conversation, the two men realize that they went to the same college and have a nostalgic conversation about school while the landowner walks with the man for one acre until they get to the edge of the property; lastly, the two men stand on the property's edge and speak for another ten minutes about school. If the real-estate agent was injured while they were walking off the property, what is his classification? Surely, he is no longer a trespasser, but did his status change from invitee to licensee once the business conversation ended? What if he was hurt while the two men were talking at the property's edge? Does it matter how long they were talking?

The Supreme Court of Wisconsin made a similar argument in *Antoniewicz* when it asked whether there is any reason why one who invites a guest to a party should have less concern for that individual's well-being than he has for the safety of an insurance salesman delivering a policy to his home. *See Antoniewicz*, 70 Wis. 2d at 854, 236 N.W.2d at 10. The court then inquired whether the life or welfare of the guest should be regarded in a more sacred manner. *Id.* Moreover, it queried whether we realistically can say that reasonable people vary their conduct based upon the status of the entrant. *Id.*

The preceding illustrations demonstrate the complexity associated with the trichotomy. Moreover, they demonstrate that the trichotomy often forces the trier of fact to focus upon irrelevant factual gradations instead of the pertinent question of whether the landowner acted reasonably toward the injured entrant. For instance, in the real-estate agent hypothetical posed above, the trier of fact would be focused on determining the agent's purpose for being on the land at the time of injury instead of addressing the pertinent question of whether the landowner acted as a reasonable person would under the circumstances.

Corresponding to this argument is the fact that "in many instances, recovery by an entrant has become largely a matter of chance, dependent upon the pigeonhole in which the law has put him, e.g., 'trespasser,' 'licensee,' or 'invitee' — each of which has radically different consequences in law." *Peterson*, 294 Minn. at 166, 199 N.W.2d at 643. Significantly, this pigeonholing is essentially an attempt to transmute propositions of fact into propositions of law — a transmutation that has only distracted the jury's vision away from the proper consideration of whether the defendant acted reasonably. For instance, the three experienced Court of Appeals judges who initially decided this case — Judge Smith, Chief Judge Arnold, and Judge Walker — disagreed not only with respect to whether plaintiff was an invitee or a licensee, but also as to whether this case involved a question of law or fact.

Lastly, we note that the trichotomy has been criticized because its underlying landowner-immunity principles force many courts to reach unfair and unjust results disjunctive to the modern fault-based tenets of tort law. For example, the Kansas Supreme Court noted that "modern times demand a recognition that requiring all to exercise reasonable care for the safety of others is the more humane approach." *Jones*, 254 Kan. at 504, 867 P.2d at 307. Likewise, the California Supreme Court noted that using the trichotomy to determine whether a landowner owed the injured plaintiff a duty of care "is contrary to our modern social mores and humanitarian values." *Rowland*, 69 Cal. 2d at 118, 443 P.2d at 567, 70 Cal. Rptr. at 104. Indeed, modern thought dictates that "[a] man's life or limb does not become less worthy of protection by the law nor a loss less worthy of compensation . . . because he has come upon the land of another without permission or with permission but without a business purpose." *Id.*

Significantly, the fact that judges and justices cannot agree as to whether a landowner's conduct is actionable — as evidenced by dissents in prior cases — evidences that the trichotomy fails to clearly articulate a landowner's standard of care. This confusion is most disturbing when considered in light of the comparatively simplistic approach set forth in the modern tort principle of negligence and its accompanying standard of reasonable care under the circumstances.

In sum, there are numerous advantages associated with abolishing the trichotomy. First, it is based upon principles which no longer apply to today's modern industrial society. Further, the preceding cases demonstrate that the trichotomy has failed to elucidate the duty a landowner owes to entrants upon his property. Rather, it has caused confusion amongst our citizens and the judiciary — a confusion exaggerated by the

Principles

The Washington Supreme Court's decision to retain the traditional trichotomy classifications was multifaceted: "The reasons proffered for continuing the distinctions include that the distinctions have been applied and developed over the years, offering a degree of stability and predictability and that a unitary standard would not lessen the confusion. . . . Some courts fear a wholesale change will delegate social policy decisions to the jury with minimal guidance from the court. We find these reasons to be compelling. As noted by the Kansas Supreme Court, 'The traditional classifications were worked out and the exceptions were spelled out with much thought, sweat and even tears.' We are not ready to abandon them for a standard with no contours."

Younce v. Ferguson, 724 P.2d 991 (Wash. 1986).

numerous exceptions and subclassifications engrafted into it. Lastly, the trichotomy is unjust and unfair because it usurps the jury's function either by allowing the judge to dismiss or decide the case or by forcing the jury to apply mechanical rules instead of focusing upon the pertinent issue of whether the landowner acted reasonably under the circumstances. Thus, we conclude that North Carolina should join the twenty-four other jurisdictions which have modified or abolished the trichotomy in favor of modern negligence principles.

Given the numerous advantages associated with abolishing the trichotomy, this Court concludes that we should eliminate the distinction between licensees and invitees by requiring a standard of reasonable care toward all lawful visitors. Adoption of a true negligence standard eliminates the complex, confusing, and unpredictable state of premises-liability law and replaces it with a rule which focuses the jury's attention upon the pertinent issue of whether the landowner acted as a reasonable person would under the circumstances.

In so holding, we note that we do not hold that owners and occupiers of land are now insurers of their premises. Moreover, we do not intend for owners and occupiers of land to undergo unwarranted burdens in maintaining their premises. Rather, we impose upon them only the duty to exercise reasonable care in the maintenance of their premises for the protection of lawful visitors.

Further, we emphasize that we will retain a separate classification for trespassers. We believe that the status of trespasser still maintains viability in modern society, and more importantly, we believe that abandoning the status of trespasser may place an unfair burden on a landowner who has no reason to expect a trespasser's presence. Indeed, whereas both invitees and licensees enter another's land under color of right, a trespasser has no basis for claiming protection beyond refraining from willful injury.

Given that we are convinced that the common-law trichotomy is no longer viable, we should put it to rest. By so doing, we align North Carolina premises-liability law with all other aspects of tort law by basing liability upon the pillar of modern tort theory: negligence. Moreover, we now join twenty-four other jurisdictions which have carefully examined and analyzed this issue, ultimately determining that the trichotomy is no longer applicable in the modern world.

Accordingly, plaintiff Nelson is entitled to a trial at which the jury shall be instructed under the new rule adopted by this opinion. Specifically, the jury must determine whether defendant Freeland fulfilled his duty of reasonable care under the circumstances. This case is therefore remanded to the Court of Appeals for further remand to the Superior Court, Guilford County, for proceedings consistent with this opinion.

REVERSED AND REMANDED.

NOTES AND PROBLEMS

1. *Frustration with Trichotomy.* Some of the criticisms of the trichotomy are that it is confusing, complex, and leads to unpredictable results. With regard to the facts in *Freeland*, the court says the uncertain classification of the plaintiff made it unclear whether the defendant might be liable to the plaintiff. With regard to the dangerous condition (i.e. the left-behind stick on the steps) do you understand why the defendant's lack of actual knowledge might be critically important if the court found the plaintiff to be a mere licensee? If so, would the defendant have any potential liability? What does the trichotomy advise about whether the landowner must inspect the property for the benefit of a licensee? Is this unpredictable and uncertain? By contrast, under the holding of the court in *Freeland*, what will be the outcome? Does the unified system adopted by the court answer the question whether a duty to inspect applied?

2. *Judges vs. Juries.* In the system first adopted by California — which treats all injured victims the same — who ultimately determines what the landowner should have done under the circumstances? How is this different from the traditional system? Are jury outcomes more predictable? Which system allows for entry of summary judgment at times? Which system is more efficient? Which system do you prefer?

3. Yania *Revisited.* This chapter began with the *Yania* case in which the defendant landowner asked the plaintiff to come upon his land to assist him. After doing so, the plaintiff fell into the water-filled cut and drowned when the defendant failed to come to his aid. The court there held there was no affirmative duty to act. Could you now make the argument that the defendant landowner did owe some duty to affirmatively act with reasonable care to provide some rescue effort? Was that case wrongly decided based upon the special status of the plaintiff and the defendant?

Upon Further Review

Currently, the largest divide among the various jurisdictions in premises liability cases is whether to accept the traditional trichotomy (where duty depends upon classifying the plaintiff as trespasser, licensee, or invitee), to break down the categories into only two (trespassers and those legally entitled to enter the land), or to simply charge the jury in all premises liability cases with a "reasonable care" instruction and let the jury decide on a case by case basis what this should mean. About half of the states still swear allegiance to the traditional classifications. The circumstances of the plaintiff's entry will still potentially impact expectations for the landowner in every case; the difference is whether to have the judge declare differing duties based upon the classifications, or to let the jury intuitively take this factor into account as merely one of the "circumstances" for applying the reasonable care standard. Under the traditional system, legal analysis essentially involves two steps: (1) classifying the plaintiff; and (2) analyzing the facts with the applicable duty to see if a breach of duty has occurred.

 DUTY BASED UPON DEFENDANT'S STATUS: PROFESSIONALS

Our final set of special duty rules deals with the situation where the alleged tortfeasors are professionals practicing their craft. In this regard, we have seen in Chapter 4 two relevant sets of rules with respect to understanding the objective, reasonable person standard. In *Cervelli*, the court stated that an actor's superior gifts, talents, knowledge, and skills are taken into consideration in judging whether negligence has occurred. This concept hints at the possibility that professionals might be viewed somewhat differently than others in applying negligence standards given their relatively elevated levels of knowledge, experience, and skills. On the other hand, in *The T.J. Hooper* case Judge Hand indicated that industry customs are not controlling on the issue of whether an actor's conduct has conformed to the reasonable person standard. Yet does it make sense to allow lay juries to sit in judgment over doctors and lawyers' complex judgment decisions regarding their practices when those professions may have established their own expectations? A primary issue this section begins with, therefore, is how these concepts apply when the alleged negligence arises in someone's professional practice. Is a professional's duty of care higher than someone else's and, if so, how do the industry custom rules apply to a professional industry? The following two cases show the majority view — one in a medical injury case (*Osborn*) and the other (*Hodges*) in a legal malpractice context.

A. The Professional Standard of Care

1. *Professional Custom*

OSBORN v. IRWIN MEMORIAL BLOOD BANK

5 Cal. App. 4th 234 (Cal. App. 1992)

PERLEY, J.

The trial in this case has been reported as the first in the nation where a blood bank was found liable in connection with transmission of the acquired immune deficiency syndrome (AIDS) virus by a blood transfusion.

In February of 1983, at the age of three weeks, Michael Osborn contracted the AIDS virus from a blood transfusion in the course of surgery on his heart at the University of California at San Francisco Medical Center. The blood used in the operation was supplied by the Irwin Memorial Blood Bank. Michael and his parents, Paul and Mary Osborn, sued Irwin and the University for damages on various theories .... [The jury returned a 9-3 decision against Irwin, awarding damages of $550,000 to Michael and $200,000 to his parents.] After the jury returned a general verdict for plaintiffs, the court granted Irwin's motion for judgment notwithstanding the verdict on the ... negligence claims.

...

The most significant issue on appeal is whether Irwin was entitled to judgment notwithstanding the verdict on the issue of negligence. Qualified experts opined for plaintiffs that Irwin's blood testing and donor screening practices prior to Michael's surgery were negligent [for failure to perform certain tests on the blood] in light of concerns about AIDS at the time. On matters such as these that are outside common knowledge, expert opinion is ordinarily sufficient to create a prima facie case. Here, however, there was uncontradicted evidence that Irwin was doing as much if not more in the areas of testing and screening than any other blood bank in the country, and there is no question that it followed accepted practices within the profession. We hold that Irwin cannot be found negligent in these circumstances.

Most of the evidence at trial concerned the actions Irwin took, or allegedly should have taken, to safeguard its blood supply in early 1983 in light of concerns at the time that AIDS might be transmissible by blood. The issue on appeal is whether, in light of that evidence, Irwin was entitled to judgment notwithstanding the verdict on plaintiffs' claim of negligence.

Plaintiffs' principal theory of negligence is that Irwin should have started anti-HBc surrogate testing for AIDS prior to Michael's operation

The form of their experts' testimony suggests that plaintiffs assumed their case against Irwin was one of ordinary negligence. Plaintiffs' experts did not couch their opinions in terms of the standard of care for blood banks in early 1983. They simply said what Irwin "should" have done, or what a "reasonable person" would have done, in light of what was known about AIDS at the time. We ultimately conclude that this distinction is one of substance as well as form, but the threshold question is whether Irwin should be held to a professional standard of care.

We note that this appears to be a point of first impression in California. The precedents indicating that blood banks are not subject to strict liability for providing contaminated blood (*see Health & Saf. Code, §1606* [distribution of blood is a service rather than a sale]) have observed that blood banks may be sued for negligence but have not undertaken to define the standard of care. (*See McDonald v. Sacramento Medical Foundation Blood Bank*, 62 Cal. App. 3d 866 (1976); *Klaus v. Alameda- Contra Costa Medical Assn. Blood Bank, Inc.*, 62 Cal. App. 3d 417, 419 (1976). We have determined that Irwin is a "health care provider" within the meaning of MICRA and there is no question that donor screening and blood testing are "professional services" for purposes of MICRA (defining "professional negligence" in pertinent part as "a negligent act or omission to act by a health care provider in the rendering of professional services").

We conclude that the adequacy of a blood bank's actions to prevent the contamination of blood is a question of professional negligence and fulfillment of a professional standard of care. As another court has observed, the "activities of [the blood bank] at issue here — the collection, processing, and testing of blood for transfusion — no doubt require the exercise of professional expertise and professional judgment." *Doe v. American Red Cross Blood Services, S.C. Region*, 125 F.R.D. 637, 642 (D.S.C. 1989).

This conclusion is consistent with most of the cases in other jurisdictions that have considered negligence claims against blood banks. This conclusion is also consistent with California cases that have applied a professional standard to activities involving special training and skill.

Plaintiffs contend that custom and practice are relevant, but not conclusive, on the standard of care. This is the general rule in cases of ordinary negligence. *See* Kinney & Wilder, *Medical Standard Setting in the Current Malpractice Environment: Problems and Possibilities* (1989) 22 U.C. Davis L. Rev. 421, 439-40; Keeton, *Medical Negligence — The Standard of Care* 10 Tex. Tech L. Rev. 351, 354 (1979). The leading case for this rule is *The T.J. Hooper* (2d Cir. 1932) 60 F.2d 737, 740, where Learned Hand wrote that "in most cases reasonable prudence is in fact common prudence; but strictly it is never its measure; a whole calling may have unduly lagged in the adoption of new and available devices. It never may set its own tests, however persuasive be its usages. Courts must in the end say what is required; there are precautions so imperative that even their universal disregard will not excuse their omission." There is no question that California follows this rule in ordinary negligence cases.

This is a case of professional negligence, however, and we must assess the role of custom and practice in that context. The question presented here is whether California law permits an expert to second-guess an entire profession. We have found no definitive precedent on this issue and it is not one that is likely to arise.

Custom and practice are not controlling in cases, unlike ours, where a layperson can infer negligence by a professional without any expert testimony. In *Leonard v. Watsonville Community Hosp.* (1956) 305 P.2d 36, for example, where a clamp was left in the plaintiff's body after surgery, the lack of an "'established practice'" of counting clamps did not preclude a finding of negligence: "Defendants seek to avoid liability on the theory that they were required to exercise only that degree of skill employed by other hospitals and nurses in the community. It is a matter of common knowledge, however, that no special skill is required in counting instruments. Although *under such circumstances* proof of practice or custom is some evidence of what should be done and may assist in the determination of what constitutes due care, it does not conclusively establish the standard of care." (*Id.*, at 519 [italics added].)

On the other hand, in cases like ours where experts are needed to show negligence, their testimony sets the standard of care and is said to be "conclusive." "Ordinarily, where a professional person is accused of negligence in failing to adhere to accepted standards within his profession the accepted standards must be established only by qualified expert testimony [citations] unless the standard is a matter of common knowledge. [Citation.] However, when the matter in issue is within the knowledge of experts only and not within common knowledge, expert evidence is conclusive and cannot be disregarded." *Huber, Hunt & Nichols, Inc. v. Moore* (1977) 136 Cal. Rptr. 603. Qualified expert opinion will thus generally preclude a directed verdict in a professional negligence case.

This case, however, is distinguishable .... Here it is undisputed that no blood bank in the country was doing what the plaintiffs' experts' standard of care would require of Irwin, and we have an unusual situation where we are called upon to address the significance of a universal practice.

While it may be true that "an increasing number of courts are rejecting the customary practice standard in favor of a reasonable care or reasonably prudent doctor standard" (Prosser & Keeton, The Law of Torts (5th ed., 1988 pocket supp.) p. 30, fn. 53 [citing cases outside California]), numerous commentaries have noted that custom generally sets the standard of care. *See*, e.g., King, *In Search of a Standard of Care for the Medical Profession: The "Accepted Practice" Formula* (1975) 28 Vand. L. Rev. 1213, 1235, 1245-1246.

Most commentators have urged that a customary or accepted practice standard is preferable to one that allows for the disregard of professional judgment. Indeed, the more recent commentaries are not concerned with whether customary practices should be the maximum expected of medical practitioners, but rather with whether those practices should continue to set a minimum standard in a time of increasing economic constraints.

The basic reason why professionals are usually held only to a standard of custom and practice is that their informed approach to matters outside common knowledge should not be "evaluated by the ad hoc judgments of a lay judge or lay jurors aided by hindsight." *King, supra,* 28 Vand. L. Rev. at p. 1249. In the words of a leading authority, "When it can be said that the collective wisdom of the profession is that a particular course of action is the desirable course, then it would seem that the collective wisdom should be followed by the courts." Keeton, *supra,* 10 Tex. Tech L. Rev. at pp. 364-365.

The "most famous & judicial departure from the usual rule" is *Helling v. Carey* (1974) 519 P.2d 981. In that case, the Washington Supreme Court held ophthalmologists negligent as a matter of law for failing to administer routine glaucoma tests to a patient under the age of 40, despite expert testimony from both sides that the standards of the profession did not require such testing of patients that age. The court reached this decision by balancing its perception of the seriousness of the disease against the cost of the test.

Most of the commentary on this case has been unfavorable. A contemporary observer wrote that the *Helling* court had "unwisely ... arrogated to itself medical decisions, superimposing its medical judgment upon the collective experience of the medical profession. Can it really be said that medical judgments of the courts will be 'right' more often than those guided by approved medical practices?" *King, supra,* 28 Vand. L. Rev. at p. 1250; *see also,* Keeton, *supra,* 10 Tex. Tech L. Rev. at pp. 367-68. Such concerns may have been borne out by subsequent medical research: "It is a telling commentary on the judicial performance in the *Helling* case that medical research taking all relevant factors into account provides no convincing evidence for the cost-effectiveness of even the customary practice of screening all patients over age 40 for glaucoma. The Washington court, which held on the basis of its own intuition that it was negligence not to screen the plaintiff because she was *under* 40, is thus left with egg on its face." Havighurst, *Private Reform of Tort- Law Dogma: Market Opportunities and Legal Obstacles* (1986) 49 Law & Contemp. Probs. 143, 159, fn. 45.

[Prevailing sentiments in other jurisdictions, and some prior cases from this state confirm] that professional prudence is defined by actual or accepted practice within a profession, rather than theories about what "should" have been done.

It follows that Irwin cannot be found negligent for failing to perform tests that no other blood bank in the nation was using. Judgment notwithstanding the verdict was properly granted to Irwin on the issue of anti-HBc testing because there was no substantial evidence that failure to conduct the tests was not accepted *practice* for blood banks in January and February of 1983.

HODGES v. CARTER

80 S.E.2d 144 (N.C. 1954)

Civil action to recover compensation for losses resulting from the alleged negligence of defendant D.D. Topping and H.C. Carter, now deceased, in prosecuting, on behalf of plaintiff, certain actions on fire insurance policies.

On 4 June 1948 plaintiff's drugstore building located in Belhaven, N.C., together with his lunch counter, fixtures, stock of drugs and sundries therein contained, was destroyed by fire. At the time plaintiff was insured under four policies of fire insurance against loss of, or damage to, said mercantile building and its contents. He filed proof of loss with each of the four insurance companies which issued said policies. The insurance companies severally rejected the proofs of loss, denied liability, and declined to pay any part of the plaintiff's losses resulting from said fire.

H.C. Carter and D.D. Topping were at the time attorneys practicing in Beaufort and adjoining counties. As they were the ones from whom plaintiff seeks to recover, they will hereafter be referred to as the defendants.

On 3 May 1949 defendants, in behalf of plaintiff, instituted in the Superior Court of Beaufort County four separate actions — one against each of the four insurers. Complaints were filed and summonses were issued, directed to the sheriff of Beaufort County. In each case the summons and complaint, together with copies thereof, were mailed to the Commissioner of Insurance of the State of North Carolina. The Commissioner accepted service of summons and complaint in each case and forwarded a copy thereof by registered mail to the insurance company named defendant therein.

Thereafter each defendant made a special appearance and moved to dismiss the action against it for want of proper service of process for that the Insurance Commissioner was without authority, statutory or otherwise, to accept service of process issued against a foreign insurance company doing business in this State. When the special appearance and motion to dismiss came on for hearing at the February Term 1950, the judge presiding concluded that the acceptance of service of process by the Insurance Commissioner was valid and served to subject the movants to the jurisdiction of the court. Judgment was entered in each case denying the motion therein made. Each defendant excepted and appealed. This Court reversed. *Hodges v. Insurance Co.*, 61 S.E.2d 372.

[In the North Carolina Supreme Court's reversal, the Court stated that: "At the time defendant entered its motion to dismiss the original action, the plaintiff still had more than sixty days in which to sue out an alias summons and thus keep his action alive. He elected instead to rest his case upon the validity of the service had. The unfortunate result is unavoidable." By the time of the Supreme Court's reversal, the applicable statute of limitations had run and no new suit could be brought.]

On 4 March 1952 plaintiff instituted this action in which he alleges that the defendants were negligent in prosecuting his said actions in that they failed to (1) have process properly served, and (2) sue out *alias* summonses at the time the insurers filed their motions to dismiss the actions for want of proper service of summons, although they then had approximately sixty days within which to procure the issuance thereof.

Defendants, answering, deny negligence and plead good faith and the exercise of their best judgment.

At the hearing in the court below the judge, at the conclusion of plaintiff's evidence in chief, entered judgment of involuntary nonsuit. Plaintiff excepted and appealed.

Barnhill, J.

This seems to be a case of first impression in this jurisdiction. At least counsel have not directed our attention to any other decision of this Court on the question here presented, and we have found none.

Ordinarily when an attorney engages in the practice of the law and contracts to prosecute an action in behalf of his client, he impliedly represents that (1) he possesses the requisite degree of learning, skill, and ability necessary to the practice of his profession and which others similarly situated ordinarily possess; (2) he will exert his best judgment in the prosecution of the litigation entrusted to him; and (3) he will exercise reasonable and ordinary care and diligence in the use of his skill and in the application of his knowledge to his client's cause.

An attorney who acts in good faith and in an honest belief that his advice and acts are well founded and in the best interest of his client is not answerable for a mere error of judgment or for a mistake in a point of law which has not been settled by the court of last resort in his State and on which reasonable doubt may be entertained by well-informed lawyers.

Conversely, he is answerable in damages for any loss to his client which proximately results from a want of that degree of knowledge and skill ordinarily possessed by others of his profession similarly situated, or from the omission to use reasonable care and diligence, or from the failure to exercise in good faith his best judgment in attending to the litigation committed to his care.

When the facts appearing in this record are considered in the light of these controlling principles of law, it immediately becomes manifest that plaintiff has failed to produce a scintilla of evidence tending to show that defendants breached any duty the law imposed upon them when they accepted employment to prosecute plaintiff's actions against his insurers or that they did not possess the requisite learning and skill required of an attorney or that they acted otherwise than in the utmost good faith.

The Commissioner of Insurance is the statutory process agent of foreign insurance companies doing business in this State, G.S. 58-153, and when defendants mailed the process to the Commissioner of Insurance for his acceptance of service thereof, they were following a custom which had prevailed in this State for two decades or more. Foreign insurance companies had theretofore uniformly ratified such service, appeared in response thereto, filed their answers, and made their defense. The right of the Commissioner to accept [mailed] service of process in behalf of foreign insurance companies doing business in this State had not been tested in the courts. Attorneys generally, throughout the State, took it for granted that under the terms of G.S. 58-153 such acceptance of service was adequate. And, in addition, the defendants had obtained the judicial declaration of a judge of our Superior Courts that the acceptance of service by the Commissioner subjected the defendants to the jurisdiction of the court. Why then stop in the midst of the stream and pursue some other course?

Doubtless this litigation was inspired by a comment which appears in our opinion on the second appeal [set forth above]. However, what was there said was pure *dictum*, injected — perhaps ill advisedly — in explanation of the reason we could afford plaintiff no relief on that appeal. We did not hold, or intend to intimate, that defendants had been in any wise neglectful of their duties as counsel for plaintiff.

The judgment entered in the court below is affirmed.

NOTES AND PROBLEMS

1. ***Professional Negligence Analysis.*** According to the *Osborn* court, professional malpractice claims are typically analyzed under the professional standard, which affords absolute weight to any professional customs. If professionals have recognized certain customs for actions under certain circumstances, these become the standard of care. When this occurs, the jury does not utilize the considerations normally associated with the Learned Hand formula to determine if a breach of duty has occurred. Instead, the jury merely

applies the applicable custom to the defendant professional's conduct to see if they met this alternative standard of care. The only exception is when the professional's action does not involve matters over which a layperson lacks understanding. For example, if a patient in a hospital slips and falls on a wet floor, the hospital's negligence would not rely upon application of the professional standard. If a surgeon forgets to remove a piece of surgical hardware from the patient (a so-called "sponge" case), the jury need not hear expert testimony about whether a custom exists to remove a scalpel. Or if a lawyer forgets to file a lawsuit and the statute of limitations runs on the claim, even a lay juror can understand easily how this would amount to negligence. But in any area requiring professional expertise and judgment, the custom within the profession governs the analysis.

2. *Rejection of* The T.J. Hooper. The professional standard is a stark departure from what we discovered in Chapter 4 in the case of *The T.J. Hooper*. The idea from that case of industry custom being relevant but not controlling seemed to make sense. But with respect to professionals, most courts have held that it would be nonsensical to allow jurors to second-guess the views of an entire profession. This conclusion makes the issue of who is considered a professional very important. In the next case we will consider this issue squarely. In the context of that case, you will discover why courts are willing to trust professionals to set their own standard of care when we don't allow tug boat owners to do likewise. Application of the professional standard of care, despite the perhaps good reason for its use, sometimes means that plaintiffs that appear to have been harmed by a professional have no remedy. For example, in *Osborn*, the trial was conducted on the basis of the normal breach analysis with expert evidence offered as to the feasibility of performing blood tests at a low cost (burden) in the face of increasing awareness of the devastating impact of tainted blood being given to unsuspecting patients (the foreseeable risk of harm). One can easily view the case as exemplifying the observation from *The T.J. Hooper* of an entire industry lagging behind the care that a reasonable person would adhere to in a given circumstance. The same observations might be made of the lawyers effectuating service of process in a rather informal manner in *Hodges* when serving process the lawful way would impose no great burden. Critics of the professional standard would thus use both of these cases as examples of why the reasonable person standard, as applied in *The T.J. Hooper*, should always be applied. But, the majority of courts continue to apply the professional standard to professional groups.

3. *Expert Witnesses.* When the professional standard applies, the jury needs information about the applicable professional customs. The only persons with personal knowledge of these customs are experts practicing within that profession. In this way, courts have held that expert testimony is essential in such cases to inform the jury of the governing standard. Interestingly, a defendant in a malpractice case necessarily qualifies as such an expert witness and is permitted to offer testimony on their own behalf—presumably always testifying that they met the standard (or else the case needs to settle). Plaintiffs in malpractice cases need the testimony of another professional setting forth an applicable custom to which the defendant did not adhere in order to have a potential claim of malpractice for a jury to even consider. Many malpractice cases involve defendants filing motions for summary judgment attacking the adequacy of the plaintiff's evidence of deviation from a professional custom. Plaintiffs can either hire a testifying expert witness from within the profession or, in some cases, offer the opinions from another professional who has dealt with the plaintiff. For example, in some medical malpractice cases a subsequent doctor has treated the plaintiff to remedy a complication from the original doctor's treatment. So long as that other doctor is practicing in the same specialty area as the defendant, if the subsequent treating doctor has critical opinions concerning noncompliance with the governing customs, this can form a sufficient basis for the malpractice claim. A cottage industry has arisen for certain professionals to make themselves available for hire as expert witnesses (for either side) in malpractice cases. When juries hear testimony from dueling expert witnesses as to prevailing customs, the jury needs to determine as a factual matter whom to believe.

4. ***Competing Schools of Thought.*** In a given situation, a profession may not uniformly act in one particular way. When a certain type of cancer is diagnosed in a patient, for example, the specialists involved in treating the cancer may have differences of opinion regarding surgical intervention, radiation and/or chemotherapy. In other words, there may be multiple *schools of thought* within a profession as to the proper course of treatment. In such cases, so long as the defendant doctor has adhered to one of the recognized schools of thought, the doctor has met the duty of care and is not liable for malpractice. There is a lot of potential for dispute as to whether a practice constitutes a recognized school of thought or whether it merely evidences a handful of doctors committing malpractice. These matters are usually left for the jury to decide upon hearing the testimony from the competing expert witnesses.

Watch "Professional Standard of Care" video on Casebook Connect.

2. *Who Is a Professional?*

Doctors and lawyers have always been considered professionals for purposes of analyzing their potential negligence. For this reason, negligence claims against them are called "malpractice" cases. Who else is a professional? Does the professional standard apply to anyone practicing a craft that seems complicated? How about pharmaceutical companies or automobile manufacturers? If we are too liberal in allowing different industries to qualify for professional status, then the well-reasoned opinion in *The T.J. Hooper* becomes meaningless. Even tug boat owners will simply declare themselves professionals and lag behind the expectations for reasonable care with impunity. The *Rossell* case below does an excellent job discussing this question and suggests a framework for analyzing how the courts should define the word "professional." As you read the following case, consider why this issue is so important to the outcome of the case and why the court rejects the professional label for the defendant.

ROSSELL v. VOLKSWAGEN OF AMERICA

709 P.2d 517 (Ariz. 1985)

FELDMAN, J.

This is a product liability action brought by Phyllis A. Rossell, as guardian ad litem on behalf of her daughter, Julie Ann Kennon (plaintiff), against the manufacturer and the North American distributor of Volkswagen automobiles. The defendants will be referred to collectively as "Volkswagen." The case involves the design of the battery system in the model of the Volkswagen automobile popularly known as the "Beetle" or "Bug." The jury found for the plaintiff and awarded damages in the sum of $1,500,000. The court of appeals held that the plaintiff had failed to establish a prima facie case of negligence . . . and that the trial judge had erred in denying Volkswagen's motion for judgment n.o.v.

This action arises from a 1970, one-vehicle accident. At the time of the accident Julie, then eleven months old, was sleeping in the front passenger seat of a 1958 Volkswagen driven by her mother. At approximately 11:00 p.m., on State Route 93, Ms. Rossell fell asleep and the vehicle drifted to the right, off the paved roadway. The sound of the car hitting a sign awakened Rossell, and she attempted to correct the path of the car, but oversteered. The car flipped over, skidded off the road and landed on its roof at the bottom of a cement culvert. The force of the accident dislodged and fractured the battery which was located inside the passenger compartment. In the seven hours it took Rossell to regain full consciousness and then extract herself and her daughter from the car, the broken battery slowly dripped sulfuric acid on Julie. The acid severely burned her face, chest, arm, neck, part of her back and shoulder, and both hands. Since the accident Julie has undergone extensive corrective surgery but remains seriously disfigured and in need of additional surgery.

Plaintiff filed the complaint in May, 1978. She alleged . . . negligent design of the battery system [among other claims]. [At trial,] the case was submitted to the jury only on the question of Volkswagen's negligence in locating the battery inside the passenger compartment.

Plaintiff argued at trial that battery placement within the passenger compartment created an unreasonable risk of harm and that alternative designs were available and practicable. In their trial motions and later motion for judgment n.o.v., Volkswagen argued that plaintiff had failed to make a prima facie case. First, it claimed that in a negligent design case the defendant must comply with the standard of a reasonably prudent designer of automobiles and that

> knowledge of automobile design principles and engineering practices often is beyond the knowledge of laymen, [so that] plaintiff in a case such as this must produce expert testimony establishing the minimum standard of care and deviation therefrom in designing the automobile....

The trial judge characterized Volkswagen's position as a contention that plaintiff could not prevail in the

> absence of testimony... from a qualified expert as opposed to simply permitting the jury to infer it, ... that the standard of care required of a prudent manufacturer would require that the battery be placed elsewhere [or that] it was negligent ... not to have placed it outside of the passenger compartment.

The trial judge disagreed with Volkswagen and denied the motion for judgment n.o.v. However, a majority of the court of appeals held that such evidence was required for a prima facie case.

...

We turn, then, to the central issue presented. What type of proof must plaintiff produce in order to make a prima facie case of negligent design against a product manufacturer? What is the standard of care? In the ordinary negligence case, tried under the familiar rubric of "reasonable care," plaintiff's proof must provide facts from which the jury may conclude that defendant's behavior fell below the "reasonable man" standard. Prosser, *supra* §31 at 169. This question is ordinarily decided without providing the jury with any direct evidence about the details of what may or may not comply with the standard of care. The risk/benefit analysis involved in deciding what is reasonable care under the circumstances is generally left to the jury....

Thus, in the usual negligence case the jury is left to reach its own conclusion on whether defendant's conduct complied with the legal standard of reasonable care. There need be no opinion testimony on the subject; the jury is encouraged, under proper instruction, to consider the circumstances, use its own experience and apply community standards in deciding what is or is not negligence.

Volkswagen claims that negligent design cases are an exception. They contend that product manufacturers are held to an expert's standard of care, as are professionals such as lawyers, doctors and accountants. In professional malpractice cases the reasonable man standard has been replaced with the standard of "what is customary and usual in the profession." Prosser, *supra* §32, at 189. This, of course, requires plaintiff to establish by expert testimony the usual conduct of other practitioners of defendant's profession and to prove, further, that defendant deviated from that standard.

> It has been pointed out often enough that this gives the medical profession, and also the [other professions], the privilege, *which is usually emphatically denied to other groups*, of setting their own legal standards of conduct, merely by adopting their own practices.

Id. (emphasis supplied) (citations omitted).

Should we adopt for manufacturers in negligent design cases a rule "emphatically denied to other groups" but similar to those applied to defendants in professional malpractice cases? Such a rule, of course, would require — not just permit — plaintiff to present explicit evidence of the usual conduct of other persons in the field of design by offering expert evidence of what constitutes "good design practice." Plaintiff would also be required to establish that the design adopted by the defendant deviated from such "good practice." We believe that such a rule is inappropriate.

The malpractice requirement that plaintiff show the details of conduct practiced by others in defendant's profession is not some special favor which the law gives to professionals who may be sued by their clients. It is, instead, a method of holding such defendants to an even higher standard of care than that of an ordinary, prudent person. Prosser, *supra* §32 at 185. Such a technique has not been applied in commercial settings, probably because the danger of allowing a commercial group to set its own standard of what is reasonable is not offset by professional obligations which tend to prevent the group from setting standards at a low level in order to accommodate other interests. Thus, it is the general law that industries are not permitted to establish their own standard of conduct because they may be influenced by motives of saving "time, effort or money." Prosser, *supra* §33 at 194. Long ago, Judge Learned Hand expressed the rule in a case in which the defendant claimed that it had not been negligent in failing to put Mr. Marconi's invention on its tugboats:

> Is it then a final answer that the business had not yet generally adopted receiving sets? . . . Indeed in most cases reasonable prudence is in fact common prudence; but strictly it is never its measure; a whole calling may have unduly lagged in the adoption of new and available devices. It never may set its own tests, however persuasive be its usages. Courts must in the end say what is required; there are precautions so imperative that even their universal disregard will not excuse their omission.

The T.J. Hooper, 60 F.2d 737, 740 (2d Cir.1932). This, of course, is not to say that evidence of custom and usage is inadmissible.

Volkswagen argues that case law already recognizes that in negligent design cases a manufacturer is not liable absent a showing that he failed to conform to the standard of care in design followed by other manufacturers. We do not agree.

In view of public policy and existing law, we decline to transform defective design cases into malpractice cases. We believe the law is best left as it is in this field. Special groups will be allowed to create their own standards of reasonably prudent conduct only when the nature of the group and its special relationship with its clients assure society that those standards will be set with primary regard to protection of the public rather than to such considerations as increased profitability. We do not believe that automobile manufacturers fit into this category. This is no reflection upon automobile manufacturers, but merely a recognition that the necessities of the marketplace permit manufacturers neither the working relationship nor the concern about the welfare of their customers that the professions generally permit and require from their practitioners.

Therefore, in Arizona the rule in negligence cases shall continue to be that evidence of industry custom and practice is generally admissible as evidence relevant to whether defendant's conduct was reasonable under the circumstances. In determining what is reasonable care for manufacturers, the plaintiff need only prove the defendant's conduct presented a foreseeable, unreasonable risk of harm. As in all other negligence cases, the jury is permitted to decide what is reasonable from the common experience of mankind. We do not disturb the rule that in determining what is "reasonable care," expert evidence may be required in those cases in which factual issues are outside the common understanding of jurors. However, unlike most malpractice cases, there need not be explicit expert testimony establishing the standard of care and the manner in which defendant deviated from that standard. With these principles in mind, we now turn to a consideration of the evidence in order to determine whether plaintiff did prove a prima facie case.

Plaintiff presented two experts, Jon McKibben, an automotive engineer, and Charles Turnbow, a safety engineer. Their testimony established that the great majority of cars on the road at the time the Beetle in question was designed had batteries located outside the passenger compartment, usually in the engine compartment and occasionally in the luggage compartment. There was evidence from which the jury could find that from both an engineering and practical standpoint the 1958 Volkswagen could have been designed with the battery outside the passenger compartment, as was the Karmann Ghia, an upscale model which used the same chassis as the Beetle. There was further testimony that placement of the battery inside the passenger compartment was unreasonably dangerous because "batteries do fracture in crashes, not infrequently."

We conclude that the plaintiff did present expert evidence that the battery design location presented a foreseeable, unreasonable risk of harm, that alternative designs were available and that they were feasible from a technological and practical standpoint. We reject Volkswagen's contention that in addition to the evidence outlined above, plaintiff was compelled to produce expert opinion evidence that the standard of "good design practice" required Volkswagen to design the car so that the battery system was located outside the passenger compartment. Unlike a malpractice case, the jury was free to reach or reject this conclusion on the basis of its own experience and knowledge of what is "reasonable," with the assistance of expert opinion describing only the dangers, hazards and factors of design involved.

The opinion of the court of appeals is vacated. The judgment is affirmed.

NOTES AND PROBLEMS

1. *Trust as the Distinction Between Industry and Professions.* The court in *Rossell* clarifies that the professional standard is not a courtesy offered to certain special groups as a favor but instead reflects the fact that certain groups can be trusted to set relatively high standards for themselves. In this regard, it gives two primary considerations for determining that a group deserves the status as a profession: (1) the nature of the group, and (2) whether it has special relationships with its clients. With respect to the nature of the group, the court observes that professional groups have self-imposed "professional obligations" and also tend to be somewhat insulated from "motives of saving time, effort, or money" in setting customs. The court then determines that automobile manufacturers lack the same relationships with their customers that doctors and lawyers have with their patients and clients, and that such manufacturers are driven by profit (presumably from their shareholders) without offsetting professional obligations (e.g., rules of professional responsibility for lawyers and the Hippocratic oath for doctors). Ultimately, what the courts say about commercial industry groups is that they cannot be trusted to set their own standards for fear that the care necessary to protect their customers will be lacking. Viewed in this manner, the court in *Rossell* reaffirms the principles underlying Judge Hand's decision in *The T.J. Hooper* while revealing why a departure from this principle is applicable to true professionals.

2. *Problem.* Given the analytical framework from *Rossell*, practice articulating how each of the following groups should be treated in a negligence case:

Group	Independent professional obligations?	Influenced by commercial profit motives?	Special relationship with clients?
Doctors			
Lawyers			
Automakers			
Drug makers			

B. Informed Consent

One unique subset of medical malpractice cases involves a physician who treats a patient without obtaining their *informed consent.* In such a case, the patient suffers some side effect from the treatment and claims that they would not have agreed to the treatment if the doctor had disclosed such risk as an inherent potential aspect of the treatment. If the bad outcome arises from faulty treatment it would be a normal medical malpractice case. But sometimes even when the treatment is appropriate and performed in conformance with applicable medical customs there may still be certain inherent risks of some side effects. It is in such instances, when a patient who experiences such a side effect from otherwise proper treatment, that an informed consent claim may be available when the physician has failed to disclose this risk. Of course, if the doctor truly obtains no consent before treating a patient, the doctor may have committed a battery. What we are instead analyzing is the instance when the patient does give consent to the treatment but complains that it was not informed. Courts have recognized this type of claim as a subset of medical negligence but have had some difficulty analyzing the standard for determining what information must be disclosed and how to prove actual causation on this unique cause of action. The *Scott* case below illustrates a state's decision to recognize this cause of action and determine the proper method to analyze it.

SCOTT v. BRADFORD

606 P.2d 554 (Okla. 1979)

DOOLIN, J.

This appeal is taken by plaintiffs in trial below, from a judgment in favor of defendant rendered on a jury verdict in a medical malpractice action.

Mrs. Scott's physician advised her she had several fibroid tumors on her uterus. He referred her to defendant surgeon. Defendant admitted her to the hospital where she signed a routine consent form prior to defendant's performing a hysterectomy. After surgery, Mrs. Scott experienced problems with incontinence. She visited another physician who discovered she had a vesicovaginal fistula which permitted urine to leak from her bladder into the vagina. This physician referred her to an urologist who, after three surgeries, succeeded in correcting her problems.

Mrs. Scott, joined by her husband, filed the present action alleging medical malpractice, claiming defendant failed to advise her of the risks involved or of available alternatives to surgery. She further maintained had she been properly informed she would have refused the surgery.

The case was submitted to the jury with instructions to which plaintiffs objected. The jury found for defendant and plaintiffs appeal.

The issue involved is whether Oklahoma adheres to the doctrine of informed consent as the basis of an action for medical malpractice, and if so did the present instructions adequately advise the jury of defendant's duty.

Anglo-American law starts with the premise of thoroughgoing self-determination, each man considered to be his own master. This law does not permit a physician to substitute his judgment for that of the patient by any form of artifice. The doctrine of informed consent arises out of this premise.

Consent to medical treatment, to be effective, should stem from an understanding decision based on adequate information about the treatment, the available alternatives, and the collateral risks. This requirement, labeled "informed consent," is, legally speaking, as essential as a physician's care and skill in the *performance* of the therapy. The doctrine imposes a duty on a physician or surgeon to inform a patient of his options and their attendant risks. If a physician breaches this duty, patient's consent is defective, and physician is responsible for the consequences.

If treatment is completely unauthorized and performed without any consent at all, there has been a battery. However, if the physician obtains a patient's consent but has breached his duty to inform, the patient has a cause of action sounding in negligence for failure to inform the patient of his options, regardless of the due care exercised at treatment, assuming there is injury.

Until today, Oklahoma has not officially adopted this doctrine.

[I]n perhaps one of the most influential informed consent decisions, *Canterbury v. Spence*, 464 F.2d 772 (D.C. Cir. 1972) cert. den, 409 U.S. 1064, the doctrine received perdurable impetus. Judge Robinson observed that suits charging failure by a physician adequately to disclose risks and alternatives of proposed treatment were not innovative in American law. He emphasized the fundamental concept in American jurisprudence that every human being of adult years and sound mind has a right to determine what shall be done with his own body. True consent to what happens to one's self is the informed exercise of a choice. This entails an opportunity to evaluate knowledgeably the options available and the risks attendant upon each. It is the prerogative of every patient to chart his own course and determine which direction he will take.

The decision in *Canterbury* recognized the tendency of some jurisdictions to turn this duty on whether it is the custom of physicians practicing in the community to make the particular disclosure to the patient. That court rejected this standard and held the standard measuring performance of the duty of disclosure is conduct which is reasonable under the circumstances: "[We cannot] ignore the fact that to bind disclosure obligations to medical usage is to arrogate the decision on revelation to the physician alone." We agree. A patient's right to make up his mind whether to undergo treatment should not be delegated to the local medical group. What is reasonable disclosure in one instance may not be reasonable in another. We decline to adopt a standard based on the professional standard. We, therefore, hold the scope of a physician's communications must be measured by his patient's need to know enough to enable him to make an intelligent choice. In other words, full disclosure of all *material risks* incident to treatment must be made. There is no bright line separating the material from the immaterial; it is a question of fact. A risk is material if it would be likely to affect patient's decision. When non-disclosure of a particular risk is open to debate, the issue is for the finder of facts.

This duty to disclose is the first element of the cause of action in negligence based on lack of informed consent. However, there are exceptions creating a privilege of a physician not to disclose. There is no need to disclose risks that either ought to be known by everyone or are already known to the patient. Further, the primary duty of a physician is to do what is best for his patient and where full disclosure would be detrimental to a patient's total care and best interests a physician may withhold such disclosure, for example, where disclosure would alarm an emotionally upset or apprehensive patient. Certainly too, where there is an emergency and the patient is in no condition to determine for himself whether treatment should be administered, the privilege may be invoked.

The patient has the burden of going forward with evidence tending to establish prima facie the essential elements of the cause of action. The burden of proving an exception to his duty and thus a privilege not to disclose, rests upon the physician as an affirmative defense.

The cause of action, based on lack of informed consent, is divided into three elements: the duty to inform being the first, the second is causation, and the third is injury. The second element, that of causation, requires that plaintiff patient would have chosen no treatment or a different course of treatment had the alternatives and material risks of each been made known to him. If the patient would have elected to proceed with treatment had he been duly informed of its risks, then the element of causation is missing. In other words, a causal connection exists between physician's breach of the duty to disclose and patient's injury when and only when disclosure of material risks incidental to treatment would have resulted in a decision against it. A patient obviously has no complaint if he would have submitted to the treatment if the physician had complied with his duty and informed him of the risks. This fact decision raises the difficult question of the correct standard on which to instruct the jury.

The court in *Canterbury v. Spence, supra,* although emphasizing principles of self-determination permits liability only if non-disclosure would have affected the decision of a fictitious "reasonable patient," even though actual patient testifies he would have elected to forego therapy had he been fully informed.

Decisions discussing informed consent have emphasized the *disclosure* element but paid scant attention to the consent element of the concept, although this is the root of causation. Language in some decisions suggest the standard to be applied is a subjective one, i.e., whether that particular patient would still have consented to the treatment, reasonable choice or otherwise. *See Woods v. Brumlop, supra, n.8*; *Wilkinson v. Vesey, supra, n.3*; *Gray v. Grunnagle,* 223 A.2d

663 (Pa. 1966); *Poulin v. Zartman*, 542 P.2d 251 (Alas. 1975) reh. den., 548 P.2d 1299 (Alas. 1976).

Although the *Canterbury* rule is probably that of the majority, its "reasonable man" approach has been criticized by some commentators as backtracking on its own theory of self-determination. The *Canterbury* view certainly severely limits the protection granted an injured patient. To the extent the plaintiff, given an adequate disclosure, would have declined the proposed treatment, and a reasonable person in similar circumstances would have consented, a patient's right of self-determination is *irrevocably lost.* This basic right to know and decide is the reason for the full-disclosure rule. Accordingly, we decline to jeopardize this right by the imposition of the "reasonable man" standard.

If a plaintiff testifies he would have continued with the proposed treatment had he been adequately informed, the trial is over under either the subjective or objective approach. If he testifies he would not, then the causation problem must be resolved by examining the credibility of plaintiff's testimony. The jury must be instructed that it must find plaintiff would have refused the treatment if he is to prevail.

Although it might be said this approach places a physician at the mercy of a patient's hindsight, a careful practitioner can always protect himself by insuring that he has adequately informed each patient he treats. If he does not breach this duty, a causation problem will not arise.

The final element of this cause of action is that of injury. The risk must actually materialize and plaintiff must have been injured as a result of submitting to the treatment. Absent occurrence of the undisclosed risk, a physician's failure to reveal its possibility is not actionable.

In summary, in a medical malpractice action a patient suing under the theory of informed consent must allege and prove:

1) defendant physician failed to inform him adequately of a material risk before securing his consent to the proposed treatment;
2) if he had been informed of the risks he would not have consented to the treatment;
3) the adverse consequences that were not made known did in fact occur and he was injured as a result of submitting to the treatment.

Because we are imposing a new duty on physicians, we hereby make this opinion prospective only, affecting those causes of action arising after the date this opinion is promulgated.

The trial court in the case at bar gave rather broad instructions upon the duty of a physician to disclose. The instructions objected to did instruct that defendant should have disclosed material risks of the hysterectomy and feasibility of alternatives. Instructions are sufficient when considered as a whole they present the law applicable to the issues. Jury found for defendant. We find no basis for reversal.

NOTES AND PROBLEMS

1. ***Standard for Determining the Duty.*** Courts have recognized the informed consent cause of action based upon the principle of autonomy of the individual to make their own medical decisions. If the doctor obtains your consent without advising you of the possible negative aspects of treatment, courts conclude that the doctor has committed a form of medical malpractice. Originally, as courts recognized this type of malpractice claim they naturally utilized the professional standard of care as they would with any other malpractice claim. That is, the governing standard was what other similar medical professionals advised their patients about the side effects of the treatment. In the case above, the *Scott* court rejects this standard for several reasons, but most importantly because the professional standard is inconsistent with the autonomy at the heart of the informed consent claim. The professional standard applied in this context seems inappropriately paternalistic to most modern courts. Instead, the courts have adopted the objective, reasonably prudent patient standard in deciding what side effects of treatment are "material." The biggest criticism of this standard is that it leaves doctors in an awkward gray zone where it may not be clear (until after a malpractice case is filed and tried to a jury) to a doctor what possible ill effects need to be disclosed. It can result in the defensive practice of medicine with doctors disclosing every far-flung remote side effect possible. As a consequence, patients may have a hard time deciphering the significant risks from the theoretical risks.

2. ***Causation Analysis.*** The second issue the courts adopting this cause of action have to determine is what standard should be used in assessing actual but-for causation. After all, just because the patient suffers the side effect does not establish causation by itself because the malpractice is not in the manner of treatment but in the failure to let the patient make the treatment decision. If the patient would have opted for the treatment even with full disclosure it is difficult to see how the malpractice has caused any harm. Courts have chosen between the objective, reasonably prudent patient standard or the actual subjective statements of the plaintiff. Many courts have opted for the objective standard for causation out of practical recognition that any informed consent plaintiff, aided by hindsight, is likely to testify that she would have declined the treatment if only she had known of the risk. Even with this possibility, the *Scott* court still rejects this objective standard for causation because the plaintiff ultimately has the choice to accept or reject treatment and this choice is so personal that it should not matter if the decision was reasonably made. The jury, of course, can still reject a plaintiff's self-serving testimony if they do not find the plaintiff credible.

3. ***Emergency Consent.*** As the court observes in *Scott*, in emergency scenarios where the patient is not able to give consent to necessary treatment,

courts have allowed doctors the privilege to provide medical care given in good faith. Of course, if the treatment itself falls below the professional standard, the doctor can still be subject to a malpractice suit.

C. Limitations on a Professional's Duty

Another important issue courts have faced is how far the duty of care stretches for professionals. Specifically, courts have sometimes faced malpractice claims brought by a non-client of the professional. In the *Elliott* case below, one state's highest court has to determine whether a lawyer can be subject to a legal malpractice suit brought by individuals who claim to have been adversely impacted by the lawyer's possible mistakes in performing some estate planning for his client. There are powerful reasons given to permit this claim to go forward, as many courts have done in similar circumstances, but this court determines that it is more important to limit the duty of the lawyer.

BARCELO, III v. ELLIOTT

923 S.W.2d 575 (Tex. 1996)

Phillips, C.J.

The issue presented is whether an attorney who negligently drafts a will or trust agreement owes a duty of care to persons intended to benefit under the will or trust, even though the attorney never represented the intended beneficiaries. The court of appeals held that the attorney owed no duty to the beneficiaries, affirming the trial court's summary judgment for the defendant-attorney. Because the attorney did not represent the beneficiaries, we likewise conclude that he owed no professional duty to them. We accordingly affirm the judgment of the court of appeals.

After Frances Barcelo retained attorney David Elliott to assist her with estate planning, Elliott drafted a will and inter vivos trust agreement for her. The will provided for specific bequests to Barcelo's children, devising the residuary of her estate to the inter vivos trust. Under the trust agreement, trust income was to be distributed to Barcelo during her lifetime. Upon her death, the trust was to terminate, assets were to be distributed in specific amounts to Barcelo's children and siblings, and the remainder was to pass to Barcelo's six grandchildren. The trust agreement contemplated that the trust would be funded by cash and shares of stock during Barcelo's lifetime, although the grandchildren contend that this never occurred. Barcelo signed the will and trust agreement in September 1990.

Barcelo died on January 22, 1991. After two of her children contested the validity of the trust, the probate court, for reasons not disclosed on the record before us, declared the trust to be invalid and unenforceable. Barcelo's grandchildren — the intended remainder beneficiaries under the trust — subsequently agreed to settle for what they contend was a substantially smaller share of the estate than what they would have received pursuant to a valid trust.

Barcelo's grandchildren then filed the present malpractice action against Elliott and his law firm (collectively "Elliott"). Plaintiffs allege that Elliott's negligence caused the trust to be invalid, resulting in foreseeable injury to the plaintiffs. Elliott moved for summary judgment on the sole ground that he owed no professional duty to the grandchildren because he had never represented them. The trial court granted Elliott's motion for summary judgment.

The court of appeals affirmed, concluding that under Texas law an attorney preparing estate planning documents owes a duty only to his or her client — the testator or trust settlor — not to third parties intended to benefit under the estate plan.

The sole issue presented is whether Elliott owes a duty to the grandchildren that could give rise to malpractice liability even though he represented only Frances Barcelo, not the grandchildren, in preparing and implementing the estate plan.

At common law, an attorney owes a duty of care only to his or her client, not to third parties who may have been damaged by the attorney's negligent representation of the client. *See Savings Bank v. Ward*, 100 U.S. 195, 200 (1879); Annotation, *Attorney's Liability, to One Other Than Immediate Client, for Negligence in Connection with Legal Duties*, 61 A.L.R. 4th 615, 624 (1988). Without this "privity barrier," the rationale goes, clients would lose control over the attorney-client relationship, and attorneys would be subject to almost unlimited liability. Texas courts of appeals have uniformly applied the privity barrier in the estate planning context. *See Thomas v. Pryor*, 847 S.W.2d 303, 304-05 (Tex. App. — Dallas 1992), *judgm't vacated by agr.*, 863 S.W.2d 462 (Tex. 1993).

Plaintiffs argue, however, that recognizing a limited exception to the privity barrier as to lawyers who negligently draft a will or trust would not thwart the rule's underlying rationales. They contend that the attorney should owe a duty of care to persons who were specific, intended beneficiaries of the estate plan. We disagree.

The majority of other states addressing this issue have relaxed the privity barrier in the estate planning context. *See Lucas v. Hamm*, 56 Cal. 2d 583, 364 P.2d 685, 689, 15 Cal. Rptr. 821 (Cal. 1961), *cert. denied*, 368 U.S. 987, 7 L. Ed. 2d 525, 82 S. Ct. 603 (1962); *Stowe v. Smith*, 184 Conn. 194, 441 A.2d 81, 83 (Conn. 1981); *Needham v. Hamilton*, 459 A.2d 1060, 1062 (D.C. 1983); *DeMaris v. Asti*, 426 So. 2d 1153, 1154 (Fla. Dist. Ct. App. 1983); *Ogle v. Fuiten*, 102 Ill. 2d 356, 466 N.E.2d 224, 226-27, 80 Ill. Dec. 772 (Ill. 1984); *Walker v. Lawson*, 526 N.E.2d 968, 968 (Ind. 1988); *Schreiner v. Scoville*, 410 N.W.2d 679, 682 (Iowa 1987); *Pizel v. Zuspann*, 247 Kan. 54, 795 P.2d 42, 51 (Kan. 1990); *In re Killingsworth*, 292 So. 2d 536, 542 (La. 1973); *Hale v. Groce*, 304 Ore. 281, 744 P.2d 1289, 1292-93 (Or. 1987); *Guy v. Liederbach*, 501 Pa. 47, 459 A.2d 744, 751-53 (Pa. 1983); *Auric v. Continental Cas. Co.*, 111 Wis. 2d 507, 331 N.W.2d 325, 327 (Wis. 1983). *But see Lilyhorn v.*

Dier, 214 Neb. 728, 335 N.W.2d 554, 555 (Neb. 1983); *Viscardi v. Lerner*, 125 A.D.2d 662, 510 N.Y.S.2d 183, 185 (N.Y. App. Div. 1986); *Simon v. Zipperstein*, 32 Ohio St. 3d 74, 512 N.E.2d 636, 638 (Ohio 1987).

While some of these states have allowed a broad cause of action by those claiming to be intended beneficiaries, others have limited the class of plaintiffs to beneficiaries specifically identified in an invalid will or trust. *See Ventura County Humane Society v. Holloway*, 40 Cal. App. 3d 897, 115 Cal. Rptr. 464, 468 (Cal. Dist. Ct. App. 1974); *DeMaris*, 426 So. 2d at 1154; *Schreiner*, 410 N.W.2d at 683; *Kirgan v. Parks*, 60 Md. App. 1, 478 A.2d 713, 718-19 (Md. Ct. Spec. App. 1984) (holding that, if cause of action exists, it does not extend to situation where testator's intent as expressed in the will has been carried out); *Ginther v. Zimmerman*, 195 Mich. App. 647, 491 N.W.2d 282, 286 (Mich. Ct. App. 1992) (same); *Guy*, 459 A.2d at 751-52. The Supreme Court of Iowa, for example, held that

> a cause of action ordinarily will arise only when as a direct result of the lawyer's professional negligence the testator's intent as expressed in the testamentary instruments is frustrated in whole or in part and the beneficiary's interest in the estate is either lost, diminished, or unrealized.

Schreiner v. Scoville, 410 N.W.2d 679, 683 (Iowa 1987).

We agree with those courts that have rejected a broad cause of action in favor of beneficiaries. These courts have recognized the inevitable problems with disappointed heirs attempting to prove that the defendant-attorney failed to implement the deceased testator's intentions. Certainly allowing extrinsic evidence would create a host of difficulties. In *DeMaris v. Asti*, 426 So. 2d 1153, 1154 (Fla. Dist. Ct. App. 1983), for example, the court concluded that "there is no authority — the reasons being obvious — for the proposition that a disappointed beneficiary may prove, by evidence totally extrinsic to the will, the testator's testamentary intent was other than as expressed in his solemn and properly executed will." Such a cause of action would subject attorneys to suits by heirs who simply did not receive what they believed to be their due share under the will or trust. This potential tort liability to third parties would create a conflict during the estate planning process, dividing the attorney's loyalty between his or her client and the third-party beneficiaries.

Moreover, we believe that the more limited cause of action recognized by several jurisdictions also undermines the policy rationales supporting the privity rule. These courts have limited the cause of action to beneficiaries specifically identified in an invalid will or trust. Under these circumstances, courts have reasoned, the interests of the client and the beneficiaries are necessarily aligned, negating any conflict, as the attorney owes a duty only to those parties which the testator clearly intended to benefit. *See, e.g., Needham*, 459 A.2d at 1062.

In most cases where a defect renders a will or trust invalid, however, there are concomitant questions as to the true intentions of the testator. Suppose, for example, that a properly drafted will is simply not executed at the time of the testator's death. The document may express the testator's true intentions, lacking signatures solely because of the attorney's negligent delay. On the other hand, the testator may have postponed execution because of second thoughts regarding the distribution scheme. In the latter situation, the attorney's representation of the testator will likely be affected if he or she knows that the existence of an unexecuted will may create malpractice liability if the testator unexpectedly dies.

The present case is indicative of the conflicts that could arise. Plaintiffs contend in part that Elliott was negligent in failing to fund the trust during Barcelo's lifetime, and in failing to obtain a signature from the trustee. These alleged deficiencies, however, could have existed pursuant to Barcelo's instructions, which may have been based on advice from her attorneys attempting to represent her best interests. An attorney's ability to render such advice would be severely compromised if the advice could be second-guessed by persons named as beneficiaries under the unconsummated trust.

In sum, we are unable to craft a bright-line rule that allows a lawsuit to proceed where alleged malpractice causes a will or trust to fail in a manner that casts no real doubt on the testator's intentions, while prohibiting actions in other situations. We believe the greater good is served by preserving a bright-line privity rule which denies a cause of action to all beneficiaries whom the attorney did not represent. This will ensure that attorneys may in all cases zealously represent their clients without the threat of suit from third parties compromising that representation.

We therefore hold that an attorney retained by a testator or settlor to draft a will or trust owes no professional duty of care to persons named as beneficiaries under the will or trust.

Plaintiffs also contend that, even if there is no tort duty extending to beneficiaries of an estate plan, they may recover under a third-party-beneficiary contract theory. While the majority of jurisdictions that have recognized a cause of action in favor of will or trust beneficiaries have done so under negligence principles, some have allowed recovery in contract.

In Texas, however, a legal malpractice action sounds in tort and is governed by negligence principles. *See Cosgrove v. Grimes*, 774 S.W.2d 662, 664 (Tex. 1989); *Willis v. Maverick*, 760 S.W.2d 642, 644 (Tex. 1988). *Cf. Heyer v. Flaig*, 70 Cal. 2d 223, 449 P.2d 161, 164, 74 Cal. Rptr. 225 (Cal. 1969) (recognizing that third-party-beneficiary contract theory "is conceptually superfluous since the crux of the action must lie in tort in any case; there can be no recovery without negligence"). Even assuming that a client who retains a lawyer to draft an estate plan intends for the lawyer's work to benefit the will or trust beneficiaries, the ultimate question is whether, considering the competing policy implications, the lawyer's professional duty should extend to persons whom the lawyer never represented. For the reasons previously discussed, we conclude that the answer is no.

For the foregoing reasons, we affirm the judgment of the court of appeals.

NOTES AND PROBLEMS

1. *Privity as a Limit on Duty.* The *Elliott* court begins by recognizing the general rule that permits only clients to sue lawyers for malpractice. This privity rule helps to clarify to whom the lawyer owes a duty of care and helps to avoid a potential division of loyalties by the lawyer. The rule also facilitates the unhindered zealous representation of clients by lawyers without fear for the consequences of their representation on third parties. Against these good reasons for the limitation on duty, however, the court admits that the majority of courts in this estate-planning context are willing to recognize some claims by beneficiaries despite the lack of privity of contract with the lawyer. The broad exception permits any stranger to a will to argue that the lawyer's neglect explains their absence from being named a beneficiary. Obviously recognizing such claims is potentially troublesome because anyone might make such a claim after the death of a wealthy individual. The narrow exception is more limited — it only applies to permit a malpractice claim by named beneficiaries when the will or trust instrument is declared invalid due to the lawyer's negligence. The *Elliott* court says that trusts and wills are often held invalid for technical reasons that cast doubt on whether the instruments prepared by the lawyer accurately reflect the testator/client's true intentions; the court was, therefore, unwilling to permit any exception to the strict privity rule for limiting the lawyer's duty. This general issue comes up in other professional malpractice claims with most courts typically limiting the duty in a similar way. Generally only patients can sue doctors for malpractice. (Though recall under *Tarasoff* that third parties hurt by the patient can sometimes sue the patient's doctor, but these are not technically considered malpractice claims.) This issue also comes up in accountant claims for negligent misrepresentation when investors claim the accountant's errors misstated a company's true financial picture. There is a wide body of conflicting case law in this accountant malpractice area with the traditional rule being one of strict privity but modern courts being willing to consider a somewhat broader rule of duty owed to known potential investors. *See e.g.*, Grant Thornton LLP v. Prospect High Income Fund, 314 S.W.3d 913 (Tex. 2010) (outlining the various approaches taken by courts on the extent of an accountant's duty of care in negligent misrepresentation cases). This area of law is covered in Chapter 13 Business Torts.

2. *Causation in a Legal Malpractice Claim.* If a lawyer is accused of mishandling a case for a client, proof of actual causation of harm must be predicated on proof that the client would have won the underlying case but for the lawyer's negligence. To determine causation in the malpractice case, the jury has to decide not only the merits of the malpractice claim but the merits of the underlying suit as well. This concept of proving causation is referred to sometimes as the *trial within the trial.* In such a suit, much of the evidence offered will pertain to the merits of the initial suit, which the malpractice jury will necessarily have to hear to determine if the lawyer's mishandling of the initial case actually made any difference.

3. *No Mention of Mere Economic Harm Rule.* You may have wondered, as you read the foregoing decision denying recovery to the grandchildren, why the court did not just cite to the *mere economic harm* rule to reject a duty of care. Indeed, would not this doctrine preclude almost all legal malpractice claims — because lawyers' mistakes usually do not result in physical injuries? For such claims, courts do not apply this doctrine because it is designed to provide a limit to otherwise unlimited potential liabilities. Because malpractice claims are already generally limited by the privity rule — a much narrower duty — there is no concern for far-flung unlimited liabilities rippling out from a lawyer's mistakes. This is also true in other malpractice or negligent misrepresentation claims against other professionals, such as accountants. This is discussed further in Chapter 13 Business Torts.

Upon Further Review

Negligence claims against professionals raise interesting issues in analyzing the breach of duty as well as causation. To the extent a defendant is part of a special group that, due to its nature and special relationships with clients/patients, can be trusted to set relatively high standards for itself, courts recognize a departure from the doctrine in *The T.J. Hooper* that we encountered in Chapter 4. Rather than utilize the reasonable man as the standard of care, courts instead look exclusively to industry custom. Where the professional is operating within a recognized school of thought in her profession, she operates in a safe harbor zone and cannot be proven to have breached her professional duty. If a breach of custom can be demonstrated, plaintiffs often have unique causation issues with which to contend. In medical malpractice cases, the plaintiff might have trouble proving but-for causation if the doctor's negligence merely deprived the plaintiff of a somewhat better chance of recovery. If the negligence probably made no difference, some courts will reject any recovery and others will offer a reduced recovery based upon the percentage reduction times the actual harm actually experienced. In claims for failure to give informed consent, the plaintiff will need to demonstrate that either she or a reasonable patient would not have undergone the procedure with proper information about the inherent side effects. And in legal malpractice claims involving the mishandling of prior litigation, the jury will need to determine the merits of not only the malpractice allegations but also the merits of the underlying lawsuit — for unless the lawyer's negligence turned a victory into a loss, the professional blunder would be considered nothing more than "negligence in the air" and would impose no liability on the lawyer.

Pulling It All Together

George lived in a suburban house by himself. Being an avid athlete, he purchased an in-ground basketball goal for his driveway and began to install this goal. He was pretty gifted with his hands and did not feel the need to consult the instructional manual. He worked on the goal for several hours and believed it was complete. There were some extra nuts and bolts left over. He considered testing the strength of the goal but ran out of time, as he desired to attend a floral exhibition at the community garden center.

Dennis was a six-year-old boy that lived with his parents Henry and Alice, next door to George. He had a way of getting into trouble. George was constantly having to run Dennis off of his property, as Dennis was a cause of much consternation to George. On this particular date, Dennis was watching from a distance as George was building the new basketball goal. Dennis stood across the street bouncing a basketball, eagerly anticipating the chance to shoot baskets. As George drove off, Dennis ran onto George's property and began shooting baskets. Dennis noticed a mini-trampoline in George's garage. He had seen mascots at basketball games jump from such trampolines to dunk a basketball and decided to do likewise. On his first attempt, he soared into the air, dunked the basketball, and then grabbed the rim for dear life. His weight was too much for the new goal. As it turns out, some necessary screws had been left unsecured in the goal. The entire apparatus fell over on top of poor Dennis. Dennis lay on the ground screaming in agony. A few minutes later, a schoolmate named Tommy came walking by. He saw Dennis in pain and ran to his assistance. Tommy had seen CPR performed on television and, despite the fact that Dennis was conscious, he began pounding on Dennis's chest. This caused Dennis's sternum to crack and made Dennis' condition worse.

Eventually an ambulance arrived. The paramedics secured Dennis into their vehicle and rushed toward the hospital. At the hospital, the emergency room physician set some open fractures in Dennis's arm and provided him with pain medication. She did not, however, prescribe any antibiotics for the open wound. A few days after his discharge, Dennis's wounds became horribly infected and he went to see a different doctor at the same hospital. This doctor, a surgeon, ultimately determined that the arm could not be saved and amputated it. The surgeon indicated that his personal practice would be to always give antibiotics for compound fractures. While this would not absolutely prevent all infections, it made them less likely to occur.

Analyze any tort causes of action — 45 minutes

CHAPTER 7

Affirmative Defenses

I INTRODUCTION

Even when the plaintiff in a tort suit can prove the elements of her cause of action, this does not necessarily mean that the war is over. Tort law has recognized a number of doctrines that can still serve to defeat (or sometimes lessen) the plaintiff's attempted recovery. These are considered "affirmative defenses" — defenses that, in effect, say "even though you have proven my negligent conduct was the legal cause of your harm, I still win because ________." This chapter will fill in that blank with a variety of potential affirmative defenses. Chapter 3 introduced some affirmative defenses unique to intentional torts. This chapter covers affirmative defenses of a more general application, including defenses to negligence claims. Whereas a plaintiff has the burden of proving the elements of her claim, a defendant has the burden of proving any affirmative defenses. A number of these defenses have been modified by relatively recent developments in the law, some of them late in coming. Often, changes to these affirmative defenses have been driven by state legislatures rather than the common law. Mastering these defenses and understanding the rationale behind them are the twin goals of this chapter.

We begin with some *blame the plaintiff* defenses that have been recognized to defeat the plaintiff's recovery when the plaintiff has misbehaved in some fashion or has acted in a way that relieves the defendant's duty of care. Contributory negligence is a concept we have already seen on the periphery when we learned about the duty of reasonable care and the concept of proving breach

CHAPTER GOALS

☑ Understand not only the different ways jurisdictions today punish a plaintiff for the plaintiff's own negligent conduct but also appreciate the differing balance of policies underlying each competing alternative set of rules.

☑ Become familiar with the two true affirmative defense varieties of assumption of the risk (versus primary assumption of the risk seen in Chapter 6 Special Duty Rules) and whether they are compatible with the evolutionary transition to a comparative fault scheme.

☑ Learn how certain special relationships traditionally serve to defeat a duty of care (rather than create one as we saw in Chapter 6 Special Duty Rules) in scenarios involving citizens and their government, spousal relationships, and the parent/child relationship.

☑ Recognize that every civil tort claim comes with an expiration date — a statute of limitations — requiring it be filed within a certain period of time and learn the differing rules for when the clock begins ticking and what might interrupt its running.

In Practice

Under Federal Rule of Civil Procedure 8(c), a party must "affirmatively state any avoidance or affirmative defense" or else it is waived. Defense counsels' ability to spot possible defenses and to plead them at the beginning of the lawsuit can be critically important.

of the duty. For example, you will recall Judge Cardozo in the case of *Martin v. Herzog*, declared that the plaintiff could not possibly recover because he had driven his buggy at night without the lights required by statute. In that context, the doctrine of negligence *per se* proved contributory negligence. Contributory negligence in its classic sense is a harsh doctrine; a silver bullet defense so severe that all but a handful of states have now replaced it with *comparative fault* which often just serves to reduce, rather than eliminate, the plaintiff's recovery. We will also delve into two additional varieties of *assumption of the risk* — express assumption of the risk and secondary implied assumption of the risk. Unlike primary assumption of the risk, which we saw was merely another way of finding that the defendant acted reasonably with regard to inherent risks, these two varieties of assumption of risk are true affirmative defenses based on the plaintiff's decision to confront willingly the danger created by the defendant's negligence.

II CONTRIBUTORY NEGLIGENCE AND COMPARATIVE FAULT

A. Contributory Negligence

Butterfield v. Forrester is the first known case to hold that the plaintiff's own negligence served to relieve the defendant of liability for his unreasonable conduct, which also contributed to causing the plaintiff's harm. Following this case is a more modern application (substituting automobiles for horses) of this ancient defense doctrine. As you read the following cases, consider what justifications would support a doctrine that yields the pro-defendant results below.

BUTTERFIELD v. FORRESTER

103 Eng. Rep. 926 (1809)

This was an action on the case for obstructing a highway, by means of which obstruction the plaintiff, who was riding along the road, was thrown down with his horse, and injured. At the trial before Bayley, J. at Derby, it appeared that the defendant, for the purpose of making some repairs to his house, which was close by the road side at one end of the town, had put up a pole across this part of the road, a free passage being left by another branch or street in the same direction. That the plaintiff left a public house not far distant from the place in question at 8 o'clock in the evening in August, when they were just beginning to light candles, but while there was light enough left to discern the obstruction at 100 yards distance: and the witness, who proved this, said that if the plaintiff had not been riding very hard he might have observed and avoided it: the plaintiff however, who was riding violently, did not observe it, but rode against it, and fell with his horse and was much hurt in consequence of the accident; and there was no evidence of his being intoxicated at the time. On this evidence Bayley J. directed the jury, that if a person riding with reasonable and ordinary care could have seen and avoided the obstruction; and if they were satisfied that the plaintiff was riding along the street extremely hard, and without ordinary care, they should find a verdict for the defendant, which they accordingly did. [Plaintiff requested a new trial; referred to as a "Rule," which was denied for the reasons set forth in the following two opinions.]

Bayley, J. The plaintiff was proved to be riding as fast as his horse could go, and this was through the streets of Derby. If he had used ordinary care he must have seen the obstruction; so that the accident appeared to happen entirely from his own fault.

Lord Ellenborough, C.J. A party is not to cast himself upon an obstruction which has been made by the fault of another, and avail himself of it, if he do not himself use common and ordinary caution to be in the right. In cases of persons riding upon what is considered to be the wrong side of the road, that would not authorize another purposely to ride up against them. One person being in fault will not dispense with another's using ordinary care for himself. Two things must concur to support this action, an obstruction in the road by the fault of the defendant, and no want of ordinary care to avoid it on the part of the plaintiff.

HARRIS v. MEADOWS

477 So. 2d 374 (Ala. 1985)

Almon, J.

This case involves a claim for damages for injuries resulting from an automobile collision.

First Avenue North in Birmingham, Alabama, is a five-lane street consisting of two eastbound lanes, two westbound lanes and a center turn lane.

The plaintiff, Carol P. Harris, was driving east in the far right lane, and the defendant, Dora Stubbs Meadows, was in the center lane facing west, preparing to turn left. As Harris neared Meadows, Meadows began to turn in front of Harris. Harris testified that she blew her horn, applied her brakes, and "moved over to the right a little bit." Meadows's vehicle then collided with the left side of Harris's vehicle in the area of the front fender and driver's door. As a result of the collision, Harris suffered a cervical sprain and a contusion, or bruise, to her left hip.

Harris's complaint contained counts alleging that the collision was a result of negligent and wanton conduct on the part of Meadows. The wanton count was dismissed upon a motion by Meadows at the close of all the evidence.

At trial Meadows admitted that she was guilty of negligence but contended that Harris should not recover because Harris was guilty of contributory negligence. Harris appeals from a judgment on the jury's verdict for Meadows, and a denial of her motion for a new trial.

Harris argues that the judgment should be reversed because the verdict upon which it is based is unsupported by facts and is contrary to law.

A jury verdict is presumed correct and will not be set aside unless it is without supporting evidence or is so contrary to the evidence as to render it wrong and unjust. Where the jury verdict is not plainly erroneous, we cannot consider other possible conclusions that might have been reached. *Kent v. Singleton*, 457 So. 2d 356 (Ala. 1984).

In reviewing the record we note the following testimony by Harris:

Q. How far from her vehicle would you say you were when you really came down on your brakes in an attempt to stop?
A. I didn't really come down on my brakes in an attempt to stop. I slowed down to see that maybe she could get on across there and not hit me. But that was not possible. She was already on me at that point.
Q. Did you make any attempt to put on your brakes and come to a stop and let this lady turn in front of you to go into Kelly's?
A. There wasn't time.
Q. But you never did come down hard on your brakes, lock your brakes, skid, and attempt to stop. You were going to see if she had time to come in front of you?
A. There was not time to make all those decisions. I just slowed down thinking she would see me coming at that point and stop her turn.
Q. Did you ever try to mash your brakes to the floor to try to stop your vehicle to keep from hitting the Chevrolet that was turning in front of you?
A. No, sir."

We are of the opinion that there was sufficient evidence before the jury for it to conclude that Harris was guilty of contributory negligence in failing to act reasonably under the circumstances to avoid the collision. This case is perhaps illustrative of the harshness of the contributory negligence doctrine, a doctrine which, like the scintilla evidence rule, seems to be firmly established in our jurisprudence.

There appearing no reversible error, the judgment is affirmed.

AFFIRMED.

NOTES AND PROBLEMS

1. ***All or Nothing.*** Under the common law doctrine of contributory negligence, the defense was an all or nothing proposition. Either the plaintiff's claim was completely unblemished by fault and the plaintiff deemed worthy of recovery of all her damages from the defendant, or she could recover nothing despite proving the elements of the defendant's own negligence. Under this doctrine, the relative degrees of fault between the plaintiff and the defendant were immaterial. *Any* fault by the plaintiff destroyed her cause of action.

2. ***Justifications.*** In both of the foregoing cases, did the plaintiffs appear to have sufficient evidence of the defendant's negligence? Did the defendant's negligence in each of the two cases appear to be both an actual and proximate cause of each plaintiff's harm as well? If so, what would justify denying all recovery to the plaintiffs and permitting the defendants to avoid any responsibility? What tort purposes are served by such a rule? Are any tort purposes undermined? Observe, by the way, that in the *Meadows* case, the defendant likely incurred some harm during the car accident and could have asserted her own counterclaim for negligence against the plaintiff. What would be the likely result of such a counterclaim if it were filed?

3. ***Analysis of Contributory Negligence.*** Determining whether the doctrine of contributory negligence is applicable requires application of the same elements we have already covered with respect to proving a defendant's liability—proof of a duty, breach, cause (both actual and proximate), and harm. All doctrines previously encountered, and everything we have learned about the reasonable person, applies with equal force to the analysis of a plaintiff's fault.

4. ***Problems.*** Would each defendant in the following scenarios appear to have a viable contributory negligence defense?

   A. While driving on the interstate at 9:00 a.m., Plaintiff is driving faster than the posted speed limit for the sheer joy of driving fast. Seeing a police car by the side of the road, Plaintiff slows down. A few minutes later, at 9:05 a.m., Defendant swerves into Plaintiff's lane of traffic and causes a collision.

B. The same Plaintiff from the above problem is distracted when she receives a text message on her phone. She takes her eyes off the road to read the text message. At that moment, Defendant swerves into Plaintiff's lane of traffic and sideswipes Plaintiff's car.

C. Despite having an important business meeting at 8:00 a.m., Plaintiff carelessly forgets to set his alarm clock the night before and oversleeps. He misses his meeting and is driving to work at 8:30 a.m. when he drives his car into a controlled intersection with a green light. Defendant has a red light but ignores it and drives into the same intersection at the same moment as Plaintiff and broadsides Plaintiff's car. Had Plaintiff awoken on time, he would not have been in that intersection at the same moment that Defendant ran the red light.

B. The Comparative Fault Reform

The phrase "tort reform" commonly brings to mind the current movement's predominant form — efforts to curtail the ability of plaintiffs to bring tort claims and to recover for all of their harm. A few decades ago, tort reform was just as likely to embody opposite goals. Courts and legislatures alike began to express discomfort with the harshness of contributory negligence and to wonder whether that *all or nothing* doctrine truly epitomized the tort principles of compensation, deterrence, and punishment, with the defense's single-minded focus on denying all rewards to negligent plaintiffs. The tide has now turned with most, but not all, jurisdictions abandoning contributory negligence for one of the three different variations of a *comparative fault* system. The following case explores this twentieth century variety of pro-plaintiff tort reform.

1. The Decision to Switch to Comparative Fault

McINTYRE v. BALENTINE

833 S.W.2d 52 (Tenn. 1992)

Drowota, J.

In this personal injury action, we granted Plaintiff's application for permission to appeal in order to decide whether to adopt a system of comparative fault in Tennessee. We now replace the common law defense of contributory negligence with a system of comparative fault.

In the early morning darkness of November 2, 1986, Plaintiff-Harry Douglas McIntyre and Defendant-Clifford Balentine were involved in a motor vehicle accident resulting in severe injuries to Plaintiff. The accident occurred in the vicinity of Smith's Truck Stop in Savannah, Tennessee. As Defendant-Balentine was traveling south on Highway 69, Plaintiff entered the highway (also traveling south) from the truck stop parking lot. Shortly after Plaintiff entered the highway, his pickup truck was struck by Defendant's Peterbilt tractor. At trial, the parties disputed the exact chronology of events immediately preceding the accident.

Both men had consumed alcohol the evening of the accident. After the accident, Plaintiff's blood alcohol level was measured at .17 percent by weight. Testimony suggested that Defendant was traveling in excess of the posted speed limit.

Plaintiff brought a negligence action against Defendant-Balentine and Defendant-East-West Motor Freight, Inc. Defendants answered that Plaintiff was contributorily negligent, in part due to operating his vehicle while intoxicated. After trial, the jury returned a verdict stating: "We, the jury, find the plaintiff and the defendant equally at fault in this accident; therefore, we rule in favor of the defendant."

After judgment was entered for Defendants, Plaintiff brought an appeal alleging the trial court erred by refusing to instruct the jury regarding the doctrine of comparative negligence. The Court of Appeals affirmed holding that comparative negligence is not the law in Tennessee.

The common law contributory negligence doctrine has traditionally been traced to Lord Ellenborough's opinion in *Butterfield v. Forrester*, 11 East 60, 103 Eng. Rep. 926 (1809). There, plaintiff, "riding as fast as his horse would go," was injured after running into an obstruction defendant had placed in the road. Stating as the rule that "one person being in fault will not dispense with another's using ordinary care," plaintiff was denied recovery on the basis that he did not use ordinary care to avoid the obstruction.

The contributory negligence bar was soon brought to America as part of the common law, *see Smith v. Smith*, 19 Mass. 621, 624 (1824), and proceeded to spread throughout the states. *See* H.W. Woods, The Negligence Case: Comparative Fault §1:4 (1978). This strict bar may have been a direct outgrowth of the common law system of issue pleading; issue pleading posed questions to be answered "yes" or "no," leaving common law courts, the theory goes, no choice but to award all or nothing. *See* J.W. Wade, W.K. Crawford, Jr., and J.L. Ryder, *Comparative Fault in Tennessee Tort Actions: Past, Present and Future*, 41 Tenn. L. Rev. 423, 424-25 (1974). A number of other rationalizations have been advanced in the attempt to justify the harshness of the "all-or-nothing" bar. Among these: the plaintiff should be penalized for his misconduct; the plaintiff should be deterred from injuring himself; and the plaintiff's negligence supersedes the defendant's so as to render defendant's negligence no longer proximate. *See* W. Keeton, *Prosser and Keeton on the Law of Torts*, §65, at 452 (5th ed. 1984); J.W. Wade, *supra*, at 424.

In Tennessee, the rule as initially stated was that "if a party, by his own gross negligence, brings an injury upon himself, or contributes to such injury, he cannot recover;" for, in such cases, the party "must be regarded as the author of his own misfortune." *Whirley v. Whiteman*, 38 Tenn. 610, 619 (1858). In subsequent decisions, we have continued to follow the general rule that a plaintiff's contributory negligence completely bars recovery. *See, e.g., Hudson v. Gaitan*, 675 S.W.2d 699, 704 (Tenn. 1984).

Equally entrenched in Tennessee jurisprudence are exceptions to the general all-or-nothing rule: contributory negligence does not absolutely bar recovery where defendant's conduct was intentional, *see, e.g., Stagner v. Craig*, 19 S.W.2d 234, 234-35 (1929); where defendant's conduct was "grossly" negligent, *see, e.g., Ellithorpe v. Ford Motor Co.*, 503 S.W.2d 516, 522 (Tenn. 1973); where defendant had the "last clear chance" with which, through the exercise of ordinary care, to avoid plaintiff's injury, *see, e.g., Roseberry v. Lippner*, 574 S.W.2d 726, 728 (Tenn. 1978); or where plaintiff's negligence may be classified as "remote." *See, e.g., Arnold v. Hayslett*, 655 S.W.2d 941, 945 (Tenn. 1983).

In contrast, comparative fault has long been the federal rule in cases involving injured employees of interstate railroad carriers, *see* Federal Employers' Liability Act, ch. 149, §3, 35 Stat. 66 (1908) (codified at 45 U.S.C. §53 (1988)), and injured seamen. *See Death on the High Seas Act*, ch. 111, §6, 41 Stat. 537 (1920) (codified at 46 U.S.C. §766 (1988)); Jones Act, ch. 250, §33, 41 Stat. 1007 (1920) (codified as amended at 46 U.S.C. §688 (1988)).

Between 1920 and 1969, a few states began utilizing the principles of comparative fault in all tort litigation. *See* C. Mutter, *Moving to Comparative Negligence in an Era of Tort Reform: Decisions for Tennessee*, 57 Tenn. L. Rev. 199, 227 n.127 (1990). Then, between 1969 and 1984, comparative fault replaced contributory negligence in 37 additional states. In 1991, South Carolina became the 45th state to adopt comparative fault, *see Nelson v. Concrete Supply Co.*, 303 S.C. 243, 399 S.E.2d 783 (1991), leaving Alabama, Maryland, North Carolina, Virginia, and Tennessee as the only remaining common law contributory negligence jurisdictions.

Eleven states have judicially adopted comparative fault.[1] Thirty-four states have legislatively adopted comparative fault.[2]

We recognize that this action could be taken by our General Assembly. However, legislative inaction has never prevented judicial abolition of obsolete common law doctrines, especially those, such as contributory negligence,

---

1. In the order of their adoption, these states are Florida, California, Alaska, Michigan, West Virginia, New Mexico, Illinois, Iowa, Missouri, Kentucky, and South Carolina. Nine courts adopted pure comparative fault. In two of these states, legislatures subsequently enacted a modified form. Two courts adopted a modified form of comparative fault. *See Bradley v. Appalachian Power Co.*, 163 W. Va. 332, 256 S.E.2d 879 (1979) (plaintiff may recover if his negligence is less than defendants'); *Nelson v. Concrete Supply Co.*, 303 S.C. 243, 399 S.E.2d 783 (1991) (plaintiff may recover if his negligence is not greater than defendants').

2. Six states have legislatively adopted pure comparative fault: Mississippi, Rhode Island, Washington, New York, Louisiana, and Arizona; eight legislatures have enacted the modified "49 percent" rule (plaintiff may recover if plaintiff's negligence *is less than* defendant's): Georgia, Arkansas, Maine, Colorado, Idaho, North Dakota, Utah, and Kansas; eighteen legislatures have enacted the modified "50 percent" rule (plaintiff may recover so long as plaintiff's negligence *is not greater than* defendant's): Wisconsin, Hawaii, Massachusetts, Minnesota, New Hampshire, Vermont, Oregon, Connecticut, Nevada, New Jersey, Oklahoma, Texas, Wyoming, Montana, Pennsylvania, Ohio, Indiana, and Delaware; two legislatures have enacted statutes that allow a plaintiff to recover if plaintiff's negligence is slight when compared to defendant's gross negligence: Nebraska and South Dakota.

conceived in the judicial womb. *See Hanover v. Ruch*, 809 S.W.2d 893, 896 (Tenn. 1991) (citing cases). Indeed, our abstinence would sanction "a mutual state of inaction in which the court awaits action by the legislature and the legislature awaits guidance from the court," *Alvis v. Ribar*, 421 N.E.2d 886, 896 (Ill. 1981), thereby prejudicing the equitable resolution of legal conflicts.

Nor do we today abandon our commitment to *stare decisis.* While "confidence in our courts is to a great extent dependent on the uniformity and consistency engendered by allegiance to *stare decisis*, . . . mindless obedience to this precept can confound the truth and foster an attitude of contempt." *Hanover*, 809 S.W.2d at 898.

Two basic forms of comparative fault are utilized by 45 of our sister jurisdictions, these variants being commonly referred to as either "pure" or "modified." In the "pure" form, a plaintiff's damages are reduced in proportion to the percentage negligence attributed to him; for example, a plaintiff responsible for 90 percent of the negligence that caused his injuries nevertheless may recover 10 percent of his damages. In the "modified" form, plaintiffs recover as in pure jurisdictions, but only if the plaintiff's negligence either (1) does not exceed ("50 percent" jurisdictions) or (2) is less than ("49 percent" jurisdictions) the defendant's negligence.

In Practice

In many tort cases (e.g., car accidents) where the plaintiff also appears to be at fault and defendant has also been harmed, a defendant can assert this both as an affirmative defense as well as the basis for a counterclaim for the defendant's own damages.

Although we conclude that the all-or-nothing rule of contributory negligence must be replaced, we nevertheless decline to abandon totally our fault-based tort system. We do not agree that a party should necessarily be able to recover in tort even though he may be 80, 90, or 95 percent at fault. We therefore reject the pure form of comparative fault.

We recognize that modified comparative fault systems have been criticized as merely shifting the arbitrary contributory negligence bar to a new ground. *See, e.g., Li v. Yellow Cab Co.*, 532 P.2d 1226 (Cal. 1975). However, we feel the "49 percent rule" ameliorates the harshness of the common law rule while remaining compatible with a fault-based tort system. We therefore hold that so long as a plaintiff's negligence remains less than the defendant's negligence the plaintiff may recover; in such a case, plaintiff's damages are to be reduced in proportion to the percentage of the total negligence attributable to the plaintiff.

In all trials where the issue of comparative fault is before a jury, the trial court shall instruct the jury on the effect of the jury's finding as to the percentage of negligence as between the plaintiff or plaintiffs and the defendant or defendants. The attorneys for each party shall be allowed to argue how this instruction affects a plaintiff's ability to recover.

Turning to the case at bar, the jury found that "the plaintiff and defendant [were] equally at fault." Because the jury, without the benefit of proper instructions by the trial court, made a gratuitous apportionment of fault, we find that their "equal" apportionment is not sufficiently trustworthy to form the basis of a final determination between these parties. Therefore, the case is remanded for a new trial in accordance with the dictates of this opinion.

We recognize that today's decision affects numerous legal principles surrounding tort litigation. For the most part, harmonizing these principles with comparative fault must await another day.

NOTES AND PROBLEMS

1. ***Principled Reform.*** The *Balentine* decision does a good job of summarizing the transformation of the vast majority of jurisdictions to some form of comparative fault. The court refers to four primary reasons behind the old contributory negligence rule: (1) that courts used to deal exclusively in black and white, "yes or no" jury verdicts; (2) that negligent plaintiffs must be punished; (3) that plaintiffs must be deterred from misconduct; and (4) that the plaintiff's negligence supersedes a defendant's prior act of negligence and, as a matter of law, negates proximate causation. Other changes in tort law have shown that both courts and juries can thrive in systems that permit something other than yes and no answers. In Chapter 9, Apportionment, for example, we will explore a related change from joint and several liability to several liability that similarly invites more nuanced jury findings in determining the tortfeasors' fault. And while it is true that a plaintiff's negligent conduct that contributes to their harm cannot be ignored (or else principles of punishment and deterrence are rendered impotent), lawmakers have recognized that the problem with contributory negligence is that it completely ignores the fault of the defendant and provides a windfall to that bad actor. Finally, as you should appreciate from the facts in *Balentine*, it is often simply incorrect to label the plaintiff's misconduct as "superseding" because the conduct might be quite foreseeable — as was the plaintiff's careless horse riding in *Butterfield* and the plaintiff's failure to take appropriate corrective actions in *Meadows*. Do you also see how relying upon proximate cause doctrines to account for a plaintiff's negligence is just another "all or nothing" approach?

2. ***Other Mitigation Doctrines Under Contributory Negligence.*** Under contributory negligence, many jurisdictions sometimes felt discomfort with eliminating all recovery by the plaintiff in certain situations despite the plaintiff's negligence. One of these mentioned in *Balentine* was the doctrine of *last clear chance*; this doctrine declared that even if a plaintiff's own fault placed the plaintiff in a situation of peril, this could be ignored if the defendant had a chance to avoid causing the accident and failed to do so through its own misconduct. The *last clear chance* doctrine applied when the defendant had seen the plaintiff and failed to avoid inflicting the injury, despite having a good opportunity to do so at a point when the plaintiff had no such chance. In

Principles

One scholar observed that most *courts* adopting comparative fault have chosen the "pure" system over a "modified" system because only pure comparative fault directly and completely ties the consequences of one's negligence to the jury's allocation of responsibility for the harm. By contrast, legislatures have tended to choose a modified form as a compromise between the perceived extremes of contributory negligence and pure comparative fault. For a good discussion of the reform movement away from the traditional system of contributory negligence, see Arthur Best, *Impediments to Reasonable Tort Reform: Lessons from the Adoption of Comparative Negligence*, 40 Ind. L. Rev. 1 (2007).

addition to this plaintiff friendly doctrine, many jurisdictions also refused to recognize the defense of contributory negligence when the defendant's misconduct rose to the level of either gross negligence or an intentional tort. These devices are no longer seen as necessary under modern comparative fault systems because of their rejection of the harsh all or nothing consequences. Instead, the jury considers all of these circumstances in apportioning fault among the parties.

3. ***Problems. Different Types of Comparative Fault Statutes.*** The following are examples of statutes from states that have moved away from contributory negligence by legislative action. Which system of comparative fault is adopted by each of the following statutes? Imagine a case where the plaintiff has suffered $100,000 in harm. With respect to the jury's allocation of fault set forth in the table below, what result is reached in each of these three states? What result in a contributory negligence state? Practice by filling out the table.

A. **New York.** In any action to recover damages for personal injury, injury to property, or wrongful death, the culpable conduct attributable to the claimant or to the decedent, including contributory negligence or assumption of the risk, shall not bar recovery, but the amount of damages otherwise recoverable shall be diminished in the proportion which the culpable conduct attributable to the claimant or decedent bears to the culpable conduct which caused the damages. (New York's McKinney's Civ. Prac. Law §1411 (1976))

B. **Colorado.** Contributory negligence shall not bar recovery in any action by any person or his legal representative to recover damages for negligence resulting in death or in injury to person or property, if such negligence was not as great as the negligence of the person against whom recovery is sought, but any damages allowed shall be diminished in proportion to the amount of negligence attributable to the person for whose injury, damage, or death recovery is made. (Colo. Rev. Stat. §13-21-111 (2009))

C. **Wisconsin.** Contributory negligence does not bar recovery in an action by any person or the person's legal representative to recover damages for negligence resulting in death or in injury to person or property, if that negligence was not greater than the negligence of the person against whom recovery is sought, but any damages allowed shall be diminished in the proportion to the amount of negligence attributed to the person recovering. (Wisconsin Stat. Ann. §895.045 (1983))

Plaintiff's Fault	Defendant's Fault	Pure CF	50% CF	49% CF	Contrib. Negligence
99%	1%				
51%	49%				
50%	50%				
49%	51%				
1%	99%				

2. *The Apportionment Problem*

In states that have rejected the all or nothing approach of contributory negligence and adopted a form of comparative fault, the issue becomes *how exactly is the jury supposed to decide the percentages of fault or responsibility*? Is it a function of comparing the reprehensibility of each party's misconduct; or should the jury be apportioning the causal role that each party's conduct played in bringing about the plaintiff's injury? In other words, is the jury comparing how negligent each of the parties was, or is the jury deciding which party's negligence played a greater causal role in bringing about the accident? This problem has been exacerbated by the law's development of a strict liability theory of recovery in defective products cases — a so-called "liability without fault." (We will be exploring strict liability and products liability in Chapters 10 and 11.) Because most states adopting products liability recognize comparative negligence as an affirmative defense in such cases, how can the jury apportion "fault" between the parties or compare the relative fault between the parties and the defective product? The following case illustrates a mainstream approach to the problem of how juries should play the blame game.

SANDFORD v. CHEVROLET

642 P.2d 624 (Or. 1982)

LINDA, J.

Plaintiff suffered extensive burns when a pickup truck that she was driving overturned and caught fire. She brought an action for damages against a number of defendants in which she alleged, among other things, that the accident was caused by a defective tire manufactured by defendant Uniroyal, Inc., and mounted on the truck by The Tire Factory. The defendants filed answers alleging that plaintiff's own negligence caused her injuries. The jury found defendants Uniroyal, Inc. and The Tire Factory at fault to the extent of 55 percent and plaintiff to the extent of 45 percent and awarded plaintiff a corresponding fraction of her total damages.

The Court of Appeals reversed. We allowed review in this case . . . primarily to decide whether and how the proportionate fault law applies when a dangerously defective product and a plaintiff's negligence together resulted in the plaintiff's injuries.

[The Court first held that a plaintiff's ordinary negligence could be considered as an affirmative defense even in a case brought on the basis of strict products liability rather than negligent conduct by the defendants.]

Another problem posed by the [comparative fault] statute is the question exactly what is to be assessed in determining the "percentage of fault attributable to the person" seeking recovery, and whether that person's fault was "greater than the combined fault of the person or persons against whom recovery is sought." The question has puzzled commentators as well as courts. At least three views are possible.

A. QUANTIFYING "FAULT"

The first is that the formula calls upon the factfinder to assess the relative magnitude of the parties' respective "fault." As stated by a leading textbook on these laws: "The process is *not* allocation of physical causation, which could be scientifically apportioned, but rather of allocating *fault*, which cannot be scientifically measured." Schwartz, *Comparative Negligence* 276 (1974). It has been recognized that fault is an evaluation that does not lend itself to quantification, so that a comparison of fault magnifies the subjective elements already intrinsic to the ordinary judgment of negligence. This is true even in assigning proportions to two or more distinct types of negligence, but critics have found a greater theoretical obstacle when the responsibility of one party is grounded in fault other than negligence, or in no fault at all. The obstacle is greater where strict products liability is explained as a device for spreading losses from economic activity regardless of fault. . . . Whether the "fault" in products liability inheres in the defective product or in the act of placing it on the market, however, difficulties of comparison with the injured party's fault undeniably remain.

B. "COMPARATIVE CAUSATION"

Some courts, applying comparative negligence law to products liability under statutes different from ours or under no statute, have tried to escape the difficulty by stating that the allocation of damages is to reflect relative causation, that is to say, an assessment of the proportion in which the plaintiff's injuries were caused by the product defect on the one hand and by plaintiff's own negligence on the other. *See, e.g., Murray v. Fairbanks Morse*, 610 F.2d 149 (3d Cir. 1979) (applying Virgin Island comparative negligence statute); *Pan-Alaska Fisheries, Inc. v. Marine Const. & Design Co.*, 565 F.2d 1129 (9th Cir. 1977) (admiralty law). They have done so in the belief that this is conceptually more logical or pragmatically easier than to compare the defect of a product with the negligence of one whom it has injured. In *Murray v. Fairbanks Morse*, for instance, Judge Rosenn wrote for the Third Circuit:

> The key conceptual distinction between strict products liability theory and negligence is that the plaintiff need not prove faulty *conduct* on the part of the defendant in order to recover. The jury is not asked to determine if the defendant deviated from a standard of care in producing his product. There is no proven faulty conduct of the defendant to compare with the faulty conduct of the plaintiff in order to apportion the responsibility for an accident. Although we may term a defective product "faulty," it is qualitatively different from the plaintiff's conduct that contributes to his injury. A comparison of the two is therefore inappropriate.
>
> We believe that if the loss for a particular injury is to be apportioned between the product defect and the plaintiff's misconduct, the only conceptual basis for comparison is the causative contribution of each to the particular loss or injury. In apportioning damages we are really asking how much of the injury was caused by the defect in the product versus how much was caused by the plaintiff's own actions.

610 F.2d at 159. With due respect to these courts, however, we are not persuaded that the concept of "comparative causation" is more cogent or meaningful than comparative fault, if by "causation" is meant some relation of cause and effect in the physical world rather than the very attribution of responsibility for which "causation" is to serve as the premise.

Both the defect and the plaintiff's fault must in fact be causes of one injury before a question of apportionment of fault arises. Although defendants in this case had completed all acts necessary for liability when they manufactured and mounted a dangerously defective tire that might blow out and overturn the Sandford pickup, they obviously would not be liable if the pickup overturned for some unrelated reason. Similarly, it would not matter that a driver operated his car unlawfully or recklessly if he was injured by an explosion due to an electrical defect that would have occurred with the same harmful consequences if the car had been standing still. In less obvious situations where the physical course of events is in doubt, if either party convinces the factfinder that its misconduct in fact was not a cause of the injury, there is no occasion for allocating partial damages.

The concept of apportioning causation must be tested on the assumption that both causes had to join to produce the injury for which damages are to be allocated. Once it is assumed, however, that two or more distinct causes had to occur to produce an indivisible injury, we doubt that the purpose of the proportional fault concept is to subject the combined causation to some kind of vector analysis, even in the rare case of simultaneous, physically commensurable forces. In most cases, it would be a vain exercise.

C. MIXING "FAULT" WITH "PROXIMATE" CAUSATION

A third view considers it futile to attempt to explain what is to be compared, because it is equally illogical to compare strict liability with negligence and to quantify the relative causative effect of either when it would have caused no harm in the absence of the other. Thus Dean Twerski, in the cited article, describes the technical problems of making the comparison as a "red herring": "The short answer to the dilemma of how one can compare strict liability and negligence is that one must simply close one's eyes and accomplish the task." 10 Ind. L. Rev. 796, 806-808. The opinion in *Pan-Alaska, supra*, similarly questions the significance of theoretical distinctions when it states:

> In any event, whether we use the term comparative fault, contributory negligence, comparative causation, or even comparative blameworthiness, we are merely beating around the semantical bush seeking to achieve an equitable method of allocating the responsibility for an injury or loss.

565 F.2d at 1139. In part this second view rests on the assumption that rational analysis in tort cases dissolves in the collegial judgment of juries. That is probably an unwarranted generalization; ability and effort to decide in accordance with law can be expected to differ from one jury to the next with such variables as the makeup of the particular jury, with the quality of evidence and advocacy, and not least with the rationality of the legal formulations in which the court explains the jury's task to it.

In any event, the assumption does not let us escape the need to state coherent rules of liability. Some tort cases are tried to the court without a jury, as *Pan-Alaska, supra*, illustrates. Trial judges must know on what findings an apportionment of damages depends, whether these are to be made by the judge or by a jury. Our system of appeal as well as trial predicates that jurors will conscientiously attempt to apply the law if it is explained in comprehensible terms. A juror who wants to know how to treat cause and how to treat fault is entitled to an answer, whatever comes of it in a collective decision. Counsel need to know whether to address the relative gravity of the parties' fault or to seek expert testimony on the relative impact of their respective fault in causing the asserted harm. We cannot dismiss the question as a distinction without a difference.

The National Conference of Commissioners on Uniform State Laws attempted to overcome the distinction, or perhaps split the difference, in a proposed Uniform Comparative Fault Act, by calling on the factfinder, in determining the percentages of fault, to "consider both the nature of the conduct of each party at fault and the extent of the causal relation between the conduct and the damages claimed." *See* Wade, *Products Liability and Plaintiff's Fault—The Uniform Comparative Fault Act,* 29 Mercer L Rev 373 (1978). This might add the difficulties of comparing causation to those of comparing fault if causation in fact were meant, especially since the act also calls for special findings. But the comments indicate that "the extent of the causal relation" does not mean causation in fact but what has traditionally been labeled "proximate cause." In *Murray v. Fairbanks Morse, supra,* also, "proximate" causation rather than factual causation turns out to be what the court means by "comparative causation."

Proportionate fault under ORS 18.470. ORS 18.470, *supra,* by its terms applies whenever "the fault attributable to the person seeking recovery was not greater than the combined fault of the person or persons against whom recovery is sought." If there was such fault, "any damages allowed shall be diminished in the proportion to the percentage of fault attributable to the person recovering." There is no reference to causation, or to any question how much the fault of each contributed to the injury. Indeed, the reference to negligence "contributing to the injury" in former ORS 18.470 was removed in the 1975 amendment. We do not mean that the allegedly faulty conduct or condition need not have affected the event for which recovery is sought; as we have said, it must have been a cause in fact. But the statute does not call for apportioning damages by quantifying the contribution of several causes that had to coincide to produce the injury.

Rather, ORS 18.470 falls within the first of the different approaches that we have reviewed. It calls upon the factfinder to assess and quantify fault. If the plaintiff's conduct is not faultless, the assessment has two purposes: To determine whether her fault is "not greater than" that of defendants, and if it is not, then to reduce the plaintiff's recovery of damages "in the proportion to the percentage of fault attributable to" the plaintiff.

[I]f the plaintiff's behavior which was one cause of the injury is alleged to have been negligent or otherwise "fault," it is to be measured against behavior that would have been faultless under the circumstances. The factfinder is to determine the degree to which the plaintiff's behavior fell short of that norm and express this deficit as a numerical percentage, which then is applied to diminish the recoverable damages. There necessarily must be some comparable assessment of the fault attributable to defendants as a departure from the norm invoked against them (which, in products liability, will involve the magnitude of the defect rather than negligence or moral "blameworthiness") in order to determine which is greater. In this comparison, the benchmark for assessing a defendant's fault for marketing a product which is dangerously defective in design, manufacture, or warning is what the product should have been without the defect. The benchmark for the injured claimant's fault is conduct which would not be unlawful or careless in any relevant respect. This corresponds to views expressed by the Supreme Judicial Court of Maine:

> [A]pportionment is on the basis of fault or blame. This involves a comparison of the culpability of the parties, meaning by culpability not moral blame but the degree of departure from the standard of a reasonable man. [C]omparison is invited between degrees of fault which may range from trivial inadvertence to the grossest recklessness. In judging the conduct of an actor it should be considered complete carefulness is at one end, a deliberate intention to bring about the result is at the other. Negligence ranges from the least blameworthy type, namely, inadvertence and negligent errors of judgment up to a state where knowledge or more complete knowledge supervenes and the negligence of obstinacy, self-righteousness or reckless is reached. The factfinder must be told then under our statute, it should give consideration to the relative blameworthiness of the causative fault of the claimant and of the defendant."

Wing v. Morse, 300 A.2d 491, 500 (Me. 1973).

Accordingly, after determining whether and how far each party's conduct was at fault, measured against the norm governing that party's conduct, these respective degrees of fault are to be converted into a percentage which will be applied to the plaintiff's total damages to determine his actual recovery.

To summarize: When an injured claimant's misconduct is a cause in fact of the injury, it can defeat a products liability claim if the claimant's fault is "greater than" the defendants' combined fault involved in marketing the defective product. If it is not greater, plaintiff's fault proportionately reduces her recoverable damages.

NOTES AND PROBLEMS

1. *The Choice of Apportionment Theories.* Although the *Sandford* court acknowledges that the precise formula for apportioning responsibility may not matter to a real jury, it reaffirms that this is more than a question of semantics. In bench trials, the judge needs to know what it is she is apportioning, and appellate courts, in reviewing the sufficiency of evidence, need to know what it is they are looking for in the evidence. And juries, attempting their best to listen to the court's instructions and the arguments of counsel, need to have some basis upon which to act. In short, the issue matters in the real world where juries are frequently asked to apportion between the claimant and the defendant. The *Sandford* court embraces the idea of comparing the blameworthiness of the parties (or product), in part, because comparing the causal role makes no sense when actual "but for" cause demands that the parties' conduct (or product) played an essential role in order to create liability in the first instance.

2. *Third Restatement View.* Section 8 of the Restatement (Third) of Torts (2000) appears to advocate for option three, mixing the concepts of fault and comparative *proximate* causation:

> **Factors for Assigning Shares of Responsibility**
>
> Factors for assigning percentages of responsibility to each person whose legal responsibility has been established include:
>
> (a) the nature of the person's risk-creating conduct, including any awareness or indifference with respect to the risks created by the conduct and any intent with respect to the harm created by the conduct; and
> (b) the strength of the causal connection between the person's risk-creating conduct and the harm.

3. *Problems.* Utilizing the foregoing view from the Third Restatement on apportioning fault, where both fault and relative proximate cause are considered, how would you argue the apportionment question to the jury as an advocate for both the plaintiff and the defendant in the following scenarios?

A. The custodian at a law school was tired one evening and failed to clean up a puddle of coffee that had spilled on the tile floor in the hallway. Plaintiff, a law student, is rushing to get to her torts class the next morning and is literally running around the corner of the hallway when her foot hits the puddle. She slips and falls, breaking her wrist. Plaintiff sues the school on a premises liability claim. The school contends she fell so violently only because she was running around a blind corner.

B. Defendant supplies barrels of flammable chemicals to Plaintiff corporation. Defendant failed to inspect the barrels on a recent shipment and, therefore, did not notice one of the barrels was leaking dangerous vapors into the air. After its delivery, one of Plaintiff's employees decided (against company policy) to light a cigarette in the chemical storage room where the barrels were kept. The vapors exploded, causing massive property damage to Plaintiff's building and inventory.

3. *Multiple Tortfeasors in Modified Comparative Fault*

The other apportionment-related issue arises in modified comparative fault jurisdictions — those of either the 49 percent or 50 percent varieties. The statutes are quite clear that the plaintiff's fault must be compared to that of the person against whom judgment is sought in order to determine if it is *no greater than* (50 percent rule) or *less than* (49 percent rule) the defendant's fault. But how does this comparison work in a case with *multiple tortfeasor defendants*? Should the comparison be made multiple times, between the plaintiff and each single defendant? Or should the fault of the defendants be lumped together and then, as a unit, compared with that of the plaintiff? That issue is dealt with head on in the following case.

BEAUDOIN v. TEXACO, INC.

653 F. Supp. 512 (D.N.D. 1987)

VAN SICKLE, J.

A collision of legal principles renders a truly equitable result in this case impossible. The difficult decision confronting this court is which inequitable result is most proper.

Mark Beaudoin, the plaintiff, was an employee of Wood Wireline. Texaco, Inc., the defendant, hired Wireline to conduct a pressure gradient check on Texaco's well, CM Loomer #13 near Keene, North Dakota.

Beaudoin and a co-worker arrived on the unlighted site before dawn on February 21, 1983, to prepare their equipment for the job. Beaudoin was uncoiling wire from a large spool mounted on the wireline rig when he was struck in the left eye by the end of the wire. He is now legally blind in that eye.

Texaco's employee John Spain arrived after the incident occurred to supervise the work being done on the site.

On March 29, 1985, Beaudoin brought an action for damages against Texaco. Beaudoin alleged that the injury was the result of Texaco's negligence in requiring the work to commence at an hour that would require the equipment to be set up in darkness, in failing to provide proper lighting, and in failing to properly supervise the work. Texaco alleged that the injury was the result of Beaudoin's negligence in handling the wire carelessly. Both parties denied the negligence alleged against them. Testimony was presented at trial that could have led to the conclusion that Wood Wireline was negligent in failing to provide proper equipment and training for its employees. Wood Wireline is immune from liability under the provisions of North Dakota's worker's compensation law, NDCC §65-04-28, and is not a defendant in the action.

The jury found damages of $44,057.04, and apportioned the negligence causing the injury as follows: 60% to Wood Wireline, 30% to Beaudoin, and 10% to Texaco. This court must now determine what judgment results from this verdict.

That determination depends on the proper interpretation and application of North Dakota's comparative negligence statute.

> Contributory negligence shall not bar recovery in an action by any person or his legal representative to recover damages for negligence resulting in death or in injury to person or property, if such negligence was not as great as the negligence of the person against whom recovery is sought, but any damages allowed shall be diminished in proportion to the amount of negligence attributable to the person

> recovering. . . . Upon the request of any party, this section shall be read by the court to the jury and the attorneys representing the parties may comment to the jury regarding this section.

NDCC §9-10-07.

The narrow question before this court is whether in cases involving a negligent plaintiff and more than one other negligent actor this statute allows recovery only against those defendants more negligent than the plaintiff or against all negligent defendants so long as the plaintiff's negligence is less than the combined negligence of the other negligent actors. The North Dakota Supreme Court has not ruled on this issue, and the other jurisdictions are divided.

This court must first determine how a federal district court sitting with diversity jurisdiction should properly approach resolving a legal issue not yet settled by the highest court of the law-determining state.

This court will not presume to divine the thinking or inclinations of the justices of the North Dakota Supreme Court, but will attempt to examine and weigh the persuasive authority as that court would if this issue were before it. Those sources include the case law of sister states, the case law of the other states, the majority rule and modern trend if there are such, and principles of justice and equity. It is the opinion of this court that there is no conflict between the goal of seeking the best legal conclusion and the goal of seeking the conclusion that the North Dakota Supreme Court would reach.

As the states have abandoned the harsh and outdated rule of contributory negligence they have replaced it with one of two general types of comparative negligence. A number of jurisdictions have adopted "pure" comparative negligence. Under this rule, every party is liable for its own share of the negligence. If, for example, a plaintiff bears 60% of the responsibility for the injuries he has suffered, he will bear 60% of the cost, while the negligent defendant whose responsibility is 40% will be liable for 40% of the cost. Other jurisdictions, including North Dakota, have opted for a system of "modified" comparative negligence. These systems vary in detail, but all prohibit a plaintiff who is assigned more than 50% of the causal negligence from recovering any damages. Following this approach the 40% negligent defendant in the example above would be completely free from any liability. Whatever the merits of the policy reasons for the adoption of modified comparative negligence, such systems lead to a number of unavoidable complications, one of which confronts this court today.

Modified comparative negligence jurisdictions follow one of two rules for determining the damage award in cases with multiple tortfeasors at least one of which is less negligent than the plaintiff: the "Wisconsin rule" and the "unit rule." Under the Wisconsin rule the plaintiff's share of the negligence is compared in turn with the negligence apportioned to each individual defendant. Any defendant whose percentage of the negligence is lower than, or, in North Dakota, equal to, the plaintiff's, is dismissed from the case. Under the unit rule the plaintiff's share of the negligence is compared to the sum of the shares of negligence apportioned to the other negligent actors. If the plaintiff's share is less than that sum, then the plaintiff can recover from each of the defendants. This court must determine which of these rules should, from the perspective of the North Dakota Supreme Court, be applied in this case.

Minnesota follows, and Wisconsin initiated, the Wisconsin rule. *Marier v. Memorial Rescue Service, Inc.*, 296 Minn. 242, 207 N.W.2d 706, 707, 708 (1973), *Walker v. Kroger Grocery & Baking Co.*, 214 Wis. 519, 252 N.W. 721, 727, 728 (1934). Absent any countervailing considerations, that rule should be applied in this case. There are, however, a number of countervailing considerations.

The Wisconsin rule is the minority rule. This court has discovered fourteen states that follow the unit rule, but only six that follow the Wisconsin rule.

The unit rule is the modern trend. Of the six Wisconsin rule states, four adopted the rule ten or more years ago. Seven states have had to choose between the alternative rules in the last five years, and all seven have chosen the unit rule.

It is evident that the weight of authority is heavily in favor of the unit rule. Furthermore, even the states that have adopted the Wisconsin rule do not appear to strongly support it. None of the six opinions in which state high courts chose the Wisconsin rule was based on arguments supporting the rule on its merits. As the Utah Supreme Court observed, "almost without variation, those states that have adopted the Wisconsin rule have done so on the rather wooden analysis that the Legislature must have intended to adopt the court decisions construing the Wisconsin statute as a part of that state's law." 679 P.2d at 909. This approach, based only on a canon of statutory construction, has been thoroughly repudiated. *See, e.g.*, 642 P.2d at 632, 679 P.2d at 905, 624 P.2d at 388-394 (Bistline, J., dissenting). Suffice to say that, as discussed above, the North Dakota Supreme Court gives serious consideration to the judicial gloss of the source state of a statute, but does not abdicate its judicial and intellectual responsibilities in doing so. Following the supreme court's approach, the fact that North Dakota derived §9-10-07 from Wisconsin by way of Minnesota creates a presumption in favor of Wisconsin case law, but it does not settle the question without further inquiry.

The other argument generally relied on by courts adopting the Wisconsin rule is that their comparative negligence statute is phrased in terms of a single defendant, as is North Dakota's: "if such negligence was not as great as the negligence of the person against whom recovery is sought. . . ." NDCC §9-10-07. The Code contains a provision aimed at preventing this kind of misplaced reliance. "Words used in the singular number include the plural and words used in the plural number include the singular, except when a contrary intention plainly appears." NDCC §1-01-35. The intention appearing from the text of §9-10-07 is, of course, not plain. It is not clear whether the legislature intended to excuse all defendants whose negligence is less than the plaintiff's or to limit recovery only to those plaintiffs who bear less than half the fault for their own injuries. In the absence of a plain meaning of §9-10-07's text, §1-01-35 becomes operative, and the term "person" in §9-10-07 must be taken to include both the singular and the plural. This statutorily mandated rule of construction requires the adoption of the unit rule, as it aggregates the negligence of the other parties at fault for comparison with the negligence of the plaintiff.

Perhaps the most telling strike against the Wisconsin rule is that it is no longer supported by the Wisconsin Supreme Court.

> This case is one of many cases which have come before this court involving multiple party tortfeasors. . . . The majority of the court has become convinced that comparing the negligence of the individual plaintiff to that of each individual tortfeasor — rather than comparing the negligence of the individual plaintiff to that of the combined negligence of the several tortfeasors who have collectively contributed to plaintiff's injuries — leads to harsh and unfair results. . . .

May v. Skelley Oil Co., 83 Wis. 2d 30, 264 N.W.2d 574, 578 (1978). It appears that at present the Wisconsin Supreme Court adheres to the rule because it considers itself bound by its prior holdings and the state legislature's failure to counteract them. *Reiter v. Dyken*, 95 Wis. 2d 461, 290 N.W.2d 510, 515-517 (1980). The North Dakota Supreme Court is not caught in such a trap, and so those considerations do not apply in this state.

The factors leading to the adoption of the unit rule are numerous and compelling. This court has considered the following factors in weighing its decision: the unit rule is the majority rule and the modern trend; those courts that have most thoroughly reviewed the arguments of policy and law have chosen the unit rule, while those courts opting for the Wisconsin rule have generally done so because of undue deference to a canon of statutory construction or misplaced reliance on statutory phraseology; application of the unit rule in North Dakota is mandated by §1-01-35. Further arguments against the Wisconsin rule and in favor of the unit rule have been made. *See, e.g.*, 483 A.2d at 483-489, 679 P.2d at 904-909.

Following this approach, this court concludes that the North Dakota Supreme Court would profit from the misfortune of Wisconsin, and avoid placing itself in the trap in which that court finds itself. This court is convinced that the correct decision is to apply the unit rule in this case, and that that is the decision the North Dakota Supreme Court would reach.

Application of the unit rule in this case raises the issue of whether "the person against whom recovery is sought" includes statutorily immune employers who were not made parties to a suit. Other states have reviewed this issue and determined that they are to be included. In this case, therefore, Beaudoin's negligence, 30%, will be compared against the negligence of Texaco and Wireline, 70%. Since Beaudoin's negligence is less, he can recover.

In North Dakota a joint tortfeasor is liable for the share of negligence attributed to a statutorily immune employer. *Layman v. Braunschweigische Maschinenbauanstalt, Inc.*, 343 N.W.2d 334, 344-350 (N.D. 1983). In this case, then,

Texaco, which was only 10% contributorily negligent, will be forced to pay 70% of the damages. This is clearly an inequitable result, but given the current state of the law it is unavoidable.

If the Wisconsin rule were applied to the facts of this case, Beaudoin, who was only 30% contributorily negligent, would be denied any recovery. This would be an inequitable result. Further, it would be an inequitable result imposed by the operation of the comparative negligence provision of §9-10-07. The result actually reached is also inequitable, but the inequity is imposed by the operation of the joint and several liability provision of §9-10-07 and the immunity provision of §65-04-28. As was noted at the opening of this order, it is a collision of legal principles that renders an equitable result in this case impossible. This court has declined to adopt an outmoded rule that works inequity, but another outmoded and inequitable rule, joint and several liability, still remains to prevent a just outcome. Some states have abolished this rule as a part of their statutory system of comparative negligence, *see, e.g., Teepak, Inc. v. Learned*, 237 Kan. 320, 699 P.2d 35, 38 (1985), but the North Dakota Legislature has not yet done so. If it were to adopt a several liability rule, then the combination of that rule and the unit rule would produce more nearly equitable results than can be achieved if either the Wisconsin rule or the joint and several liability rule is present.

Therefore it is ORDERED:

> That plaintiff Mark Chris Beaudoin shall have judgment against defendant Texaco, Inc. in the sum of 70% of $44,057.04, that is $30,839.93, plus interest thereon from the date of judgment and costs and disbursements as taxed by the clerk and added to the judgment. The clerk shall prepare and enter the judgment.

NOTES AND PROBLEMS

1. ***Problem Unique to Modified Comparative Fault.*** Given the jury's apportionment in the *Texaco* case, what would be the outcome in each of the following jurisdictions?

A. In contributory negligence?
B. In pure comparative fault?

The dilemma the court faced in *Texaco* would not matter in either a contributory negligence or a pure comparative fault jurisdiction because no comparison between (or among) the claimant and the defendant(s) is needed to implement the doctrine. Either the plaintiff recovers nothing (in contributory negligence) or the plaintiff recovers something (in pure comparative fault). But in modified comparative fault, the court must consider whether *any* recovery is permitted in light of the plaintiff's apportionment. Unfortunately, many of the modified comparative fault statutes are written in a manner similar to the North

Dakota statute in *Texaco*. That is, the statutes are often worded as if the only parties being apportioned fault are a single plaintiff and a single defendant. When that is not the case, the court must ascertain the appropriate method by which to compare fault levels.

2. ***Other Rationales for Rejection of the Wisconsin Rule.*** The federal district court in *Texaco* alludes to other public policy reasons for rejecting the Wisconsin rule. One is based upon the conceptual math problems. For example, consider if a jury apportioned fault 30 percent to the plaintiff, 60 percent to Defendant 1, and 10 percent to Defendant 2. Under the Wisconsin rule, the court would first compare the plaintiff's fault of 30 percent with Defendant 1's fault of 60 percent (and permit recovery). Then the court would compare plaintiff's 30 percent fault with Defendant 2's 10 percent (and reject any recovery against that defendant). But all of this comparison would involve a total of 130 percent fault rather than limiting the universe of fault to 100 percent. The other problem with the Wisconsin rule is more pragmatic — the more tortfeasors that cause the plaintiff's harm (and are included in the apportionment question) the more likely the plaintiff will be unable to recover. For example, if there are three defendants who contribute to the plaintiff's injury and the jury assesses fault against all three and plaintiff equally, they will each be 25 percent at fault — plaintiff will be unable to recover in a 49 percent modified comparative fault state (since plaintiff's fault is not less than any defendant). But if there was only one defendant apportioned the 75 percent fault, plaintiff could easily recover something in a modified comparative fault state. Courts often cite these additional arguments for rejecting the Wisconsin rule.

3. ***Problems. Can a Better Modified Comparative Fault Statute Be Built?***

A. Read the following statute and ask yourself whether this statute renders moot the unit rule vs. Wisconsin rule debate. In other words, what would the result be under this statute using the jury's findings from the *Texaco* case?

> Sec. 33.001. Proportionate Responsibility. In an action to which this chapter applies, a claimant may not recover damages if his percentage of responsibility is greater than 50 percent.

Tex. Civ. Prac. & Rem. Code §33.001. Does this rule implicitly embrace a unit rule result or a Wisconsin rule result?

B. The Oregon proportionate fault statute at issue in the Sandford v. Chevrolet case permits a plaintiff to recover whenever "the fault attributable to the person seeking recovery was not greater than the combined fault of the person or persons against whom recovery is sought." Does this statute expressly incorporate a Wisconsin rule or unit rule? Is the statute more clear than the North Dakota statute in *Texaco*?

III ASSUMPTION OF THE RISK

We have previously explored primary assumption of the risk — the "no duty" doctrine that declares that a reasonable person would not make special efforts to reduce or eliminate "inherent risks" of certain activities. That doctrine is not an affirmative defense but a particular way of concluding that the defendant who provided the activity was not negligent. In terms of true affirmative defenses, tort law has traditionally recognized two varieties of assumption of the risk: (a) *express* assumption of the risk, where the plaintiff has promised not to hold the defendant liable for its own negligence prior to the injury; and (b) *secondary implied* assumption of the risk, where the plaintiff has knowingly and voluntarily decided to encounter a risk previously created by the defendant's negligence.

A. Express Assumption of the Risk

When a defendant pleads that the plaintiff has previously agreed to assume the risk of injury due to the defendant's negligence, that defendant must overcome two hurdles: (1) that the exculpatory clause does not offend the court's view of public policy in terms of its enforcement, and (2) that the clause was worded with sufficient clarity to release the defendant from liability for the plaintiff's actual injuries. We will take up these issues in that order.

1. Public Policy Hurdle

TUNKL v. REGENTS OF THE UNIVERSITY OF CALIFORNIA

383 P.2d 441 (Cal. 1963)

TOBRINER, J.

This case concerns the validity of a release from liability for future negligence imposed as a condition for admission to a charitable research hospital. For the reasons we hereinafter specify, we have concluded that an agreement between a hospital and an entering patient affects the public interest and that, in consequence, the exculpatory provision included within it must be invalid under Civil Code section 1668.

Hugo Tunkl brought this action to recover damages for personal injuries alleged to have resulted from the negligence of two physicians in the employ of the University of California Los Angeles Medical Center, a hospital operated and maintained by the Regents of the University of California as a nonprofit charitable institution. Mr. Tunkl died after suit was brought, and his surviving wife, as executrix, was substituted as plaintiff.

The University of California at Los Angeles Medical Center admitted Tunkl as a patient on June 11, 1956. The Regents maintain the hospital for the primary purpose of aiding and developing a program of research and education in the field of medicine; patients are selected and admitted if the study and treatment of their condition would tend to achieve these purposes. Upon his entry to the hospital, Tunkl signed a document setting forth certain "Conditions of Admission." The crucial condition number six reads as follows:

> Release: The hospital is a nonprofit, charitable institution. In consideration of the hospital and allied services to be rendered and the rates charged therefor, the patient or his legal representative agrees to and hereby releases The Regents of the University of California, and the hospital from any and all liability for the negligent or wrongful acts or omissions of its employees, if the hospital has used due care in selecting its employees.

Plaintiff stipulated that the hospital had selected its employees with due care. The trial court ordered that the issue of the validity of the exculpatory clause be first submitted to the jury and that, if the jury found that the provision did not bind plaintiff, a second jury try the issue of alleged malpractice. When, on the preliminary issue, the jury returned a verdict sustaining the validity of the executed release, the court entered judgment in favor of the Regents.[3] Plaintiff appeals from the judgment.

In one respect, as we have said, the decisions [regarding the enforceability of exculpatory provisions] are uniform. The cases have consistently held that the exculpatory provision may stand only if it does not involve "the public interest."[6] In *Stephens* v. *Southern Pac. Co.* (1895) 109 Cal. 86 [41 P. 783, 50 Am. St. Rep. 17, 29 L.R.A. 751], a railroad company had leased land, which adjoined its depot, to a lessee who had constructed a warehouse upon it. The lessee covenanted that the railroad company would not be responsible for damage from fire "caused from any . . . means." This exemption, under the court ruling, applied to the lessee's damage resulting from the railroad company's carelessly burning dry grass and rubbish. Declaring the contract not "violative of sound public policy," the court pointed out "As far as this transaction was concerned, the parties when contracting stood upon common ground, and dealt with each other as

3. Plaintiff at the time of signing the release was in great pain, under sedation, and probably unable to read. At trial plaintiff contended that the release was invalid, asserting that a release does not bind the releasor if at the time of its execution he suffered from so weak a mental condition that he was unable to comprehend the effect of his act. The jury, however, found against plaintiff on this issue. Since the verdict of the jury established that plaintiff either knew or should have known the significance of the release, this appeal raises the sole question of whether the release can stand as a matter of law.

6. The view that the exculpatory contract is valid only if the public interest is not involved represents the majority holding in the United States. Only New Hampshire, in definite opposition to "public interest" test, categorically refuses to enforce exculpatory provisions.

A and B might deal with each other with reference to any private business undertaking." The court concluded "that the *interests of the public* in the contract are more sentimental than real" and that the exculpatory provision was therefore enforceable.

In applying this approach and in manifesting their reaction as to the effect of the exemptive clause upon the public interest, some later courts enforced, and others invalidated such provisions.... Thus in *Nichols* v. *Hitchcock Motor Co.* (1937) 70 P.2d 654, the court enforced an exculpatory clause on the ground that "the public neither had nor could have any interest whatsoever in the subject-matter of the contract, considered either as a whole or as to the incidental covenant in question. The agreement between the parties concerned 'their private affairs' only."

In *Barkett* v. *Brucato* (1953) 264 P.2d 978, which involved a waiver clause in a private lease, Justice Peters summarizes the previous decisions in this language: "These cases hold that the matter is simply one of interpreting a contract; that both parties are free to contract; that the relationship of landlord and tenant *does not affect the public interest*; that such a provision *affects only the private affairs of the parties...*" (Italics added.)

On the other hand, courts struck down exculpatory clauses as contrary to public policy in the case of a contract to transmit a telegraph message (*Union Constr. Co.* v. *Western Union Tel. Co.* (1912) 125 P. 242) and in the instance of a contract of bailment (*England* v. *Lyon Fireproof Storage Co.* (1928) 271 P. 532). In *Hiroshima* v. *Bank of Italy* (1926) 248 P. 947, the court invalidated an exemption provision in the form used by a payee in directing a bank to stop payment on a check. The court relied in part upon the fact that "the banking public, as well as the particular individual who may be concerned in the giving of any stop-notice, is interested in seeing that the bank is held accountable for the ordinary and regular performance of its duties and, also, in seeing that direction in relation to the disposition of funds deposited in [the] bank are not heedlessly, negligently, and carelessly disobeyed and money paid out, contrary to directions given."

In placing particular contracts within or without the category of those affected with a public interest, the courts have revealed a rough outline of that type of transaction in which exculpatory provisions will be held invalid. Thus the attempted but invalid exemption involves a transaction which exhibits some or all of the following characteristics. It concerns a business of a type generally thought suitable for public regulation. The party seeking exculpation is engaged in performing a service of great importance to the public, which is often a matter of practical necessity for some members of the public. The party holds himself out as willing to perform this service for any member of the public who seeks it, or at least for any member coming within certain established standards. As a result of the essential nature of the service, in the economic setting of the transaction, the party invoking exculpation possesses a decisive advantage of bargaining strength against any member of the public who seeks his services. In exercising a superior bargaining power the party confronts the public with a standardized adhesion contract of exculpation, and makes no provision whereby a purchaser may pay additional reasonable fees and obtain protection against negligence. Finally, as a result of the transaction, the person or property of the purchaser is placed under the control of the seller, subject to the risk of carelessness by the seller or his agents.

While obviously no public policy opposes private, voluntary transactions in which one party, for a consideration, agrees to shoulder a risk which the law would otherwise have placed upon the other party, the above circumstances pose a different situation. In this situation the releasing party does not really acquiesce voluntarily in the contractual shifting of the risk, nor can we be reasonably certain that he receives an adequate consideration for the transfer. Since the service is one which each member of the public, presently or potentially, may find essential to him, he faces, despite his economic inability to do so, the prospect of a compulsory assumption of the risk of another's negligence. The public policy of this state has been, in substance, to posit the risk of negligence upon the actor; in instances in which this policy has been abandoned, it has generally been to allow or require that the risk shift to another party better or equally able to bear it, not to shift the risk to the weak bargainer.

In the light of the decisions, we think that the hospital-patient contract clearly falls within the category of agreements affecting the public interest. To meet that test, the agreement need only fulfill some of the characteristics above outlined; here, the relationship fulfills all of them. Thus the contract of exculpation involves an institution suitable for, and a subject of, public regulation. That the services of the hospital to those members of the public who are in special need of the particular skill of its staff and facilities constitute a practical and crucial necessity is hardly open to question.

The hospital, likewise, holds itself out as willing to perform its services for those members of the public who qualify for its research and training facilities. While it is true that the hospital is selective as to the patients it will accept, such selectivity does not negate its public aspect or the public interest in it. The hospital is selective only in the sense that it accepts from the public at large certain types of cases which qualify for the research and training in which it specializes. But the hospital does hold itself out to the public as an institution which performs such services for those members of the public who can qualify for them.

In insisting that the patient accept the provision of waiver in the contract, the hospital certainly exercises a decisive advantage in bargaining. The would-be patient is in no position to reject the proffered agreement, to bargain with the hospital, or in lieu of agreement to find another hospital. The admission room of a hospital contains no bargaining table where, as in a private business transaction, the parties can debate the terms of their contract. As a result, we cannot but conclude that the instant agreement manifested the characteristics of the so-called adhesion contract. Finally, when the patient signed the contract, he completely placed himself in the control of the hospital; he subjected himself to the risk of its carelessness.

In brief, the patient here sought the services which the hospital offered to a selective portion of the public; the patient, as the price of admission and as a result of his inferior bargaining position, accepted a clause in a contract of adhesion waiving the hospital's negligence; the patient thereby subjected himself to control of the hospital and the possible infliction of the negligence which he had thus been compelled to waive. The hospital, under such circumstances, occupied a status different than a mere private party; its contract with the patient affected the public interest. We see no cogent current reason for according to the patron of the inn a greater protection than the patient of the hospital; we cannot hold the innkeeper's performance affords a greater public service than that of the hospital.

We must note, finally, that the integrated and specialized society of today, structured upon mutual dependency, cannot rigidly narrow the concept of the public interest. From the observance of simple standards of due care in the driving of a car to the performance of the high standards of hospital practice, the individual citizen must be completely dependent upon the responsibility of others. The fabric of this pattern is so closely woven that the snarling of a single thread affects the whole. We cannot lightly accept a sought immunity from careless failure to provide the hospital service upon which many must depend. Even if the hospital's doors are open only to those in a specialized category, the hospital cannot claim isolated immunity in the interdependent community of our time. It, too, is part of the social fabric, and prearranged exculpation from its negligence must partly rend the pattern and necessarily affect the public interest.

The judgment is reversed.

Principles

With regard to the willingness to enforce an express assumption of the risk, one court commented: "More than one hundred years ago, it was noted that 'the right of parties to contract as they please is restricted only by a few well defined and well settled rules, and it must be a very plain case to justify a court in holding a contract to be against public policy.'"

Seigneur v. National Fitness Institute, Inc., 752 A.2d 631 (Md. Ct. Spec. App. 2000).

NOTES AND PROBLEMS

1. ***Exculpatory Clauses at Intersection of Different Aims.*** One might wonder, from a torts perspective, why a court would ever enforce an exculpatory clause. It undermines the tort purpose of compensating deserving victims as well as the goal of deterring avoidable injuries. On the other hand, exculpatory clauses are governed to an extent by contract law, which generally permits parties the autonomy to structure their personal affairs as they see fit. Courts have essentially compromised — they will enforce such clauses as an express assumption of the risk so long as the clauses do not violate public policy. Despite the non-exhaustive yet lengthy list of factors utilized in *Tunkl*, courts seem to enforce these clauses to the extent they merely express the voluntary decision on a private matter to assign (or diminish) duties between those

parties. Thus, some of the factors relate to whether the activity or transaction is truly just a private matter, and others relate to whether the plaintiff actually and voluntarily agreed to the clause.

2. ***Other Examples of Void Exculpatory Clauses.*** In addition to the provision of hospital services, courts have also refused to uphold an express assumption of the risk in a variety of other circumstances, including the following examples:

A. Requiring parents of high school students to sign a release in connection with school athletic programs. Wagenblast v. Odessa School District, 758 P.2d 968 (Wash. 1988).

B. Exculpatory agreement by employee releasing employer from negligence in the workplace environment. Brown v. Soh, 909 A.2d 43 (Conn. 2006).

C. An express assumption of the risk barring recovery even for grossly negligent or intentional misconduct. City of Santa Barbara v. Superior Court, 161 P.3d 1095 (Cal. 2007).

3. ***Rationale for Public Policy Exception to Enforcement.*** One court summarized this body of law, following the *Tunkl* case, as follows:

> Responding to changes in economic and social necessities, courts then went beyond this rule of construction [applying strict scrutiny to an express assumption of the risk] and found that in certain situations and relations express agreements by which one party assumes the risk of another's conduct could not, in good conscience, be accepted. Where a disparity of bargaining power has grown out of economic necessity for certain goods or services or from a monopolistic position of a seller, courts have found exculpatory agreements inimical to the public interest. Where an agreement does not represent a free choice on the part of the plaintiff, where he is forced to accept the clause by the necessities of the situation, courts have refused to enforce such agreements as contrary to public policy. This rule has been applied broadly in the employer-employee relationship; in situations where one party is charged with a duty of public service; to agreements which attempt to exculpate one from liability for the violation of statute or regulation designed to protect human life; and elsewhere, e.g., Uniform Commercial Code §2-719(3), provides that the limitation of consequential damages for injury to the person in the case of consumer goods is prima facie unconscionable.

Phillips Home Furnishings, Inc. v. Continental Bank, 331 A.2d 840, 944 (Pa. Super. Ct. 1974).

4. ***Problems.*** In light of the factors adopted by the *Tunkl* court for considering the public policy issue of enforcement of an exculpatory clause, should a court agree to enforce an express assumption of the risk in the following hypothetical scenarios?

A. General Dynamics, a defense contractor to the United States, includes an express assumption of the risk in its procurement contract with the United States for its sale of tanks.

B. Acme Tire and Valve Company includes a release in its supply contracts with Ford Motor Company exonerating itself from liability for any defective tires sold to the automobile manufacturer.

C. A manufacturer of trampolines includes a release on its website that a purchaser must accept when ordering one of its products online.

D. A lease between a landlord and tenant includes an express assumption of the risk clause that excuses the landlord from liability for negligence in maintaining the common areas of the rental property.

E. A scuba diving school requires its students to sign a release agreement in order to receive instruction.

2. *The Drafting Hurdle*

Even if the defendant's reliance upon a release survives the public policy scrutiny under the *Tunkl* factors, the court may still refuse to enforce the release if it is not drafted with sufficient clarity. The following case involves an attempted utilization of a release as a defense by a health club. As you read this case, consider why the *Tunkl* factors might permit the enforcement of a properly worded release for health club members. But note why this particular release was nevertheless found invalid due to its drafting.

ALACK v. VIC TANNY INTERNATIONAL OF MISSOURI, INC.

923 S.W.2d 330 (Mo. 1996)

Price, Jr., J.

Plaintiff was injured while using health club facilities. He had signed a two-page, seventeen-paragraph "Retail Installment Contract" containing a general exculpatory clause. The clause, however, did not expressly release the health club from injuries resulting from its own negligence. The trial court ruled that the exculpatory clause did not bar plaintiff's negligence action as a matter of law, but the trial court allowed the contract as evidence and submitted the issue to the jury as a matter of fact. The jury returned a verdict for plaintiff in the amount of $17,000.

We hold that the exculpatory clause was ambiguous and that defendant health club did not insulate itself from liability for future negligence because the exculpatory clause did not use the word "negligence" or "fault" or their equivalents so that a clear and unmistakable waiver occurred. The judgment of the trial court is affirmed.

In 1982, Charles Alack became a member of Vic Tanny International of Missouri, Inc., a health club facility. Alack was encouraged to engage in a specific cardiovascular workout routine known as the "Super Circuit." During this routine, a member was instructed to exercise on ten different weight machines while running a lap between each exercise. The weight machines used during a "Super Circuit" were specifically chosen because they required only a selection of weight amount prior to their use and would not interrupt the cardiovascular nature of the routine.

While using an upright row machine during a "Super Circuit," the machine's handle disengaged from the weight cable and smashed into Alack's mouth and jaw. Alack suffered injuries to his mouth and lips, including several loose and broken teeth. As of the trial, Alack had seen his dentist over 20 times, had undergone two surgeries, and was scheduled for a third surgery. While the surgeries relieved some of Alack's pain, his temporomandibular joint remained displaced. Alack testified that he will be subject to additional jaw problems, including arthritic changes, and might require additional surgery in the future. Alack had already incurred, or was committed to incur, $17,000 in medical expenses for these surgical and dental procedures.

The handle of the machine was connected without the necessary clevis pin placed between the cable and the pigtail hook. The manufacturer originally designed, manufactured, and shipped the machine with the clevis pin in place. The manufacturer also provided a user manual warning that keeping the equipment correctly assembled was "critically important to user safety." At trial, maintenance employees of Vic Tanny acknowledged that the work-out machine could be dangerous if used without the clevis pin. It was also acknowledged that Vic Tanny did not require periodic inspections by any specifically designated employee to make certain that the clevis pin was in place. [Plaintiff's product liability claim against the manufacturer was dismissed because the evidence showed the defect occurred after it had already been shipped to Defendant intact.]

On cross-examination, Alack was questioned about his Vic Tanny "Retail Installment Contract," including a paragraph purporting to release Vic Tanny from "any and all claims" against it.[2] At no place in the membership contract does Alack expressly agree to release Vic Tanny from its own future negligence or fault. All seventeen of the paragraphs on the form-contract were printed with

---

2. "By the use of the facilities of Seller and/or by the attendance at any of the gymnasiums owned by Seller, the Member expressly agrees that Seller shall not be liable for any damages arising from personal injuries sustained by the Member or his guest in, on or about the premises of the said gymnasiums or as a result of their using the facilities and the equipment therein. By the execution of this agreement Member assumes full responsibility of any such injuries or damages which may occur to the Member or guest in, on or about the said gymnasiums and further agrees that Seller shall not be liable for any loss or theft of personal property. Member assumes full responsibility for any injuries, damages or losses which may occur to Member or guest, in, on or about the premises of said gymnasiums and does hereby fully and forever release and discharge Seller and all associated gymnasiums, their owners, employees and agents from any and all claims, demands, damages, rights of action, or causes of action, present or future, whether the same be known or unknown, anticipated, or unanticipated, resulting from or arising out of the Member's or his guests use or intended use of the said gymnasium or the facilities and equipment thereof." [Paragraph G.]

the same-sized lettering. Nothing made Paragraph G, or any of the language contained therein, conspicuously stand out. Alack signed the contract near the bottom of the first page. Paragraph G was on the back side of the contract.

During trial, Vic Tanny initially used the exculpatory paragraph to demonstrate that Alack was aware that injuries could occur during a workout session. Then Alack used the paragraph to explain that he believed he was only releasing Vic Tanny from any injuries caused if he attempted to lift too much weight or workout for too long of a period. Alack explained what the clause meant to him during direct examination:

Q. (By Alack's attorney) And having read that language what was your understanding as to what that language meant?

A. (By Alack) That language to me meant that if — It's somewhat of a limitation of liability intended. And to me it meant that if I did something, sprained my back, which I have done, sprained ankle or whatever in working out with the weights that they're not liable.

Q. Did you understand that language to mean that if Vic Tanny was negligent and that negligence resulted in injury to you that you could not bring a claim against Vic Tanny for negligence?

A. No, that was not my understanding.

Finally, Vic Tanny argued that the exculpatory clause entitled it to a directed verdict because Paragraph G bars any negligence claim by Alack as a matter of law. The trial judge decided to submit the issue to the jury. The jury was instructed that it could find in favor of Vic Tanny only if it believed that, when Alack signed the membership agreement, he had agreed to release Vic Tanny from the type of claim involved in this case. The jury returned a verdict against Vic Tanny on Alack's negligence count, and awarded Alack $17,000.00 in damages. Vic Tanny filed a motion for judgment notwithstanding the verdict [which was overruled by the trial court].

Vic Tanny appeals, alleging that the trial court erred in denying Vic Tanny a directed verdict as a matter of law on Alack's negligence claim because of the exculpatory membership contract. . . .

Although exculpatory clauses in contracts releasing an individual from his or her own future negligence are disfavored, they are not prohibited as against public policy. *Rock Springs Realty, Inc. v. Waid*, 392 S.W.2d 270, 272 (Mo. 1965). However, contracts exonerating a party from acts of future negligence are to be "strictly construed against the party claiming the benefit of the contract, and clear and explicit language in the contract is required to absolve a person from such liability." *Hornbeck v. All American Indoor Sports, Inc.*, 898 S.W.2d 717, 721 (Mo.

In Practice

A clause disclaiming liability for negligence signed *prior* to any tort is referred to in Fed. R. Civ. P. 8 as an "assumption of risk," whereas a clause in a contract disclaiming liability for negligence signed *after* a tort has already occurred is referred to as a "release" (i.e., a settlement).

App. 1995). It is a "well-established rule of construction that a contract provision exempting one from liability for his or her negligence will never be implied but must be clearly and explicitly stated." *Poslosky v. Firestone Tire and Rubber Co.*, 349 S.W.2d 847, 850 (Mo. 1961).

Most states have enforced exculpatory clauses when they include specific references to the negligence or fault of the drafter. In *Dresser Industries, Inc. v. Page Petroleum*, Inc., 853 S.W.2d 505, 508-509 (Tex. 1993), the Texas Supreme Court applied an "express negligence doctrine" that requires a release to specifically express the intent of a party to be relieved from his or her own negligence. The court explained that indemnity agreements, releases, exculpatory agreements, or waivers are extraordinary methods of shifting the risk of negligent conduct. Therefore, individuals wishing to protect themselves from their own negligence "must express that intent in specific terms within the four corners of the contract."

In *Gross v. Sweet*, 400 N.E.2d 306, 309 (N.Y. 1979), the New York Court of Appeals first noted the following principles of law regarding the construction of exculpatory language:

> As the cases make clear, the law's reluctance to enforce exculpatory provisions of this nature has resulted in the development of an exacting standard by which courts measure their validity. So, it has been repeatedly emphasized that unless the intention of the parties is expressed in unmistakable language, an exculpatory clause will not be deemed to insulate a party from liability for his own negligent acts [citations omitted]. Put another way, it must appear plainly and precisely that the "limitation of liability extends to negligence or other fault of the party attempting to shed his ordinary responsibility" [citations omitted].
>
> Not only does this stringent standard require that the drafter of such an agreement make its terms unambiguous, but it mandates that the terms be understandable as well. Thus, a provision that would exempt its drafter from any liability occasioned by his fault should not compel resort to a magnifying glass and lexicon. [Citations omitted.]

The court then held that a release providing that "I . . . waive any and all claims," language remarkably similar to that used in the present case, was insufficient to bar a personal injury action for negligence because the release "nowhere expresses any intention to exempt the defendant from liability for injury or property damages which may result from his failure to use due care." 400 N.E.2d at 311. In requiring the use of the word "negligence" or "words conveying a similar import" the court noted that while one might accept the risks inherently associated with any particular activity, "it does not follow that he was aware of, much less intended to accept, any *enhanced* exposure to injury occasioned by the carelessness of the very persons on which he depended for his safety." 400 N.E.2d at 310-11 (emphasis in original). *See also Schlobohm v. Spa Petite, Inc.*, 326 N.W.2d 920, 923 (Minn. 1982) (barring claim when "negligence" stated in release); *Doyle v. Bowdoin College*, 403 A.2d 1206, 1208 (Me. 1979) (holding the release must use the "greatest particularity" to extinguish negligence liability and there must be an express reference to liability for negligence); *Geise v. County of Niagara*, 117 Misc. 2d 470, 458 N.Y.S.2d 162, 164 (Sup. 1983) (explaining that a negligence claim was not barred unless words referring to the "neglect" or "fault" of the defendant were used in the release); *Haugen v. Ford Motor Co.*, 219 N.W.2d 462, 470 (N.D. 1974) (holding that there is no "plain and precise" limitation of liability without a reference to "negligence"); *Blum v. Kauffman*, 297 A.2d 48, 49 (Del. 1972) (explaining that the word "negligence" was not in release and, therefore, did not "clearly and unequivocally" spell out the intent to grant such protection from liability for negligence); *Ciofalo v. Vic Tanney Gyms, Inc.*, 10 N.Y.2d 294, 177 N.E.2d 925, 926, 220 N.Y.S.2d 962 (N.Y. 1961) (barring claim when "negligence" stated in release).

Other states have said that the word "negligence" is not necessarily required in an agreement in order to release a party from his or her own negligence. In *Audley v. Melton*, 640 A.2d 777 (N.H. 1994), a model was bitten by a lion during a photography shoot. The model had signed a release stating she realized working with wild animals was potentially dangerous and that she released "the photographer, his/her agents or assigns from any and all liability whatsoever." The trial court granted the photographer summary judgment on the model's negligence claim. However, the New Hampshire Supreme Court reversed because the clause failed to bring particular attention "to the notion of releasing the defendant from liability for his own negligence." While the magic word "negligence" is not required, the language must "put plaintiff on clear notice of such intent."

In *Boehm v. Cody Country Chamber of Commerce*, 748 P.2d 704 (Wyo. 1987), a member of a gun club was injured during a mock gunfight. Because he had signed a release, the trial court granted summary judgment in favor of the defendant gun club, and the Wyoming Supreme Court affirmed. The release stated that the member shall "hold harmless and release [defendant], its agents and employees . . . from any and all claims and damages which [plaintiff] may incur from participating in any and all activities sanctioned by [defendant]." The court held that such language was a "clear and unambiguous" release of defendant from its own negligence liability even without the use of the word "negligence" in the release.

Historically, Missouri appellate courts have required that a release from one's own future negligence be *explicitly* stated. In *Poslosky v. Firestone Tire and Rubber Co.*, 349 S.W.2d 847 (Mo. 1961), this Court held that a tenant was not released from liability for negligently starting a fire when the lease did not contain clear language referring to exemption from negligence. Instead, the lease stated only that "Lessor agrees that it will . . . keep the improvements on the said premises insured against fire . . . and all moneys collected from such insurance shall be used toward the full compliance of the obligation of Lessor [to repair or restore the damaged premises]." In holding this language inadequate, the Court noted the traditional rule of construction particular to exculpatory clauses by stating that "a contract provision exempting one from liability for his negligence will never be implied but must be explicitly stated."

We are persuaded that the best policy is to follow our previous decisions and those of other states that require clear, unambiguous, unmistakable, and conspicuous language in order to release a party from his or her own future negligence. The exculpatory language must effectively notify a party that he or she is releasing the other party from claims arising from the other party's own negligence. Our traditional notions of justice are so fault-based that most people might not expect such a relationship to be altered, regardless of the length of an exculpatory clause, unless done so explicitly. General language will not suffice.

"A determination as to whether a [contract] is ambiguous is a question of law to be decided by the court." Royal Banks of Missouri v. Fridkin, 819 S.W.2d 359, 361 (Mo. banc 1991). "An ambiguity arises when there is duplicity, indistinctness, or uncertainty in the meaning of the words used in the contract." *Rodriguez v. General Accident Insurance Company of America*, 808 S.W.2d 379, 382 (Mo. banc 1991). In this case, the exculpatory clause purports to shield Vic Tanny from liability for "*any* damages," "*any* . . . injuries" and "*any* and *all* claims, demands, damages, rights of action, present or future . . . resulting from or arising out of the Member's . . . use . . . of said gymnasium or the facilities and equipment thereof." (Emphasis added.) Vic Tanny argues that this language is clear and unambiguous. In a theoretical vacuum, the words "any and "all" might appear unambiguous: "all" means "every" and "any" means "all." Webster's Third New International Dictionary 54, 97 (1976).

When viewed in the context of the law governing exculpatory clauses, however, this clause is ambiguous. As extensive as it is, the exculpatory clause at issue in this case is ambiguous because it did not specifically state that a member was releasing Vic Tanny for its own future negligence. Additionally, there is no question that one may never exonerate oneself from future liability for intentional torts or for gross negligence, or for activities involving the public interest. *See Liberty Financial Management Corp. v. Beneficial Data Processing Corp.*, 670 S.W.2d 40, 48 (Mo. App. 1984). Yet the words used here would purport to include these claims, which cannot be waived. Although these claims were not asserted here, they demonstrate the ambiguity of the contractual language. A contract that purports to relieve a party from any and all claims but does not actually do so is duplicitous, indistinct and uncertain.

Alack testified that he did not understand that he was releasing Vic Tanny from its own future negligence. Additionally, the twelve jurors found, as a matter of fact, that the exculpatory clause did not so release Vic Tanny. While this issue is to be decided as a matter of law, and should not have been submitted to the jury, our law on such an important point cannot be so out of step with the understanding of our citizens. The better rule is one that establishes a bright-line test, easy for courts to apply, and certain to alert all involved that the future "negligence" or "fault" of a party is being released. The words "negligence" or "fault" or their equivalents must be used conspicuously so that a clear and unmistakable waiver and shifting of risk occurs.[4] There must be no doubt that a reasonable person agreeing to an exculpatory clause actually understands what future claims he or she is waiving.

The trial court did not err in denying Vic Tanny's request for a directed verdict because the exculpatory clause at issue did not meet the requirements discussed above.

NOTES AND PROBLEMS

1. ***Strict Scrutiny.*** While courts hearing tort claims will permit an express assumption of the risk (also known as an exculpatory agreement) if it does not offend public policy, most courts do apply strict scrutiny to such agreements and construe them against the party invoking their protections. Typically, the party invoking the protection of the clause is also the party that drafted the clause and insisted upon its execution. Certainly a lack of clarity will invalidate a particular exculpatory clause. In the *Vic Tanny* case, the court demanded, as a matter of law, that the agreement expressly indicate that the claims being released included claims based upon the health club's own negligence — the so-called *express negligence* rule. Beyond this, the court also alluded to other courts' demands when scrutinizing releases, such as that the language be clear and unmistakable as well as conspicuous. Beyond the failure to meet the express negligence rule, do you see other potential problems with the release in *Vic Tanny*?

2. ***Restatement (Second) View.*** Second Restatement §496B generally provides that: "A plaintiff who by contract or otherwise expressly agrees to accept a risk of harm arising from the defendant's negligent . . . conduct cannot recover for such harm, unless the agreement is invalid as contrary to public policy." In addition, the Restatement (Second) also comments on the need for a showing that the plaintiff was aware of and freely agreed to the release:

> In order for an express agreement assuming the risk to be effective, it must appear that the plaintiff has given his assent to the terms of the agreement. Particularly where the agreement is drawn by the defendant, and the plaintiff's conduct with respect to it is merely that of a recipient, it must appear that the terms were in fact brought home to him and understood by him, before it can be found that he has accepted them.

Restatement (Second) §496B, cmt. c. (1965).

---

4. This case does not involve an agreement negotiated at arms length between equally sophisticated commercial entities. Less precise language may be effective in such situations, and we reserve any such issues.

FREE CRUNCHY TACO

Offer good at participating Taco Shacks!

IMPORTANT: PLEASE READ. PUBLIC CONSUMPTION OF ALCOHOL AT THE ARENA IS PROHIBITED. This ticket is a revocable license granted by The University to the ticket holder. The University reserves the right to refuse admission or change the start time of the event. The person using this ticket assumes all risk of personal injury and loss of property. This ticket may not be resold at a premium. Ticket good for admission only.
NO REFUNDS OR EXCHANGES

3. ***Problems.***

A. A college basketball fan purchases season tickets to a local university's basketball games. At the time of the purchase the fan had not yet looked at any tickets. A week before the season was to begin, the packet of tickets arrived in the mail. The back of each ticket includes some exculpatory language (see adjacent box).

While attending the game, the fan slipped and fell on a puddle of inconspicuous grease that had been left for several hours. Can the fan hold the university liable for its negligence or will the express assumption of the risk defense prevail? Even when such clauses are unlikely to be upheld, do you see any advantage to businesses or other entities including this type of language?

B. A gravel truck driver overfills his truck so that the gravel is piled high above the edges of the truck bed. Speeding down a bumpy road, some gravel falls out and breaks the window of the car following him, causing that driver to lose control of his car and crash. Does this sticker on the back of the truck preclude a negligence claim by the driver of the car?

WARNING
STAY BACK 200 FEET!

NOT RESPONSIBLE
FOR BROKEN
WINDSHIELDS!!

B. Secondary Implied Assumption of the Risk

While express assumption of the risk arises because of courts' willingness to permit contract principles to supply the defense to a negligence claim, secondary implied assumption of the risk has nothing to do with any contractual relationship between the parties. We will begin by observing the traditional application of the doctrine in two different cases. The latter of the two demonstrates a very broad application of the doctrine. Following those cases, we will see a court wrestle with the question of whether it makes sense to continue to recognize secondary implied assumption of the risk as a viable separate defense in the age of comparative fault.

The *Riddle* case set forth immediately below applies both express and secondary implied assumption of the risk to find against the plaintiff. Observe differences between these two types of assumption of risk in the court's discussion. The next case, *Schroyer*, discusses *unqualified* assumption of the risk as opposed to the *qualified* variety involved in *Riddle*. What is the essential difference between these two versions of secondary implied assumption of the risk?

1. *Qualified Secondary Implied Assumption of the Risk*

RIDDLE v. UNIVERSAL SPORT CAMP

786 P.2d 641 (Kan. App. 1990)

Per Curiam.

Theresa Riddle appeals from summary judgment denying her personal injury claim and holding that Tennessee law was applicable and that Riddle had . . . assumed the risk of her injury. We affirm as modified.

Theresa Riddle was a cheerleader for Kansas State University during the 1983-84 and 1984-85 academic years. She signed a release to the University in 1983, but apparently signed no such release in 1984. As a condition to her participation in cheerleading, she was required to attend the Universal Sport Camp d/b/a Universal Cheerleaders Association (Universal) in Memphis, Tennessee. Bea Pray and Scott Shell supervised the cheer leading squad at the camp.

In August 1984, Riddle was involved in building a "toe-touch pyramid" on which she was to be the top person. Two men from the camp gave her a boost, pushing on the bottom of her feet. The men tossed her "a little too hard," causing her to overrotate and fall forward, missing the people on whom she was supposed to land. She fell approximately fifteen feet and landed on her face. Camp employees told her she probably had a hyperextended back and did not recommend medical treatment. The next day Riddle participated in pyramid formations despite pain and back spasms.

Three days later, Riddle's back was x-rayed, and she was diagnosed as suffering from a fractured vertebra. She received injections, medication, and therapy. She eventually was released to return to cheerleading, which she continued to do in a limited capacity to the end of the 1984-85 basketball season.

UNIVERSAL SPORT CAMP

The trial court elected to apply Tennessee substantive law pursuant to *Brown v. Kleen Kut Mfg. Co.*, 714 P.2d 942 (1986) (a tort action is governed by the laws of the state where the injuries are sustained). Riddle does not raise the choice of law issue on appeal.

Prior to participating in the camp, Riddle signed a "Medical Treatment Form," Section A of which provided for insurance, and Section B of which reads:

"I, the undersigned parent or guardian, do hereby grant permission for my daughter/son [daughter circled] Theresa M. Riddle to attend the above Universal camp. . . .

"I further acknowledge and understand and agree that in participating in this camp there is a possibility of physical illness or injury and that my daughter/son *is assuming the risk* of such illness or injury by his/her participation. Payment of any medical bills incurred by my daughter/son will be paid by myself or our insurance company." (Emphasis added.)

Riddle signed in her own capacity as a camper over the age of eighteen. During her deposition, Riddle stated she did not read the above section and did not intend to release Universal from liability. She acknowledged, however, that all the handwriting on the form was hers, including the circle around the word "daughter" in the exculpatory clause.

Tennessee, with limited exceptions, recognizes the validity of such exculpatory clauses.

[The court held that because participation in a sports camp was not an area of public interest, the exculpatory clause was not void. Further, Tennessee does not require that such clauses expressly refer to a release from the defendant's own "negligence" in order to be enforced. The court noted that Tennessee "has elected not to follow the lead of jurisdictions strictly construing exculpatory contracts against the party acting in reliance on such contracts and requiring mention of negligence in the contract. *Trailmobile, Inc. v. Chazen*, 51 Tenn. App. 576, 584; 370 S.W.2d 840 (1963). The public policy of Tennessee favors freedom to contract against liability for negligence."]

Riddle signed a statement to Universal Sport Camp expressly assuming the risk of injury and agreeing to pay medical bills herself or from insurance money. Tennessee recognizes the validity of such releases, and summary judgment is appropriate with respect to the defendant Universal.

THE OTHER DEFENDANTS

The trial court found that Riddle expressly assumed the risk of injury when she signed the medical treatment release and liability release prior to attending camp and thus her claims were barred against all the defendants. It is uncontroverted that this release was required by Universal. The form was apparently provided by Universal; the other defendants are not named in the document nor are they claiming that they required the release.

As to Universal, the release constituted a contractual release of liability under Tennessee law. As to the other defendants, the release was written evidence of Riddle's voluntary exposure to the known dangers involved in participating in the cheerleading camp. Under Tennessee law, the assumption of risk defense is not dependent upon a contractual relationship.

"At the commencement of any analysis of the doctrine of assumption of risk, we must recognize that we deal with a potpourri of labels, concepts, definitions, thoughts, and doctrines. The confusion of labels does not end with the indiscriminate and interchangeable use of the terms 'contributory negligence' and 'assumption of risk.' In the case law and among text writers, there have developed categories of assumption of risk. Distinctions exist between *express* and *implied;* between primary and secondary; and between reasonable and unreasonable or, as sometimes expressed, *strict* and *qualified.*" *Blackburn v. Dorta*, 348 So. 2d 287, 290 (Fla. 1977).

In express assumption of risk, the plaintiff expressly contracts that defendant shall have no duty of care toward plaintiff. The courts continue to hold that an action for negligence is barred under these circumstances. See, *e.g.*, *Coates v. Newhall Land & Farming, Inc.*, 236 Cal. Rptr. 181 (1987).

Implied assumption of risk exists when a plaintiff has impliedly consented to assume risks. Prosser and Keeton on the Law of Torts §68, 484 (5th ed. 1984). Implied assumption of risk is divided into primary and secondary assumption of risk. Primary assumption of risk is basically a principle of no negligence where there is no duty or no breach. *Blackburn v. Dorta*, 348 So. 2d at 290. This would include the ordinary risks of an activity where no negligence exists. Assumption of risk would still exist in that situation, but its utility is small as it could more properly be explained as non-negligence without reference to assumption of risk. Without a breach of duty by the defendant there is nothing left to compare with any misconduct of the plaintiff.

Secondary assumption of risk contemplates a voluntary encounter with a known and obvious risk created by the negligent conduct of another. *Blackburn v. Dorta*, 348 So. 2d at 291. It is further broken down into reasonable and unreasonable assumption of such risk. The distinction between the two is determined by weighing the utility of the conduct in comparison with the risk involved.

One example of a reasonable secondary assumption of risk would be a tenant who is injured when he enters his burning apartment to save his child and it is determined that the fire was due to the landlord negligently allowing the premises to become highly flammable. An example of an unreasonable secondary assumption of risk would be when a tenant, under the same circumstances, enters his burning apartment to retrieve his hat. See *Blackburn v. Dorta*, 348 So. 2d at 291.

Absent an express contract with the defendants other than Universal, we must determine if there was an implied assumption of risk.

"The elements of assumption of the risk are: (1) actual knowledge of the danger; (2) appreciation of the gravity of the danger; and (3) voluntary exposure to the danger. Knowledge of the danger can be established if the danger was so obvious that one was bound to know of it." *Frazier v. Moore*, 651 S.W.2d at 242.

Considering the first element, Riddle knew of the risks of injury related to cheerleading. Riddle was an experienced cheerleader in her second year for Kansas State University, this was her second year at the camp, she had moved from alternate to full-time cheerleader in 1983 because another girl was injured, and she had also been previously injured in 1984, which required surgery.

Likewise, Riddle's experience would lead her to appreciate the danger (the second element) involved in any number of routines, including the "toe-touch pyramid" in which she is literally flung some ten to fifteen feet into the air, where she lands on the backs of two men who are in turn standing on the shoulders of two other men. The risk of falling is obvious.

Finally, Riddle voluntarily assumed the risk (the third element), as evidenced by her becoming and remaining a cheerleader, her attendance at the camps, and her written release to Universal. Riddle assumed the risk.

Riddle contends that the defendants were negligent in not having a spotter in front of the pyramid.

Assuming for purposes of summary judgment the defendants were negligent in failing to place a spotter in front of the pyramid, then Riddle's assumption of risk would not be classified as an implied primary assumption of risk in which the defendant neither owes a duty to plaintiff nor is negligent.

Secondary (reasonable or unreasonable) assumption of risk contemplates a voluntary encounter with a known and obvious risk created by the negligence of the defendant. Again, assuming the defendants were negligent in failing to place a spotter in front of the pyramid, this would have been obvious to Riddle before and during the routine, and, notwithstanding defendants' negligence, it would be unreasonable as a matter of law for Riddle to risk a fall of approximately fifteen feet knowing there was no spotter. Under Tennessee law, the defendants' negligence, then, would not preclude the assumption of risk defense as a bar to Riddle's claims.

The trial court correctly concluded that the risk of falling was a specific risk known to Riddle and voluntarily encountered. When undisputed facts reveal knowledge of danger and voluntary participation in the hazardous activity, there is no jury question, and judgment for the defendant is appropriate. *Pearce v. Canady*, 52 Tenn. App. at 354.

Summary judgment in favor of Universal based upon Riddle's express assumption of risk is affirmed. Summary judgment in favor of the other defendants is affirmed as modified based upon Riddle's implied assumption of risk.

2. *Unqualified Secondary Implied Assumption of the Risk*

SCHROYER v. McNEAL

592 A.2d 1119 (Md. App. 1991)

Bell, J.

The genesis of this case was a slip and fall accident which occurred on the parking lot of the Grantsville Holiday Inn in Garrett County, Maryland. Frances C. McNeal (McNeal), the respondent, sustained a broken ankle in the accident and, as a result, sued Thomas Edward Schroyer and his wife, Patricia A. Schroyer (the Schroyers), the petitioners, in the Circuit Court for Garrett County, alleging both that they negligently maintained the parking lot and negligently failed to warn her of its condition. The jury having returned a verdict in favor of McNeal for $50,000.00 and their motion for judgment notwithstanding the verdict or for new trial having been denied, the Schroyers appealed to the Court of Special Appeals, which affirmed. In its opinion, the intermediate appellate court directly addressed the Schroyers's primary negligence and McNeal's contributory negligence; however, although it was properly presented, that court did not specifically address whether McNeal had assumed the risk of her injury. We issued the writ of certiorari at the request of the Schroyers and now reverse. We hold that, as a matter of law, McNeal assumed the risk of the injury. We need not and, therefore, do not, reach the other issues presented.

The events surrounding McNeal's accident and her subsequent complaint against the Schroyers are largely not in dispute. McNeal arrived at the Grantsville Holiday Inn at approximately 5:30 p.m. on January 9, 1985. At that time, although approximately four inches of sleet and ice had accumulated, she observed that the area in front of, and surrounding, the main lobby area, where hotel guests registered, had been shoveled and, thus, was reasonably clear of ice and snow. She also noticed, however, that the rest of the parking lot had neither been shoveled nor otherwise cleared of the ice and snow. McNeal parked her car in front of the hotel while she registered. While registering, she requested a room closest to an exit due to her need to "cart" boxes and paperwork back and forth to her room. She was assigned a room close to the west side entrance, which was at the far end of the hall, away from the lobby. This was done notwithstanding the hotel's policy of not assigning such rooms during inclement weather. Also, contrary to policy, McNeal was not advised that she should not use the west entrance and, of course, no warnings to that effect were posted near that entrance.

Having registered, McNeal drove her car from the main entrance to within ten to fifteen feet of the west side entrance. She parked on packed ice and snow. Moreover, as she got out of her car, she noticed that the sidewalk near the entrance had not been shoveled and, furthermore, that the area was slippery. Nevertheless, she removed her cat from the car and crossed the ice and snow carefully, and without mishap. On the return trip to her car to retrieve the remainder of her belongings, she slipped and fell, sustaining the injury previously described.

Concerning her knowledge of the parking lot's condition, McNeal testified that, in the immediate vicinity of where she parked her car, the "packed ice and snow" was slippery and that, as a result, she entered the building "carefully." She denied, however, that it was unreasonable for her, under the circumstances, to try to traverse the parking lot; she "didn't think it was that slippery. I didn't slip the first time in."

The Schroyers moved for judgment, both at the end of McNeal's case in chief and at the conclusion of all the evidence. That McNeal had assumed the risk of her injury was one of the grounds advanced in support of those motions. Both motions were denied. The jury having returned its verdict in favor of McNeal, the Schroyers filed a motion for judgment notwithstanding the verdict or a new trial. As in the case of the motions for judgment, they argued that respondent was barred from recovery by the doctrine of assumption of the risk. The trial court denied that motion.

As indicated earlier, the Court of Special Appeals did not directly address whether McNeal assumed the risk of injury. Although it recognized that she "knew of the dangerous condition" and, presumably, acted voluntarily when she started to cross the ice and snow covered parking lot and sidewalk, the court perceived the question to be "whether she acted reasonably under the circumstances." It concluded that whether McNeal was contributorily negligent, *i.e.*, acted reasonably in light of the known risk, was a question appropriately left to the jury for decision.

Assumption of the risk and contributory negligence are closely related and often overlapping defenses. They may arise from the same facts and, in a given case, a decision as to one may necessarily include the other.

The relationship between the defenses has also been addressed in the Restatement (Second) of Torts:

> The same conduct on the part of the plaintiff may . . . amount to both assumption of risk and contributory negligence, and may subject him to both defenses. His conduct in accepting the risk may be unreasonable and thus negligent, because the danger is out of all proportion to the interest he is seeking to advance, as where he consents to ride with a drunken driver in an unlighted car on a dark night, or dashes into a burning building to save his hat. Likewise, even after accepting an entirely reasonable risk, he may fail to exercise reasonable care for his own protection against that risk.

§496A, comment d, at 562. The overlap between assumption of the risk and contributory negligence is a complete one where "the plaintiff's conduct in voluntarily encountering a known risk is itself unreasonable. . . ." §496A, comment c 4. When that occurs, the bar to recovery is two-pronged: 1) because the plaintiff assumed the risk of injury and 2) because the plaintiff was contributorily negligent.

There is, however, a distinction, and an important one, between the defenses of assumption of the risk and contributory negligence. That distinction was stated in *Warner v. Markoe*, 189 A.2d 260, 264 (Md. 1937), thusly:

> The distinction between contributory negligence and voluntary assumption of the risk is often difficult to draw in concrete cases, and under the law of this state usually without importance, but it may be well to keep it in mind. Contributory negligence, of course, means negligence which contributes to cause a particular accident which occurs, while assumption of risk of accident means voluntary incurring that of an accident which may not occur, and which the person assuming the risk may be careful to avoid after starting. Contributory negligence defeats recovery

> because it is a proximate cause of the accident which happens, but assumption of the risk defeats recovery because it is a previous abandonment of the right to complain if an accident occurs.

189 A. at 264. The distinction is no less clearly made by reference to the rationale underlying the doctrine of assumption of the risk. We explicated that rationale in *Gibson v. Beaver*, 226 A.2d 273, 275 (1967) (quoting W. Prosser, *Handbook of the Law of Torts* §55 at 303 (2d ed. 1955)):

> The defense of assumption of risk rests upon the plaintiff's consent to relieve the defendant of an obligation of conduct toward him, and to take his chances of harm from a particular risk. Such consent may be found: . . . by implication from the conduct of the parties. When the plaintiff enters voluntarily into a relation or situation involving obvious danger, he may be taken to assume the risk, and to relieve the defendant of responsibility. Such implied assumption of risk requires knowledge and appreciation of the risk, and a voluntary choice to encounter it.

See also Restatement (Second) of Torts §496A, comment d, at 562 and §496C, at 569-574. Assumption of the risk, then, "implies an intentional exposure to a known danger which may or may not be true of contributory negligence." *Burke v. Williams*, 223 A.2d at 189.

Whether they overlap or not, the critical distinction between contributory negligence and assumption of the risk is that, in the latter, by virtue of the plaintiff's voluntary actions, any duty the defendant owed the plaintiff to act reasonably for the plaintiff's safety is superseded by the plaintiff's willingness to take a chance. Consequently, unlike the case of contributory negligence, to establish assumption of the risk, negligence is not an issue — proof of negligence is not required. The plaintiff need only be aware of the risk, which he or she then voluntarily undertakes. Restatement (Second) of Torts, §496A, comment d, at 562; *Prosser and Keeton* §68 at 485-86; *Keenan*, 193 A.2d at 36; *Bull Steamship Lines v. Fisher*, 77 A.2d at 146.

It is, in short, the willingness of the plaintiff to take an informed chance that distinguishes assumption of the risk from contributory negligence. Thus, just as the facts of a given case may warrant the same result on either theory, the facts in another may warrant conflicting results. In other words, "either may constitute a defense, with or without the other." *Evans*, 167 A.2d at 594. A plaintiff who proceeds reasonably, and with caution, after voluntarily accepting a risk, not unreasonable in itself, may not be guilty of contributory negligence, but may have assumed the risk. *See Pinehurst Co. v. Phelps*, 163 Md. 68, 72, 160 A. 736, 737 (1932) ("A risk, while obvious, may not be so imminently dangerous that a prudent man would necessarily avoid it, yet if it shall be freely encountered it will in general be held to be so far assumed that no recovery for consequent injury is possible."). That plaintiff may be barred from recovery on the ground of assumption of the risk, while he or she would recover were the defense theory contributory negligence.

While, ordinarily, application of either defense will produce the same result, that is not always the case. Especially is that so in the instant case. The record reflects, and the Court of Special Appeals held, a matter not in dispute on this appeal, that McNeal was fully aware of the dangerous condition of the premises. She knew that the area was ice and snow covered and that the ice and snow were slippery. Nevertheless, she parked in the area and, notwithstanding, according to her testimony, that she proceeded carefully, she took a chance and walked over the ice and snow covered parking lot and sidewalk because she did not think it was "that" slippery.

It is clear, on this record, that McNeal took an informed chance. Fully aware of the danger posed by an ice and snow covered parking lot and sidewalk, she voluntarily chose to park and traverse it, *albeit* carefully, for her own purposes, *i.e.* her convenience in unloading her belongings. Assuming that the decision to park on the ice and snow covered parking lot and to cross it and the sidewalk was not, itself, contributory negligence, McNeal's testimony as to how she proceeded may well have generated a jury question as to the reasonableness of her actions. On the other hand, it cannot be gainsaid that she intentionally exposed herself to a known risk. With full knowledge that the parking lot and sidewalk were ice and snow covered and aware that the ice and snow were slippery, McNeal voluntarily chose to park on the parking lot and to walk across it and the sidewalk, thus indicating her willingness to accept the risk and relieving the Schroyers of responsibility for her safety. Consequently, while the issue of her contributory negligence may well have been for the jury, the opposite is true with respect to her assumption of the risk. We hold, as a matter of law, that McNeal assumed the risk of her own injuries.

NOTES AND PROBLEMS

1. ***Express vs. Implied Assumption of the Risk.*** In *Riddle*, the camp defendant was entitled to summary judgment because it had a valid exculpatory clause in its camp contract signed by the plaintiff. Tennessee law, which applied to the case, does not follow the *express negligence* rule and the court found that this clause was clear enough, since strict scrutiny was not applied. This defense would not be applicable to the remaining defendants, including Kansas State University, as they were not parties to the contract. However, the court found that the separate doctrine of *secondary implied assumption of the risk* did apply and served as a complete bar to recovery. What were the elements of this defense? Why, on the facts of the case, did the court find this defense to be valid?

2. ***Qualified vs. Unqualified Secondary Implied Assumption of the Risk.*** The *Riddle* court indicated that some jurisdictions apply secondary implied assumption of the risk in an *unqualified* manner, while others (including Tennessee) apply it with the qualification that the doctrine is only applicable when the decision by the plaintiff to voluntarily encounter a known risk was an

unreasonable decision. In this limited manner, what is the difference between traditional contributory negligence and secondary implied assumption of the risk? While this variety of assumption of the risk requires subjective awareness and appreciation by the plaintiff of the risk, if the court limits its application to situations where that decision was unreasonable, contributory negligence (if still observed by the court) likewise would bar the claim; so limited, the doctrine is unnecessary baggage. However, in its traditional application, not all courts limited the doctrine in this manner. Many courts applied the doctrine regardless of how reasonable the plaintiff's conduct may have been, so long as the remaining elements of secondary implied assumption of the risk were present — this is *unqualified secondary implied assumption of the risk.* This was true in the *McNeal* case where the court demonstrated that, even though the plaintiff's decision to encounter the snow and ice was reasonable (according to the jury), the evidence was undisputed that she nevertheless voluntarily chose to encounter the known risk; this decision barred her claim.

3. ***Problems.*** Would secondary implied assumption of the risk apply in the following scenarios?

- **A.** A chef notices that his toaster is starting to emit a strange, burning odor and that excessive amounts of smoke accompany its recent usage. He continues to use it. The toaster catches on fire, and the chef suffers a burned hand trying to extinguish the flames.
- **B.** A motorist recently had the brakes replaced on his automobile. The mechanic who repaired the brakes neglected to completely refill the brake fluid necessary for the hydraulics on the brake to work properly. The motorist notices that the brakes are somewhat mushy in the days following the repair. He continues to drive the car. As he approaches a red light, he applies the brakes. Suddenly, they fail altogether and he is involved in an accident.
- **C.** A tourist pays a fee at a riding stable to ride a horse for the afternoon in the mountains. She notices that the saddle appears loose, but continues to ride the horse. As the horse is galloping around a curve, the saddle falls off and the rider falls to the ground and is hurt.

3. *Does Comparative Fault Abolish Secondary Implied Assumption of the Risk?*

Given the frequent overlap between secondary implied assumption of the risk and contributory negligence, many courts have had to confront the legal question of whether their rejection of contributory negligence in favor of comparative fault necessitates an abandonment of secondary implied assumption of the risk as well. The following court discusses the divergent views on this important question.

DAVENPORT v. COTTON HOPE PLANTATION HORIZONTAL PROPERTY REGIME

508 S.E.2d 565 (S.C. 1998)

TOAL, J.

This is a comparative negligence case arising out of an accident in which respondent, Alvin Davenport, was injured while descending a stairway near his apartment. We affirm as modified.

Alvin Davenport is a resident of Cotton Hope Plantation located on Hilton Head Island. The plantation is organized under state law as Cotton Hope Plantation Horizontal Regime ("Cotton Hope"). Cotton Hope is composed of ninety-six condominium units located in multiple buildings. Each building consists of three levels. The buildings have three stairways each, one in the middle and two on either side. Davenport's unit is on the top level, approximately five feet from a stairway. Davenport leases his unit from the owner.

Cotton Hope employed Property Administrators, Incorporated ("PAI") to maintain the grounds at Cotton Hope Plantation. In April 1991, PAI, as Cotton Hope's agent, hired Carson Landscaping Company, Inc., ("Carson") to perform landscaping and general maintenance work at the condominiums. Carson's duties included checking the outdoor lights and changing light bulbs as needed.

In June 1991, Davenport began reporting that the floodlights at the bottom of the stairway he used were not working. Davenport testified he made several phone calls to PAI complaining about the problem. Davenport nevertheless continued to use the stairway during this time. On the evening of August 12, 1991, Davenport fell while descending the stairway closest to his apartment. Davenport testified he fell after attempting to place his foot on what appeared to be a step but was really a shadow caused by the broken floodlights. He admitted not using the handrail in the stairway.

Davenport sued Cotton Hope for his injuries. At the close of all the evidence, the trial court directed a verdict against Davenport, finding he had assumed the risk of injury. The trial court also held that even if assumption of risk were abrogated by the adoption of comparative negligence, Davenport was more than fifty-percent negligent. Davenport appealed the trial court's ruling.

The threshold question we must answer is whether assumption of risk survives as a complete bar to recovery under South Carolina's comparative negligence system. In *Nelson v. Concrete Supply Company*, 303 S.C. 243, 399 S.E.2d 783 (1991), we adopted a modified version of comparative negligence. Under this system, "for all causes of action arising on or after July 1, 1991, a plaintiff in a negligence action may recover damages if his or her negligence is not greater than that of the defendant." *Nelson* made clear that a plaintiff's contributory negligence would no longer bar recovery unless such negligence exceeded that of the defendant. Not so clear was what would become of the defense of assumption of risk.

Currently in South Carolina, there are four requirements to establishing the defense of assumption of risk: (1) the plaintiff must have knowledge of the facts constituting a dangerous condition; (2) the plaintiff must know the condition is dangerous; (3) the plaintiff must appreciate the nature and extent of the danger; and (4) the plaintiff must voluntarily expose himself to the danger.

As noted by the Court of Appeals, an overwhelming majority of jurisdictions that have adopted some form of comparative negligence have essentially abolished assumption of risk as an absolute bar to recovery. In analyzing the continuing viability of assumption of risk in a comparative negligence system, many courts distinguish between "express" assumption of risk and "implied" assumption of risk. *See* W. Page Keeton et al., Prosser and Keeton on the Law of Torts, §68 at 496 (5th ed. 1984). Implied assumption of risk is further divided into the categories of "primary" and "secondary" implied assumption of risk. *Id.* We will discuss each of these concepts below.

Express assumption of risk applies when the parties expressly agree in advance, either in writing or orally, that the plaintiff will relieve the defendant of his or her legal duty toward the plaintiff. Thus, being under no legal duty, the defendant cannot be charged with negligence. Even in those comparative fault jurisdictions that have abrogated assumption of risk, the rule remains that express assumption of risk continues as an absolute defense in an action for negligence. The reason for this is that express assumption of risk sounds in contract, not tort, and is based upon an express manifestation of consent.

Express assumption of risk is contrasted with implied assumption of risk, which arises when the plaintiff implicitly, rather than expressly, assumes known risks. As noted above, implied assumption of risk is characterized as either primary or secondary. Primary implied assumption of risk arises when the plaintiff impliedly assumes those risks that are *inherent* in a particular activity. Primary implied assumption of risk is not a true affirmative defense, but instead goes to the initial determination of whether the defendant's legal duty encompasses the risk encountered by the plaintiff. In *Perez*, the Tennessee Supreme Court summarized the doctrine in the following way:

> In its primary sense, implied assumption of risk focuses not on the plaintiff's conduct in assuming the risk, but on the defendant's general duty of care. . . . Clearly, primary implied assumption of risk is but another way of stating the conclusion that a plaintiff has failed to establish a prima facie case [of negligence] by failing to establish that a duty exists.

872 S.W.2d at 902. In this sense, primary implied assumption of risk is simply a part of the initial negligence analysis.

Secondary implied assumption of risk, on the other hand, arises when the plaintiff knowingly encounters a risk created by the defendant's negligence. It is a true defense because it is asserted only after the plaintiff establishes a *prima facie* case of negligence against the defendant. Secondary implied assumption of risk may involve either reasonable or unreasonable conduct on the part of the plaintiff.

Since express and primary implied assumption of risk are compatible with comparative negligence, we will refer to secondary implied assumption of risk simply as "assumption of risk."

As alluded to in *Litchfield*, assumption of risk and contributory negligence have historically been recognized as separate defenses in South Carolina. However, other courts have found assumption of risk functionally indistinguishable from contributory negligence and consequently abolished assumption of risk as a complete defense.

To date, the only comparative fault jurisdictions that have retained assumption of risk as an absolute defense are Georgia, Mississippi, Nebraska, Rhode Island, and South Dakota. Only the Rhode Island Supreme Court has provided a detailed discussion of why it believes the common law form of assumption of risk should survive under comparative negligence. In *Kennedy v. Providence Hockey Club, Inc.*, 376 A.2d 329 (R.I. 1977), the Rhode Island Supreme Court distinguished between assumption of risk and contributory negligence, emphasizing the former was measured by a subjective standard while the latter was based on an objective, reasonable person standard. The court further noted that it had in the past limited the application of assumption of risk to those situations where the plaintiff had actual knowledge of the hazard. The court then rejected the premise that assumption of risk and contributory negligence overlap:

> Contributory negligence and assumption of the risk do not overlap; the key difference is, of course, the exercise of one's free will in encountering the risk. Negligence analysis, couched in reasonable hypotheses, has no place in the assumption of the risk framework. When one acts knowingly, it is immaterial whether he acts reasonably.

Kennedy, 376 A.2d at 333.

Rhode Island's conclusions are in sharp contrast with the West Virginia Supreme Court's opinion in *King v. Kayak Manufacturing Corp.*, 182 W. Va. 276, 387 S.E.2d 511 (W. Va. 1989). Like Rhode Island, the West Virginia Supreme Court in *King* recognized that assumption of risk was conceptually distinct from contributory negligence. The court specifically noted that West Virginia's doctrine of assumption of risk required actual knowledge of the dangerous condition, which conformed with the general rule elsewhere in the country. In fact, the court cited Rhode Island's decision in *Kennedy* as evidence of this general rule. Nevertheless, the West Virginia court concluded that the absolute defense of assumption of risk was incompatible with its comparative fault system. The court therefore adopted a *comparative assumption of risk* rule, stating, "a plaintiff is not barred from recovery by the doctrine of assumption of risk unless his degree of fault arising therefrom equals or exceeds the combined fault or negligence of the other parties to the accident." The court explained that the absolute defense of assumption of risk was as repugnant to its fault system as the common law rule of contributory negligence.

A comparison between the approaches in West Virginia and Rhode Island is informative. Both jurisdictions recognize that assumption of risk is conceptually distinct from contributory negligence. However, Rhode Island focuses on the objective/subjective distinction between the two defenses and, therefore, retains assumption of risk as a complete bar to recovery. On the other hand, West Virginia emphasizes that the main purpose of its comparative negligence system is to apportion fault. Thus, West Virginia rejects assumption of risk as a total bar to recovery and only allows a jury to consider the plaintiff's negligence in assuming the risk. If the plaintiff's total negligence exceeds or equals that of the defendant, only then is the plaintiff completely barred from recovery.

Like Rhode Island and West Virginia, South Carolina has historically maintained a distinction between assumption of risk and contributory negligence, even when the two doctrines appear to overlap. Thus, the pertinent question is whether a plaintiff should be completely barred from recovery when he voluntarily assumes a known risk, regardless of whether his assumption of that risk was reasonable or unreasonable. Upon considering the purpose of our comparative fault system, we conclude that West Virginia's approach is the most persuasive model.

In *Nelson*, we adopted Chief Judge Sanders's analysis of comparative negligence [because]: "It is contrary to the basic premise of our fault system to allow a defendant, who is at fault in causing an accident, to escape bearing any of its cost, while requiring a plaintiff, who is no more than equally at fault or even less at fault, to bear all of its costs." By contrast, the main reason for having the defense of assumption of risk is not to determine fault, but to prevent a person who knowingly and voluntarily incurs a risk of harm from holding another person liable. Cotton Hope argues that the justification behind assumption of risk is not in conflict with South Carolina's comparative fault system. We disagree.

[I]t is contrary to the premise of our comparative fault system to require a plaintiff, who is fifty-percent or less at fault, to bear all of the costs of the injury. In accord with this logic, the defendant's fault in causing an accident is not diminished solely because the plaintiff knowingly assumes a risk. If assumption of risk is retained in its current common law form, a plaintiff would be completely barred from recovery even if his conduct is reasonable or only slightly unreasonable. In our comparative fault system, it would be incongruous to absolve the defendant of all liability based only on whether the plaintiff assumed the risk of injury. Comparative negligence by definition seeks to assess and compare the negligence of both the plaintiff and defendant. This goal would clearly be thwarted by adhering to the common law defense of assumption of risk.

We therefore hold that a plaintiff is not barred from recovery by the doctrine of assumption of risk unless the degree of fault arising therefrom is greater than the negligence of the defendant. To the extent that any prior South Carolina cases are inconsistent with this approach, they are overruled. Express and primary implied assumption of risk remain unaffected by our decision.

Cotton Hope argues that even if this Court abrogates assumption of risk as a complete defense, the trial court's directed verdict should be upheld [because] as a matter of law, Davenport's negligence exceeded that of Cotton Hope. We disagree.

The trial court based its ruling on the fact that Davenport knew of the danger weeks before his accident, and he had a safe, alternate route. However, there was also evidence suggesting Cotton Hope was negligent in failing to properly maintain the lighting in the exterior stairway. In the light most favorable to Davenport, it could be reasonably concluded that Davenport's negligence in proceeding down the stairway did not exceed Cotton Hope's negligence. Thus, it is properly submitted for jury determination.

NOTES AND PROBLEMS

1. ***Express, Primary Implied, and Secondary Implied.*** The court in *Davenport* begins by observing differences between these three varieties of assumption of the risk. What are the essential differences? Why does the court believe that express and primary implied assumption of the risk should be unaffected by a jurisdiction's movement from contributory negligence to comparative fault? Why does this not hold true as well (for most courts) with regard to secondary implied assumption of the risk?

2. ***The Rescue Doctrine Revisited.*** You may recall that one of the two functions of the rescue doctrine (covered in Chapter 6, Special Duty Rules) is to invalidate any attempted application of the defense of secondary implied assumption of the risk in the case of a rescuer. Do you see how a rescuer might be deemed to have knowingly and voluntarily encountered a risk by engaging in certain rescue efforts? For this reason, the law traditionally has held that this defense should not apply to rescuers. Because most states have now shifted to comparative fault and, accordingly, eliminated the doctrine of secondary implied assumption of the risk, this aspect of the rescue doctrine has little utility. You may recall that the rescue doctrine only applied to rescuers whose decision to engage in a rescue effort was "reasonable." With unqualified secondary implied assumption of the risk effectively abolished in most states, only unreasonable conduct applied through comparative fault would be a defense against an injured rescuer. And, by definition, whenever the rescue doctrine applies there has been no such unreasonable conduct. Accordingly, the only remaining viable defense of comparative fault would not apply anyway.

Upon Further Review

Reflecting courts' judgment that an express assumption of the risk can constitute private parties' freedom to delineate their respective rights and responsibilities on private matters, courts will enforce such exculpatory clauses when they clear these two hurdles: (i) they do not touch upon public concerns, and (ii) are drafted with sufficient clarity so that there is no doubt that the agreement truly represents the intention of the plaintiff prior to the accident. Secondary implied assumption of the risk, by contrast, is premised more on the apparent inconsistency between a plaintiff knowingly and voluntarily encountering a risk created by defendant's negligence, and then trying to hold the defendant responsible post-accident. When this decision by the plaintiff is unreasonable (i.e., qualified secondary implied assumption of the risk), it looks essentially the same as contributory negligence. As states began to abandon contributory negligence in favor of comparative fault, it made sense to eliminate qualified assumption of the risk as a separate defense doctrine. With respect to the unqualified application of the doctrine, courts appreciated the particular anomaly that would result if a plaintiff's reasonable decision to encounter the risk created by defendant's negligence were barred under that doctrine, even though comparative fault would not reduce the plaintiff's award. As a result, modern courts in states that have moved to comparative fault tend to permit a defense only when the jury finds the decision unreasonable (i.e. negligent), and then this fault is apportioned. In other words, in most states today there is no longer any secondary implied assumption of the risk — only comparative fault.

Watch "Assumption of the Risk" video on Casebook Connect.

IMMUNITIES

Another set of affirmative defenses arise, based not upon the agreement or the conduct of the plaintiff, but upon the status of the defendant or the special status of the relationship between the plaintiff and the defendant. These are immunities to suit that exist to prevent liability for very different reasons. The first is *sovereign immunity*, a common law doctrine originally premised upon the quaint idea that "the king can do no wrong." This doctrine, which applies to both the federal and state and local governments, has some exceptions that are frequently the subject of litigation. There are also *intrafamilial immunities* that have existed, both (a) between spouses and (b) between parents and their children.

A. Sovereign Immunity

1. The Federal Government

CESTONARO v. UNITED STATES

211 F.3d 749 (3d Cir. 2000)

SCIRICA, J.

This appeal requires us to interpret the "discretionary function" exception to the Federal Tort Claims Act's general waiver of sovereign immunity. The District Court dismissed a wrongful death complaint against the United States, finding that the discretionary function exception to the Federal Tort Claim Act's waiver of sovereign immunity, 28 U.S.C. §2680(a), applied. We will reverse.

The underlying facts are undisputed. In December 1993, Daniele Cestonaro, his wife Giovanna, and their daughter, all Italian citizens and residents, were vacationing in St. Croix, Virgin Islands. On the evening of December 28, the Cestonaros parked their rental car in a lot on Hospital Street in Christiansted. Upon returning to their car after dinner, the Cestonaros were confronted by two armed gunmen. Daniele Cestonaro was shot and died almost immediately.

The Hospital Street lot falls within the boundaries of the Christiansted National Historic Site owned and controlled by the United States Department of the Interior, National Park Service. At the time of the murder, the Hospital Street lot was not an official parking lot. There were no signs designating or even indicating that it was a parking lot; it was neither paved nor striped. The lot's appearance, however, differed from the surrounding area in the Christiansted National Historic Site in terms of grade and surface, as it consisted of broken asphalt from a previous paving. Since the 1940s, the general public had used the Hospital Street lot as a parking area. Furthermore, the National Park Service was aware that crimes had occurred in the lot before December 28, 1993. In addition to crime incidents reports from the Virgin Island Police Department and its own park rangers, the National Park Service also received regular complaints about safety in the Hospital Street lot from local business owners.

It is undisputed that the National Park Service had done nothing to deter nighttime parking in the Hospital Street lot. It had not posted signs prohibiting parking, nor signs warning of dangers of nighttime parking, nor issued tickets for illegal parking. In fact, the lot was lighted at night. Some time after the lot came into the government's possession, five lights were installed illuminating the Hospital Street lot. It is undisputed the National Park Service maintained those lights.

Giovanna Cestonaro filed a wrongful death action against the United States under the Federal Tort Claims Act and the Virgin Islands Wrongful Death Statute. In her complaint, Mrs. Cestonaro alleged that "defendant was negligent in failing to provide adequate lighting and correct the known dangerous condition and to warn others about the existence of the dangerous condition" at the Hospital Street lot. The United States filed a motion to dismiss under Fed. R. Civ. P. 12(b)(1) asserting the District Court lacked subject matter jurisdiction because the challenged National Park Service actions fell under the discretionary function exception to the FTCA's waiver of sovereign immunity.

The District Court dismissed the complaint, finding the National Park Service's decisions concerning the Hospital Street lot were grounded in its mission to "safeguard the natural and historic integrity of national parks" and in its policy "to minimally intrude upon the setting of such parks." Mrs. Cestonaro appealed.

The Federal Tort Claims Act is a partial waiver of the sovereign immunity that would otherwise protect the United States from tort liability stemming from the actions of its employees. The express purpose of the FTCA is to make the United States liable "in the same manner and to the same extent as a private individual under like circumstances. . . ." 28 U.S.C. §2674. But the FTCA's waiver is tempered by several exceptions. For our purposes, the relevant exception is the "discretionary function exception" that withdraws the waiver of sovereign immunity with regard to:

> Any claim based upon . . . the exercise or performance or the failure to exercise or perform a discretionary function or duty on the part of a federal agency or an employee of the Government whether or not the discretion involved be abused.

28 U.S.C. §2680(a).

The exception "marks the boundary between Congress' willingness to impose tort liability upon the United States and its desire to protect certain governmental activities from exposure to suit by private individuals." *United States v. S.A. Empresa de Viação Aérea Rio Grandense (Varig Airlines)*, 467 U.S. 797 (1984). The FTCA does not, however, define "discretionary function." As a result there has arisen a trove of case law identifying the contours of the government's tort liability.

The analytical framework of the discretionary function exception has been laid out by the Supreme Court in a trilogy of cases — *United States v. S.A. Empresa de Viação Aérea Rio Grandense (Varig)*, 467 U.S. 797 (1984); *Berkovitz v. United States*, 486 U.S. 531 (1988); and *United States v. Gaubert*, 499 U.S. 315 (1991).

The first issue is whether "a federal statute, regulation, or policy specifically prescribes a course of action for an employee to follow." *Berkovitz*, 486 U.S. at 536. If so, the exception cannot apply. If not, the question is whether the governmental action or inaction "is of the kind that the discretionary function exception was designed to shield." Id. If it is, the action constitutes the exercise of protected discretion, and the United States is immune from suit.

The touchstone of the second step of the discretionary function test is susceptibility to policy analysis. As we have previously stated, a plaintiff's claim can only survive if "the challenged actions cannot 'be grounded in the policy of the regulatory regime.'" *Gotha*, 115 F.3d at 179. The Court in *Gaubert* underscored the importance of the relationship between the discretionary decision and policy considerations, noting the exception applies only if the challenged actions can "be said to be based on the purposes that the regulatory regime seeks to accomplish."

Before proceeding to apply the discretionary function analysis to the facts of this case, there is one remaining preliminary issue — we must identify the challenged action. In effect, plaintiff challenges the National Park Service's decisions concerning lighting and warning in the Hospital Street lot.

As noted, the first step in our analysis is whether there was discretion over the challenged action, that is, whether a federal regulation or policy specifically prescribes a course of action. Plaintiff contends the National Park Service, by virtue of a 1985 agreement with the Virgin Islands, had no discretion with respect to the Hospital Street lot. According to the plaintiff, the 1985 Addendum mandated the removal of the Hospital Street lot by 1988, thereby eliminating any National Park Service discretion.

The District Court addressed the argument in two ways. First, it expressed skepticism that the 1985 Addendum constituted the kind of mandate that prevented the government's recourse to the discretionary function exception. Second, it held the plaintiff did not allege negligence on the part of the National Park Service for failing to close the parking lot, but rather for failing to provide adequate lighting or to warn of known dangers associated with nighttime parking in the lot.

Given the qualification "subject to the availability of funds" [within the Addendum, this] does not appear to be the kind of express mandate that precludes coverage by the discretionary function exception. *See, e.g., Berkovitz*, 486 U.S. at 536 ("The discretionary function exception will not apply when a federal statute, regulation, or policy specifically prescribes a course of action for an employee to follow."). Here, the National Park Service's determination whether there were funds available seems to be the kind of judgment or choice inherent in the discretionary function exception.

But we need not determine whether the 1985 Addendum eliminates the National Park Service's discretion regarding the use of the Hospital Street lot. We agree with the District Court that the 1985 Addendum does not mandate a specific course of conduct and cannot be dispositive with respect to lighting and warning decisions in the Hospital Street lot. The lighting and warning decisions here, therefore, remain discretionary.

But this does not end our inquiry. We must determine whether the discretionary lighting and warning decisions are susceptible to policy analysis and therefore enjoy the protection of the discretionary function exception. *See, e.g., Gaubert*, 499 U.S. at 322-23 ("Even assuming the challenged conduct involves an element of judgment, it remains to be decided whether that judgment is of the kind that the discretionary function exception was designed to shield.").

The National Park Service contends its decisions (or non-decisions) not to add lighting nor to post warning signs were grounded in its overarching objective of returning the area to its historic appearance. The government points to several documents to ground this policy concern. First, it relies on the original 1952 Memorandum of Agreement, which established the National Historic Site with the purpose of preserving the integrity of the historic structures and grounds. It also points to a 1972 Memorandum of Agreement which recited that its "basic objective in the management of Christiansted National Historic Site is to retain the architectural and historical integrity of the structures and their environment." The National Park Service also argues it is not expressly required to add lighting or post warning signs in the Hospital Street lot.

The National Park Service's arguments are inapposite. It may be arguable that the initial decision to maintain parking at the Hospital Street lot was protected by the discretionary function exception. But assuming this were so, subsequent decisions concerning the Hospital Street lot were not necessarily protected. *See, e.g., Indian Towing Co., Inc. v. United States,* 350 U.S. 61 (1955); *George v. United States,* 735 F. Supp. 1524 (M.D. Ala. 1990).

Indian Towing involved alleged negligence by the United States Coast Guard in its failure to properly maintain the light on a lighthouse it had established. Despite the Coast Guard's claim of sovereign immunity, the Court found the United States could be held liable under the FTCA for the negligent operation of the lighthouse even though the initial decision to establish a lighthouse was discretionary. The Court explained

> The Coast Guard need not undertake the lighthouse service. But once it exercised its discretion to operate a light on Chandeleur Island and engendered reliance on the guidance afforded by the light, it was obligated to use due care to make certain that the light was kept in good working order; and, if the light did become extinguished, then the Coast Guard was further obligated to use due care to discover this fact and to repair the light or give warning that it was not functioning. If the Coast Guard failed in its duty and damage was thereby caused to petitioners, the United States is liable under the Tort Claims Act.

Indian Towing Co., 350 U.S. at 69.

In *George*, a District Court rejected the National Forest Service's attempt to invoke the discretionary function exception when Mr. George was attacked by an alligator while swimming in a recreational swimming area designated by the Forest Service. The court held that although the decision to establish the swimming area was discretionary, the subsequent failure to warn the public of known dangers was not covered by the exception.

Even if there was protected discretion for the National Park Service's decision to maintain parking at the Hospital Street lot, that does not answer whether subsequent decisions were also protected.

The National Park Service fails to show how providing some lighting, but not more, is grounded in the policy objectives with respect to the management of the National Historic Site. Similarly, the National Park Service has not presented a viable argument as to how its alleged failure to warn is rooted in its policy objectives.

Accordingly, we see no tension between our decision and those reached in the cases cited. Under proper circumstances, the National Park Service may balance aesthetic and safety interests and avoid liability through the discretionary function exception. To properly invoke an aesthetic interest, there must be a reasonable relationship between that interest and the challenged action.

In our view, plaintiff's suit does not put the District Court in the position of second guessing a National Park Service administrative decision that is "grounded in social, economic, and political policy." We are unable to find a rational nexus between the National Park Service's lighting or warning decisions (or non-decisions) and social, economic and political concerns. Nor will plaintiff's claim seriously impede the National Park Service's proper functions or operations.

For the reasons stated, we hold the discretionary function exception does not apply to the National Park Service's decisions concerning the Hospital Street lot. We will reverse the judgment of the District Court and remand for proceedings consistent with this opinion.

NOTES AND PROBLEMS

1. *FTCA and DFE.* The common law says that citizens cannot sue the government in tort unless the government permits it. It used to be that, at the federal government level, citizens hurt due to government neglect would petition a local congressman to try to get a bill passed by Congress permitting their particular claim. Eventually Congress decided to pass a broad statutory waiver called the Federal Tort Claims Act ("FTCA"):

> [T]he district courts . . . shall have exclusive jurisdiction of civil actions on claims against the United States, for money damages . . . for injury or loss of property, or personal injury or death caused by the neglect or wrongful act or omission of any employee of the Government while acting within the scope of his office or employment, under circumstances where the United States, if a private person, would be liable to the claimant in accordance with the law of the place where the act or omission occurred.

28 U.S.C. §1346(b)(1) (2009). One major restriction on this waiver of immunity is the so-called *discretionary function exception* ("DFE"), which states that the waiver in §1346(b)(1) does not apply to any claim "based upon the exercise or performance or the failure to exercise or perform a discretionary function or duty on the part of a federal agency or an employee of the Government, whether or not the discretion involved be abused." 28 U.S.C. §2680(a) (2009).

2. ***Other Limitations on Federal Government Liability.*** Other federal statutes make clear that, even for claims permitted by the FTCA, there is no governmental liability for pre-judgment interest or for punitive damages. Furthermore, there is no liability for strict liability torts or intentional torts. Finally, all suits under the FTCA are within the federal courts' exclusive subject matter jurisdiction, and the claimant is not entitled to a jury trial. How can such limitations be constitutional? Because the federal government need not permit *any* suits (and none were permitted at common law when the U.S. Constitution was adopted), and so such limitations are permissible. In other words, it is only by the grace of the king that any suit at all may be maintained.

3. ***Problems.*** With regard to the following fact patterns, would the challenged actions of the federal government likely be within the DFE's exception (and thus immune)?

- **A.** Assume there is a federal regulation that declares that no doctor at a Veteran's Administration hospital may work more than 20 hours in a day. The plaintiff is hurt when a tired VA doctor in her 23rd consecutive hour cuts an artery during surgery and kills the patient. The local VA administrator permitted the doctor to work that many hours despite the regulation because he felt that this doctor could work extraordinary hours.
- **B.** A Bureau of Prisons regulation requires that all exercise equipment be checked on a regular cycle to ensure it is in good working order. The warden at a Federal Correctional Institute decides that an examination once a quarter will be sufficient due to concerns about staff resources. A prisoner is hurt when a pull-down bar collapses. This bar had not been checked since the last quarterly cycle.
- **C.** A postal worker driving his route is in a hurry and decides to speed through a school zone, neglecting to see a child step out in front of him. He runs over the child.

2. *State and Local Governments*

While the common law has applied sovereign immunity, or governmental immunity, to not only the federal government but also to state and local governments, there have been some important differences. First, in many states the common law has evolved into a dichotomy between *governmental* vs. *proprietary* services of the government. That is, when a state or local government is performing a service or task that is considered governmental, immunity from suit exists; however, it does not exist when the government is performing in a proprietary capacity. In at least some states, the lack of a coherent way to determine what is proprietary and what is governmental has caused some wholesale reexamination of the immunity doctrine.

CAMPBELL v. INDIANA

284 N.E. 733 (Ind. 1973)

ARTERBURN, J.

These cases were consolidated for the purposes of appeal. The facts in the two cases are somewhat different, but the outcome of both is dependent on the same question of law. The cases were decided separately in the Court of Appeals and were consolidated upon transfer to the Supreme Court.

In the *Campbell* case the appellants sustained personal injuries as a result of a head-on collision with an automobile traveling in appellant's lane of traffic upon a state-maintained highway. In their complaint appellants alleged negligence on the part of the state in that, after repaving the highway, it failed to: (a) mark with a yellow line the aforesaid State Road 221 where it is unsafe to pass; and (b) carelessly and negligently failed to install no passing signs along Road 221 or any other signs indicating to the traveling public that the public highway was unsafe for passing. Appellants also contended that the road as maintained constituted a nuisance.

In the *Knotts* case, the appellant sued the City of Indianapolis and the State of Indiana complaining that he sustained $100,000 in damages because of personal injuries incurred as the result of a fall on a crosswalk in Indianapolis. Appellant alleged that the injuries were the result of the negligent state of repair of the crosswalk. The fall occurred on the crosswalk at the intersection of Market Street and Monument Circle in Indianapolis. Monument Circle is a part of the state highway system and as such, the State of Indiana is responsible for its care and maintenance. In both *Campbell* and *Knotts* the state filed a motion to dismiss in the trial court alleging that there was no basis upon which relief could be granted premised upon the doctrine of sovereign immunity. In both cases the trial court sustained the motion and the Court of Appeals affirmed the rulings. Thereafter, both appellants petitioned this court for transfer to resolve the status of the doctrine of sovereign immunity in Indiana.

Both the *Campbell* and *Knotts* briefs raise the issue of whether the State of Indiana still recognizes the common law doctrine of sovereign immunity. The doctrine in its present form is a far cry from the original common law principle which exempted the sovereign from liability in court on the basis that "the king could do no wrong." The doctrine has been amended and eroded until the most that remains is an abstract and confusing principle which finds literally no continuity between jurisdictions. The purpose for which the doctrine was created has long since vanished and it is now time to finally reexamine the basis of the rule.

The original adoption of the doctrine in America following the Revolutionary War was founded on the premise that the new government was not financially secure enough to face claims of negligence in its governmental activities. Therefore, the English Common Law was adopted and the same immunity which protected the King from liability was adopted to protect the states.

The first inroad in Indiana to limit the doctrine occurred in the case of *City of Goshen v. Myers* (Ind. 1889), 21 N.E. 657, where the court held that:

> In our opinion, it was the duty of the city of Goshen to keep the bridge under consideration in repair. The public bridges within the limits of the cities of the State, located upon the streets and public highways of the cities — and such cities, where they take charge of the same, are liable to persons suffering injury or loss. . . ."

Id. at 658-59.

Out of early forms of municipal liability grew the current governmental-proprietary standard which has been applied to the state and its subdivisions. This is in essence a court-made distinction as to the types of activities which governmental bodies perform, created to ameliorate the harshness of total governmental immunity. It is generally held that if a governmental body is negligent in performing a proprietary function, it will be liable for its negligence; while, if its activity is classified as governmental, the defense of sovereign immunity shall apply.

Exactly what constitutes a proprietary function as opposed to a governmental function has never been clearly enunciated by the courts, and this failure to establish a criteria has led to the generally confused state of the bench and bar in the application of the doctrine of sovereign immunity. Deciding on useful guidelines between rather obscure, whimsical notions enunciated by the appellate courts throughout the country has caused enormous conflicts in the courts in the past decade. However, the fact that the doctrine is beyond the scope of explicit definition has not halted its application. In the case of *Flowers v. Board of Commissioners of County of Vanderburgh* (Ind. 1960), 168 N.E.2d 224, this court held, in regard to appellant recovering for injuries sustained in a skating rink operated by the county and for use of which admission was charged [that the defendant was liable to the plaintiff because its activity was proprietary rather than governmental in nature].

Further erosion of the doctrine followed in the case of *Brinkman v. City of Indianapolis* (Ind. 1967), 231 N.E.2d 169, in which the Appellate Court abolished the right of a city to claim the defense of sovereign immunity regardless of whether the nature of the act was governmental or proprietary. The court reasoned:

> The governmental-proprietary rule, however, often produces legalistic distinctions that are only remotely related to the fundamental considerations of municipal tort responsibility. As for example, it does not seem to be good policy to permit the chance that a school building may or may not be producing rental income at the time determine whether a victim may recover for a fall into a dark and unguarded basement stairway or elevator shaft. Neither does it seem to be good policy to find that a municipal garbage truck is engaged in a *nonimmune* proprietary function when en route from a wash rack to the garage while the same truck is engaged in an *immune* governmental function when enroute to a garbage pickup.
>
> The extent to which a municipal corporation should be held liable for torts committed by its officers or employees in the course of the employment is a perplexing problem that has been the subject of litigation on many occasions. There has been a general apprehension that fraud and excessive litigation would result in

> unbearable cost to the public in the event municipal corporations were treated as ordinary persons for purposes of tort liability. On the other hand the unfairness to the innocent victim of a principle of complete tort immunity and the social desirability of spreading the loss — a trend now evident in many fields — have been often advanced as arguments in favor of extending the scope of liability. It is doubtful whether the purposes of tort law are well served by either the immunity rule or its exceptions. After careful consideration we are of the opinion that *the doctrine of sovereign immunity has no proper place in the administration of a municipal corporation.*" (Emphasis added)

Id. at 172.

The next logical step was taken in the case of *Klepinger v. Board of Commissioners* (Ind. 1968), 239 N.E.2d 160. The court abrogated immunity for all counties in Indiana. In the aftermath of *Klepinger* all that remained was immunity to the state. The court in *Klepinger* made it clear that the governmental-proprietary distinction was to be completely disregarded in cases involving city or county immunity.

In *Perkins* v. *State* (1969), 252 Ind. 549, 251 N.E.2d 30, the Supreme Court utilized the governmental-proprietary function to limit the application of the doctrine on the state level. In *Perkins*, the appellants fell ill due to the contamination of a lake with raw sewage. They had rented a lakeside cottage in a state park for which the maintenance thereof was the duty of the state. The trial court sustained the state's motion to dismiss on the ground that the court did not have jurisdiction due to the sovereign immunity of the state. The Supreme Court reversed, holding that such operation was a proprietary activity, and, therefore, the state could not avail itself of the immunity privilege. Following the holding in *Perkins*, all that remained of sovereign immunity was immunity on the part of the state from negligent acts occurring while the state was in performance of a solely "governmental function." Exactly what a governmental function constituted was not yet clearly defined.

With only a mere fraction of the original doctrine remaining, we are faced with the task of attempting to eliminate the confusion surrounding the doctrine.

The argument has been presented that elimination of the doctrine of sovereign immunity will impose a disastrous financial burden upon the state. Assuming there is any relevancy to this contention, we point out that the abrogation of sovereign immunity on the state level is consistent with conditions already existing in cities and counties in this state. If city and county governments can withstand the consequences of such liability, where traffic hazards seemingly are greater, the state should be able to also bear such burden.

We may also add that the elimination of sovereign immunity means a more equitable distribution of losses in society caused by the government unto members of society, rather than forcing individuals to face the total loss of the injury.

The state argues that abolition of sovereign immunity will result in a great number of problems for the state. Inability to collect payment for claims against the state, inability of the state to secure adequate insurance, and prospective legal chaos are cited as examples of some of these problems. The arguments which the state presents are questions which properly belong to the legislature in facing and solving the problems of liability.

We do not mean to say by this opinion that all governmental units can be held liable for any and all acts or omissions which might cause damage to persons. For example, one may not claim a recovery because a city or state failed to provide adequate police protection to prevent crime. *Simpson's Food Fair v. City of Evansville* (Ind. 1971), 272 N.E.2d 871. Nor may one recover damages because a state official made an appointment of an individual whose incompetent performance gives rise to a suit alleging negligence on the part of the state official for making such an appointment. Likewise the United States Supreme Court has recognized a judicial immunity. *Pierson v. Ray* (1967), 386 U.S. 547. On this subject matter Professor Prosser, in his treatise, stated the following:

> At the very outset it was more or less obvious that some vestige of the governmental immunity must be retained. It was, for example unthinkable that either state [or] a municipality should be held liable for a wrong decision of its courts, for an erroneous evaluation of property by a tax assessor. In several of the decisions abrogating the immunities, there was language used which reserved the possibility that there might still be immunity as to 'legislative' or 'judicial' functions, or as to acts or omissions of government employees which were 'discretionary.'

Prosser, *Law of Torts* §131, at 986 (4th ed. 1971.)

Therefore, it appears that in order for one to have standing to recover in a suit against the state there must have been a breach of duty owed to a private individual.

Finding no basis for the continuation of the doctrine of sovereign immunity as applicable to the state any more than it is applicable to municipal corporations and counties, we hold that such a defense by the state is not available to any greater extent than it is now available to municipal corporations and counties of this state. Judgment of the trial court is reversed with directions to vacate by ruling on the motion to dismiss in each case and to enter an order overruling such motion and for further proceedings in conformity with this opinion.

NOTES AND PROBLEMS

1. ***Proprietary vs. Governmental.*** Though Indiana repudiated this common law distinction, many states still retain the rule that immunity at the state and local level exists for governmental functions but not proprietary functions. The standard for judging between the two is often vague. For example, here is one court's articulation of the test: "[W]hether in providing such services, the governmental entity is exercising the powers and duties of government conferred by law for the general benefit and well being of its citizens." Edwards v. City of Portsmouth, 375 S.E.2d 747, 750 (Va. 1989). This is an incredibly nebulous test that affords little predictability in deciding, for

example, whether an ambulance service run by a municipality is proprietary or governmental. In such states where this dichotomy still prevails, one can only be safe in finding published decisions that are on point.

2. ***Statutory Waiver at the State/Local Level.*** Even for activities that are governmental, a state might have statutes that permit partial waivers of immunity. Unlike the FTCA, which provides a broad waiver of immunity subject to some exceptions (like the DFE), most states retain a broad immunity with statutes that provide limited waivers. For example, many state waivers of immunity apply where someone's injury arises out of the state government's use of real or personal property. Much litigation ensues, of course, over what such phrases actually mean. Again, it is imperative to resort to the decisional law of such jurisdictions to understand the application of such statutes.

B. Spousal and Parental Immunity

At common law, one spouse was not permitted to sue the other in tort. In application, this rule of law was applied if the tort claim arose during the marriage or if the spouses were married at the time of the lawsuit's filing. So entrenched was this rule that even after the demise of the original justification — that the wife was indistinct from her husband — courts continued to apply this doctrine based upon new justifications. In most states, this immunity has been abolished, in whole or in part, for reasons similar to those set forth below in *Price*. The court's discussion and abandonment of the doctrine exemplifies the process by which an antiquated tort doctrine eventually passes away. With respect to parental immunity, though the doctrine has less bite than it used to have, most courts continue to recognize some vitality in the limited doctrine. As you read the next two cases, consider why most courts have rejected spousal immunity but continue to give credence to some level of parental immunity.

1. Spousal Immunity

PRICE v. PRICE

732 S.W.2d 316 (Tex. 1987)

KILGARLIN, J.

This case presents us with the opportunity to re-examine the validity of the doctrine of interspousal immunity. The case originated as a civil action of negligence for personal injuries brought by Kimberly Parmenter Price against her husband, Duane Price. Duane Price's motion for summary judgment was granted. The court of appeals affirmed that judgment. We reverse the judgment of the court of appeals and remand this cause to the trial court.

In July of 1983, Kimberly Parmenter, at the time a *feme sole*, was injured when a motorcycle on which she was riding collided with a truck. The motorcycle was driven by Duane Price. Six months after the accident, Duane and Kimberly were married. After marriage, Kimberly brought this action seeking recovery from her husband, Duane, and from the driver of the truck, claiming that the negligence of these drivers had caused her injuries. The driver of the truck and his employer settled. The trial court, in granting summary judgment for Duane, relied on the doctrine that one spouse could not sue another for negligent conduct.

The doctrine of interspousal immunity is a part of the common law, having been judicially created. Its origins are shrouded in antiquity, but the basis of the doctrine is *"that a husband and wife are one person." Firebrass v. Pennant*, 2 Wils. 255, 256 (C.P. 1764) (emphasis in original).

A woman's disability during coverture was an essential ingredient in fostering the doctrine. As was stated in *Thompson v. Thompson*, 218 U.S. 611, 614-15 (1910):

> At common law the husband and wife were regarded as one, — the legal existence of the wife during coverture being merged in that of the husband; and, generally speaking, the wife was incapable of making contracts, of acquiring property or disposing of the same without her husband's consent. They could not enter into contracts with each other, *nor were they liable for torts committed by one against the other* (emphasis added).

An earlier thesis on American law expanded the concept of superiority of the husband over the wife even to the extent of restraining her liberty or disciplining her. 2 Kent's Com. 174 (8th ed. 1854). While in this, the last quarter of the twentieth century, such views seem preposterous, recognition that those views were prevalent in the law makes easily understandable why suits by wives against husbands were not permitted.

However, the husband/wife unity argument as grounds for the doctrine was severely impeded by the adoption of what were known as Married Women Acts. These legislative acts occurred principally in the latter half of the nineteenth century and early twentieth century. These acts, while varying from state to state, generally gave wives the rights to own, acquire and dispose of property; to contract; and, to sue in respect to their property and contracts. Most importantly, many of the statutes specifically abolished the doctrine of the oneness of husband and wife.

With the demise of the legal fiction of the merger of husband and wife into a single entity, the doctrine of interspousal immunity found support in considerations of marital harmony, as well as the potential for collusive lawsuits. Restatement (Second) of Torts §895F, comment d (1979).

American jurisdictions, in upholding the doctrine, early on espoused the premise that a civil suit by one spouse against another would destroy the harmony of the home. One court, in a fire and brimstone opinion upholding the prohibition against suits between spouses, foresaw all manner of evil should the immunity doctrine be terminated. In *Ritter v. Ritter*, 31 Pa. 396 (1858), that court, while observing that a favorite maxim at common law was that marriage makes a man and woman one person at law, also said:

> Nothing could so complete that severance [of the marriage relationship] and degradation, as to throw open litigation to the parties. The maddest advocate for woman's rights, and for the abolition on earth of all divine institutions, could wish for no more decisive blow from the courts than this. The flames which litigation would kindle on the domestic hearth would consume in an instant the conjugal bond, and bring on a new era indeed—an era of universal discord, of unchastity, of bastardy, of dissoluteness, of violence, cruelty, and murders.

The second argument for barring interspousal suits, the possibility of collusive lawsuits, is entirely inconsistent with the subjugation of wife to husband and preservation of happy homes theses. Nevertheless, such inconsistency did not seem to trouble the courts. The possibility of collusion was alluded to in *Abbott v. Abbott*, 67 Me. 304 (1877), where it was suggested that a widow could raid her deceased husband's estate by claiming all sorts of wrongs by him during his lifetime. The fraud theory expanded into vogue with the advent of insurance to cover vehicular accidents. In *Newton v. Weber*, 119 Misc. Rep. 240, 196 NYS 113, 114 (1922), the court said of allowing a tort action by a wife against her husband, "the maintenance of an action of this character, unless the sole purpose be a raid upon an insurance company, would not add to conjugal happiness and unison."

Without ascribing any reasons for doing so, Texas adopted the doctrine of interspousal immunity one hundred years ago in *Nickerson and Matson v. Nickerson*, 65 Tex. 281 (1886). *Nickerson* barred all civil actions for tort between husband and wife.

The doctrine remained firmly established as Texas law until *Bounds v. Caudle*, 560 S.W.2d 925 (Tex. 1977). *Bounds* abrogated the rule as to intentional torts. In *Bounds*, this court concluded that suits for willful or intentional torts would not disrupt domestic tranquility since "the peace and harmony of a home" which had "been strained to the point where an intentional physical attack could take place" could not be further impaired by allowing a suit to recover damages.

Is there today any policy justification for retaining this feudal concept of the rights of parties to a marriage? Apparently, our colleagues on the Court of Criminal Appeals have decided "no" in respect to the marital discord argument. The Fourth Court of Appeals questioned the justification of the policy when it observed:

> While the new legislation [the Married Women Acts] forced recognition of the rights of a married woman to recover from her husband if he broke the leg of her mule, the courts continued to clothe him with immunity if he tortiously broke his wife's leg.

> It has never been satisfactorily explained how permitting the wife to recover for her husband's conduct which tortiously injures her property would not disrupt domestic harmony, while allowing her to recover for bodily injury would.

Sneed v. Sneed, 705 S.W.2d 392, 394 (Tex. App.—San Antonio 1986, writ ref'd n.r.e.).

Dean William Prosser, a preeminent commentator on tort law, certainly agreed that the doctrine is indefensible. He has stated:

> Stress has been laid upon the danger of fictitious and fraudulent claims, on the very dubious assumption that a wife's love for her husband is such that she is more likely to bring a false suit against him than a genuine one; and likewise the possibility of trivial actions for minor annoyances, which might well be taken care of by finding consent to all ordinary fictions of wedlock—or at least assumption of risk! The chief reason relied upon by all these courts, however, is that personal tort actions between husband and wife would disrupt and destroy the peace and harmony of the home, which is against the policy of the law. This is on the bald theory that after a husband has beaten his wife, there is a state of peace and harmony left to be disturbed; and that if she is sufficiently injured or angry to sue him for it, she will be soothed and deterred from reprisals by denying her the legal remedy.

Prosser, *Law of Torts*, §122 at 863 (4th ed. 1971). While it is true that part of this quote involves intentional rather than negligent torts, the arguments in favor of interspousal immunity are generally equally applicable, and lacking, as to both. It is difficult to fathom how denying a forum for the redress of any wrong could be said to encourage domestic tranquility. It is equally difficult to see how suits based in tort would destroy domestic tranquility, while property and contract actions do not.

As to the potential for fraud and collusion, we are unable to distinguish interspousal suits from other actions for personal injury. In *Whitworth v. Bynum*, 699 S.W.2d 194, 197 (Tex. 1985), this court "refuse[d] to indulge in the assumption that close relatives will prevaricate so as to promote a spurious lawsuit." Our system of justice is capable of ascertaining the existence of fraud and collusion. The Supreme Court of West Virginia, abolishing the rule in *Coffindaffer v. Coffindaffer*, 244 S.E.2d 338, 343 (1978), stated:

> Anyone who has confronted insurance defense counsel in personal injury cases knows that it is a rare occasion when the false or collusive claim escapes their searching examination. We do an injustice not only to the intelligence of jurors, but to the efficacy of the adversary system, when we express undue concern over the quantum of collusive or meritless lawsuits. There is, to be sure, a difference between the ability to file a suit and to achieve a successful result. It is upon the anvil of litigation that the merit of a case is finally determined. Forged in the heat of trial, few but the meritorious survive.

In regards to both the domestic tranquility and fraud arguments, Prosser and Dean Page Keeton have said "almost no legal writer has had any use for these arguments, and under repeated criticisms and reiterated attacks on them in the courts, judicial perception of these arguments has slowly shifted." W. Prosser & P. Keeton, *Law of Torts* §122 at 902 (5th ed. 1984).

Other jurisdictions have preceded us in either completely or partially abolishing the doctrine of interspousal immunity.

The doctrine of interspousal immunity has previously been abrogated as to some causes of action in this jurisdiction. We now abolish that doctrine completely as to any cause of action. We do not limit our holding to suits involving vehicular accidents only, as has been done by some jurisdictions and as has been urged upon us in this case. To do so would be to negate meritorious claims such as was presented in *Stafford v. Stafford*, 726 S.W.2d 14 (Tex. 1987). In that case a husband had transmitted a venereal disease to his wife, resulting in an infection that ultimately caused Mrs. Stafford the loss of her ovaries and fallopian tubes, ending for all time her ability to bear children. While we ruled for her, the issue of interspousal immunity had not been preserved for our review. To leave in place a bar to suits like that of Mrs. Stafford or other suits involving non-vehicular torts would amount to a repudiation of the constitutional guarantee of equal protection of the laws. This we will not do.

Our result today is compelled by the fundamental proposition of public policy that the courts should afford redress for a wrong, and the failure of the rationale supporting the doctrine to withstand scrutiny. We therefore reverse the judgment of the court of appeals upholding the trial court's summary judgment, and remand this cause to the trial court for further proceedings.

2. Parental Immunity

SANDOVAL v. SANDOVAL

623 P.2d 800 (Az. 1981)

CAMERON, J.

We must answer the following question on appeal: Does the parental immunity doctrine, as it presently exists in Arizona, bar a suit by a minor child against his parents for negligence in leaving a gate open through which the minor child drove his tricycle and was injured by a passing automobile?

On 22 January 1977, four-year-old Ramero Sandoval rode his tricycle from his front yard into the street in front of his home and was run over by an automobile driven by Mr. Noe Perez Lopez. Ordinarily, the gate to the fenced front yard is closed and the child rides his tricycle inside the yard, but in this case the child's father, Antonio Sandoval, negligently forgot to close the gate when he left the house prior to the accident.

Mr. Perez was an uninsured motorist. The parents of Ramero did not have uninsured motorist insurance, but did have a homeowner's insurance policy which they believed would pay a judgment that might be obtained by the minor child against the parents.

The child, through his guardian ad litem, filed a complaint against his parents alleging that the cause of his injuries was their negligence. The superior Court of Maricopa County granted the parents' motion for summary judgment based upon the doctrine of parental immunity.

The principles of parental immunity were formulated in the landmark case of *Hewlett v. George (Ragsdale)*, 9 So. 885 (1891). In that case the Mississippi Supreme Court stated the following rationale:

> The peace of society, and of the families composing society, and a sound public policy, designed to subserve the repose of families and the best interests of society, forbid to the minor child a right to appear in court in the assertion of a claim to civil redress for personal injuries suffered at the hands of the parent.

This case has been followed by a majority of state courts because of the need to preserve family unity and prevent collusion between family members against their insurance companies. See Annotation, Liability of Parent for Injury to Unemancipated Child Caused by Parent's Negligence, 41 A.L.R.3d 904. However, with the advent of the automobile and the increasing presence of insurance, a minority of jurisdictions has abrogated parental immunity where the minor has been injured as a result of the negligent driving of a parent. E.g., *Hebel v. Hebel*, 435 P.2d 8 (Alaska 1967); *Briere v. Briere*, 224 A.2d 588 (N.H. 1966); *Goller v. White*, 122 N.W.2d 193 (Wisc. 1963). Prior to 1970, Arizona clearly followed *Hewlett*, supra, see *Purcell v. Frazer*, 435 P.2d 736 (1967), but in 1970 we overruled *Purcell*, and partially abrogated the immunity doctrine in the case of *Streenz v. Streenz*, 471 P.2d 282 (Az. 1970). Both the *Purcell* and *Streenz* cases involved minor children injured in automobile accidents through the negligent driving of a parent. Our two reasons for abrogating parental immunity in *Streenz* were: (1) That the common law has long allowed suits by a child against a parent in property and contract actions. Therefore, it is reasonable that the law should protect the rights of the child in a personal injury action as well. (2) The existence of liability insurance to compensate the plaintiff, particularly in automobile accident cases, negates the possibility of disrupting family unity. After balancing the potential for disruptive suits against the need to compensate injured parties, we held that the minor child could sue her parents for injuries sustained through the negligent driving of her mother. We did not, however, abolish the doctrine in its entirety. We stated:

> Our holding today is not a total abrogation of the parental immunity doctrine. Rather we agree . . . that 'the role of *paterfamilias* should not be usurped by the judiciary as to intrafamilial activities involving parental discipline, care and control.'

In *Streenz* we cited with approval *Goller v. White*, supra, which held that parents would not be immune from suit in personal injury actions brought by their children against them *except* in two situations:

> (1) Where the alleged negligent act involves an exercise of parental authority over the child; and (2) where the alleged negligent act involves an exercise of ordinary parental discretion with respect to the provision of food, clothing, housing, medical and dental services, and other care. *Goller v. White*, supra, 20 Wis. 2d at 413, 122 N.W.2d at 198.

In *Streenz* we also cited with approval a later case of the same Wisconsin court. *Lemmen v. Servais*, 158 N.W.2d 341 (Wisc. 1968). In *Lemmen*, a child was injured when she was struck by a car after she alighted from a school bus. The child sued the driver of the car, who then filed a third-party claim against the parents for contribution to any recovery obtained by the child. The basis of the driver's claim was that the parents were negligent in failing to properly instruct their child on safety procedures in crossing the street. The court held that the second exception stated in *Goller*, supra, applied to make the parents immune from suit, because they were acting within their discretion as parents with respect to the "other care" of their child. The court stated:

> The two exceptions set forth in *Goller* are directed toward preserving, fostering and maintaining a proper and wholesome parent-child relationship in a family. The immunity granted by these two exceptions is accorded the parent, not because he is a parent, but because as a parent he pursues a course within the family constellation which society exacts of him and which is beneficial to the state. The parental nonliability is not granted as a reward, but as a means of enabling the parents to discharge the duties which society exacts.

Lemmen, at 343-344.

In *Streenz*, we did not delineate precisely the areas in which parental immunity would continue to be a bar to suit by a minor for the negligence of his parents, though it is apparent that automobile cases are ones in which the doctrine of parental immunity is abolished. This, however, is not an automobile case in the usual sense in that the parent's obligation did not arise out of his driving of an automobile. The direct cause of Ramero's injuries was the impact of the Perez automobile, not the act of leaving the gate open. We distinguish this act from the act of the parents in *Streenz*, supra, in which the parent, as a driver, had a duty to the world at large to drive carefully. If an accident resulted because of the parent's negligent driving, any passenger in the vehicle could have been injured, and the driver should be liable to that passenger regardless of the fact that the passenger is the child of the driver.

A case with similar facts is the Illinois case of *Cummings v. Jackson*, 372 N.E.2d 1127 (Ill. App. 1978). There the parent, in violation of a city ordinance, failed to trim the trees between the edge of the street and the parent's property line. This obstructed the view of a driver who ran over the minor child. The Illinois Court of Appeals stated:

> [A] suit charging a breach of a duty owed the general public is not as disruptive to a family unity as one charging breach of duty owed primarily to family members and thus bringing into contention the inner workings of the family.
>
> In the instant case the duty alleged to have been breached by the mother concerned the maintenance of trees on the area immediately adjacent to the home. The duty was owed primarily to the general public, however, and only incidentally to the members of the family living in the house. Although the question is a close one, we conclude that the injury to plaintiff was not alleged to arise out of the family relationship.

372 N.E.2d at 1128.

We believe that *Cummings* is distinguishable from the instant case in that the mother had a duty to the public (imposed by city ordinance) to keep the trees trimmed, and insofar as her failure was the proximate cause of the minor child's injuries, she could be liable. In the instant case, the closing of the gate was a duty owed to the child alone and a part of the parental "care and control" or "other care" to be provided by the parents.

> The familial obligations imposed by nature because of the parental relationship, imperfect though they may sometimes be because of the ever present common denominator of human behavior, are quite distinct from the general obligation which the law imposes upon every one in all his relations to his fellow men, and for the breach of which it gives a remedy.
>
> A new and heavy burden would be added to the responsibility and privilege of parenthood, if within the wide scope of daily experiences common to the upbringing of children a parent could be subjected to a suit for damages for each failure to exercise care and judgment commensurate with the risk.

Lemmen v. Servais, Id. 344.

Regrettably, the injured child may be foreclosed from recovery. Assuming the driver was negligent, the lack of recovery results more from the fact that the driver of the automobile which injured the child was uninsured than from the fact of parental immunity. We hold that the act of leaving a gate open should not subject the plaintiff's parents to suit and that the trial court properly granted summary judgment to the defendants.

We do not, by this case, limit the abrogation of the parental immunity doctrine to automobile negligence cases. We will continue to consider, on a case by case basis, the actual cause of the injury and whether the act of the parent breached a duty owed to the world at large, as opposed to a duty owed to a child within the family sphere.

Judgment affirmed.

NOTES AND PROBLEMS

1. ***Abrogation of Spousal Immunity.*** In the vast majority of states, spousal immunity no longer exists. The doctrine's original rationale was conceptual and based upon a legal fiction — that the husband and wife were one person (i.e., the husband). While that flawed premise eventually became too obvious to ignore, courts continued to recognize the doctrine based upon one of two inconsistent premises: (1) that the suit was a legitimate legal dispute between the spouses and would destroy the marriage; or (2) that the suit was a fraudulent attempt to reach into the pockets of an insurance policy. Why did the court in *Price* determine that neither of these arguments supported the doctrine any longer?

2. ***Partial Abrogation of Parental Immunity.*** Courts have frequently mentioned similar concerns regarding a child's suit against her parent — disruption to family harmony and the potential for insurance fraud. Yet notwithstanding this similarity, most courts continue to recognize at least a limited version of the parental immunity doctrine. Notice in *Sandoval* that the court makes a distinction between cases involving negligent driving or negligent tree maintenance and those involving alleged negligent supervision of the children. Given this distinction, what seems to be the remaining concern with completely abrogating parental immunity?

3. ***Parental Discipline Privilege and Immunity.*** The *Sandoval* court was concerned with whether a negligence claim might still be covered by immunity. When a parent spanks a child or places the child in "time out," what prevents the child from suing for an intentional tort? Courts have long held that there is a privilege or immunity for such conduct — that would otherwise qualify as an intentional tort — so long as it involves the good faith use of reasonable force or imposition of punishment in a way that is necessary to control, train, and educate the child. As one court described this immunity to discipline:

> Not every spanking is a battery and not every 'time out' in one's bedroom is a false imprisonment. The parent's prerogative to exercise authority and attend to a child's needs must be exercised within reasonable limits. When her conduct so far exceeds the discharging of normal parental duties and responsibilities, the public policies of peace, tranquility and discipline in the home are no longer served by this doctrine of immunity.

Brozdowski v. Southern Conn. Gas Co., 192 Conn. Super. LEXIS 2534 (Conn. Sup. 1992). In extreme cases of unreasonable punishments, neither the court nor agencies of the state have a problem declaring the conduct extreme and wrongful and offering sanctions in the forms of civil tort suits, criminal prosecution, or other regulatory sanctions such as removing the child from the home. Might spanking become so taboo that eventually this immunity will no longer permit such battery to occur?

4. ***Problems.*** Should the following claims against the victims' parents be barred by parental immunity?

A. A father allows his 13-year-old daughter to stay out late without a curfew, and she is injured while running around town with her friends after midnight.

B. A mother is watching out her living room window while her 5-year-old plays a game in the alley behind their house with other children. A car coming down the alley hits the child.

C. A mother purchases a new lawn mower and decides to remove the deflector shield from the side of the mower. As a result, while the mother is mowing the yard one day, some rocks shoot out the side of the mower and hit her son in the eye — causing him to become blind.

D. A famous NFL player disciplines his pre-school son by using a wooden spoon to spank him causing cuts, marks, and bruising to his thigh and back.

Watch "Parental Immunity" video on Casebook Connect.

Upon Further Review

Advising a client that her otherwise strong tort claim is barred because the target defendant is immune from a civil lawsuit can be daunting. Most lay people are shocked to hear of the concept of civil immunity. While some immunities have ancient origins, whether or not the immunity will have modern vitality often depends upon whether currently acceptable alternative justifications exist. "The king can do no wrong" might suffice in the eighteenth century, but twentieth-century Americans would not tolerate such a rationale for federal governmental immunity. Instead, the concept of not using taxpayer funds to benefit isolated individuals can instead justify the doctrine. And while few states cling to spousal immunity, most still recognize a legitimate need to continue to protect certain uniquely parental decisions from judicial oversight or second-guessing.

STATUTES OF LIMITATION AND REPOSE

Like the immunity defenses and unlike comparative fault, statutes of limitation defenses have nothing to do with the factual merits of the lawsuit. Even the best tort claim will be "dead on arrival" if filed in an untimely manner. Every civil cause of action, including all tort claims, has a limited shelf life as set by a statute. Many personal injury claims, for example, must be brought within two or three years. Many defamation claims are time-barred after one year. Lawyers must be careful in several respects when planning their tort litigation. First, a careful understanding of the applicable statute is required to ensure that counsel knows exactly what starts the running of the clock. Second, counsel must be aware of the availability of (and the limits on) equitable doctrines that are sometimes utilized by courts to provide additional time to bring a claim. When applicable, these equitable doctrines can stop the clock for a period of time. Finally, counsel also needs to distinguish between a statute of *limitation* and a statute of *repose*; the latter sometimes has harsh results by declaring a claim time-barred before the plaintiff even owns a tort cause of action.

A. Statutes of Limitation

1. Accrual of a Claim

CRUMPTON v. HUMANA, INC.

661 P.2d 54 (N.M. 1983)

Payne, J.

This is a frivolous appeal. We also note that there is a strong indication in the record that counsel for the appellant ineptly and perhaps negligently handled his client's case. Counsel for the appellant failed to file suit before the applicable statute of limitations had run. We are disappointed when members of our State Bar betray the trust and confidence of their clients by engaging in careless and unprofessional practice.

On February 8, 1979, Wanda Crumpton underwent surgery at Llano Estacado Medical Center in Hobbs. She alleged that she sustained injuries to her neck and legs when an attending nurse attempted to lower her hospital bed on February 11, 1979. Her suit was filed more than three years later on February 15, 1982. The trial court granted a motion for summary judgment on the ground that the suit was barred by the three-year statute of limitations. Crumpton now appeals and argues that the exact date of her injury may not be ascertainable.

Crumpton argues that her injury was not ascertainable until some time after the accident occurred. Further, she contends that the statute of limitations should have been tolled during the time the parties were negotiating.

These arguments are entirely without merit. In her deposition, Crumpton plainly testified that her injuries occurred on February 11, 1979. She also testified that she is still having problems in her shoulders, legs and sides which she attributed to the February 11, 1979 incident. Crumpton offers no evidence to contradict the fact that the alleged negligent act and injury occurred simultaneously on February 11, 1979. In our view, the fact that she had continuing treatments and hospitalizations after the injury does not necessarily make the date of the injury unascertainable.

Under . . . the general three-year statute of limitations, Section 37-1-8, Crumpton's suit is barred. [This statute of limitation] clearly indicates that the statute of limitations commences running from the *date of injury*. . . . In *Peralta v. Martinez*, 90 N.M. 391, 564 P.2d 194 (Ct. App. 1977), *cert. denied*, 90 N.M. 636, 567 P.2d 485 (1977), the Court of Appeals stated at page 394:

> 'The injury is done when the act heralding a possible tort inflicts a damage which is physically objective and ascertainable'. . . . We hold the limitation period begins to run from the time the injury manifests itself in a physically objective manner *and* is ascertainable.

Crumpton cites no authority for her argument that the statute of limitations should be tolled during the time when the parties were negotiating a settlement. The record indicates that defendants did not fraudulently lead Crumpton to believe that the case would be settled at some future date. In fact, the record indicates that in May 1981, defendants sent Crumpton a letter wherein defendants made a final offer for a compromise settlement of the case.

Accordingly, we affirm the trial court's grant of summary judgment against Crumpton. Because we determine this appeal to be frivolous and entirely without merit, costs and attorneys fees are to be borne by appellants.

IT IS SO ORDERED.

2. *The Legal Injury Rule and the Discovery Rule Exception*

S.V. v. R.V.

933 S.W.2d 1 (Tex. 1996)

HECHT, J.

R. intervened in her parents' divorce proceeding, alleging that her father, S., was negligent by sexually abusing her until she was seventeen years old. (Given the sensitive nature of these allegations, we refer to the parties only by initials to avoid the use of proper names.) Because R. did not sue her father within two years of her eighteenth birthday as required by the applicable statutes of limitations, her action is barred as a matter of law unless the discovery rule permits her to sue within two years of when she knew or reasonably should have known of the alleged abuse. R. contends that the discovery rule should apply in this case because she repressed all memory of her father's abuse until about a month after she turned twenty, some three months before she intervened in the divorce action. The district court directed a verdict against R. on the grounds that the discovery rule does not apply in this case, and that R. adduced no evidence of abuse. A divided court of appeals reversed and remanded for a new trial. We reverse the judgment of the court of appeals and affirm the judgment of the district court on limitations grounds.

Before we review the evidence in this case it is important to have clearly in mind the issue that is crucial in determining whether to apply the discovery rule. To pose that issue we begin with an analysis of our discovery rule jurisprudence.

We have long recognized the salutary purpose of statutes of limitations. In *Gautier v. Franklin*, 1 Tex. 732, 739 (1847), we wrote that statutes of limitations are justly held

> as statutes of repose to quiet titles, to suppress frauds, and to supply the deficiencies of proof arising from the ambiguity, obscurity and antiquity of transactions. They proceed upon the presumption that claims are extinguished, or ought to be held extinguished whenever they are not litigated in the proper forum at the prescribed period. They take away all solid ground of complaint, because they rest on the negligence or laches of the party himself; they quicken diligence by making it in some measure equivalent to right. . . .

Joseph P. Story, Conflicts of Law 482.

More recently, we explained:

> Limitations statutes afford plaintiffs what the legislature deems a reasonable time to present their claims and protect defendants and the courts from having to deal with cases in which the search for truth may be seriously impaired by the loss of evidence, whether by death or disappearance of witnesses, fading memories, disappearance of documents or otherwise. The purpose of a statute of limitations is to establish a point of repose and to terminate stale claims.

Murray v. San Jacinto Agency, Inc., 800 S.W.2d 826, 828 (Tex. 1990).

The enactment of statutes of limitations is, of course, the prerogative of the Legislature. At the time this case was filed and tried, the applicable statute was the one governing personal injury actions generally, which provided: "A person must bring suit for . . . personal injury . . . not later than two years after the day the cause of action accrues." Tex. Civ. Prac. & Rem. Code §16.003(a). The code contains two other provisions relevant to this case. One is: "If a person entitled to bring a personal action is under a legal disability when the cause of action accrues, the time of the disability is not included in the limitations period." Tex. Civ. Prac. & Rem. Code §16.001(b). The other is: "For the purposes of this subchapter, a person is under a legal disability if the person is: (1) younger than 18 years of age." *Id.* §16.001(a). Thus, a person has until his or her twentieth birthday (or the next business day, §16.072) to bring suit for personal injury from sexual assault if — and here we come to the root of the problem in the case before us — the cause of action "accrued" while the person was a minor.

Many other statutes peg the beginning of the limitations period on the date the cause of action "accrues." Occasionally the date of accrual is defined. *E.g.*, Tex. Civ. Prac. & Rem. Code §16.003(b) (a wrongful death cause of action "accrues on the death of the injured person"). More often, however, the definition of accrual is not prescribed by statute and thus has been left to the courts. As a rule, we have held that a cause of action accrues when a wrongful act causes some legal injury, even if the fact of injury is not discovered until later, and even if all resulting damages have not yet occurred. *Trinity River Auth. v. URS Consultants, Inc.*, 889 S.W.2d 259, 262 (Tex. 1994). We have not applied this rule without exception, however, and have sometimes held that an action does not accrue until the plaintiff knew or in the exercise of reasonable diligence should have known of the wrongful act and resulting injury.

Accrual of a cause of action is deferred in two types of cases. In one type, those involving allegations of fraud or fraudulent concealment, accrual is deferred because a person cannot be permitted to avoid liability for his actions by deceitfully concealing wrongdoing until limitations has run. The other type, in which the discovery rule applies, comprises those cases in which "the nature of the injury incurred is inherently undiscoverable and the evidence of injury is objectively verifiable." These two elements of inherent undiscoverability and objective verifiability balance the conflicting policies in statutes of limitations: the benefits of precluding stale or spurious claims versus the risks of precluding meritorious claims that happen to fall outside an arbitrarily set period. Restated, the general principle is this: accrual of a cause of action is deferred in cases of fraud or in which the wrongdoing is fraudulently concealed, and in discovery rule cases in which the alleged wrongful act and resulting injury were inherently undiscoverable at the time they occurred but may be objectively verified. This principle, while not expressed in every deferred accrual case, is derived from them and best defines when the exception to the legal injury rule has been and should be applied.

We have considered the "inherently undiscoverable" element of the discovery rule in several cases. *Willis*, 760 S.W.2d at 645 (lawyer's error could not be discovered by client who was ignorant of the law); *Nelson*, 678 S.W.2d at 923 (malpractice in muscular dystrophy gene screening could not be discovered by parents until child showed symptoms); *Kelley*, 532 S.W.2d at 949 (false credit report could not be discovered until credit denied); *Hays*, 488 S.W.2d at 414 ("One who undergoes a vasectomy . . . and then after tests is told that he is sterile, cannot know that he is still fertile . . . until either his wife becomes pregnant or he is shown to be fertile by further testing."); *Gaddis*, 417 S.W.2d at 578 ("it is often difficult, if not impossible, to discover that a foreign object has been left within the body within the statutory period of limitation"). The common thread in these cases is that when the wrong and injury were unknown to the plaintiff because of their very nature and not because of any fault of the plaintiff, accrual of the cause of action was delayed.

To be "inherently undiscoverable," an injury need not be absolutely impossible to discover, else suit would never be filed and the question whether to apply the discovery rule would never arise. Nor does "inherently undiscoverable" mean merely that a particular plaintiff did not discover his injury within the prescribed period of limitations; discovery of a particular injury is dependent not solely on the nature of the injury but on the circumstances in which it occurred and plaintiff's diligence as well. An injury is inherently undiscoverable if it is by nature unlikely to be discovered within the prescribed limitations period despite due diligence.

We have also considered the "objectively verifiable" element of the rule in a number of cases. In *Gaddis*, a patient claimed that her doctors were negligent in leaving a sponge inside her body after surgery. The presence of the sponge in her body — the injury — and the explanation for how it got there — the wrongful act — were beyond dispute. The facts upon which liability was asserted were demonstrated by direct, physical evidence. In contrast, *Robinson* involved a claim by a patient against his doctors for misdiagnosis of his back condition. We summarized the issue this way:

> Plaintiff, to prove his cause of action, faces the burden of proving both a mistake in professional judgment and that such mistake was negligent. Expert testimony would be required. Physical evidence generally is not available when the primary issue relevant to liability concerns correctness of past judgment. Unlike *Gaddis v. Smith* there exists in the present case no physical evidence which in-and-of-itself establishes the negligence of some person. What physical evidence was to the cause of action alleged in *Gaddis v. Smith*, expert testimony is to the cause of action in the present case. Even the fact of injury is a matter of expert testimony.

Expert testimony, we concluded, did not supply the objective verification of wrong and injury necessary for application of the discovery rule.

In the present case plaintiff R. claims that her father sexually abused her and that she unconsciously repressed all memory of it for years. If the legal injury rule were applied, R.'s claims against S. would each have accrued on the date the alleged incident of abuse occurred. In applying the statute of limitations, however, the years of her minority are not included. In effect, then, under the legal injury rule, R. is in the same position as if her claims all accrued on her eighteenth birthday and limitations began to run on that date, expiring about four months before she filed suit. R.'s claims are therefore barred unless she is entitled to an exception to the legal injury rule. R. does not allege fraud or fraudulent concealment, nor could she. R. was not deceived into thinking that she was not being abused when she was. To the contrary, R.'s contention is that she was fully aware of the episodes of abuse, so painfully so that she repressed all memory of them for years. Thus, for accrual to be deferred the discovery rule must apply. For the discovery rule to apply, R.'s claim must have been inherently undiscoverable within the limitations period and objectively verifiable.

We have twice held a fiduciary's misconduct to be inherently undiscoverable. *Willis*, 760 S.W.2d at 645 (attorney); *Slay*, 187 S.W.2d at 394 (trustee). The reason underlying both decisions is that a person to whom a fiduciary duty is owed is either unable to inquire into the fiduciary's actions or unaware of the need to do so. While a person to whom a fiduciary duty is owed is relieved of the responsibility of diligent inquiry into the fiduciary's conduct, so long as that relationship exists, when the fact of misconduct becomes apparent it can no longer be ignored, regardless of the nature of the relationship. Because parents generally stand in the role of fiduciaries toward their minor children, *see Thigpen v. Locke*, 363 S.W.2d 247, 253 (Tex. 1962), R. was not obliged to watch for misconduct by her father as long as she was a minor. Again, however, R. does not claim to have been misled.

Nevertheless, given the special relationship between parent and child, and the evidence reviewed in detail below that some traumas are by nature impossible to recall for a time, we assume without deciding that plaintiff can satisfy the inherent undiscoverability element for application of the discovery rule. We therefore focus on the second element of objective verifiability. The question is whether there can be enough objective verification of wrong and injury in childhood sexual abuse cases to warrant application of the discovery rule.

The literature on repression and recovered memory syndrome establishes that fundamental theoretical and practical issues remain to be resolved. These issues include the extent to which experimental psychological theories of amnesia apply to psychotherapy, the effect of repression on memory, the effect of screening devices in recall, the effect of suggestibility, the difference between forensic and therapeutic truth, and the extent to which memory restoration techniques lead to credible memories or confabulations. Opinions in this area simply cannot meet the "objective verifiability" element for extending the discovery rule.

Accordingly, we conclude that the discovery rule does not apply in this case.

We do not, of course, impose any additional requirements on proof of a childhood sexual abuse case brought within the applicable limitations period. The objective verifiability requirement of the discovery rule does not apply in proving the case on the merits.

Nor are we insensitive to the terrible wrong of childhood sexual abuse and the strong public policies condemning it as reflected in the criminal statutes. False accusations of abuse are equally devastating to families, however. As several state legislatures have already realized, the law must approach these difficult cases with an appreciation of all the interests affected. We believe the best approach is to apply the discovery rule in the same manner that we have applied it today . . . and would apply it in any other case.

The judgment of the court of appeals is reversed and the judgment of the district court is affirmed.

NOTES AND PROBLEMS

1. ***Interpreting the Word "Accrue."*** When analyzing any statute of limitation issue, it is important to understand that the judicial history of interpreting a particular statute may impact its meaning in a significant way. Many statutes of limitation — which are frequently phrased to run from the time a claim "accrues" — are interpreted in light of the *legal injury rule.* This means, as the court held above, that because a cause of action is complete when injury has occurred, the claim accrues upon the happening of the physical injury

regardless of whether the plaintiff realizes she has been injured. *See e.g.*, Rod v. Farrell, 291 N.W.2d 568 (Wis. 1980) (interpreting the medical malpractice statute of limitation use of the word "accrue" to refer to the date of the injury and finding the claim barred even though plaintiff had no way to discover the claim until 17 years later). Sometimes, however, a court will interpret a statute of limitation to implicitly incorporate a discovery rule so that the claim does not "accrue" under it until the plaintiff knew or should have known he had a possible claim. *See e.g.*, Hanley v. Citizens Bank of Massachusetts, 2001 W.L. 717106 (Mass. Super. 2001) (interpreting a statute of limitation that granted a plaintiff "three years after the cause of action accrues" to mean the plaintiff had until three years after an event took place that would "reasonably likely put the plaintiff on notice that someone may have caused her injury"). Some statutes of limitation expressly incorporate a discovery rule into the text of the statute. For example, Tex. Civ. Prac. & Rem. Code §16.010 provides that in a claim for misappropriation of trade secrets, the claim must be brought within "three years after the misappropriation is discovered or by the exercise of reasonable diligence should have been discovered." What is significant is that a lawyer should not assume, in the absence of express statutory language, that a client is entitled to the benefit of a discovery rule.

2. *Alternative Definitions of "Accrue" in Statutes.* Sometimes the legislature will draft particular statutes of limitation that expressly contain an alternative definition for when the claim accrues. For example, many wrongful death claims are governed by statutes of limitation that expressly state that the claim accrues on the death of the injured person. In cases where, following an accident, the primary victim does not die for an extended period of time, the normal time to file suit could significantly increase.

3. *Limitations in Repressed Sexual Abuse Cases.* Other courts have reached similar conclusions as the Texas Supreme Court did in *S.V.* For example, in Doe v. Maskell, 679 A.2d 1087, 1093 (Md. 1996), the court found that plaintiff's claims of repressed memory of sexual abuse as a minor by a chaplain at a parochial school were barred by the applicable statute of limitations and that the discovery rule was inapplicable: "[W]e are unconvinced that repression exists as a phenomenon separate and apart from the normal process of forgetting. Therefore we hold that the mental process of repression of memories of past sexual abuse does not activate the discovery rule."

4. *Problems.* Should the applicable statutes of limitation bar the following claims?

A. A statute of limitation provides that all personal injuries claims must be filed within three years of the accrual of the claim. Plaintiff uses Defendant's insecticide in her garden to protect her tomato plants from certain bugs. Her repeated exposure to the chemical over five years results in increasing levels of fatigue and dizziness. In year five, her doctor diagnoses her condition as resulting from the chemical exposure. She discontinues use of the product and sues due to her permanent neurological impairment.

B. Plaintiff is kidnapped by Defendant and held hostage in his basement in Cleveland for 10 years. She finally escapes and sues him for all of her injuries. The applicable statute of limitation provides for a two-year period to bring all claims for personal injuries upon their accrual.

B. Statutes of Repose

Statutes of limitation typically run from the date a cause of action "accrues," which is either the date of injury (damage or legal injury being the last element of a tort cause of action) or, when the discovery rule applies, the date that the plaintiff knew or should have known of a possible claim. Sometimes the legislature is concerned that a case might be filed against a defendant long after the defendant's conduct giving rise to the claim has occurred. This could happen if the defendant's negligence sets in motion a sequence of events that does not harm the plaintiff for many years. For example, if you negligently exposed your workers to asbestos but it did not result in injury for two decades, a worker's suit against you might still be timely under a two-year statute of limitation so long as the sick worker filed suit soon after becoming ill. Or, in cases where the discovery rule is applied to a statute of limitation, the plaintiff's lengthy delay in bringing suit might be justified where the plaintiff's injury was inherently undiscoverable for a period of time.

For these reasons, legislatures sometimes will craft a *statute of repose* — an additional or alternative requirement for bringing a suit within a period of time running from the date of a particular event, such as the date of the defendant's negligence. These are increasingly enacted in many states for medical malpractice cases, product liability cases, and construction defect cases. Although the terms of the particular statutes ultimately guide the analysis, courts typically find that the discovery rule is inapplicable to statutes of repose. To apply a discovery rule would undermine the definite deadline offered by such a statutory scheme. In this instance, the only avenue around missing such a deadline might be through the doctrine of *fraudulent concealment* — that the defendant concealed the existence of the claim. The *Kern* case below discusses this equitable tolling doctrine in a statute of repose scenario. Statutes of repose also raise the possibility that someone might be barred from bringing a claim based upon a deadline that had already passed prior to the plaintiff even being injured or owning a cause of action. Efforts to attack the unconstitutionality of such statutes of repose are often difficult, as we will see.

KERN v. ST. JOSEPH HOSPITAL

697 P.2d 135 (N.M. 1985)

FEDERICI, J.

This medical malpractice action is before us on writ of certiorari. [Plaintiff's decedent Dale Kern appealed from the affirmance of the trial court's summary judgment in favor of defendants Dr. Doyle Simmons and X-Ray Associates based upon the statute of repose.] We reverse the Court of Appeals and the trial court.

Dale Kern received external beam radiation therapy for cancer of the bladder at St. Joseph Hospital in Albuquerque, New Mexico. The treatments were administered by defendant Dr. Simmons, an employee of defendant-respondent, X-Ray Associates, from August 16, 1977, through September 22, 1977. Kern and his wife were told by Dr. Simmons that Kern's therapy would consist of 30 treatments of radiation. After Kern had received 25 treatments, however, the therapy was discontinued without explanation. When Kern and his wife asked Dr. Simmons the reason for the early termination of the therapy, Dr. Simmons did not respond and appeared to stare off in the other direction. After the radiation treatments, Kern experienced problems with frequency of urination and the passing of blood in his bowel movements and urine. Kern died on August 30, 1982. The cause of death listed on the death certificate was sepsis-urinary tract infection due to or as a consequence of irradiation cystitis and proctitis and/or urinary bladder cancer.

Both Kern and his wife believed that the problems Kern experienced after the radiation therapy were acceptable complications of the treatments. They were never informed that Kern had received an excessive amount of radiation. However, after reading a newspaper article in 1981 regarding excessive radiation having allegedly been administered at St. Joseph Hospital, they began to suspect the propriety of Kern's treatment. Kern and his wife employed a lawyer to investigate whether Kern's radiation therapy had been administered properly.

This lawsuit was filed on March 21, 1983, by Kern's widow in her capacity as personal representative of her husband's estate. She alleged that her husband's death was due to the negligent administration and calculation of external beam radiation therapy. Dr. Simmons and X-Ray Associates filed a motion for summary judgment contending that petitioner's lawsuit was barred by NMSA 1978, Section 41-5-13. The trial court and the Court of Appeals agreed.

Section 41-5-13 requires that a claim be filed "within three years after the date that the act of malpractice occurred. . . ." Petitioner argues that there is no malpractice until there is injury and that the statute, therefore, should not start to run until the injury has manifested itself in a physically objective manner and is ascertainable. She argues that *Peralta v. Martinez*, 564 P.2d 194 (N.M. Ct. App.), *cert. denied*, 567 P.2d 485 (1977) and the general rules of statutory construction compel such an interpretation. We disagree.

Prior to the enactment of the Medical Malpractice Act in 1976, malpractice actions were governed by the general statute of limitations applicable to all personal injury actions, NMSA 1953, Section 23-1-8, which is now NMSA 1978, Section 37-1-8. This statute reads, in applicable part, "for an injury to the person or reputation of any person, within three years." Primarily because of the use of the word "injury," *Peralta* interpreted this statute of limitations "to run from the time the injury manifests itself in a physically objective manner *and* is ascertainable." *Peralta v. Martinez* at 394, 564 P.2d at 197 (emphasis in original). *Peralta* is not controlling in the present case, therefore, for two reasons. First, it construes a different statute of limitations. Second, Section 41-5-13 makes no reference to "injury" or any such comparable term. In fact, *Peralta* recognized this significant wording difference between the general statute of limitations it was construing and NMSA 1953, Section 58-33-13 (Int. Supp. 1976), the precursor of Section 41-5-13.

We agree with the Court of Appeals that the meaning of Section 41-5-13 is clear and unambiguous. If the language of a statute is not ambiguous, the literal meaning of the words must be applied. The statute clearly starts to run from the time of the occurrence of the act giving rise to the cause of action. Since we find the meaning of this statute unambiguous, there is no need to resort to rules of construction.

We recognize that this statute may be harsh when applied to latent injury cases. Although the "wrongful act rule," as our type of statute has become known, was once the general rule, it is now generally disfavored and many states have enacted some form of discovery provision which typically provides for the cause of action not to accrue until the patient discovers or should have discovered the injury. Any changes to our statute, however, should be made by the Legislature and not by the courts.

In the present case, petitioner's lawsuit was filed more than three years after Kern's last radiation treatment and is barred by Section 41-5-13 unless the statute was tolled by the doctrine of fraudulent concealment. New Mexico recognizes the doctrine of fraudulent concealment in medical malpractice actions. *Hardin v. Farris*, 530 P.2d 407 (N.M. Ct. App. 1974). The doctrine is based not upon a construction of the statute, but rather upon the principle of equitable estoppel. The theory is premised on the notion that the one who has prevented the plaintiff from bringing suit within the statutory period should be estopped from asserting the statute of limitations as a defense.

In *Hardin*, the court recognized the estoppel nature of fraudulent concealment and stated:

> We therefore conclude that where a party against whom a cause of action accrues prevents the one entitled to bring the cause from obtaining knowledge thereof by fraudulent concealment . . . the statutory limitation on the time for bringing the action will not begin to run until the right of action is discovered, or, by the exercise of ordinary diligence, could have been discovered.

Id. at 410. Silence may sometimes constitute fraudulent concealment where a physician breaches his fiduciary duty to disclose material information concerning a patient's treatment. The statute of limitations, however, is not tolled if the patient knew, or through the exercise of reasonable diligence should have known, of his cause of action within the statutory period. If tolled by fraudulent concealment, the statute commences to run again when the patient discovers, or through the exercise of reasonable diligence should have discovered, the malpractice.

Fraus Omnia Corrumpit

"Fraud vitiates everything it touches."

To toll the statute of limitations under the doctrine of fraudulent concealment, a patient has the burden, therefore, of showing (1) that the physician knew of the alleged wrongful act and concealed it from the patient or had material information pertinent to its discovery which he failed to disclose, *and* (2) that the patient did not know, or could not have known through the exercise of reasonable diligence, of his cause of action within the statutory period.

When we consider the record, we find that petitioner did present sufficient evidence to raise an issue of material fact regarding Dr. Simmons' knowledge of excessive radiation having been administered to Kern. The record reveals that in opposition to [defendants'] motion for summary judgment, [Kern] presented the affidavit of a doctor knowledgeable in the field of therapeutic radiology who stated that although the intended treatment plan for Kern conformed with the customary standards at that time, the dose levels given did not follow the plan and were greatly excessive and that such dose levels "will cause unacceptable complications such as those recorded in the medical records as being suffered by Dale Kern, deceased." In addition, the affidavit of a radiation physicist stated, "Whoever calculated the treatment times needed to implement this treatment plan performed a *gross calculation error*." (Emphasis added.) Petitioner also presented her own affidavit which contained the facts set forth at the beginning of this opinion.

In support of his motion for summary judgment, Dr. Simmons filed an affidavit denying knowledge of any malpractice and denying concealment of any material facts. Resolving, however, all doubts in favor of petitioner, we find the evidence sufficient to create a fact issue. The early termination of the treatments without explanation, Dr. Simmons' failure to answer the Kerns' question concerning the early termination, and the statements in the affidavits filed by petitioner lend possible support to petitioner's claims of excessive radiation having been given to Kern, and of "a gross calculation error" having been made in implementing Kern's treatment plan.

Summary judgment was improperly granted. The trial court and the Court of Appeals are reversed. The case is remanded to the trial court for proceedings consistent with this opinion.

NOTES AND PROBLEMS

1. ***Statute of Repose.*** Statutes of repose are intended to operate in a stricter fashion than statutes of limitation. This is often accomplished in one of two ways. First, the statute often begins the running of the deadline from a more specific date, such as the date of the alleged medical malpractice, the date a manufacturer sold a product, or the date a construction project was completed. Second, such statutes are generally considered to be exempt from possible application of any discovery rule, unless the plaintiff facing a possibly stale claim is able to plead and prove fraudulent concealment as in *Kern.*

2. ***Fraudulent Concealment.*** As discussed by the court in *Kern*, fraudulent concealment might consist of the defendant affirmatively covering up information that would reveal a cause of action, perhaps by lying to the plaintiff about certain facts. On the other hand, where there is a fiduciary or special relationship between the parties, fraudulent concealment is possible where the defendant is merely silent. Either way, courts generally hold that the equitable doctrine of fraudulent concealment can be a defense to the application of either a statute of limitation or a statue of repose. By contrast, the discovery rule typically is only available (if at all) as a defense to a statute of limitation.

3. ***Constitutionality of Statutes of Repose.*** Some plaintiffs particularly aggrieved by the harsh application of a statute of repose have challenged its legality, either under a due process or equal protection argument. One noteworthy example is Sedar v. Knowlton Construction Co., 551 N.E.2d 938 (Ohio 1990) in which the plaintiff was injured in a dormitory at Kent State University. In 1985, his arm was injured in a panel of wire-reinforced glass due to alleged faulty design and construction. Unfortunately for the plaintiff, the trial court dismissed his lawsuit filed less than two years later because of the applicable statute of repose for cases involving construction or improvement defects. This statute of repose precluded all claims brought "more than ten years after . . . the furnishing [of construction] services." Because the dormitory was completed in 1966, all claims for defective construction were required to be brought by 1976 — nine years before plaintiff was even hurt. The only way the plaintiff's suit could have been timely was to bring it nearly a decade before he had any injuries. Of course, no such suit was possible then. Nevertheless, the court upheld the statute as a rational exercise of the legislature's power to limit the liability of architects and builders to "encourage [them] to experiment with new designs and materials." By contrast, in Kennedy v. Cumberland Engineering Co., 471 A.2d 195 (R.I. 1984), the Rhode Island Supreme Court held unconstitutional a 10-year statute of repose for product manufacturers — the statute required all claims to be brought within 10 years of the initial sale of the product. The plaintiff was first injured by defendant's product 9 years after its

initial sale; plaintiff had no way of discovering when the product was first sold until after filing suit several years later and obtaining the sales history of the product during discovery. The court held that such harsh application — even to the point where one might not be injured until long after the deadline for suits had passed — violated the right to a forum guaranteed by the state constitution, stating: "[A] product with a life expectancy much greater than ten years can unfairly enjoy a total immunity from the effect of its defect for a great part of the product's useful life. The application of this statute to this plaintiff is no less harsh and unjust." *Id.* at 200.

4. ***Problems.*** Using the same general facts and the statute of repose from the *Kern* case, consider whether the following variations would alter the outcome the court reached:

A. After discontinuing the radiation therapy, neither Kern nor his wife have any conversations with their doctor about the reasons for the premature stopping of his treatments.

B. In response to being questioned by the Kerns about why the treatments were abruptly stopped, their doctor says, "We were concerned that your levels of radiation might be such that you would be at too high of a risk of suffering some complications, and we would rather err on the side of safety."

C. A month after the actual conversation with their doctor about the abrupt termination of Mr. Kern's radiation, Mr. Kern overhears a nurse say, "I sure hope none of our patients were hurt from their exposure to radiation." Mr. Kern is not completely sure what this means and is concerned, but he fails to inquire about it any further.

Upon Further Review

There are few worse feelings for a plaintiff's lawyer than the realization that she has been tardy in filing a client's case. The transformation of a good tort claim into one fraught with a technical deficiency is not only a cause for concern for the lawyer, but also for the lawyer's legal malpractice insurance carrier. Whether as a plaintiff's lawyer trying to screen a new case to be sure it is still viable, or as a defense lawyer reading a new complaint and trying to identify possible affirmative defenses, all trial lawyers need to be able to accurately determine the timetable during which a particular claim must be filed. Generalities will not suffice. Instead, counsel needs to isolate the applicable statute, determine if it is a statute of limitation or a statute of repose, clarify what stops the applicable time period from commencing, and identify if any equitable tolling doctrines might extend the time period during which the claim must be filed.

Pulling It All Together

Paula is on the rooftop of her Colorado home installing Christmas lights on an early December morning. A low-flying military F-18 fighter jet flies overhead circling the mountain on which Paula's home was built. Paula was amazed by the sight of the aircraft, though alarmed at how low it was flying. Rather than leaving her rooftop, however, she decided to stay where the view was good and take photographs of it with her smartphone. Finally it headed directly toward her home; Paula was giddy at the prospect of the image she might capture. However, as it passed overhead, the wind gust generated by the plane's movement through the air literally knocked Paula off her feet, causing her to roll off the edge of the roof and suffer a serious neck fracture. Paula incurred extensive medical bills and it will take her years of therapy to regain the ability to walk. In the meantime, she complained to the Department of Defense within a month of the accident about the low flight of the aircraft. The government official, in response to Paula's complaints, erroneously advised her that the aircraft was never lower than 300 feet—well above the 200-foot ceiling for aircraft practicing combat maneuvers over residential areas dictated by Department of Defense regulations. Three years pass since the accident. Out of desperation to pay her continuing medical bills, she finally consults a lawyer. The lawyer obtains the actual flight records for that F-18's operations on the day of the incident (through a Freedom of Information Act request) and learns that the aircraft was recorded flying as low as 150 feet and that his commander had authorized the low flight as "good training." Assume that there is a governing statute that states, "Any claims for personal injuries caused by aircraft must be brought within two years of the date of the flight."

Analyze any legal impediments to Paula's claims against the United States—30 minutes.

CHAPTER 8

Damages

I. Introduction
II. Actual, Compensatory Damages
III. Limitations on Actual Damages
IV. Nominal Damages
V. Punitive Damages

I INTRODUCTION

CHAPTER GOALS

- ☑ Understand the difference between economic and non-economic damages, the way courts review their award by juries, the necessity to reduce to present value awards of future economic losses, and limitations on court's recognition of certain possible categories of damages.
- ☑ Become familiar with certain damage limiting doctrines and statutes, including failure to mitigate, changes to the collateral source rule, and statutory limits on actual damages.
- ☑ Recognize the limited role for awards of nominal damages.
- ☑ Learn the unique role that punitive damages play in a civil tort system, the prerequisites for imposing such punishment, and the limits on a jury's discretion.

We have spent significant time exploring the details of various tort mainstay causes of action, including a wide variety of intentional torts as well as the behemoth known as negligence law. Then we delved into a number of different affirmative defenses — doctrines that could cause a plaintiff to lose a suit despite being able to prove each and every element of her claim. You might think that you are done, but the fun is just beginning. Because almost all civil tort claims are brought for the recovery of damages, no analysis of a tort claim is fully complete without considering the damages to which a plaintiff might be entitled. Stated another way, without the recovery of damages, there would be virtually no tort litigation. This chapter will demonstrate both the principles governing and the process of ascertaining damages for which a plaintiff might seek recovery. We will begin with a discussion of actual damages, both economic and non-economic, and discover certain rules setting parameters for both the nature and scope of recovery of these compensatory damages, as well as some of the procedures available for proving such damages to the jury. And though they are rarely awarded, no discussion of tort remedies would be complete without considering the prospect of a punitive damage recovery. With regard to such exemplary damages, we will consider both the issue of what misconduct is sufficiently perverse in the eyes of the law to justify the doling out of punishment in a civil suit, and what limits (either constitutional or statutory) might restrict the jury's discretion.

"LADIES AND GENTLEMEN OF THE JURY . . ."

5th Circuit Pattern Jury Instructions (Civil Cases) 15.2 Compensatory Damages:

"If you find that the defendant is liable to the plaintiff, then you must determine an amount that is fair compensation for all of the plaintiff's damages. The purpose of compensatory damages is to make the plaintiff whole — that is, to compensate the plaintiff for the damage that the plaintiff has incurred."

II ACTUAL, COMPENSATORY DAMAGES

A. Special (Economic) Damages

Actual damages awards are designed to make the victim whole by compensating the victim for the harm that has been suffered (past damages) as of the time of trial and all damages likely to be suffered after the trial (future damages). This remedial purpose is why actual damages also go by the name compensatory damages. The two categories of actual damages are often referred to as *special* and *general.* Special damages are economic harms caused by the defendant's misconduct. These are called economic because the items in this category relate to matters for which there are objective economic values in the marketplace. For example, economic losses include lost wages or earning capacity, medical expenses, and property repairs (or lost fair market value of property). Every day medical expenses are, in effect, bought and sold in doctors' offices and hospitals. Medicines have a particular purchase price. When someone has been unable to work due to the accident, the fact finder can ascertain what that person would have earned from their job had they not been hurt. For future lost earning capacity (if the plaintiff's injuries will prevent her from doing some jobs in the future) it is possible to estimate what her earning power would have been in the market but for the injuries. Many times, some of these items of

In Practice

The Federal Rules of Civil Procedure require that if "an item of special damage" is being sought by a plaintiff, "it must be specifically stated" in the complaint.

Fed. R. Civ. P. 9(g).

damages are relatively non-controversial. Simply keeping receipts for certain expenses incurred from injuries can suffice to prove elements of such a loss. Other times, the parties may end up going to trial over disputed issues of economic losses. The *Martin* case below offers a good foray into a fact finder's analysis in setting compensatory damages. We get to peek into the mind of the fact finder because it was a bench trial (due to being a FTCA claim against the U.S. government), and the judge has written findings of fact supporting the entry of a damage award. As you read this opinion, pay close attention to the details of how the court goes about calculating the special damages.

MARTIN v. UNITED STATES

471 F. Supp. 6 (D. Ariz. 1979)

Burns, J.

This is a Federal Tort Claims case tried in the District of Arizona while I was sitting there, by assignment, in February. On February 14, 1979, by oral opinion, I found in favor of plaintiffs on the issue of the government's negligence; in addition, I found against the government on the issue of contributory negligence. Liability having been established, I requested the parties to submit post-trial memoranda concerning damages, so as to permit me to decide the damage issue upon my return to the District of Oregon.

The facts of this near-fatal accident are simple. [Melvin E. Burrows II, one of the two plaintiffs in this case,] . . . a grade school youngster, [was] riding home from school on a motorbike [as a passenger] at about 6:00 P.M. on September 21, 1977, when [the bike] struck a sagging or "down" power line negligently maintained by the government. [Plaintiff suffered] tragically severe and permanent injuries.[1] The damage elements are:

1) Past medical expenses, which are agreed;
2) Future medical expenses, also agreed, save for minor aspects;
3) Present value of lost future earning capacity;
4) Pain and suffering, and interference with normal and usual activities.

1. While my description of plaintiffs' injuries may seem clinical and detached, I did not view their plight without compassion. But it would serve little purpose to adorn this description with emotional adjectives. And my task, in any event, is to make an award based upon the facts, freed from inappropriate considerations such as sympathy, passion or prejudice. This I have tried to do.

Plaintiff Burrows sustained severe burns to his face, head, back, buttocks, arms and legs.

PAST MEDICAL EXPENSES

[P]laintiff has submitted uncontested documentation of past medical expenses totaling $48,130.97.

FUTURE MEDICAL EXPENSES

[P]laintiff originally sought an award of $55,000 for future medical expenses based upon the testimony of Dr. Alan Sacks that each of 11 further contemplated plastic surgeries will cost about $3,000; that the operations should be performed at intervals of approximately six months; that hospital costs have doubled over the past five years; and that future cost increases will be about 12-15% per year. The defendant objected to plaintiff's suggestion that I take judicial notice of the asserted rate of inflation in hospital costs. Defendant also noted that the award could be immediately invested by the plaintiff to generate a return that would at least partially offset future medical care cost inflation. Following my letter of March 20, 1979, to the parties seeking clarification of this matter, the parties agreed to entry of an award for future medical expenses of $48,629. In addition, I award $5,000 for psychological treatments to accompany Melvin's additional surgeries, as recommended by Dr. Aaron Canter, a clinical psychologist who treated Melvin during and after his stay at the Maricopa County Hospital.

LOSS OF EARNING CAPACITY

Probable Earning Capacity Absent the Accident

Clarence Martin is principal of the Florence middle school, owner of a roofing business that employs Melvin Burrows' father, and uncle of the other plaintiff in this case. He testified upon the basis of his observation of Melvin during the seven years he has known him and the month and a half that Melvin had attended the middle school prior to the accident. He believed that Melvin was average or above average in intelligence and probably would have become a skilled worker, perhaps a mechanic or a carpenter. Dr. Glenn Wilt, an associate professor of finance at Arizona State University and an investment counselor, stated:

> [I]t can be reasonably presumed that, but for their injuries, both Melvin and Jeffrey would have gravitated into positions in one of the construction trades. Clearly, that is exactly what most of their uninjured classmates will do, and considering the general demand in this territory, due to the growth of population and need for

attendant services in the construction field, a strong demand can be forecast for these jobs.

Dr. David Yandell, a clinical psychologist and vocational rehabilitation counselor called by the defendant, testified that the intelligence and aptitude tests administered by Dr. Donald Guinoud show that Melvin could not have pursued a career in the skilled crafts but instead probably would have become a laborer. Defendant's other witness, Dr. John Buehler, chairman of the department of economics at the University of Arizona, expressed his opinion that neither plaintiff probably would have become a worker in the skilled trades, but rather each would have earned average wages.[2]

Based upon my evaluation of the testimony and the expertise and credibility of the witnesses, I conclude that Melvin Burrows probably would have become a skilled worker. Dr. Wilt stated that a carpenter would, at 1978 wage rates, earn about $9,450 per year during a four-year apprenticeship and during a subsequent 42-year career as a journeyman carpenter would earn about $18,900 annually in wages and $3,900 annually in fringe benefits. I accept these figures as reasonable approximations of Melvin's lifetime earnings had he not experienced this accident.

Probable Earning Capacity

Dr. Guinourd testified that Melvin might be employable as a night watchman or night diesel mechanic not involved with the public interaction aspect of either business. Dr. Wilt concluded that, because of Melvin's disfigurement and intolerance to sunlight and perspiration, he would probably be unable to find a job suited to his handicap. Dr. Canter testified that Melvin would benefit psychologically from working even at a lowly position.

Based upon the testimony and my own observation of Melvin Burrows, I conclude that he probably will be able to work at an entry-level position for at least half of his normal working life. According to Dr. Wilt, such work would generate an annual income of $3,120 in 1978 dollars. Thus, Melvin is entitled to recover in 1978 dollars $6,330 per year for four years (apprenticeship period), then $19,680 per year for the following 42 years (journeyman period).

---

2. Plaintiff Burrows was born November 30, 1963; thus, he was 12 years old and an eighth grader at the time of the accident. Neither, therefore, has had any work history, making it necessary for damages purposes to predict what each plaintiff's future earnings would have been if the accident hadn't happened. Prediction also is necessary as to actual future earnings in light of the disabilities suffered from the accident. Neither side suggested that either plaintiff would likely become a member of the professions or work in a managerial or entrepreneurial capacity. Thus, each side, in submitting opinions as to the vocational future of the plaintiffs, assumed that each would enter the workforce at 19, upon completion of high school. Plaintiffs' experts, in predicting a skilled worker future, assumed a four-year apprenticeship period, with, thereafter, a 42-year journeyman career in effect, assuming retirement from the workforce at age 65. Defendant's expert made similar assumptions, except that defendant did not agree that either plaintiff would have become a member of a skilled craft.

Inflation Rate and Return on Investment

Dr. Wilt testified that it is reasonable to expect an annual wage inflation rate of 7% over Melvin's working lifetime and that a sum of money in the hundreds of thousands of dollars could earn 7% annually in relatively riskless investments.[3] Dr. Buehler, on the other hand, stated that wages should be expected to increase only 5.5% annually over this period and that the award could presently be invested with essentially no risk yet earn more than 9% annually.

I find that the award can presently be invested at very little risk and return 7.5% compounded annually. I find that 5.5% is a reasonable annual rate of wage inflation to be expected during Melvin's working lifetime.

Amount of the Award

I award an amount for the loss of Melvin's earning capacity sufficient when invested at a 7.5% annual rate of return to generate in 1978 dollars $6,330 per year for the four years 1983-86 (hypothetical apprenticeship period) and $19,680 per year for the following 42 years 1987-2028 (hypothetical journeyman period). These amounts in 1978 dollars are to be converted to current dollars for each year by application of a 5.5% expected annual rate of wage inflation, then discounted at 7.5% per year back to 1979. By this method of calculation, the award for loss of Melvin's earning capacity amounts to $548,029.

[The court reviewed the evidence regarding the extensive burns to the plaintiff's body, the painful removal of charred layers of skin from his face, head, and buttocks, the permanent contortion of his mouth into a sneer, and his psychological and sociological suffering (e.g, the taunting and ridicule he has faced from schoolmates and strangers) in reaching a finding of an additional $1,000,000 in damages for pain and suffering.

The court went through a similar analysis in finding actual damages for similar components of harm for the other plaintiff.]

The foregoing shall constitute findings of fact and conclusions pursuant to Rule 52, Fed. R. Civ. P., together with earlier findings and conclusions set out in my oral opinion on February 14, 1979.

---

3. Each side recognized, of course, the necessity to reduce to present value the projected stream of lost future earnings. The method may be stated simply. The estimator (fact finder) must predict what inflation will occur in the wage rate during the working lifetime of each plaintiff and what return (or interest) could be earned from investment of the lump sum award over that same period. The fact finder then must calculate the amount of an award that would return a stream of earnings over the plaintiff's working lifetime equal to the amount of earnings that the plaintiff will lose over that period as a result of his injury. In simple, non-expert lingo, the higher the assumed rate of investment return (interest) compared to the assumed rate of wage inflation, the lower is the present lump-sum amount of the award. Conversely, the lower the assumed rate of investment return (discount to present value) compared to the assumed rate of wage inflation, the higher is the present lump-sum amount of the award. If the assumed interest rate is equal to the assumed wage inflation rate, then no adjustment to ascertain present value is necessary. It is not entirely surprising, therefore, that plaintiffs' experts expressed opinions calling for the use of factors producing large present-day amounts, and that defendant's experts expressed opinions calling for the use of factors producing small present-day amounts.

NOTES AND PROBLEMS

1. ***Medical Expenses.*** Tortfeasors are required to pay for the medical expenses incurred in good faith for injuries caused by a tortfeasor's misconduct. Courts frequently speak in terms of medical expenses that were "reasonable and necessary" as proper items for inclusion in a damage award. When the services are obviously necessary there may be little dispute about this item of damages. But where it is unclear that treatment was associated solely with the injury caused by the tortfeasor, there may be a greater need for expert testimony (usually the treating health care provider) to prove the causal link between the expense and the incident. Future medical expenses almost always require expert testimony to prove that they will in "reasonable probability" be incurred in the future for the underlying condition.

2. ***Lost Earning Capacity.*** For past lost wages, reference for the amount lost is typically made to the job plaintiff actually had at the time of the incident. Where the injuries have prevented the plaintiff from working, often a simple mathematical calculation yields the past lost wages amount. Future lost earning capacity can be quite a bit trickier. One can obtain damages for future lost earning capacity even if not presently employed, so long as the evidence shows that the injuries will prevent employment that otherwise would have been forecast as likely to have occurred. In the *Martin* case, this required extrapolation, based upon the character traits of the minor plaintiff and the surrounding circumstances, as to what he likely would have done after reaching adulthood. This is, of course, inherently speculative, but it is a necessary exercise if the goal is to attempt to provide full compensation. *See* Feldman v. Allegheny Airlines, 382 F. Supp. 1271 (D. Conn. 1974) (approving the practice of extrapolating based upon the evolving pattern of the claimant's life). A minority of courts will not permit such speculation into areas of employment never before achieved by a plaintiff. These courts tend to restrict generally future earning capacity to the same type of employment plaintiff has already achieved (subject to increases based upon seniority). *See* State v. Guinn, 555 P.2d 530 (Alaska 1976).

3. ***Inflation.*** The court in *Martin* had to increase the future earnings calculation based upon the assumption that cost of living raises in the applicable area of likely employment would increase during the work life expectancy of the plaintiff. Failure to take such inflationary pressures on earnings into account would otherwise result in not compensating the plaintiff for all of his actual losses. Courts used to refuse to use inflation to increase such future special damage awards because they felt that this was too speculative. But economists recognize the need to include inflationary adjustments, and courts have shifted positions on this issue today.

4. ***Discounting to Present Value.*** Also, in *Martin*, the court had to take the future special damages award and discount it so that the award today of future losses would not overcompensate the plaintiff. Without discounting to present

value, awards of future special damages would overcompensate a plaintiff because $1 today is worth more than $1 in the future due to the ability to invest that money. One legal scholar has explained the principle of reducing future awards of special damages to present value as follows:

> [I]t is assumed that the plaintiff will invest the sum awarded and receive interest thereon. That interest accumulated over the number of relevant years will be available, in addition to the capital, to provide the plaintiff with his future support until the total is exhausted at the end of the period. The projected interest must therefore be allowed in reduction of capital lest it be claimed that the plaintiff is overcompensated.

Fleming, *Inflation and Tort Compensation*, 26 Am. J. Comp. Law 51, 66 (1977). Note the difference in opinions in *Martin* between experts as to the appropriate discount rate to use; the job of the fact finder is to employ a discount rate that reflects a reasonably safe investment. While the need to reduce to present value and the principles governing this calculation are clear, the proper rates to use can become a topic on which competing expert witnesses disagree in particular cases. Courts do not require that future awards of general, non-economic damages be discounted to present value.

5. ***Total Offset Alternative.*** If you are paying close attention to the math in the two foregoing notes, the thought should occur to you that on future special damages, we first increase the damages using a percentage (for inflation) and then decrease the damages using a percentage (the discount to present value number). Some courts believe that it is simpler and fairer to simply declare these two computations a "total offset" and to neither increase the future damages for inflation nor decrease them to present value. *See generally* Kaczkowski v. Bolubasz, 421 A.2d 1027 (Pa. 1980) (discussing the differences between the minority "total offset" position and the majority approach of increasing for inflation and then decreasing to present value). In most scenarios, the total offset approach is more plaintiff-friendly than the majority approach. This is because the discount rate is usually higher than the rate of inflation (or else people would not bother to invest money).

6. ***Taxation of Damages.*** Under current federal tax laws, awards of actual, compensatory damages for personal injury cases are not subject to federal income tax. This is true even for past lost wages and future lost earning capacity. Many states permit the fact finder to take into account the non-taxation on this element of recovery (by reducing the award to after-tax estimates of earnings) in order to avoid a windfall recovery to the plaintiff and the defendant paying an excessive amount of actual damages.

7. ***Problem.*** Trial courts have discretion as to whether to submit one damage question to the jury or to break up the damages into multiple questions or blanks to fill in, as in the following example. If you were the defense counsel would you prefer one approach to the other?

"LADIES AND GENTLEMEN OF THE JURY . . ."

Texas PJC 8.2 Personal Injury Damages — Basic Question

What sum of money, if paid now in cash, would fairly and reasonably compensate *Paul Payne* for his injuries, if any, that resulted from the occurrence in question?

Consider the elements of damages listed below and none other. Consider each element separately. Do not award any sum of money on any element if you have otherwise, under some other element, awarded a sum of money for the same loss. That is, do not compensate twice for the same loss, if any. Do not include interest on any amount of damages you find.

Answer separately, in dollars and cents, for damages, if any. Do not reduce the amounts, if any, in your answers because of the negligence, if any, of *Paul Payne.*

a. Physical pain and mental anguish sustained in the past.
Answer: $________________________

b. Physical pain and mental anguish that, in reasonable probability, *Paul Payne* will sustain in the future.
Answer: $________________________

c. Loss of earning capacity sustained in the past.
Answer: $________________________

d. Loss of earning capacity that, in reasonable probability, *Paul Payne* will sustain in the future.
Answer: $________________________

e. Disfigurement sustained in the past.
Answer: $________________________

f. Disfigurement that, in reasonable probability, *Paul Payne* will sustain in the future.
Answer: $________________________

g. Physical impairment sustained in the past.
Answer: $________________________

h. Physical impairment that, in reasonable probability, *Paul Payne* will sustain in the future.
Answer: $________________________

i. Medical care expenses incurred in the past.
Answer: $________________________

j. Medical care expenses that, in reasonable probability, *Paul Payne* will incur in the future.
Answer: $________________________

B. General (Non-Economic) Damages

General damages are another category of actual damages designed to compensate for *non-economic* harms — injuries for which there is no actual market value. It is conceptually difficult to quantify physical pain and suffering or emotional anguish in dollars and cents. These damages are simply incapable of exact mathematical calculation and this is qualitatively different than what we encountered with special damages. Yet money is the language of tort law no matter the type of harm involved. The tort goals we first encountered in Chapter 1 — compensating worthy victims, deterring conduct that is likely to cause harm, and punishing misconduct — are all furthered through the auspices of a court order requiring a tortfeasor to pay a victim a certain amount of money. The primary dilemma with general damages is ascertaining when a jury's award is appropriate. While juries are not permitted to receive evidence of other jury awards of general damages, the judges (both trial and appellate) frequently compare jury awards of general damages in order to determine if a challenged award seems appropriate. The *Miraglia* case below is an example of a trial court judge conducting such an analysis in a tragic case. You will notice perhaps that this analysis seems more akin to art than science.

Because it is difficult for juries to find general damages and tougher yet for judges reviewing such verdicts to understand how a jury determined the dollar value of such intangible loss, the law of general damages often focuses upon controlling the type of evidence and arguments juries are permitted to hear on the topic. While their deliberations are, essentially, a "*black box*" into which we cannot peer to understand their findings, we can control which matters go into that black box. In this way, tort law hopes to promote rational and reasonable general damage findings by juries. We will explore some of these black box input rules.

Finally, we will consider the possibility of juries awarding, under different labels, damages for essentially the same harms. General damages include harms referred to by labels such as pain and suffering, emotional anguish (or mental distress), disfigurement, physical impairment or disability, loss of reputation, and loss of spousal or parental consortium. A classic example of the potential for double dipping in these losses comes with the additional item of general damages referred to as *hedonic losses* — loss of the intrinsic joy of life. We will encounter one court's attempt to control the potential for juries making cumulative awards due to a request for compensation of this type of loss.

Principles

"We disagree with those students of tort law who believe that pain and suffering are not real costs and should not be allowable items of damages in a tort suit. No one likes pain and suffering and most people would pay a good deal of money to be free of them. If they were not recoverable in damages, the cost of negligence would be less to the tortfeasors and there would be more negligence, more accidents, more pain and suffering, and hence higher social costs."

Kwasny v. United States, 823 F.2d 194, 197-98 (7th Cir. 1987) (Posner, J.).

1. Review of Jury's Award

Of all of the categories of general damages, by far the one that receives the most attention (and criticism) is an award for *pain and suffering.* Consider the words of one famous California jurist regarding the enigma of awards for pain and suffering:

> It would hardly be possible ever to compensate a person fully for pain and suffering. "No rational being would change places with the injured man for an amount of gold that would fill the room of the court, yet no lawyer would contend that such is the legal measure of damages." Translating pain and anguish into dollars can, at best, be only an arbitrary allowance, and not a process of measurement, and consequently the judge can, in his instructions give the jury no standard to go by; he can only tell them to allow such amount as in their discretion they may consider reasonable. The chief reliance for reaching reasonable results in attempting to value suffering in terms of money must be the restraint and common sense of the jury.

Seffert v. Los Angeles Transit Lines, 364 P.2d 337, 345 (Cal. 1961) (Traynor, J., dissenting from affirmance of jury's pain and suffering award). Consider whether you agree with the jury's or the trial judge's determination of what a reasonable award of pain and suffering damages should be for the victim in the following case.

MIRAGLIA v. H&L HOLDING CORP.

799 N.Y.S.2d 162 (N.Y. Sup. 2004)

SALERNO, J.

Lane &Sons Construction Corp., (Lane), (third party defendant) moves to reduce the damages awarded to the plaintiff, after a jury trial, contending that the award is excessive and materially deviates from fair and reasonable compensation.

The plaintiff sustained serious and catastrophic injuries when he fell while traversing a trench at a construction site in the Bronx. As a result of plaintiff's fall into a trench at the job site he became impaled on a reinforcement bar (rebar) that was surgically removed several hours after his admission to the hospital. It is in this setting that the jury, after a trial and after hearing testimony from plaintiff's physicians and other experts (that was largely uncontroverted) regarding the devastating and traumatic nature of the injuries he sustained, rendered a verdict in the sum of $86 million including $20 million for past pain and suffering and $55 million for future pain and suffering.

Plaintiff's treating physician Dr. Carrano, the Director of Spinal Cord Services at Helen Hayes Hospital, described in explicit detail the nature and effect of the injuries plaintiff incurred. Dr. Carrano provided the court and jury with a graphic picture of plaintiff's suffering, stating in part, that the pain plaintiff continues to experience "is of two types. He has nerve pain in his legs, and that nerve pain is perhaps one of the worst pains that you could think of. Imagine somebody stabbing you with a knife, a gazillion times, or with a pin all over the place. That numbness, that tingling, that stabbing sensation" [is] "present all the time. But it is a constant pain and that pain will not go away." Dr. Carrano depicted plaintiff's chronic pain by providing the jury with a vivid description of the damage to plaintiff's spinal column when the rebar went into the area of his spinal cord and the compression fracture also caused by the pipe entering his body. Dr. Carrano described the emotional pain sustained by the plaintiff caused by the distress of no longer having the ability to walk and the nerve pain emanating from his legs which Dr. Carrano testified was permanent. The jury also heard testimony regarding plaintiff's chronic bed sores, his catherization in order to urinate, his inability to control bowel movements, constant urinary track infections and repeated hospitalization for the conditions described by Dr. Carrano.

Manifestly, pain and suffering awards are not subject to precise standards that permit a purely mathematically evaluation in order to determine whether a verdict deviates materially from what is reasonable compensation. CPLR §5501 requires that:

> In reviewing a money judgment in an action in which . . . it is contended that the award is excessive or inadequate and that a new trial should have been granted unless a stipulation is entered to a different award, the appellate division shall determine that an award is excessive or inadequate if it deviates materially from what would be reasonable compensation.

It is well established that the language quoted, although specifically directed to the appellate courts, also applies to the trial court mandating the trial court to review jury awards to determine whether the award is excessive or inadequate. Consequently, review under CPLR 5501 requires the trial court to evaluate whether the award deviates from comparable awards and as the court observed in *Donlon v. City of New York*, 284 A.D.2d 13, reviewing comparable awards "cannot, due to the inherently subjective nature of non-economic awards, be expected to produce mathematically precise results, much less a per diem pain and suffering rate." It is also evident that review of jury verdicts for personal injuries to ascertain whether the award is reasonable, involves questions of fact and is the peculiar function of the jury. If such principles are to be accorded weight, when reviewing the sufficiency or excessiveness of jury awards, the trial court should not blindly substitute its judgment for that of the jury without affording considerable deference to the jury's interpretation of the evidence.

Defendant Lane referred this Court to several cases in an effort to convince the Court that the award, in the instant case, is not fair and reasonable. The

Court also heard the arguments raised by counsel for each party and reviewed the cases cited by counsel which purport to support each party's position regarding the verdict. At the outset, this court acknowledges that the verdict rendered by the jury in the case at bar is unprecedented in view of the evidence presented regarding plaintiff's injuries and the jury award clearly exceeds what can be considered fair and reasonable.

Lane's counsel submitted approximately eighteen (18) prior verdicts to "enlighten the court and in a sense, may constrain it" *Senko v. Fonda*, 53 A.D.2d 638, 639, to support the contention that the award for pain and suffering cannot be justified. As previously stated, this Court recognizes that the jury award which approximates $86 million deviates from what can be considered fair and reasonable. However, this recognition regarding the size of the verdict in the instant case does not automatically carry with it the court's determination that the award falls within the boundaries which Lane suggests would be a fair and reasonable award for the plaintiff, who concededly is a paraplegic experiencing constant pain.

[The court first reduced the jury's award of $10 million for future medical expenses to $8,294,669, which was the actual amount testified to by plaintiff's expert witnesses, a medical doctor, and an economist.]

With respect to Lane's contention that the award for pain and suffering deviates from reasonable compensation, counsel direct the Court's attention to several cases where the plaintiff purportedly sustained similar or more significant injuries than the plaintiff in the instant action such as *Schifelbine*, where the award of $23,218.586 was substantially reduced; *Coniker v. State*, 181 Misc. 2d 801 (N.Y. Ct. of Claims 1999), 23-year-old quadriplegic, verdict of $10 million reduced to $6 million; *Auer v. State of New York*, 289 A.D.2d 626 (3d Dept., 2001), future pain and suffering award raised from $750,000 to $1,500,000; *Driscoll v. New York City Transit Authority*, 262 A.D.2d 271 (2d Dept. 1999), injured plaintiff a paraplegic, awarded $10 million for past and future pain and suffering, reduced to $2 million; *Dimarco v. NYC Health & Hospitals Corporation*, 247 A.D.2d 574 (2d Dept., 1998), plaintiff sustained brain damage, verdict reduced to $1,300,000 for past pain and suffering and $1,500,000 for future pain and suffering; *Eccleston v. New York City Health & Hospitals Corp.*, 266 A.D.2d 426 (2d Dept. 1999), plaintiff sustained serious neurological injuries causing sensory paralysis to the lower half of the infant's body, verdict for past and future pain and suffering reduced from $7 million to $1,425,000; *Karney v. Arnot-Ogden Memorial Hospital*, 251 A.D.2d 780, 674 N.Y.S.2d 449 (3d Dept. 1998), infant plaintiff sustained neurological injuries including cerebral palsy and spastic diplegia, verdict reduced to $2 million; *Brown v. City of New York*, 275 A.D.2d 726 (N.Y.2d Dept. 2000), quadriplegic plaintiffs, separate verdicts for past and future pain and suffering reduced to $4 million; *Harvey v. Mazal American Partners*, 165 A.D.2d 242 [N.Y. 1st Dept. 1991], plaintiff construction worker fell two stories, suffered incomplete parapeglia, incontinency, $10 million verdict for past and future pain and suffering reduced and $10 million for future medical expenses reduced to $7 million; *Nowlin v. City of New York,* 182 A.D.2d 376 (N.Y. 1st Dept. 1992), $7,450,000 verdict for past and future pain and suffering reduced (by stipulation) to $2.5 million and the economic loss reduced to $5 million; *Bebee v. City of New York,* 231 A.D.2d 481 (2d Dept. 1996), plaintiff suffered paraplegia, $22 million verdict including $10 million for pain and suffering reduced to $3,015,000; *Pahuta v. Massey-Ferguson Inc.,* 997 F. Supp. 379 (W.D.N.Y. 1998), a 21-year-old plaintiff sustained paralysis of the lower half of her body, jury award of $2.4 million affirmed; *Barnes v. City of New York,* N.Y. L.J., Jan. 5, 1999, at 27 col 1, Sup. Ct. Bronx County, plaintiff was shot by a police officer, paraplegia injury, $76.4 million verdict reduced to $1 million for past pain and suffering and $7.5 million for future pain and suffering; *Torres v. City of New York,* 259 A.D.2d 693, the plaintiff who sustained a gun shot wound to his back which caused motor and sensory paralysis of the entire lower half of his body was awarded $11 million for pain and suffering and reduced to $2.5 million.

[I]t is self-evident that reviewing prior verdicts furnishes "to the judicial mind some indication of the consensus of opinion of jurors and courts to the proper relation between the character of the injured and the amount of compensation awarded" (*Senko v. Fonda,* 53 A.D.2d 638). Evaluation of prior awards, in similar personal injury cases is intended to provide guidance to the court in resolving disputed contentions regarding the adequacy or inadequacy of a verdict so that issues such as prejudice or sympathy do not become the motivating factor for the award. The trial court, therefore, in reviewing a jury award must consider the nature of the injury sustained by the plaintiff, the plaintiff's age, the physical condition of the plaintiff prior to the occurrence, the permanency of the injury sustained, plaintiff's ability to return to gainful employment, the pain, both physical and emotional, experienced and to be experienced in the future, the extent of future hospitalization and ascertain whether the award in part was generated by the devastating effect of plaintiff's injury. Here, x rays introduced at the trial showing the presence of the rebar that entered plaintiff's body clearly invoked sympathy by the jury causing in part, a huge verdict that was intended to compensate the plaintiff not only for pain and suffering he sustained but the grief experienced by the impact of the steel rod entering his body. Manifestly, modification of damages awards cannot be based on past precedents alone and as the Appellate Division appropriately stated in *PoYee So v. Wing Tat Realty*:

> Although possessing the power to set aside an excessive jury verdict, a trial court should nonetheless be wary of substituting its judgment for that of a panel of fact finders whose peculiar function is the fixation of damages. Modification of damages, which is a speculative endeavor, cannot be based upon case precedent alone, because comparison of injuries in different cases is virtually impossible.

In contrast to the cases cited by the defendant Lane, plaintiff's counsel submits several cases where jury's award were significantly larger than the awards presented by the defendant. In *Bondi v. Bambrick*, 308 A.D.2d 330 (1st Dept.), plaintiff was severely injured when she was struck by the defendant who was operating his motor vehicle while intoxicated. Plaintiff was 35 years of age at the time of the accident and lost part of one leg, underwent nine surgeries, including skin grafts, two surgeries involving removal and relocation of muscle tissue with pervasive scarring and a wound at the area of the amputation that may never heal. The court held that the "total pain and suffering award of $9,750,000" *did not deviate from reasonable compensation.* In *Weigl v. Quincy Specialties Co.*, 735 N.Y.S.2d 729, the jury awarded plaintiff $20 million for pain and suffering that was reduced by the trial court to $8 million *and sustained by the appellate division*, (N.Y. 1st Dept. 2003). *Barnes v. City of New York* involved an action brought by a 22-year-old plaintiff to recover damages sustained when he was shot in the back by a police officer. The gunshot wound rendered Barnes a paraplegic with multiple psychological disorders. The trial court in Barnes reduced the jury award of $15 million for past pain and suffering and $35 million for future pain and suffering to a total of $9,750,000. The Court in *Mundy v. New York City Transit Authority*, 299 A.D.2d 243 (N.Y. 1st Dept. 2002) reviewed a verdict for $20 million for past pain and suffering and $10 million for future pain and suffering that was reduced to $3 million and $5 million respectively. This Court has also reviewed the award of $14 million to the plaintiff in *Waldron v. City of New York*, NYLJ, June 7, 2004, vol. 108; p. 5, who sustained a spinal injury that rendered him a paraplegic. The injuries he sustained which also included a T1 fracture, fractured ribs and a punctured lung were caused when he was shot by a police officer. The Court denied the city's motion to set aside the verdict.

This Court's review of the cases set forth in this opinion denotes the factors which are considered in assessing what would be reasonable compensation. This process, now completed, does not however provide a clear picture that permits the application of some formula that identifies the limits of compensation for injuries that parallel plaintiff's suffering. It is undisputed that plaintiff who at one time was a strong and vibrant man is now a wheelchair-bound paraplegic. The devastating injury he sustained was caused by the pipe that upon entering his body destroyed his bowel requiring a colostomy bag to collect his waste matter and he is required to manage his bladder with catheters. Plaintiff's nerve pain in his legs is continuous and permanent. Such injuries, including those previously described, including the permanency of his injuries and his inability to return to gainful employment, are the factors that this court has applied in determining what would be reasonable compensation.

For the foregoing reasons, this Court grants defendant's motion to set aside the verdict as excessive unless within 30 days after service of a copy of this decision and order with notice of entry plaintiff stipulates to reduce the jury award for past pain and suffering from $20 million to $5 million; for future pain and suffering from $55 million to $10 million, and for future medical related expenses from $10 million to $8,295,000.

This constitutes the decision and order of the Court.

NOTES AND PROBLEMS

1. ***Comparison of Prior Jury Awards.*** While it is customary for judges, both trial and appellate, to consider other juries' awards in comparable cases to determine the reasonableness of general damage awards, courts forbid counsel from informing the jury of such awards. This might strike you as somewhat hypocritical, but the prevailing thought is that it would misdirect the jury's attention away from the facts of the particular case before them. Not all courts agree that it is appropriate to consider, even on appeal, whether a jury's award is consistent with other comparable cases. *See e.g.*, Ritter v. Stanton, 745 N.E.2d 828, 847-49 (Ind. Ct. App. 2001) (suggesting that aggressive comparability analysis by a court in review of a jury's damage findings might violate at least the spirit of the 7th Amendment's right to a jury trial).

2. ***Remittitur and Additur.*** The order of the court in *Miraglia* is an example of a remittitur. This is when the trial court advises the plaintiff that the plaintiff can either accept a reduction in the damages or else the trial court will grant a new trial. All courts have the power of remittitur. Additur is a related concept — when the court gives the defendant a choice of either accepting an increase to the damage award (when the jury's award is too low in light of the evidence) or else the court will grant the plaintiff's motion for a new trial. Federal courts do not have the power of additur.

3. ***Attorney's Fees.*** U.S. courts follow the "American Rule" which generally requires litigants to pay for their own attorney's fees. The only primary exceptions to this are when either a statute directs that the prevailing party recover their attorney's fees (often in consumer rights and employment discrimination statutes) or if a governing contract between the litigants so provides. But in most tort claims, even the prevailing plaintiff often recovers only 50 percent to 60 percent of the actual amount awarded by the jury, and that assumes the defendant has the funds to satisfy the judgment. The remainder of the award is often taken up by attorney's fees and other expenses (e.g., expert witness fees). There is some thought among plaintiffs' counsel that one of the pragmatic purposes behind awards of general damages is to increase the total recovery enough to help the plaintiff pay off the attorney's fees while still yielding a sufficient net recovery to help compensate for more tangible harms.

4. ***Evidentiary Support for Future Pain and Suffering.*** Where there is objective evidence that, due to the physical nature of the plaintiff's injury, it is plainly apparent that she will likely suffer future pain and suffering, the plaintiff is not required to offer expert testimony to support such an award. On the other hand, where the injury is more subjective and less obvious to cause ongoing pain and suffering, most courts require expert medical testimony to support an award of future pain and suffering. For example, in Krause, Inc. v. Little, 34 P.3d

566, 572 (Nev. 2001), the court held that it was common knowledge that broken bones can cause continued pain and that no expert testimony was needed to permit a jury award of future pain and suffering damages. The court stated that the injury itself was objective, being observable and understandable without expert assistance. Another plaintiff complaining of sexual dysfunction, headaches, and backaches after having ten stitches in his head was not permitted such an award of future pain and suffering damages where the only evidence to support an inference of future pain and suffering was from the plaintiff's subjective complaints. Thompson v. Port Authority of New York, 284 A.2d 232, (N.Y. App. Div. 2001).

2. *Per Diem Awards*

Given the uncertainty and lack of mathematical precision regarding how the fact finder should translate non-economic harms into monetary awards, trial lawyers have been creative in trying to help the jury with this endeavor. Some controversies have arisen regarding certain practices that plaintiffs' counsel have crafted to help the jury understand the seriousness of such harms. Consider the following jury argument regarding a hypothetical case with alleged pain and suffering as an item of possible damages:

> Ladies and gentlemen, the judge has instructed you that one of the items of damage for your consideration in this case, after you have found the defendant negligent, concerns my client Paul's pain and suffering. This item actually refers to two related, serious harms — his physical pain that he endures constantly, twenty-four hours each and every day since the date the defendant's careless driving caused the horrendous accident. You have also heard Paul's personal family physician's expert opinion that this type of pain will likely be a permanent part of the remaining twenty-five years of his expected life. Imagine that — 25 years of ever-present pain. And there is also the associated mental horror of knowing that his life will be spent enduring such pain. Imagine the toll this will take. The best physicians can offer him no prospect of relief despite the best medical practices.
>
> You are asked to do something difficult, which is to determine a monetary award for this lifetime of hurt. Let me suggest one technique that might help you a bit. Imagine what one day looks like for Paul. Better yet, imagine a single hour of his life. You've seen him grimace while testifying on the stand for about an hour, after walking slowly to the stand aided by his walking cane and his persistent limp. Now you have to decide what this pain is worth in terms of dollars. Let me just suggest a possible figure of $5 per hour. A pretty small sum isn't it? Surely his pain is far worse than that, but we want to be reasonable. You, of course, might decide a smaller or larger sum is more appropriate. But if you start with a premise of $5 per hour, in one day he would suffer $120 dollars. In a month that would add up to merely $3,600 — not a huge sum, considering a whole month of unrelenting pain and anguish. Even a whole year of that is $43,200. Anyway, you can do the rest of the math. Just take the annual figure and multiple it by Paul's undisputed

remaining life expectancy to reach a possible award for his future pain and suffering. Perhaps this is helpful for you.

Notice how this argument breaks down the victim's lifetime of suffering into easily manageable units. Do you think such an argument would be more effective than standing in front of the jury and suggesting they award $1,000,000 to the plaintiff for his pain and suffering? The *Beagle* case explores some of the pros and cons of this practice and joins the majority view in ruling upon its legality.

BEAGLE v. VASOLD

417 P.2d 673 (Cal. 1966)

MOSK, J.

Plaintiff brought an action against defendants for personal injuries suffered by him as the result of an automobile accident. The jury returned a verdict in his favor in the sum of $1,719.48, and he appeals from the judgment entered thereon, contending that the damages awarded are inadequate as a matter of law. The only issue raised on this appeal by any of the parties is whether the trial court erred in prohibiting plaintiff's counsel from stating in argument to the jury the amount of general damages claimed by plaintiff, either in terms of a total sum or of a sum for a time segment. We conclude it was error to restrict counsel's arguments in that regard.

Plaintiff's injuries resulted from an accident in which a car driven by Kenneth Vasold went over an embankment while rounding a curve in the road. Vasold died as a result of his injuries. Plaintiff and two other occupants of the car were injured. In the complaint, plaintiff prayed for $61,025.18 in general damages, as well as compensation for medical expenses, loss of earnings, and costs of suit.

The trial court informed plaintiff's attorney in chambers that he would not be permitted to mention to the jury "the value of his action in dollars" in a lump sum or as to "any per diem damages such as so many dollars per day, or so many dollars per month" because "[Such] is not evidence." In accordance with this request, counsel confined his arguments on the question of damages to the amount of past and anticipated medical expenses and loss of earnings, a description of plaintiff's injuries, and general statements to the effect that plaintiff was entitled to recover for past and future pain and suffering resulting from the accident.

One of the most difficult tasks imposed upon a jury in deciding a case involving personal injuries is to determine the amount of money the plaintiff is to be awarded as compensation for pain and suffering. No method is available to the jury by which it can objectively evaluate such damages, and no witness may express his subjective opinion on the matter. In a very real sense, the jury is asked to evaluate in terms of money a detriment for which monetary compensation cannot be ascertained with any demonstrable accuracy. As one writer on the subject has said, "Translating pain and anguish into dollars can, at best, be only an arbitrary allowance, and not a process of measurement, and consequently the judge can, in his instructions, give the jury no standard to go by; he can only tell them to allow such amount as in their discretion they may consider reasonable. . . . The chief reliance for reaching reasonable results in attempting to value suffering in terms of money must be the restraint and common sense of the jury. . . ." (McCormick on Damages, §88, pp. 318-319.)

Before turning to the question of the propriety of the so-called "per diem" argument [whereby counsel in argument segments the damages into a stated amount of money representing a certain time period, such as $5 for each day] it is significant to note that, while no case has been found specifically holding an attorney may inform the jury as to the total amount of the general damages sought by the plaintiff, there is a clear implication that such a statement may be made by an attorney, and defendants here do not seriously challenge plaintiff's assertion that the trial court erred in limiting counsel's argument in this regard.

It has long been a courtroom practice of attorneys in this state to tell the jury the total amount of damages the plaintiff seeks, and no questioning of the technique has come to our attention. Moreover, an attorney may and frequently does read the complaint, including the prayer, to the jury.

The question whether an attorney may argue to the jury that his client's damages for pain and suffering may be measured in terms of a stated number of dollars for specific periods of time presents a more difficult problem. Few issues in the area of tort law have evoked more controversy in the last decade. While no California case has decided the matter, the controversy has been resolved in most of our sister states and in some federal jurisdictions.

Twenty-one jurisdictions which have passed on the issue permit an attorney to make the "per diem" argument. [*See e.g.,*] *Baron Tube Co. v. Transport Ins. Co.*, 365 F.2d 858 (5th Cir. 1966); *Atlantic Coast Line R.R. Co. v. Kines*, 160 So. 2d 869 (Ala. 1963); *Vanlandingham* v. *Gartman*, 367 S.W.2d 111 (Ark. 1963); *Newbury v. Vogel*, 379 P.2d 811 (Colo. 1963); *Evening Star Newspaper Co. v. Gray*, 179 A.2d 377 (D.C. Mun. Ct. App. 1962); *Ratner v. Arrington* 111 So. 2d 82 (Fla. App. 1959); *Southern Indiana Gas & Elec. Co. v. Bone*, 180 N.E.2d 375 (Ind. App. 1962; *Grossnickle v. Village of Germantown* 209 N.E.2d 442 (Oh. 1965); and *Hernandez v. Baucum*, 344 S.W.2d 498 (Tex. Civ. App. 1961).

In 11 jurisdictions the argument is not permitted. [*See e.g.,*] *Henne v. Balick*, 146 A.2d 394 (Del. 1958); *Franco v. Fujimoto*, 390 P.2d 740 (Haw. 1964); *Caley v. Manicke*, 182 N.E.2d 206 (Ill. 1962); *Botta v. Brunner*, 138 A.2d 713 (N.J. 1958); and *Caylor v. Atchison, Topeka & Santa Fe Ry. Co.*, 374 P.2d 53 (Kan. 1962).

The conflict has also been thoroughly debated in the law reviews. An examination of a large number of articles on the subject indicates that a substantial majority of the authors are of the view that it is desirable to permit "per diem" argument.

We believe the reasons hereinafter discussed persuasively require California to align itself with the majority of jurisdictions on this issue.

The opening guns in the battle to prohibit an attorney from arguing damages on a "per diem" basis were sounded in *Botta v. Brunner* and every decision since *Botta* holding such argument to be improper has followed, at least in part, the reasoning employed in that case. In *Botta* the Supreme Court of New Jersey upheld the trial court's refusal to permit plaintiff's attorney to suggest that his client's damages for pain and suffering be measured by a stated number of dollars for each day, essentially on the rationale that such statements of counsel are not evidence and have no foundation in the evidence, but in the minds of jurors they substitute "unproven, speculative and fanciful standards of evaluation for evidence."

We do not find the reasoning of *Botta* convincing. It is, of course, axiomatic that pain and suffering are difficult to measure in monetary terms. Yet the inescapable fact is that this is precisely what the jury is called upon to do. As one critic of *Botta* has noted: "The plaintiff sues for money. The defendant defends against an award of money. The jury is limited to expressing its findings in terms of money. Nevertheless, the jury must be precluded from hearing any reference whatever to money. It must retire to the jury room *in vacuo* on this essential of the case where the unmentionable and magical conversion from broken bones to hard cash may then take place." 12 Rutgers L. Rev. 522 (1958).

It is undeniable that the argument of counsel does not constitute evidence. However, it does not follow, as averred in *Botta*, that the suggestion of a sum for damages can have no foundation in the evidence. Indeed it is necessarily inferred from observation of the plaintiff in the courtroom and from expert testimony regarding the nature of his injuries and their consequences. If the jury must infer from what it sees and hears at the trial that a certain amount of money is warranted as compensation for the plaintiff's pain and suffering, there is no justification for prohibiting counsel from making a similar deduction in argument. An attorney is permitted to discuss all reasonable inferences from the evidence. It would be paradoxical to hold that damages in totality are inferable from the evidence but that when this sum is divided into segments representing days, months or years, the inference vanishes.

Thus, an attorney who suggests that his client's damages for pain and suffering be calculated on a "per diem" basis is not presenting evidence to the jury but is merely drawing an inference from the

In Practice

Examples of different types of special and general damages frequently sought in tort litigation include the following:

Special Damages

- Lost Wages
- Loss of Earning Capacity
- Lost Profits
- Medical Expenses
- Loss of Fair Market Value
- Cost of Repair
- Cost of Maintenance

General Damages

- Pain and Suffering
- Emotional Distress
- Disfigurement
- Disability

evidence given at the trial. Of course, the trial court has the power and duty to contain argument within legitimate bounds and it may prevent the attorney from drawing inferences not warranted by the evidence. For example, counsel should not be permitted to argue future damages for pain and suffering on a "per diem" basis where the evidence would not justify an inference that the plaintiff will suffer pain in the future.

Another dubious aspect of *Botta* is its conclusion that an attorney who employs the "per diem" argument invades the province of the jury. It seems patently clear that an attorney does not interfere with a jury's decision-making powers to any greater extent when he suggests that damages be measured on a segmented basis than when he exhorts the jury to find the defendant negligent. It has never been contended that the jury forsakes its duty of determining whether the defendant acted as a reasonable man because counsel is permitted to discuss the participants' conduct and the inferences to be drawn therefrom.

Many of the authorities, including *Botta*, point out that it is logically inconsistent to permit counsel to inform the jury of the lump sum amount claimed by the plaintiff or to suggest that a certain sum be awarded, while shielding the jury from the suggestion that the total amount may be fragmented to represent periods of time. These cases reason that discussion of a "per diem" amount involves no more speculation than a total figure. Indeed, in a Nevada case the court stated that, while it found the reasoning of *Botta* very persuasive, it felt compelled to allow "per diem" argument because of the practice in Nevada of telling the jury the total amount of damages sought by the plaintiff. *Johnson v. Brown*, 345 P.2d 754, 759 (Nev. 1959). Moreover, the jury itself may calculate the segmented amount of a verdict which it has under discussion from the figures available since, in addition to the lump sum amount sought, it is customarily told the life expectancy of the plaintiff where it is claimed there will be future detriment.

Some legal scholars indicate the actual subjective basis for decisions which hold the "per diem" argument improper is the belief such argument results in excessive verdicts and that courts which prohibit the "per diem" argument demonstrate a lack of confidence in the jury system. Even if it can be established that larger verdicts result on occasions when the "per diem" argument is employed, it does not necessarily follow that these awards are excessive under the circumstances of the particular cases since, as pointed out hereinafter, both the trial and the appellate courts have the power and the duty to reduce verdicts which are unreasonably large. As was stated in one case, "if the evil feared is excessive verdicts, then the cure ought to be directed against the product, not the practice." *Johnson v. Colglazier* (1965) 348 F.2d 420, 425, 429 (dissenting opinion; the majority opinion in *Johnson* was overruled in *Baron Tube Co. v. Transport Ins. Co.*, 365 F.2d 858 (5th Cir. 1966)).

Some of the cases which cite the danger of excessive damages as a basis for disapproving the "per diem" argument point to a Florida case (*Braddock v. Seaboard Airline R.R. Co.*, 80 So. 2d 662 (Fla. 1955)) in which "per diem" damages were argued and the jury returned a verdict of $248,439, the exact amount requested by plaintiff's counsel. But even where the amount awarded is identical to the sum suggested, the verdict is not excessive as a matter of law. The circumstances may indicate the prescience of the attorney or his accurate evaluation of the case.

Other objections made to the use of a mathematical formula are that it produces an illusion of certainty which appeals to the jury but can only mislead it and that it can result in grossly magnifying the total damages by shrewd manipulation of the unit of time employed. In *Affett v. Milwaukee & Suburban Transport Corp.* (1960) *supra*, 106 N.W.2d 274, 280, it is said that the absurdity of using a mathematical formula is demonstrated by the fact that an attorney could, instead of using a day as the unit of time for measurement, ask the jury to calculate his client's pain and suffering in terms of seconds. Thus, one cent for each second of pain may not seem unreasonable, but if the damages were to be calculated on this basis it would result in $86.40 for a 24-hour day, $31,536 for each year, and an absurdly high figure *in toto*.

There are at least two answers to the foregoing objections. First, whatever manner of calculation is proposed by counsel or employed by the jury, the verdict must meet the test of reasonableness. The "per diem" argument is only a suggestion as to one method of reaching the goal of reasonableness, not a substitute for it. If the jury's award does not meet this test, the trial court has the duty to reduce it, and the appellate court has the authority to review the result. To be sure, the standard of reasonableness permits the jury a wide latitude of discretion, but there is no convincing assurance that the accuracy of its evaluation would be enhanced by prohibiting counsel from suggesting that the plaintiff's compensation for pain and suffering be measured in aggregates of short periods of time rather than by a total sum award for a longer period.

Second, there exist meaningful safeguards to prevent the jury from being misled. As expected of him by his client, plaintiff's attorney will urge the jury to award the maximum amount of damages which the evidence plausibly justifies, but he has the best of reasons for refraining from grossly exaggerating his claim since, by doing so, he may so tax the credulity of the jury that it will disregard his entire argument. If he overstates his claim by the device described in *Affett*, there is nothing to prevent defense counsel from pointing out this stratagem or to argue that the amount suggested is excessive and emphasize that the jury's duty is to award only a reasonable sum as compensation. More important, the trial court can and should instruct the jury that the argument of counsel as to the amount of damages claimed by the plaintiff is not evidence and that its duty is only to award such damages as will reasonably compensate the plaintiff for his pain and suffering. The court may also, if it deems appropriate, advise the jury it is not bound by any particular method of calculation in assessing damages for pain and suffering.

Every case which has considered the issue before us has emphasized the difficulty faced by a jury in attempting to measure in monetary terms compensation for injuries as subjective as pain, humiliation and embarrassment. The cases abound in broad statements such as that the matter is entrusted to the "impartial conscience and judgment of jurors who may be expected to act reasonably, intelligently and in harmony with the evidence," and that they are to award "fair and reasonable compensation" and be guided by "their observation, experience and sense of fairness and right." These homilies provide little assistance to the jury. Under some circumstances, the concept of pain and suffering may become more meaningful when it is measured in short periods of time than over a span of many years, perhaps into infinity. The "worth" of pain over a period of decades is often more difficult to grasp as a concept of reality than is the same experience limited to a day, a week or a month. It is this very consideration which underlies much of the controversy over the issue before us. The fact that the "per diem" argument provides a more explicit comprehension and humanization of the plaintiff's predicament to lay jurors makes this approach an effective tool in the hands of his attorney. This alone is not, however, a sufficient reason to condemn it.

We pause to note that the "per diem" device is not beneficial exclusively to plaintiffs seeking damages. It is a double-edged sword with equal availability and utility in argument by defendant's counsel who may employ the technique of dividing plaintiff's total demand into time segments in order to illustrate how exaggerated or ludicrous the claim may be.

Denial of the "per diem" argument deprives counsel of the full fruits of effective advocacy on the issue of damages, which is not infrequently the crucial conflict in the trial of an action for personal injuries. Only the most persuasive reasons justify handcuffing attorneys in the exercise of their advocacy within the bounds of propriety. We do not find them here.

Defendant and amici curiae urge that even if we do not adhere to the *Botta* prohibitory rule, we should hold that the "per diem" argument is not available as a matter of right but, rather, the entire question should be subject to the discretion of the trial court. We believe this would be an undesirable solution, creating more problems than it would solve. The inevitable results would be peremptory challenges to judges on the basis of whether or not they were inclined to permit argument on a mathematical basis, and the proliferation of appeals on the complex question of whether the court's discretion was abused in a particular case. Existing rules relating to the trial court's control over the scope of counsel's argument are sufficient to protect the integrity of the jury's decision-making role. There is no justification for holding that the "per diem" argument is governed by special standards not applicable to other types of argument.

We come, finally, to the question whether the trial court's error in limiting counsel's argument in the present case resulted in prejudice. Plaintiff, a carpenter by trade, was 39 years old at the time of the accident. He was hospitalized for 12 days. He suffered cuts on his head and hands, a sliver of wood became lodged under his eyelid, and one of his front teeth was chipped in the mishap. Subsequently, his vision became impaired. He had not worn eyeglasses prior to the accident but was required to obtain a pair shortly thereafter, and a few weeks after receiving the first pair of glasses he suffered another change in his vision, requiring a different prescription for his eyeglasses.

Plaintiff did not have any pains in his back before the accident, but subsequent thereto he had severe back pains which radiated down his thighs to the knees. He was required to wear a back brace and had been unable to work in his trade as a carpenter since the accident. A medical doctor testified that plaintiff was suffering from a congenital back defect known as spondylolisthesis and, although there is some conflict in the evidence on the issue, the expert testimony strongly indicates that this condition became symptomatic as a result of the accident. The doctor also testified that an operation costing $2,000 would be necessary in order to relieve plaintiff's condition. After an examination of the entire record, we are compelled to conclude that it is reasonably probable that a result more favorable to plaintiff would have been reached if the trial court had not limited counsel's argument on the question of damages for pain and suffering.

When prejudicial error appears in the determination of the issue of damages, "It has been held that on an appeal from a judgment where the evidence as to liability is 'overwhelming' a retrial may be limited to the issue of damages. Where, however, the evidence as to liability is in sharp and substantial conflict, and the damages awarded are so grossly inadequate as to indicate a compromise on the issues of liability and damages, the case should be remanded for a retrial of both issues." *Cliffordv. Ruocco*, 246 P.2d 651 (Cal. 1952).

The judgment is reversed.

NOTES AND PROBLEMS

1. ***The Per Diem Debate.*** Though the majority of courts permit *per diem* arguments, many such courts expect the trial judge to remind the jurors that they are hearing mere arguments of counsel and that they get to decide what the facts are in the case. Nevertheless, this admonition from the judge does little to offer solace to defense counsel, who generally do not want the jury thinking in per diem terms. Why is it that defendants are so opposed to the per diem argument, given that it could be used by either side to suggest a possible award (large or small)? Which objections to this type of jury argument discussed in *Beagle* seemed the most persuasive?

2. ***Golden Rule Arguments.*** What if, in addition to the hypothetical closing argument set forth just before *Beagle*, plaintiff's counsel also said something such as: "Now when I suggest the sum of $5 per hour for this pain you may think that's quite a large figure. You would likely not feel this way if it were you experiencing an hour of my client's pain. Would you take on a lifetime of the

pain and suffering my client is expected to have for a measly $5 per hour?" In another portion of the opinion, the court contrasted its ruling on per diem arguments with prohibited golden rule arguments:

> In holding that counsel may properly suggest to the jury that plaintiff's pain and suffering be measured on a "per diem" basis, we do not imply that we also approve the so-called "golden rule" argument, by which counsel asks the jurors to place themselves in the plaintiff's shoes and to award such damages as they would "charge" to undergo equivalent pain and suffering. *Id.* at 182 n.11.

The overwhelming judicial sentiment regarding golden rule arguments is that they improperly attempt to shift the focal point from the actual victim to the jurors in assessing damages. The ultimate prejudice with golden rule arguments is that they appeal to the sentiment alluded to by Justice Traynor in the quote at the beginning of this section on general damages — that no sane person would voluntarily take on a serious injury in exchange for even a room full of gold. To use such a device to ask the jury to award a room full of gold is universally condemned.

3. *Problem.* Does the following jury argument from a plaintiff's lawyer seem appropriate in light of the above concerns with per diem and golden rule arguments? Are these types of arguments effective in your opinion? As a defense counsel, how might you counter such an argument?

> There is extensive evidence in this case that my client suffered a tremendous injury to her left knee, which has, and almost certainly will in the future, impair her ability to walk, jog, or even get around the house very easily. When she puts weight on her leg, the doctors have found that she experiences a sharp pain that begins in her knee, extends up her leg, and culminates in a burning sensation in her lower back. This isn't just pain she must tolerate every once in awhile. It's pain she feels with each and every step she takes. She has no choice but to live with this pain. But that is no life that you or I would ever choose to live for any amount of money. How much will it take to compensate her fully for this pain and limitation on her daily life? That's for you to decide. But as you make this decision, I would ask you what it's worth in terms of dollars and cents, for each and every step she must take not only this afternoon, and tomorrow, but next month, next year, and nearly every moment of every day for the rest of her life on this earth. I would urge you to calculate for each step what the proper compensation should be and then to consider how many steps each of us takes on a daily basis, multiplying that amount by 365 for the number of days in a year, and then multiplying that amount by the estimated 35 years my client is expected to live after this trial. My client and I will accept your judgment as to that amount, whatever your calculations yield.

Watch "Per Diem" video on Casebook Connect.

"LADIES AND GENTLEMEN OF THE JURY . . ."

5th Circuit Pattern Jury Instructions (Civil Cases), Preliminary Instructions 1.1:

> "Soon, the lawyers for each of the parties will make what is called an opening statement. Opening statements are intended to assist you in understanding the evidence. What the lawyers say is not evidence. After all the evidence is completed, the lawyers will again address you to make final arguments."

3. *Day in the Life Videos*

Another arrow in plaintiff's counsel's quiver is a videotaped depiction of a "day-in-the-life" of the plaintiff introduced to support the plaintiff's claim to pain and suffering damages. While courts have broad discretion under the rules of evidence regarding such videos, counsel frequently dispute the admissibility of particular videos. Whether or not the videotape is a useful piece of demonstrative evidence or a calculated appeal to the prejudices and sympathies of a jury is a question trial courts have to answer in many cases. Below is one court's review of such a decision.

DONNELLAN v. FIRST STUDENT, INC.

891 N.E.2d 463 (Ill. App. 2008)

MURPHY, J.

On February 11, 2002, plaintiff Vincent Donnellan's cargo van was rear-ended by a school bus driven by an employee of defendant First Student, Inc. Plaintiff, 31 years old on the date of the accident, had no adverse health issues at the time. Plaintiff alleged in his complaint that, as a result of the accident, he suffered numerous permanent physical and mental injuries. Defendant conceded its negligence in the accident, but disputed that the accident was the proximate cause of plaintiff's alleged injuries.

On April 7, 2006, following several days of trial, the jury returned a verdict in favor of plaintiff for $6 million. Defendant seeks reversal of the jury verdict or, alternatively, reversal of the damages award and remand for new trial on damages or substantial remittitur. Defendant argues that the trial court abused its discretion and committed prejudicial error in allowing plaintiff's day-in-the-life video as demonstrative evidence. For the following reasons, we affirm the verdict of the jury.

On September 11, 2002, plaintiff filed a complaint against defendant and Earl F. McClendon for injuries allegedly suffered due to defendant's negligence in the February 11, 2002, accident. At the time, McClendon was defendant's employee and driving the school bus that rear-ended plaintiff. Prior to trial, McClendon was voluntarily dismissed and defendant admitted negligence.

Prior to the commencement of trial on the issues of causation and damages, the trial court heard the parties' motions *in limine.* At issue on appeal [is the trial court's decision] regarding plaintiff's day-in-the-life video.

The parties and the trial court watched the day-in-the-life video that the trial court described as a 4.5-minute video of plaintiff arriving at his therapist's office and going through physical therapy. Defendant argued that the video was not demonstrative, but substantive medical evidence, and that the audio and video depicted plaintiff in pain during his therapy session. Defendant claimed that it was at a disadvantage from the late disclosure as it could not depose the therapist or videographer before trial. The trial court found that, with the proper foundation from someone with personal knowledge that the video truly and accurately depicts what it shows, the video would be allowed as demonstrative evidence without audio. The trial court further granted defendant the right to depose the physical therapist in the video.

Plaintiff testified that [at the scene of the accident] he was dizzy and had a headache, but he refused treatment at the scene of the accident. A friend drove him home, where he went to bed. Later that day, plaintiff felt great pain and continued to have a headache so he went to the emergency room. Plaintiff was diagnosed with a cervical strain. Two days later, plaintiff returned to the emergency room due to pain in the lower back and neck.

Plaintiff testified to the years of consultations, treatments, and physical therapy he had received, and continued to receive, to treat his headaches and pain and sleep and vision problems and to work on regaining mobility. Plaintiff takes several medications but could not recall which types. For a period of time, plaintiff received painful steroid shots in the base of his neck to treat his headaches. While these treatments seemed to work, they were discontinued as plaintiff began to feel pain beyond the treatment time in the area that he received the shots. Plaintiff also continued to receive Botox treatments to try and strengthen his leg.

Plaintiff testified to his typical day and week. On Monday and Thursday, plaintiff attends therapy. On the other days of the week, plaintiff works for his friend Gavin Nicholas, as his health allows. Plaintiff works in a supervisory capacity at construction sites, assuring that the laborers, tradesmen and contractors are coordinated. After the accident, plaintiff obtained his commercial driver's license on his fourth attempt. While he still drives his car short distances, plaintiff can no longer drive trucks or operate heavy machinery. Plaintiff testified that he often has to close one eye and tilt his head to see properly when driving.

Plaintiff's wife, Rosanne Donnellan, a pediatrician, testified that she and plaintiff were engaged on December 24, 2001, and married on May 25, 2002, and that she was pregnant with their first child. Rosanne testified that she first noticed plaintiff's leg starting to turn in a few months after the accident until it eventually was turned in at all times. Rosanne stated that plaintiff had regular headaches, back spasms, vomiting due to pain, and sleep problems. In addition, plaintiff complained of double vision and, as a result, he no longer reads for enjoyment.

Rosanne testified that plaintiff suffers serious memory lapses. She testified that she was worried that this was a danger to plaintiff and their household. Rosanne also testified that plaintiff's problems have resulted in a drastic decrease in the couple's attendance at social functions because plaintiff does not want to suffer pain or people looking at him.

Dr. Gary M. Yarkony, board certified in physical medicine and rehabilitation since 1982, first saw plaintiff on July 12, 2002. Plaintiff complained of neck and back pain when he visited Yarkony. Yarkony suspected that plaintiff was suffering from a brain injury, including a cranial nerve injury that was causing a problem with plaintiff's eye muscle. Yarkony stated that this type of injury is typically associated with traumatic brain damage and he ordered an MRI of plaintiff's brain. Yarkony testified that the MRI did not demonstrate any issues and he utilized the later SPECT scan, which identified a brain injury, in his diagnosis. Yarkony also noted that he first observed plaintiff walking with an unusual gait on July 16, 2003, during his visit. Using a "little rehab doctor trick," he observed plaintiff walking in the parking lot as he left the examination to assure it was not an act.

Yarkony testified that plaintiff suffered a *coup contre coup* injury, meaning an injury to the brain at the site of impact, the back of plaintiff's brain, and the opposite side, the front of his brain. In addition, Yarkony diagnosed plaintiff with fourth nerve palsy, dystonia, myofascial pain, allodynia, occipital neuralgia, and depression. The result of these ailments are hypersensitivity to pain, cognitive dysfunctions, double vision, headaches, sleeping and mood problems and decreased ability to walk. Yarkony opined that plaintiff's symptoms will all naturally worsen as plaintiff ages and his body deteriorates.

[The jury returned a verdict of $6 million for the plaintiff, including] $82,500 for the stipulated past medical expenses, $3,417,500 for disability experienced and expected in the future, $500,000 for disfigurement, and $2 million for past and future pain and suffering. The trial court denied defendant's posttrial motion and this appeal followed.

Defendant first argues that the trial court erred in admitting plaintiff's physical therapy video as demonstrative evidence. Defendant asserts that the video was not timely disclosed, an insufficient foundation was laid, and it improperly focused on plaintiff's discomfort to elicit sympathy from the jury. Defendant argues that the failure to bar the video . . . resulted in reversible error. We review a trial court's admission of a day-in-the-life video for an abuse of discretion, which occurs only when no reasonable person would agree with the decision of the trial court.

Plaintiff's video, shot on March 17, 2006, is approximately five minutes long and contains footage of plaintiff exiting his car, walking into the rehabilitation center, and undergoing therapy on his leg and foot. Plaintiff produced the video to defense counsel on March 29, 2006, the day before trial pro[illegible] Defendant argues that because the video was not disclosed un[illegible] date, in addition to the failure to disclose the physical therap[illegible] witness, it was deprived of any opportunity to challenge the eviden[illegible]

Defendant continues to argue that plaintiff's video was not a day-[illegible] video as it did not simply demonstrate plaintiff's daily tasks and fu[illegible] *Velarde*, 354 Ill. App. 3d at 535. Defendant points to several instances [illegible] video where plaintiff grimaces and presents expressions of pain whil[illegible] foot is manipulated by the therapist.

Defendant points out that this case is unlike *Georgacopoulos v. University* [illegible] *Chicago Hospitals & Clinics*, 504 N.E.2d 830 (Ill. App. 1987). In *Georgacopoulos*, this court affirmed the admission of a day-in-the-life video that included a portion where the plaintiff undergoes a painful physical therapy session. The court noted that the therapy session was only a portion of the 19-minute video and that the trial court described the tape as "'tasteful.'" The court further distinguished that case from a federal case that found a day-in-the-life video more prejudicial than probative because it only showed a physical therapy session of the plaintiff that had suffered severe burns. *Thomas v. C.G. Tate Construction Co.*, 465 F. Supp. 566, 569 (D.S.C. 1979). Defendant argues that, as in the *Thomas* case, plaintiff's video was only of his physical therapy session and the display of pain by plaintiff was therefore more prejudicial than probative.

Plaintiff asserts that the trial court properly rejected defendant's argument that the video was more documentation of a medical examination than demonstrative day-in-the-life evidence. Plaintiff notes that our courts have stated that day-in-the-life videos constitute demonstrative evidence which helps jurors understand witness testimony. *Cisarik v. Palos Community Hospital*, 579 N.E.2d 873 (Ill. App. 1991). Plaintiff contends that defendant's argument rests on the inaccurate claim that the video so focused on plaintiff's pain and effort that it was prejudicial as the video distinguished by *Georgacopoulos*.

Plaintiff concludes that a proper foundation was laid by Rosanne, who testified that she had attended two physical therapy sessions in the past. She testified that the video accurately depicted how plaintiff exits his car, how he walks, and how his physical therapy is administered. Plaintiff argues that this is all that is required by *Spyrka* and *Cryns* to properly lay a foundation for demonstrative video evidence.

First, we agree that *Velarde* provides that day-in-the-life videos are demonstrative and not substantive videos. In addition, the very purpose of these videos is to illustrate evidence regarding a party's life at the time of trial. Accordingly, the disclosure prior to trial was not prejudicial. As succinctly outlined in *Cisarik*, a day-in-the-life video is akin to a photograph and admissible if a foundation is laid by someone having personal knowledge of the filmed object and that the video is an accurate portrayal of that. The video's probative value also must not be substantially outweighed by the danger of prejudice.

Rosanne certainly knew plaintiff and could testify to his ability to drive, get out of a car and how he walked. She testified that she had attended plaintiff's he physical therapist twice and that the video was an accurate plaintiff and his therapy session. As with a photograph, Rosanne knowledge of the contents of the video and the trial court properly his as a foundation.

rial court also found the danger of any prejudice did not outweigh its e value. The video in this case is unlike those in *Spyrka* and *French*. In , the video that was found to be prejudicial was a step-by-step animation at happened to the plaintiff, not a general demonstrative exhibit to under- d the medical condition suffered. Furthermore, the testifying doctor stated t he could not say the video accurately represented what happened to the aintiff. Likewise, in *French*, the video in question purported to familiarize the jury with the scene of an accident that occurred at night. The video, however was filmed in the day and in a fashion that mirrored the alleged chain of events in the case. Accordingly, in both cases, the videos were prejudicial because they preconditioned the minds of the jury to accept the plaintiffs' theories in each case.

As in *Georgacopoulos*, the video in this case was "tastefully" produced. The video was not produced to improperly precondition the jury on plaintiff's theory. Having viewed the video, it does not present a focus on plaintiff's pain and discomfort to the exclusion of anything else. While plaintiff does wince and/or grimace in different spots in the video, he also smiles and talks with the therapist. There is no undue focus on his pain, it simply focuses on a typical therapy session that the evidence at trial indicated would be required for the rest of plaintiff's life.

Finally, defendant contends that the jury award of $6 million was excessive and should be reversed with remand for further proceedings on that issue or a substantial remittitur must be entered. The question of damages is specifically reserved for the trier of fact, and we will not substitute our judgment lightly. We may reverse or modify a damages award as excessive only if it is unfair and unreasonable, if it results from passion or prejudice, or it is so excessively large that it shocks the conscience.

Defendant argues that the jury's award is radically disproportionate to the economic loss such that the award bears no relationship to plaintiff's losses. Defendant notes that the noneconomic loss determined by the jury was over 70 times greater than the economic loss of the stipulated medical bills. Defendant argues that this fact alone makes the verdict shocking and excessive as a matter of law.

Plaintiff responds by highlighting the great discretion granted to the jury in setting the amount of a verdict. Plaintiff notes that *Velarde* also cites several factors that may be used in reviewing compensatory damages, including the permanency of the condition, the possibility of future deterioration, the extent of medical expenses, and the restrictions imposed due to the injuries suffered. Plaintiff also argues that Illinois does not require any particular ratio of economic loss to non-economic loss and that the evidence presented at trial supported the jury's award.

While a damage award for noneconomic damages such
plaintiff is subject to even less precision than economic damag
still must be a product of the evidence and not passion such th
excessive. As defendant indicated, a "plethora of medical evid
sented at trial. That evidence indicated plaintiff's life will be nega
for the remainder of his life, with a life expectancy of more than 4

While it is true that plaintiff has retained a certain amount o
function since the accident as defendant enumerates, the evidence als
that each of those activities listed by defendant is limited by plaintiff's lo
ity, increased pain, and depression. Furthermore, testimony was given inc
that, as plaintiff aged and his body deteriorated, his symptoms would
worsen. While $6 million is a large sum, it is by no means so large as to s
the conscience as compensation for the lifetime of consequences that plaintiff a
his family face due to the physical and mental limitations posed by his injurie

Accordingly, for the aforementioned reasons, the decision of the trial court is affirmed.

NOTES AND PROBLEMS

1. *The Evidentiary Debate.* The Federal Rules of Evidence (which also provide a model for most states' evidentiary rules as well) generally provide that evidence that is "relevant" is admissible (Rule 401) so long as it is not unduly "prejudicial" (Rule 403). Though most courts are willing to consider the admission into evidence of a day-in-the-life video as relevant evidence of a plaintiff's pain and suffering as well as of a plaintiff's physical limitations from a disability, courts frequently have to consider whether the evidence is too prejudicial and panders to the jury's emotions. In the above case, the court found that the video's depiction of the plaintiff was tastefully done and supported by appropriate evidence.

2. *Problem.* Imagine that you are plaintiff's counsel for a client who suffered a serious spinal cord injury resulting in paralysis below the shoulders. With the admonition from the *Donnellan* court in mind — that a video depicting your client's daily life and limitations must be accurate, tasteful, and without "undue focus on his pain" — consider what aspects of your client's daily life would be suitable to show to a jury in order to demonstrate the seriousness of his condition. Which specific portions of his daily life might you seek to include in the video? How long is an appropriate length for the video depiction, considering that you want the jury to award appropriately high damages without offending the jury? Which aspects that you might want to depict would be most objectionable to defense counsel?

Watch "Day in the Life" video on Casebook Connect.

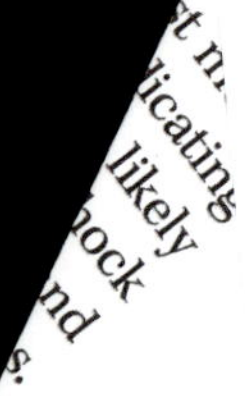

, the 1980s, plaintiffs' counsel, concerned that the existing categories damages (e.g., pain and suffering, disfigurement, impairment, mental might allow other harm to fall through the compensatory cracks, ıvocating for recognition of another category of general damages — the oyment of life or *hedonic damages.* As you might imagine, defendants are ırilled about adding yet another damage line to verdict forms and have ced this urging from the plaintiffs' bar. In the case below the court wrestles ı whether it is fair to recognize this additional category of damages. It adopts e majority approach.

> "Hedonism" comes from the Greek word for "delight" or "pleasure."

McDOUGALD v. GARBER

536 N.E.2d 372 (N.Y. 1989)

WACHTLER, J.

This appeal raises fundamental questions about the nature and role of nonpecuniary damages in personal injury litigation. By nonpecuniary damages, we mean those damages awarded to compensate an injured person for the physical and emotional consequences of the injury, such as pain and suffering and the loss of the ability to engage in certain activities. Pecuniary damages, on the other hand, compensate the victim for the economic consequences of the injury, such as medical expenses, lost earnings and the cost of custodial care.

The specific questions raised here deal with the assessment of nonpecuniary damages and are (1) whether some degree of cognitive awareness is a prerequisite to recovery for loss of enjoyment of life and (2) whether a jury should be instructed to consider and award damages for loss of enjoyment of life separately from damages for pain and suffering. We answer the first question in the affirmative and the second question in the negative.

On September 7, 1978, plaintiff Emma McDougald, then 31 years old, underwent a Caesarean section and tubal ligation at New York Infirmary. Defendant Garber performed the surgery; defendants Armengol and Kulkarni provided anesthesia. During the surgery, Mrs. McDougald suffered oxygen deprivation which resulted in severe brain damage and left her in a permanent comatose condition. This action was brought by Mrs. McDougald and her husband, suing derivatively, alleging that the injuries were caused by the defendants' acts of malpractice.

A jury found all defendants liable and awarded Emma McDougald a total of $9,650,102 in damages, including $1,000,000 for conscious pain and suffering and a separate award of $3,500,000 for loss of the pleasures and pursuits of life. The balance of the damages awarded to her were for pecuniary damages — lost earnings and the cost of custodial and nursing care. Her $1,500,000 on his derivative claim for the loss of his wife

[On appeal, the primary dispute] is the award to s awarded for nonpecuniary damages. At trial, defendants sougl Mrs. McDougald's injuries were so severe that she was in ougald experiencing pain or appreciating her condition. Plaintiffs, on that introduced proof that Mrs. McDougald responded to certain sti ther cient extent to indicate that she was aware of her circumstan d, extent of Mrs. McDougald's cognitive abilities, if any, was sharply -

The parties and the trial court agreed that Mrs. McDougald recover for pain and suffering unless she were conscious of the pain. D maintained that such consciousness was also required to support an a loss of enjoyment of life. The court, however, accepted plaintiffs' view th of enjoyment of life was compensable without regard to whether the pl was aware of the loss. Accordingly, because the level of Mrs. McDougald's nitive abilities was in dispute, the court instructed the jury to consider loss enjoyment of life as an element of nonpecuniary damages separate from pai and suffering.

We conclude that the court erred, both in instructing the jury that Mrs. McDougald's awareness was irrelevant to their consideration of damages for loss of enjoyment of life and in directing the jury to consider that aspect of damages separately from pain and suffering.

We begin with the familiar proposition that an award of damages to a person injured by the negligence of another is to compensate the victim, not to punish the wrongdoer. The goal is to restore the injured party, to the extent possible, to the position that would have been occupied had the wrong not occurred. To be sure, placing the burden of compensation on the negligent party also serves as a deterrent, but purely punitive damages — that is, those which have no compensatory purpose — are prohibited unless the harmful conduct is intentional, malicious, outrageous, or otherwise aggravated beyond mere negligence.

Damages for nonpecuniary losses are, of course, among those that can be awarded as compensation to the victim. This aspect of damages, however, stands on less certain ground than does an award for pecuniary damages. An economic loss can be compensated in kind by an economic gain; but recovery for noneconomic losses such as pain and suffering and loss of enjoyment of life rests on "the legal fiction that money damages can compensate for a victim's injury." We accept this fiction, knowing that although money will neither ease the pain nor restore the victim's abilities, this device is as close as the law can come in its effort to right the wrong. We have no hope of evaluating what has been lost, but a monetary award may provide a measure of solace for the condition created.

Our willingness to indulge this fiction comes to an end, however, when it ceases to serve the compensatory goals of tort recovery. When that limit is met, further indulgence can only result in assessing damages that are punitive. The

d by this case, then, is whether an award of damages for loss of
life to a person whose injuries preclude any awareness of the loss
npensatory purpose. We conclude that it does not.

put, an award of money damages in such circumstances has no or utility to the injured person. An award for the loss of enjoyment annot provide [such a victim] with any consolation or ease any burden on him. He cannot spend it upon necessities or pleasures. He cannot ience the pleasure of giving it away." *Flannery v. United States*, 718 F.2d 108, *cert denied* 467 U.S. 1226.

We recognize that, as the trial court noted, requiring some cognitive awareess as a prerequisite to recovery for loss of enjoyment of life will result in some cases "in the paradoxical situation that the greater the degree of brain injury inflicted by a negligent defendant, the smaller the award the plaintiff can recover in general damages." The force of this argument, however — the temptation to achieve a balance between injury and damages — has nothing to do with meaningful compensation for the victim. Instead, the temptation is rooted in a desire to punish the defendant in proportion to the harm inflicted. However relevant such retributive symmetry may be in the criminal law, it has no place in the law of civil damages, at least in the absence of culpability beyond mere negligence.

Accordingly, we conclude that cognitive awareness is a prerequisite to recovery for loss of enjoyment of life. With respect to pain and suffering, the trial court charged simply that there must be "some level of awareness" in order for plaintiff to recover. We think that this is an appropriate standard for all aspects of nonpecuniary loss. No doubt the standard ignores analytically relevant levels of cognition, but we resist the desire for analytical purity in favor of simplicity. A more complex instruction might give the appearance of greater precision but, given the limits of our understanding of the human mind, it would in reality lead only to greater speculation.

We turn next to the question whether loss of enjoyment of life should be considered a category of damages separate from pain and suffering.

There is no dispute here that the fact finder may, in assessing nonpecuniary damages, consider the effect of the injuries on the plaintiff's capacity to lead a normal life. Traditionally, in this State and elsewhere, this aspect of suffering has not been treated as a separate category of damages; instead, the plaintiff's inability to enjoy life to its fullest has been considered one type of suffering to be factored into a general award for nonpecuniary damages, commonly known as pain and suffering.

Recently, however, there has been an attempt to segregate the suffering associated with physical pain from the mental anguish that stems from the inability to engage in certain activities, and to have juries provide a separate award for each.

We do not dispute that distinctions can be found or created between the concepts of pain and suffering and loss of enjoyment of life. If the term "suffering" is limited to the emotional response to the sensation of pain, then the emotional response caused by the limitation of life's activities may be considered qualitatively different. But suffering need not be so limited — it can easily encompass the frustration and anguish caused by the inability to participate in activities that once brought pleasure. Traditionally, by treating loss of enjoyment of life as a permissible factor in assessing pain and suffering, courts have given the term this broad meaning.

If we are to depart from this traditional approach and approve a separate award for loss of enjoyment of life, it must be on the basis that such an approach will yield a more accurate evaluation of the compensation due to the plaintiff. We have no doubt that, in general, the total award for nonpecuniary damages would increase if we adopted the rule. That separate awards are advocated by plaintiffs and resisted by defendants is sufficient evidence that larger awards are at stake here. But a larger award does not by itself indicate that the goal of compensation has been better served.

The advocates of separate awards contend that because pain and suffering and loss of enjoyment of life can be distinguished, they must be treated separately if the plaintiff is to be compensated fully for each distinct injury suffered. We disagree. Such an analytical approach may have its place when the subject is pecuniary damages, which can be calculated with some precision. But the estimation of nonpecuniary damages is not amenable to such analytical precision and may, in fact, suffer from its application. Translating human suffering into dollars and cents involves no mathematical formula; it rests, as we have said, on a legal fiction. The figure that emerges is unavoidably distorted by the translation. Application of this murky process to the component parts of nonpecuniary injuries (however analytically distinguishable they may be) cannot make it more accurate. If anything, the distortion will be amplified by repetition.

Principles

Though still a minority position, there has been a trend toward recognizing hedonic damages as a separate category of damages. One scholarly article urges retrenchment on this trend for a number of reasons, but most notably because: "[a]mong the gravest risks hedonic damages pose is the risk of double counting."

Victor E. Schwartz and Cary Silverman, Hedonic Damages: The Rapidly Bubbling Cauldron, 69 Brooklyn L. Rev. 1037, 1044 (2004).

Thus, we are not persuaded that any salutary purpose would be served by having the jury make separate awards for pain and suffering and loss of enjoyment of life. We are confident, furthermore, that the trial advocate's art is a sufficient guarantee that none of the plaintiff's losses will be ignored by the jury.

The errors in the instructions given to the jury require a new trial on the issue of nonpecuniary damages to be awarded to plaintiff Emma McDougald. Defendants' remaining contentions are either without merit, beyond the scope of our review or are rendered academic by our disposition of the case.

NOTES AND PROBLEMS

1. *Conceptual Purity vs. Practicality.* In rejecting hedonic damages as a separate item of general recovery, the New York court agrees that it is possible to conceptualize a difference between pain and suffering harm and the harm for loss of enjoyment of life's activities. If this is the case, why does the court ultimately reject this category as a separate item of compensation?

2. *Awareness of Suffering.* With respect to some of the plaintiff's losses, whether or not the plaintiff is conscious makes no difference in terms of her right to recover for it. Why does it make sense to require consciousness for some items of damage but not all?

3. *Majority View.* The opinion of the New York court on the issue of whether hedonic damages constitute a separate item apart from pain and suffering represents the clear majority view among courts in the United States. Some courts, however, permit a separate line on the verdict form for hedonic damages, but most consider loss of enjoyment to be a part of the broader recovery for pain and suffering. Yet other courts have held that such items are not recoverable under *any* category of recognized general damages. In terms of the closing arguments that might be presented at the conclusion of a personal injury trial, does the New York court's holding substantially impact how the attorneys will approach the issue? If not, what is the real consequence of the holding in most cases?

C. Wrongful Death and Survival Claims

At common law the death of a victim was paradoxically a cause for celebration for the tortfeasor because the claims expired with the victim. That is, no cause of action survived the death of the victim. Ironically, this meant that it was cheaper for a defendant to kill a victim than just to injure him. This began to change in the first half of the nineteenth century by certain acts of legislatures. Today every state has enacted wrongful death statutes and survival statutes. A survival cause of action is owned by the estate of the decedent and provides for recovery for damages suffered by the decedent from the time of the tort until his death; such damages might include pain and suffering damages as well as medical expenses and lost wages. This claim survives for the benefit of the estate. A wrongful death cause of action provides for recovery by certain statutory beneficiaries (typically the immediate family) to compensate for their losses associated with the death of their loved one; that is, a wrongful death claim covers the harm to others beginning at the moment of the victim's death. Exactly what forms of damages are recoverable, and who is entitled to bring suit, are ultimately governed by the terms of the applicable statute. Many wrongful death statutes have been interpreted to provide for recovery of only "pecuniary" losses. What this means and whether a wrongful death beneficiary might be able to sue for an item of general damages has been the subject of many lawsuits, such as the following case.

JORDAN v. BAPTIST THREE RIVERS HOSPITAL

984 S.W.2d 593 (Tenn. 1999)

HOLDER, J.

We granted this appeal to determine whether spousal and parental consortium losses should be permissible in wrongful death actions. Tennessee law previously permitted the anomalous result of allowing spousal consortium losses in personal injury cases but not in cases of wrongful death. Upon review of the modern trend of authority and careful scrutiny of our statutory scheme, we hold that loss of consortium claims should not be limited to personal injury suits. We hold that the pecuniary value of a deceased's life includes the element of damages commonly referred to as loss of consortium.

This cause of action arises out of the death of Mary Sue Douglas ("decedent"). The plaintiff, Martha P. Jordan, is a surviving child of the decedent and the administratrix of the decedent's estate. The plaintiff, on behalf of the decedent's estate, filed a medical malpractice action against the defendants, Baptist Three Rivers Hospital, Mark W. Anderson, M.D., Noel Dominguez, M.D., and Patrick Murphy, M.D. The plaintiff has alleged that the defendants' negligence caused the decedent's death.

The plaintiff's complaint sought damages for loss of consortium [among other items of damage incurred by the decedent]. The defendants filed a motion to strike and a motion for judgment on the pleadings asserting that Tennessee law does not permit recovery for loss of parental consortium.

The trial court granted the defendants' motion to strike and granted the plaintiff permission to file an interlocutory appeal. The Court of Appeals [denied the application for an interlocutory appeal]. We granted appeal to determine whether claims for loss of spousal and parental consortium in wrongful death cases are viable in Tennessee under Tenn. Code Ann. §20-5-113.

A wrongful death cause of action did not exist at common law. Pursuant to the common law, actions for personal injuries that resulted in death terminated at the victim's death because "in a civil court the death of a human being could not be complained of as an injury." W. Page Keeton et al., Prosser and Keeton on the Law of Torts §127, at 945 (5th ed. 1984) ("Prosser"). "The [legal] result was that it was cheaper for the defendant to kill the plaintiff than to injure him, and that the most grievous of all injuries left the bereaved family of the victim . . . without a remedy." Id. This rule of non-liability for wrongful death was previously the prevailing view in both England and in the United States. *East Tennessee V. & G. Ry. Co. v. Lilly*, 18 S.W. 243, 244 (Tenn. 1891).

In 1846, the British Parliament enacted a wrongful death statute designed to abrogate the common law rule's harsh effect of denying recovery for personal injuries resulting in death. The English statute was referred to as "Lord Campbell's Act" and created a cause of action for designated survivors that accrued upon the tort victim's death.

Jurisdictions in the United States were quick to follow England's lead. In 1847, New York became the first American jurisdiction to enact a wrongful death statute. Presently, every jurisdiction in the United States has a wrongful death statute. These statutes, including that of Tennessee, embody the substantive provisions of Lord Campbell's Act and permit designated beneficiaries to recover losses sustained as a result of the tort victim's death.

Because a cause of action for wrongful death is a creation of statute, recoverable damages must be determined by reference to the particular statute involved. Although all states have abolished the rule of non-liability when personal injury results in death, the statutory methods of doing so fall into two distinct categories — wrongful death statutes and survival statutes.

The majority of states have enacted "survival statutes." These statutes permit the victim's cause of action to survive the death, so that the victim, through the victim's estate, recovers damages that would have been recovered by the victim had the victim survived. Survival statutes do not create a new cause of action; rather, the cause of action vested in the victim at the time of death is transferred to the person designated in the statutory scheme to pursue it, and the action is enlarged to include damages for the death itself. Prosser, §126, at 942-43. "The recovery is the same one the decedent would have been entitled to at death, and thus included such items as wages lost after injury and before death, medical expenses incurred, and pain and suffering," and other appropriate compensatory damages suffered by the victim from the time of injury to the time of death. Id. at 943.

In contrast to survival statutes, "pure wrongful death statutes" create a new cause of action in favor of the survivors of the victim for their loss occasioned by the death. These statutes proceed "on the theory of compensating the individual beneficiaries for the loss of the economic benefit which they might reasonably have expected to receive from the decedent in the form of support, services or contributions during the remainder of [the decedent's] lifetime if [the decedent] had not been killed." Prosser, §127, at 949. Hence, most wrongful death jurisdictions have adopted a "pecuniary loss" standard of recovery, allowing damages for economic contributions the deceased would have made to the survivors had death not occurred and for the economic value of the services the deceased would have rendered to the survivors but for the death.

Tennessee's approach to providing a remedy for death resulting from personal injury is a hybrid between survival and wrongful death statutes, resulting in a statutory scheme with a "split personality." 27 Tenn. L. Rev. at 454. The pertinent damages statute, Tenn. Code Ann. §20-5-113, has been in existence in one form or another since 1883. It provides:

> Where a person's death is caused by the wrongful act, fault, or omission of another, and suit is brought for damages . . . the party suing shall, if entitled to damages, have the right to recover the mental and physical suffering, loss of time, and necessary expenses resulting to the deceased from the personal injuries, **and also the damages resulting to the parties for whose use and benefit the right of action survives from the death consequent upon the injuries received.**

Tenn. Code Ann. §20-5-113 (emphasis added).

The plain language of Tenn. Code Ann. §20-5-113 reveals that it may be classified as a survival statute because it preserves whatever cause of action was vested in the victim at the time of death. The survival character of the statute is evidenced by the language "the party suing shall have the right to recover [damages] resulting to **the deceased from the personal injuries.**" *Thrailkill v. Patterson*, 879 S.W.2d 836, 841 (Tenn. 1994) (emphasis added). Tennessee courts have declared that the purpose of this language is to provide "for the continued existence and passing of the right of action of the deceased, and not for any new, independent cause of action in [survivors]." *Whaley v. Catlett*, 53 S.W. 131, 133 (Tenn. 1899); see also *Herrell v. Haney*, 341 S.W.2d 574, 576 (Tenn. 1960). Accordingly, Tenn. Code Ann. §20-5-113 "in theory, preserve[s] the right of action which the deceased himself would have had, and . . . [has] basically been construed as falling within the survival type of wrongful death statutes for over a century" because it continues that cause of action by permitting recovery of damages for the death itself. Jones, 539 S.W.2d at 123-25.

Notwithstanding the accurate, technical characterization of Tenn. Code Ann. §20-5-113 as survival legislation, the statute also creates a cause of action that compensates survivors for their losses. The statute provides that damages may be recovered "**resulting to the parties for whose use and benefit the right of action survives from the death.**" Id. (emphasis added). Hence, survivors of the deceased may recover damages for their losses suffered as a result of the death as well as damages sustained by the deceased from the time of injury to the time of death. Our inquiry shall focus on whether survivors should be permitted to recover consortium losses.

The defendant argues that this Court has previously held that Tenn. Code Ann. §20-5-113 is a survival statute and that survival statutes generally do not permit recovery under consortium theories. While this Court in *Jones v. Black*, 539 S.W.2d 123 (Tenn. 1976), previously classified Tennessee's wrongful death statute as a survival statute for purposes of limitations of action, we are not confined to interpret the statute according to the strictures of a judicially imposed classification when such an interpretation would ignore unambiguous statutory language. Accordingly, our analysis of Tenn. Code Ann. §20-5-113 shall focus on the statute's language and not on what damages "survival" statutes in other states generally permit. It must be remembered that, notwithstanding the accurate, technical characterization of Tenn. Code Ann. §20-5-113 as survival legislation, the statute also provides for a cause of action that compensates survivors for *their* losses.

Damages under our wrongful death statute can be delineated into two distinct classifications. The first classification permits recovery for injuries sustained by the deceased from the time of injury to the time of death. Damages under the first classification include medical expenses, physical and mental pain and suffering, funeral expenses, lost wages, and loss of earning capacity.

The second classification of damages permits recovery of incidental damages suffered by the decedent's next of kin. Incidental damages have been judicially defined to *include* the pecuniary value of the decedent's life. Pecuniary value has been judicially defined to include "the expectancy of life, the age, condition of health and strength, capacity for labor and earning money through skill, any art, trade, profession and occupation or business, and personal habits as to sobriety and industry." Id. Pecuniary value also takes into account the decedent's probable living expenses had the decedent lived. *Wallace v. Couch*, 642 S.W.2d 141 (Tenn. 1982).

The wrongful death statute neither explicitly precludes consortium damages nor reflects an intention to preclude consortium damages. The statute's language does not limit recovery to purely economic losses. To the contrary, the statute's plain language appears to encompass consortium damages.

Indeed, this Court has recognized that pecuniary value cannot be defined to a mathematical certainty as such a definition "would overlook the value of the [spouse's] personal interest in the affairs of the home and the economy incident to [the spouse's] services." Thrailkill, 879 S.W.2d at 841. We further believe that the pecuniary value of a human life is a compound of many elements. An individual family member has value to others as part of a functioning social and economic unit. This value necessarily includes the value of mutual society and protection, i.e. human companionship. Human companionship has a definite, substantial and ascertainable pecuniary value, and its loss forms a part of the value of the life we seek to ascertain. Moreover, it seems illogical and absurd to believe that the legislature would intend the anomaly of permitting recovery of consortium losses when a spouse is injured and survives but not when the very same act causes a spouse's death.

The wrongful death statute precludes neither a minor child nor an adult child from seeking compensation for the child's consortium losses.

A review of case law in other jurisdictions indicates a trend to expand consortium claims to include the impairment of a child's relationship with a parent. In cases involving a parent's death, "the general rule . . . followed is that a child's loss of nurture, education and moral training which it probably would have received from a parent wrongfully killed is a pecuniary loss to be considered as an element of the damages suffered by the child." Recovery for Wrongful Death at §3:47 (listing thirty-four jurisdictions so holding). See also 94 Va. L. Rev. at 266 ("Most states . . . allow a surviving . . . child . . . to recover for loss of consortium where a parent is tortiously killed."); Prosser, §127, at 952 ("Even jurisdictions that have rejected the loss of society or consortium claim, as such, have permitted one form of it, namely a loss of guidance and advice that the decedent would have provided [to the child].").

A basis for placing an economic value on parental consortium is that the education and training which a child may reasonably expect to receive from a parent are of actual and commercial value to the child. Accordingly, a child sustains a pecuniary injury for the loss of parental education and training when a defendant tortiously causes the death of the child's parent.

The additional considerations employed for spousal consortium may be applicable to parental consortium claims. We agree with the observation of one court that "companionship, comfort, society, guidance, solace, and protection . . . go into the vase of family happiness [and] are the things for which a wrongdoer must pay when he shatters the vase." *Spangler v. Helm's New York-Pittsburgh Motor Exp.*, 153 A.2d 490 (Penn. 1959).

Adult children may be too attenuated from their parents in some cases to proffer sufficient evidence of consortium losses. Similarly, if the deceased did not have a close relationship with any of the statutory beneficiaries, the statutory beneficiaries will not likely sustain compensable consortium losses or their consortium losses will be nominal. The age of the child does not, in and of itself, preclude consideration of parental consortium damages. The adult child inquiry shall take into consideration factors such as closeness of the relationship and dependence (i.e., of a handicapped adult child, assistance with day care, etc.).

We hold that consortium-type damages may be considered when calculating the pecuniary value of a deceased's life. This holding does not create a new cause of action but merely refines the term "pecuniary value." Consortium losses are not limited to spousal claims but also necessarily encompass a child's loss, whether minor or adult. Loss of consortium consists of several elements, encompassing not only tangible services provided by a family member, but also intangible benefits each family member receives from the continued existence of other family members. Such benefits include attention, guidance, care, protection, training, companionship, cooperation, affection, love, and in the case of a spouse, sexual relations. Our holding conforms with the plain language of the wrongful death statutes, the trend of modern authority, and the social and economic reality of modern society.

The decision of the trial court granting the defendants' motion to strike is reversed.

NOTES AND PROBLEMS

1. ***Wrongful Death and Survival Statutes.*** In *Jordan*, the court devotes time to distinguishing between wrongful death and survival statutes — these differences relate to (a) who owns the claim, (b) who is the "victim" who is the focal point in assessing damages, (c) the timing of when the recoverable damages are incurred, and (d) the types of damages recoverable. To a large

extent, the intricate answers to these questions are found in each state's respective statutes. In general though, how did *Jordan* answer these questions? As between wrongful death and survival claims, do you believe one will tend to be of greater value than the other?

2. ***Loss of Consortium Recovery.*** The court in *McDougald* mentioned that the husband received a jury award of $1.5 million for loss of household services of his wife. Courts have traditionally permitted a spouse's right to recover for the personal loss arising from the serious disability of a husband or wife. Typically referred to as *loss of consortium* damages, such recovery is intended to provide compensation for harms to the relationship as well as the loss of personal services provided by that spouse. In *Jordan,* the court confronted the issue of whether the state's wrongful death statute permitted a loss of consortium claim and whether this should allow an adult child to recover for the wrongful death of a parent. Many courts now recognize such claims by one whose parent is killed. Courts have also recently recognized a loss of "filial" consortium claim for the parent of a deceased child. Most courts, however, refuse to extend loss of consortium claims to cover other relationships, such as grandparent-grandchild, siblings, friends, or even a fiancée.

3. ***Derivative Nature of Claim.*** Where a loss of consortium claim is recognized, it is *derivative* of the primary victim's claim. This means that any defense the defendant may have to the primary victim's claim also applies with equal force to the loss of consortium claim (including comparative fault or the primary victim's assumption of the risk). If the primary victim is apportioned a level of fault, the owner of the derivative cause of action for loss of consortium is equally impacted by this apportionment (this could result in either a reduction or elimination of their claim, depending upon the type of comparative fault system and the levels of apportioned fault). Wrongful death claims are similarly derivative of the decedent's survival cause of action and subject to the same affirmative defenses.

4. ***Overlap Between Bystander Injury and Lost Consortium.*** Previously in Chapter 6 on Special Duty Rules, we explored courts' willingness to permit a claim, in *Dillon* jurisdictions, for the emotional distress of witnessing the death or serious injury of a loved one. In such a scenario, the family member witnessing the tragic accident would likely also have a loss of consortium claim if the victim were either a spouse or a parent/child of the witness. Significant potential overlap exists between one's bystander claim for emotional anguish and the loss of consortium arising from the same accident. The difference between them is that the bystander claim remedies the harm from witnessing the event while the consortium claim arises from the ensuing negative impact on the relationship between the witness and victim. In the real world of a jury box, one wonders how easily a typical juror could maintain such distinction in assessing damages.

5. *Problems.* Imagine a traffic accident occurs on an interstate freeway, causing severe injuries to the plaintiff. The plaintiff is taken to a hospital and treated for a week prior to her death. With respect to the Tennessee wrongful death and survival statute interpreted by the court in *Jordan*, try to classify each of the following components of harm as either appropriate damages for a wrongful death claim or for a survival claim:

- **A.** The cost of an ambulance taking the plaintiff-decedent from the scene of the accident to the hospital.
- **B.** Hospital bills incurred in treating the plaintiff-decedent's injuries, including medicines, room costs, treatment expenses, MRI exams, etc.
- **C.** Disfigurement to the plaintiff's face from burns received in the accident.
- **D.** Funeral and burial expenses.
- **E.** Pain experienced by plaintiff-decedent once she became conscious until she passed away.
- **F.** Lost wages of the plaintiff-decedent during the week between the accident and her death.
- **G.** The lost future earnings that would likely have been used to provide support to the plaintiff-decedent's immediate family.
- **H.** The loss associated with the plaintiff-decedent's spouse and children in losing the plaintiff-decedent.
- **I.** The cost of the household services likely to be incurred in the future that would have normally been performed by the plaintiff-decedent (e.g., mowing the lawn regularly).
- **J.** The loss of enjoyment of the daily activities of life experienced by the plaintiff-decedent prior to her death.

D. Property Damages

Where the defendant's misconduct has caused property damage, a typical method of calculating this item of special damage is to use the difference between the market value of the property prior to the tort and after the tort. The reduction in the amount is the lost fair market value of the property. Of course, where the property is completely destroyed due to the defendant's tort, the entire market value at the time of its destruction becomes recoverable. Market value is what the property could have been sold for on the open market in a voluntary sale to a willing buyer. Where the property is merely damaged and it is unclear how this damage has impacted the market value, courts often permit consideration of the costs of repair of the item as a substitute method for calculating the damage. Generally, costs of repair as an alternative calculation of damage should not exceed the actual market value of the unimpaired item. When the plaintiff cannot use the property for a significant period of time as a result of the defendant's tort, courts will permit recovery of a reasonable rental cost as a way to determine the damages for the loss of use of the item. Each of these calculations of actual damage would be in the nature of special or economic losses. As to these items of damage, little controversy exists in terms of the principles governing providing a remedy.

While these damage models are relatively straightforward in tort cases involving harm to personal property, plaintiffs in some such cases have made creative attempts to recover for additional items of loss. The following recent case involving an injury to someone's dog portrays such an attempt. As you read the opinion, consider the rationales behind courts' reluctance to permit recovery of general damages for injury to most types of personal property.

STRICKLAND v. MEDLEN

56 Tex. Sup. J. 470 (Tex. 2013)

WILLETT, J.

Beauty without Vanity,
Strength without Insolence,
Courage without Ferocity,
And all the Virtues of Man without his Vices[4]

Texans love their dogs. Throughout the Lone Star State, canine companions are treated — and treasured — not as mere personal property but as beloved friends and confidants, even family members. Given the richness that companion animals add to our everyday lives, losing "man's best friend" is undoubtedly sorrowful. Even the gruffest among us tears up (every time) at the end of *Old Yeller.*

This case concerns the types of damages available for the loss of a family pet. If a cherished dog is negligently killed, can a dollar value be placed on a heartsick owner's heartfelt affection? More pointedly, may a bereaved dog owner recover emotion-based damages for the loss? In 1891, we effectively said no, announcing a "true rule" that categorized dogs as personal property, thus disallowing non-economic damages. In 2011, however, a court of appeals said yes, effectively creating a novel — and expansive — tort claim: loss of companionship for the wrongful death of a pet.

In today's case, involving a family dog that was accidentally euthanized, we must decide whether to adhere to our restrictive, 122-year-old precedent classifying pets as property for tort-law purposes, or to instead recognize a new common-law loss-of-companionship claim that allows non-economic damages rooted solely in emotional attachment, a remedy the common law has denied those who suffer the wrongful death of a spouse, parent, or child,[5] and is available in Texas only by [the enactment of a wrongful death] statute.

---

4. Lord Byron, *Inscription on the Monument of a Newfoundland Dog*, in 7 The Works of Lord Byron: with His Letters and Journals, and His Life 292-93 n.2 (Thomas Moore ed., 1832).

5. *See Russell v. Ingersoll-Rand Co.*, 841 S.W.2d 343, 345 (Tex. 1992) ("common law rule" was that "no cause of action [could] be brought for the death of another person").

We acknowledge the grief of those whose companions are negligently killed. Relational attachment is unquestionable. But it is also uncompensable. We reaffirm our long-settled rule, which tracks the overwhelming weight of authority nationally, plus the bulk of amicus curiae briefs from several pet-welfare organizations (who understand the deep emotional bonds between people and their animals): Pets are property in the eyes of the law, and we decline to permit noneconomic damages rooted solely in an owner's subjective feelings. True, a beloved companion dog is not a fungible, inanimate object like, say, a toaster. The term "property" is not a pejorative but a legal descriptor, and its use should not be misconstrued as discounting the emotional attachment that pet owners undeniably feel. Nevertheless, under established legal doctrine, recovery in pet-death cases is, barring legislative reclassification, limited to loss of value, not loss of relationship.

We reverse the court of appeals' judgment and render judgment in favor of the [defendant].

FACTUAL BACKGROUND

In June 2009, Avery, a mixed-breed dog owned by Kathryn and Jeremy Medlen, escaped the family's backyard and was promptly picked up by Fort Worth animal control. Jeremy went to retrieve Avery but lacked enough money to pay the required fees. The shelter hung a "hold for owner" tag on Avery's cage to alert employees that the Medlens were coming for Avery and ensure he was not euthanized. Despite the tag, shelter worker Carla Strickland mistakenly placed Avery on the euthanasia list, and he was put to sleep.

Jeremy and his two children learned of Avery's fate a few days later when they returned to retrieve him. Devastated, the Medlens sued Strickland for causing Avery's death and sought "sentimental or intrinsic value" damages since Avery had little or no market value but was irreplaceable. Strickland specially excepted, contending such damages are unrecoverable in pet-death cases. The trial court directed the Medlens to amend their pleadings to "state a claim for damages recognized at law." The Medlens amended their petition to drop the words "sentimental value" but realleged damages for Avery's "intrinsic value." Strickland specially excepted on the same basis, and the trial court, sure that Texas law barred such damages, dismissed the suit with prejudice.

The court of appeals reversed, becoming the first Texas court to hold that a dog owner may recover intangible loss-of-companionship damages in the form of intrinsic or sentimental-value property damages. Addressing our 1891 decision in *Heiligmann v. Rose* [16 S.W. 931], which pegged dog-loss damages to market value or a value ascertained from the dog's "usefulness and services," the court of appeals stated, "Texas law has changed greatly since 1891" and "sentimental damages may now be recovered for . . . all types of personal property." Reinstating the Medlens' claim, the court of appeals concluded: "Because an owner may be awarded damages based on the sentimental value of lost personal property, and because dogs are personal property, the trial court erred in dismissing the Medlens' action against Strickland."

This appeal followed, posing a single, yet significant, issue: whether emotional-injury damages are recoverable for the negligent destruction of a dog.

DISCUSSION

America is home to 308 million humans and 377 million pets. In fact, "American pets now outnumber American children by more than four to one." In a nation with about 78 million pet dogs and 86 million pet cats (and 160 million pet fish), where roughly 62% of households own a pet, it is unsurprising that many animal owners view their pets not as mere personal property but as full-fledged family members, and treat them as such:

- A study found that 70% of pet owners thought of their pets as family members.
- 45% of dog owners take their pets on vacation.
- Over 50% of pet owners say they would rather be stranded on a deserted island with a dog or cat than with a human.
- 50% of pet owners report being "very likely" to put their own lives in danger to save their pets, and 33% are "somewhat likely" to risk their lives.
- In 2012, Americans spent roughly $53 billion on their pets.

The human-animal bond is indeed powerful. As the Medlens' second amended petition states: "The entire Medlen family was devastated by the loss of Avery, who was like a family member to them." Countless Texas families share this pets-as-family view, but Texas law, for a century-plus, has labeled them as "property" for purposes of tort-law recovery.

Our analysis begins with *Heiligmann v. Rose*, our 1891 case upholding $75 in damages for the poisoning of three "well trained" Newfoundland dogs. *Heiligmann* articulated some key valuation principles for animal cases. First, we classified dogs as personal property for damages purposes, not as something giving rise to personal-injury damages. Second, we declared a "true rule" for damages that flags two elements: (1) "market value, if the dog has any," or (2) "some special or pecuniary value to the owner, that may be ascertained by reference to the usefulness and services of the dog."

In *Heiligmann*, the dogs "were of fine breed, and well trained," with one using different barks to signal whether an approaching person was a man, woman, or child. While the owner could sell each dog for $5, they had no market value beyond that, but the Court upheld damages of $25 each:

> There is no evidence in this case that the dogs had a market value, but the evidence is ample showing the usefulness and services of the dogs, and that they were of special value to the owner. If the jury from the evidence should be satisfied that the

> dogs were serviceable and useful to the owner, they could infer their value when the owner, by evidence, fixes some amount upon which they could form a basis.

The Medlens insist that *Heiligmann* does not limit recovery to an amount based *solely* on the dog's economic usefulness and services. Rather, when the Court mentioned certain dogs lacking market value but having "a special value to the owner," we meant something far broader and distinct from the dogs' commercial attributes. Similarly, argue the Medlens, when the Court in *Heiligmann* noted a dog's "special or pecuniary value to the owner," the word "or" indicates two distinct categories of non-market value dogs — those with a special value to the owner, and those with a pecuniary value to the owner. We disagree.

Given its ordinary, contextual meaning, *Heiligmann* tied the recovery of "special or pecuniary value" to the dogs' "usefulness and services" — their economic value, not their sentimental value. While we referenced evidence "showing the usefulness and services of the dogs, and that they were of a special value to the owner," the next conditional sentence pegs the jury's valuation decision to the dogs' economic attributes: "If the jury from the evidence should be satisfied that the dogs were serviceable and useful to the owner. . . ." The decision never references, even by implication, any evidence regarding companionship or owner affection.

Thus, a dog's "special or pecuniary value" refers not to the dog-human bond but to the dollars-and-cents value traceable to the dog's usefulness and services. Such value is economic value, not emotional value based on affection, attachment, or companionship. In short, *Heiligmann's* use of the word "special" does not authorize "special damages" and does not refer generically to a dog's ability to combat loneliness, ease depression, or provide security. The valuation criteria is not emotional and subjective; rather it is commercial and objective.

Alternatively, the Medlens assert that [the] post-*Heiligmann* decision [in] *Brown v. Frontier Theatres, Inc.* [369 S.W.2d 299 (Tex. 1963)] entitles property owners to seek intrinsic or sentimental-value damages for certain destroyed property that lacks market value or "special or pecuniary" value. Because dogs are considered property under Texas law, they should be treated no differently, argue the Medlens. Accordingly, Avery's intrinsic value to them, including companionship, is recoverable. We decline to stretch our post-*Heiligmann* decisions this far.

Our decision a half-century ago in *Brown* involved irreplaceable family heirlooms such as a wedding veil, pistol, jewelry, hand-made bedspreads and other items going back several generations — in other words, family keepsakes that "have their primary value in sentiment." Such one-of-a-kind heirlooms have a "special value . . . to their owner," and damages may factor in "the feelings of the owner for such property." Notably, on the same day we decided *Brown* fifty years ago, we reaffirmed in another case the default damages rule for destroyed non-heirloom property lacking market or replacement value: "the actual worth or value of the articles to the owner . . . excluding any fanciful or sentimental considerations." [*Crisp v. Sec. Nat'l Ins. Co.*, 369 S.W.2d 326, 328 (Tex. 1963)].

Heiligmann remains our lone case directly on point, and after a century-plus we are loathe to disturb it. An owner's attachment to a one-of-a-kind family keepsake as in *Brown* is sentimental, but an owner's attachment to a beloved pet is more: It is emotional. Pets afford here-and-now benefits — company, recreation, protection, etc. — unlike a passed-down heirloom kept around chiefly to commemorate past events or passed family members. We agree with the amicus brief submitted by the American Kennel Club (joined by several other pet-welfare groups): "While no two pets are alike, the emotional attachments a person establishes with each pet cannot be shoe-horned into keepsake-like sentimentality for litigation purposes." Finally, . . . permitting sentiment-based damages for destroyed heirloom property portends nothing resembling the vast public-policy impact of allowing such damages in animal-tort cases.

Loss of companionship, the gravamen of the Medlens' claim, is fundamentally a form of *personal-injury* damage, not property damage. It is a component of loss of consortium, including the loss of "love, affection, protection, emotional support, services, companionship, care, and society." Loss-of-consortium damages are available only for a few especially close family relationships, and to allow them in lost pet cases would be inconsistent with these limitations. Therefore, like courts in the overwhelming majority of other states, the Restatement of the Law of Torts, and the other Texas courts of appeals that have considered this question, we reject emotion-based liability and prohibit recovery for loss of the human-animal bond.

> Columnist George Will expressed pleasure in the *Strickland* court's decision to stick with its 1891 "true value" doctrine:
>
> > By this judicial statesmanship, the trial bar was muzzled, for now, and denied a fresh arena for mischief. So Texas' Supreme Court is, for now, man's best friend.
>
> *George F. Will, Texas Court Limits Lawyers in Pet-Related Suits, Washington Post (May 29, 2013).*

We do not dispute that dogs are a special form of personal property. That is precisely why Texas law forbids animal cruelty generally (both civilly and criminally), and bans dog fighting and unlawful restraints of dogs specifically — because animals, though property, are unique. Most dogs have a simple job description: provide devoted companionship. We have no need to overrule *Brown*'s narrow heirloom exception today; neither do we broaden it to pet-death cases and enshrine an expansive new rule that allows recovery for what a canine companion meant to its owner. The Medlens find it odd that Texas law would permit sentimental damages for loss of an heirloom but not an Airedale. Strickland would find it odd if Texas [common] law permitted damages for loss of a Saint Bernard but not for a brother Bernard. The law is no stranger to incongruity, and we need not jettison *Brown* in order to refuse to extend it to categories of property beyond heirlooms.

The "true rule" in Texas remains this: Where a dog's market value is unascertainable, the correct damages measure is the dog's "special or pecuniary value" (that is, its actual value) — the economic value derived from its "usefulness and services," not value drawn from companionship or other non-commercial considerations.

CONCLUSION

To his dog, every man is Napoleon;
hence the constant popularity of dogs.[73]

It is an inconvenient, yet inescapable, truth: "Tort law . . . cannot remedy every wrong." Lines, seemingly arbitrary, are required. No one disputes that a family dog — "in life the firmest friend" — is a treasured companion. But it is also personal property, and the law draws sensible, policy-based distinctions between types of property. The majority rule throughout most of America — including Texas since 1891 — leavens warm-heartedness with sober-mindedness, applying a rational rule rather than an emotional one. For the reasons discussed above, we decline to (1) jettison our 122-year-old precedent classifying dogs as ordinary property, and (2) permit non-economic damages rooted in relational attachment.

We reverse the court of appeals' judgment and render judgment in favor of Strickland.

NOTES AND PROBLEMS

1. ***Personal Injury vs. Property Damages.*** The court in *Strickland* distinguishes between the items of damage recoverable in personal injury litigation versus property damage cases. Are you persuaded by the court's distinction between the two? What is the justification for refusing to allow recovery of emotional distress damages (or any other general damage category) for the loss of a family pet despite the court's acknowledgement that such harm is likely to occur? Is this rule of law consistent with the tort goal of providing full compensation to injured parties?

2. ***Negligent Infliction of Emotional Distress.*** Where a defendant has negligently caused primary harm to another and this harm has caused secondary and indirect loss to bystanders, we have seen the courts find different doctrinal methods to limit recovery, with the majority of courts adopting the *Dillon* rule and only permitting close family members who actually witness the death or serious harm to recover for their emotional losses (Chapter 6, Special Duty Rules). If the plaintiff's argument in *Strickland* were accepted, what would this do to the sanctity behind the *Dillon* limitations? *Strickland* can, therefore, be

73. Aldous Huxley, *as quoted* in Robert Andrews, The Concise Columbia Dictionary of Quotations 83 (1990).

viewed both as a case limiting the nature of damages recoverable when the primary harm was to one's personal property, as well as a case reaffirming that a *Dillon*-type of recovery is limited to human family members.

3. ***Heirloom Exception.*** As the *Strickland* court acknowledges, one deviation from the general rule limiting damages for loss of personal property to market value arises in the case of items considered family heirlooms that may have no recognizable market value but have great sentimental value. This exception has been found applicable when the item damaged or destroyed was clothing, books, pictures, furniture, or other household goods that had unique personal value to the owner but to no one else. In such cases, courts have recognized that the market value recovery would fail to offer compensation for the real loss and so they permit the jury to assess damages based upon the emotional injury to the owner. On the other hand, is it difficult to conceptualize a legitimate reason for permitting exceptional, emotional-related recovery for damage to an heirloom but not to a pet?

Upon Further Review

While some students might be tempted to view damage issues as an uninteresting after-thought in tort cases, questions regarding what sums should be paid by the tortfeasor often dominate tort litigation. Indeed, in many cases the liability issues are very straightforward and the jury's primary job is to determine actual damages. Many out-of-court settlement discussions and mediations focus upon the parties' disparate views of the proper amounts that should be paid to the victim. With regard to special or economic losses, the determination is often aided by relatively concrete formulas approved by the courts to help determine the economic losses suffered due to the defendant's tortious misconduct. Where the nature of the loss does not involve something that is typically bought or sold in the marketplace — such as disfigurement or pain or emotional distress — the law has had a much more difficult time providing any concrete formulas. Instead, courts often are only able to give the juries vaguely worded principles to guide their deliberations, and appellate courts frequently find their analysis limited to comparing one jury's award of general damages with other juries' awards in similar cases. It is rough justice. On the other hand, courts have come up with a variety of concrete rules in cases involving general damages that govern the types of evidence and arguments that lawyers are permitted to present to the jury. In this way, courts try to reign in potential abuses by juries in finding general damages disproportionate to the injuries suffered by plaintiffs. The next section will deal with other potential limits on the recovery of actual damages.

 LIMITATIONS ON ACTUAL DAMAGES

Thus far we have focused upon differentiating between the various types of actual damages and understanding particular analytical issues arising under some of these varieties. A complete understanding of tort law's treatment of actual damages demands consideration of three additional issues that potentially impact the actual size of compensatory damage recovery in a tort case. First, the doctrine of *failure to mitigate damages* imposes a post-tort duty upon the plaintiff to exercise reasonable care to treat or lessen the ultimate harm plaintiff suffers and for which plaintiff can expect to receive compensation from the tortfeasor. We will begin with two cases that illustrate the two different analytical approaches to this duty. We will then take up consideration of a hotly debated topic — whether an accident victim's failure to anticipate a crash and wear a seat belt should have any damage recovery reduced as either evidence of a failure to mitigate or comparative fault. Second, a long established doctrine called *the collateral source rule* declares that the plaintiff's receipt of benefits from someone other than the tortfeasor (e.g., health insurance) to help pay or reimburse plaintiff for some of her losses should not work to lessen the tortfeasor's liability for all of the harm caused. This doctrine has come under attack in recent decades, and some courts (or legislatures) have abandoned it. We will encounter a court considering such a change to the doctrine. Finally, we will consider the epicenter of the tort reform movement — statutory ceilings on a plaintiff's recovery of actual damages. Many states now have legislatively imposed limits on tort recovery; this has led to constitutional challenges regarding such limits, with mixed results.

A. Failure to Mitigate Damages

The doctrine of *failure to mitigate damages* — sometimes called the "avoidable consequences rule" — places an obligation on the victim to exercise reasonable care to reduce or "mitigate" her actual damages. Given that so much of tort law deals with the goal of avoiding or deterring losses, placing the duty on the victim makes a lot of sense. Further, to the extent the plaintiff could have minimized some of her losses through exercising reasonable care after the initial injury, tort law believes it inappropriate to reward the plaintiff by awarding full damages. In this instance, the tort goal of providing compensation to worthy victims only demands compensating the plaintiff for unavoidable losses. While all courts place this expectation — or duty — upon the plaintiff, there are two different conceptual ways of implementing this doctrine. The traditional method of enforcing this obligation is for courts to consider the failure to mitigate damages to be a *damage limiting doctrine* by which the jury is merely instructed in finding the actual damages to not include any sums that the plaintiff could have avoided by exercising reasonable care in responding to the injuries. Some other courts, however, after moving away from contributory negligence to some form of comparative fault, have chosen to consider a breach of the duty to exercise reasonable care in minimizing harm to be a type of *fault* (negligence) and will apportion this fault and reduce damages post-verdict by judicial action. See how the two courts below follow each of these two models, and consider whether it makes a difference which conceptual approach a state chooses.

1. Failure to Mitigate as "Fault"

MILLER v. EICHHORN

426 N.W.2d 641 (Iowa 1988)

SACKETT, J.

Plaintiffs appeal a damage award in their favor for injuries resulting from an automobile accident. Plaintiffs claim . . . there were errors in the instructions. We affirm.

A car driven by Plaintiff-Appellant Connie M. Miller collided with a car driven by Defendant-Appellee Harold Eichhorn. The collision occurred when defendant backed his car from his driveway into the street. Plaintiffs sued defendants for injuries Connie allegedly received in the accident. Plaintiff Keith Miller is Connie's husband. His claim was for loss of consortium. The case was tried to a jury which found Connie's damages to be $3,569.70. The jury found no damages for Keith. The jury determined Connie's fault to be fifteen percent and Harold's fault to be eighty-five percent.

Plaintiff challenges the trial court's submission of an instruction on mitigation of damages. Plaintiff objected to the mitigation of damage instruction claiming the failure to mitigate damages is not fault. We disagree. Iowa Comparative Fault Act, Iowa Code section 668.1, provides:

> As used in this chapter . . . the term ["fault"] also includes . . . unreasonable failure to avoid an injury or to mitigate damages.

Section 668.3 provides:

> In determining the percentages of fault, the trier of fact shall consider both the nature of the conduct of each party and the extent of the causal relation between the conduct and the damages claimed.

The statute clearly provides the unreasonable failure to mitigate damages means fault as used in the statute.

Defendant argues it was not error to give the instruction because there is substantial evidence plaintiff failed to mitigate damages. Defendant also argues there is substantial evidence because plaintiff claimed medical problems and the need to employ substitute labor in her business from the time of the accident to the time of trial. There were periods of time when Connie did not see a doctor regularly. We reject defendant's argument on these grounds. For the failure to consult a doctor on a regular basis to be evidence of failure to mitigate damages there must be a showing consultations on a regular basis would have mitigated damages. Connie's duty is to use ordinary care in consulting a physician. There is, however, testimony by one of Connie's doctors that additional chiropractic treatments would have helped Connie's condition. This evidence supports the submission of the mitigation of damage issue and is evidence from which the jury could find she did not use due care in following her doctor's advice.

We affirm.

In Practice

Fed. R. Civ. P. 8(c) requires a defendant to plead any affirmative defenses. This includes contributory negligence (or comparative fault). Limitations on damages, however, are not typically considered to be affirmative defenses but merely inferential rebuttals of an element (damages) of the plaintiff's claim. How a state classifies failure to mitigate implicates whether it must be pled or is subject to waiver.

2. Failure to Mitigate as a Damage Consideration

KLANSECK v. ANDERSON SALES & SERVICE, INC.

393 N.W.2d 356 (Mich. 1986)

WILLIAMS, J.

This motorcycle accident case presents [the question of] whether it was error for the court to instruct the jury regarding the plaintiff's duty to mitigate damages. Since evidence was presented that the plaintiff did not follow the course of action recommended by his physician, we find the court's instruction was warranted.

Plaintiff, Stephen Klanseck, brought this action, seeking damages for injuries suffered in a motorcycle accident which occurred May 27, 1976. Mr. Klanseck had that day purchased a Honda GL 1000 motorcycle from defendant Anderson Sales & Service, Inc., and was heading for home with his new cycle when the machine began to "fishtail." Plaintiff applied the brakes and the motorcycle slid sideways and went down, resulting in plaintiff's injuries.

Principles

The Restatement (Second) of Torts §918 (1965) provides the following succinct statement concerning mitigation: "One injured by the tort of another is not entitled to recover damages for any harm that he could have avoided by the use of reasonable effort of expenditure after the commission of the tort."

Following the accident, plaintiff received sutures in his left arm, was x-rayed and released. Twelve days later, a fracture of plaintiff's right wrist was diagnosed and treated. Plaintiff, who was employed as an auto mechanic, claimed that his injuries resulted in chronic pain and numbness in his left arm and hand, which interfered with his work and eventually resulted in a serious mental disorder.

With regard to plaintiff's alleged failure to mitigate damages, the court gave the following instruction:

> Now, a person has a duty to use ordinary care to minimize his own damages after he has been injured, and it is for you to decide whether the Plaintiff failed to use such ordinary care and, if so, whether any damages resulted from such failure.
>
> You may not compensate the Plaintiff for any portion of his damages which resulted from his failure to use ordinary care.

Plaintiff contends that this instruction was erroneous because no evidence was presented that would create an issue as to plaintiff's failure to mitigate his damages. Defendant points to the testimony of Dr. Gary W. Roat, and claims that it creates an issue on the question of mitigation. Dr. Roat, a neurologist, testified that the plaintiff had come to him on referral from another physician about a year after the accident and that he had treated the plaintiff a number of times for numbness and tingling in his hand as well as back and leg pain. After trying several medications, Dr. Roat recommended that plaintiff undergo additional diagnostic tests, including nerve conduction studies, an electromyelographic examination, and a myelogram to determine whether he had a herniated disk. According to Dr. Roat's testimony, plaintiff decided against taking these tests unless his symptoms worsened.

It is well settled that an injured party has a duty to exercise reasonable care to minimize damages, including obtaining proper medical or surgical treatment. It is also settled that the charge of the court must be based upon the evidence and should be confined to the issues presented by the evidence.

Although the evidence of plaintiff's alleged failure to mitigate damages was weak, there was evidence that plaintiff had not followed the recommendation of Dr. Roat. Even scant evidence may support an instruction where it raises an issue for the jury's decision. The trial court's instruction on failure to mitigate damages was proper.

Affirmed.

NOTES AND PROBLEMS

1. ***Does the Different Treatment Matter?*** While *Miller* treats the mitigation issue as one of comparative fault, the *Klanseck* court treats it as an issue of damages for the jury to consider in assessing the actual damages award. Do you see how the difference in approach might lead to the exact same result? Can you think of an instance where it might matter? Consider a situation where the plaintiff suffers a compound fracture in an auto accident due to the defendant's fault and is treated at an emergency room. Among other things, the plaintiff is given antibiotics to take for possible infection. Plaintiff fails to take the medicine, the wound is horribly infected and she ultimately loses the limb. In her suit for all of her damages from the other driver, do you see why a jury might consider that a significant percentage of her injuries were her own fault? If so, and if the state treats a failure to mitigate as a type of "fault" to be apportioned, what percentage might the jury apply? What happens if the state is a 49 percent or 50 percent modified comparative fault jurisdiction and the jury translates the plaintiff's failure to mitigate into an apportionment of fault, giving the plaintiff 75 percent of the total fault and the defendant driver only 25 percent? How much does the plaintiff recover? If the state, however, treats the plaintiff's failure to mitigate as merely a damages issue, how much might the plaintiff recover? This possibility of the failure to mitigate acting as a complete bar to recovery (despite the defendant being solely to blame for the accident itself) might be a good reason for a state to reject the treatment of mitigation as a comparative fault proposition.

2. ***Problems.*** With respect to the mitigation doctrine's prohibition on a victim recovering damages for harms that could have been avoided following an accident, do you believe a failure to mitigate damages argument exists in the following two scenarios?

A. Plaintiff suffers a compound fracture in an accident, and her doctors advise her that surgery is available to treat her condition. Due to religious objections, however, plaintiff declines medical treatment. Her limb develops necrosis and has to be amputated. *See* Loomis, *Thou Shalt Take Thy Victim as Thou Findest Him: Religious Conviction as a Pre-Existing State Not Subject to the Avoidable Consequences Rule*, 14 Geo. Mason L. Rev. 473 (2007).

B. Plaintiff sues for the wrongful death of his spouse who was killed when a roof at a restaurant collapsed on her as she dined. Plaintiff seeks loss of consortium damages, among other items. Plaintiff and his wife were 25 years old at the time of the accident. Plaintiff has since begun dating another woman but refuses to ever consider remarrying. Compare Benwell v. Dean, 57 Cal. Rptr. 394 (Cal. App. 1967) with Jensen v. Heritage Mutual Ins. Co., 127 N.W.2d 228 (Wis. 1974).

"LADIES AND GENTLEMEN OF THE JURY . . ."

5th Circuit Pattern Jury Instructions (Civil Cases) 15.15 Mitigation of Damages:

"A person who claims damages resulting from the wrongful act of another has a duty under the law to use reasonable diligence to mitigate — to avoid or minimize those damages.

If you find the defendant is liable and the plaintiff has suffered damages, the plaintiff may not recover for any item of damage which he could have avoided through reasonable effort."

3. *Seat-Belt Defense*

NABORS WELL SERVICES v. ROMERO

456 S.W.3d 553 (Tex. 2015)

Brown, J.

For more than forty years evidence of a plaintiff's failure to use a seat belt has been inadmissible in car-accident cases. That rule, which this Court first announced in 1974, offered plaintiffs safe harbor from the harshness of an all-or-nothing scheme that barred recovery for even the slightest contributory negligence. Moreover, the Court reasoned that although a plaintiff's failure to use a seat belt may exacerbate his injuries, it cannot *cause* a car accident, and therefore should not affect a plaintiff's recovery.

In 1985 the Legislature jumped in to statutorily prohibit evidence of use or nonuse of seat belts in all civil cases. It repealed that law in 2003, leaving our rule to again stand alone. But much has changed in the past four decades. The Legislature has overhauled Texas' system for apportioning fault in negligence cases — a plaintiff's negligence can now be apportioned alongside a defendant's without entirely barring the plaintiff's recovery. And unlike in 1974, seat belts are now required by law and have become an unquestioned part of daily life for the vast majority of drivers and passengers.

These changes have rendered our prohibition on seat-belt evidence an anachronism. The rule may have been appropriate in its time, but today it is a vestige of a bygone legal system and an oddity in light of modern societal norms. Today we overrule it and hold that relevant evidence of use or nonuse of seat belts is admissible for the purpose of apportioning responsibility in civil lawsuits.

I

This case arises from a collision between a Nabors Well Services, Ltd. transport truck and a Chevrolet Suburban with eight occupants — three adults and five children. Both vehicles were traveling southbound on two-lane U.S. Highway 285 in rural West Texas. As the transport truck slowed to make a left turn into a Nabors facility, Martin Soto, the Suburban's driver, pulled into the opposing traffic lane and attempted to pass the transport truck. As Soto passed, the transport truck began its left turn and clipped the Suburban, which careened off the highway and rolled multiple times. The evidence is disputed as to whether the transport truck used a turn signal and for how long and whether Soto could have passed the transport truck within the legal passing zone.

Aydee Romero, an adult passenger, was killed in the accident. Martin, his wife Esperanza Soto, and all five children — Esperanza, Guadalupe, and Marielena Soto, and Edgar and Saul Romero — suffered injuries. There is conflicting evidence as to which occupants were belted and which were ejected from the Suburban. A responding state trooper wrote in his report that all occupants were unrestrained except Marielena and the elder Esperanza. But both of them, along with the younger Esperanza, testified they did not use seat belts, while Martin and Guadalupe testified they wore theirs. Guadalupe testified all occupants were ejected except for Martin and Edgar, but Edgar testified he was ejected. And an EMS report stated one of the family members reported at the scene that seven of eight occupants were ejected.

The Soto and Romero families sued Nabors and its truck driver. At trial, Nabors sought to offer expert testimony from a biomechanical engineer, James Funk, Ph.D., that seven of the eight Suburban occupants were unbelted (all except Martin, the driver), that five of those seven were ejected from the vehicle, and that the failure to use seat belts caused the passengers' injuries and the one fatality. Nabors also hoped to introduce evidence of a citation issued to Soto for driving without properly restraining the child passengers as well as testimony from the plaintiffs as to who was unbelted and who was ejected.

Following our precedent in *Carnation Co. v. Wong*, 516 S.W.2d 116 (Tex. 1974), the trial court excluded all evidence of nonuse of seat belts. The jury found Nabors 51% and Soto 49% responsible for the accident, and awarded the Soto and Romero families collectively just over $2.3 million. The court of appeals affirmed the trial court's judgment based solely on the *Carnation* prohibition on seat-belt evidence. We granted review to consider the current viability of *Carnation* in light of the Legislature's repeal of its statutory ban on seat-belt evidence.

II

A

Texas's earliest cases on the admissibility of seat-belt evidence first appeared in the late 1960s. The context within which these cases arose is instructive. First, there was no law requiring seat-belt use; in fact, a federal mandate that seat belts be installed as standard equipment on all new passenger vehicles was barely in its infancy. And second, Texas courts operated under an unforgiving all-or-nothing rule in negligence cases that entirely barred a plaintiff from recovery if the plaintiff himself was negligent in any way.

This Court first encountered the issue in *Kerby v. Abilene Christian College*, in which the driver of a linen truck, Kerby, was ejected through the open sliding door of his truck after colliding with an ACC bus. 503 S.W.2d 526, 526 (Tex. 1973). The jury found Kerby negligent and 35% responsible for his injuries. The trial court accordingly reduced Kerby's recovery by 35%, but the court of appeals tossed his award entirely because under the law at the time his contributory negligence barred any recovery whatsoever. This Court reversed both lower courts and restored Kerby's recovery in full, reasoning that "[c]ontributory negligence must have the causal connection with the accident that but for the conduct the accident would not have happened." Accordingly, "negligence that merely increases or adds to the extent of the loss or injury occasioned by another's negligence is not such contributory negligence as will defeat recovery." In so holding, the Court drew "a sharp distinction between negligence contributing to the accident and negligence contributing to the damages sustained." The Court further likened the facts of *Kerby* to earlier cases in which courts of appeals held the failure to use a seat belt was not "actionable negligence" or "contributory negligence such that would bar recovery," and underscored the "conceptual difficulty of applying the mitigation of [damages concept to Plaintiff's conduct antedating the negligence of the Defendant." *Id.* In so doing, the Court declared seat-belt evidence incompatible with the only two legal doctrines — contributory negligence and failure to mitigate damages — that arguably could accommodate it.

A year later in *Carnation v. Wong*, the jury found plaintiffs involved in a car accident negligent for failing to use seat belts. The jury attributed 50% of the fault for the husband's injuries against him and 70% of the fault for the wife's injuries against her. The trial court reduced the Wongs' awards correspondingly, but the court of appeals overturned those reductions. Finding no reversible error, this Court announced: "We now hold that . . . persons whose negligence did not contribute to an automobile accident should not have the damages awarded to them reduced or mitigated because of their failure to wear available seat belts."

B

About a decade after *Carnation*, the federal government began to push seat-belt-use initiatives that would give rise to the first seat-belt laws in Texas. The Texas Legislature, along with many others, responded, and in 1985 for the first time made it a criminal offense for anyone fifteen years or older to ride in a front seat unbelted, and further placed on drivers a responsibility to properly restrain children under fifteen riding in a front seat. The new law further provided that: "Use or nonuse of a safety belt is not admissible evidence in a civil trial." And with that prohibition, *Carnation* was mothballed — not stricken from the books but preempted by a stricter statutory prohibition. The prohibition against seat-belt evidence in civil trials remained intact throughout the law's evolution until 2003, when the Legislature repealed the provision as part of the sweeping tort-reform legislation. The Legislature did not replace the prohibition with any language affirming the use of seat-belt evidence — it simply struck the provision altogether.

III

Everyone in this case agrees the statutory repeal revived this Court's holding in *Carnation*, a common-law rule subsumed for eighteen years by a broader statutory prohibition but never overruled. The question is whether that rule, established more than forty years ago, should still stand today. While the Legislature now says nothing about seat-belt evidence specifically, it has said much since *Carnation* about the assignment of responsibility in negligence lawsuits.

At the time *Kerby* and *Carnation* were tried, Texas followed the all-or-nothing system of contributory negligence. Under contributory negligence, if a plaintiff was even one percent at fault, he or she could not recover. [Beginning in 1973, the legislature adopted a 50% comparative responsibility system which is now embodied in Chapter 33 of Texas' Civil Practice & Remedies Code.] Gone is the "harsh system of absolute victory or total defeat." *See Parker*, 565 S.W.2d at 518. Under [the current law a plaintiff who is no more than 50% at fault merely has damages reduced according to the plaintiff's percentage of fault]. And the statute casts a wide net over conduct that may be considered in this determination, including negligent acts or omissions as well as any conduct or activity that violates an applicable legal standard. The directive is clear — fact-finders should consider each person's role in causing, "in any way," harm for which recovery of damages is sought. The question we now face is whether the "sharp distinction" between occurrence-causing and injury-causing negligence this Court drew in *Kerby* is still viable in light of the Legislature's current mandate. In other words, can a plaintiff's failure to use a seat belt, though it did not cause the car accident, limit his recovery if it can be shown that the failure to use a seat belt caused or contributed to cause his injuries?

The systematic elimination of outmoded ameliorative doctrines has led to speculation about the continued viability of the "sharp distinction" we recognized in *Kerby*. The Third Restatement has specifically cited *Carnation* as an example of how "[s]ome courts used to forgive a plaintiff of *pre-accident* negligence that merely aggravated the injury." Restatement (Third) of Torts: Apportionment of Liab. §3 Reporter's Note, cmt. b at 39 (2000) (emphasis in original). Of such decisions, the Restatement observes:

> They gave various rationales for this rule, including that the legislature had not mandated the conduct, that counting the conduct would constitute a windfall for the defendant, and that a plaintiff should not have to foresee and guard against the possibility of a defendant's negligence. None of these rationales provides an adequate account for the rule, because each of them could be applied with equal force to ordinary contributory negligence. The most satisfactory explanation is that courts were hostile to the harsh consequences of contributory negligence as an absolute bar to recovery and developed the rule as an ameliorative device. Comparative responsibility eviscerates that rationale.

Our precedents holding that a plaintiff's injury-causing negligence cannot reduce a plaintiff's recovery cannot stand if today's proportionate-responsibility statute contradicts those precedents. And we hold it does. We recently observed in *Dugger* that the proportionate-responsibility statute "indicates the Legislature's desire to compare responsibility for *injuries* rather than bar recovery, even if the claimant was partly at fault or violated some legal standard." *Dugger*, 408 S.W.3d at 832.

Furthermore, [our current comparative responsibility laws] focus the fact-finder on assigning responsibility for the "harm for which recovery of damages is sought" — two examples of which are "personal injury" and "death" — and not strictly for the underlying occurrence, such as a car accident. This distinction recognizes plaintiffs do not sue simply because they were involved in a car accident; they sue because they suffered damages for which they have not been compensated. Accordingly, the question is not simply who caused the car accident, but who caused the plaintiff's injuries.

We believe most reasonable people considering who caused a plaintiff's injuries in a car accident would not lean on a logical distinction between occurrence-causing and injury-causing conduct. Rather, most would say a plaintiff who breaks the law or otherwise acts negligently by not using a seat belt is at least partially responsible for the harm that befalls him. This is true even if he did not cause the car accident, provided it can be shown the failure to buckle up exacerbated his injuries.

Given the statute's plain language, we conclude that, for purposes of the proportionate-responsibility statute, the Legislature both intends and requires fact-finders to consider relevant evidence of a plaintiff's pre-occurrence, injury-causing conduct. This comports with the modern trend in tort law toward "abolishing doctrines that give all-or-nothing effect to certain types of plaintiff's negligence based on the timing of the plaintiff's and defendant's negligence" and instead considering "the timing of the plaintiff's and defendant's negligence [as] factors for assigning percentages of responsibility." Restatement (Third) of Torts: Apportionment of Liab. §3, Reporter's Note, cmt. b at 41.

Today's holding opens the door to a category of evidence that has never been part of our negligence cases, but we need not lay down a treatise on how and when such evidence should be admitted. Seat-belt evidence has been unique only in that it has been categorically prohibited in negligence cases. With that prohibition lifted, our rules of evidence include everything necessary to handle the admissibility of seat-belt evidence. As with any evidence, seat-belt evidence is admissible only if it is relevant. The defendant can establish the relevance of seat-belt nonuse only with evidence that nonuse caused or contributed to cause the plaintiff's injuries. And the trial court should first consider this evidence, for the purpose of making its relevance determination, outside the presence of the jury.

The fact-finder may consider relevant evidence of a plaintiff's failure to use a seat belt as a "negligent act or omission" or as a violation of "an applicable legal standard" in cases where the plaintiff was personally in violation of an applicable seat-belt law. And in cases in which an unrestrained plaintiff was not personally in violation of a seat-belt law, the fact-finder may consider whether the plaintiff was negligent under the applicable standard of reasonable care. This scenario is likely to arise when children are among the passengers of the plaintiff's vehicle. Most children do not violate seat-belt laws by failing to restrain themselves; rather, it is the driver upon whom the law places the responsibility to properly restrain them. Nonetheless, a minor is still held to the degree of care that would be exercised by an "ordinarily prudent child of [the same] age, intelligence, experience and capacity . . . under the same or similar circumstances." *Rudes v. Gottschalk*, 159 Tex. 552, 324 S.W.2d 201, 204 (Tex. 1959). The jury may further apportion third-party responsibility to the person upon whom the law places the burden to properly restrain the child.

There also should be no confusion on the relationship of this holding with the existing failure-to-mitigate-damages doctrine. A plaintiff's failure to mitigate his damages traditionally occurs post-occurrence and the doctrine does not readily translate in the pre-occurrence context. That distinction remains. A plaintiff's post-occurrence failure to mitigate his damages operates as a reduction of his damages award and is not considered in the responsibility apportionment. It is only the plaintiff's *pre*-occurrence, injury-causing conduct that should be considered in the responsibility apportionment.

IV

Today's holding is rooted in statutory interpretation and the unavoidable conclusion that our proportionate-responsibility statute both allows and requires fact-finders to consider pre-occurrence, injury-causing conduct. But the arguments against allowing seat-belt evidence, including some urged by the families in this case, transcend statutory interpretation and touch on themes of general fairness and fundamental principles of tort law. We respond to them because we believe our holding is not merely correct statutory interpretation; it also promotes sound public policy.

Attitudes toward use of seat belts have evolved drastically since the early 1970s. When we decided *Kerby* and *Carnation*, seat-belt use was not required by law. Seat-belt laws are now in effect in every state, and the vast majority of Texans buckle up on a regular basis. Yet until today a contradictory legal system punished seat-belt nonuse with criminal citations while allowing plaintiffs in civil lawsuits to benefit from juries' ignorance of their misconduct.

Some argue that admitting seat-belt evidence violates the principle that a plaintiff is not required to anticipate the negligent or unlawful conduct of another. *See Humble Oil & Refining Co. v. Martin*, 148 Tex. 175, 222 S.W.2d 995, 1001 (Tex. 1949) (noting the "general axiom that a person is not bound to anticipate the negligence of others"). But this has never been a steadfast rule of tort law. Rather, it is a guiding principle the law has balanced with the duty everyone has to guard against foreseeable risks — a duty that has been recognized at least since *Palsgraf v. Long Island R. Co.*, 248 N.Y. 339, 162 N.E. 99 (N.Y. 1928). The general danger of driving is obvious to everyone. So when it comes to foreseeing the general hazard of automobile travel, "[t]here is nothing to anticipate; the negligence of other motorists is omnipresent." *Law v. Superior Court*, 157 Ariz. 147, 755 P.2d 1135, 1141 (Ariz. 1988). Indeed, by enacting seat-belt laws, the Legislature has required motorists to anticipate the negligence of others.

Finally, some insist that admitting seat-belt evidence provides a windfall for defendants who will be relieved of paying the full damages caused by their negligence. But the reverse is equally arguable — a plaintiff whose injuries were exacerbated by failure to use a seat belt benefits from the jury's ignorance of his own conduct. The result is certainly an oddity: the unbelted plaintiff is likely to be punished with a criminal citation carrying a monetary fine from the police officer investigating the accident, but in the civil courtroom his illegal conduct will be rewarded by monetary compensation. There are no windfalls under the rule we announce today. Even when trial courts properly admit seat-belt evidence, defendants will still be held liable for the damages they caused, but not the injuries the plaintiff caused by not using a seat belt.

We hold relevant evidence of use or nonuse of seat belts, and relevant evidence of a plaintiff's pre-occurrence, injury-causing conduct generally, is admissible for the purpose of apportioning responsibility under our proportionate-responsibility statute, provided that the plaintiff's conduct caused or was a cause of his damages. Accordingly, we reverse the court of appeals' judgment and remand this case to the court of appeals for further proceedings consistent with this opinion.

NOTES AND PROBLEMS

1. ***Trend In Recognizing Seat-Belt Defense.*** The court in *Nabors* discusses the fact that traditional tort concepts — like the duty to protect oneself from foreseeable dangers — argue in favor of permitting jury consideration of seat-belt non-use to reduce damages. In doing so, the court admits, however, that seat-belt non-use cannot be considered a classic form of failure to mitigate because it happens before the injury rather than constituting an unreasonable response to an injury. On the other hand, the court no longer finds a disconnect in applying comparative fault principles to seat belt non-use. The court reasons that the jury is being asked to apportion between the collision-causing defendant's fault in causing the accident and the plaintiff's fault in enhancing the injuries beyond what would have been suffered. It helped in that case that the jurisdiction's comparative fault statute asks jurors to apportion fault for the *injuries or harm* rather than for causing the accident itself. Further, the court mentions two other changes in the legal context that prompted the court to re-visit the matter: (1) the switch away from contributory negligence (that would have completely barred a claim if seat-belt non-use had been considered negligence) to a comparative fault system that still permits some reduced recovery despite a plaintiff's negligence; and (2) the fault of the plaintiff

in failing to wear a seat belt is typically more stark now in light of statutes in every state generally mandating seat belt usage. Does the court limit its holding, however, to scenarios where a statute has been violated by the plaintiff?

2. ***Problems.*** How might the following scenarios be handled when a jurisdiction decides to permit a seat-belt defense?

A. In Texas, where *Nabors* was decided, the court acknowledges that the state has adopted a 50 percent comparative fault rule. What if Bill broadsides into Jim's vehicle by wrongfully running a red light? The impact causes Jim's car to roll over and he is ejected due to not wearing a seat belt and, as a result, suffers a fractured neck and becomes a quadriplegic. Despite undisputed evidence that Bill was solely responsible for the collision and the ensuing roll-over, the jury apportions the total fault (taking into account the seat belt non-use) as follows: Jim 75 percent and Bill 25 percent. The total damages are $10 million. How much will Jim recover from Bill?

B. In the same accident as the preceding hypothetical, a five-year-old child, Freddy, is also unrestrained in the back seat of Jim's vehicle. Freddy likewise is ejected during the roll-over. May the jury assess fault against Freddy though the applicable seat-belt statute does not impose a statutory duty on the child to wear a seat belt (only on the adult driver to have the child restrained)? May the jury reduce the damages awardable to Freddy from his failure to wear a seat belt?

C. Hillary is riding her motorcycle when she is side-swiped by Donald, the driver of a pick-up truck, who fails to notice the motorcyclist next to him. Hillary suffers a severe brain injury as she was not wearing a helmet. (Her state does not mandate a helmet for riders who have taken a training course.) She also suffers multiple fractures in her arms and legs, but they heal. The brain injury will be a lifelong disability, however, and the evidence suggests that had Hillary worn a helmet she would not have suffered a permanent brain injury. Does the rule from *Nabors* also allow Donald to reduce or escape responsibility for paying for all the damages from the accident he caused? Consider Jones v. Harley-Davidson, Inc., 2016 U.S. Dist. LEXIS 123225 (E.D. Tex. 2016).

D. Paul loves to drive his vintage 1965 Ford Mustang convertible. Of course, it has no air bag because this technology didn't exist when the car was manufactured. Paul bought it (paying a high price) at a recent auction. Unfortunately, when Ringo swerves across the center yellow line on a country highway and causes a head-on collision with Paul late one evening, Paul is killed due to the force of the impact despite wearing his seat belt. Defendant proffers an expert witness at trial who says that if Paul had been driving a car with an air bag, he would have likely survived the collision with treatable injuries. May the jury be permitted to reduce the damage recovery of his estate in the ensuing wrongful death and survival claim due to his failure to drive a vehicle with air bags?

B. Collateral Source Rule

The *collateral source rule* forbids the reduction of the claimant's actual damages by virtue of the claimant's receipt of any benefit from a third party (e.g., a health insurance company) that offset the harms for which the claimant seeks recovery from the tortfeasor. To many first confronting this doctrine, the initial reaction is shock. Why should the defendant be forced to pay the plaintiff for certain damages for which he has been reimbursed? Doesn't this act as a potentially huge windfall for the plaintiff and unnecessarily increase tort judgments and the defendant's litigation losses? This common law rule was not fashioned without acknowledgment of these arguments, and many courts still find the doctrine to be sound despite the challenges to it. However, some courts and legislatures have abandoned or limited the doctrine as a type of tort reform. As you read the following case, consider who might benefit from the windfall under both the existing doctrine and its alternative.

HELFEND v. SOUTHERN CALIFORNIA RAPID TRANSIT DISTRICT

465 P.2d 61 (Cal. 1970)

Tobriner, J.

Defendants appeal from a judgment of the Los Angeles Superior Court entered on a verdict in favor of plaintiff, Julius J. Helfend, for $16,400 in general and special damages for injuries sustained in a bus-auto collision that occurred on July 19, 1965, in the City of Los Angeles.

We have concluded that the judgment for plaintiff in this tort action against the defendant governmental entity should be affirmed. The trial court properly followed the collateral source rule in excluding evidence that a portion of plaintiff's medical bills had been paid through a medical insurance plan that requires the refund of benefits from tort recoveries.

Shortly before noon on July 19, 1965, plaintiff drove his car in central Los Angeles east on Third Street approaching Grandview. At this point Third Street had six lanes, four for traffic and one parking lane on each side of the thoroughfare. While traveling in the second lane from the curb, plaintiff observed an automobile driven by Glen A. Raney, Jr., stopping in his lane and preparing to back into a parking space. Plaintiff put out his left arm to signal the traffic behind him that he intended to stop; he then brought his vehicle to a halt so that the other driver could park.

At about this time Kenneth A. Mitchell, a bus driver for the Southern California Rapid Transit District, pulled out of a bus stop at the curb of Third Street and headed in the same direction as plaintiff. Approaching plaintiff's and Raney's cars which were stopped in the second lane from the curb,

Mitchell pulled out into the lane closest to the center of the street in order to pass. The right rear of the bus sideswiped plaintiff's vehicle, knocking off the rear-view mirror and crushing plaintiff's arm, which had been hanging down at the side of his car in the stopping signal position.

An ambulance took plaintiff to Central Receiving Hospital for emergency first aid treatment. Upon release from the hospital plaintiff proceeded to consult Dr. Saxon, an orthopedic specialist, who sent plaintiff immediately to the Sherman Oaks Community Hospital where he received treatment for about a week. Plaintiff underwent physical therapy for about six months in order to regain normal use of his left arm and hand. He acquired some permanent discomfort but no permanent disability from the injuries sustained in the accident. At the time of the injury plaintiff was 67 years of age and had a life expectancy of about 11 years. He owned the Jewel Homes Investment Company which possessed and maintained small rental properties. Prior to the accident plaintiff had performed much of the minor maintenance on his properties including some painting and minor plumbing. For the six-month healing period he hired a man to do all the work he had formerly performed and at the time of the trial still employed him for such work as he himself could not undertake.

Plaintiff filed a tort action against the Southern California Rapid Transit District, a public entity, and Mitchell, an employee of the transit district. At trial plaintiff claimed slightly more than $2,700 in special damages, including $921 in doctor's bills, a $336.99 hospital bill, and about $45 for medicines.[5] Defendant requested permission to show that about 80 percent of the plaintiff's hospital bill had been paid by plaintiff's Blue Cross insurance carrier and that some of his other medical expenses may have been paid by other insurance. The superior court thoroughly considered the then very recent case of *City of Salinas* v. *Souza & McCue Constr. Co.*, 424 P.2d 921 (Cal. 1967), distinguished the *Souza* case on the ground that *Souza* involved a contract setting, and concluded that the judgment should not be reduced to the extent of the amount of insurance payments which plaintiff received. The court ruled that defendants should not be permitted to show that plaintiff had received medical coverage from any collateral source.

After the jury verdict in favor of plaintiff in the sum of $16,400, defendants appealed, raising [as their primary argument that] trial court committed prejudicial error in refusing to allow the introduction of evidence to the effect that a portion of the plaintiff's medical bills had been paid from a collateral source.

We must decide whether the collateral source rule applies to tort actions . . . in which the plaintiff has received benefits from his medical insurance coverage.

The Supreme Court of California has long adhered to the doctrine that if an injured party receives some compensation for his injuries from a source wholly

5. The plaintiff claimed special damages of $2,737.99 of which $1,302.99 represented medical expenses, $35 repair of plaintiff's watch, about $1,350 expenses and costs incurred as a result of hiring another man to do the work plaintiff normally performed, and $50 plaintiff's share of the automobile repair costs.

independent of the tortfeasor, such payment should not be deducted from the damages which the plaintiff would otherwise collect from the tortfeasor. See, e.g., *Peri* v. *Los Angeles Junction Ry. Co.*, 137 P.2d 441 (Cal. 1943) [(plaintiff victim of auto accident was entitled to undiminished recovery for lost past wages despite having insurance that reimbursed plaintiff for $2 per day for time off of work because the "[d]amages recoverable for a wrong are not diminished . . . by [being] indemnified for his loss by insurance effected by him, and to the procurement of which the defendant did not contribute)]. As recently as August 1968 we unanimously reaffirmed our adherence to this doctrine, which is known as the "collateral source rule."

Although the collateral source rule remains generally accepted in the United States, nevertheless many other jurisdictions have restricted or repealed it. In this country most commentators have criticized the rule and called for its early demise. In *Souza* we took note of the academic criticism of the rule, characterized the rule as "punitive," and held it inapplicable to the governmental entity involved in that case. [The court then noted that *Souza* was a breach of contract case and not a tort case and that the receipt of benefits did not truly come from an independent source.]

The collateral source rule as applied here embodies the venerable concept that a person who has invested years of insurance premiums to assure his medical care should receive the benefits of his thrift. The tortfeasor should not garner the benefits of his victim's providence.

The collateral source rule expresses a policy judgment in favor of encouraging citizens to purchase and maintain insurance for personal injuries and for other eventualities. Courts consider insurance a form of investment, the benefits of which become payable without respect to any other possible source of funds. If we were to permit a tortfeasor to mitigate damages with payments from plaintiff's insurance, plaintiff would be in a position inferior to that of having bought no insurance, because his payment of premiums would have earned no benefit. Defendant should not be able to avoid payment of full compensation for the injury inflicted merely because the victim has had the foresight to provide himself with insurance.

Some commentators object that the above approach to the collateral source rule provides plaintiff with a "double recovery," rewards him for the injury, and defeats the principle that damages should compensate the victim but not punish the tortfeasor. We agree with Professor Fleming's observation, however, that "double recovery is justified only in the face of some exceptional, supervening reason, as in the case of accident or life insurance, where it is felt unjust that the tortfeasor should take advantage of the thrift and prescience of the victim in having paid the premium." Fleming, *Introduction to the Law of Torts* (1967) p. 131. As we point out *infra*, recovery in a wrongful death action is not defeated by the payment of the benefit on a life insurance policy.

Furthermore, insurance policies increasingly provide for either subrogation or refund of benefits upon a tort recovery, and such refund is indeed called for in the present case. See Fleming, *The Collateral Source Rule and Loss Allocation in*

Tort Law, supra, 54 Cal. L. Rev. 1478, 1479. Hence, the plaintiff receives no double recovery; the collateral source rule simply . . . permits a proper transfer of risk from the plaintiff's insurer to the tortfeasor by way of the victim's tort recovery. The double shift from the tortfeasor to the victim and then from the victim to his insurance carrier can normally occur with little cost in that the insurance carrier is often intimately involved in the initial litigation and quite automatically receives its part of the tort settlement or verdict.

Even in cases in which the contract or the law precludes subrogation or refund of benefits,[17] or in situations in which the collateral source waives such subrogation or refund, the rule performs entirely necessary functions in the computation of damages. For example, the cost of medical care often provides both attorneys and juries in tort cases with an important measure for assessing the plaintiff's general damages. To permit the defendant to tell the jury that the plaintiff has been recompensed by a collateral source for his medical costs might irretrievably upset the complex, delicate, and somewhat indefinable calculations which result in the normal jury verdict.

We also note that generally the jury is not informed that plaintiff's attorney will receive a large portion of the plaintiff's recovery in contingent fees or that personal injury damages . . . are normally deductible by the defendant. Hence, the plaintiff rarely actually receives full compensation for his injuries as computed by the jury. The collateral source rule partially serves to compensate for the attorney's share and does not actually render "double recovery" for the plaintiff. Indeed, many jurisdictions that have abolished or limited the collateral source rule have also established a means for assessing the plaintiff's costs for counsel directly against the defendant rather than imposing the contingent fee system.[19] In sum, the plaintiff's recovery for his medical expenses from both the tortfeasor and his medical insurance program will not usually give him "double recovery," but partially provides a somewhat closer approximation to full compensation for his injuries.

If we consider the collateral source rule as applied here in the context of the entire American approach to the law of torts and damages, we find that the rule

17. "Certain insurance benefits are regarded as the proceeds of an investment rather than as an indemnity for damages. Thus it has been held that the proceeds of a life insurance contract made for a fixed sum rather than for the damages caused by the death of the insured are proceeds of an investment and can be received independently of the claim for damages against the person who caused the death of the insured. The same rule has been held applicable to accident insurance contracts. As to both kinds of insurance it has been stated: 'Such a policy is an investment contract, giving the owner or beneficiary an absolute right, independent of the right against any third person responsible for the injury covered by the policy.' An insurer who fully compensates the insured, however, is subrogated to the rights of the insured against [or may receive a refund of benefits from] one who insured his property if the insurance was for the protection of the property of the insured, and was therefore an indemnity contract. In such cases subrogation [or refund of benefits] is the means by which double recovery by the owner is prevented and the ultimate burden shifted to the wrongdoer where it belongs." *Anheuser-Busch, Inc.* v. *Starley, supra*, 28 Cal. 2d 347, 355 (dissenting op. of Traynor, J.). One Court of Appeal has, however, upheld the refund of benefits provision in a Blue Shield medical insurance contract similar to the one at issue here. *Block* v. *California Physicians' Service*, 53 Cal. Rptr. 51 (Cal. App. 1966).

19. Under workmen's compensation, subrogation normally prevents double recovery by shifting the loss to the tortfeasor. In actions to recover against a tortfeasor, the court sets a reasonable attorney's fee.

presently performs a number of legitimate and even indispensable functions. Without a thorough revolution in the American approach to torts and the consequent damages, the rule at least with respect to medical insurance benefits has become so integrated within our present system that its precipitous judicial nullification would work hardship. In this case the collateral source rule lies between two systems for the compensation of accident victims: the traditional tort recovery based on fault and the increasingly prevalent coverage based on non-fault insurance. Neither system possesses such universality of coverage or completeness of compensation that we can easily dispense with the collateral source rule's approach to meshing the two systems. The reforms which many academicians propose cannot easily be achieved through piecemeal common law development; the proposed changes, if desirable, would be more effectively accomplished through legislative reform. In any case, we cannot believe that the judicial repeal of the collateral source rule, as applied in the present case, would be the place to begin the needed changes.

Although in the special circumstances of *Souza* we characterized the collateral source rule as "punitive" in nature, we have pointed out the several legitimate and fully justified compensatory functions of the rule. In fact, if the collateral source rule were actually punitive, it could apply only in cases of oppression, fraud, or malice and would be inapplicable to most tort, and almost all negligence, cases regardless of whether a governmental entity were involved. We therefore reaffirm our adherence to the collateral source rule in tort cases in which the plaintiff has been compensated by an independent collateral source — such as insurance, pension, continued wages, or disability payments — for which he had actually or constructively paid or in cases in which the collateral source would be recompensed from the tort recovery through subrogation, refund of benefits, or some other arrangement. Hence, we conclude that in a case in which a tort victim has received partial compensation from medical insurance coverage entirely independent of the tortfeasor the trial court properly followed the collateral source rule and foreclosed defendant from mitigating damages by means of the collateral payments.

The judgment is affirmed.

NOTES AND PROBLEMS

1. ***Subrogation.*** The court discusses subrogation, which was applicable to the plaintiff's recovery in that case, as one justification for maintaining the collateral source rule. Although the plaintiff might theoretically receive a windfall if it recovers as medical expenses from a tortfeasor sums for which a health insurer has already reimbursed it, when the insurer has a right to subrogation that windfall is eliminated. Subrogation typically exists either due to the contractual terms of the insurance policy (as a matter of contract law) or by operation of a statute that expressly provides for subrogation rights in

certain instances. For example, worker's compensation insurers are typically granted a right to subrogation when the hurt employee has a claim against a tortfeasor. These insurers frequently intervene in litigation brought by worker's compensation beneficiaries in order to protect their subrogation interest. In those cases, the insurer typically gets to keep the first fruits on the applicable recovered damages until the amount of their subrogation lien has been satisfied. For this reason, such insurers are often present during pre-trial settlement conferences and mediation because no deal resolving the litigation can be obtained without their participation and acquiescence.

2. ***Windfall Arguments.*** No matter what system is used, there is a windfall available to someone. Under the collateral source rule the windfall either goes to the plaintiff, or, if there is subrogation permitted by a health insurance company, to the insurer (which has received premiums to pay for losses but ends up not paying out on a loss). When the collateral source rule is legislatively eliminated, the tortfeasor (and its liability insurance company) receives a windfall because its tort liability is reduced as a result of the plaintiff's foresight to arrange for insurance coverage.

3. ***Legislative Repeal.*** Some legislative bodies have disagreed with the *Helfend* arguments for retaining the common law collateral source rule. In fact, the California legislature ultimately enacted a statute that abrogates the collateral source rule in medical malpractice cases, allowing doctors to offer evidence to the jury of the plaintiff's receipt of benefits (such as health insurance) in order to reduce the damages awarded. *See* Calif. Civ. Code §3333.1; Fein v. Permanente Medical Group, 695 P.2d 665 (Cal. 1985) (upholding the constitutionality of this statutory reversal of the collateral source rule, saying it was within the legislature's discretion to retain or dispense with the common law rule). Nearly half of the states have repealed, or limited, the collateral source rule in some manner. Interestingly, even in some cases where the legislature has overturned the collateral source rule, some health insurers have still tried to assert subrogation rights against the plaintiff's receipt of a tort judgment. Of course, permitting such subrogation would go further than eliminating a windfall to the plaintiff because, if allowed, the plaintiff would not even theoretically be fully compensated. The courts have rebuffed such attempts. *See* Perreira v. Rediger, 778 A.2d 429 (N.J. 2001) (New Jersey, which legislatively repealed the collateral source rule by permitting defendant to offer evidence of collateral benefits in order to reduce its tort liability, would not recognize any subrogation rights otherwise claimed by health insurer).

C. Statutory Limits

The poster child for tort reform involves legislatively imposed limits on certain plaintiffs' entitlement to some or all categories of compensatory damages. The chief rationale is that "runaway" jury verdicts are windfalls for plaintiffs and trial lawyers but bad for business and the economy in general (by driving up costs for everyone), or at least bad for certain segments — chiefly medical doctors and hospitals. With respect to medical malpractice caps on damages, reformers have successfully urged many legislators to limit recovery because our "unrestrained" tort system has driven up health care costs for everyone, caused doctors' malpractice insurance premiums to go through the roof and resulted in many doctors abandoning practice altogether — or at least in certain "litigation magnet" states. In essence, the argument goes that the combination of our tort common law and the constitutional jury system has conspired to cause a "tort crisis" that demands innovative solutions.

1. Examples of Statutory Limits

There are a variety of statutes that limit recovery of actual damages. The majority of these statutes only apply to a narrow category of claims — chiefly medical malpractice suits. The California and Texas statutes set forth below are so limited. The Maryland statute is much broader in this sense as it applies to all personal injury tort claims. Many of the statutes only limit *noneconomic general damages* while imposing no limits on *special economic losses.* The Texas medical malpractice wrongful death statute (§74.303), however, limits both general and special damages — as well as exemplary damages — to $500,000.

California Civ. Code §333.2 (1975)

(a) In any action for injury against a health care provider based on professional negligence, the injured plaintiff shall be entitled to recover noneconomic losses to compensate for pain, suffering, inconvenience, physical impairment, disfigurement and other nonpecuniary damage.

(b) In no action shall the amount of damages for noneconomic losses exceed two hundred fifty thousand dollars ($250,000).

Maryland Code Ann., Ct. & Jud. Proc. §11-108 (1997)

(a) In this section: (1) "noneconomic damages" means pain, suffering, inconvenience, physical impairment, disfigurement, loss of consortium, or other nonpecuniary injury; and (2) "noneconomic damages" does not include punitive damages.

(b) In any action for damages for personal injury . . . an award for noneconomic damages may not exceed $350,000.

(c)(1) In a jury trial, the jury may not be informed of the limitation established under subsection (b) of this section. (2) If the jury awards an amount for noneconomic damages that exceeds the limitation established under subsection (b) of this section, the court shall reduce the amount to conform to the limitation.

Texas Civ. Prac. & Rem. Code §74.301 (2003)

(a) In any action on a health care liability claim where final judgment is rendered against a physician or health care provider . . . the limit of civil liability for noneconomic damages . . . shall be limited to an amount not to exceed $250,000 for each claimant, regardless of the number of defendant physicians or health care providers . . . against whom the claim is asserted or the number of separate causes of action on which the claim is based.

Texas Civ. Prac. & Rem. Code §74.303 (2003)

(a) In a wrongful death or survival action on a health care liability claim where final judgment is rendered against a physician or health care provider, the limit of civil liability for all damages, including exemplary damages, shall be limited to an amount not to exceed $500,000 for each claimant, regardless of the number of defendant physicians or health care providers against whom the claim is asserted or the number of separate causes of action on which the claim is based.

(b) [Contains a provision to permit inflationary adjustment on the ceiling in this subsection.]

(c) Subsection (a) does not apply to the amount of damages awarded on a health care liability claim for the expenses of necessary medical, hospital, and custodial care received before judgment or required in the future for treatment of the injury.

2. *Constitutionality of Limits on Actual Damages*

While all of the damage-limiting statutes are subject to potential interpretational disputes (as are most statutes), the most serious legal questions arising out of these statutes focus upon their legality. Do legislative efforts intended to limit a tort claimant's recovery of all jury-awarded damages violate the claimant's constitutional rights? There are several primary constitutional attacks: (1) substantive due process arguments contend that the legislature has acted irrationally by taking away a portion of the plaintiff's cause of action; (2) equal protection arguments assert that, when the legislature imposes limits on only some personal injury claimants (e.g., medical malpractice victims), the statute violates the claimant's right to be treated the same as all other personal injury victims; and (3) Seventh Amendment right to jury trial arguments claim that, by superimposing legislative determinations over the actual damages to which a claimant might have recovery, the statutes disregard the jury's function and render a portion of the jury's job moot. The courts vary widely regarding these challenges. Sometimes the disagreement concerns whether the court believes there is a true "tort crisis" to justify such legislation. Sometimes the differing legal conclusions of the courts can be attributed to varying levels of judicial scrutiny over legislation. And sometimes the difference in results can be explained by different conceptual views of the jury's role in our judicial process. Below is a good example of two courts' reactions to such arguments.

SAMSEL v. WHEELER TRANSPORT SERVICES, INC.

789 P.2d 541 (Kan. 1990)

LOCKETT, J.

Chief Judge Earl E. O'Connor of the United States District Court for the District of Kansas has certified the following question for resolution: Does K.S.A. 1987 Supp. 60-19a01 violate the Kansas Constitution?

The majority of our legislature voted to limit the traditional role of the jury to determine the monetary value for loss of the quality of life in Kansas by setting a limit on the recovery of noneconomic damages. The majority of this court recognizes that the legislature's decision to modify the common law, by setting a limit on noneconomic damages, is a legislative decision that does not violate our state constitution.

A great change in tort doctrine has taken place over the past century. The primary function of damages is no longer seen as deterrence or retribution for harm caused; damages are now seen as compensation. In large part, this shift has been caused by the modern availability of affordable liability insurance, the purchase of which has occasionally been required by legislation.

It is the availability of liability insurance which critics warn is threatened by the present tort system. If insurance goes, so will compensation to many plaintiffs, no matter how favorable the laws are in their favor. In reality, "[j]ustice is not achieved when deserved compensation is granted by a court; it is achieved when that compensation is paid to the plaintiff." *Citizens Committee Report* 52.

The insurance crisis of the 1970s, referred to in the *Citizens Committee Report,* was partially caused by the industry's increased market at lower premiums due to its remarkably high rate of return on investments. The crisis was especially hard-felt in the malpractice insurance area. In response to this crisis and to ensure the continued availability of medical liability insurance, every state enacted some type of tort reform; the statutes number over 300.

In the case before this court, the question certified by the United States District Court for the District of Kansas arises out of a personal injury action wherein the plaintiff, Douglas Samsel, claims that one of the defendants, Don Hilgenfeld, negligently caused an automobile accident by driving left of the center line. Samsel was rendered a quadriplegic as a result of this accident. Other defendants are Wheeler Transport Services, Inc., Hilgenfeld's employer, and Great West Casualty Co., Wheeler's insurance company. Douglas Samsel is a resident of Kansas; Hilgenfeld of Nebraska. Wheeler has its principal place of business in Nebraska and Great West is organized under Nebraska law. The case was filed in federal court based on diversity of citizenship pursuant to 28 U.S.C. §1332 (1982).

When the accident occurred on May 16, 1988, K.S.A. 1987 Supp. 60-19a01 was in effect. This statute caps damages in personal injury actions for pain and suffering [or other non-economic losses] at $250,000.

The certified question limits our review to an analysis of the Kansas Constitution. The federal court will decide whether the contested statute offends the federal constitution. Specifically, plaintiff argues that the statutory cap violates §§5 and 18 of the Bill of Rights in the Kansas Constitution. Section 5 states: "The right of trial by jury shall be inviolate." Section 18 is almost as succinct: "All persons, for injuries suffered in person, reputation or property, shall have remedy by due course of law, and justice administered without delay."

We have previously said that §18 protects the right to "reparation for injury, ordered by a tribunal having jurisdiction, in due course of procedure and after a fair hearing." *Ernest v. Faler*, 697 P.2d 870 (Kan. 1985).

The certified question requires us to review our state constitution, the role of the common law, legislative and judicial power vis-a-vis the common law, and the separation of powers doctrine. It is also essential that we analyze the doctrine of stare decisis and the consequences of our prior decisions.

Our constitution is a written charter enacted by the direct action of the citizens of Kansas. It is a compilation of the fundamental laws of the state and embodies the principles upon which the state government was founded. The object of our constitution is to provide a government of law and not of men, while insuring the protection of life, liberty, and property.

The state constitution establishes the form of our government. Like the Constitution of the United States, the Constitution of Kansas contains no express provision requiring the separation of governmental powers, but all decisions of this court have taken for granted the constitutional doctrine of separation of powers between the three branches of the state government—legislative, executive, and judicial.

Our constitution does not make this court the critic of the legislature; rather, this court is the guardian of the constitution and every legislative act comes before us with a presumption of constitutionality. A statute will not be declared unconstitutional unless its infringement on the superior law of the constitution is clear, beyond substantial doubt. In determining whether a statute is constitutional, courts must guard against substituting their views on economic or social policy for those of the legislature. Courts are only concerned with the legislative power to enact statutes, not with the wisdom behind those enactments.

The common law can be determined only from decisions in former cases bearing upon the subject under inquiry. As distinguished from statutory or written law, the common law embraces that great body of unwritten law founded upon general custom, usage, or common consent, and based upon natural justice or reason. It may otherwise be defined as custom long acquiesced in or sanctioned by immemorial usage and judicial decision.

Our constitution provides that the common-law right to a jury trial includes the right to have the jury determine the amount of the damages in personal injury actions. Statutory modification of the common law must meet due process requirements and be reasonably necessary in the public interest to promote the general welfare of the people of the state.

Section 5 of the Kansas Bill of Rights protects the right to jury trial as it existed under common law at the time the constitution was adopted. Under the common law, jury verdicts have always been subject to the concurrence of the trial judge and the trial judge's power to grant a new trial. The right of the trial court and the appellate court to grant a remittitur or a new trial does not violate the individual's right to a jury trial guaranteed by the United States Constitution. See *Capital Traction Co. v. Hof,* 174 U.S. 1 (1899).

A court may refuse to accept a jury's finding of damages in a personal injury case if, in the light of the evidence, the amount is either so high or so low as to shock the conscience of the court. The court, in such a case, may offer the affected party the opportunity to accept a damage verdict more in line with the evidence. If the party consents to the altered verdict, the party loses the right to appeal as to the amount of damages. If the party refuses to accept the altered verdict, the court may order a new trial, in which the party again faces the court's discretion to refuse to order damages in the amount found by the jury.

If the Kansas Constitution prohibits the legislature from . . . limiting recovery for economic or noneconomic losses, this court would have been required to declare the Workers Compensation Act . . . unconstitutional. We did not. Because we did not, we must now adhere to the doctrine of stare decisis. In the past, we have recognized that the legislature, under its power to act for the general welfare, may alter common-law causes of action.

The statute is a cap only on noneconomic damages and does not limit the court's power to reduce any other portion of the award it deems excessive. The duty of a court to protect parties from unjust verdicts arising from ignorance of the rules of law and of evidence, from impulse of passion or prejudice, or from any other violation of their lawful rights in the conduct of the trial is still maintained. *Pleasants v. Fant,* 89 U.S. 116 (1875).

Denying those with the greatest pain and suffering a full remedy in order to ease insurance rates for those who cause injury was considered and approved by a majority of the legislature. The legislature is aware that the cap on noneconomic loss will affect the right to recover by those most severely injured in Kansas. Laws that restrict those who suffer the greatest pain, mental anguish, and disfigurement from a case-by-case determination of individual damages by jury are harsh. However, our determination is that, under proper circumstances, the legislature may limit recovery of noneconomic losses of those individuals whose quality of life has been most affected.

To be consistent with our prior decisions . . . the answer to the certified question is that K.S.A. 1988 Supp. 60-19a01 [does] not violate §5 (right to a jury) or §18 (right to due course of law for injuries suffered) of the Kansas Bill of Rights.

KNOWLES v. UNITED STATES

544 N.W.2d 183 (S.D. 1996)

SABERS, J.

Parents brought suit for severe injuries suffered by minor son while under care of Air Force hospital. The United States admitted liability and invoked the $1 million cap on medical malpractice damages. The federal district court held the cap was constitutional under the South Dakota and United States Constitutions. On appeal to the Eighth Circuit Court of Appeals, four certified questions were presented and accepted by the South Dakota Supreme Court. For the reasons set forth herein, we hold that the damages cap of SDCL 21-3-11 is unconstitutional.

Kris Knowles was twelve days old when he was admitted for treatment of a fever at the Ellsworth Air Force Base Hospital, near Rapid City, South Dakota. Medical Service Specialists, the Air Force's equivalent to nurses' aides, recorded Kris' temperature. On the night before his discharge, the specialists failed to report to nurses or physicians that Kris' temperature had been dropping throughout that night. Kris developed hypoglycemia and suffered respiratory arrest resulting in severe, permanent brain damage.

William and Jane Knowles brought suit on their own behalf and for Kris for medical malpractice, emotional distress, and loss of consortium. The United States admitted liability for medical malpractice and filed a motion for entry of judgment of $1 million based on SDCL 21-3-11[6], which limits damages in medical malpractice actions to $1 million. The United States District Court of South Dakota, Western Division, ruled that SDCL 21-3-11 was constitutional and entered judgment for $1 million. Knowles appealed. The Eighth Circuit Court of Appeals certified [to this court the issue of the statute's constitutionality under the South Dakota Constitution].

In Practice

Some scholars have argued that legislative caps on non-economic damages have a disproportionate adverse impact upon female claimants who are allegedly more likely than men to suffer emotional injuries. *See* Lisa Ruder, Comment, *Caps on Noneconomic Damages and the Female Plaintiff*, 44 Case W. Res. L. Rev. 197 (1993), and Koenig and Rustad, *His and Her Tort Reform: Gender Injustice in Disguise*, 70 Wash. L. Rev. 1 (1995).

Initially, we note that many courts have invalidated limitations on damages based on their respective state constitutions. *Moore v. Mobile Infirmary Ass'n*, 592 So. 2d 156, 158 (Ala. 1991) (invalidating a damages cap on personal injury awards);

6. In any action for damages for personal injury or death alleging malpractice against any physician, chiropractor, dentist, hospital, registered nurse, certified registered nurse anesthetist, licensed practical nurse or other practitioner of the healing arts under the laws of this state, whether taken through the court system or by binding arbitration, the total damages which may be awarded may not exceed the sum of one million dollars.

Wright v. Central Du Page Hosp. Ass'n, 347 N.E.2d 736 (Ill. 1976); *Brannigan v. Usitalo*, 587 A.2d 1232 (N.H. 1991); *Arneson v. Olson*, 270 N.W.2d 125 (N.D. 1978); *Morris v. Savoy*, 576 N.E.2d 765 (Ohio 1991); *Lucas v. United States*, 757 S.W.2d 687 (Tex. 1988); *Condemarin v. Univ. Hosp.*, 775 P.2d 348 (Utah 1989); *Sofie v. Fibreboard Corp.*, 771 P.2d 711 (Wash. 1989) (invalidating a damages cap on all personal injury actions).

Other jurisdictions have upheld a damages cap: *Fein v. Permanente Medical Group*, 695 P.2d 665 (Calif. 1985); *Johnson v. St. Vincent Hosp., Inc.*, 404 N.E.2d 585 (Ind. 1980); *Samsel v. Wheeler Transp. Serv., Inc.*, 789 P.2d 541 (Kan. 1990); *Etheridge v. Medical Center Hosp.*, 376 S.E.2d 525 (Va. 1989).

However, the questions presented herein generally turn on the particular constitutional provisions of the state and the case law precedent interpreting those provisions. Because the provisions of the South Dakota Constitution guaranteeing the right to jury trial . . . and due process are dispositive, we do not reach [any of] the other constitutional questions.

South Dakota Constitution article VI, §6 guarantees the right of trial by jury:

> The right of trial by jury shall remain inviolate and shall extend to all cases at law without regard to the amount in controversy[.]

"Inviolate" has been defined as "free from change or blemish: pure, unbroken . . . free from assault or trespass: untouched, intact[.]" *Sofie*, 771 P.2d at 721-22. In discussing the role of the jury, the United States Supreme Court has stated:

> Maintenance of the jury as a fact-finding body is of such importance and occupies so firm a place in our history and jurisprudence that any seeming curtailment of the right to a jury trial should be scrutinized with the utmost care.

Dimick v. Schiedt, 293 U.S. 474 (1935) (assessment of damages is a "matter so peculiarly within the province of the jury[.]").

"A jury is the tribunal provided by law to determine the facts and to fix the amount of damages." *Schaffer v. Edward D. Jones & Co.*, 521 N.W.2d 921, 927 n.9 (S.D. 1994). "The amount of damages to be awarded is a factual issue to be determined by the trier of fact[.]" *Sander v. The Geib, Elston, Frost Pro. Ass'n*, 506 N.W.2d 107, 119 (S.D. 1993) (citation omitted). With any jury award for personal injuries, we "have allowed [the jury] 'wide latitude'" in making its award. *Id.* (citation omitted).

> We are unwilling to allow the trial court authority to limit a damages award as a matter of law. . . . *A jury determination of the amount of damages is the essence of the right to trial by jury*—to go beyond the procedural mechanisms now in place [remittitur] for reduction of a verdict and to bind the jury's discretion is to deny this constitutional right.

Moore, 592 So. 2d at 161 (emphasis in original). The damages cap is unconstitutional because it limits the jury verdict "automatically and absolutely" which makes the jury's function "*less* than an advisory status." *Id.* at 164 (emphasis in original).

SDCL 21-3-11 arbitrarily and without a hearing imposes a limitation of one million dollars on all damages in all medical malpractice actions. It does so without provisions for determining the extent of the injuries or resulting illness, or whether these injuries or illness resulted in death. It purports to cover even those cases where the medical costs occasioned by the malpractice alone exceed one million dollars. In other words, the damages recovered in these cases could actually be payable to the wrongdoers for medical expenses, not to the victims. It does so in all cases, even when a judicial determination of damages above one million dollars results from an adversarial hearing after notice.

For these reasons, we hold that the damages cap violates the right to a jury trial under South Dakota Constitution article VI, §6.

Under South Dakota Constitution article VI, §2, "no person shall be deprived of life, liberty or property without due process of law." People have a right to be free from injury. *Swanson v. Ball*, 67 S.D. 161, 290 N.W. 482 (1940). We apply a more stringent test than the federal courts' rational basis test. *Katz v. Bd. of Med. & Osteopathic Exam.* 432 N.W.2d 274, 278 n.6 (S.D. 1988). The statute must "bear a real and substantial relation to the objects sought to be attained." *Id.* (citation omitted).

The arbitrary classification of malpractice claimants based on the amount of damages is not rationally related to the stated purpose of curbing medical malpractice claims. The legislation was adopted as a result of "some perceived malpractice crisis.[6]" Many courts and commentators have argued that there

In Practice

A scholarly survey of Texas trial judges discovered that most sitting judges in Texas failed to perceive rampant instances of juries awarding too much in actual or punitive damages. Surprisingly, a bigger problem perceived by the judges was juries awarding *too little* in actual damages or being too reluctant to award any punitive damages. A number of the judges in the survey believed that media coverage of tort reform contributed to the problem of jury awards being too low. *See* Lyon, Toben, Underwood and Wren, *Straight From the Horse's Mouth: Judicial Observations of Jury Behavior and the Need for Tort Reform,* 59 Baylor L. Rev. 419 (2007).

6. SDCL 21-3-11 was adopted as a result of recommendations by the 1975 South Dakota Legislature's Special Committee on Medical Malpractice. As noted by one commentator:

> Statements made by insurance representatives before the [Committee], referring to the low number of medical malpractice claims brought in the state, can only create significant doubt that South Dakota was experiencing a genuine insurance crisis at that time. Startling data on medical malpractice claims in South Dakota, North Dakota, and Minnesota, collected by the Minnesota Department of Commerce from 1982-1987 [the Hatch Study], also tends to call into question the basis for cries of *any* insurance crisis; if claim frequency and severity did not change significantly in those years, and if in those same six years only one-half of one percent of all medical malpractice plaintiffs were awarded any damages, why then did physicians' insurance premiums *triple* in that same time period?

Eiesland, *infra*, at 703 (emphasis in original).

was no "crisis" at all. Gail Eiesland, note, *Miller v. Gilmore: The Constitutionality of South Dakota's Medical Malpractice Statute of Limitations*, 38 S.D. L. Rev. 672, 703 (1993); *Hoem v. State*, 756 P.2d 780, 783 (Wyo. 1988) (holding that medical malpractice tort reform violated equal protection under the rational basis standard). As noted by the court in *Hoem*:

> It cannot seriously be contended that the extension of special benefits to the medical profession and the imposition of an additional hurdle in the path of medical malpractice victims relate to the protection of the public health.

756 P.2d at 783.

In *Arneson*, 270 N.W.2d at 136, the North Dakota Supreme Court upheld the trial court's finding that no medical malpractice insurance availability or cost crisis existed:

> The Legislature was advised that malpractice insurance rates were determined on a national basis, and did not take into account the state-wide experience of smaller States such as North Dakota. Thus, premiums were unjustifiably high for States such as North Dakota with fewer claims and smaller settlements and judgments.

Id. Similar evidence on how rates are calculated was presented to the 1975 South Dakota Committee.

Before SDCL 21-3-11 was amended in 1986, the statute only capped general or noneconomic damages. Now, the $1 million cap applies to all damages, noneconomic and economic. 1986 S.D. Sess. Laws ch. 172. This record provides no reasons for amending the statute or making the cap apply to all damages. Therefore, even if the legislative record and findings were sufficient to support the existence of an insurance crisis and the reasonableness of the cap on noneconomic damages at $500,000, they would not support the reasonableness of placing a cap on all damages, economic and noneconomic, at $1 million. No justifiable reason appears to cap economic damages.

SDCL 21-3-11 does not treat each medical malpractice claimant uniformly. It divides claimants into two classes: those whose damages are less than $1 million and those whose damages exceed $1 million. Those who have awards below the statutory cap shall be fully compensated for their injury while those exceeding the cap are not.

Therefore, SDCL 21-3-11 does not bear a "real and substantial relation to the objects sought to be obtained" and we hold that the damages cap violates due process guaranteed by [the] South Dakota Constitution.

The Hatch Study concluded that "despite unchanging claim frequency and declining loss payments and loss expense, on average, physicians paid approximately triple the amount of premiums for malpractice insurance in 1987 than in 1982." Hatch Study, at 31.

Evidence presented to the 1975 Committee indicated that only two jury verdicts in the last few years had been obtained against doctors in South Dakota. One verdict was for $1 and the other was for $10,000.

We are not saying that the state cannot subsidize health practitioners or even the health insurance industry. We are simply saying that it cannot be done in this manner to the sole detriment of the injured. Obviously, fewer constitutional objections would exist if the state would pay the difference to the injured; or, before the fact, to the insurer or health care provider; or, in all personal injury actions, all damages, economic and noneconomic, were limited in reasonable proportions for all those wrongfully injured for the benefit of all wrongdoers. We decline to comment on the wisdom, as opposed to the constitutionality of such approach.

NOTES AND PROBLEMS

1. ***Rationales for Differing Decisions.*** The Kansas and South Dakota Supreme Courts reached remarkably different decisions regarding essentially the same questions. With regard to the right to a jury trial, why do the two courts disagree? With regard to the due process arguments, is the difference between the two decisions more because of disparate views over the existence of a tort crisis or because of the degree to which they were each willing to scrutinize the wisdom behind the legislation?

2. ***Debate over Tort Crisis.*** Beginning in the 1970s, renewed in the 1980s, and repeated in the first decade of the twenty first century have been cries by business and insurance interests of a "tort crisis" demanding reforms to limit juries' abilities to award large damages in tort cases. Whether such a crisis has ever really existed is the subject of much scholarly debate. *See e.g.*, Michael A. Allen, *A Survey and Some Commentary on Federal "Tort Reform,"* 39 Akron L. Rev. 909 (2006); Michael J. Saks, *Do We Really Know Anything About the Behavior of the Tort Litigation System — And Why Not?*, 140 U. Pa. L. Rev. 1147 (1992); Johnson, *The Attack on Trial Lawyers and Tort Law*, A Commonwealth Institute Report (2003). Perhaps the poster child for a need for tort reform was the McDonald's hot coffee case where media reports on the multi-million dollar jury award were widely disseminated and repeated. The jury verdict became a punch line for many late-night comedians and the inspiration for an episode of *Seinfeld.* A recent HBO documentary entitled *Hot Coffee* attempted to debunk many of the perceived myths commonly held by the public regarding this case. Ironically, one possible unintended consequence of the media-driven tort reform movement might be to cause juries to *increase* their awards of damages. One empirical study of juror behavior found a correlation between jurors' belief in the frequency of million-dollar verdicts and their willingness to similarly award at least a million dollars in actual damages. Edith Green, Jane Goodman, and Elizabeth F. Loftus, *Jurors' Attitudes About Civil Litigation and the Size of Damage Awards*, 40 American U. L. Rev. 805 (1991).

NOMINAL DAMAGES

Where the defendant violates the rights of the plaintiff but actually causes no harm for which actual damage can be determined, it would seem obvious that the plaintiff cannot recover actual damages from the tortfeasor. But is it still worth the court's time to entertain a claim for damages in name only? That is, should the court consider awarding *nominal* damages for technical violations of rights? The following case illustrates just such a scenario, where the jury apparently found no harm caused by the defendant's good faith act of trimming the plaintiff's trees. Upon entry of a take nothing judgment in favor of the defendant, the plaintiff appealed seeking some vindication of its claim. Consider the possible public policy served by permitting such a suit as you read the following case.

LONGENECKER v. ZIMMERMAN

267 P.2d 543 (Kan. 1954)

WERTZ, J.

This was an action to recover damages for an alleged trespass. Plaintiff (appellant) in her petition alleged she was the owner of certain described real estate, and defendant (appellee) without her permission hired and caused the Arborfield Tree Surgery Company, its agents and employees, to go upon her property and top off, injure and in effect destroy three cedar trees of the value of $150 each, which trees were growing upon plaintiff's property and were both shade and ornamental in their presence. Plaintiff further stated she was entitled . . . to recover from the defendant by reason of the matters hereinbefore [for the] value of the plaintiff's property thus injured and destroyed. Defendant answered by way of a general denial.

Plaintiff's evidence disclosed that she and defendant owned adjoining residences and were neighbors for about five years. On September 8, 1950, defendant without her permission employed a tree surgery company to go upon plaintiff's property and top three cedar trees. The trees were located some two or three feet north of plaintiff's south boundary line. The trees before being topped were 20 to 25 feet high, and were as she wanted them on her property. About 10 feet were cut off the tops of the trees, and from such topping the trees would never grow any higher, and she didn't want them to stop growing. Cedars are not pruned from the top, but are feathered and shaped and not cropped. She considered the trees were, in effect, destroyed by improper pruning. She attached a sentimental value to them as they stood; they served a special purpose, were both shade and ornamental trees and were worth $150 to $200 each.

Defendant's evidence was to the effect that the trees, prior to the time they were topped, seemed to be dying out at the top and they also contained bagworms; that two or three feet were taken out of the top of one tree and about a foot or so out of the other two; that the work done was beneficial to the trees and that they were not injured. The work consisted of cutting out dead branches and cleaning out bagworms. One of defendant's expert witnesses testified on direct examination that the cutting away of dead wood would not injure the physical condition of the tree. However, on cross-examination he testified that if the top is taken out, it is the ambition of every bud on the tree to try to take the place of the terminal bud which has been sacrificed, but the trunk itself is no longer going to grow in height. Defendant stated that she was mistaken as to the boundary line and believed the trees were on her property.

In Practice

Sometimes a plaintiff will seek an award of nominal damages in order to be declared a "prevailing party" in light of a statute that awards attorney's fees to prevailing parties. This issue has been the subject of much debate in the context of certain so-called "constitutional tort" claims against government officials where plaintiff's rights were invaded but no compensable harm occurred. *See* Mark T. Morrell, *Who Wants Nominal Damages Anyway? The Impact of an Automatic Entitlement to Nominal Damages Under §1983*, 13 Regent U. L. Rev. 225 (2001).

The case was submitted to a jury which returned a general verdict for the defendant. Plaintiff's motion for a new trial was overruled and the court rendered judgment against plaintiff from which she appeals.

At the outset it may be stated that defendant admits the trespass upon plaintiff's property. The determinative question on this appeal is whether the trial court erred in refusing plaintiff's requested instruction to the effect that defendant had admitted the trespass upon plaintiff's property by topping the three cedar trees and, therefore, she was liable to the plaintiff in damages. In lieu of this requested instruction, the court gave the following instruction:

> You are instructed that the motive of the defendant is not material, and is not necessary that the defendant be acting with malice or wrongful intent in order for plaintiff to recover damages to her trees, *if any*.
>
> The defendant has admitted that she had plaintiff's trees topped and therefore she has admitted the trespass and is liable in damages *for such sum, if any, as you find from a preponderance of the evidence plaintiff has sustained.*
>
> In arriving at the value of said trees you may, *if you find from a preponderance of the evidence they have been damaged, injured or destroyed,* and should take into consideration the cost of replacement and also the sentimental and utility value of the trees. (Italics supplied.)

From every direct invasion of the person or property of another, the law infers some damage, without proof of actual injury. In an action of trespass the plaintiff is always entitled to at least nominal damages, even though he was actually benefited by the act of the defendant. 52 Am. Jur. 872, 873, Trespass,

§47; 63 C.J. 1035, §225. Since from every unauthorized entry into the close of another, the law infers some damage, nominal damages are recoverable therefor even though no substantial damages result and none are proved. In *Craig v. St. Louis-San Francisco R. Co.*, 120 Kan. 105, 106, 242 P. 117, 118, it was said:

> For present purposes it may be said that an invasion of a legally protected interest imports injury, and injury is redressed by damages. Quantum of damages depends on extent of injury caused by the invasion. If nothing but the invasion appears, the injury is technical, and is compensated by nominal damages.

It is apparent the trial court erred in including the italicized portion in the mentioned instruction, thereby submitting the question to the jury whether plaintiff had suffered any damage by reason of the unlawful trespass, when in fact the jury should have been instructed that damages, in some amount, resulted as a matter of law.

The petition alleges the facts constituting trespass at common law, that is, that the plaintiff was the owner of certain property and that the defendant without permission or other just cause hired third persons to go upon a portion of plaintiff's property and top, injure and, in effect, destroy three cedar trees, each of the value of $150. . . . It cannot be said that the erroneous instruction given by the trial court was not prejudicial to the rights of plaintiff. The judgment of the trial court is reversed and the cause is remanded with instructions to grant the plaintiff a new trial.

NOTES AND PROBLEMS

1. *Justification for Nominal Damages.* There are a fair number of cases, primarily older cases, where the court recites the black letter law that nominal damages are available for an intentional invasion of another's rights, even if no actual harm occurs. There is a legal injury brought about by intentional conduct and for this the law affords a remedy at least in the form of nominal damages. In a world of crowded court dockets, what sense does this make? One justification offered relates to permitting nominal recovery if only to declare the rights of the respective parties in the event of later disputes:

> Thus, the allowance of nominal damages is generally based on the ground either that every injury from its very nature legally imports damage, or that the injury complained of would in the future be evidence in favor of the wrongdoer, where, if continued for a sufficient length of time, the invasion of the plaintiff's rights would ripen into a prescriptive right in favor of the defendant. The maxim "de minimis non curat lex" [the law cares not about trifles] will not preclude the award of nominal damages in such cases. However, if there is no danger of prescription, no proof of substantial loss or injury, or willful wrongdoing by the defendant, it

> has been said that there is no purpose for allowing nominal damages, and judgment should be rendered for the defendant.

22 Am. Jur. 2d, Damages, §9 (1996). Accordingly, one can fairly safely assume that any intentional tort (except for a harmless intermeddling as discussed under Trespass to Chattels in Chapter 2) should at least give rise to a *possible* claim for nominal damages. On the other hand, courts would dismiss a case for negligence where the misconduct inflicted no harm, as there is no purpose to be served in awarding nominal damages where the defendant's carelessness amounted to "negligence in the air."

2. ***Other Motivations for Seeking Nominal Damages.*** Beyond vindicating her rights, why else might a "victim" of an intentional tort bother to sue for nominal damages? One reason might be to have a court rule upon a legal issue in which the parties have some interest. Setting precedent might be enormously valuable in one setting even if it first arose in a seemingly minor case for nominal damages. Further, when one's constitutional rights are violated, courts have sometimes declared a plaintiff who has proven a technical violation and recovered nominal damages to be the "prevailing party" under civil rights statutes that also permit such party to recover attorney's fees from the defendant. Sometimes awards of attorney's fees can be quite substantial and can offer some deterrent to the defendant continuing to engage in such misconduct. There have also been instances of juries awarding punitive damages on top of a nominal damage award, though this practice is prohibited in some states and has suspect continued validity in light of State Farm Mutual Automobile Insurance v. Campbell, 538 U.S. 408 (2003), discussed in the next section.

V PUNITIVE DAMAGES

While compensating victims — making them "whole" as much as money ever can — is the common refrain used to describe the primary purpose of actual damage awards, an award of punitive or exemplary damages is very different in purpose. A punitive damage award is considered "extraordinary" and is used only to provide additional punishment and deterrence for the egregious conduct in which the defendant engaged. Such an award is "additional" because even an award of actual damages provides some level of punishment and deterrence. Forcing someone to pay for harms caused is a negative consequence for having hurt another. But the thought is that the transfer of money to cover the harms may be sufficient to compensate or reimburse the plaintiff but may not be enough of a punishment for the wrongdoer. Plaintiffs' lawyers making closing arguments in punitive damage cases talk about "sending a message" to the defendant that its conduct will not be tolerated any longer. They advocate for the award to be large enough so that the defendant will remember the severe consequences the next time the defendant is tempted to repeat its antisocial behavior. Consider it the civil tort world's form of electric shock therapy.

> **In Practice**
>
> A study of hundreds of federal court cases found that punitive damages were awarded only in 2 % of the cases tried.
>
> *William Landes and Richard Posner, Punitive Damages in Products Liability Litigation, 74 Mich. L. Rev. 1257, 1329 (1976).*

We have already spent considerable time exploring expansion and contraction in tort law based upon waxing and waning sentiment regarding the degree to which the law fulfills its purposes of compensating, deterring, and punishing, balanced against providing windfall recoveries for plaintiffs with runaway jury verdicts of excessive damages. These same debates often focus upon awards of punitive damages because, while they are not routinely handed out in most tort cases, the headlines regarding particularly large exemplary damage awards can garner much attention. Large punitive damage awards may be hard to justify at times because of the reality that such an award is truly a windfall to the victim who has already received the law's best estimate of full compensatory damages, and then may also receive a punitive award many times greater than his actual damages.

The other aspect of punitive damage law that makes it a natural center of legal debate is that it occupies a gray land somewhere between the civil and criminal sides of our justice system. Criminal law places its primary focus upon retribution — punishing unlawful conduct in a way that satisfies citizens and makes it less likely that criminal behavior will be repeated. While that is criminal law's primary focus, judges frequently also enter judgments in criminal law cases requiring the convicted criminal to make restitution payments to compensate their victims. Overlap exists between these two worlds in two places — in criminal cases when restitution is required and in civil cases when punitive damages are awarded. But the punitive damage context is where the controversy exists because civil cases do not offer the same heightened constitutional protections for citizens accused of crimes — the constitutional rights to counsel, to not have to testify against oneself, and for the prosecution to have to prove the crime beyond a reasonable doubt. Is it appropriate to award potentially large "fines" in the form of punitive damages in a civil case without such procedural protections? These concerns underlie various legal issues that abound in recent tort cases where punitive damages are being considered.

In this section we will begin by reviewing some of the common law's conclusions regarding when compensatory awards may be insufficient and punitive damages necessary to offer complete justice in response to the tortfeasor's misconduct. After that we will explore statutory and constitutional limitations upon the amount of punitive damages.

A. When Civil Punishment Is Permitted

1. Malicious Conduct

Many cases of punitive damages involve intentional torts. But as the following case demonstrates, not every intentional tort circumstance warrants an additional award as punishment against the tortfeasor.

SHUGAR v. GUILL

283 S.E.2d 507 (N.C. 1981)

Plaintiff instituted this civil action on 5 January 1979 seeking damages for injuries allegedly caused by an assault and battery committed by defendant. At trial defendant duly moved to dismiss plaintiff's claim for punitive damages on the ground that plaintiff had failed properly to plead or prove such claim. The trial judge denied these motions and submitted to the jury the issues of liability, punitive damages, and compensatory damages.

Plaintiff's evidence tended to show that on 19 October 1978 around 9:25 a.m. he entered the defendant's restaurant in Tarboro known as "Cotton's Grill" for the purpose of joining several regular customers for coffee. After serving himself a cup of coffee, he joined the group. Plaintiff moved toward the table where the men sat without paying for his cup of coffee. Defendant was seated at the table, and as plaintiff took a seat at the table, he said to defendant, "This cup of coffee is on the house." Plaintiff then told defendant to "charge it against the formica that you owe me for."

Plaintiff's remarks were in reference to a dispute between himself and defendant regarding a piece of formica that a contractor had removed from a job at plaintiff's place of business with his permission to use it in the completion of a job at defendant's restaurant in March, 1978. Plaintiff had billed defendant twice for the formica, but the $6.25 bill remained unpaid at the time of the October 1978 incident. Defendant had refused to pay for the formica and had in turn sent plaintiff a bill for what defendant claimed was lost time for a painter who had been conversing with plaintiff while he was working on a job for defendant. Plaintiff had not honored defendant's request to reimburse him for the painter's lost time although defendant had offered to pay plaintiff for the formica after plaintiff had paid defendant for the claimed lost time.

Following plaintiff's comment regarding the charging of the coffee against the formica cost, defendant commented on plaintiff's cheapness and demanded that plaintiff leave the restaurant immediately. Plaintiff responded by saying, "Make me." Defendant then picked plaintiff up in a "bear hug" and started toward the door. Plaintiff managed to free himself and blows were exchanged. Plaintiff was struck about the eyes twice, and defendant's glasses were broken when he was hit in the face during the scuffle. A bystander attempted to intervene, and plaintiff, apparently thinking the melee over, dropped his hands to his side at which point defendant struck plaintiff squarely in the face breaking his nose and causing it to bleed profusely.

Plaintiff lost consciousness momentarily after being struck in the nose. The entire incident lasted less than sixty seconds. Later that day, plaintiff visited a Tarboro physician who referred him to a specialist in Greenville.

Plaintiff's nose was treated by straightening, packing, and bandaging. The medical treatment involved was quite painful, and plaintiff experienced a partial loss of breathing capacity as a result of the blow to the nose. Plaintiff's medical expenses totalled $234.

The jury answered the issue of liability in plaintiff's favor and awarded him $2,000 in compensatory damages and $2,500 in punitive damages.

Branch, J.

The rationale permitting recovery of punitive damages is that such damages may be awarded in addition to compensatory damages to punish a defendant for his wrongful acts and to deter others from committing similar acts. A civil action may not be maintained solely for the purpose of collecting punitive damages but may only be awarded when a cause of action otherwise exists in which at least nominal damages are recoverable by the plaintiff. *Worthy v. Knight*, 187 S.E. 771 (N.C. 1936).

It is well established in this jurisdiction that punitive damages may be recovered for an assault and battery but are allowable *only* when the assault and battery is accompanied by an element of aggravation such as malice, or oppression, or gross and wilful wrong, or a wanton and reckless disregard of plaintiff's rights. *Oestreicher v. American Nat. Stores, Inc.*, 225 S.E.2d 797 (N.C. 1976).

Some jurisdictions permit the recovery of punitive damages on the theory of *implied* or *imputed* malice when a person intentionally does an act which naturally tends to be injurious. These jurisdictions thus infer the malice necessary to support recovery of punitive damages from *any* assault and battery. *Barker v. James*, 486 P.2d 195 (Ariz. 1971); *Robbs v. Missouri Pac. Ry. Co.*, 242 S.W. 155 (Mo. 1922); *Custer v. Kroeger*, 209 Mo. App. 450, 240 S.W. 241 (1922); *Mecham v. Foley*, 235 P.2d 497 (Utah 1951). We do not adhere to this rule. To justify the awarding of punitive damages in North Carolina, there must be a showing of *actual* or *express* malice, that is, a showing of a sense of personal ill will toward the plaintiff which activated or incited a defendant to commit the alleged assault and battery. *Baker v. Winslow*, 113 S.E. 570 (N.C. 1922).

[In reviewing the punitive damage award here, we] find it helpful to review the *types* of cases in which punitive damages have been allowed. Punitive damages were recovered in cases where a clergyman while peacefully walking down a street was attacked by the defendant and severely injured; where the plaintiff while eating in a hotel dining room was compelled to sign a retraction by a show of violence, accompanied with offensive and threatening language;

where defendant assaulted a weak and old person with a stick loaded with lead for the reason that defendant *thought* plaintiff was a trespasser; [and] where a twelve-year-old boy was assaulted in public in the presence of others without justification or excuse. We note that all of these cases contain a thread of unprovoked humiliating assaults, assaults on children, assaults on weaker persons, or assaults where a deadly weapon was callously used. Such is not the case before us.

The case of *Riepe v. Green*, 65 S.W.2d 667 (Mo. App. 1933), is most instructive toward decision because of its strong factual similarity to the case before us. There plaintiff brought a civil action against defendant seeking compensatory and punitive damages. The evidence of the plaintiff disclosed that there had been some difficulty between plaintiff and defendant and that plaintiff "had no good feeling toward him (defendant) for over a year." *Id.* at 668. On the day that the incident complained of occurred, defendant was talking to some men on the street when plaintiff called him and asked "have you found any more victims?" Plaintiff then drove his wagon across the sidewalk so that defendant could not move. After some further conversation, plaintiff told defendant that he did not want any dealings with him because of his refusal to pay for some cow pasture. Plaintiff testified that he might have called defendant an "S.O.B." and a damned crook. Thereafter, a fight ensued which resulted in plaintiff's alleged injuries. The jury answered issues awarding plaintiff compensatory and punitive damages, and defendant appealed. In reversing and remanding, the Kansas City Court of Appeals reasoned:

> The general rule, as to punitive damages, is to the effect that the question is one for the jury and not for the court. This general rule is predicated upon the presumption that wantonness, recklessness, oppression, or express malice be shown by some fact or circumstance in evidence from which one of these elements may be inferred. (Citation omitted.)
>
> We fail to find any evidence in the record before us that justifies the submission of the issue of punitive damages. In so far as words and conduct could provoke such a state of mind as above, the plaintiff is shown to be the aggressor. One who drives a wagon across the pathway of another with the intent expressed by plaintiff furnishes a poor subject for smart money. While foul words and epithets do not justify assault, yet such words and epithets mitigate, and, in the absence of any showing that defendant was actuated by willfull, wanton, and malicious state of mind, it was error to submit the issue of punitive damages.

Id. at 669.

Applying the above-stated principles of law to the facts presented by this appeal, we conclude that the evidence presented was not sufficient to permit the jury reasonably to infer that defendant's actions were activated by personal ill will toward plaintiff or that his acts were aggravated by oppression, insult, rudeness, or a wanton and reckless disregard of plaintiff's rights. To the contrary, the evidence shows that two adults acting as adolescents engaged in an affray which was precipitated by plaintiff's "baiting" of defendant and plaintiff's invitation that he be ejected from defendant's premises. Thus, the trial court erred by denying defendant's motion to dismiss on the ground that there was not sufficient evidence to carry the issue of punitive damages to the jury. We affirm the Court of Appeals' action in vacating for the reasons set forth herein.

NOTES AND PROBLEMS

1. ***Proving Elements of Tort Not Necessarily Enough.*** While intentional tort claims are often the subject of punitive damage awards, most states refuse to make the possibility of such an award automatic. Rather, in most jurisdictions the plaintiff must prove — in addition to the elements of the intentional tort — aggravating circumstances referred to as "malice." A minority of courts assume this bad intent when an intentional tort is proven. The problem with this approach is that many intentional torts might not involve any ill will (for example, a simple trespass where the defendant has taken a shortcut across the landowner's property).

2. ***Nominal Damages as Anchor.*** Some courts have permitted punitive damage claims when the defendant's intentional tort was coupled with "malice" despite the fact that no actual harm was caused, so long as there was an award of at least nominal damages. *See e.g.*, Peete v. Blackwell, 504 So. 2d 222 (Ala. 1986) (upholding award of $10,000 in punitive damages where angry doctor struck the arm of a nurse during an emergency procedure despite the fact that the jury only awarded $1 in nominal damages). This practice is called into serious question both by constitutional due process issues (*see* State Farm v. Campbell below) and under certain states' statutory modifications to punitive damages.

3. ***Problems.*** In light of the *Shugar* opinion, would the following scenarios appear to be appropriate for awards of punitive damages?

- **A.** A music teacher walks up behind a student of his in a social setting and taps his fingers on the student's back as if to simulate how to play the piano. The student recoils in pain as the contact causes a dislocation in her vertebrae. Assume this is a single intent battery jurisdiction (where only an intent to cause contact that turns out to be harmful, is required).
- **B.** A neighbor mistakenly believes a tree is on his property and hires a trimming service to trim some unsightly and unhealthy branches. It turns out the tree belongs to a neighbor.
- **C.** A debt collector repeatedly hits a debtor over the head with the butt end of a handgun in order to compel full payment of the debt. As the collector raises his hand to swing at the debtor again, the gun discharges and shoots the debtor in the abdomen causing serious injuries.

2. *Corporate Liability for Reckless Conduct*

In addition to a showing of "malice" accompanying the commission of an intentional tort, most courts have also recognized reckless misconduct (or gross negligence) as an additional path to punitive damages. In Chapter 3, we explored gross negligence as an alternative standard to ordinary negligence in *Mobil Oil v. Ellender*. In that case, the court discussed the two-pronged nature of a showing of gross negligence: (1) that, viewed objectively, the defendant's conduct created a substantial *probability* of *serious danger* to the plaintiff; and (2) that the defendant had a subjective awareness of the risk of harm arising from its actions but made the conscious decision to disregard this risk. Many cases of gross negligence arise in the corporate context, such as *Mobil Oil*. In such cases, courts have to determine precisely *whose reckless misconduct* suffices to justify punishing the corporate entity. In other words, when does the reckless misconduct of an employee count as recklessness by the corporation itself? Below is an additional excerpt from *Mobil Oil* discussing and applying the gross negligence standard to a punitive damage award in the corporate context.

MOBIL v. ELLENDER

968 S.W.2d 917 (Tex. 1998)

Baker, J.

[Plaintiff decedent died from exposure to benzene while working as an independent contractor at defendant's plant for many years. Defendant permitted plaintiff, and other independent contractors working at the facility, to work around benzene without gloves. In fact, benzene was provided to such workers to wash their hands. The jury found the defendant liable for negligence, also found gross negligence against the corporation, and assessed actual damages of $622,000 and punitive damages in the amount of $6 million. The Texas Supreme Court found that the evidence showed gross negligence in the defendant's mistreatment of independent contractors. Defendant also claimed, however, that there was insufficient showing that the recklessness was properly attributable to the corporation itself, as opposed to mere employees.]

A corporation may be liable in punitive damages for gross negligence only if the corporation itself commits gross negligence. *See Fort Worth Elevators, Co. v. Russell*, 70 S.W.2d 397, 406 (Tex. 1934), *overruled on other grounds by Wright v. Gifford-Hill & Co.*, 725 S.W.2d 712 (Tex. 1987). Because a corporation can "act only through agents of some character," *Fort Worth Elevators*, 70 S.W.2d at 402, this Court has developed tests for distinguishing between acts that are solely attributable to agents or employees and acts that are directly attributable to the corporation. *See Hammerly Oaks, Inc. v. Edwards*, 958 S.W.2d 387 (Tex. 1997). A corporation is liable for punitive damages if it authorizes or ratifies an agent's gross negligence or if it is grossly negligent in hiring an unfit agent. *See King v. McGuff*, 149 Tex. 432, 234 S.W.2d 403, 405 (Tex. 1950) (adopting the Restatement of Torts section 909).

A corporation is also liable if it commits gross negligence through the actions or inactions of a vice principal. *See Hammerly Oaks*, 958 S.W.2d at 389. "Vice principal" encompasses:

> (a) corporate officers; (b) those who have authority to employ, direct, and discharge servants of the master; (c) those engaged in the performance of nondelegable or absolute duties of the master; and (d) those to whom the master has confided the management of the whole or a department or a division of the business.

See Hammerly Oaks, 958 S.W.2d at 391.

In determining whether acts are directly attributable to the corporation, the reviewing court does not simply judge individual elements or facts. Instead, the court should review all the surrounding facts and circumstances to determine whether the corporation itself is grossly negligent. Whether the corporation's acts can be attributed to the corporation itself, and thereby constitute corporate gross negligence, is determined by reasonable inferences the factfinder can draw from what the corporation did or failed to do and the facts existing at relevant times that contributed to a plaintiff's alleged damages.

[The court found that the evidence showed there was a significant health risk that was known throughout the industry, and within Mobil, to prolonged or repeated exposure to benzene. The evidence also showed that the exposure of workers at defendant's plant was at dangerously high levels.]

Mobil counters that because there is no evidence that *a vice principal's conduct* involved an extreme degree of risk to contract workers like Ellender, Mobil cannot be liable for gross negligence. However, in reviewing all the facts and circumstances, we conclude that there is evidence that Mobil's own acts and omissions involved an extreme degree of risk to contract workers like Ellender.

David B. Dunham, a Mobil industrial hygienist, testified that although Mobil monitored its employees, it had an "unwritten practice or policy" not to monitor contract workers and that when he attempted to monitor contract workers, he was told not to. Ellender's co-workers testified that they never saw any signs warning them of benzene hazards at Mobil and that Mobil did not monitor them for exposure or provide them with protective gear when they worked around benzene. Moreover, Mobil did not include any reference to benzene or other chemicals in its 1967 pamphlet entitled "Mobil Safety and Security Regulations for Contract Workers." Dr. Josh Esslinger, a former medical consultant for Mobil in Beaumont, testified that he knew workers washed their hands in benzene and that such a practice indicated that workers were not adequately warned of benzene hazards. Dr. Dement testified that Mobil's industrial hygiene program was poor and practically nonexistent for contractors. This is evidence from which the jury could reasonably infer that Mobil had a company policy of not monitoring contract workers for benzene exposure, not warning them of the dangers of such exposure, and not providing them with protective gear and that this policy involved an extreme degree of risk to those workers. *See generally McPhearson*, 463 S.W.2d at 176. Thus, there is evidence that acts and omissions of Mobil itself involved an extreme degree of risk to contract workers like Ellender.

[The court affirmed the punitive damage award.]

NOTES AND PROBLEMS

1. ***Gross Negligence as Basis for Punitive Damages.*** While the vast majority of courts have traditionally accepted the possibility of a jury's award of punitive damages in accidental injury cases where the defendant's conduct amounts to gross negligence, reckless, or "wilful and wantonness," a minority of courts have dismissed this possibility—instead insisting on a showing of "actual malice" as a motivation for the wrongful conduct as the needed threshold. *See e.g.*, Owens-Illinois, Inc. v. Zenobia, 601 A.2d 633 (Md. 1992) (rejecting gross negligence as a basis for punitive damages and instead insisting upon a finding of "evil motive, intent to injure, ill will, or fraud, i.e., 'actual malice.'").

2. ***Gross Negligence of the Corporation Itself.*** An artificial legal entity, such as a corporation, can only act through its employees and agents. But just because one of those employees has engaged in misconduct warranting punitive damages does not automatically mean the corporation should be punished. In the next chapter on Apportionment, we will discuss vicarious liability—a type of guilt by association — for actual damages. But the ease by which a corporation might be liable for its employees' ordinary negligence in a suit for compensatory damages does not apply to exemplary damages. In *Mobil*, the court acknowledges various bases for corporate liability for punitive damages — authorization or ratification of the employees' malicious or grossly negligent conduct, or where the bad-acting employee is part of management, as a *vice principal.* The court also mentions the gross negligence in hiring a bad-acting employee as a basis for corporate liability for punitive damages, but this is redundant because such conduct would necessarily involve the gross negligence of a vice principal.

3. ***Problems.*** In light of the court's opinion in *Mobil Oil*, would there be a potential for punitive damages against the corporate entity below?

A. A pizza delivery person is heavily intoxicated while driving to deliver a pizza and runs over the plaintiff pedestrian.

B. The same pizza delivery person was visibly intoxicated in front of the pizza store manager while picking up the pizza for delivery.

B. The Amount of Punitive Damages

Under the common law, there is no real measure for the amount of punitive damages other than that the jury should find a suitable amount in light of the following considerations:

- The nature of the wrong;
- The character of the conduct involved;
- The degree of culpability of the wrongdoer;
- The situation and sensibilities of the parties concerned;
- The extent to which such conduct offends a public sense of justice and propriety; and
- The net worth of the defendant.

Tex. Civ. Prac. & Rem. Code §41.011 (listing the factors the trier of fact "shall consider" in "determining the amount of exemplary damages, if any"). As further examples of tort reform, both the U.S. Supreme Court and various state legislatures have placed limits on the traditionally great discretion given to juries. We will discuss each of these types of limits in order. In State Farm Insurance v. Campbell, the Supreme Court applies new constitutional Due Process limits to a case where the jury found the insurance company's conduct reprehensible and awarded an extraordinary amount of punitive damages. The Supreme Court discusses and applies a three-factored analysis for determining whether the verdict was constitutionally impermissible.

1. Due Process Limits

For centuries, federal courts have left the world of punitive damages to the control of state common law. Recently as a type of judicial tort reform, the U.S. Supreme Court has recognized as a Due Process limitation that excessively high punitive damage awards may violate the rights of the tortfeasor. In *State Farm*, the Court applies this new constitutional standard to a rather large award against an insurer whose conduct "merits no praise." The issue was whether the state court jury had doled out an excessive punishment in its exemplary damage award.

STATE FARM MUTUAL v. CAMPBELL

538 U.S. 408 (2003)

KENNEDY, J.

We address once again the measure of punishment, by means of punitive damages, a State may impose upon a defendant in a civil case. The question is whether, in the circumstances we shall recount, an award of $145 million in punitive damages, where full compensatory damages are $1 million, is excessive and in violation of the Due Process Clause of the Fourteenth Amendment to the Constitution of the United States.

In 1981, Curtis Campbell (Campbell) was driving with his wife, Inez Preece Campbell, in Cache County, Utah. He decided to pass six vans traveling ahead of them on a two-lane highway. Todd Ospital was driving a small car approaching from the opposite direction. To avoid a head-on collision with Campbell, who by then was driving on the wrong side of the highway and toward oncoming traffic, Ospital swerved onto the shoulder, lost control of his automobile, and collided with a vehicle driven by Robert G. Slusher. Ospital was killed, and Slusher was rendered permanently disabled. The Campbells escaped unscathed.

In the ensuing wrongful death and tort action, Campbell insisted he was not at fault. Early investigations did support differing conclusions as to who caused the accident, but [the investigators quickly agreed that Campbell's unsafe pass caused the crash]. Campbell's insurance company, State Farm, nonetheless decided to contest liability and declined offers by Slusher and Ospital's estate to settle the claims for the policy limit of $50,000. State Farm also ignored the advice of one of its own investigators and took the case to trial, assuring the Campbells that [their assets were safe, that they had no liability for the accident, and that State Farm would take care of them so they need not hire their own separate counsel]. To the contrary, a jury determined that Campbell was 100 percent at fault, and a judgment was returned for $185,849, far more than the amount offered in settlement.

Principles

Concerns have been raised about the disconnect potential in permitting punishment unrelated to compensation to be handed out in a civil proceeding: "Perhaps most troubling . . . is the fact that although punitive damages are quasi-criminal in nature, they are imposed in the course of civil litigation without many of the procedural safeguards that accompany criminal penalties."

Pace, Recalibrating the Scales of Justice Through National Punitive Damage Reform, 46 Am. U. L. Rev. 1573, 1576 (1997).

At first State Farm refused to cover the $135,849 in excess liability. Its counsel made this clear to the Campbells: "You may want to put for sale signs on your property to get things moving." Nor was State Farm willing to post a supersedeas bond to allow Campbell to appeal the judgment against him. Campbell obtained his own counsel to appeal the verdict. During the pendency of the appeal, in late 1984, Slusher, Ospital, and the Campbells reached an agreement whereby Slusher and Ospital agreed not to seek satisfaction of their claims against the Campbells. In exchange the Campbells agreed to pursue a bad faith action against State Farm and to be represented by Slusher's and Ospital's attorneys. The Campbells also agreed that Slusher and Ospital would have a right to play a part in all major decisions concerning the bad faith action. No settlement could be concluded without Slusher's and Ospital's approval, and Slusher and Ospital would receive 90 percent of any verdict against State Farm.

In 1989, the Utah Supreme Court denied Campbell's appeal in the wrongful death and tort actions. State Farm then paid the entire judgment, including the amounts in excess of the policy limits. The Campbells nonetheless filed a complaint against State Farm alleging bad faith, fraud, and intentional infliction of emotional distress. State Farm moved *in limine* to exclude evidence of alleged conduct that occurred in unrelated cases outside of Utah, but the trial court denied the motion. At State Farm's request the trial court bifurcated the trial into two phases conducted before different juries. In the first phase the jury determined that State Farm's decision not to settle was unreasonable because there was a substantial likelihood of an excess verdict.

Before the second phase of the action against State Farm we decided *BMW of North America, Inc. v. Gore*, 517 U.S. 559 (1996), and refused to sustain a $2 million punitive damages award which accompanied a verdict of only $4,000 in compensatory damages. Based on that decision, State Farm again moved for the exclusion of evidence of dissimilar out-of-state conduct. The trial court denied State Farm's motion.

The second phase addressed State Farm's liability for fraud and intentional infliction of emotional distress, as well as compensatory and punitive damages. The Utah Supreme Court aptly characterized this phase of the trial:

> State Farm argued during phase II that its decision to take the case to trial was an 'honest mistake' that did not warrant punitive damages. In contrast, the Campbells introduced evidence that State Farm's decision to take the case to trial was a result of a national scheme to meet corporate fiscal goals by capping payouts on claims company wide. To prove the existence of this scheme, the trial court allowed the Campbells to introduce extensive expert testimony regarding fraudulent practices by State Farm in its nation-wide operations. Although State Farm moved prior to phase II of the trial for the exclusion of such evidence and continued to object to it at trial, the trial court ruled that such evidence was admissible to determine whether State Farm's conduct in the Campbell case was indeed intentional and sufficiently egregious to warrant punitive damages.

Evidence pertaining to the [scheme] concerned State Farm's business practices for over 20 years in numerous States. Most of these practices bore no relation to third-party automobile insurance claims, the type of claim underlying the Campbells' complaint against the company. The jury awarded the Campbells $2.6 million in compensatory damages and $145 million in punitive damages, which the trial court reduced to $1 million and $25 million respectively. Both parties appealed.

The Utah Supreme Court [reinstated the $145 million punitive damage verdict. State Farm appealed from the judgment of $1 million in actual damages and $145 million in punitive damages].

We recognized in *Cooper Industries, Inc. v. Leatherman Tool Group, Inc.*, 532 U.S. 424 (2001), that in our judicial system compensatory and punitive damages, although usually awarded at the same time by the same decisionmaker, serve different purposes. Compensatory damages "are intended to redress the concrete loss that the plaintiff has suffered by reason of the defendant's wrongful conduct." By contrast, punitive damages serve a broader function; they are aimed at deterrence and retribution. See *Gore, supra,* at 568 ("Punitive damages may properly be imposed to further a State's legitimate interests in punishing unlawful conduct and deterring its repetition").

While States possess discretion over the imposition of punitive damages, it is well established that there are procedural and substantive constitutional limitations on these awards. The Due Process Clause of the Fourteenth Amendment prohibits the imposition of grossly excessive or arbitrary punishments on a tortfeasor. The reason is that "elementary notions of fairness enshrined in our constitutional jurisprudence dictate that a person receive fair notice not only of the conduct that will subject him to punishment, but also of the severity of the penalty that a State may impose." *Id.,* at 574. To the extent an award is grossly excessive, it furthers no legitimate purpose and constitutes an arbitrary deprivation of property. *Haslip, supra,* at 42 (O'Connor, J., dissenting) ("Punitive damages are a powerful weapon. Imposed wisely and with restraint, they have the potential to advance legitimate state interests. Imposed indiscriminately, however, they have a devastating potential for harm. Regrettably, common-law procedures for awarding punitive damages fall into the latter category").

Although these awards serve the same purposes as criminal penalties, defendants subjected to punitive damages in civil cases have not been accorded the protections applicable in a criminal proceeding. This increases our concerns over the imprecise manner in which punitive damages systems are administered. We have admonished that "punitive damages pose an acute danger of arbitrary deprivation of property. Jury instructions typically leave the jury with wide discretion in choosing amounts, and the presentation of evidence of a defendant's net worth creates the potential that juries will use their verdicts to express biases against big businesses, particularly those without strong local presences." *Honda Motor, supra,* at 432.

In light of these concerns, in Gore we instructed courts reviewing punitive damages to consider three guideposts: (1) the degree of reprehensibility of the defendant's misconduct; (2) the disparity between the actual or potential harm suffered by the plaintiff and the punitive damages award; and (3) the difference between the punitive damages awarded by the jury and the civil penalties authorized or imposed in comparable cases.

Under the principles outlined in *BMW of North America, Inc. v. Gore,* this case is neither close nor difficult. It was error to reinstate the jury's $145 million punitive damages award. We address each guidepost of *Gore* in some detail.

"[T]he most important indicium of the reasonableness of a punitive damages award is the degree of reprehensibility of the defendant's conduct." *Gore, supra,* at 575. We have instructed courts to determine the reprehensibility of a defendant by considering whether: the harm caused was physical as opposed to economic; the tortious conduct evinced an indifference to or a reckless disregard of the health or safety of others; the target of the conduct had financial vulnerability; the conduct involved repeated actions or was an isolated incident; and the harm was the result of intentional malice, trickery, or deceit, or mere accident. It should be presumed a plaintiff has been made whole for his injuries by compensatory damages, so punitive damages should only be awarded if the defendant's culpability, after having paid compensatory damages, is so reprehensible as to warrant the imposition of further sanctions to achieve punishment or deterrence.

Applying these factors in the instant case, we must acknowledge that State Farm's handling of the claims against the Campbells merits no praise. The trial court found that State Farm's employees altered the company's records to make Campbell appear less culpable. State Farm disregarded the overwhelming likelihood of liability and the near-certain probability that, by taking the case to trial, a judgment in excess of the policy limits would be awarded. State Farm amplified the harm by at first assuring the Campbells their assets would be safe from any verdict and by later telling them, postjudgment, to put a for-sale sign on their house. While we do not suggest there was error in awarding punitive damages based upon State Farm's conduct toward the Campbells, a more modest punishment for this reprehensible conduct could have satisfied the State's legitimate objectives, and the Utah courts should have gone no further.

This case, instead, was used as a platform to expose, and punish, the perceived deficiencies of State Farm's operations throughout the country. The Utah Supreme Court's opinion makes explicit that State Farm was being condemned for its nationwide policies rather than for the conduct direct toward the Campbells.

The Campbells contend that State Farm has only itself to blame for the reliance upon dissimilar and out-of-state conduct evidence. The record does not support this contention. From their opening statements onward the Campbells framed this case as a chance to rebuke State Farm for its nationwide activities. ("You're going to hear evidence that even the insurance commission in Utah and around the country are unwilling or inept at protecting people against abuses.") This was a position maintained throughout the litigation.

A State cannot punish a defendant for conduct that may have been lawful where it occurred. Nor, as a general rule, does a State have a legitimate concern in imposing punitive damages to punish a defendant for unlawful acts committed outside of the State's jurisdiction. Any proper adjudication of conduct that occurred outside Utah to other persons would require their inclusion, and, to those parties, the Utah courts, in the usual case, would need to apply the laws of their relevant jurisdiction.

For a more fundamental reason, however, the Utah courts erred in relying upon this and other evidence: The courts awarded punitive damages to punish and deter conduct that bore no relation to the Campbells' harm. A defendant's dissimilar acts, independent from the acts upon which liability was premised, may not serve as the basis for punitive damages. A defendant should be punished for the conduct that harmed the plaintiff, not for being an unsavory individual or business. Due process does not permit courts, in the calculation of punitive damages, to adjudicate the merits of other parties' hypothetical claims against a defendant under the guise of the reprehensibility analysis, but we have no doubt the Utah Supreme Court did that here. Punishment on these bases creates the possibility of multiple punitive damages awards for the same conduct; for in the usual case nonparties are not bound by the judgment some other plaintiff obtains.

The same reasons lead us to conclude the Utah Supreme Court's decision cannot be justified on the grounds that State Farm was a recidivist. Although "our holdings that a recidivist may be punished more severely than a first offender recognize that repeated misconduct is more reprehensible than an individual instance of malfeasance," *Gore*, at 577, in the context of civil actions courts must ensure the conduct in question replicates the prior transgressions.

The Campbells have identified scant evidence of repeated misconduct of the sort that injured them. Nor does our review of the Utah courts' decisions convince us that State Farm was only punished for its actions toward the Campbells. Although evidence of other acts need not be identical to have relevance in the calculation of punitive damages, the Utah court erred here because evidence pertaining to claims that had nothing to do with a third-party lawsuit was introduced at length. For example, the Utah Supreme Court criticized State Farm's investigation into the personal life of one of its employees and, in a broader approach, the manner in which State Farm's policies corrupted its employees. The reprehensibility guidepost does not permit courts to expand the scope of the case so that a defendant may be punished for any malfeasance, which in this case extended for a 20-year period. In this case, because the Campbells have shown no conduct by State Farm similar to that which harmed them, the conduct that harmed them is the only conduct relevant to the reprehensibility analysis.

Turning to the second *Gore* guidepost, we have been reluctant to identify concrete constitutional limits on the ratio between harm, or potential harm, to the plaintiff and the punitive damages award. We decline again to impose a bright-line ratio which a punitive damages award cannot exceed. Our jurisprudence and the principles it has now established demonstrate, however, that, in practice, few awards exceeding a single-digit ratio between punitive and compensatory damages, to a significant degree, will satisfy due process. In *Haslip*, in upholding a punitive damages award, we concluded that an award of more than four times the amount of compensatory damages might be close to the line of constitutional impropriety. We cited that 4-to-1 ratio again in *Gore*. The Court further referenced a long legislative history, dating back over 700 years and going forward to today, providing for sanctions of double, treble, or quadruple damages to deter and punish. While these ratios are not binding, they are instructive. They demonstrate what should be obvious: Single-digit multipliers are more likely to comport with due process, while still achieving the State's goals of deterrence and retribution, than awards with ratios in range of 500 to 1, or, in this case, of 145 to 1.

Nonetheless, because there are no rigid benchmarks that a punitive damages award may not surpass, ratios greater than those we have previously upheld may comport with due process where "a particularly egregious act has resulted in only a small amount of economic damages." The converse is also true, however. When compensatory damages are substantial, then a lesser ratio, perhaps only equal to compensatory damages, can reach the outermost limit of the due process guarantee. The precise award in any case, of course, must be based upon the facts and circumstances of the defendant's conduct and the harm to the plaintiff.

In sum, courts must ensure that the measure of punishment is both reasonable and proportionate to the amount of harm to the plaintiff and to the general damages recovered. In the context of this case, we have no doubt that there is a presumption against an award that has a 145-to-1 ratio. The compensatory award in this case was substantial; the Campbells were awarded $1 million for a year and a half of emotional distress. This was complete compensation. The harm arose from a transaction in the economic realm, not from some physical assault or trauma; there were no physical injuries; and State Farm paid the excess verdict before the complaint was filed, so the Campbells suffered only minor economic injuries for the 18-month period in which State Farm refused to resolve the claim against them. The compensatory damages for the injury suffered here, moreover, likely were based on a component which was duplicated in the punitive award. Much of the distress was caused by the outrage and humiliation the Campbells suffered at the actions of their insurer; and it is a major role of punitive damages to condemn such conduct. Compensatory damages, however, already contain this punitive element.

The third guidepost in *Gore* is the disparity between the punitive damages award and the "civil penalties authorized or imposed in comparable cases."

Here, we need not dwell long on this guidepost. The most relevant civil sanction under Utah state law for the wrong done to the Campbells appears to be a $10,000 fine for an act of fraud, an amount dwarfed by the $145 million punitive damages award. The Supreme Court of Utah speculated about the loss of State Farm's business license, the disgorgement of profits, and possible imprisonment, but here again its references were to the broad fraudulent scheme drawn from evidence of out-of-state and dissimilar conduct. This analysis was insufficient to justify the award.

An application of the *Gore* guideposts to the facts of this case, especially in light of the substantial compensatory damages awarded (a portion of which contained a punitive element), likely would justify a punitive damages award at or near the amount of compensatory damages. The punitive award of $145 million, therefore, was neither reasonable nor proportionate to the wrong committed, and it was an irrational and arbitrary deprivation of the property of the defendant. The proper calculation of punitive damages under the principles we have discussed should be resolved, in the first instance, by the Utah courts.

The judgment of the Utah Supreme Court is reversed, and the case is remanded for proceedings not inconsistent with this opinion.

DISSENT

SCALIA, J., *dissenting*

I adhere to the view expressed in my dissenting opinion in *BMW of North America, Inc. v. Gore*, 517 U.S. 559, 598-99 (1996), that the Due Process Clause provides no substantive protections against "excessive" or "unreasonable" awards of punitive damages. I am also of the view that the punitive damages jurisprudence which has sprung forth from *BMW v. Gore* is insusceptible of principled application; accordingly, I do not feel justified in giving the case *stare decisis* effect. I would affirm the judgment of the Utah Supreme Court.

GINSBURG, J., *dissenting*

When the Court first ventured to override state-court punitive damages awards, it did so moderately. The Court recalled that "in our federal system, States necessarily have considerable flexibility in determining the level of punitive damages that they will allow in different classes of cases and in any particular case." *Gore*, 517 U.S. at 568. Today's decision exhibits no such respect and restraint. No longer content to accord state-court judgments "a strong presumption of validity," *TXO*, 509 U.S. at 457, the Court announces that "few awards exceeding a single-digit ratio between punitive and compensatory damages, to a significant degree, will satisfy due process." In a legislative scheme or a state high court's design to cap punitive damages, the handiwork in setting single-digit and 1-to-1 benchmarks could hardly be questioned; in a judicial decree imposed on the States by this Court under the banner of substantive due process, the numerical controls today's decision installs seem to me boldly out of order.

Justice Ginsburg

I remain of the view that this Court has no warrant to reform state law governing awards of punitive damages. Even if I were prepared to accept the flexible guides prescribed in *Gore*, I would not join the Court's swift conversion of those guides into instructions that begin to resemble marching orders. For the reasons stated, I would leave the judgment of the Utah Supreme Court undisturbed.

2. *Statutory Limits*

Justice Ginsburg had earlier dissented from the majority's opinion in the *BMW v. Gore* case on the grounds that the Supreme Court was violating principles of traditional federalism by imposing unnecessary federal court oversight to state court jury decisions. She observed that many states had already passed legislation placing appropriate limits on the size of punitive damage verdict. Since then, additional states have followed suit. The majority of states now place statutory limits on the jury's ability to award exemplary damages. Some examples include:

- **Colorado**: Generally caps punitive damages in an amount equal to the actual damages. Colo. Rev. Stat. §§13-21-102(1)(a) and (3) (1987).
- **Delaware**: Limits punitive damages to greater of three times the actual damages or $250,000 — whichever is greater. H.R. 237, 138th Gen. Ass. (1995).
- **Florida**: Limits punitive damages to three times the compensatory damages. Fla. Stat. §§768.73(1)(a)-(b) (1992).
- **Georgia**: Limits punitive damages to $250,000 for certain tort actions. Ga. Code Ann. §51-12-5.1 (1995).
- **Illinois**: Limits punitive damages to three times actual damages. H. 20, 89th Gen. Ass. (1995).
- **New Jersey**: Caps exemplary damages at greater of five times actual damages or $350,000. §1496, 206th Leg. 2d Ann. Sess. (1995).
- **North Dakota**: Limits punitive damages to two times the compensatory damages or $250,000. N.D. Cent. Code §32-03.2-11(4) (1995).
- **Texas**: Caps punitive damages in most cases at two times the actual damages plus up to $750,000 in general damages. Tex. Civ. Prac. & Rem. Code §4 (1995).
- **Virginia**: Caps punitive damages at $350,000. Va. Code Ann. §8.01-38.1 (1992).

NOTES AND PROBLEMS

1. *No Entitlement to Award of Punitive Damages.* Courts have consistently held that a plaintiff has no vested right or entitlement to an award of

punitive damages. No matter how despicable the behavior of the tortfeasor, a jury can decide that only actual damages should be awarded. This makes it extremely difficult for a plaintiff to complain about a punitive damage cap's application under any constitutional right analysis.

2. *Impact of Statutory Limits on* BMW *Factors.* Given that so many states now have statutory limits on punitive damages, such as those examples above, does this add weight to the concerns of Justice Scalia that the federal courts have no business meddling in a state's punitive damage jurisprudence? If a punitive damage award complies with any of the foregoing statutes, is it likely to be held unconstitutional under *State Farm*? If not, is it worth the incursion into state law matters?

"LADIES AND GENTLEMEN OF THE JURY . . ."

5th Circuit Pattern Jury Instructions (Civil Cases) 15.13 Punitive Damages:

"If you determine that the defendant's conduct was so shocking and offensive as to justify an award of punitive damages, you may exercise your discretion to award those damages. In making any award of punitive damages, you should consider that the purpose of punitive damages is to punish a defendant for shocking conduct, and to deter the defendant and others from engaging in similar conduct in the future. The law does not require you to award punitive damages, however, if you decide to award punitive damages, you must use sound reason in setting the amount of the damages. The amount of an award must not reflect bias, prejudice, or sympathy toward any party. However, the amount can be as large as you believe necessary to fulfill the purposes of punitive damages. You may consider the financial resources of the defendant in fixing the amount of punitive damages and you may impose punitive damages against one or more of the defendants, and not others, or against more than one defendant in different amounts."

CHAPTER 9

Apportionment

I INTRODUCTION

Even after adjudicating the merits of the plaintiff's tort claim and determining the amount of damages, the court may not yet be ready to close the file and send it to storage. Many modern cases involve multiple alleged tortfeasors that played a role in bringing about the plaintiff's harm. We have already seen a number of instances of such claims. Examples include two boys firing paper clips at another scout's eye during a pack meeting (*McQuiggan v. Boy Scouts of America*), a woman attacked by a rapist at her hotel (*McCarty v. Pheasant Run*), and a rescuer being hit in a secondary collision (*McCoy v. American Suzuki Motor Corp.*). This increased frequency of cases involving multiple tortfeasors is partly due to greater complexity in our lives that leave us interacting with greater numbers of people in varying ways and capacities. For example, in the nineteenth century, a vehicular accident was likely to involve two (slow moving) wagons. On today's congested, speedy highways, one gaffe often involves many vehicles and drivers. A driver may have been inattentive to his steering and veered into the path of another car. That other car may not have responded in a timely fashion, causing a collision that spilled over to the next lane where an innocent motorist was hit. The possibilities for multi-tortfeasor scenarios are endless.

Another reason for this phenomenon is tort law's expanding recognition of new duties and even new causes of action previously not known or permitted. For example, while a criminal engaging in an armed assault and robbery is nothing new, tort law recognition of a premises owner's duty to sometimes anticipate and prevent that crime is relatively novel. The result of this expansion is that a victim may have more than one tortfeasor to blame for her harm. Finally, evolving concepts in tort law invite greater potential for holding

CHAPTER GOALS

- ☑ In multiple tortfeasor scenarios, understand why the common law developed the doctrine of joint and several liability to aid the innocent victim in recovering all of her damages. Appreciate the corollary doctrines of contribution and credits for settlement needed to fully apportion fault and to further the one satisfaction principle.
- ☑ Understand why most jurisdictions have gone away from a pure system of joint and several liability. Understand the options of either a pure several liability system or some other mixed or hybrid system for apportioning responsibility in multiple tortfeasor scenarios.
- ☑ Gain deeper understanding of certain complexities that arise when adopting several liability, including how to handle absent or immune actors and whether to adopt the negligent enabling doctrine as an exception to several liability.
- ☑ Learn two other equitable doctrines creating a joint liability: (a) vicarious liability and (b) concert of action.

multiple bad actors accountable. For example, when most courts applied the *direct cause* test for proximate cause, there were fewer instances where courts would find multiple tortfeasors to have each been a direct cause. The evolution of proximate cause to adopt primarily the tests of foreseeability or substantial factor necessarily lends itself to embrace holding several tortfeasors liable for the same harm.

The foregoing examples of multi-tortfeasor scenarios illustrate the concept of *conceptual indivisibility*—that is, there is no way to allocate the one set of harms based upon notions of causation because all of the misconduct was a necessary link in the chain of causation that led to the *one accident* with its one set of losses. By contrast, if one motorist is involved in two different accidents that occur at different times and places and each accident results in separately identifiable damage to the car (e.g. one rear-ender hurts the back bumper and a subsequent accident damages the driver's door), obviously each tortfeasing driver will be separately liable for the divisible harm associated with their misconduct. Nevertheless, when someone is harmed today, there is often increased risk and recognition of the role of multiple wrongdoers being involved in causing a *singular harm* for which the issue of apportionment of liability is raised. In other words, how much responsibility will each tortfeasor bear for the single harm?

We have already seen some of these multiple tortfeasor scenarios. One as-yet unexplored issue that has been lurking in the darkened corners of our prior coverage involves the actual entry of judgment in these multiple tortfeasor scenarios. What if there are multiple defendants found liable to the plaintiff? How much of the plaintiff's actual damages does each defendant have to pay?

Further, if the plaintiff has settled with one tortfeasor but gone to trial and won against another joint tortfeasor, does the plaintiff get to collect more than 100 percent of her damages? If apportionment of responsibility is called for, how should this be conducted and who should be included in the apportionment analysis? To what extent are employers subject to the entry of judgment against them based upon the misconduct of someone under their control? What is the result when tortfeasors are not acting independently but actually working together in bringing about the plaintiff's harm?

These are far from clerical or administrative issues. Rather, answering these remaining questions involves incredible complexity and important policy debates that are not academic. Until they are addressed, a trial court often cannot enter the final judgment needed to finish the process of civil adjudication of a tort claim. And looking even further back, the resolution of these issues impacts the strategy decisions made by a claimant's attorney in determining who to name as a defendant in a lawsuit. Confronting these difficult issues and mastering them are the audacious goals of this chapter.

II JOINT AND SEVERAL LIABILITY

When the plaintiff has proven the elements of her cause of action against more than one tortfeasor, from which tortfeasor does the plaintiff actually recover damages? The common law traditionally sought to help the victim recover as much of her losses as possible by creating the apportionment doctrine known as *joint and several liability*. This doctrine is easily articulated — any tortfeasor found to have been a cause of the plaintiff's harm could be liable to the plaintiff for *all* of the compensable damages. The procedural rules have never required a plaintiff to sue all possible tortfeasors in one action. A plaintiff could, for any reason, decide to file suit against only one or some of the joint tortfeasors that caused the plaintiff's singular harm. Under this doctrine, if one of the tortfeasors has inadequate assets to pay damages, the plaintiff can simply recover the entirety of her judgment for actual damages from another tortfeasor with deeper pockets. It is referred to as "joint and several" because, as a group, the tortfeasors are jointly responsible and liable to the plaintiff and, individually (or severally), any of the tortfeasors can be liable to the plaintiff for the entire amount of damages.

In Practice

The U.S. Supreme Court has held that the procedural joinder rules (i.e. Rules 19 and 20) do *not* require a plaintiff to sue all tortfeasors in order to recover a claim for all her damages:

> A tortfeasor with the usual "joint-and-several" liability is merely a permissive party to an action against another with like liability.
>
> *Temple v. Synthes Corp., Ltd.,* *498 U.S. 5, 7 (1990).*

Two interesting scenarios developed under this doctrine. First, how should the loss be spread as between the tortfeasors? If the plaintiff recovers all of her damages from only one of the joint tortfeasors, what recourse does that defendant have to seek reimbursement (known as *contribution*) from the other joint tortfeasors? Second, what is the effect under joint and several liability when the plaintiff has already reached a pre-trial settlement for a portion of the plaintiff's damages with one of the joint tortfeasors? May the plaintiff still recover 100 percent of her demonstrated losses from any other non-settling tortfeasors? Concern with overcompensating victims led joint and several liability courts to create the concept of a *settlement credit* to avoid such result.

The following case illustrates the common law operation of joint and several liability as well as courts' recognition of the right of contribution and analysis of how such a claim should be valued.

SITZES v. ANCHOR MOTOR FREIGHT, INC.

289 S.E.2d 679 (W. Va. 1982)

MILLER, J.

We have accepted [a] certain certified question from the United States District Court for the Southern District of West Virginia. Generally, we are asked to state what effect our adoption of comparative negligence . . . has upon . . . the rules of contribution among joint tortfeasors.

The facts of the case have been presented to us as follows:

> Plaintiffs in this action, Arnold L. Sitzes and Edward L. Rucks, are administrators of the estate of Patricia Ann Roberson. Mrs. Roberson was killed in an automobile accident on January 19, 1977. At the time, she was a passenger in a pick-up truck driven by her husband, James R. Roberson, which collided with a motor truck driven by Oswald R. Carter, an agent and employee of the defendant Anchor Motor Freight, Inc. Mrs. Roberson is survived by her husband and her son, Joseph Eugene Roberson.
>
> Plaintiffs commenced this action against the defendant on November 23, 1977. With leave of court, defendant filed a third-party complaint for contribution against Mr. Roberson on February 12, 1980. This court, perceiving a potential conflict between West Virginia's normal rules of contribution (which would apportion damages equally among joint tortfeasors) and the state's newly-adopted rule of comparative negligence (which requires a jury to 'assign the proportion or degree of this total negligence among the various parties,' *Bradley v. Appalachian Power*, 163 W. Va. 332, 256 S.E.2d 879, 885 (1979), and which denies recovery to a plaintiff whose negligence equals or exceeds 50% of the combined negligence of the parties to the accident), instructed the jury to assign percentages of fault to the third-party plaintiff and third-party defendant if it found that both had been negligent.

Plaintiffs' defendant was not negligent, and was therefore excluded from the apportioning.

On March 31, 1981, the jury returned a verdict for the plaintiffs and against the defendants and assessed plaintiffs' damages in the amount of $100,000.

On the third-party claim, the jury found both the third-party plaintiff and the third-party defendant negligent, and found that the degree of negligence attributable to Anchor Motor Freight was 70% and the degree attributable to James R. Roberson was 30%.

Thus, in summary, the jury concluded that the accident was caused by the combined negligence of the defendant (70% negligent) and the third-party defendant (30% negligent); that the amount of damages was $100,000.

This jurisdiction is committed to the concept of joint and several liability among tortfeasors. *Tennant v. Craig*, 195 S.E.2d 727 (W. Va. 1973); *Hutcherson v. Slate*, 142 S.E. 444 (W. Va. 1928). A plaintiff may elect to sue any or all of those responsible for his injuries and collect his damages from whomever is able to pay, irrespective of their percentage of fault. Our adoption of a modified rule for contributory negligence in *Bradley* did not change our adherence to joint and several liability:

> Neither our comparative negligence rule nor *Haynes* [*v. City of Nitro*, 240 S.E.2d 544 (W. Va. 1977)] is designed to alter our basic law which provides for joint and several liability among joint tortfeasors after judgment. Most courts which have considered the question after either a statutory or judicial adoption of some form of comparative negligence have held that the plaintiff can sue one or more joint tortfeasors, and if more than one is sued and a joint judgment is obtained, he may collect the entire amount from any one of the defendants.

It is clear from the foregoing quotation that the concept of joint and several liability after judgment relates primarily to the liability of all of the joint tortfeasors to the plaintiff. We decline here, as we did in *Bradley*, to alter our rule permitting joint and several liability as against joint tortfeasors after judgment. This concept of joint and several liability after judgment runs throughout other areas of our judgment law.[9]

In the present case, the trial court permitted the jury to apportion the two joint tortfeasors. The jury concluded that the defendant, Anchor was 70% at fault while the third-party defendant, Mr. Roberson, was found to be 30% at fault.[10] The certified question inherently demands consideration of whether we recognized that primary fault or negligence should be apportioned among joint tortfeasors in accordance with their degrees of fault.

---

9. Here, the plaintiff in the wrongful death action elected to sue only Anchor and it is therefore liable to the plaintiff for the entire $100,000 jury verdict.

10. In our decision in *Haynes v. City of Nitro*, 240 S.E.2d 544 (W. Va. 1977), we held if a plaintiff does not elect to sue all of the joint tortfeasors, those that have been sued may bring in the absent joint tortfeasors in a third-party suit for contribution.

The basic purpose of the joint and several liability rule is to permit the injured plaintiff to select and collect the full amount of his damages against one or more joint tortfeasors. This rule however need not preclude a right of comparative contribution between the joint tortfeasors *inter se.* The purpose of this latter rule is to require the joint tortfeasors to share in contribution based upon the degree of fault that each has contributed to the accident. There is a definite trend in the field of tort law toward allocation of judgmental liability between the joint tortfeasors *inter se.* It is thought to be fairer to require them to respond in damages based on their degrees of fault.

Historically, at common law, there was no right of contribution between joint tortfeasors on the theory that the law should not aid wrongdoers. The historic development of this point is contained in *Northwest Airlines, Inc. v. Transport Workers Union of American, AFL-CIO, et al.*, 451 U.S. 77 (1981), where Justice Stevens states in note 17:

> Thirty-nine States and the District of Columbia recognize to some extent a right to contribution among joint tortfeasors. In 10 jurisdictions, the common-law rule was initially changed by judicial action.

The right of contribution developed because it was thought unfair to have one of several joint tortfeasors pay the entire judgment and not be able to obtain contribution from any of his fellow wrongdoers. It would seem proper social policy that a wrongdoer should not escape his liability on the fortuitous event that another paid the entire joint judgment.

In this State since 1872, by virtue of W. Va. Code, 55-7-13, we have permitted a right of contribution between joint tortfeasors. Thus, our cases . . . have utilized the phrases "joint and several liability" and the "right of contribution" if the judgment debtor pays more than his *pro tanto* share of the liability. The traditional method of assigning *pro tanto* liability was to divide the judgment by the number of debtors who were liable on the judgment.

Once a right of contribution was recognized between joint tortfeasors, courts and commentators began to realize that a more equitable method of handling the right of contribution *inter se* would be to allocate it according to the degrees of fault attributable to each tortfeasor. This concept arose from the fact that in many cases involving joint tortfeasors, the tortfeasors were vastly unequal in their degrees of fault or negligence.

In Practice

The Federal Rules of Civil Procedure still reflect the common law's willingness to let the plaintiff be the master of her own lawsuit:

- *Rule 20*: Permits a plaintiff to add multiple defendants to a case if the claims arise out of one occurrence.
- *Rule 19*: Compels joinder of multiple defendants in some isolated instances but has always been interpreted to *not* require joinder of all joint tortfeasors.
- *Rule 14*: Permits the filing of any derivative claim that a defendant might have against another for contribution or indemnity in the event the defendant is found liable to the plaintiff.

One of the catalysts for adopting a system of comparative contribution was the relaxation of the common law rule that a plaintiff's contributory negligence completely barred his recovery. With the adoption of comparative negligence statutes and case decisions allowing allocation of negligence between plaintiffs and defendants, the allocation of fault among joint tortfeasors seemed the next logical step.

Comparative contribution makes the right of contribution equitable to the degree of fault between each tortfeasor. This is in keeping with the trend toward reducing substantial artificiality or unfairness in tort law. A number of states by statute now base contribution on relative fault.

Over the last twenty years there has been a noticeable trend in our tort decisions to ameliorate the rigidity of many common law rules.

We have attempted not only substantively but procedurally to fashion a more equitable allocation of fault and its attendant liability in our tort law. Our seminal decision of *Haynes v. City of Nitro, supra*, recognized the right of a joint tortfeasor to bring in a fellow joint tortfeasor by way of a third-party complaint under Rule 14 of our Rules of Civil Procedure. The purpose of this rule was to modify the strict common law principle that prevented a right of contribution among joint tortfeasors before judgment. The old common law rule enabled the plaintiff to sue one of several joint tortfeasors and hold him responsible for the entire damage claim, even though other joint tortfeasors had contributed to the damages. Because the defendant had no right prior to *Haynes, supra*, to bring in by way of contribution another joint tortfeasor, he became liable for the entire judgment.

In the present case, the third-party defendant, Roberson, was not a co-defendant. Thus, insofar as the plaintiff is concerned, his entire judgment of $100,000 is collectible only against the defendant, Anchor. On the other hand, in the third-party action filed by Anchor against Roberson, the third-party defendant, was found to be 30% at fault. This means that Anchor is entitled to collect $30,000 from the third-party defendant Roberson.

The certified question having been answered, this case is dismissed from the docket.

NOTES AND PROBLEMS

1. ***Joint and Several Liability.*** While joint and several liability was universally accepted at common law, many courts and legislatures have abandoned it in recent decades either in whole or at times. Some courts continue to retain the doctrine even after a switch to comparative fault. In *Sitzes*, the court declares its continued fealty to the doctrine that seeks to maximize the plaintiff's ability to recover all of her compensable damages. In the next section we will see other courts take a different view.

2. ***One Satisfaction Rule.*** A concern that occurs to many law students first encountering the doctrine of joint and several liability is the possibility of the plaintiff recovering more than 100 percent of its damages. If the plaintiff is permitted to sue one tortfeasor after another in separate actions for the same harm, what prevents a plaintiff from receiving redundant awards of damages and realizing a windfall? The answer is the *one satisfaction rule*, which declares that a plaintiff who has received full satisfaction of a tort judgment for one harm cannot continue to recover against other joint tortfeasors for that same harm:

> It is elementary that one who has been injured by the joint wrong of several parties may recover his damages against either or all; but, although there may be several suits and recoveries, there can be but *one satisfaction*. The reason of the rule is that while there may be many perpetrators of a wrongful act, each of whom is separately liable, yet the act and its consequences are indivisible, and the injured person is, therefore, limited to a single satisfaction.

Bundt v. Embro, 265 N.Y.S.2d 872, 875 (N.Y. Sup. 1965) (emphasis added). If the plaintiff recovers a judgment in the first suit but is unhappy with the jury's finding of damages and the subsequent judgment, plaintiff cannot seek to recover more by filing a second suit against another tortfeasor for the same harm on the hope of convincing a second jury to award greater damages. The one-bite-at-the-apple civil procedure doctrine of *collateral estoppel* will preclude the plaintiff from having this fact issue determined a second time in order to improve the outcome. *See e.g.*, Nielson v. Spanaway General Medical Clinic, Inc., 956 P.2d 312 (Wash. 1998).

3. ***Contribution as a Necessary Byproduct.*** While some courts traditionally refused to permit one tortfeasor to sue another for contribution because of the view that the court should not lend its hand to a wrongdoer, modern courts retaining joint and several liability have come to embrace contribution as an appropriate method to assure that all wrongdoers feel the adverse consequences for causing a harm. Thus, contribution assures that deterrence is provided for all tortfeasors who contributed to causing a singular harm. It is also considered more fair to the defendant who originally paid all of the plaintiff's damages. Most courts, therefore, see contribution as a necessary corollary to the doctrine of joint and several liability. It is available to any defendant who has been forced to pay for *more than its own share* of the harm. It permits an action for partial reimbursement against other joint tortfeasors. The plaintiff in the main suit may have sued these other tortfeasors, but the plaintiff chose to enforce the judgment against another defendant. Or the plaintiff may have never bothered to sue all of the joint tortfeasors. If neither the plaintiff nor the defendant (through a third-party action) has brought the contribution defendant into the original suit, a subsequent suit for contribution will be necessary. In that new lawsuit, the findings of the original jury (including any apportionment findings) will not be binding on the contribution defendant because it has not yet had its

day in court and due process demands a new fact finding. Further, courts have held that the statute of limitations on a contribution claim does not begin to run until after the entry of judgment against the original defendant. *See e.g.*, Cooper v. Philadelphia Dairy Products Co., 112 A.2d 308, 309-10 (N.J. Super. 1955) (the cause of action owned by the victim is distinct from the cause of action for contribution arising out of the duty of the joint tortfeasor to reimburse the original defendant).

Principles

Contribution assures that deterrence is provided for all tortfeasors who contributed to causing a singular harm.

4. *Credits for Settlement.* What if by the time the plaintiff goes to trial against one tortfeasor, the plaintiff has already received partial compensation for the same injuries by virtue of a pretrial settlement with a joint tortfeasor? Most states hold that a claim for contribution is not permitted against the settling party; else, a defendant would never agree to settle in instances where less than all of the tortfeasors have joined into the agreement. Furthermore, allowing the plaintiff to receive partial satisfaction from a settling party and then permitting a full recovery for 100 percent of the plaintiff's harm against the non-settling joint tortfeasor at trial would seem to violate the principles behind the one satisfaction rule. To avoid all of this unfairness, courts instead have held that some type of *credit* is due to the remaining defendant based upon the prior settlement. The credit is calculated either as a dollar-per-dollar set-off against the total award of actual damages or, if there has been some apportionment of responsibility at trial against the settling tortfeasor, sometimes a credit is given based upon the settling party's percentage of responsibility for the harm. Whether to calculate the credit on a dollar-per-dollar basis or by the percentage-of-fault method is either up to the court or is determined by statutory interpretation where the legislature has addressed the issue. This is an important consideration for counsel discussing settlement, as it can affect settlement strategies.

Principles

The doctrine of joint and several liability necessarily requires courts to either permit: (1) a right of contribution against other joint tortfeasors or, (2) when the other tortfeasors have settled with the plaintiff, a credit against the entry of judgment against the non-settling tortfeasor.

III SEVERAL LIABILITY

Most courts (and legislatures) came to view the transition from the all or nothing world of contributory negligence to the modern scheme of comparative fault as a catalyst for reconsidering joint and several liability. At the opposite end of the spectrum was the new doctrine of *several liability,* by which a tortfeasor only is liable for his share of the fault that led to the plaintiff's harm. This doctrine shifts the risk of insolvency from the tortfeasors to the victim. It also has created some of its own interesting dilemmas, including whether and how to apportion fault between a negligent and an intentional tortfeasor as well as the question of how to apportion responsibility in scenarios where some of the tortfeasors are incapable of being sued for legal or practical reasons.

1. Rejection of Joint and Several Liability in Favor of Several Liability

Despite the view of some courts, as illustrated by *Sitzes,* that joint and several liability should be retained, other courts have struggled with the apparent disharmony between a comparative fault system — whereby a negligent plaintiff is permitted to recover a portion of her damages — and the doctrine of joint and several liability. This led some courts to reject joint and several liability and to adopt instead the doctrine of several liability — in which a tortfeasor is only liable for his own percentage of fault. In Chapter 7, Affirmative Defenses, we previously explored a portion of the Tennessee Supreme Court's decision in *McIntyre v. Balentine,* in which that court judicially abandoned contributory negligence in favor of comparative fault. The *Balentine* court believed that the issues of contributory negligence/comparative fault and joint and several liability were necessarily linked; in another portion of its opinion, *Balentine* also abandoned joint and several liability, for the reasons set forth below.

McINTYRE v. BALENTINE

833 S.W.2d 52 (Tenn. 1992)

DROWOTA, J.

[In a personal injury action arising out of collision on Highway 69 in which both the plaintiff and defendant drivers had been consuming alcohol, the plaintiff pulled out in front of the defendant, and the defendant failed to stop or avert the accident. The court rejected the "all or nothing" rule of contributory negligence. In its place, the court adopted the 49 percent modified comparative fault rule.]

We recognize that today's decision affects numerous legal principles surrounding tort litigation. For the most part, harmonizing these principles with comparative fault must await another day. However, we feel compelled to provide some guidance to the trial courts charged with implementing this new system.

First, and most obviously, the new rule makes the doctrine of last clear chance obsolete. [This was discussed in Chapter 7 as a type of common law mitigation doctrine to soften some of the harshness of contributory negligence.] The circumstances formerly taken into account by [that doctrine] will henceforth be addressed when assessing relative degrees of fault.

Second, in cases of multiple tortfeasors, plaintiff will be entitled to recover so long as plaintiff's fault is less than the combined fault of all tortfeasors. [This holding is the same as that of the court in *Beaudoin v. Texaco*, in Chapter 7, rejecting the "Wisconsin rule" in favor of the unit rule in a modified comparative fault system.]

Third, today's holding renders the doctrine of joint and several liability obsolete. Our adoption of comparative fault is due largely to considerations of fairness: the contributory negligence doctrine unjustly allowed the entire loss to be borne by a negligent plaintiff, notwithstanding that the plaintiff's fault was minor in comparison to defendant's. Having thus adopted a rule more closely linking liability and fault, it would be inconsistent to simultaneously retain a rule, joint and several liability, which may fortuitously impose a degree of liability that is out of all proportion to fault.[7]

Further, because a particular defendant will henceforth be liable only for the percentage of a plaintiff's damages occasioned by that defendant's negligence, situations where a defendant has paid more than his "share" of a judgment will no longer arise, and therefore [there will no longer be a general need for any right to contribution].

Fourth, fairness and efficiency require that defendants called upon to answer allegations in negligence be permitted to allege, as an affirmative defense, that a nonparty caused or contributed to the injury or damage for which recovery is sought. In cases where such a defense is raised, the trial court shall instruct the jury to assign this nonparty the percentage of the total negligence for which he is responsible. However, in order for a plaintiff to recover a judgment against such additional person, the plaintiff must have made a timely amendment to his complaint and caused process to be served on such additional person. Thereafter, the additional party will be required to answer the amended complaint. The procedures shall be in accordance with the Tennessee Rules of Civil Procedure.

NOTES AND PROBLEMS

1. ***Rationale for Rejection of Joint and Several Liability.*** Most courts reconsidering the doctrine of joint and several liability after their jurisdiction's

---

7. Numerous other comparative fault jurisdictions have eliminated joint and several liability. *See, e.g.*, Alaska Stat. §09.17.080(d) (Supp. 1991); Colo. Rev. Stat. §13-21-111.5(1) (1987); Kan. Stat. Ann. §60-258a(d) (Supp. 1991); N.M. Stat. Ann. §41-3A-1 (1989); N.D. Cent. Code §32-03.2-02 (Supp. 1991); Utah Code Ann. §78-27-38, -40 (1992); Wyo. Stat. Ann. §1-1-109(d) (1988).

abandonment of contributory negligence have tended to likewise embrace several liability. A primary conceptual reason for this is the perceived inconsistency between rejecting the all or nothing doctrine of contributory negligence and retaining the all-or-nothing apportionment doctrine of joint and several liability. Both comparative fault and several liability illustrate the prevailing modern view that one's rights and responsibilities in a tort suit should reflect the actual extent to which one was at fault and nothing more. Rather than seeing litigants wearing either white or black hats, these cases tend to see the tort world in various shades of gray. Further, many jurisdictions have embraced several liability as a type of tort reform based upon the belief that it is simply unfair to hold a tortfeasor accountable to the plaintiff for all damages, despite being apportioned as little as one percent of the responsibility. Advocates of several liability see it as custom-tailored justice rather than the rough and harsh justice doled out by joint and several liability.

2. ***When the Choice Matters.*** Given the right of contribution available to a tortfeasor under joint and several liability who has paid for more than his own share of the harm, why is the choice between joint and several liability versus several liability so hotly debated? Either way, the plaintiff can receive full compensation and a tortfeasor will ultimately only be out-of-pocket to the extent of his own share of fault. The choice ultimately matters in instances where some of the tortfeasors are either *insolvent* or *not amenable* to a tort suit and entry of judgment. In this scenario, the choice between the two systems reflects a value judgment by the state as to whether the risk of such insolvency should be borne by the victim or by another tortfeasor. Under the common law where the victim was necessarily blameless, the decision to impose this risk upon the tortfeasor seemed obvious. Under modern comparative fault systems, however, the issue is not always quite as clear or compelling. But make no mistake: Whether a jurisdiction retains joint and several liability or adopts several liability in its stead, it is making a values-based decision as to whether to favor the victim or the tortfeasor in allocating the risk of insolvency.

3. ***Several Liability Negates Contribution and Credits for Settlement.*** Because a tortfeasor in a several liability system is only paying for his own share of the harm (a simple calculation of the tortfeasor's percentage of fault multiplied by the actual damages), logically there can be no right of contribution — in such a system a tortfeasor never pays more than his own share. *See e.g.*, Kottler v. Washington, 963 P.2d 834 (Wash. 1998) (no contribution claim against settling defendants who settled their own proportionate shares of liability, absent joint and several liability, remaining defendant would only be paying for his own personal share of liability). Further, it would be illogical to grant a non-settling defendant in a several liability scenario any right to a credit based upon the distinct potential liability of a settling tortfeasor. The liability of each toward the plaintiff is distinct, like a separate debt. *See e.g.*, Neil v. Kavena, 859 P.2d 203 (Ariz. App. 1993) (credit not applicable if settling and non-settling

parties are not jointly and severally liable). Indeed, to reduce one judgment debtor's several liability based upon a credit for another tortfeasor's settlement would only penalize a plaintiff for compromising her claim against the settling tortfeasor. Not only would this be illogical but it would practically render partial settlements extinct. Courts desire to encourage settlements rather than impede them. Thus, it is now clear that both contribution and credits — while an integral aspect of joint and several liability systems — are not recognized when several liability is being imposed against a defendant.

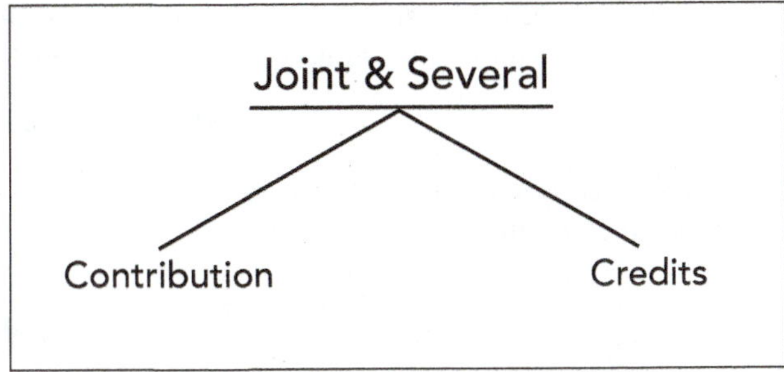

2. *Threshold Level Joint and Several Liability Statutes*

The *Balentine* case involved a judicial decision to abandon the common law rule of joint and several liability. In many states this decision has been made legislatively. As a result of both judicial declaration and legislative enactment, the majority of jurisdictions no longer recognize pure joint and several liability. The majority of jurisdictions have either generally embraced several liability or created a hybrid system as a sort of compromise on the issue. Some statutes create a default rule of several liability but still permit joint and several liability when a particular tortfeasor's level of apportioned fault rises to a specific level. Others will impose several liability except as to certain categories of cases or categories of actual damages, for which joint and several liability will apply. Consider how each of the following statutes creates such a hybrid set of apportionment rules:

New Jersey Stat. §2A:15-53 (2009)

Except as provided in subsection (d) [regarding environmental tort claims], the party so recovering may recover as follows:

(a) The full amount of the damages from any party determined by the trier of fact to be 60% or more responsible for the total damages.

(b) . . .

(c) Only that percentage of the damages directly attributable to that party's negligence or fault from any party determined by the trier of fact to be less than 60% responsible for the total damages.

Texas Civ. Prac. & Rem. Code §33.013 (2003)

(a) Except as provided in Subsection (b), a liable defendant is liable to a claimant only for the percentage of the damages found by the trier of fact equal to that defendant's percentage of responsibility with respect to the personal injury, property damage, death, or other harm for which the damages are allowed.

(b) Notwithstanding Subsection (a), each liable defendant is, in addition to his liability under Subsection (a), jointly and severally liable for the damages recoverable by the claimant under Section 33.012 with respect to a cause of action if:

(1) the percentage of responsibility attributed to the defendant with respect to a cause of action is greater than 50 percent.

Hawaii Rev. Stat. §663-10.9 (1995)

Joint and several liability for joint tortfeasors . . . is abolished except in the following circumstances:

(1) For the recovery of economic damages against joint tortfeasors in actions involving injury or death to persons;

(2) For the recovery of economic and noneconomic damages against joint tortfeasors in actions involving:

a. Intentional torts;

b. Torts relating to environmental pollution;

c. Toxic and asbestos-related torts;

d. Torts relating to aircraft accidents;

e. Strict and products liability torts.

f. Torts relating to motor vehicle accidents . . . ;

(3) For the recovery of noneconomic damages in actions, other than those enumerated in paragraph (2), involving injury or death to persons against those tortfeasors whose individual degree of negligence is found to be twenty-five percent or more. . . .

NOTES AND PROBLEMS

1. ***Problems.*** In each of the following scenarios, analyze whether joint and several liability would exist under each of the three statutes set forth above. How should the trial court enter judgment? Is there any other information the court might require in order to make these decisions?

A. Trespass claim arising out of fire accidentally set by four defendant trespassers on plaintiff's business property late at night. Jury apportions 25 percent fault to each of the four defendants with damages based on diminished market value of property of $100,000.

B. Plaintiff hurt when a screw on a medical implant device comes loose after surgery. Plaintiff sues surgeon and implant manufacturer. Jury finds the defective implant manufacturer to be 50 percent at fault, the doctor 30 percent at fault and plaintiff 20 percent at fault. Plaintiff's special damages are $50,000, and her general damages are $50,000.

C. Plaintiff pedestrian is hit crossing a street with the right of way by two drivers approaching the intersection from opposite directions, each of whom ignored the red light and struck the plaintiff. The jury finds the plaintiff's pain and suffering damages to be $1,000,000 and economic losses to be $250,000. The jury apportions the fault equally between the two drivers.

2. ***Legislative Values.*** As you consider each of the following examples of legislative reform of the common law doctrine of joint and several liability, consider what value statements are reflected by the particular reform. When a state switches generally to several liability, what value is reflected by this decision? With regard to Hawaii's statute, what seems to be the legislature's view of general damages and of intentional tortfeasors? With regard to the threshold levels in the New Jersey and Texas statutes, what seems to be the legislators' view regarding when it is appropriate to hold a tortfeasor liable for all of the plaintiff's harm? Do there appear to be common values reflected by all three statutes or might their provisions simply reflect legislative compromise?

"LADIES AND GENTLEMEN OF THE JURY . . ."

Texas PJC 4.3 Proportionate Responsibility

If you answered "Yes" to Question[s] _______ [applicable liability question(s)] for more than one of those named below, then answer the following question.

Assign percentages of responsibility only to those you found caused or contributed to cause the [occurrence or injury]. The percentages you find must total 100 percent. The percentages must be expressed in whole numbers. The percentage of responsibility attributable to any one is not necessarily measured by the number of acts or omissions found.

3. Apportionment with Absent or Immune Actors

Several important interpretational issues have arisen in several liability jurisdictions. While it is clear that a jury should apportion the fault of any of the tortfeasors that plaintiff might have sued or been able to sue, does it make sense to allow a jury to consider apportioning some of the fault to parties that cannot be sued? This is an important issue because in a several liability jurisdiction, any fault apportioned to an absent or immune party necessarily reduces the liability of a named defendant from whom the plaintiff might actually receive compensation. Further, plaintiff obviously does not receive a judgment against any absent party. And in threshold level joint and several liability jurisdictions, reducing the fault of a named defendant might prevent that tortfeasor from reaching the threshold level of fault necessary to trigger joint and several liability. Often this question is answered by resort to the appropriate statute in the jurisdiction. Below is one court's attempt to divine legislative intent on this matter.

SULLIVAN v. SCOULAR GRAIN CO.

853 P.2d 877 (Utah 1993)

Durah, J.

This case comes to us pursuant to rule 41 of the Utah Rules of Appellate Procedure as a question certified from the United States District Court for the District of Utah. Two issues have been accepted on certification:

> 1. Under the Utah Comparative Fault Act, Utah Code Annot. §78-27-38, et seq., can a jury apportion the fault of the plaintiff's employers that caused or contributed to the accident although said employers are immune from suit under Utah Workers' Compensation Act, Utah Code Ann. §35-1-60, et seq.
> 2. Under the Utah Comparative Fault Act, Utah Code Ann. §78-27-38, et seq., can a jury apportion the fault of an individual or entity that has been dismissed from the litigation but against whom it is claimed that they have caused or contributed to the accident.

We hold that the purpose and intent of the Utah Liability Reform Act require that a jury account for the relative proportion of fault of a plaintiff's employer that may have caused or contributed to an accident, even though the employer is immune from suit. Apportionment of fault does not of itself subject the employer to civil liability. Rather, the apportionment process merely ensures that no defendant is held liable to any claimant for an amount of damages in excess of the percentage of fault attributable to that defendant.

We also hold that an individual or entity dismissed from a case pursuant to an adjudication on the merits of the liability issue may not be included in the apportionment. When a defendant is dismissed due to a determination of lack of fault as a matter of law, the defendant's exclusion from apportionment does not subject the remaining defendants to liability for damages in excess of their proportionate fault.

The following facts are taken from the federal district court's certification order. In October 1986, plaintiff Kenneth Sullivan lost his left arm and left leg in an accident on the railroad tracks at the Freeport Center in Clearfield, Utah. At the time of his injury, Sullivan was assigned to unload grain from rail cars into warehouses. He was employed by Scoular Grain Company, Freeport Center Associates, and Scoular Grain Company of Utah ("the Scoular parties").

Sullivan filed this action against the Scoular parties, Union Pacific Railroad Company, Denver & Rio Grande Western Railroad Company, Oregon Short Line Railroad Company, Utah Power & Light Company, Trackmobile, Inc., and G.W. Van Keppel Company. In 1989, the federal district court found the Scoular parties immune from plaintiff's claim under the exclusive remedy provision of Utah's Workers' Compensation Law and dismissed them from the action. That court also found that defendant Denver & Rio Grande Western Railroad had no legal duty to Sullivan and dismissed it from the lawsuit. The remaining defendants in the case are Utah Power & Light, Trackmobile, G.W. Van Keppel, Union Pacific Railroad, and Oregon Short Line Railroad. A motion to dismiss Utah Power & Light for lack of jurisdiction is pending at this time.

Defendant Trackmobile moved to have the jury apportion and compare the fault of all the originally named defendants, whether dismissed or present at trial. Plaintiff opposed this motion, claiming that only the fault of parties who are defendants at trial may be compared.

The court's principal duty in interpreting statutes is to determine legislative intent, and the best evidence of legislative intent is the plain language of the statute. *Jensen v. Intermountain Health Care, Inc.*, 679 P.2d 903, 906 (Utah 1984).

Plaintiff argues that his former employers must be excluded from the apportionment process because they are not "defendants" under the Liability Reform Act's definition. Section 68-3-11 of the Utah Code states that "words and phrases . . . [which] are defined by statute, are to be construed according to such peculiar and appropriate meaning or definition." Under section 78-27-39 of the Liability Reform Act, a jury may be instructed "to find separate special verdicts determining the total amount of damages sustained and the percentage or proportion of fault attributable to each person seeking recovery and to each defendant." Section 78-27-37(1) defines "defendant" as "any person *not immune from suit* who is claimed to be liable because of fault to any person seeking recovery." (Emphasis added.) Therefore, plaintiff argues, because the district court found the Scoular parties to be "immune from suit" under the exclusive remedy provision of Utah Workers' Compensation Act, Utah Code Ann. §35-1-60, they are not defendants and are excluded from apportionment under the plain language of the Act.

Excluding plaintiff's employers from the apportionment process, however, would directly conflict with the language of other sections of the Act which require that no defendant be held liable for damages in excess of its proportion of fault. The relevant portions of sections 78-27-38 and -40 read as follows:

> 78-27-38. Comparative negligence. The fault of a person seeking recovery shall not alone bar recovery by that person. He may recover from any defendant or group of defendants whose fault exceeds his own. However, *no defendant is liable to any person seeking recovery for any amount in excess of the proportion of fault attributable to that defendant.*
>
> 78-27-40. Amount of liability limited to proportion of fault–No contribution. Subject to Section 78-27-38, *the maximum amount for which a defendant may be liable to any person seeking recovery is that percentage or proportion of the damages equivalent to the percentage or proportion of fault attributed to that defendant.* No defendant is entitled to contribution from any other person. (Emphasis added.)

If the Scoular parties, who allegedly contributed to the accident, are not included on the special verdict form, the remaining defendants will be potentially liable to plaintiff for an amount in excess of their proportion of fault. For example, if the Scoular parties were 90% at fault and the defendants remaining in the action were 10% at fault, the remaining defendants would be apportioned 100% of any damages awarded even though they were only 10% at fault. Such a result would violate the plain language of sections 78-27-38 and -40.

Thus, we are faced with two arguably contradictory statutes within the same article. Section 78-27-37 defines "defendant" in a way that appears to preclude the inclusion of an employer from apportionment. But excluding employers from apportionment would violate the mandate of section 78-27-40 that no defendant be held liable for damages greater than its proportion of fault. This conflict creates an ambiguity that requires the court to make a policy inference as to the overall purpose and intent of the Act.

"When interpreting an ambiguous statute, we first try to discover the underlying intent of the legislature, guided by the purpose of the statute as a whole and the legislative history." *Hansen v. Salt Lake County*, 794 P.2d 838, 841 (Utah 1990) (citations omitted). We then try to harmonize ambiguous provisions accordingly. *Clover v. Snowbird Ski Resort*, 808 P.2d 1037, 1045 (Utah 1991).

In the 1986 session of the Utah Legislature, Substitute Senate Bill No. 64 proposed that a jury may determine the "total amount of damages sustained and a percentage or proportion of fault attributable to each person seeking recovery, to each defendant, *and to each other person whose fault contributed to the injury or damages.*" (Emphasis added.) Before being enacted, the bill was amended by deleting the part underlined above and inserting the word "and" before "to each defendant." The result is codified at Utah Code Ann. §78-27-39:

> The trial court may, and when requested by any party shall, direct the jury, if any, to find separate special verdicts determining the total amount of damages sustained and the percentage or proportion of fault attributable to each person seeking recovery and to each defendant.

Sullivan argues that this amendment shows that the legislature did not intend to include nonparties in the apportionment process.

Trackmobile counters that the *reason* for the amendment is not clear and argues that, by contrast, the intent of the comparative negligence statute to limit a defendant's liability to his or her proportion of fault *is* clear. That purpose is to ensure that "no defendant is liable to any person seeking recovery for any amount in excess of the proportion of fault attributable to that defendant." Utah Code Ann. §78-27-38.

"The primary rule of statutory interpretation is to give effect to the intent of the legislature in light of the purpose the statute was meant to achieve." *Reeves v. Gentile*, 813 P.2d 111, 115 (Utah 1991). Thus, failing to include immune employers in the apportionment violates the main purpose of the Act by improperly subjecting the remaining defendants to liability in excess of their proportion of fault.

Other portions of the Act's history support this conclusion. First, during a floor debate prior to the adoption of the bill, one senator observed that "it is the basic fairness concept we're driving at. The defendant ought to be on the hook only for its own percentage of damages, but ought not be the guarantor for everyone else's damages." Floor Debate, Utah Senate, 46th Leg. 1986, General Sess., Senate Day 31, Records No. 63 (Feb. 12, 1986). Second, each preliminary draft of Senate Bill 64 states in the title that the purpose of the Act was, among other things, "abolishing joint and several liability." If the jury is prevented in this case from considering the relative fault of the Scoular parties in the apportionment process, Trackmobile and the other defendants will be held liable in the event of a verdict for plaintiff, not only for their own proportionate share of fault, but also for the proportionate share of fault attributable to the Scoular parties. Thus, one of the major evils of joint and several liability would result, and the stated purpose of the legislature in abolishing it would be frustrated.

Any judicial or legislative decision concerning tort liability requires a balancing of competing interests and a policy decision as to which party should bear the risks of an immune or insolvent tort-feasor. Prior to 1986, under joint and several liability, a tortfeasor bore the risk of paying not only his or her share of the plaintiff's damages, but also the shares of other tortfeasors who were impecunious or immune from suit. The 1986 Utah Liability Reform Act shifted the risks caused by impecunious or immune tort-feasors to the plaintiffs by abolishing joint and several liability and contribution among tortfeasors.

Principles

The wisdom of joint and several liability versus some modern adoption of several liability is still hotly debated by scholars, such as in the following critique of the several liability experiment:

> I contend that the legislative attempts to abolish joint and several liability have perpetuated and worsened the problem of unfair and inaccurate damage assessments that the legislation was intended to remedy. Both "pure" and modified proportional fault allocation systems intended to replace joint and several liability have created complex and daunting obstacles for courts and litigants . . . [including] phantom party problems.

Nancy C. Marcus, Phantom Parties and Other Practical Problems with the Attempted Abolition of Joint and Several Liability, 60 Ark. L. Rev. 437, 442-43 (2007).

Plaintiff correctly asserts that if his employer's actions are included in apportionment, his recovery may be significantly reduced. Plaintiff's recovery from nonemployer defendants would be reduced directly in proportion to the percentage of fault, if any, the jury attributes to the employer.

On the other hand, in Trackmobile's view, fairness to the defendants requires that each defendant pay only its proportionate share of the plaintiff's damages. If the Scoular parties are not included in apportionment, Trackmobile and the other defendants would be liable for damages in excess of their proportion of fault. "There is nothing inherently fair about a defendant who is [for example] 10% at fault paying 100% of the loss. . . ." *Brown v. Keill,* 224 Kan. 195, 580 P.2d 867, 874 (Kan. 1978).

General comparative negligence theory also supports the inclusion of non-party employers in apportionment. For example, according to Heft and Heft:

> It is accepted practice to include all tortfeasors in the apportionment question. This includes nonparties who may be unknown tortfeasors, phantom drivers, and persons alleged to be negligent but not liable in damages to the injured party such as in the third party cases arising in the workmen's compensation area. . . .
>
> The reason for such rules is that true apportionment cannot be achieved unless that apportionment includes all tortfeasors guilty of causal negligence either causing or contributing to the occurrence in question, whether or not they are parties to the case.

Carroll R. Heft & C. James Heft, *Comparative Negligence Manual,* §8.100, at 14 (John J. Palmer & Stephen M. Flanagan eds., rev. ed. 1992) (footnote omitted). Thus, it is accepted practice for the jury to apportion the comparative fault of all tortfeasors when comparative negligence is at issue.

Based on the foregoing analysis, our answers to the questions certified from the federal court are as follows:

> 1. A jury may apportion the fault of employers under Utah Code Ann. §78-27-38 to -43 notwithstanding their immunity under Utah Code Ann. §35-1-60.
> 2. A jury may not apportion the fault of a party that has been dismissed from the lawsuit pursuant to an adjudication on the merits of the liability issue.

DISSENT

STEWART, Justice (Dissenting)

The majority opinion holds that an immune non-defendant should be included in the apportionment of fault to defendants under the Liability Reform Act. I submit that the majority, in direct defiance of the specific language of the Act and its legislative history, completely reverses the intended effect of the Act as to how fault should be apportioned when one of the parties whose negligence contributed to the plaintiff's injuries is immune from liability.

The majority rejects clear and consistent statutory language and its compelling legislative history with the extraordinary argument that "failing to include immune employers in the apportionment violates the main purpose of the Act by improperly subjecting the remaining defendants to liability in excess of their proportion of fault." I see nothing improper in the legislative scheme. The fact is that it is for the Legislature — not this Court — to decide how to deal with the fault of an immune party in a multi-defendant comparative negligence case.

While it is true that the Act abolishes joint and several liability, that was not its sole purpose. The Act also provides the manner in which fault should be allocated in comparative negligence cases and how the universe of actionable fault should be apportioned when one party is immune.

The damage the majority does to the legislative scheme and to a plaintiff's rights is exacerbated by the provision in the Workers' Compensation Act that gives an employer (whose fault may have contributed to a plaintiff's injuries) a lien against the plaintiff's damage recovery for benefits paid out of workers' compensation. Thus, not only is the plaintiff made responsible for the employer's proportionate share of fault, but he must also reimburse his employer out of his diminished recovery for any workers' compensation benefits received. This is not only unjust and inequitable, but might well be unconstitutional.

PROBLEM

1. ***Statutory Interpretation.*** The Utah court agrees with the proposition that it should interpret the relevant statute according to its plain meaning. The court then declares two statutory provisions to be in conflict and resorts to considering legislative goals and policies. As a result, it concludes that excluding an immune and absent tortfeasor from the apportionment would result in the named defendant being held liable for more than its share of the fault. Do you see any flaws with this analysis? As the dissent alludes to, the legislature seems to be addressing two separate questions. First, *how* should the apportionment of fault be handled — by including all who may have been at fault, even if they cannot be sued? Second, once the jury answers the apportionment question, *what are the effects* of that finding? By switching to several liability, which of the two questions was the legislature actually addressing? Was there a separate statute that addressed the first question? What did it say? Nevertheless, the Utah court adopts a policy for a several liability jurisdiction that most other several liability statutes also adopt after tort reform — that even where the plaintiff is legally precluded from suing someone (due to immunity) or is practically unable to sue (due to being unknown or having unknown whereabouts), statutes today are often interpreted to permit the jury to consider the fault of such absent or immune actors, in addition to the named parties. Can you explain why this issue does not really matter to a plaintiff in a joint and several liability jurisdiction?

4. Negligent Enabling

While the concept and application of several liability would appear to be fairly straightforward — a tortfeasor should only be liable according to his own percentage of apportioned fault — many courts have found some equitable exceptions to this rule. One such scenario involves the concept of negligent enabling, where one defendant's duty of care is to prevent another from committing a subsequent tort. For example, under the *Tarasoff* rule (covered in Chapter 6, Special Duty Rules), a medical doctor sometimes owes an obligation to prevent her patient from intentionally causing harm to third parties. Or consider the burglar alarm company who installs an alarm for the purpose of helping to prevent a burglary (the Chapter 5 *Emmittee* case). If the doctor or alarm company breaches their duty, should the jury be permitted to apportion the fault between the negligent actor and the intentional tortfeasor who was more directly responsible for the plaintiff's harm? This concept of negligent enabling is not limited to scenarios involving subsequent intentional tortfeasing. For example, how should apportionment in a several liability jurisdiction work when a car's owner hands the keys over to an obviously intoxicated friend who carelessly injures a pedestrian? Consider the arguments for and against apportioning fault in a case of negligent enabling.

TURNER v. JORDAN, M.D.

957 S.W.2d 815 (Tenn. 1997)

ANDERSON, C.J.

We granted this [to decide] whether the patient's intentional conduct should be considered in determining comparative fault under *McIntyre v. Balentine*, 833 S.W.2d 52 (Tenn. 1992).

The trial court determined that the psychiatrist in this case owed a duty of care to the nurse, and instructed the jury to consider the intentional conduct of the patient, a non-party, in determining the psychiatrist's comparative fault. The jury returned a verdict for the nurse in the amount of $1,186,000. It allocated the fault as 100 percent to the psychiatrist and zero percent to the patient. The trial court approved the jury's verdict except as to the allocation of fault, and granted a new trial. The Court of Appeals affirmed, finding that a duty was owed, that the patient's intentional conduct should be compared with the psychiatrist's negligence, and that a new trial should have been granted.

We agree that the psychiatrist owed a duty of care because he knew or should have known that his patient posed an unreasonable risk of harm to a foreseeable, readily identifiable third party. We have also determined that the trial court erred in instructing the jury to compare the patient's intentional conduct with the defendant's negligence in allocating fault. We, however, consider the error harmless because the jury allocated 100 percent of the fault to the negligent defendant psychiatrist.

In March of 1993, the plaintiff, Emma Turner, a nurse at Hubbard Hospital in Nashville, was attacked and severely beaten by Tarry Williams, a psychiatric in-patient at the hospital. The defendant, Harold Jordan, M.D., was the attending psychiatrist.

Williams, who had been diagnosed as bipolar and manic, had been a patient at Hubbard on five prior occasions; three of these times he was found to be a danger to himself or others and was committed to the Middle Tennessee Mental Health Institute. On one occasion, in April of 1990, Williams tried to attack Dr. Jordan with a table leg, but hospital staff intervened.

On March 4, 1993, Williams was again admitted to Hubbard's psychiatric ward and examined by a resident physician. Williams's history indicated that he had not taken his prescribed lithium, which was used to control his bipolar disorder, for over a week. Williams also reported that he had met with "Gorbachev and Saddam Hussein" and that he had "classified information" about space flights and nuclear science. The resident physician determined that Williams had illogical and disorganized thinking, flight of ideas, grandiosity, and delusional thinking. Lithium was prescribed, which takes five to seven days to reach a therapeutic level.

The next day, on March 5, 1993, Dr. Jordan reviewed and approved the resident physician's orders. He and members of a treatment team then attempted to interview Williams, who refused to cooperate and left the interview. The treatment team then discussed the case for thirty to forty-five minutes, after which Dr. Jordan wrote:

> This patient presents no behavior or clinical evidence suggesting that he is suicidal. He is *aggressive, grandiose, intimidating, combative, and dangerous.* We will discharge him soon by allowing him to sign out AMA [Against Medical Advice].

(Emphasis added.) That evening, according to notes, Williams, although quiet and non-disruptive, had an "angry and hostile" affect. Around 11:30 p.m., after requesting a cigarette and asking the nurse, Emma Turner, about being discharged, Williams attacked Turner, inflicting severe head injuries.

Thereafter, Emma Turner sued Dr. Jordan for medical negligence, alleging he violated his duty to use reasonable care in the treatment of his patient, which proximately caused her injuries and damages. At trial, Dr. David Sternberg, a psychiatric expert witness, testified that Jordan's failure to medicate, restrain, seclude or transfer Williams fell below the standard of care for psychiatrists.

After the completion of the proof, the trial court instructed the jury on the law of comparative fault, and it provided the jury with a verdict form indicating it could allocate the fault, if any, between the alleged negligence of Dr. Jordan and the alleged intentional conduct of patient Williams.[2] The jury returned a

2. Prior to trial, the trial court had overruled the plaintiff's motion in limine asking that the negligent conduct of the defendant not be compared with the intentional act of Williams. At trial there was no allegation or proof that the plaintiff herself was negligent in any way.

verdict for the plaintiffs, Emma and Rufus Turner, allocating 100 percent of the fault to defendant Jordan. The trial court approved all of the jury's verdict except the allocation of fault. As a result, it granted the defendant's motion for new trial, but thereafter granted an interlocutory appeal. The Court of Appeals affirmed.

We granted the appeal to consider [among other things, the] comparison of fault between a negligent actor and an intentional actor.

[The court reaffirmed the legal duty in Tennessee, based upon the doctor's special relationship with a known dangerous patient to warn others foreseeably endangered by the patient, citing Bradshaw v. Daniel, 854 S.W.2d 865, 869 (Tenn. 1993) covered in Chapter 6, Special Duty Rules.]

Having determined that a duty of care exists in this case, we now turn to the issue of whether the defendant psychiatrist's negligence should have been compared with the intentional act of the non-party patient Williams in determining the extent of the defendant's liability to the plaintiffs.

The plaintiffs' argument is twofold: a psychiatrist's liability should not be reduced by the occurrence of a foreseeable act he had the duty to prevent; and as a matter of practice and policy, the negligent act of a tortfeasor should not be compared to the intentional act of another tortfeasor. The defendant maintains that comparison is proper because it limits his liability to his percentage of fault in causing harm to the plaintiff.

In *McIntyre v. Balentine*, we adopted a modified form of comparative fault under which a plaintiff whose negligence is less than that of a defendant may recover damages in an amount reduced in proportion to the percentage of the plaintiff's own negligence. Based on notions of fairness and justice, we abolished the outdated doctrine of contributory negligence and yet stressed that "a particular defendant [is] liable only for the percentage of a plaintiff's damages occasioned by that defendant's negligence." *McIntyre*, 833 S.W.2d at 58. Moreover, to provide guidance in future cases, we said that a defendant is permitted to show that a non-party caused or contributed to the damages for which the plaintiff seeks recovery.

Accordingly, in determining comparative fault, we have considered cases in which the negligence of a tortfeasor was compared with the negligence of other tortfeasors. *Volz v. Ledes*, 895 S.W.2d 677 (Tenn. 1995); *Bervoets v. Harde Ralls Pontiac-Olds, Inc.*, 891 S.W.2d 905 (Tenn. 1994). We have also considered the question of comparing the negligence of a defendant with the strict liability of third-party defendants. *Owens v. Truckstops of America*, 915 S.W.2d at 431-33. This case presents our first opportunity to determine whether the negligent act of a defendant should be compared with the intentional act of another in determining comparative fault.

Other jurisdictions have addressed the issue. In *Veazey v. Elmwood Plantation Assoc., Ltd.*, 650 So. 2d 712 (La. 1994), the plaintiff was sexually assaulted by an intruder and filed a negligence action against her apartment complex for failing to maintain adequate security; the defendant apartment complex, in turn, defended on the basis of the intentional act by the assailant. The Louisiana

Supreme Court declined to compare the negligent act of the defendant with the intentional act of the third party primarily because it believed the negligent defendant should not be allowed to reduce its fault by relying on an intentional act it had the duty to prevent. It also expressed several public policy concerns that supported its conclusion: that comparison would reduce the plaintiff's recovery because juries will likely allocate most if not all fault to the intentional actor; that allocating fault to the intentional party may reduce the incentive for the negligent actor to act with due care; and that comparison is impractical because intentional and negligent torts are different "not only in degree but in kind, and the social condemnation attached to it." *Id.* at 719, quoting, Prosser §65 at 462.

In another sexual assault case, *Kansas State Bank & Trust Co. v. Specialized Transportation Services, Inc.*, 249 Kan. 348, 819 P.2d 587 (Kan. 1991), the parents of a child who was sexually assaulted by a school bus driver filed a negligence suit against the school and the bus company. The Kansas Supreme Court held that a negligent defendant should not be permitted to reduce its liability by intentional acts they had a duty to prevent.

The Kansas Supreme Court followed its holding in *Gould v. Taco Bell*, 722 P.2d 511 (Kan. 1986), in which it said the question of comparing negligent and intentional acts depends on "the nature of the duty owed in each instance." In *Gould*, an assailant physically and verbally abused the plaintiff in a restaurant in full view of the restaurant's managers. The court held that the restaurant's negligent failure to maintain security under the facts of the case should not have been compared with the intentional conduct of the assailant.

A similar approach was suggested by the New Jersey Supreme Court in *Blazovic v. Andrich*, 590 A.2d 222 (N.J. 1991). There the jury was permitted to compare the negligence of a restaurant owner in failing to maintain adequate lighting and security in the parking lot with the intentional act of a patron who attacked the plaintiff. While the court upheld the comparison, it recognized that apportionment of fault between tortfeasors may be precluded "when the duty of one encompassed the obligation to prevent the specific misconduct of the other." It distinguished the facts before it on the basis that "the events that allegedly took place in the parking lot neither were sufficiently foreseeable nor bore an adequate causal relationship to [the negligent defendant's] alleged fault to justify the imposition on [the defendant] of the entire responsibility for the resultant injury." 590 A.2d at 233; *compare Gould*, 722 P.2d at 511-13.

Other courts take a different view. In *Reichert v. Atler*, 117 N.M. 623, 875 P.2d 379 (N.M. 1992), a bar patron was killed when assaulted by another customer. The bar owners were sued for failing to provide adequate security, and the bar owners relied on the intentional act of the third party to reduce their liability. The court held that the bar owner may reduce his liability by the percentage of fault attributable to a third party. They reasoned that this principle was most consistent with the rejection of joint and several liability in comparative fault cases and that each individual tortfeasor should be held responsible only for his or her percentage of fault. 875 P.2d at 381. *See also Barth v. Coleman*, 878 P.2d 319 (N.M. 1994) (following Reichert).

Likewise, in *Weidenfeller v. Star & Garter*, 2 Cal. Rptr. 2d 14 (Cal. App. 4 Dist. 1991), an assault victim sued a bar owner for failing to have adequate lighting and security. The jury allocated 75 percent of the fault to the assailant. On appeal, the court said that the argument that negligent acts should not be compared with intentional acts "violated the common sense notion that a more culpable party should bear the financial burden caused by its intentional act."

Accordingly, the concern in cases that compare the negligence of a defendant with the intentional act of a third party is not burdening the negligent tortfeasor with liability in excess of his or her fault; conversely, the primary concern in those cases that do not compare is that the plaintiff not be penalized by allowing the negligent party to use the intentional act it had a duty to prevent to reduce its liability.

In our view, the conduct of a negligent defendant should not be compared with the intentional conduct of another in determining comparative fault where the intentional conduct is the foreseeable risk created by the negligent tortfeasor. As other courts have recognized, comparison presents practical difficulties in allocating fault between negligent and intentional acts, because negligent and intentional torts are different in degree, in kind, and in society's view of the relative culpability of each act. Such comparison also reduces the negligent person's incentive to comply with the applicable duty of care. Moreover, while a negligent defendant may, of course, raise a third party's intentional act to refute elements of the plaintiff's negligence claim such as duty and causation, fairness dictates that it should not be permitted to rely upon the foreseeable harm it had a duty to prevent so as to reduce its liability.

Principles

Negligent enabling is when one breaches the duty specifically of preventing the subsequent tort from occurring.

Our holding also comports with the principles underlying *McIntyre.* The plaintiff here was not negligent. On the other hand, the defendant was negligent, and his breach of care led to the plaintiff's injuries. Thus, the defendant's liability to the plaintiff is linked to his degree of fault as required by *McIntyre*, and he should not be permitted to reduce his liability by relying on the occurrence of the foreseeable risk of harm he had a duty to prevent. As one commentator has written: "the *McIntrye* principle of holding the tortfeasor liable for only his own percentage of fault is not abrogated by nonapportionment when the nature of the tortfeasor's breach is that he created the risk of the second tortfeasor's [intentional] act." Entman, *The Nonparty Tortfeasor*, 23 Mem. St. U. L. Rev. 105, 107 (1992).[9]

9. We do not reach the issues of whether, and under what circumstances, a negligent defendant may be entitled to contribution or indemnity from the intentional actor. *See* Restatement of Restitution, §§94 and 97.

Accordingly, we conclude that the lower courts incorrectly determined that the negligence of the defendant should have been compared with the intentional act of the defendant's patient. In this case, however, the error was harmless in that the jury apportioned 100 percent of the fault to the defendant. Thus, we remand the case to the trial court for entry of a judgment consistent with the jury's verdict.

NOTES AND PROBLEMS

1. ***Practical and Conceptual Issues.*** Do you see why the difficult apportionment issue addressed in *Turner* does not arise in the context of joint and several liability? In instances where joint and several liability applies, there is no need to apportion between tortfeasors (unless to determine the amount of a possible contribution claim between them) because each tortfeasor is already liable to the plaintiff for the entire harm. In several liability jurisdictions, of course, any percentage apportioned to the intentional tortfeasor will directly reduce the liability of the negligent tortfeasor. Some courts conclude that this is acceptable, premised upon their belief that this was the desired outcome when rejecting joint and several liability. However, the majority of several liability courts (like the above opinion in *Turner*) in addressing the issue of negligent enabling — where the duty of the negligent party was specifically to prevent the subsequent tort — conclude otherwise; these courts believe that it makes no sense to create a duty only to lessen liability upon its breach. This is practical policymaking. Often the intentional tortfeasor is judgment proof or cannot be found. Reducing the liability of the negligent enabler results in the plaintiff receiving only fractional compensation. Beyond this, the majority of courts also stress the conceptual difficulty of asking a jury to apportion between fundamentally different types of fault — between those who accidentally injure another and those who strive to do so. At least one court has suggested a creative way to both honor the explicit language of its several liability statute and avoid the unsavory result of denying full compensation to the plaintiff. In Bedford v. Moore, 166 S.W.3d 454 (Tex. App. — Fort Worth, 2005), the court held the jury should first apportion between both the negligent enabler and the subsequent tortfeasor, but that the negligent actor should be liable for both percentages of fault as a joint liability. And if this combined percentage exceeds a jurisdiction's threshold level for imposing joint and several liability, then the negligent enabler would face joint and several liability. Whether the direct tortfeasor would also face several or joint and several liability would depend upon how much fault was apportioned to that tortfeasor.

2. ***Right of Contribution or Indemnity.*** Near the end of the opinion above, the court in footnote nine observed that it had no need to decide whether there should be contribution or indemnity rights by the negligent enabler against the

intentional tortfeasor. Most courts in this scenario believe that a right to *indemnity should exist* because the negligent enabler is being held jointly liable for both its percentage of fault and that of the intentional tortfeasor. Further, to deny such a right would be to allow the intentional tortfeasor to escape liability altogether in favor of imposing the full loss at the feet of the actor less culpable. *See e.g.*, Degener v. Hall Contracting Corp., 27 S.W.3d 775 (Ky. 2000) (while negligent enablers were liable for the fault of the subsequent intentional tortfeasors, they were entitled to a common law indemnity action for the fault attributable to the intentional tortfeasors).

3. ***Problems.*** Under the holding of *Turner*, would a court likely find the initial negligent actor responsible for all of the victim's harm in each of the following scenarios?

A. A security company is hired by a nightclub to prevent anyone from entering the club with a weapon. A company employee assigned to the front door one evening fails to check a patron for a weapon. That patron gets angry later in the evening while at the club and shoots another customer.
B. A car owner gives her car keys to an obviously intoxicated driver who takes the car and hurts another person while driving carelessly.
C. An electrical company secures a contract with the city to install streetlights on a busy road in town. The company fails to install the poles properly, making them less secure. A driver fails to control his car and hits the pole causing it to fall over (due to its improper installation) and crush a nearby pedestrian.

Upon Further Review

At common law, plaintiff's award of damages in multiple tortfeasor cases was always based upon joint and several liability — this facilitated easier recovery of all damages by the innocent plaintiff. The adoption of comparative fault has caused most states to modify their rules so that several liability predominates. Notwithstanding this shift, no state has completely abandoned joint and several liability in all instances. Regardless of one's position on the debate between these two systems of apportioning liability, the switch to several liability has created certain interpretational dilemmas that were not a concern at common law, including apportionment in cases of absent or immune tortfeasors, comparisons between negligent and intentional tortfeasors, and what to do with a negligent actor whose fault has permitted a subsequent actor's tort to occur. How a state answers these questions involves important public policy debates and, on a very practical level, impacts a plaintiff's decision as to who to sue and which theories to adopt in presenting a tort claim.

EQUITABLE DOCTRINES CREATING JOINT LIABILITY

A. Introduction

In addition to the negligent enabling scenario discussed in the previous section, there are a few other instances where courts have crafted other doctrines that result in one being liable not just for his own fault but also for the fault of another. *Vicarious liability* is a doctrine that imposes liability upon one, however innocent, based solely upon that party's relationship with the actual tortfeasor. When applicable, both the tortfeasor and the vicariously liable defendant share a joint liability. The *concert of action* doctrine creates a joint liability for those actors who are found to be involved in the tortious misconduct that has harmed the plaintiff, either by virtue of a common scheme or some acts of encouragement. While applying in very different contexts and supported by different principles, in application these two doctrines operate in a similar fashion — by creating a joint liability not only on the part of the primary tortfeasor, but also with those connected with the tortfeasor either by their relationship or by their incriminating conduct. Both doctrines have the effect of providing additional defendants against whom a victim might be able to recover. In this way, the doctrines further the tort purpose of providing compensation to tort victims.

B. Vicarious Liability

An important doctrine that can impact the court's entry of a final judgment for damages is the common law doctrine of *vicarious liability* or *respondeat superior*. The term "vicarious" refers generally to the related concepts of standing in place for another or to a type of shared experience. Both of these non-legal meanings are appropriate for the tort doctrine of vicarious liability because this doctrine involves one being held lawfully responsible for the tortious harm inflicted by another. Vicarious liability is, at its core, *guilt by association* with a tortfeasor. It is manifest in various forms, including the liability of one business partner for the torts of another, the liability of any member of a "joint enterprise" for the tort of another member, the liability of one family member for the tort of another conducted in pursuing the family affairs, and the liability (under some state statutes) of the owner of a vehicle loaned to a tortfeasor who causes an accident. But the most prevalent application of vicarious liability is in the master-servant (nowadays the

Respondeat Superior

Latin term that literally means "let the master pay." This term is a synonym for vicarious liability.

employer-employee) context. The following case introduces vicarious liability in a case where the plaintiff seeks to impose liability on the defendant employer in two ways, one involving a direct liability claim and the other for vicarious liability.

TRAHAN-LAROCHE v. LOCKHEED SANDERS, INC.

657 A.2d 417 (N.H. 1995)

Horton, J.

The plaintiffs, Rita Trahan-Laroche and Lucien Laroche, appeal a decision of the Superior Court granting the motion of the defendant, Lockheed Sanders, Inc., [to dismiss] on their respondeat superior and negligent supervision claims. We reverse and remand.

On October 24, 1990, a flatbed trailer separated from the pickup truck towing it and collided with the plaintiffs' vehicle. Patrick J. Maimone, employed by the defendant as a maintenance mechanic, was the driver as well as the owner of both the truck and the trailer. One of his tasks was to hay the fields at the defendant's facilities in Hudson and Litchfield. Maimone provided most of the haying equipment, most of which he towed to the defendant's premises with his truck and trailer. The defendant did not compensate Maimone for the use of the equipment or the time spent transporting it, but did pay him his normal wages while haying the fields and permitted him to keep any hay he removed. Prior to the day of the accident, Maimone had completed haying the fields at the defendant's Litchfield facility, but had not removed his trailer or all of the farming equipment. After work on October 24, 1990, but before leaving the defendant's premises, Maimone hitched his trailer to his truck for use in transporting hay from his farm to the Agway store to sell that evening. He planned to return the trailer to remove the remaining farm machinery. The trailer separated from the truck during the drive from the defendant's Litchfield facility to Maimone's farm.

The plaintiffs sued the defendant under theories of respondeat superior and negligent supervision. They argued that Maimone was acting within the scope of his employment at the time of the accident. Alternatively, they argued that while on the defendant's property and under the defendant's supervision and control, Maimone negligently attached his trailer and used inadequate safety chains in violation of the common law. The defendants moved for summary judgment, arguing that no disputed issues of material fact existed and that the plaintiffs failed to state a claim upon which relief may be granted because Maimone was not acting within the scope of his employment.

The trial court ruled as a matter of law that Maimone acted outside the scope of his employment. Treating the defendant's motion as a motion to dismiss, the court concluded that "even taking the facts and reasonable inferences drawn therefrom in the light most favorable to them, the plaintiffs have failed to state a claim that would permit them to recover."

Under the doctrine of respondeat superior, an employer may be held vicariously responsible for the tortious acts of an employee committed incidental to or during the scope of employment. Here, the plaintiff has alleged that the movement of Maimone's trailer for temporary personal use was understood to be part of the agreement between Maimone and the defendant regarding Maimone's provision of the farming equipment and removal of the hay, and therefore incidental to Maimone's employment. This allegation could lead to a finding that would support recovery based on the doctrine of respondeat superior if found to be true by a jury.

An employer may be directly liable for damages resulting from the negligent supervision of its employee's activities. Restatement (Second) of Agency §213 (1958). The employer's duty to exercise reasonable care to control its employee may extend to activities performed outside the scope of employment. Restatement (Second) of Torts §317 (1965). The plaintiffs alleged that although Maimone was involved in several accidents involving vehicles and equipment while in the defendant's employ, his activities were not closely supervised, and his equipment and vehicles were not regularly inspected. This allegation and the reasonable inferences therefrom raise a jury issue as to whether the defendant negligently supervised Maimone. We therefore hold that it was error to dismiss the plaintiffs' claims.

In Practice

The vicarious liability doctrine exists to provide a deep pocket to enhance the plaintiff's ability to collect on a tort judgment. It does not relieve the servant of any liability toward the plaintiff but rather provides an *additional* defendant against whom the plaintiff can secure and collect upon a tort judgment.

A review of the record, including the depositions, reveals evidence from which conflicting inferences could be drawn both as to whether Maimone was acting incidental to or within the scope of his employment when he moved his trailer for temporary personal use and whether the defendant was independently negligent in supervising Maimone and in inspecting his truck and his trailer. We conclude that [defendant is not] entitled to judgment as a matter of law on either the plaintiff's respondeat superior or negligent supervision claims.

NOTES AND PROBLEMS

1. ***Respondeat Superior Claim.*** The basic rule of vicarious liability in the master-servant context is quite easy to articulate — a master is liable for the torts committed by his servant in the course and scope of employment. *See* Restatement (Second) of Agency §219. (1958) Thus, there are two basic

components to the doctrine's application. First, the relationship needs to be one of employer-employee. Employment relationships come in all shapes and sizes. A corporate officer can be an employee, and so can the janitor who empties the officer's trashcan each evening. There are many published decisions analyzing whether someone who seems to be acting for the benefit of the defendant is an employee or a mere "independent contractor." We will see a multi-factored list of considerations courts utilize to make this distinction. The chief factor will be the extent of control the defendant has over the details of the tortfeasor's work. Second, even if an employment relationship exists, vicarious liability only attaches when the employee commits the tort in the "course and scope" of employment. When the employee is "off the clock," the relationship ceases as far as vicarious liability is concerned. There is, again, a plethora of cases giving meaning to the phrase "course and scope of employment." Notice that the employer's liability exists absent proof of fault against the employer. Some have suggested that vicarious liability is, therefore, a type of strict liability or liability without fault. This thought may be somewhat misleading because various liability, for it to attach, certainly requires that the plaintiff prove the fault of the employee. True strict liability requires no traditional proof of fault against anyone. In *Trahan-Laroche*, there appeared to be no dispute about the employer-employee relationship that existed between defendant Lockheed Sanders and Patrick Maimone. With respect to the second element, the court believed that there were both sufficient allegations and evidence to submit to the jury the issue of whether Maimone was acting in the course and scope of employment at the time of his alleged negligent act. The next two cases will further explore the law related to these two elements of vicarious liability.

2. ***Negligent Supervision Claim.*** You may recall seeing in Chapter 6, Special Duty Rules (in connection with the *Otis Engineering* case), that employers have their own duty to supervise their employees for the protection of third parties. If an employer breaches its own duty through poor hiring, supervision of its employee, or the negligent entrustment of dangerous materials or machinery to an employee, then it has its own independent basis for liability. Breaching its own duty of care imposes *direct liability* on the employer based upon its own fault and is distinct from vicarious liability concepts. For example, if an employer knowingly permits an intoxicated employee to use a company vehicle to make a delivery, it has breached its own duty of care. If that employee drives carelessly and hits a pedestrian, the employer is also subject to vicarious liability. In such instances, it would be appropriate to submit for apportionment purposes the fault of both the employee (for driving poorly) and the employer (for letting a drunk drive its truck) — but the employer would face a judgment for the combined percentage of fault. In *Trahan-Laroche*, the appellate court believed that the allegations and evidence were sufficient to demonstrate a possible breach of duty of care owed by Lockheed Sanders, which arose out of a failure to supervise the actions of Maimone in connecting the trailer while on the defendant's premises. In cases such as this, one has to be careful to analyze separately the fault of the employer as well as the vicarious liability of the employer for the employee's fault.

3. *Effect of Vicarious Liability Doctrine.* It is important to consider the impact of the vicarious liability doctrine on the entry of judgment in a torts case. The doctrine exists to provide a deep pocket to enhance the plaintiff's ability to collect on a tort judgment. If the plaintiff proves the two prerequisites for the doctrine *and* proves that the defendant's employee committed a tort against the plaintiff, the plaintiff can recover against the employer to the same extent as she could against the employee. Of course, to recover against either, the plaintiff has to name that party as a defendant in the lawsuit and serve them with process. The plaintiff can sue both or either of the two. In terms of apportionment issues, in cases of pure vicarious liability there is no reason to apportion between the employee and the employer — the employer is not accused of being separately at fault itself; it merely stands in the shoes of its employee and *bears a joint liability* to the same extent as the employee. If the employee is apportioned 25 percent of the total fault in a several liability jurisdiction, the plaintiff can seek to collect on that 25 percent of the total damages from the employee, the employer, or a combination of the two. If the plaintiff collects the judgment from the vicariously liable employer, that employer may pursue a common law *indemnification* claim against the employee. Indemnification is the right to seek *full reimbursement* for all damages paid by virtue of the tort caused by another for whom the vicariously liable actor was held responsible. Although it operates similarly to a contribution claim, it is technically distinct. A right to contribution is a claim between joint tortfeasors in a joint and several liability context where one has paid beyond his own level of fault and seeks a *partial* reimbursement. In a case of pure vicarious liability, the employer is not a joint tortfeasor and so instead owns a right to indemnification rather than contribution. Can you understand why the vicariously liable actor should be entitled to be fully indemnified from the tortfeasor employee?

"LADIES AND GENTLEMEN OF THE JURY . . ."

Florida Standard Jury Instruction 3.3: Issues as to Vicarious Liability

The first issue for your determination on the claim of claimant against defendant on account of the alleged negligence of [third party] is whether [the third party] was an agent of defendant and was acting within the scope of his employment at the time and place of the incident complained of. An agent is a person who is employed to act for another, and whose actions are controlled by his or her employer or are subject to his or her employer's right of control. An employer is responsible for the negligence of its agent if such negligence occurs while the agent is performing services

> which he or she was employed to perform or while the agent is acting at least in part because of a desire to serve his or her employer and is doing something that is reasonably incidental to his or her employment or something the doing of which was reasonably foreseeable and reasonably to be expected of persons similarly employed.
>
> But a person is not responsible for the negligence of an independent contractor. An independent contractor is a person who is engaged by another to perform specific work according to his or her own methods and whose methods of performing the work are not controlled by the person engaging him or her and are not subject to that person's right of control.

1. Employees v. Independent Contractors

Sometimes in vicarious liability claims, it is clear that the direct tortfeasor was involved in performing a task for the benefit of another but it is unclear whether an employer-employee relationship existed. Absent this relationship, there is no guilt by association. In the following case, plaintiff fails in her attempt to invoke vicarious liability as a basis for seeking judgment against the corporate entity. What was lacking, according to the court?

THROOP v. F.E. YOUNG & CO.

382 P.2d 560 (Az. 1963)

McCarthy, J.

The plaintiff, Mrs. Marie D. Throop, a widow, brought a wrongful death action for the benefit of herself and her minor children, against defendants Robert D. Stauffer, as administrator of the estate of Peter J. Hennen, deceased, and the F.E. Young and Company.

Vernon Throop, husband of the plaintiff, Marie Throop, was a counter-intelligence officer of the United States Army working out of Tucson, Arizona. On October 10, 1957, Throop, with a passenger, was driving west towards Tucson on U. S Highway 80 near Benson. On a level and straight highway in broad daylight the vehicle occupied by Peter Hennen, proceeding in an easterly direction, suddenly swerved into Throop's lane of traffic causing a violent head-on collision. Both Throop and Hennen were found dead in their cars by witnesses to the accident.

At the conclusion of the evidence, both defendants moved for a directed verdict. The court directed a verdict for the defendant F.E. Young and Company and denied the motion of Robert D. Stauffer, as administrator. The jury returned a verdict for plaintiff in the sum of $50,400.00 against the administrator.

Plaintiff has appealed from the directed verdict in favor of the F.E. Young and Company, and the defendant Stauffer, as administrator of the estate of Hennen, has appealed from the verdict in favor of plaintiff.

[With respect to the plaintiff's recovery against the estate of the other driver, Hennen, the court found the trial court's use of the doctrine of res ipsa loquitur was appropriate and that the evidence was sufficient to support the jury's decision in favor of the plaintiff.

Plaintiff appealed from the entry of a directed verdict on her claims against defendant F.E. Young and Company.]

Plaintiff's first assignment of error is that there was sufficient evidence from which the jury could have found that the defendant controlled or had the right to control the actions of its deceased salesman.

The uncontradicted evidence of Hennen's employment by F.E. Young and Company showed that Violet Jennings, 48, a widow, was president of the Company which caused to be manufactured various medical testing kits and sold them to wholesalers throughout the country. The company employed the services of only two office employees other than the services of Peter J. Hennen. Hennen had been with the company 15 years and during the lifetime of William Jennings (deceased husband of Violet Jennings), a letter was drawn up by Mr. Jennings outlining the terms of the contract between the company and Hennen. Mrs. Jennings testified that the manner in which Mr. Hennen performed the services for the company was that he would come to the company office from time to time, pull cards on wholesale houses, and pick out the ones he desired to visit; or, if one of the two office employees would make a list of wholesalers for Hennen to visit, he would modify the list as he saw fit. He took care of his own hotel and traveling expenses out of his commissions; 1¼ cents per mile was paid on his automobile which he owned. He had no power to fix prices but he often gave more discounts than were on the discount cards furnished wholesalers and the company accepted these. He arranged his selling visits in accordance with the times he wished to visit relatives in various parts of the country and stayed with his relatives for varying periods of time as he desired. Hennen sold the goods of at least one other company while on his trips, in particular, novelty glass vases and paper weights for the St. Clair Glass Works. The amount of his commissions with the defendant company never exceeded $1,200 in any one year as Hennen was receiving social security and did not wish to jeopardize this status. The company made deductions from payments to Hennen for federal withholding tax and paid federal employment compensation. He was carried the same way on personnel records as the two office employees. Hennen visited the office an average of only four or five times a year.

The test to determine if the doctrine of "respondeat superior" applies to charge an employer with liability for negligence of his employee is whether, with respect to the physical conduct of the employee and the performance of his service, he is subject to the employer's control or right of control. This principle is stated in Restatement of the Law, Agency 2d, §220 in part as follows:

§220. Definition of Servant

(1) A servant is a person employed to perform services in the affairs of another and who with respect to the physical conduct in the performance of the services is subject to the other's control or right to control.

(2) In determining whether one acting for another is a servant or an independent contractor, the following matters of fact, among others, are considered:

(a) the extent of control which, by the agreement, the master may exercise over the details of the work;

(b) whether or not the one employed is engaged in a distinct occupation or business;

* * *

(e) whether the employer or the workman supplies the instrumentalities, tools, and the place of work for the person doing the work;

* * *

(g) the method of payment, whether by the time or by the job."

* * *

The foregoing test has been approved and followed in Arizona in the cases of *Consolidated Motors, Inc. v. Ketcham*, 66 P.2d 246 (Ariz.), and *Lee Moor Contracting Co. v. Blanton*, 65 P.2d 35 (Ariz.).

The following discussion from the *Consolidated Motors* case is controlling in the instant case:

> But the ultimate fact, which these evidentiary facts are merely intended to assist the jury or court in determining, is whether the alleged servant is subject to the other's control or right to control in the manner in which he reaches the desired result. The distinction is well set forth as follows:
>
> It is important to distinguish between a servant and an agent who is not a servant, since ordinarily a principal is not liable for the incidental acts of negligence in the performance of duties committed by an agent who is not a servant. One who is employed to make contracts may, however, be a servant. Thus, a shop girl or a traveling salesman may be a servant and cause the employer to be liable for negligent injuries to a customer or for negligent driving while traveling to visit prospective customers. The important distinction is between service in which the actor's physical activities and his time are surrendered to the control of the master, and service under an agreement to accomplish results or to use care and skill in accomplishing results. . . . For the purpose of determining liability, they are . . . "independent contractors" and do not cause the person for whom the enterprise is undertaken to be responsible. . . .

Plaintiff contends that by virtue of the contract signed by Hennen and Mr. Jennings prior to his death, at least seven years before the accident, Mr. Hennen was clearly a servant and not an independent contractor by reason of the mandatory provisions of the contract. This contract provided that Hennen was to do the following: "You are to call on accounts or prospects in person and not by telephone. You are to present all items that we sell to each dealer. You are to submit a written report on each prospect called on, giving reasons where an order is not obtained for each item." The letter further provided that Hennen would make collections, pick up stock from customers, put out display cards to dealers and perform other duties. This letter was later copied by Mrs. Jennings but was never signed and was apparently used as a memorandum of the method of computing commissions due Hennen.

The uncontradicted testimony is that Hennen never made any written reports or put out display cards. There is no testimony as to the manner he called on customers. Hennen did pick up and return some unsalable items. Mrs. Jennings testified that when she took over the business on her husband's death she just continued things as they were and never discussed any changes in procedure with Mr. Hennen. Hennen had no office duties and when he would return from his trips he would report to Mrs. Jennings, his "superior" but not his "supervisor."

Of significance to the control or right to control issue is the testimony that Hennen represented other companies, such as the St. Clair Glass Works, but the extent of this representation was unknown. Some of the samples of the St. Clair Glass Works were found in Hennen's car after his death.

There is no evidence of actual control over Hennen's use of his car or methods of selling. Any right to control selling procedures, if such still existed by virtue of the original letter-contract, would not justify an inference of any right to control the time, method or manner of the operation of Hennen's automobile. This was a matter of Hennen's uncontrolled discretion within the United States at large, for business, for pleasure, representing defendant's company or other companies as he chose.

Plaintiff next states as a "signpost" that the fact either party may terminate the employment at any time without liability, raises a strong inference that the workman is a servant. Plaintiff [argues the power to discharge gives the power to direct the smallest details of the work].

Rather than unnecessarily extend this opinion by a discussion of all the "signposts" set forth in plaintiff's assignments of error it suffices to state that the ultimate issue in the servant-independent contractor disputes is "control or right to control". The "matters of fact" or "signposts" listed in the Restatement are but matters to be considered.

An examination of the facts in the instant case makes readily apparent the correctness of the trial court's ruling in directing a verdict in favor of defendant F.E. Young and Company for there is no evidence from which to reasonably infer that the defendant had a right to control Hennen in the operation of his automobile. The whole of the United States and anywhere he chose to go in it was Hennen's territory. He visited prospects at whatever time he chose and he selected the prospects, visiting the office only four or five times a year. Clearly, no inference of control could stand the scrutiny of a motion for judgment notwithstanding the verdict had the case been submitted to the jury. There being no control or right of control, the reason for imposing vicarious liability upon this employer is wanting.

The judgment is affirmed.

NOTES AND PROBLEMS

1. ***Multiple Criteria Used to Determine Control.*** The court references some of the factors identified by the Restatement (Second) of Agency as useful in determining if the tortfeasor was an employee or a mere independent contractor. The court notes that the key is the extent of "control" one has over the details of the other's work, whether exercised or not. Other courts have identified other *additional* relevant criteria in this inquiry, including (a) the extent of specialized skills necessary to perform the assigned tasks, (b) the provision of materials needed for the tasks and the place of the work, (c) the relationship of the work to the regular business of the alleged employer, and (d) the belief of the parties as to their relationship as well as the belief of third parties dealing with them. None of these lists are exhaustive, as courts will consider any relevant circumstances. One potential criteria courts discount, however, is language in the parties' contract labeling the agent as an "independent contractor." While this language is relevant to the belief of the parties, it is not controlling and certainly not binding on the third-party victim of the tort. *See e.g.*, Anton v. Industrial Commission, 688 P.2d 192, 194 (Ariz. 1984) (contract language is not determinative of the issue but rather the "objective nature of the relationship, determined upon an analysis of the totality of the facts and circumstances of each case.").

2. ***Court Rejects Vicarious Claims.*** The court in *Throop* determined that the requisite employer-employee relationship was missing on the vicarious liability claim. What facts were most essential to the court's conclusion that the tortfeasor was an independent contractor rather than an employee of the defendant corporation? Would it have changed the outcome, for example, if the driver were not permitted to represent any other companies in his travels for the defendant?

3. ***Rationale for Vicarious Liability.*** Most courts have traditionally focused upon the right to control the assigned tasks as creating a fair argument in favor of imposing vicarious liability. What is it about someone's control over another that makes it fairer to impose guilt by association upon them?

4. ***Problems.*** Consider whether the following relationships would meet the criteria for an employer-employee relationship. Use the Restatement criteria to articulate your answer. What additional information might you want to know before reaching a firm conclusion in each instance?

A. While delivering the defendant's newspapers to customers, a delivery person speeds in his car and hits a patch of ice. He loses control of his vehicle and drives through the plaintiff's living room.

B. Defendant hires a nanny to care for her child, including driving the child to and from school and other extracurricular events. The nanny has an accident during one of these trips for which she is at fault.

C. Defendant hires a plumber to install a new gas line to his fireplace. The plumber accidentally errs in performing his work and this leads to an explosion that not only destroys the defendant's home, but also the neighbor's home. The neighbor sues defendant.

2. Course and Scope of Employment

Even if the direct tortfeasor is proven to be the employee of the defendant employer, vicarious liability is not automatic. Unless the tort occurs while the employee is acting in the *course and scope of employment* there is no guilt by association. The following case discusses the criteria used by courts to determine this issue when it is disputed.

FRUIT v. EQUITABLE LIFE ASSURANCE SOCIETY

502 P.2d 133 (Alaska 1972)

Boochever, J.

This case arises from a tragic accident in which the appellee, John Schreiner, was crushed between his parked automobile and the colliding vehicle owned and driven by the appellant, Clay Fruit. Schreiner's left leg was amputated and the muscle tissue of the right leg so destroyed as to leave him crippled and permanently disabled.

At the time of the accident, Fruit, a life insurance salesman, was attending a sales convention of his employer, Equitable Life Assurance Society (Equitable). The annual convention was being conducted at the resort location of Land's End near Homer on July 10-13, 1969. Sales employees of the company were required to attend the convention. After discussing with district managers the possibility of transporting the Anchorage insurance salesmen to the convention by bus, the agency manager decided that participants should travel by private transportation, and that they would be reimbursed a lump sum for their expenses. Clay Fruit chose to drive his own automobile, accompanied by his wife, another insurance agent and the wife and child of the latter.

Insurance experts from California and Washington were also invited as guests to the convention, and the Alaska salesmen were encouraged to mix freely with these guests to learn as much as possible about sales techniques during the three-day gathering. Scheduled events included business meetings during morning hours, evening dinners and at least two cocktail parties. District managers entertained their own sales personnel at other cocktail parties.

On the first evening of the convention, Thursday, July 10, 1969, the out-of-state guests and the agency manager dined at the Waterfront Bar and Restaurant in downtown Homer, approximately five miles from the convention headquarters at Land's End. They were joined a few hours later by a number of sales agents, including Fruit, for drinks and socializing. At other times during the first two days of the convention, the participants made occasional visits in small groups to the Salty Dawg Bar located about a half-mile from the convention center at Land's End.

A desk clerk at Land's End testified that loud and sometimes disorderly partying continued around the room of the agency manager and the adjoining porch and stairway until the early hours of the morning on Friday, July 11, 1969. One of the district managers testified that he complained about the noise to the agency manager.

A business meeting on Friday morning proceeded on schedule followed by a cocktail party and hors d'oeuvres in the room and adjoining spaces of the agency manager. Fruit went to the room of an out-of-state guest with whom he talked business and had drinks. Testimony indicates that by mid-afternoon Fruit was asleep on the floor. That evening, a scheduled cocktail party and seafood dinner on the beach proceeded without Fruit who was still asleep in a room adjacent to that of the out-of-state guest.

At some time between 10:00 and 11:30 p.m. following the seafood dinner other members of the group awoke Fruit who, accompanied by his wife and two couples, walked to the Salty Dawg Bar and returned shortly. The others were tired and went to bed but Fruit decided to go to Homer as he was under the impression that the out-of-state guests were at the Waterfront Bar and Restaurant. Fruit then drove his car to Homer but departed when he did not find any of his colleagues.

His return route to Land's End took him past the Salty Dawg Bar where Schreiner's automobile was disabled on or immediately off the side of the road opposite Fruit's lane. While the facts of the particular moment of the accident which occurred at approximately 2:00 a.m. on July 12, 1969, are unclear, it appears that Fruit applied his brakes and skidded across the dividing line of the highway, colliding with the front of Schreiner's car. The hood of Schreiner's automobile had been raised and Schreiner was standing in front of his car. The collision crushed his legs.

The subsequent amputation and crippling of Schreiner was exacerbated by a urinary disorder resulting from exploratory surgery necessitated by the accident. Schreiner sued Fruit and his employer, Equitable, for damages including pain and suffering, mental anguish, interference with normal activities, continuing medical expenses, loss of income and financial losses incurred from the forced sale of his home, a lot and securities. The jury found on special interrogatories that Fruit's negligence was the proximate cause of the accident; that he was acting within the course and scope of his employment for Equitable; that Equitable was directly negligent in planning and conducting the convention, which negligence was a proximate cause of the accident; and that Schreiner was not contributorily negligent. The jury awarded damages of $635,000 against both defendants. Both moved for a judgment notwithstanding the verdict and presently appeal from the respective denials of the motions.

Equitable contends that the evidence was insufficient to establish that Fruit was acting within the course and scope of his employment at the time of the accident; that Equitable cannot be held directly liable for the manner in which it conducted the summer conference; and that Equitable did not receive a fair trial because the facts adduced by the plaintiff in support of its direct negligence claim "tainted the jury's consideration of respondeat superior."

The jury found that Fruit was an employee acting within the course and scope of his employment for Equitable at the time and place of the accident. Under the doctrine of *respondeat superior* (which simply means "let the employer answer") Equitable would thus be liable for Fruit's acts of negligence despite lack of fault on Equitable's part.

Equitable argues, however, that the evidence was insufficient to establish that Fruit was acting within the course and scope of his employment. Equitable contends that any business purpose was completed when Fruit left the Waterfront Bar and Restaurant. It cites cases holding that an employee traveling to his home or other personal destination cannot ordinarily be regarded as acting in the scope of his employment. But Fruit was not returning to his home. He was traveling to the convention headquarters where he was attending meetings as a part of his employment.

In addition, Equitable seeks to narrow the scope of *respondeat superior* to those situations where the master has exercised control over the activities of employees. Disposition of this issue requires an analysis of the doctrine of *respondeat superior*, one of the few anomalies to the general tort doctrine of no liability without fault.

Principles

"Vicarious liability occupies a mysterious place in the common law. Our system of wrongs is premised upon fault as justifying why the apparatus of the state is to be marshaled against the assets of one person for the benefit of another. Yet despite this general conception, the law has recognized for centuries that in some cases one person may be vicariously liable for the fault of another. Rather than excising this anomaly on its march toward modernity, as had been suggested by some, the common law continued to develop and rely upon vicarious liability to such an extent that it is now generally assumed that any complete theory of tort law must be able to account for its presence."

J.W. Neyers, A Theory of Vicarious Liability, 43 Alberta L. Rev. 287, 288 (2005).

The origins of the principle whereby an employer may be held vicariously liable for the injuries wrought by his employee are in dispute. Justice Holmes traces the concept to Roman law while Wigmore finds it to be of Germanic origin. The doctrine emerged in English law in the 17th Century. Initially a master was held liable for those acts which he commanded or to which he expressly assented. This was expanded to include acts by implied command or authority and eventually to acts within the scope of employment. The modern theory evolved with the growth of England's industry and commerce.

A truly imaginative variety of rationale[s] have been advanced by courts and glossators in justification of this imposition of liability on employers. Among the suggestions are the employer's duty to hire and maintain a responsible staff of employees, to "control" the activities of his employees and thus to insist upon appropriate safety measures; the belief that the employer should pay for the inherent risks which result from hiring others to carry on his business; the observation that the employer most often has easier access to evidence of the facts surrounding the injury; and the metaphysical identification of the employer and employee as a single "persona" jointly liable for the injury which occurred in the context of the business.

Baty more cynically states: "In hard fact, the reason for the employers' liability is the damages are taken from a deep pocket."

The two theories which carry the greatest weight in contemporary legal thought are respectively, the "control" theory which finds liability whenever the act of the employee was committed with the implied authority, acquiescence or subsequent ratification of the employer, and the "enterprise" theory which finds liability whenever the enterprise of the employer would have benefited by the context of the act of the employee but for the unfortunate injury.

Since we are dealing with vicarious liability, justification may not be found on theories involving the employer's personal fault such as his failure to exercise proper control over the activities of his employees or his failure to take proper precautions in firing or hiring them. Lack of care on the employer's part would subject him to direct liability without the necessity of involving *respondeat superior.*

The concept of vicarious liability is broad enough to include circumstances where the master has been in no way at fault; where the work which the servant was employed to do was in no sense unlawful or violative of the plaintiff's rights; where there has been no delegation of a special duty; where the tortious conduct of the servant was neither commanded nor ratified; but nevertheless the master is made responsible. This liability arises from the relationship of the enterprise to society rather than from a misfeasance on the part of the employer.

The aspect of the relationship most commonly advanced to delimit the theory is the "scope of employment" of the employee-tortfeasor. While the factual determination generally is left to the jury, many cases lying in the penumbras of "scope of employment" have produced confusing and contradictory legal results in the development of an otherwise worthy doctrine of law. To assist in delineating the areas of tortious conduct imposing liability, it is helpful to consider what we believe to be the correct philosophical basis for the doctrine.

There was a time when the artisans, shopkeepers and master craftsmen could directly oversee the activities of their apprentices and journeymen. Small, isolated communities or feudal estates evinced a provincial sense of social interaction which ensured that many enterprises would conduct their businesses with a careful concern for the community of its patrons. But in the present day when hundreds of persons divide labors under the same corporate roof and produce a single product for market to an unidentified consumer, the communal spirit and shared commitment of enterprises from another age is sacrificed to other efficiencies. At the same time, the impersonal nature of such complex enterprises and their mechanization make third parties considerably more vulnerable to injury incidentally arising from the pursuit of the business. Business corporations are granted a personal identification in legal fiction to limit liability of the investors, but not to insulate the corporate entity itself from liability for the unfortunate consequences of its enterprise.

"Scope of employment" as a test for application of *respondeat superior* would be insufficient if it failed to encompass the duty of every enterprise to the social community which gives it life and contributes to its prosperity.

> The meaning of the legal sword of Damocles forged for [the enterprises'] penalization is rightly to be found, not in the particular relation they bear to their charge, but in the general relation to society into which their occupation brings them.

The basis of *respondeat superior* has been correctly stated as the desire to include in the costs of operation inevitable losses to third persons incident to carrying on an enterprise, and thus distribute the burden among those benefited by the enterprise.

The desirability of the result is readily discernible when an employee obviously engaged in his employer's business causes injury to a third party as a result of the employee's negligence. Thus, if an employee is engaged in trucking merchandise for an employer and through negligence in driving injures a pedestrian, it appears more socially desirable for the employer, although faultless itself, to bear the loss than the individual harmed. Insurance is readily available for the employer so that the risk may be distributed among many like insureds paying premiums and the extra cost of doing business may be reflected in the price of the product.

Although not usually enunciated as a basis for liability, in essence the enterprise may be regarded as a unit for tort. Employees' acts sufficiently connected with the enterprise are in effect considered as deeds of the enterprise itself. Where through negligence such acts cause injury to others it is appropriate that the enterprise bear the loss incurred.

Consistent with these considerations, it is apparent that no categorical statement can delimit the meaning of "scope of employment" once and for all times. Applicability of *respondeat superior* will depend primarily on the findings of fact in each case. In this particular case, Clay Fruit's employment contract required that he attend the sales conference. Each employee was left to his own resources for transportation, and many of the agents, including Fruit, chose to drive their own automobiles. By the admission of Equitable's agency manager, the scope of the conference included informal socializing as well as formal meetings. Social contact with the out-of-state guests was encouraged, and there is undisputed evidence that such associations were not limited to the conference headquarters at Land's End. Some agents, including Fruit, gathered with the guests in Homer the evening before the accident, and groups of agents and their wives visited the Salty Dawg on various occasions.

When Fruit left for the Waterfront Bar and Restaurant his principal purpose was to join the out-of-state guests. This testimony of his was further confirmed by the fact that once he discovered that they were not present at the Waterfront he departed immediately. Had he been engaged in a "frolic of his own" it would appear likely that he would have remained there. There was evidence from which the jury would find that he was at least motivated in part by his desire to meet with the out-of-state guests and thus to benefit from their experience so as to improve his abilities as a salesman.

Because we find that fair-minded men in the exercise of reasonable judgment could differ as to whether Fruit's activities in returning from Homer to the convention headquarters were within the scope of his employment, we are not disposed to upset the jury's conclusion that liability for damages may be vicariously imputed to Equitable.

The judgment below is affirmed.

NOTES AND PROBLEMS

1. ***Course and Scope.*** Courts have an obligation to review the factual evidence relating to a vicarious liability claim in order to determine if there are sufficient facts by which a jury might reasonably find that a defendant's employee was acting in the course and scope of employment. The issue is ultimately an issue of fact, however, and frequently is left to the jury's judgment as in the *Fruit* case above. One relatively concise statement of relevant criteria on this issue, however, is found in the Restatement (Second) of Agency §228(a):

Conduct of a servant is within the scope of employment if, but only if:

(A) it is of the kind he is employed to perform;
(B) it occurs substantially within the authorized time and space limits;
(C) it is actuated, at least in part, by a purpose to serve the master; and
(D) if force is intentionally used by the servant against another, the use of force is not unexpected by the master.

2. ***Frolic and Detour.*** In analyzing this issue courts frequently resort to the use of certain phrases in reaching conclusions. For example, when an employee has substantially deviated from his appropriate duties such that he is no longer within the course and scope of employment courts will often say that he has engaged in a "frolic" — a temporary abandonment of the relationship that is the basis for the imposition of vicarious liability. When the deviation is not

substantial enough to destroy vicarious liability, courts refer to it as a mere "detour."

3. ***Going and Coming Rule.*** Courts have generally held as a matter of black letter law that employees are not within the scope of employment when they are engaged in a routine commute to and from work. If they commit a tort while driving home from the office, they are typically not considered to be within the course and scope of employment. This rule applies unless the employee is engaged in a "special errand" for her employer that requires the travel, such as when an associate at a law firm is instructed to drive to the courthouse on the way to work to review a case file. If the young lawyer has an accident while driving to the court, this will be considered a special errand and thus falls within the course and scope of employment.

4. ***Intentional Misconduct.*** Courts have struggled at times with employees who, while engaged in the work of the employer, have engaged in an intentional tort such as battering a customer at a store. Many courts refuse to recognize the employee as being within the course and scope of employment during the commission of an intentional tort because the employee is not actuated by any sense of furthering the employer's business in such instances. *See e.g.*, Lisa M. v. Henry Mayo Newhall Memorial Hospital, 907 P.2d 358 (Cal. 1995) (sexual assaults not within course and scope of employment generally). Yet there is no absolute rule cutting off vicarious liability for intentional torts. *See e.g.*, Patterson v. Blair, 172 S.W.3d 361 (Ky. 2005) (affirming vicarious liability verdict when employee shot a gun at car's tires while attempting to repossess the vehicle); Fearing v. Bucher, 977 P.2d 1163, 1168 (Or. 1999) (pastor of church who engaged in sexual abuse could be within scope of employment if the assaults were an "outgrowth of and were engendered by conduct that was within the scope" of his duties). In a similar vein, courts have generally held that the fact that an employee's tortious misconduct was committed in violation of the employer's rules does not automatically disqualify the doctrine of vicarious liability from attaching. Otherwise, employers could categorically avoid any vicarious liability by simply having a rule that employees were not permitted to commit any torts.

5. ***Problems.*** How would you analyze whether the tortious actions of each employee in the following scenarios was committed within the course and scope of employment?

A. A beer company advises its delivery drivers to always obey the speed limits. One driver flaunts this rule and continues to drive at much higher speeds. One afternoon during a delivery, the speeding driver hits a pedestrian.

B. An employee is instructed by her boss to deliver a package to a customer an hour's drive north of town. After driving for fifteen minutes toward the customer, the employee takes an exit to get a cup of coffee. While exiting the freeway, the employee carelessly rear-ends another car.

C. An employee at a manufacturing facility is feeling drowsy and steps outside to get some fresh air and enjoy smoking a cigarette. The employee negligently drops the cigarette into a trash dumper while it is still lit. This causes a fire, which spread to the plaintiff's property next door.

D. A manager's assistant at defendant's restaurant comes into work after hours one evening when the restaurant is closed to catch up on completing some paperwork. The assistant falls asleep at his desk during the middle of the night and is awakened by a startled housekeeper who is present to empty the trashcans from the office. The assistant misperceives what is happening and violently punches the housekeeper in the face.

E. An installer for a cable TV company arrives at the Kennedy mansion to upgrade their service to the new premium level. While in the house installing the new boxes, the installer begins to notice all of the fine jewels laying around. He also discovers the family is headed to Maine for a long weekend stay. So after finishing the job, he returns late that night when the house is empty. He sneaks inside of it using a window he had unlatched, and makes off with hundreds of thousands of dollars in jewels. A security video camera captures the installer doing this, but he has fled to Costa Rica.

C. Concert of Action

Many courts will impose liability on a defendant for the tort of another when there is proof that the defendant was *acting in concert* with the primary tortfeasor. This theory of liability is analogous to the criminal law concepts of *conspiracy*, and *aiding and abetting*. In a tort suit, the effect of a finding that one was acting in concert with a tortfeasor is to impose liability jointly on both actors. This is true even if the plaintiff would be unable to prove each of the elements of any other tort cause of action against the defendant. Concert of action is similar to vicarious liability in that one is being held responsible for the tortious harms caused by another. This theory is distinguishable from vicarious liability, however, because there is some level of wrongdoing here rather than simply being guilty by association. The court below discusses different ways that one might be considered to be liable under the concert of action theory. As you read the following cases, ask yourself why the plaintiff had to resort to relying upon the concert of action doctrine and why this doctrine was available in *Herman* but unavailing to create liability in *Shinn*. After *Shinn*, we will also see lawyers for a very sympathetic pair of victims of a car accident attempt to impose liability on someone not who was not physically involved in the accident, but had texted the driver at fault moments before the accident.

1. Conduct Creating Joint Liability

HERMAN v. WESGATE

464 N.Y.S.2d 315 (N.Y. App. Div. 1983)

MEMORANDUM OPINION

Plaintiff was injured while a guest at a stag party to celebrate the impending marriage of defendant Thomas Hauck. The party was held on-board a barge owned by defendant Donald Wesgate and Thomas Rouse. Following a three-hour cruise, the barge was anchored near the shoreline of Irondequoit Bay. The depth of the water off the bow of the barge was approximately two feet. Several guests began "skinny dipping" and, within a brief period of time, some in the party began to throw others still clothed off the bow into the water. Two or more individuals escorted plaintiff to the bow of the barge where, unwillingly, he went overboard. Trauma to his head or neck resulted in injury to his spinal cord.

[The trial court granted the summary judgment motions of defendants John Hauck and James Hauck. Plaintiff appealed from this order.]

It was improper to grant the motions of defendants John Hauck and James Hauck. Plaintiff's complaint alleges concerted action by all of the defendants.

> Concerted action liability rests upon the principle that "[all] those who, in pursuance of a common plan or design to commit a tortious act, actively take part in it, or further it by cooperation or request, or who lend aid or encouragement to the wrongdoer, or ratify and adopt his acts done for their benefit, are equally liable with him" (Prosser, Torts [4th ed], §46; see, also Restatement, Torts 2d, §876). An injured plaintiff may pursue any one joint tort-feasor on a concerted action theory. Such tort-feasor may, in turn, seek contribution from others who acted in concert with him.

Here, the conduct of the defendants alleged to be dangerous and tortious is the pushing or throwing of guests, against their will, from the barge into the water. Liability of an individual defendant will not depend upon whether he actually propelled plaintiff into the water; participation in the concerted activity is equivalent to participation in the accident resulting in the injury. Whether codefendants acted in concert is generally a question for the jury. The complaint states a cause of action against each of the defendants and the record presents questions of fact as to whether defendants John Hauck and James Hauck acted in concert with the other defendants. Thus summary judgment should not have been granted.

SHINN v. ALLEN

984 S.W.2d 308 (Tex. App. 1998)

Wilson, J.

Appellant, Marjorie Gail Shinn, individually and as representative/sole heir of the estate of Robert Wayne Shinn, appeals the rendition of summary judgment in favor of appellee, Russell Martin Allen.

In December 1994, a vehicle driven by Jeremy Michael Faggard, in which Allen was a passenger, collided with a vehicle driven by Robert Wayne Shinn, Gail Shinn's husband. Robert Shinn was killed in the accident, and Gail Shinn was seriously injured.

Gail Shinn sued Allen for negligence, alleging Allen substantially assisted or encouraged an intoxicated person to drive an automobile on public roads that resulted in the collision which killed Robert Shinn and injured her. Allen moved for summary judgment contending he owed no duty to Gail Shinn. The summary judgment was granted.

In her sole point of error, Gail Shinn alleges the trial court erred in granting Allen's motion for summary judgment because the evidence established the existence of both a duty and a question of material fact under the concert-of-action theory of liability.

The summary judgment evidence consists of Allen's affidavit, his deposition, his answers to interrogatories, and a copy of the judgment in Faggard's driving-while-intoxicated case.

On the day of the accident, Faggard picked Allen up from his parents' home at approximately 3:00 p.m. to go and "hang out." Allen and Faggard were acquaintances who had met playing volleyball. Allen stated that Faggard was not a "close buddy of mine." Both Allen and Faggard were under 21 years of age; however, about an hour before the accident Faggard decided to buy some beer. Faggard and Allen went to the convenience store where Faggard bought a twelve-pack of beer. Allen did not pay for the beer or arrange for the purchase of the beer. Allen stated he did not plan on drinking that day and did not know that Faggard drank. After buying the beer, Faggard and Allen went to Faggard's house and talked and drank the beer. Allen consumed four or five beers, and Faggard consumed six or seven. Allen and Faggard did not eat anything while drinking the beer, and the last time Allen ate was at "lunchtime."

Sometime before 7:00 p.m., Allen asked Faggard to take him home because his parents wanted him home by 7:00 p.m. to eat dinner. During the ride home, Allen did not think Faggard was speeding.

The summary judgment evidence indicates Allen did not exercise any control over the operation of Faggard's vehicle. Allen affirmatively stated that he did not know what Faggard's tolerance level to alcohol was. Allen did not observe anything indicating Faggard was intoxicated before the accident. Faggard did not slur his words and was not stumbling or walking in a way that would indicate he was intoxicated. Allen, however, did state that he (Allen) was drunk. Faggard was later convicted of driving while intoxicated.

Gail Shinn asserts that the summary judgment should be reversed because there is a fact issue regarding whether Allen is liable under the concert-of-action theory. The Texas Supreme Court has stated that, "whether such a theory of liability is recognized in Texas is an open question." *Juhl v. Airington*, 936 S.W.2d 640, 643 (Tex. 1996). A version of the theory has been articulated by Professor Keeton as follows:

> All those who, in pursuance of a common plan or design to commit a tortious act, actively take part in it, or further it by cooperation or request, or who lend aid or encouragement to the wrongdoer, or ratify and adopt the wrongdoer's acts done for their benefit, are equally liable.

W. Page Keeton Et Al., Prosser and Keeton on The Law of Torts §46, at 323 (5th ed. 1984).

The Restatement (Second) of Torts also incorporates this principle, imposing liability on a person for the conduct of another which causes harm. Section 876 states:

> **§876 Persons Acting in Concert**
>
> For harm resulting to a third person from the tortious conduct of another, one is subject to liability if he
>
> (a) does a tortious act in concert with the other or pursuant to a common design with him, or
>
> (b) knows that the other's conduct constitutes a breach of duty and gives substantial assistance or encouragement to the other so to conduct himself, or
>
> (c) gives substantial assistance to the other in accomplishing a tortious result and his own conduct, separately considered, constitutes a breach of duty to the third person.

Restatement (Second) of Torts §876 (1977).

Gail Shinn argues that the facts of this case fall under section 876(b). Subsection (b) imposes liability not for an agreement, but for substantially assisting and encouraging a wrongdoer in a tortious act. This subsection requires that the defendant have "an unlawful intent, i.e., knowledge that the other party is breaching a duty and the intent to assist that party's actions." *Juhl*, 936 S.W.2d at 644 (quoting *Payton v. Abbott Labs*, 512 F. Supp. 1031, 1035 (D. Mass. 1981)).

Comment d to section 876 lists five factors that can be relevant to whether the defendant substantially assisted the wrongdoer. These include: (1) the nature of the wrongful act; (2) the kind and amount of the assistance; (3) the relation of the defendant and the actor; (4) the presence or absence of the defendant at the occurrence of the wrongful act; and (5) the defendant's state of mind.

1. NATURE OF THE WRONGFUL ACT

The purpose of the concert-of-action theory is to deter antisocial or dangerous behavior that is likely to cause serious injury or death to a person or certain harm to a large number of people. *Juhl*, 936 S.W.2d at 644-45. It is commonly recognized that driving while intoxicated is an antisocial and dangerous behavior, likely to cause serious injury or death to a person.

2. THE KIND AND AMOUNT OF THE ASSISTANCE

Gail Shinn relies on *Cooper v. Bondoni*, 841 P.2d 608 (Okla. Ct. App. 1991), to support her position. The court in *Cooper* recognized that the non-acting person must give *substantial* assistance or encouragement to the tortfeasor in order to affix Section 876 liability. *Id.* at 612 (emphasis added). There is no evidence Allen purchased the beer, ordered the beer, paid for the beer, encouraged Faggard to consume the beer, or encouraged Faggard to drive recklessly. Allen asked for a ride home. Allen's request was gratuitous. There is no evidence that Faggard's decision to drive in an intoxicated condition was more than his alone.

3. RELATION OF THE PARTIES

There is no special relationship between Allen and Faggard, such as an employee/employer relationship, that would place one party in a position of control over the other. Allen and Faggard were just acquaintances who decided to "hang out" one afternoon.

4. PRESENCE OR ABSENCE OF THE DEFENDANT

Although we are not bound by out-of-state decisions, we find *Olson v. Ische*, 343 N.W.2d 284 (Minn. 1984), informative on this issue. In *Olson*, the court held that "the mere presence of the particular defendant at the commission of the wrong, or his failure to object to it, is not enough to charge him with responsibility." It is uncontroverted that Allen was riding in Faggard's car as a passenger when the accident occurred.

5. DEFENDANT'S STATE OF MIND

The summary judgment evidence shows Allen stated he did not think Faggard was intoxicated. While a fact issue exists as to whether Allen had knowledge that Faggard was intoxicated, that issue alone does not create a fact issue as to whether Allen substantially assisted or encouraged Faggard. Rather, Allen's state of mind is merely one of five factors that can be relevant to whether Allen substantially assisted Faggard.

In reviewing the summary judgment evidence in the context of the above five factors, we conclude Gail Shinn did not raise a material fact issue that Allen substantially assisted or encouraged Faggard in operating the vehicle.

[W]e conclude that the evidence conclusively disproves that Allen breached the concert-of-action theory of duty to Gail Shinn.

NOTES AND PROBLEMS

1. *Conspirators and Aiders and Abettors.* Restatement (Second) of Torts §876 describes three scenarios where the concert of action doctrine will create a joint liability. Subpart (a)'s reference to a tort committed pursuant to a "common design" describes a conspiracy carried out by direct tortfeasors but to which the defendant has also attached himself perhaps by being a part of the planning of the tort. Subparts (b) and (c) are more analogous to aiding and abetting because they each involve conduct by the defendant to offer "substantial assistance" or "encouragement" to the primary tortfeasor. In the *Shinn* case, there was obviously no plan to be involved in a car accident or to engage in careless driving. Why did the court reject imposing the doctrine under subpart (b) despite the fact that the defendant asked the drunk driver to give him a ride home? Why was this not considered enough encouragement to create joint liability? By contrast, the relatively brief involvement by the defendants in *Herman* was considered adequate to potentially amount to acting in concert. What was different about the defendants' conduct in the two cases?

2. *Role and Effect of Doctrine.* If a plaintiff cannot prove the elements of the underlying tort against all of the actors, she can still impose a joint liability for the harm done through resort to the concert of action doctrine. In the *Shinn* case, the defendant had moved for summary judgment on the basis of a no duty argument — that he had no duty to the plaintiff for the negligent operation of the car by the drunken acquaintance. Plaintiff responded to this argument by pointing to the concert of action doctrine as a basis for maintaining the lawsuit against the passenger. Why did the court reject the possible application of the concert of action doctrine in *Shinn* but determine in *Herman* that the plaintiff presented a jury question? If you could change one fact in *Shinn* that might change the outcome, which fact would it be?

3. *Problems.* Would Restatement §876 concert of action liability apply in the following scenarios? Which provision would provide the best argument in each case?

A. Two teenage boys pull up to a red light late at night. They each start revving their engines in an apparent challenge to a street race. As the light turns green, both cars speed into the night. One car hits a pedestrian in the process but the driver of that car has no assets or insurance. Can the other driver be held liable to the plaintiff despite the fact that he did not hit her?

B. A crowd of people gathers on a street corner around a potential fistfight after the high school lets out in the afternoon. After the fight is apparently finished (when one of the combatants is knocked unconscious and is lying down), someone in the crowd yells to the victor, "give him another kick to be sure he's not going to get back up and continue!" Others in the crowd join in the refrain of "Kick him! Kick him!" Giving in to the peer pressure, the victorious fighter kicks the loser, fracturing several ribs and puncturing the other boy's lung. Can the beaten boy sue members of the crowd as well as the victorious fighter?

KUBERT v. BEST

432 N.J. Super. 495 (N.J. App. 2013)

Ashrafi, J.

Plaintiffs Linda and David Kubert were grievously injured by an eighteen-year-old driver who was texting while driving and crossed the center-line of the road. Their claims for compensation from the young driver have been settled and are no longer part of this lawsuit. Plaintiffs appeal the trial court's dismissal of their claims against the driver's seventeen-year-old friend who was texting the driver much of the day and sent a text message to him immediately before the accident.

New Jersey prohibits texting while driving. A statute under our motor vehicle laws makes it illegal to use a cell phone that is not "hands-free" while driving, except in certain specifically-described emergency situations. For future cases like this one, the State Legislature enacted a law, called the "Kulesh, Kubert, and Bolis Law," to provide criminal penalties for those who are distracted by use of a cell phone while driving and injure others.

The issue before us is not directly addressed by these statutes or any case law that has been brought to our attention. We must determine as a matter of civil common law whether one who is texting from a location remote from the driver of a motor vehicle can be liable to persons injured because the driver was distracted by the text.

On the afternoon of September 21, 2009, David Kubert was riding his motorcycle, with his wife, Linda Kubert, riding as a passenger. As they came south around a curve on Hurd Street in Mine Hill Township, a pick-up truck being driven north by eighteen-year-old Kyle Best crossed the double-center line of the roadway into their lane of travel. David Kubert attempted to evade the pick-up truck but could not. The front driver's side of the truck struck the Kuberts and their motorcycle. The collision severed, or nearly severed, David's left leg. It shattered Linda's left leg, leaving her fractured thighbone protruding out of the skin as she lay injured in the road.

Best stopped his truck, saw the severity of the injuries, and called 911. The time of the 911 call was 17:49:15, that is, fifteen seconds after 5:49 p.m. Best, a volunteer fireman, aided the Kuberts to the best of his ability until the police and emergency medical responders arrived. Medical treatment could not save either victim's leg. Both lost their left legs as a result of the accident.

After the Kuberts filed this lawsuit, their attorney developed evidence to prove Best's activities on the day of the accident. In September 2009, Best and Colonna were seeing each other socially but not exclusively; they were not boyfriend and girlfriend. Nevertheless, they texted each other many times each day. Best's cell phone record showed that he and Colonna texted each other sixty-two times on the day of the accident, about an equal number of texts originating from each.

The accident occurred about four or five minutes after Best began driving home from the YMCA [where he worked]. At his deposition, Best testified that he did not text while driving — meaning that it was not his habit to text when he was driving. He testified falsely at first that he did not text when he began his drive home from the YMCA on the day of the accident. But he was soon confronted with the telephone records, which he had seen earlier, and then he admitted that he and Colonna exchanged text messages within minutes of his beginning to drive.

The sequence of texts between Best and Colonna indicates the precise time of the accident — within seconds of 5:48:58. Seventeen seconds elapsed from Best's sending a text to Colonna and the time of the 911 call after the accident. Those seconds had to include Best's stopping his vehicle, observing the injuries to the Kuberts, and dialing 911. It appears, therefore, that Best collided with the Kuberts' motorcycle immediately after sending a text at 5:48:58. It can be inferred that he sent that text in response to Colonna's text to him that he received twenty-five seconds earlier. Finally, it appears that Best initiated the texting with Colonna as he was about to and after he began to drive home.

Missing from the evidence is the content of the text messages.

After plaintiffs learned of Colonna's involvement and added her to their lawsuit, she moved for summary judgment. Her attorney argued to the trial court that Colonna had no liability for the accident because she was not present at the scene, had no legal duty to avoid sending a text to Best when he was driving, and further, that she did not know he was driving. [The trial judge granted the motion, dismissing the claims against Colonna.]

In this case, plaintiffs argue that a duty of care should be imposed upon Colonna because she aided and abetted Best's violation of the law when he used his cell phone while driving. To support their argument, plaintiffs cite §876 of the Restatement (Second) of Torts, a compilation of common law principles. Under §876, an individual is liable if he or she knows that another person's "conduct constitutes a breach of duty and gives substantial assistance or encouragement to the other."

To illustrate this concept, the *Restatement* provides the following hypothetical example:

> A and B participate in a riot in which B, although throwing no rocks himself, encourages A to throw rocks. One of the rocks strikes C, a bystander. B is subject to liability to C.

Restatement §876, comment d, ill. 4.

The example illustrates that one does not actually have to be the person who threw a rock to be liable for injury caused by the rock. In *Tarr v. Ciasulli*, 853 A.2d 921 (N.J. 2004), the New Jersey Supreme Court adopted the principle stated in Restatement §876 as applicable to determine joint liability when persons act in concert and cause harm to another.

In this case, plaintiffs assert that Colonna and Best were acting in concert in exchanging text messages. Although Colonna was at a remote location from the site of the accident, plaintiffs say she was "electronically present" in Best's pickup truck immediately before the accident and she aided and abetted his unlawful use of his cell phone.

In *Champion ex rel. Ezzo v. Dunfee*, 939 A.2d 825 (N.J. App. 2008), we analyzed §876 in a context where the defendant was actually present at the site of the accident. In *Champion*, the injured plaintiff was a backseat passenger in a car driven by a friend who had been drinking. The driver's girlfriend was also a passenger in the car, sitting in the front seat. The car approached speeds of 100 miles per hour as the driver tried to prove the performance capabilities of his car. The car hit a bump and crashed, severely injuring the backseat passenger. He sued the driver, and subsequently, added the driver's girlfriend as a defendant in his lawsuit on a theory that she had a duty to prevent her boyfriend from driving because she knew he had been drinking.

We reviewed common law precedents from other jurisdictions where passengers in a car had encouraged the driver to consume alcohol or drugs or otherwise to drive dangerously, and we compared those precedents to others where the passengers were present but neither encouraged nor prevented the negligent conduct of the driver. We concluded that the law permits recovery against a passenger under two conditions. One is a "special relationship" that gave the passenger control over the driver's conduct, such as an employer-employee or parent-child relationship. The second is "that the defendant passenger *actively encouraged* the driver to commit" the negligent act. Mere failure to prevent wrongful conduct by another is ordinarily not sufficient to impose liability. In *Champion*, the girlfriend could not be held liable merely for failing to prevent her boyfriend's negligent driving.

In this case, Colonna did not have a special relationship with Best by which she could control his conduct. Nor is there evidence that she actively encouraged him to text her while he was driving. Colonna sent two texts to Best in the afternoon of September 21, 2009, one about two hours and the second about twenty-five seconds before the accident. What she said in those texts is unknown. Even if a reasonable inference can be drawn that she sent messages requiring responses, the act of sending such messages, by itself, is not active encouragement that the recipient read the text and respond immediately, that is, while driving and in violation of the law.

Another case decided by this court, *Podias v. Mairs*, 926 A.2d 859 (N.J. App. 2007), also provides some guidance on liability of a passenger for aiding and abetting a driver's wrongful conduct. In *Podias*, we reviewed claims against two passengers who were present when an eighteen-year-old driver who had been drinking struck and injured a motorcyclist at 2:00 a.m. on the Garden State Parkway. Rather than calling for medical aid for the unconscious motorcyclist, the passengers discussed how to prevent detection of their own involvement in the incident. They had cell phones, but they did not call the police, and they also told the driver not to call the police and not to get them involved. The driver and passengers all fled the scene of the accident. The motorcyclist was killed by another driver who did not see him lying injured in the roadway.

We reviewed Restatement §876 and held that the passengers could be found liable for giving "substantial assistance" to the driver in failing to fulfill his legal duty to remain at the scene of the accident and to notify the police. We found "an aiding and abetting theory" to be viable because the passengers had taken "affirmative steps in the immediate aftermath [of the accident] to conceal their involvement" and to encourage the driver's violation of the law.

Unlike the facts of *Podias*, the evidence in this case is not sufficient for a jury to conclude that Colonna took affirmative steps and gave substantial assistance to Best in violating the law. Plaintiffs produced no evidence tending to show that Colonna urged Best to read and respond to her text while he was driving.

The evidence available to plaintiffs is not sufficient to prove Colonna's liability to the Kuberts on the basis of aiding and abetting Best's negligent driving while using a cell phone.

Principles

Regarding §876 (a) and (b)'s varieties of concert of action liability, one commentator described them as follows:

> The first variety is indistinguishable from traditional conspiracy, requiring all actors to knowingly join a tortious venture, while not requiring each member to actually engage in the injurious act. The second variety is similarly indistinguishable from classical aiding and abetting, requiring that all actors knowingly give substantial assistance to the wrongdoer, while again not requiring that each actor engage directly in the injurious act.

E. Dana Neacsu, Concert of Action by Substantial Assistance: Whatever Happened to Unconscious Aiding and Abetting?, 16 Touro L. Rev. 25, 27 (2000).

NOTES AND PROBLEMS

1. ***Separating Causation from Liability.*** In *Kubert*, there was at least inferential evidence that the driver of the pick-up truck was distracted by receiving and sending text messages with his friend Colonna. This should provide

sufficient evidence that defendant Colonna was a but-for cause of the accident — that without her sending text messages to the driver moments before the accident, he would not have been distracted and struck the plaintiffs on their motorcycle. But merely being a cause of harm does not suffice to impose liability. One avenue of possible attack was to argue that the defendant Colonna had her own independent duty of reasonable care to prevent another driver from texting while driving. But the plaintiff's primary efforts to impose liability involved utilizing the concert of action theory from Restatement §876. The appellate court affirmed the trial court's grant of summary judgment, rejecting the application of this doctrine under the facts of the case. What evidence was missing that would have permitted the doctrine to apply to Colonna? Do you agree with the court's use of the *Podias* and *Champion* cases to explain its decision?

2. ***Problem.*** Would any of the three varieties of concert of action liability embodied in §876 apply in the following scenario? Juanita is a sophomore in college and a close college friend of hers, Frederick, is hanging out with Juanita at her apartment one afternoon. Juanita demonstrates to Frederick how she is able to download music for free from a questionable website. She advises Frederick that, even though it is not legal, there is no way they would ever get caught doing it. Frederick goes home that night and begins downloading hundreds of pirated songs from the website. The owner of the copyright on the songs eventually discovers the identity of Frederick. The owner also wants to sue Juanita under §876 for her role in Frederick's conversion of its music.

2. *Extent of Liability for Acting in Concert*

When one is cheering on the commission of a tort that is taking place immediately in full view, it seems reasonable to hold the one acting in concert fully liable for the harm caused. But what if the one that is acting in concert does not know about some of the primary tortfeasor's conduct and does not know about the full extent of the harms being caused by the others involved? Is it fair to hold all of the actors fully liable for the full extent of the harms? The *Grim* case below discusses the extent of one's liability when found to be acting in concert with other tortfeasors who cause harms.

AMERICAN FAMILY MUT. INS. CO. v. GRIM

440 P.2d 621 (Kan. 1968)

O'Connor, J.

This is a subrogation action by the American Family Mutual Insurance Company (plaintiff) to recover from a thirteen-year-old boy (defendant) a portion of a fire loss paid to the Derby Methodist Church, the company's insured, as the result of a fire occurring August 16, 1965. Following a trial without a jury, the lower court entered judgment in favor of the insurance company, and defendant has appealed.

The issues raised on appeal relate to the sufficiency of the evidence and the liability of the defendant as a joint tortfeasor.

On the evening of August 15, 1965, the defendant and three companions, ages thirteen and fourteen, gathered at the home of one of the boys to spend the night. They planned to sleep in the backyard in sleeping bags, as they had done several times previously during the summer. About ten o'clock the four lads decided to go downtown to a filling station to get some Cokes. They left the yard through a back gate and proceeded down the alley. The home was located about three houses south of the church, and as they passed the church, one of the boys remarked that Cokes were kept in a refrigerator in the kitchen and maybe they could get some there.

The boys entered the building through the unlocked door of the main entrance to the sanctuary, which is the east wing of the church. The kitchen is located in the north part of the west wing. [The boys went to the west wing and found the kitchen doors locked. They began to look for other ways into the kitchen.] The defendant and his three companions . . . went into the furnace room located on the south side of the west wing. From here two of the boys went up into the attic through a trap door that opened into the area above the hallway. The defendant and his other companion remained behind. Upon entering the attic, the two boys found some paper material which, without the defendant's knowledge, they rolled up, lighted with a match, and used as torches to light their way. As the torches burned down during the search in the attic, the two boys extinguished one over the hallway area and the second over the area north of the hallway into which they had gained admittance through a small opening in the wall. One torch was extinguished by "stomping" it on a board lying across the rafters; the other burned rapidly and was permitted to fall between the rafters onto the ceiling. [T]he two youths, believing the torches to be fully extinguished, left the attic and descended to the furnace room. From the time the two boys entered the attic until they returned to the furnace room the defendant was in the hallway obtaining a drink at the water fountain.

The four youths then left the church through the same door by which they had entered and proceeded to a filling station where they drank Cokes. After walking around for a while, they returned to their sleeping bags around midnight. In the early morning hours of August 16 the church was discovered to be on fire, and the local fire department was called to the scene. When the firemen arrived they found extensive fire, with smoke coming out from under the eaves of the building and through the roof at one point on the south side of the west wing. Defendant and his three companions were awakened about 5:00 a.m. by the fire alarm activity and went over to the church to help remove Boy Scout equipment from a storage room located in the southeast corner of the east wing.

The trial court found that the fire was started as a result of the torches, either one or both, that were lighted in the attic; that the cause of the fire was the lighting of the torches and the attempt to extinguish them; that defendant knew nothing about the lighting of the torches, but that he and the other three boys were in the church, and two of the boys were in the attic, for the purpose of attempting to find an entrance into the kitchen in order to get, or attempt to get, Cokes therefrom. The court concluded that defendant was jointly and severally liable, and entered judgment for the plaintiff insurance company in the sum of $25,000.

Defendant vigorously argues he cannot be held liable, either jointly or severally, for the damage caused by the fire. He observes there was no evidence his companions had any discussion with him about using torches and the trial court specifically found that he knew nothing about the lighting of the torches in the attic. Although plaintiff's petition recites, "Defendant and three other persons engaged in a joint venture," it appears the case was actually tried and submitted without objection to the lower court on the theory that the four boys were jointly engaged in the commission of an unlawful tortious act — gaining entrance to the kitchen in order to obtain Cokes — and all were liable as joint tort feasors for any wrongful act done in attempting to accomplish their objective.

One who aids, abets and encourages others in the commission of an unlawful act is guilty as a principal, and all are jointly and severally liable in a civil action for any damages that may have resulted from their act. Defendant argues this rule does not apply, because he had nothing to do with the use of the torches, nor did he know they were being used. The weakness of his argument lies in defendant's disregard of the fact the torches were used in the four boys' attempt to carry out their original unlawful plan.

The rule of joint and several liability . . . prevails where tortfeasors act in concert in the execution of a common purpose. The tort liability of persons acting in concert is expressed in the Restatement of the Law of Torts, §876:

> For harm resulting to a third person from the tortious conduct of another, a person is liable if he. . . .
>
> (b) knows that the others conduct constitutes a breach of duty and gives substantial assistance or encouragement to the other so to conduct himself.

Germane to our case is the comment [to subsection (b)] that a person who encourages another to commit a tortious act may also be responsible for other foreseeable acts done by such other person in connection with the intended act. To illustrate the point, the following example is given:

> A and B conspire to burglarize C's safe. B, who is the active burglar, after entering the house and without A's knowledge of his intention to do so, burns the house in order to conceal the burglary. A is liable to C, not only for the conversion of the contents of the safe, but also for the destruction of the house.

A fortiori, the same result would obtain had B negligently set fire to the house while using a match or torch to find the safe.

Here, the boys entered the church for the common purpose of obtaining Cokes from the kitchen. Finding their way thwarted by the locked door, the boys sought a means of entry through the attic to an area over the kitchen where entrance could be accomplished through the ceiling. In their attempt to reach that area, the need for adequate lighting could reasonably be anticipated. The use of the torches served that purpose. From the time the boys entered the church to the time of departure, defendant was more than an innocent bystander. Although he actually did not enter the attic or have anything to do with the use of the torches, there was evidence from which it could be inferred that he actively participated and lent encouragement and cooperation to the successful accomplishment of their over-all mission. At no time did he make any attempt to withdraw from participation in the agreed-on objective or plan. In fact, it would appear he intended to reap the same benefits, once the mission was completed, as would be forthcoming to his companions.

The judgment is affirmed.

NOTES AND PROBLEMS

1. ***Basis for Liability.*** The trial and appellate courts in *Grim* reference Restatement §876(b) as the basis for finding that the defendant had acted in concert with the other boys who negligently set fire to the church. Can you make an argument that §876(a) could also apply to this factual scenario?

2. ***Liability Limited by Foreseeability.*** As we have seen in many other instances in the law of torts, the court adopts a rule of foreseeability in order to limit the potential liability of one found to be acting in concert. Exactly what must the defendant foresee in order to be fully liable for all of the resulting harms? Did the defendant in *Grim* have any ideas that the other members of the group were going to use torches? If not, what did the defendant foresee that the court found to be sufficient?

3. ***Problems.***

A. Multiple manufacturers of the drug DES employ an identical formula for their drug and market it as safe for use in pregnant women. When it is revealed that the drug causes birth defects, may the plaintiffs employ the concert of action doctrine to hold them all jointly liable (and thus avoid potentially difficult issues of identifying which manufacturer actually caused each plaintiff's harm)? What did the court say about this in *Sindel v. Abbott Laboratories*?

B. Recall the *Wawanesa Mutual Ins. v. Matlock* case from Chapter 4 Negligence: Breach of Duty of Reasonable Care. Timothy purchased cigarettes for the younger Eric and together they trespassed on the Woodman Pole Company's lot, smoking and roughhousing atop a large stack of wooden telephone poles. This led to an accidental fire and the loss of $100,000 in property. Could Timothy have been considered jointly liable with Eric due to the concert of action doctrine?

Upon Further Review

Even in a world of several liability, courts still employ the equitable doctrines of vicarious liability and concert of action to create joint liability against one for the misconduct of another. In each instance, the victim is permitted to sue either the primary tortfeasors, the deeper pockets employing the tortfeasors, or both. Though these doctrines have different conceptual bases for their utilization, they operate in similar ways and ultimately for the similar purpose of permitting a victim to be more likely to have a full recovery. Further, when joint liability attaches to one for the misconduct of another, a right to indemnification will be created so that ultimately the risk of loss might be borne by the direct tortfeasor.

Pulling It All Together

HomeResource, Inc. is in the business of supplying home health nurses to elderly homebound patients. The company screens the nurses by confirming their degree and credentials and running a criminal records history on their candidates. The nurses receive as compensation an hourly rate tied to whatever amount the elderly patients' insurers agree to reimburse for their time. HomeResource keeps the balance to offset its operating expenses and profits. The nurses they provide to the patients use their own vehicles and all of their own equipment (scrubs, gloves, stethoscope, etc.). The company does perform periodic in-home checks on patients and also checks the record-keeping practices of the nurses to ensure they conform to industry standards.

HomeResource hired Jillian as a new home health nurse. They checked her educational and licensing records but never got around to checking her criminal record — they missed a prior conviction she had in another state for theft of a dwelling. HomeResouce assigned Jillian to work with an elderly man named Trent who was suffering the early stages of dementia and had limited mobility. She worked in Trent's home full-time, Monday through Friday during the daytime. During the three months she worked there she began stealing cash from Trent, as well as jewelry (watches, primarily, and a few gold chains), and taking blank checks and using them to pay some of her personal expenses. Trent had many indications of these missing items but he did not want to believe that Jillian would do such a thing. He also ignored his bank statements for those three months, which showed the illicit check-writing activities of Jillian. When Trent's adult daughter was visiting, she looked at one of Trent's bank statements and discovered Jillian's illicit activities. Jillian was arrested. Trent hired a lawyer who sued HomeResource, Inc. and Jillian. He sued Jillian for conversion with losses of $10,000. He also alleged emotional distress and said he could never trust another nurse again. He alleged HomeResource was liable as her employer and also that it was negligent in hiring and supervising her activities.

The case went to trial and the jury found in favor of Trent and against HomeResource and Jillian on all legal theories. The jury found actual damages of $60,000 ($10,000 in stolen items and $50,000 in emotional distress related to the loss of property). The jury also found punitive damages against Jillian for $250,000. The jury apportioned fault as follows: Jillian, 50 percent; HomeResource, 25 percent; and Trent, 25 percent. The state has a statute providing that a plaintiff found to be at fault is still permitted to recover "so long as the claimant's fault is less than the fault of the person against whom they seek to recover. In such instances, the claimant's recovery is reduced proportionally. Tortfeasors are only severally liable unless apportioned greater than 50 percent of the fault."

If you are the trial judge, how should you enter judgment in this case — against whom and for what amounts? 30 minutes.

CHAPTER 10

Strict Liability

I INTRODUCTION

In Chapter 1, we discussed the hierarchy of tort claims in terms of their relative degrees of fault. Intentional torts were listed at the top as *generally* involving the most anti-social variety of misconduct. Below that were accidental torts involving either recklessness or carelessness. The final category involves *strict liability* torts. Often, these torts are referred to as *no fault* causes of action or as involving the imposition of *absolute liability*. In a technical sense, strict liability does not require any finding of negligence by the defendant as a precondition on imposing tort liability — in this classic sense the phrase "no fault" might be appropriate. When true strict liability is applied, a defendant can be found liable no matter how great the defendant's precautions may have been to try to prevent the plaintiff's harm. In other words, the reasonableness of one's conduct provides no safe harbor for such a defendant. Rather than requiring a search for traditional notions of fault, strict liability attaches when the defendant has been involved in something the law determines involves non-reciprocal dangers. That is, the defendant has chosen to be involved in an activity that creates unique and significant risks for others; this choice demands that the defendant, in essence, act as an insurer for victims.

CHAPTER GOALS

- ☑ Gain introduction to the concept of liability without traditional notions of fault (i.e., without at least negligence).
- ☑ Understand how certain unusual (i.e., non-reciprocal) and ultrahazardous activities give rise to liability for all resulting harms.
- ☑ See these non-reciprocal risks illustrated by certain types of activities involving explosives or other highly dangerous activities or materials.
- ☑ Learn about strict liability for possessors of wild animals or animals that have demonstrated ultrahazardous personality traits.

Strict liability in tort was historically reserved for harms caused by a defendant's wild animals or unusually dangerous activities. In this chapter, we will study strict liability by reviewing cases involving these two categories of strict liability. In each category, note exactly what the defendant must do to subject itself to liability without a showing of negligence. We will also discuss how strict liability is fundamentally different from a traditional, fault-based approach to tort liability. This study is important not only because people are still hurt today by wild animals and by defendants' unusually dangerous activities, but also because this form of strict liability was the genesis for the concept of strict liability for defective products — the topic we take up next in Chapter 11.

II UNUSUALLY DANGEROUS ACTIVITIES

Modern common law abandoned a requirement for proving fault in cases involving unusually dangerous activities, beginning in the nineteenth century English case of *Rylands v. Fletcher.* In that case, the defendants constructed a reservoir on land located above some vacant mine shafts. As the reservoir began to fill with water, it burst through one of these mine shafts, flooding the plaintiff's adjacent property. The defendants were unaware of the shafts, and there was no negligence proven against them. Nevertheless, the court found the defendants liable due to the nature of their activity and despite the lack of fault. The court stated that "the true rule of law is, that the person who for his own purposes brings on his lands and collects and keeps there anything likely to do mischief if it escapes must keep it in at his peril, and, if he does not do so, is prima facie answerable for all the damage which is the natural consequence of its escape." Blackburn, J., Exchequer Chamber: L.R. 1 Exch. 265, 266 (1866). Upon appeal, Lord Cairns imposed strict liability based upon the defendant's "non-natural use" of the land. This holding has generally been accepted in the United States in the form of courts imposing strict liability on "ultrahazardous" and "extraordinary" activities. *See e.g.*, Ainsworth v. Lakin, 180 Mass. 397 (Mass. 1902).

When strict liability is found to apply to an activity, the defendant is liable for all of the harmful consequences of the activity regardless of how much care was employed to avoid the harm. The major question involves the type of activities for which the doctrine will apply. The first case below, *Exner*, involves the defendant's storage of blasting materials. Courts have had little difficulty determining that blasting activities involve "unusual and extraordinary" conduct. The second case, *Martin*, involves a more modern and aggressive attempt to apply the doctrine against the manufacturer and seller of handguns.

EXNER v. SHERMAN POWER CONST. CO.

54 F.2d 510 (2d Cir. 1931)

A. HAND, J.

This is an action in tort, brought by Delia H. Exner to recover damages to her person, property, and business which were caused by the explosion of dynamite kept by the defendant company in connection with work upon a hydroelectric development at Bellows Falls, Vt., in which it was engaged. The plaintiff Frederick Exner, the husband of Delia H. Exner, was joined as a plaintiff because he sought to recover damages for injuries to his marital rights.

The defendant kept dynamite in a small hut on the westerly bank of the Connecticut River located conveniently to its work. This hut was approximately 935 feet from the dwelling of the plaintiffs, in which they rented rooms and apartments and carried on a restaurant and lunchroom. The dynamite hut was located close to a thickly settled part of Bellows Falls, and within fifty rods of five dwelling houses, a hotel, several factories, and business buildings belonging to persons other than the plaintiffs.

Mildred Wolfel, one of defendant's witnesses, who observed the explosion from the New Hampshire side of the river, 300 or 400 feet from where it occurred, said that she saw two men coming out of the dynamite hut carrying boxes; that she saw a flash and a ball of fire and then another flash, and experienced an explosion so severe as to throw her across the road. The hut was blown to atoms by the explosions, and three men engaged in getting the cases of dynamite to take down to the place along the river where the blasting was to be done were killed.

There was evidence that Mrs. Exner, the plaintiff, who was in bed in her house at the time of the explosion, was thrown out of bed and received injuries, that her house was so badly shattered as to require extensive repairs, and that her business was damaged. The accident occurred on February 18, 1928.

The principal storehouse of the dynamite was on the eastern or New Hampshire side of the river. From that, dynamite was brought in an automobile across the bridge and placed in the hut to be warmed so as to be in condition for use when needed for blasting. Evidence was introduced that twenty cases of dynamite, weighing fifty pounds each, were sent from the storehouse across the river to the hut the day before the explosion, and that three such cases were still on hand in the hut before the additional twenty cases were brought to it. There was evidence that after the explosion one of the witnesses picked up as much as two fifty-pound cases of unexploded dynamite at the scene of the explosion and found four or five more in a tool box thirty to fifty feet from the hut. The general foreman of the defendant testified that about one thousand pounds of dynamite were ordinarily required for daily use in blasting, but on some days when the company was not doing much drilling much less than one thousand pounds would be used.

The defendant's president testified that there was no place where the dynamite hut could be located that would be accessible to the work that would not be within fifty rods from an inhabited dwelling, and, if it had been placed beyond that limit, the dynamite would necessarily have been too cold for use before it reached the job and would have been carried more frequently than was the case through the streets of Bellows Falls, to the greater peril of the inhabitants. He also said that the hut was adopted as a place to store a supply of dynamite for daily use after a hearing before the deputy fire marshal of the state, and with his consent.

There is a statute of Vermont (Rev. Laws 1880, §4323), the consideration of which is involved in this case, which reads as follows:

> Keeping Explosives. A person who keeps or suffers to be kept upon premises owned or occupied by him, within fifty rods of an inhabited building of another person, more than fifty pounds of gunpowder or nitroglycerine at one time, or more than one pound, unless contained in sound canisters of tin or other metal, or a package containing more than fifty pounds of dynamite, shall be fined twenty-five dollars, and twenty-five dollars additional for each day that it is so kept after notice from an inhabitant of such town to remove the same.

The plaintiffs [alleged, among other things, that defendant was liable for having violated the statute by storing] an amount of dynamite in excess of fifty pounds within fifty rods of a building inhabited by another than the defendant.

Upon the case as submitted to the jury we must determine whether, under section 4323, or under the common law, the defendant became liable, irrespective of any fault, for the damage arising from the explosion.

The defendant was not, in our opinion, liable to the plaintiffs for a violation of section 4323. It is well established that only members of a class to be benefited can invoke a civil remedy by reason of such a statute as we have here. The plaintiffs inhabited a dwelling more than fifty rods from the dynamite hut, and the act in terms covers only an area within a radius of fifty rods from the place of storage. It is impossible to see how the plaintiffs were of the class intended to be benefited by a law forbidding storage of dynamite within an area in which they were not included. The plaintiffs were not of the class to be benefited.

The question remains whether there was an absolute liability for the damage caused by the explosion at common law. We may say at the outset that we have been referred to nothing relevant as to this in the Vermont decisions, but they would not control in any event, because the matter is one in which we are at liberty to gather the principle to be applied from the general field of jurisprudence.

Dynamite is of the class of elements which one who stores or uses in such a locality, or under such circumstances as to cause likelihood of risk to others, stores or uses at his peril. He is an insurer, and is absolutely liable if damage results to third persons, either from the direct impact of rocks thrown out by the explosion (which would be a common-law trespass) or from concussion.

For the reasons already given in discussing the Vermont statute, we assume that the storage of dynamite in the case at bar was not an act of which the plaintiffs could complain. There was uncontradicted proof that the place of storage and the quantities stored were approved by the deputy fire marshal of the state. While such approval would be no protection against claims of persons inhabiting dwellings within the prescribed zone, the plaintiffs were not of that class and could not have enjoined the storage. The liability of the defendant is not founded on illegal storage or on negligence, which was not proved, but upon the ground that the use of dynamite is so dangerous that it ought to be at the owners' risk.

In *Bradford Glycerine Co. v. St. Marys Woolen Mfg. Co.*, 54 N.E. 528 (Ohio), the defendant manufactured and stored nitroglycerine which exploded and caused damage to the plaintiff. The Supreme Court of Ohio held that the defendant was liable though there was no proof of negligence. To the same effect was the decision in *French v. Center Creek Powder Mfg. Co.*, 158 S.W. 723 (Mo). These cases followed *Rylands v. Fletcher, L.R. 3 H.L.* 330, which has found considerable explicit support in this country.

It is true that some courts have distinguished between liability for a common-law trespass, occasioned by blasting, which projects rocks or debris upon the property or the person of the plaintiff, and liability for so-called consequential damages arising from concussion, and have denied liability for the latter where the blasting itself was conducted at a lawful time and place and with due care. Yet in every practical sense there can be no difference between a blasting which projects rocks in such a way as to injure persons or property and a blasting which, by creating a sudden vacuum, shatters buildings or knocks down people. In each case, a force is applied by means of an element likely to do serious damage if it explodes. The distinction is based on historical differences between the actions of trespass and case and, in our opinion, is without logical basis.

We can see no reason for imposing a different liability for the results of an explosion, whether the dynamite explodes when stored or when employed in blasting. To be sure there is a greater likelihood of damage from blasting than from storage, but in each case the explosion arises from an act connected with a business conducted for profit and fraught with substantial risk and possibility of the gravest consequences. As Justice Holmes has said in The Common Law, p. 154: "The possibility of a great danger has the same effect as the probability of a less one, and the law throws the risk of the venture on the person who introduces the peril into the community."

Frequently as much as one thousand pounds of dynamite were stored by the defendant near a group of dwellings, factories, and a hotel. The fact that the explosion was severe enough to kill three men, blow up the hut, unsettle and damage the plaintiff's house, over nine hundred feet away, and that even then, one hundred pounds of dynamite still remained unexploded, shows that there must have been a large amount of dynamite in or about the hut at the time of the accident. When a person engages in such a dangerous activity, useful though it be, he becomes an insurer.

It is argued that transportation of the dynamite through the town in small quantities would have increased the risk to the public. This seems to be true, and no reason is shown for taking such a course, because it would have added to the danger without relieving the defendant from absolute liability, had an explosion occurred while the dynamite was on the way.

It the case at bar, the court decided that the Vermont statute made the storage illegal and afforded the plaintiffs a remedy. With this we differ, for the reasons already stated. Nevertheless, as we hold that the defendant acted at its own risk in storing a large amount of dynamite at the particular locality chosen, the error was harmless.

Judgment affirmed.

MARTIN v. HARRINGTON & RICHARDSON, INC.

743 F.2d 1200 (7th Cir. 1984)

PELL, J.

During January of 1981, Donovan and James Barnes shot and killed Larry Martin and wounded Kenneth Jackson. Plaintiffs seek to recover for the injuries suffered by the two men, but not from the Barnes brothers, who have little or no money. Plaintiffs have instead filed this diversity action against Harrington and Richardson (H&R), the manufacturer of the gun used by the Barnes's, alleging that H&R was strictly liable for the damage caused by the weapon. The district court found no support for plaintiffs' theory in Illinois law and dismissed the suit for failure to state a cause of action.

Before examining the district court's conclusion we should clarify the nature of plaintiffs' claim, which is not clear from either the complaint or the briefs filed in this court. Although plaintiffs refer to the gun as an unreasonably dangerous instrument and complain of H&R's conduct in selling the gun to the public, it becomes clear from examining plaintiffs' arguments that they do not, and cannot, seek recovery under products liability or negligence. Products liability requires a defect of some sort in the gun, a claim that plaintiffs expressly disavow. [Plaintiffs further do not allege any negligence against H&R and, at oral argument, conceded that H&R could have done nothing to prevent the shootings here except refrain from selling guns altogether. Plaintiffs' claims are solely grounded in strict liability.] Plaintiffs instead claim that H&R's liability stems solely from "the manufacture of an inherently dangerous, nondefective instrument." Plaintiffs' claim, in essence, is that manufacturing and selling handguns to the public is an ultrahazardous activity that gives rise to strict liability for any damage done by the guns. The district court dismissed plaintiffs' claim after finding:

> There is no case or statutory law demonstrating that such a cause of action exists in Illinois, and we decline to create such a new cause of action. In the present state of

> law, a manufacturer of a nondefective handgun is not liable for injury caused by use of the gun, whether that use be lawful or unlawful. *Accord Bennet v. The Cincinnati Checker Cab Co., Inc.*, 353 F. Supp. 1206, 1210 (E.D. Ky. 1973) (holding that a firearms dealer was under no duty to protect plaintiff, who was shot by a gun imported by dealer, from criminal attack). If a cause of action such as the one proposed by plaintiffs is to become recognized in Illinois, it must be done by the Illinois legislature or the Illinos courts, not by a federal court in a diversity action.

Plaintiffs claim that the district court shirked its responsibility to decide the case presented to it as an Illinois court and that, had the district court fulfilled this responsibility, it would have concluded that a cause of action exists. Plaintiffs ask that we either reverse the district court's finding that no cause of action exists or at least remand the case to the district court with instructions to determine whether such an action would be recognized by an Illinois court.

Although the district court's opinion, which we have quoted in its entirety, may be Spartan, we do not think that it reflects a failure to determine how an Illinois court would decide the issue. The duty of a district court sitting in diversity faced with a novel claim such as plaintiffs' is to predict, as best as possible, how an Illinois court would decide the issue. We turn now to examine the accuracy of that prediction.

Illinois recognizes strict liability under two theories: unreasonably dangerous defective products and ultrahazardous activities. Strict products liability in Illinois follows the formulation set forth in §402A of the Restatement (Second) of Torts (1965), which imposes strict liability upon one "who sells any product in a defective condition unreasonably dangerous to the user or consumer or to his property."

Plaintiff has not directly pursued a products liability approach here because the gun involved in the shootings was not defective and posed an obvious danger that required no warning, and thus was not unreasonably dangerous.

Plaintiffs attempt to circumvent the problems posed by products liability by urging that the sale of handguns to the public is an ultrahazardous activity. Under section 519 of the Restatement (Second) of Torts: "One who carries on an abnormally dangerous activity is subject to liability for harm to the person, land or chattels of another resulting from the activity, although he has exercised the utmost care to prevent the harm." Section 520 of the Restatement sets forth the following factors to be considered in determining whether an activity is abnormally dangerous:

> (a) existence of a high degree of risk of some harm to the person, land or chattels of others;
>
> (b) likelihood that the harm that results from it will be great;
>
> (c) inability to eliminate the risk by the exercise of reasonable care;
>
> (d) extent to which the activity is not a matter of common usage;
>
> (e) inappropriateness of the activity to the place where it is carried on; and
>
> (f) extent to which its value to the community is outweighed by its dangerous attributes.

Illinois has long recognized strict liability for damage caused by engaging in an abnormally dangerous or ultrahazardous activity, although it has never explicitly relied upon the Restatement factors in determining whether a given activity is abnormally dangerous. In *City of Joliet v. Harwood*, 86 Ill. 110 (1877), the Illinois Supreme Court held that blasting with dynamite in a residential area was intrinsically dangerous and gave rise to strict liability for the blaster. A similar result was reached in *FitzSimmons & Connell Co. v. Braun*, 65 N.E. 249 (Ill. 1902), and *Opal v. Material Service Corp.*, 133 N.E.2d 733 (Ill. App. 1956). More recently, the court in *Snow v. Judy*, 239 N.E.2d 327 (Ill. App. 1968), found that the use of barbed wire was not abnormally dangerous, although the negligent use could be the basis for liability. Finally, a federal district court sitting in diversity held that shipping acrylonitrile, a hazardous and toxic substance, was an ultrahazardous activity that subjected the shipper to strict liability under Illinois law. *Indiana Belt Harbor Railroad Co.*, 517 F. Supp. 314. In so holding, the court relied upon the Restatement formulation of abnormally dangerous activities.

If plaintiffs were claiming that the *use* of a handgun was an ultrahazardous activity the argument would clearly fit within the parameters of Illinois law. However, plaintiffs' attempt to impose strict liability for engaging in an ultrahazardous activity upon the *sale* of a nondefective product is unprecedented in Illinois, and in fact is only supported by a recent district court decision from the Eastern District of Louisiana. *Richman v. Charter Arms Corp.*, 571 F. Supp. 192 (E.D. La. 1983). Balanced against *Richman* is the recent decision of the Circuit Court of Cook County, Illinois, rejecting a claim identical to plaintiffs'. *Riordan v. International ArmamentCorp.*, 81 L 27923 (Circuit Court Cook County, Law Division, July 21, 1983). Although a trial court decision is not determinative, the reasoning of *Riordan* and our own misgivings about the result in *Richman* provide persuasive support for rejecting plaintiffs' claim.

Riordan rejected the claim that selling handguns is an ultrahazardous activity after observing that:

> Cases requiring liability impose liability for the ultrahazardous activity as a result of the *use* of the product. To recognize liability of a manufacturer or distributor would virtually make them the insurer for such products as explosives, hazardous chemicals or dangerous drugs even though such products are not negligently made nor contain any defects. Although such a social policy may be adopted by the legislature, it ought not to be imposed by judicial decree.

Riordan, slip op. at 3 (emphasis in original).

Plaintiff would have us ignore the concerns expressed in *Riordan*, the only Illinois decision directly on point, and instead adopt the reasoning of *Richman*. In *Richman*, the court found that a nondefective handgun was not unreasonably dangerous, but held that selling such a gun to the public could constitute an ultrahazardous activity. The court recognized that possession of handguns is legal in Louisiana, which indicated that "the legislature does not think handgun manufacturers act unreasonably (are negligent per se) when they market their product to the general public. The legislators do not think marketing handguns for sale to the general public is an 'unreasonably dangerous' activity." Nonetheless, the court found that selling guns could constitute an ultrahazardous activity. The court observed that an ultrahazardous activity is not an unreasonably dangerous one, but rather simply an activity that poses a high degree of risk that is justified by the value of the enterprise. In this situation, the actor is not negligent in engaging in the activity, but nonetheless must bear the risk of damages caused by the activity. Such is clearly the case with blasting or transporting toxic substances, but we have found no decision other than *Richman* that has held that the lawful sale of a nondefective product can be an ultrahazardous activity.

Our primary misgiving with *Richman* is that it blurs the distinction between strict liability for selling unreasonably dangerous *products* and strict liability for engaging in ultrahazardous *activities* by making the sale of a product an activity. Accepting plaintiffs' argument would run counter to Illinois' long-standing requirement that strict liability for the sale of a product be limited to unreasonably dangerous products. Illinois has never imposed liability upon a non-negligent manufacturer of a product that is not defective.

A change in this policy, as observed in *Riordan*, would require that manufacturers of guns, knives, drugs, alcohol, tobacco and other dangerous products act as insurers against all damages produced by their products. Whatever the economic wisdom of such a policy might be, there is no basis for assuming that Illinois wishes to adopt it.

We are also concerned that plaintiffs' argument would thwart Illinois' policy regarding possession of handguns. The right of private citizens in Illinois to bear arms is protected, at least against all restrictions except those imposed by the police power, by the Illinois Constitution. The State of Illinois regulates, but does not ban, the possession of handguns by private citizens. As *Richman* recognized, this express policy is a strong indication that handguns should not be considered unreasonably dangerous. *See also Mavilia v. Stoeger Industries*, 574 F. Supp. 107 (D. Mass. 1983) (Massachusetts' decision to allow possession of handguns precludes imposing strict liability on handgun manufacturer under products liability). Imposing liability for the sale of handguns, which would in practice drive manufacturers out of business, would produce a handgun ban by judicial fiat in the face of the decision by Illinois to allow its citizens to possess handguns.

Nor do we believe Illinois is ready to adopt a theory which in essence would hold that whenever someone is injured there must be someone also answerable in damages.

One is reminded, if the contention of the appellants were carried to its logical conclusion, of a figmental, perhaps allegorical, nation called Litigatia described in the article by Paul B. Horton, *How Lawsuits Brought the World's Greatest Nation to Ruin*, Medical Economics, February 21, 1977, 142:

> Throughout the economy, new ventures disappeared. New factories were not built, since no locations could be found where it was legally possible to build them. [T]he

> U.S. Supreme Court promulgated the "omnia culpa" doctrine which in plain language meant that whenever a person suffered injury through use of a product, *all* persons or corporations who had any contact with the product, from raw material to delivery van, were equally liable to damage claims. It soon became very difficult to get anyone to make or sell anything, and most people went back to the ancient art of making things for themselves.

Id. at 149. Hopefully, the dire thought expressed is not prophetic for our jurisprudence.

In conclusion, we agree with the district court that there is no support for plaintiffs' claim in Illinois law and no basis for predicting that an Illinois court would expand existing law to accommodate plaintiffs' claim. Accordingly, the decision of the district court is AFFIRMED.

CUDAHY, C.J., *concurring*

I agree that there is little reason to believe that the Illinois Supreme Court would enforce a theory of strict liability against handgun manufacturers at this time. That is the question presented by this diversity case and I think Judge Pell has answered it correctly.

Our analysis may be incomplete, however, if we lose sight of the fact that, in a broad economic sense, death and injury from bullet wounds are an external cost of handgun manufacture and sale, imposed on gun victims or on society as a whole. The central reality is that these costs exist in fact, and the only question is who should bear them. The imposition of strict liability on the manufacturer or seller of handguns should not be viewed as an attempt to drive handguns from the market — for the courts, an improper goal. Rather, it is an effort to place the costs inherent in handguns on the users rather than on the victims.

If a victim has been injured and attempts to recover damages from the user of the handgun, the user is frequently unreachable or judgment-proof. Strict liability for the manufacturer or marketer of handguns, on the other hand, places the costs of injury on a party who is able to spread those costs widely among all users through higher prices. An argument can be made for thus internalizing the costs in the price of handguns and thereby distributing them to all users rather than imposing them on shooting victims, which is the alternative. As we have noted, the costs exist and *someone* must pay them.

The justification for the imposition of strict manufacturer liability is that the manufacturer, "by marketing a product, has assumed a special responsibility to the public and should bear the costs of accidents, as a cost of doing business." Note, *Manufacturers' Liability to Victims of Handgun Crime: A Common-Law Approach*, 51 Fordham L. Rev. 771, 778 (1983). *See also* Turley, *Manufacturers' and Suppliers' Liability to Handgun Victims*, 10 N. Ky. L. Rev. 41, 45 (1981). In practice, however, neither the manufacturer nor even an insurance company would ultimately bear the costs; these enterprises would simply serve as distributors of the risks and costs associated with handgun use among those who use handguns.

Strict manufacturer or seller liability might be imposed under Restatement (Second) of Torts, §§519-20, following the reasoning of *Richman v. Charter Arms Corp.*, 571 F. Supp. 192 (E.D. La. 1983). Whatever may be said for or against this approach, however, it is not now the law of Illinois. And that is where, for present purposes, the analysis must end.

NOTES AND PROBLEMS

1. ***Distinction Between Defendant's Activity and Others.*** The *Martin* court lists the Restatement (Second)'s proposed factors for finding strict liability based upon the defendant's activity. Were these factors present in *Exner* when the defendant chose to store a thousand pounds of dynamite close to town? Notice in *Exner* that the court imposed liability against the defendant despite the fact that plaintiff had no theory as to a better course of behavior for the defendant's use and storage of the dynamite. Arguably, the defendant was storing the dynamite in the way *least likely to cause harm* while still permitting the public works project that apparently had great value to the community. Would it appear the defendant acted unreasonably? With respect to *Martin*, practice this analysis by considering (a) the activity of *selling* a weapon and (b) the activity of *using* a weapon. Do you understand why most courts have rejected the attempted imposition of strict liability against sellers of handguns based upon the careful use of these criteria in light of the actual activity undertaken by the gun manufacturer? The court's secondary argument is that imposing liability would implicate Second Amendment concerns. How persuasive do you find this argument?

2. **Richman** ***Reversed.*** The *Martin* court above refutes the reasoning of the federal district court in *Richman* that ruled against the gun manufacturer and held that strict liability might be applicable against one who engaged in the dangerous activity of selling firearms. The Fifth Circuit later reversed the district court's holding in *Richman* for reasons similar to those outlined by the *Martin* court. *See* Perkins v. F.I.E. Corp., 762 F.2d 1250, 1267 (5th Cir. 1985).

3. ***Reducing the Restatement Factors to Two.*** As illustrated above, the Restatement (Second) offers six factors for courts considering whether to apply strict liability to certain activities. These factors can be grouped into two key questions that pay homage to the origins of this area of the law: (a) "to what extent is the activity dangerous?" and (b) "how uncommon is the activity?" The more the activity reflects an unusual degree of potential harm and is not carried out by many others in the community, the more likely courts are to conclude that those who choose to engage in such an unusually dangerous activity should be forced to internalize the cost for it through application of strict liability. Positive answers to these two questions evidence a dangerous, non-reciprocal risk that the law declares should impose liability when the risks are realized.

Indeed, the Restatement (Third) of Torts §20 reduces the six factors down to these two, inquiring only as to an activity's risks and whether it is a matter of "common usage." The only additional factor from the Second Restatement that does not fall neatly into either of these considerations is factor (f), which asks about the value of the activity to the community. Courts have been very mixed in applying this last consideration, unclear as to whether the activity's high value should insulate the actor from liability or whether its high value means the actor should be able to afford to pay for its true costs on the community. In other words, if the activity has significant value, those carrying it out should be able to charge higher prices to absorb the costs imposed by strict liability. However,

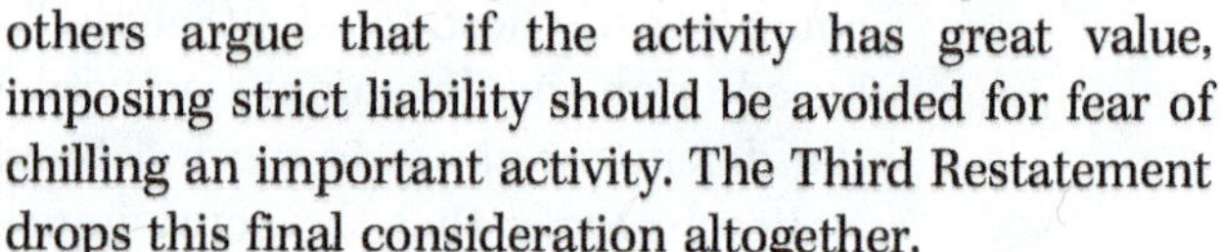

others argue that if the activity has great value, imposing strict liability should be avoided for fear of chilling an important activity. The Third Restatement drops this final consideration altogether.

Judge August Hand

3. ***Famous Jurists.*** If you were attentive in your reading, you might have noticed that the author of the *Exner* opinion for the Second Circuit had a familiar last name. Judge Augustus Noble Hand was the older first cousin of our ubiquitous Judge Learned Hand. Judge Augustus Hand was perhaps known most for his decision in 1934 declaring that the sale of contraceptives to physicians for use by their patients did not involve any immoral or obscene devices. United States v. One Package, 86 F.2d 737 (2d Cir. 1934).

4. ***Problems.*** Using the Restatement (Second) factors, should a court apply strict liability in the following circumstances?

A. Every Halloween, Defendant sets up and runs a haunted house in which customers walk through a darkened facility with creepy, costumed characters that jump out and chase the customers. One customer trips and falls while being chased through the dark facility, suffering a broken leg.

B. Defendant conducts public fireworks displays, typically on the 4th of July, in public places such as parks, stadiums, or riverfront properties. During one display, for unknown reasons, one of the cannons misfires and causes the firework to blast horizontally into a crowd. Plaintiff suffers severe burns.

C. Defendant operates a driving range for golfers adjacent to a roadway, which has a large volume of traffic. Golfers frequently hit bad golf shots that veer onto the road. Plaintiff is driving a convertible down this road when he is hit by an errant golf shot in his eye that causes partial blindness.

D. Defendant runs a shipping line and is unwittingly transporting nitroglycerin in an unmarked crate. Upon arriving at the port in San Francisco, the defendant discovers a leak coming from the crate and, upon taking a hammer to the crate to open it, causes a massive explosion that kills nearby people and destroys buildings.

III WILD AND TRESPASSING ANIMALS

The common law has similarly held that owners or possessors of animals may be strictly liable for harms caused by those animals. In the *Byram* case below, the court outlined three classes of cases in which the owners of animals are strictly liable. As you read this opinion, pay close attention to why the defendant's possession of the animal that caused the plaintiff's harm should not create strict liability. Following this case, in *Clark*, the plaintiff contends that the animal responsible for her injuries should be declared "wild" and that strict liability should be applied. Note the alternative arguments the plaintiff also employs to attempt to invoke strict liability. As you read these cases, ask yourself what similarity there is in the law between strict liability's application to dangerous activities and its application to certain animal-inflicted harms.

BYRAM v. MAIN

523 A.2d 1387 (Me. 1987)

McKusick, J.

Defendant Peter Main appeals from a judgment entered on August 22, 1986 in the amount of $27,483.52 for plaintiff Ray Byram. After a jury-waived trial the court found Main strictly liable for damages to Byram's tractor-trailer rig caused in the early morning hours of July 22, 1981, when Byram's rig struck Meadow, the pet donkey of Main's daughter, which had escaped from its enclosure and wandered onto Interstate 95 in Orono. The judgment here on review was entered following a second trial in this case, on remand from plaintiff Byram's earlier appeal to this court. On that first appeal we held that the Superior Court had improperly directed a verdict for Main on Byram's negligence claim, because the evidence presented by Byram concerning the adequacy of the fence used to contain the donkey had generated a question for the jury as to Main's negligence. Before the second trial Byram amended his complaint to add a strict liability count, and by stipulation of the parties the original negligence count was dismissed with prejudice.

The sole issue presented by this second appeal is whether the owner of a domestic animal that has escaped and wandered onto a high-speed public highway is strictly liable for harm resulting from a motor vehicle's collision with that animal. Main urges us that the Superior Court erred in relying upon *Decker v. Gammon*, 44 Me. 322 (1857), as authority for imposing strict liability upon him and that there is no basis in common law for finding strict liability on the facts of this case. We agree, and therefore vacate the judgment for Byram. In doing so we adopt for application to the present facts the rule of liability set forth in the *Restatement (Second) of Torts* §518 (1977).

Decker defines three classes of cases in which the owners of animals are liable for harm done by them to others:

> 1. The owner of wild beasts, or beasts that are in their nature vicious, is, *under all circumstances*, liable for injuries done by them.
> 2. If domestic animals, such as oxen and horses, injure any one, . . . *if they are rightfully in the place where they do the mischief*, the owner of such animals is not liable for such injury, unless he knew that they were accustomed to do mischief.
> 3. The owner of domestic animals, *if they are wrongfully in the place where they do any mischief*, is liable for it, though he had no notice that they had been accustomed to do so before.

The Superior Court found that the case at bar fell within the third class.

The Superior Court misinterpreted the *Decker* court's use of the word "wrongfully" when it included in that term the donkey's extremely inappropriate presence on the interstate. Viewing *Decker* against the backdrop of the common law, we read that opinion to say that cases involving trespass by domestic animals are the only cases imposing strict liability encompassed in the third class. Under common law both in 1857 and today, an owner of a domestic animal not known to be abnormally dangerous is strictly liable only for harms caused by that animal while trespassing; if the animal causes harm in a public place, no liability is imposed upon the owner without a finding that the owner was at fault. *Restatement (Second) of Torts* §§504, 509, 518 (1977); W. Keeton, *Prosser and Keeton on Torts* §76, at 538-42 (5th ed. 1984). The *Decker* court, in defining three classes of cases, set forth the whole common law of animal owner liability so as to fit the particular case before it into that general framework. The holding of the *Decker* case was limited to its facts. The *Decker* court decided only that strict liability applies in a fact situation that supports a trespass action. The 1857 Law Court specifically noted that:

> In the case before us, though the declaration is not technically for trespass *quare clausum*, it is distinctly alleged that the defendant's horse, "being so unlawfully at large, broke and entered the plaintiff's close, and injured the plaintiff's horse," which was there peaceably and of right depasturing.

Therefore, *Decker* cannot properly be interpreted to extend by dictum strict liability to harm caused by an animal in a public place. In fact, the *Decker* court specifically noted that "if the owner puts a horse or an ox to grass in his field, and the horse or ox breaks the hedge, and runs into the highway, and gores or kicks some passenger, an action will not lie against the owner unless he had notice that they had done such a thing before."

We realize that since 1857 radical changes have occurred in the nature and use of public highways, particularly those with limited access and high-speed motor traffic. Despite those changes, however, we do not read *Decker*'s words "wrongfully in the place" to apply to the facts of the case at bar. The general development of the law has not been in that direction. In fact, *Decker,* when its third class is correctly interpreted to include animal trespass cases but not cases where the animal is in a merely inappropriate place when it causes harm, is still a remarkably good statement of the common law as it remains today, as reflected by the *Restatement.*

Furthermore, the considerations that support the strict liability rules in animal trespass and wild animal cases do not apply to the present facts. The liability imposed by courts in cases described by the third *Decker* category and by section 504 of the *Restatement* and the comments following developed as an extension of liability for trespass by persons; the possessor of a domestic animal was identified with the animal, so that when it trespassed the owner trespassed. *Prosser and Keeton on Torts* §76, at 539. The imposition of strict liability for trespass protects the crucial right of the possessor of land to its exclusive use and control. Strict liability could not serve that same purpose in the case at bar because no individual has the right to the exclusive use and control of a public highway.

The first *Decker* rule, now set forth in *Restatement (Second) of Torts* §507, imposes strict liability for the consequences of keeping a wild animal, an activity that, while not wrongful, exposes the community to an obvious abnormal danger.[7] The keeper of a wild animal "takes the risk that at any moment the animal may revert to and exhibit" "the dangerous propensities normal to the class to which it belongs." *Restatement (Second) of Torts* §507 comment c, at 11-12. Nonetheless, strict liability is not applied to all damages caused by wild animals. Even a wild animal that goes astray and causes damage to a highway traveler in circumstances similar to those of the case at bar would not at common law bring strict liability down upon its keeper.

> [The possessor of a wild animal] is liable for only such harm as the propensities of the animal's class or its known abnormal tendencies make it likely that it will inflict. Thus if [a tame] bear, having escaped, goes to sleep in the highway and is run into by a carefully driven motor car on a dark night, the possessor of the bear is not liable for harm to the motorist in the absence of negligence in its custody.

---

7. The keeping of wild animals is categorized with such dangerous activities as blasting, pile driving, storing inflammable liquids, and accumulating sewage. *Prosser and Keeton on Torts* §76 and §78.

Id. comment e, at 12. The rationale for imposing strict liability upon the owners of wild animals thus does not support applying anything beyond a negligence rule on the facts presented to us here.

For the purposes of this decision, therefore, we adopt the approach of *Restatement (Second) of Torts* §518, which is supported by the case law in Maine and elsewhere:

> Except for animal trespass, one who possesses or harbors a domestic animal that he does not know or have reason to know to be abnormally dangerous, is subject to liability for harm done if, but only if,
>
> (a) he intentionally causes the animal to do the harm, or
>
> (b) he is negligent in failing to prevent the harm.

We, as does the *Restatement*, leave the highway traveler who is injured by colliding with a stray domestic animal solely to his remedy in negligence. The degree of care required of the animal owner is of course commensurate with the propensities of the particular domestic animal and with the location, including proximity to high-speed highways, of the place where the animal is kept by its owner. Whether the owners of large domestic pets should be required to bear more stringent responsibilities for those animals than are imposed by common law is a question the public policy makers of the other branches of state government may well wish to address.

Judgment vacated. Remanded with directions to enter judgment for defendant.

CLARK v. BRINGS

169 N.W.2d 407 (Minn. 1969)

PETERSON, J.

While working as a babysitter for respondents' three young children, appellant was without warning attacked and bitten by their pet Siamese cat. She brought this action to recover for the extensive injuries which allegedly resulted, and she appeals . . . after the court below directed a verdict for respondents. These alternative contentions are argued: (1) That the common-law cause of action for injuries by animals should be changed, or the statute covering injuries by dogs judicially extended, to hold owners of cats strictly liable for the acts of their pets; [or] (2) that the evidence in this case should be held sufficient to prove a cause of action under the common law as it now stands, that is, to show that respondents' cat was dangerous and that they were aware of the fact.

Most of the problems in this appeal fall within the ambit of the common-law's system of distributing the costs of misbehavior by animals. The relevant cause of action in tort, sometimes called "the scienter action," which is not . . .

based on negligence, divides animals held as property into two classes: Domesticated animals, or those *mansuetae* or *domitae naturae*, and wild beasts, or those *ferae naturae*. In the case of injury by one of the first class, the plaintiff must prove that the particular animal was abnormal and dangerous, and that its owner or harborer let it run unfettered though he actually or constructively had knowledge of its harmful propensities — knowledge usually found to have been gleaned from specific acts of the animal prior to the injury sued upon. The possessor of an animal within the second class, on the other hand, is conclusively presumed to know of the danger, so a person injured need not prove such knowledge before he can recover.

This judicial distinction between classes of animals was clearly announced, at least by dicta, as early as 1730. The scienter action as it has come down to us is not without its modern critics, who would apply the simpler rules of liability for negligence to some or all of the situations it covers, but the ancient doctrine has long been given continuous approval and application in Minnesota.

Appellant first contends that this distinction is based on comparative economic utility, the owners of "useful" animals being somewhat protected as an encouragement to maintaining them and the owners of "useless" animals receiving no protection whatever. Although the cat may once have served rural society as a "mouser," it is argued, in modern cities it is merely a dispensable pet, the owner of which ought to be held, as would the owner of a tiger, liable for any damage it causes.

So far as this argument may be based on the relative productivity of animals, it is not well founded. It is true that the economic contribution made by certain animals has been considered by the courts in the difficult cases of animals whose tameness has seemed in doubt. Thus, holding bees to be domesticated, the court in *Earl v. Van Alstine*, 8 Barb. (N.Y.) 630, 636, said that "the law looks with more favor upon the keeping of animals that are useful to man, than such as are purely noxious and useless." It is also true that many of the animals which have been held to be of a harmless nature, such as milk cows are obviously more economically

Principles

Matters are different when risks are non-reciprocal even if injurers exercise due care. Some risks are reasonable because they are to the long-run advantage of those imperiled by them, but they are not mutually beneficial in the sense that reciprocal risks are. For example, given the importance of driving to our daily lives, each of us may benefit from the transport of large quantities of gasoline over the roads, even though this method of transporting gasoline creates risks of massive explosion, and even though most of us never expect to make use of the legal right to transport vast quantities of gasoline in this manner. It follows that the prospective victims of non-reciprocal risk impositions are not fully compensated for bearing these risks by the right to impose equal risks in turn. The imposition of non-reciprocal risks is not part of a normal life, and the value of the right to impose such risks does not offset the disvalue of having to bear exposure to them. Subjecting non-reciprocal risks to strict liability offsets this unfairness. By ensuring that those injured by non-reciprocal risk impositions are — so far as possible — fully compensated for their injuries, strict liability affects a more robust mutuality of benefit.

Gregory C. Keating, Philosophy and the Law of Torts 32 (Cambridge Univ. Press 2001).

productive and, in that narrow sense, more useful to society than are cats.

The example of the horse, however, belies the suggestion that this is the primary ground on which the common law distinguishes. The position of the horse has changed with the times, however, as perhaps has that of the cat; yet the law has continued to apply the same rules to these animals when in service only for amusement and exercise.

So far as appellant's argument may proceed on any broader theory of utility, we find no basis for distinguishing between species of animals. The courts have indeed held animals *ferae naturae* to include such worthless predators as coyotes, and wolves, but they have made the same finding as to chimpanzees, elephants, and, proverbially, tigers. All of these are animals of undoubted value to society in science, education, and entertainment, on the keepers of which the law must have some reason other than uselessness for imposing a special burden of care.

A close examination of the authorities shows that the law's division of animals into those domesticated and those dangerous is based rather on "[e]xperience as interpreted by the English law." Holmes, The Common Law, p. 157. Horses, cows, and other animals have been regarded by the courts as *domitae naturae* because "years ago, and continuously to the present time, the progeny of these classes has been found by experience to be harmless, and so the law assumes the result of this experience to be correct without further proof." *Filburn v. People's Palace and Aquarium Co.* L.R. 25 Q.B. 258, 260.

"[I]t appears," moreover, "that as soon as an animal is placed in the harmless class by judicial decision, judicial notice will be taken of the fact in any future case." Williams, Liability for Animals, p. 295. In the few apposite cases, the courts have without exception explicitly held or implicitly regarded the cat as a domesticated animal, one "that is dealt with by mankind on the footing that a person may safely keep it." *Clinton v. J. Lyons & Co.* [1912] 3 K.B. 198, 207. As was stated by Chief Justice Rugg in *Goodwin v. E.B. Nelson Grocery Co.* 132 N.E. 51, 53 (Mass.): "The domestic cat is by nature ordinarily harmless and docile."

William Blake's famous poem, "The Tiger" begins with the following memorable lines:

"Tiger, Tiger, burning bright
In the forest of the night,
What immortal hand or eye
Could frame thy fearful symmetry?"

We should be most reluctant, therefore, to be the first to observe judicially in this little house pet, the cat, the "fearful symmetry" which the poet, William Blake, saw in the tiger. If the law has erred in interpreting mankind's experience with cats, or if this animal's value to society strikes an inadequate balance against whatever damage and injury it might cause, then it is for the legislature, which can best assess the total dimension of the problem, to change the common law by statute.

This change, appellant asserts alternatively, has in fact been accomplished by the legislature. She argues that Minn. St. 347.22, which makes the owner of a dog liable for the bites which it might without provocation inflict on those rightfully coming near it, by necessary implication includes cats — that is, if the owner of one pet is thus to be held liable, then the same statutory policy should be applied to the owner of another.

Minn. St. 347.22 (L. 1951, c. 315, §1) was the first statute on this subject and provides:

> If a dog, without provocation, attacks or injures any person who is peaceably conducting himself in any place where he may lawfully be in any urban area, the owner of the dog is liable in damages to the person so attacked or injured to the full amount of the injury sustained. The term "owner" includes any person harboring or keeping a dog. The term "dog" includes both male and female of the canine species.

Before 1951, a person bitten by a dog in Minnesota could recover only through the scienter action.

Whatever the theory on which this statute was enacted, its close wording would seem to preclude any extension of its severe provisions to the owners of other animals, even those others of the "leisured classes" of pets. This court has not so extended this statute in other cases, for since its enactment we have continued to apply the common law in cases involving all other beasts.

If the Minnesota Legislature had in 1951 intended to revise the common law as to cats in the same manner as it abolished it as to dogs, there would have been no difficulty in doing so expressly, and there would be no apparent barrier to amending the statute now. Absent legislative action, we decline to hold that Minn. St. 347.22 applies to the owners of cats.

We must consider, then, whether appellant made out a jury issue as to her scienter action. To prove that respondents' cat had committed prior acts of viciousness, known to them, appellant's evidence was threefold: First, the cat had once before bitten a babysitter; second, the cat had scratched several members of the household; and third, the cat was usually confined to the basement.

The biting incident, although not without significance, is less significant than appellant would acknowledge. The babysitter who had been bitten testified that the incident occurred when she and the children were playing with the cat by pulling a spool across the basement floor on a string. The cat became excited from chasing it, she related, and inflicted a "superficial" bite on her ankle. The respondents, moreover, were not informed of this "attack" incident.

It is true that a pet's owner need not "have notice that the animal has frequently 'broken through the tameness of his nature' into acts of aggression," and that the notice is sufficient should the animal just once "throw off the habits of domesticity and tameness, and put on a savage nature." *Kittredge v. Elliott*, 16

N.H. 77, 81. "It is not true, as has often been stated, that 'the law allows a dog his first bite,' for if the owner has good reason to apprehend, from his knowledge of the nature and propensity of the animal, that he has become evilly inclined, the duty of care and restraint attaches." *Cuney v. Campbell*, 78 N.W. 878, 879 (Minn.). Here, however, the testimony shows that the cat was provoked and excited by play when it inflicted the first injury, and the authorities universally hold that "[s]uch an attack is no evidence of viciousness in the animal and is insufficient to render the owner liable." *Erickson v. Bronson*, 83 N.W. 988 (Minn). At best, to say that this bite "was vicious is merely conjecture," and the testimony thus cannot withstand a motion for a directed verdict.

The evidence that the cat had several times scratched respondents themselves, their children, and their other babysitters is scarcely more significant. The cat usually scratched them on their hands, it appears, when they were picking it up or playfully handling it. We would agree that it is the mere dangerousness of an animal's character, and not any intentional malevolence, which must be proved to render its owner liable — that the "propensity is vicious if it tends to harm, whether manifested in play or in anger, or in some outbreak of untrained nature which, from want of better understanding, must remain unclassified." *Hill v. Moseley*, 17 S.E.2d 676, 678. But many of these incidents of scratching would seem necessarily to be excused as provoked, under the rule discussed *supra*; in any event, injuries of so slight a nature as those shown, unaccompanied by any indications of a propensity of the cat to cause greater harm, are inadequate to prove that it was dangerous and ought to have been caged or destroyed.

Appellant relies upon evidence that respondents kept their cat confined in their basement to establish knowledge and acknowledgment by respondents that their cat was dangerous. There is indeed authority to the effect that such restraint of a pet may be proof that the animal was, as its owner knew, vicious. The sort of confinement shown in the case at bar, however, could hardly support an inference that respondents knew of any danger from their cat. It was kept in the basement, they testified, simply to prevent its scratching their living room furniture, not to protect against attack upon people. Respondents' three children, the youngest only about 3 years old, shared with the cat a furnished basement recreation room, where many of their toys were kept and where they often played. The precautions taken to keep the cat downstairs were minimal, consisting largely of a catch on the basement door, and the restraint was not continuously effective. The trial court, in our opinion, rightly considered the whole of this evidence far too tenuous for submission to the jury.

Affirmed.

NOTES AND PROBLEMS

1. ***Wild vs. Domestic Animals.*** What is the justification for imposing liability on owners and possessors of wild animals without a showing of fault? Consider the phrase "abnormal danger" as used by the court in *Byram*. How does this justification compare with the principle supporting strict liability for ultrahazardous activities? How would the Restatement (Second)'s factors for imposing liability for ultrahazardous activities apply to the activity of keeping a tiger in one's backyard?

2. *Different Pathways to Imposing Strict Liability.* *Byram* does a good job discussing the three ways in which animal owners can be subject to strict liability for harm caused by their animals: (a) characterization of their animal as wild; (b) the scienter action, in which a particular domesticated animal has previously displayed to its owner aberrational character traits of a propensity for violence; and (c) the animal causing harm while on the victim's property without consent. *Clark* also demonstrates that a legislature may modify the common law by enacting statutes that impose strict liability under certain circumstances for harms inflicted by domesticated animals, such as the Minnesota law creating strict liability for dog owners. In *Clark*, the plaintiff's various arguments for imposing strict liability essentially raised three questions for the court: (a) Are cats tantamount to tigers? (b) Are cats tantamount to dogs? and (c) Had the defendant's cat acted like a tiger in the past? Notice that the first two questions concern the cat species generally while the last question, relevant to the scienter action, only concerns the defendant's pet. Why did the court answer each question in the negative?

3. *Negligence vs. Scienter Action.* In *Clark*, the court describes the scienter action as imposing strict liability once it is shown that the defendant had actual or constructive knowledge from specific acts of its domesticated animal of dangerous propensities abnormal to its species. Focusing on the actual or constructive knowledge of the defendant to impose liability appears to come close to describing a fault-based negligence cause of action. But notice that in a scienter action, once this level of awareness by the owner of a domesticated animal is demonstrated, the owner becomes absolutely liable for the harm inflicted by its pet regardless of what measures the owner undertook to prevent such harm. In this way, the scienter action still imposes strict liability rather than requiring negligence as a basis for liability. Once Fluffy has been shown to be a very bad kitty, no amount of care by its owner will preclude liability for the harm Fluffy inflicts on others. Of course, if a pet's owner makes no efforts to protect others from its animal despite foreseeable knowledge of the animal's propensity to inflict injuries, a victim can always assert a negligence action as well. And when the pet owner's acts or omissions display gross negligence, an action for punitive damages might be warranted. The point is that the availability of a strict liability cause of action for wild animals does not displace other fault-based claims that might be available based on the circumstances.

4. *Problems.* Should strict liability apply in the following circumstances?

A. Defendant lives in a semi-rural area and keeps exotic animals on his property, which a large fence surrounds. Vandals cut a hole in his fence one evening and a zebra escapes. The zebra runs through an intersection in a nearby town, causing two cars to collide.

B. A local college keeps a bear in a caged enclosure on campus as its mascot. The bear escapes the enclosure and urinates on the plaintiff's new car parked on a public street, ruining its paint job.

C. A city ordinance requires dog owners to keep their pets on a leash when walking on public property. The defendant's unleashed dog is chasing Frisbees in a public park when it spots the plaintiff's dog (on a leash) and attacks it.

D. Defendant has a pit bull, which has never displayed a propensity for viciousness. However, it is provoked one day while sitting in the defendant's driveway by youths on their bikes throwing rocks toward the dog. The pit bull attacks one of the teens on his bike and inflicts significant wounds to the teen's leg.

E. Defendant owns a ranch and has horses. One of the horses, Ginger, has a bit of a short fuse and becomes annoyed when ridden for long periods of time. She has a tendency in such instances to refuse to be ridden any further, as she stubbornly will simply stop moving. She has also tried on a few occasions to turn her head back toward a rider's leg and bump the leg to indicate her annoyance. Becoming tired while being ridden by a guest of the ranch, Ginger turned her head and tried to bump the rider's leg. When the rider responded by kicking the horse in her ribs, Ginger got angry and bit the rider's foot.

Upon Further Review

For most of our usual activities, such as mowing the lawn, driving to work, shopping in the local market, building a tree-house, keeping a family pet, or playing tennis, the law does not make one liable unless found to be at fault in causing another's injuries — either through an intentional tort or an act of carelessness. But when conduct creates non-reciprocal risks because it is so unusual, and when those risks are considered significant, the law has for a long time dispensed with a showing of fault as a condition of imposing liability. So, for example, actors who use explosives in their business or keep a pet cobra can be held strictly liable when their conduct causes harm to another. Such liability can attach regardless of how much care was employed by the actor — they become insurers of others hurt by their conduct. While this body of law is important in its own right, it was considered a fairly niche area of tort law until the recognition of strict products liability.

CHAPTER 11

Products Liability

I INTRODUCTION

An individual is making toast one morning when her toaster overheats and explodes. She suffers horrific skin burns. What recourse does the consumer have? Before the adoption of strict liability for defective product sellers, an injured consumer had to resort to either a claim for negligence or breach of warranty. Each theory was fraught with some peril and significant obstacles to overcome. Much of the early history of strict liability for products cases involves courts recognizing these barriers and deciding that they could no longer be tolerated. Within a few years of the California Supreme Court's decision to offer a strict liability remedy to users of flawed products, nearly every other state followed suit based upon Restatement (Second) of Torts §402A — arguably the most influential provision in the entire Restatement of Torts. The pendulum swung far with the adoption of strict liability, sweeping aside many possible defenses otherwise available to product sellers. The law over the years has become more complex and sophisticated in terms of the proper analysis of each variety of products case. In modern strict products liability, many have begun to question whether the pendulum has

CHAPTER GOALS

- ☑ Appreciate the dual heritage of strict products liability law from the laws of warranty and torts.
- ☑ Learn how barriers of duty and fault were overcome to facilitate compensation to injured consumers of faulty goods.
- ☑ See how Restatement of Torts (Second) §402A shaped strict products liability.
- ☑ Discover the different tests for manufacturing defects, design defects, and marketing defects. Compare and contrast strict products liability from negligence law.
- ☑ Appreciate how issues of comparative fault might involve a different balancing of interests than in negligence cases.
- ☑ Encounter the limitation on the concept of a seller's duty to design around (or warn of) risks associated only with product misuses.

swung back the opposite direction with increasingly familiar notions of fault injected into the supposedly "absolute" theory of liability. Aside from negligence law, strict products liability might be one of the most common civil tort claims filed today. Entire elective courses in law school are frequently devoted to the intricacies in this specialty area of the law. Nevertheless, this foray into the law of strict products liability should enable you to perceive differences and similarities between this uniquely twentieth century theory of recovery and older causes of action. Product liability law continues to evolve through judicial decisions as well as legislative modifications arising out of a perceived need for tort reform. It nevertheless remains a favorite theory of recovery for many plaintiffs' counsel.

II HISTORICAL DEVELOPMENT AND ADOPTION

A. Limitations on Duty

At one point in time, courts uniformly applied a limited special duty rule in negligence cases that recognized a duty of care to a consumer injured by a product only if the seller was in contractual privity with the plaintiff. That is, the consumer could only assert a negligence claim against her *immediate seller* of the product. If the plaintiff bought directly from the manufacturer, she could sue if the manufacturer could be shown to be at fault. On the other hand, most consumer products are not sold directly by the manufacturer to the consumer but through wholesalers, distributors, and then retailers. Under this scenario, the only entity owing the consumer a duty of care would be the retailer from whom the plaintiff purchased the item. Unfortunately, retailers are less likely to have acted negligently than manufacturers — after all, retailers rarely exercise any control over the design or building of such goods. The retailer might also have no indication, until the plaintiff's injury and suit, of the existence of any problem. Thus, the only one in the stream of commerce owing a duty of care toward the plaintiff would be the one least likely to be culpable of any wrongdoing. Courts increasingly desired to make it easier for consumers damaged by defective products to find recourse against sellers of such goods. This limited duty rule was a major obstacle in the path of easing restrictions on suits brought by injured consumers. A case with enormous influence in torts was decided in 1916 in an opinion written by Judge Cardozo. In the *MacPherson* case below, note how Judge Cardozo masterfully and dramatically changes the law while making it look like less than a wholesale shift in the law of torts.

MACPHERSON v. BUICK MOTOR COMPANY

111 N.E. 1050 (N.Y. 1916)

CARDOZO, J.

The defendant is a manufacturer of automobiles. It sold an automobile to a retail dealer. The retail dealer resold to the plaintiff. While the plaintiff was in the car, it suddenly collapsed. He was thrown out and injured. One of the wheels was made of defective wood, and its spokes crumbled into fragments. The wheel was not made by the defendant; it was bought from another manufacturer. There is evidence, however, that its defects could have been discovered by reasonable inspection, and that inspection was omitted. There is no claim that the defendant knew of the defect and willfully concealed it. The charge is one, not of fraud, but of negligence. The question to be determined is whether the defendant owed a duty of care and vigilance to any one but the immediate purchaser.

The foundations of this branch of the law, at least in this state, were laid in *Thomas v. Winchester* (6 N.Y. 397). A poison was falsely labeled. The sale was made to a druggist, who in turn sold to a customer. The customer recovered damages from the seller who affixed the label. "The defendant's negligence," it was said, "put human life in imminent danger." A poison falsely labeled is likely to injure any one who gets it. Because the danger is to be foreseen, there is a duty to avoid the injury. Cases were cited by way of illustration in which manufacturers were not subject to any duty irrespective of contract. The distinction was said to be that their conduct, though negligent, was not likely to result in injury to any one except the purchaser. We are not required to say whether the chance of injury was always as remote as the distinction assumes. Some of the illustrations might be rejected today. The *principle* of the distinction is for present purposes the important thing.

Thomas v. Winchester became quickly a landmark of the law. In the application of its principle there may at times have been uncertainty or even error. There has never in this state been doubt or disavowal of the principle itself. The chief cases are well known, yet to recall some of them will be helpful. *Loop v. Litchfield* (42 N.Y. 351) is the earliest. It was the case of a defect in a small balance wheel used on a circular saw. The manufacturer pointed out the defect to the buyer, who wished a cheap article and was ready to assume the risk. The risk can hardly have been an imminent one, for the wheel lasted five years before it broke. In the meanwhile the buyer had made a lease of the machinery. It was held that the manufacturer was not answerable to the lessee. *Loop v. Litchfield* was followed in *Losee v. Clute* (51 N.Y. 494), the case of the explosion of a steam boiler. That decision has been criticised (Thompson on Negligence, 233; Shearman & Redfield on Negligence [6th ed.], §117); but it must be confined to its special facts. It was put upon the ground that the risk of injury was too remote. The buyer in that case had not only accepted the boiler, but had tested it. The manufacturer knew that his own test was not the final one. The finality of the test has a bearing on the measure of diligence owing to persons other than the purchaser (Beven, Negligence [3d ed.], pp. 50, 51, 54; Wharton, Negligence [2d ed.], §134).

These early cases suggest a narrow construction of the rule. Later cases, however, evince a more liberal spirit. First in importance is *Devlin v. Smith* (89 N.Y. 470). The defendant, a contractor, built a scaffold for a painter. The painter's servants were injured. The contractor was held liable. He knew that the scaffold, if improperly constructed, was a most dangerous trap. He knew that it was to be used by the workmen. He was building it for that very purpose. Building it for their use, he owed them a duty, irrespective of his contract with their master, to build it with care.

From *Devlin v. Smith* we pass over intermediate cases and turn to the latest case in this court in which *Thomas v. Winchester* was followed. That case is *Statler v. Ray Mfg. Co.* (195 N.Y. 478, 480). The defendant manufactured a large coffee urn. It was installed in a restaurant. When heated, the urn exploded and injured the plaintiff. We held that the manufacturer was liable. We said that the urn "was of such a character inherently that, when applied to the purposes for which it was designed, it was liable to become a source of great danger to many people if not carefully and properly constructed."

It may be that *Devlin v. Smith* and *Statler v. Ray Mfg. Co.* have extended the rule of *Thomas v. Winchester*. If so, this court is committed to the extension. The defendant argues that things imminently dangerous to life are poisons, explosives, deadly weapons — things whose normal function it is to injure or destroy. But whatever the rule in *Thomas v. Winchester* may once have been, it has no longer that restricted meaning. A scaffold is not inherently a destructive instrument. It becomes destructive only if imperfectly constructed. A large coffee urn may have within itself, if negligently made, the potency of danger, yet no one thinks of it as an implement whose normal function is destruction. We are not required at this time either to approve or to disapprove the application of the rule that was made in these cases. It is enough that they help to characterize the trend of judicial thought.

We hold, then, that the principle of *Thomas v. Winchester* is not limited to poisons, explosives, and things of like nature, to things which in their normal operation are implements of destruction. If the nature of a thing is such that it is reasonably certain to place life and limb in peril when negligently made, it is then a thing of danger. Its nature gives warning of the consequences to be expected. If to the element of danger there is added knowledge that the thing will be used by persons other than the purchaser, and used without new tests, then, irrespective of contract, the manufacturer of this thing of danger is under a duty to make it carefully. That is as far as we are required to go for the decision of this case. There must be knowledge of a danger, not merely possible, but probable. It is *possible* to use almost anything in a way that will make it dangerous if defective. That is not enough to charge the manufacturer with a duty independent of his contract. Whether a given thing is dangerous may be sometimes a question for the court and sometimes a question for the jury. There must also be knowledge that in the usual course of events the danger will be shared by others than the buyer. Such knowledge may often be inferred from the nature of the transaction. But it is possible that even knowledge of the danger and of the use will not always be enough. The proximity or remoteness of the relation is a factor to be considered. We are dealing now with the liability of the manufacturer of the finished product, who puts it on the market to be used without inspection by his customers. If he is negligent, where danger is to be foreseen, a liability will follow.

We are not required at this time to say that it is legitimate to go back of the manufacturer of the finished product and hold the manufacturers of the component parts. To make their negligence a cause of imminent danger, an independent cause must often intervene; the manufacturer of the finished product must also fail in *his* duty of inspection. It may be that in those circumstances the negligence of the earlier members of the series is too remote to constitute, as to the ultimate user, an actionable wrong. We leave that question open. We shall have to deal with it when it arises. The difficulty which it suggests is not present in this case. There is here no break in the chain of cause and effect. In such circumstances, the presence of a known danger, attendant upon a known use, makes vigilance a duty. We have put aside the notion that the duty to safeguard life and limb, when the consequences of negligence may be foreseen, grows out of contract and nothing else. We have put the source of the obligation where it ought to be. We have put its source in the law.

From this survey of the decisions, there thus emerges a definition of the duty of a manufacturer, which enables us to measure this defendant's liability. Beyond all question, the nature of an automobile gives warning of probable danger if its construction is defective. This automobile was designed to go fifty miles an hour. Unless its wheels were sound and strong, injury was almost certain. It was as much a thing of danger as a defective engine for a railroad. The defendant knew the danger. It knew also that the car would be used by persons other than the buyer. This was apparent from its size; there were seats for three persons. It was apparent also from the fact that the buyer was a dealer in cars, who bought to resell. The maker of this car supplied it for the use of purchasers from the dealer just as plainly as the contractor in *Devlin v. Smith* supplied the scaffold for use by the servants of the owner. The dealer was indeed the one person of whom it might be said with some approach to certainty that by him the car would not be used. Yet the defendant would have us say that he was the one person whom it was under a legal duty to protect. The law does not lead us to so inconsequent a conclusion. Precedents drawn from the days of travel by stage coach do not fit the conditions of travel to-day. The principle that the danger must be imminent does not change, but the things subject to the principle do change. They are whatever the needs of life in a developing civilization require them to be.

In this view of the defendant's liability there is nothing inconsistent with the theory of liability on which the case was tried. It is true that the court told the jury that "an automobile is not an inherently dangerous vehicle." The meaning, however, is made plain by the context. The meaning is that danger is not to be expected when the vehicle is well constructed. The court left it to the jury to say whether the defendant ought to have foreseen that the car, if negligently constructed, would become "imminently dangerous." Subtle distinctions are drawn by the defendant between things inherently dangerous and things imminently dangerous, but the case does not turn upon these verbal niceties. If danger was to be expected as reasonably certain, there was a duty of vigilance, and this whether you call the danger inherent or imminent. In varying forms that thought was put before the jury. We do not say that the court would not have been justified in ruling as a matter of law that the car was a dangerous thing. If there was any error, it was none of which the defendant can complain.

We think the defendant was not absolved from a duty of inspection because it bought the wheels from a reputable manufacturer. It was not merely a dealer in automobiles. It was a manufacturer of automobiles. It was responsible for the finished product. It was not at liberty to put the finished product on the market without subjecting the component parts to ordinary and simple tests (*Richmond & Danville R.R. Co. v. Elliott*, 149 U.S. 266, 272). Under the charge of the trial judge nothing more was required of it. The obligation to inspect must vary with the nature of the thing to be inspected. The more probable the danger, the greater the need of caution. Both by its relation to the work and by the nature of its business, it is charged with a stricter duty.

The judgment should be affirmed with costs.

NOTES AND PROBLEMS

1. *Eradication of Special Duty Limit.* The plaintiff in *MacPherson* encountered a duty problem with respect to its attempted negligence claim against Buick. As an example of a special duty rule (similar to those we encountered in Chapter 6, Special Duty Rules) sellers of goods who were not in direct privity of contract with the plaintiff generally had no duty of care toward the plaintiff. Can you imagine why the law had come up with this limitation to protect remote sellers? This special duty rule was first announced in Winterbottom v. Wright, 152 Eng. Rep. 402 (1842) where the court stated that a coach driver hurt by a defect in the stagecoach he was hired to drive could not sue for negligence because he lacked privity of contract. You will recall encountering Judge Cardozo in the *Palsgraf* case, where he declared that the concept of a duty of care was premised upon a foreseeable risk of harm to the plaintiff from the defendant's conduct. In *MacPherson*, Cardozo determined to run the historic no-duty rule for sellers of goods lacking privity of contract with victims through this crucible of foreseeability. Judge Cardozo first noted that an exception to the general no-duty rule had become the trend based upon the foreseeability of significant harm to remote users of negligently designed and manufactured goods. How does Cardozo use this exception to establish a new rule? What are the two aspects of foreseeability that Cardozo declares are necessary to remove the privity barrier in a particular case?

2. ***Liability of Retailer.*** Near the end of his opinion in *MacPherson*, Judge Cardozo turns his attention to the second issue of whether there was evidence of any fault against Buick. He contrasts the potential requirement for an inspection of the finished goods against a manufacturer such as Buick with the subsequent retailer of the car. He observes that Buick was "not merely a dealer in automobiles. It was a manufacturer of automobiles. It was not at liberty to put the finished product on the market without subjecting the component parts to ordinary and simple tests." The negative implication of this observation is that an ordinary retailer, having no part in the design or manufacture of a finished good, might not have any obligation — as part of its duty of reasonable care — to inspect or test a car before selling it. This observation highlights a significant importance of the decision in *MacPherson* because, prior to this case, the only seller in the stream of commerce owing the plaintiff a duty of care was the one least likely to be found to have breached such a duty. *MacPherson* fixes this anomaly and opens the door to suits by victims against those likely to have deeper pockets than the retailer with whom the plaintiff dealt.

3. ***Liability of Remote Component Manufacturer.*** On the other end of the stream of commerce from the retailer, Cardozo briefly speculates about the potential liability of the remote manufacturer of the defective wheel used on the Buick. While not absolving that remote seller of a duty of care, Cardozo wonders whether proximate cause will be a stumbling block for an injured consumer under his direct cause view of proximate cause: "It may be that in those circumstances the negligence of the earlier members of the series is too remote to constitute, as to the ultimate user, an actionable wrong. We leave that question open." Do you understand why under a direct cause test for proximate cause the subsequent negligence of Buick might be considered an independent intervening cause?

4. ***Paving the Way for Strict Liability Against Sellers.*** Though Cardozo conditioned a finding of duty on Buick being able to foresee the special dangers of a negligently constructed car to users other than immediate purchasers, courts eventually quit asking these questions and began to routinely assume a *duty* on all product manufacturers owed toward any user or victim of a negligently built product. Thus, *Macpherson* paved the way toward easing one of the two major impediments toward recovery by victims of products. The *Escola* case below suggested a pathway around the other hurdle — establishing *fault*, or negligence, against a product seller.

B. Rejection of Fault or Contract Breach as Prerequisites to Recovery

The *MacPherson* case was enormously important in terms of making manufacturers who were careless about designing or building goods accountable to remote injured consumers. But it still left intact certain other hurdles to recovery, either on a tort theory or a breach of warranty theory. In the following case of *Escola v. Coca Cola,* Justice Traynor in his famous concurring opinion proposed that courts find a new, simpler pathway toward an injured consumer's recovery that is neither shackled with the burden of proving fault nor subject to the intricacies of the law of sales (for a warranty recovery). Although it was "just" a concurring opinion, the strength of his arguments resonated and ultimately became the basis nearly two decades later for the adoption of strict products liability. Consider the multifaceted arguments Justice Traynor gives for this proposed fundamental change in the law.

ESCOLA v. COCA COLA BOTTLING CO. OF FRESNO

150 P.2d 436 (Cal. 1944)

GIBSON, J.

Plaintiff, a waitress in a restaurant, was injured when a bottle of Coca Cola broke in her hand. She alleged that defendant company, which had bottled and delivered the alleged defective bottle to her employer, was negligent in selling "bottles containing said beverage which on account of excessive pressure of gas or by reason of some defect in the bottle was dangerous and likely to explode." This appeal is from a judgment upon a jury verdict in favor of plaintiff.

Defendant's driver delivered several cases of Coca Cola to the restaurant, placing them on the floor, one on top of the other, under and behind the counter, where they remained at least thirty-six hours. Immediately before the accident, plaintiff picked up the top case and set it upon a nearby ice cream cabinet in front of and about three feet from the refrigerator. She then proceeded to take the bottles from the case with her right hand, one at a time, and put them into the refrigerator. Plaintiff testified that after she had placed three bottles in the refrigerator and had moved the fourth bottle about eighteen inches from the case "it exploded in my hand." The bottle broke into two jagged pieces and inflicted a deep five-inch cut, severing blood vessels, nerves and muscles of the thumb and palm of the hand. Plaintiff further testified that when the bottle exploded, "It made a sound similar to an electric light bulb that would have dropped. It made a loud pop." Plaintiff's employer testified, "I was about twenty feet from where it actually happened and I heard the explosion." A fellow employee, on the opposite side of the counter, testified that plaintiff "had the bottle, I should judge, waist high, and I know that it didn't bang either the case or the door or another bottle . . . when it popped. It sounded just like a fruit jar would blow up." The witness further testified that the contents of the bottle "flew all over herself and myself and the walls and one thing and another."

The top portion of the bottle, with the cap, remained in plaintiff's hand, and the lower portion fell to the floor but did not break. The broken bottle was not produced at the trial, the pieces having been thrown away by an employee of the restaurant shortly after the accident. Plaintiff, however, described the broken pieces, and a diagram of the bottle was made showing the location of the "fracture line" where the bottle broke in two.

One of defendant's drivers, called as a witness by plaintiff, testified that he had seen other bottles of Coca Cola in the past explode and had found broken bottles in the warehouse when he took the cases out, but that he did not know what made them blow up.

Plaintiff then rested her case, having announced to the court that being unable to show any specific acts of negligence, she relied completely on the doctrine of res ipsa loquitur.

Although it is not clear in this case whether the explosion was caused by an excessive charge or a defect in the glass, there is a sufficient showing that neither cause would ordinarily have been present if due care had been used. Further, defendant had exclusive control over both the charging and inspection of the bottles. Accordingly, all the requirements necessary to entitle plaintiff to rely on the doctrine of res ipsa loquitur to supply an inference of negligence are present.

The judgment is affirmed.

Traynor, J., *concurring*

I concur in the judgment, but I believe the manufacturer's negligence should no longer be singled out as the basis of a plaintiff's right to recover in cases like the present one. In my opinion it should now be recognized that a manufacturer incurs an absolute liability when an article that he has placed on the market, knowing that it is to be used without inspection, proves to have a defect that causes injury to human beings. *McPherson v. Buick Motor Co.* established the principle, recognized by this court, that irrespective of privity of contract, the manufacturer is responsible for an injury caused by such an article to any person who comes in lawful contact with it. In these cases the source of the manufacturer's liability was his negligence in the manufacturing process or in the inspection of component parts supplied by others. Even if there is no negligence, however, public policy demands that responsibility be fixed wherever it will most effectively reduce the hazards to life and health inherent in defective products that reach the market. It is evident that the manufacturer can anticipate some hazards and guard against the recurrence of others, as the public cannot. Those who suffer injury from defective products are unprepared to meet its consequences. The cost of an injury and the loss of time or health may be an overwhelming misfortune to the person injured, and a needless one, for the risk of injury can be insured by the manufacturer and distributed among the public as a cost of doing business. It is to the public interest to discourage the marketing of products having defects that are a menace to the public. If such products nevertheless find their way into the market it is to the public interest to place the responsibility for whatever injury they may cause upon the manufacturer, who, even if he is not negligent in the manufacture of the product, is responsible for its reaching the market. However intermittently such injuries may occur and however haphazardly they may strike, the risk of their occurrence is a constant risk and a general one. Against such a risk there should be general and constant protection and the manufacturer is best situated to afford such protection.

The injury from a defective product does not become a matter of indifference because the defect arises from causes other than the negligence of the manufacturer, such as negligence of a submanufacturer of a component part whose defects could not be revealed by inspection, or unknown causes that even by the device of res ipsa loquitur cannot be classified as negligence of the manufacturer. The inference of negligence may be dispelled by an affirmative showing of proper care. If the evidence against the fact inferred is "clear, positive, uncontradicted, and of such a nature that it cannot rationally be disbelieved, the court must instruct the jury that the nonexistence of the fact has been established as a matter of law." (*Blank v. Coffin*, 126 P.2d 868 (Cal.)) An injured person, however, is not ordinarily in a position to refute such evidence or identify the cause of the defect, for he can hardly be familiar with the manufacturing process as the manufacturer himself is. In leaving it to the jury to decide whether the inference has been dispelled, regardless of the evidence against it, the negligence rule approaches the rule of strict liability. It is needlessly circuitous to make negligence the basis of recovery and impose what is in reality liability without negligence. If public policy demands that a manufacturer of goods be responsible for their quality regardless of negligence there is no reason not to fix that responsibility openly.

In the case of foodstuffs, the public policy of the state is formulated in a criminal statute. The statute imposes criminal liability not only if the food is adulterated, but if its container, which may be a bottle has any deleterious substance or renders the product injurious to health. The criminal liability under the statute attaches without proof of fault, so that the manufacturer is under the duty of ascertaining whether an article manufactured by him is safe. Statutes of this kind result in a strict liability of the manufacturer in tort to the member of the public injured.

The statute may well be applicable to a bottle whose defects cause it to explode. In any event it is significant that the statute imposes criminal liability without fault, reflecting the public policy of protecting the public from dangerous products placed on the market, irrespective of negligence in their manufacture. While the Legislature imposes criminal liability only with regard to food products and their containers, there are many other sources of danger. It is to the public interest to prevent injury to the public from any defective goods by the imposition of civil liability generally.

The retailer, even though not equipped to test a product, is under an absolute liability to his customer, for the implied warranties of fitness for proposed use and merchantable quality include a warranty of safety of the product. This warranty is not necessarily a contractual one for public policy requires that the buyer be insured at the seller's expense against injury. The courts recognize, however, that the retailer cannot bear the burden of this warranty, and allow him to recoup any losses by means of the warranty of safety attending the wholesaler's or manufacturer's sale to him. Such a procedure, however, is needlessly circuitous and engenders wasteful litigation. Much would be gained if the injured person could base his action directly on the manufacturer's warranty.

The liability of the manufacturer to an immediate buyer injured by a defective product follows without proof of negligence from the implied warranty of safety attending the sale. Ordinarily, however, the immediate buyer is a dealer who does not intend to use the product himself, and if the warranty of safety is to serve the purpose of protecting health and safety it must give rights to others than the dealer. In the words of Judge Cardozo in the *McPherson* case: "The dealer was indeed the one person of whom it might be said with some approach to certainty that by him the car would not be used. Yet, the defendant would have us say that he was the one person whom it was under a legal duty to protect. The law does not lead us to so inconsequent a solution." While the defendant's negligence in the *McPherson* case made it unnecessary for the court to base liability on warranty, Judge Cardozo's reasoning recognized the injured person as the real party in interest and effectively disposed of the theory that the liability of the manufacturer incurred by his warranty should apply only to the immediate purchaser. It thus paves the way for a standard of liability that would make the manufacturer guarantee the safety of his product even when there is no negligence.

Principles

"Most students of the field, including myself, having witnessed the extraordinary expansion of liability since the first adoption of the strict liability concept and having witnessed, especially in recent years, the widespread withdrawal of products from markets on liability grounds, have concluded that products liability standards should be substantially rolled back."

George L. Priest, Can Absolute Manufacturer Liability Be Defended?, 9 Yale J. on Reg. 237, 238 (1992).

This court and many others have extended protection according to such a standard to consumers of food products, taking the view that the right of a consumer injured by unwholesome food does not depend "upon the intricacies of the law of sales" and that the warranty of the manufacturer to the consumer in absence of privity of contract rests on public policy. Dangers to life and health inhere in other consumers' goods that are defective and there is no reason to differentiate them from the dangers of defective food products.

In the food products cases the courts have resorted to various fictions to rationalize the extension of the manufacturer's warranty to the consumer: that a warranty runs with the chattel; that the cause of action of the dealer is assigned to the consumer; that the consumer is a third party beneficiary of the manufacturer's contract with the dealer. They have also held the manufacturer liable on a mere fiction of negligence: "Practically he must know it [the product] is fit, or bear the consequences if it proves destructive." Such fictions are not necessary to fix the manufacturer's liability under a warranty if the warranty is severed from the contract of sale between the dealer and the consumer and based on the law of torts as a strict liability. Warranties are not necessarily rights arising under a contract. An action on a warranty "was, in its origin, a pure action of tort," and only late in the historical development of warranties was an action in assumpsit allowed.

As handicrafts have been replaced by mass production with its great markets and transportation facilities, the close relationship between the producer and consumer of a product has been altered. Manufacturing processes, frequently valuable secrets, are ordinarily either inaccessible to or beyond the ken of the general public. The consumer no longer has means or skill enough to investigate for himself the soundness of a product, even when it is not contained in a sealed package, and his erstwhile vigilance has been lulled by the steady efforts of manufacturers to build up confidence by advertising and marketing devices such as trade-marks. Consumers no longer approach products warily but accept them on faith, relying on the reputation of the manufacturer or the trademark. Manufacturers have sought to justify that faith by increasingly high standards of inspection and a readiness to make good on defective products by way of replacements and refunds. The manufacturer's obligation to the consumer must keep pace with the changing relationship between them; it cannot be escaped because the marketing of a product has become so complicated as to require one or more intermediaries. Certainly there is greater reason to impose liability on the manufacturer than on the retailer who is but a conduit of a product that he is not himself able to test.

The manufacturer's liability should, of course, be defined in terms of the safety of the product in normal and proper use, and should not extend to injuries that cannot be traced to the product as it reached the market.

NOTES AND PROBLEMS

1. *Subsequent Adoption.* In 1963, Justice Traynor wrote the majority opinion in Greenman v. Yuba Power Products, Inc., 377 P.2d 897 (Cal. 1963) formally adopting the same theory of strict liability he endorsed in *Escola* for identical reasons. In *Greenman*, a power lathe manufactured by the defendant hurt the plaintiff. One of the legal problems the plaintiff had with recovering under a warranty theory was that state law demanded that a plaintiff give a timely notice of breach of warranty to anyone he intended to pursue on a warranty theory. The plaintiff, not realizing the possible claim against the remote manufacturer, failed to comply with this notice obligation. The court nevertheless permitted the plaintiff to recover on this new tort theory of strict liability due to the defect in the product that rendered it dangerous. The court summarized the plaintiff's right to recover under this theory of absolute liability, as follows:

> Implicit in the machine's presence on the market . . . was a representation that it would safely do the jobs for which it was built. Under these circumstances, it should not be controlling whether plaintiff selected the machine because of statements in [a] brochure, or because of the machine's own appearance of excellence that belied the defect lurking beneath the surface, or because he merely assumed that it would safely do the jobs it was built to do. It should not be controlling whether the details of the sales from manufacturer to retailer and from retailer to plaintiff's wife were such that one or more of the implied warranties of the sales act arose. To establish the manufacturer's liability, it was sufficient that plaintiff proved that he was injured while using the [lathe] in a way it was intended to be used as a result of a defect in design and manufacture of which plaintiff was not aware that made the [lathe] unsafe for its intended use.

Id. at 901.

2. *Restatement (Second) §402A (1965).* Within just a few years after the formal adoption of the legal theory of strict products liability in *Greenman*, Restatement (Second) §402A was published. It was quickly adopted by most jurisdictions. It has become the most cited and influential provision in the entire Restatement. It contemplates liability as follows:

> §402A *Special Liability of Seller of Product for Physical Harm to User or Consumer*
>
> (1) One who sells any product in a defective condition unreasonably dangerous to the user or consumer or to his property is subject to liability for physical harm thereby caused to the ultimate user or consumer, or to his property, if
>
> (a) the seller engaged in the business of selling such a product, and
>
> (b) it is expected to and does reach the user or consumer without substantial change in the condition in which it is sold.
>
> (2) The rule stated in Subsection (1) applies although
>
> (a) the seller has exercised all possible care in the preparation and sale of his product, and
>
> (b) the user or consumer has not bought the product from or entered into any contractual relation with the seller.

How are the decisions in *MacPherson* and *Escola/Greenman* reflected by §402A? In the stream of commerce, which sellers would face strict liability under its provisions? What sorts of losses create strict liability? There has more recently been published a Restatement (Third) of Torts: Products Liability (1998), but its provisions have not been as widely received or embraced as §402A from the Second Restatement.

3. ***Liability for "Sellers" of Defective Products.*** Restatement (Second) 402A establishes liability for any seller of a defective product within the stream of commerce — manufacturers, wholesalers, distributors, and retailers. So long as the defendant is regularly engaged in the sale of goods, and the product is proven to have contained an unreasonably dangerous "defect" at the time the defendant sold the item, that seller is liable. In effect, the common law recognizes a joint liability for all sellers of the defective product that hurt the plaintiff. The common law also has recognized, within the stream of commerce, that there is an implied right to be indemnified by a seller further upstream from the defendant seller held liable to the plaintiff. For example, if a retailer is liable to the plaintiff for a defective good received (in that same condition) from a wholesaler, the retailer can sue the wholesaler for complete indemnification. Of course, the wholesaler can then sue the manufacturer for indemnification as well, so long as the defective condition existed when the manufacturer initially sold the product. In this way, the plaintiff has multiple sources for redress for injuries caused by defective products, and (due to the indemnity rights) the loss theoretically will be borne by the seller that was the original source of the defect. In cases where the only allegations against various sellers involve their conduct in selling the defective good (as contrasted with some other act of negligence), there is no reason to have the jury apportion fault among the sellers. If there is any apportionment question, there would simply be a line item for the product itself. The percentage fault attributed to the product would create a joint liability for the sellers of the product (much like vicarious liability creates a joint liability for both employee and employer). Of course, in reality, the ultimate economic loss likely is not left on the shoulders of even the manufacturer. As Justice Traynor argued in *Escola*, manufacturers can pass on such losses to the consumers of their products by simply raising the price on the good to reflect such liabilities. Some states, by statute, provide immunity for "innocent retailers" who were not the source of a product defect, requiring plaintiffs to generally sue the manufacturer except in instances where the manufacturer is insolvent, beyond the jurisdiction of the court, or where the retailers are not so innocent (e.g. having knowledge of the defect, or contributing in some way to causing the defect).

4. ***Who Is a Seller?*** Two interesting issues have arisen concerning who qualifies as a product "seller." First, some plaintiffs have attempted to hold service providers strictly liable when their service involved the use of a product that contained a defect. For example, in Newmark v. Gimbel's, Inc., 258 A.2d 697 (N.J. 1969), the plaintiff was hurt while receiving service at a beauty parlor by allegedly defective permanent wave solution. The salon owner resisted the strict liability claim, arguing that she was selling services rather than products. The New Jersey court permitted the strict liability claim. The court distinguished beauty parlors from other professional service providers. Two years earlier, in Magrine v. Krasnica, 227 A.2d 539 (N.J. 1967) the same court held that strict products liability could not be applied to a claim against a dentist who attempted to use a hypodermic needle to inject anesthetic into the plaintiff's gums when it broke off

and caused injury to the patient. The court found that the dentist was providing professional services predominantly rather than selling products. It found that the rationales behind imposing strict liability on product sellers had no application to professionals. Other courts tend to agree that when the *primary purpose* behind the transaction is to bestow a professional service rather than sell a product, strict liability should be inapplicable. *See e.g.*, Easterly v. HSP of Texas, Inc., 772 S.W.2d 211, 213 (Tex. App.—Dallas 1989) (hospital could not be held strictly liable for defective catheter used at hospital on patient as it was an integral part of the professional services, not a separate product sale). Courts have also debated whether commercial lessors of products could be strictly liable as a product "seller" with most concluding that strict liability should be applicable. *See e.g.*, Cintrone v. Hertz Truck Leasing & Rental Service, 212 A.2d 769 (N.J. 1965) (reversing dismissal of strict liability claim against Hertz which leased truck that was not in good working order).

5. ***New vs. Used Goods.*** An individual who resells a used automobile or a used appliance at a garage sale will not face strict liability for a defect in those goods because they are not considered to be in the regular business of selling goods. Whether someone who engaged in the commercial re-sale of used products should face strict liability is a disputed matter. Compare Realmuto v. Straub Motors, 322 A.2d 440 (N.J. 1974) (strict liability applies to dealer who sells used products) with La Rosa v. Superior Court, 176 Cal. Rptr. 224 (1981) (refusing to apply strict liability to sellers of used goods).

6. ***Warranty Law, Negligence Law, and Strict Liability.*** While one might read the foregoing cases and conclude that strict liability law has wholly displaced any continued role for warranty or negligence law when a consumer is hurt by a product, this would be misleading. While an injured party might not *need* to resort to the "intricacies of the law of sales" in order to seek recompense, that avenue can still be available. Both claims for breach of express and implied warranties are generally governed today by Article 2 of the U.C.C. On such claims, the U.C.C. does not stake out a certain position on the privity requirement, instead leaving three options to courts, with a range from (a) only the purchaser and immediate family and household guests being allowed to sue for breach of warranty to (b) all those foreseeably injured by the breach of warranty for the product being permitted to sue. Why would someone jump through the extra hoops necessary to bring a warranty claim? Sometimes the remedies might be broader (including the possibility of recovering for purely economic losses) or the breach might help to facilitate a broader attack against the seller under a state's deceptive trade practices statute (which might permit recovery of attorney's fees or trebled damages). Finally, it might be that under a state's particular definitions of a product "defect" that a warranty claim might be subject to a different standard than a strict liability claim. (We will see this latter scenario later in this chapter in the *Denny v. Ford Motor Co.* case.) Also, negligence claims can likewise be brought in addition to a strict liability claim. It

may be that the plaintiff is able to conjure up evidence of traditional fault against a product seller and might want the jury to be able to receive this incriminating evidence. Further, the consumer might even be able to offer evidence of gross negligence to justify a submission on punitive damages to the jury. Thus, while the emergence of strict products liability law has freed consumers of the *necessity* of relying upon warranty and negligence causes of action, these alternative claims are still available in some circumstances.

7. ***Defects that Are Unreasonably Dangerous.*** Comment g to Restatement (Second) 402A describes a "defective condition" as follows:

> The rule stated in this Section applies only where the product is, at the time it leaves the seller's hands, in a condition not contemplated by the ultimate consumer, which will be unreasonably dangerous to him. The seller is not liable when he delivers the product in a safe condition, and subsequent mishandling or other causes make it harmful by the time it is consumed. The burden of proof that the product was in a defective condition at the time that it left the hands of the particular seller is upon the injured plaintiff; and unless the evidence can be produced which will support the conclusion that it was then defective, the burden is not sustained.

In the next three sections, we will dig deeper into the analytical models employed by courts to determine whether particular defects exist.

III DEFECTS

A. Manufacturing

Restatement (Second) §402A does not specify particular types of defects that may exist in a product. Nevertheless, courts have settled upon three categories of product defects—manufacturing, design, and marketing (i.e., warnings). A design defect occurs when the idea or plans for a product render it unreasonably dangerous. Imagine an automobile designer drawing up the plans for a new vehicle with wheels held in place by only two lug nuts. The plans might be followed perfectly but the wheel will likely fail because it is not designed to withstand enough physical forces on it to be able to hold it securely to the vehicle over time. This ill-conceived *design* for a wheel might permit the ultimate characterization that it was unreasonably dangerous and, therefore, defective. On the other hand, the design might have called for five lug nuts (a standard number for a passenger vehicle) but somewhere during the actual assembly of a particular unit on the assembly line, one car went through and only received four lug nuts. In other words, the plans were not followed. If that missing lug nut resulted in a wheel coming loose and causing an accident with injuries, the claimant would assert a *manufacturing* defect. Finally, if you assume that even the best designed and properly manufactured automobile wheels might, over time, come loose due to the physics of their movement, it might be necessary for the seller to provide a warning accompanying the automobile warning that, for example, the tightness of the lug nuts needs to be checked every 25,000 miles to guarantee they remain tight. A failure to provide this warning could be evidence of a *marketing* defect.

Most would agree that identifying a manufacturing defect is, of the three categories, the most straightforward analysis. This does not always mean that it will be easy to determine; that is dependent upon how clear the facts may be. But courts generally agree as to what they are looking for when testing for a manufacturing defect. A manufacturing defect is described in the Restatement of Products Liability as a "physical departure from a product's intended design." Section 1, comment a (1998). In such cases, one is merely comparing the plans with the actual output of the unit that hurt the plaintiff. If the deviation from the plans caused the plaintiff's injury, plaintiff has a good manufacturing defect case. Observe that the issue of how or why the defect occurs is irrelevant. Further, it makes no difference how hard the manufacturer tried to prevent such errors. Liability is very strict.

The first case we will review, involving a claim by a smoker against a tobacco company, will apply this straightforward analysis by comparing the product that hurt the plaintiff with the plans for that product. This case actually involved manufacturing, design, and marketing defect claims. We will revisit this case again, therefore, in each of the next two sections as we encounter those types of defects. The second case, involving a chair that was apparently not strong enough to hold the plaintiff, concerns an attempted use of circumstantial evidence to prove the requisite departure from the plans in a case where the plaintiff's expert could not identify any specific deviation.

AMERICAN TOBACCO CO. v. GRINNELL

951 S.W.2d 420 (Tex. 1997)

CORNYN, J.

In 1952, nineteen-year-old Wiley Grinnell began smoking Lucky Strikes, cigarettes manufactured by the American Tobacco Company. Almost a year later, Grinnell changed to Pall Malls, also manufactured by American. After smoking for approximately thirty-three years, Grinnell was diagnosed with lung cancer in July 1985. Shortly thereafter, he filed this lawsuit. He died less than a year later. Grinnell's family continued this suit after his death, adding wrongful death and survival claims. The family alleges that American failed to warn of, and actively concealed, facts that it knew or should have known, including the facts that Grinnell could quickly become addicted to cigarettes and that his smoking could result in injury or death from the cancer-causing ingredients if he used the cigarettes as American intended. They also allege that, even though American knew or should have known that its cigarettes were dangerous and could not be used safely, American represented to consumers that cigarettes were not harmful, dangerous, or capable of causing injury.

The Grinnells assert [among other claims] strict liability design, marketing, and manufacturing defect [claims].

The trial court granted [defendant's motions for summary judgment] and dismissed the Grinnells' suit. The court of appeals reversed the trial court's judgment and remanded the entire case.

The Grinnells allege that cigarettes are both defective and unreasonably dangerous under section 402A of the *Restatement (Second) of Torts.* Specifically, they assert that American's cigarettes are (1) defectively designed because ingredients found in cigarettes cause cancer, addiction, and disease, (2) defectively marketed, because the cigarette packages contain inadequate warnings, and (3) defectively manufactured because cigarettes contain pesticide residue. In his deposition taken one month before his death, Grinnell testified that had he known of the dangers inherent in cigarettes he would never have started smoking in the first place.

In Texas, section 402A of the Restatement (Second) of Torts governs claims for strict liability in tort. *Firestone Steel Prods. Co. v. Barajas,* 927 S.W.2d 608, 613 (Tex. 1996); *McKisson v. Sales Affiliates, Inc.,* 416 S.W.2d 787, 788-89 (Tex. 1967). Section 402A provides:

> (1) one who sells any product in a defective condition unreasonably dangerous to the user or consumer or to his property is subject to liability for physical harm thereby caused to the ultimate user or consumer, or to his property, if
>
> (a) the seller is engaged in the business of selling such a product, and
>
> (b) it is expected to and does reach the user or consumer without substantial change in the condition in which it is sold.

Restatement (Second) of Torts §402A (1965). A product may be unreasonably dangerous because of a defect in marketing, design, or manufacturing. *Caterpillar, Inc. v. Shears,* 911 S.W.2d 379, 382 (Tex. 1995); *Technical Chem. Co. v. Jacobs,* 480 S.W.2d 602, 604-05 (Tex. 1972). The Grinnells allege that the cigarettes sold by American were unreasonably dangerous due to each of the three types of defect.

MANUFACTURING DEFECT

We turn . . . to the Grinnells' strict liability claim based on a manufacturing defect. The Grinnells assert that American's products were defectively manufactured because they contained carcinogens and other toxic chemicals, including pesticide residue. During discovery, the Grinnells obtained internal documents showing that American fumigated its Turkish tobacco with Acritet 34, a chemical composed of acrylonitrile and carbon tetrachloride. American uses Turkish tobacco in all of its cigarettes. In 1978, American circulated a memorandum noting new government regulations requiring all materials containing acrylonitrile to be affixed with a "Cancer Hazard" warning label. Likewise, the Grinnells allege that American knew that methyl bromide pesticide residue remained in its tobacco after fumigation. The Grinnells alleged that this potentially cancerous pesticide residue contributed to Grinnell's cancer and resulting death.

Under Texas law, a plaintiff has a manufacturing defect claim when a finished product deviates, in terms of its construction or quality, from the specifications or planned output in a manner that renders it unreasonably dangerous. *SeeFord Motor Co. v. Pool*, 688 S.W.2d 879, 881 (Tex. App. — Texarkana 1985), *aff'd in part and rev'd in part on other grounds*, 715 S.W.2d 629 (Tex. 1986); *see also Lucas v. Texas Indus., Inc.*, 696 S.W.2d 372, 377-78 (Tex. 1984); *Morgan v. Compugraphic Corp.*, 675 S.W.2d 729, 732-33 (Tex. 1984); *Darryl v. Ford Motor Co.*, 440 S.W.2d 630, 632 (Tex. 1969). The common-knowledge defense does not apply to this type of claim because a user does not anticipate a manufacturing defect. This type of defect is a deviation from the planned output.

American, conceding that its cigarettes contain pesticide residue, argues that summary judgment was proper because all cigarette manufacturers fumigate their tobacco with some type of pesticide, and residue inevitably remains after fumigation. Thus, American concludes that the Grinnells' claims based on the presence of pesticide residue are actually design defect claims masquerading as manufacturing defect claims.

According to the undisputed facts, pesticide residue is incidentally, yet normally, found in tobacco after it is fumigated. The presence of pesticide residue is not an anomaly attributable only to the cigarettes Grinnell smoked. Nevertheless, the fact that all cigarettes potentially contain pesticide residue does not transform the Grinnells' manufacturing defect claim into a design defect claim subject to the common-knowledge defense. Simply because certain precautions or improvements in manufacturing technology, which could eliminate pesticide residue from cigarettes, are universally disregarded by an entire industry does not excuse their omission. *See T.J. Hooper*, 60 F.2d 737, 740 (2d Cir.), *cert. denied*, 287 U.S. 662 (1932). Although pesticide residue may be found in many if not all cigarettes, it is not an ingredient American intended to incorporate into its cigarettes. Analyzed in this light, the presence of pesticide residue could be a manufacturing defect, not a design defect. Therefore, American did not conclusively negate the existence of a defect in its cigarettes.

We hold that summary judgment was improper on the manufacturing defect claim.

NOTES AND PROBLEMS

1. ***Distinct Test for Manufacturing Defects.*** The test for manufacturing defects assumes that the manufacturer had a good design, recipe, or plan for the product but something went awry in the details of actually making the particular product that hurt the plaintiff. This is normally demonstrated by comparing the original plans or specifications with the product that hurt the plaintiff to determine if there is any deviation. Alternatively, the plaintiff can compare the product causing her injuries with other ostensibly identical products made by the same manufacturer to determine if there were any flaws that led to the plaintiff's injury. How did the plaintiffs in the tobacco case above demonstrate that something went awry in the manufacture of the cigarettes? Was the manufacturer really surprised by the cigarettes that it produced?

2. ***Tainted Food Products.*** Sometimes manufacturers of some processed food will be sued when a contaminant is found inside their finished product that has injured someone. For example, in Jackson v. Nestle-Beich, Inc., 589 N.E.2d 547 (Ill. 1992), the plaintiff purchased a chocolate pecan-caramel candy made by the defendant. When the plaintiff bit into the candy, she broke her tooth due to the presence of a hard pecan shell within the piece of candy. Under the normal analysis for a manufacturing defect, one would easily conclude that unless the recipe calls for a shell in the finished product, the candy that hurt the plaintiff had a manufacturing defect. Nevertheless, the defendant attempted to invoke a doctrine recognized by a number of courts — the *foreign-natural doctrine.* Under this doctrine, manufacturing defects only exist when the unintended ingredient is wholly foreign to the items intended for the final prepared food item. For example, a hair from a rat found in a can of soup would be foreign to any of the intended ingredients. On the other hand, because the candy purchased by the plaintiff was supposed to have pecans, the shell from a pecan would be considered a natural (though unintended) ingredient and would not create a manufacturing defect. Many courts, including the Illinois Supreme Court in that case, reject this doctrine because it seems to inject issues of fault into what is supposed to be a strict liability analysis.

3. ***Problems.*** Would there appear to be a good claim for a manufacturing defect in the following scenarios?

- **A.** A carbonated can of cola contains a shard of loose, sharp metal that damages the plaintiff's throat when she attempts to take a drink from the can.
- **B.** A manufacturer of latex gloves makes different models of the gloves for use in hospitals. One model contains extra amounts of latex to provide greater protection from germs. Another model is made that contains less latex in recognition that certain users of the gloves might be prone to allergic reactions to high concentrations of latex. Plaintiff is a nurse at

a hospital who uses the higher concentration latex gloves and suffers a bad allergic reaction to the gloves.

C. Defendant manufactures artificial hip joints for surgical implantation in patients with bad hips. A competitor decides that bad publicity for the defendant company would help him regain lost market share. The competitor sneaks into defendant's facility late at night and loosens some of the parts on a number of the artificial hips. When those hips are later implanted into patients, the parts become loose due to the vandalism and the patients suffer personal injuries, requiring removal of the hip implants and the implantation of new devices. A number of the patients file a class action against defendant citing the loosened parts as manufacturing defects. Surveillance videos at defendant's plant reveal the source of the problem.

MYRLAK v. PORT AUTHORITY OF NEW YORK & NEW JERSEY

723 A.2d 45 (N.J. 1999)

Coleman, J.

In this strict products liability case involving one defendant, the primary issue is whether the doctrine of *res ipsa loquitur* should be applied when liability is based upon an alleged manufacturing defect. The trial court declined to instruct the jury regarding *res ipsa loquitur.* The Appellate Division held that the trial court should have given such an instruction. We disagree and reverse. We hold that the traditional negligence doctrine of *res ipsa loquitur* generally is not applicable in a strict products liability case. We adopt, however, the "indeterminate product defect test" established in Section 3 of the *Restatement (Third) of Torts: Products Liability* as the more appropriate jury instruction in cases that do not involve a shifting of the burden of persuasion.

On July 6, 1991, plaintiff, John Myrlak, was injured when his chair collapsed while he was at work. At that time, plaintiff was forty-three years old, six feet six inches tall, and weighed approximately 325 pounds. Plaintiff was employed as an assistant trainmaster for the Port Authority Trans-Hudson Corporation (PATH). He worked at the Hoban Control Center at Journal Square in Jersey City. Plaintiff usually performed his duties while seated in a movable desk chair that was positioned at a semicircular console, approximately eight feet long and three feet high.

At the time of the accident, plaintiff had been seated in the chair performing his duties for approximately one hour and forty-five minutes. He suddenly heard a loud noise, and the back of his chair cracked and gave way. Plaintiff and the chair fell backwards, causing both to land parallel to the floor. Plaintiff grabbed the arms of the chair and pulled himself forward as he was falling. He injured his lower back and was hospitalized.

Although no one other than the plaintiff actually saw the accident, several PATH employees testified that they heard either a clicking or ratcheting sound, or a loud noise like a grinding of gears. After the accident, those employees observed that the back of the chair had collapsed and was parallel to the floor.

The chair involved in the accident was manufactured by defendant Girsberger Industries, Inc. It was one of five hundred chairs purchased by PATH at the same time from the same company. All of the chairs were delivered to PATH either on November 1, 1990, or on May 1, 1991, and were placed in use at the Hoban Control Center on June 1, 1991. Thus, the chair that caused plaintiff's accident had been in use for five weeks.

The chair had a high backed seat with a triple joint construction that allowed the seat to follow the user's movement by adjusting two levers. One of the levers positioned the chair in either a locked or a "free flow" mode; the other lever adjusted the height of the chair. The chair was also equipped with a tension control mechanism underneath the seat to adjust the tension of the chair's back according to the user's need or desire. Plaintiff was familiar with the chair and its operation.

There was no evidence that the chair had been misused by plaintiff or any other PATH employee. The chair, however, was not used exclusively by plaintiff. On the contrary, it was customarily used by several different PATH employees twenty-four hours each day. Although some of the PATH employees who used the chair were similar in size to plaintiff, none of them ever reported any similar incidents or complaints with regard to the chair.

Plaintiff filed products liability claims against the manufacturer of the chair alleging a manufacturing theory of liability.

Plaintiff's expert was unable to duplicate the accident with the chair that was presented as evidence. The expert was unable to identify a specific defect in the chair; nor could he state that a defect caused the accident.

At the close of all of the evidence, plaintiff requested the court to charge the jury on *res ipsa loquitur* regarding the manufacturing defect claim. In denying the requested charge, the trial court stated that it wanted to avoid that phrase even though plaintiff relied on circumstantial evidence to infer that there was a manufacturing defect. The jury found that plaintiff failed to establish a manufacturing defect in the chair.

In a reported opinion, the Appellate Division reversed the verdict in favor of the manufacturer, concluding that the trial court should have instructed the jury on *res ipsa loquitur*. We granted defendant Girsberger's petition for certification, limited to the issue whether *res ipsa loquitur* should apply to this strict products liability case.

The *res ipsa loquitur* doctrine derives its roots from the common law of England. The first reported decision to apply the doctrine in a case not involving railway collisions between two trains on the same line was *Byrne v. Boadle*, 159 Eng. Rep. 299, 300 (Exch. of Pleas 1863). The court permitted a presumption of negligence, reasoning that it was "apparent that the barrel was in the custody of the defendant who occupied the premises, and the fact of its falling is *prima facie* evidence of negligence, but if there are any facts inconsistent with negligence it is for the defendant to prove them."

Res ipsa loquitur, which in Latin means "the thing speaks for itself," is a rule of law that has its origin in negligence and "governs the availability and adequacy of evidence of negligence in special circumstances." *Brown v. Racquet Club of Bricktown*, 471 A.2d 25 (N.J. 1984). *Res ipsa loquitur* is not a theory of liability; rather, it is an evidentiary rule that governs the adequacy of evidence in some negligence cases. Specifically, the doctrine permits an inference of defendant's want of due care when the following three conditions have been met: "(a) the occurrence itself ordinarily bespeaks negligence; (b) the instrumentality was within the defendant's exclusive control; and (c) there is no indication in the circumstances that the injury was the result of the plaintiff's own voluntary act or neglect." *Bornstein v. Metropolitan Bottling Co.*, 139 A.2d 404 (N.J. 1958).

Whether an occurrence ordinarily bespeaks negligence is based on the probabilities in favor of negligence. Hence, *res ipsa* is available if it is more probable than not that the defendant has been negligent.

In the typical manufacturing defect case, a plaintiff is not required to establish negligence. In other words, a plaintiff must impugn the product but not the conduct of the manufacturer of the product.

The Act defines a manufacturing defect as a deviation "from the design specifications, formulae, or performance standards of the manufacturer or from otherwise identical units manufactured to the same manufacturing specifications or formulae." *N.J.S.A.* 2A:58C-2a. The Restatement defines a manufacturing defect as one in which "the product departs from its intended design though all possible care was exercised in the preparation and marketing of the product." *Restatement (Third) of Torts: Products Liability* §2(a). The Act's and the Restatement's definitions of a manufacturing defect both emphasize the safety of the product rather than the reasonableness of the manufacturer's conduct.

Simply because a plaintiff is not required to prove fault in a strict liability case does not mean that absolute liability will be imposed upon a manufacturer. Although a plaintiff is relieved of proving fault, that plaintiff must nonetheless prove that the product was defective under our common law jurisprudence that was incorporated into the Act. Based on our well-established case law in this area, a plaintiff must prove that the product was defective, that the defect existed when the product left the manufacturer's control, and that the defect proximately caused injuries to the plaintiff, a reasonably foreseeable or intended user.

As noted previously, a manufacturing defect under the Act occurs when the product comes off the production line in a substandard condition based on the manufacturer's own standards or identical units that were made in accordance with the manufacturing specifications.

To prove both the existence of a defect and that the defect existed while the product was in the control of the manufacturer, a plaintiff may resort to direct evidence, such as the testimony of an expert who has examined the product, or, in the absence of such evidence, to circumstantial proof. *Scanlon v. General Motors Corp.*, 326 A.2d 673 (N.J. 1974). The mere occurrence of an accident and the mere fact that someone was injured are not sufficient to demonstrate the existence of a defect.

Under the *Scanlon* circumstantial evidence method of proving a product defect, the fact that a product is relatively new does not suffice by itself to establish a defective condition. The age and prior usage of the product in relation to its expected life span are factors to consider in conjunction with other evidence presented. Generally, the older a product is, the more difficult it is to prove that a defect existed while in the manufacturer's control.

Based on the foregoing legal principles synthesized from our products liability and *res ipsa loquitur* jurisprudence, it is evident that there are some technical differences between using *res ipsa loquitur* as a method of proving negligence and using that doctrine to prove a product defect in strict products liability cases. *Res ipsa loquitur* is a doctrine created under the fault theory of negligence as a means of circumstantially proving a defendant's lack of due care. Strict products liability, on the other hand, is a theory of liability based upon allocating responsibility regardless of a defendant's unreasonableness, negligence, or fault. Nonetheless, except in those rare cases in which the application of *res ipsa loquitur* also involves a shifting of the burden of persuasion, there may be sound reasons to adopt a *res ipsa*-like method of circumstantially proving a product defect.

We agree with the majority of jurisdictions that, ordinarily, the traditional *res ipsa loquitur* jury charge should not be used in strict products liability actions. As noted previously, *res ipsa loquitur* is a negligence doctrine; it is a circumstantial means of proving a defendant's lack of due care. Strict liability, on the other hand, is a theory of liability based on allocating responsibility regardless of a defendant's unreasonableness, negligence or fault. Thus, while *res ipsa* might demonstrate a manufacturer's negligence in failing to inspect or appropriately assemble a particular product, strict liability merely questions whether there is a defect in that product that existed before it left the manufacturer's control.

We recognize that as an alternative to a traditional *res ipsa loquitur* instruction, various states and commentators have advocated an intermediate-type approach for circumstantially proving the existence of a product defect. That approach appears to best serve the interest of all parties and is not inconsistent with the Act.

The *Scanlon* rule regarding circumstantial proof of a defect in a strict products liability case was adopted recently in the *Restatement (Third) of Torts: Products Liability*. It provides:

> It may be inferred that the harm sustained by the plaintiff was caused by a product defect existing at the time of sale or distribution, without proof of a specific defect, when the incident that harmed the plaintiff:

> (a) was of a kind that ordinarily occurs as a result of a product defect; and
> (b) was not, in the particular case, solely the result of causes other than product defect existing at the time of sale or distribution.

[Restatement (Third) of Torts §3 (1997).]

Although Section 3 of the Restatement is based on a *res ipsa* model, it permits the jury to draw two inferences: that the harmful incident was caused by a product defect, and that the defect was present when the product left the manufacturer's control. The *res ipsa loquitur* doctrine, on the other hand, creates the single inference of negligence. Nevertheless, Section 3 of the Restatement parallels the elements of our *res ipsa loquitur* doctrine.

Section 3 of the Restatement has been referred to as the "indeterminate product test" because its use is limited to those product liability cases in which the plaintiff cannot prove a specific defect. A plaintiff can satisfy the requirements of Section 3 of the Restatement the same way as in the case of *res ipsa loquitur*, by direct and circumstantial evidence as well as evidence that negates causes other than product defect.

Other jurisdictions have adopted similar circumstantial methods for establishing an inference of a product defect in strict products liability cases. We agree with those states that in some cases, "common experience indicates that certain accidents do not occur absent some defect," and therefore an inference of a defect under specific circumstances should be permitted. Matthew R. Johnson, Note, *Rolling the "Barrel" a Little Further: Allowing Res Ipsa Loquitur to Assist in Proving Strict Liability in Tort Manufacturing Defects*, 38 Wm. & Mary L. Rev. 1197, 1225 (1997). *See also Crump v. MacNaught P.T.Y. Ltd.*, 743 S.W.2d 532, 535 (Mo. Ct. App. 1987) (finding that common sense suggests handles do not usually fly off pumps); *Bombardi v. Pochel's Appliance & TV Co.*, 518 P.2d 202, 204 (Wash. Ct. App. 1975) (implying that common sense would lead jury to conclude that television set was defective because it caught on fire). Fifteen other states have adopted the principles incorporated into Section 3 of the Restatement. We also adopt the indeterminate product defect test announced in Section 3 of the Restatement.

Our independent review of the record, including a consideration of the jury charge as a whole, *State v. Wilbely*, 307 A.2d 608 (1973); *State v. Kamienski*, 603 A.2d 78 (N.J. App. Div.), *certify. denied*, 130 N.J. 18, 611 A.2d 656 (1992), convinces us that the trial court adequately informed the jury that it could rely on circumstantial evidence to "infer that there was a defect by reasoning from circumstances and the facts shown." Hence, plaintiff was not prejudiced by the absence of a *res ipsa loquitur* jury charge even if one had been required. Moreover, the circumstantial evidence charge that was given was equivalent to the indeterminate product test charge under Section 3 of the Restatement.

[The court determined that the trial court had erred in excluding certain opinion testimony offered in support of the plaintiff's claims. This error necessitated a new trial.]

Because we have adopted Section 3 of the Restatement, upon retrial, plaintiff need not prove a specific defect in the chair if he can establish that the incident that harmed him is of the kind that ordinarily occurs as a result of a product defect, and that the incident was not solely the result of causes other than product defect existing at the time the chair left Girsberger's control. *Restatement (Third) of Torts* §3(a) and (b). If plaintiff cannot satisfy those requirements, he is not entitled to have the jury charged regarding an inference of a product defect, and plaintiff would be obligated to establish one or more manufacturing defects required by the Act.

That part of the Appellate Division's judgment requiring a *res ipsa loquitur* charge on the manufacturing defect claim is reversed. The matter is remanded to the Law Division for further proceedings as otherwise directed by the Appellate Division.

NOTES AND PROBLEMS

1. ***Res Ipsa and the Indeterminate Product Defect Theory.*** The plaintiff in *Myrlak* desired a *res ipsa* instruction advising the jury of his right to rely upon circumstantial evidence to prove a manufacturing defect. On appeal, the court determined that a *res ipsa* instruction would be inappropriate because that was a negligence concept utilized to show fault through circumstantial evidence. Because the plaintiff was suing on a strict liability theory rather than negligence, such an instruction would be inappropriate. Nevertheless, citing the *indeterminate product defect test* from the Restatement (Third) of Torts §3, the court ultimately endorsed a jury instruction that likewise permitted the jury to rely upon circumstantial evidence to prove a manufacturing defect. Compare the prerequisites of each doctrine and the resulting inferences created. In reality, how different are these doctrines?

2. ***Circumstantial Evidence Appropriate Absent Direct Proof.*** As we saw previously in the material on proving breach of the duty of reasonable care, the doctrine of *res ipsa loquitur* is unavailable when direct proof of the defendant's questioned conduct is available. Thus, the indeterminate product defect test only makes sense in application when comparison of the product to the manufacturer's plans is not available. Additionally, because evidence of a manufacturer's designs and warnings for its products is always available for scrutiny, this doctrine necessarily is limited to potential manufacturing defect theories.

3. ***Problem.*** Imagine that plaintiff is a waitress at a restaurant transferring bottles of soft drinks from their original crates into a refrigerator. One of the bottles inexplicably explodes, causing severe injuries to her hand. Her employer throws away the pieces of the bottle while she is at the hospital. Can the plaintiff rely upon the indeterminate product defect theory to prove a manufacturing

defect? Because strict liability for manufacturing defects might involve invocation of similar rules of circumstantial evidence as a negligence suit, how different is strict liability today in such circumstances from 1944 in the *Escola* case?

Upon Further Review

If one assumes a manufacturer's ideas for a product are safe and appropriate, any unplanned deviations from that idea constitute a manufacturing or construction defect. If that deviation leads to physical harm to the plaintiff it would be considered an unreasonably dangerous manufacturing defect that makes sellers of that product strictly liable — regardless of any care undertaken to avoid that outcome. Even if the defendant has production protocols that eliminate 99.9 percent of all possible errors, the one flawed unit that falls through the cracks and injures the plaintiff still creates liability for the seller. It is the best example of truly strict liability as the focus is entirely upon the traits of the product and whether its production results in some surprising and undesired feature. In most cases, the analysis is very concrete, as one simply compares the original plans with the actual unit that hurt the plaintiff. Where such direct analysis is not possible — for example, where the unit is destroyed in the accident — resort to circumstantial evidence of a defect is permissible as well.

B. Design Defects

In manufacturing defects, a particular unit in the defendant's production has deviated from the original plans. By contrast, design defect claims involve accusations that the entire product line was ill conceived. Recall the example of the automobile manufacturer who designs a wheel held in place by only two lug nuts. After these wheels begin falling off of customers' cars and causing injuries, an expert might opine that such design was destined to cause these accidents because of insufficient support for the weight of the wheels on the vehicle. The focus in design defect claims is not upon just the one automobile that plaintiff was driving, but upon the *entire line* of identically designed cars containing this same defect. Courts emphasize frequently that the design of the product is scrutinized rather than the designer, to contrast strict liability from negligence. Yet under the analysis of many courts, the line between negligence and strict liability can be easily obscured. As you will see in the following cases, some courts utilize a *consumer expectation test* to identify a design defect, while others resort to a balancing analysis referred to as the *risk utility test*. The difference in origin and operation of these two analytical models reflects the dual heritage (warranty and negligence law) of strict products liability.

1. The Consumer Expectation Test

Reflecting its warranty law heritage, the consumer expectation test for design defects focuses upon the expectations for the product's performance by the ordinary consumer of the product. The origin of this particular test comes from comments contained within the Restatement (Second) of Torts §402A: "The rule stated in this Section applies only where the defective condition of the product makes it unreasonably dangerous to the user or consumer. The article sold must be dangerous to an extent beyond that which would be contemplated by the ordinary consumer who purchases it, with the ordinary knowledge common to the community as to its characteristic." In the *Sparks* case below, the California appellate court discusses when this test is appropriately used in a design defect case and what evidence is appropriately used to analyze its application. Pay close attention to the evidence utilized by the plaintiffs to substantiate their claims of a design defect and also observe the evidence defendant unsuccessfully argued should instead be the focal point.

SPARKS v. OWENS-ILLINOIS, INC.

32 Cal. App. 4th 461 (1995)

PHELAN, J.

Owens-Illinois, Inc. (Owens-Illinois or appellant), timely appeals from a judgment entered after a jury trial, by which it was held 100 percent responsible for personal injuries to Charles Wayne Sparks (Sparks) and his wife, Betty Raley Sparks, respondents herein. The jury found that an Owens-Illinois product, an asbestos-containing thermal insulation known as Kaylo, was defective, and that the defect was the sole legal cause of injury to Sparks. Appellant contends that . . . [t]here was no evidence that Kaylo was defective because plaintiffs failed to show that it could have been designed more safely, i.e., without asbestos as a component.

Owens-Illinois made and sold a product known as "Kaylo" between 1948 and 1958. Kaylo was a calcium silicate insulation, made with 13 to 20 percent asbestos, which was sold in pipe-covering and block forms, and intended to be used for "industrial high[-]temperature thermal insulation." The asbestos used in Kaylo was predominantly of the chrysotile variety but amosite was also used to a lesser extent. Owens-Illinois sold its Kaylo operation to Owens-Corning Fiberglass in April 1958. Owens-Corning Fiberglass continued to make and sell Kaylo pipe covering and block insulation after April 1958.

Charles Sparks joined the United States Navy in 1959, when he was 20 years old. Although he originally intended to obtain training as a draftsman, he was instead sent for training as a metalsmith. Also in 1959, Sparks met and married his wife, Betty. Shortly after he was married, Sparks was sent out on a six-month cruise aboard the heavy cruiser U.S.S. Bremerton.

The Bremerton operated on steam turbines and, therefore, had many pipes, valves, condensers, heat exchangers, generators, boilers, and other machinery which had to be insulated against high temperatures. There was no significant work on the insulation during the cruise but, in January or February of 1960, the Bremerton was sent to Long Beach for a decommissioning overhaul, which lasted approximately six months. Sparks's duty aboard the Bremerton during the decommissioning was to remove and inspect the valves in the various pipelines. In order for Sparks to do this, the insulation had to be sawed or cut, and removed from the pipes. A great deal of dust was generated by the procedures Sparks followed to remove the insulation and the valves. At the same time, the boilers and other machinery were being overhauled by procedures that also generated dust to which Sparks was exposed. Regular cleanup procedures during the decommissioning involved the use of compressed air and fox-tail brooms, both of which generated a large amount of dust.

Plaintiffs presented the deposition testimony of another insulator who worked at the Puget Sound Shipyard. That witness, Ralph David, testified that he had no idea that his workplace exposure to asbestos could be dangerous to his health. Mr. David further stated that both he and the other workers who ripped out and installed asbestos-containing insulation simply assumed that it was part of their job and that there was no particular danger in it.

Several medical experts testified on behalf of the Sparkses. Dr. Barry Horn testified that . . . the exposure which Charles Sparks experienced on the Bremerton was the most intense of his lifetime and was "certainly" sufficient, "in and of itself," to have caused his mesothelioma.

Dr. Samuel Hammar, a pathologist, also testified that the exposure Sparks incurred on the Bremerton was "easily great enough" to have caused his mesothelioma. More specifically, Dr. Hammar opined that exposure to Kaylo fibers during the decommissioning of the Bremerton was, by itself, sufficient to cause his disease.

[In addition,] Samuel Schillaci, the Owens-Illinois employee who was responsible for overseeing the Kaylo division in the 1950's, testified that he had observed workers in the field using Kaylo. These workers would saw the Kaylo and generate dust, but would not be using respirators at the time.

The Sparkses filed their complaint for personal injuries and loss of consortium on April 11, 1991. Prior to trial, both plaintiffs and defendants filed a large number of motions *in limine*. Plaintiffs . . . prevailed on their motion to exclude evidence on a "state-of-the-art" defense, on the ground that the case was to be tried solely on a

Principles

"Recent events in consumer product markets — in particular, the withdrawal of some products and price increases for others — are largely the welcome result of efficient changes in products liability law. Expanded manufacturer liability has resulted in the internalization of . . . significant externalities."

Steven Croley and Jon Hanson, "What Liability Crisis? An Alternative Explanation for Recent Events in Product Liability," 8 Yale J. on Reg. 1, 9 (1991).

"consumer expectation" theory and all claims for punitive damages were being waived.

Both Owens-Illinois and the plaintiffs submitted jury instructions specifying the "consumer expectation test" for determining whether a given product was defectively designed . . . and Owens-Illinois joined in the plaintiffs' request for [an instruction on multiple, independent, sufficient causes: "Where two or more causes combine to bring about an injury and any of them operating alone would have been sufficient to cause the injury, each cause is considered to be a legal cause of the injury if it is a material element and a substantial factor in bringing it about, even though the result would have occurred without it"].

As to the [plaintiff's defective design claim, the jury was instructed that:] "Charles and Betty Sparks have the burden of proving by a preponderance of the evidence all of the facts necessary to establish: 1. That defendant Owens-Illinois, Inc.'s product failed to perform as safely as an ordinary consumer of that product would expect; 2. That the defect in design existed when the product left the defendant's possession; 3. That the design of the product was a legal cause of Mr. Sparks['s] injury; 4. That the product was used in a manner reasonably foreseeable by the defendant; [and 5.] the nature and extent of Charles Sparks['s] and Betty Spark[s's] injuries."

Owens-Illinois contends that the jury verdict must be reversed because there was no showing that Kaylo was a defective product. That is, Owens-Illinois contends plaintiffs were required to show that high-temperature insulation such as Kaylo could have been more safely designed, i.e., without asbestos, for use aboard Navy ships. Respondent argues that it was not required to make such a showing in this case, in which the jury was properly instructed to apply only the "consumer expectation" test to determine whether appellant's product was defectively designed. Respondent has the better of this argument.

It is well settled in California that a manufacturer may be held strictly liable in tort for placing a defective product on the market if that product causes personal injury, provided that the injury resulted from a use of the product that was reasonably foreseeable by the defendant. This doctrine of strict liability extends to products which have design defects, manufacturing defects, or "warning defects."

The instant case involves only allegations of design defects. It is, thus, governed by *Barker* [*v. Lull Engineering Co.*, 573 P.2d 443 (Cal. 1978)], where our Supreme Court held that a product may be found defective in design under either of two alternative theories. "First, a product may be found defective in design if the plaintiff establishes that the product failed to perform as safely as an ordinary consumer would expect when used in an intended or reasonably foreseeable manner. Under this first, so-called "consumer expectation test," a plaintiff is required to produce evidence of the "objective conditions of the product" as to which the jury is to employ its "own sense of whether the product meets ordinary expectations as to its safety under the circumstances presented by the evidence."

The second prong of the *Barker* test for design defects is as follows: "[A] product may alternatively be found defective in design if the plaintiff demonstrates that the product's design proximately caused his injury and the defendant fails to establish, in light of the relevant factors, that, on balance, the benefits of the challenged design outweigh the risk of danger inherent in such design." In order to satisfy its burden under this so-called "risk-benefit" theory, the defendant manufacturer may — but is not required to — present evidence of the feasibility of a safer alternative design, the financial cost of an improved design, and any adverse consequences to the product or the consumer from the alternative design.

The plaintiffs in this case limited their theory of recovery by electing to proceed only under the "consumer expectation test" for design defects. Owens-Illinois contends, however, that it was error to allow the plaintiffs to proceed in this fashion because the "consumer expectation test" is inappropriate in this case in that the undisputed evidence establishes that Kaylo was "the best possible product that could have been manufactured." Owens-Illinois further contends that plaintiffs were required — and failed — to prove that there was a safer alternative design for Kaylo. We reject these arguments, which are devoid of factual and legal support.

Our Supreme Court recently analyzed the circumstances under which the "consumer expectation test" should, and should not, be employed. *Soule v. General Motors Corp.*, 882 P.2d 298 (Cal. 1994). The court held that "the consumer expectations test is reserved for cases in which the *everyday experience* of the product's users permits a conclusion that the product's design violated *minimum* safety assumptions, and is thus defective *regardless of expert opinion about the merits of the design.*" The *Soule* court further held that where the consumer expectation test applies, evidence of the relative risks and benefits of the design is irrelevant and inadmissible: "If the facts permit such a conclusion, and if the failure resulted from the product's design, a finding of defect is warranted without any further proof. The manufacturer *may not defend* a claim that a product's design failed to perform as safely as its ordinary consumers would expect by presenting expert evidence of the design's relative risks and benefits."

On the other hand, our Supreme Court held that the "consumer expectation test" should *not* be used where the alleged injury resulted from products whose characteristics or performance are beyond the understanding or common experience of those who ordinarily use them. . . . Such "instances" include claims involving "complex" products which "cause injury in a way that does not engage its ordinary consumers' reasonable minimum assumptions about safe performance."

The *Soule* case provides a good example of a situation in which the consumer expectation test is not appropriate. There, the court was confronted with a complicated claim that General Motors' defective design of the wheel assembly and front floorboard enhanced the injuries the plaintiff suffered when another car collided with the left front wheel area of her automobile. As the court explained, "Plaintiff's theory of design defect was one of technical and mechanical detail. It sought to examine the precise behavior of several obscure components of her car under the complex circumstances of a particular accident. The collision's exact speed, angle, and point of impact were disputed. It seems settled, however, that plaintiff's Camaro received a substantial oblique blow near the left front wheel, and that the adjacent frame members and bracket assembly absorbed considerable inertial force." The court held that the consumer expectation test should not have been used: "An ordinary consumer of automobiles cannot reasonably expect that a car's frame, suspension, or interior will be designed to remain intact in any and all accidents. Nor would ordinary experience and understanding inform such a consumer how safely an automobile's design should perform under the esoteric circumstances of the collision at issue here. Indeed, both parties assumed that quite complicated design considerations were at issue, and that expert testimony was necessary to illuminate these matters."

There were neither "complicated design considerations," nor "obscure components," nor "esoteric circumstances" surrounding the "accident" in the instant case. Kaylo was a common type of asbestos-containing block insulation. It was a simple, stationary product in its ordinary uses. Because it was made of friable material that had to be cut and shaped to perform its insulating function on irregularly shaped objects, it generated large amounts of asbestos-laden dust during normal installation, inspection, removal, and replacement processes. The design failure was in Kaylo's emission of highly toxic, respirable fibers in the normal course of its intended use and maintenance as a high-temperature thermal insulation. It is a reasonable inference from the evidence that this emission of respirable fibers, which were capable of causing a fatal lung disease after a long latency period, was a product failure beyond the "legitimate, commonly accepted minimum safety assumptions of its ordinary consumers."

The instant case is analogous to *West v. Johnson & Johnson Products, Inc.* (1985) 174 Cal. App. 3d 831. In *West*, the plaintiff became seriously ill during her menstrual period. At the time, there were growing indications that tampon use sometimes caused toxic shock syndrome (TSS). After reading medical reports, plaintiff's physicians belatedly concluded that she had suffered TSS caused by tampons produced by the defendant. At trial, experts debated the nature of plaintiff's illness, and disputed whether the tampon design and materials used by the defendant encouraged TSS. The trial court instructed the jury only on the "consumer expectation test" prong of *Barker*, and the jury returned a verdict in favor of the plaintiff.

On appeal, the defendant contended that the risk-benefit test alone was proper. The Court of Appeal . . . reasoned that, in a time before there was general awareness and warnings about TSS, the plaintiff "had every right to expect" that use of such a seemingly innocuous product "would not lead to a serious (or perhaps fatal) illness."

The same is true here. Plaintiffs presented ample evidence that, when used in the intended manner, Kaylo violated the minimum safety expectations of its ordinary consumers. For example, Ralph David testified that he and other insulators freely manipulated asbestos-containing insulation products such as Kaylo during both installation and removal procedures, all the while assuming that it was innocuous, just part of their job. Samuel Schillaci, the Owens-Illinois employee who was responsible for the Kaylo division in the 1950's, testified that he frequently observed workers in the field sawing Kaylo, generating dust, but not wearing respirators. Plaintiff himself testified that he and all the other workers around him on the Bremerton worked with asbestos-containing insulation and cleaned up after such projects in a manner that caused large amounts of dust to circulate throughout the work area, without any special precautions against the generation, distribution or inhalation of the asbestos fibers, and without any expectation that the respirable fibers could cause serious illness. The jury could infer from this and other testimony that the ordinary users of Kaylo in the late 1950's and early 1960's did not expect to develop a fatal disease from simply breathing Kaylo dust and, thus, that the product's performance did not meet the "minimum safety assumptions of its ordinary consumers." We conclude that the trial court did not err by instructing the jury only on the "consumer expectation test," and that there was substantial evidence to support the jury finding of a design defect in Kaylo.

For all the foregoing reasons, the judgment of the trial court is affirmed in its entirety.

NOTES AND PROBLEMS

1. ***Relevant Evidence Under Consumer Expectation Test.*** As the court clarifies in *Sparks*, when the consumer expectation test is utilized, the plaintiff offers evidence of the circumstances surrounding the product and its usage. The jury then resorts to its "own sense" of whether the product meets the expectations of ordinary consumers. What evidence did the plaintiff in *Sparks* offer the jury that the court concluded enabled the jury to find a design defect? By contrast, the court held that expert testimony regarding the risks and benefits of the design chosen and the availability of other possible designs would be irrelevant under this analysis. Given the nature of the evidentiary inquiry, do you understand the appeal of this test for a design defect to a plaintiff's lawyer? Consider the cost and ease of offering the evidence of a design defect given the limited nature of the inquiry and the evidence ruled irrelevant.

In Practice

Motions *in limine* literally refer to being "at the threshold" of a proceeding. These are evidentiary motions made before the jury is seated to resolve known evidentiary disputes prior to a jury hearing any evidence or arguments that might be highly prejudicial or inappropriate. Sometimes such motions raised fundamental legal questions for the court.

2. ***State of the Art Evidence.*** The trial court had granted the plaintiff's pretrial *motion in limine* ruling that the defendant's proffered "state-of-the-art defense" evidence was inappropriate under the consumer expectation test. In design defect cases analyzed under the alternative risk utility test, as we shall see, courts focus upon a cost-benefit analysis of the details of the defendant's chosen design, taking into account the

state of the art of knowledge available. In such cases, defendants sometimes defend these claims on the grounds that, at the time of the product's design, the state of the art did not include knowledge of the risks of using the product. Some states even have statutes that provide a "state of the art defense" in instances when the defendant can show that it used a design that was, at the time, as technologically advanced as was reasonably possible. One fundamental difference between the consumer expectation test and the risk utility test is that the former focuses exclusively upon the awareness of risks by the *consumers* of the product; knowledge on the part of the manufacturer is irrelevant.

3. ***Consumer Expectation as Preferred Test.*** Some jurisdictions prefer the consumer expectation test as its primary design defect analysis, and many reject it. Other jurisdictions, such as California, offer more of a hybrid system that requires the consumer expectation test to be utilized in cases involving non-complex goods but mandates the risk utility test where the product is so esoteric or complex that ordinary consumers would have no particular expectations regarding its safety under the circumstances of the case. Why does the *Sparks* court believe that the consumer expectation test is more appropriate in claims involving asbestos-infused insulation and tampons but not appropriate in the case involving the design of a car's floorboard? Also, note that under the consumer expectation test the controlling standard is *not* the subjective beliefs of the injured claimant but the objective viewpoint of the ordinary users of the product.

2. *The Risk Utility Test*

Embodying more of the negligence heritage behind strict liability law, the majority of jurisdictions have adopted the *risk utility* test for analyzing alleged design defects. This test involves a balancing of the benefits of the product's existing design with the risks of that design in light of other possible alternatives. Courts look to multiple factors in applying this test as is evidenced by the *Dawson* case below. As you consider the application of this analysis, see if you can still find differences between this test for a strict liability design defect and ordinary negligence concepts.

DAWSON v. CHRYSLER CORP.

630 F.2d 950 (3d Cir. 1980)

Adams, J.

This appeal from a jury verdict and entry of judgment in favor of the plaintiffs arises out of a New Jersey automobile accident in which a police officer was seriously injured. The legal questions in this diversity action, that are governed by New Jersey law, are relatively straight-forward. The public policy questions, however, which are beyond the competence of this Court to resolve and with which Congress ultimately must grapple, are complex and implicate national economic and social concerns.

In adjudicating this appeal, we first decide the question whether the district court erred in denying the defendant's motion for judgment notwithstanding the verdict. [We will also] address the troubling public policy dilemma namely, that under existing federal law individual juries in the various states are permitted, in effect, to establish national automobile safety standards. The result of such an arrangement, predictably, is not only incoherence in the safety requirements set by disparate juries, but also the possibility that a standard established by a jury in a particular case will conflict with other policies regarding the economics of the automobile industry as well as energy conservation programs.

On September 7, 1974, Richard F. Dawson, while in the employ of the Pennsauken Police Department, was seriously injured as a result of an automobile accident that occurred in Pennsauken, New Jersey. As Dawson was driving on a rain-soaked highway, responding to a burglar alarm, he lost control of his patrol car a 1974 Dodge Monaco. The car slid off the highway, over a curb, through a small sign, and into an unyielding steel pole that was fifteen inches in diameter. The car struck the pole in a backwards direction at a forty-five degree angle on the left side of the vehicle; the point of impact was the left rear wheel well. As a result of the force of the collision, the vehicle literally wrapped itself around the pole. The pole ripped through the body of the car and crushed Dawson between the seat and the "header" area of the roof, located just above the windshield. The so-called "secondary collision" of Dawson with the interior of the automobile dislocated Dawson's left hip and ruptured his fifth and sixth cervical vertebrae. As a result of the injuries, Dawson is now a quadriplegic. He has no control over his body from the neck down, and requires constant medical attention.

Dawson, his wife, and their son brought suit in the Court of Common Pleas of Philadelphia against the Chrysler Corporation, the manufacturer of the vehicle in which Dawson was injured. Chrysler removed the case to the United States District Court for the Eastern District of Pennsylvania on the grounds of diversity, and subsequently had the case transferred to the District Court for the District of New Jersey. The plaintiffs' [strict products liability theory was] that the patrol car was defective because it did not have a full, continuous steel frame extending through the door panels, and a cross-member running through the floor board between the posts located between the front and rear doors of the vehicle. Had the vehicle been so designed, the Dawsons alleged, it would have "bounced" off the pole following relatively slight penetration by the pole into the passenger space.

Expert testimony was introduced by the Dawsons to prove that the existing frame of the patrol car was unable to withstand side impacts at relatively low speed, and that the inadequacy of the frame permitted the pole to enter the passenger area and to injure Dawson. The same experts testified that the improvements in the design of the frame that the plaintiffs proposed were feasible and would have prevented Dawson from being injured as he was. According to plaintiffs' expert witnesses, a continuous frame and cross-member would have deflected the patrol car away from the pole after a minimal intrusion into the passenger area and, they declared, Dawson likely would have emerged from the accident with only a slight injury.

In response, Chrysler argued that it had no duty to produce a "crashproof" vehicle, and that, in any event, the patrol car was not defective. Expert testimony for Chrysler established that the design and construction of the 1974 Dodge Monaco complied with all federal vehicle safety standards, and that deformation of the body of the vehicle is desirable in most crashes because it absorbs the impact of the crash and decreases the rate of deceleration on the occupants of the vehicle. Thus, Chrysler's experts asserted that, for most types of automobile accidents, the design offered by the Dawsons would be less safe than the existing design. They also estimated that the steel parts that would be required in the model suggested by the Dawsons would have added between 200 and 250 pounds to the weight, and approximately $300 to the price of the vehicle. It was also established that the 1974 Dodge Monaco's unibody construction was stronger than comparable Ford and Chevrolet vehicles.

After all testimony had been introduced, Chrysler moved for a directed verdict, which the district judge denied. The jury thereupon returned a verdict in favor of the plaintiffs. The jury awarded Mr. Dawson $2,064,863.19 for his expenses, disability, and pain and suffering, and granted Mrs. Dawson $60,000.00 for loss of consortium and loss of services. After the district court entered judgment, Chrysler moved for judgment notwithstanding the verdict or, alternatively for a new trial. The court denied both motions.

At the outset, it is important, indeed crucial, to point out, that the substantive issues of this diversity case are controlled by the law of New Jersey. [W]e proceed with the adjudication of this appeal pursuant to the rubric of strict liability.

Chrysler urges that . . . it had no obligation to manufacture a vehicle that would protect a passenger against the type of harm suffered by Dawson. As we understand Chrysler's argument, however, it appears to be directed, not to Chrysler's duty vis-a-vis Dawson, but rather to the question whether the patrol car was defective inasmuch as it did not adequately prevent Dawson from sustaining serious injury. For, as we stated in *Huddell*, it is "beyond peradventure that an automobile manufacturer today has some legal obligation to design and produce a reasonably crashworthy vehicle. Rephrased in the terminology of strict liability, the manufacturer must consider accidents as among the "intended uses of its products," and passengers injured in such accidents as among the group of reasonably foreseeable plaintiffs.

Thus, the controlling issue in the case is whether the jury could be permitted to find, under the law of New Jersey, that the patrol car was defective.

The determination whether a product [contains a design defect] is to be informed by what the New Jersey Supreme Court has termed a "risk/utility analysis." *Cepeda v. Cumberland Engineering Co., Inc.*, 386 A.2d 816, 825-29

(N.J. 1978). Under this approach, a product is defective if "a reasonable person would conclude that the magnitude of the scientifically perceivable danger as it is proved to be at the time of trial outweighed the benefits of the way the product was so designed and marketed." *Id.* at 826. The court in *Cepeda* identified seven factors that might be relevant to this balancing process:

> (1) The usefulness and desirability of the product its utility to the user and to the public as a whole.
>
> (2) The safety aspects of the product the likelihood that it will cause injury, and the probable seriousness of the injury.
>
> (3) The availability of a substitute product which would meet the same need and not be as unsafe.
>
> (4) The manufacturer's ability to eliminate the unsafe character of the product without impairing its usefulness or making it too expensive to maintain its utility.
>
> (5) The user's ability to avoid danger by the exercise of care in the use of the product.
>
> (6) The user's anticipated awareness of the dangers inherent in the product and their avoidability, because of general public knowledge of the obvious condition of the product, or of the existence of suitable warnings or instructions.
>
> (7) The feasibility, on the part of the manufacturer, of spreading the loss by setting the price of the product or carrying liability insurance.

The court suggested that the trial judge first determine whether a balancing of these factors precludes liability as a matter of law. If it does not, then the judge is to incorporate into the instructions any factor for which there was presented specific proof and which might be deemed relevant to the jury's consideration of the matter.

Chrysler maintains that, under these standards, the district court erred in submitting the case to the jury because the Dawsons failed, as a matter of law, to prove that the patrol car was defective. Specifically, it insists that the Dawsons did not present sufficient evidence from which the jury reasonably might infer that the alternative design that they proffered would be safer than the existing design, or that it would be cost effective, practical, or marketable. In short, Chrysler urges that the substitute design would be less socially beneficial than was the actual design of the patrol car. In support of its argument, Chrysler emphasizes that the design of the 1974 Dodge Monaco complied with all of the standards authorized by Congress in the National Traffic and Motor Vehicle Safety Act of 1966, Pub. L. 89-563, tit. I, §107, 80 Stat. 718, codified in 15 U.S.C. §1396 (1976), and set forth in accompanying regulations, 49 C.F.R. §571.1 (1979).

Compliance with the safety standards promulgated pursuant to the National Traffic and Motor Vehicle Safety Act, however, does not relieve Chrysler of liability in this action. For, in authorizing the Secretary of Transportation to enact these standards, Congress explicitly provided, "Compliance with any Federal motor vehicle safety standard issued under this subchapter does not exempt any person from any liability under common law." 15 U.S.C. §1397(c) (1976).

Thus, consonant with this congressional directive, we must review Chrysler's appeal on the question of the existence of a defect under the common law of New Jersey that is set forth above.

Our examination of the record persuades us that the district court did not err in denying Chrysler's motion for judgment notwithstanding the verdict. The Dawsons demonstrated that the frame of the 1974 Dodge Monaco was noncontinuous that is, it consisted of a front portion that extended from the front of the car to the middle of the front passenger seat, and a rear portion that ran from the middle of the rear passenger seat to the back end of the vehicle. Thus, there was a gap in the seventeen-inch side area of the frame between the front and rear seats. The plaintiffs also proved that, after colliding with the pole, the car slid along the left side portion of the rear frame until it reached the gap in the frame. At that point, the pole tore through the body of the vehicle into the passenger area and proceeded to push Dawson into the header area above the windshield.

Three experts, a design analyst, a mechanical engineer, and a biochemical engineer also testified on behalf of the Dawsons. These witnesses had examined the patrol car and concluded that it was inadequate to withstand side impacts. They testified that there was an alternative design available which, had it been employed in the 1974 Monaco, would have prevented Dawson from sustaining serious injuries. The substitute design called for a continuous frame with an additional cross member running between the so-called B-posts the vertical posts located at the side of the car between the front and rear seats. According to these witnesses, this design was known in the industry well before the accident and had been tested by a number of independent testing centers in 1969 and in 1973.

The mechanical engineer conducted a number of studies in order to ascertain the extent to which the alternative design would have withstood the crash. On the basis of these calculations, he testified that the pole would have penetrated only 9.9 inches into the passenger space, and thus would not have crushed Dawson. Instead, the engineer stated, the car would have deflected off the pole and back into the highway. Under these circumstances, according to the biochemical engineer, Dawson would have been able to "walk away from the accident" with but a bruised shoulder.

Also introduced by the Dawsons were reports of tests conducted for the United States Department of Transportation, which indicated that, in side collisions with a fixed pole at twenty-one miles per hour, frame improvements similar to those proposed by the experts presented by the Dawsons reduced intrusion into the passenger area by fifty percent, from sixteen inches to eight inches. The study concluded that the improvements, "in conjunction with interior alterations, demonstrated a dramatic increase in occupant protection." There was no suggestion at trial that the alternative design recommended by the Dawsons would not comply with federal safety standards. On cross-examination, Chrysler's attorney did get the Dawsons' expert witnesses to acknowledge that the alternative design would add between 200 and 250 pounds to the vehicle and would cost an additional $300 per car. The Dawsons' experts also conceded that the heavier and more rigid an automobile, the less able it is to absorb energy upon impact with a fixed object, and therefore the major force of an accident might be transmitted to the passengers. Moreover, an expert for Chrysler testified that, even if the frame of the patrol car had been designed in conformity with the plaintiffs' proposals, Dawson would have sustained injuries equivalent to those he actually incurred. Chrysler's witness reasoned that Dawson was injured, not by the intrusion of the pole into the passenger space, but as a result of being thrown into the header area of the roof by the vehicle's initial contact with the pole that is, prior to the impact of the pole against the driver's seat.

On the basis of the foregoing recitation of the evidence presented respectively by the Dawsons and by Chrysler, we conclude that the record is sufficient to sustain the jury's determination . . . that the design of the 1974 Monaco was defective. The jury was not required to ascertain that all of the factors enumerated by the New Jersey Supreme Court in *Cepeda* weighed in favor of the Dawsons in order to find the patrol car defective. Rather, it need only to have reasonably concluded, after balancing these factors, that, at the time Chrysler distributed the 1974 Monaco, the car was "not reasonably fit, suitable and safe for its intended or reasonably foreseeable purposes." *Suter*, 406 A.2d at 149.

Although we affirm the judgment of the district court, we do so with uneasiness regarding the consequences of our decision and of the decisions of other courts throughout the country in cases of this kind.

As we observed earlier, Congress, in enacting the National Traffic and Motor Vehicle Safety Act, provided that compliance with the Act does not exempt any person from liability under the common law of the state of injury. The effect of this provision is that the states are free, not only to create various standards of liability for automobile manufacturers with respect to design and structure, but also to delegate to the triers of fact in civil cases arising out of automobile accidents the power to determine whether a particular product conforms to such standards. In the present situation, for example, the New Jersey Supreme Court has instituted a strict liability standard for cases involving defective products, has defined the term "defective product" to mean any such item that is not "reasonably fit, suitable and safe for its intended or reasonably foreseeable purposes," and has left to the jury the task of determining whether the product at issue measures up to this standard.

The result of such arrangement is that while the jury found Chrysler liable for not producing a rigid enough vehicular frame, a factfinder in another case might well hold the manufacturer liable for producing a frame that is too rigid. Yet, as pointed out at trial, in certain types of accidents head-on collisions it is desirable to have a car designed to collapse upon impact because the deformation would absorb much of the shock of the collision, and divert the force of deceleration away from the vehicle's passengers. In effect, this permits individual juries applying varying laws in different jurisdictions to set nationwide automobile safety standards and to impose on automobile manufacturers conflicting requirements. It would be difficult for members of the industry to alter their design and production behavior in response to jury verdicts in such cases, because their response might well be at variance with what some other jury decides is a defective design. Under these circumstances, the law imposes on the industry the responsibility of insuring vast numbers of persons involved in automobile accidents.

Equally serious is the impact on other national social and economic goals of the existing case-by-case system of establishing automobile safety requirements. As we have become more dependent on foreign sources of energy, and as the price of that energy has increased, the attention of the federal government has been drawn to a search to find alternative supplies and the means of conserving energy. More recently, the domestic automobile industry has been struggling to compete with foreign manufacturers which have stressed smaller, more fuel-efficient cars. Yet, during this same period, Congress has permitted a system of regulation by ad hoc adjudications under which a jury can hold an automobile manufacturer culpable for not producing a car that is considerably heavier, and likely to have less fuel efficiency.

In sum, this appeal has brought to our attention an important conflict that implicates broad national concerns. Although it is important that society devise a proper system for compensating those injured in automobile collisions, it is not at all clear that the present arrangement of permitting individual juries, under varying standards of liability, to impose this obligation on manufacturers is fair or efficient. Inasmuch as it was the Congress that designed this system, and because Congress is the body best suited to evaluate and, if appropriate, to change that system, we decline today to do anything in this regard except to bring the problem to the attention of the legislative branch.

Bound as we are to adjudicate this appeal according to the substantive law of New Jersey, and because we find no basis in that law to overturn the jury's verdict, the judgment of the district court will be affirmed.

NOTES AND PROBLEMS

1. ***Similarities to Negligence.*** The comparison of the product's utility with the risks associated with the product's intended or foreseeable uses, appears strangely familiar to the Learned Hand analysis for breach of duty in a negligence case (see Chapter 4). You might say that a reasonable automobile designer would necessarily take into account the same factors that courts utilize in applying the risk utility analysis. This has led to the observation by some that strict liability design defect claims are functionally the equivalent of a negligence claim.

2. ***Differences from Negligence.*** Despite similarities between negligence analysis and the risk utility test, many theoretical and some practical differences demonstrate that they are not identical. For example, the "state of the art" of an industry's knowledge can be utilized in determining the risk portion of the risk utility test, even if there is no proof that a reasonable manufacturer did or should have known of the risk. Furthermore, some courts explicitly (and others implicitly) permit hindsight to be considered in applying the risk utility test; whereas this application of hindsight would be abhorrent to a court evaluating a negligence claim. In addition, the jury considers the qualitative aspects of the product in a strict liability claim rather than the conduct of the defendant seller — evidence of what the defendant knew is theoretically not germane in a strict liability case. Finally, when the risk utility test is applied in the case of a non-manufacturing commercial seller of a product (for which liability is just as broad under Restatement (Second) of Torts §402A), the fact that the seller was not involved with the design of the product is no defense.

3. ***Crashworthiness as a Design Defect.*** Many auto manufacturers have argued that a car need not be designed to perform in any particular way during a crash because the car's intended purpose is not to be involved in an accident. They argue that being in a crash constitutes a type of product "misuse" that need not be taken into account in designing the product. Most (though not all) courts have rejected this argument because of the inevitability of car accidents. These courts have held that such use is a foreseeable, even if not desired, use of the product and that this foreseeability compels consideration of the risks involved in designing the car. *See e.g.*, Larsen v. General Motors Corp., 391 F.2d 495, 502 (8th Cir. 1968). In applying this crashworthy doctrine, most courts put the burden on the defendant, once a defect is proven, to differentiate between the underlying damages from the accident itself and the enhancement of the injuries from the car not being safe in the event of a crash. If the defendant cannot provide a basis for the jury separating out the initial harm from the secondary injury, the defendant is liable for all of the harm incurred in the accident.

4. ***Federal Issue: Preemption of State Law Claims.*** The court above refused the defense offered by the defendant that its compliance with federal regulations in designing the product offered a safe harbor of immunity. There are instances where courts have found that congressional legislation evidences either an express or implied *preemption* of any state law to the contrary. If the court believes that Congress did not intend to tolerate any standard for the defendant's conduct different than a federal standard, preemption would sometimes preclude a state law tort claim where the defendant's design (or warning) for a product finds federal approval. Because the federal statute in the above case expressly stated otherwise, there was no federal preemption of the claims. In an important and relatively recent opinion, the U.S. Supreme Court held in Wyeth v. Levine, 555 U.S. 555 (2009), that the FDA's approval of certain drug labels did not preempt any state law strict liability claim asserting a marketing (warning) defect. In its opinion written by Justice Stevens, the court said that there is a strong presumption against preemption, which could only be

rebutted by a "clear and manifest purpose" in the legislation to supersede the historic police powers of the state.

5. ***State Law Issue: Weight to Be Given Compliance.*** Even where there is no federal preemption (a question of federal law), it is up to each state to determine what weight, if any, to give to the fact that the federal government has approved a design or warning for a particular product. While some courts expressly hold that such a circumstance is irrelevant to the state law inquiry into a possible product defect (*see* Edwards v. Basel Pharmaceuticals, 933 P.2d 298 (Okla. 1997)), other states have ruled otherwise, often by virtue of tort reform statutes giving great weight to evidence of federal approval of the product. For example, Texas has enacted a statute creating a rebuttable presumption that there is no defective design or warning when the manufacturer has "complied with mandatory safety standards or regulations adopted and promulgated by the federal government." Tex. Civ. Prac. & Rem. Code §82.008(a). Such a presumption is only rebuttable upon proof that the federal regulations were inadequate to protect the public or that the manufacturer lied to the government to obtain approval for the design or warning.

3. The Alternative Feasible Design Requirement

As the court in the *Dawson* case mentioned, under the risk utility analysis, a jury need not find that each factor favors the existence of a defect. Instead, a balancing of the totality of these considerations is supposed to drive the jury's verdict. Notwithstanding the general agreement with most courts of this concept, some jurisdictions have held that under the risk utility analysis a mandatory prerequisite for finding a design defect is the plaintiff's proof of an alternative feasible product design. The *Grinnell* case, which we have previously reviewed in part with respect to manufacturing defects, addresses this evidentiary requirement in ruling upon the summary judgment granted to the tobacco company on the design defect claim.

AMERICAN TOBACCO CO. v. GRINNELL

951 S.W.2d 420 (Tex. 1997)

PART 2 — DESIGN DEFECT

[As set forth previously in this chapter as Part I, the decedent began smoking the defendant's cigarettes in 1952 and contracted cancer 33 years later. In the wrongful death and survival action against the manufacturer, plaintiff asserted defective manufacturing, design, and marketing theories of liability, among others. Part II of the opinion, set forth below, contains the Court's analysis of the summary judgment granted against the plaintiff on her defective design claim.]

The duty to design a safe product is "an obligation imposed by law." *McKisson v. Sales Affiliates, Inc.*, 416 S.W.2d 787, 789 (Tex. 1967). Whether a seller has breached this duty, that is, whether a product is unreasonably dangerous, is a question of fact for the jury. *See Turner v. General Motors Corp.*, 584 S.W.2d 844, 848 (Tex. 1979). In determining whether a product is defectively designed, the jury must conclude that the product is unreasonably dangerous as designed, taking into consideration the utility of the product and the risk involved in its use.

In *Turner* we held that evidence of the following factors of risk and utility were admissible in design defect cases: (1) the utility of the product to the user and to the public as a whole weighed against the gravity and likelihood of injury from its use; (2) the availability of a substitute product which would meet the same need and not be unsafe or unreasonably expensive; (3) the manufacturer's ability to eliminate the unsafe character of the product without seriously impairing its usefulness or significantly increasing its costs; (4) the user's anticipated awareness of the dangers inherent in the product and their avoidability because of general public knowledge of the obvious condition of the product, or of the existence of suitable warnings or instructions; and (5) the expectations of the ordinary consumer. *Id.* at 846, 847. *See also Caterpillar, Inc.*, 911 S.W.2d at 384; *Boatland of Houston, Inc. v. Bailey*, 609 S.W.2d 743, 746 n.2 (Tex. 1980).

American argues that the common-knowledge defense bars the Grinnells' design defect claims as a matter of law. But, as we stated in *Turner*, "the user's anticipated awareness of the dangers inherent in the product and their avoidability because of general public knowledge of the obvious condition of the product," and "the expectations of the ordinary consumer," are but two factors for the jury to consider when determining whether a product was defectively designed. American's attempt to invoke the common-knowledge defense is actually an attempt to invoke the "open and obvious defense" or "patent danger rule," which this Court has rejected in design defect cases:

> A number of courts are of the view that obvious risks are not design defects which must be remedied. *See, e.g., Gray*, 771 F.2d 866, 870 (applying Mississippi law); *Delvaux v. Ford Motor Co.*, 764 F.2d 469, 474 (7th Cir. 1985) (applying Wisconsin law); *Young v. Tide Craft, Inc.*, 270 S.C. 453, 242 S.E.2d 671, 680 (1978). However, our Court has held that liability for a design defect may attach even if the defect is apparent. *Turner*, 584 S.W.2d at 850. Determining if a design is unreasonably dangerous requires balancing the utility of the product against the risks involved in its use. *Id.* at 847 & n.1.

Caterpillar, Inc., 911 S.W.2d at 383-84. Accordingly, American's attempt to invoke the common-knowledge defense in the context of an alleged design defect is without merit.

Alternatively, American argues that it is entitled to summary judgment because no safer alternative cigarette design exists. In *Turner,* we held that "the availability of a substitute product which would meet the same need and not be unsafe or unreasonably expensive," was one factor for juries to consider when determining whether a product was defectively designed. We reaffirmed this holding in *Caterpillar, Inc. v. Shears* by stating that "if there are no safer alternatives, a product is not unreasonably dangerous as a matter of law.[1]" 911 S.W.2d at 384. Accordingly, if there is no safer alternative to the cigarette manufactured by American, then its cigarettes are not unreasonably dangerous as a matter of law.

The Grinnells assert that American's cigarettes could have been made reasonably safer by filtration, and by reducing the amount of tobacco, tar, nicotine, and toxins in them. In making its argument that no reasonably safer alternative design exists, American relies on the testimony of the Grinnells' experts, Drs. Greenberg, Stevens, and Ginzel. These experts testified that Grinnell would have developed cancer and died regardless of whether filters, lower tar, or less tobacco had been used. Specifically, Dr. Greenberg testified:

Q: It didn't matter to you and your opinion would not have changed as to the cause of the lung cancer, regardless of the brand, whether it was filtered or nonfiltered, short or long cigarette. Is that right?
A: That's correct.

Dr. Ginzel testified similarly:

Q: Doctor, is there any safe cigarette with respect to lung cancer?
A: Not that I know of.
Q: Is there any design for a cigarette that Mr. Grinnell could have smoked that would have avoided his claimed lung cancer?
A: Not during his lifetime, no.

Ultimately, the Grinnells essentially concede that no reasonably safer alternatives exist, but argue that all cigarettes are defective and unreasonably dangerous nonetheless.[2] Because American conclusively proved that no reasonably safer alternative design exists for its cigarettes, we hold that summary judgment

---

1. Although not applicable to the present case, the Texas Legislature has codified the "safer alternative" requirement. Tex. Civ. Prac. & Rem. Code §82.005 (safer alternative design must be shown by preponderance of the evidence in design defect case).

2. By arguing for liability even in the absence of a reasonably safer alternative design, the Grinnells effectively propose that we adopt a system of categorical liability with respect to cigarettes. Categorical liability is not only an unworkable solution, but also a position repeatedly rejected by courts. *See generally* Grossman, *Categorical Liability: Why the Gates Should be Kept Closed,* 36 S. Tex. L. Rev. 385, 392 (1995) (noting that categorical liability has been advocated, unsuccessfully, for alcoholic beverages, handguns and cigarettes); Henderson & Twerski, *Closing the American Products Liability Frontier: The Rejection of Liability Without Defect,* 66 N.Y.U. L. Rev. 1263, 1307 (1991) (courts should not abandon traditional risk/utility test in favor of categorical exclusion).

was proper on all of the Grinnells' design defect claims, including those based on the addictive quality of cigarettes.

NOTES AND PROBLEMS

1. *Differing List of Factors.* Note that in the *Grinnell* case, the court identifies itself as a risk utility jurisdiction for purposes of analyzing a design defect case. Not all such jurisdictions recite an identical list of considerations, though they all tend to overlap significantly. The last factor identified by *Grinnell* actually incorporates the consumer expectation test into the risk utility analysis as one of the considerations. It thus represents a hybrid approach.

2. *Mandatory Proof of Alternative Feasible Design.* The court indicates that both the court and the legislature had demanded that in design defect cases, the plaintiff offer evidence of an alternative feasible design that would provide essentially the same functions of the product, but in a safer and economically and technologically feasible manner. Courts that require this as an element of a design defect claim have held that the plaintiff need not actually build a prototype of the proposed alternative design but simply offer expert testimony showing the feasibility of such a design. See General Motors v. Sanchez, 997 S.W.2d 584, 592 (Tex. 1999) ("[P]laintiffs did not have to build an automobile transmission to prove a safer alternative design. A design need only prove 'capable of being developed.'"). Not all courts agree that this one factor in the risk utility analysis requires proof of an alternative feasible design as a prerequisite for finding a defect. *See e.g.*, Potter v. Chicago Pneumatic Tool Co., 694 A.2d 1319 (Conn. 1997).

4. Comparing the Consumer Expectation and Risk Utility Tests

In some cases, the choice between the consumer expectation test and the risk utility test might make no difference — when products are either so obviously flawed or well-designed that either test should yield the same verdict. But in other cases, the choice between the two tests might change the verdict. The following case offers a unique opportunity to gain one court's insight into the difference between the two tests in the context of an actual case. In *Denny*, the plaintiff asserted both a strict liability design defect claim as well as a breach of warranty claim. The court found the two claims different enough to permit submission of both theories to the jury. New York utilizes the risk utility test for strict liability design defect claims but, in effect, uses a consumer expectation test for breach of warranty claims. Pay close attention to why the appellate court finds that the jury may have properly found for the defendant manufacturer on the risk utility test but in favor of the plaintiff using the consumer expectation test.

DENNY v. FORD MOTOR CO.

662 N.E.2d 730 (N.Y. 1995)

TITONE, J.

Are the elements of New York's causes of action for strict products liability and breach of implied warranty always coextensive? If not, can the latter be broader than the former? These are the core issues presented by the questions that the United States Court of Appeals for the Second Circuit has certified to us in this diversity action involving an allegedly defective vehicle. On the facts set forth by the Second Circuit, we hold that the causes of action are not identical and that, under the circumstances presented here, it is possible to be liable for breach of implied warranty even though a claim of strict products liability has not been satisfactorily established.

As stated by the Second Circuit, this action arises out of a June 9, 1986 accident in which plaintiff Nancy Denny was severely injured when the Ford Bronco II that she was driving rolled over. The rollover accident occurred when Denny slammed on her brakes in an effort to avoid a deer that had walked directly into her motor vehicle's path. Denny and her spouse sued Ford Motor Co., the vehicle's manufacturer, asserting claims for negligence, strict products liability and breach of implied warranty of merchantability. The case went to trial in the District Court for the Northern District of New York in October of 1992.

The trial evidence centered on the particular characteristics of utility vehicles, which are generally made for off-road use on unpaved and often rugged terrain. Such use sometimes necessitates climbing over obstacles such as fallen logs and rocks. While utility vehicles are traditionally considerably larger than passenger cars, some manufacturers have created a category of down-sized "small" utility vehicles, which are designed to be lighter, to achieve better fuel economy and, presumably, to appeal to a wider consumer market. The Bronco II in which Denny was injured falls into this category.

Plaintiffs introduced evidence at trial to show that small utility vehicles in general, and the Bronco II in particular, present a significantly higher risk of rollover accidents than do ordinary passenger automobiles. Plaintiffs' evidence also showed

In Practice

Rule 18 of the Federal Rules of Civil Procedure permits a plaintiff to join as many claims as desired against a particular defendant. When a product hurts the plaintiff, the plaintiff might join to her strict products liability action a count of negligence as well as a count for breach of warranty, depending upon whether the state utilizes different tests for these claims.

that the Bronco II had a low stability index attributable to its high center of gravity and relatively narrow track width. The vehicle's shorter wheelbase and suspension system were additional factors contributing to its instability. Ford had made minor design changes in an effort to achieve a higher stability index, but, according to plaintiffs' proof, none of the changes produced a significant improvement in the vehicle's stability.

Ford argued at trial that the design features of which plaintiffs complained were necessary to the vehicle's off-road capabilities. According to Ford, the vehicle had been intended to be used as an off-road vehicle and had not been designed to be sold as a conventional passenger automobile. Ford's own engineer stated that he would not recommend the Bronco II to someone whose primary interest was to use it as a passenger car, since the features of a four-wheel-drive utility vehicle were not helpful for that purpose and the vehicle's design made it inherently less stable.

Despite the engineer's testimony, plaintiffs introduced a Ford marketing manual which predicted that many buyers would be attracted to the Bronco II because utility vehicles were "suitable to contemporary life styles" and were "considered fashionable" in some suburban areas. According to this manual, the sales presentation of the Bronco II should take into account the vehicle's "suitab[ility] for commuting and for suburban and city driving." Additionally, the vehicle's ability to switch between two-wheel and four-wheel drive would "be particularly appealing to women who may be concerned about driving in snow and ice with their children." Plaintiffs both testified that the perceived safety benefits of its four-wheel-drive capacity were what attracted them to the Bronco II. They were not at all interested in its off-road use.

At the close of the evidence, the District Court Judge submitted both the strict products liability claim and the breach of implied warranty claim, despite Ford's objection that the two causes of action were identical. [The jury rejected the negligence claim and no appeal was taken as to it.] With respect to the strict products liability claim the court told the jury that "[a] manufacturer who places a product on the market in a defective condition is liable for injury which results from use of the product when the product is used for its intended or reasonably foreseeable purpose." Further, the court stated:

> A product is defective if it is not reasonably safe. It is not necessary for the plaintiffs to prove that the defendant knew or should have known of the product['ls potential for causing injury to establish that the product was not reasonably safe. Rather, the plaintiffs must prove by a preponderance of the evidence that a reasonable person . . . who knew of the product's potential for causing injury and the existence of available alternative designs . . . would have concluded that such a product should not have been marketed in that condition. Such a conclusion should be reached after balancing the risks involved in using the product against the product[']s usefulness and its costs against the risks, usefulness and costs of the alternative design as compared to the product defendant did market.

With respect to the breach of implied warranty claim, the court told the jury:

> The law implies a warranty by a manufacturer which places its product on the market that the product is reasonably fit for the ordinary purpose for which it was intended. If it is, in fact, defective and not reasonably fit to be used for its intended purpose, the warranty is breached.
>
> The plaintiffs claim that the Bronco II was not fit for its ordinary purpose because of its alleged propensity to rollover and lack of warnings to the consumer of this propensity.

Neither party objected to the content of these charges.

In response to interrogatories, the jury found that the Bronco II was not "defective" and that defendant was therefore not liable under plaintiffs' strict products liability cause of action. However, the jury also found that defendant had breached its implied warranty of merchantability and that the breach was the proximate cause of Nancy Denny's injuries. Following apportionment of damages, plaintiff was awarded judgment in the amount of $1.2 million.

In this proceeding, Ford's sole argument is that plaintiffs' strict products liability and breach of implied warranty causes of action were identical and that, accordingly, a defendant's verdict on the former cannot be reconciled with a plaintiff's verdict on the latter. This argument is, in turn, premised on both the intertwined history of the two doctrines and the close similarity in their elements and legal functions. Although Ford recognizes that New York has previously permitted personal injury plaintiffs to simultaneously assert different products liability theories in support of their claims, it contends that the breach of implied warranty cause of action, which sounds in contract, has been subsumed by the more recently adopted, and more highly evolved, strict products liability theory, which sounds in tort. Ford's argument has much to commend it. However, in the final analysis, the argument is flawed because it overlooks the continued existence of a separate *statutory* predicate for the breach of warranty theory and the subtle but important distinction between the two theories that arises from their different historical and doctrinal root.

When products liability litigation was in its infancy, the courts relied upon contractual warranty theories as the only existing means of facilitating economic recovery for personal injuries arising from the use of defective. Eventually, the contractually based implied warranty theory came to be perceived as inadequate in an economic universe that was dominated by mass-produced products and an impersonal marketplace. Its primary weakness was, of course, its rigid requirement of a relationship of privity between the seller and the injured consumer — a requirement that often could not be satisfied. However, the warranty approach remained unsatisfactory, and the courts shifted their focus to the development of a new, more flexible tort cause of action: the doctrine of strict products liability.

The establishment of this tort remedy has, as this Court has recognized, significantly diminished the need to rely on the contractually based breach of implied warranty remedy as a means of compensating individuals injured because of defective products. Further, although the available defenses and applicable limitations principles may differ, there is a high degree of overlap between the substantive aspects of the two causes of action. Indeed, on an earlier occasion, this Court observed, in dictum, that "strict liability in tort and implied warranty in the absence of privity are merely different ways of describing the very same cause of action."

Nonetheless, it would not be correct to infer that the tort cause of action has completely subsumed the older breach of implied warranty cause of action or that the two doctrines are now identical in every respect.

Although the products liability theory sounding in tort and the breach of implied warranty theory authorized by the UCC coexist and are often invoked in tandem, the core element of "defect" is subtly different in the two causes of action. Under New York law, a design defect may be actionable under a strict products liability theory if the product is not reasonably safe. [T]he New York standard for determining the existence of a design defect has required an assessment of whether "if the design defect were known at the time of manufacture, a reasonable person would conclude that the utility of the product did not outweigh the risk inherent in marketing a product designed in that manner."

The adoption of this risk/utility balance as a component of the "defectiveness" element has brought the inquiry in design defect cases closer to that used in traditional negligence cases, where the reasonableness of an actor's conduct is considered in light of a number of situational and policy-driven factors. While efforts have been made to steer away from the fault-oriented negligence principles by characterizing the design defect cause of action in terms of a product-based rather than a conduct-based analysis, the reality is that the risk/utility balancing test is a "negligence-inspired" approach, since it invites the parties to adduce proof about the manufacturer's choices and ultimately requires the fact finder to make "a judgment about [the manufacturer's] judgment." In other words, an assessment of the manufacturer's conduct is virtually inevitable, and, as one commentator observed, "[i]n general, . . . the strict liability concept of 'defective design' [is] functionally synonymous with the earlier negligence concept of unreasonable designing."

It is this negligence-like risk/benefit component of the defect element that differentiates strict products liability claims from UCC-based breach of implied warranty claims in cases involving design defects. While the strict products concept of a product that is "not reasonably safe" requires a weighing of the product's dangers against its over-all advantages, the UCC's concept of a "defective" product requires an inquiry only into whether the product in question was "fit for the ordinary purposes for which such goods are used." The latter inquiry focuses on the expectations for the performance of the product when used in the customary, usual and reasonably foreseeable manners. The cause of action is one involving true "strict" liability, since recovery may be had upon a showing that the product was not minimally safe for its expected purpose — without regard to the feasibility of alternative designs or the manufacturer's "reasonableness" in marketing it in that unsafe condition.

This distinction between the "defect" analysis in breach of implied warranty actions and the "defect" analysis in strict products liability actions is explained by the differing etiology and doctrinal underpinnings of the two distinct theories. The former class of actions originates in contract law, which directs its attention to the purchaser's disappointed expectations; the latter originates in tort law, which traditionally has concerned itself with social policy and risk allocation by means other than those dictated by the marketplace.

[Some] criticize the consumer-expectation-based tests for product defect and argue instead for the use of a risk/utility approach. . . . One of the cited commentators, for example, argues that the consumer expectation test is a "blunt instrument" "when it comes to recognizing and maximizing the . . . goals, objectives, interests and values *important to modern tort law*" (Kennedy, *The Role of the Consumer Expectation Test Under Louisiana's Products Liability Tort Doctrine*, 69 Tul. L. Rev. 117, 152 [emphasis supplied]).

Significantly, the consumer-expectation test has its advocates as well as its critics. In view of the "rigors of the risk-utility test," it has been suggested that it is "worthwhile" to retain the consumer-expectation test . . . rather than simply abandoning it.

In any event, while the critics and commentators may debate the relative merits of the consumer-expectation and risk/utility tests, there is no existing authority for the proposition that the risk/utility analysis is appropriate when the plaintiff's claim rests on a claimed breach of implied warranty under UCC 2-314(2)(c) and 2-318. Further, . . . the negligence-like risk/utility approach is foreign to the realm of contract law.

As a practical matter, the distinction between the defect concepts in tort law and in implied warranty theory may have little or no effect in most cases. In this case, however, the nature of the proof and the way in which the fact issues were litigated demonstrates how the two causes of action can diverge. In the trial court, Ford took the position that the design features of which plaintiffs complain, i.e., the Bronco II's high center of gravity, narrow track width, short wheel base and specially tailored suspension system, were important to preserving the vehicle's ability to drive over the highly irregular terrain that typifies off-road travel. Ford's proof in this regard was relevant to the strict products liability risk/utility equation, which required the fact finder to determine whether the Bronco II's value as an off-road vehicle outweighed the risk of the rollover accidents that could occur when the vehicle was used for other driving tasks.

On the other hand, plaintiffs' proof focused, in part, on the sale of the Bronco II for suburban driving and everyday road travel. Plaintiffs also adduced proof that the Bronco II's design characteristics made it unusually susceptible to rollover accidents when used on paved roads. All of this evidence was useful in showing that routine highway and street driving was the "ordinary purpose" for which the Bronco II was sold and that it was not "fit" — or safe — for that purpose.

Thus, under the evidence in this case, a rational fact finder could have simultaneously concluded that the Bronco II's utility as an off-road vehicle outweighed the risk of injury resulting from rollover accidents *and* that the vehicle was not safe for the "ordinary purpose" of daily driving for which it was marketed and sold. Under the law of this State such a set of factual judgments would lead to the concomitant legal conclusion that plaintiffs' strict products liability cause of action was not viable but that defendant should nevertheless be held liable for breach of its implied promise that the Bronco II was "merchantable" or "fit" for its "ordinary purpose." Importantly, what makes this case distinctive is that the "ordinary purpose" for which the product was marketed and sold to the plaintiff was *not* the same as the utility against which the risk was to be weighed. It is these unusual circumstances that give practical significance to the ordinarily theoretical difference between the defect concepts in tort and statutory breach of implied warranty causes of action.

From the foregoing it is apparent that the causes of action for strict products liability and breach of implied warranty of merchantability are not identical in New York and that the latter is not necessarily subsumed by the former. It follows that, under the circumstances presented, a verdict such as the one occurring here — in which the manufacturer was found liable under an implied warranty cause of action and not liable under a strict products cause of action — is theoretically reconcilable under New York law.

In Practice

While some fret that strict liability has made it too easy for product sellers to be found liable, and that this has had a chilling impact on commerce, one empirical study discovered that plaintiffs prevailed in only one of five design defect cases that went to trial.

D. Merritt and K. Barry, Is the Tort System in Crisis? New Empirical Evidence, 670 Ohio St. L.J. 315 (1999).

NOTES AND PROBLEMS

1. ***Different Heritage.*** The court in *Denny* describes how the risk utility test is similar to and derived from the law of negligence; while the consumer expectation test derives from warranty law. Although the court believed there was substantial overlap between a strict liability design defect claim and a breach of warranty claim, it indicated that they had different definitions of "defect" — at least under the laws of many jurisdictions. If that jurisdiction had employed a consumer expectation test for a design defect, would it have made sense to submit a separate issue on the breach of warranty claim? Regarding the court's suggestion that strict liability and negligence were almost one and the same, some scholars would agree. Some have suggested that it is foolishness to believe that a design defect claim is analyzed differently than a negligence claim, at least when the risk utility test is employed. Judge Posner made this argument in the context of Indiana law requiring proof of negligence in a design defect case:

> Expressly requiring proof of negligence in a design-defect case, as Indiana law does, though unusual really isn't much of a legal innovation, since "defect" always implied something that should not have been allowed into the product — something, in other words, that could have been removed at a reasonable cost in light of the risk that it created.

Mesman v. Crane Pro Services, Inc., 409 F.3d 846, 849 (7th Cir. 2005).

2. ***Problem.*** Consider whether the risk utility and the consumer expectation tests would yield similar results in the following scenarios:

A. A bulletproof vest is designed in a way that makes it susceptible to permitting a bullet to strike the person wearing the vest, because there are obvious circular areas cut out along the sides. A police office wearing one of these vests is struck in the ribs by a bullet that hits in the area of one of these cutouts.

B. A well-known chef on the Food Network sells a set of knives that are very sharp, for use in chopping vegetables. The plaintiff cuts off her finger using this knife.

C. Marketing Defects

There are instances where a product has great utility accompanied with risks for which no better design is available. While such products would not generally be considered to have a design defect, strict products liability law also recognizes that a marketing defect can exist when needed warnings are not properly given to consumers. In these cases, two primary areas of dispute concern (a) when is a warning required, and (b) what exactly must the warning say? When the plaintiff has suffered an injury from an intended or foreseeable use of the product, and no warning of this risk was given, the issue of liability for a marketing or warning defect is concentrated solely on the former issue. In some instances, however, the defendant has provided a warning of a known risk, but the plaintiff complains that the warning was not good enough. These two issues tend, in practice, to be mutually exclusive because it is difficult for a defendant who has given some warning of a particular risk to argue that no warning was necessary. In the following case, what is the nature of the defendant's defense to the argument that the product was defective in its marketing?

1. The Duty to Warn

RICHTER v. LIMAX INTERNATIONAL

45 F.3d 1464 (10th Cir. 1995)

LAY, J.

Dearmedia Richter appeals from the district court's grant of judgment as a matter of law to Limax International, Inc. and LMX-Manufactures Consultants, Inc. (collectively Limax). Richter claimed that repetitive use of a mini-trampoline manufactured by Limax caused stress fractures in her ankles. In March 1991, Richter sued Limax alleging the mini-trampoline was defectively designed and came with an inadequate warning. The jury found, in a special verdict, that the mini-trampoline was not defectively designed. However, it nonetheless found Limax was liable under theories of strict liability and negligence for its failure to warn and determined damages to be $472,712 reduced by Richter's percentage of fault of thirty-eight percent.

Limax then moved for judgment as a matter of law, which the court granted. The court concluded the defendant had no duty to warn because the plaintiff had failed to prove that Limax had knowledge of the danger of stress fractures or that the danger was known in the state of the art. The court further concluded that under these circumstances Kansas law does not impose a duty on manufacturers to warn about dangers they might have discovered by conducting reasonable tests. Richter appealed. We reverse and remand to the district court with instructions to reinstate the jury's verdict and enter a judgment on the verdict.

Richter purchased a mini-trampoline from Limax on February 1, 1989. There were no instructions in or on the box containing the mini-trampoline, although the trampoline did have sticker on it stating: "This product was designed to be used only as an exercise device. It is not designed to be used for acrobatics, trampolining or any springboard type activities." Richter stated she only used the trampoline for jogging. She began by jogging for short periods of time but eventually increased her time up to sixty minutes per day. She used the product until March 10, 1989. The next day she experienced severe pain in her ankles while walking. A doctor diagnosed her as having stress fractures in her ankles. Richter testified the pain forced her to discontinue her work as a sales representative for a furniture manufacturer.

The plaintiff produced expert testimony which established relatively simple tests would have revealed that because the surface of a mini-trampoline depresses furthest in the center and decreasingly towards the edges, as a jogger's feet strike the trampoline's surface and it gives way, the inside of each foot drop further than the outside. This rotation of the foot, which is termed "eversion," occurs to a lesser degree in normal jogging, but rebound jogging markedly accentuates the degree of rotation.

Further testimony established it has long been known that lateral pulling on a bone by ligaments or muscles can cause microscopic fractures. If the bone is not allowed time to heal and the stress on the bone continues, these tiny fractures can coalesce into a stress fracture. The eversion of the feet caused by the mini-trampoline results in certain tissues pulling laterally on particular ankle bones. Richter's expert witnesses testified that long-term use of the trampoline could cause stress fractures in the affected anklebones.

Limax admitted it conducted no tests relating to the long-term effects of jogging on the mini-trampoline and did not systematically review published studies of mini-trampolines by sports medicine and exercise specialists. The CEO of Limax testified the company had sold approximately two million mini-trampolines world-wide and Richter's complaint about stress fractures was the first Limax had received. Further, although mini-trampolines had been in use since 1975, by the time of Richter's purchase no one had yet suggested their use entailed a risk of stress fractures. No expert testifying at trial could identify any study or article on rebound jogging or mini-trampolines that reported ankle stress fractures or pointed out the risk joggers faced of incurring such an injury.

Richter, however, produced testimony by experts that observations from very simple tests, interpreted in light of well-established knowledge about the structure of the foot and the causes of stress fractures, would have made it apparent that the repetitive use of the mini-trampoline for jogging could cause stress fractures. Two experts testified the danger was well within the state of society's knowledge about such matters. One of Richter's experts pointed out that although there were no known reports concerning mini-trampolines as a cause of stress fractures, sport and exercise magazines as well as scientific and medical journals have long published articles establishing that repetitive jogging can cause stress fractures. The testimony verified that such repetitive jogging on a mini-trampoline exaggerates the stresses that result from repetitive jogging on a flat surface. Although the mini-trampoline was found by the jury not to have a defective design, Richter's expert witness testimony established that the marked accentuation of eversion caused by the design of the mini-trampoline could result in her kind of injury developing from her repetitive jogging.

Richter contends Kansas law imposes a duty on manufacturers to test their products and warn consumers appropriately. In *Wooderson v. Ortho Pharmaceutical Corp.*, the Kansas Supreme Court held an ethical drug company had a duty to warn the medical profession about what "it knows, has reason to know, or should know, based upon its position as an expert in the field, upon its research, upon cases reported to it, and upon scientific development, research, and publications in the field." 681 P.2d 1038, 1057 (Kan.), *cert. denied*, 469 U.S. 965 (1984). Richter interprets the language "upon its research," to require manufacturers to test their products for their potential to injure consumers.

The district court held, "though not without misgivings," that Kansas law does not require a manufacturer to test its products for dangers not otherwise known in *the state of the art.* The court held that because the evidence indicated that prior to Richter's injuries, no one was aware of the possibility that jogging on a mini-trampoline could cause stress fractures, there was nothing to give rise to a duty warn.

We find the district court's restrictive interpretation is contrary to Kansas law on the duty of a manufacturer to warn consumers of foreseeable dangers. An earlier district court decision summed up Kansas law relating to the duty to warn consumers:

> Ordinarily, a manufacturer has a duty under Kansas law to warn consumers and users of its products when it knows or has reason to know that its product is or is likely to be dangerous during normal use. The duty to warn is a continuous one, requiring the manufacturer to keep abreast of the current state of knowledge of its products as acquired through research, adverse reaction reports, scientific literature, and other available methods. A manufacturer's failure to adequately warn of its product's reasonably foreseeable dangers renders that product defective under the doctrine of strict liability.

Pfeiffer v. Eagle Mfg. Co., 771 F. Supp. 1133, 1139 (D. Kan. 1991).

Kansas applies the same test to whether a manufacturer met his duty to warn under negligence as it does under strict liability.[5]

Kansas law makes clear this general duty to warn consumers of foreseeable dangers is not limited to ethical drug companies. In 1976, Kansas adopted the rule set out in the Restatement (Second) of Torts §402A (1965) in *Brooks v. Dietz*, 545 P.2d 1104, 1108 (Kan. 1976), an adoption that has been repeatedly affirmed. Section 402A establishes strict liability for a seller of a product whose defective condition makes the product unreasonably dangerous. Comment *h* to section 402A states that where a seller "has reason to anticipate that danger may result from a particular use . . . he may be required to give adequate warning of the danger (see Comment *j*), and a product sold without such warning is in a defective condition." Kansas courts have relied on both comments *j* and *k* to section 420A in concretizing the duty to warn announced in comment *h*.[7]

---

5. In determining warning issues, the test is reasonableness. . . . "In all warning cases [either negligence or strict liability] — even if the plaintiff or the court claims to analyze failure to warn or inadequacy of warning in the context of a strict products liability claim — the tests actually applied condition imposition of liability on the defendant's having actually or constructively known of the risk that triggers the warning." *Johnson v. American Cyanamid Co.*, 718 P.2d 1318, 1324 (Kan. 1986), *aff'd*, 243 Kan. 291, 758 P.2d 206 (Kan. 1988).

7. Comment *j* reads, in pertinent part:

> Directions or warning. In order to prevent the product from being unreasonably dangerous, the seller may be required to give directions or warning, on the container, as to its use. . . .
>
> Where warning is given, the seller may reasonably assume that it will be read and heeded; and a product bearing such a warning, which is safe for use if it is followed, is not in defective condition, nor is it unreasonably dangerous.

Comment *k* reads:

> Unavoidably unsafe products. There are some products which, in the present state of human knowledge, are quite incapable of being made safe for their intended and ordinary use. . . . Such a product, properly prepared,

See Cott, 856 P.2d at 931; *Humes v. Clinton,* 246 Kan. 590, 792 P.2d 1032, 1039 (Kan. 1990); *Johnson,* 718 P.2d at 1323. These comments make clear that a product may not be defectively designed, but may nonetheless be defective because the manufacturer failed to adequately warn the users of the product of a reasonably foreseeable hazard. The Kansas Supreme Court in *Savina* stated this proposition as follows:

> Under the strict liability theory, a plaintiff is not required to establish misconduct by the maker or seller but, instead, is required to impugn the product. The plaintiff must show the product is in "a defective condition unreasonably dangerous," which means that it must be defective in a way that subjects persons or tangible property to an unreasonable risk of harm. Prosser and Keeton, Law of Torts §99, p. 695 (5th ed. 1984) A product can be defective in one of the following three ways: (1) a flaw is present in the product at the time it is sold; (2) *the Producer or assembler of the product fails to adequately warn of a risk or hazard related to the way the product was designed;* or (3) the product, although perfectly manufactured, contains a defect that makes it unsafe. Prosser, §99, pp. 695-98.

795 P.2d at 923 (emphasis added).

The district court's restriction of the general duty to warn to specific design defects overlooks that under Kansas law of strict liability, even if a product does not have a design defect, failure to warn of a foreseeable danger arising from the product's normal use makes the product defective.

The mini-trampoline was specifically intended for exercise, and in particular, for jogging. When used for this purpose, however, the mini-trampoline's design results in the foot turning in a way that places stress on the anklebones. That the design is not defective, within the state of the known art, does not detract from the manufacturer's duty to warn the consumer of foreseeable dangers that can arise from normal use.

Given that repetitive jogging on the mini-trampoline could cause stress fractures, the question becomes whether Richter presented sufficient evidence that a jury could permissibly conclude reasonable tests would have been effective in bringing this danger to light. Richter presented a substantial amount of expert testimony to the effect that visual observation of a person jogging on the mini-trampoline by someone with expertise in biomechanics, would reveal eversion and further that relatively simple tests could measure the degree of eversion. A comparison of that measurement with a measurement of the eversion caused by jogging on a flat surface would have revealed mini-trampolines cause users' feet to evert to a markedly greater degree. Testimony established that it is well known that such stresses, experienced on a repetitive basis, could cause

---

and accompanied by proper directions and warning, is not defective, nor is it unreasonably dangerous. . . . The seller of such products, again with the qualification that they are properly prepared and marketed, and proper warning is given, where the situation calls for it, is not to be held to strict liability for unfortunate consequences attending their use, merely because he has undertaken to supply the public with an apparently useful and desirable product, attended with a known but apparently reasonable risk.

fractures. We hold the jury could have reasonably found Richter's injury was causally related to repetitive jogging on the mini-trampoline, the use for which Limax's product was intended. The jury could also reasonably have concluded Limax should have warned users of this danger because the danger was eminently knowable given the state of the art and Limax should have known of it.

Under Kansas law, both strict liability and negligence require warnings only for dangers which are reasonably foreseeable in light of the intended use of a product. The jury could reasonably have concluded that a simple consultation with a biomechanics expert would have given Limax sufficient information to arrange for appropriate testing of the mini-trampoline. No expert witness for either side expressed any doubt that the mini-trampoline accentuates eversion of the ankles or that eversion could cause stress fractures. It is true that no one appears to have considered the problem until Richter's injury occurred, but it is also true that plaintiff's evidence demonstrated that the danger was patently obvious to any expert who had a reason to look for it. The jury could permissibly conclude Limax should reasonably have foreseen that design of the mini-trampoline could result in the harm produced. Limax conceded that it did no testing or research to consider foreseeable harm arising out of the uses to which the mini-trampoline would be put.

Notable Warning Labels

Liquid Plumr:
"Do not reuse the bottle to store beverages."
Windex:
"Do not spray in eyes."
BIC lighter:
"Ignite lighter away from face."
Pine Mountain Fire Logs:
"Caution: Risk of Fire."
RCA Television Remote Control:
"Not Dishwasher Safe."
Auto-Shade Windshield Visor:
"Do not drive with sunshade in place. Remove from windshield before starting ignition."

Manufacturers do not have a duty to test for inconceivable dangers, nor do they have a duty to test for every conceivable danger. They do have a duty to warn of dangers of harmful effects arising from the foreseeable use and misuse of a product that are known or are readily foreseeable in the state of art. In any given case, plaintiff's evidence must sufficiently demonstrate that the harm incurred should have been reasonably foreseeable to the manufacturer of the product. Absent such proof a manufacturer cannot be held liable for harm that no reasonable person could anticipate.

Every case must turn on its own evidentiary facts. In the present case, plaintiff's experts testified that the accentuated eversion of the foot caused by prolonged jogging on the mini-trampoline made Richter's injury foreseeable and that the manufacturer should have warned the user of the product of the possible foreseeable harm she encountered. We do not make this ruling as a matter of law. We simply find that there existed substantial evidence in the record from which the jury could find that the harm was foreseeable. As earlier stated, we must review the evidence in the light most favorable to the verdict holder. A fair and impartial jury concluded under the evidence that because of the specific design of the mini-trampoline, Richter's harm was foreseeable. We simply conclude there was sufficient evidence to allow the jury to make that finding.

We find that the district court erred in granting a judgment as a matter of law and we therefore hold that the verdict and judgment in favor of the plaintiff should be reinstated.

On cross appeal, Limax . . . contends Richter made no showing as to whether the warning would have been effective in avoiding her injury.

[Under] Kansas law, an inadequate warning creates a "presumption of causation." *O'Gilvie v. International Playtex, Inc.*, 821 F.2d 1438, 1442 (10th Cir. 1987) (citing *Wooderson*, 681 P.2d at 1057). Limax insists that because the jury heard no evidence as to what an adequate warning might have been, the jury had no basis for deciding a warning would have been effective. Limax contends that to establish causation, Richter should have had to testify she would have behaved differently had she been warned. Kansas does not require such self-serving testimony from plaintiffs and Limax's argument entirely ignores that the effect of the presumption is to place the burden on Limax to rebut it. The trial court did not err in submitting the issue to the jury.

Reversed and remanded to the district court to reinstate the jury's verdict and enter a judgment on the verdict.

NOTES AND PROBLEMS

1. ***Duty to Warn.*** According to the Restatement (Third), a product has a marketing defect "because of inadequate instructions or warnings when the foreseeable risks of harm posed by the product could have been reduced or avoided by the provision of reasonable instructions or warnings by the seller or other distributor . . . and the omission of the instructions or warnings renders the product not reasonably safe." §2(c) (1998).

2. ***Negligence Revisited.*** Of all of the areas of strict products liability, the defective marketing (or warning) area overlaps most with negligence law. The court above quotes Kansas courts as holding that negligence and strict liability for marketing defects are one and the same. With respect to manufacturing and design defects, where would those fit on the continuum of negligence law versus true strict (no fault) liability?

3. ***Design and Marketing Defect Claims.*** A defective marketing claim might be made in conjunction with a design defect claim or independently. In the *Limax* case above, the plaintiff sued on both theories though the jury rejected the defective design claim. Can you understand why, at least in a risk-utility jurisdiction, it might be difficult to prevail on a defective design of a min-trampoline claim? Exactly how else could a mini-trampoline be designed to avoid the "eversion" referred to in the case? On the other hand, even a product

with a proper design might still have foreseeable risks associated with its use. In these instances, the product will still be considered defective if it lacks a reasonably adequate warning of those foreseeable risks.

4. ***Read and Heed Presumption.*** Courts have recognized a "read and heed" presumption to help facilitate the plaintiff's proof of causation in cases where no warning has been given. Because plaintiff must demonstrate that any defect caused the plaintiff's physical harm, this doctrine provides that if the required warning had been given, the plaintiff would have read it and abided by the warning to protect herself from the injury. This presumption thus helps the plaintiff in such a case to prove actual causation from the failure to warn. However, it is a *rebuttable* presumption, meaning that defendants are allowed to try to persuade the fact finder that, had the necessary warning been given, a particular plaintiff would have still disregarded it, making the failure to warn immaterial. In such instances, there is no causal link between the product defect and the plaintiff's harm and so no liability attaches.

5. ***Learned Intermediary Doctrine.*** In most cases, the duty to warn is satisfied when a reasonably adequate warning is given to the consumer (often with instructions accompanying the product or on the packaging itself). However, under the learned intermediary doctrine, the duty to warn is satisfied with respect to *prescription* drugs and devices by providing the warning to the physician instead. The law presumes that the physician can decipher such warnings and decide in her professional judgment what information needs to be shared with the patient when prescribing the drugs or device:

> Although ordinarily warnings must be given to the ultimate user of a product, a different approach has been developed for prescription drugs. It is settled in a substantial majority of jurisdictions that the duty a manufacturer of ethical drugs owes to the consumer is to warn only physicians (or other medical personnel permitted by state law to prescribe drugs) of any risks or contra-indications associated with that drug.

Stanback v. Parke, Davis & Co., 657 F.2d 642, 644 (4th Cir. 1981). Interestingly, some courts have held that the learned intermediary doctrine no longer insulates sellers of prescription drugs from liability where they have engaged in the direct marketing of such drugs to the consumers (through advertisements) because the sellers are trying to influence the consumers directly. *See e.g.*, Perez v. Wyeth Laboratories, 734 A.2d 1245 (N.J. 1999) ("The direct marketing of drugs to consumers generates a corresponding duty requiring manufacturers to warn of defects in the product"). *But cf.* In re Norplant Contraceptive Prods. Liab. Litig., 165 F.3d 374 (5th Cir. 1999) (applying Texas' learned intermediary doctrine despite aggressive marketing of drugs by defendants).

2. Common Knowledge Exception

Tort law has a practical component to many of its doctrines. One of those practical principles concerns a disdain for requiring unnecessary action. In Chapter 6, Special Duty Rules, we encountered the *open and obvious danger doctrine* that eliminates any duty by a premises owner to eliminate or warn about dangerous conditions on the land of which an ordinary person would obviously be aware. With respect to strict liability claims for defecting marketing, tort law has come up with an analogous exception to the normal duty to provide warnings about the risks arising from the intended or foreseeable uses of products. This *common knowledge* defense is applied in the *Grinnell* case, which we have already encountered in both the manufacturing defect and design defect sections. Pay close attention to the subtle distinction the court makes between two different risks of smoking as we visit this case one final time.

AMERICAN TOBACCO CO. v. GRINNELL

951 S.W.2d 420 (Tex. 1997)

PART 3 — MARKETING DEFECT

Opinion [As set forth previously in this chapter, the decedent began smoking the defendant's cigarettes in 1952 and contracted cancer 33 years later. In the wrongful death and survival action against the manufacturer, the plaintiff asserted defective manufacturing, design and marketing theories of liability, among others. Part III of the opinion, set forth below, contains the Texas Supreme Court's analysis of the summary judgment granted against the plaintiff on her defective marketing (or warning) claim.]

A defendant's failure to warn of a product's potential dangers when warnings are required is a type of marketing defect. *Caterpillar, Inc.*, 911 S.W.2d at 382; *Lucas v. Texas Indus., Inc.*, 696 S.W.2d 372, 377 (Tex. 1984). The existence of a duty to warn of dangers or instruct as to the proper use of a product is a question of law. *Firestone Steel*, 927 S.W.2d at 613; *General Motors Corp. v. Saenz*, 873 S.W.2d 353, 356 (Tex. 1993). Generally, a manufacturer has a duty to warn if it knows or should know of the potential harm to a user because of the nature of its product. *Bristol-Myers Co. v. Gonzales*, 561 S.W.2d 801, 804 (Tex. 1978). Nevertheless, this Court has recognized that there is no duty to warn when the risks associated with a particular product are matters "within the ordinary knowledge common to the community." *Joseph E. Seagram & Sons, Inc. v. McGuire*, 814 S.W.2d 385, 388 (Tex. 1991) (holding that no legal duty exists to warn of the health risks of alcohol consumption because such risks are common knowledge). American argues that it had no duty to warn Grinnell of the risks associated with smoking its cigarettes because the dangers of smoking were common knowledge when Grinnell began smoking in 1952.

Comments i and j to *Restatement* section 402A incorporate common knowledge into the analysis of whether a product is "unreasonably dangerous" under that section Comment i, which defines "unreasonably dangerous," forecloses liability against manufacturers unless a product is dangerous to an extent beyond that which would be contemplated by the ordinary consumer with knowledge common to the community:

> Many products cannot possibly be made entirely safe for all consumption, and any food or drug necessarily involves some risk of harm, if only from over-consumption. . . . That is not what is meant by "unreasonably dangerous" in this Section. *The article sold must be dangerous to an extent beyond that which would be contemplated by the ordinary consumer who purchases it, with the ordinary knowledge common to the community as to its characteristics. . . . Good tobacco is not unreasonably dangerous merely because the effects of smoking may be harmful; but tobacco containing something like marijuana may be unreasonably dangerous.*

Restatement (Second) of Torts §402A cmt. i (1965) (emphasis added). Comment j excuses a seller from the duty to warn about dangers that are generally known and recognized:

> In order to prevent the product from being unreasonably dangerous, the seller may be required to give directions or warning, on the container, as to its use. . . . But a seller is not required to warn with respect to products, or ingredients in them, which are only dangerous, or potentially so, when consumed in excess quantity, or over a long period of time, *whenthe danger, or potentiality of danger, is generally known and recognized.* . . . The dangers of alcoholic beverages are an example. . . .

Id. §402A cmt. j (1965) (emphasis added).

Common knowledge, in the context of comments i and j, connotes a general societal understanding of the risks inherent in a specific product or class of products. *Seagram*, 814 S.W.2d at 388. In *Seagram* we also emphasized that the standard for finding common knowledge as a matter of law is a strict one. First holding that the term "common knowledge" encompasses "those facts that are so well known to the community as to be beyond dispute," *id.*, we then noted:

> Because Seagram is asking this court to determine common knowledge as a matter of law, we find the judicial notice rule helpful in providing a standard. Compare 33 S. Goode, O. Wellborn, III & M. Sharlot, Guide to Texas Rules of Evidence §201.2 (Tex. Prac. 1988) (requiring "high degree of indisputability" as prerequisite to judicial notice) with *Brune v. Brown Forman Corp.*, 758 S.W.2d 827, 830-31 (Tex. App. — Corpus Christi 1988, writ denied) ("common knowledge is information known by the public generally based upon indisputable facts").

814 S.W.2d at 388 n.6.

Thus, common knowledge is an extraordinary defense[3] that applies only in limited circumstances. As the court in *Brune* noted, common knowledge encompasses only those things "so patently obvious and so well known to the community generally, that there can be no question or dispute concerning their existence." *Brune*, 758 S.W.2d at 830-31. We will find common knowledge as a matter of law only when the standard set out in *Seagram* is met. It is not met in all respects here.

For example, we do not find the dangers of alcohol and cigarettes, or the public's awareness of those respective dangers, to be commensurate. Unlike Seagram & Sons, which did not dispute the health dangers of prolonged alcohol use, the tobacco industry, including American, actively disputed that cigarettes posed any health risk at the time Grinnell began smoking in 1952. Indeed, the industry continues to dispute the health risks of smoking and the addictive nature of cigarettes, before Congress, in the national press, and even at oral argument before the Court in this case. Despite this ongoing "dispute," we are bound to apply the rule that whether knowledge has become common to the community is an objective determination. *See Caterpillar, Inc. v. Shears*, 911 S.W.2d 379, 383 (Tex. 1995).

The party asserting the common-knowledge defense must establish that the dangers attributable to alcohol, tobacco, or other products were a matter of common knowledge when the consumer began using the product. Based on the summary judgment record, we hold American established that the general ill-effects of smoking were commonly known when Grinnell started smoking in 1952. However, we also hold that American did not establish that the addictive quality of cigarettes was commonly known when Grinnell began smoking in 1952.

Regarding the general health risks associated with smoking, the Tennessee Supreme Court held as early as 1898 that these risks were "generally known." *Austin v. State*, 101 Tenn. 563, 48 S.W. 305, 306 (Tenn. 1898), *aff'd as modified sub nom. Austin v. Tennessee*, 179 U.S. 343, 45 L. Ed. 224, 21 S. Ct. 132 (1900). On certiorari, the United States Supreme Court observed:

> We should be shutting our eyes to what is constantly passing before them were we to affect an ignorance of the fact that a belief in [cigarettes'] deleterious effects, particularly upon young people, *has become very general*, and that communications are constantly finding their way into the public press denouncing their use as fraught with great danger.

---

3. As we have stated, whether the risks associated with a product are common knowledge is one factor courts consider when determining the existence of a duty to warn. Common knowledge is referred to as a defense, *see Seagram*, 814 S.W.2d at 388 n.5, because the product user has the burden to prove that the seller had a duty warn of a product's danger, while the product seller may assert that no such duty existed because of the common knowledge regarding such danger.

179 U.S. at 348 (emphasis added). Other early courts also recognized the harmful effects of smoking cigarettes. *Gundling v. City of Chicago*, 176 Ill. 340, 52 N.E. 44, 45 (Ill. 1898) (cigarettes are "deleterious" and "injurious"), *aff'd*, 177 U.S. 183, 44 L. Ed. 725, 20 S. Ct. 633 (1900); *State v. Nossaman*, 107 Kan. 715, 193 P. 347, 348 (Kan. 1920) (dangers of smoking and deleterious effects of cigarettes are common knowledge); *Liggett & Myers Tobacco Co. v. Cannon*, 132 Tenn. 419, 178 S.W. 1009, 1010 (Tenn. 1915) (cigarettes are "possessed of no virtue, being bad inherently").

Moreover, by 1962, when the Surgeon General's advisory committee began examining the health risks associated with smoking, there were already more than seven thousand publications of professional and general circulation examining the relationship between smoking and health. Of these publications, articles published in nationally circulated magazines dating back to the early 1900s informed readers about the deleterious effects of smoking. Brown, *Is a Tobacco Crusade Coming?*, Atlantic Monthly, Oct. 1920, at 447 (adverse medical science findings on smoking have been brought before the public for the past thirty years); *Does Tobacco Make One Tired?*, The Literary Digest, Apr. 15, 1922, at 27 (noting the effect of heavy smoking, light smoking, and nonsmoking on workers' efficiency); Hirshberg, *Truth About Tobacco*, Harper's Weekly, Jan. 4, 1913 (consumer awareness of claims linking smoking to cancer, health disease, and bronchitis is pervasive); Norr, *Cancer by the Carton*, Reader's Digest, Dec. 1952, at 7 (examining data and projecting the number of future lung cancer deaths from smoking).

During this same period, many books examined the health risks associated with smoking and argued against the use of cigarettes. . . . These books and articles published before 1952 indicate that the general dangers of smoking were common knowledge even before Grinnell began smoking. *See, e.g.*, Crist & Majoras, *The "New" Wave in Smoking and Health Litigation — Is Anything Really So New?*, 54 Tenn. L. Rev. 551, 553 (1987) ("Even prior to the beginning of this century, . . . the public [was] constantly exposed to innumerable reports associating smoking with health risks."); Henderson & Twerski, *Closing the American Products Liability Frontier: The Rejection of Liability Without Defect*, 66 N.Y.U. L. Rev. 1263, 1325 (1991) ("The amount of information available to American consumers about the dangers of smoking is, and for some while has been, staggering.").

Not only does historical evidence illustrate the public's pre-1952 awareness of smoking's dangerous effects, but the Grinnells' experts also confirmed that the health hazards of smoking were common knowledge when Grinnell began smoking. Dr. Ravenholt, an expert on cancer and its causes, testified that the dangers of smoking were well known by the 1950s: "I think the majority [of people] would have been aware, you know, an adult, reasonably intelligent." He also testified that, in 1950, "evidence emerged of the lung cancer producing capability of smoking" and that the dangers attributable to smoking were extensively published and frequently front-page news stories in the 1950s. Dr. Greenberg likewise testified that the decision to smoke or refrain from smoking cigarettes is a matter of "individual personal responsibility" in light of the health risks.

We conclude that the general health dangers attributable to cigarettes were commonly known as a matter of law by the community when Grinnell began smoking. *See Caterpillar, Inc. v. Shears*, 911 S.W.2d at 383 (common knowledge is usually determined as a matter of law).

We cannot conclude, however, that the specific danger of nicotine addiction was common knowledge when Grinnell began smoking. Addiction is a danger apart from the direct physical dangers of smoking because the addictive nature of cigarettes multiplies the likelihood of and contributes to the smoker's ultimate injury, in Grinnell's case, lung cancer. *See* Garner, *Cigarette Dependency and Civil Liability: A Modest Proposal*, 53 S. Cal. L. Rev. 1423, 1430 (1980) ("Dependency adds a new dimension to smoking, for it greatly increases the likelihood of high volume, long term use which leads to disease, disability, and early death."). This Court has also recognized the seriousness of addiction and the need for manufacturers to warn of this danger in the context of prescription drugs. *Crocker v. Winthrop Labs.*, 514 S.W.2d 429, 432-33 (Tex. 1974) (holding drug manufacturer liable under *Restatement (Second) of Torts* §402B for misrepresenting that drug "was free and safe from all dangers of addiction"); *see also Carlisle v. Philip Morris, Inc.*, 805 S.W.2d 498, 516 (Tex. App. — Austin 1991, writ denied) ("Indeed, the failure to warn of cigarettes' addictive nature could be the essence of a plaintiff's complaint."). We acknowledge that some authorities support the proposition that some members of the community associated addiction with smoking cigarettes earlier in this century. *Ploch v. City of St. Louis*, 345 Mo. 1069, 138 S.W.2d 1020, 1023 (Mo. 1940) (cigarettes have "harmful properties" and it is common knowledge that nicotine produces "tobacco addicts"); Wiley, *The Little White Slaver*, Good Housekeeping, Jan. 1916, at 91 (people can become "slaves" to the cigarette habit and cigarette smoking can "shorten their lives").

The Surgeon General spoke to the addictive nature of tobacco in the most recent and comprehensive report on the subject in 1988. In that report, the Surgeon General concluded that: (1) cigarettes and other forms of tobacco are addicting, (2) nicotine is the drug in tobacco that causes addiction, and (3) the pharmacologic and behavioral processes that determine tobacco addiction are similar to those that determine addiction to drugs such as heroin and cocaine. More recently, the Food and Drug Administration has concluded that tobacco products are addictive.

But we cannot simply assume that common knowledge of the general health risks of tobacco use naturally includes common knowledge of tobacco's addictive quality. Indeed, as David Kessler, former head of the FDA, has pointed out:

> Before 1980, when FDA last considered its jurisdiction over tobacco products, *no* major public health organization had determined that nicotine was an addictive drug. Today, however, *all* major public health organizations in the United States and abroad with expertise in tobacco or drug addiction recognize that the nicotine delivered by cigarettes and smokeless tobacco is addictive.

The FDA based its 1996 assertion of jurisdiction on "a wealth of epidemiologic and laboratory data establishing that tobacco users display the clinical symptoms of addiction and that nicotine has the characteristics of other addictive drugs." Thus, unlike the general dangers associated with smoking, as late as 1988 and certainly in 1952, the danger of addiction from smoking cigarettes was not widely known and recognized in the community in general, or, particularly, by children or adolescents. The FDA has explained that because of tobacco's addictive effects, the only way to prevent the ensuing disease and death is to prevent children and adolescents from starting to use tobacco: "Most people who suffer the adverse health consequences of using cigarettes and smokeless tobacco begin their use before they reach the age of 18, an age when they are not prepared for, or equipped to, make a decision that, for many, will have lifelong consequences."

Because the community's knowledge concerning the danger of nicotine addiction associated with cigarettes was not beyond dispute in 1952, the *Seagram* standard for finding common knowledge as a matter of law has not been met. We agree with the court in *Rogers v. R.J. Reynolds Tobacco Co.*:

> There is no basis for our judicially noticing what the ordinary consumer's knowledge concerning the addictive qualities of cigarettes may have been when [the plaintiff] began smoking in 1940. The state of knowledge attributable to the community of individuals consuming cigarettes has changed over time and will continue to do so. It was not until 1988 that the Surgeon General published a report informing of the addictive nature of cigarettes.

557 N.E.2d 1045, 1054 (Ind. Ct. App. 1990). Accordingly, we hold that American did not establish as a matter of law that the danger of addiction associated with cigarettes was commonly known in 1952.

Because we conclude that American did not conclusively establish that the danger of addiction to nicotine was common knowledge, the Grinnells may maintain their strict liability marketing defect claims to the extent they are based on the addictive qualities of cigarettes, if no other defenses defeat those claims.

The Grinnells assert that American breached its duty to warn users about it product's addictive nature because before January 1, 1966, the product's packages contained no warnings. A manufacturer is required to give an adequate warning if it knows or should know that potential harm may result from use of the product. *Bristol-Myers Co. v. Gonzales*, 561 S.W.2d 801, 804 (Tex. 1978). In the absence of a warning, a *rebuttable* presumption arises that the "user would have read and heeded such warnings and instructions." *Magro v. Ragsdale Bros., Inc.*, 721 S.W.2d 832, 834 (Tex. 1986) (citing *Technical Chem. Co. v. Jacobs*, 480 S.W.2d 602, 606 (Tex. 1972)). A manufacturer may rebut the presumption with evidence that the plaintiff did not heed whatever warnings were given, or would not have heeded any proposed warnings. *See Magro*, 721 S.W.2d at 834; *see also GeneralMotors Corp. v. Saenz*, 873 S.W.2d 353, 358-59 (Tex. 1993).

The Grinnells assert that when Grinnell started smoking in 1952 he did not know and had heard nothing about any risk of addiction associated with smoking. The Grinnells further assert that American's failure to warn of the addictive nature of cigarettes caused Grinnell's eventual death because Grinnell testified that had he known what he later learned, he would never have started smoking. In rebuttal, American cites testimony that in the late 1950s and the 1960s, Grinnell continued smoking despite warnings from his father, coaches, and friends.

At most, the evidence relied on by American establishes that some people warned Grinnell about the general dangers of smoking. It does not conclusively establish that had Grinnell been warned that cigarettes were addictive *before* he began smoking he would have refused to follow the warnings. Grinnell testified at his deposition that if he had known of the dangers associated with smoking, including addiction, he never would have *started* smoking. At the very least, this testimony creates a fact issue regarding whether Grinnell would have heeded warnings had they been given to him before he began smoking. Dr. Grabowski, an expert on addiction, testified that Grinnell was addicted to cigarettes by the late 1950s and early 1960s and could not have stopped smoking without "intensive intervention." In short, American's summary judgment evidence does not conclusively establish that adequate warnings would not have been followed and thus would not have "made a difference in the outcome." Summary judgment on the Grinnells' marketing defect theory related to the addictive nature of cigarettes was therefore improper.

Thus, to the extent we hold that the general health risks of smoking were within the knowledge common to the community even before Grinnell began smoking in 1952, American has established that its cigarettes were not unreasonably dangerous. Summary judgment was, therefore, proper to the extent the Grinnells' strict liability claims relate to the general health risks associated with smoking. However, we also hold that American did not establish as a matter of law that the specific danger of addiction from smoking was knowledge common to the community. Therefore, we hold that the Grinnells' marketing defect claim survives to the extent it is based on the allegation that the addictive nature of cigarettes rendered American's products unreasonably dangerous, and to the extent it is not preempted by federal law.

NOTES AND PROBLEMS

1. ***Common Knowledge as a Defense.*** The court indicates that the common knowledge exception to the duty to warn only arises when it is beyond dispute that a risk was a matter of common knowledge at the relevant period of time and place. The Restatement (Third) articulates this exception, and its rationale, as follows:

> A product seller is not subject to liability for failing to warn regarding risks . . . that should be obvious to, or generally known by, foreseeable product users. . . .

> Warnings of an obvious or generally-known risk in most instances will not provide an effective additional measure of safety. Furthermore, warnings that deal with obvious or generally known risks may be ignored by users and consumers and may diminish the significance of warnings about non-obvious, not-generally-known risks.

Section 2, comment j. (1998). While this is a fairly high threshold for invocation of the no-duty doctrine, the court above finds the common knowledge defense applicable to the risk of cancer but not applicable to the risk of addiction. Why does the court distinguish between these two risks in terms of the viability of this defense?

2. *Knowledge as a Creator and Destroyer of Duty.* The foreseeability of a risk of harm associated with the use of a product can be seen on a continuum as both the creator and destroyer of a duty to warn. On the one hand, tort law requires there to be some foreseeable risk of harm associated with the product — at least in the so-called "state of the art" — as a prerequisite for imposing any obligation (or duty) to warn about the uses of the product. But where that knowledge rises to the level of undisputed common knowledge, the duty to warn is eviscerated.

3. *Problems.* Would the common knowledge exception apply to any of the following risks?

A. The risks associated with intoxication from drinking alcoholic beverages.
B. The risks associated with falling off of a trampoline while jumping on it.
C. The risk of death from being shot with a firearm.
D. The risk of liver or kidney dysfunction from taking the herb kava root.

IV DEFENSES ARISING OUT OF PLAINTIFF'S MISCONDUCT

Some defenses apply equally to strict products liability claims as they do to any other tort claim. For example, a plaintiff's delinquency in filing a strict liability claim gives rise to a defense under the applicable statute of limitations (as covered in Chapter 7). Other defenses are unique to products claims. As was discussed in *Dawson*, a federal statute might be interpreted to expressly or implicitly preempt the availability of state law products liability claims. Or a state might give presumptive or controlling weight to the federal government's approval of a manufacturer's design or warning. All of these defenses, both general to any tort suit and unique to a products liability claim, have already been discussed. What remains for our consideration, however, is the extent to which defenses based upon a claimant's *misconduct* might be recognized in a strict liability products suit.

Initially at common law, courts uniformly refused to recognize any general act of negligence by a claimant as even a partial defense to a claim for strict liability. Punishing the plaintiff for her misconduct seemed repugnant to the goal of holding the defendant absolutely liable — such refusal to recognize contributory negligence applying with equal force to *all varieties of strict liability claims*, whether involving wild animals, unusually dangerous activities or defective products. This rule of law was adopted at a time when any degree of negligence by the claimant acted as a complete defense. Nevertheless, courts were willing to recognize qualified (i.e., unreasonable) secondary implied assumption of risk as a complete defense. Further, in a strict products liability lawsuit, courts likewise recognized product misuse as an additional complete defense.

With almost all jurisdictions shifting to comparative fault, courts began to reexamine these traditional rules for blaming the plaintiff. Some courts have steadfastly refused to change their view of defenses in strict liability cases while others have embraced the application of comparative fault (and the elimination of secondary implied assumption of the risk as a separate defense) to strict liability suits. This section will first examine the ongoing debate over whether to recognize negligence as a defense to a strict liability claim. The *Bowling* and *Daly* cases contain excellent contrary opinions on this question. Finally, we will look at the continuing role that the defense of product misuse has in strict products liability suits.

A. Is Negligence a Defense to Strict Liability?

BOWLING v. HEIL CO.

511 N.E.2d 373 (Ohio 1987)

Appellant, Emma K. Bowling, brought this action against appellee, the Heil Company ("Heil"), among others, in her representative capacity as the administratrix of the estate of her husband, David B. Bowling, seeking to recover damages for his alleged wrongful death. Bowling died when he was crushed between the chassis of a truck and the dump bed mounted onto it.

Heil is engaged in the business of manufacturing and selling dump truck beds and hydraulic dump hoist systems designed to be installed on the chassis of trucks produced by various truck manufacturers. Heil does not install its dump beds and hoist systems; rather, it sells them to authorized distributors who install them onto the chassis of trucks selected by their customers.

In May 1979, Ralph Rogers purchased the dump truck at issue for use in his backhoe business. The truck was equipped with a Heil 1617 DL dump hoist system, which included a dump bed, a hydraulic hoist, and a hydraulic pump valve assembly.

As originally mounted, the 1617 DL system utilized a cable control system linking the truck cab controls to the hydraulic pump valve. Rogers was dissatisfied with the operation of the cable control system, however, and returned the truck to [the seller,] Sweeney, requesting that a lever control system be installed. Sweeney contacted Robco, Inc. ("Robco"), another Heil distributor, and Robco replaced the cable control system with a lever control system, which had also been manufactured by Heil. The failure of one of Robco's welds made while installing the lever control system triggered the tragic series of events culminating in David Bowling's death.

On April 26, 1980, [the truck was being used to move five tons of gravel. One of the individuals using the truck] pushed the in-cab control lever forward to lower the dump bed, but due to the failure of Robco's weld, the bed would not come down. David Bowling, [who was present and assisting in the job], leaned over the chassis, underneath the raised bed, to investigate the problem. Bowling reached in with his hand and grabbed the control lever on the pump valve assembly, and when he manually manipulated it the dump bed rapidly descended upon him, killing him instantly.

Appellant proceeded against Heil on [a theory of] strict liability in tort. The jury returned a verdict in favor of appellant against Heil and assessed damages at $1.75 million. Upon written interrogatories, the jury determined that Heil was strictly liable, that Bowling was contributorily negligent but that he had not assumed a known risk, and [apportioned 30% of the loss to Bowling].

Based on the jury's findings, the trial court entered judgment against Heil for $1.75 million plus funeral costs, less those amounts previously received by appellant by way of settlement with [Sweeney and Robco]. On appeal by Heil, the court of appeals affirmed the jury's verdict, but remanded the case with directions to enter judgment against Heil in the amount of $700,000 only, representing forty percent of $1.75 million.

Brown, J.

[This case presents the issue of] whether principles of comparative negligence or comparative fault are applicable to a products liability action based upon strict liability in tort. For the reasons that follow, we answer [this question] in the negative.

Included in the body of Ohio law governing products liability is an analysis of the defenses available in actions involving allegedly defective products. Currently, two affirmative defenses based upon a plaintiff's misconduct are recognized. First, an otherwise strictly liable defendant has a complete defense if the plaintiff voluntarily and knowingly assumed the risk occasioned by the defect. Second, such a defendant is also provided with a complete defense if the plaintiff misused the product in an unforeseeable manner.

The court of appeals below, construing Comment *n* to Section 402A, attempted to distinguish between negligent "affirmative action" by a plaintiff and negligent *passive* conduct by him in failing either to discover a defect or to guard against the possibility of its existence. The court held that although a plaintiff's passive contributory negligence provides no defense to a products liability action, his contributorily negligent "affirmative action" does provide a defense, and that such affirmative negligence should be compared by a jury to the fault of a strictly liable manufacturer of a defective product, in a manner similar to the principles of comparative negligence.

Comment *n* to Section 402A provides:

> Contributory negligence of the plaintiff is not a defense when such negligence consists merely in a failure to discover the defect in the product, or to guard against the possibility of its existence. On the other hand the form of contributory negligence which consists in voluntarily and unreasonably proceeding to encounter a known danger, and commonly passes under the name of assumption of risk, is a defense under this Section as in other cases of strict liability. If the user or consumer discovers the defect and is aware of the danger, and nevertheless proceeds unreasonably to make use of the product and is injured by it, he is barred from recovery.

The court of appeals has carved out a middle ground, to wit: contributory negligence consisting of "affirmative action," theoretically located between a plaintiff's failure to discover or guard against a defect and his voluntary assumption of a known risk. There is no such middle ground. Comment *n* covers the entire spectrum of conduct which can be termed "contributory negligence," as applicable to products liability actions. That spectrum begins with a mere failure to discover a defect in a product, continues with a failure to guard against the existence of a defect, and concludes with an assumption of the risk of a known defect. "Affirmative action" by the plaintiff is not left uncovered. Failure to guard against a defect can be "affirmative action." Indeed such would describe the conduct of David Bowling in this case.

Under Comment *n*, either a plaintiff's contributory negligence amounts to a voluntary assumption of a known risk, or it does not. If it does, then that conduct provides an otherwise strictly liable defendant with a complete defense. If it does not, the contributory negligence of the plaintiff provides no defense.[3]

In the case *sub judice*, the jury found that Bowling was contributorily negligent but that he had not assumed a known risk. Therefore, his contributory negligence did not provide Heil with a defense to appellant's strict liability claim.

Of course, the absence of support in either the Restatement or existing Ohio law for the recognition of comparative negligence as a defense to strict liability does not preclude this court from adopting comparative negligence principles as part of the law of products liability. This court, having developed that body of

---

3. Here, we discuss only the language of Comment *n*, which does not mention the defense consisting of a plaintiff's misuse of a product in an unforeseeable manner. In some sense, such misuse is an act of contributory negligence. Nonetheless, it remains a defense to a products liability action based upon strict liability in tort.

law, remains inherently vested with the power to modify it. We now turn to a consideration of the public policy underlying the application of strict liability in tort to products liability cases, in order to demonstrate why such modification is not appropriate.

Dean Prosser has [explained the goals of strict products liability in these] terms:

> The costs of damaging events due to defectively dangerous products can best be borne by the enterprisers who make and sell these products. *Those who are merchants and especially those engaged in the manufacturing enterprise have the capacity to distribute the losses of the few among the many who purchase the products.* It is not a 'deep pocket' theory but rather a 'risk-bearing economic' theory. The assumption is that the manufacturer can shift the costs of accidents to purchasers for use by charging higher prices for the costs of products.

(Emphasis added.) Prosser & Keeton, Law of Torts (5 Ed. 1984) 692-693, Section 98.

Under negligence principles, on the other hand, liability is determined according to *fault.* In negligence, we seek to make the person or persons responsible for causing a loss pay for it. In other words, we "blame" the loss on the negligent party or parties because it was they who could have avoided the loss by conforming to due care. Conversely, in strict liability in tort we hold the manufacturer or seller of a defective product responsible, not because it is "blameworthy," but because it is more able than the consumers to spread that loss among those who use and thereby benefit from the product.

We recognize that strict liability cannot be absolutely divorced from traditional concepts of fault. In a sense we "blame" the loss on the manufacturer or seller because it introduced the defective product into the marketplace. However, it must be reemphasized that strict liability is at odds with traditional notions of due care.

In sum, the public policy and goals underlying strict liability differ in important respects from those underlying the law of negligence.

Comparative negligence or comparative fault has been applied in products liability cases by a number of courts, both in states that have comparative negligence statutes and in states where comparative negligence was judicially adopted. See, *e.g., Duncan v. Cessna Aircraft Co.* (Tex. 1984), 665 S.W.2d 414; *Mulherin v. Ingersoll-Rand Co.* (Utah 1981), 628 P.2d 1301; *Daly v. General Motors Corp.*, 575 P.2d 1162 (Cal. 1978). On the other hand, numerous courts have refused to apply comparative negligence principles to products liability cases. See, e.g., *Young's Machine Co. v. Long*, 692 P.2d 24 (Nev. 1984); *Correia v. Firestone Tire & Rubber Co.*, 446 N.E.2d 1033 (Mass. 1983); *Seay v. Chrysler Corp.*, 609 P.2d 1382 (Wash. 1980); *Smith v. Smith*, 278 N.W.2d 155 (S.D. 1979).

We believe that the better-reasoned decisions are those that decline to inject a plaintiff's negligence into the law of products liability. We agree with

Justice Mosk of the California Supreme Court, who stated in his *dissent* in *Daly v. General Motors Corp.*:

> The defective product is comparable to a time bomb ready to explode; it maims its victims indiscriminately, the righteous and the evil, the careful and the careless. Thus when a faulty design or otherwise defective product is involved, the litigation should not be diverted to consideration of the negligence of the plaintiff. The liability issues are simple: was the product or its design faulty, did the defendant inject the defective product into the stream of commerce, and did the defect cause the injury? The conduct of the ultimate consumer-victim who used the product in the contemplated or foreseeable manner is wholly irrelevant to those issues.

Id. at 1183-1184.

Therefore, when we search the decisions from other jurisdictions, we find no rationale which persuades us that comparative negligence or comparative fault principles should be applied to products liability actions.

We therefore reverse the judgment of the court of appeals with respect to its reduction of appellant's verdict by the thirty percent found by the jury to be attributable to Bowling's contributory negligence.

DALY v. GENERAL MOTORS CORP.

575 P.2d 1162 (Cal. 1978)

Richardson, J.

[The family of a man killed in a one-car accident brought a strict products liability action against the manufacturer of the car and other companies who were sellers in the chain of distribution. The car hit a metal freeway divider at more than 50 miles per hour, and the decedent had been thrown through the door and suffered fatal head injuries. It was undisputed that had he remained inside the car his injuries would have been minor. Plaintiffs proved that an exposed push button on the exterior door handle, which had caused the door to open, constituted a design "defect." Over plaintiffs' objection, defendants introduced evidence that the car was fitted with a safety belt and door-lock, neither of which, despite a warning in the owner's manual, was being used by the decedent. Defendants also introduced evidence that the decedent was intoxicated. Defendants' theory was that this evidence showed either product misuse or an assumption of the risk by the decedent, either of which was a complete defense under the existing law. The jury delivered a verdict in favor of the defendants and judgment was entered accordingly.]

The sole theory of plaintiffs' complaint was strict liability for damages allegedly caused by a defective product, namely, an improperly designed door latch claimed to have been activated by the impact. It was further asserted that, but for the faulty latch, decedent would have been restrained in the vehicle and, although perhaps injured, would not have been killed. Thus, the case involves a so-called "second collision" in which the "defect" did not contribute to the original impact, but only to the "enhancement" of injury.

Over plaintiffs' objections, defendants were permitted to introduce evidence [of the decedent's intoxication and failure to utilize either the seat belt or the door locks].

In response to plaintiffs' assertion that the "intoxication-nonuse" evidence was improperly admitted, defendants contend that the deceased's own conduct contributed to his death. Because plaintiffs' case rests upon strict products liability based on improper design of the door latch and because defendants assert a failure in decedent's conduct, namely, his alleged intoxication and nonuse of safety equipment, without which the accident and ensuing death would not have occurred, there is thereby posed the overriding issue in the case, should comparative principles apply in strict products liability actions?

It may be useful to refer briefly to certain highlights in the historical development of the two principles — strict and comparative liability. Tort law has evolved from a legal obligation initially imposed without "fault," to recovery which, generally, was based on blameworthiness in a moral sense. For reasons of social policy and because of the unusual nature of defendants' acts, liability without fault continued to be prescribed in a certain restricted area, for example, upon keepers of wild animals, or those who handled explosives or other dangerous substances, or who engaged in ultrahazardous activities.

General dissatisfaction continued with the conceptual limitations which traditional tort and contract doctrines placed upon the consumers and users of manufactured products, this at a time when mass production of an almost infinite variety of goods and products was responding to a myriad of ever-changing societal demands stimulated by wide-spread commercial advertising. From an historic combination of economic and sociological forces was born the doctrine of strict liability in tort.

We, ourselves, were perhaps the first court to give the new principle judicial sanction. In *Greenman v. Yuba Power Products, Inc.*, 377 P.2d 897 (Cal. 1963), [w]e rejected both contract and warranty theories, as the basis for liability. Strict liability, we said, did not rest on a consensual foundation but, rather, on one created by law. The liability was created judicially because of the economic and social need for the protection of consumers in an increasingly complex and mechanized society, and because of the limitations in the negligence and warranty remedies. Subsequently, the *Greenman* principle was incorporated in §402A of the Restatement Second of Torts, and adopted by a majority of American jurisdictions.

From its inception, however, strict liability has never been, and is not now, *absolute* liability. As has been repeatedly expressed, under strict liability the manufacturer does not thereby become the insurer of the safety of the product's user. On the contrary, the plaintiff's injury must have been caused by a "defect" in the product. Thus the manufacturer is not deemed responsible when injury results from an unforeseeable use of its product. Furthermore, we have recognized that though most forms of contributory negligence do not constitute a defense to a strict products liability action, plaintiff's negligence is a complete defense when it comprises assumption of risk.

In *Li v. Yellow Cab Co.*, 532 P.2d 1226 (Cal. 1975), we introduced the other doctrine with which we are concerned, comparative negligence. We examined the history of contributory negligence, the massive criticism directed at it because its presence in the slightest degree completely barred plaintiff's recovery, and the increasing defection from the doctrine. [W]e announced in *Li* the adoption of a "pure" form of comparative negligence which, when present, reduced but did not prevent plaintiff's recovery. We held that the defense of assumption of risk, insofar as it is no more than a variant of contributory negligence, was merged into the assessment of liability in proportion to fault.

We stand now at the point of confluence of these two conceptual streams, having been greatly assisted by the thoughtful analysis of the parties and the valuable assistance of numerous amici curiae. We are by no means the first to consider the interaction of these two developing principles. As with the litigants before us, responsible and respected authorities have reached opposing conclusions stressing in various degrees the different considerations which we now examine.

Those counseling against the recognition of comparative fault principles in strict products liability cases vigorously stress, perhaps equally, not only the conceptual, but also the semantic difficulties incident to such a course. The task of merging the two concepts is said to be impossible, that "apples and oranges" cannot be compared, that "oil and water" do not mix, and that strict liability, which is not founded on negligence or fault, is inhospitable to comparative principles. The syllogism runs, contributory negligence was only a defense to negligence, comparative negligence only affects contributory negligence, therefore comparative negligence cannot be a defense to strict liability. While fully recognizing the theoretical and semantic distinctions between the twin principles of strict products liability and traditional negligence, we think they can be blended or accommodated.

The inherent difficulty in the "apples and oranges" argument is its insistence on fixed and precise definitional treatment of legal concepts. In the evolving areas of both products liability and tort defenses, however, there has developed much conceptual overlapping and interweaving in order to attain substantial justice. The concept of strict liability itself, as we have noted, arose from dissatisfaction with the wooden formalisms of traditional tort and contract principles in order to protect the consumer of manufactured goods. Similarly, increasing social awareness of its harsh "all or nothing" consequences led us in *Li* to moderate the impact of traditional contributory negligence in order to accomplish a fairer and more balanced result. We acknowledged an intermixing of defenses of contributory negligence and assumption of risk and formally effected a type of merger: "We think it clear that the adoption of a system of comparative negligence should entail the merger of the defense of assumption of risk into the general scheme of assessment of liability in proportion to fault in those particular cases in which the form of assumption of risk involved is no more than a variant of contributory negligence."

Furthermore, the "apples and oranges" argument may be conceptually suspect. We think, accordingly, the conclusion may fairly be drawn that the terms "comparative negligence," "contributory negligence" and "assumption of risk" do not, standing alone, lend themselves to the exact measurements of a micrometer-caliper, or to such precise definition as to divert us from otherwise strong and consistent countervailing policy considerations. Fixed semantic consistency at this point is less important than the attainment of a just and equitable result. The interweaving of concept and terminology in this area suggests a judicial posture that is flexible rather than doctrinaire.

The [goals sought to be achieved by strict products liability] will not be frustrated by the adoption of comparative principles. Plaintiffs will continue to be relieved of proving that the manufacturer or distributor was negligent in the production, design, or dissemination of the article in question. Defendant's liability for injuries caused by a defective product remains strict. The principle of protecting the defenseless is likewise preserved, for plaintiff's recovery will be reduced *only* to the extent that his own lack of reasonable care contributed to his injury. The cost of compensating the victim of a defective product, albeit proportionately reduced, remains on defendant manufacturer, and will, through him, be "spread among society." However, we do not permit plaintiff's own conduct relative to the product to escape unexamined, and as to that share of plaintiff's damages which flows from his own fault we discern no reason of policy why it should, following *Li*, be borne by others. Such a result would directly contravene the principle announced in *Li*, that loss should be assessed equitably in proportion to fault.

We conclude, accordingly, that the expressed purposes which persuaded us in the first instance to adopt strict liability in California would not be thwarted were we to apply comparative principles. What would be forfeit is a degree of semantic symmetry. However, in this evolving area of tort law in which new remedies are judicially created, and old defenses judicially merged, impelled by strong considerations of equity and fairness we seek a larger synthesis. If a more just result follows from the expansion of comparative principles, we have no hesitancy in seeking it, mindful always that the fundamental and underlying purpose of *Li* was to promote the equitable allocation of loss among all parties legally responsible in proportion to their fault.

In passing, we note one important and felicitious result if we apply comparative principles to strict products liability. This arises from the fact that under present law when plaintiff sues in negligence his own contributory negligence, however denominated, may diminish but cannot wholly defeat his recovery. When he sues in strict products liability, however, his "assumption of risk" *completely bars* his recovery. Under *Li*, as we have noted, "assumption of risk" is merged into comparative principles. The consequence is that after *Li* in a negligence action, plaintiff's conduct which amounts to "negligent" assumption of risk no longer defeats plaintiff's recovery. Identical conduct, however, in a strict liability case acts as a complete bar under rules heretofore applicable. Thus, strict products liability, which was developed to free injured consumers from the constraints imposed by traditional negligence and warranty theories, places a consumer plaintiff in a worse position than would be the case were his claim founded on simple negligence. This, in turn, rewards adroit pleading and selection of theories. The application of comparative principles to strict liability obviates this bizarre anomaly by treating alike the defenses to both negligence and strict products liability actions. In each instance the defense, if established, will reduce but not bar plaintiff's claim.

We note that the majority of our sister states which have addressed the problem, either by statute or judicial decree, have extended comparative principles to strict products liability.

Having examined the principal objections and finding them not insurmountable, and persuaded by logic, justice, and fundamental fairness, we conclude that a system of comparative fault should be and it is hereby extended to actions founded on strict products liability. In such cases the separate defense of "assumption of risk," to the extent that it is a form of contributory negligence, is abolished. While, as we have suggested, on the particular facts before us, the term "equitable apportionment of loss" is more accurately descriptive of the process, nonetheless, the term "comparative fault" has gained such wide acceptance by courts and in the literature that we adopt its use herein.

[The court ruled that the admission of evidence of the decedent's intoxication and failure to use safety equipment was improper because it was not germane to showing any assumption of the risk or product misuse — the only blame-the-plaintiff defenses available at the time of trial. The court said the introduction of such evidence was instead a "thinly disguised" attempt to inject issues of general contributory negligence into the case — a defense not yet available as of the time of trial. The court believed it was this evidence that led to the jury's defense verdict. This improper admission of evidence, therefore, necessitated a new trial. In the event of the new trial, such evidence could be offered but only as relevant to the issue of the decedent's comparative fault under the newly applicable pure comparative fault system.]

NOTES AND PROBLEMS

1. ***Apples and Oranges.*** As illustrated by the two cases above, courts have disagreed over whether comparative fault principles should apply to strict products liability suits. The traditional rule, preserved by Ohio, is that contributory negligence is no defense to strict products liability, but secondary implied assumption of the risk and product misuse are complete defenses. One reason these courts refuse to apply contributory negligence to strict liability is because of the harsh consequences of its application. However, once most jurisdictions abandoned contributory negligence for comparative fault, the

pressure mounted to recognize this partial defense. In response, some courts continued to resist the argument for application of comparative fault due to the notion that the disparate concepts of "negligence" and "strict liability" are like apples and oranges and impossible to compare to one another. Of course, some scholars (and most courts) observe that even strict liability contains some notion of fault:

> In the case of products liability, the fault inheres primarily in the nature of the product. The product is "bad" because it is not duly safe; it is determined to be defective and (in most jurisdictions) unreasonably dangerous. [S]imply maintaining the bad condition or placing the bad product on the market is enough for liability. . . . One does not have to stigmatize conduct as negligent in order to characterize it as fault.

Wade, *Products Liability and Plaintiff's Fault*, 29 Mercer L. Rev. 373, 377 (1978). Do you find the opinion of the Ohio court or the California court more persuasive?

2. *Is Application of Comparative Fault Pro-Plaintiff?* As you read the Ohio Supreme Court's decision adamantly refusing to apply comparative fault to strict liability, the impression given is that the court's holding is designed to protect the ability of injured consumers to recover — by refusing to permit their misconduct to be used as even a partial defense. On the other hand, retaining the traditional rules also leaves intact the defense of secondary implied assumption of the risk as a *complete* defense. In the California decision, the court stressed that one advantage of applying comparative fault principles to strict products liability cases was that this permitted cases involving conduct amounting to a secondary implied assumption of the risk to no longer raise a total defense; instead, it would merely permit the jury to apportion any fault associated with such an assumption and to reduce the damage recovery accordingly. Thus, the decision whether to retain the traditional defense rules or to apply comparative fault principles is neither purely pro-consumer nor pro-seller. Which set of rules is better for a plaintiff is dependent upon the particular circumstances of the plaintiff's case.

B. When, and How, Does Product Misuse Provide a Defense?

In Justice Traynor's concurring opinion in *Escola* advocating for the adoption of strict products liability, his final caveat was that the seller's liability "should, of course, be defined in terms of the safety of the product in *normal and proper use*." Similarly, in his majority opinion in *Greenman* adopting strict liability, he summarized the plaintiff's burden of proof as follows: "To establish the manufacturer's liability it was sufficient that plaintiff proved that he was injured while using the [product] in a *way it was intended to be used* as a result of a defect in design and manufacture." Seizing upon such language, courts have refused to hold product sellers liable for injuries associated with some misuses of products. On the other hand, as we have already seen in *Dawson*, where the court rejected the manufacturer's argument that an automobile need not be crashworthy because crashing is not the intended purpose of a car, the misuse defense has its limits. A product "misuse" technically might entail any use of the product not intended by the manufacturer or seller. The *Daniell* case below involves a particularly notorious misuse of the allegedly defective product. Observe what role the plaintiff's misconduct plays in the court's analysis of whether a defect existed in the product. What is most instructive about this case is the court's determination about what factor will determine whether a consumer's misuse provides a complete defense to the strict liability claim. You will also observe that the defendant could potentially have used the consumer's misuse to its legal advantage in two different ways. In the *Tokai* case that follows *Daniell*, the court considers how to correctly analyze a claim of a possible design defect when the product hurt an unintended, yet foreseeable, user.

DANIELL v. FORD MOTOR CO.

581 F. Supp. 728 (D.N.M. 1984)

BALDOCK, J.

This matter comes on for consideration of defendant's Motion for Summary Judgment pursuant to Fed. R. Civ. P. 56(c). The court, having considered the accompanying memoranda submitted by the parties, the deposition and affidavits relied upon by the parties, and the relevant law, finds that the motion is well taken and should be granted. Summary judgment is a severe remedy that should be cautiously applied. It should not be used for resolution of factual issues appearing on the record. Summary judgment is appropriate in this case, however, because certain uncontroverted facts bar plaintiff's recovery.

In 1980, the plaintiff became locked inside the trunk of a 1973 Ford LTD automobile, where she remained for some nine days. Plaintiff now seeks to recover for psychological and physical injuries arising from that occurrence. She contends that the automobile had a design defect in that the trunk lock or latch did not have an internal release or opening mechanism. She also maintains that the manufacturer is liable based on a failure to warn of this condition. Plaintiff advances several theories for recovery: (1) strict products liability under §402A of the Restatement 2d of Torts, (2) negligence, and (3) breach of express warranty and implied warranties of merchantability and fitness for a particular purpose.

Three uncontroverted facts bar recovery under any of these theories. First, the plaintiff ended up in the trunk compartment of the automobile because she felt "overburdened" and was attempting to commit suicide. Second, the purposes of an automobile trunk are to transport, stow and protect items from elements of the weather. Third, the plaintiff never considered the possibility of exit from the inside of the trunk when the automobile was purchased. Plaintiff has not set forth evidence indicating that these facts are controverted.

The overriding factor barring plaintiff's recovery is that she intentionally sought to end her life by crawling into an automobile trunk from which she could not escape. This is not a case where a person inadvertently became trapped inside an automobile trunk. The plaintiff was aware of the natural and probable consequences of her perilous conduct. Not only that, the plaintiff, at least initially, sought those dreadful consequences. Plaintiff, not the manufacturer of the vehicle, is responsible for this unfortunate occurrence.

Recovery under strict products liability and negligence will be discussed first because the concept of duty owed by the manufacturer to the consumer or user is the same under both theories in this case. As a general principle, a design defect is actionable only where the condition of the product is unreasonably dangerous to the user or consumer. Under strict products liability or negligence, a manufacturer has a duty to consider only those risks of injury which are foreseeable. A risk is not foreseeable by a manufacturer where a product is used in a manner which could not reasonably be anticipated by the manufacturer and that use is the cause of the plaintiff's injury. The plaintiff's injury would not be foreseeable by the manufacturer.

The purposes of an automobile trunk are to transport, stow and secure the automobile spare tire, luggage and other goods and to protect those items from elements of the weather. The design features of an automobile trunk make it well near impossible that an adult intentionally would enter the trunk and close the lid. The dimensions of a trunk, the height of its sill and its load floor and the efforts to first lower the trunk lid and then to engage its latch, are among the design features which encourage closing and latching the trunk lid while standing outside the vehicle. The court holds that the plaintiff's use of the trunk compartment as a means to attempt suicide was an unforeseeable use as a matter of law. Therefore, the manufacturer had no duty to design an internal release or opening mechanism that might have prevented this occurrence.

Nor did the manufacturer have a duty to warn the plaintiff of the danger of her conduct, given the plaintiff's unforeseeable use of the product. Another reason why the manufacturer had no duty to warn the plaintiff of the risk inherent in crawling into an automobile trunk and closing the trunk lid is because such a risk is obvious. There is no duty to warn of known dangers in strict products liability or tort. Moreover, the potential efficacy of any warning, given the plaintiff's use of the automobile trunk compartment for a deliberate suicide attempt, is questionable.

The court notes that the automobile trunk was not defective under these circumstances. The automobile trunk was not unreasonably dangerous within the contemplation of the ordinary consumer or user of such a trunk when used in the ordinary ways and for the ordinary purposes for which such a trunk is used. *Skyhook Corp. v. Jasper*, 90 N.M. 143, 147, 560 P.2d 934, 938 (1977); Restatement 2d of Torts §402A, comment i.

Having held that the plaintiff's conception of the manufacturer's duty is in error, the court need not reach the issues of the effect of comparative negligence or other defenses such as assumption of the risk on the products liability claim. *See Scott v. Rizzo*, 634 P.2d 1234 at 1240-41 (N.M. 1981) (In adopting comparative negligence, the New Mexico Supreme Court indicated that in strict products liability a plaintiff's "misconduct" would be a defense, but not a complete bar to recovery). The court also does not reach the comparative negligence defense on the negligence claim.

Having considered the products liability and negligence claims, plaintiff's contract claims for breach of warranty are now analyzed. Plaintiff has come forward with no evidence of any express warranty regarding exit from the inside of the trunk. [The implied warranty of merchantability claim also is flawed.] [T]he usual and ordinary purpose of an automobile trunk is to transport and store goods, including the automobile's spare tire. Plaintiff's use of the trunk was highly extraordinary, and there is no evidence that that trunk was not fit for the ordinary purpose for which it was intended.

Lastly, plaintiff's claim for a breach of implied warranty of fitness for a particular purpose, cannot withstand summary judgment because the plaintiff has admitted that, at the time she purchased the automobile neither she nor her husband gave any particular thought to the trunk mechanism. Plaintiff has admitted that she did not even think about getting out from inside of the trunk when purchasing the vehicle. Plaintiff did not rely on the seller's skill or judgment to select or furnish an automobile suitable for the unfortunate purpose for which the plaintiff used it.

IT IS ORDERED that defendant's Motion for Summary Judgment is granted.

NOTES AND PROBLEMS

1. ***Unforeseeable Misuse.*** In *Daniell* there was no real dispute that the plaintiff's use of the vehicle's trunk to attempt suicide was not the manufacturer's intended use for the product. It was a clear case of misuse. But in terms of whether the defendant had an obligation (or duty) to take the risks of being trapped in the trunk into consideration in designing the car, or in preparing instructions or warnings for its use, the key determination was whether the misuse was *foreseeable* or not. Given the characteristics of the car's trunk and the rather bizarre nature of the plaintiff's conduct, the court concludes as a matter of law that her misuse was unforeseeable. This conclusion alone was sufficient to permit the conclusion that no product defect existed. The duty to design or provide warnings does not encompass risks that arise only out of unforeseeable misuses of the product. Would this conclusion change if the manufacturer of the vehicle starts receiving numerous reports of others attempting suicide in the same manner?

2. *Problems with Duty to Warn Claim.* The unforeseeable misuse of the product meant that the defendant was under no duty to provide a warning for the product. The court also concludes that the danger of being locked inside the trunk would have been obvious. This conclusion would remove any duty to warn because of the *common knowledge doctrine*. As if those two fatal flaws were not enough, the court also observes that any warning about the danger of being locked in the trunk would have been ineffective in preventing this plaintiff's harm since the plaintiff desired to kill herself. This is an example of the facts rebutting the read and heed presumption. Any one of these three rationales would have been sufficient to warrant the grant of the defendant's motion for summary judgment on this claim.

3. *Negligent Misuse.* The court's conclusion that the plaintiff's misuse was unforeseeable ended the necessary analysis of the strict liability claims. The court stated, therefore, that it need not consider the possible negligence by the plaintiff in her misuse of the product. Like the majority of jurisdictions, New Mexico has applied comparative fault to strict liability claims (whether the misconduct relates to negligently assuming a known risk or involves some other general act of carelessness). Had the plaintiff's misuse been foreseeable, the plaintiff might have still been able to prove a defect existed. This is true in automobile defect cases involving allegations that the car was not crashworthy. As we have already seen in that context, most courts hold that such foreseeable misuse does not relieve the sellers of potential liability for defects related to the car's crashworthiness. But in such instances, if the plaintiff's misuse involves any negligence on the plaintiff's part, the misuse can give rise to demonstrating comparative fault which will serve at least as a partial defense by reducing the recoverable damages. Thus, the two questions any defendant must consider in cases of product misuse are (1) was the misuse foreseeable to the seller, and if so, (2) did the plaintiff's misuse involve negligence?

4. *Problems.* Consider whether a product manufacturer or seller has a duty to attempt to reduce or warn about the following risks in either their design or marketing of these products:

- **A.** A teenager uses a can of aerosol hairspray to get high by breathing the inhalant. He goes into a coma and dies.
- **B.** A manufacturer of a modeling compound called "Ply-Doh" is sued after a toddler playing with the toy decides to eat the brightly colored substance and suffers a severe allergic reaction.
- **C.** Some boys take their steel-tipped lawn darts and decide to use them to play tag. One of the boys is hit in the eye with the dart. It penetrates his brain and kills him instantly.

HERNANDEZ v. TOKAI CORP.

2 S.W.3d 251 (Tex. 1999)

HECHT, J.

The United States Court of Appeals for the Fifth Circuit has certified to us the following question:

> Under the Texas Products Liability Act of 1993 [Tex. Civ. Prac. & Rem. Code Ch. 82] can the legal representative of a minor child injured as a result of the misuse of a product by another minor child maintain a defective-design products liability claim against the product's manufacturer where the product was intended to be used only by adults, the risk that children might misuse the product was obvious to the product's manufacturer and to its intended users, and a safer alternative design was available?

In the context of this case, the question, more specifically, is whether a disposable butane lighter, intended only for adult use, can be found to be defectively designed if it does not have a child-resistant mechanism that would have prevented or substantially reduced the risk of injury from a child's foreseeable misuse of the lighter.

The factual circumstances in which the certified question comes to us are these.

Rita Emeterio bought disposable butane lighters for use at her bar. Her daughter, Gloria Hernandez, took lighters from the bar from time to time for her personal use. Emeterio and Hernandez both knew that it was dangerous for children to play with lighters. They also knew that some lighters were made with child-resistant mechanisms, but Emeterio chose not to buy them. On April 4, 1995, Hernandez's five-year-old daughter, Daphne, took a lighter from her mother's purse on the top shelf of a closet in a bedroom in her grandparents' home and started a fire in the room that severely burned her two-year-old brother, Ruben.

Hernandez, on Ruben's behalf, sued the manufacturers and distributors of the lighter, Tokai Corporation and Scripto-Tokai Corporation (collectively, "Tokai"), in the United States District Court for the Western District of Texas, San Antonio Division. Hernandez alleged that the lighter was defectively designed and unreasonably dangerous because it did not have a child-resistant safety mechanism that would have prevented or substantially reduced the likelihood that a child could have used it to start a fire. Tokai does not dispute that mechanisms for making disposable lighters child-resistant were available when the lighter Daphne used was designed and marketed, or that such mechanisms can be incorporated into lighters at nominal cost.

Tokai moved for summary judgment on the grounds that a disposable lighter is a simple household tool intended for adult use only, and a manufacturer has no duty to incorporate child-resistant features into a lighter's design to protect unintended users — children — from obvious and inherent dangers.

Tokai also noted that adequate warnings against access by children were provided with its lighters, even though that danger was obvious and commonly known. In response to Tokai's motion, Hernandez argued that, because an alternative design existed at the time the lighter at issue was manufactured and distributed that would have made the lighter safer in the hands of children, it remained for the jury to decide whether the lighter was defective under Texas' common-law risk-utility test.

The federal district court granted summary judgment for Tokai, and Hernandez appealed.

A product's utility and risk under the common-law test must both be measured with reference to the product's intended users. A product intended for adults need not be designed to be safe for children solely because it is possible for the product to come into a child's hands.

A child may hurt himself or others with a hammer, a knife, an electrical appliance, a power tool, or a ladder; he may fall into a pool, or start a car. The manufacturers and sellers of such products need not make them childproof merely because it is possible for children to cause harm with them and certain that some children will do so. The risk that adults, for whose use the products were intended, will allow children access to them, resulting in harm, must be balanced against the products' utility to their intended users.[23]

Even if an alternative design does not [overly] restrict a product's utility . . . it still may not be sufficient for defective-design liability if it overly restricts consumer choice. The *Restatement (Third) of Torts: Products Liability* offers [an example]: a smaller car that is not as crashworthy as a larger car merely because it is not as large. A chemistry set designed for the ordinary teenager is not unreasonably dangerous solely because it is possible that a younger sibling could get into it and harm himself or others. Products liability law does not force experienced carpenters to use only nail guns that are safe for the garage workshop. To make such products safe for the least apt, and unintended, user would hold other users hostage to the lowest common denominator.

A disposable lighter without a child-resistant mechanism is safe as long as its use is restricted to adults, as its manufacturer and users intend. Tokai makes lighters with and without child-resistant devices. Adults who want to minimize the possibility that their lighter may be misused by a child may purchase the child-resistant models. Adults who prefer the other model, as Hernandez and Emeterio did, may purchase it [though such products have since been banned by the federal Consumer Product Safety Commission]. Whether adult users of lighters should [have been] deprived of this choice of product design because of the risk that some children will obtain lighters that are not child-resistant and cause harm is the proper focus of the common-law risk-utility test.

---

23. "Texas law does not require a manufacturer to destroy the utility of his product in order to make it safe." *Hagans v. Oliver Mach. Co.*, 576 F.2d 97, 101 (5th Cir. 1978).

The utility of disposable lighters must be measured with reference to the intended adult users. Consumer preference — that is, that users like Hernandez and Emeterio simply prefer lighters without child-resistant features — is one consideration. Tokai also argues that adults whose dexterity is impaired, such as by age or disease, cannot operate child-resistant lighters, but Hernandez disputes this. If Tokai were shown to be correct, then that would be an additional consideration in assessing the utility of non-child-resistant lighters.

The relevant risk includes consideration of both the likelihood that adults will allow children access to lighters and the gravity of the resulting harm. The risk is not that a child who plays with a lighter may harm himself. We assume that that risk is substantial. As Hernandez and Emeterio both acknowledged in this case, they would not allow a child to have a lighter and would discipline a child caught playing with one. Rather, the risk is that a lighter will come into a child's hands. The record before us suggests that children will almost certainly obtain access to lighters, that this will not happen often in comparison with the number of lighters sold, but that when it does happen the harm caused can be extreme. Each of these considerations is relevant in assessing the risk of non-child-resistant lighters.

In sum, a manufacturer's intention that its product be used only by adults does not insulate it from liability for harm caused by a child who gains access to the product, but liability standards must be applied in the context of the intended users.

■ ■ ■

Whether in the present case the issue is one of fact or law is not for us to decide. The Fifth Circuit has asked whether a defective-design claim can be maintained under stated conditions. We respond that it can, depending on the evidence, but there will also be cases — the present case may or may not be one — in which a claim cannot be maintained as a matter of law, for the reasons we have explained.

A few other arguments remain to be addressed.

Tokai contends that a defective-design claim cannot be maintained in the circumstances before us because a manufacturer has no duty whatsoever to make products intended solely for adults child-proof. As we have explained, a product that is safely designed for its intended users is not unreasonably dangerous solely because someone else may obtain the product. But we think the issue should be resolved by applying the standard risk-utility analysis rather than as a matter of legal policy, at least in the circumstances of this case.

Tokai also contends that simple tools, like hammers and knives, whose essential utility involves intrinsic and obvious dangers to children, should not, as a matter of law, be unreasonably dangerous. [W]e do not think [this suggested approach is] helpful. The obviousness of the risk of harm and the inherent nature of the danger are, as we have explained, important factors to be considered in determining whether a product is unreasonably dangerous, and in a given case they may be conclusive of that issue. But that depends on an assessment of all the relevant considerations in the risk-utility analysis, not on whether a product can be called a simple tool. Many simple tools are not defectively designed merely because they are not child-proof, but the reason is because they are not unreasonably dangerous under the risk-utility test, not because they are simple tools.

Tokai argues that the risk-utility analysis is ill-suited for cases like this when the utility of a product design is largely satisfaction of consumer preference and the risk of harm, while improbable relative to the number of products sold, is often calamitous. We recognize that such circumstances make the use of the risk-utility test difficult. But we are reluctant to carve out exceptions to the risk-utility test that we have employed for years and that has been adopted by the *Restatement*, especially when consumer expectation is a factor to be considered in applying the risk-utility test and may in some cases outweigh all other considerations. We believe that the risk-utility test, properly focused, can be applied in a case like this.

Tokai argues that the weight of authority in other jurisdictions is to reject disposable lighter design-defect claims as a matter of law. This is true, but there is more to it. Courts in jurisdictions that employ a consumer-expectation test for determining defect have mostly held that disposable lighters without child-proof features are not defectively designed because they function in the manner expected by the intended adult consumers. But courts in jurisdictions employing a risk-utility analysis have mostly concluded that the determinative considerations are usually matters for the jury.

In sum: a claimant can maintain a defective-design claim in the circumstances posited by the certified question if, but only if, with reference to the product's intended users, the design defect makes the product unreasonably dangerous, a "safer alternative design" as defined by statute is available, and the defect is the producing cause of the injury.

NOTES AND PROBLEMS

1. ***Foreseeable but Unintended Users and Uses.*** The *Tokai* case involves the misuse (playing with a lighter) of a product by one not intended to be using the product. But as with the *Daniell* case, whether or not such unintended use creates an automatic defense to liability depends on whether this misuse is unforeseeable. The Texas Supreme Court was unwilling to say that a child getting hold of a lighter is unforeseeable. In fact, the manufacturer concedes as much with its own observation that the danger of access by children to lighters is "obvious and commonly known." Given this concession, it is difficult for the court to rule as a matter of law that a manufacturer of such lighters need not take into account the risk of injury to a child.

2. ***A Refined Application of the Risk Utility Test.*** The court in *Tokai* is careful to differentiate how the court (or factfinder) should apply the risk utility test in the circumstance of a foreseeable but unintended user of the product. It states that the risk utility test should be applied with reference to the intended adult users with the caveat that the product might end up in the hands of a child. If the court had instead indicated that the test should be applied with reference solely to child users, do you see why the risk utility test would obviously declare the lack of childproof features to be defective? Given the proper focus, why is the question of a defective design here much closer?

3. ***Risk Utility vs. Consumer Expectation Test.*** Near the end of the opinion, the court explains that most of the cases ruling in favor of lighter manufacturers in this factual circumstance come from states that employ the alternative consumer expectation test. Why under that test is the product's design not defective? Although as a general rule, plaintiff's lawyers often prefer the consumer expectation test (due to its simplicity and the lower cost of proving a defect since experts may not be necessary), this case illustrates that there are exceptions to this generalization. Which test might be more likely to lead to the conclusion that a design defect exists ultimately depends upon the facts of the particular case and the identity of the product involved?

4. ***Problem.*** An unlicensed 14-year-old obtains the key to the family sedan and goes joy riding on the interstate at 90 m.p.h. Due to vibrations in the steering mechanism, he loses control of the car and is injured. What role will the child's inappropriate use of the car play in determining whether the car was defectively designed to handle being driven at such speeds?

Upon Further Review

Even when a product is well-built according to the original plans, sellers may face liability either because the design rendered the product unreasonably dangerous or because the product was unsafe absent some appropriate warnings regarding its safe use. Analysis of design defects is either done using the warranty-like consumer expectation test or the negligence-like risk-utility test, depending upon jurisdiction and the circumstances. Marketing defect claims are analyzed in a manner closest to negligence analysis — some would argue identically to negligence analysis. Even the language used by courts in marketing defects cases — *duty, breach, constructive or actual knowledge, reasonably adequate* — all allude to negligence-based concepts.

In terms of affirmative defenses, general forms of negligence were not permitted to be used at all at common law in a strict liability case. The only silver-bullet defenses were related to the consumer's misuse of the product or secondary implied assumption of the risk. The shift away from contributory negligence to forms of comparative fault has convinced many jurisdictions to now permit the plaintiff's negligence to be a partial defense — something to be apportioned with the tortfeasors' conduct and which will at least reduce the claimant's recovery. Some courts are adamant in refusing to permit any ordinary negligence to constitute a defense, however. In most jurisdictions that permit comparative fault as a defense, they require the factfinder to apportion as merely another type of fault any conduct amounting to an unreasonable secondary implied assumption of the risk or unreasonable misuse. Of course, unforeseeable misuses of the product need not be taken into account when designing a product or providing warnings about the risks associated with its foreseeable uses.

🎥 Watch "Liability" video on Casebook Connect.

CHAPTER 12

Defamation

I INTRODUCTION

"Sticks and stones may break my bones, but names may never hurt me." We teach our kids to live by this credo, spurning attention to the ill words that others may have for them. And this old advice may have legs when the listener is the subject of the scorn. But what if whispers are made behind your client's back — words spoken in secret and designed to tear apart the reputation of the target? Your client may never even have the opportunity to set the record straight. All who have heard the accusations and innuendo may treat your client differently in the future. Job offers may be withheld based upon the gossip disseminated in the community. As the rumors spread, their original source (and the basis for the accusations) may become unclear, making any defense by your client of her formerly good name an impossibility. Your client may despair because the intangible nature of the tort increases its perniciousness. In the real world, injury to one's reputation is deemed by society to be an interest worthy of protection and retribution.

CHAPTER GOALS

- ☑ Gain awareness of the defamation cause of action and its interest in protecting against a lowering of one's reputation through false statements.
- ☑ Learn the distinction between libel and slander and ascertain when the distinction makes a profound difference in terms of recoverable items of damage and the necessary proof of damage.
- ☑ Discover common law qualified and absolute privileges and appreciate the balancing of competing policies at play in the application of such privileges.
- ☑ Encounter the First Amendment's application to this speech-based cause of action as a constitutional qualified privilege.

II ELEMENTS OF CLAIM

Defamation — which can involve claims of either *libel* or *slander* — arises from ancient roots, has undergone many changes throughout its history, and illustrates great complexity in the law. It can be viewed as an intentional tort, a strict liability tort, or a tort requiring negligence depending upon the era, the circumstances, and the possible application of privileges (arising under the common law, statutes, or the U.S. Constitution). The following three cases give us a chance to decipher the essential ingredients of a defamation claim. We will begin by comparing and contrasting two courts' views of the essentials of a defamation claim — one written by Judge Learned Hand during the Great Depression and the other a much more modern and evolved application of the common law claim. As you read the opinions below in *Burton* and *Busch*, identify the fundamental components of the tort of defamation and ask yourself whether these two opinions are consistent with one another. Specifically, under the elements explained by the federal district court in *Busch*, would there exist a cognizable claim under the facts from the *Burton* case below?

A. False and Defamatory Statements

1. Early Application

BURTON v. CROWELL PUB. CO.

82 F.2d 154 (2d Cir. 1936)

L. Hand, J.

This appeal arises upon a judgment dismissing a complaint for libel upon the pleadings. The complaint alleged that the defendant had published an advertisement made up of text and photographs; that one of the photographs was "susceptible of being regarded as representing plaintiff as guilty of indecent exposure and as being a person physically deformed and mentally perverted"; that some of the text, read with the offending photograph, was "susceptible of being regarded as falsely representing plaintiff as an utterer of salacious and obscene language"; and finally that "by reason of the premises plaintiff has been subjected to frequent and conspicuous ridicule, scandal, reproach, scorn, and indignity." The advertisement was of "Camel" cigarettes; the plaintiff was a widely known gentleman steeple-chaser, and the text quoted him as declaring that "Camel" cigarettes "restored" him after "a crowded business day." Two photographs were inserted; the larger, a picture of the plaintiff in riding shirt and breeches, seated apparently outside a paddock with a cigarette in one hand and a cap and whip in the other. This contained the legend, "Get a lift with a Camel"; neither it, nor the photograph, is charged as part of the libel, except as the legend may be read upon the other and offending photograph. That represented him coming from a race to be weighed in; he is carrying his saddle in front of him with his right hand under the pommel and his left under the cantle; the line of the seat is about twelve inches below his waist. Over the pommel hangs a stirrup; over the seat at his middle a white girth falls loosely in such a way that it seems to be attached to the plaintiff and not to the saddle. So regarded, the photograph becomes grotesque, monstrous, and obscene; and the legends, which without undue violence can be made to match, reinforce the ribald interpretation. That is the libel. The answer alleged that the plaintiff had posed for the photographs and been paid for their use as an advertisement; a reply, that they had never been shown to the plaintiff after they were taken. On this showing the judge held that the advertisement did not hold the plaintiff up to the hatred, ridicule, or contempt of fair-minded people, and that in any event he consented to its use and might not complain.

We dismiss at once so much of the complaint as alleged that the advertisement might be read to say that the plaintiff was deformed, or that he had indecently exposed himself, or was making obscene jokes by means of the legends. Nobody could be fatuous enough to believe any of these things; everybody would at once see that it was the camera, and the camera alone, that had made the unfortunate mistake. If the advertisement is a libel, it is such in spite of the fact that it asserts nothing whatever about the plaintiff, even by the remotest implications. It does not profess to depict him as he is; it does not exaggerate any part of his person so as to suggest that he is deformed; it is patently an optical illusion, and carries its correction on its face as much as though it were a verbal utterance which expressly declared that it was false. It would be hard for words so guarded to carry any sting, but the same is not true of caricatures, and this is an example; for, notwithstanding all we have just said, it exposed the plaintiff to overwhelming ridicule. The contrast between the drawn and serious face and the accompanying fantastic and lewd deformity was so extravagant that, though utterly unfair, it in fact made of the plaintiff a preposterously ridiculous spectacle; and the obvious mistake only added to the amusement. Had such a picture been deliberately produced, surely every right-minded person would agree that he would have had a genuine grievance; and the effect is the same whether it is deliberate or not. Such affects a man's reputation, if by that is meant his position in the minds of others; the association so established may be beyond repair; he may become known indefinitely as the absurd victim of this unhappy mischance. Literally, therefore, the injury falls within the accepted rubric; it exposes the sufferer to "ridicule" and "contempt." Nevertheless, we have not been able to find very much in the books that is in point, for although it has long been recognized that pictures may be libels, and in some cases they have been caricatures, in nearly all they have impugned the plaintiff at least by implication, directly or indirectly uttering some falsehood about him.

The defendant answers that every libel must affect the plaintiff's character; but if by "character" is meant those moral qualities which the word ordinarily includes, the statement is certainly untrue. Thus, it is a libel to say that a man is insane, or that he has negro blood if he professes to be white, or is too educated to earn his living, or is desperately poor, or that he is a eunuch, or that he has an infectious disease, even though not venereal, or that he is illegitimate, or that his near relatives have committed a crime, or that he was mistaken for Jack Ketch, or that a woman was served with process in her bathtub. It is indeed not true that all ridicule or all disagreeable comment is actionable; a man must not be too thin-skinned or a self-important prig; but this advertisement was more than what only a morbid person would not laugh off; the mortification, however ill deserved, was a very substantial grievance.

In all wrongs we must first ascertain whether the interest invaded is one which the law will protect at all; that is indeed especially important in defamation, for the common law did not recognize all injuries to reputation, especially when the utterance was oral. But the interest here is by hypothesis one which the law does protect; the plaintiff has been substantially enough ridiculed to be in a position to complain. The defendant must therefore find some excuse, and truth would be an excuse if it could be pleaded. The only reason why the law makes truth a defense is . . . because the utterance of truth is in all circumstances an interest paramount to reputation; it is like a privileged communication, which is privileged only because the law prefers it conditionally to reputation. When there is no such countervailing interest, there is no excuse; and that is the situation here. In conclusion therefore we hold that because the picture taken with the legends was calculated to expose the plaintiff to more than trivial ridicule, it was prima facie actionable.

Finally, the plaintiff's consent to the use of the photographs for which he posed as an advertisement was not a consent to the use of the offending photograph; he had no reason to anticipate that the lens would so distort his appearance. If the defendant wished to fix him with responsibility for whatever the camera might turn out, the result should have been shown him before publication. Possibly anyone who chooses to stir such a controversy in a court cannot have been very sensitive originally, but that is a consideration for the jury, which, if ever justified, is justified in actions for defamation.

Judgment reversed; cause remanded for trial.

2. *Modern Application*

BUSCH v. VIACOM INTERNATIONAL

477 F. Supp. 2d 764 (N.D. Tex. 2007)

LINDSAY, J.

Before the court is Defendants' Motion to Dismiss. After careful consideration of the motion, response, reply, record, legal briefing and applicable authority, the court grants Defendants' Motion to Dismiss.

This is an action for defamation and misappropriation of image. *Pro se* Plaintiff Phillip Busch ("Plaintiff" or "Busch"), a bodybuilder who resides in Addison, Dallas County, Texas, brings this action against Defendants Viacom International Inc. ("Viacom") and Jon Stewart ("Stewart"), the anchor of *The Daily Show with Jon Stewart* (*"The Daily Show"*), a nightly news satire that airs on Comedy Central, owned and operated by Viacom. Plaintiff's allegations arise from an October 2005 broadcast of *The Daily Show*, specifically a satiric segment involving a "fake endorsement" of a dietary shake promoted by television evangelist Pat Robertson ("Robertson"). At the end of the segment, *The Daily Show* featured a brief replay of an episode of *The 700 Club*, a talk show hosted by

Robertson, which included Plaintiff's image. On or about July 13, 2005, Plaintiff had appeared as a guest on *The 700 Club*, filmed in Virginia Beach, Virginia, to discuss his weight loss and Robertson's diet shake following his more than 200-pound weight loss over a 15-month period where he had used elements of Robertson's weight-loss program featured on *The 700 Club*, as well as "Pat's Great Tasting Diet Shake," a diet shake based on a recipe developed by Robertson.

According to the Complaint, "On or about October 15, 2005, *The Daily Show* aired a fake endorsement by Pat's Diet Shake. The fake endorsement included a segment from General Nutrition Corporation's television commercial for the product, some commentary by one of *The Daily Show* correspondents, and, at the end, a clip from *The 700 Club* that clearly showed Pat Robertson shaking hands with Mr. Busch and [Robertson] exclaiming 'thanks for using the shake!'"

On February 16, 2006, Busch filed this lawsuit in the 192nd District Court of Dallas County, Texas, seeking compensatory and punitive damages. Defendants removed the action to this court based on diversity of citizenship. On April 18, 2006, Defendants filed their motion to dismiss.

[The court first granted Jon Stewart's motion to dismiss for lack of personal jurisdiction. Defendant Viacom had not challenged jurisdiction and the court addressed the merits of its Rule 12(b)(6) motion to dismiss the defamation claim.]

A motion to dismiss for failure to state a claim under Fed. R. Civ. P. 12(b)(6) "is viewed with disfavor and is rarely granted." *Lowrey v. Texas A&M Univ. Sys.*, 117 F.3d 242, 247 (5th Cir. 1997). A district court "may dismiss a complaint only if it is clear that no relief could be granted under any set of facts that could be proved consistent with the allegations." *Swierkiewicz v. Sorema*, 534 U.S. 506, 514 (2002).

The elements of a cause of action for defamation under Texas law are that:

1. the challenged broadcast contains assertions of fact about the plaintiff;
2. the challenged assertions of fact are defamatory, injuring the plaintiff's reputation;
3. the challenged assertions of fact are false; and
4. [in cases where the plaintiff is a public figure, the constitution demands proof of "actual malice"].

WFAA-TV, Inc. v. McLemore, 978 S.W.2d 568, 571 (Tex. 1998). *See generally New York Times v. Sullivan*, 376 U.S. 254, 279-80 (1964).

In support of its motion to dismiss Plaintiff's defamation claim, Viacom contends that Plaintiff's defamation claim fails as to each and every element of Texas defamation law. Specifically, Viacom argues that: (1) the challenged broadcast contains no assertions of fact about Plaintiff; (2) the broadcast contains no defamatory statements about Plaintiff; (3) the broadcast contains no false statements about Plaintiff; (4) Plaintiff has failed to allege that Defendants acted with negligence or actual malice regarding the truth of the broadcast; and (5) the broadcast constitutes parody and satire fully protected by the First Amendment to the United States Constitution.

Viewing all the allegations in the complaint as true, and after viewing the DVD of the challenged segment, the court determines that Plaintiff has failed to state a claim for defamation. First, Plaintiff has failed to allege that Viacom made any false statements about him. A review of the approximately six-second segment confirms that Plaintiff was never mentioned in the broadcast segment, and his appearance in the clip from *The 700 Club* was never identified. As Viacom correctly argues, in the challenged broadcast it does not make any assertions of fact, false or otherwise, concerning Plaintiff that could even serve as the basis for his defamation claim. *See generally New Times, Inc. v. Isaacks*, 146 S.W.3d 144, 157 (Tex. 2004) (publication must "be reasonably understood as describing actual facts" about the plaintiff in order to state a claim for defamation). The court further determines that, as a matter of law, because Plaintiff's image appears in a "fake endorsement" of Robertson's diet shake on *The Daily Show*, a satiric program, no reasonable viewer would have believed that the challenged clip contained assertions of fact about Plaintiff. *See generally Hustler Magazine v. Falwell*, 485 U.S. 46, 53-57 (1988) (no liability where parody could not reasonably be understood as describing actual facts about the plaintiff); *cf. Isaacks*, 146 S.W.3d at 157 (the "appropriate inquiry is objective, not subjective. Thus, the question is not whether some actual [viewers] were misled, as they inevitably will be, but whether the hypothetical reasonable [viewer] could be"). In short, because Plaintiff has failed to allege the first element of a claim for defamation, namely, that the challenged broadcast contains assertions of fact about him, and because no reasonable viewer would have believed that the challenged clip in an October 2005 broadcast of *The Daily Show* contained assertions of fact about him, Plaintiff's defamation claim must be dismissed for failure to state a claim. Moreover, the Complaint contains no factual allegations from which the court could reasonably infer that the challenged broadcast contains defamatory statements about Plaintiff.

For the reasons set forth above, the court grants Defendants' Motion to Dismiss.

NOTES AND PROBLEMS

1. ***Defamatory Statements.*** In *Burton*, Judge Learned Hand was willing to recognize a claim for defamation even in the absence of any factual assertions regarding the jockey. The court believed that because the advertisement's photo made a caricature of the plaintiff, causing him to be the subject of ridicule and contempt, the publisher was liable for defamation. Most courts today would not share this view. In *Busch*, the court refused to recognize a defamation claim, in part, because the satirical television episode made no factual assertions regarding the plaintiff. The court further held that parody and satire were not grounds for defamation. While courts do define a defamatory statement as one that tends to expose the plaintiff to "hatred, contempt, or aversion," to be actionable this must be accomplished through the utterance of factual information about the plaintiff that is false.

2. ***Concerning the Plaintiff.*** Unless the defamatory statement would be understood by the reasonable listener to pertain to the plaintiff, the plaintiff has no cause of action. This does not mean that the defendant only faces liability, however, when he explicitly uses the plaintiff's name in making the defamatory statement. Under the right circumstances, the reasonable listener might have no problem understanding that the statement is about the plaintiff despite the plaintiff's name never being uttered. If someone stands in front of the plaintiff's house holding a placard falsely declaring that "the occupant of this house is a pedophile," anyone seeing the sign who can later figure out who lives in the house has been the recipient of a defamatory publication concerning the plaintiff.

3. ***Truth or Falsity.*** Under the common law, states have taken different positions on whether the plaintiff must prove the defamatory statement's falsity as an element of her claim or whether the defendant is instead relegated to pleading and proving truth as an affirmative defense. In many instances this may not be critical because, whether considered an element of the claim or a defense, if the jury finds the statement to be true all modern courts agree that no liability can attach for defamation. Where the evidence is equivocal on the

issue of truthfulness, of course, who bears the burden of proof might be critically important. Further, in jurisdictions where truth is considered an affirmative defense, the defendant has an obligation to plead truth or else waives the defense.

4. ***Consent.*** As with many other tort claims, consent can be an affirmative defense to a defamation claim. This is rarely invoked as a successful defense, however, because the circumstances of the defendant falsely uttering defamatory statements concerning a plaintiff are usually not invited. In *Burton*, the defendant raised this as a defense to the print advertisement because the plaintiff had willingly permitted his name and appearance to be used. Yet the court held that consent was not available because the facts did not show that the plaintiff was aware of how he would be depicted when he gave his consent.

HENDERSON v. HENDERSON

1996 LEXIS 60 (R.I. Super. 1996)

WILLIAMS, J.

On July 3, 1996 and July 5, 1996, an evidentiary hearing was held before this Court regarding Brian R. Henderson's (defendant) motion to strike Susan R. Henderson's (plaintiff) claim for punitive damages.

The plaintiff is the ex-wife of the defendant. The parties were married in 1967 and had two children, Jill Henderson (daughter) and Brett Henderson (son), both of whom are now adults. The parties subsequently separated on October 28, 1989, and were officially divorced on May 15, 1991.

After the parties were separated in October 1989, the defendant began to send a steady stream of correspondences to the plaintiff at her sister Sarah Mancini's residence, where she was living at the time, and later to a home she shared with their daughter. These correspondences were addressed to the plaintiff, referring to her as "wacco" and "Sue T. Whore" on the envelope. The defendant also wrote numerous letters and correspondences to the parties' daughter referring to the plaintiff as "wacco" and "the whore." Additionally, the defendant sent copies of a letter to the plaintiff's father and her sister referring to the plaintiff as "Sue the whore," and copies of other letters to the plaintiff's father and stepmother claiming the plaintiff had mental problems. Moreover, the defendant initialized checks that were sent to the plaintiff, that allegedly had obscene connotations.

On September 22, 1992, the plaintiff filed suit against the defendant accusing him of defamation. On June 5, 1996, the plaintiff made a motion for an order permitting discovery on the issue of punitive damages. The defendant responded by moving to strike the plaintiff's claim for punitive damages. An evidentiary hearing was held before this court on the motion to strike.

The standard in Rhode Island for imposing punitive damages is rigorous and will be satisfied only in instances wherein a defendant's conduct required deterrence and punishment over and above that provided in an award of compensatory damages. [A] showing that the defendant acted with malice or in bad faith must be made for the Court to award punitive damages.

In Rhode Island, an action for defamation requires proof of

(a) a false and defamatory statement concerning another;
(b) an unprivileged communication to a third party;
(c) fault amounting at least to negligence on the part of the publisher; and
(d) damages.

Lyons v. R.I. Public Employees Council 94, 516 A.2d 1339, 1342 (R.I. 1986). Restatement (Second) Torts §558 (1977). "Any words, if false and malicious, imputing conduct which injuriously affects a man's reputation, or which tends to degrade him in society or bring him into public hatred and contempt are in their nature defamatory." *Elias v. Youngken*, 493 A.2d 158, 161 (R.I. 1985).

On the evidence before it, this Court concludes that the plaintiff has made a prima facie showing that defendant's statements are defamatory. The plaintiff has shown that the defendant's numerous references to the plaintiff as being mentally unstable and a "whore" are false and defamatory statements. There is no competent evidence in the record that these statements are true. This Court is also of the opinion that the initials the defendant placed on checks made out to the defendant, would be found not only to be false and defamatory but possibly obscene. These statements and terms were published on envelopes, letters, checks and postcards that were communicated to third parties, including the parties' daughter and the plaintiff's sister who testified to this at the hearing. Additionally, the evidence indicates that there was fault amounting at least to negligence on the part of the defendant, and that the plaintiff suffered damages. The statements made about the plaintiff clearly impute the kind of conduct which injuriously affects a person's reputation.

The plaintiff argues that the weight of the testimonial evidence of the plaintiff, the parties' daughter and the plaintiff's sister, as well as the exhibits introduced, answers by the defendant to requests for admissions, and the portions of the deposition transcript read into the record, more than demonstrate facts sufficient to establish a prima facie showing of egregious conduct to warrant the imposition of punitive damages. This Court agrees.

> A statement is defamatory "if it tends to expose a person to hatred, contempt or aversion, or to induce an evil or unsavory opinion of him in the minds of a substantial number of the community."
>
> *Mencher v. Chelsey, 297 N.Y. 94, 100 (1947).*

This Court believes that a prima facie showing has been made that defendant's actions arose from spite or ill will, with willful and wanton disregard of the rights and interest of the plaintiff. This Court is also of the opinion that the competent evidence of record could support a finding that the defendant's statements were published with such malice and wickedness that they rise to the level of requiring punishment over and above that provided in an award of compensatory damages.

The defendant refers this Court to *Johnson v. Johnson*, 654 A.2d 1212 (R.I. 1995), a Rhode Island case in which punitive damages were denied when an ex-husband called his ex-wife a "whore." However, in this Court's opinion, the *Johnson* case is entirely different from than the present matter. In *Johnson*, unlike here, the trial justice found that the ex-husband's statements were essentially truthful. Furthermore, the defamatory statements in *Johnson* consisted of one incident, while here the defamatory statements occurred continuously over a period of almost three years, even after the plaintiff had initially brought this defamation suit.

This Court concludes that there are adequate facts to support an award of punitive damages in this case. This Court holds that the plaintiff established in the evidentiary hearing that a prima facie case for punitive damages exists. Accordingly, the defendant's motion to strike is denied, and the plaintiff may conduct discovery on the issue of punitive damages.

NOTES AND PROBLEMS

1. ***Elements Applied.*** Using the *Henderson* court's recitation of the elements of defamation, can you explain why the court believed that the plaintiff might have a good case for defamation on the facts of the case? In connection with that, is it clear that the defendant was asserting any statements of fact concerning the plaintiff?

2. ***Publication.*** Defamation requires proof that the defendant "published" the defamatory statements to a third party. Publication should be understood in its broadest sense, however, as any utterance made to another or any written statement shown to a third party constitute publications. Publication of a defamatory statement solely to the plaintiff does not give rise to a defamation claim because it would not taint the plaintiff's reputation. Hurt feelings, on their own, do not give rise to a claim for defamation. Further, the *self-publication rule* holds that a plaintiff's own repetition of the defamatory speech to third parties cannot create a claim for defamation. For example, if John tells Paula that she is a thief, and Paula then says to her friends, "Can you believe that John called me a thief?", this would not make John liable for defamation. John would only be liable if he uttered the accusation himself to the friends. Most courts have held that a publication to a third party has occurred if the defendant makes the statement either intending for third parties to hear it or when it would be reasonably foreseeable that third parties would hear (or see) the defamatory statement.

3. ***Republication.*** Under the common law, someone who repeats or "republishes" a defamatory statement may be just as liable to the plaintiff as

the original publisher. Someone hearing as gossip a defamatory statement concerning the plaintiff and deciding to share this gossip with others is liable for defamation, in addition to the person who first started the gossip. In the section on constitutional privileges later in this chapter, we will see an example of this in *Khawar v. Globe International, Inc.*, where the defendant published a written report of a book that had previously included some defamatory statements regarding the plaintiff. While the report was accurate, it repeated the defamatory statements and created liability for the paper's publisher.

4. *Fault.* At common law, defamation was considered a strict liability tort in the sense that plaintiffs were not required to prove that the defendant uttered the defamatory statement with any knowledge of its falsity. If the factfinder found the statement untrue (and defamatory) the defendant was liable no matter how much good faith he possessed when making the statement. In the subsection on privileges, we will encounter courts demanding some proof of fault in various situations where either common law, statutory, or constitutional privileges might otherwise protect the publisher from liability. For now, understand that, historically, no evidence of fault was necessary, but that in many modern applications of this cause of action the law might now demand some type of fault be proven.

5. *Damages.* In *Henderson*, the court lists proof of damages as one of the elements of a claim for defamation. In cases where the defamatory speech has resulted in special economic losses (e.g., a loss of a job) all courts recognize a right to recover such damages. In some situations, however, courts are willing to permit a recovery of actual "presumed" damages to one's reputation even without any proof of such reputational injury. This issue is at the very heart of the parties' dispute in the *Agriss* case in the next subsection.

6. *Punitive Damage Submission.* As we learned in Chapter 8, Damages, punitive damages require not only the commission of a tort but aggravating circumstances, such as the defendant acting with "malice" or "gross negligence." Defamation claims often include claims for punitive damages when the plaintiff can demonstrate that the defendant's utterance of the false speech was motivated by ill will toward the plaintiff or resulted from a grossly negligent lack of concern for the truthfulness of the statement. In the *Henderson* case, the court found that the facts warranted permitting the plaintiff to attempt to persuade the jury that punitive damages were appropriate in light of the evidence of the former husband's multiple utterances of obviously false and defamatory statements about the plaintiff to her relatives.

7. *Distinguished from Other Related Causes of Action.* Defamation, as a tort cause of action, is a much older and well-established relative of another group of torts arising under the concept of a *right to privacy*. These other legal cousins of defamation include such tort claims as (1) false light, (2) publication of private facts, (3) intrusion into another's private affairs, and (4) misappropriation of one's name or likeness. Each of these four claims is understood to arise out of concern for individuals' right of privacy — the right to be left alone. A false light claim might exist if the defendant announced false information about the plaintiff. Technically, such a claim can exist even if the false information does not rise to the level of being defamatory. Not all jurisdictions recognize a claim for false light. Publication of private facts may create liability when someone reveals private information about the plaintiff to the public. Liability exists here, even if the information is true, if the court determines that the public did not have a legitimate need to be aware of such private facts. A claim for intruding into another's private affairs has been recognized by some courts for conduct such as spying on the plaintiff. Finally, if a defendant utilizes the plaintiff's name or likeness for commercial exploitation, courts have recognized a cause of action so long as the plaintiff has not consented to the use and the defendant was capitalizing on the name or likeness rather than reporting on some newsworthy event or engaged in some other protected use (e.g., parody, satire, political commentary, etc.). Defamation claims, while conceivably capable of arising in similar scenarios, can be distinguished from these claims as they involve a right to have one's reputation not falsely disparaged, and not a mere right to be left alone. It is also worth noting that, in the business world, additional related common law tort claims that many courts have recognized include (a) business disparagement and (b) commercial defamation. Business disparagement applies when the defendant makes false factual assertions regarding the plaintiff's business products and this causes financial harm. Commercial defamation applies when a corporate entity is the subject of false reports concerning either its financial health or business ethics — but does not arise if the statement concerns any other topic.

8. *Problems.* With each of the elements of defamation in mind, consider whether a defamation claim should be recognized in the following scenarios:

- **A.** While sitting in the staff cafeteria at work, Elaine tells co-workers that their boss, Mr. Peterman, is a "jerk."
- **B.** George steals a loaf of bread from the parents of his girlfriend. When confronted by her parents on the front steps of their Manhattan apartment, George points to a teenager running down the street and shouts "He's the one!"
- **C.** Jerry is having dinner with his friend Kramer at a diner. In a voice loud enough that it could be heard at the next table, Jerry says "Chef Poppy at this restaurant did not wash his hands after using the bathroom." The nearby diners are horrified and leave the diner immediately. As it turns out, Poppy had only been in the bathroom to comb his hair.
- **D.** Newman brags to Kramer about the beautiful model he had a first date with the night before. When Kramer asks if Newman "got lucky," Newman just smiles a very broad smile. Of course, this only occurred in Newman's dreams.

E. Jerry's father, Morty, is running for election to be the president of his condominium association. When asked about his opponent during a candidate debate, Morty says, "He's a Republican!" The opponent has never once voted for a Republican presidential candidate.

B. Libel vs. Slander

As mentioned at the outset of this chapter, the law of defamation involves claims for libel and claims for slander. In many respects the two claims look almost identical — up until now we have made no distinction between the two. But in some circumstances, the difference between libel and slander can be outcome determinative. In the following case, the court gives an excellent historical recapitulation of the two tort claims and clarifies the obscurity concerning when the characterization of a defamation claim as libel or slander makes a difference and when it does not. As you read the following opinion, pay close attention to the two mistakes made by the trial court — one involving the application of law to the facts of the case and the other involving the purely legal distinction between libel and slander.

AGRISS v. ROADWAY EXPRESS, INC.

483 A.2d 456 (Pa. Super. Ct. 1984)

CIRILLO, J.

> The security of his reputation or good name from the arts of detraction and slander, are rights to which every man is entitled by reason and natural justice; since without these, it is impossible to have the perfect enjoyment of any other advantage or right.

1 W. Blackstone, Commentaries 134.

Appellant William Agriss sued his employer, Roadway Express, Inc., for what he considered a slight to his good name. A jury trial was held in the Monroe County Court of Common Pleas. After appellant had presented his evidence the court entered a nonsuit. This appeal followed.

Appellant had been employed by Roadway Express since 1976 as a truck driver. In February 1979 he was elected as a shop steward for Teamsters Local 229, the union representing Roadway employees based at Roadway's facility in Tannersville, Pennsylvania.

On December 21, 1979, Agriss returned from a round trip to Hartford, Connecticut, and entered the Tannersville terminal. He was scheduled to begin his vacation that day, and went to the dispatcher's window to collect his vacation paycheck. The dispatcher told Agriss to see the driver foreman, Steve Versuk, before leaving. Versuk handed Agriss a company "warning letter," signed by Versuk and initialed by Roadway relay manager Joe Moran. The letter read:

> By reason of your conduct as described below, it is necessary to issue this notice of warning. On 12/21/79 at Tannersville, Pennsylvania you violated our policy (or contract) by opening company mail. Subsequent violations of any company policy or contract will result in your receiving more severe disciplinary action up to and including discharge in accordance with Article 44 of the Central Pa. Over-the-road and Local Cartage Supplemental Agreement.

The accusation in the letter was false, as Agriss had never, on that or any other day, opened company mail.

Agriss immediately took the letter to Joe Moran and denied the charge. Moran refused to withdraw the warning. Agriss then wrote out and presented to Moran a formal protest, which Moran rejected. Under the contractual grievance procedure between Roadway and the Teamsters, such a protest was the only remedial step open to an employee receiving a warning letter.

Shortly thereafter, Agriss flew with his girlfriend to Hawaii to spend the holidays. While Agriss was in Hawaii, Roadway driver Joseph Verdier heard stories about the warning circulating in the drivers' room at the Tannersville terminal. He heard other drivers and a Roadway dispatcher saying that Agriss was going to be fired for looking into company mail.

When Agriss returned to work on the 7th or 8th of January, 1980, several drivers asked him about the warning letter, and he heard the charge against him bandied over the CB radio. Aside from Versuk, Moran, and Brophy, Agriss had mentioned the charge only to his girlfriend.

Over the next year Agriss continued to receive comments and questions about the warning letter from Roadway workers and union officials. Agriss instituted this suit, claiming that Roadway had defamed him. Trial began on January 23, 1981. After the plaintiff rested his case, the court granted the defendant's motion for compulsory nonsuit, ruling that the plaintiff's evidence failed to prove a cause of action for defamation.

The threshold question in an action for defamation is whether the communication at issue is capable of a defamatory meaning. It is for the court in the first instance to make this determination; but if the communication could be understood as defamatory then it is for the jury to determine whether it was so understood by the recipient.

A publication is defamatory if it tends to blacken a person's reputation or expose him to public hatred, contempt, or ridicule, or injure him in his business or profession. The court should read an allegedly libelous statement in context. The nature of the audience seeing or hearing the remarks is also a critical factor in assessing whether a communication is capable of a defamatory meaning.

With these principles in mind we turn to the parties' arguments on the defamatory character of the charge "opening company mail."

Appellant contends that the words could have been understood to impute to him at least dishonesty, lack of integrity, and untrustworthiness, and at worst the crime of illegally opening another's United States mail. He argues that the charge therefore had the potential to damage his reputation among fellow workers, especially in his capacity as a union official entrusted with handling employee grievances against the company.

For its part appellee argues that, "Taken at its worst, the warning issued in this case implies that Agriss is nosey or is eavesdropping on company affairs. There is no accusation of crime [and that the words] were not calculated to demean Agriss; they were intended to communicate to him a warning not to violate company policy."

Appellant proved, for purposes of overcoming a motion for nonsuit, that when he returned from his vacation speculation was rampant among his fellow employees and union men about what exactly he had done and whether he would be discharged for it. Obviously the charge of "opening company mail" implied more to some people than that he had received a benign reprimand. For a Roadway employee to be charged with opening company mail was highly uncommon. Appellant testified that in all his time as a union steward, during which he had dealt with "thousands" of grievances, he had never heard of an employee's being warned or cited for opening company mail. Moreover, the specific misconduct alleged — opening mail he had no right to open — reasonably could be interpreted to call in question appellant's general character for honesty, integrity, or trustworthiness. In fact, appellant testified that the accusation prompted people to ask him what he was accused of stealing. Giving appellant the benefit of inferences to which he is entitled, the charge "opening company mail" was capable of impugning appellant's good name or reputation in the popular sense, and these are the interests that defamation law seeks to protect.

[The court agreed with appellant that the evidence was sufficient to permit a jury to find that the Roadway employees were responsible for publishing the defamatory statements contained in the letter by showing it to third parties who had no business seeing the letter.]

We have touched on the newest constitutional frontiers of the law of defamation, and now must backtrack to its oldest shibboleths. The trial court held that the charge "opening company mail" was not "libel per se," and that because it was not the plaintiff was obliged to prove special damages in order to recover. Appellant proved no special damages; thus the court's fourth ground for entering nonsuit.

Appellant quarrels mainly with the trial court's holding that the words "opening company mail" were not "libel per se." However, we are concerned also with what the court meant by "libel per se," and with the rule it applied upon determining that the words complained of in this case were not "libel per se." Implicit in the court's decision to grant nonsuit is a distinction between "libel per se" and "libel per quod," and between different burdens of proof which these two forms of libel are thought to require. We have come to the conclusion that the "per se/per quod" distinction is without validity in the modern law of libel, and should be abolished as a means of allocating the plaintiff's burden of proof in a libel case. We also conclude that the trial court erred in nonsuiting appellant on the grounds of a rule based on the "libel per se" concept. However, our task of correcting the error is difficult because the very meaning of "libel per se," let alone its legal significance, is an enigma in this jurisdiction.

The import of "per se" in a defamation case is a problem that has kept Pennsylvania courts going in circles for generations. Originally the term meant one thing when attached to slander, and something entirely different when attached to libel. In the courts these separate meanings and the separate rules they entailed gradually drifted toward, into, and among one another, until nowadays "per se" is used so inconsistently and incoherently in the defamation context that any lawyer or judge about to use it should pause and replace it with the English words it is intended to stand for.

It is time to exert state court control over the "per se" concept, if only because it is primarily our responsibility, not the federal courts', to say what a plaintiff in defamation must plead and prove under Pennsylvania law. Here the plaintiff was thrown out of court on the ground that the libel he complained of was not "libel per se." To discharge our duty to pass on the propriety of the trial court's ruling, we must pull "libel per se" up by the roots and examine it. We cannot dispel completely the confusion that has been accreting for decades, but we can separate terminological chaff from kernels of legal principle.

The difficulty the courts have had with "per se" springs directly from the historical distinction between libel and slander. Before going further, we should make that distinction. Libel may be defined conveniently as "A method of defamation expressed by print, writing, pictures, or signs." Black's Law Dictionary 824 (5th ed. 1979). Slander, broadly, is usually understood to mean oral defamation.[6]

"Per se" first cropped up in defamation law in connection with slander. At early common law a person generally could not recover for slanderous utterances unless they caused him "special harm," meaning

Principles

The history of libel and slander illustrates "a perversion of evolutionary processes" resulting in "a rather heterogeneous pile which should normally have gone to form a consistent body of legal doctrine, but which on the contrary, comprises many disconnected fragments moving in a confused way under the impulse of different principles."

Thomas Atkins Street, Foundations of Legal Liability, 273 (1960).

6. In the present case evidence of the precise "method" used to publish the charge "opening company mail" was sorely lacking. The only thing clear is that the words at one point were expressed in print in a warning letter. Perhaps in reliance on this one certain fact, the court and parties throughout have treated this as a libel case. To avoid unwarranted complexity, we will continue to do so. The approach makes sense, considering the libelous form of the warning letter and the rule that subsequent oral repetition of a libel does not change it to slander and vice versa. We are told that the substantive differences between the law of libel and the law of slander are relics of the ancient past serving no useful purpose, but to this day they wield dead-hand influence over the law of defamation. Nowhere is the pervasive, perverse sway of the distinction more evident than where "per se" enters the discussion.

> harm of a material and generally of a pecuniary nature . . . result[ing] from conduct of a person other than the defamer or the one defamed which conduct is itself the result of the publication or repetition of the slander. Loss of reputation to the person defamed is not sufficient to make the defamer liable under the rule . . . unless it is reflected in material harm.

Restatement of Torts §575, Comment b (1938). The common law courts' insistence that a plaintiff in slander prove "material harm" in turn "goes back to the ancient conflict of jurisdiction between the royal and ecclesiastical courts, in which the former acquired jurisdiction over some kinds of defamation only because they could be found to have resulted in 'temporal' rather than 'spiritual' damage.' Restatement (Second) of Torts §575, Comment b (1977).

Early exceptions to the requirement of proving special harm were carved for slanders imputing crime, loathsome disease, shortcomings affecting the plaintiff in his business, trade, profession, or calling, or (later) unchastity to a woman. Prosser, *supra*, §112 at 754; 3 W. Blackstone, Commentaries 123-24. These "per se" slanders were supposed to be so naturally injurious that the law allowed recovery of general or presumed damages for loss of reputation, even without proof of actual injury.

"Per se" and its counterpart "per quod" were common law pleading devices used to indicate whether the plaintiff's cause of action depended on general or special damages. Francis Murnaghan, in *From Figment to Fiction to Philosophy—the Requirement of Proof of Damages in Libel Actions*, 22 Cath. U. L. Rev. 1, 13 (1972), explains:

> In common law pleading, the right to recover general damages meant that the portion of the writ employed for institution of the suit devoted to specification of damage, and introduced by the words "per quod," became inapplicable whenever damages were presumed. To fill the void, and to signify that something had not been overlooked, the draftsmen in such cases would simply insert "per se" where the allegations of damages, headed by the phrase 'per quod' otherwise would be expected.

> We are told that the substantive differences between the law of libel and the law of slander are relics of the ancient past serving no useful purpose, but to this day they wield dead-hand influence over the law of defamation.

These archaic pleading terms stuck so hardily to slander actions that today "slander per quod" and "slander per se" retain their original meanings as, respectively, slander actionable only on a showing of special harm to the plaintiff, and slander actionable even without special harm. The substantive law of defamation continues to recognize the original four categories of slander "actionable per se," *see* Restatement (Second), *supra*, §570, with all other slanders actionable only on a showing of special harm.

The per se/per quod distinction in libel originated differently. It was used to distinguish libel defamatory on its face ("libel per se") from libel not defamatory on its face ("libel per quod"). "Libel per quod" required a showing of facts and circumstances imparting a defamatory meaning to otherwise innocent or neutral words.[7] The plaintiff in libel per quod had to plead and prove the extrinsic facts (the "inducement") imparting defamatory meaning, and the defamatory meaning (the "innuendo") imparted.

Originally, the per se/per quod distinction in slander, by which some slanders were actionable without proof of special damages while others were not, had no parallel application to libel. Any libel, whether libelous on its face or libelous only upon proof of extrinsic circumstances, was actionable with or without proof of special damages. The willingness of the law to presume damages for all libels as opposed to all slanders arose partly from the greater permanency, dissemination, and credence, and hence the greater harm, supposed naturally to attend defamations in printed or written form.

Inevitably, use of the identical per se/per quod terminology in two torts so similar in nature led to the distinct rules for libel and slander being blurred and melded together in the courts. The rule of slander per quod, requiring proof of special damages for any slander not coming under one of the four time-honored exceptions, came to be applied to "libel per quod" (i.e., libel not defamatory on its face). Under this "hybrid" rule of libel per quod, a libel not defamatory on its face was not actionable without proof of special harm. As a further twist to the hybrid scheme, a libelous imputation of crime, loathsome disease, unfitness for business or calling, or unchastity (the four imputations actionable without proof of special harm in slander) was held to be actionable without proof of special harm in libel, even if the libel were "per quod" (proven libelous through extrinsic facts).

The trial court en banc evidently applied this hybrid rule of libel per quod. It found appellant's evidence deficient for failure to show either "libel per se" or special harm. We agree that appellant's case did not establish that he suffered any economic or material loss amounting to "special harm." On the other hand, we believe that the words "opening company mail" did not require such proof of special damages under the hybrid rule because the charge imputed to appellant unfitness for business or calling and, arguably, criminal activity. We would, therefore, find that the trial court erroneously applied the hybrid rule to the facts of this case. However, we would be shirking our responsibility as an appellate court if we did not decide also whether the hybrid rule was the correct one to apply in the first place.

Although Prosser believed the hybrid rule of libel per quod to be the majority rule in America, the American Law Institute, in both the First and Second Restatements of Torts, consistently has adhered to the traditional rule that all libels are actionable "per se," irrespective of special harm. Restatement of Torts §569; Restatement (Second) of Torts §569. The Institute views

7. Prosser's "classic case" of libel per quod is *Morrison v. Ritchie & Co.*, [1902] 4 Fr. 645, 39 Scot. L. Rep. 432. Defendant's newspaper published a report that the plaintiff had given birth to twins. There were readers who knew she had been married only one month.

Prosser's hybrid rule as the "minority position." *See* Restatement (Second) of Torts §569, Comment b.

[T]here are sound policy reasons for allowing a plaintiff to recover for any libel even where he cannot prove special harm in the form of direct economic or pecuniary injury. As Justice Eagen said in *Gaetano v. Sharon Herald Co., supra* note 8, 426 Pa. at 183, 231 A.2d at 755,

> The most important function of an action for defamation is to give the innocent and injured plaintiff a public vindication of his good name. Its primary purpose is to restore his unjustly tarnished reputation, and "reputation is the estimation in which one's character is held by his neighbors or associates." Restatement, Torts §577, comment b (1938).

By its very nature, injury to reputation does not work its greatest mischief in the form of monetary loss.

Where an individual is made the victim of a false, malicious, and defamatory libel published to third persons, it is unfair to hold that vindication of his good name in the courts depends upon proof that the injury to his reputation has injured him economically as well. Once reputational damage alone is proven, the plaintiff in libel has proven his entitlement to recovery, and to make that recovery contingent on whether the damage was done by words "defamatory on their face" merely adds another irrelevant factor to the equation.

By its very nature, injury to reputation does not work its greatest mischief in the form of monetary loss.

The perceived requirement of "special damages" has been narrowly interpreted by trial courts in Pennsylvania. It is seen as a complete bar to relief in defamation if the plaintiff fails to prove that reputational injury has caused concrete economic loss computable in dollars. These cases are disapproved to the extent they conflict with the rule we announce today: a plaintiff in libel in Pennsylvania need not prove special damages or harm in order to recover; he may recover for any injury done his reputation and for any other injury of which the libel is the legal cause. *See* Restatement (Second), *supra*, §621 & Comments. Courts in libel cases should be guided by the same general rules regarding damages that govern other types of tort recovery.

The order of the court en banc refusing to take off nonsuit is reversed; appellant to receive a new trial in accordance with this opinion; jurisdiction relinquished.

NOTES AND PROBLEMS

1. *When Does the Distinction Matter?* According to the *Agriss* court in its rejection of the hybrid rule, all claims for libel permit recovery for both general, presumed reputational injury, as well as for special damages in the form of economic losses (if any) caused by the libelous statement. Furthermore, claims for slander per se receive equal treatment. Only claims for slander per quod — slander that is defamatory but not involving any of the four most serious categories — limit recovery to economic losses. What is the justification for not recognizing slander per quod claims in the absence of economic injury?

2. ***Distinguishing Libel from Slander.*** The *Agriss* court quotes Black's Law Dictionary's definition for libel as "defamation expressed by print, writing, pictures, or signs." By contrast, slander is typically in the form of oral utterances or bodily gestures. Because libel involves a more permanent and arguably more damaging form of defamation than slander, it has generally been considered the more serious infringement. It was for this reason that historically all libel claims permitted recovery of general presumed damages. In cases where the libel versus slander distinction matters, courts have had to grapple with applying these historic categories to modern forms of communication, such as defamatory utterances made on the Internet, television, and radio broadcasts. While not unanimous, the trend has been to treat defamation appearing in these forms of media as libel, which is arguably appropriate given the power, permanence, and ability to spread the injurious defamation contained in these forms of communication. Some courts have distinguished, however, between utterances made on radio and television that were read from a written script and utterances made without such a script — only finding the former to be libel and the latter slander. Yet the Restatement supports the majority approach: "Broadcasting of defamatory matter by means of radio or television is libel, whether or not it is read from a manuscript." Restatement (Second) of Torts §568A (1965)

3. ***Special and General Damages.*** In Chapter 8, Damages, we explored the two branches of actual compensatory damages — general damages and special damages. Defamation law recognizes these same two categories. Every type of defamation suit permits recovery of special damages. These are for economic losses caused by the defamatory statements — for lost jobs, lost business opportunities, loss of contractual relationships, and any other out-of-pocket losses incurred by the plaintiff. When general reputational damages are available, courts permit the jury great latitude in assessing the amount once it is clear that some injury to reputation has occurred. Proof of the publication of defamatory statements concerning the plaintiff permits a presumption of the existence of general damages. Many other circumstances might impact the *amount* of general damages a jury might award for such presumed injuries, including matters such as the plaintiff's prior reputation in the community, the nature of the defamatory utterances, how widespread the publication of the statements was, whether the audience for the publication tended to believe the publication's truth, and whether the plaintiff was able to redeem her reputation through any mitigating acts or communications.

4. ***Single-Publication Rule.*** Most states have adopted a *single-publication rule* in defamation actions, holding that the defendant's singular publication gives rise to one defamation claim no matter how many people view the publication and regardless of when they view the publication. Thus, a defendant's publication of one edition of a book can give rise to only one claim against that defendant rather than a separate suit arising each time another person reads the book. This prevents defendants from repeated suits over the same publication, and it also permits the plaintiff to recover all of her damages in one lawsuit. Newly issued editions of the book, however, would give rise to a new defamation claim because this is considered a new publication. Commentators have debated whether an entry on a website gives rise to a single defamation suit or a new count of defamation every day that the publication remains on the website. Courts have not resolved application of the single-publication rule to the Internet.

5. ***Defamation-Proof Plaintiffs.*** There are a small number of cases where courts have denied any recovery of compensatory damages to the plaintiff because the court has found that the plaintiff's reputation was already so poor in the community that the defendant's defamatory statements could not have caused any harm. In one case, the plaintiff had multiple prior criminal convictions. When the National Enquirer falsely reported that he had an affair with Elizabeth Taylor, he sued for libel. Rejecting his claim for actual damages, the court stated: "When . . . an individual engages in conspicuously anti-social or even criminal behavior, which is widely reported to the public, his reputation diminishes proportionately. Depending upon the nature of the conduct, the number of offenses, and the degree and range of publicity received, there comes a time when . . . he can recover only nominal damages for subsequent defamatory statements." Wynberg v. National Enquirer, Inc., 564 F. Supp. 924, 928 (D. Cal. 1982). In Guccione v. Hustler Magazine, Inc., the plaintiff (publisher of Penthouse magazine) was denied recovery for the defendant's libel of him despite its false accusation of him as an adulterer. *See also*, Kevorkian v. American Medical Ass'n, 602 N.W.2d 233 (Mich. Ct. App. 1999) (plaintiff, famous for his physician-assisted suicides, was not permitted to recover for defendant's accusations that he was a "killer" and a "criminal"). Can you think of any other notorious people in our society that might have trouble recovering for certain types of false and defamatory statements? How would you feel if a court held that you were defamation-proof? For further discussion of this doctrine, compare Note, *The Libel-Proof Plaintiff Doctrine*, 98 Harv. L. Rev. 1909 (1985) (surveying the law concerning the libel-proof plaintiff doctrine and arguing that it "serves the legitimate purpose of barring — in narrowly defined circumstances — suits that serve no productive juridical purpose.") and King, Jr., *The Misbegotten Libel-Proof Doctrine and the "Gordian Knot" Syndrome*, 29 Hofstra L. Rev. 343 (2000) (arguing that the issue of the plaintiff's reputation should merely be evaluated by the jury in assessing damages rather than justifying dismissal of the suit).

6. ***Problems.*** Would plaintiffs appear to have viable defamation claims in the following scenarios? In each, would the statement involve slander or libel, and per se or per quod? And in which of the following instances would the libel versus slander distinction appear to make a difference?

- **A.** After interviewing Sheldon for a job at a nuclear research facility, Raj looks at Sheldon's Facebook page and finds an entry written by Howard, one of Sheldon's prior co-workers, saying: "Sheldon, sorry you were fired for plagiarizing the results of your research." Howard was confused about the real reasons for Sheldon's termination. Raj decides not to hire Sheldon for the new position.
- **B.** Bernadette is jealous over Penny's career achievements and writes on the public bathroom stall at Penny's apartment complex that, "Penny is such a floozy, who knows what germs she has?" Penny hears whispers about these allegations everywhere she goes.
- **C.** Leonard, an aspiring astronaut, hears that his former friend Stuart told a NASA administrator that Leonard gets motion sickness easily. Leonard loses his chance to be selected for a space mission. A book publisher who had once offered him a chance to write an autobiography about his potential space adventure loses interest in the project.
- **D.** A newspaper writes a headline in large font — "Amy Confesses Guilt." Within the body of the story, it describes how Amy is starting her own ice cream business and admits to having an addiction for chocolate ice cream that she indulges in daily.
- **E.** The local news does a story about Leslie, erroneously attributing a quote to her that says, "I hate the outdoors; if given the chance to go for a walk or sit in a dentist's chair, I'd pick the drill any day." Leslie is the head of the local parks department and her staff now ridicules her.

III PRIVILEGES

Privileges play an important role as affirmative defenses in defamation lawsuits. Even a plaintiff who has proven that the defendant's intentional publication of a defamatory statement about the plaintiff is false might still face defeat due to the operation of a legal privilege. The common law has long recognized that certain communications are so highly valued that speech that might otherwise be actionable as defamation might be subject to particular privileges. Some of these common law privileges are absolute — when the privilege attaches there can be no defamation claim based upon the communication. Other privileges are only qualified — that is, that the circumstances may or may not warrant immunity from a defamation claim. The *Johnson* and *Powers* cases below contain examples of both absolute and qualified privileges. Consider as you read them why the law would recognize privileges in their different contexts.

Beginning in the 1960s, the U.S. Supreme Court determined that the First Amendment applied to certain state law defamation claims and, when applicable, necessarily required some constitutional "breathing space" for the speaker. The contours and application of this First Amendment privilege have been the subject of numerous lengthy published opinions. As you will see in the *Khawar* case, the level of protection varies with both the categorization of the plaintiff and the nature of the speech involved. In certain circumstances, the level of protection also varies based upon whether the plaintiff is seeking to recover actual proven damages, presumed damages, or punitive damages. Finally, in the *Dun & Bradstreet* case, the Supreme Court will loosen First Amendment protections for certain plaintiffs suing over certain types of communications based upon their content and the public's interest in hearing the communication.

A. Common Law

JOHNSON v. QUEENAN

12 Mass. L. Rptr. 461 (Mass. Super. Ct. 2000)

GRABAU, J.

Plaintiff Johnson [defendant-in-counterclaim] brought this action against defendant Christopher Queenan [plaintiff-in-counterclaim] for assault and battery after defendant allegedly raped her at a party that both attended on November 29, 1996. In response, Queenan filed a counterclaim against Johnson alleging defamation. Plaintiff now moves for summary judgment on [the defamation counterclaim]. For the reasons set forth below, Plaintiff's motion for summary judgment is *ALLOWED.*

The undisputed material facts as established by the summary judgment record are as follows. Johnson alleges that Queenan raped and assaulted her in a bedroom at a private party that both Johnson and Queenan attended on November 29, 1996 in Westford, Massachusetts. Johnson acknowledges being in the bedroom and kissing Queenan. Johnson, however, contends that although she repeatedly told Queenan that she did not want to have intercourse, he held her down on the bed and raped her. Queenan denies raping Johnson, but acknowledges that Johnson was crying when he left the bedroom.

Upon leaving the bedroom, Johnson located her friend Ryan Dadmun (Dadmun) who was also at the party and told him that Queenan had just raped her. Johnson asked Dadmun to drive her home. She did not report the rape to anyone else that evening.

The next morning, Johnson telephoned Dadmun and asked him to help her make arrangements to see a doctor. After several telephone calls to various health care providers, Johnson realized that her only treatment option was the emergency room. Reluctant to go to the emergency room, Johnson asked

Dadmun to bring her to her friend, Staci Scolovino's (Scolovino) home. After Johnson explained to Scolovino that Queenan raped her, Scolovino brought her to the Emerson Hospital emergency room. Johnson was not treated immediately and left the emergency room with Scolovino because the rape specialist at the emergency room was not on duty and Johnson was scheduled to work later that afternoon.

Later that evening, Dadmun again drove Johnson to Emerson Hospital's emergency room. Dr. Ingrid Balcolm and Nurse Heidi Crim (Nurse Crim) examined and treated Johnson in accordance with Massachusetts sexual assault protocol. Pursuant to G.L.c. 112 §12A½, Nurse Crim reported the alleged incident to the Westford Police Department, however, at Johnson's request Nurse Crim did not provide the police with Johnson's name. Nurse Crim encouraged Johnson to discuss the incident with her parents or a close family friend.

Based on Nurse Crim's report, the Westford Police Department began a criminal investigation of the alleged incident. On December 5, 1996, as part of this investigation, Detective Michael Perron (Detective Perron) met with the Dean of Students, Carla Scuzzarella (Scuzzarella) at Johnson's school and told her that he needed to speak with Johnson. Scuzzarella arranged to have Johnson meet privately with Detective Perron. During the meeting, Johnson gave Detective Perron her account of the events of November 29, 1996. Detective Perron also encouraged Johnson to talk to her parents and accompanied her home, where Johnson told her mother about the incident involving Queenan.

As a result of the investigation, the Westford Police charged Queenan with rape and assault and battery. While the criminal case was pending in Ayer District Court, the Commonwealth made a presentment to a Middlesex County Grand Jury. Both Johnson and Queenan testified before the Grand Jury. The Grand Jury, however, did not issue an indictment to Queenan.

The moving party bears the burden of affirmatively demonstrating the absence of a triable issue and that the summary judgment record entitles it to judgment as a matter of law. Courts favor the use of summary judgment in cases in which defamation is alleged.

The plaintiff bears the initial burden of proving prima facie elements of a slander claim — "the publication of a false and defamatory statement by spoken words of and concerning the plaintiff." *Ellis v. Safety Ins. Co.*, 672 N.E.2d 979 (Mass. 1996), citing Restatement (Second) of Torts §§558 and 568 (1977).

STATEMENTS MADE TO DETECTIVE PERRON, ADA BEDROSIAN, AND THE MIDDLESEX GRAND JURY

Johnson asserts that various statements made to Detective Perron, ADA Bedrosian and the Middlesex Grand Jury are privileged under Massachusetts law. Once the plaintiff meets its initial burden, the defendant has the burden to show that a privilege applies. *See Jones v. Taibbi*, 512 N.E.2d 260 (Mass. 1987). "An absolute privilege provides a defendant with complete defense to a defamation suit even if the defamatory statement is uttered maliciously or in bad faith. A qualified or conditional privilege, on the other hand, immunizes a defendant from liability unless he or she acted with actual malice, or unless there is 'unnecessary, unreasonable or excessive publication,' and the plaintiff establishes that the defendant published the defamatory information recklessly." *Mulgrew v. Taunton*, 574 N.E.2d 389 (Mass. 1991) (citations omitted). Johnson contends that her statements to Detective Perron, ADA Bedrosian and the Middlesex Grand Jury fall under an absolute privilege, thus immunizing her from any claim of defamation.

Statements made in the course of judicial proceedings which pertain to the proceeding are absolutely privileged and cannot support a claim of defamation, even if communicated with malice or in bad faith. *See Correllas v. Viveiros*, 572 N.E.2d 7 (Mass. 1991) (statements made to investigating police officers and prosecutor during the course of the investigation are privileged); *Hahn v. Sargent*, 388 F. Supp. 445, 452 (D. Mass. 1975), *affd*, 523 F.2d 461 (1975), *cert. denied*, 425 U.S. 904 (1976) (testimony before a grand jury privileged). Therefore, I find that all statements Johnson made to Detective Perron, ADA Bedrosian, and the Middlesex Grand Jury are protected under an absolute privilege because they pertain to the judicial proceeding and were made in the course of that proceeding.

STATEMENTS MADE TO NURSE CRIM, DADMUN, SCOLOVINO, AND JOHNSON'S MOTHER

Johnson also contends that her statements to Nurse Crim, Dadmun, Scolovino and her mother are conditionally privileged and thus protected against Queenan's defamation claim. Massachusetts recognizes certain privileges that are conditioned upon the manner in which they are exercised. *See Sheehan v. Tobin*, 93 N.E.2d 524 (Mass. 1950). One type of conditional privilege protects statements "where the publisher and the recipient have a common interest, and the communication is of a kind reasonably calculated to protect or further it." *Sheehan*, 326 Mass. at 190-91. Where there is no dispute about the existence of the facts surrounding the publication, a judge must determine whether or not the privilege applies.

Here, after Johnson told Dadmun that she had been raped, he immediately brought her home. The next morning, Dadmun and Scolovino assisted Johnson in seeking medical care. Johnson told Nurse Crim about the alleged rape in order to receive the appropriate medical treatment. Johnson later confided in her mother after both Nurse Crim and Detective Perron encouraged her to do so, presumably to enable her to get proper emotional support. Thus, Johnson's publication to her two close friends Dadmun and Scolovino, Nurse Crim, and her mother are protected by a qualified privilege because the communications were reasonably calculated to further a common interest, namely Johnson's physical and emotional well-being.

Once a defendant asserts a claim of privilege, it is plaintiff's burden to prove abuse of the privilege or actual malice. Plaintiff provides no evidence to support a claim that Johnson abused the privilege through unnecessary, unreasonable or excessive publication, nor does he indicate that he can produce any evidence to enable him to reach the jury on the issue of malice. Based on the foregoing, Queenan has failed to provide sufficient evidence for a jury to infer that Johnson, without a privilege to do so, published a false and defamatory statement about Queenan. Thus, Johnson is entitled to summary judgment on Queenan's defamation counterclaim.

For the foregoing reasons, it is hereby *ORDERED* that plaintiff, defendant-in-counterclaim, Johnson's motion for summary judgment be *ALLOWED*.

LESTER v. POWERS

596 A.2d 65 (Me. 1991)

COLLINS, J.

Lewis F. Lester appeals from a summary judgment in the Superior Court. The court concluded Lester could have no recovery on his claims for libel [or] slander against his former student, Mary Jane E. Powers. We affirm.

Powers was a Colby College undergraduate majoring in psychology. In early 1985, during her junior year, she took a class in abnormal psychology from Lester, then an associate professor. One of the classes was a discussion of homosexuality — specifically, the appropriateness of classifying homosexuality as a disorder when the person is unhappy about his or her sexual orientation, but not when the person is happy. [Powers had recently concluded that she was a lesbian but was not open yet about it.]

In the class discussion, at least one student made comments to the effect that "gays are sick"; Lester questioned the appropriateness of the differential classification of the two classifications of homosexuality, and said that he had gay friends in the mental health profession who themselves did not understand why they were "that way." Powers understood his tone of voice to indicate disapproval.

Whether or not Powers overreacted, however, she undisputedly was upset. After the class, she went immediately to an assistant dean and complained that she had found Lester's handling of the subject offensive. She repeated that assertion later to various students, faculty members, and members of the college administration.

Lester had previously been affiliated with Colby in a non-tenure-track position, as a part-time faculty member and part-time clinical psychologist, for over ten years. He then started working toward tenure; this process culminated in a tenure review in the fall of 1986, after Powers graduated from Colby. As a part of the tenure review process, the Committee on Promotion and Tenure solicited letters from former students. Powers did not respond to this invitation to comment before the Committee's deadline, October 15.

Following a visit to Colby after the deadline, however, Powers contacted the Dean of the Faculty and asked if it was too late to comment. The Dean invited her to do so, even though the deadline had passed. Powers then wrote the letter that underlies the present case. The letter primarily related Powers' version of the class discussion that upset her, together with several other minor incidents involving Lester that she found distasteful, and concluded:

> I don't want to use this letter as a way to "get even" with Professor Lester. I have found him to be entirely knowledgeable and competent in his field, and I have received valuable assistance from him on one or two occasions in my work. But as an ex-member of the college committee on sexual harassment, I know that a student should not ever be made to feel uncomfortable or intimidated in her/his learning on account of gender or sexual orientation, and I sadly feel this was definitely the case for me. I also know of others who still feel intimidated, much as I have and for the same reasons, and who have not written to add their input to this decision; I thank this Committee for the opportunity to express my (and their) opinion that Professor Lewis Lester should not be tenured.

[After receiving the letter, the University decided to deny tenure to Lester. He then filed this lawsuit. Among other possible defenses, Powers argued that her comments were non-actionable opinions as well as statements made during the tenure process and protected by a qualified privilege.]

Following a hearing [on Powers' motion for summary judgment], the court granted summary judgment. With regard to the letter, the court concluded that defendant would have a conditional privilege regarding her comments made in the tenure consideration process. Frank and sometimes critical evaluations of a person's job performance are vital to employee rating, promotion or job change processes. If those who know most about one's job performance are deterred from frank evaluations by fear of defamation actions, and recommendations then come to be discounted as benign pablum, we all lose. Job movers and seekers will be left to the gut and necessarily arbitrary instincts of employment decisionmakers who act without confidence that they have the accurate evaluation history so vital to predicting future performance. To avoid this problem and bolster the integrity of the job evaluation process, persons who are expected to make comments on employment qualifications and do so in the normal channels of an employment review are entitled to a conditional privilege.

Examining the record, the [trial] court found no factual support for the suggestion that Powers made the statements in the letter knowing them to be false or recklessly disregarding whether they were true or false; instead, the court found that the record could support only the conclusion that Powers sincerely believed the statements in the letter.

Lester now appeals.

A defamation claim requires a statement — i.e. an assertion of fact, either explicit or implied, and not merely an opinion, provided the opinion does not imply the existence of undisclosed defamatory facts. The statement must be false. It must also be "of and concerning" the plaintiff. The statements in the letter were undisputedly "of and concerning" Lester and tended to injure his professional reputation, and thus if false were actionable at common law irrespective of actual damages to him.

A conditional privilege against liability for defamation arises in settings where society has an interest in promoting free, but not absolutely unfettered, speech. If a conditional privilege exists, liability for defamation attaches only if the person who made the defamatory statements loses the privilege through abusing it. Such an abuse occurs when the person either knows the statement to be false or recklessly disregards its truth or falsity. [Unlike First Amendment privileges, a plaintiff may create liability notwithstanding a common law privilege by showing its abuse by a preponderance of the evidence standard, rather than by clear and convincing evidence.]

Lester argues that the Superior Court erred in deciding that Powers' statements were made under conditions giving rise to a conditional privilege. He asserts that Maine law recognizes such a privilege only within an employment relationship. We disagree. Conditional privilege is based upon the circumstances of "the occasion upon which the defendant published defamatory matter," and we use the *Restatement* approach when determining the existence of such circumstances.

The Restatement does not prescribe a list of particular settings to which conditional privileges are restricted. Instead, it uses a weighing approach based on the totality of the circumstances, in view of the interests of the publisher and the recipient. *See Restatement* §§594-598. Any situation in which an important interest of the recipient will be furthered by frank communication may give rise to a conditional privilege. *See* Restatement §595, comment j.

Powers wrote the letter in connection with tenure review, an occasion in which the need for candid speech is apparent. She did so in response to a request by Colby College and in furtherance of Colby's interests in the tenure review process. As a recent alumna, she had a close and ongoing relationship with Colby. Under these circumstances, her letter was subject to a conditional privilege.

Lester asserts that even if Powers' letter would ordinarily have been subject to a conditional privilege, she lost the privilege through abuse because her publication of it was outside ordinary channels, excessive, improper, and not calculated to further the college's interests. *See* Restatement §599. He contends the letter was "outside ordinary channels" because Powers submitted it after the October 15 deadline for comments. We find his argument unpersuasive. The college solicited the letter and assured Powers that her comments were desired even if they were late. She submitted the letter to the Committee, which reviewed it in the course of its tenure review deliberations. Lester similarly argues that Powers lost the privilege through abuse because she submitted the letter out of ill will toward him. Contrary to his assertion, however, a publication of defamatory matter upon an occasion giving rise to a privilege, if made solely from spite or ill will, is an abuse and not a use of the privilege. However, if the publication is made for the purpose of protecting the interest in question, *the fact that the publication is inspired in part by resentment or indignation at the supposed misconduct of the person defamed does not constitute an abuse of the privilege.* Because the record does not support Lester's contention that Powers submitted the letter *solely* out of spite or ill will and not to further the tenure review process, we cannot conclude that she lost her conditional privilege through abuse.

Powers [also] argues that because her letter expressed only her opinion and no statements of fact, it is not actionable. Although Maine's common law of defamation does not allow recovery for statements of opinion alone, deciding whether a statement expresses "fact" or "opinion" is not always an easy task. Our standard looks to the totality of the circumstances: "[A] comment . . . is an opinion if it is clear from the surrounding circumstances that the maker of the statement did not intend to state an objective fact but intended rather to make a personal observation on the facts. *Caron*, 470 A.2d at 784. Under the *Caron* test, Powers' letter expresses her personal observations, and thus is a statement of opinion rather than of fact. It conveys her subjective evaluation that Lester was homophobic, and that his manner was offensive, insensitive, and occasionally intimidating; these are not statements of fact but rather her personal observations. The letter itself makes it clear that Powers was conveying her subjective impressions; it states at the outset that it expresses "my strong opinions on this matter." Finally, the context in which the letter was written indicates that the kinds of statements solicited in the tenure review process are evaluations — i.e., statements of opinion as to the tenure candidate's merit. We are persuaded that the letter was an expression of opinion.

A statement of opinion may be actionable, however, if it implies the existence of undisclosed defamatory facts. Assuming that a jury could reasonably understand the letter to imply undisclosed defamatory facts, we must decide whether the record before us could support a finding that Powers knew any such factual implications to be false, or recklessly disregarded their truth or falsity.

Knowledge or disregard of falsity is a purely subjective state of mind. Although Lester contends numerous statements in Powers' letter are false, "there must be sufficient evidence to permit the conclusion that the defendant *in fact entertained serious doubts as to the truth of his publication.*" *Michaud*, 381 A.2d at 1114. Evidence that some of Powers' factual premises were objectively false, or even that no reasonable person could have believed them to be true, does not show that she knew or disregarded their falsity.

Lester contends a jury could infer that Powers knew the statements in her letter were false, however, because after she learned that Lester had been denied tenure, she destroyed or discarded her notes from his abnormal psychology class, including whatever notes she took during the class discussion of homosexuality. Although Powers explained this action as her way of turning the page psychologically on "unfinished business," Lester argues a jury might fairly infer that she destroyed the notes because they did not support the version of the class portrayed in her letter, and therefore that she was consciously untruthful.

He also suggests a jury could rationally draw the same inference from the fact that Powers submitted the letter after the deadline.

We disagree. Even though Lester is entitled to "the full benefit of all favorable inferences that may be drawn from [the] evidence," he is not entitled to the benefit of unsupported speculation. The trial court properly concluded that Lester failed to generate a factual issue as to whether Powers abused the conditional privilege afforded her letter, and accordingly Powers was entitled to a summary judgment as a matter of law.

NOTES AND PROBLEMS

1. ***Absolute Privileges.*** For speech that is so essential that courts will not tolerate the chill of any defamation claim, the common law has created an *absolute* or *unconditional privilege.* In these instances, courts have concluded that the interest in undeterred speech far outweighs the interests of the victim in vindicating her name and in being compensated for her reputational injury. As you might guess, instances where the common law has recognized such a broad privilege to defame another are quite limited. Two primary contexts generate such a privilege: (1) the operation of the various branches of government; and (2) the operation of the institution of marriage. For speech that arises in the "course of" judicial, legislative, or executive functions of government, an absolute privilege generally attaches. Absolute privileges are quite absolute — when applicable, no amount of bad faith or ill will by the publisher of the defamatory statements will give rise to a meritorious defamation claim. Is this too much protection? Does it invite perjured testimony? *Johnson* involved various forms of speech related to the investigation and attempted prosecution of a criminal case against the alleged rapist. The court had no problem concluding that each of the plaintiff/counter-defendant's statements was so closely associated with the potential criminal case that the absolute privilege should attach. Can you make an argument that only some of the plaintiff's speech protected by the absolute privilege in *Johnson* should have been considered so protected? Some states treat an alleged crime victim's statements to criminal enforcement personnel as not sufficiently related to a criminal lawsuit for the absolute privilege to attach, instead only applying a qualified privilege conditioned upon good faith. *Johnson* applied a broader view of when this absolute privilege attaches, applying it to each of the plaintiff's statements made to the police, district attorney, and grand jury.

2. ***Qualified Common Interest Privilege.*** The common law has also recognized a *common interest privilege* according to *Johnson,* where the "publisher and recipient have a common interest, and the communication is of a kind reasonably calculated to protect or further it." Taken literally, this broad description could apply in any instance where even a prurient interest

motivated a conversation between the defamer and a third party. In *Powers*, the court explains that this privilege only will apply where the court believes the communication has sufficient value to justify protection: "A conditional privilege against liability for defamation arises in settings where society has an interest in promoting free, but not absolutely unfettered, speech." What was so important in *Johnson* about the plaintiff/counter-defendant's speech with her friends, health care providers, and family to warrant qualified or conditional protection? In *Powers*, how did the court describe the need for a qualified privilege in the context of the tenure decision? Can you think of other areas of communication in our society where courts might want to apply the common interest privilege? In terms of defeating the invocation of a conditional privilege, courts generally look for evidence of some type of malice (stated as either ill-will or knowledge of the speech's falsity), or the overuse or abuse of the privilege. Can you think of circumstances where an alleged rape victim's allegations of rape might be considered excessive under the common interest privilege?

3. ***Statutory Privileges, Codifications, and Modifications of Common Law.*** Perhaps not having sufficient faith that the courts will recognize the importance of some speech and provide it with the protection of a common law privilege, legislatures sometimes enact statutory privileges or modify the common law to limit liability. A few examples follow. With respect to each statute, why do you think the legislators perceived that the speech needed protection? How broad is the protection?

Florida Stat. §768.095 (1999):

An employer who discloses information about a former or current employee to a prospective employer of the former or current employee upon request of the prospective employer or of the former or current employee is immune from civil liability for such disclosure or its consequences unless it is shown by clear and convincing evidence that the information disclosed by the former or current employer was knowingly false.

Louisiana Rev. Stat. §14.50 (1950):

There shall be no prosecution for defamation in the following situations:

(1) When a statement is made by a legislator or judge in the course of his official duties.

(2) When a statement is made by a witness in a judicial proceeding, or in any other legal proceeding where testimony may be required by law, and such statement is reasonably believed by the witness to be relevant to the matter in controversy.

(3) Against the owner, licensee or other operator of a visual or sound broadcasting station or network of stations by one other than such owner, licensee, operator, agents or employees.

Texas Civ. Prac. & Rem. Code §73.002 (1985):

(a) The publication by a newspaper or other periodical of a matter covered by this section is privileged and is not a ground for a libel action. This privilege does not extend to the republication of a matter if it is proved that the matter was republished with actual malice after it had ceased to be of public concern.

(b) This section applies to:

(1) A fair, true, and impartial account of:

a. A judicial proceeding, unless the court has prohibited publication of a matter because in its judgment the interests of justice demand that the matter not be published;

b. An official proceeding, other than a judicial proceeding, to administer the law;

c. An executive or legislative proceeding (including a proceeding of a legislative committee), a proceeding in or before a managing board of an educational institution supported from the public revenue, of the governing body of a city or town, of a county commissioners court, and of a public school board or a report or debate and statements made in any of those proceedings; and

(2) Reasonable and fair comment on or criticism of an official act of a public official or other matter of public concern published for general information.

Texas Civ. Prac. & Rem. Code §73.004 (1985):

A broadcaster is not liable in damages for a defamatory statement published or uttered in or as part of a radio or television broadcast by one other than the broadcaster unless the complaining party proves that the broadcaster failed to exercise due care to prevent the publication or utterance of the statement in the broadcast.

Federal Communications Decency Act 47 U.S.C.A. §230(c)(1996):

(1) Treatment of publisher or speaker: No provider or user of an interactive computer service shall be treated as the publisher or speaker of any information provided by another information content provider.

(2) Civil Liability: No provider or user of an interactive computer service shall be held liable on account of

a. Any action voluntarily taken in good faith to restrict access to or availability of material that the provider or user considers to be obscene, lewd, lascivious, filthy, excessively violent, harassing, or otherwise objectionable, whether or not such material is constitutionally protected;

[Courts have concluded that the foregoing CDA does *not protect* the person who posts a defamatory message on an Internet site or sends a defamatory email. Too Much Media, LLC v. Hale, 20 A.3d 364 (N.J. 2011).]

Wisconsin Stat. Ann. §895.05:

> (1) The proprietor, publisher, editor, writer or reporter upon any newspaper published in this state shall not be liable in any civil action for libel for the publication in such newspaper of a true and fair report of any judicial, legislative or other public official proceeding authorized by law or of any public statement, speech, argument or debate in the course of such proceeding.
>
> (2) Before any civil action shall be commenced on account of any libelous publication in any newspaper, magazine or periodical, the libeled person shall first give those alleged to be responsible or liable for the publication a reasonable opportunity to correct the libelous matter [through printing a retraction upon notice of the libel]. A correction, timely published, without comment, in a position and type as prominent as the alleged libel, shall constitute a defense against the recovery of any damages except actual damages, as well as being competent and material in mitigation of actual damages to the extent the correction published does so mitigate them.

4. ***Opinions vs. Facts.*** We have previously seen in *Busch* that statements of opinion will not support a defamation claim — which demands instead publication of false statements of "factual information" regarding the plaintiff. In *Powers*, the court deals with one exception to this rule, in instances where the opinion falsely implies additional facts supporting the opinion that would be considered defamatory. Can you think of any such speech?

5. ***Problems.*** Would any common law or statutory privileges preclude defamation claimants from recovering in the following circumstances?

- **A.** Two teenagers are eating lunch in the cafeteria. Susan wants to deter Bethany from going out with Felix, the quarterback of the school football team. Therefore, Susan tells Bethany to "stay away from Felix for your own good because he has a venereal disease."
- **B.** One law student advises another that, "In my opinion, I've concluded that Joshua [another law student] is likely a pedophile. Stay away from him."
- **C.** Isabella was hurt in her Chevrolet Camaro when the brakes failed. She writes a letter to the C.E.O. of General Motors (the manufacturer) demanding that the company pay her the sum of $1,000,000 for her injuries, alleging that the C.E.O. "purposely produced a defective car." To show how serious she was, she sent a copy of the letter to her local television news station asking them to air a story about the incident.
- **D.** After Isabella's demand letter goes unnoticed, Isabella hires a lawyer and files a lawsuit against General Motors and its C.E.O. She personally schedules a press conference on the courthouse steps moments after filing the

lawsuit in the district clerk's office and reads from her complaint. The complaint repeats the allegations of the two defendants knowingly producing defective cars.

E. During the trial of Isabella's product liability suit against General Motors and its C.E.O., Isabella testifies about the accident and her resulting injuries. After watching her testimony, the judge turns to the jury and says, "It's up to you to judge the credibility of each witness, but I found Isabella's testimony to be bordering on perjury."

F. After losing her lawsuit against General Motors, Isabella posts comments on the Chevrolet website under "Customer Reviews." In her review she repeats her accusations that General Motors and its C.E.O. were purposefully selling defective cars and states that their "continued conduct shows their corporate arrogance."

G. Alejandro is a major league baseball player known as a home run hitter. In the wake of media reports of steroid abuse in baseball, a congressional sub-committee holds an inquiry into steroid abuse in professional sports and invites Alejandro to testify. Alejandro testifies before Congress that another famous home run hitter, Peter, was a steroid abuser and claims that he had personally witnessed Peter injecting himself when they played on the same team. It turns out that this information was false and that Alejandro was testifying against Peter because both were competing for a lucrative free agent contract with the New York Yankees.

H. Destiny lives in a small town and was recently the victim of a burglary while away on vacation. She suspected her neighbor Jada might be the thief. The next time she saw Jada was at church on a Sunday morning. Destiny pointed her finger at Jada during the middle of the service and said, "Jada it's time for you to confess and repent from your sins. You know you broke into my house!"

B. Constitutional Privilege

As if the state law of privileges did not adequately complicate the traditional common law defamation claim, the U.S. Supreme Court in 1964 found that state courts imposing defamation liability for speech implicated the First Amendment's concern for freedom of speech. In *New York Times v. Sullivan*, the Court found that public officials had to prove by clear and convincing evidence both the falsity of the defamatory speech (in states that made truth an affirmative defense) and that the speaker published the comments with *actual malice* — that is, with knowledge of the falsity of the speech or with gross negligence as to the truth or falsity of the speech. In this application of the First Amendment, the Court was providing a qualified or conditional constitutional privilege for certain speech involving certain victims. Subsequent decisions have further refined this analysis by defining what actual malice means under different circumstances, by clarifying who qualifies as a public official, by broadening the rule's application to public figures, and by coming up with other protections for suits brought by private figures concerning matters of public importance. The *Khawar* case involves a good discussion and application of much of this area of the law. The *Dun & Bradstreet* case in the next section demonstrates the Court placing limits on the application of the First Amendment's reach into purely private matters of speech. As you read these two opinions, try to visualize the delicate balancing of competing interests embodied by the case law in this field.

1. Speech About Public Officials, Public Figures, and Public Matters

KHAWAR v. GLOBE INTERNATIONAL, INC.

965 P.2d 696 (Cal. 1998)

KENNARD, J.

We granted review to decide certain issues concerning the federal Constitution's guarantees of freedom of speech and of the press insofar as they restrict a state's ability to impose tort liability for the publication of defamatory falsehoods. More specifically, we address the definition of a "public figure" for purposes of tort and First Amendment law . . . and the showings required to support awards of compensatory and punitive damages for the republication of a defamatory falsehood.

In November 1988, Roundtable Publishing, Inc., (Roundtable) published a book written by Robert Morrow (Morrow) and entitled The Senator Must Die: The Murder of Robert Kennedy (the Morrow book). The Morrow book alleged that the Iranian Shah's secret police (SAVAK), working together with the Mafia, carried out the 1968 assassination of United States Senator Robert F. Kennedy (Kennedy) in California and that Kennedy's assassin was not Sirhan Sirhan, who had been convicted of Kennedy's murder, but a man named Ali Ahmand, whom the Morrow book described as a young Pakistani who, on the evening of the Kennedy assassination, wore a gold-colored sweater and carried what appeared to be a camera but was actually the gun with which Ahmand killed Kennedy. The Morrow book contained four photographs of a young man the book identified as Ali Ahmand standing in a group of people around Kennedy at the Ambassador Hotel in Los Angeles shortly before Kennedy was assassinated.

Globe International, Inc., (Globe) publishes a weekly tabloid newspaper called Globe. Its issue of April 4, 1989, contained an article on page 9 under the headline: *Former CIA Agent Claims: Iranians Killed Bobby Kennedy for the Mafia* (the Globe article). Another headline, appearing on the front page of the same issue, stated: *Iranian secret police killed Bobby Kennedy.* The Globe article, written by John Blackburn (a freelance reporter and former Globe staff reporter), gave an abbreviated, uncritical summary of the Morrow book's allegations. The Globe article included a photograph from the Morrow book showing a group of men standing near Kennedy; Globe enlarged the image of these individuals and added an arrow pointing to one of these men and identifying him as the assassin Ali Ahmand.

In August 1989, Khalid Iqbal Khawar (Khawar) brought this action against Globe, Roundtable, and Morrow, alleging that he was the person depicted in the photographs and identified in the Morrow book as Ali Ahmand, and that the book's accusation, repeated in the Globe article, that he had assassinated Kennedy was false and defamatory and had caused him substantial injury.

Morrow defaulted, and Roundtable settled with both Khawar and Ahmad before trial. A jury trial ensued on the claims against Globe.

The evidence at trial showed that in June 1968, when Kennedy was assassinated, Khawar was a Pakistani citizen and a freelance photojournalist working on assignment for a Pakistani periodical. At the Ambassador Hotel's Embassy Room, he stood on the podium near Kennedy so that a friend could photograph him with Kennedy, and so that he could photograph Kennedy. He was aware that television cameras and the cameras of other journalists were focused on the podium and that his image would be publicized. When Kennedy left the Embassy Room, Khawar did not follow him; Khawar was still in the Embassy Room when Kennedy was shot in the hotel pantry area. Both the Federal Bureau of Investigation (FBI) and the Los Angeles Police Department questioned Khawar about the assassination, but neither agency ever regarded him as a suspect.

In April 1989, 21 years later, when the Globe article was published, Khawar was a naturalized United States citizen living with his wife and children in Bakersfield, California, where he owned and operated a farm. After Khawar read the Globe article, he became very frightened for his own safety and that of his family. He received accusatory and threatening telephone calls about the article from as far away as Thailand, he and his children received death threats, and his home and his son's car were vandalized. A Bakersfield television station interviewed Khawar about the Globe article.

[T]he jury returned [a verdict, finding that] the Globe article contained statements about Khawar that were false and defamatory; [and that] (2) Globe published the article negligently and with malice or oppression. The jury awarded Khawar [actual damages, presumed damages and punitive damages].

Globe appealed from the judgment.

We consider first Globe's contention that the trial court and the Court of Appeal erred in concluding that Khawar is a private rather than a public figure for purposes of this defamation action.

The federal Constitution's First Amendment, made applicable to the states by the Fourteenth Amendment guarantees freedom of speech and of the press.

In *New York Times Co.* v. *Sullivan* (1964) 376 U.S. 254, the United States Supreme Court for the first time construed these constitutional guarantees as imposing limitations on a state's authority to award damages for libel. Specifically, the court held that the First Amendment "prohibits a public official from recovering damages for a defamatory falsehood relating to his official conduct unless he proves [through clear and convincing evidence] that the statement was made with 'actual malice'—that is, with knowledge that it was false or with reckless disregard of whether it was false or not." The court later explained that the publisher of a defamatory statement acts with reckless disregard amounting to actual malice if, at the time of publication, the publisher "in fact entertained serious doubts as to the truth of his publication." *St. Amant v. Thompson* (1968) 390 U.S. 727, 731. In *Curtis Publishing Co.* v. *Butts* (1967) 388 U.S. 130, 134, the high court held that this "actual malice" requirement for defamation actions brought by public officials applied also to defamation actions brought by "public figures."

"One of the things I'm going to do if I win, and I hope we do and we're certainly leading. I'm going to open up our libel laws so when they write purposely negative and horrible and false articles, we can sue them and win lots of money. We're going to open up those libel laws. So when The New York Times writes a hit piece which is a total disgrace or when The Washington Post, which is there for other reasons, writes a hit piece, we can sue them and win money instead of having no chance of winning because they're totally protected."

Donald Trump

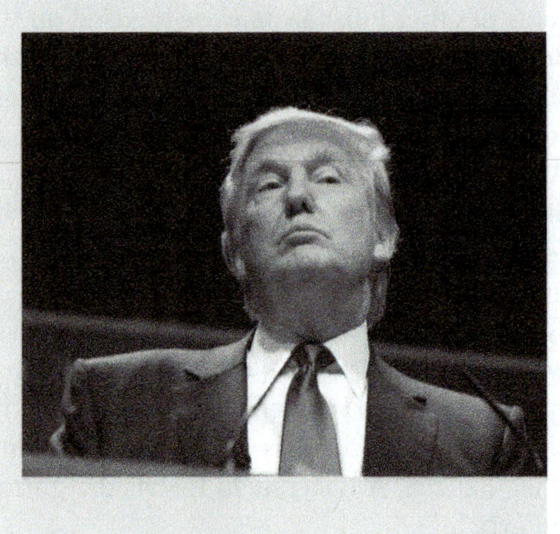

In *Gertz* v. *Robert Welch, Inc.* (1974) 418 U.S. 323, the court explained that it had imposed the actual malice requirement on defamation actions by both public officials and public figures because such persons "usually enjoy significantly greater access to the channels of effective communication and hence have a more realistic opportunity to counteract false statements than private individuals normally enjoy" and because they "have voluntarily exposed themselves to increased risk of injury from defamatory falsehood concerning them." Concerning the latter justification, the court stated: "Hypothetically, it may be possible for someone to become a public figure through no purposeful action of his own, but the instances of truly involuntary public figures must be exceedingly rare."

The court then explained that there are two types of public figures: "Some occupy positions of such persuasive power and influence that they are deemed public figures for all purposes. More commonly, those classed as public figures have thrust themselves to the forefront of particular public controversies in order to influence the resolution of the issues involved. In either event, they invite attention and comment." The court reiterated the distinction in these words: "[The public figure] designation may rest on either of two alternative bases. In some instances an individual may achieve such pervasive fame or notoriety that he becomes a public figure for all purposes and in all contexts. More commonly, an individual voluntarily injects himself or is drawn into a particular public controversy and thereby becomes a public figure for a limited range of issues. In either case such persons assume special prominence in the resolution of public questions."

At trial, whether a plaintiff in a defamation action is a public figure is a question of law for the trial court. On appeal, the trial court's resolution . . . of the ultimate question of public figure status is subject to independent review for legal error.

Applying the standard here, we note, first, that Globe does not contend that Khawar is a public figure for all purposes but merely that he is a public figure for limited purposes relating to particular public controversies. Globe's main argument appears to be that publication of the Morrow book drew Khawar into public controversies surrounding Kennedy's assassination and that Khawar is therefore an involuntary public figure for the limited purpose of a report on that book. In making this argument, Globe relies on the language in *Gertz, supra*, 418 U.S. 323, that it is possible for a person "to become a public figure through no purposeful action of his own" and that a person can become a public figure by being "drawn into a particular public controversy." Thus, Globe concedes, at least for purposes of this one argument, that Khawar did not intentionally thrust himself into the vortex of any public controversy.

We find Globe's argument unpersuasive because characterizing Khawar as an involuntary public figure would be inconsistent with the reasons that the United States Supreme Court has given for requiring public figures to prove actual malice in defamation actions. As we have explained, the high court imposed the actual malice requirement on defamation actions by public figures and public officials for two reasons: They have media access enabling them to effectively defend their reputations in the public arena; and, by injecting themselves into public controversies, they may fairly be said to have voluntarily invited comment and criticism. By stating that it is theoretically possible to become a public figure without purposeful action inviting criticism, the high court has indicated that purposeful activity may not be essential for public figure characterization. But the high court has never stated or implied that it would be proper for a court to characterize an individual as a public figure in the face of proof that the individual had neither engaged in purposeful activity inviting criticism nor acquired substantial media access in relation to the controversy at issue. We read the court's decisions as precluding courts from affixing the public figure label when neither of the reasons for applying that label has been demonstrated. Thus, assuming a person may ever be accurately characterized as an *involuntary* public figure, we infer from the logic of *Gertz* that the high court would reserve this characterization for an individual who, despite never having *voluntarily* engaged the public's attention in an attempt to influence the outcome of a public controversy, nonetheless has acquired such public prominence in relation to the controversy as to permit media access sufficient to effectively counter media-published defamatory statements.

We find in the record no substantial evidence that Khawar acquired sufficient media access in relation to the controversy surrounding the Kennedy assassination or the Morrow book to effectively counter the defamatory falsehoods in the Globe article. After the assassination and before publication of the Morrow book, no reporter contacted Khawar to request an interview about the assassination. Nor was there any reason for a reporter to do so: Khawar was not a suspect in the investigation, he did not testify at the trial of the perpetrator of the assassination, and, so far as the record shows, his own views about the assassination were never publicized.

Nothing in the record demonstrates that Khawar acquired any significant media access as a result of publication of either the Morrow book or the other book, RFK Must Die (1970) by Robert Blair Kaiser, in which, according to Globe, questions were raised about Khawar's activities in relation to the assassination. There is no evidence that either book enjoyed substantial sales or was reviewed in widely circulated publications. Indeed, the evidence showed that when the Globe article appeared, Roundtable had sold only 500 of the 25,000 printed copies of the Morrow book, and that although Roundtable had sent 150 copies of the Morrow book to various media entities, only Globe published a report concerning it. Before publication of the Globe article, no reporter contacted Khawar to interview him about either book, and he remained unaware of their publication.

The interview by the Bakersfield television station, which was the only interview in which Khawar ever participated that related in any way to the Kennedy assassination, the Morrow book, or the Globe article, occurred *after and in response to* the publication of the Globe article. Although this single interview demonstrates that Khawar enjoyed some media access, it is only the media access that would likely be available to any private individual who found himself the subject of sensational and defamatory accusations in a publication with a substantial nationwide circulation (Globe distributed more than 2.7 million copies of the issue containing the Globe article). If such access were sufficient to support a public figure characterization, any member of the media — any newspaper, magazine, television or radio network or local station — could confer public figure status simply by publishing sensational defamatory accusations against any private individual. This the United States Supreme Court has consistently declined to permit. As the court has repeatedly said, "those charged with defamation cannot, by their own conduct, create their own defense by making the claimant a public figure." *Hutchinson v. Proxmire, supra,* 443 U.S. 111, 135 (1979).

Although Globe's primary argument is that publication of the Morrow book made Khawar an involuntary public figure, Globe may be understood to argue further that Khawar's involvement with the Kennedy assassination controversies was not entirely involuntary because, immediately before the assassination, Khawar sought and obtained a position close to Kennedy on the podium knowing that there would be substantial media coverage of the event. For a variety of reasons, this conduct does not demonstrate that Khawar voluntarily elected to encounter an increased risk of injury from defamatory falsehoods in publications like the Globe article.

First, Khawar's conduct occurred before any relevant controversy arose. The controversies discussed in the Globe article related to Kennedy's assassination and the particular theory concerning it that was proposed in the Morrow book. Khawar's conduct in standing near Kennedy at the hotel was not a voluntary association with either of those controversies because the conduct occurred before the assassination and before the Morrow book's publication. Khawar did not know, nor should he have known, that Kennedy would be assassinated moments later, much less that a book would be published 20 years thereafter containing the theory proposed in the Morrow book. We do not disagree with Globe that Kennedy's campaign for his party's nomination to the presidency may be described as a public issue or controversy, nor do we disagree that Khawar voluntarily associated himself with this public issue or controversy by allowing himself to be photographed with Kennedy at a campaign press conference. But these facts have no legal significance for purposes of this libel action. The subject of the Globe article was not Kennedy's candidacy as such, but rather Kennedy's assassination and the theory put forward in the Morrow book.

Second, even as to the public issues or controversies relating to Kennedy's candidacy, the role in these controversies that Khawar voluntarily assumed by standing near Kennedy on the podium was trivial at best. Khawar's conduct in standing near Kennedy foreseeably resulted in his being photographed with Kennedy, but a journalist who is photographed with other journalists crowded around a political candidate does not thereby assume any special prominence in relation to the political campaign issues.

Third, appearing on the podium was not conduct by which Khawar "engaged the attention of the public *in an attempt to influence* the resolution of the issues involved." *Wolston, supra*, 443 U.S. 157, 168. Khawar, who was an admirer of Kennedy, wanted to be photographed with Kennedy because the resulting photographs would have a strictly personal value as souvenirs. Khawar did not anticipate, nor did he have reason to anticipate, that inclusion of his image would make the photographs more newsworthy or would in any way affect the resolution of any public issue related to Kennedy's run for the presidency. In brief, by appearing in close proximity to Kennedy, Khawar did not engage in conduct that was "calculated to draw attention to himself in order to invite public comment or influence the public with respect to any issue."

Having concluded that Khawar did not voluntarily elect to encounter an increased risk of media defamation and that before publication of the Globe article he did not enjoy media access sufficient to prevent resulting injury to his reputation, we agree with the trial court and the Court of Appeal that, for purposes of this defamation action, Khawar is a private rather than a public figure.

The First Amendment to the federal Constitution, as authoritatively construed by the United States Supreme Court, does not require a private figure plaintiff to prove actual malice to recover damages for actual injury caused by publication of a defamatory falsehood. *Gertz, supra*, 418 U.S. 323, 347. Rather, in this situation, the individual states may define the appropriate standard of liability for defamation, provided they do not impose liability without fault. See also *Dun & Bradstreet, Inc. v. Greenmoss Builders, Inc.* (1985) 472 U.S. 749, 761 [private figure plaintiff need not prove actual malice to recover presumed or punitive damages if the defamatory publication was not on a matter of public concern]. In California, this court has adopted a negligence standard for private figure plaintiffs seeking compensatory damages in defamation actions.

There is a different rule, however, for recovery of either punitive damages or damages for presumed injury. The United States Supreme Court has held that to recover such damages, even a private figure plaintiff must prove actual malice if the defamatory statement involves matters of public concern. We agree with Globe that the Kennedy assassination is a matter of public concern.

Because in this defamation action Khawar is a private figure plaintiff, he was required to prove only negligence, and not actual malice, to recover damages for actual injury to his reputation. But Khawar was required to prove actual malice to recover punitive or presumed damages for defamation involving the Kennedy assassination. Because Khawar sought punitive and presumed damages as well as damages for actual injury, the issues of both actual malice and negligence were submitted to the jury. The jury found that in publishing the Globe article Globe acted both negligently and with actual malice. Globe challenged both findings on appeal. In this court, Globe contends that the Court of Appeal erred in rejecting its challenges to these two findings.

Having independently reviewed the full record, we agree with the Court of Appeal that clear and convincing proof supports the jury's finding of actual malice.

In this context, actual malice means that the defamatory statement was made "with knowledge that it was false or with reckless disregard of whether it was false or not." *New York Times Co. v. Sullivan, supra*, 376 U.S. 254, 280. Reckless disregard, in turn, means that the publisher "in fact entertained serious doubts as to the truth of his publication." *St. Amant v. Thompson, supra*, 390 U.S. 727, 731. To prove actual malice, therefore, a plaintiff must "demonstrate with clear and convincing evidence that the defendant realized that his statement was false or that he subjectively entertained serious doubts as to the truth of his statement." *Bose Corp. v. Consumers Union of U.S., Inc., supra*, 466 U.S. 485, 511, fn. 30.

To prove this culpable mental state, the plaintiff may rely on circumstantial evidence, including evidence of motive and failure to adhere to professional standards. When, as in this case, a finding of actual malice is based on the republication of a third party's defamatory falsehoods, "failure to investigate before publishing, even when a reasonably prudent person would have done so, is not sufficient." *Harte-Hanks Communications v. Connaughton, supra*, 491

U.S. 657. Nonetheless, the actual malice finding may be upheld "where there are obvious reasons to doubt the veracity of the informant or the accuracy of his reports" and the republisher failed to interview obvious witnesses who could have confirmed or disproved the allegations or to consult relevant documentary sources.

There were, to say the least, obvious reasons to doubt the accuracy of the Morrow book's accusation that Khawar killed Kennedy. The assassination of a nationally prominent politician, in the midst of his campaign for his party's nomination for the presidency, had been painstakingly and exhaustively investigated by both the FBI and state prosecutorial agencies. During this massive investigation, these agencies accumulated a vast quantity of evidence pointing to the guilt of Sirhan as the lone assassin. As a result, Sirhan alone was charged with Kennedy's murder. At Sirhan's trial, "it was undisputed that [Sirhan] fired the shot that killed Senator Kennedy" and "[t]he evidence also established conclusively that he shot the victims of the assault counts." *People v. Sirhan, supra*, 7 Cal. 3d 710, 717. The jury returned a verdict finding beyond a reasonable doubt that Sirhan was guilty of first degree murder. On Sirhan's appeal from the resulting judgment of death, this court carefully reviewed the evidence and found it sufficient to sustain the first degree murder conviction. In asserting that Khawar, and not Sirhan, had killed Kennedy, the Morrow book was making the highly improbable claim that results of the official investigation, Sirhan's trial, and this court's decision on Sirhan's appeal, were all fundamentally mistaken.

Because there were obvious reasons to doubt the accuracy of the Morrow book's central claim, and because that claim was an inherently defamatory accusation against Khawar, the jury could properly conclude that Globe acted with actual malice in republishing that claim if it found also, as it impliedly did, that Globe failed to use readily available means to verify the accuracy of the claim by interviewing obvious witnesses who could have confirmed or disproved the allegations or by inspecting relevant documents or other evidence. The evidence at trial supports the jury's implied finding that neither Blackburn (who wrote the Globe article) nor Globe's editors made any such effort.

Preliminarily, we note that this was not a situation in which time pressures made it impossible or impractical to investigate the truth of the accusation. Kennedy had been assassinated in 1968. In November 1988, when Roundtable published the Morrow book, and in April 1989, when Globe published its article, the Kennedy assassination had long ceased to be an issue that urgently engaged the public's attention. Before publishing an article accusing a private figure of a sensational murder, Globe could well have afforded to take the time necessary to investigate the matter with sufficient thoroughness to form an independent judgment before republishing an accusation likely to have a devastating effect on the reputation of the person accused. But Globe did not do so.

Neither Blackburn nor Globe's editors contacted any of the eyewitnesses to the assassination, some of whom were prominent individuals who could easily have been located. At the trial, for example, Roosevelt Grier, a well-known former professional football player and volunteer Kennedy security aide who was present in the pantry area where Kennedy was shot, testified that after the assassination he had remained active in public life and was not "real difficult to find," but that no one from Globe had contacted him. As the United States Supreme Court [has held] "[a]lthough failure to investigate will not alone support a finding of actual malice, the purposeful avoidance of the truth is in a different category." [*Harte-Hanks Communications v. Connaughton*, 491 U.S. 657, 692.]

Globe argues generally that it had no duty to verify the claims, no matter how improbable, of a prominent and responsible source like Morrow, and that as a result its failure to conduct any investigation whatsoever of Morrow's highly improbable claims does not establish that it acted with actual malice in republishing Morrow's accusation against Khawar. We are not persuaded.

Having independently reviewed the record, we agree with the Court of Appeal that the evidence at trial strongly supports an inference that Globe purposefully avoided the truth and published the Globe article despite serious doubts regarding the truth of the accusation against Khawar. In short, we conclude that clear and convincing evidence supports the jury's finding that in republishing the Morrow book's false accusation against Khawar, Globe acted with actual malice — that is, with reckless disregard of whether the accusation was false or not.

Globe's challenge to the sufficiency of the evidence to support the finding of negligence merits little consideration.

Because actual malice is a higher fault standard than negligence, a finding of actual malice generally includes a finding of negligence, and evidence that is sufficient to support a finding of actual malice is usually, and perhaps invariably, sufficient also to support a finding of negligence. In any event, we are satisfied that the evidence we previously reviewed, and which we have concluded clearly and convincingly establishes actual malice in the form of reckless disregard, is sufficient also to sustain the finding of negligence.

The judgment of the Court of Appeal is affirmed.

NOTES AND PROBLEMS

1. *Public Officials.* The U.S. Supreme Court has clearly applied the First Amendment to require public officials (and candidates for the office of a public official) to prove by clear and convincing evidence the falsity of the defamatory statement and the publisher's actual malice regarding the issue of falsity. Obviously the president of the United States, any state's governor, or other such prominent office holders will qualify as a public official. But how far down the ranks of government bureaucrats will the public official designation apply? In Rosenblatt v. Baer, 383 U.S. 75 (1966), the Court held in this regard: "[T]he 'public official' designation applies at the very least to those among the hierarchy of government employees who have, or appear to the public to have, substantial responsibility for or control over the conduct of governmental affairs." Clarifying further, the Court stated that when the government position has such "apparent importance that the public has an independent interest in the qualifications and performance of the person who holds it, beyond the general public interest in the qualifications and performance of all government employees" that the public interest in being able to criticize such influential persons demands application of the actual malice standard. The Court held in that case that it was possible that a *former* supervisor of a county recreation area might qualify as a public official, whereas the Court noted in a footnote that a night watchman at the Pentagon would not qualify (in a hypothetical case accusing the night watchman of stealing government secrets). *Id.* at 86 n.13.

2. ***Public vs. Private Figures.*** The court in *Khawar* discussed the extension of the actual malice standard to plaintiffs who were not government office holders, yet who were considered *public figures*—individuals who generally thrust themselves into the limelight and who had sufficient access to the media (before being defamed). The court held that they could protect their own reputation through making their personal defense to the media. With respect to public figures, the courts have further determined that there are some who are so famous that they would be considered a public figure regardless of the subject matter of the defamatory statements. These *general-purpose public figures* tend to be one-name household celebrities who get attention whenever they want and for any purpose. Can you imagine such people? Courts have also recognized that some people are well known but only regarding particular issues or matters. These are often people, such as Dr. Jack Kervorkian, who may have been well known, but only in the context of particular issues of debate or policy. If Dr. Kervorkian had tried to schedule a press conference to discuss his views on the Internal Revenue Code, would anyone have shown up? With regard to these *limited purpose public figures*, the actual malice rules only apply when the subject of the defamatory speech relates to the issue for which they are famous. Otherwise, they would be considered a private figure.

3. ***Private Figures Defamed by Speech Concerning Public Matters.*** Reflecting the delicate balance between the First Amendment's concern with protecting important speech and the interest of the states and defamation victims in protecting reputation, the Supreme Court in Gertz v. Robert Welch, 418 U.S. 323 (1974) and the court in *Khawar* have held that with respect to a private plaintiff's suit for defamation where the speech related to matters of legitimate public importance, actual malice would be required in order to justify an award of either punitive damages or presumed, general damages but that any lower level of fault (i.e., ordinary negligence) could justify an award of actual damages. Applying these standards to the re-publication by the defendant in *Khawar*, why did the court find that the jury's various awards were consistent with the First Amendment?

4. ***Problems.*** Would the following victims of false, defamatory speech be required by the First Amendment to prove any particular level of fault by the defendant?

A. Tiger Woods is accused by a newspaper reporter of cheating on his taxes by failing to report income earned in certain golf tournaments.

B. Former Vice President and presidential candidate Al Gore is accused by defendant Internet blogger of incurring extraordinarily high energy bills on his personal residence.

C. Cindy Sheehan (founder of Camp Casey who demanded an audience with former President George W. Bush to discuss why her son had to die in the Middle East war effort) is accused by a prominent citizen of Waco, Texas in a newspaper letter to the editor of having a "questionable criminal background."

D. The author of a conservative book includes within his book a chapter on U2's Bono stating that he fathered several children out of wedlock.

E. A county dogcatcher running for re-election is accused by his opponent of bungling the finances of his office and causing unnecessary deficit spending.

F. The student body president of a state university is accused by the university president of improperly vandalizing school property with graffiti attacking the administration.

LADIES AND GENTLEMEN OF THE JURY . . .

Idaho J.I. 4.82 Elements of Defamation

In order to prove a claim of defamation, the plaintiff has the burden of proving each of the following elements:

1. The defendant communicated information concerning the plaintiff to others; and
2. The information impugned the honesty, integrity, virtue or reputation of the plaintiff or exposed the plaintiff to public hatred, contempt or ridicule; and
3. The information was false; and
4. The plaintiff suffered actual injury because of the defamation; and
5. The amount of damages suffered by the plaintiff.

2. *Private Matters*

Until the U.S. Supreme Court's decision in *Dun & Bradstreet*, First Amendment jurisprudence regarding defamation suits contained a blind spot in the area of suits brought by private plaintiffs on matters that did not seem to implicate matters of significant public interest. In *Khawar*, while the plaintiff was a private figure, the subject of the defamatory speech concerned a matter of great public interest — who shot a U.S. presidential candidate. What if the private plaintiff was defamed by speech that was not so noteworthy? Did the First Amendment still put limitations on a court's ability to award damages based upon the defendant's speech?

DUN & BRADSTREET, INC. v. GREENMOSS BUILDERS, INC.

472 U.S. 749 (1985)

POWELL, J.

In *Gertz*, we held that the First Amendment restricted the damages that a private individual could obtain from a publisher for a libel that involved a matter of public concern. More specifically, we held that in these circumstances the First Amendment prohibited awards of presumed and punitive damages for false and defamatory statements unless the plaintiff shows "actual malice," that is, knowledge of falsity or reckless disregard for the truth. The question presented in this case is whether this rule of *Gertz* applies when the false and defamatory statements do not involve matters of public concern.

Petitioner Dun & Bradstreet, a credit-reporting agency, provides subscribers with financial and related information about businesses. All the information is confidential; under the terms of the subscription agreement the subscribers may not reveal it to anyone else. On July 26, 1976, petitioner sent a report to five subscribers indicating that respondent, a construction contractor, had filed a voluntary petition for bankruptcy. This report was false and grossly misrepresented respondent's assets and liabilities. That same day, while discussing the possibility of future financing with its bank, respondent's president was told that the bank had received the defamatory report. He immediately called petitioner's regional office, explained the error, and asked for a correction. In addition, he requested the names of the firms that had received the false report in order to assure them that the company was solvent. Petitioner promised to look into the matter but refused to divulge the names of those who had received the report.

After determining that its report was indeed false, petitioner issued a corrective notice on or about August 3, 1976, to the five subscribers who had received the initial report. The notice stated that one of respondent's former employees, not respondent itself, had filed for bankruptcy and that respondent "continued in business as usual." Respondent told petitioner that it was dissatisfied with the notice, and it again asked for a list of subscribers who had seen the initial report. Again petitioner refused to divulge their names.

Respondent then brought this defamation action in Vermont state court. It alleged that the false report had injured its reputation and sought both compensatory and punitive damages. The trial established that the error in petitioner's report had been caused when one of its employees, a 17-year-old high school student paid to review Vermont bankruptcy pleadings, had inadvertently attributed to respondent a bankruptcy petition filed by one of respondent's former employees. Although petitioner's representative testified that it was routine practice to check the accuracy of such reports with the businesses themselves, it did not try to verify the information about respondent before reporting it.

After trial, the jury returned a verdict in favor of respondent and awarded $50,000 in compensatory or presumed damages and $300,000 in punitive damages. Petitioner moved for a new trial. It argued that in *Gertz*, this Court had ruled broadly that "the States may not permit recovery of presumed or punitive damages, at least when liability is not based on a showing of knowledge of falsity or reckless disregard for the truth," and it argued that the judge's instructions in this case permitted the jury to award such damages on a lesser showing.

[The trial court granted the motion for new trial but the Vermont Supreme Court reversed this order.] It held that the balance between a private plaintiff's right to recover presumed and punitive damages without a showing of special fault and the First Amendment rights of "nonmedia" speakers "must be struck in favor of the private plaintiff defamed by a nonmedia defendant." Accordingly, the court held "that as a matter of federal constitutional law, the media protections outlined in *Gertz* are inapplicable to nonmedia defamation actions."

Recognizing disagreement among the lower courts about when the protections of *Gertz* apply, we granted certiorari. We now affirm, although for reasons different from those relied upon by the Vermont Supreme Court.

We have never considered whether the *Gertz* balance obtains when the defamatory statements involve no issue of public concern. To make this determination, we must employ the approach approved in *Gertz* and balance the State's interest in compensating private individuals for injury to their reputation against the First Amendment interest in protecting this type of expression. This state interest is identical to the one weighed in *Gertz*. There we found that it was "strong and legitimate."

The First Amendment interest, on the other hand, is less important than the one weighed in *Gertz*. We have long recognized that not all speech is of equal First Amendment importance. It is speech on "matters of public concern" that is "at the heart of the First Amendment's protection." *First National Bank of Boston v. Bellotti*, 435 U.S. 765, 776 (1978).

As a number of state courts, including the court below, have recognized, the role of the Constitution in regulating state libel law is far more limited when the concerns that activated *New York Times* and *Gertz* are absent. In such a case,

> [there] is no threat to the free and robust debate of public issues; there is no potential interference with a meaningful dialogue of ideas concerning self-government; and there is no threat of liability causing a reaction of self-censorship

> by the press. The facts of the present case are wholly without the First Amendment concerns with which the Supreme Court of the United States has been struggling.

Harley-Davidson Motorsports, Inc. v. Markley, 568 P.2d 1359, 1363 (Ore. 1977).

While such speech is not totally unprotected by the First Amendment, its protections are less stringent. In *Gertz*, we found that the state interest in awarding presumed and punitive damages was not "substantial" in view of their effect on speech at the core of First Amendment concern. This interest, however, *is* "substantial" relative to the incidental effect these remedies may have on speech of significantly less constitutional interest. The rationale of the common-law rules has been the experience and judgment of history that "proof of actual damage will be impossible in a great many cases where, from the character of the defamatory words and the circumstances of publication, it is all but certain that serious harm has resulted in fact." W. Prosser, Law of Torts §112, p. 765 (4th ed. 1971). As a result, courts for centuries have allowed juries to presume that some damage occurred from many defamatory utterances and publications. This rule furthers the state interest in providing remedies for defamation by ensuring that those remedies are effective. In light of the reduced constitutional value of speech involving no matters of public concern, we hold that the state interest adequately supports awards of presumed and punitive damages — even absent a showing of "actual malice."

The only remaining issue is whether petitioner's credit report involved a matter of public concern. In a related context, we have held that "[whether] . . . speech addresses a matter of public concern must be determined by [the expression's] content, form, and context . . . as revealed by the whole record." These factors indicate that petitioner's credit report concerns no public issue. It was speech solely in the individual interest of the speaker and its specific business audience. This particular interest warrants no special protection when — as in this case — the speech is wholly false and clearly damaging to the victim's business reputation. Moreover, since the credit report was made available to only five subscribers, who, under the terms of the subscription agreement, could not disseminate it further, it cannot be said that the report involves any "strong interest in the free flow of commercial information." There is simply no credible argument that this type of credit reporting requires special protection to ensure that "debate on public issues [will] be uninhibited, robust, and wide-open."

In addition, the speech here, like advertising, is hardy and unlikely to be deterred by incidental state regulation. It is solely motivated by the desire for profit, which, we have noted, is a force less likely to be deterred than others. Arguably, the reporting here was also more objectively verifiable than speech deserving of greater protection. In any case, the market provides a powerful incentive to a credit-reporting agency to be accurate, since false credit reporting is of no use to creditors. Thus, any incremental "chilling" effect of libel suits would be of decreased significance.

We conclude that permitting recovery of presumed and punitive damages in defamation cases absent a showing of "actual malice" does not violate the First Amendment when the defamatory statements do not involve matters of public concern. Accordingly, we affirm the judgment of the Vermont Supreme Court.

It is so ordered.

NOTES AND PROBLEMS

1. ***Wholly Without First Amendment Concerns.*** Citing prior case law that characterized purely private speech as being "wholly without First Amendment concerns," the U.S. Supreme Court held in *Dun & Bradstreet* that, in such instances, the private plaintiff need not prove actual malice even to recover presumed or punitive damages (unless state law requires it). The Court did not address whether any fault was required, as a matter of constitutional interest balancing, to recover presumed or punitive damages. Some commentators believe that an argument exists that at least a negligence standard would still be required by the First Amendment in all defamation cases — but the Court has never reached this holding. As of today, whether a state should always require some level of fault in a defamation suit is left to the states themselves as a matter of their common or statutory law. Different states have reached different conclusions with some embracing the traditional common law view of strict liability (for example, look at the Idaho pattern jury charge at the end of the prior subsection) and others requiring negligence for any recovery of damages by a defamation plaintiff. Do you have an opinion as to whether it is better policy to require some level of fault in any defamation case or do you believe that when you intentionally publish a defamatory statement about another that you should bear the risk of your statement's falsity?

2. ***Problems.*** Does the following defamatory speech concern a public or a purely private matter?

   A. Plaintiff sues a local radio station because its disc jockey falsely stated on the air that plaintiff, a janitor in town, was the likely culprit in a series of robberies that had been committed at businesses where plaintiff had accounts.

   B. Plaintiff, a restaurant owner, sues the defendant, a former customer at the restaurant, of falsely stating on Yelp's Internet restaurant review site that the plaintiff's restaurant had "mold in the ice machine."

   C. Plaintiff is the former spouse of the defendant who stood outside the plaintiff's residence during their divorce proceedings, with a handmade sign stating "Cheater!"

Upon Further Review

Defamation claims demonstrate the full array of different tort levels of fault. At common law, defamation required no showing of fault against the defendant so long as she published defamatory statements concerning the plaintiff. One who published negative statements about another took the risk that if the information was wrong they would have to compensate the plaintiff for any recoverable damages to reputation. When the law has determined, however, that the nature of the speech was important enough to deserve some protection, the common law created both absolute and qualified privileges for the publisher. Whether an absolute or qualified privilege would attach reflected the law's view on how critical the nature of the communication tended to be considered; speech necessary for the effective operation of the affairs of government or a married couple's household has received maximum protection. For such speech, even actual malice by the publisher will not create defamation liability. For conditional privileges, both at common law and under the actual malice standard of the First Amendment, the courts have determined that while the speech is deserving of some protection, that protection can be lost and recovery permitted for defamation when the circumstances of the publication are more egregious. In such instances, the individual's interest in being compensated outweighs the potential chilling effect on the speech by imposition of a monetary judgment. As of now, whether any level of fault is required for purely private speech having no First Amendment connection, is a matter left to the various state courts and legislatures.

CHAPTER 13

Business Torts

I INTRODUCTION

The claims we have studied thus far involve torts that manifest themselves chiefly in terms of causing personal injuries or property damage rather than purely economic injuries. Assaults, batteries, false imprisonments, defamation, and product liability claims typically involve harm to the claimant's body and/or mind. Trespass and conversion involve harm to the claimant's property. And negligence can give rise to either type of physical injury — to one's body or property. In any of these various claims there may also be economic injuries (i.e., special damages) but those are secondary to the physical harm caused by the tort. For example, a woman physically injured in a car accident may also be unable to work for some period of time and lose income. Were we to end our coverage of tort law at this point, we would be missing a whole branch of tort law involving misconduct arising in business transactions that results in purely economic harms.

A burgeoning area of tort law involves the common law's adoption and application of tort claims that tend to arise in business transactions. The losses in these circumstances typically involve financial injury alone. There are many such tort causes of action and, indeed, there are entire elective classes in law schools devoted to exploring the nuances of the many types of common law business torts. For brevity's sake, we will confine ourselves to an introduction to some of the stalwart theories of recovery in this field — fraud, negligent misrepresentation, and tortious interference with contract or prospective business relations. We will conclude, finally, with consideration of a key issue that can arise in many business tort cases — when the defendant's actionable conduct that gives rise to the tort claim also involves the breach of an agreement, should

CHAPTER GOALS

- ☑ Acquire basic knowledge of some of the most ubiquitous common law tort causes of action arising from disputed business transactions.
- ☑ Learn how different types of misrepresentations can serve as the basis for a fraud cause of action, including misstatements of fact, concealment of material information, and making a promise to perform with no present intention of performing.
- ☑ Compare and contrast a negligent misrepresentation claim with a fraud claim, including the important limitations on the concept of duty in a negligent misrepresentation cause of action.
- ☑ Encounter the ancient claim for intentional interference with an existing contractual relationship and how it differs significantly from a more recently recognized claim for interference with a mere prospective contractual relationship.
- ☑ Learn the tests used by courts to divine when certain conduct that amounts to a breach of contract can simultaneously be considered a business tort.

the court recognize a tort claim or limit the scope of the action to a breach of contract recovery? In this manner, we ironically end up coming full circle with the beginning of this textbook. We will conclude with the question, "What is a tort?"

II FRAUD

Fraud is an ancient tort — at one time called an action for *deceit* — that is designed to protect the integrity of business transactions. The right to recover for fraud is premised upon the notion of a right to trust or rely upon certain statements or assurances from others. Fraud is recognized across many areas of the law and can yield varying remedies and results. In a breach of contract action, for example, a defendant might plead fraud as an affirmative defense to enforcement of the obligation. In a federal bankruptcy matter, a creditor might prove a fraudulent transaction as a basis to avoid the extinguishment of the debtor's liability. We saw in Chapter 7, Affirmative Defenses, that fraudulent concealment can be pled as a way to escape the impact of a statute of limitations or statute of repose defense. Fraud can also be used affirmatively to seek a rescission of a contract. Our focus will be upon a claimant pleading the tort claim of common law fraud in an effort to recover for economic losses associated with a business transaction.

A. Misrepresentations

All fraud claims involve proof of a misrepresentation by the defendant to the plaintiff, typically to induce the plaintiff into entering a contract. Of course, many sales pitches involve nuanced representations that might be called into question long after the consummation of a business deal. Courts are sensitive to not allowing "buyer's remorse" to give rise to easy claims for fraud and, therefore, the commonly understood elements of a fraud claim take this hesitation into account. There are volumes of case reporters filled with opinions trying to determine if the defendant's words or actions might be considered an actionable

"There are three things in the world that deserve no mercy—hypocrisy, fraud, and tyranny."

Frederick W. Robertson

misrepresentation. We will begin our foray into fraud by examining different types of misrepresentation that can be considered fraudulent.

1. *Existing Facts or Opinions Based Upon Facts*

As we learned in the preceding chapter on defamation, the law often makes a distinction between opinions and statements of fact. This is true in the law of fraud, with courts generally declaring that only false statements of fact are actionable. There are exceptions to this precept, of course. As you read the *Trenholm* case, pay close attention to each of the elements of fraud and ask yourself why the court characterized the land developer's sales pitch as fraudulent.

TRENHOLM v. RATCLIFF

646 S.W.2d 927 (Tex. 1983)

SPEARS, J.

Trenholm, a homebuilder, sued Ratcliff, a developer [for common law fraud].

The cause before us involves the appeal from the trial for fraud. After the jury returned its answers to the special issues, both parties moved for judgment on the verdict, and Ratcliff, in the alternative, filed a motion for judgment *non obstante veredicto.* The trial court rendered judgment for Ratcliff, and rendered a take nothing judgment against Trenholm. The court of appeals affirmed the judgment, holding the evidence established, as a matter of law, that Trenholm did not rely on Ratcliff's representations. We reverse the judgment of the court of appeals and render judgment for plaintiff Trenholm.

George and Robert Trenholm were the principal stockholders in Oxford Building Systems, a corporation engaged in the building of custom homes. Robert sold his interest to George prior to the filing of this lawsuit. Respondent, Raymond Ratcliff is the principal owner of Ratcliff Investments and Ramahal Development Corporation.

Ratcliff, a land developer, entered into a joint venture agreement with Richardson Savings & Loan to develop and sell lots in the Greenhollow subdivision in West Plano, Texas. In November 1975, Ratcliff held a "draw meeting" to solicit local builders. The meeting was attended by several builders, including George Trenholm. At the meeting Ratcliff discussed the Greenhollow development, and invited the builders to purchase lots in the subdivision. During the presentation, Ratcliff stated a mobile home park located near Greenhollow would be a future shopping center. At the conclusion of his presentation, Ratcliff invited questions. George Trenholm asked:

> Ray, you talked in, around and about this mobile home park through your presentation, and you definitely left me with the impression that its going to be moved, but before I buy any lots I specifically want to know what disposition is going to be made on that property.

Ratcliff answered:

> Don't worry about it, that's zoned commercial, and that property has already been sold. Those people have been notified that their leases will not be renewed, so the park should close up sometime in April and after that, why, after they get everything moved out over there, they will come in and bulldoze it down so by June or July it will be like there's never been a park there, and that will coincide actually just fine with the grand opening out there.

Trenholm built eighteen houses in the Greenhollow development. Six houses were built for his account, and twelve were built pursuant to a joint venture with Richardson Savings & Loan. Richardson Savings & Loan would furnish the money, and Trenholm would build and sell the houses. The profits or losses of the joint venture would be split 50/50 between them.

The mobile home park was not owned by Ratcliff or by Richardson Savings & Loan, but rather by a third party. The mobile home park was not moved by the time the houses were completed for sale. The Greenhollow subdivision did poorly, and on June 23, 1976, a meeting was held by Ratcliff to discuss the slow sales. Trenholm asked about the continued presence of the mobile home park, and he was told that the park would not be moved. The houses were ultimately sold at a net loss, and Trenholm settled his joint venture losses with Richardson Savings & Loan.

In the trial for common law fraud the jury found: (1) that Ratcliff made false representations to Trenholm as to material facts with the intent to induce Trenholm to purchase Greenhollow lots, and which were relied on by Trenholm; (2) that the representations concerning the trailer park were not known by Ratcliff to be false, but were made recklessly and with a purported special knowledge; (3) that the false representations were made with malice; (4) that Trenholm did not waive his claim against Ratcliff; (5) that Trenholm could not have discovered the falsity of the false representation by reasonable investigation; (6) that Trenholm suffered $68,750 out-of-pocket losses on the six Oxford homes, $37,500 lost net profits on the twelve joint venture homes and $37,500 lost net profits on the

Oxford homes; and (7) that $250,000 exemplary damages should be awarded. Both parties moved for judgment on the verdict. Ratcliff contended the jury's finding of recklessness would not support a cause of action for fraud. In the alternative, Ratcliff asked for judgment *non obstante veredicto.* The trial court rendered judgment for Ratcliff and that Trenholm take nothing.

The trial court's take nothing judgment, as we construe it, was based on one of two grounds: that a finding of recklessness would not support a cause of action for fraud concerning a future prediction, or that there was no evidence to support the jury findings in Trenholm's favor.

Ratcliff contends the necessary elements of a common law fraud action have not been established, and therefore, the jury verdict does not support a judgment for Trenholm. The elements of actionable fraud in Texas were stated in *Wilson v. Jones,* 45 S.W.2d 572, 574 (Tex. Comm. App. 1932, holding app'd) as follows:

> (1) that a material representation was made; (2) that it was false; (3) that, when the speaker made it, he knew it was false or made it recklessly without any knowledge of its truth and as a positive assertion; (4) that he made it with the intention that it should be acted upon by the party; (5) that the party acted in reliance upon it; and (6) that he thereby suffered injury.

Ratcliff argues the "trailer park representations" are matters of opinion or predictions of future events, and therefore, Trenholm must prove that Ratcliff knew they were false at the time they were made. The jury, in answer to special issue number two did not find that Ratcliff knew his representations were false. Ratcliff argues, therefore, he could not and did not make fraudulent representations.

Pure expressions of opinion are not actionable. It has been held that a representation, to be actionable, must be a representation of a material fact. *Wilson v. Jones, supra* at 574; W. Prosser, *Law of Torts* §109 at p. 720-724 (4th ed. 1971). There are exceptions to this general rule that an expression of an opinion cannot support an action for fraud. An opinion may constitute fraud if the speaker has knowledge of its falsity. An expression of an opinion as to the happening of a future event may also constitute fraud where the speaker purports to have special knowledge of facts that will occur or exist in the future. Additionally, when an opinion is based on past or present facts, an action for fraud may be maintained. Thus, the Texas courts have held a jury finding of recklessness or special knowledge establishes a basis for fraud in the last two exceptions.

Ratcliff's representation was not merely an expression of an opinion that the trailer park would be moved in the future. He falsely represented that the trailer park had been sold, and that notices had been given to the tenants. These are direct representations of present facts, which are so intertwined with his future prediction that the whole statement amounts to a representation of facts. A jury finding of recklessness is sufficient to establish a basis for misrepresentation of facts.

NOTES AND PROBLEMS

1. ***Elements of Fraud.*** Most courts have long agreed the basic elements of a fraud consist of the following: (a) a material misrepresentation, (b) falsity, (c) that was made with knowledge of the falsity or in reckless disregard of the truth, (d) intending for the plaintiff to rely upon the misrepresentation, (e) actual and justifiable (or reasonable) reliance by the plaintiff, and (f) actual harm suffered by the plaintiff in relying upon the misrepresentation. Courts adopted this cause of action with business transactions in mind, though occasionally you can find a court willing to consider its application to claims for personal injury. *See generally* Jane Doe v. Elizabeth Dilling, 888 N.E.2d 24 (Ill. 2008) (discussing the possible application of fraud to a fiancée's contracting HIV). The primary issues in the foregoing *Trenholm* case were whether an actionable misrepresentation had occurred and whether recklessness would suffice as adequate mens rea. How did the court resolve those concerns?

2. ***Scienter Needed for Fraud.*** Traditionally courts state that the scienter necessary to hold a defendant liable for damages in a fraud case involves either knowledge of the falsity of the representation or recklessness regarding the issue of falsity. As you may recall from Chapter 12, Defamation, this is what is referred to as *actual malice* in the context of the First Amendment's application to libel and slander actions involving public officials and public figures. Proof of knowledge of falsity often involves circumstantial proof of information, or other statements by the defendant, such that the jury can conclude that the defendant must have known that his representation was untrue at the time of making it. With regard to the alternative standard of recklessness, proof that the defendant had sufficient information available at the time of making the representation to cast significant doubt on the truth of the statement can be considered adequate to uphold a jury verdict. Lacking evidence to support either form of scienter, a claimant might consider negligent misrepresentation, covered in the next section of this chapter, as a possible alternative claim.

3. ***Availability of Punitive Damages.*** Because the common law requires proof of the defendant stating a known falsehood or being reckless about it, courts have long allowed juries to consider punitive damages in common law fraud actions. Perhaps fearing that it was too easy to allege a misrepresentation and to engage in punitive damage discovery, the drafters of Federal Rule of Civil Procedure 9 (governing the pleading of fraud claims) have required that claims for fraud be plead with "particularity." This is typically considered to include pleading the specific misrepresentation, the name and circumstances of the speaker making the statement, the facts demonstrating why the statement was false, as well as the other elements of the claim. What is it

about an act of fraud that has led courts to universally permit punitive damages when it is proven?

4. *Opinions vs. Facts.* As the court discusses in *Trenholm*, courts have also been willing in the right context to permit a fraud claim based upon a misrepresented opinion, but these are limited to specific varieties: (a) false opinion as to future events when the speaker claims to have special insight, (b) opinions given that are insincere, and (c) opinions that are premised upon past or present facts when these underlying facts are false. Which of these was involved in *Trenholm*? Outside of these three exceptional categories, courts reject fraud claims that are premised solely upon pure opinions stated by the defendant. What is it about an opinion that would lead to this conclusion?

5. *Puffery as a Form of Opinion.* Sometimes the defendant is sued for making statements designed to "puff up" the perceived value of the subject of the contemplated transaction. The use of adjectives in the negotiations often leads to inquiry as to whether the statements could be considered potentially false statements of fact or mere opinions that should not be actionable. Use of phrases such as "fine," "first-class," "land of gold," "a hot buy," a "good one," "excellent," and "perfect" raise such an issue. If the court concludes that the statement is a mere opinion, it will refer to it as "puffery" and dismiss the fraud claim. *See e.g.*, Miller v. William Chevrolet, 762 N.E.2d 1 (Ill. App. Ct. 2001) ("puffing is defined as a bare and naked statement as to value of a product and is considered a nonactionable assertion of opinion"). Frankly, a survey of cases involving this issue reveals courts within the same jurisdictions that are often inconsistent in analyzing such adjectives. *Compare, e.g.*, Pennington v. Singleton, 606 S.W.2d 682 (Tex. 1980) ("excellent" was a representation of fact), *with* Buckingham v. Thompson, 135 S.W. 652 (Tex. Civ. App. 1911, no writ) ("good one" was mere puffery). In cases where there is doubt as to whether the representation amounted to a factual statement or puffery, the court will submit the issue to a jury with an instruction along the lines that "puffery is an expression of opinion by a seller not made as a representation of fact." One scholar lamented the lack of a coherent legal analysis of this issue:

> We are constantly exposed to speech . . . encouraging us to buy goods, invest in stocks, and transact for services. This speech is often intentionally misleading, is usually vivid and memorable, and induces many of us to rely upon it. But the law, which normally punishes lies for profit, encourages this speech by immunizing it as "mere puffery." "Puffery" is an increasingly important defense . . . in common law settings, resulting in thousands of citations in cases and law reviews. However, puffery doctrine, a major element of the law of fraud . . . is missing an explanatory theory.

David A. Hoffman, *The Best Puffery Article Ever*, 91 Iowa L. Rev. 1395, 1396 (2006).

6. ***Problems.*** Would the following circumstances seem to involve actionable claims for common law fraud? In each, consider carefully the nature of the alleged misrepresentation and why it may or may not qualify as sufficient. What issues regarding the fairness of permitting a fraud claim might exist in each situation?

A. Nadine goes to a used car lot to purchase a 2005 BMW 3-Series that has 85,00 miles. The dealer offers it to her for $15,000 and says, "This is a better deal than you'll find anywhere else in the city. I just need to clear my lot to make room for some additional inventory." Nadine buys the car at the requested price. Later that day, she decides to look online at used cars and, much to her dismay, finds similar BMWs for several thousand dollars less.

B. Barney agrees to buy an outline for a torts class from a more senior student who claims to have received the highest grade in her prior torts class. After buying her outline, Barney discovers that she did not have the highest grade in the class but still received an "A."

C. Carlos goes to a famous chain restaurant and orders a pork chop dinner that has a heart symbol next to it. At the bottom of the menu it indicates that meals with a heart symbol are "carefully prepared with customers' health in mind." After purchasing and eating the meal, Carlos later is bothered when he discovers that his dinner had more fat and calories than a Big Mac.

D. Travis owns a trucking company and is negotiating to sell it because he is tired of dealing with increased federal regulations and having to provide health insurance for his employees. These things make it difficult for Travis to meet his payroll many months, though he has always managed to get by with some occasional cash advances from his banker. During negotiations the buyer, Bill, asks if there are any "cash flow problems," which Travis denies. After the sale of the business, Bill decides the company cannot make a profit and sues Travis.

2. Affirmative Acts of Concealment

The obvious claim for fraud involves the verbally expressed lie. But courts have also recognized circumstances where fraud arises out of the unspoken word or action. In other words, silence can sometimes constitute fraud. In the *Lindberg Cadillac* case below, the plaintiff is not able to point to an express misrepresentation by the defendant. At first glance, it would appear that no claim for fraud would be recognized. Yet the court below treats the deceitful conduct as being another type of actionable misrepresentation.

LINDBERG CADILLAC CO. v. ARON

371 S.W.2d 651 (Mo. 1963)

CLOYD, J.

This is an action in fraud in which the defendant is charged by the plaintiff with concealing defects in an automobile, which he traded to plaintiff in part payment of the purchase price of a new car, which the plaintiff sold to him. The trial was to the court, which found for the plaintiff in the sum of $759.00 and costs. After an unavailing motion for a new trial, the defendant appealed.

The plaintiff company was engaged in the sale of automobiles. Its business was located in the City of St. Louis. The defendant was in the vending machine business in St. Louis. He had some trucks and a Cadillac and Imperial automobiles, which he used in connection with his business.

He decided to trade in his 1957 Imperial on another Cadillac. In June of 1959 the Imperial was brought into the plaintiff's place of business and was appraised by the sales manager in charge of such work. He examined the automobile and appraised its value to be $2,165 at that time. No deal was made then because the parties were unable to reach a trade-in figure that was agreeable to both.

In the month of October, 1959, during a cold spell, the coolant in the Imperial froze. The car was taken to a filling station which Aron, the defendant, patronized. According to the testimony of the filling station operator, defendant told him that the motor had frozen and he wanted it checked to see if it had cracked. The filling station operator thawed out the motor and placed the car on a grease rack to check it over. He testified that he found two cracks on each side of the motor block. He said that the told Aron, the defendant, that the block was cracked. He estimated the cost of a new block to be in the neighborhood of four or five hundred dollars. He told Aron that he could put a "K and W sealer" in the cracks, but that it would be "strictly temporary." He also suggested that if the car was to be traded in, the cracks filled with the sealer could be covered with Permatex, which would conceal the filled cracks. Permatex is a gasket sealer and could serve no purpose other than to conceal the filled cracks in the motor block. He said that Aron told him to do this work, and that he did a "pretty smooth job" and that the Permatex concealed the cracks.

About the 20th of November, 1959, Aron drove the Imperial into the Lindberg Cadillac Company's service department for appraisal as a trade-in. It was there about half an hour, and he then drove it away. Aron had not driven the Imperial after the crack sealer was put in until the time he drove it to the plaintiff's place of business for the purpose of a trade-in. Defendant Aron testified that he discussed the condition of the Imperial in plaintiff's office when they were attempting to close the deal. He said that they agreed that it needed floor mats, that the motor was leaking oil and needed repair, and that the fenders needed fixing. He did not tell either the salesman or the sales manager about the cracked block. Thus the car which had been appraised in June was reappraised on November 20th, and an agreement was eventually reached to allow $2,290 for the Imperial on the purchase price of a new Cadillac. There was testimony that the actual value of the Imperial as traded in, assuming that the block was not cracked, was appraised at $1,720.00, and $259.00 was later spent by the plaintiff on reconditioning it for sale. There was also testimony that the book value of the car was $1,979.00.

The sales manager for the plaintiff company, who made the appraisal of the car, drove it for a few minutes on November 20th. He checked the heat gauge to see if it was overheating. This would normally disclose a cracked motor block. He also checked for water leaks, and found none. After the appraisal and sale, the car was reconditioned in the normal course of business for sale. This usually took about 30 days.

On December 21st, the Imperial as reconditioned was sold for $2,476.08. The purchaser returned the next day and complained that it was overheating. The car was taken to the plaintiff's shop to verify the purchaser's complaint. It was found that the motor block had the cracks in it, and the plaintiff refunded to the purchaser the money he had paid for the car. The plaintiff then sold the Imperial, known to the buyer to have a cracked motor block, for $1,200.

The defendant, testifying in his own behalf, said that he did not know what a motor block was. He said that when the Imperial was frozen, he took it to the filling station because they were supposed to have put anti-freeze in the radiator. He testified that the station attendant said that he would take care of what was wrong, and kept the car for about a day. The attendant said nothing to him about the cracked motor block. He said that after he was informed of the cracked block by the plaintiff, he never went to the filling station attendant about the matter nor had any communication with him in relation to it. Defendant also testified that he had been sentenced to three and one-half years for counterfeiting cigarette tax stamps, and at the time of trial he was on probation for a period of seven years.

As stated, the court found for the plaintiff in the sum of $759.00, and the defendant appealed.

The first point he raises is that the appellant failed to make a prima facie showing of fraud, and that the court should have found for the defendant. The appellant asserts in support of this that he made no misrepresentation, and that his mere silence cannot be held to have been fraudulent where the matter was open to investigation by the party alleged to have been defrauded. This constitutes a complete disregard of the facts. Silence can be an act of fraud. In one of our earliest cases, *McAdams v. Cates*, 24 Mo. 223, 225, our Supreme Court stated:

> If, in a contract of sale, the vendor knowingly allows the vendee to be deceived as to the thing sold in a material matter, his silence is grossly fraudulent in a moral point of view, and may be safely treated accordingly in the law tribunals of the country. Although he is not required to give the purchaser all the information he possesses himself, he can not be permitted to be silent when his silence operates virtually as a fraud. If he fails to disclose an intrinsic circumstance that is vital to the contract, knowing that the other party is acting upon the presumption that no such fact

> exists, it would seem to be quite as much a fraud as if he had expressly denied it, or asserted the reverse, or used any artifice to conceal it, or to call off the buyer's attention from it.

The reason for the rule is that since matters are not what they appear to be and the true state of affairs is not discoverable by ordinary diligence, deceit is accomplished by suppression of the truth. 23 Am. Jur. Fraud and Deceit, §84, p. 863.

We have in the facts before us more than a failure to speak. There is also a positive fraudulent concealment. In the case of *Jones v. West Side Buick Auto Co.*, 93 S.W.2d 1083, decided by this court, we had before us facts quite similar in effect to those here under consideration. There a fraudulent seller turned back the speedometer in the car sold to 22,400 miles, when the car had in fact been driven 48,800 miles. There was no verbal or written representation by the seller, but the buyer, relying upon the mileage registered on the speedometer, purchased the car. We held that the buyer had been defrauded by the deception, stating: "a representation is not confined to words or positive assertions; it may consist as well of deeds, acts, or artifices of a nature calculated to mislead another and thereby to allow the fraud-feasor to obtain an undue advantage over him." See, also, *Hutchings v. Tipsword*, 363 Mo. App., 363 S.W.2d 40, 45. The acts of the defendant as stated above were designed to, and did, defraud the plaintiff, and there is no merit to the contention that a case in fraud was not made.

The second point raised is that the court erred in its finding as to damages. The court reached the sum of $759.00 as damages by allowing $500.00 for the motor block and $259.00 for the sum spent by the plaintiff in reconditioning the car. It is asserted that the proper measure of damages is the difference between the actual value and the value the car would have had if the representation had been true. We agree that such generally is the proper measure of damages.

In applying the rule we must consider the nature of the fraud committed as it reflects upon the value of the property as fraudulently represented. A trade was made here with the full knowledge that the car was to be reconditioned for sale. It was represented as a car that could be so reconditioned by certain minor repairs caused by normal use. It was known by the defendant that the expenditures that the plaintiff intended to make would not make the car serviceable for resale, as the car, after such repairs, could not honestly be sold for its intended use. The fact that the court, in reaching the amount of damages, found the cost of the block and the cost of the repairs to be the

Principles

"In the present stage of the law, the decisions show a drawing away from this idea [that nondisclosure is not actionable], and there can be seen an attempt by many courts to reach a just result in so far as possible, but yet maintaining the degree of certainty which the law must have."

Dean Keeton, Fraud—Concealment and Nondisclosure, 15 Tex. L. Rev. 1, 31 (1936).

total, was not erroneous, as both went to the value of the car as represented and its actual value.

We find no error present, and the judgment is affirmed.

NOTES AND PROBLEMS

1. ***Concealment as a Misrepresentation.*** In the above case the defendant tried to argue that mere silence would not support a fraud cause of action. Did the court agree that, at worst, the defendant could be accused of the sin of omission or failing to do something that would have placed the plaintiff in a more advantageous position? When did the court indicate that silence could still constitute a misrepresentation of the truth to justify a cause of action based upon deceit?

2. ***Other Instances Where Silence Is Fraud.*** Most fraud claims permitted by courts involve affirmative statements proven to be false. The *Lindberg Cadillac* case involved an exception to this norm. Beyond active concealment of relevant information involved in the foregoing case, courts have also been willing to permit fraud claims when a defendant has been silent in circumstances where an affirmative duty to disclose is recognized. One such situation involves transactions entered into among those in a confidential or fiduciary relationship. For example, when one retains an attorney, an accountant, or a similar professional, courts typically hold that the professional owes a duty of loyalty to the client and is held to the utmost standard of fair dealing, including an affirmative obligation to disclose any material information before engaging in a transaction involving the client. Many other courts have also held that when one conveys partial information that creates a misleading impression, there is a duty triggered to supply the rest of the material information. In other words, a half-truth is a complete falsehood. Some courts have recognized a duty of the seller in the context of a real estate sale to affirmatively disclose material information about the real estate which the buyer would not otherwise be in a position to uncover. Finally, some courts have agreed with Restatement (Second) of Torts §551 (1965), which requires a general duty to disclose facts in a commercial setting when the defendant knows that the plaintiff is ignorant about the fact and does not have an equal opportunity to discover the truth. Many courts have refused to accept the Restatement's potentially broad exception to the normal requirement of an affirmative misrepresentation. Because it is unclear when disclosure is required outside of special relationships, litigants and courts are often left with a "somewhat nebulous standard, praiseworthy as looking toward more stringent business ethics, but possibly difficult of practical application." Note, *Fraudulent Concealment — Vendor & Purchaser — Duty to Disclose,* 36 Wash. L. Rev. 202, 204 (1961).

3. ***Damages for Fraud.*** The *Lindberg Cadillac* court stated that the normal measure of damages in a fraud case was the difference in value between the subject of the transaction as represented versus its actual market value. While courts often utilize such measures, they have been quite flexible in permitting other calculations in a fraud case where justice demanded it. In fact, in *Lindberg Cadillac* the court also permitted recovery of some out-of-pocket expenses incurred by the plaintiff in getting the automobile ready for resale. In general, courts have recognized damages for the (1) out-of-pocket damages incurred by the victim, the (2) loss of the benefit of the bargain, (3) a restitution type of recovery designed to remove any unjust enrichment gained by the defendant from the fraud, as well as (4) other consequential damages not otherwise covered. There are some courts that have recognized emotional distress damages in certain fraud cases, but such recovery is not typical.

4. ***Materiality of Information.*** The common law only imposes liability for fraud when the misrepresentation is considered "material" to the parties' transaction. *See* Restatement (Second) of Torts §538 (1965) (reliance upon fraudulent misrepresentation not justifiable unless the matter misrepresented is material). One issue that courts have had to consider is whether the issue of materiality should be resolved by resorting to an objective or subjective standard. For example, if most purchasers of defendant's widget would not care about the color of the product (perhaps some piece of industrial equipment), should the defendant's knowing falsehood that the crane was "bright yellow" when it was actually a dull mustard color still give rise to liability if the plaintiff attached considerable importance to the color of the equipment being purchased? Most courts have utilized an *objective measure* of materiality — whether reasonable people in the circumstance would have attached significance to the matter — except when the defendant has knowledge of the plaintiff's own subjective view of the importance of the matter. As one court described the proposition, a representation is material if:

> A reasonable man would attach importance to its existence or nonexistence in determining his choice of action in the transaction in question; or the maker of the representation knows or has reason to know that its recipient regards or is likely to regard the matter as important in determining his choice of action, although a reasonable man would not so regard it.

Watts v. Krebs, 962 P.2d 387, 391 (Idaho 1998).

5. ***Problems.*** Would the following scenarios give rise to valid claims for fraud?

A. A used car dealer fails to inform buyer that the car was previously in an accident requiring cosmetic repairs to the car's exterior body.

B. A jeweler advises the purchaser of a diamond ring that it had "exceptional cut and clarity," though on the jeweler's internal inventory records the ring was categorized as "dull and unimpressive."

C. Business partners for over twenty years decided to wrap up their business affairs in preparation for retirement. The elder of the two who had more day-to-day experience with the inventory and equipment fails to inform his partner about the actual condition of certain equipment when they negotiate to divide up assets of the company.

3. Promissory Fraud

Where the misrepresentation that procured the parties' agreement is separate from the promises within the agreement, courts have had no problem recognizing an actionable fraudulent misrepresentation. What if the defendant's promise to perform is the fraudulent misrepresentation because the defendant never plans to perform as promised? Is this a mere broken promise — a breach of contract case — or is it fraud? For example, if the defendant agrees upon receipt of $10,000 to deliver an automobile to the plaintiff but instead takes the money (and the car) and drives to Canada, has the defendant committed a tort or just breached an agreement? The *Smehlik* case below explores the concept of *promissory fraud* as a type of fraudulent misrepresentation.

SMEHLIK v. ATHLETES AND ARTISTS, INC.

861 F. Supp. 1162 (W.D.N.Y. 1994)

Curtin, J.

Plaintiff Richard Smehlik, a Czechoslovakian hockey player now under contract with the Buffalo Sabres hockey club ("the Sabres"), brought this action against defendant Athletes and Artists ("A&A"), a New York corporation retained by Smehlik to act as his representative in negotiating professional hockey contracts with the Sabres or with other National Hockey League ("NHL") teams. Smehlik's [amended complaint alleged common law fraudulent misrepresentation. Defendant A&A has filed a Rule 12(b)(6) motion to dismiss asserting that no claim for fraud has been adequately pled].

Smehlik was drafted by the Sabres in the 1990 NHL draft. On August 28, 1990, while still in Czechoslovakia, he signed an agreement with A&A under which, inter alia, A&A was to act as his exclusive representative in the negotiation of professional hockey contracts with the Sabres, or with whichever team held his rights. The agreement had an initial term of two years, or until such time as A&A had completed the negotiation of Smehlik's next professional hockey contract, whichever was longer.

A&A claims that it commenced contract negotiations with the Sabres on behalf of Smehlik in the summer of 1990. The negotiations, which were conducted entirely via telephone and fax, continued periodically until about April 1992. At that time, A&A received a letter from Smehlik stating that he was terminating his agreement with A&A, and/or that he believed the agreement to be invalid. Subsequently, in August 1992, Smehlik entered into a contract with the Sabres. That contract was negotiated by Rich Winter of The Entertainment & Sports Corporation, Smehlik's current agent.

Smehlik alleges that in order to induce him to enter into the contract at issue in this case, A&A "misrepresented to plaintiff its abilities, capabilities and what it would do for plaintiff pursuant to the agreement so as to induce plaintiff to enter the agreement with it." More specifically, he alleges that on or about August 28, 1990, A&A's representative Carl Hron told him:

> (1) that A&A could obtain a contract for him with the Sabres for the 1991/92 season;
> (2) that it could "make a deal right away";
> (3) that it would arrange for him to participate in the Sabres' 1991 training camp; and
> (4) that it would make all necessary arrangements to enable him to attend the Sabres' 1991 training camp, which required, inter alia, obtaining a release from his Czech hockey club, T.J. Vitkovice.

He alleges that these representations were made with the intent to deceive him, and to induce him to sign an agreement with A&A that he would not otherwise have signed. He maintains that he reasonably relied on the representations in deciding to sign the agreement. He asserts that A&A failed to obtain a contract with the Sabres for him for the 1991/92 season or to "make a deal right away," and that it failed to follow up on Hron's promises relating to his attendance at the Sabres' 1991 training camp. Finally, he alleges that A&A "misrepresented, concealed or failed to disclose material facts including that it either did not have sufficient knowledge and/or experience in dealing with Czechoslovak laws and practices and/or that if it had adequate knowledge and/or experience with respect to same, that it would fail to utilize same."

A&A has moved to dismiss [the fraud claim on the ground that it] simply alleges that A&A made a false promise to perform under the contract, a promise which, it maintains, cannot, under New York law, convert a breach of contract claim into one for fraud. In response, Smehlik contends that the specific oral representations made by Hron, devised for the purpose of inducing him to enter into the agreement, included promises that went beyond A&A's general obligation under the written contract to "use its best efforts to secure offers" from the Sabres or other NHL clubs. He argues that under New York law, one who is fraudulently induced to enter into a contract may maintain a cause of action for fraud separate from his breach of contract cause of action, when the fraud allegations are, as he claims they are here, distinct from the breach of contract claim.

It is well established in the New York courts that when a plaintiff alleges both breach of contract and fraud, "[the] cause of action in fraud may be maintained where the allegations of wrongdoing are distinct from those giving rise to the breach of contract claim and relate to facts extraneous thereto." *Steigerwald v. Dean Witter Reynolds, Inc.*, 107 A.D.2d 1026 (N.Y. 4th Dept. 1985). A mere "promissory statement as to what will be done in the future" may give rise only to a breach of contract claim. *See Stewart v. Jackson and Nash*, 976 F.2d 86, 89 (2d Cir. 1992). However, a false representation of a present fact may give rise to a separable claim for fraudulent inducement, and generally speaking, if a promise is "made with a preconceived and undisclosed intention of not performing it, it constitutes a misrepresentation of material existing fact" upon which an action for fraudulent inducement may be predicated. Thus, it is clear that a cause of claim for fraudulent inducement may be sustained on the basis of an allegation that the defendant made a promise to undertake some action separate and apart from his obligations under the express terms of the contract, if it is also alleged that he made the promise with no intention of making good on that commitment.

What is much less clear is whether a cause of action for fraud may properly be sustained on the basis of an allegation that the defendant made a promise to perform under the express terms of the contract while intending not to abide by its terms. The New York courts are split on this issue. *See Kenevan v. Empire Blue Cross and Blue Shield*, 791 F. Supp. 75, 80 (S.D.N.Y. 1992); *Bower v. Weisman*, 650 F. Supp. 1415, 1422-1423 (S.D.N.Y. 1986). The Second Department has recently stated, for example, that where a fraud claim "is premised upon an alleged breach of contractual duties and the supporting allegations do not concern representations which are collateral or extraneous to the terms of the parties' agreement, a cause of action sounding in fraud does not lie." *McKernin v. Fanny Farmer Candy Shops, Inc.*, 176 A.D.2d 233, 574 N.Y.S.2d 58, 59 (2d Dept. 1991) (citing *Mastropieri v. Solmar Construction Co., Inc.*, 159 A.D.2d 698, 553 N.Y.S.2d 187 (2d Dept. 1990); *Tuck Industries, Inc. v. Reichhold Chemicals, Inc.*, 151 A.D.2d 565, 542 N.Y.S.2d 701 (2d Dept. 1989); *Manshul Construction Corp. v. City of New York*, 143 A.D.2d 333, 532 N.Y.S.2d 419 (2d Dept. 1988); *Edwil Industries, Inc. v. Stroba Instruments Corp.*, 131 A.D.2d 425, 516 N.Y.S.2d 233 (2d Dept. 1987); *Spellman v. Columbia Manicure Manufacturing Co., Inc.*, 111 A.D.2d 320, 489 N.Y.S.2d 304 (2d Dept. 1985)). The First Department takes a similar approach. See *Caniglia v. Chicago Tribune-New York News Syndicate, Inc.*, 612 N.Y.S.2d 146, 147 (1st Dept. 1994) ("a cause of action does not lie where . . . the only fraud alleged merely relates to a contracting party's alleged intent to breach a contractual obligation"); *Comtomark, Inc. v. Satellite Communications Network, Inc.*, 116 A.D.2d 499, 497 N.Y.S.2d 371 (1st Dept. 1986). On the other hand, the Third Department has recently held that "a party who is fraudulently induced to enter a contract may join a cause of action for fraud with one for breach of the same contract" where the misrepresentations alleged are "misstatements of material fact or promises [to perform under the contract] made with a present, albeit undisclosed, intent not to perform them." *Shlang v. Bear's Estates*

Development of Smallwood N.Y., Inc., 194 A.D.2d 914, 599 N.Y.S.2d 141, 142-143 (3d Dept. 1993); *Bibeau v. Ward*, 193 A.D.2d 875, 596 N.Y.S.2d 948, 950 (3d Dept. 1992) (citing *Deerfield Communications Corp. v. Chesebrough-Ponds, Inc.*, 68 N.Y.2d 954, 510 N.Y.S.2d 88, 502 N.E.2d 1003).

In its Rule 12(b)(6) motion, A&A asks that I first make a determination, from the face of the amended complaint and the written agreement between A&A and Smehlik, that the oral statements allegedly made by Hron to Smehlik must be regarded as promises encompassed by the contractual arrangement between A&A and Smehlik. This I cannot do. The written contract required only that A&A use its "best efforts" on behalf of Smehlik. Whether or not A&A's "best efforts" would have encompassed the oral promises allegedly made by Hron is a matter of factual dispute.

Even if I were able to find that Hron's representations were nothing more than promises to perform under the contract, I would not be able to grant A&A's motion because Smehlik has adequately pleaded an undisclosed intent by A&A not to perform, and there is a split in the New York case law as to whether or not a cause of action for fraud may be sustained under such circumstances. It is not "'beyond doubt that [Smehlik] can prove no set of facts in support of his claim which would entitle him to relief.'" *Goldman v. Belden*, 754 F.2d at 1065 (quoting Conley v. Gibson, 355 U.S. 41, 45-46 (1957)).

For the reasons given above, A&A's motions are denied. It is time now to move ahead with resolution of the substantive issues in this action.

So ordered.

NOTES AND PROBLEMS

1. ***Promissory Fraud as a Tort Claim.*** While some courts have been relatively slow to recognize a broad form of promissory fraud as a viable type of actionable misrepresentation, it has actually been around for quite a long time. The claim was recognized as early as 1885 in the old English case of Edgington v. Fitzmaurice, 29 Ch. D. 459, where an investor was swindled through a promise that the directors would use his investment for a particular business purpose without ever so intending. The court found the directors liable based upon their lack of an intention to ever perform as promised. The court stated that:

> The state of a man's mind is as much a fact as the state of his digestion. It is true that it is very difficult to prove what the state of man's mind at a particular time is, but if it can be ascertained it is as much a fact [capable of being misrepresented] as anything else. A misrepresentation as to the state of a man's mind is, therefore, a misstatement of fact.

Id. at 461. Similar to the insincere opinion that can count as a misrepresentation of fact, promissory fraud can be viewed as an insincere promise that misrepresents the defendant's actual state of mind. Most courts have now recognized a broad form of promissory fraud — that even as to promises contained within the express terms of the contract, a failure by the defendant to intend to perform such promises at the time of entering into the contract counts as an actionable misrepresentation of fact. One entering into a contract without the intent to carry through on his promises now subjects himself not only to a breach of contract claim but a tort claim for fraud.

Texas PJC on Fraud

Texas Pattern Jury Charge 105.1-105.3

Fraud occurs when —

a. a party makes a material misrepresentation,

b. the misrepresentation is made with knowledge of its falsity or made recklessly without any knowledge of the truth and as a positive assertion,

c. the misrepresentation is made with the intention that it should be acted on by the other party, and

d. the other party relies on the misrepresentation and thereby suffers injury.

"Misrepresentation" means:

105.3 A false statement of fact [or]

105.3B A promise of future performance with an intent, at the time the promise was made, not to perform as promised [or]

105.3C A statement of opinion based on a false statement of fact [or]

105.3D A statement of opinion that the maker knows to be false [or]

105.3E An expression of opinion that is false, made by one claiming or implying to have special knowledge of the subject matter of the opinion.

2. ***Distinctions Between Suing on Contract vs. Fraud.*** Despite near universal willingness by courts to recognize promissory fraud, courts are also quite clear that a "mere breach of contract" alone does not constitute fraud and does not give rise to a tort cause of action. But where plaintiff can prove the lack of present intent to perform a promise, a tort cause of action for fraud will lie. Whether the claimant can sue on the contract only or also in tort can impact the applicable statute of limitations, the appropriate damages, whether a liquidated damage clause will govern, the scope of discovery and admissibility of certain evidence at trial, and the recovery of punitive damages.

3. ***Evidence of Lack of Intent to Perform.*** In addition to the normal proof of the other elements of a fraud claim, a plaintiff in a promissory fraud claim must demonstrate that, at the time of making the enforceable promise, the defendant had no intention of performing as represented. While a failure to perform is circumstantial evidence supporting this finding, the failure to perform *alone* can never transform the breach of contract into a fraud claim. On the other hand, where the defendant denies the existence of the contract, this is strong evidence of a lack of intent to perform — assuming the jury finds the disputed agreement was made. Further, evidence that performance was not possible at the time the promise was made can be strong evidence in support of a promissory fraud claim.

4. ***Problem.*** Jack manufactures rocking chairs for a living. Normally he can build four chairs per day when working fairly hard. Jill comes to see Jack in urgent need of 50 rocking chairs for a "Rock-A-Thon" she is organizing involving 50 senior citizens who will attempt to set a new world record by rocking for

three straight days in a fundraiser. Jill advises Jack of this and says she needs the chairs in seven days. Jack knows this will be difficult to meet, but he is inspired to give it his best effort. Unfortunately, despite building as fast as possible he is unable to finish the 50 chairs on time. Jill has to cancel the event. Does Jill have a good fraud claim against Jack?

B. Justifiable Reliance

Like other tort claims we have examined previously, fraud requires proof that the defendant's misconduct was the cause of the plaintiff's harm. Despite the defendant lying to the plaintiff, if the plaintiff does not care about the challenged representation or does not rely upon that misinformation in choosing to transact business with the defendant, is there any reason to hold the defendant liable for fraud? Further, if the plaintiff is foolishly duped into entering the transaction should this provide a defense to the deceitful party? The court in the following case explores the concept of *justifiable reliance* as an additional element of a fraud cause of action and helps define when the intentional tortfeasor can rely upon the plaintiff's own misconduct as a defense.

JUDD v. WALKER

215 Mo. 312 (1908)

LAMM, J.

Judd, the plaintiff, resides in Brookline, Massachusetts, but is in business at Dwight, Illinois. Bourland resides at Pontiac, Illinois. The defendants, Walker and Naxera, reside in Buffalo township, Pike county, Missouri. Naxera owned two tracts of land in Pike county, Illinois. Walker was Naxera's agent to sell them. Bourland was Judd's agent to buy them. So acting, at a certain time Bourland purchased from Walker said tracts of Illinois land. Judd and Bourland were strangers in that vicinity and unfamiliar with the lands. Walker and Naxera were familiar with the lands and Walker made false representations as to the acreage. After the deed passed from Naxera to Judd, it was ascertained there was a serious discrepancy in the amount of land conveyed by the deed, whereby Judd paid over $1,000 for land he did not get and which Naxera did not own and knew he did not own. Thereupon Judd sued Naxera and Walker for damages [for] fraud and deceit. No question is made on the pleadings and the facts seem to be of such sort that the law should throw no mere captious obstacle on dry technicality in the road of recovery — to the contrary, should put its benediction on the effort if it can be done without overturning settled principles.

The laws of hospitality seem to require that strangers should be taken in in a good sense, but courts should be astute to not permit such a "taking in" as appears here.

At a trial in that court with the aid of a jury, at the close of plaintiff's evidence, he was cast by a peremptory instruction. Thereafter he appealed to the St. Louis Court of Appeals. That court, speaking through Nortoni, J., handed down a unanimous opinion reversing and remanding the case, but certified it here, being of mind that its opinion was in conflict with [another intermediate appellate court].

The statement of facts by Judge Nortoni and his conclusions of law follow:

"This is an action at law on an allegation of fraud and deceit for the sale of lands. The evidence was to the effect that the plaintiff, Curtis J. Judd, treasurer of the Keeley Company of Dwight, Illinois, is a man of means and invests surplus money in lands. One Bourland, a banker of Pontiac, Illinois, and Mr. Judd have an arrangement whereby Bourland looks around for lands out of which money can be made by buying and reselling, and upon locating such lands, Mr. Judd furnishes the money and the land is purchased in the name of Judd as a speculation. The business is all done by Bourland, subject to Judd's approval. On the occasion in question, Bourland, as agent of Judd, came to Louisiana, Missouri, in search of lands and met the defendant Walker, a real estate agent at that place, who drove him across the Mississippi river into Pike county, Illinois, and upon the lands of the defendant Naxera, which he then had for sale as agent for Naxera. The land was irregular in shape, being bounded on one side by the Sny and running to a dull point on the north end. Walker, Naxera's agent, informed Bourland, Judd's agent, that the two pieces of land which were adjacent and owned by Naxera, contained one hundred and seventy-eight acres, one piece containing eighty acres and the other ninety-eight acres, and offered the tract at forty dollars per acre. Bourland looked at the land and they then drove on and viewed other properties. Returning to Louisiana, both Bourland and one Sims, a friend of Bourland who was accompanying him on the trip, informed Walker that Bourland was acting for Judd and that he would wire Judd for consent to buy the Naxera lands, which he did and received Judd's permission by wire, which was communicated to Walker. On the following day, Bourland drove to and upon the lands in order to locate a certain slough thereon, and that evening paid Walker $200 earnest money and entered into a contract in writing, whereby he agreed to purchase said lands as soon as Walker could procure satisfactory abstracts, conveyances, etc. At the time of executing this contract, Walker said he was not sure of the number of acres in excess of ninety in the irregular-shaped tract adjacent to the Sny and therefore they had better put in the contract the round number of ninety acres and would ascertain definitely thereafter. A month later Walker drew up a deed which was executed by his principal, Naxera, and acknowledged before Walker as a notary public, which deed purported to convey to Judd the two tracts of land mentioned, one hundred and seventy-eight acres, for which a draft payable to Walker, covering the balance due at $40 per acre, was delivered to the bank in payment therefor, and the deed was thereupon delivered to Judd.

"It was shown by the evidence both of Walker and Naxera, as well as otherwise, that each of them knew there was not one hundred and seventy-eight acres of the land; that Naxera claimed to own one hundred and sixty acres only, and that he refused to execute the deed for one hundred and seventy-eight acres at Walker's request and advised with friends about it before signing the same, and finally consented to do so upon the agent Walker giving him a written obligation to hold him harmless in event the shortage of acres was discovered and he would be called upon to make good; that Naxera received pay for one hundred and sixty acres of the land at forty dollars per acre, less Walker's commission, a total of $640, and that Walker appropriated to his own use, with Naxera's consent and approval, forty dollars per acre for the remaining eighteen acres, besides his commission. Some time thereafter, Judd caused the land to be surveyed, whereby it was ascertained that it contained 153.24 acres only, instead of one hundred and seventy-eight acres, there being a shortage of 24.76 acres. One witness also testified that between the time of the negotiation of the land and the making of the deed, Walker told him in his (Walker's) office that Bourland was going to take the land and that he was getting paid for a number of acres, something like twenty-seven acres, more than there was in the tract. Upon this state of facts, this suit for fraud and deceit was instituted to recover this shortage at forty dollars per acre."

"At the conclusion of the evidence for the plaintiff, the court peremptorily instructed the jury that the finding should be for the defendant. In obedience thereto, the jury returned a verdict as directed. After unsuccessful motions to set the same aside and for new trial, plaintiff appeals.

"1. There are cases which hold that where the parties go upon the land during negotiations and the seller points out the true boundaries thereof to the purchaser, with the statement of the number of acres contained therein, and upon this statement of the acreage the purchaser relies and purchases the land, no action of deceit can be maintained by the injured party on account thereof. The reason assigned in these cases seems to be two-fold: first, that parties ought not rely on such statements; and, second, that the parties were upon the land and the means of information were equally open to both, therefore the rule *caveat emptor* applies, as the true number of acres could be ascertained by ordinary vigilance on the part of the purchaser. . . . After much careful and painstaking investigation, we are satisfied that the law is quite generally established throughout those jurisdictions where the common law obtains, to the effect that false statements and representations made by the vendor, positively as of his own knowledge, as to the number of acres in a certain tract of land when the tract is being negotiated by the acre, are not regarded as expressions of opinion, but on the contrary, are considered statements of fact, and as such constitute fraud. . . . This view has become almost universally recognized and adopted by the courts throughout the country. The generally accepted doctrine on the subject is thus announced in 14 Am. and Eng. Ency. Law (2 Ed.), 45: 'There are some cases in which it has been held or said that a false statement as to the boundaries of a tract of land, or as to the number of acres which it contains, will not support an action of deceit, but they base the rule on the ground that such statements ought not to be relied upon, and not on the ground that they are expressions of opinion. Statements as to such matters, if made by a person positively, and as of his own knowledge, are statements of fact, and have often been held to constitute fraud.'

"In fact, the rule announced above is the same which applies in cases of fraud and deceit generally and is to the effect that the party owning the property or article, is presumed to know the facts. No one has prevented him from knowing them and one dealing with him has the right to rely upon the positive statements and representations of fact pertaining thereto, even though the means of knowledge were specially open to him, provided the representations were relied upon and were sufficient to and did actually induce action, for the law will not hear the guilty party say, 'You were yourself guilty of negligence,' or 'You ought not to have trusted me.' Bigelow on Fraud, 523, 524; Kerr on Fraud (2 Ed.)

"2. This case reeks with fraud. The evidence shows conclusively that Walker made positive representations to Bourland as to the number of acres in the tract from the inception of the trade up to the time of drawing the contract, at which time he suggested that as he was not sure of the exact number of acres in excess of ninety, they would call the irregular tract ninety acres in round numbers, leaving the impression that in the interim, prior to the making of the deed, he would ascertain the true acreage. Bourland relied upon what he said and trusted to him to make good his representations. Walker himself drew the deed for one hundred and seventy-eight acres, and procured his principal's signature thereto by giving to him an obligation of indemnity as mentioned, and collected the cash for the full number of acres as represented by him in the first instance, knowing at the time that he was then and there perpetrating a heinous fraud upon the purchaser. It would seem that in a case of such gross deception a recovery should be had without much difficulty. The respondent contends, however, that inasmuch as Bourland went upon the land twice and viewed the same, the parties were then upon an equal footing, and means of knowledge being open to him, the rule of *caveat emptor* applies; that it was the purchaser's duty to use his senses and vigilance and ascertain for himself the true facts, and not having done so, a recovery is precluded. The cases of *Mires v. Summerville, Mooney v. Miller, Gordon v. Parmelee,* and *Credle v. Swindell,* supra, are cited and relied upon as supporting this contention.

"Chancellor Kent says: 'The common law affords to every one reasonable protection against fraud in dealing; but it does not go to the romantic length of giving indemnity against the consequences of indolence and folly, or a careless indifference to the ordinary and accessible means of information. It reconciles the claims of convenience with the duties of good faith, to every extent compatible with the interests of commerce. This it does by requiring the purchaser to apply his attention to those particulars which may be supposed within the *reach of his observation and judgment*; and the vendor to communicate those particulars and defects which cannot be supposed *to be immediately within the reach of such attention.* If the purchaser be wanting of attention to these points, where attention would have been sufficient to protect him from surprise or imposition, the maxim, *caveat emptor,* ought to apply.' 2 Kent's Comm. (14 Ed.), 484, 485.

"The true test of the application of the rule *caveat emptor,* is the liability of the defect complained of to the observation and judgment of one exercising ordinary and usual business attention, care and circumspection, that is, such care and attention as is usually exercised by ordinarily prudent men in like business affairs. The law requires this much and no more. It does not require nor expect the purchaser to exercise a degree of care and prudence greater than business men ordinarily exercise in like transactions. The rule is a reasonable one and its chief purpose is to require men to see and know such things as are open and patent to their senses upon penalty. It is where the defect complained of is open and patent to the senses of one exercising ordinary business care and attention only that the rule of *caveat emptor* applies. . . . The rule mentioned has been carried to its full extent in this State. In *Morse v. Rathburn*, 49 Mo. 91, the alleged false representations were that certain unimproved portions of the farms were well-timbered and that the soil was good, whereas most of the timber had been cut off and the land was broken and rocky. The plaintiff having been over the land during negotiations, the court very properly denied a recovery by the application of the rule aforesaid, on the ground that the matters and things about which the alleged false representations were made were open to the observation of the purchaser. To the same effect is the case of *McFarland v. Carver*, 34 Mo. 195, in which case the fraud and deceit alleged was as to certain representations regarding the quality of lands and it appeared that one hundred and twenty acres thereof were subject to overflow. The court held that if the defect was patent to observation, no recovery could be had therefor.

"Entertaining these views, we are fully persuaded that the case under consideration is not one where the rule should find application. To apply it here, we must find that the alleged shortage of acres in the tract was open and patent to the observation of the purchaser and within the range of his senses while viewing the lands. This we cannot do as it is a matter of common knowledge that a man cannot view a tract of land and arrive at anything like an accurate estimate of its contents. As said by the Supreme Court of Michigan: 'It cannot be generally true that a person can judge of the contents of a piece of land by the eye.' *Starkweather v. Benjamin*, 32 Mich. 305.

"3. Considering the next proposition, that Bourland having viewed the lands, he should have used vigilance to ascertain the fact of acreage. To follow out this suggestion, a survey would have been necessary. The rule only requires that Bourland should use that degree of business circumspection usually exercised by prudent men in like transactions. This being true, he would be chargeable with neglect in that behalf only in event that prudent men usually cause surveys to be made under like circumstances. In dealing with this suggestion, we must apply a degree of common sense commensurate with the case in hand and view it in the light of common knowledge and every-day experience pertaining to like affairs. From these bearings, we all know that land in large tracts is bought and sold almost daily by the acre in this country without surveys. This arises no doubt from the fact that the original Government surveys are usually accurate and men rely thereon, together with the presumption usually indulged that he who owns the land knows the acreage, and the negotiations are generally had on the faith of prior surveys, and representation of the owner. The citizens of Missouri from time immemorial have been accustomed to deal with the utmost good faith in matters of this kind, and it would be a sad commentary indeed upon the moral sense and integrity of the State for the courts to say even by inference that our citizens can no longer be trusted in this behalf. Our conclusion is that in case of positive representation of a given number of acres in a tract, ordinary business prudence does not require a survey and measurement thereof and that the party relying upon such representations of fact is not precluded from recovery by not causing measurements to be made in advance of the purchase.

"The words 'means of knowledge easily within reach' employed in some of the cases ought not to be construed to require the purchaser to seek out and employ a survey or for the purpose of verifying a fact positively asserted by the seller.

"4. There is yet an additional reason why this case should have gone to the jury. Respondents were in no position to avail themselves of appellant's want of care and

> lack of attention. The general rule seems to be well settled that where the parties deal fairly or at arm's length, the rule of *caveat emptor* as above indicated applies, but when fair dealing is departed from by the vendor making false statements of fact as of his own knowledge, the falsity of which is not palpable to the purchaser, the purchaser has the undoubted right to rely implicitly upon such statements and the principle has no application (Authorities supra), and in event the purchaser is entrapped thereby and afterwards calls upon the vendor in a court of justice to make compensation for his deceit, the law will not permit him to escape by urging the folly of his dupe nor by admitting that he, the seller, was a knave and a scoundrel, and averring the defrauded party was negligent and careless in thus believing and trusting him, for this would be equivalent to saying, 'You trusted me, therefore I have a right to betray you.' *Cottrill v. Krum*, 100 Mo. 397, 13 S.W. 753.
>
> "Mr. Kerr, in his work on Fraud (2 Ed.), 40, 41, says: 'If a definite or particular statement be made as to the contents of property, and the statement be untrue, it is not enough that the party to whom the representation was made may have been acquainted with the property. A very intimate knowledge with the premises will not necessarily imply knowledge of their exact contents, while the particularity of the statement will naturally convey the notion of exact admeasurement. The fact that he had the means of knowing or of obtaining information of the truth which he did not use is not sufficient. . . . He is not bound to inquire unless something has happened to excite suspicion, or unless there is something in the case or in the terms of the representation to put him on inquiry. . . .'
>
> "For the reasons above given, the judgment is reversed and the cause remanded to be proceeded with as herein indicated."

We approve the [foregoing] statement of facts by the learned judge and his conclusions of law. Would it not be a shame to jurisprudence if, on the facts found, the conclusions drawn did not irresistibly follow? True, Naxera made no false representations of material facts in person to either Judd or Bourland, but his mouthpiece, Walker, did, and Naxera after notice adopted the transaction and either shared in the polluted gains or aided Walker in pocketing them. True, the written contract preceding the deed was signed by Bourland as a party thereto. But Walker knew at that time that Bourland represented another, and, if he did not know it at that time, both he and Naxera knew it before the deed was made by Naxera to Judd. True, the false representations relating to acreage antedated the written contract and the deed, but the fraud was not merged in those instruments.

As we read the record, there is present here a typical case of actionable fraud and deceit. For instance: False representations of the vendor on material facts leading up to the sale, with his knowledge of their falsity and a present intention they should be believed and acted on by the vendee, coupled with the vendee's ignorance of their falsity and his reliance and acting on such representations to his resulting damage. The fraud, resting in parol, may be proved by parol, and the written documents were mere steps in that proof.

It is elementary that a grantee, defrauded as was Judd, is not obliged to sue on the covenants of warranty in his deed nor need he go into equity to rescind the contract, but he may hold what he got under the contract and sue at law for his damages. That is what Judd did in this case.

The premises considered, the judgment of the [trial court] is reversed and the cause is remanded to be retried in accordance with the views expressed in the opinion of Nortoni, J., and in this. All concur.

NOTES AND PROBLEMS

1. ***Plaintiff's Misconduct Negating Justifiable Reliance.*** Assuming that a plaintiff *actually relies* upon the defendant's misrepresentation, another possible issue concerns whether that reliance was *justifiable* under the circumstances. In the *Judd* case the defendant contended that reliance was not justifiable because the size of the land was open and ascertainable, and the plaintiff should have paid for a formal survey to ascertain the actual acreage. The court stated that the test for justifiable reliance was whether "one exercising ordinary and usual business attention, care and circumspection" would have relied upon the misrepresentation. In applying this somewhat general test of reasonableness, the court elaborated that when the "defect was open and patent to the senses," that reliance could not be justified and the rule of *caveat emptor* — or buyer beware — would instead apply. While courts sometimes refer to this justification test as one asking whether the plaintiff's reliance was "reasonable" — indicating an ordinary negligence standard — in application it appears that most courts are really applying more of a gross negligence standard for the issue of justification. As the court in *Judd* summarized: "The fact that he had the means of knowing or of obtaining information of the truth which he did not use is not sufficient [to negate justified reliance]. . . . He is not bound to inquire unless something has happened to excite suspicion, or unless there is something in the case or in the terms of representation to put him on inquiry." Ultimately, the issue of justification turns on whether the fact-finder determines that there were any "red flags" to make the reliance unjustified. What facts would have to have been different for the buyer's reliance in that case to have been unjustified?

2. ***Disclaimer of Reliance Clause in Contracts.*** Recently, enterprising transaction lawyers have tried to insulate their clients from claims for fraud by use of inventive disclaimer language within the terms of a written contract. Referred to as "disclaimer of reliance" clauses, these are often worded so as to negate any actual reliance by the parties to a contract on any representation made beyond the four corners of the agreement. Under the right circumstances, courts have shown a willingness to enforce such waivers of reliance, particularly among parties of equal bargaining strength and sophistication, and when represented by counsel. Some courts have held, however, that a mere "merger" clause — that recites that no representations or promises outside the terms of the written contract have been made — does not preclude a claim for fraudulent

inducement. *See* Italian Cowboy Partners, Ltd. v. Prudential Ins. Co. of America, 341 S.W.3d 323 (Tex. 2011).

3. ***Problems.*** Would the claimants below appear to have justifiably relied upon the other actor's misrepresentations?

A. A mattress salesperson tells Rachel that the mattress on sale is one of the softest mattresses they sell. It is actually quite firm. Rachel has available all of the store's mattresses on display to try out but trusts the salesperson instead and buys the mattress. She later regrets the purchase after sleeping on the mattress and concluding that it was firm rather than soft.

B. The seller of a house tells James that the house has no problems. James relies upon this and foregoes an inspection, failing to notice spots along the side of the house where the existing bricks are crumbling.

III NEGLIGENT MISREPRESENTATION

Given its name, you may be tempted to assume that a claim for negligent misrepresentation is identical to a fraud claim except with a lower *mens rea* (i.e. carelessness). If that were entirely true, of course, there would be no need for courts to recognize separately a fraud claim. If anyone could recover just as easily by proving the lower *mens rea* for negligent misrepresentation, it would make no sense to attempt to prove greater fault than required to recover. Negligent misrepresentation does have a degree of overlap with a fraud cause of action, but its elements reveal a more limited application in terms of the types of instances where courts will recognize this cause of action.

A. Introduction

STAGGS v. SELLS

82 S.W.3d 219 (Ct. App. Tenn. 2001)

This case involves a claim of negligent misrepresentation in the sale of a home. The trial court found that Defendants' statements and actions constituted negligent misrepresentation of the condition of the property resulting in $25,000.00 in damages to Plaintiff. However, the trial court also found, applying principles of comparative fault, that Defendants were 60% at fault and Plaintiff was 40% at fault. A judgment of $15,000 was, thus, assessed against Defendants. Defendants appeal the court's finding of negligent misrepresentations, as well as the amount of damages determined by the court to be suffered by Plaintiff. We affirm.

In 1987, Defendants/Appellants, William E. and Betty Jean Sells, purchased a home in which their daughter lived until 1995, when they placed this house up for sale. Defendants never actually lived in the home, but lived close by and visited their daughter regularly. Plaintiff/Appellee, Christell Staggs, viewed the home on three occasions and negotiated a purchase price for the house of $71,000.00. A contract was signed with Defendants to purchase the house for that amount. This contract also provided "that [the] Property has not been damaged or affected by flood or storm run-off and that [the] Property does / does not require flood insurance." The box next to the phrase "does not" in this sentence was checked. No other explanation was provided by Defendants.

Although Defendants accepted the offer, they never saw the contract and authorized their agent to sign it for them. Their agent never read the terms of the contract to them and did not inquire regarding any flooding which might have occurred on the property.

Plaintiff inspected the property herself. She also had the property appraised and inspected by professionals. The appraisal came in at $71,000.00; however, the appraiser noted that the property was in a low-lying area and could be subject to minor flooding. He recommended having a surveyor check for flooding, but issued the appraisal, which was accepted by the bank, without obtaining a survey on the assumption that the property did not flood. A flood certification was obtained that established that the property, like the majority of property in Putnam County, was in flood zone C. Flood insurance could be purchased but was not required.

At the closing, Plaintiff inquired of her agent what 'flood zone C' was. She was told by her agent that "it was a flood zone, but it is a low flood zone, it wasn't supposed to flood." She never ask Defendants about any flooding, and Defendants, who were present at the closing, never mentioned any flooding to her.

Over the next few years, water came up flooding the yard around 15 times. In some cases the flooding was so severe that the house was completely surrounded by water rendering it a virtual island. However, water has never come into the house and has not yet caused any structural damage to the dwelling. Testimony showed that no residents have had to spend significant time away from the house since the water usually recedes quickly, allowing access to the house within a few hours and completely clearing the property within a day or two.

In his findings of fact, the judge determined that the paragraph regarding storm run-off and flood insurance was marked at the time the contract was signed and held that, when Defendant's agent signed this contract, a guarantee was made by Defendants in that agreement. Said the court:

> I don't think there's an intentional misrepresentation here. I don't think that the proof rises to that level. But I think it does rise to the level of recklessness when that provision was in the contract when he and Mrs. Sells had authorized the agent to sign the contract for them, you're guaranteeing that there's no water problem on

> this property. Putting that kind of authority in the hands of the agent without carefully looking at the contract itself, does amount to recklessness, and I'm satisfied that there was a misrepresentation.
>
> The Court finds that Mr. and Mrs. Sells, not intentionally, but recklessly through their agent, misrepresented that this property did not — was not affected by flood or storm runoff.
>
> I find that that representation was not true. I find that the defendants made that representation in this contract without exercising reasonable care. . . . And that this did in fact have the affect (sic) of causing Mrs. Staggs to rely on it.
>
> For the purpose of this lawsuit the comparison of fault is appropriate. I find that the defendants were 60 percent at fault. I find that the plaintiff was 40 percent at fault. I find that the damages were suffered in this matter when you consider all the proof, including the photographs, the appraisals and the testimony of the plaintiff was in the amount of $25,000.
>
> I find that because of the fault of Mrs. Staggs and her 40 percent of the fault that that judgment must be reduced to $15,000."

Defendants essentially presented three issues for review: (1) how should the principles of comparative fault be applied to negligent misrepresentation; (2) whether the evidence preponderates against the judge's finding of negligent misrepresentation; and (3) whether the evidence preponderates against the amount of damages found to be suffered by Plaintiff.

The trial judge found that Defendants negligently represented in the contract that the property was not affected by flood or storm runoff and that this representation was false. Tennessee recognizes the tort of negligent misrepresentation, *Tartera*, 224 Tenn. 262, 453 S.W.2d 780 at 784, the law of which was set out in the American law Institute, Restatement of Torts (Second), §552, Tentative Draft Number 11, as quoted by the supreme court:

> (1) One who, in the course of his business, profession or employment, or a transaction in which he has a pecuniary interest, supplies false information for the guidance of others in their business transactions, is subject to liability for pecuniary loss caused to them by their justifiable reliance upon such information, if he fails to exercise reasonable care or competence in obtaining or communicating the information.
>
> (2) The liability stated in subsection (1) is limited to loss suffered
>
> (a) By the person or one of the persons for whose benefit and guidance he knows the information to be intended; and
>
> (b) Through reliance upon it in a transaction in which it is intended to influence his conduct.

Id.; *See also*, *Hunt v. Walker*, 483 S.W.2d 732, 735 (Tenn. Ct. App. 1971). Thus, to prevail, the plaintiff must establish that "(1) the defendant supplied information to the plaintiff; (2) the information was false; (3) the defendant did not exercise reasonable care in obtaining or communicating the information; and (4) the plaintiff justifiably relied on the information." *Atkins v. Kirkpatrick*, 823

S.W.2d 547, 552 (Tenn. Ct. App. 1991). Further, Defendants, as principal, are liable for the negligent misrepresentations of their agent. *Haynes v. Cumberland Builders, Inc.*, 546 S.W.2d 228, 232 (Tenn. Ct. App. 1976).

Even though Defendants did not actually read or sign the contract themselves, they are responsible for the actions and representation of their agent, who was authorized to review and sign the contract on their behalf. The court made a finding that, at the time the contract was signed by Defendants' agent, it represented that the property was not affected by flood or storm runoff. The court also weighed the credibility of the witnesses and, based on testimony at trial, determined that Defendants were well aware of the flooding problems and the extent thereof at the time the contract was signed by their agent. We find the testimony in the record more than sufficient to support these findings.

"Before a seller makes a representation, he is required to exercise reasonable care to make sure that it is correct." *Akbari v. Horn*, 641 S.W.2d 506, 508 (Tenn. Ct. App. 1982). The statement regarding flooding and storm runoff was patently false. Defendants' agent had an obligation to use reasonable care in determining that all representations made in the contract were true and correct. Such care was not used, and Defendants, as the principal, are now responsible for the negligence of their agent.

Defendants also argue that there was no reasonable reliance on the information supplied in the contract since Plaintiff was free to, and did, perform her own inspection of the building and property. However, as the flooding problem only occurred during periods of very heavy or prolonged rain, it was not readily discoverable by visual inspection. The flood zone was no different than that of the surrounding houses, and the inspection revealed no telltale water damage to the house. Although the appraiser recommended a survey due to the low lying nature of the property, the statement in the contract that there was no flooding or storm runoff diminished the necessity for such survey, and the appraisal was accepted by the bank without question. Plaintiff also testified that she relied on the representation made in the contract that the property was not affected by flooding or storm runoff, and the court accepted her testimony as credible. The facts, as found by the court, support the court's determination that Plaintiff reasonably relied on the representations made by Defendants, and this evidence certainly does not preponderate against the finding of negligent misrepresentation.

Defendants/Appellants argued that Tennessee law does not provide for applying comparative fault to negligent misrepresentation cases since, in these cases, Plaintiff must show that she justifiably relied on the misrepresentation, and if Plaintiff was negligent in performing reasonable inspections and inquiries, it cannot be said that she justifiably relied on the representations of Defendant. We find this argument unsound.

The doctrine of comparative fault in Tennessee is applied to negligence cases, and negligent misrepresentation is an action "in tort determined by the general principles of the law of negligence." *Tartera v. Palumbo*, 224 Tenn. 262, 453 S.W.2d 780, 784 (Tenn. 1970). "If the plaintiff meets the burden of establishing the defendant's duty in a particular case, as well as the other elements of the negligence claim, the trier or fact must apply the [49 percent comparative fault principles of *McIntyre v. Balentine* (See Chapter 7, Defenses)].

It is axiomatic that a plaintiff could commit negligence which might have contributed to the amount of damage suffered, but still have justifiably relied on the defendants' representations. Justifiable reliance is one of the elements that must be established to the satisfaction of the trial judge by a preponderance of the evidence before the tort of negligent misrepresentation can be established by a plaintiff. Such a finding is not inconsistent with comparative fault on the part of the plaintiff. The trial judge found just such a situation here, and the evidence does not preponderate against that finding. We further find that the judge correctly applied Tennessee's comparative fault law to these facts and properly reduced the award of damages by the amount of fault attributable to Plaintiff.

With regard to damages, there was very little evidence introduced other than Plaintiff's own testimony. She testified, pursuant to Rule 701 of the Tennessee Rules of Evidence, that the value of the property as a result of the flooding was between $32,000.00 and $35,000.00 and asked the court for a judgment of $38,500.00 representing the difference between what she believed she could sell the property for and the $71,000.00 she paid. The judge also viewed the very telling pictures, which showed the house completely surrounded by water only inches away from actually entering the house, and heard the testimony of several real estate agents who articulated their belief that the property would be extremely difficult sell.

The plaintiffs have a right to recover for all losses proximately caused by [defendant's] tortious conduct. The evidence does not preponderate against the finding of damages in the amount of the $25,000.00.

Based on the foregoing findings, we affirm the trial court's Ruling in its entirety.

NOTES AND PROBLEMS

1. ***Negligent Misrepresentation Elements.*** While both fraud and negligent misrepresentation require a false representation there are significant other differences, one of which was alluded to by the court above. Fraud requires knowledge of the falsity, or at least recklessness regarding truth. Negligent misrepresentation only requires the defendant to be careless regarding the truthfulness of the information shared. This tort is also narrower in that it is only to be applied in situations where the defendant provides the information in the course of her business or a transaction in which the defendant has a pecuniary interest. Technically one can by liable for fraud for influencing the plaintiff to enter into a transaction with a third party even if the defendant had no interest in the transaction. In this way, this tort can be viewed as somewhat narrow in application. Further, the defendant in a negligent misrepresentation

case should only be liable toward someone whom the defendant intended to influence in providing the representation. The full meaning of this will be discussed in the next section under Duty Revisited. Finally, many courts hold that a plaintiff in a negligent misrepresentation case may only recover for pecuniary harm, as opposed to lost profits from the transaction. In other words, expenses incurred or sums lost out of pocket might be proper recoveries in a negligent misrepresentation case. In *Staggs*, what evidence supported the finding in favor of plaintiff on each of these elements?

2. ***Silence as Negligent Misrepresentation?*** Many courts have been reluctant to apply the tort of negligent misrepresentation to instances of silence — in effect, often holding that there is no duty to affirmatively disclose information under this theory. Jurisdictions are fairly mixed on this issue, with some courts holding that silence can never give rise to a negligent misrepresentation claim (*see* Eberts v. Goderstad, 569 F.3d 757 (7th Cir. 2009) (following the logic that the Restatement only refers to "supply[ing] false information" rather than to silence) and others reaching contrary holdings (*See* In re Agrobiotech, Inc., 291 F. Supp. 2d 1186 (D. Nev. 2003).

3. ***Justifiable Reliance and Comparative Fault.*** The court in *Staggs* found that there was no inconsistency between the finding that plaintiff had justifiably relied on the misrepresentations yet had committed comparative fault in relying upon the misrepresentations. To the extent that a court applies a "reasonable person" standard to the justifiable reliance issue (as was discussed earlier under the Fraud section) do you see any inconsistency here? On the other hand, if courts essentially apply a gross negligence standard (i.e., did the plaintiff ignore obvious red flags?) to the justifiable reliance issue and an ordinary care standard to comparative fault, there would be no such potential inconsistency. This is an area of the law that remains undeveloped. With regard to express disclaimers of reliance, as we saw in fraud cases in the prior section, courts have been willing under the proper circumstances to allow an express provision in the parties' contract disclaiming reliance on any representations to negate a cause of action for negligent misrepresentation.

B. Duty Revisited

Negligent misrepresentation is a very particular subspecies of a negligence cause of action, applicable in only particular instances and providing relief only for pecuniary losses. As with other negligence causes of action, however, a significant issue in many negligent misrepresentation claims is the fundamental question of duty. Clearly when a professional represents a client there will be no serious question about any duty of care. In fact, when the client is hurt by bad advice or "representations," courts will often just treat it as a "malpractice" claim. But what about someone who has not hired the professional but foreseeably relies upon representations carelessly made by the professional? Does the professional owe a duty of care regarding her representations toward this non-client? Courts around the country have taken, and continue to take, three different views regarding this duty issue. The *Bily* case below represents the majority view and offers a very comprehensive discussion of the matter. As you read the court's description of the three competing schools of thought on the issue of duty, which one do you prefer?

BILY v. ARTHUR YOUNG & CO.

834 P.2d 745 (Cal. 1992)

LUCAS, C.J.

[Investors in Osborne Computer Corporation — a computer manufacturing company — brought this litigation against Arthur Young. The business was founded in 1980 by the entrepreneur Adam Osborne and put on the market the first portable personal computer.

By fall of 1982, sales of the company's Osborne I computer were quite good and the firm began planning for initial public offering in 1982. To assist with this IPO, the company hired Arthur Young to prepare audit reports for the recent two years. Arthur Young issued an unqualified opinion on February 11, 1983. However, at the suggestion of underwriters, the offering was postponed.

In the meantime, in order to obtain needed financing, the company issued warrants to investors (individuals and venture capitals) in exchange for direct loans. The warrants entitled their holders to purchase blocks of the company's stock at favorable prices.

As the warrant transactions closed on April 8, 1983, the company's performance began to deteriorate. Sales declined sharply, promotion of the new "Executive" computer model turned out to be a disaster. Public offering never materialized. The company had to file for bankruptcy on September 13, 1983. Plaintiffs, who ultimately lost their investments, claimed that in their investments they relied heavily on Arthur Young's unqualified audit opinion.

Plaintiffs' principal expert witness found more than 40 deficiencies in Arthur Young's performance amounting in his view, to gross professional negligence. It was discovered that Arthur Young was aware of material weaknesses in the company's controls, yet failed to disclose them as a qualification to its audit report or report to management.]

The case was tried to a jury for 13 weeks. At the close of the evidence and arguments, the jury received instructions and special verdict questions including three theories of recovery: fraud, negligent misrepresentation, and professional negligence. The fraud instructions required proof of an intentional misrepresentation made by defendant "with intent to defraud the plaintiff or a particular class of persons to which plaintiff belonged." Similarly, the negligent misrepresentation instructions required a negligent misrepresentation made "with the intent to induce plaintiff or a particular class of persons to which plaintiff belongs to rely on it."

The negligence instructions stated in part that an independent auditor has a duty to have the degree of skill and learning possessed by reputable certified public accountants in the same community and to use "reasonable diligence and its best judgment in the exercise of its professional skill."

With respect to liability to third parties, negligence instructions were to the effect that: "An accountant owes a further duty of care to those third parties who reasonably and foreseeably rely on an audited financial statement prepared by the accountant. A failure to fulfill any such duty is negligence."

We granted review to consider whether and to what extent an accountant's duty of care in the preparation of an independent audit of a client's financial statements extends to persons other than the client.

Since Chief Judge Cardozo's seminal opinion in *Ultramares Corp. v. Touche*, 174 N.E. 441 (N.Y. 1931) (*Ultramares*), the issue before us has been frequently considered and debated by courts and commentators. Different schools of thought have emerged. At the center of the controversy are difficult questions concerning the role of the accounting profession in performing audits, the conceivably limitless scope of an accountant's liability to nonclients who may come to read and rely on audit reports, and the effect of tort liability rules on the availability, cost, and reliability of those reports.

We will analyze these questions by discussing the purpose and effect of audits and audit reports, the approaches taken by courts and commentators, and the basic principles of tort liability announced in our prior cases. We conclude that an auditor owes no general duty of care regarding the conduct of an audit to persons other than the client. An auditor may, however, be held liable for negligent misrepresentations in an audit report to those persons who act in reliance upon those misrepresentations in a transaction which the auditor intended to influence, in accordance with the rule of §552 of the Restatement (Second) of Torts, as adopted and discussed below. Finally, an auditor may also be held liable to reasonably foreseeable third persons for intentional fraud in the preparation and dissemination of an audit report.

THE AUDIT FUNCTION IN PUBLIC ACCOUNTING

Although certified public accountants (CPA's) perform a variety of services for their clients, their primary function, which is the one that most frequently generates lawsuits against them by third persons, is financial auditing. "In an audit engagement, an accountant reviews financial statements prepared by a client and issues an opinion stating whether such statements fairly represent the financial status of the audited entity." Siliciano, *supra*, 86 Mich. L. Rev. at p. 1931.

In a typical audit, a CPA firm may verify the existence of tangible assets, observe business activities, and confirm account balances and mathematical computations. It might also examine sample transactions or records to ascertain the accuracy of the client company's financial and accounting systems.

For practical reasons of time and cost, an audit rarely, if ever, examines every accounting transaction in the records of a business. The planning and execution of an audit therefore require a high degree of professional skill and judgment.

The end product of an audit is the audit report or opinion. The report is generally expressed in a letter addressed to the client. The body of the report refers to the specific client-prepared financial statements which are attached. In the case of the so-called "unqualified report" (of which Arthur Young's report on the company's 1982 financial statements is an example), two paragraphs are relatively standard.

In a scope paragraph, the CPA firm asserts that it has examined the accompanying financial statements in accordance with GAAS. GAAS are promulgated by the American Institute of Certified Public Accountants (AICPA), a national professional organization of CPA's, whose membership is open to persons holding certified public accountant certificates issued by state boards of accountancy.

In an opinion paragraph, the audit report generally states the CPA firm's opinion that the audited financial statements, taken as a whole, are in conformity with GAAP and present fairly in all material respects the financial position, results of operations, and changes in financial position of the client in the relevant periods.

APPROACHES TO THE PROBLEM OF AUDITOR LIABILITY TO THIRD PERSONS

The complex nature of the audit function and its economic implications has resulted in different approaches to the question whether CPA auditors should be subjected to liability to third parties who read and rely on audit reports. Although three schools of thought are commonly recognized, there are some variations within each school and recent case law suggests a possible trend toward merger of two of the three approaches.

A substantial number of jurisdictions follow the lead of Chief Judge Cardozo's 1931 opinion for the New York Court of Appeals in *Ultramares, supra*, 174 N.E. 441, by denying recovery to third parties for auditor negligence in the absence of a third party relationship to the auditor that is "akin to privity." In contrast, a handful of jurisdictions, spurred by law review commentary, have recently allowed recovery based on auditor negligence to third parties whose reliance on the audit report was "foreseeable."

Most jurisdictions, supported by the weight of commentary and the modern English common law decisions cited by the parties, have steered a middle course based in varying degrees on Restatement Second of Torts §552, which generally imposes liability on suppliers of commercial information to third persons who are intended beneficiaries of the information. Finally, the federal securities laws have also dealt with the problem by imposing auditor liability for negligence-related conduct only in connection with misstatements in publicly filed and distributed offering documents.

A. Privity of Relationship

In *Ultramares*, plaintiff made three unsecured loans totalling $165,000 to a company that went bankrupt. Plaintiff sued the company's auditors, claiming reliance on their audit opinion that the company's balance sheet "present[ed] a true and correct view of the financial condition of [the company]." Although the balance sheet showed a net worth of $1 million, the company was actually insolvent. The company's management attempted to mask its financial condition; the auditors failed to follow paper trails to "off-the-books" transactions that, if properly analyzed, would have revealed the company's impecunious situation.

The jury, precluded by the trial judge from considering a fraud cause of action, returned a verdict in plaintiff's favor based on the auditor's negligence in conducting the audit. The New York Court of Appeals, speaking through Chief Judge Cardozo, reinstated the fraud cause of action but set aside the negligence verdict.

With respect to the negligence claim, the court found the auditor owed no duty to the third party creditor for an "erroneous opinion." In an often quoted passage, it observed: "If liability for negligence exists, a thoughtless slip or blunder, the failure to detect a theft or forgery beneath the cover of deceptive entries, may expose accountants to a liability in an indeterminate amount for an indeterminate time to an indeterminate class. The hazards of a business conducted on these terms are so extreme as to enkindle doubt whether a flaw may not exist in the implication of a duty that exposes to these consequences."

Although acknowledging the demise of privity of contract as a limitation on tort liability in the context of personal injury and property damage, the court distinguished between liability arising from a "physical force" and "the circulation of a thought or the release of the explosive power resident in words."

In summarizing its holding, the court emphasized that it was not releasing auditors from liability to third parties for fraud but merely for "honest blunder." It questioned "whether the average business man receiving a certificate without paying for it, and receiving it as one of a multitude of possible investors, would look for anything more."

From the cases cited by the parties, it appears at least nine states purport to follow privity or near privity rules restricting the liability of auditors to parties with whom they have a contractual or similar relationship. In five states, this result has been reached by decisions of their highest courts. In four other states, the rule has been enacted by statute. Federal court decisions have held that the rule represents the law of three additional states whose highest courts have not expressly considered the question.

B. Foreseeability

Arguing that accountants should be subject to liability to third persons on the same basis as other tortfeasors, Justice Howard Wiener advocated rejection of the rule of *Ultramares* in a 1983 law review article. (Wiener, *Common Law Liability of the Certified Public Accountant for Negligent Misrepresentation* (1983) 20 San Diego L. Rev. 233 [hereafter Wiener].) In its place, he proposed a rule based on foreseeability of injury to third persons. Criticizing what he called the "anachronistic protection" given to accountants by the traditional rules limiting third person liability, he concluded: "Accountant liability based on foreseeable injury would serve the dual functions of compensation for injury and deterrence of negligent conduct. Moreover, it is a just and rational judicial policy that the same criteria govern the imposition of negligence liability, regardless of the context in which it arises. The accountant, the investor, and the general public will in the long run benefit when the liability of the certified public accountant for negligent misrepresentation is measured by the foreseeability standard." Under the rule proposed by Justice Wiener, "[f]oreseeability of the risk would be a question of fact for the jury to be disturbed on appeal only where there is insufficient evidence to support the finding."

[The supreme courts in New Jersey, Wisconsin, Mississippi, and an intermediate court of appeals in California have since adopted the foreseeability approach first advocated by Justice Wiener. Nevertheless, in] the nearly 10 years since it was formally proposed, the foreseeability approach has not attracted a substantial following. And at least four state supreme courts have explicitly rejected the foreseeability approach in favor of the Restatement's "intended beneficiary" approach since the New Jersey court's decision in *Rosenblum*.

The foreseeability approach has also encountered substantial criticism from commentators, who have questioned, among other matters, its failure to consider seriously the problem of indeterminate liability and its prediction of a significant deterrent effect that will improve the quality of audit reporting. Other commentators have disagreed. The body of scholarly and practical literature is substantial.

C. The Restatement: Intent to Benefit Third Persons

Restatement (Second) of Torts §552 covers "Information Negligently Supplied for the Guidance of Others." It states a general principle that one who negligently supplies false information "for the guidance of others in their business transactions" is liable for economic loss suffered by the recipients in justifiable reliance on the information. But the liability created by the general principle is expressly limited to loss suffered: "(a) [B]y the person or one of a limited group of persons for whose benefit and guidance he intends to supply the information or knows that the recipient intends to supply it; and (b) through reliance upon it in a transaction that he intends the information to influence or knows that the recipient so intends or in a substantially similar transaction." To paraphrase, a supplier of information is liable for negligence to a third party only if he or she intends to supply the information for the benefit of one or more third parties in a specific transaction or type of transaction identified to the supplier.

Comment (h) observes that the liability of a negligent supplier of information is appropriately more narrowly restricted than that of an intentionally fraudulent supplier. It also notes that a commercial supplier of information has a legitimate concern as to the nature and scope of the client's transactions that may expand the supplier's exposure liability. As the comment states: "In many situations the identity of the person for whose guidance the information is supplied is of no moment to the person who supplies it, although the number and character of the persons to be reached and influenced, and the nature and extent of the transaction for which guidance is furnished may be vitally important. *This is true because the risk of liability to which the supplier subjects himself by undertaking to give the information, while it may not be affected by the identity of the person for whose guidance the information is given, is vitally affected by the number and character of the persons, and particularly the nature and the extent of the proposed transaction.*" (Italics added.)

To offer a simple illustration of comment (h), an auditor engaged to perform an audit and render a report to a third person whom the auditor knows is considering a $10 million investment in the client's business is on notice of a specific potential liability. It may then act to encounter, limit or avoid the risk. In contrast, an auditor who is simply asked for a generic audit and report to the client has no comparable notice.

Although the parties debate precisely how many states follow the Restatement rule, a review of the cases reveals the rule has somewhat more support than the privity of relationship rule and much more support than the foreseeability rule. At least 17 state and federal decisions have endorsed the rule in this and related contexts. Whatever the exact number of states that have endorsed it, the Restatement rule has been for many, if not most, courts a satisfactory compromise between their discomfort with the traditional privity approach and the "specter of unlimited liability."

In attempting to ascertain the presence of an intent to benefit third parties from the facts of particular audit engagements and communications with auditors, the Restatement rule inevitably results in some degree of uncertainty. Dean William L. Prosser, the Reporter for the Restatement, reflected on the difficulty of formulating a comprehensive rule in this area:

> The problem is to find language which will eliminate liability to the very large class of persons whom almost any negligently given information may foreseeably reach and influence, and limit the liability, not to a particular plaintiff defined in advance, but to the comparatively small group whom the defendant expects and intends to influence. Neither the Reporter, nor, it is believed, the Advisers nor the Council, is entirely satisfied with the language of Subsection (2); and if anyone can do better, it will be most welcome.

Rest. 2d Torts, Tent. Draft No. 11 (Apr. 15, 1965) §552.

ANALYSIS OF AUDITOR'S LIABILITY TO THIRD PERSONS FOR AUDIT OPINIONS

The threshold element of a cause of action for negligence is the existence of a duty to use due care toward an interest of another that enjoys legal protection against unintentional invasion. Whether this essential prerequisite to a negligence cause of action has been satisfied in a particular case is a question of law to be resolved by the court.

A judicial conclusion that a duty is present or absent is merely "a shorthand statement . . . rather than an aid to analysis. . . . [D]uty, is not sacrosanct in itself, but only an expression of the sum total of those considerations of policy which lead the law to say that the particular plaintiff is entitled to protection." *Dillon v. Legg*, 441 P.2d 912 (Cal. 1968).

We have employed a checklist of factors to consider in assessing legal duty in the absence of privity of contract between a plaintiff and a defendant:

> The determination whether in a specific case the defendant will be held liable to a third person not in privity is a matter of policy and involves the balancing of various factors, among which are the extent to which the transaction was intended to affect the plaintiff, the foreseeability of harm to him, the degree of certainty that the plaintiff suffered injury, the closeness of the connection between the defendant's conduct and the injury suffered, the moral blame attached to the defendant's conduct, and the policy of preventing future harm.

Biakanja v. Irving, 320 P.2d 16 (Cal. 1958).

Viewing the problem before us in light of the factors set forth above, we decline to permit all merely foreseeable third party users of audit reports to sue the auditor on a theory of professional negligence. Our holding is premised on three central concerns: (1) Given the secondary "watchdog" role of the auditor, the complexity of the professional opinions rendered in audit reports, and the difficult and potentially tenuous causal relationships between audit reports and economic losses from investment and credit decisions, the auditor exposed to negligence claims from all foreseeable third parties faces potential liability far out of proportion to its fault; (2) the generally more sophisticated class of plaintiffs in auditor liability cases (e.g., business lenders and investors) permits the effective use of contract rather than tort liability to control and adjust the relevant risks through "private ordering"; and (3) the asserted advantages of more accurate auditing and more efficient loss spreading relied upon by those who advocate a pure foreseeability approach are unlikely to occur; indeed, dislocations of resources, including increased expense and decreased availability of auditing services in some sectors of the economy, are more probable consequences of expanded liability.

In a broad sense, economic injury to lenders, investors, and others who may read and rely on audit reports is certainly "foreseeable." Foreseeability of injury, however, is but one factor to be considered in the imposition of negligence liability. Even when foreseeability was present, we have on several recent occasions declined to allow recovery on a negligence theory when damage awards threatened to impose liability out of proportion to fault or to promote virtually unlimited responsibility for intangible injury.

In placing explicit limits on recovery for negligent infliction of emotional distress by accident bystanders, we commented: "'[F]oreseeability' 'is endless because [it], like light, travels indefinitely in a vacuum.' [It] proves too much. . . . Although it may set tolerable limits for most types of physical harm, it provides virtually no limit on liability for non-physical harm.' . . . It is apparent that reliance on foreseeability of injury alone in finding a duty, and thus a right to recover, is not adequate when the damages sought are for an intangible injury. In order to avoid limitless liability out of all proportion to the degree of a defendant's negligence, and against which it is impossible to insure without imposing unacceptable costs on those among whom the risk is spread, the right to recover for negligently caused emotional distress must be limited." *Thing v. La Chusa*, 71 P.2d 814 (Cal. 1989).

Emphasizing the important role of policy factors in determining negligence, we observed that "there are clear judicial days on which a court can foresee forever and thus determine liability but none on which that foresight alone provides a socially and judicially acceptable limit on recovery of damages for [an] injury." *Id.* In line with our recent decisions, we will not treat the mere presence of a foreseeable risk of injury to third persons as sufficient, standing alone, to impose liability for negligent conduct.

In view of the factors discussed above, judicial endorsement of third party negligence suits against auditors limited only by the concept of foreseeability raises the spectre of multibillion-dollar professional liability that is distinctly out of proportion to: (1) the fault of the auditor (which is necessarily secondary and may be based on complex differences of professional opinion); and (2) the connection between the auditor's conduct and the third party's injury (which will often be attenuated by unrelated business factors that underlie investment and credit decisions).

As a matter of economic and social policy, third parties should be encouraged to rely on their own prudence, diligence, and contracting power, as well as other informational tools. This kind of self-reliance promotes sound investment and credit practices and discourages the careless use of monetary resources. If, instead, third parties are simply permitted to recover from the auditor for mistakes in the client's financial statements, the auditor becomes, in effect, an insurer of not only the financial statements, but of bad loans and investments in general.

For the reasons stated above, we hold that an auditor's liability for general negligence in the conduct of an audit of its client financial statements is confined to the client, i.e., the person who contracts for or engages the audit services. Other persons may not recover on a pure negligence theory.

One difficulty in considering the problem before us is that neither the courts (ourselves included), the commentators, nor the authors of the Restatement Second of Torts have made clear or careful distinctions between the tort of negligence and the separate tort of negligent misrepresentation. The distinction is important not only because of the different statutory bases of the two torts, but also because it has practical implications for the trial of cases in complex areas such as the one before us.

Negligent misrepresentation is a separate and distinct tort, a species of the tort of deceit. "Where the defendant makes false statements, honestly believing that they are true, but without reasonable ground for such belief, he may be liable for negligent misrepresentation, a form of deceit." 5 Witkin, Summary of Cal. Law (9th ed. 1988) Torts, §720 at p. 819.

Under certain circumstances, expressions of professional opinion are treated as representations of fact. When a statement, although in the form of an opinion, is "not a casual expression of belief" but "a deliberate affirmation of the matters stated," it may be regarded as a positive assertion of fact. Moreover, when a party possesses or holds itself out as possessing superior knowledge or special information or expertise regarding the subject matter and a plaintiff is so situated that it may reasonably rely on such supposed knowledge, information, or expertise, the defendant's representation may be treated as one of material fact. There is no dispute that Arthur Young's statements in audit opinions fall within these principles.

But the person or "class of persons entitled to rely upon the representations is restricted to those to whom or for whom the misrepresentations were made. Even though the defendant should have anticipated that the misinformation might reach others, he is not liable to them." 5 Witkin, Summary of Cal. Law, *supra*, Torts, §721 at p. 820.

Of the approaches we have reviewed, §552 of the Restatement (Second) of Torts subdivision (b) is most consistent with the elements and policy foundations of the tort of negligent misrepresentation. The rule expressed there attempts to define a narrow and circumscribed class of persons to whom or for whom representations are made. In this way, it recognizes commercial realities by avoiding both unlimited and uncertain liability for economic losses in cases of professional mistake and exoneration of the auditor in situations where it clearly intended to undertake the responsibility of influencing particular business transactions involving third persons. The Restatement rule thus appears to be a sensible and moderate approach to the potential consequences of imposing unlimited negligence liability which we have identified.

We recognize the rule expressed in the Restatement Second of Torts has been criticized in some quarters as vague and potentially arbitrary. In his article advocating a foreseeability rule, Justice Wiener generally criticized the Restatement rule as resting "solely on chance considerations" and "fortuitousness" (e.g., the "state of the mind of the accountant" and the scope of his engagement) having, in his view, nothing to do with increasing the flow of accurate information.

We respectfully disagree. In seeking to identify a specific class of persons and a transaction that the supplier of information "intends the information to influence," the authors of the Restatement Second of Torts have applied basic factors of tort liability recognized in this state and elsewhere. By confining what might otherwise be unlimited liability to those persons whom the engagement is designed to benefit, the Restatement rule requires that the supplier of information receive notice of potential third party claims, thereby allowing it to ascertain the potential scope of its liability and make rational decisions regarding the undertaking. The receipt of such notice justifies imposition of auditor liability for conduct that is merely negligent.

The Restatement Second of Torts approach is also the only one that achieves consistency in the law of negligent misrepresentation. Accountants are not unique in their position as suppliers of information and evaluations for the use and benefit of others. Other professionals, including attorneys, architects, engineers, title insurers and abstractors, and others also perform that function. And, like auditors, these professionals may also face suits by third persons claiming reliance on information and opinions generated in a professional capacity.

By allowing recovery for negligent misrepresentation (as opposed to mere negligence), we emphasize the indispensability of justifiable reliance on the statements contained in the report. As the jury instructions in this case illustrate, a general negligence charge directs attention to defendant's level of care and compliance with professional standards established by expert testimony, as opposed to plaintiff's reliance on a materially false statement made by defendant. The reliance element in such an instruction is only implicit–it must be argued and considered by the jury as part of its evaluation of the causal relationship between defendant's conduct and plaintiff's injury. In contrast, an instruction based on the elements of negligent misrepresentation necessarily and properly focuses the jury's attention on the truth or falsity of the audit report's representations and plaintiff's actual and justifiable reliance on them. Because the audit report, not the audit itself, is the foundation of the third person's claim, negligent misrepresentation more precisely captures the gravamen of the cause of action and more clearly conveys the elements essential to a recovery.

Based on our decision, the California standard jury instructions concerning negligent misrepresentation should be amended in future auditor liability cases to permit the jury to determine whether plaintiff belongs to the class of persons to whom or for whom the representations in the audit report were made.

DISPOSITION

This case was tried on the assumption that the general negligence rule and foreseeability approach represented California law. The jury was instructed in accordance with that approach. For the reasons stated above, we have rejected [those rules] in favor of a negligent misrepresentation rule substantially in accord with §552 of the Restatement (Second) of Torts. As a result, plaintiffs' judgment based on the general negligence rule must be set aside. Because plaintiffs were not clients of Arthur Young, they were not entitled to recover on a general negligence theory.

The jury also rejected plaintiffs' causes of action for negligent misrepresentation and intentional fraud. Although it was not instructed in accordance with the rules we have announced here, the jury was told Arthur Young could be held liable for misrepresentation to "plaintiff or a particular class of persons to which plaintiff belonged." If anything, these general instructions are more favorable to plaintiffs than the ones required by our decision, which more narrowly and specifically defines the "class of persons" entitled to recover.

NOTES AND PROBLEMS

1. *Negligence and Negligent Misrepresentation.* The court spends some time separately considering the negligence (i.e., malpractice) claim from the negligent misrepresentation claim, holding that the former can only apply to clients. With respect to the duty regarding negligent misrepresentation the court also applies a limitation, but expands the scope of the duty potentially beyond one's clients.

2. *Three Competing Views.* The court separately describes and assesses three competing views regarding to whom a duty of care would be owed for a negligent misrepresentation cause of action: (1) the near strict-privity rule from *Ultramares* limiting the duty to those in privity of contract with the professional supplier of information; (2) a broader, more flexible rule of foreseeability, holding that the professional owes a duty of care toward anyone that might foreseeably receive (even indirectly) the representations and rely upon them; and (3) the intermediate, and majority view, reflected by the Restatement (Second) that duty is only owed toward those that the defendant knows and intends to receive and rely upon it. What are the relative merits of each position on this issue? Do you agree with the court that the intermediate position makes the most sense? Which one is the most concrete and easy for courts to apply?

3. *Problems.* How would courts utilizing the three different duty tests view the liability of the potential defendants below?

- **A.** Recall the hypothetical from the Fraud section regarding the builder of rocking chairs who sincerely, but incorrectly, promises a purchaser that he can build 50 chairs within a week's time and fails to deliver. Would the buyer have a good claim for negligent misrepresentation in lieu of a fraud claim?
- **B.** Dell, a farmer, seeks a business loan to help his ailing farm operation and the lender agrees, subject to the receipt of a letter from a lawyer stating that a lien search has been done and representing that there are no outstanding liens on any of Dell's equipment that will be used to secure the loan. Dell hires Juan, a lawyer, to do this task. Juan sends such a letter of

assurance to the creditor but fails to accomplish the lien search and thereby misrepresents that the equipment is unencumbered.

C. Ramses, a financial analyst, appears on the Tonight Show and tells the audience that the stock market is going to plummet and that they should buy gold. A member of the television audience watches this episode, sells all their stock and puts all of their investment money into gold. The gold market falls while the stock market increases.

"LADIES AND GENTLEMEN OF THE JURY . . ."

Iowa Civil Jury Instruction 800.1

Negligent Misrepresentation

The plaintiff must prove the following propositions:

1. The defendant on or about the [date], negligently supplied (as set forth in detail the information supplied) to plaintiff (or plaintiff as one of the limited group of person), which was false.
2. The defendant had a financial interest in supplying the information.
3. The defendant intended to supply the information for the benefit and guidance of plaintiff [or the defendant knew the person who received the information intended to supply the information for the benefit and guidance of plaintiff].
4. The defendant intended the information to influence the transaction for which the information was supplied [or a transaction substantially similar to the transaction for which the information was supplied].
5. The plaintiff acted in reliance on the truth of the information supplied and was justified in relying on the information.
6. The negligently supplied information was a proximate cause of the plaintiff's damage.
7. The amount of damage.

TORTIOUS INTERFERENCE WITH CONTRACT

Claims for tortious interference with business relationships have fairly ancient legal roots. Nevertheless, the multi-billion dollar recovery in *Pennzoil v. Texaco* did much to bring this somewhat obscure cause of action to the forefront of the business and legal communities. Regardless of the age of this legal theory and its recent ascendance in attempted application, there has been significant confusion regarding two different branches of this area of law — (a) intentional interference with existing contracts, versus (b) intentional interference with merely prospective contractual relations. Before we address that confusion head on, it is worth pausing at the famous case of *M/V Testbank* to see the court's rejection of any claim for *negligent* interference with a contract, as well as to greet (again) the *mere economic harm rule* first encountered in Chapter 6, Special Duty Rules.

A. Rejection of Negligent Interference

STATE OF LOUISIANA v. M/V TESTBANK

752 F.2d 1019 (5th Cir. 1985)

HIGGINBOTHAM, J.

We are asked to abandon physical damage to a proprietary interest as a prerequisite to recovery for economic loss in cases of unintentional maritime tort. We decline the invitation.

I

In the early evening of July 22, 1980, the M/V Sea Daniel, an inbound bulk carrier, and the M/V Testbank, an outbound container ship, collided at approximately mile forty-one of the Mississippi River Gulf outlet. At impact, a white haze enveloped the ships until carried away by prevailing winds, and containers aboard Testbank were damaged and lost overboard. The white haze proved to be hydrobromic acid and the contents of the containers which went overboard proved to be approximately twelve tons of pentachlorophenol, PCP, assertedly the largest such spill in United States history. The United States Coast Guard closed the outlet to navigation until August 10, 1980 and all fishing, shrimping, and related activity was temporarily suspended in the outlet and four hundred square miles of surrounding marsh and waterways.

Forty-one lawsuits were filed and consolidated before the same judge in the Eastern District of Louisiana. These suits presented claims of shipping interests, marina and boat rental operators, wholesale and retail seafood enterprises not actually engaged in fishing, seafood restaurants, tackle and bait shops, and recreational fishermen. They proffered an assortment of liability theories, including maritime tort, private actions pursuant to various sections of the Rivers & Harbors Appropriation Act of 1899 and rights of action under Louisiana law. Jurisdiction rested on the proposition that the collision and contamination were maritime torts and within the court's maritime jurisdiction. *See* 28 U.S.C. §1333.

Defendants moved for summary judgment as to all claims for economic loss unaccompanied by physical damage to property. The district court granted the requested summary judgment as to all such claims except those asserted by commercial oystermen, shrimpers, crabbers and fishermen who had been making a commercial use of embargoed waters. The district court found these commercial fishing interests deserving of a special protection akin to that enjoyed by seamen.

On appeal a panel of this court affirmed, concluding that claims for economic loss unaccompanied by physical damage to a proprietary interest were not recoverable in maritime tort. The panel, as did the district court, pointed to the doctrine of *Robins Dry Dock & Repair Co. v. Flint*, 275 U.S. 303 (1927), and its development in this circuit. Judge Wisdom specially concurred, agreeing that the denial of these claims was required by precedent, but urging reexamination en banc. We then took the case en banc for that purpose. After extensive additional briefs and oral argument, we are unpersuaded that we ought to drop physical damage to a proprietary interest as a prerequisite to recovery for economic loss. To the contrary, our reexamination of the history and central purpose of this pragmatic restriction on the doctrine of foreseeability heightens our commitment to it. Ultimately we conclude that without this limitation foreseeability loses much of its ability to function as a rule of law.

II

Plaintiffs first argue that the "rule" of *Robins Dry Dock* is that "a tort to the property of one which results in the negligent interference with contractual relationships of another does not state a claim," and that so defined, *Robins Dry Dock* is here inapplicable. Next and relatedly, plaintiffs urge that physical damage is not a prerequisite to recovery of economic loss where the damages suffered were foreseeable. Third, plaintiffs argue that their claims are cognizable in maritime tort because the pollution from the collision constituted a public nuisance and violated the Rivers and Harbors Appropriation Act of 1899, as well as Louisiana law.

Defendants urge the opposite: that *Robins Dry Dock* controls these cases; [and] that the physical damage limitation on foreseeability ought to be retained.

III

The meaning of *Robins Dry Dock v. Flint* is the flag all litigants here seek to capture. We turn first to that case and to its historical setting.

Robins broke no new ground but instead applied a principle, then settled both in the United States and England, which refused recovery for negligent interference with "contractual rights." Stated more broadly, the prevailing rule denied a plaintiff recovery for economic loss if that loss resulted from physical damage to property in which he had no proprietary interest. *See, e.g., Byrd v. English*, 43 S.E. 419 (Ga. 1903); *Cattle v. Stockton Waterworks Co.*, 10 Q.B. 453, 457 (C.A. 1875). *See also* James, *Limitations on Liability for Economic Loss Caused by Negligence: A Pragmatic Appraisal*, 25 Vand. L. Rev. 43, 44-46 (1972) (discussing history of the rule); Carpenter, *Interference with Contract Relations*,

41 Harv. L. Rev. 728 (1928). Professor James explains this limitation on recovery of pure economic loss: "The explanation . . . is a pragmatic one: the physical consequences of negligence usually have been limited, but the indirect economic repercussions of negligence may be far wider, indeed virtually open-ended." James, *supra*, at 45.

Robins broke no new ground but instead applied a principle, then settled both in the United States and England, which refused recovery for negligent interference with "contractual rights."

Decisions such as *Stockton* illustrate the application of this pragmatic limitation on the doctrine of foreseeability. The defendant negligently caused its pipes to leak, thereby increasing the plaintiff's cost in performing its contract to dig a tunnel. The British court, writing fifty-two years before *Robins*, denied the plaintiff's claim. The court explained that if recovery were not contained, then in cases such as *Rylands v. Fletcher*, 1 L.R. — E.X. 265 (1866), the defendant would be liable not only to the owner of the mine and its workers "but also to . . . every workman and person employed in the mine, who in consequence of its stoppage made less wages than he would otherwise have done."

In *Robins*, the time charterer of a steamship sued for profits lost when the defendant dry dock negligently damaged the vessel's propeller. The propeller had to be replaced, thus extending by two weeks the time the vessel was laid up in dry dock, and it was for the loss of use of the vessel for that period that the charterer sued. The Supreme Court denied recovery to the charterer, noting:

> no authority need be cited to show that, as a general rule, at least, a tort to the person or property of one man does not make the tortfeasor liable to another merely because the injured person was under a contract with that other unknown to the doer of the wrong. The law does not spread its protection so far.

275 U.S. at 309. Justice Holmes did not stop with this Delphic language, but with a citation to three cases added a further signal to his meaning:

> A good statement, applicable here, will be found in *Elliott Steam Tug Co., Ltd. v. The Shipping Controller*, 1 K.B. 127, 139, 140 (1922); *Byrd v. English*, 43 S.E. 419 (Ga.); *The Federal No. 2*, 21 F.2d 313 (C.C.A. 1927).

Id.

The plaintiff in *Elliott Steam Tug* was a charterer of a tug boat who lost profits when the vessel was requisitioned by the admiralty under wartime legislative powers. In applying an indemnity statute that authorized recovery, the court noted that the charterer could not have recovered at common law: "the charterer in collision cases does not recover profits, *not because the loss of profits during repairs is not the direct consequence of the wrong*, but because the common law rightly or wrongly does not recognize him as able to sue for such an injury to his mere contractual rights." *Id.* at 140. (emphasis supplied). In

Byrd v. English, recovery of lost profits was denied when a utility's electrical conduits were negligently damaged by defendant, cutting off power to plaintiff's printing plant. In *The Federal No. 2*, the third case cited by Justice Holmes, the defendant tug negligently injured plaintiff's employee while he was working on a barge. The Second Circuit denied the employer recovery from the tug for sums paid to the employee in maintenance and cure. The court (Manton, Swan and Augustus Hand) explained:

> It is too indirect to insist that this may be recovered, where there is neither the natural right nor legal relationship between the appellant and the tug, even though the alleged right of action be based upon negligence.

21 F.2d at 314.

The principle that there could be no recovery for economic loss absent physical injury to a proprietary interest was not only well established when *Robins Dry Dock* was decided, but was remarkably resilient as well. Its strength is demonstrated by the circumstance that *Robins Dry Dock* came ten years after Judge Cardozo's shattering of privity in *MacPherson v. Buick Motor Co.*, 111 N.E. 1050 (N.Y. 1916). Indeed this limit on liability stood against a sea of change in the tort law. Retention of this conspicuous bright-line rule in the face of the reforms brought by the increased influence of the school of legal realism is strong testament both to the rule's utility and to the absence of a more "conceptually pure" substitute. The push to delete the restrictions on recovery for economic loss lost its support and by the early 1940's had failed. *See* W. Prosser, *Law of Torts* §129, at 938-940 (4th ed. 1971). In sum, it is an old sword that plaintiffs have here picked up.

Plaintiffs would confine *Robins* to losses suffered for inability to perform contracts between a plaintiff and others, categorizing the tort as a species of interference with contract. When seen in the historical context described above, however, it is apparent that *Robins Dry Dock* represents more than a limit on recovery for interference with contractual rights. Apart from what it represented and certainly apart from what it became, its literal holding was not so restricted. If a time charterer's relationship to its negligently injured vessel is too remote, other claimants without even the connection of a contract are even more remote.

In a sense, every claim of economic injury rests in some measure on an interference with contract or prospective advantage. It was only in this sense that profits were lost in *Byrd v. English* when the electrical power to plaintiffs printing plant was cut off. The printing company's contractual right to receive power was interfered with, and in turn, its ability to print for its customers was impinged. That the printing company had a contract with the power company did not make more remote the relationship between its loss of profits and the tortious acts. To the contrary, the contract reduced this remoteness by defining an orbit of predictable injury smaller than if there were no contract between the power company and the printer. When the loss is economic rather than physical, that the loss caused a breach of contract or denied an expectancy is of no moment. If a plaintiff connected to the damaged chattels by contract cannot recover, others more remotely situated are foreclosed *a fortiori.* Indisputably, the *Robins Dry Dock* principle is not as easily contained as plaintiff would have it. We turn to our application of the principle, its application in other circuits, and the tort law of our Gulf states before returning to the doctrine itself.

This circuit has consistently refused to allow recovery for economic loss absent physical damage to a proprietary interest. In *Kaiser Aluminum & Chemical Corp. v. Marshland Dredging Co., Inc.*, 455 F.2d 957 (5th Cir. 1972), the plaintiff lost gas supplies when the defendant negligently broke a gas pipeline. We held that because the interference with Kaiser's business was only negligently inflicted, recovery was precluded as a matter of law. In *Dick Meyers Towing Service, Inc. v. United States,* 577 F.2d 1023 (5th Cir. 1978), we denied recovery to a tug boat operator for damages suffered when a lock on Alabama's Warrior River was closed as a result of defendant's negligence. We explained:

> The law has traditionally been reluctant to recognize claims based solely on harm to the interest in contractual relations or business expectancy. The critical factor is the character of the interest harmed and not the number of parties involved.

Id. at 1025.

In *Union Oil,* vast quantities of raw crude were released when the defendant oil company negligently caused an oil spill. The oil was carried by wind, wave, and tidal currents over large stretches of the California coast disrupting, among other things, commercial fishing operations. While conceding that ordinarily there is no recovery for economic losses unaccompanied by physical damage, the court concluded that commercial fishermen were foreseeable plaintiffs whose interests the oil company had a duty to protect when conducting drilling operations. The opinion pointed out that the fishermen's losses were foreseeable and direct consequences of the spill, that fishermen have historically enjoyed a protected position under maritime law, and suggested that economic considerations also supported permitting recovery.

Yet *Union Oil's* holding was carefully limited to commercial fishermen, plaintiffs whose economic losses were characterized as "of a particular and special nature." 501 F.2d at 570. The *Union Oil* panel expressly declined to "open the door to claims that may be asserted by . . . other[s] . . . whose economic or personal affairs were discommoded by the oil spill" and noted that the general rule denying recovery for pure economic loss had "a legitimate sphere within which to operate."

A substantial argument can be made that commercial fishermen possess a proprietary interest in fish in waters they normally harvest sufficient to allow recovery for their loss. Whether the claims of commercial fishermen ought to be analyzed in this manner or simply carved from the rule today announced, in the fashion of *Union Oil,* or allowed at all, we leave for later. That is, today's decision does not foreclose free consideration by a court panel of the claims of commercial fishermen.

In sum, the decisions of courts in other circuits convince us that *Robins Dry Dock* is both a widely used and necessary limitation on recovery for economic losses. The holdings in *Kinsman* and *Union Oil* are not to the contrary. The courts in both those cases made plain that restrictions on the concept of foreseeability ought to be imposed where recovery is sought for pure economic losses.

Jurisprudence developed in the Gulf states informs our maritime decisions. It supports the *Robins* rule. Courts applying the tort law of Texas, Georgia, Florida, Alabama, Mississippi and Louisiana have consistently denied recovery for economic losses negligently inflicted where there was no physical damage to a proprietary interest.

IV

Plaintiffs urge that the requirement of physical injury to a proprietary interest is arbitrary, unfair, and illogical, as it denies recovery for foreseeable injury caused by negligent acts. At its bottom the argument is that questions of remoteness ought to be left to the trier of fact. Ultimately the question becomes who ought to decide — judge or jury — and whether there will be a rule beyond the jacket of a given case. The plaintiffs contend that the "problem" need not be separately addressed, but instead should be handled by "traditional" principles of tort law. Putting the problem of which doctrine is the traditional one aside, their rhetorical questions are flawed in several respects.

Those who would delete the requirement of physical damage have no rule or principle to substitute. Their approach fails to recognize limits upon the adjudicating ability of courts. We do not mean just the ability to supply a judgment; prerequisite to this adjudicatory function are preexisting rules, whether the creature of courts or legislatures. Courts can decide cases without preexisting normative guidance but the result becomes less judicial and more the product of a managerial, legislative or negotiated function.

Review of the foreseeable consequences of the collision of the Sea Daniel and Testbank demonstrates the wave upon wave of successive economic consequences and the managerial role plaintiffs would have us assume. The vessel delayed in St. Louis may be unable to fulfill its obligation to haul from Memphis, to the injury of the shipper, to the injury of the buyers, to the injury of their customers. Plaintiffs concede, as do all who attack the requirement of physical damage, that a line would need to be drawn — somewhere on the other side, each plaintiff would say in turn, of its recovery. Plaintiffs advocate not only that the lines be drawn elsewhere but also that they be drawn on an ad hoc and discrete basis. The result would be that no determinable measure of the limit of foreseeability would precede the decision on liability. We are told that when the claim is too remote, or too tenuous, recovery will be denied. Presumably then, as among all plaintiffs suffering foreseeable economic loss, recovery will turn on a judge or jury's decision. There will be no rationale for the differing results save the "judgment" of the trier of fact. Concededly, it can "decide" all the claims presented, and with comparative if not absolute ease. The point is not that such a process cannot be administered but rather that its judgments would be much less the products of a determinable rule of law. In this important sense, the resulting decisions would be judicial products only in their draw upon judicial resources.

The bright line rule of damage to a proprietary interest, as most, has the virtue of predictability with the vice of creating results in cases at its edge that are said to be "unjust" or "unfair." Plaintiffs point to seemingly perverse results, where claims the rule allows and those it disallows are juxtaposed — such as vessels striking a dock, causing minor but recoverable damage, then lurching athwart a channel causing great but unrecoverable economic loss. The answer is that when lines are drawn sufficiently sharp in their definitional edges to be reasonable and predictable, such differing results are the inevitable result — indeed, decisions are the desired product. But there is more. The line drawing sought by plaintiffs is no less arbitrary because the line drawing appears only in the outcome — as one claimant is found too remote and another is allowed to recover. The true difference is that plaintiffs' approach would mask the results. The present rule would be more candid, and in addition, by making results more predictable, serves a normative function. It operates as a rule of law and allows a court to adjudicate rather than manage.

VII

In conclusion, having reexamined the history and central purpose of the doctrine of *Robins Dry Dock* as developed in this circuit, we remain committed to its teaching. Denying recovery for pure economic losses is a pragmatic limitation on the doctrine of foreseeability, a limitation we find to be both workable and useful.

Accordingly, the decision of the district court granting summary judgment to defendants on all claims for economic losses unaccompanied by physical damage to property is AFFIRMED.

DISSENT

Wisdom, J., with whom Rubin, J. Politz, J., Tate, J. and Johnson, J., join dissenting

Robins is the Tar Baby of tort law in this circuit. And the brier-patch is far away. This Court's application of *Robins* is out of step with contemporary tort doctrine, works substantial injustice on innocent victims, and is unsupported by the considerations that justified the Supreme Court's 1927 decision.

Robins was a tort case grounded on a contract. Whatever the justification for the original holding, this Court's requirement of physical injury as a condition to recovery is an unwarranted step backwards in torts jurisprudence. The resulting bar for claims of economic loss unaccompanied by any physical damage conflicts with conventional tort principles of foreseeability and proximate cause. I would analyze the plaintiffs' claims under these principles, using the "particular damage" requirement of public nuisance law as an additional means of limiting claims. Although this approach requires a case-by-case analysis, it comports with the fundamental idea of fairness that innocent plaintiffs should receive compensation and negligent defendants should bear the cost of their tortious acts. Such a result is worth the additional costs of adjudicating these claims, and this rule of liability appears to be more economically efficient. Finally, this result would relieve courts of the necessity of manufacturing exceptions totally inconsistent with the expanded *Robins* rule of requiring physical injury as a prerequisite to recovery.

ALTERNATE STATEMENT OF THE CASE

A. Factual Background

On July 22, 1980, at 8:44 p.m., the inbound bulk carrier M/V Sea Daniel collided with the outbound container ship M/V Testbank at Mile 41 of the Mississippi River Gulf Outlet Channel. This channel is a 66-mile, man-made shortcut between New Orleans and the Gulf of Mexico. Immediately following the collision, a cloud of hydrobromic acid mist enveloped the ships from ruptured containers onboard the Testbank. The prevailing winds carried the acid cloud to Shell Beach, Louisiana, a little town downwind of the collision. The collision damaged several containers on the Testbank, which were then lost overboard. One of these containers held about twelve tons of pentachlorophenol (PCP) in fifty-pound bags. This was the largest PCP spill in the United States history. [The PCP involved here is distinct from "angel dust," which is also often designated by the initials PCP.]

The same day, Civil Defense and local authorities evacuated all residents within a ten-mile radius of the collision. The Coast Guard closed the Outlet to vessel navigation. Health officials suspended all fishing, shrimping, and associated activities on the Outlet and within about 400 square miles of surrounding Louisiana waterways and marshes. They also embargoed seafood and shellfish caught in the area and widely broadcast notice of this embargo. The closure and suspensions lasted through mid-August.

The commercial fishing industry in the area sustained serious losses, primarily from the depressed market in that industry in southern Louisiana. Other businesses suffered losses. Numerous parties filed suit against the vessels and their owners, seeking compensation for their expenses and their lost profits caused by the collision, pollution, and bans to navigation and fishing. The claimants may be classified as follows:

(1) commercial fishermen, crabbers, oystermen, and shrimpers who routinely operated in and around the closed area;
(2) fishermen, crabbers, oystermen, and shrimpers who engaged in these practices only for recreation;
(3) operators of marinas and boat rentals, and marine suppliers;
(4) tackle and bait shops;
(5) wholesale and retail seafood enterprises not actually engaged in fishing, shrimping, crabbing, or oystering in the closed area;
(6) seafood restaurants;
(7) cargo terminal operators;
(8) an operator of railroad freight cars seeking demurrage;
(9) vessel operators seeking expenses (demurrage, crew costs, tug hire) and losses of revenues caused by the closure of the outlet.

B. Difficulties with Subsequent Extensions

It is a long step from *Robins* to a rule that requires *physical damage* as a prerequisite to recovery in maritime tort. The majority believes that the plaintiff's lack of any contractual connection with an injured party, taken with the *Robins* rule, forecloses liability: "If a plaintiff connected to the damaged chattels by contract cannot recover, others more remotely situated are foreclosed *a fortiori.*" This conclusion follows readily from the reasoning that if uninjured contracting parties are barred from recovery, and if contracting parties have a closer legal relationship than non-contracting parties, then a party who is not physically injured and who does not have a contractual relation to the damage is surely barred.

This argument would be sound in instances where the plaintiff suffered no loss *but for a contract* with the injured party. We would measure a plaintiff's connection to the tortfeasor by the only line connecting them, the contract, and disallow the claim under *Robins.* In the instant case, however, some of the plaintiffs suffered damages whether or not they had a contractual connection with a party physically injured by the tortfeasor. These plaintiffs do not need to rely on a contract to link them to the tort: The collision proximately caused their losses, and those losses were foreseeable. These plaintiffs are therefore freed from the *Robins* rule concerning the recovery of those who suffered economic loss because of an injury to a party with whom they have contracted.

CONCLUSION

The *Robins* approach restricts liability more severely than the policies behind limitations on liability require and imposes the cost of the accident on the victim, who is usually not in a superior position to obtain insurance to cover this loss. I would apply a rule of recovery based on conventional tort principles of proximate cause and foreseeability and limit eligibility only by the requirement that a claimant prove "particular" damages.

NOTES AND PROBLEMS

1. ***Overlap Between the Mere Economic Harm Rule and Failure to Recognize Negligent Interference with Contract.*** This case can be understood in light of two parallel, but not identical, doctrines. One is the fairly stubborn refusal by courts to recognize a cause of action for negligent interference by a third party with another's contractual performance, even where it is foreseeable that such unintended interference might cause losses to another in privity of contract. The other is the fairly rigid adherence to the "mere economic loss" rule that we encountered in Chapter 6, Special Duty Rules. Part of the Fifth Circuit's discussion in the foregoing case concerns its view on whether the *Robins* decision was just an application of the rule rejecting negligent interference with contract as a recognized cause of action or, rather, whether it involved application of the broader mere economic loss rule. Do you see how either rule would have hurt the plaintiff's claims in *Robins*, but how application of the latter rule was necessary to dismiss most of the plaintiffs' claims here?

2. ***Modern Adherence to Mere Economic Harm Rule.*** Do you prefer the bright-line approach reaffirmed by the Fifth Circuit or the dissent's approach of just employing traditional tort stalwarts of foreseeability and proximate cause to determine, on a case-by-case approach, how far liability should extend? Is one approach better or worse for commerce?

3. ***Strict Products Liability Application.*** Another common manifestation of the economic loss rule is in the area of strict products liability. Courts uniformly hold that where the defect in a product only causes injury to the product itself — rather than also causing personal injuries or harm to other property — the only cause of action lies in contract law (i.e. warranty) rather than tort law. As one court surmised, after surveying holdings from many jurisdictions, "the United States Supreme Court, the overwhelming majority of state courts, and legal scholars have recognized the unfairness of imposing on a seller [of defective goods] tort liability for economic loss." Alloway v. General Marine Industries, L.P., 695 A.2d 264, 271 (N.J. 1997) (plaintiff's attempt to recover for lost value/repairs to defective boat on tort theories held invalid). The thought seems to be that tort theories were made more for unreasonable risks of harm to persons and other property than for unmet expectations regarding the subject of the transaction. The draft of the Third Restatement of Torts also concurs in this line of reasoning.

4. ***Policy Justifications?*** We will next be turning to a discussion of the cause of action entitled tortious interference with contract, which is an

intentional tort. Why would courts be so reluctant to recognize as actionable interference that is merely negligent as opposed to intentional?

B. Intentional Interference with Contract

A relatively old business tort exists for "tortious interference with a contractual relationship." The Restatement (Second) describes this tort as follows:

> One who intentionally and improperly interferes with the performance of a contract (except a contract to marry) between another and a third person by inducing or otherwise causing the third person not to perform the contract, is subject to liability to the other for the pecuniary loss resulting to the other from the failure of the third person to perform the contract.

Restatement (Second) of Torts §766 (1965). This is an interesting concept because contract law does not consider the intentional breach by a contracting party as a tort subject to tort remedies. On the other hand, when one who is a stranger to the contract interferes with the performance of the contract, courts consider this to be actionable in tort. Consider the justification for imposing such liability as you read the facts from the famous old English case of *Lumley v. Gye* below.

LUMLEY v. GYE

118 Eng. Rep. 749 (1853)

[Plaintiff was the lessee and manager of the Queen's Theatre, which hosted performing operas for the plaintiff's profit. Plaintiff alleged that he had contracted with Johanna Wagner to perform at the theatre for a certain time with the stated condition that she should "not sing nor use her talents elsewhere during the term without plaintiff's consent in writing." Notwithstanding these terms, and despite the defendant's knowledge of this contract, the plaintiff alleged that the defendant maliciously and intentionally enticed and procured Wagner to refuse to perform for the plaintiff, and to perform for the defendant instead. Plaintiff alleged special damages from this intentional act of interference with Wagner's performance of her contact. The court held for the plaintiff.]

Principles

"[I]n connection with the tort of interference, precedents are only suggestive . . . and the fact that a situation is one in which a remedy for interference has never previously been granted does not deter the courts from granting a remedy."

Torbett v. Wheeling Dollar Sav. & Trust, 314 S.E.2d 166, 173 (W. Va. 1983).

Erle, J.

The question raised upon this demurrer is, Whether an action will lie by the proprietor of a theatre against a person who maliciously procures an entire abandonment of a contract to perform exclusively at that theatre for a certain time; whereby damage was sustained? And it seems to me that it will. The authorities are numerous and uniform, that an action will lie by a master against a person who procures that a servant should unlawfully leave his service. The principle involved in these cases comprises the present; for, there, the right of action in the master arises from the wrongful act of the defendant in procuring that the person hired should break his contract, by putting an end to the relation of employer and employed; and the present case is the same. If it is objected that this class of actions for procuring a breach of contract of hiring rests upon no principle, and ought not to be extended beyond the cases heretofore decided, and that, as those have related to contracts respecting trade, manufactures or household service, and not to performance at a theatre, therefore they are no authority for an action in respect of a contract for such performance; the answer appears to me to be, that the class of cases referred to rests upon the principle that the procurement of the violation of the right is a cause of action, and that, when this principle is applied to a violation of a right arising upon a contract of hiring, the nature of the service contracted for is immaterial. It is clear that the procurement of the violation of a right is a cause of action in all instances where the violation is an actionable wrong, as in violations of a right to property, whether real or personal, or to personal security: he who procures the wrong is a joint wrong-doer, and may be sued, either alone or jointly with the agent, in the appropriate action for the wrong complained of.

This principle is supported by good reason. He who maliciously procures a damage to another by violation of his right ought to be made to indemnify; and that, whether he procures an actionable wrong or a breach of contract. He who procures the non-delivery of goods according to contract may inflict an injury, the same as he who procures the abstraction of goods after delivery; and both ought on the same ground to be made responsible. The remedy on the contract may be inadequate, as where the measures of damages is restricted; or in the ease of non-payment of a debt where the damage may be bankruptcy to the creditor who is disappointed, but the measure of damages against the debtor is interest only; or, in the case of the non-delivery of the goods, the disappointment may lead to a heavy forfeiture under a contract to complete a work within a time, but the measure of damages against the vendor of the goods for non-delivery may be only the difference between the contract price and the market value of the goods in question at the time of the breach. In such cases, he who procures the damage maliciously might justly be made responsible beyond the liability of the contractor.

The result is that there ought to be, in my opinion, judgment for the plaintiff.

NOTES AND PROBLEMS

1. ***Adoption of* Lumley *Tort.*** The above decision in *Lumley* is the most famous decision recognizing a tort cause of action for intentionally interfering with the plaintiff's contract with a third party. The court recognized that the third party (the opera singer) might be liable for breach of contract but that the actor who instigated the failure to perform would be liable in tort for the damages caused through his intentional act of interference. This principle for liability, while novel in 1853, was fully embraced by both English and American courts over time. While some of the judges in *Lumley* premised their verdict upon the showing that the defendant had acted maliciously, others believed this was not critical to proving the claim. This dispute has been ongoing. Most courts traditionally identify the elements of tortious interference with contract as follows:

A. The existence of a contract subject to interference;
B. A willful and intentional act of interference by the defendant;
C. The intentional act was a proximate cause of the plaintiff's damage; and
D. Actual damages or loss occurred.

One continuing bone of contention has been whether plaintiff must prove a form of "malice" — which is often seen as the opposite of being justified in one's action by legitimate business interests or rights. Many courts treat this issue as an affirmative defense. Rather than having the plaintiff bear the burden of proving "malice," the defendant must affirmatively plead and prove that it was justified in its act of interference in order to defeat the claim that otherwise satisfied the foregoing elements. There are still jurisdictions, however, that require the plaintiff to prove malice as an element of the claim (and in effect, to negate any justification or privilege for the defendant's act of interference).

2. ***Factors Utilized in Assessing the Impropriety.*** The Restatement (Second) §766 (1965) offers the following list of factors to consider (whether as an element of the plaintiff's claim or as relevant to the defendant's affirmative defense of "privilege") in determining if the act of interference warrants imposition of liability:

A. The nature of the actor's conduct,
B. The actor's motive,
C. The interests of the other with which the actor's conduct interferes,
D. The interests sought to be advanced by the actor,
E. The social interests in protecting the freedom of action of the actor and the contractual interests of the other,
F. The proximity or remoteness of the actor's conduct to the interference, and
G. The relations between the parties.

With respect to an intentional act of interfering with the plaintiff's existing contract with a third party, however, courts do not typically consider the mere right of "competition" to be sufficient justification. Utilizing these factors, how might you justify the decision by the court in *Lumley* to hold the defendant liable to the plaintiff?

3. *Billion Dollar Cause of Action.* One of the largest tort judgments in history involved this cause of action. Pennzoil sued Texaco in Texas state court for interfering with Pennzoil's contractual relations with Getty Oil Co. Getty and Pennzoil had agreed to Pennzoil's takeover of Getty through a stock acquisition. Subsequently, Texaco offered (and Getty accepted) a deal to pay a higher dollar amount per share to permit Texaco to take over Getty instead of Pennzoil. Pennzoil sued Texaco and the jury returned a verdict for Pennzoil of $7.53 billion in compensatory damages and $3 billion in punitive damages. On appeal the punitive damages were reduced to $1 billion but the compensatory damages were left intact. The Texas Supreme Court refused to hear any further appeals and Texaco filed for bankruptcy while seeking further appellate review from the U.S. Supreme Court. While these matters were pending, the parties settled the case for a total of $3 billion — a pretty good day at the office for any attorney with a contingency fee interest.

4. *Triangular Relationships Required.* Courts have held that a mere breach of contract does not give rise to a cause of action for tortious interference against the breaching party. In other words, one cannot tortiously interfere with one's own contract. A third party, who is a stranger to the contract, is the only one capable of committing this tort. *See* In re James E. Bashaw & Co., 2009 Tex. App. LEXIS 5745 (Tex. App. — Houston [1st Dist.] 2009, no pet.). In other words, you need a triangular relationship to have this tort. Merely failing to perform, or somehow interfering with the performance of a contract to which the actor is a party, subjects that party only to a breach of contract claim and not a tort claim. *See e.g.*, Applied Equipment Corp. v. Litton Saudi Arabia Ltd., 869 P.2d 454 (Cal. 1994).

5. *Problem.* During the summer of 2010, there were news reports that Marist College filed a lawsuit against James Madison University for luring its men's basketball coach (Matt Brady) away while the coach was in the middle of a multi-year deal (with no buyout clause). Brady spent four years as the coach at Marist before accepting the offer from James Madison. In the suit, Marist alleged that the coach was induced to leave with three years remaining on his current contract. James Madison did not file a timely answer in the suit and a default judgment was entered by New York State Supreme Court Justice Charles D. Wood, who stated that James Madison University had committed "tortious interference" with the contract of employment between Marist and Brady. A subsequent hearing was scheduled to determine the damages. (The school also sued the coach for breach of contract, including violating a provision in the contract stating that if Brady left, he would not solicit any current Marist players to leave with him.) The coach filed an answer denying any liability for breach of contract. Did James Madison University have a viable defense to the claim for tortious interference?

"LADIES AND GENTLEMEN OF THE JURY . . ."

Idaho J.I. 4.70: Tortious Interference with Contract

With respect to the plaintiff's claim for tortious interference with contract, the plaintiff has the burden of proving each of the following propositions:

(1) The plaintiff was a party to an existing contract;
(2) The defendant knew of the contract;
(3) The defendant intentionally interfered with the contract, causing a breach;
(4) The plaintiff was damaged as a proximate result of the defendant's interference; and
(5) The nature and extent of damages, and the amount thereof.

C. Interference with Prospective Contractual Relations

In a parallel line of cases, courts have also recognized a tort for intentional interference with a *merely prospective* contractual relationship. While the preceding case specifically rejected the concept of a competition privilege when an actor intentionally interferes with an *existing* contractual relationship, courts and commentators have long agreed that when the actor's conduct merely interferes with a claimant's *possible* contractual relationship with a third party, competition should not be prohibited. For example, consider two competing manufacturers of soft drink products. When one advertises that its product is better than the other in order to attract customers to its own product and away from the other, do you see how this might appear to be an intentional act of interference with a prospective contractual relationship? In such a scenario, courts in fact find such conduct commendable rather than actionable:

> "Iron sharpens iron" is ancient wisdom, and the law is in accord in favoring free competition, since ordinarily it is essential to the general welfare of society, notwithstanding [that] competition is not altruistic but is fundamentally the play of interest against interest, and so involves the interference of the successful competitor with the interest of his unsuccessful competitor in the matter of their common rivalry. Competition is the state in which men live and is not a tort, unless

> the nature of the method employed is not justified by public policy, and so supplies the condition to constitute a legal wrong. Accordingly, we have made clear in our cases that acting to pursue one's own business interests at the expense of others is not, in itself, tortious.

Goldman v. Building Ass'n, 133 A. 843, 846 (Md. 1926). Thus, while expressly embracing competition as a generally acceptable privilege, courts have also embraced the concept that there should be limits to this privilege and that sometimes the act of interference is actionable. The first and second Restatements have struggled to provide a bright line articulating when the act of interference is privileged and when it is not justified "by public policy" and, therefore, provides grounds for legal redress. The following opinion provides historical perspective on the related tort claims of interference with an existing contract versus interference with a mere prospective contact. It also offers an arguably brighter line for determining when competition is justified and when it is not.

WAL-MART STORES, INC. v. STURGES, III

52 S.W.3d 711 (Tex. 2001)

HECHT, J.

Texas, like most states, has long recognized a tort cause of action for interference with a prospective contractual or business relation even though the core concept of liability — what conduct is prohibited — has never been clearly defined. Texas courts have variously stated that a defendant may be liable for conduct that is "wrongful," "malicious," "improper," of "no useful purpose," "below the behavior of fair men similarly situated," or done "with the purpose of harming the plaintiff," but not for conduct that is "competitive," "privileged," or "justified," even if intended to harm the plaintiff. Repetition of these abstractions in the case law has not imbued them with content or made them more useful, and tensions among them, which exist not only in Texas law but American law generally, have for decades been the subject of considerable critical commentary.

This case affords us the opportunity to bring a measure of clarity to this body of law. From the history of the tort in Texas and elsewhere, and from the scholarly efforts to analyze its boundaries, we conclude that to establish liability for interference with a prospective contractual or business relation the plaintiff must prove that it was harmed by the defendant's conduct that was either independently tortious or unlawful. By "independently tortious" we mean conduct that would violate some other recognized tort duty. We must explain this at greater length, but by way of example, a defendant who threatened a customer with bodily harm if he did business with the plaintiff would be liable for interference because his conduct toward the customer — assault — was independently tortious, while a defendant who competed legally for the customer's business would not be liable for interference. Thus defined, an action for interference with a prospective contractual or business relation provides a remedy for injurious conduct that other tort actions might not reach (in the example above, the plaintiff could not sue for assault), but only for conduct that is already recognized to be wrongful under the common law or by statute.

Because the defendant's conduct in this case was not independently tortious or unlawful, and because the defendant did not breach its contract, we reverse the court of appeals' judgment and render judgment for the defendant.

I

Plaintiff Harry W. Sturges, III contracted for himself and plaintiffs Dick Ford, Bruce Whitehead, and J.D. Martin, III to purchase from Bank One, Texas a vacant parcel of commercial property in Nederland, Texas, referred to as Tract 2. The contract, dated December 29, 1989, gave purchasers the right to terminate if within sixty days they were unable to lease the property and "to secure the written approval of Wal-Mart Corporation to the intended use of the Property, in accordance with the right so given to Wal-Mart pursuant to certain restrictions on the Property." The right referred to was the right to approve modifications in a site plan for the property that Wal-Mart Stores, Inc. and Wal-Mart Properties, Inc. (collectively, "Wal-Mart") held under two recorded instruments, each entitled "Easements with Covenants and Restrictions Affecting Land" ("ECRs"), one filed in 1982 and the other in 1988. The purpose of the ECRs was to assure the commercial development of Tract 2 and an adjacent tract, Tract 1, according to a prescribed plan.

The 1982 ECR was between Wal-Mart, which owned Tract 2 at the time, and the State Teachers Retirement System of Ohio ("OTR"), which owned Tract 1, having acquired it from Wal-Mart under a sale and leaseback agreement. OTR leased Tract 1 to Wal-Mart to use for a store. In 1984, Wal-Mart sold Tract 2 to a joint venture that included a partnership, Gulf Coast Investment Group. Gulf Coast later acquired Tract 2 from the joint venture. The 1988 ECR, made by Gulf Coast, OTR, and Wal-Mart, modified the site plan for the tracts and otherwise incorporated the terms of the 1982 ECR.

Gulf Coast's efforts to develop Tract 2 failed, and in 1989 Bank One acquired the property by foreclosure. Two of Gulf Coast's partners, plaintiffs Whitehead and Martin, along with two other investors, plaintiffs Sturges and Ford, continued to look for a way to develop the property. When Sturges learned that Fleming Foods of Texas, Inc. was interested in building a food store in the area, he contracted with Bank One to purchase Tract 2 for the plaintiffs in hopes of leasing the property to Fleming Foods.

As soon as the agreement with Bank One was executed, Sturges contacted Wal-Mart to request a modification of the 1982/1988 ECRs to permit construction on Tract 2 of a food store to Fleming's specifications. A modification was necessary in part because Fleming wanted to construct a 51,000-square-foot store, and the site plan permitted only a 36,000-square-foot structure. A manager in Wal-Mart's property management department, DeLee Wood, told Sturges to submit a revised site plan, and though she did not have authority to approve the modification herself, she indicated to Sturges that Wal-Mart would approve it. About the same time, Sturges obtained from Fleming a non-binding memorandum of understanding that it would lease Tract 2.

Unbeknownst to Wood, a manager in another Wal-Mart department, Sandra Watson, had been evaluating the possibilities for expanding stores at various locations, including the Nederland store. If a store could not be expanded, Watson's assignment was to consider relocating the store. In July 1989 Watson hired a realtor, Tom Hudson, to help Wal-Mart acquire Tract 2 for purposes of expansion. When Hudson learned of Sturges's contract with Bank One, he suggested to Watson that Wal-Mart could thwart Sturges's efforts to purchase the property by refusing to approve the requested modification of the 1982/1988 ECRs. At the time, neither Watson nor Hudson knew of Wood's conversations with Sturges.

When Wood's and Watson's conflicting activities came to the attention of the head of Wal-Mart's property management department, Tony Fuller, he agreed with Watson that Wal-Mart should try to acquire Tract 2 and told Wood to deny Sturges's request to modify the ECR, which she did in a letter to Sturges without explanation. Fuller then instructed Hudson to contact Fleming and communicate Wal-Mart's desire to expand onto Tract 2. Hudson complied, telling L. G. Callaway, Fleming's manager of store development who had been working on the deal with Sturges, that if Wal-Mart could not acquire Tract 2, it would close its store on Tract 1 and relocate. Since Fleming was not interested in Tract 2 without a Wal-Mart store next door, Callaway took Hudson's call to be an ultimatum not to move forward on the proposed lease with Sturges. Consequently, Fleming canceled its letter of intent with Sturges, and the plaintiffs opted out of their contract with Bank One. Several months later, Wal-Mart purchased Tract 2 and expanded its store.

The plaintiffs sued Wal-Mart for tortiously interfering with their prospective lease with Fleming and for breaching the 1982/1988 ECRs by unreasonably refusing to approve the requested site plan modification. The plaintiffs' actual damages claim under both theories was the same — the profits the plaintiffs would have made on the Fleming lease. The jury found Wal-Mart liable on both theories. Concerning the plaintiffs' interference claim, the district court submitted to the jury two questions with accompanying instructions as follows:

> Did Wal-Mart wrongfully interfere with Plaintiffs' prospective contractual agreement to lease the property to Fleming?
>
> Wrongful interference occurred if (a) there was a reasonable probability that Plaintiffs would have entered into the contractual relation, and (b) Wal-Mart intentionally prevented the contractual relation from occurring with the purpose of harming Plaintiffs.
>
> Was Wal-Mart's intentional interference with Plaintiffs' prospective lease agreement with Fleming justified?

> An interference is "justified" if a party possesses an interest in the subject matter equal or superior to that of the other party, or if it results from the good faith exercise of a party's rights, or the good faith exercise of a party's mistaken belief of its rights.

The jury answered "yes" to the first question and "no" to the second. Wal-Mart offered no objection to this part of the jury charge that is relevant to our consideration of the case. The jury assessed $1 million actual damages on the contract claim and on the interference claim, assessed $500,000 punitive damages on the interference claim, and found that reasonable attorney fees for each side were $145,000. At the plaintiffs' election, the trial court rendered judgment on the interference claim, awarding actual and punitive damages but not attorney fees.

All parties appealed. The court of appeals affirmed the award of actual damages but remanded for a retrial of punitive damages, holding that the trial court had improperly excluded evidence offered by the plaintiffs during the punitive damages phase of the trial.

II

Wal-Mart argues that there is no evidence to support the jury's verdict that it wrongfully interfered with the plaintiffs' prospective lease with Fleming or that it was not justified in acting as it did. Our analysis of these arguments is complicated because it must be made in light of the jury charge that the district court gave without objection, even though, as we conclude, the charge's statement of the law was not entirely correct. We will focus on Wal-Mart's argument that there is no evidence of wrongful interference: that is, in the language of the jury charge, no evidence that Wal-Mart acted "with the purpose of harming Plaintiffs." To resolve this issue, we must understand what kind of conduct is legally harmful and constitutes tortious interference. Whenever two competitors vie for the same business advantage, as Wal-Mart and Sturges did over the acquisition of Tract 2, one's success over the other can almost always be said to harm the other. Wal-Mart's evidentiary challenge here raises the question of what harm must be proved to constitute tortious interference. To answer this question, we look to the historical development of the interference torts in other jurisdictions and in Texas and survey every Texas case involving a claim of intentional interference with prospective relations. We then analyze the evidence in this case.

The origins of civil liability for interference have been traced to Roman law that permitted a man to sue for violence done to members of his household. The common law also recognized such liability as early as the fourteenth century and extended it to include driving away a business's customers or a church's donors. But a common-law cause of action was strictly limited to cases in which actual violence or other such improper means were used. For centuries the common law continued to allow civil actions for interference with one's customers or other prospective business relationships, but as the *Restatement (Second) of Torts* summarizes, "in all of them the actor's conduct was characterized by violence, fraud or defamation, and was tortious in character."

The common law departed from this requirement in 1853 in the English case of *Lumley v. Gye*, which held that liability could be imposed for interference with a contract if the defendant acted "wrongfully and maliciously," even if the defendant's conduct was not tortious or illegal. In that case, Gye induced an opera singer to sing for him instead of Lumley, for whom she had contracted to perform, not with threats of violence but by offering her a higher fee. Forty years later in *Temperton v. Russell*, the English court reaffirmed its decision in *Lumley*, holding that trade union officials could be liable to a building materials supplier for threatening his customers with labor disturbances if they continued to purchase supplies from him. The court announced that the rule in *Lumley* would apply not only to interference with all contracts, regardless of the subject matter, but to interference with prospective or potential relations as well.

Temperton's treatment of interference with prospective relations as simply another aspect of interference with contract was a mistake. It is one thing for *A* and *B* to compete for *C*'s business, and quite another for *A* to persuade or force *C* to break his contract with *B*. Tortious interference with contract contemplates that competition may be lawful and yet limited by promises already made. Absent any such promises, competitors should be free to use any lawful means to obtain advantage. As one commentator has observed:

> Although one who interferes with the stability of a contractual relationship may be seen as an interloper and possibly a tortfeasor, one who interferes merely with a "prospective business advantage" may be essentially a competitor. In an economic system founded upon the principle of free competition, competitors should not be liable in tort for seeking a legitimate business advantage.[17]

Lumley's holding that unlawful conduct was not a prerequisite for liability for tortious interference with contract was understandable; *Temperton*'s extension of the same rule to situations involving only prospective relations was not.

The use of "malice" to denote the touchstone of liability for tortious interference with contract was not well explained in *Lumley* and the cases that followed. "Malice" appeared at first to signify malevolence, although it soon became apparent that that definition would not work. As we have explained in a similar context, lawful conduct is not made tortious by the actor's ill will towards another, nor does an actor's lack of ill will make his tortious conduct any less so. "Malice" obviously meant that character of conduct that would not justify inducing a breach of contract, but that was an obviously circular definition (a person is not justified in inducing a breach of contract if he acts with malice, that is, if he acts in such a way that does not justify inducing a breach of contract). Exactly what conduct was culpable, and therefore "malicious," went undefined.

As clumsy as the idea of "malice" was in describing liability for tortious interference with contract, it made no sense at all in trying to describe liability for tortious interference with prospective advantage. Competitors could quite naturally be expected, well within the bounds of law, to try to achieve the best for themselves and, consequently, harm to each other. In a society built around business competition, interference with prospective business relations has never been thought to be wrongful in and of itself. That some liability factor was essential has never been in doubt. If that factor was not unlawful conduct, discarded by *Lumley* for tortious interference with contract, then it was not clear what it should be.

These two problems — the misassociation of the two torts and the confusion regarding their standards of liability — may have been due to, and were certainly exacerbated by, the concept of a prima facie tort that was being advanced about the same time. As explained by Justice Holmes: "It has been considered that, prima facie, the intentional infliction of temporal damages is a cause of action, which, as a matter of substantive law, whatever may be the form of pleading, requires a justification if the defendant is to escape." In other words, intentionally inflicting harm is tortious unless justified. Consistent with this idea, and with the association of the two interference torts, the 1939 *Restatement of Torts* defined tortious interference as simply this:

> One who, without a privilege to do so, induces or otherwise purposely causes a third person not to (a) perform a contract with another, or (b) enter into or continue a business relation with another is liable to the other for the harm caused thereby.

In determining the existence of a privilege, the *Restatement* called for consideration of:

> (a) the nature of the actor's conduct, (b) the nature of the expectancy with which his conduct interferes, (c) the relations between the parties, (d) the interest sought to be advanced by the actor and (e) the social interests in protecting the expectancy on the one hand and the actor's freedom of action on the other hand.

The *Restatement* also stated a privilege for competition when, among other things, "the actor does not employ improper means." The *Restatement*'s broad statements did almost nothing to define the parameters of tortious conduct. What was it about the nature of an actor's conduct, or of the expectancy at issue, or of any of the other considerations that should or should not result in liability in specific circumstances? Were the considerations the same for interference with a contract and interference with a prospective business relation? When were means of competition "improper"? The *Restatement*'s provisions gave no more guidance than the concept of prima facie tort. Not surprisingly, when the second *Restatement* was published forty years later, it commented:

> There is no clear cut distinction between the requirements for a prima facie case and the requirements for a recognized privilege. Initial liability depends upon the interplay of several factors and is not reducible to a single rule; and privileges, too, are not clearly established but depend upon a consideration of much the same factors. Moreover, there is considerable disagreement on who has the burden of pleading and proving certain matters, such for example, as the existence and effect of competition for prospective business.
>
> This has occurred for two reasons. First, the law in this area has not fully congealed but is still in a formative stage. The several forms of the [interference] tort . . . are often not distinguished by the courts, and cases have been cited among them somewhat indiscriminately. This has produced a blurring of the significance of the factors involved in determining liability.
>
> The second reason grows out of use of the term "malicious" in [*Lumley v. Gye*] and other early cases. It soon came to be realized that the term was not being used in a literal sense, requiring ill will toward the plaintiff as a requirement for imposing liability. Many courts came to call this "legal malice," and to hold that in this sense the requirement means that the infliction of the harm must be intentional and "without justification." "Justification" is a broader and looser term than "privilege," and the consequence has been that its meaning has not been very clear.

Having recognized these problems, the *Restatement* did little to solve them. Concluding that "it has seemed desirable to make use of a single word that will indicate for this tort the balancing process expressed by the two terms, 'culpable and not justified,'" the *Restatement* chose "improper" as a word "neutral enough to acquire a specialized meaning of its own" for purposes of defining the interference torts. The *Restatement* separated interference with contract and interference with prospective business relations, previously combined as one, but it used the same new standard — "improper" — to define liability for each.

Thus, the second *Restatement* abandoned the confusing and overlapping notions of "malice," "privilege," and "justification," but it made little more than a formal distinction between the two interference torts, setting the liability standard for both at "improper" conduct, and it continued the idea that the considerations for determining what was improper were, except for lawful competition, similar for both torts. Commentators since have criticized the *Restatement* as overstating case law. Professor Perlman's analysis of the cases suggests that the interference tort [with prospective relations] should be limited to cases in which the defendant's acts are independently unlawful and that if improper motivation is to give rise to liability, it should be based only on objective indicia of activity producing social loss. In most cases, tort law will provide the standard for judging the unlawfulness of the means. At the same time, those courts that have emphasized unlawful means have recognized that sources other than traditional tort law also might define the lawfulness of the defendant's behavior. Incorporation of such sources seems right.

Likewise, Professor Keeton summarized:

> Violence or intimidation, defamation, injurious falsehood or other fraud, violation of the criminal law, and the institution or threat of groundless civil suits or criminal prosecutions in bad faith, all have been held to result in liability, and there is some authority which limits liability to such cases.

Two recent cases of note have echoed the same idea after surveying existing case law. In *Della Penna v. Toyota Motor Sales, Inc.*, a car manufacturer required dealers not to sell its vehicles for resale outside the United States in order to protect its dealership network. An exporter sued the manufacturer for tortious interference with his business prospects. The Supreme Court of California rejected the claim as a matter of law, concluding that the manufacturer's conduct was not actionable. Abandoning notions of "malice" and "justification," the court held that a plaintiff seeking to recover for an alleged interference with prospective contractual or economic relations must plead and prove as part of its case-in-chief that the defendant not only knowingly interfered with the plaintiff's expectancy, but engaged in conduct that was wrongful by some legal measure other than the fact of interference itself.

The "legal measures" identified by the court were existing tort law and statutes.

Similarly, in *Speakers of Sport, Inc. v. Proserv, Inc.*, the Seventh Circuit concluded that under Illinois law, actionable interference requires conduct that is independently tortious by nature. In that case, one sports agency sued another for interference in obtaining Texas Rangers' catcher Ivan Rodriguez as a client by promising him more than it could deliver. The plaintiff agency sought damages alleging that the defendant agency's conduct was unfair, unethical, and deceitful. The court rejected the argument that actionable interference could be based on conduct that was not independently tortious or otherwise unlawful. As Judge Posner explained in the court's opinion, no other workable basis exists for distinguishing between tortious interference and lawful competition:

It can be argued . . . that competition can be tortious even if it does not involve an actionable fraud . . . or other independently tortious act, such as defamation, or trademark or patent infringement, or a theft of a trade secret; that competitors should not be allowed to use "unfair" tactics; and that a promise known by the promisor when made to be unfulfillable is such a tactic, especially when used on a relatively unsophisticated, albeit very well to do, baseball player. Considerable support for this view can be found in the case law. But the Illinois courts have not as yet embraced the doctrine, and we are not alone in thinking it pernicious. *Della Penna v. Toyota Motor Sales, U.S.A., Inc.*, 902 P.2d 740, 760- 763 (Cal. 1995) (concurring opinion). We agree with Professor Perlman that the tort of interference with business relationships should be confined to cases in which the defendant employed unlawful means to stiff a competitor, and we are reassured by the conclusion of his careful analysis that the case law is generally consistent with this position as a matter of outcomes as distinct from articulation.

Expressly endorsing the legal commentary critical of the development of the law of tortious interference, *Della Penna* and *Speakers of Sport* demonstrate the importance of decoupling interference with contract from interference with prospective relations, and of grounding liability for the latter in conduct that is independently tortious by nature or otherwise unlawful.

We therefore hold that to recover for tortious interference with a prospective business relation a plaintiff must prove that the defendant's conduct was independently tortious or wrongful. By independently tortious we do not mean that the plaintiff must be able to prove an independent tort. Rather, we mean only that the plaintiff must prove that the defendant's conduct would be actionable under a recognized tort. Thus, for example, a plaintiff may recover for tortious interference from a defendant who makes fraudulent statements about the plaintiff to a third person without proving that the third person was actually defrauded. If, on the other hand, the defendant's statements are not intended to deceive, as in *Speakers of Sport*, then they are not actionable. Likewise, a plaintiff may recover for tortious interference from a defendant who threatens a person with physical harm if he does business with the plaintiff. The plaintiff need prove only that the defendant's conduct toward the prospective customer would constitute assault. Also, a plaintiff could recover for tortious interference by showing an illegal boycott, although a plaintiff could not recover against a defendant whose persuasion of others not to deal with the plaintiff was lawful. Conduct that is merely "sharp" or unfair is not actionable and cannot be the basis for an action for tortious interference with prospective relations, and we disapprove of cases that suggest the contrary. These examples are not exhaustive, but they illustrate what conduct can constitute tortious interference with prospective relations.

The concepts of justification and privilege are subsumed in the plaintiff's proof, except insofar as they may be defenses to the wrongfulness of the alleged conduct. For example, a statement made against the plaintiff, though defamatory, may be protected by a complete or qualified privilege. Justification and privilege are defenses in a claim for tortious interference with prospective relations only to the extent that they are defenses to the independent tortiousness of the defendant's conduct. Otherwise, the plaintiff need not prove that the defendant's conduct was not justified or privileged, nor can a defendant assert such defenses.

In reaching this conclusion we treat tortious interference with prospective business relations differently than tortious interference with contract. It makes sense to require a defendant who induces a breach of contract to show some justification or privilege for depriving another of benefits to which the agreement entitled him. But when two parties are competing for interests to which neither is entitled, then neither can be said to be more justified or privileged in his pursuit. If the conduct of each is lawful, neither should be heard to complain that mere unfairness is actionable. Justification and privilege are not useful concepts in assessing interference with prospective relations, as they are in assessing interference with an existing contract.

III

With this understanding of what conduct is prohibited by the tort of interference with prospective contractual or business relations and what conduct is not prohibited, we return to the evidence of this case. As we have already noted, we must assess Wal-Mart's argument that no evidence supports a finding of wrongful interference with the plaintiffs' prospective agreement with Fleming Foods in light of the jury charge to which Wal-Mart did not object, even though the charge does not correctly state the law. We must therefore consider whether the plaintiffs offered any evidence from which the jury could find, as the trial court instructed them, that Wal-Mart acted "with the purpose of harming Plaintiffs." As we have shown, however, harm that results only from lawful competition is not compensable by the interference tort. We must look to see whether there is evidence of harm from some independently tortious or unlawful activity by Wal-Mart.

The plaintiffs tell us that their interference claim is based on the telephone conversation between Hudson, Wal-Mart's relator, and Callaway, Fleming's manager of store development. Specifically, the plaintiffs complain of Hudson's "ultimatum" to Callaway that if Wal-Mart were not able to acquire Tract 2 for expansion, it would relocate its store. The plaintiffs contend that Hudson's statement was false and therefore fraudulent. To be fraudulent a statement must be material and false, the speaker must have known it was false or acted recklessly without regard to its falsity, the speaker must have intended that the statement be acted on, and hearer must have relied on it. The plaintiffs do not dispute that Wal-Mart had undertaken to identify stores which could not be expanded and to relocate them, that it attempted to acquire Tract 2 as an alternative to relocating the Nederland store, and that as Hudson told Callaway, if Wal-Mart could not acquire Tract 2 it would relocate. The only evidence the plaintiffs cite in support of their contention is that at the time Hudson called Callaway Wal-Mart had not begun efforts to relocate; that as a general matter Wal-Mart preferred to expand rather than relocate; and that there was room on Tract 1 for some expansion of the store. The fact that Wal-Mart had not begun to relocate its store when Hudson talked with Callaway is no evidence that his statement was false. The plaintiffs point to no evidence that Wal-Mart's general preference for expansion over relocation, or the possibilities for some expansion on Tract 1, would have made it decide not to relocate. Indeed, if Tract 1 had been adequate for Wal-Mart's intended expansion, it would not have needed to acquire Tract 2.

Thus, no evidence supports the plaintiffs' contention that Hudson's statement to Callaway was fraudulent or that Hudson intended to deceive Callaway, and the plaintiffs do not contend that Wal-Mart's conduct was otherwise illegal or tortious. The record contains no evidence to indicate that Wal-Mart intended the plaintiffs any harm other than what they would necessarily suffer by Wal-Mart's successful acquisition of Tract 2, which they were both pursuing, by entirely lawful means. We therefore conclude that there is no evidence to support a judgment for the plaintiffs on their interference claim.

NOTES AND PROBLEMS

1. ***Decoupling the Two Interference Torts.*** The above court "decouples" these two related tort claims in the opinion, indicating that the concept of "justification" makes sense for a defendant to attempt to explain its intentional interference with an existing contractual relationship, but that no such burden should be placed on a defendant who has merely interfered with a prospective relationship. In the latter case, to recover, the plaintiff must also demonstrate that the *means employed* by the defendant involved conduct that was *independently unlawful or tortious* — in other words, one must find a tort within the tort.

2. ***Breach of Contract as Wrongful Conduct.*** In another portion of the opinion, the *Wal-Mart* court also finds (as a matter of contract interpretation) that the defendant had not committed any breach of contract through the alleged "unreasonable" failure to agree to the modification of the easements and covenants. Interestingly, the court only appeared to reach this issue for the purpose of evaluating the jury's finding of a cause of action for contract breach, rather than suggesting that an intentional act of interference involving the defendant's own breach of a separate contract might be sufficient evidence of "wrongful" conduct. This is consistent with the holdings of some other courts — the fact that the defendant breached a contract with a third party in the course of interfering with the plaintiff's prospective relationship does not itself make the interference tortious. Breach of a contract is not illegal, improper, wrongful, or unjustified under the law of tort, but instead simply gives rise to a claim for breach of contract. *See* Windsor Securities, Inc. v. Hartford Life Ins. Co., 986 F.2d 655, 664 (3d Cir. 1993).

3. ***At-Will Employment Relationships.*** Most courts treat contracts terminable at will as the equivalent of a prospective contractual relationship because there is no assurance the relationship would continue. Given the *Wal-Mart* court's distinction between the torts of interference with an existing contract versus interference with a prospective contract, do you understand why characterizing the at-will relationship in this manner is so important? Consider this scenario. Competitor calls at-will Employee and recruits her to quit her job with Employer and go to work for Competitor. Analyze the liability of

Competitor toward Employer depending upon whether the employment relationship is considered an existing contract or merely a prospective contractual relationship.

4. ***Privilege to Compete.*** Under the Restatement (Second), there is a separately recognized "competition" privilege, which can be used by a defendant to justify interference with a prospective contractual relationship. This privilege is set forth, in part, below:

> One who intentionally caused a third person not to enter into a prospective contractual relation with another who is his competitor or not to continue an existing contract terminable at will does not interfere improperly with the other's relation if
>
> **A.** the relation concerns a matter involved in the competition between the actor and the other and
> **B.** the actor does not employ wrongful means and
> **C.** his action does not create or continue an unlawful restraint of trade and
> **D.** his purpose is at least in part to advance his interest in competing with the other.

Restatement (Second) §768 (1965). Note that this privilege to compete is expressly limited to interference with *prospective* and not existing contractual relations. The *Wal-Mart* court found this articulation of a privilege unwieldy in terms of differentiating between acceptable and unacceptable conduct. Many courts still analyze interference with prospective contractual relations, however, utilizing this foregoing Restatement (Second)'s list of factors. In adhering to this Restatement test some courts have focused more upon a finding of an improper *motive*, and others upon whether the defendant utilized improper *means* in the act of interference. The Restatement itself does not say which of the multiple factors is most important, much less how a court should go about considering these factors. To that extent, the Restatement is less of a test and more of a list of variables. By contrast, the modern trend illustrated by the *Wal-Mart* case narrows the analysis considerably and likely creates an actual test that can be more predictive of outcomes. Which analysis do you find more helpful — the Restatement (Second)'s list of factors, or the *Wal-Mart* court's limitation of the tort to acts of interference involving conduct independently recognized as tortious or wrongful?

5. ***Problem.*** Plaintiff is a company maintaining a retail sales website offering discounted prices on many products. Plaintiff pays considerable sums to advertise its website. Defendant also sells identical products on its own website. Defendant promotes its products not through independent television advertisements (like the plaintiff), but instead by utilizing "pop-up" ads that appear on the plaintiff's website. If a consumer clicks on the pop-up ad, the consumer is directed away from the plaintiff's website and to the defendant's

competing website. Should the defendant be liable to the plaintiff for interfering with potential sales to those customers that click on the pop-up ad? *See* Overstock.com v. SmartBargains, Inc., 192 P.3d 858 (Utah 2008).

DISTINGUISHING TORT VS. CONTRACT CLAIMS

In several instances in this chapter we have briefly discussed how a business tort cause of action might be preferable to a breach of contract action for the aggrieved claimant. Plaintiff lawyers have recognized this as well and have increasingly become more aggressive in attempting to plead tort claims rather than, or in addition to, their contract causes of action. At some level, for example, you might argue that many broken promises stem from a lack of care taken by the promisor. In that event, can one argue that the contract breach could also be considered negligent performance of the contract? Or could the breach also involve grossly negligent performance? In the following case the court grappled with how to distinguish between a tort and a contract action in instances where the proof of the tort claim necessarily also involved conduct constituting a contract breach.

SOUTHWESTERN BELL TELEPHONE v. DELANNEY

809 S.W.2d 493 (Tex. 1991)

Phillips, J.

We consider whether a cause of action for negligence is stated by an allegation that a telephone company negligently failed to perform its contract to publish a Yellow Pages advertisement. The court of appeals held that the company's failure to perform its contract was a basis for recovery in tort as well as contract, and that the clause limiting the telephone company's liability could not apply to limit tort damages. We reverse the judgment of the court of appeals and render judgment in favor of Bell.

Eugene DeLanney advertised his real estate business in the Galveston Yellow Pages for several years. For the 1980-1981 directory, he again contracted with Bell for a Yellow Pages advertisement. At this time DeLanney had two business phones, a rotary line and a single line. Prior to publication of the 1980-1981 directory, DeLanney's wife asked Bell to cancel the single line and add a third number to their existing rotary line. The Yellow Pages advertisement was billed to DeLanney's single line. When that line was canceled, DeLanney's

Yellow Pages advertisement was automatically deleted from the directory due to Bell's internal procedures.

When the advertisement was not published as promised, DeLanney sued Bell alleging negligence. Bell answered and urged by special exception that DeLanney's petition failed to state a cause of action for negligence. No ruling was made on this special exception, and DeLanney proceeded to trial. [After plaintiff Delanney rested his case in chief, defendant Bell moved for a directed verdict, but the trial court denied the motion as to the negligence claim and submitted the case to the jury.]

The jury found that Bell was negligent in omitting DeLanney's advertisement from the Yellow Pages and that such negligence was a proximate cause of damages to DeLanney. The jury assessed these damages at $109,000 for lost profits in the past and $40,000 for lost profits in the future. After ordering a partial remittitur which reduced future lost profits to $21,480, the trial court rendered judgment for DeLanney. Bell appealed.

The court of appeals, with one justice concurring and one justice dissenting, affirmed. A majority of the court held that Bell's cancellation of DeLanney's Yellow Pages advertisement was correctly submitted as a negligence claim. The dissenting justice argued that because DeLanney sought damages for breach of a duty created under the contract, rather than a duty imposed by law, the claim sounded only in contract. We agree with the dissent.

The majority below relied on *Montgomery Ward & Co. v. Scharrenbeck*, 204 S.W.2d 508, 510 (Tex. 1947), where we quoted from 38 Am. Jur. Negligence §20 (1941) as follows:

> Accompanying every contract is a common-law duty to perform with care, skill, reasonable expedience and faithfulness the thing agreed to be done, and a negligent failure to observe any of these conditions is a tort, as well as a breach of the contract.

In *Scharrenbeck*, the defendant agreed to repair a water heater in plaintiff's home. A short time after repair, the heater ignited the roof, destroying the house and its contents. Although the contract obligated the defendant to put the water heater back in good working order, the law also implied a duty to the defendant to act with reasonable skill and diligence in making the repairs so as not to injure a person or property by his performance. In failing to repair the water heater properly, the defendant breached its contract. In burning down plaintiff's home, the defendant breached a common-law duty as well, thereby providing a basis for plaintiff's recovery in tort.

The principle recognized in *Scharrenbeck* has also been recognized by commentators in this area. As one prominent authority has explained: "Tort obligations are in general obligations that are imposed by law — apart from and independent of promises made and therefore apart from the manifested intention of the parties — to avoid injury to others." W. Keeton, D. Dobbs, R. Keeton & D. Owen, Prosser and Keeton on The Law of Torts §92 at 655 (5th Ed. 1984) [hereinafter "Prosser and Keeton"]. If the defendant's conduct — such as negligently burning down a house — would give rise to liability independent of the fact that a contract exists between the parties, the plaintiff's claim may also sound in tort. Conversely, if the defendant's conduct — such as falling to publish an advertisement — would give rise to liability only because it breaches the parties' agreement, the plaintiff's claim ordinarily sounds only in contract.

In determining whether the plaintiff may recover on a tort theory, it is also instructive to examine the nature of the plaintiff's loss. When the only loss or damage is to the subject matter of the contract, the plaintiff's action is ordinarily on the contract. *See* Prosser and Keeton at 656; 1 J. Edgar, Jr. & J. Sales, Texas Torts and Remedies §1.03[4][b] at 1-36 (1990). We applied this analysis in *Jim Walter Homes, Inc. v. Reed*, 711 S.W.2d 617, 618 (Tex. 1986), where we wrote:

> The acts of a party may breach duties in tort or contract alone or simultaneously in both. The nature of the injury most often determines which duty or duties are breached. When the injury is only the economic loss to the subject of a contract itself the action sounds in contract alone.

Bell's duty to publish DeLanney's advertisement arose solely from the contract. DeLanney's damages, lost profits, were only for the economic loss caused by Bell's failure to perform. Although DeLanney pleaded his action as one in negligence, he clearly sought to recover the benefit of his bargain with Bell. We hold that Bell's failure to publish the advertisement was not a tort. Under our analysis in Reed, DeLanney's claim was solely in contract. [The court found that the plaintiff had waived any contract claim by failing to submit jury questions on that cause of action.]

For the foregoing reasons, the judgment of the court of appeals is reversed, and judgment is rendered that DeLanney take nothing.

GONZALEZ, J., *concurring*

I agree with the court that Bell's failure to publish the advertisement was not a tort and that it sounded solely in contract. I also agree that DeLanney failed to discharge his burden to obtain affirmative findings to jury questions on the contract. However, I do not fault the court of appeals for its confusion. We have muddled the law of "contorts" and an all encompassing bright line demarcation of what constitutes a tort distinct from breach of contract has proven to be elusive. See generally W. Prosser & W. Keeton, The Law of Torts §1 (5th ed. 1984).

DeLanney and the court of appeals rely heavily on the statement in *Montgomery Ward & Co. v. Scharrenbeck*, 146 Tex. 153, 204 S.W.2d 508, 510 (Tex. 1947), that:

> Accompanying every contract is a common-law duty to perform with care, still, reasonable expedience and faithfulness the thing agreed to be done, and a negligent failure to observe any of these conditions is a tort, as well as a breach of the contract.

Despite this broad language, not every breach of contract accompanied by negligence creates a cause of action in tort. In *International Printing Pressman & Assistants' Union v. Smith*, 145 Tex. 399, 198 S.W.2d 729, 735 (Tex. 1946), we acknowledged that no single concise rule will define the rights of parties in every situation. We nonetheless wrote:

> Generally speaking, "actions in contract and in tort are to be distinguished in that an action in contract is for the breach of a duty arising out of a contract either express or implied, while an action in tort is for a breach of duty imposed by law. . . ." "If the action is not maintainable without pleading and proving the contract, where the gist of the action is the breach of the contract, either by malfeasance or nonfeasance, it is, in substance an action on the contract, whatever may be the form of the pleading." (citations omitted).

Id. at 735. I believe that this formulation comes closer than *Scharrenbeck* to stating a general rule to distinguish contract from tort and that the broad language in *Scharrenbeck* must be read in light of the particular circumstances of that case. The opinion in *Scharrenbeck* is correct in its observation that a contract may be the occasion that brings the parties together, but it is the relationship or situation of the parties that gives rise to a duty in law, the breach of which is a tort. Had Montgomery Ward repaired the water heater gratuitously, it would have owed *Scharrenbeck*a duty not to create a dangerous condition. Thus the duty to not create a dangerous condition existed independent of any contractual relationship.

In summary, when a party must prove the contents of its contract and must rely on the duties created therein, the action is "in substance an action on the contract, even though it is denominated an action for negligent performance of the contract." *Bernard Johnson, Inc. v. Continental Constructors, Inc.*, 630 S.W.2d 365, 368 (Tex. App.—Austin 1982, writ ref'd n.r.e.).

NOTES AND PROBLEMS

1. ***Why Contract vs. Tort Matters.*** In the *Southwestern Bell* case, why was the plaintiff attempting to pursue a tort claim rather than a contract claim? Notice the reference early in the opinion to a liquidated damages clause in the Yellow Pages contract. On a tort claim this would not cap the recovery of full compensatory damages like it might in a contract breach action. In other instances, the tort versus contract issue may arise because the claimant might try to sue on a tort theory in order to try to justify a submission of a punitive damage question to the jury.

2. ***Negligent Performance of a Contract Duty.*** Much of the foregoing opinion revolves around trying to determine if this case was distinguishable from the *Sharrenbeck* decision discussed by the court. How convinced are you

by the majority's distinction? How clear is that distinction? What analysis should be employed going forward after *Southwestern Bell*?

3. ***Acts vs. Omissions.*** Do you find it useful to distinguish between cases of non-performance of a contractual duty and cases of poor performance of a contractual duty? Would this dichotomy help to explain the difference in outcomes between *Sharrenbeck* and *Southwestern Bell*?

4. ***Problems.*** Using the two-part test from *Southwestern Bell* (analyzing whether a separate tort duty existed independent of the contract and whether any separate tort damages were incurred), analyze the following scenarios to determine if a tort claim might be maintainable:

A. A defendant water heater repairperson agrees to fix the plaintiff's water heater but never shows up. By virtue of this lack of repair, the water heater explodes and destroys the house.

B. Southwestern Bells agrees to place a Yellow Pages advertisement knowing at the time of doing so that it was already at 100 percent capacity and would not be able to include the plaintiff's ad within its publication.

C. Defendant employer agrees to provide health insurance to the plaintiff. After the plaintiff is diagnosed with cancer and begins receiving expensive chronic medical treatment, the employer decides to increase the deductible of only that sick employee to astronomical heights. This conduct causes great anguish and emotional disturbance. The plaintiff alleges intentional infliction of emotional anguish in addition to contract breach.

Upon Further Review

While many law students (and members of the public) perceive torts as solely related to personal injury or property damage claims, in fact there are increasing numbers of tort suits filed by businesses against other businesses. For the lawyer who enjoys having clients rich enough to pay high hourly fees, yet yearns to represent plaintiffs, the world of business torts can be quite enticing, because corporations are just as likely to be claimants as defendants in this area. Many, though not all, of the business torts litigated today arise in the context of contractual relationships; a recurring theme, therefore, in business torts concerns whether and when to recognize a tort claim rather than relegating the parties to the world of contract law. Despite many business tort causes of action being quite ancient, their modern adaptation and interpretation had led to this area being uniquely in flux. For those students of the law who enjoy grappling with complex issues, business torts can be very enjoyable. While there are many business tort causes of action that we simply do not have time to encounter here (e.g., misappropriation of trade secrets, business disparagement, breach of fiduciary duty, commercial defamation), the claim that has long predominated in this field concerns a common law claim for fraud. Fraud permeates the law and its study can be endless. Understanding what types of statements (or conduct) are considered misrepresentations is the beginning point in any fraud analysis. Further, fault and justifiable reliance are elements that can be daunting in many factual scenarios. And while negligent misrepresentation can often be brought in cases that involve conduct close to fraud, this cause of action has some significant limitations in its application — most notably, concerning the issue of duty. Finally, while it is clear that only intentional and not negligent claims of interference with contract will be considered by the courts, the analytical distinctions between interference with existing contracts and interference with prospective contracts has caused great angst for lawyers and litigants trying to understand their rights.

TABLE OF CASES

The primary cases are in bold. Other cases include those cited in the text and notes. Cases merely cited within the primary cases are not included.